Oracle PL/SQL Programming

Feng Sun

Oracle PL/SQL Programming

Second Edition

Steven Feuerstein

with Bill Pribyl

O'REILLY®

Beijing · Cambridge · Köln · Paris · Sebastopol · Taipei · Tokyo

Oracle PL/SQL Programming, Second Edition
by Steven Feuerstein with Bill Pribyl

Published by O'Reilly & Associates, Inc. 101 Morris Street, Sebastopol, CA 95472.

Editor: Deborah Russell

Production Editor: Jane Ellin

Printing History:

September 1995:   First Edition.

September 1997:   Second Edition.

ISBN: 1-56592-335-9   [3/99]

I dedicate this book to my parents, Sheldon and Joan Feuerstein, and to the children in my life: the babies at the Columbus Maryville Reception Center, Nikolas Silva, Ian and Michaela McCauseland, Danielle and Benjamin DeUrso, Adam and Jay Bartell, Ciera, Brian, and Michael Daniels, Timnah and Masada Sela, and of course my own boys, Eli and Chris.

—Steven Feuerstein

To my father, who told me "that's no hill for a stepper" enough times that it finally sank in.

—Bill Pribyl

Table of Contents

Foreword

The world is always changing for applications developers. In the early 1990s the emphasis was on the user interface, and the demand was overwhelming for PC clients with buttons, pop-up lists, tab folders, and other fancy GUI elements. We learned Visual Basic, PowerBuilder, SQL Windows, Access, and Paradox to meet that demand, or we suffered through the evolution of the Developer/2000 tools from Oracle Corporation. We were able to create instant legacy applications in just a matter of weeks—legacy applications with a pretty interface and some of the ugliest, undocumented, nonoptimized, spaghetti code that you have ever seen. We could quickly build unreadable, unmaintainable code with all the application logic wrapped up in the interface elements.

Now it's Java, Java, Java, and more Java. Our clients want elegant multi-tier applications that run on any client from thin-client network computers to overstuffed NT workstations with hundreds of megabytes of memory, with that same instantaneous response they expected from client/server systems. Now our applications must support not hundreds of users on a local area network but thousands of users on the Internet. Oracle is even promising that you will be able to execute Java in the database server itself and write stored procedures in Java rather than PL/SQL. So why aren't we rushing off to learn Java? Because even with all of the hoopla over Java, PL/SQL is still the best way to build programs to access data in Oracle7 and Oracle8 databases. After Oracle began using PL/SQL to build its own tools for replication, the open APIs for Designer/2000 and Developer/2000, and the HTML generators, it began to pay a lot more attention to performance characteristics, and PL/SQL8 includes a number of significant enhancements to speed execution of complex PL/SQL logic. With these new improvements, PL/SQL8 assumes even more importance as the principal data access language for Oracle8.

Oracle has been methodically enhancing the capabilities of PL/SQL to make it the language of choice for developing distributed computing environments. When Oracle finally delivers client-side PL/SQL with the full characteristics of server-side code (effectively turning all clients into mini-servers for certain purposes), we will be able to build truly distributed environments for maximizing the effectiveness of our limited computing resources. We already can use PL/SQL packages and procedures from most good front-end tools, and that integration should get better over time. Almost every Java-based middleware connectivity tool is being released with support for PL/SQL. That should help make it easier to build the complex rules in a portable language that we can run in most popular hardware or software environments.

PL/SQL is a complex and powerful programming language that you can use to build a new generation of multi-tier systems—systems that can scale up past the department LAN to enable world-wide enterprise systems on the Internet with the same reliability that we expect from old mainframe applications. The ability to build those systems does not mean that we will be able to manage our development environments effectively. You can be sure that the tools to help us cope with the complexity of truly distributed business objects will be slower to emerge, and we will all be in pretty deep before they are really ready.

We can start to get ready now as we begin to take advantage of the new power and sophistication of Oracle8's PL/SQL. We can start writing modular code that can be developed in a top-down manner with program names that truly describe their function. We can start to write PL/SQL code that we can reuse within and among our applications. We can apply the principles of good structured design to our development of PL/SQL packages, procedures, functions, etc. And we can use *Oracle PL/SQL Programming* as our source of the right way to write efficient and effective PL/SQL code.

Many of us have already adopted *Oracle PL/SQL Programming* as our programming "bible." Steven's no-nonsense approach to minimizing the amount of code he needs to write and maintain; his naming conventions that maximize the documentation content of his code; his innate ability to sniff out ways to make coding PL/SQL less drudgery and more creative—all of these characteristics should be extremely useful and inspiring to good developers. The first edition of this book is one of the very few titles in my Oracle collection of more than 70 books that is actually dog-eared from use. All of my colleagues already know the book intimately.

I have known Steven Feuerstein and his work for a long time through my publishing of Oracle technical publications: the NY Oracle Users newsletter in 1989; the Oracle User Resource newsletter from 1990 to 1994; the International *Oracle Users Journal* from 1990 to 1992; the Proceedings of the East Coast Oracle

Developers Conference from 1991 to 1996; and since 1994, Pinnacle Publishing's *Oracle Developer.* Steven has been my most prolific and admired writer for more than seven years.

Now that Steven (with the able help of Bill Pribyl) has updated the original version of *Oracle PL/SQL Programming*, I advise every Oracle developer to replace his or her own well-utilized copy with this new edition. They'll start out checking the new Oracle8 additions and the additional chapters on performance tuning, debugging, and tracing. But I think every one of them should have a copy of the new edition handy so they'll be prepared when someone comes to them with the inevitable questions about PL/SQL. Oracle8 is going to be the database behind many of the biggest systems on the Internet, and PL/SQL is going to be the language that makes it happen. The most successful Oracle developers and DBAs will be up to their ears in PL/SQL code—and they'll be eternally grateful if that code is written in accordance with Steven and Bill's teachings.

As an extra treat, you should also find the book to be readable and entertaining, not easy adjectives to apply to most technical tomes. You will enjoy this book! I did.

Tony Ziemba
Editor, *Oracle Developer*
New York, NY
August 1997

Preface

Thousands of application developers and database administrators around the world use software provided by Oracle Corporation to build complex systems that manage vast quantities of data. At the heart of much of Oracle's software is PL/SQL—a programming language that provides procedural extensions to the SQL relational database language and an ever-growing range of Oracle development tools.

PL/SQL figures prominently as an enabling technology in almost every new product released by Oracle Corporation. Developers can use PL/SQL to perform many kinds of programming functions, including:

- Implementing crucial business rules in the Oracle Server with PL/SQL-based stored procedures and database triggers

- Enhancing powerful and easy-to-use GUI interfaces of products like Oracle Developer/2000 with detailed, programmatic control

- Employing object-oriented design principles in Oracle-based applications

- Linking a World Wide Web page to an Oracle database

Perhaps most importantly, PL/SQL plays a crucial role in the design of successful client-server applications because it provides the foundation for the code used to distribute processing and transactions across the network.

PL/SQL was modeled after Ada,[*] a programming language designed for the United States Department of Defense. Ada is a high-level programming language which

---

[*] The language was named "Ada" in honor of Ada Lovelace, a mathematician who is regarded by many to have been the world's first computer programmer.

emphasizes data abstraction, information hiding, and other key elements of modern design strategies.

PL/SQL is a powerful language which incorporates many of the most advanced elements of procedural languages, including:

- A full range of datatypes

- Explicit block structures

- Conditional and sequential control statements

- Loops of various kinds

- Exception handlers for use in event-based error handling

- Constructs that help in the development of modular code—functions, procedures, and packages (collections of related programs and variables); packages are often referred to as "poor man's objects"

- User-defined datatypes such as objects and nested tables (with the Oracle objects option)

PL/SQL is integrated tightly into Oracle's SQL language: you can execute SQL statements directly from your procedural program. Conversely, you can also call PL/SQL functions from within a SQL statement.

Oracle developers who want to be successful in the 1990s and beyond must learn to use PL/SQL to full advantage. This is a two-step process: first, learn how to use the language's full set of features; and second, after mastering those individual features, learn how to put these constructs together to build complex applications.

How can you best learn PL/SQL? The usual way is to struggle with the software tool and, through trial and error, discover the best implementation techniques. With PL/SQL, a slow and uncertain process is made worse by several factors:

- PL/SQL is still a relatively new language; there are few resources outside of Oracle manuals that will help you learn more. Classes tend to focus on the flashy side of the new GUI tools, and they ignore the more complicated programming that is so necessary in production applications. Books on Oracle technology try to cover too much territory and as a result cannot support developers as they move past the most basic requirements.

- PL/SQL is just now maturing to the point where it offers and is supported by a comprehensive set of features and programmer utilities. For years, developers have complained about a lack of a debugger, the inability to read from and write to operating system files, no support for arrays, and other issues. Oracle Corporation has finally released versions of PL/SQL which address these complaints and are robust enough to support large-scale application development. To complement this robustness, third-party vendors are also beginning to offer useful programming environments.

- PL/SQL is an island of procedurality in a sea of declarative or "fill-in-the-form" products; you have to figure out how to blend these two different approaches when you develop your code. It is one thing to click on a button in a designer interface and create a widget. It is quite another thing to learn how to manipulate that widget and handle the event-based interactions between widgets with procedural code.

For all of these reasons and more, Oracle developers need a solid, comprehensive resource for all things PL/SQL. You need to know about the basic building blocks of PL/SQL, but you also need to learn by example, so you can skip as much of the trial-and-error as possible. As with any programming language, there is a right way and many wrong ways (or at least "not as right" ways) in PL/SQL to handle just about every requirement you will meet. It's my hope that this book will help you learn how to use the PL/SQL language in the most effective and efficient way possible.

Objectives of This Book

What, specifically, will this book help you do?

Take full advantage of PL/SQL. The reference manuals may describe all the features of the PL/SQL language, but they don't tell you how to apply the technology. In fact, in some cases, you'll be lucky to even understand how to use a given feature after you've made your way through the railroad diagrams. Books and training courses tend to cover the same standard topics in the same limited way. In this book, we'll venture beyond to the edges of the language, to the nonstandard ways in which a particular feature can be tweaked to achieve a desired result.

Use PL/SQL to solve your problems. You don't spend your days and nights writing PL/SQL modules so that you can rise to a higher plane of existence. You use PL/SQL to solve problems for your company or your customers. In this book, I try hard to help you tackle real-world problems, the kinds of issues developers face on a daily basis (at least those problems that can be solved with mere software). To do this, I've packed the book with examples—not just small code fragments, but complete application components you can apply immediately to your own situations. There is a good deal of code in the book itself, and much more on the disk that accompanies the book. In this book I guide you through the analytical process used to come up with a solution. In this way I hope you'll see, in the most concrete terms, how to apply PL/SQL features and undocumented applications of those features to a particular situation.

Write efficient, maintainable code. PL/SQL and the rest of the Oracle products offer the potential for incredible development productivity. If you aren't careful, however, this rapid development capability will simply let you dig yourself into a deeper, darker hole than you've ever found yourself in before. I would consider this book a failure if it only ended up helping programmers write more code in less time than ever before. I want to help you develop the skills and techniques that give you the time to build modules which readily adapt to change and are easily understood and maintained. I want to teach you to use comprehensive strategies and code architectures which allow you to apply PL/SQL in powerful, general ways to many of the problems you will face.

Structure of This Book

This second edition has changed from the first edition in a number of significant ways. Before listing the individual parts of the book, I want to explain the overall restructuring.

About the Second Edition

We (the authors and O'Reilly & Associates) are committed to providing comprehensive, useful coverage of the PL/SQL language over the life of this language. The first edition of this book covered *most* of PL/SQL's features as it existed through PL/SQL Release 2.3. With the release of Oracle8, however, we faced a challenge: how do we fit all the new technologies of PL/SQL8 into *Oracle PL/SQL Programming* and fill out coverage of existing elements of PL/SQL without creating a tome so unwieldy that reading the book becomes as much a physical as a mental workout?

Furthermore, if we look ahead a few years, we can easily expect that Oracle will continue to roll out expanded functionality in the objects area, as well as providing new and enhanced built-in packages. Given this situation, it quickly became clear to us that it was not practical to offer a single text which covered "all things PL/SQL."

Two questions then arose: what do we cut and what do we do with the stuff that we cut? The answers are as follows:

- Move the package examples from the printed text to the disk. The second edition's disk offers a Windows-based interface designed by RevealNet, Inc. (*www.revealnet.com*) allowing you rapid access to the many utilities and samples. Now, instead of having to look through a directory listing and then using an editor to view those files, you will be able to mouse-click and drill-down your way to the topics in which you are interested. We take advantage of this interface to give you an easy way to examine the many examples of packages I built for the book.

- Remove the chapter on built-in packages and expand it into a complete book. This chapter in the first edition offered lots of good information, but it was not comprehensive and simply couldn't keep growing to absorb all the new technology issuing forth from Oracle headquarters. Moving coverage of built-in packages to its own book will give us room to provide more and better information about this key element of the PL/SQL language. Appendix C, *Built-In Packages*, of this edition of *Oracle PL/SQL Programming* will still provide a quick reference to the more common built-in packages. As I write this, I am hard at work on the new book, *Oracle Built-in Packages*. Watch for it in early 1998.

About the Contents

The second edition of *Oracle PL/SQL Programming* is divided into seven parts.:

Part I, Programming in PL/SQL

Chapters 1 through 3 explain what it means to program in PL/SQL and in Oracle-based applications in general. This part of the book introduces you to the main features of the PL/SQL language and gives you some general advice on programming habits and effective coding style.

Part II, PL/SQL Language Elements

Chapters 4 through 10 describe the basic PL/SQL programming components— variables, cursors, conditional and sequential control statements, loops, exception handlers, PL/SQL records, and PL/SQL tables. These chapters contain numerous examples, along with tips on how, when, and where to apply these programming constructs most effectively. When you complete this section of the book you will know how to apply all the constructs of the PL/SQL language. You will also be able to examine the complex requirements in your own applications and use the different parts of PL/SQL to implement those requirements.

Part III, Built-In Functions

Chapters 11 through 14 present the many built-in (predefined) PL/SQL functions and procedures, which you can put to use immediately in your applications. One of the key barometers of your success with PL/SQL will be the extent to which you know how to leverage all of the capabilities that Oracle Corporation provides. (You don't want to have to reinvent the wheel when so many functions and procedures are provided for you.) Appendix C supplements Part III by summarizing the syntax of Oracle's built-in packages.

Part IV, Modular Code

Chapters 15 through 17 take you past the individual components of the PL/SQL language to explore modular construction in PL/SQL. You will learn how to build procedures, functions, and packages; more than that, you will learn how to build them correctly. More than with any other aspect of code, the way you design your modules has an enormous impact on your applications' development time, reusability, and maintainability.

Part V, New PL/SQL8 Features

Chapters 18 through 21 contain the main discussion of the new features of Oracle8—in particular, object types, new types of collections (nested tables and VARRAYs), object views, and external procedures. Although we describe Oracle8 enhancements as appropriate in other sections of the book, we localize the major discussion here. Doing so allows developers new to Oracle8 to learn about the features in a coordinated way. It also lets developers still working on Oracle7 systems to skip over much of the discussion until it is more relevant to them.

Part VI, Making PL/SQL Programs Work

Chapters 22 through 26 tell you how to manage your PL/SQL code and debug, tune, and trace the execution of your programs. This part of the book also contains a summary of particularly helpful tips for effective PL/SQL programming in the real world.

Part VII, Appendixes

Appendixes A through C summarize what's on the companion disk, how to call stored procedures from PL/SQL Version 1.1, and how to call Oracle's built-in packages.

If you are new to PL/SQL, reading this book from beginning to end should improve your skills and help your understanding widen in a gradual, natural process. If you're already a proficient PL/SQL programmer, you'll probably want to dip into the appropriate sections in order to extract particular techniques for immediate application. Whether you use this book as a teaching guide or as a reference, I hope that it will have a significant impact on your ability to use PL/SQL most effectively.

Long as this book is, it doesn't do everything. The Oracle environment is a huge and complex one, and in this book I've focused my attention on PL/SQL itself. Some topics are outside the logical scope of this book. Therefore, this book does not cover:

- *Administration of Oracle databases*. While the DBA can use this book to learn how to write the PL/SQL needed to build and maintain databases, this book does not explore all the nuances of the Data Definition Language (DDL) of Oracle's SQL.

- *Application and database tuning.* I don't cover detailed tuning issues in this book, though the second edition does add a chapter on PL/SQL tuning. *Oracle Performance Tuning* by Peter Corrigan and Mark Gurry (O'Reilly & Associates, Second Edition, 1997) gives you all the information you need about tuning your Oracle applications.

- *Oracle tool-specific technologies independent of PL/SQL.* This book won't teach you everything you need to know about such technologies as SQL*Forms and Oracle Forms triggers. Similarly, you won't find detailed discussions of repeating frames of Oracle Reports in here. Nevertheless, many of the techniques offered in this book certainly do apply to the Oracle Developer/2000 environment.

- *Third-party application development software.* There are many alternatives to using PL/SQL and the tools supplied by Oracle to build your applications. This book does not address these options, nor does it attempt to compare PL/SQL to these third-party products.

- *National Language Support in Oracle.* This book does not offer comprehensive coverage of Oracle's National Language Support (NLS) capabilities for developing applications for multiple languages.

- *Trusted Oracle.* Oracle Corporation has developed a special version of its Oracle7 Server for high-security environments. This book does not detail the additional datatypes and features available only for Trusted Oracle.

Audience

This book was designed to be used by anyone who needs to develop Oracle-based applications using the PL/SQL programming language. There are a number of distinct audiences:

Role	How to Use the Book
Information systems manager	The application development or database administration manager in an Oracle shop needs a thorough grasp of the technology used in the development groups. Familiarity with the technology will help the manager to better understand the challenges faced by the team members and the ability of that team to solve problems. These managers will want to pay particular attention to Part IV, *Modular Code*, for the big picture of structuring PL/SQL-based applications.
One-person information systems shop	Oracle licenses are frequently sold into small companies or departments where the supporting information systems organization consists of little more than a single manager and single developer (or perhaps both of those functions rolled into one). These small organizations do not have the time to search through multiple manuals or sets of training notes to find the solution to their problems. This book offers one-stop shopping for these people—a consolidated reference and solutions source.

Role	How to Use the Book
Database administrator	The DBA in the world of Oracle7 needs to build database triggers and stored procedures in order to manage business rules at the RDBMS levels and implement distributed databases. The DBA will use this book to strengthen his or her understanding of how to write efficient RDBMS-level objects. This book will also discuss constructing packages of related objects which will reduce the resources required to maintain these objects.
New developer in the Oracle Developer/2000 environment	Many developers arrive fresh on the Oracle scene through the use of the new Oracle Developer/2000 tools in the Windows environment. These developers will be comfortable manipulating the various widgets in the GUI world, but will find PL/SQL to be a strange, new partner for development. This book will quickly bring them up to speed and make them more productive users of Oracle Developer/ 2000 software.
Experienced Oracle developer	Many thousands of programmers have spent years writing, debugging, and maintaining programs written in SQL*Forms, SQL*Reportwriter, SQL*Plus, and SQL*Menu. While their PL/SQL skills have progressed to meet the needs of specific applications, most could expand both their PL/SQL knowledge and their awareness of its subtleties. In addition, as developers move into the Oracle Developer/2000 generation, PL/SQL plays a significantly more central role; the developer will have to gain new expertise to meet the demands of this change.
Consultant	Consultants must offer a high level of service and quality to their customers. This added value is measured in productivity and in the application of skills not currently held by the client. Consultants should find this book an invaluable aid in deepening their understanding of PL/SQL technology.

Conventions Used in This Book

The following conventions are used in this book:

Italic
> is used for file and directory names.

`Constant width`
> is used for code examples.

`Constant width bold`
> In some code examples, highlights the statements being discussed.

`Constant width italic`
> In some code examples, indicates an element (e.g., a filename) that you supply.

UPPERCASE
> In code examples, indicates PL/SQL keywords.

lowercase

> In code examples, indicates user-defined items such as variables, parameters, etc.

punctuation

> In code examples, enter exactly as shown.

indentation

> In code examples, helps to show structure but is not required.

-- In code examples, a double hyphen begins a single-line comment, which extends to the end of a line.

/* and */

> In code examples, these characters delimit a multiline comment, which can extend from one line to another.

. In code examples and related discussions, a dot qualifies a reference by separating an object name from a component name. For example, dot notation is used to select fields in a record and to specify declarations within a package.

< > In syntax descriptions, angle brackets enclose the name of a syntactic element.

[ ] In syntax descriptions, square brackets enclose optional items.

... In syntax descriptions, an ellipsis shows that statements or clauses irrelevant to the discussion were left out.

Indicates that the code example described in the text appears on the companion disk.

Which Platform or Version?

In general, all of the discussions and examples in this book apply regardless of the machine and/or operating system you are using. In those few cases where a feature is in any way system-dependent, I note that in the text.

There are many versions of PL/SQL, and you may even find that you need to use multiple versions in your development work. Chapter 1 describes in detail the many versions of PL/SQL and what you need to know about them; see the section called "PL/SQL Versions."

About the Disk

You'll find a high-density Windows disk included with this book. This disk contains the Companion Utilities Guide for *Oracle PL/SQL Programming*, an online tool developed by RevealNet, Inc. that gives you point-and-click access to more than 100 files of source code and documentation that we developed. Many of the code examples are also printed in the book. We've included these to give you a jump start on writing your own PL/SQL code and to keep you from having to type many pages of PL/SQL statements from printed text.

Throughout the book, disk icons (see the "Conventions Used in This Book" section above) will indicate where a code example shown or mentioned in the text is included on the disk. Appendix A, *What's on the Companion Disk?*, describes how to install the Windows-based interface. You can run the software in any Microsoft Windows environment (3.1, 95, NT 3.5, NT 4.0). If you are working in a non-Windows environment, you can obtain a compressed file containing the utilities on the desk from the RevealNet PL/SQL Pipeline Archives at *www.revealnet.com/plsql-pipeline.*

Comments and Questions

Please address comments and questions concerning this book to the publisher:

> O'Reilly & Associates
> 101 Morris Street
> Sebastopol, CA 95472
> 1-800-998-9938 (in the U.S. or Canada)
> 1-707-829-0515 (international or local)
> 1-707-829-0104 (FAX)

You can also send us messages electronically. See the insert in the book for information about O'Reilly & Associates' online services.

For corrections and amplifications for the book, check out *www.oreilly.com/catalog/oraclep2/.*

If you have any questions about the disk supplied with this book, contact RevealNet Inc. at *www.revealnet.com.*

Acknowledgments

We're determined not to miss anyone here. Here are the original acknowledgments from the first edition (because we're still grateful to you all), the new acknowledgments from Steven, and the acknowledgments from Bill.

First Edition (Steven)

As a teenager and young man, I wrote many poems, works of short fiction, and uncompleted novels. I dreamed of being an author and sent out my share of manuscripts and self-addressed, stamped envelopes. I never thought that my first book would be on software programming techniques, but here it is! I have tried to keep the fictional content down to an absolute minimum.

I was assisted by many people as I conceived of, wrote, and then polished this text. I would like to thank the following individuals for reviewing draft versions of this book: Jennifer Blair of Blair Technical Training, Eric Camplin of SSC, Joe Celko of OSoft Development Corporation, Avery Cohen of Synectics, Thomas Dunbar, Computer System Engineer at Virginia Tech, R. James Forsythe of PCS Technologies, Mike Gangler of Sharidionne, Gabriel Hoffman of PCS Technologies, Karen Peiser of SSC, Pete Schaffer of SSC, and David Thompson of Spectrum Group.

While all of the people listed above made a contribution, I received particularly detailed and insightful feedback from three people: David Thompson, who saved me much embarrassment from technical glitches in Part III and singlehandedly recoded an obtuse example into a well-thought-out illustration of concepts; Thomas Dunbar, who helped me liberate this book from the confines of the Oracle development tools; and Avery Cohen, whose sharp eye and organized mind greatly improved Part IV.

One of the most dramatic improvements at Oracle Corporation in the last few years is its eagerness to work with those of us outside of the company to help utilize fully its technology. Many individuals at Oracle Corporation have supported the writing of this book. Technical reviewers from Oracle Corporation included Cailein Barclay, Sunil Bhargava, Boris Burshteyn, Gray Clossman, Radhakrishna Hari, James Mallory, Nimesh Mehta, Jeff Muller, Dave Posner, Chris Racicot, Peter Vasterd, and Zona Walcott. These reviews were especially helpful in clarifying language and concepts and in improving technical accuracy. I am grateful for their time and attention.

Two Oracle employees made a special effort on my behalf and I offer them my warmest thank-yous: Peter Vasterd, Product Manager of Server Technologies, who responded rapidly to each of my questions, coordinated the technical review of my book by Oracle Corporation employees, and was especially helpful in the final stages of the book; and Nimish Mehta, Vice-President of the Desktop Products Division and a friend from the early days of SQL*Reportwriter, who was more than generous in providing early releases of software I needed to test and develop the code for this book.

In addition to the reviewing process, many other Oracle employees gave of their time, knowledge, and resources to strengthen this book, including Sohaib Abassi, Per Brondum, Ivan Chong, Bill Dwight, Steve Ehrlich, Bushan Fotedar, Ken Jacobs, Nimish Mehta, Steve Muench, Sri Rajan, and Mark Richter.

Of course, the universe of people who provide a support network for this kind of project goes far beyond those directly involved in the writing and reviewing. For the past three years I have been very fortunate to have been a consultant in SSC, a systems management consulting firm led by Bill Hinman. Bill has created a unique, empowering professional environment. Rather than try to bind his employees to SSC, Bill has sought to offer a guild-like atmosphere in which we each are encouraged to cultivate our own interests, develop a vision, and, of course, hone our technical skills. My time with SSC has exceeded all expectations and we are still just cranking up the model! Hugo Toledo, a fellow SSC consultant, has also been especially supportive of my work. He is one of the most helpful, generous, and intelligent people I have ever met, with a breadth and depth of knowledge about data processing technology that continually astonishes me. For three years, he has always been ready to lend a hand and answer a question, and I am grateful to him for his friendship and commitment.

As I became more active in writing articles and papers for the Oracle User Group community, two editors provided encouragement and steady outlets for my work: Tony Ziemba, editor of Pinnacle's *Oracle Developer* newsletter, and Bill Pribyl, former and outstanding editor of the IOUG *Select* magazine. They have both had a wide and lasting impact on improving the flow of quality technical information to Oracle users around the world.

Of course, I would not have been able to write this book without the invaluable experience I gained during my years at Oracle Corporation. I want to thank, in particular, John Cordell, who brought me into Oracle Corporation and guided me through the shoals of Oracle politics and technology, and Beverly Gibson, who worked hard to create special opportunities for so many talented technicians in the sales force. I had the privilege of working with many other incredibly smart, funny, dedicated, and energetic people at Oracle between 1987 and 1992 and I will always treasure that experience.

Thanks to all the people at O'Reilly & Associates who turned my manuscript into a finished book: to Debby Russell, my time-slicing, parallel-processing editor who managed to wrestle this book down to publishable size; Mike Sierra, whose wizardry converted hundreds of pages of Microsoft Word files to FrameMaker; Gigi Estabrook, who read and edited the book several times to prepare drafts for technical review and the East Coast Developer's Conference; Edie Freedman, who designed the cover, and Nancy Priest, who designed the interior layout; Donna Woonteiler, who copyedited the final draft of the book and brought order to the fonts; Chris Reilley and Michelle Willey, who prepared the diagrams; Debby Cunha, Michael Deutsch, John Files, and Juliette Muellner, who edited the files; Cory Willing, who did a final proofreading; Seth Maislin, who prepared the index; Kismet McDonough Chan, who did the final quality control on the book; and

Clairemarie Fisher O'Leary, drill sergeant, who pulled together all the pieces of final production.

Finally, I thank my wife, Veva Silva Feuerstein, for her support and tolerance of the absorption of so many of our evenings and weekends in the past year.

Second Edition (Steven)

I know! Instead of saying "Finally, I thank my wife" at the end of this section, I will do it first: Thanks, Veva, for being a fantastic partner and wonderful mother. Sure, I could have written this book without you (actually, I *did* write this book without you. You don't know anything about PL/SQL...), but without you my life would be empty, so I wouldn't *care* that I wrote the book.

Wow, what a fast and fascinating trip this has been! The first edition of this book was published in September 1995 and it certainly changed my life. Clearly, the book touched a nerve and filled a need. The book's reception showed that Oracle developers have been desperate for both clear reference information on the PL/SQL language and, perhaps more importantly, tips on how best to take full advantage of this core Oracle technology. From what my readers have told me, *Oracle PL/SQL Programming* has been a big help. I am very glad that all those trees were not chopped down in vain. I furthermore feel a real obligation to my readers to maintain this text, and my growing series on PL/SQL, so that you may continue to get the most out of this important language. (Who knows? It might even outlive Java!)

The human most responsible for making this second edition possible is Bill Pribyl. When it became clear that Oracle would finally release Oracle8 and that PL/SQL would be changed in fundamental ways, I started to panic. How could I learn everything I needed to learn about object-oriented programming, as well as PL/SQL8, and then write all that down to be published in the fall of 1997, on top of everything else I was doing? It just didn't seem possible. So I sent a plea for help out to a few select people whom I knew were solid writers and outstanding Oracle technicians. Bill quickly exposed a masochistic sliver of his personality by agreeing to cover many of the new features of PL/SQL8 for this edition. He also proved to be a great writer, infused with discipline and enthusiasm for the project. I believe his text (and sense of humor) meshes well with the existing content of the book; I am sure you will feel the same.

This second edition is much more a product of the worldwide PL/SQL developer community than the first edition. I have received hundreds of messages from readers over the past two years, pointing out errors in the text, asking for clarification, and offering suggestions for improvements. I love to hear from you and I do read every single critique, so please keep the comments coming. I am particularly indebted to Eric Givler, Systems Analyst, Department of Environmental Protection, State of Pennsylvania. He pored over my first edition with a devotion and fanaticism that was totally unsolicited and deeply appreciated. He uncovered many, many errors in my first text (I am embarrassed to admit to their volume), and has therefore contributed mightily to the much-improved quality of this second edition. I therefore forgive him his occasional wisecrack at my expense.

Many others helped in ways large and small. Bert Scalzo, Senior DBA/Data Architect at Analysts International Corp (AIC) provided quick reference material for Appendix C. John Beresniewicz of Savant has offered advice and support since the day I met him at the ECO96 conference in Washington, DC. Tom White and Steve Hilker of RevealNet have not only been wonderfully supportive, but they have established a viable commercial outlet for my software, PL/Vision, and for that I am deeply grateful.

At Oracle Corporation, Thomas Kurian made certain that we got the software, support, and answers we needed to make this book technically sound. Also among the contributors were some extremely helpful folks on the Oracle8 development team, approximately 15 of whom fielded our questions at one point or another. In particular, Radhakrishna Hari provided solid and helpful reviews of the Oracle8 material. Shirish Puranik and Kannan Muthukkaruppan assisted with the performance tuning tips in Chapter 25.

As with the first edition, Debby Russell of O'Reilly & Associates carried this book through to publication. I have greatly enjoyed working with Debby and hope to do so for a good many other books. This second edition was prepared in record time, in no small part due to Debby's professionalism and competence, not to mention the skills and devotion of the rest of her team: Jane Ellin, the production editor who also copyedited the manuscript; Mike Sierra, who converted the new files to Frame and helped in many other ways; Kimo Carter, who entered edits into the files; Madeleine Newell, who provided extensive production support; Rob Romano, who created the new figures; Edie Freedman, who designed the cover, and Nancy Priest, who designed the interior format; and Seth Maislin, who prepared the index.

Many of the people who helped me in the first edition also stood by me for the second edition. Without repeating all of their names again, I once again thank them.

Second Edition (Bill)

When Steven asked me if I would write a few chapters for this new edition of the book, I was, for once, speechless. Not long before, my citation of Steven as "one of my all-time heroes" had appeared on the back of his second book—and here he was on the phone, asking me for help! It took me a long time—about 1.2 seconds—to give him an answer.

And now, untold hours of "is this a bug or a feature?" later, I'm even more delighted to have collaborated with Steven; not only do I appreciate his willingness to assume the risk of adding a second author to his magnum opus, but I have also thoroughly enjoyed his insightful reviews and astute criticisms of my text. My first acknowledgment goes to Steven.

There is no way that the Oracle8 material would have been acceptable for publication without a brilliant supporting cast. First, fellow consultant Fred Polizo of FP Systems in San Jose, California (*fredp@ricochet.net*), one of the finest C programmers I know, developed all of the C-based examples in the *External Procedures* chapter. He, like Steven and I, slogged through the beta, producing test after test and revision after revision of the material until it was just right—and then came the production version! Words cannot express the respect I have for Fred's programming talents, nor the amazement I felt when I received immediate answers to questions emailed to him at 2 A.M. I think you'll find his crystal-clear C code to be both educational and immediately useful.

I second Steven's ode of gratitude to the folks at Oracle Corporation for their help with this edition, and there are two special thank yous from me. A major supporter of the entire effort was Donald Herkimer, who fielded question after question gracefully and tirelessly, even when it must have gotten way past the fun stage. Don works in Oracle's "Center of Excellence for Applications Development and Productivity with Object-oriented Technology" (they must have won the longest-name award!). When he didn't happen to have the answer himself, Don somehow knew the incantations required to extract answers from deep within the email jungle at Oracle. Ervan Darnell was a tremendous help with the chapter on *Nested Tables and VARRAYs*, gently convincing me to bury one of my sillier examples, and injecting a bit of precision into my treatment of some of the new SQL functions.

I'd also like to acknowledge Gary Cernosek, an old friend and OO wizard at Rational Corporation, for checking the sanity of the *Object Types* chapter; and my brother, Patrick Pribyl, C++ programmer extraordinaire, for doing the same. Separate conversations with longtime acquaintances Bill Watkins and Debra Luik were also very enlightening and helped shape the *Object Types* chapter.

Thanks also go to the staff and clients of my firm, DataCraft, who were more than patient while I went into writing mode. I appreciate their tolerance and moral support, especially from Leo and the rest of the gang.

But my most heartfelt gratitude has to go to my immediate family, for putting up with my writing into the wee hours ("Mommy, Daddy fell asleep at the computer again!") and remaining a constant source of love and good humor.

I

Programming in PL/SQL

Part I of this book introduces PL/SQL and presents the basics of how to program in Oracle-based applications.

- Chapter 1, *Introduction to PL/SQL*, introduces PL/SQL and explains where it came from. It describes the various PL/SQL versions and environments you might be using and the differences among the implementations of PL/SQL. It also presents some basic PL/SQL programming principles.

- Chapter 2, *PL/SQL Language Fundamentals*, introduces the PL/SQL character set, identifiers, literals, and other basic elements of the language.

- Chapter 3, *Effective Coding Style*, presents guidelines for coding style and discusses how the decisions you make about the formatting of your programs can determine how readable and useful those programs can be.

1

Introduction to PL/SQL

This chapter introduces PL/SQL, its origins, and its various versions. It also introduces you to what it means to be a PL/SQL programmer, and how PL/SQL programming differs from the kind of programming with which you may be familiar.

What Is PL/SQL?

PL/SQL stands for "Procedural Language extensions to SQL." PL/SQL is available primarily as an "enabling technology" within other software products; it does not exist as a standalone language. You can use PL/SQL in the Oracle relational database, in the Oracle Server, and in client-side application development tools, such as Oracle Forms. PL/SQL is closely integrated into the SQL language, yet it adds programming constructs that are not native to this standard relational database language. As you can see from the following code example, PL/SQL allows you to combine SQL statements with "standard" procedural constructs. This single program can either insert a company into or delete a company from the database. It relies on the IF statement (not a SQL statement) to determine which action to take:

```
PROCEDURE maintain_company
   (action_in IN VARCHAR2,
    id_in IN NUMBER,
    name_in IN VARCHAR2 := NULL)
IS
BEGIN
   IF action_in = 'DELETE'
   THEN
      DELETE FROM company WHERE company_id = id_in;
```

```
    ELSIF action_in = 'INSERT'
    THEN
        INSERT INTO company (company_id, name)
        VALUES (id_in, name_in);
    END IF;
END;
```

PL/SQL is an unusual—and an unusually powerful—programming language. You can write programs that look just like traditional 3GL modules, but you can also include calls to SQL statements, manipulate data through cursors, and take advantage of some of the newest developments in programming languages. PL/SQL supports packages which allow you to perform object-oriented design. PL/SQL provides a powerful mechanism for trapping and, with exception handlers, resolving errors. The tight integration of PL/SQL with SQL provides developers with the best of both worlds—declarative and procedural logic.

Figure 1-1 shows how PL/SQL fits within the client-server architecture of Oracle-based applications. It shows both an Oracle Forms client and a non-Oracle tool client, both executing against an Oracle Server database. Notice that the Oracle Forms client makes use of two versions of PL/SQL:

- PL/SQL Release 1.1: a client-side PL/SQL engine that allows the application to execute local PL/SQL programs

- PL/SQL Release 2.X: the server-based PL/SQL engine that executes stored programs

The third-party tool executes calls to stored programs, which are then run on the server.

Because PL/SQL is used both in the database (for stored procedures and database triggers) and in the application code (to implement logic within a form, for example), you can leverage the same programming language for both client-side and server-side development. You can even move programs from one component of the configuration to another.[*] For example, you might decide that a function which was originally coded for a single screen could be shared by all of the modules in an application. To make this happen, you simply move that function from the client-side screen component to the server-side database environment. You have to change neither the PL/SQL code nor any of the programs that call that function.

Of course, as an underlying technology in the Oracle constellation of products, PL/SQL is just one element of the total programming experience. In fact, building an Oracle-based application requires a combination of technology and techniques, as you'll see in the next section.

---

[*] As long as there are no conflicts between different versions of PL/SQL.

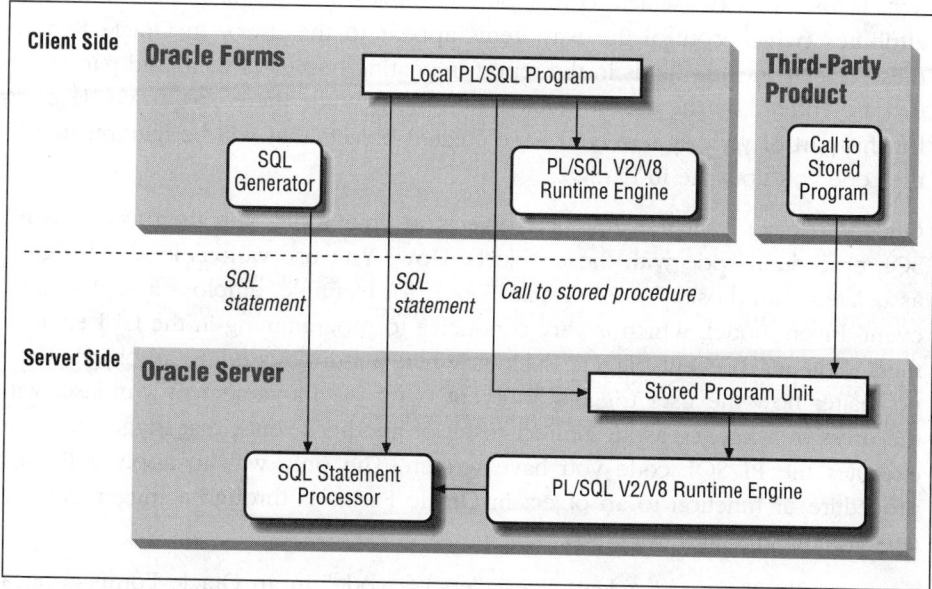

Figure 1-1. PL/SQL within the Oracle client-server architecture

The Concept of Programming in Oracle Applications

The whole idea of "programming" in Oracle-based applications has a somewhat different meaning from what you might be used to in a third-generation, or even a wholly procedural fourth-generation, language.

Programming in Oracle generally entails a blending of technologies and programming styles. Suppose, for example, that you are building an application to maintain invoice information. You will first design and create a database, relying mostly on the declarative SQL language. However, you might also create database triggers, coded in PL/SQL, to implement complex business rules at the database level. From there you build the screens, charts, and reports that make up the user interface. You could use third-party tools, or you could rely on Oracle Developer/ 2000 (formerly the Cooperative Development Environment, or CDE), with such products as Oracle Forms, Oracle Graphics, and Oracle Reports.

Each of the Oracle Developer/2000 tools employs a nondeclarative or "fill-in-the-blanks" approach to development. Without writing any code in the traditional sense, you create a full-functioned screen with buttons, radio groups, menus, and pictures. These objects are, more or less, the graphical pieces of the program that the user views, touches, and acts upon. They are somewhat different in each tool. In Oracle Forms, these objects include items on the screen (buttons, radio groups, text fields), blocks (which correspond to tables in the database), and visual attributes (which control the way items appear to the user). In Oracle Reports, these objects include fields in the report, repeating frames of data, and parameters that are entered by the user to initiate the report. While there isn't any code *per se* for this part of your system, you have created objects that will be manipulated by the code you do write in PL/SQL.

Once you have built the graphical objects in your tools, you then associate PL/SQL procedural code with those objects. How? You use various kinds of triggers associated with those objects. Oracle Forms, for example, employs a sophisticated event-driven model, which is very conducive to programming in the GUI environment. You attach event triggers, such as When-Button-Pressed, to an object. Then, no matter how the user triggers an event (with the movement of a mouse, with the press of a key, or as an indirect result of another event), that trigger fires and executes the PL/SQL code you have written. The only way to apply a PL/SQL procedure or function to an object in Oracle Forms is through a trigger. All triggers are implemented in PL/SQL.

Conceptually, there are at least five layers of "code" in an Oracle Forms application, as Table 1-1 shows. Each of these different kinds of code requires a different approach to programming.

Table 1-1. Layers of Code in an Oracle Forms Application

Code Level	Role of Code in Application
Graphical objects	Accessed directly by the user. (You can, of course, create objects which are "view only.")
Event triggers	Triggered by user activity; triggers are usually attached to events associated with a specific graphical object
Form-based PL/SQL	Executed by a trigger; implements nondeclarative, non-default functions in an application
RDBMS-based PL/SQL	Stored procedures and database triggers executed in response to actions initiated in the form
SQL	The data definition and data manipulation statements used to create and maintain the data in the Oracle Server

You may find the blend of technologies and programming environments that make up Oracle-based applications to be a challenge. If you are an experienced programmer, you might have worked for years in a 100% procedural language environment like COBOL. There, you've learned methodologies for designing and building your code. If you are asked to review a program, you can display those lines of text on a screen and do your analysis. In Oracle, you cannot.

If you are new to computer programming, the situation can be even worse. Introduced to powerful new technologies without any formal grounding in development, you may find yourself churning out screen after screen, report upon report, with little regard for code reusability, quality assurance, and development methodologies. And why should you? No one ever told you these issues were important. Instead, you received a week of training and were expected to move immediately to "rapid application development."

How can you apply your knowledge and experience to the world of Oracle? No matter where you came from, you will need to reconcile the different kinds of code and programming techniques. In this book we will try to help you do that.

The Origins of PL/SQL

Oracle has a history of leading the software industry in providing declarative, nonprocedural approaches to designing both databases and applications. The Oracle Server technology is among the most advanced, powerful, and stable relational databases in the world. Its application development tools, such as Oracle Forms, offer high levels of productivity, precisely by relying heavily on a "paint-your-screen" approach in which extensive default capabilities allow developers to avoid heavy customized programming efforts.

In Oracle's early years, this declarative approach, combined with its groundbreaking relational technology, was enough to satisfy developers. But as the industry matured, expectations and requirements became more demanding. Developers needed to get under the skin of the products. They needed to build complicated formulas, exceptions, and rules into their forms and database procedures.

In 1991, Oracle Corporation released Oracle Version 6.0, a major advance in its relational database technology. A key component of Oracle Version 6.0 was the so-called "procedural option" or PL/SQL. At roughly the same time, Oracle released its long-awaited upgrade to SQL*Forms Version 2.3. SQL*Forms V3.0 incorporated the PL/SQL engine for the first time on the tool side, allowing developers to code their procedural logic in a natural, straightforward manner.

This first release of PL/SQL was very limited in its capabilities. On the server side, you could use PL/SQL only to build "batch-processing" scripts of procedural and SQL statements. In other words, you could not store procedures or functions for execution at some later time. You could not construct a modular application or store complex business rules in the server. On the client side, SQL*Forms V3.0 did allow you to create procedures and functions, though support for functions was not documented and therefore not used by many developers for years. In addition, this release of PL/SQL did not implement array support and could not interact with the operating system (for input or output). It was a far cry from a full-fledged programming language.

For all its limitations, PL/SQL was warmly, even enthusiastically, received in the developer community. The hunger for the ability to code a simple IF statement inside SQL*Forms was strong. The need to perform multi-SQL statement batch processing was overwhelming.

What few developers realized at the time was that the original motivation and driving vision behind PL/SQL extended beyond the desire to offer programmatic control within products like SQL*Forms. Very early in the life cycle of Oracle's database and tools, Oracle Corporation had recognized two key weaknesses in their architecture: lack of portability and problems with execution authority.

Improved Application Portability with PL/SQL

The concern about portability might seem odd to those of us familiar with Oracle Corporation's marketing and technical strategies. One of the hallmarks of the Oracle solution from the early 1980s was its portability. At the time that PL/SQL came along, the C-based RDBMS ran on many different operating systems and hardware platforms. SQL*Plus and SQL*Forms adapted easily to a variety of terminal configurations. Yet for all that coverage, there were still many applications which needed the more sophisticated and granular control offered by host languages like COBOL, C, and FORTRAN. As soon as a developer stepped outside of the port-neutral Oracle tools, the resulting application would no longer be portable.

The PL/SQL language was (and is) intended to widen the range of application requirements which can be handled entirely in operating-system independent programming tools.

Improved Execution Authority and Transaction Integrity with PL/SQL

Even more fundamental an issue than portability was that of execution authority. The RDBMS and SQL language give you the capability to tightly control access to, and changes in, any particular table. For example, with the GRANT command you can make sure that only certain roles and users have the ability to perform an UPDATE on a given table. On the other hand, this GRANT statement can't ensure that the full set of UPDATEs performed by a user or application is done correctly. In other words, the database can't guarantee the integrity of a transaction that spans more than one table.

Let's look at an example. In a typical banking transaction, you might need to transfer funds from account A to account B. The balance of account B must be incremented, and that of account A decremented. Table access is necessary, but not sufficient, to guarantee that both of these steps are always performed by all programmers who write code to perform a transfer. Without stored objects, the best you can do is require extensive testing and code review to make sure that all transactions are properly constructed. With stored objects, on the other hand, you can guarantee that a funds transfer either completes successfully or is completely rolled back—regardless of who executes the process.

The secret to achieving this level of transaction integrity is the concept of *execute authority* (also known as *run authority*). Instead of granting to a role or user the authority to update a table, you grant privileges to only execute a procedure. This procedure controls and provides access to the underlying data structures. The procedure is owned by a separate Oracle RDBMS account, which, in turn, is granted the actual update privileges on those tables needed to perform the transaction. The procedure therefore becomes the "gatekeeper" for the transfer transaction. The only way a program (whether it's an Oracle Forms application or a Pro*C executable) can execute the transfer is through the procedure. The result is that transaction integrity is guaranteed.

The long-term objective of PL/SQL, realized with PL/SQL Version 2.0, was to provide a programming environment which would allow developers both to create reusable, callable modules and also to grant authority to those modules. Given Oracle Corporation's strategic technical investment in relational databases, it's only logical that these programs would reside in the database itself. This way, the same data dictionary that controls access to data could control access to the programs.

PL/SQL has come a long way from its humble beginnings. It is a rapidly maturing programming language that will play a prominent role in all future Oracle application development and database management efforts.

PL/SQL Versions

One thing that may complicate using PL/SQL is that it is not a single product. There are several distinct, supported versions out there. Table 1-2 summarizes the various versions; the following sections describe the main features available in each of the versions in use today.

Table 1-2. PL/SQL Versions

Version/Release	Characteristics
Version 1.0	First available in SQL*Plus as a batch-processing script. Oracle Version 6.0 was released at approximately the same time. PL/SQL was then implemented within SQL*Forms Version 3, the predecessor of Oracle Forms.

Table 1-2. PL/SQL Versions (continued)

Version/Release	Characteristics
Release 1.1	Available only in the Oracle Developer/2000 Release 1 tools. This upgrade supports client-side packages and allows client-side programs to execute stored code transparently.
Version 2.0	Available with Release 7.0 (Oracle Server). Major upgrade to Version 1. Adds support for stored procedures, functions, packages, programmer-defined records, PL/SQL tables, and many package extensions, including DBMS_OUTPUT and DBMS_PIPE.
Release 2.1	Available with Release 7.1 of the Oracle Server Version. Supports programmer-defined subtypes, enables the use of stored functions inside SQL statements, and offers dynamic SQL with the DBMS_SQL package. With Version 2.1, you can now execute SQL DDL statements from within PL/SQL programs.
Release 2.2	Available with Release 7.2 of the Oracle Server Version. Implements a binary "wrapper" for PL/SQL programs to protect source code, supports cursor variables for embedded PL/SQL environments such as Pro*C, and makes available database-driven job scheduling with the DBMS_JOB package.
Release 2.3	Available with Release 7.3 of the Oracle Server Version. Enhances functionality of PL/SQL tables, offers improved remote dependency management, adds file I/O capabilities to PL/SQL, and completes the implementation of cursor variables.
Version 8.0	Available with Oracle8 Release 8.0. The drastic change in version number reflects Oracle's effort to synchronize version numbers across related products. PL/SQL8 is the version of PL/SQL which supports the many enhancements of Oracle8, including large objects (LOBs), object-oriented design and development, collections (VARRAYs and nested tables), and Oracle/AQ (the Oracle/Advanced Queueing facility).

Working with Multiple Versions of PL/SQL

All of the releases of PL/SQL Version 2 are linked directly to the release of the Oracle Server on which they run. PL/SQL Release 1.1 is available only with the Oracle Developer/2000 Release 1 tools. The presence of these different versions can make your life complicated. Consider the following scenarios:

- You want to take full advantage of all the latest features of the Oracle software family, from the frontend tools to the backend RDBMS and stored procedures. You will therefore use PL/SQL Release 1.1 (until Oracle makes available the second version of its Oracle Developer/2000 toolset) to build client-side programs and will use PL/SQL Release 2.X through PL/SQL8 for your stored programs.

- You develop applications in a distributed environment and support different versions of the Oracle Server on different platforms. If you need to build stored programs to run in each of these databases, you will need to work with more than one release of PL/SQL.

Given this complexity, you need to be aware of the differences between the releases, as well as restrictions on PL/SQL development in Release 1.1 of PL/SQL.

How This Book Handles Different Versions of PL/SQL

This book uses Version 2.0 of the PL/SQL language as the "base" version for purposes of presenting the technology. If you are using any of the more recent releases of the PL/SQL language (2.1, 2.2, 2.3, or 8.0), you will be able to take advantage of all the standard features of PL/SQL and, in addition, leverage the enhancements of that release. If you are using Release 1.1 of PL/SQL, you will not be able to use *all* the features of Versions 2.0 through Version 8.0.

The new Oracle8-related functionality (delivered in PL/SQL8) is covered primarily in Part V. Additional coverage of PL/SQL8-specific features is provided in chapters which cover that area of technology. For example, Chapter 4, *Variables and Program Data*, introduces the new datatypes of PL/SQL8, including large objects (LOBs).

I will note explicitly throughout the book when a particular feature is available only in a specific PL/SQL version or release. If this book does not cover a particular feature, that is mentioned as well.

The following sections summarize the new features of each PL/SQL release, as well as the restrictions placed on the use of PL/SQL Release 1.1. Review these sections now so you can more easily identify and use them later in your programming efforts.

NOTE   If you are using the Oracle Developer/2000 suite of development tools, then you will be using PL/SQL Release 1.1 for all local PL/SQL programs. You may also run PL/SQL Version 2-based programs stored in the database from the Oracle Developer/2000 application. See the section below for those features of PL/SQL Version 2.0 that may be used in programs based on PL/SQL Release 1.1.

PL/SQL Version 2.0

PL/SQL Version 2.0 was first released with the Oracle Server and expanded significantly the ability of PL/SQL to support large-scale, complex, distributed application development efforts. With Version 2.0, you can modularize your programs into procedures, functions, and—most importantly—packages. You can store your modules in the database and call them from any Oracle session, on both the client and server sides of distributed applications.

The features of PL/SQL Version 2.0 are described in the following sections.

Integration with SQL

PL/SQL was originally designed to provide procedural extensions to the SQL language. From within PL/SQL you can execute any DML statement (SELECT, UPDATE, INSERT, and DELETE). You cannot, however, execute a DDL statement, such as CREATE TABLE. This capability is available only in later releases through the use of specially provided packages, such as DBMS_SQL.

This integration with SQL also means that from within the native PL/SQL language you can make full use of all SQL operators, predicates, and built-in functions. Outside a SQL statement you can call the TO_CHAR function to convert a date to a string and check to see if one string is LIKE another string (an operator usually found in the WHERE clause of a SQL statement).

In addition to DML statements, you can use SQL's transaction-oriented statements to commit and roll back transactions. You can also mark SAVEPOINTs and roll back to those intermediate phases in a transaction.

Because the SQL is called from within PL/SQL, you can make use of PL/SQL constructs in the SQL statement. The following example references the PL/SQL variable last_hire_date in the WHERE clause of a SELECT statement:

```
SELECT employee.last_name    -- Database column
    INTO new_hire_name       -- Local PL/SQL variable
    FROM employee            -- Name of table
    WHERE hire_date =        -- References column and PL/SQL variable
            last_hire_date;
```

With Version 2.0, PL/SQL also supports the syntax required to perform distributed SQL. The following update changes the data in a remote table by selecting information from a second remote table:

```
UPDATE employee@NEW_YORK
    SET salary = (SELECT MAX(salary)
                    FROM employee@TORONTO);
```

NEW_YORK and TORONTO are database links to employee tables in different database instances (presumably in those cities).

PL/SQL Version 2.0 also lets you include hints to the optimizer (structured as comments within the SQL statement, enclosed by the /* and */ delimiters) to modify the execution plan used by the optimizer.

Expanded set of datatypes for variables and constants

PL/SQL lets you declare local variables and constants and then use those identifiers in your PL/SQL program. You can declare the variables and constants to be a datatype known to the RDBMS, such as NUMBER or VARCHAR2. However, you can also make use of PL/SQL-specific data structures such as:

BOOLEAN

A true Boolean datatype whose value is TRUE, FALSE, or NULL.

BINARY_INTEGER

Similar to NUMBER, BINARY_INTEGER datatype represents values as signed binary numbers of virtually any size. Because signed binary is the internal format for numeric values, you can perform calculations with this datatype that do not require any conversions.

PL/SQL record

A record contains one or more fields and is similar to a row in a database table. You can assign values to variables and SELECT information from the database into these variables.

In addition to these datatypes, PL/SQL Version 2.0 has added ROWID, RAW, LONG RAW, and MLSLABEL (for Trusted Oracle). PL/SQL Version 2.0 also predefines a set of "subtypes," which applies constraints to an existing "base" subtype. These subtypes include NATURAL (all integers greater than zero, a subtype of BINARY_INTEGER), and REAL (a subtype of NUMBER).

Programmer-defined records

A *record* is a composite data structure, consisting of one or more fields or columns. A record in PL/SQL roughly corresponds to a row in a database table. With earlier versions of PL/SQL, you can create records using the %ROWTYPE attribute; however, these records can only reflect the structure of a table or cursor. With PL/SQL Version 2.0, you can create records with whatever structure you decide upon, completely independent of any particular table or cursor. A programmer-defined record may even have another record as a field in its record, thereby allowing nested records and the ability to represent real-world structures in your programs.

Here is an example of the definition of a record type, followed by a declaration of the actual record:

```
DECLARE
    /* Create a record to hold four quarters of sales data. */
    TYPE sales_quarters_rectype IS RECORD
        (q1_sales NUMBER,
         q2_sales NUMBER,
         q3_sales NUMBER,
```

```
            q4_sales NUMBER);
    /*
    || Create a record to hold sales information for a customer.
    || Notice the nested record.
    */
    TYPE customer_sales_rectype IS RECORD
        (customer_id NUMBER (5),
         customer_name customer.name%TYPE,
         total_sales NUMBER (15,2),
         sales_by_quarter sales_quarters_rectype);

    /* Create a record for use in the program of this record type. */
    customer_sales_rec customer_sales_rectype;
BEGIN
```

You can pass records as parameters and perform aggregate assignments with records—that is, with a single assignment operation you can assign all the values of one record to another, compatible record.

PL/SQL tables

One of the first questions I ever heard posed about PL/SQL Version 1.1 was, "Where are the arrays?" Programmers who coded in the nonprocedural interface of SQL*Forms, after spending a decade with languages like FORTRAN and C, got all excited when they heard about PL/SQL: they thought they'd get all the good stuff they had in their 3GL environments—particularly arrays. Imagine the shock and disappointment when PL/SQL not only lacked the ability to read and write disk files, but also did not support arrays!

The designers of the PL/SQL language recognized the need to manipulate data in array-like structures in memory, but they also wanted to make sure to maintain PL/SQL's nature as an extension to SQL. The result is the PL/SQL table, available with Version 2.0.

The PL/SQL table is a memory-resident object that gives you array-like access to rows of information. It is similar to, but not the same as, a database table. Currently, a PL/SQL table may contain only one column (with the datatype of your choice) and one primary key (with a mandatory datatype of BINARY_INTEGER). The following declaration section contains the definition of a table type, followed by the declaration of a table, that can be used in a program:

```
DECLARE
    /* Table of strings to hold company names. */
    TYPE company_names_tabtype IS TABLE OF
        VARCHAR2(100) INDEX BY BINARY_INTEGER;

    /* Declaration of actual table to be used in code. */
    company_names company_names_tabtype;
BEGIN
```

PL/SQL tables can be passed as parameters in modules. Unlike arrays found in 3GL programs, PL/SQL tables are unconstrained and sparse. *Unconstrained* means that, as with database tables, you do not have to decide the size of a PL/SQL table in advance. *Sparse* means that the only rows defined in memory are those you create with an assignment to that row.

Built-in functions

PL/SQL Version 2.0 supports a wide range of built-in functions to manipulate data in your programs. These built-ins may be categorized as follows:

Character functions
Functions that analyze and modify the contents of CHAR and VARCHAR2 string variables

Date functions
Utilities that allow programmers to perform high-level actions on date variables, including date arithmetic

Numeric functions
A full range of functions that manipulate numbers, including trigonometric, logarithmic, and exponential functions

Conversion functions
Functions that convert from one datatype to another, often formatting the output data at the same time

Built-in packages

In addition to the built-in functions, each release of PL/SQL offers built-in packages, which bundle together related programs. These packages will prove to be invaluable in your development efforts; they are summarized in Appendix C, *Built-in Packages*. Here are some examples of built-in packages available with PL/SQL Release 2.0:

DBMS_OUTPUT
Displays information to the screen; useful for debugging PL/SQL scripts.

DBMS_PIPE
Communicates between Oracle sessions via "pipes." Oracle Corporation uses this package to parallelize their database, and you can use it to parallelize your own programs.

DBMS_LOCK
Requests and manages programmer-defined locks.

You would, for example, use the PUT_LINE procedure in the DBMS_OUTPUT package to display information to your screen (or, in the case of the World Wide Web, to your home page):

```
DBMS_OUTPUT.PUT_LINE ('Option selected is ' || option_desc);
```

Control structures

PL/SQL provides procedural extensions to SQL to implement the following types of control structures:

- *Conditional control* via IF statements
- *Iterative control* via loops, including FOR, WHILE, and simple loops
- *Sequential control* via GOTO and NULL statements

The following variations of conditional control constructs are available: IF-END IF, IF-ELSE-END IF, and IF-ELSIF-ELSE-END IF. However, PL/SQL does not support a CASE structure. All variations of the conditional structures end with an END IF statement. The result of this is a highly structured block orientation. Here is an example of an IF-ELSIF-ELSE statement:

```
IF average_salary < 10000
THEN
   bonus := 2000;

ELSIF average_salary BETWEEN 10000 AND 20000
THEN
   bonus := 1000;

ELSE
   bonus := 500;

END IF;
```

PL/SQL supports a number of different types of loops:

- WHILE loops
- FOR loops (numeric and cursor)
- Infinite or "simple" loops

These constructs allow you to execute the same code repeatedly. You can nest loops within loops. All loops end with an END LOOP statement, which results in a highly structured block orientation for your loops. Here is an example of a WHILE loop which, in turn, contains a FOR loop:

```
WHILE still_searching
LOOP
   FOR month_index IN 1 .. 12
   LOOP
      calculate_profits (month_index);
```

```
        END LOOP;
    END LOOP;
```

PL/SQL Version 2.0 also supports the GOTO statement and the NULL statement. GOTO transfers control from one executable statement to any other statement in the current program body. You can specify the NULL statement if you want to "do nothing"—and, believe it or not, there are a number of times when that is all you want to do! This example illustrates both statements:

```
    IF rooms_available = 0
    THEN
        GOTO no_rooms;
    ELSE
        reserve_a_room;
    END IF;

    <<no_rooms>>
    NULL;
```

Cursor-based access to the database

One of the most important features of PL/SQL is the ability to handle data one row at a time. SQL is a set-at-a-time database language. You cannot selectively examine or modify a single row from a SELECT statement's result set. With PL/SQL Version 2.0's cursors, however, you can attain much finer control over manipulation of information from the database. Cursors in PL/SQL can be opened, fetched from, and closed. You can use the cursor FOR loop to access all the records in a cursor quickly and easily. PL/SQL Version 1.1 also provides a useful set of cursor attributes to let you determine the current status of a cursor.

The following example declares the cursor based on a SELECT statement (along with a record to hold the information fetched from the cursor), then opens, fetches from, and closes the cursor. Before opening the cursor, the code checks the cursor attribute %ISOPEN to see if it is already open:

```
DECLARE
    CURSOR extinction_cur IS
        SELECT species_name, last_sighting
          FROM rainforest
         WHERE year = 1994
           AND number_species_left = 0;
    extinction_rec extinction_cur%ROWTYPE;

    expedition_leader VARCHAR2(100);
BEGIN
    /* Only open the cursor if it is not already open. */
    IF NOT extinction_cur%ISOPEN
    THEN
        OPEN extinction_cur;
    END IF;
```

```
      /* Fetch the next record. */
      FETCH extinction_cur INTO extinction_rec;

      /* Execute statements based on record contents. */
      IF extinction_rec.last_sighting = 'BRAZIL'
      THEN
          expedition_leader := 'RAMOS';

      ELSIF extinction_rec.last_sighting = 'BACKYARD'
      THEN
          expedition_leader := 'FEUERSTEIN';
      END IF;

      /* Close the cursor. */
      CLOSE extinction_cur;
   END;
```

Error handling

PL/SQL Version 2.0 traps and responds to errors, called *exceptions*, using an event-driven model. When an error occurs, an exception is raised. The normal processing in your program halts, and control is transferred to the separate exception handling section of your program (if it exists).

The exception handler mechanism allows you to cleanly separate your error-processing code from your executable statements. It provides an event-driven model, as opposed to a linear code model, for processing errors. In other words, no matter how a particular exception is raised, it is handled by the same exception handler in the exception section.

The following PL/SQL block attempts to select information from the employee and includes an exception handler for the case in which no data is found:

```
DECLARE
    soc_sec_number NUMBER;
BEGIN
    SELECT social_security#
      INTO soc_sec_number
      FROM employee
     WHERE last_name = 'FEUERSTEIN';
EXCEPTION
   WHEN NO_DATA_FOUND
   THEN
       INSERT INTO employee
           (last_name, first_name,
            social_security#, hire_date, department_id)
       VALUES
           ('FEUERSTEIN', 'STEVEN', '123456789', SYSDATE, 10);
END;
```

In other words, if I am not already an employee in the company, the SELECT statement fails and control is transferred to the exception section (which starts with the keyword EXCEPTION). PL/SQL matches up the exception raised with the exception in the WHEN clause (NO_DATA_FOUND is a named, internal exception that represents ORA-01403-no data found). It then executes the statements in that exception handler, so I am promptly inserted into the employee table.

Modular construction

The ability to create modules ("black boxes") which can call each other is central to any successful programming language. Modularization of code allows you to break down complex operations into smaller, more comprehensible steps. You can then combine ("plug and play") your different modules together as building blocks.

PL/SQL is itself a block-oriented language: all code is organized into one or more blocks demarked by BEGIN and END statements. These blocks provide a high degree of structure to PL/SQL-based programs, making it easier to both develop and maintain the code. PL/SQL Version 2.0 offers both unnamed blocks (also called *anonymous blocks*) and named blocks. There are two types of named blocks: procedures and functions. A *procedure* is a sequence of executable statements that performs a particular action. A *function* is a block that returns a value. Here are two examples of modules:

```
PROCEDURE display_emp_status (status_code_in IN VARCHAR2)
/* Display a message depending on the status code supplied as a parameter. */
IS
BEGIN
   IF status_code_in = 'O'
   THEN
      DBMS_OUTPUT.PUT_LINE ('Status is Open.');
   ELSE
      DBMS_OUTPUT.PUT_LINE ('Status is Closed.');
   END IF;
END;
FUNCTION total_compensation
   (salary_in IN NUMBER, commission_in IN NUMBER) RETURN NUMBER
/*
|| Calculate and return total compensation. If commission is NULL
|| then add zero to salary.
*/
IS
BEGIN
   RETURN salary_in + NVL (commission_in, 0);
END;
```

Procedures and functions are commonly found in programming languages. But PL/SQL goes beyond this level of modularization to also offer a construct called the *package*. A package is a collection of objects, including modules and other constructs, such as cursors, variables, exceptions, and records.

The package is probably the single most important and powerful addition to the PL/SQL language. With packages, PL/SQL Version 2.0 supports object-oriented design and concepts such as information hiding, encapsulation, and reusability. With packages, you can decide which code is publicly available to programmers and which code should be hidden. In addition, you can implement global variables, data structures, and values, which persist for the entire duration of a user session.

Stored procedures, functions, and packages

In combination with the expanded data dictionary of Oracle Server Version 7, you can store your modules (procedures and functions) and packages inside the database itself. These stored modules—usually referred to simply as *stored procedures*—can then be executed by any Oracle session that has access to the modules. With stored procedures, PL/SQL now also supports remote procedure calls; a program on one server or client workstation can run programs stored on different servers, connected by SQL*Net.

With the advent of stored procedures, the Oracle RDBMS becomes a repository not only for data, but for program code itself. A shared area of memory, the Shared Global Area (SGA), caches compiled PL/SQL programs and supplies those objects to the PL/SQL runtime engine when needed by an Oracle session. The database manages dependencies between code and database structures and will automatically recompile invalid modules.

Stored packages also can offer improved performance because all programs in a package are loaded into memory at the same time.

PL/SQL Release 2.1

PL/SQL Release 2.1 is the release of Version 2 that comes with Version 7.1 of the Oracle Server. It supports all the features listed for PL/SQL Release 2.0 and also adds the new capabilities described in the following sections.

Stored functions in SQL

The single most important enhancement in Release 2.1 is the ability to call stored functions (written in PL/SQL) from within a SQL statement. You can call stored functions anywhere in a SQL statement where an expression is allowed—in the SELECT, WHERE, START WITH, GROUP BY, HAVING, ORDER BY, SET, and VALUES clauses. (Stored procedures, on the other hand, are in and of themselves PL/SQL executable statements; they cannot be embedded in a SQL statement.) You can use one of your own functions just as you would a built-in SQL function, such as TO_DATE, SUBSTR, or LENGTH.

The following SELECT statement calls the total_compensation function defined earlier in this chapter. This saves you from having to code the calculation explicitly:

```
SELECT last_name, total_compensation (salary, commission)
  FROM employee
 ORDER BY total_compensation (salary, commission) DESC;
```

The ability to place PL/SQL functions inside SQL is a very powerful enhancement to the Oracle development environment. With these functions you can:

- Consolidate business rule logic into a smaller number of well-tuned and easily maintained functions. You do not have to repeat this logic across individual SQL statements and PL/SQL programs.

- Improve the performance of your SQL statements. SQL is a nonprocedural language, yet application requirements often demand procedural logic in your SQL. The SQL language is robust enough to let you get at the answer, but in many situations it is a very inefficient way to get that answer. Embedded PL/SQL can do the job much more quickly.

- Simplify your SQL statements. All the reasons you have to modularize your PL/SQL code apply to SQL as well—particularly the need to hide complicated expressions and logic behind a function specification. From the DECODE statement to nested, correlated sub-SELECTs, the readability of many SQL statements will benefit from programmer-defined functions.

Support for DDL and dynamic SQL

One of the packages provided with Oracle Server Release 7.1 is the DBMS_SQL package. The modules in this package allow you to execute dynamic SQL DDL and DML statements. A SQL statement is *dynamic* when it is not parsed and bound at compile time. Instead, the statement itself is constructed at runtime and then is passed to the SQL engine for processing.

Dynamic SQL, particularly with DDL statements, offers many possibilities. The following procedure provides a programmatic interface to drop any kind of object from the data dictionary:

```
PROCEDURE drop_object
   (object_type_in IN VARCHAR2, object_name_in IN VARCHAR2)
IS
   cursor_id INTEGER;
BEGIN
   /*
   || Open a cursor which will handle the dynamic SQL statement.
   || The function returns the pointer to that cursor.
   */
   cursor_id := DBMS_SQL.OPEN_CURSOR;
   /*
   || Parse and execute the drop command which is formed through
   || concatenation of the arguments.
```

```
      */
   DBMS_SQL.PARSE
      (cursor_id,
       'DROP ' || object_type_in || ' ' || object_name_in,
       DBMS_SQL.NATIVE);

   /* Close the cursor. */
   DBMS_SQL.CLOSE_CURSOR (cursor_id);
EXCEPTION
   /* If any problem arises, also make sure the cursor is closed. */
   WHEN OTHERS
   THEN
       DBMS_SQL.CLOSE_CURSOR (cursor_id);
END;
```

I can now drop the employee table or the total_compensation function by executing the following calls to drop_object:

```
drop_object ('table', 'employee');

drop_object ('function', 'total_compensation');
```

Entry-level ANSI SQL92 support

PL/SQL Release 2.1 lets you reference column aliases in the ORDER BY clause of a DML statement. You can also use the AS keyword to define aliases in the SELECT clause of a query. In other words, you can now write a cursor in the following way:

```
DECLARE
   CURSOR profit_cur IS
      SELECT company_id, SUM (revenue) - SUM (cost) net_profit
         FROM fin_performance
         ORDER BY net_profit DESC;
BEGIN
```

In the past, you would have had to repeat the difference of SUMs in the ORDER BY clause or simply write ORDER BY 2.

Programmer-defined subtypes

In addition to the subtypes provided by PL/SQL itself, PL/SQL Release 2.1 lets you create your own subtypes of native datatypes. Programmer-defined subtypes improve the readability and maintainability of your code. Here is an example of a definition of a subtype:

```
SUBTYPE primary_key_type IS NATURAL;
```

In this case, I create a datatype called primary_key_type of type NATURAL. Now, when I declare a variable with this type, it must be a nonzero, positive integer.

In Release 2.1, these subtypes must be unconstrained—you cannot define a subtype as VARCHAR2(30), only as VARCHAR2.

PL/SQL Release 2.2

PL/SQL Release 2.2 is the release of Version 2 that comes with Version 7.2 of the Oracle Server. It supports all of the features previously listed in this chapter and also adds the new capabilities described in the following sections.

The PL/SQL wrapper

The PL/SQL wrapper is a standalone utility that transforms PL/SQL source code into portable binary, object code. "Wrapped" or encrypted PL/SQL source code hides the internals of your application. With Release 2.2, you can distribute software without having to worry about exposing your proprietary algorithms and methods to competitors. The PL/SQL compiler automatically recognizes and loads wrapped PL/SQL program units.

Cursor variables

Prior to PL/SQL Release 2.2, you could only declare and manipulate "static" cursors—cursors that are bound at design time to a specific query and a specific cursor name. With Release 2.2, you can now declare a cursor variable and open it for any compatible query. Most importantly, you can pass and receive cursor variables as arguments to modules. Cursor variables offer tremendous new flexibility in centralizing and controlling the SQL statements in your applications.

In Release 2.2, cursor variables may only appear where PL/SQL code is embedded in a host language environment, such as the precompilers and the OCI layer. While you can OPEN a cursor with a cursor variable in your PL/SQL block, you cannot yet FETCH from that cursor. Cursor variables are made fully available within PL/SQL programs in Release 2.3, described later in this chapter.

Job scheduling with DBMS_JOB

With PL/SQL Release 2.2, Oracle Corporation offers DBMS_JOB, a new package that allows you to schedule jobs within the database itself. Oracle uses DBMS_JOB to manage its snapshot facility. You can use it to run jobs on a regular basis. A job can be any valid PL/SQL block of code, from a single SQL statement to a complex series of calls to stored procedures.

PL/SQL Release 2.3

PL/SQL Release 2.3 is the release of Version 2 that comes with Version 7.3 of the Oracle Server. It supports all of the features previously listed in this chapter and also adds the new capabilities described in the following sections.

File I/O with the UTL_FILE package

Far and away the most exciting feature of Release 2.3 is the UTL_FILE package. This collection of built-in functions and procedures allows you to read from and write to operating system files from within PL/SQL. This is a capability for which programmers have been clamoring since PL/SQL first became available.

Cursor variables for all PL/SQL environments

With Release 2.3, cursor variables (described under Release 2.2) can now be used in any PL/SQL environments, and do not rely on a host language environment. You can OPEN, FETCH from, and CLOSE cursors using standard PL/SQL syntax. In addition, all cursor attributes are now available for use with cursor variables. Release 2.3 also supports a "weak" cursor type which allows you to declare a cursor variable without having to specify its record structure.

Expanded PL/SQL table capabilities

Release 2.3 allows you to create PL/SQL tables of records, as opposed to simple scalar values, such as NUMBERs. In addition, it offers a set of operators or built-ins, which provide you with additional, heretofore unavailable, information about the PL/SQL table, including the following:

COUNT
  Returns the number of rows defined in the PL/SQL table

LAST
  Returns the number of the highest row defined in the PL/SQL table

DELETE
  Deletes rows from the table

PL/SQL tables of records are especially useful for representing database tables in memory.

Improved remote dependency model

Prior to Release 2.3 (and the underlying Oracle Server Release 7.3), PL/SQL modules that depended on remote objects (stored procedures or tables, for example) would be flagged as invalid whenever the remote object was modified. This module emphasized safety and correctness, but was also unnecessarily restrictive. For example, as long as the call interface of a procedure has not changed (its name and parameters), any program that calls that procedure should not have to be recompiled.

Release 2.3 offers a choice between the original, "timestamp" dependency model and the new, "signature" dependency model. The signature model will only flag a client-side module as invalid (requiring a recompile) if the remote stored procedure has been modified and if the signature or call interface of the program has changed.

PL/SQL Version 8.0

PL/SQL Version 8.0 (PL/SQL8) is the version of PL/SQL that comes with Oracle 8.0, the "object-relational" version of the Oracle database. PL/SQL8 incorporates numerous significant new features and many incremental improvements. PL/SQL8 features are summarized in the following sections and are covered in this book primarily in Part V. The following overview is not intended to be a comprehensive description of new Oracle8 features; it covers only those aspects of Oracle8 that have an impact on PL/SQL developers.

Support for an object-oriented model

When a mainstream vendor like Oracle Corporation ventures into new technology waters, it is virtually certain that the change will be evolutionary rather than revolutionary. True to form, Oracle8's relational capabilities are still the mainstay of Oracle Corporation's flagship database server, and they satisfy the need for compatibility with older Oracle versions. But with the objects option, Oracle8 allows programmers to use a new set of datatypes and models drawn from object programming languages, allowing persistent objects to be created in the database and accessed, via an API, from C++, Smalltalk, Object COBOL, Java, and other languages.

Contrast this "object-relational" database approach with the true "object-oriented databases" (OODBs) that first appeared commercially in the mid-1980s. Most successful in problem domains characterized by complex, often versioned, data (such as engineering, CASE, or CAD), pure OODBs typically extend the type system of object-oriented languages to allow for persistent objects. Oracle8, on the other hand, extends the programming system of the database to allow for operations, and extends conventional datatypes to include complex structures. While these object extensions to SQL and PL/SQL sometimes look as if they were designed simply to confuse the programmer, object types in Oracle8, properly implemented, can be the cornerstone of an overall object strategy.

See Chapter 18, *Object Types*, for details.

Oracle/AQ, the Advanced Queueing Facility

Oracle8 offers an "advanced queuing" facility which implements deferred execution of work. Oracle is positioning Oracle/AQ (Oracle/Advanced Queuing) as an alternative to the queuing mechanisms of teleprocessing monitors and messaging interfaces. Oracle/AQ will also serve as a foundation technology for workflow management applications.

Oracle/AQ is available from within PL/SQL programs through the DBMS_AQ built-in package. This package is described briefly in Appendix C and is covered in detail in Steven's upcoming book, *Oracle Built-in Packages*.

Variable arrays and nested tables

Oracle8 introduces two new "collection" structures that will support a wide range of application requirements. These structures are nested tables and variable-size arrays (VARRAYs). As with Oracle8's table datatype, the new structures can be used in PL/SQL programs. But what is dramatically new is the ability to use the new collections as the datatypes of fields in conventional tables and attributes of objects. While not an exhaustive implementation of user-defined datatypes, collections offer rich new physical (and, by extension, logical) design opportunities for Oracle practitioners.

Using a collection, you can actually store a "table within a table." Relational diehards may chafe at the thought, but you can use collections as a way of putting non-first-normal-form data into a table—entire sets of "detail data" can be squished into a column! No longer do columns need to be "atomic" in order to be retrievable or updateable. Why would you want to do this? Even setting aside theoretical arguments about "natural" data representations, Oracle8 collections provide a dramatic advantage from an application programmer's perspective: you can pass an entire collection between the database and PL/SQL using a single fetch. Under the right circumstances, you can even "pretend" that conventional data is a collection, and realize the same single-call advantages.

See Chapter 19, *Nested Tables and VARRAYs*, for more information.

Object views

As an "object-relational" database, Oracle8 allows both objects and relational tables to coexist. If you wish, you can read and write both objects and relations in the same PL/SQL program. Using "object views," you can even make rows or columns in relational tables look and behave like objects. Object views allow the application programmer to enjoy many of the benefits of objects—such as efficient access, convenient navigation alternatives, and consistency with new object-based applications—when working with an underlying database of conventional tables.

Oracle Corporation emphasizes the ability of object views to ease an organization's transition to object-based design and programming. In addition to this benefit, object views also provide a means of evolving object schema designs. Since you can redefine or rebuild object views at any time, a view-based object schema is much more pliable than a table-based object schema. (Oracle 8.0.3 provides virtually no support for modifying table-based object schema.)

As of Oracle 8.0, object views (and conventional views for that matter) can have their own triggers. These "INSTEAD OF" triggers allow you to write PL/SQL code to support insert, update, or delete through almost any view you can dream up.

See Chapter 20, *Object Views*, for examples and more discussion.

External procedures

This long-awaited Oracle feature allows you to call anything that you can compile into the native "shared library" format of the operating system. The external procedures feature is reliable and multi-user. Communication is bidirectional and, importantly, you can use external procedures as user-defined functions in SQL.

Under UNIX, a shared library is a shared object or *.so* file; under Windows NT, it's a DLL (dynamic linked library). You can write the external routine in any language you wish, as long as your compiler and linker will generate the appropriate shared library format that is callable from C. In Oracle 8.0, however, C will be the most common language for external procedures, since all of Oracle's support libraries are written in C.

See Chapter 21, *External Procedures*, for further details and examples.

Large object support

Oracle8 and PL/SQL8 support several variations of LOB or Large OBject datatypes. LOBs can store large amounts (up to four gigabytes) of raw data, binary data (such as images), or character text data.

Within PL/SQL you can declare LOB variables of the following datatypes:

BFILE

Declares variables which hold a file locator pointing to a large binary object in an operating system file outside the database

BLOB

Declares variables which hold a LOB locator pointing to a large binary object

CLOB

Declares variables which hold a LOB locator pointing to a large block of single-byte, fixed-width character data

NCLOB

Declares variables which hold a LOB locator pointing to a large block of single-byte or fixed-width multibyte character data

There are two types of LOBs in Oracle8: internal and external. Internal LOBs (BLOBs, CLOBs, and NCLOBs) are stored in the database and can participate in transactions in the database server. External LOBs (BFILEs) are large binary data stored in operating system files outside the database tablespaces. External LOBs cannot participate in transactions. You cannot, in other words, commit or roll back changes to a BFILE. Instead, you rely on the underlying filesystem for data integrity.

Chapter 4, *Variables and Program Data*, and Chapter 13, *Numeric, LOB, and Miscellaneous Functions*, provide additional details.

PL/SQL Release 1.1

PL/SQL Release 1.1 is only used by the tools in the Oracle Developer/2000 suite: Oracle Forms, Oracle Reports, and Oracle Graphics. Table 1-3 reviews PL/SQL Version 2.0 functionality and indicates any restrictions or special information you will need in order to determine if and how you can make use of those features under Release 1.1.

Table 1-3. PL/SQL Version 1.1 Restrictions

PL/SQL Version 2.0 Feature	Restrictions for Version 1.1
Integration with SQL	You cannot perform distributed DML statements.
Expanded set of datatypes for variables and constants	The BINARY_INTEGER datatype is only available in Version 2.0.
Programmer-defined records	This feature is undocumented in PL/SQL Version 1.1 manuals, but is available.
Built-in functions	The trigonometric, logarithmic, and other "scientific" functions are not implemented.
Built-in packages	You can make use of built-in packages both in the database and in the particular tool. Oracle Forms, for example, offers the OLE package for manipulating OLE2 objects.
Control structures	You have access to all Version 2.0 control structures.
Cursor-based access to the database	You have access to all Version 2.0 cursor features.
Error handling	Exception handling is fully implemented in Release 1.1.
Modular construction	You can build procedures, functions, and packages, but the packages do not offer the same sets of capabilities as those stored in the database.
Stored procedures, functions, and packages	Not available in PL/SQL Release 1.1. Release 1.1 is for client-side application development. The PL/SQL code for these components definitely is not stored in the database.
PL/SQL tables	You cannot declare and use PL/SQL tables in Release 1.1. You can, however, construct stored packages, which serve as interfaces to these data structures, and then call those stored modules from your client application.

Advice for Oracle Programmers

This whole book is full of advice about PL/SQL programming, but in this section I offer a few basic principles. These principles guide my own use of PL/SQL and I'd like to encourage you to adopt them as well.

Take a Creative, Even Radical Approach

We all tend to fall into ruts, in almost every aspect of our lives. People are creatures of habit: you learn to write code in one way; you come to assume certain limitations about a product; you turn aside possible solutions without serious examination because you just know it can't be done. Developers become downright prejudiced about their own tools, and often not in positive ways. "It can't run any faster than that; it's a pig." "I can't make it work the way the user wants; that'll have to wait for the next version." "If I were using X or Y or Z product, it would be a breeze. But with this stuff, everything is a struggle."

Sadly (or is it happily?), the reality is that your program could almost always run a little faster. The screen could function just the way the user wants it to. Although each product has its limitations, strengths, and weaknesses, you should never have to wait for the next version. Isn't it so much more satisfying to be able to tell your therapist that you tackled the problem head-on, accepted no excuses, and created a solution?

How do you do this? Break out of the confines of your hardened views and take a fresh look at the world (or maybe just your cubicle). Reassess the programming habits you've developed, particularly regarding fourth-generation language (4GL) development with the Oracle tools. Be creative—step away from the traditional methods, from the often limited and mechanical approaches constantly reinforced in our places of business.

Try something new: experiment with what may seem to be a radical departure from the norm. You will be surprised at how much you will learn, how you will grow as a programmer and problem-solver. Over the years, I have surprised myself over and over with what is really achievable when I stopped saying "You can't do that!" and instead simply nodded quietly and murmured "Now, if I do it this way..."

Get Ready to Establish New Habits

PL/SQL was initially a way to increase the flexibility of the ANSI-standard SQL, and soon a multi-purpose "Swiss Army Knife" for many of Oracle's tools. Suddenly, developers found they could plop function calls, IF-THEN-ELSE clauses, loops, and even GOTOs right into the midst of their otherwise pristinely declarative screen modules and batch database processing routines.

Did the appearance of PL/SQL instantly transform Oracle-based applications into shining examples for programmers of all faiths? Hardly. Sure, 4GLS are lots more productive than the older software technology: now you can dig yourself into a pretty deep hole with a 4GL much more efficiently than was ever possible with good old FORTRAN.

In fact, for a number of reasons, the level of sophistication of programming in PL/SQL has proven very uneven. While many SQL*Forms developers came out of a 3GL programming environment with a strong history in structured programming and strict guidelines, these principles have been largely forgotten or considered inapplicable in the new 4GL world of SQL and SQL*Forms. What does "structured code" mean when a screen is not composed of lines of code in a file, but rather as a series of pictures and boxes of attributes in the Designer? How do you flow-chart a SQL statement?

Many of us left our good programming manners behind when we sauntered into the world of SQL*Forms. It's been hard to return to those habits, especially given some of the limitations of PL/SQL Version 1. On the other hand, many Oracle developers are not seasoned programmers, but relative newcomers who may have little or no formal training in computer sciences and programming. They might, for example, have started out as end users who needed some *ad hoc* queries and ended up building forms.

The first release of PL/SQL (and the later versions, for that matter) was not intended to be a comprehensive procedural language in the same league as, say, C or COBOL. Officially, it existed only to provide some programming constructs around the SQL language to facilitate batch database procedures. PL/SQL did not interact with the operating system, had no debugger whatsoever, and didn't support the normal 3GL concepts of link libraries and modularized code. As soon as Oracle made PL/SQL available in SQL*Forms Version 3, however, thousands of Oracle developers moved quickly to put it to work in their forms. Suddenly they could code all (well, almost all) the fancy gizmos their users wanted.[*]

Damn the torpedoes and full speed ahead! But what about standards? What about modularization? What about reusable code? Such concerns were often ignored as the volume of PL/SQL programming exploded throughout the Oracle community. In their press to meet management expectations of extraordinary productivity, developers did what they needed to do in what little time they had. And few of us had time to take training in PL/SQL, even when it was offered. Few of us had

---

[*] And they could do so without committing the most unnatural acts (for example, user exits to provide pop-up windows or SQL*Forms Version 2.3 triggers that called themselves recursively and were impossible to debug).

time to think about whether what we wrote could be maintained or enhanced easily. Instead we just coded. And coded. And coded.

When it came time to debug a PL/SQL module, we discovered that there wasn't any debugger in PL/SQL at all, and precious little to work with in SQL*Forms and SQL*Plus. Programmers with backgrounds in established languages like COBOL or FORTRAN or C shook their heads and did what they could. The many people introduced to software development through Oracle software didn't know what they were missing. They just knew that it was very difficult to identify and then repair problems in their code.

PL/SQL has come a long way from its first hesitant offering for the RDBMS in 1990. Developers who have worked with the language since its first release must make sure to adapt to the changing features and potential of PL/SQL.

Assume that PL/SQL Has What You Need

Programmers who are new to PL/SQL often make the mistake of starting their coding efforts before they are sufficiently familiar with everything the language has to offer. I have seen and heard of many instances where a developer spends valuable time writing procedures or functions that duplicate built-in functionality provided by PL/SQL.

Please don't write a function that looks through each character in a string until it finds a match and then returns the index of that match in the string. The INSTR function does this for you. Please don't write a function to convert your string from uppercase to lowercase by performing ASCII code-table shifting. Use the LOWER function instead.

With the PL/SQL of the 1990s, you also have to keep in mind much more than these basic functions. Each new release of the database and the tools include packages that stretch the boundaries of the PL/SQL language itself. These packages extend PL/SQL by providing additional datatypes, functions, and procedures to handle more specialized situations. You can use DBMS_JOB to schedule processes from the database. You can use DBMS_PIPE to communicate information between different Oracle sessions. The ideas and the list of prebuilt code goes on and on. Take some time to stroll through Part III, *Built-In Functions*, and Appendix C, *Built-In Packages*, and get familiar with all the features that are built into the PL/SQL language.

Share Your Ideas

Oracle Corporation, along with its flavor of SQL and the PL/SQL language, has been around for close to 15 years. They have listened to user requests, kept up with the standards committees, and generally sought to create a very robust environment for developers and users. As I've said, there is a very good chance that what you need is already available in the language. If so, use it. If not, build it yourself in the most general and reusable way possible. Then share it. Share your ideas and your creations with others in your company, your Oracle User Group, even the worldwide Oracle community through the International Oracle User's Group and User's Week convention.

A Few of My Favorite (PL/SQL) Things

PL/SQL is a powerful, many-featured product. This is a lengthy book. I have gone to great lengths to make all the information within the covers highly accessible. Still, I thought it would be helpful to offer a quick review of some of my favorite aspects of the PL/SQL language.

It's all wonderful, of course, and I wouldn't trade PL/SQL for any other programming language in the world. Yet certain features and techniques have stood out for me as ways to improve the efficiency of my code and the productivity of my development effort.

The topics in the following sections offer just enough information to give you a sense of what is possible. Go to the appropriate chapter for detailed information.

Anchored declarations

You can use the %TYPE and %ROWTYPE declaration attributes to *anchor* the datatype of one variable to that of a previously existing variable or data structure. The anchoring data structure can be a column in a database table, the entire table itself, a programmer-defined record, or a local PL/SQL variable. In the following example, I declare a local variable with the same structure as the company name:

```
my_company company.name%TYPE;
```

See Chapter 4 for details.

Built-in functions

PL/SQL offers dozens of built-in functions to help you get your job done with the minimum amount of code and fuss possible. Some of them are straightforward, such as the LENGTH function, which returns the length of the specified string. Others offer subtle variations which will aid you greatly—but only when you are aware of those variations.

Two of my favorites in this category of hidden talents are SUBSTR and INSTR, both character functions. SUBSTR returns a subportion of a string. INSTR returns the position in a string where a substring is found. Most developers only use these functions to search forward through the strings. By passing a negative starting location, however, SUBSTR will count from the end of the string. And INSTR will actually scan in reverse through the string for the nth occurrence of a substring.

See the chapters in Part III for details.

Built-in packages

In addition to the many built-in functions provided by PL/SQL, Oracle Corporation also offers many built-in packages. These packages of functions, procedures, and data structures greatly expand the scope of the PL/SQL language. With each new release of the Oracle Server, we get new packages to improve our own programs.

It is no longer sufficient for a developer to become familiar simply with the basic PL/SQL functions like TO_CHAR, ROUND, and so on. Those functions have now become only the innermost layer of useful functionality. Oracle Corporation has built upon those functions, and you should do the same thing.

See Appendix C for a summary of the Application Programming Interfaces (APIs) of the built-in packages.

The cursor FOR loop

The cursor FOR loop is one of my favorite PL/SQL constructs. It leverages fully the tight and effective integration of the Ada-like programming language with the power of the SQL database language. It reduces the volume of code you need to write to fetch data from a cursor. It greatly lessens the chance of introducing loop errors in your programming—and loops are one of the more error-prone parts of a program. Does this loop sound too good to be true? Well, it isn't—it's all true!

See Chapter 7, *Loops*, for more information.

Scoping with nested blocks

The general advantage of—and motivation for—a nested block is that you create a *scope* for all the declared objects and executable statements in that block. You can use this scope to improve your control over activity in your program, particularly in the area of exception handling.

In the following procedure, I have placed BEGIN and END keywords around a sequence of DELETE statements. This way, if any DELETE statement fails, I trap the exception, ignore the problem, and move on to the next DELETE:

```
PROCEDURE delete_details
IS
BEGIN
   BEGIN
      DELETE FROM child1 WHERE ...;
```

```
    EXCEPTION
        WHEN OTHERS THEN NULL;
    END;

    BEGIN
        DELETE FROM child2 WHERE ...;
    EXCEPTION
        WHEN OTHERS THEN NULL;
    END;
END;
```

I can in this way use my nested blocks to allow my PL/SQL program to continue past exceptions.

See Chapter 15, *Procedures and Functions*, for details.

Module overloading

Within a package and within the declaration section of a PL/SQL block, you can define more than one module with the same name! The name is, in other words, overloaded. In the following example, I have overloaded the value_ok function in the body of the check package:

```
PACKAGE BODY check
IS
    /* First version takes a DATE parameter. */
    FUNCTION value_ok (date_in IN DATE) RETURN BOOLEAN
    IS
    BEGIN
        RETURN date_in <= SYSDATE;
    END;

    /* Second version takes a NUMBER parameter. */
    FUNCTION value_ok (number_in IN NUMBER) RETURN BOOLEAN
    IS
    BEGIN
        RETURN number_in > 0;
    END;
END;
```

Overloading can greatly simplify your life and the lives of other developers. This technique consolidates the call interfaces for many similar programs into a single module name. It transfers the burden of knowledge from the developer to the software. You do not have to try to remember, for example, the six different names for programs which all add values (dates, strings, Booleans, numbers, etc.) to various PL/SQL tables.

Instead, you simply tell the compiler that you want to "add" and pass it the value you want added. PL/SQL and your overloaded programs figure out what you want to do and they do it for you.

See Chapter 15 for details.

Local modules

A local module is a procedure or function defined in the declaration section of a PL/SQL block (anonymous or named). This module is considered local because it is only defined within the parent PL/SQL block. It cannot be called by any other PL/SQL blocks defined outside of that enclosing block.

See Chapter 15 for details.

Packages

A package is a collection of related elements, including modules, variables, table and record TYPEs, cursors, and exceptions. Packages are among the least understood and most underutilized features of PL/SQL. That is a shame, because the package structure is also one of the most useful constructs for building well-designed PL/SQL-based applications. Packages provide a structure in which you can organize your modules and other PL/SQL elements. They encourage proper programming techniques in an environment that often befuddles the implementation of good design.

With packages, you can:

- Create abstract datatypes and employ object-oriented design principles in your Oracle-based applications.

- Use top-down design techniques comprehensively. You can build package specifications devoid of any code and actually compile programs that call the modules in these "stub" packages.

- Create and manipulate data that persist throughout a database session. You can use variables that are declared in a package to create global data structures.

See Chapter 16, *Packages*, for details. The disk that accompanies this book contains many examples of packages. The frontend software gives you an easy-to-use interface to the code and explanations for using it.

Best Practices for PL/SQL Excellence

Since the publication of the first edition of this book, I have had the pleasure of presenting my own relatively idiosyncratic approach to building PL/SQL-based applications to thousands of developers. I have also spent an increasingly large percentage of my time writing complex PL/SQL packages. In the process, I have honed my sense of what we all need to do to write excellent PL/SQL programs which will "stand the test of time." I have, in fact, become somewhat dogmatic about these principles or "best practices," but if not me, then who?

In this second edition, I've decided to share some of my thoughts on PL/SQL best practices, in very concentrated form, to enhance your reading of the book and to give you food for thought as you venture forth with your own development projects. This is by no means a comprehensive list, but I hope it will be a good start for the construction of your own best practices.

Write as Little Code as Possible

If you can use a program that someone else wrote—someone you trust to have written it well and tested it thoroughly—why would you want to write it yourself? Seems obvious, doesn't it? The less code you yourself write, the less likely it is that you will introduce bugs into your application, and the more likely it is that you will meet deadlines and stay within budget.

The basic PL/SQL language offers tons of functionality; you need to get familiar with the built-in functions so you know what you don't have to write. At most of my trainings, I ask the attendees how many arguments the INSTR function has. Most people figure there are two (the string and the substring). A few raise their hands for three, and a special one or two believe in four arguments for INSTR— four is the correct answer. If you don't know that INSTR has four arguments, then you don't *really* know what INSTR does—and can do—for you. Investigate and discover!

Then there are the built-in packages, which greatly expand your horizons. These packages allow you to do things otherwise impossible inside PL/SQL, such as executing dynamic SQL, DDL, and PL/SQL code (DBMS_SQL), passing information through database pipes (DBMS_PIPES), and displaying information from within a PL/SQL program (DBMS_OUTPUT). It is no longer sufficient for a developer to become familiar simply with basic PL/SQL functions like TO_CHAR, ROUND, and so forth. Those functions have now become merely the innermost layer of useful functionality that Oracle Corporation has built upon (as should you). To take full advantage of the Oracle technology as it blasts its way to the 21st century, you must be aware of these packages and how they can help you.

Finally, as the PL/SQL marketplace matures, you will find that you can choose from prebuilt, third-party libraries of PL/SQL code, probably in the form of packages. These code libraries might perform specialized calculations or they might offer relatively generic extensions to the base PL/SQL language. As of the fall of 1997, there is just one commercially available PL/SQL library, PL/Vision from RevealNet (which I wrote). Soon, there will be more. Search the Web and check the advertisements in *Oracle Magazine* to find out what is available, so that you can avoid reinventing the wheel.

As you are writing your own code, you should also strive to reduce your code volume. Here are some specific techniques to keep in mind:

- Use the cursor FOR loop. Whenever you need to read through every record fetched by a cursor, the cursor FOR loop will save you lots of typing over the "manual" approach of explicitly opening, fetching from, and closing the cursor.

- Work with records. Certainly, whenever you fetch data from a cursor, you should fetch into a record declared against that cursor with the %ROWTYPE attribute (covered in next section in more detail). But if you find yourself declaring multiple variables which are related, declare instead your own record TYPE. Your code will tighten up and will more clearly self-document relationships.

- Use local modules to avoid redundancy and improve readability. If you perform the same calculation twice or more in a procedure, create a function to perform the calculation and then call that function twice instead.

Synchronize Program and Data Structures

Data analysts, data modelers, and database administrators go to great lengths to get the structures in the database *just right*. Standards for entity and attribute names, referential integrity constraints, database triggers, you name it: by the time PL/SQL developers get to work, there is (or should be) a solid foundation for their work.

Problem is, whenever you code a SQL statement in your application, you are *hardcoding* data structures and relationships into your program. What happens when those relationships change? Unless you take special precautions, your program will break. You will spend way too much of your time maintaining existing applications. Your managers will look at you funny when you have to make up all sorts of lame excuses for widespread breakdowns of code resulting from the simplest database change.

Protect your code and your reputation. As much as possible, you want to write your code so that it will "automagically" adapt to changes in underlying data structures and relationships. You can do this by taking the following steps:

- Anchor declarations of variables back to the database tables and columns they represent. Whenever you declare a variable which has *anything* to do with a database element, use the %TYPE or %ROWTYPE declaration attributes to define the datatype of those structures. If those database elements change, your compiled code is discarded. When recompiled, the changes are automatically applied to your code.

- Always fetch from an explicit cursor into a record declared with %ROWTYPE, as opposed to individual variables. Assuming that you followed my last piece of advice, that cursor is declared in a package. That cursor may, therefore, be changed without your knowledge. Suppose that another expression is added to the SELECT list. Your compiled code is then marked as being invalid. If you fetched into a record, however, upon recompiliation that record will take on the new structure of the cursor.

- Encapsulate access to your data structures within packages. I recommend, for example, that you never repeat a line of SQL in your application; that all SQL statements be hidden behind a package interface; and that most developers never write any SQL at all. They can simply call the appropriate package procedure or function, or open the appropriate package cursor. If they don't find what they need, they ask the owner of the package (who is intimate with the complex details of the data structure) to add or change an element.

This last suggestion will have the greatest impact on your applications, but it is also among the most difficult to implement. To accomplish this goal (always execute SQL statements through a procedural interface), you will want to *generate* packages automatically for a table or view. This is the only way to obtain the consistency and code quality required for this segment of your application code. By the time this second edition is published, you should be able to choose from several different package generators. You can also build your own.

Center All Development Around Packages

Little did I know when I wrote the first edition of this book how much more I was to learn about PL/SQL—and most of it was about packages. You should center all your PL/SQL development effort around packages. Don't build stand-alone procedures or functions unless you absolutely have to (some frontend tools cannot yet recognize the package syntax of dot notation: *package.program*). Expect that you will eventually construct groups of related functionality and start from the beginning with a package.

The more you use packages, the more you will discover you can do with them. The more you use packages, the better you will become at constructing clean, easy-to-understand interfaces (or APIs) to your data and your functionality. The more you use packages, the more effectively you will encapsulate acquired knowledge and then be able to reapply that knowledge at a later time—and share it with others.

My second book, *Advanced Oracle PL/SQL Programming with Packages*, offers a detailed set of "best practices" for package design and usage; highlights follow:

- Don't declare data in your package specification. Instead, "hide" it in the package body and build "get and set" programs to retrieve the data and change it.

This way, you retain control over the data and also retain the flexibility to change your implementation without affecting the programs which rely on that data.

- Build toggles into your packages, such as a "local" debug mechanisms, which you can easily turn on and off. This way, a user of your package can modify the behavior of programs inside the package without having to change his or her own code.

- Avoid writing repetitive code inside your package bodies. This is a particular danger when you overload multiple programs with the same name. Often the implementation of each of these programs is very similar. You will be tempted to simply cut and paste and then make the necessary changes. However, you will be much better off if you take the time to create a private program in the package which incorporates all common elements, and then have each overloaded program call that program.

- Spend as much time as you can in your package specifications. Hold off on building your bodies until you have tested your interfaces (as defined by the specifications) by building compilable programs which touch on as many different packages as possible.

- Be prepared to work in and enhance multiple packages simultaneously. Suppose that you are building a package to maintain orders and that you run into a need for a function to parse a string. If your string package does not yet have this functionality, stop your work in the orders package and enhance the string package. Unit-test your generic function there. When you've got it working, deploy it in the orders package. Follow this disciplined approach to modularization and you will continually build up your toolbox of reusable utilities.

- Always keep your package specifications in separate files from your package bodies. If you change your body but not your specification, then a recompile only of the body will not invalidate any programs referencing the package.

- Compile all of the package specifications for your application before any of your bodies. That way, you will have minimized the chance that you will run into any unresolved or (seemingly) circular references.

Standardize Your PL/SQL Development Environment

When you get right down to it, programming consists of one long series of decisions punctuated by occasional taps on the keyboard. Your productivity is determined to a large extent by what you spend your time making decisions on. Take some time *before* you start your programming effort to set up standards among a wide variety of aspects. Here are some of my favorite standards, in no particular order:

- Set as a rule that individual developers never write their own exception-handling code, never use the pragma EXCEPTION_INIT to assign names to error numbers, and never call RAISE_APPLICATION_ERROR with hardcoded numbers and text. Instead, consolidate exception handling programs into a single package, and predefine all application-specific exceptions in their appropriate packages. Build generic handler programs that, most importantly, hide the way you record exceptions in a log. Individual handler sections of code should *never* expose the particular implementation, such as an INSERT into a table.

- Never write implicit cursors (in other words, never use the SELECT INTO syntax). Instead, always declare explicit cursors. If you follow this advice, you will no longer spend time debating with yourself and others which course is the best. ("Well, if I use ROWNUM < 2 I never get the TOO_MANY_ROWS exception. So there!") This will improve your productivity. And you will have SQL which is more likely (and able) to be reused.

- Pick a coding style and stick to it. If you *ever* find yourself thinking things like "Should I indent three spaces or four?" or "How should I do the line breaks on this long procedure call?" or "Should I do everything in lowercase or uppercase or what?" then you are wasting time and doing an injustice to yourself. If you don't have a coding style, use mine—it is offered in detail in Chapter 3, *Effective Coding Style*.

Structured Code and Other Best Practices

Once you get beyond the "big ticket" best practices, there are many very concrete recommendations for how to write specific lines of code and constructs. Many of these suggestions have been around for years and apply to all programming languages. So if you took a good programming class in college, for example, don't throw away those books! The specific syntax may change, but the fundamental common sense motivation for what you have learned in the past will certainly work with PL/SQL as well.

Without a doubt, if you can follow these guidelines, you are sure to end up with programs which are easier to maintain and enhance:

- Never exit from a FOR loop (numeric or cursor) with an EXIT or RETURN statement. A FOR loop is a promise: my code will iterate from the starting to the ending value and will then stop execution.

- Never exit from a WHILE loop with an EXIT or RETURN statement. Rely solely on the WHILE loop condition to terminate the loop.

- Ensure that a function has a single successful RETURN statement as the last line of the executable section. Normally, each exception handler in a function would also return a value.

- Don't let functions have OUT or IN OUT parameters. The function should only return values through the RETURN clause.

- Make sure that the name of a function describes the value being returned (noun structure, as in "total_compensation"). The name of a procedure should describe the actions taken (verb-noun structure, as in "calculate_totals").

- Never declare the FOR loop index (either an integer or a record). This is done for you implicitly by the PL/SQL runtime engine.

- Do not use exceptions to perform branching logic. When you define your own exceptions, these should describe error situations only.

- When you use the ELSIF statement, make sure that each of the clauses is mutually exclusive. Watch out especially for logic like "sal BETWEEN 1 and 10000" and "sal BETWEEN 10000 and 20000."

- Remove all hardcoded "magic values" from your programs and replace them with named constants or functions defined in packages.

- Do not "SELECT COUNT(*)" from a table unless you really need to know the *total* number of "hits." If you only need to know whether there is more than one match, simply fetch twice with an explicit cursor.

- Do not use the names of tables or columns for variable names. This can cause compile errors. It can also result in unpredictable behavior inside SQL statements in your PL/SQL code. I once did a global search and replace of :GLOBAL.regcd to regcd (a local variable declared as VARCHAR2(10) but also, unfortunately, the name of a column). Our Q&A procedures were very weak and we ended up rolling out into production a program with a DELETE statement containing a WHERE clause that looked like this:

```
WHERE regcd = regcd
```

  Needless to say, this caused many headaches. If I had simply changed the global reference to v_regcd, I would have avoided all such problems.

There is lots more I could say about best practices for PL/SQL development, especially concerning the application of new Oracle8, object-oriented features. But if you follow the ideas I offer in this section, you will be writing code that is superior to just about everyone else's on this strange planet. So...read on!

2

PL/SQL Language Fundamentals

Every language—whether human or computer—has a syntax, vocabulary, and character set. In order to communicate within that language, you have to learn the rules that govern its usage. Many of us are very wary of learning a new computer language. Change is often scary, but, in general, programming languages are very simple tongues, and PL/SQL is a relatively simple programming language. The difficulty we have conversing in languages based on bytes is not with the language, but with the compiler or computer with which we are having the discussion. Compilers are, for the most part, very stupid. They are not creative, sentient beings. They are not capable of original thought. Their vocabulary is severely limited. Compilers just happen to think their dull thoughts very, very rapidly—and very inflexibly.

If I hear someone ask "gottabuck?", I can readily interpret that sentence and decide how to respond. If I instruct PL/SQL, on the other hand, to "gimme the next half-dozen records," I will not get very far in my application. To use the PL/SQL language, you must dot your i's and cross your t's—syntactically speaking. So, in this chapter, I cover the fundamental language rules that will help you converse with the PL/SQL compiler—the PL/SQL character set, lexical units, PRAGMA keyword, and block structure.

The PL/SQL Character Set

A PL/SQL program consists of a sequence of statements, each of which is made up of one or more lines of text. Text is made up of combinations of the characters shown in Table 2-1.

Table 2-1. PL/SQL Character Set

Type	Characters
Letters	A-Z, a-z
Digits	0-9
Symbols	~ ! @ # $ % & * ( ) _ - + =	[ ] { } : ; " ' < > , . ? /
Whitespace	Tab, space, carriage return

Note that PL/SQL is a case-insensitive language. Uppercase letters are treated the same way as lowercase letters except when the characters are surrounded by single quotes (when they are literal strings) or represent the value of a character variable.

Every valid statement in PL/SQL, from declaration to executable statement to keyword, is made up of various combinations of the above characters. Now you just have to figure out how to put them all together!

A number of these characters—both singly and in combination with other characters—have a special significance in PL/SQL. Table 2-2 lists these special symbols.

Table 2-2. Simple and Compound Symbols in PL/SQL

Symbol	Description
;	Semicolon: statement terminator
%	Percent sign: attribute indicator (cursor attributes like %ISOPEN and indirect declaration attributes like %ROWTYPE). Also used as multibyte wildcard symbol, as in SQL.
_	Single underscore: single-byte wildcard symbol, as in SQL
:	Colon: host variable indicator, such as :block.item in Oracle Forms
**	Double asterisk: exponentiation operator
<> and !=	"Not equals"
||	Double vertical bar: concatenation operator
<< and >>	Label delimiters
<= and >=	Relational operators
:=	Assignment operator
=>	Association operator for positional notation
--	Double dash: single-line comment indicator
/* and */	Beginning and ending multiline comment block delimiters

Characters are grouped together into lexical units, also called *atomics* of the language, because they are the smallest individual components. A lexical unit in PL/SQL is any of the following:

- Identifier

- Literal

- Delimiter

- Comment

These are described in the following sections.

Identifiers

An *identifier* is a name for a PL/SQL object, including any of the following:

- Constant

- Variable

- Exception

- Procedure

- Function

- Package

- Record

- PL/SQL table

- Cursor

- Reserved word

Properties of an identifier are summarized below:

- Up to 30 characters in length

- Must start with a letter

- Can include $ (dollar sign), _ (underscore), and # (pound sign)

- Cannot contain spaces

Remember that PL/SQL is not case-sensitive, so if the only difference between two identifiers is the case of one or more letters, PL/SQL treats those two identifiers as the same. For example, the following identifiers are all considered by PL/SQL to be the same, because the characters in the name are the same; the only difference is their case:

```
lots_of_$MONEY$
LOTS_of_$MONEY$
Lots_of_$Money$
```

The following strings are valid identifier names:

lots_of_$MONEY$	FirstName
company_id#	address_line1
primary_acct_responsibility	address_line2
First_Name	S123456

The following identifiers are all illegal in PL/SQL:

`1st_year`	`-- Starts with numeral`
`procedure-name`	`-- Contains invalid character "-"`
`minimum_%_due`	`-- Contains invalid character "%"`
`maximum_value_exploded_for_detail`	`-- Name is too long`
`company ID`	`-- Cannot have embedded spaces in name`

Identifiers are the handles for objects in your program. Be sure to name your objects carefully, so the names describe the objects and their uses. Avoid identifier names like X1 and temp; they are too ambiguous to mean anything to you or anyone else reading your code.

Reserved Words

Of course, you don't get to name all the identifiers in your programs. Many elements of your program have been named by PL/SQL itself. These are the reserved words in the language. An identifier is a reserved word if it has a special meaning in PL/SQL and therefore should not—and, in most cases, cannot—be redefined by programmers for their own use.

One very important reserved word is END. It is used to terminate programs, IF statements, and loops. If you try to declare a variable named "end", as I do below, then you will get the subsequent compile error:

```
DECLARE
    end VARCHAR2(10) := 'blip';
BEGIN
    DBMS_OUTPUT.PUT_LINE (end);
END;
/
PLS-00103: Encountered the symbol "END" when expecting one of the following:
```

The appearance of the word "end" in the declaration section signals to PL/SQL the premature termination of that anonymous block.

PL/SQL tries to be as accommodating as possible when you do redefine reserved words in your program. It makes its best effort to interpret and compile your code. You would be much better off, however, if you never redefined a reserved word for your own use. Even if you do get away with it, the resulting code will be confusing. And a later version of the PL/SQL compiler might decide that your use of that keyword is, after all, unacceptable.

In any case, finding a valid name for your identifier should be the least of your problems. There are thousands and thousands of permutations of the legal characters.

You can find a full list of all PL/SQL reserved words in an appendix of Oracle Corporation's *PL/SQL User's Guide and Reference*.

Whitespace and Keywords

Identifiers must be separated by at least one space or by a delimiter, but you can format your text by adding additional spaces, line breaks (carriage returns), and tabs wherever you can put a space, without changing the meaning of your entry.

The two statements shown below are therefore equivalent:

```
IF too_many_orders
THEN
    warn_user;
ELSIF no_orders_entered
THEN
    prompt_for_orders;
END IF;

IF too_many_orders THEN warn_user;
ELSIF no_orders_entered THEN prompt_for_orders;
END IF;
```

You may not, however, place a space or carriage return or tab within a lexical unit, such as a compound delimiter like the "not equals" symbol (!=). The following statement raises a compile error:

```
IF max_salary ! = min_salary THEN
```

because there is a space between the ! and the =.

See Chapter 3, *Effective Coding Style*, for more information on how you can use whitespace to format your code for improved readability.

Literals

A literal is a value which is not represented by an identifier; it is simply a value. A literal may be composed of one of the following types of data:

Number
    415, 21.6, or NULL

String
    'This is my sentence' or '31-JAN-94' or NULL

Boolean
    TRUE, FALSE, or NULL

Notice that there is no way to indicate a true date literal. The value '31-JAN-94' is a string literal (any sequence of characters enclosed by single quotes is a string literal). PL/SQL and SQL automatically convert such a string to a date for you (by calling TO_DATE), but a date has only an internal representation.

A string literal can be composed of zero or more characters from the PL/SQL character set. A literal of zero characters is represented as `' '` (two consecutive single quotes with no characters between them) and is defined as the NULL string. This literal has a datatype of CHAR (fixed-length string).

PL/SQL is case-sensitive within string literals. The following two literals are different:

```
'Steven'
'steven'
```

The following condition, for example, evaluates to FALSE:

```
IF 'Steven' = 'steven'
```

Embedding Single Quotes Inside a String

The trickiest part of working with string literals comes when you need to include a single quote inside a string literal (as part of the literal itself). Generally, the rule is that you write two single quotes next to each other inside a string if you want the literal to contain a single quote in that position. The following table shows the literal in one column and the resulting "internal" string in the second column:

Literal	Actual Value
`'There''s no business like show business.'`	`There's no business like show business.`
`'"Hound of the Baskervilles"'`	`"Hound of the Baskervilles"`
`'NLS_LANGUAGE=''ENGLISH'''`	`NLS_LANGUAGE='ENGLISH'`
`''''`	`'`
`'''hello'''`	`'hello'`
`''''''`	`''`

Here's a summary of how to embed single quotes in a literal:

- To place a single quote inside the literal, put two single quotes together.
- To place a single quote at the beginning or end of a literal, put three single quotes together.
- To create a string literal consisting of one single quote, put four single quotes together.
- To create a string literal consisting of two single quotes together, put six single quotes together.

Two single quotes together is not the same as a double quote character. A double quote character does not have any special significance inside a string literal. It is treated the same as a letter or number.

Numeric Literals

Numeric literals can be integers or real numbers (a number that contains a fractional component). Note that PL/SQL considers the number 154.00 to be a real number, even though the fractional component is zero and the number is actually an integer. You can also use scientific notation to specify a numeric literal. Use the letter "e" (upper- or lowercase) to raise a number times 10 to the nth power. For example: 3.05E19, 12e-5.

Boolean Literals

Remember that the values TRUE and FALSE are not strings. They are Boolean literals with the literal meaning of TRUE or FALSE. You should never place single quotes around these values. The following code will fail to compile with the error listed below:

```
DECLARE
    enough_money BOOLEAN;
BEGIN
    IF enough_money = 'TRUE'
    THEN
        . . .

    PLS-00306: wrong number or types of arguments in call to '='
```

Instead, you should reference the literal directly:

```
DECLARE
    enough_money BOOLEAN;
BEGIN
    IF enough_money = TRUE
    THEN
        . . .
```

Better yet, leave out the literal and just let the Boolean variable speak for itself in the conditional clause of the IF statement:

```
DECLARE
    enough_money BOOLEAN;
BEGIN
    IF enough_money
    THEN
        . . .
```

If you work with Oracle Forms, you may notice that some of the GET_ built-ins, such as GET_ITEM_PROPERTY, sometimes return a value of TRUE or FALSE. For example:

```
GET_ITEM_PROPERTY ('block.item', DISPLAYED)
```

returns the character string FALSE if the DISPLAYED property is set to "Off" for the specified item. Do not confuse this value with the Boolean literal. The easiest way to keep this all straight is to remember that the GET_ built-ins always return a character string.

The Semicolon Delimiter

A PL/SQL program is made up of a series of statements. A statement is terminated with a semicolon (;), not with the physical end of a line. In fact, a single statement is often spread over several lines to make it more readable. The following IF statement takes up four lines and is indented to reinforce the logic behind the statement:

```
IF salary < min_salary (1994)
THEN
    salary := salary + salary*.25;
END IF;
```

There are two semicolons in this IF statement. The first semicolon indicates the end of the single executable statement within the IF-END IF construct. The second semicolon terminates the IF statement itself. This same statement could also be placed on a single physical line (if it would fit):

```
IF salary < min_salary (1994) THEN salary := salary + salary*.25; END IF;
```

The semicolons are still needed to terminate the logical, executable statements. I suggest that you do not, however, combine the different components of the IF statement on a single line. It is much more difficult to read. I also recommend that you never place more than one executable (or declaration) statement on each line. Compare the following statements:

```
DECLARE
    continue_scanning BOOLEAN := TRUE;
    scan_index NUMBER := 1;
```

and:

```
DECLARE
    continue_scanning BOOLEAN := TRUE; scan_index NUMBER := 1;
```

In the second example, the two different statements blur into a single stream of text. It is difficult to find the semicolon in the middle of a line.

Comments

Inline documentation, otherwise known as comments, is an important element of a good program. While this book offers many suggestions on how to make your program self-documenting through good naming practices and modularization, such techniques are seldom enough by themselves to guarantee a thorough understanding of a complex program.

PL/SQL offers two different styles for comments: single-line and multiline block comments.

Single-Line Comment Syntax

The single-line comment is initiated with two hyphens (--), which cannot be separated by a space or any other characters. All text after the double hyphen, to the end of that physical line, is considered commentary and is ignored by the compiler. If the double hyphen appears at the beginning of the line, then that whole line is a comment.

Remember: the double hyphen comments out the remainder of a physical line, not a logical PL/SQL statement. In the following IF statement, I use a single-line comment to clarify the logic of the Boolean expression:

```
IF salary < min_salary (1994) -- Function returns min salary for year.
THEN
    salary := salary + salary*.25;
END IF;
```

Multiline Comment Syntax

While single-line comments are useful for documenting brief bits of code and also ignoring a line that you do not want executed at the moment, the multiline comment is superior for including longer blocks of commentary.

Multiline comments start with a slash-asterisk (/*) and end with an asterisk-slash (*/). PL/SQL considers all characters found between these two sequences of symbols to be part of the comment, and they are ignored by the compiler.

The following example of multiline comments shows a header section for a procedure. I use the double vertical bars in the left margin so that, as the eye moves down the left edge of the program, it can easily pick out the chunks of comments:

```
PROCEDURE calc_revenue (company_id IN NUMBER) IS
/*
|| Program: calc_revenue
|| Author: Steven Feuerstein
|| Change history:
||    9/23/94 - Start program
*/
```

```
BEGIN
   ...
END;
```

You can also use multiline comments to block out lines of code for testing purposes. In the following example, the additional clauses in the EXIT statement are ignored so that testing can concentrate on the a_delimiter function:

```
EXIT WHEN a_delimiter (next_char)
/*
            OR
        (was_a_delimiter AND NOT a_delimiter (next_char))
*/
;
```

The PRAGMA Keyword

The PRAGMA keyword is used to signify that the remainder of the PL/SQL statement is a *pragma*, or directive, to the compiler. Pragmas are processed at compile time; they do not execute during runtime.

A pragma is a special instruction to the compiler. Also called a *pseudoinstruction*, the pragma doesn't change the meaning of a program. It simply passes information to the compiler. It is very similar, in fact, to the tuning hints you can embed in a SQL statement inside a block comment.

PL/SQL offers the following pragmas:

EXCEPTION_INIT

Tells the compiler to associate a particular error number with an identifier you have declared as an exception in your program. See Chapter 8 for more information.

RESTRICT_REFERENCES

Tells the compiler the purity level (freedom from side effects) of a packaged program. See Chapter 17 for more information.

SERIALLY_REUSABLE

New to PL/SQL8. Tells the PL/SQL runtime engine that package-level data should not persist between references to that data. See Chapter 25 for more information.

The syntax for using the PRAGMA keyword is as follows:

```
PRAGMA <instruction>;
```

where <instruction> is a statement providing instructions to the compiler. You would call EXCEPTION_INIT as follows:

```
DECLARE
   no_such_sequence EXCEPTION;
```

```
    PRAGMA EXCEPTION_INIT (no_such_sequence, -2289);
BEGIN
   ...
END;
```

Block Structure

PL/SQL is a block-structured language. Each of the basic programming units you write to build your application is (or should be) a logical unit of work. The PL/SQL block allows you to reflect that logical structure in the physical design of your programs.

The block structure is at the core of two key concepts and features of the PL/SQL language:

Modularization
> The PL/SQL block is the basic unit of work from which modules, such as procedures and functions, are built. The ability to modularize is central to successfully developing complex applications.

Scope
> The block provides a scope or context for logically related objects. In the block, you group together declarations of variables and executable statements that belong together.

You can create anonymous blocks (blocks of code that have no name) and named blocks, which are procedures and functions. Furthermore, you can build packages in PL/SQL that group together multiple procedures and functions.

The following sections briefly examine the block structure and related concepts.

Sections of the PL/SQL Block

Each PL/SQL block has up to four different sections (some are optional under certain circumstances):

Header
> Relevant for named blocks only. The header determines the way the named block or program must be called.

Declaration section
> The part of the block that declares variables, cursors, and sub-blocks that are referenced in the execution and exception sections.

Execution section
> The part of the PL/SQL block containing the executable statements, the code that is executed by the PL/SQL runtime engine.

Exception section

> The section that handles exceptions to normal processing (warnings and error conditions).

Figure 2-1 shows the structure of the PL/SQL block for a procedure.

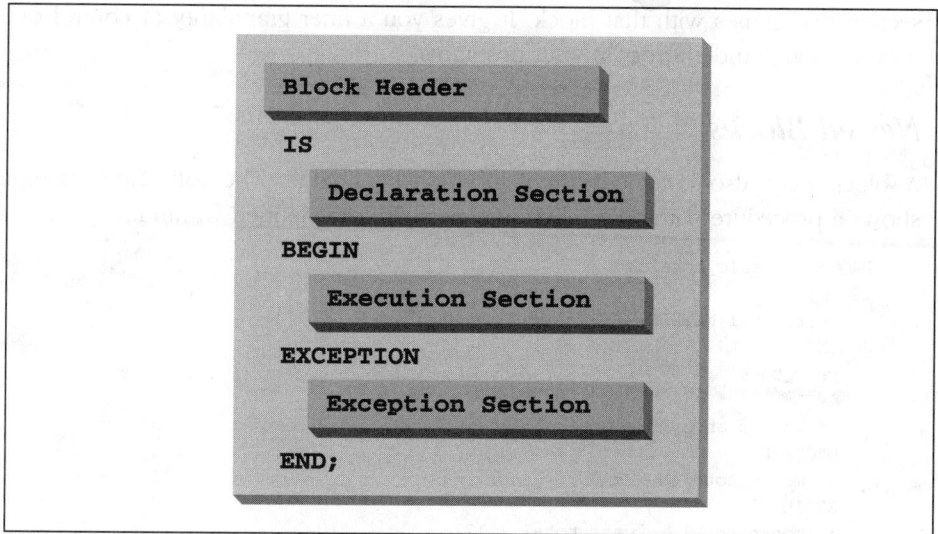

Figure 2-1. The PL/SQL block structure

The ordering of the sections in a block corresponds to the way you would write your programs and the way they are executed:

Step 1

> Define the type of block (procedure, function, anonymous) and the way it is called (header).

Step 2

> Declare any variables used in that block (declaration section).

Step 3

> Use those local variables and other PL/SQL objects to perform the required actions (execution section).

Step 4

> Handle any problems that arise during the execution of the block (exception section).

Scope of a Block

In the declaration section of the block, you may define variables, modules, and other structures. These declarations are local to that block. When the execution of the block finishes, those structures no longer exist. For example, if you open a cursor in a block, that cursor is automatically closed at the end of the block.

The block is the scope of any objects declared in that block. The block also provides the scope for exceptions that are declared and raised. In fact, one of the most important reasons to create a block is to take advantage of the exception section that comes with that block. It gives you a finer granularity of control over how you can handle errors in your programs.

Nested Blocks

A block may also contain nested sub-blocks of code. The following example shows a procedure with an anonymous, nested block defined within it:

```
PROCEDURE calc_totals
IS
    year_total NUMBER;
BEGIN
    year_total := 0;

    /* Nested anonymous block */
    DECLARE
       month_total NUMBER;
    BEGIN
       month_total := year_total / 12;
    END;

END;
```

Notice that I can reference the year_total variable inside the nested block. Any element declared in an outer block is global to all blocks nested within it. Any element declared within an inner block cannot, however, be referenced in an outer block.

Although I refer to the PL/SQL block structure throughout this book, it will figure most prominently in Part IV, *Modular Code*.

3

Effective Coding Style

You can learn everything about a programming language—its syntax, high-performance tips, and advanced features—and still write programs that are virtually unreadable, hard to maintain, and devilishly difficult to debug—even by you, the author. You can be very smart and very clever, and yet develop applications that obscure your talent and accomplishments.

This chapter addresses the "look-and-feel" of your code—the aesthetic aspect of programming. I am sure that you have all experienced the pleasure of reading well-structured and well-formatted code. You have also probably experienced a pang of jealousy at that programmer's style and effort, wondering where she or he found the time to do it right. Developers always experience a feeling of intense pride and satisfaction from carefully and artfully designing the visual layout of their code. Yet few of us take the time to develop a style and use it consistently in our work.

Of course, the impact of a coding style goes well beyond the personal satisfaction of any individual. A consistent, predictable approach to building programs makes it easier to debug and maintain that code. If everyone takes her own approach to structuring, documenting, and naming her code, every program becomes its own little pool of quicksand. It is virtually impossible for another person to put in a foot and test the water (find the source of a problem, analyze dependencies, etc.) without being pulled under.

I discuss the elements of an effective coding style in the PL/SQL language at this juncture, before we get to any code, for two reasons:

- To drive home the point that if you are going to adopt a coding style which will improve the readability and maintainability of your application, you need to do it at the beginning of your project. Programming style involves an attention to detail that can be built only during the construction process. You are not going to go back into existing code and modify the indentation, case, and documentation format after the project is done.

- To provide an explanation for the format and style which I employ throughout the book. While I can't promise that every line of code in the book will follow all of the guidelines in this chapter, I hope that you will perceive a consistent style that is easy on the eye and helpful in aiding comprehension.

Views on effective coding style are often religious in nature (similar to programmers' ideas on the use of GOTO)—that is, based largely on faith instead of rationality. I don't expect you to agree with everything in this chapter (actually, in a number of places I suggest several alternatives). Such unanimity is unrealistic and unnecessary. Rather, I hope that this chapter gets you thinking about the style in your own programming.

Fundamentals of Effective Layout

There is really just one fundamental objective of code layout:

> *Reveal and reinforce the logical structure of your program.*

You could come up with ways of writing your code that are very pleasing to the eye, but doing so is less important than choosing a format that shows the structure and intent of the program.

It is easy to address the topic of effective code layout for PL/SQL because it is such a well structured language. It benefits greatly from Ada's block structure approach. Each control construct, such as IF and LOOP, has its own terminator keyword, such as END IF and END LOOP. Each logical block of code has an explicit beginning statement and an associated ending statement. This consistent and natural block style lends itself easily and naturally to standards for indentation and whitespace, which further expose the structure of the code.

Revealing Logical Structure with Indentation

Indentation is one of the most common and effective techniques used to display a program's logic via format. As illustrated in the following examples, programs that are indented are easier to read than those that are not indented, although programs that use excessive indentation are not much more readable than unindented programs. Here is an unindented IF statement:

```
IF to_number(the_value) > 22
THEN
IF max_totals = 0
THEN
```

```
calc_totals;
ELSE
WHILE more_data
LOOP
analyze_results;
END LOOP;
END IF;
END IF;
```

The lack of indentation in this example makes it very difficult to pick out the statements that go with each clause in the IF statement. Some developers, unfortunately, go to the opposite extreme and use six or more spaces for indentation. (This usually occurs by relying on the tab key, which offers "logical" indentation—a tab can be equivalent to three spaces in one editor and eight in another. I suggest avoiding the use of tabs altogether.)

I have found that a three-space indentation not only adequately reveals the logical structure of the code but also keeps the statements close enough together to read comfortably. And, with deeply nested structures, you won't run off the right margin as quickly! Here is the three-space indented version of the previous nested IF statement:

```
IF to_number(the_value) > 22
THEN
   IF max_totals = 0
   THEN
      calc_totals;
   ELSE
      WHILE more_data
      LOOP
         analyze_results;
      END LOOP;
   END IF;
END IF;
```

The rest of this chapter presents specific techniques that I have found to be essential in writing attractive, readable code that reveals the logic of my programs.

Using Case to Aid Readability

PL/SQL code is made up of many different components: variables, form items, report fields, procedures, functions, loops, declarations, control elements, etc. But they break down roughly into two types of text: reserved words and application-specific names or identifiers.

Reserved words are those names of language elements that are reserved by PL/SQL and have a special meaning for the compiler. Some examples of reserved words in PL/SQL are:

```
WHILE
IF
```

```
BEGIN
TO_CHAR
```

Application-specific identifiers are the names that you, the programmer, give to data and program structures that are specific to your application and that vary from system to system.

The compiler treats these two kinds of text very differently. You can improve the readability of your code greatly by reflecting this difference in the way the text is displayed. Many developers make no distinction between reserved words and application-specific identifiers. Consider the following lines of code:

```
if to_number(the_value)>22 and num1 between lval and hval
then
    newval := 100;
elsif to_number(the_value) < 1
then
    calc_tots(to_date('12-jan-95'));
else
    clear_vals;
end if;
```

While the use of indentation makes it easier to follow the logical flow of the IF statement, all the words in the statements tend to blend together. It is difficult to separate the reserved words and the application identifiers in this code. Changing entirely to uppercase also will not improve matters. Indiscriminate, albeit consistent, use of upper- or lowercase for your code reduces its readability. The distinction between reserved words and application-specific identifiers is ignored in the formatting. This translates into a loss of information and comprehension for a developer.

The UPPER-lower Style

You can easily solve this problem by adopting a guideline for using a mix of upper- and lowercase to your code. I have recoded my previous example below, this time using the UPPER-lower style: all reserved words are written in UPPER-CASE and all application names are kept in lowercase:

```
IF to_number(the_value) > 22 AND
    num1 BETWEEN lval AND hval
THEN
    newval := 100;
ELSIF TO_NUMBER (the_value) < 1
THEN
    calc_tots (TO_DATE ('12-jan-95'));
ELSE
    clear_vals;
END IF;
```

Using a mixture of upper- and lowercase words increases the readability of the code by giving a sense of dimension to the code. The eye can more easily cruise over the text and pick the different syntactical elements of each statement. The uppercase words act as signposts directing the activity in the code. You can focus quickly on the lowercase words for the application-specific content. Consistent use of this method makes the program listings more attractive and accessible at a glance.

Formatting Single Statements

Most of your code consists of individual statements, such as assignments, calls to modules, and declarations. A consistent approach to formatting and grouping such statements will improve the readability of your program as a whole. This section suggests some guidelines.

Use at most one statement per line

As we discussed in Chapter 2, *PL/SQL Language Fundamentals*, PL/SQL uses the semicolon (;) as the logical terminator for a statement. As a result you can have more than one statement on a line and you can continue a single executable statement over more than one line. You will sometimes be tempted to place several statements on a single line, particularly if they are very simple. Consider the following line:

```
new_id := 15; calc_total (new_id); max_dollars := 105 * sales_adj;
```

It is very difficult to pick out the individual statements in this line, in addition to the fact that a procedure is called in the middle of the line. By placing each statement on its own line you mirror the complexity of a program—the simple lines look simple and the complex statements look complex—and reinforce the top-to-bottom logic of the program:

```
new_id := 15;
calc_total (new_id);
max_dollars := 105 * sales_adj;
```

You can scan the left margin (which will move left and right depending on the logic and corresponding indentation) and know that you are reviewing all the lines of code.

Use whitespace inside a statement

You can use all the indentation and blank lines you want to reveal the logic of a program and still end up with some very dense and unreadable code. It is also important to employ whitespace within a single line to make that one statement more comprehensible. Here are two general rules I employ in my code:

- Always include a space between every identifier and separator in a statement. Instead of this:

```
WHILE(total_sales<maximum_sales AND company_type='NEW')LOOP
```

write this:

```
WHILE (total_sales < maximum_sales AND company_type = 'NEW') LOOP
```

- Use spaces to make module calls and their parameter lists more understandable. Instead of this:

```
calc_totals(company_id,LAST_DAY(end_of_year_date),total_type);
```

write this:

```
calc_totals (company_id, LAST_DAY (end_of_year_date), total_type);
```

Formatting Your Declarations

The declaration section declares the local variables and other structures to be in your PL/SQL block. This section comes right at the top of the block, so it sets the first impression for the rest of the program. If the declaration section has no apparent order and is poorly formatted, it is unlikely that anything else in that program will be easily understood.

The declaration section in PL/SQL can contain many different kinds of declarations: simple, scalar variables; complex data structures like records and tables; exceptions; even entire subprograms which exist only in that program.

The following sections give some guidelines for creating your declaration statements.

Place one declaration on each line

You will be particularly tempted to "double up" declarations on a single line because, in general, declarations are very short in length. Resist that temptation! Which of the following sets of declarations would you prefer to try to understand at a glance?

```
DECLARE
    comp_type VARCHAR2(3); right_now DATE := SYSDATE; month_num INTEGER;
```

or:

```
DECLARE
    comp_type VARCHAR2(3);
    right_now DATE := SYSDATE;
    month_num INTEGER;
```

Ignore alignment for declarations

Many programmers like to align their declarations—for example:

```
DECLARE
    company_name      VARCHAR2(30);
    company_id        INTEGER;
```

```
employee_name      VARCHAR2(60);
hire_date          DATE;
termination_date   DATE;

min_value          NUMBER;
```

I am not convinced of the value of declaration alignment. Although alignment makes it easier to scan down the datatypes, the datatype isn't nearly as important as the identifier, which is already left-justified. A commitment to alignment also raises all kinds of questions that consume a developer's time and thought processes: If you have one long variable name, do you have to move all the other datatypes out to match that datatype declaration? What about when you add a new, very long declaration into an existing section? Do you have to go back and add a tab or two to the existing declarations?

The elegance of alignment also breaks down when you include comments above individual declarations, as shown in the following example:

```
DECLARE
    company_name       VARCHAR2(30);
    /* Primary key into company table */
    company_id         INTEGER;

    employee_name      VARCHAR2(60);
    /* Date hired; must be no greater than today's date. */
    hire_date          DATE;
    termination_date   DATE;

    min_value          NUMBER;
```

When the comment text cuts across the vast spaces of the alignment tabs, it just makes the datatype look isolated from its identifier.

I believe that you are better off ignoring alignment for declarations.[*] Keep the elements of the declaration (datatype and default value) close to the identifier.

Formatting Multiline Statements

Because a statement is terminated by a semicolon (;) rather than by the physical end of the line, statements can be continued onto additional lines without any specific continuation symbol or operator. This makes it very easy to spread a statement across more than one line, but it can also make it difficult to read across these lines.

Here are some examples of multiline statements that are hard to follow:

```
IF total_sales < maximum_sales AND company_type = 'NEW' AND (override
```

---

[*] I recognize, however, that many developers I respect greatly for their code quality and elegance differ with me strongly on this point.

```
     = 'Y' OR total_company_revenue < planned_revenue (SYSDATE))
THEN
     accept_order;
END IF;

generate_company_statistics (company_id, last_year_date
, rollup_type, total, average, variance, budgeted, next_year_plan);

total_sales := product_sales (company_id) + admin_cutbacks *
.5 - overhead - golden_parachutes;
```

The format of these continuation lines highlights a key question: How do you best break up a complex expression so the different parts can be read clearly, but still be connected to the statement as a whole? The following guidelines respond to this question and produce much cleaner code.

Use indentation to offset all continuation lines under the first line.

This is the most important guideline. The best way to identify continuation lines is to use indentation to logically subsume those lines under the main or first line of the statement. The following call to generate_company_statistics is obscured because the continuation line butts right up against the left margin with the module name:

```
generate_company_statistics (company_id, last_year_date,
rollup_type, total, average, variance, budgeted, next_year_plan);
```

If I indent the continuation line, the relationship of the second line to the first becomes clear:

```
generate_company_statistics (company_id, last_year_date,
    rollup_type, total, average, variance, budgeted, next_year_plan);
```

This attempt to recode, however, shows that simply adding an indentation isn't always enough. While it is clear that the line starting with rollup_type "belongs" to the previous line, the relationship of the text on the continuation line to that of the first line is unclear. We need more than a simple call to "Indent." There are several possible approaches:

Indent module-call continuation lines to align all parameters vertically.

You can place a single parameter on each line for maximum clarity, or include more than one parameter on a line—as long as they are properly indented. You can even break up the parameters so that related parameters go together on separate lines. If the name of the procedure is long and results in pushing the alignment column for parameters too far to the right, start the entire parameter list on the next line (indented) and then align all parameters against that second line. Here are some examples illustrating these rules:

```
gen_stats (company_id, last_year_date, rollup_type,
        total, average, variance, budgeted, next_year_plan);
```

```
   gen_stats (company_id,
             last_year_date,
             rollup_type,
             total,
             average,
             variance,
             budgeted,
             next_year_plan);

   gen_stats
      (company_id, last_year_date, rollup_type,
       total, average, variance, budgeted, next_year_plan);
```

I prefer the third alternative, in which all parameters are moved to the line following the name of the module. You can then place multiple parameters on the same line or place one parameter on each line, but the indentation is always and only the standard three spaces in from the start of the module name.

Make it very obvious that a statement is continued.

If a statement is not going to fit onto a single line, break up the statement so that it is quite obvious, with the most casual glance, that the first line could not possibly finish the statement. The following examples highlight this approach:

— The IN statement of a loop clearly needs its range:

```
FOR month_index IN
    first_month .. last_month
LOOP
    ...
```

— An assignment could not possibly end with a "+":

```
q1_sales :=
    month1_sales +
    month2_sales +
    month3_sales;
```

— The last comma in the first line of parameters indicates that other parameters follow:

```
generate_company_statistics
    (company_id, last_year_date,
     rollup_type, total, average, variance, budgeted, next_year_plan);
```

Formatting SQL Statements

Because PL/SQL is an extension to the SQL language, you can place SQL statements directly in your PL/SQL programs. You can also define cursors based on SELECT statements. This section summarizes my suggestions for formatting SQL statements and cursors for maximum readability.

PL/SQL supports the use of four SQL DML (Data Manipulation Language) statements: INSERT, UPDATE, DELETE, and SELECT. Each of these statements is composed of a series of "clauses," as in the WHERE clause and the ORDER BY clause. SQL statements can be very complex, to say the least. Without a consistent approach to indentation and alignment inside these statements, you can end up with a real mess. I have found the following guidelines useful:

Right-align the reserved words for the clauses against the DML statement.

I recommend that you visually separate the SQL reserved words which identify the separate clauses from the application-specific column and table names. The following table shows how I use right-alignment on the reserved words to create a vertical border between them and the rest of the SQL statement:

SELECT	INSERT	UPDATE	DELETE
SELECT	INSERT INTO	UPDATE	DELETE
	VALUES	SET	FROM
FROM		WHERE	WHERE
	INSERT INTO		
WHERE	SELECT		
AND	FROM		
OR	WHERE		
GROUP BY			
HAVING			
AND			
OR			
ORDER BY			

Here are some examples of this format in use:

```
SELECT last_name, first_name
  FROM employee
 WHERE department_id = 15
   AND hire_date < SYSDATE;

SELECT department_id, SUM (salary) AS total_salary
  FROM employee
 GROUP BY department_id
 ORDER BY total_salary DESC;

INSERT INTO employee
   (employee_id, ... )
VALUES
   (105 ... );

DELETE FROM employee
       WHERE department_id = 15;
```

```
UPDATE employee
   SET hire_date = SYSDATE
 WHERE hire_date IS NULL
   AND termination_date IS NULL;
```

Yes, I realize that the GROUP BY and ORDER BY keywords aren't exactly right-aligned to SELECT, but at least the primary words (GROUP and ORDER) are aligned. Notice that within each of the WHERE and HAVING clauses I right-align the AND and OR Boolean connectors under the WHERE keyword.

This right alignment makes it very easy for me to identify the different clauses of the SQL statement, particularly with extended SELECTs. You might also consider placing a blank line between clauses of longer SQL statements (this is possible in PL/SQL, but is not acceptable in "native" SQL executed in SQL*Plus).

Don't skimp on the use of line separators.

Within clauses, such separation makes the SQL statement easier to read. In particular, place each expression of the WHERE clause on its own line, and consider using a separate line for each expression in the select list of a SELECT statement. Place each table in the FROM clause on its own line. Certainly, put each separate assignment in a SET clause of the UPDATE statement on its own line. Here are some illustrations of these guidelines:

```
SELECT last_name,
       C.name,
       MAX (SH.salary) best_salary_ever
  FROM employee E,
       company C,
       salary_history SH
 WHERE E.company_id = C.company_id
   AND E.employee_id = SH.employee_id
   AND E.hire_date > ADD_MONTHS (SYSDATE, -60);

UPDATE employee
   SET hire_date = SYSDATE,
       termination_date = NULL
 WHERE department_id = 105;
```

NOTE   You can place blank lines inside a SQL statement when you are coding that SQL from within a PL/SQL block. You may not, on the other hand, embed white space in SQL statements you are executing from the SQL*Plus command line.

- *Use meaningful abbreviations for table and column aliases*

  It drives me crazy when a query has a six-table join and the tables have been assigned aliases A, B, C, D, E, and F. How can you possibly decipher the WHERE clause in the following SELECT?

```
SELECT ... select list ...
   FROM employee A, company B, history C, bonus D,
        profile E, sales F
WHERE A.company_id = B.company_id
  AND A.employee_id = C.employee_id
  AND B.company_id = F.company_id
  AND A.employee_id = D.employee_id
  AND B.company_id = E.company_id;
```

With more sensible table aliases (including no tables aliases at all where the table name was short enough already), the relationships are much clearer:

```
SELECT ... select list ...
   FROM employee EMP, company CO, history HIST, bonus,
        profile PROF, sales
WHERE EMP.company_id = CO.company_id
  AND EMP.employee_id = HIST.employee_id
  AND CO.company_id = SALES.company_id
  AND EMP.employee_id = BONUS.employee_id
  AND CO.company_id = PROF.company_id;
```

Formatting Control Structures

The control structures in your program are the most direct representation of the logic needed to implement your specifications. The format of these control structures, therefore, will have a significant impact on the readability of your code.

Indentation is the most important element of control structure layout. Always keep statements of the same "logical level" at the same indentation level. Let's see what this means for the various control structures of PL/SQL.

Formatting IF Statements

This conditional construct comes in three flavors:

IF <expression>	IF <expression>	IF <expression>
END IF;	ELSE	ELSIF <expression>
	END IF;	ELSE
		END IF;

In general, the IF statement is composed of clauses in which there is a Boolean expression or condition and a section of code executed when that condition evaluates to TRUE.

So if you want to use indentation to reveal the logical structure of the simplest form of the IF statement (IF-END IF), I suggest one of these two styles:

Notice that in both versions the executable statements are indented three spaces from the column in which the IF and END IF reserved words are found. The only difference between the two formats is the placement of the THEN reserved word.

New Line for THEN	Same Line for THEN
| ```
IF <expression>
THEN
   executable_statements;
END IF;
``` | ```
IF <expression> THEN
   executable_statements
END IF;
``` |
| ```
IF <expression>
THEN
   executable_statements;
ELSE
   else_executable_statements;
END IF;
``` | ```
IF <expression> THEN
   executable_statements
ELSE
   else_executable_statements;
END IF;
``` |
| ```
IF <expression1>1
THEN
   executable_statements1;

ELSIF <expression2>
THEN
   executable_statements2;
...

ELSIF <expressionN>
THEN
   executable_statementsN;

ELSE
   else_executable_statements;
END IF;
``` | ```
IF <expression1> THEN
   executable_statements1;

ELSIF <expression2> THEN
   executable_statements2;
...

ELSIF <expressionN>
THEN
   executable_statementsN;

ELSE
   else_executable_statements;
END IF;
``` |

I prefer the new line format, in which the THEN appears on a line by itself after the IF condition. This format provides more whitespace than the other. I could create the whitespace by using a blank, rather than indenting three spaces, but then the executable statements for the IF clause are made distinct from the condition—and they are logically connected. Let's examine some actual code to get a better sense of the differences.

The following example shows proper IF statement indentation with THEN on the same line:

```
IF max_sales > 2000 THEN
   notify_accounting ('over_limit');
   RAISE FORM_TRIGGER_FAILURE;
END IF;
```

This code has proper IF statement indentation with THEN on the next line:

```
IF max_sales > 2000
THEN
   notify_accounting ('over_limit');
   RAISE FORM_TRIGGER_FAILURE;
END IF;
```

Formatting Loops

You are going to be writing many loops in your PL/SQL programs, and they will usually surround some of the most complicated code in your application. For this reason, the format you use to structure your loops will make a critical difference in the overall comprehensibility of your programs.

PL/SQL offers the following kinds of loops:

- Infinite or simple loop
- WHILE loop
- Indexed FOR loop (numeric and cursor)

Each loop has a loop boundary (begin and end statements) and a loop body. The loop body should be indented from the boundary (again, I recommend three spaces of indentation).

As with the IF statement, you can either choose to leave the LOOP reserved word at the end of the line containing the WHILE and FOR statements or place it on the next line. I prefer the latter, because then both the LOOP and END LOOP reserved words appear at the same column position (indentation) in the program.

Here are my recommendations for formatting your loops:

- The infinite or simple loop:

```
LOOP
   executable_statements;
END LOOP;
```

- The WHILE loop:

```
WHILE condition
LOOP
   executable_statements;
END LOOP;
```

- The numeric and cursor FOR loops:

```
FOR for_index IN low_value .. high_value
LOOP
   executable_statements;
END LOOP;

FOR record_index IN my_cursor
LOOP
   executable_statements;
END LOOP;
```

Formatting Exception Handlers

PL/SQL provides a very powerful facility for dealing with errors. An entirely separate exception section contains one or more "handlers" to trap exceptions and execute code when that exception occurs. Logically, the exception section is structured like a conditional CASE statement (which, by the way, is not supported by PL/SQL).

As you might expect, the format for the exception section should resemble that of an IF statement. Here is a general example of the exception section:

```
EXCEPTION
   WHEN NO_DATA_FOUND
   THEN
       executable_statements1;

   WHEN DUP_VAL_ON_INDEX
   THEN
       executable_statements1;

   ...
   WHEN OTHERS
   THEN
       otherwise_code;
END;
```

Instead of an IF or ELSIF keyword, the exception handler uses the word WHEN. In place of a condition (Boolean expression), the WHEN clause lists an exception name followed by a THEN and finally the executable statements for that exception. In place of ELSE, the exception section offers a WHEN OTHERS clause.

Follow these guidelines:

- Indent each WHEN clause in from the EXCEPTION keyword that indicates the start of the exception section, as I've shown above. Place the THEN directly below the WHEN.

- Indent all the executable statements for that handler in from the THEN keyword.

- Place a blank line before each WHEN (except for the first).

Formatting PL/SQL Blocks

As I've outlined in Chapter 2, every PL/SQL program is structured as a block containing up to four sections:

- Header
- Declaration section

- Executable section

- Exception section

The PL/SQL block structure forms the backbone of your code. A consistent formatting style for the block, therefore, is critical. This formatting should make clear these different sections. (See Chapter 15, *Procedures and Functions*, for more information about the block structure.)

Consider the following function:

```
FUNCTION
company_name (company_id_in IN company.company_id%TYPE)      RETURN
VARCHAR2 IS cname company.company_id%TYPE; BEGIN
   SELECT name INTO cname FROM company
    WHERE company_id = company_id_in;
   RETURN cname;
EXCEPTION WHEN NO_DATA_FOUND THEN    RETURN NULL; END;
```

You know that this program is a function because the first word in the program is FUNCTION. Other than that, however, it is very difficult to follow the structure of this program. Where is the declaration section? Where does the executable section begin and end?

Here is that same function after we apply some straightforward formatting rules to it:

```
FUNCTION company_name (company_id_in IN company.company_id%TYPE)
    RETURN VARCHAR2
IS
   cname company.company_id%TYPE;

BEGIN
   SELECT name INTO cname FROM company
    WHERE company_id = company_id_in;
   RETURN cname;

EXCEPTION
   WHEN NO_DATA_FOUND
   THEN
      RETURN NULL;
END;
```

Now it is easy to see that the header of the function consists of:

```
FUNCTION company_name (company_id_in IN company.company_id%TYPE)
    RETURN VARCHAR2
```

The declaration section, which comes after the IS and before the BEGIN, clearly consists of a single declaration of the cname variable. The executable section consists of all the statements after the BEGIN and before the EXCEPTION statement; these are indented in from the BEGIN. Finally, the exception section shows a single specific exception handler and a WHEN OTHERS exception.

Generally, indent the statements for a given section from the reserved words which initiate the section. You can also include a blank line before each section, as I do above, for the executable section (before BEGIN) and the exception section (before EXCEPTION). I usually place the IS keyword on its own line to clearly differentiate between the header of a module and its declaration section.

Formatting Packages

A *package* is a collection of related objects, including variables, TYPE statements (to define structures for records, tables, and cursors), exceptions, and modules. We have already covered structuring all the different objects which make up a package. Now, let's take a look at how to structure the package itself.

A package has both a specification and a body. The package specification contains the declarations or definitions of all those objects that are visible outside of the package—the public objects. This means that the objects can be accessed by any account that has been granted EXECUTE authority on the package. The package body contains the implementation of all cursors and modules defined in the specification, and the additional declaration and implementation of all other package objects. If an object, such as a string variable, is declared in the body and not in the package, then any module in the package can reference that variable, but no program outside of the package can see it. That variable is invisible or private to the package.

The first point to make about the package structure is that all objects declared in the specification exist within the context of the package and so should be indented from the PACKAGE statement itself, as shown below:

```
PACKAGE rg_select
IS
    list_name VARCHAR2(60);

    PROCEDURE init_list
        (item_name_in IN VARCHAR2,
         fill_action_in IN VARCHAR2 := 'IMMEDIATE');
    PROCEDURE delete_list;
    PROCEDURE clear_list;

END rg_select;
```

The same is true for the package body. I suggest that you always include a label for the END statement in a package so that you can easily connect up that END with the end of the package as a whole. I place the IS keyword on a new line to set off the first declaration in the package from the name of the package. You could always use a blank line. Notice that I use blank lines in rg_select to segregate different modules which are related by function. I think that logical grouping is always preferable to an arbitrary grouping such as alphabetical order.

The other important element in formatting a package is the order in which objects are listed in the package. I generally list objects in the order of complexity of their structure, as follows:

- Scalar variables, such as a VARCHAR2 declaration

- Complex datatypes, such as records and tables

- Database-related declarations, such as cursors

- Named exceptions

- Modules (procedures and functions)

As with simple variable declarations, I sometimes have many different but related objects in my package. If so, I might group those types of objects together. But within that grouping, I still follow the above order.

Using Comments Effectively

The object of an effective coding style is to make the program more understandable and maintainable. Most programs will benefit from documentation which explains what is going on inside those programs. There are two forms of code documentation: external and internal. External documentation is descriptive information about a program which is written and stored separately from the program itself. Internal documentation, also known as inline documentation or comments, is placed within the program itself, either at the program level or the statement level. (For an introduction to inline documentation and the types of PL/SQL comments, see the section called "Comments" in Chapter 2.)

The best kind of internal documentation derives from your programming style. If you apply many of the guidelines in this chapter and throughout this book, you will be able to write code which is, to a great extent, self-documenting. Here are some general tips:

- Write straightforward code that avoids clever tricks.

- Think of names for variables and modules that accurately describe their purpose.

- Use named constants instead of literal values.

- Employ a clean, consistent layout.

Do all these things and more, and you will find that you need to write fewer comments to explain your code.

Reducing the need for comments is important. Few developers make or have the time for extensive documentation in addition to their development efforts, and, more importantly, many comments tend to duplicate the code. This raises a maintenance issue because those comments will have to be changed when the code is changed.

While it is my hope that after reading this book you will write more self-documenting code, there is little doubt that you will still need to comment your code. The following example shows the use of single- and multiline comments in PL/SQL:

```
PROCEDURE calc_totals (company_id IN NUMBER,--The company key
                       total_type IN VARCHAR2--ALL or NET
                      );

/*
|| For every employee hired more than five years ago,
|| give them a bonus and send them an e-mail notification.
*/
FOR emp_rec IN emp_cur (ADD_MONTHS (SYSDATE, -60))
LOOP
   apply_bonus (emp_rec.employee_id);
   send_notification (emp_rec.employee_id);
END LOOP;

-- IF :SYSTEM.FORM_STATUS = 'CHANGED' THEN COMMIT; END IF;

FUNCTION display_user
   (user_id IN NUMBER /* Must be valid ID */, user_type IN VARCHAR2)
```

The first example uses the single-line comment syntax to include endline descriptions for each parameter in the procedure specification. The second example uses a multiline comment to explain the purpose of the FOR loop. The third example uses the double-hyphen to comment out a whole line of code. The last example embeds a comment in the middle of a line of code using the block comment syntax.

These two types of comments offer the developer flexibility in how to provide inline documentation. The rest of this section offers guidelines for writing effective comments in your PL/SQL programs.

Comment As You Code

It is very difficult to make time to document your code after you have finished writing your program. Psychologically, you want to (and often need to) move on to the next programming challenge after you get a program working.

You may also have a harder time writing your comments once you have put some distance between your brain cells and those lines of code. Why exactly did you write the loop that way? Where precisely is the value of that global variable set? Unless you have total recall, post-development documentation can be a real challenge.

The last and perhaps most important reason to write your comments as you write your code is that the resulting code will have fewer bugs and (independent of the comments themselves) be easier to understand.

When you write a comment you (theoretically) explain what your code is meant to accomplish. If you find it difficult to come up with that explanation, there is a good chance that you lack a full understanding of what the program does or should do.

The effort that you make to come up with the right comment will certainly improve your comprehension, and may also result in code correction. In this sense, good inline documentation can be as beneficial as a review of your code by a peer. In both cases, the explanation will reveal important information about your program.

Explain the Why—Not the How—of Your Program

What do you think of the comments in the following Oracle Forms trigger code?

```
-- If the total compensation is more than the maximum...
IF :employee.total_comp > maximum_salary
THEN
    -- Inform the user of the problem.
    MESSAGE ('Total compensation exceeds maximum. Please re-enter!');

    -- Reset the counter to zero.
    :employee.comp_counter := 0;

    -- Raise the exception to stop trigger processing.
    RAISE FORM_TRIGGER_FAILURE;
END IF;
```

None of these comments add anything to the comprehension of the code. Each comment simply restates the line of code, which in most cases is self-explanatory.

Avoid adding comments simply so that you can say, "Yes, I documented my code!" Rely as much as possible on the structure and layout of the code itself to express the meaning of the program. Reserve your comments to explain the Why of your code: What business rule is it meant to implement? Why did you need to implement a certain requirement in a certain way?

In addition, use comments to translate internal, computer-language terminology into something meaningful for the application. Suppose you are using Oracle Forms GLOBAL variables to keep track of a list of names entered. Does the following comment explain the purpose of the code or simply restate what the code is doing?

```
/* Set the number of elements to zero. */
:GLOBAL.num_elements := 0;
```

Once again, the comment adds no value. Does the next comment offer additional information?

```
/* Empty the list of names. */
:GLOBAL.num_elements := 0;
```

This comment actually explains the purpose of the assignment of the global to zero. By setting the number of elements to zero, I will have effectively emptied the list. This comment has translated the "computer lingo" into a description of the effect of the statement. Of course, you would be even better off hiding the fact that you use this particular global variable to empty a list and instead build a procedure as follows:

```
PROCEDURE empty_list IS
BEGIN
    :GLOBAL.num_elements := 0;
END;
```

Then to empty a list you would not need any comment at all. You could simply include the statement:

```
empty_list;
```

and the meaning would be perfectly clear.

Make Comments Easy to Enter and Maintain

You shouldn't spend a lot of time formatting your comments. You need to develop a style that is clean and easy to read, but also easy to maintain. When you have to change a comment, you shouldn't have to reformat every line in the comment. Lots of fancy formatting is a good indication that you have a high-maintenance documentation style. The following block comment is a maintenance nightmare:

```
/*
============================================================
| Parameter          Description                          |
|                                                         |
| company_id         The primary key to company           |
| start_date         Start date used for date range       |
| end_date           End date for date range              |
============================================================
*/
```

The right-justified vertical lines and column formatting for the parameters require way too much effort to enter and maintain. What happens if you add a parameter with a very long name? What if you need to write a longer description? A simpler and more maintainable version of this comment might be:

```
/*
==============================================================
| Parameter - Description
|
| company_id - The primary key to company
| start_date - Start date used for date range
| end_date - End date for date range
==============================================================
*/
```

I like to use the following format for my block comments:

```
/*
|| I put the slash-asterisk that starts the comment on a line all by
|| itself. Then I start each line in the comment block with a double
|| vertical bar to highlight the presence of the comment. Finally,
|| I place the asterisk-slash on a line all by itself.
*/
```

On the negative side, the vertical bars have to be erased whenever I reformat the lines, but that isn't too much of an effort. On the positive side, those vertical bars make it very easy for a programmer who is scanning the left side of the code to pick out the comments.

I put the comment markers on their own lines to increase the whitespace in my program and set off the comment. That way I can avoid "heavy" horizontal lines full of delimiters, such as asterisks or dashes, and avoid having to match the longest line in the comment.

Maintain Indentation

Inline commentary should reinforce the indentation and therefore the logical structure of the program. For example, it is very easy to find the comments in the make_array procedures shown below. I do not use any double-hyphens, so the slash-asterisk sequences stand out nicely. In addition, all comments start in the first column, so I can easily scan down the left-hand side of the program and pick out the documentation:

```
PROCEDURE make_array (num_rows_in IN INTEGER)
/* Create an array of specified numbers of rows */
IS
/* Handles to Oracle Forms structures */
   col_id GROUPCOLUMN;
   rg_id RECORDGROUP;
BEGIN
/* Create new record group and column */
   rg_id := CREATE_GROUP ('array');
   col_id := ADD_GROUP_COLUMN ('col');
/*
|| Use a loop to create the specified number of rows and
|| set the value in each cell.
*/
```

```
      FOR row_index IN 1 .. num_rows_in
      LOOP
/* Create a row at the end of the group to accept data */
         ADD_GROUP_ROW (return_value, END_OF_GROUP);
         FOR col_index IN 1 .. num_columns_in
         LOOP
/* Set the initial value in the cell */
            SET_GROUP_NUMBER_CELL (col_id, row_index, 0);
         END LOOP;
      END LOOP;
   END;
```

The problem with these comments is precisely that they do all start in the first column, regardless of the code they describe. The most glaring example of this formatting "disconnect" comes in the inner loop, repeated below:

```
         FOR col_index IN 1 .. num_columns_in
         LOOP
/* Set the initial value in the cell */
            SET_GROUP_NUMBER_CELL (col_id, row_index, 0);
         END LOOP;
```

Your eye follows the three-space indentation very smoothly into the loop and then you are forced to move all the way to the left to pick up the comment. This format disrupts your reading of the code and therefore its readability. The code loses some of its ability to communicate the logical flow "at a glance," because the physical sense of indentation as logical flow is marred by the comments. Finally, you may end up writing full-line comments which are much longer than the code they appear next to, further distorting the code.

Your comments should always be indented at the same level as the code which they describe. Assuming the comments come before the code itself, those lines of descriptive text will initiate the indentation at that logical level, which will also reinforce that structure. The make_array procedure, properly indented, is shown below:

```
PROCEDURE make_array (num_rows_in IN INTEGER)
/* Create an array of specified numbers of rows */
IS
   /* Handles to Oracle Forms structures */
   col_id GROUPCOLUMN;
   rg_id RECORDGROUP;
BEGIN
   /* Create new record group and column */
   rg_id := CREATE_GROUP ('array');
   col_id := ADD_GROUP_COLUMN ('col');
   /*
   || Use a loop to create the specified number of rows and
   || set the value in each cell.
   */
   FOR row_index IN 1 .. num_rows_in
   LOOP
      /* Create a row at the end of the group to accept data */
      ADD_GROUP_ROW (return_value, END_OF_GROUP);
```

```
        FOR col_index IN 1 .. num_columns_in
        LOOP
            /* Set the initial value in the cell */
            SET_GROUP_NUMBER_CELL (col_id, row_index, 0);
        END LOOP;
    END LOOP;
END;
```

Comment Declaration Statements

I propose the following simple rule for documenting declaration statements:

Provide a comment for each and every declaration.

Does that sound excessive? Well, I must admit that I do not follow this guideline at all times, but I bet people who read my code wish I had. The declaration of a variable which seems to me to be perfectly clear may be a source of abiding confusion for others. Like many other people, I still have difficulty understanding that what is obvious to me is not necessarily obvious to someone else.

Consider the declaration section in the next example. The commenting style is inconsistent. I use double-hyphens for a two-line comment; then I use the standard block format to provide information about three variables all at once. I provide comments for some variables, but not for others. It's hard to make sense of the various declaration statements:

```
DECLARE
    -- Assume a maximum string length of 1000 for a line of text.
    text_line VARCHAR2 (1000);
    len_text     NUMBER;
    /*
    || Variables used to keep track of string scan:
    ||    atomic_count - running count of atomics scanned.
    ||    still_scanning - Boolean variable controls WHILE loop.
    */
    atomic_count NUMBER := 1;
    still_scanning BOOLEAN;
BEGIN
```

Let's recast this declaration section using my proposed guideline: a comment for each declaration statement. In the result shown below, the declaration section is now longer than the first version, but it uses whitespace more effectively. Each declaration has its own comment, set off by a blank line if a single-line comment:

```
DECLARE
    /* Assume a maximum string length of 1000 for a line of text. */
    text_line VARCHAR2 (1000);

    /* Calculate length of string at time of declaration */
    len_string NUMBER;

    /* Running count of number of atomics scanned */
    atomic_count NUMBER := 1;
```

```
     /* Boolean variable that controls WHILE loop */
     still_scanning BOOLEAN ;
  BEGIN
```

Documenting the Entire Package

A package is often a complicated and long construct. It is composed of many different types of objects, any of which may be public (visible to programs and users outside of the package) or private (available only to other objects in the package). Package structure is described in more detail in Chapter 16, *Packages*.

You can use some very simple documentation guidelines to clarify the structure of the package.

As usual when discussing packages, one must consider the specification separately from the body. As a meta-module or grouping of modules, the specification should have a standard header. This header needn't be as complicated as that of a specific module, because you do not want to repeat in the package header any information which also belongs in specific modules. I suggest using the template header shown in the following example. In the "Major Modifications" section of the header, do not include every change made to every object in the package. Instead note significant changes to the package as a whole, such as an expansion of scope, a change in the way the package and global variables are managed, etc. Place this header after the package name and before the IS statement:

```
PACKAGE package_name
/*
|| Author:
||
|| Overview:
||
|| Major Modifications (when, who, what)
||
*/
IS
   ...
END package_name;
```

Document the Package Specification

The package specification is, in essence, a series of declaration statements. Some of those statements declare variables, while others declare modules. Follow the same recommendation in commenting a package as you do in commenting a module's declaration section: provide a comment for each declaration. In addition to the comments for a specific declaration, you may also find it useful to provide a banner before a group of related declarations to make that connection obvious to the reader.

Surround the banner with whitespace (blank lines for the start/end of a multiline comment block). While you can use many different formats for this banner, use the simplest possible design that gets the point across. Everything else is clutter.

The package specification below illustrates the header and declaration-level comment styles, as well as group banners:

```
PACKAGE rg_select
/*
|| Author: Steven Feuerstein, x3194
||
|| Overview: Manage a list of selected items correlated with a
||    block on the screen.
||
|| Major Modifications (when, who, what)
||    12/94 - SEF - Create package
||    3/95  - JRC - Enhance to support coordinated blocks
||
*/
IS
    /*----------------- Modules to Define the List -------------------*/

    /* Initialize the list/record group. */
    PROCEDURE init_list (item_name_in IN VARCHAR2);

    /* Delete the list */
    PROCEDURE delete_list;

    /*----------------- Modules to Manage Item Selections -----------*/

    /* Mark item as selected */
    PROCEDURE select_item (row_in IN INTEGER);

    /* De-select the item from the list */
    PROCEDURE deselect_item (row_in IN INTEGER);

END rg_select;
```

Document the Package Body

The body is even longer and more complex than the specification. The specification contains only declarations, and only the declarations of public or global objects. The body contains the declarations of all private variables, cursors, types, etc., as well as the implementation of all cursors and modules. My suggestion for commenting declarations in the package body is, again, to provide a single line (or more) for each declaration, separated by whitespace. This takes more space, but is very legible.

Once you get beyond the variables, use banners for any and all of the following:

- The private modules of the package. These should come after the package variable declarations, but before the public module implementations. The banner alerts a reader to the fact that these modules were not in the specification.

- The public modules of the package. The package specification describes only the interface to these modules. The body contains the full code for those modules. Use a banner to let the reader know that you are done with variables and private modules.

- Groups of related modules, particularly those with the same, overloaded name. (Overloading occurs when you create multiple modules with the same name but different parameter lists.)

The banners for a package body are shown below:

```
PACKAGE BODY package_name
IS
     /*---------------------- Package Variables ----------------------*/
     ... declarations placed here

     /*---------------------- Private Modules -----------------------*/
     FUNCTION ...
     PROCEDURE ...

     /*---------------------- Public Modules ------------------------*/
     FUNCTION ...
     PROCEDURE ...

END package_name;
```

Whether in a package or an individual module, make sure that your comments add value to the code. Do not repeat what the code itself clearly states. When dealing with a structure as complicated as a package, however, you need comments which focus on communicating that structure. If your package has more than a handful of modules, and especially if it uses both private and public modules, you should make sure to use these banners to keep the reader fully informed about the context of the code they are reading in the package.

II

PL/SQL Language Elements

Part II of this book describes the essential language constructs provided by PL/SQL. It includes extensive examples of these constructs and explains how to use them most effectively.

- Chapter 4, *Variables and Program Data*, explains variables and constants in PL/SQL programs and presents the various PL/SQL datatypes.

- Chapter 5, *Conditional and Sequential Control*, describes how to use various types of IF, THEN, and ELSE constructs, as well as the NULL and GOTO statements.

- Chapter 6, *Database Interaction and Cursors*, describes how to use explicit and implicit cursors.

- Chapter 7, *Loops*, explains the different types of loops—LOOP, FOR LOOP, and WHILE LOOP.

- Chapter 8, *Exception Handlers*, discusses the various types of exceptions, including predefined, named programmer-defined, unnamed internal, and unnamed programmer-defined.

- Chapter 9, *Records in PL/SQL*, describes how to use table-based, cursor-based, and programmer-defined records.

- Chapter 10, *PL/SQL Tables*, explains how to declare and use tables, and how to apply them to a variety of tasks.

4

Variables and Program Data

Almost every PL/SQL program you write contains internal data stored as variables, constants, records, or tables. This chapter refers to these various types of storage as *variables*. Variables may be used for many purposes; for example, they may store information retrieved from columns in a table or may hold calculated values for use only in the program. Variables may be *scalar* (made up of a single value) or *composite* (made up of multiple values or components).

The *attributes* of a variable are its name, datatype, and value (or values, in a complex datatype like a record). The name indicates the part of memory you want to access or change. The datatype determines the type of information you can store in the variable. The value (or values, in the case of a composite datatype) is the set of bits stored in the variable's memory location.

This chapter describes the kinds of names you can give PL/SQL elements and the different types of scalar variables you can declare and use in your programs. It also offers tips on how best to use program data in your code.

Identifiers

Identifiers are the names given to PL/SQL elements such as variables or nested tables or cursors. Identifiers:

- Can be up to 30 characters in length

- Must start with a letter

- Can then be composed of any of the following: letters, numerals, $, #, and _

A *named constant* is a special kind of variable. A named constant has a name, datatype, and value, just like a regular variable. However, unlike a regular variable, the value of a named constant must be set when the constant is declared and may not change thereafter. Its value is constant. Unless otherwise mentioned, the information provided below for variables also applies to named constants.

NOTE   An unnamed constant is a literal value, such as 2 or Bobby McGee.
            A literal does not have a name, though it does have an implied (un-
            declared) datatype.

Choose the Right Name

The name of your identifier should describe as accurately and concisely as possible what the identifier represents. Let's take a look at choosing the name for a variable. Outside of the actual use or context of a variable, the name is all the variable's got. And if the name is bad, the context is often distorted by the bad choice of a moniker.

The first step towards choosing an accurate name is to have a clear idea of how the variable is to be used. You might even take a moment to write down—in noncomputer terms—what the variable represents. You can then easily extract an appropriate name from this statement. For example, if a variable represents the "total number of calls made about lukewarm coffee," a good name for that variable would be total_calls_on_cold_coffee—or tot_cold_calls, if you are allergic to five-word variable names. A bad name for that variable would be "totcoffee" or t_#_calls_lwcoff, both of which are too cryptic to get the point across.

You can also give each variable a name that describes the business problem that variable will be used to solve. The name should be much more than a description of the internal or computer-oriented function of the variable. If you need a Boolean variable to indicate when "the total order amount exceeds existing balance," a good name would be total_order_exceeds_balance. A poorly chosen name would be float_overflow or group_sum_too_big. You, the developer, know that you had to perform a SUM with a GROUP BY to calculate the total order, but no one else needs to know about that.

Select Readable Names

PL/SQL lets you use 30 characters, including very clear separators such as the underscore character (_), to name your variables. That gives you lots of room to come up with unambiguous names. In fact, if you have variable names of fewer than five characters in length, they are probably too short to be accurate and useful.

Resist the temptation to name a variable which stores the current date as curdat or now. Instead use the more descriptive current_date or even system_date (a logical expansion on the SQL function SYSDATE, which usually provides the value).

An excellent way to check the quality of your variable names (as well as the names of your other objects, particularly module names) is to ask for feedback from another developer on the same project. The code should, to a large extent, make sense if the variables and other identifiers are named in ways that describe the action, and not the cute programming tricks you used to meet the specifications.

Scalar Datatypes

Each constant and variable element you use in your programs has a datatype. The datatype dictates the storage format, the restrictions on how the variable can be used, and the valid values which may be placed in that variable.

PL/SQL offers a comprehensive set of predefined scalar and composite datatypes. A scalar datatype is an atomic; it is not made up of other variable components. A composite datatype has internal structure or components. The two composite types currently supported by PL/SQL are the record and table (described in Chapter 9, *Records in PL/SQL*, and Chapter 10, *PL/SQL Tables*, respectively).

The scalar datatypes fall into one of four categories or families: number, character, Boolean, and date-time, as shown in Table 4-1.

Table 4-1. Datatype Categories

Category	Datatype
Number	BINARY_INTEGER
	DEC
	DECIMAL
	DOUBLE PRECISION
	FLOAT
	INT
	INTEGER
	NATURAL
	NUMBER
	NUMERIC
	PLS_INTEGER
	POSITIVE
	REAL
	SMALLINT

Table 4-1. Datatype Categories (continued)

Category	Datatype
Character	CHAR
	CHARACTER
	LONG
	LONG RAW
	NCHAR
	NVARCHAR2
	RAW
	ROWID
	STRING
	VARCHAR
	VARCHAR2
Boolean	BOOLEAN
Date-time	DATE
Large object (LOB)	BFILE
	BLOB
	CLOB
	NCLOB

Let's take a closer look at each of the scalar datatypes.

Numeric Datatypes

PL/SQL, just like the Oracle RDBMS, offers a variety of numeric datatypes to suit different purposes. There are generally two types of numeric data: whole number and decimal (in which digits to the right of the decimal point are allowed).

Binary integer datatypes

The whole number, or integer, datatypes are:

    BINARY_INTEGER
    INTEGER
    SMALLINT
    INT
    POSITIVE
    NATURAL

The BINARY_INTEGER datatype allows you to store signed integers. The range of magnitude of a BINARY_INTEGER is $-2^{31} + 1$ through $2^{31} - 1$ (2^{31} is equal to 2147483647). BINARY_INTEGERs are represented in the PL/SQL compiler as signed binary numbers. They do not, as a result, need to be converted before PL/SQL performs numeric calculations. Variables of type NUMBER (see "Decimal numeric datatypes") do, however, need to be converted. So if you will be performing intensive calculations with integer values, you might see a performance improvement by declaring your variables as BINARY_INTEGER. In most situations, to be honest, the slight savings offered by BINARY_INTEGER will not be noticeable.

NATURAL and POSITIVE are both subtypes of BINARY_INTEGER. A subtype uses the storage format and restrictions on how the variable of this type can be used, but it allows only a subset of the valid values allowed by the full datatype. In the case of BINARY_INTEGER subtypes, we have the following value subsets:

NATURAL
   0 through 2^{31}

POSITIVE
   1 through 2^{31}

If you have a variable whose values must always be non-negative (0 or greater), you should declare that variable to be NATURAL or POSITIVE. This improves the self-documenting aspect of your code.

Decimal numeric datatypes

The decimal numeric datatypes are:

    NUMBER
    FLOAT
    DEC
    DECIMAL
    DOUBLE PRECISION
    NUMBER
    NUMERIC
    REAL

Use the NUMBER datatype to store fixed or floating-point numbers of just about any size. The maximum precision of a variable with NUMBER type is 38 digits. This means that the range of magnitude of values is 1.0E–129 through 9.999E125; you are unlikely to require numbers outside of this range.

When you declare a variable type NUMBER, you can also optionally specify the variable's precision and scale, as follows:

    NUMBER (precision, scale)

The precision of a NUMBER is the total number of digits. The scale dictates the number of digits to the right or left of the decimal point at which rounding occurs. Both the precision and scale values must be literal values (and integers at that); you cannot use variables or constants in the declaration. Legal values for the scale range from –84 to 127. Rounding works as follows:

- If the scale is positive, then the scale determines the point at which rounding occurs to the right of the decimal point.

- If the scale is negative, then the scale determines the point at which rounding occurs to the left of the decimal point.

- If the scale is zero, then rounding occurs to the nearest whole number.

- If the scale is not specified, then no rounding occurs.

The following examples demonstrate the different ways you can declare variables of type NUMBER:

- The bean_counter variable can hold values with up to ten digits of precision, three of which are to the right of the decimal point. If you assign 12345.6784 to bean_counter, it is rounded to 12345.678. If you assign 1234567891.23 to the variable, the operation will return an error because there are more digits than allowed for in the precision.

    ```
    bean_counter NUMBER (10,3);
    ```

- The big_whole_number variable contains whole numbers spanning the full range of supported values, because the default precision is 38 and the default scale is 0.

    ```
    big_whole_number NUMBER;
    ```

- The rounded_million variable is declared with a negative scale. This causes rounding to the left of the decimal point. Just as a scale of –1 (instead of +1) would cause rounding to the nearest tenth, a scale of –2 would round to the nearest hundred and a scale of –6 would round to the nearest million. If you assign 53.35 to rounded_million, it will be rounded to 0. If you assign 1,567,899 to rounded_million, it will be rounded to two million (2,000,000).

    ```
    rounded_million NUMBER (10,-6);
    ```

- In the following unusual but perfectly legitimate declaration, the scale is larger than the precision. In this case, the precision indicates the maximum number of digits allowed—all to the right of the decimal point. If you assign .003566 to small_value, it will be rounded to .00357. Because the scale is two greater than the precision, any value assigned to small_value must have two zeros directly to the right of the decimal point, followed by up to three nonzero digits.

    ```
    small_value NUMBER (3, 5);
    ```

The PLS_INTEGER datatype

This datatype is available in PL/SQL Release 2.3 and above.

Variables declared as PLS_INTEGER store signed integers. The magnitude range for this datatype is -2147483647 through 2147483647. Oracle recommends that you use PLS_INTEGER for all integer calculations which do not fall outside of its range. PLS_INTEGER values require less storage than NUMBER values, and operations on PLS_INTEGER's use machine arithmetic, making them more efficient.

Variables declared as PLS_INTEGER and BINARY_INTEGER have the same range, but they are treated differently. When a calculation involving PLS_INTEGER overflows, PL/SQL raises an exception. However, similar overflow involving BINARY_INTEGERS will not raise an exception if the result is being assigned to a NUMBER variable.

Numeric Subtypes

The remainder of the datatypes in the numeric category are all subtypes of NUMBER. They are provided in ORACLE's SQL and in PL/SQL in order to offer compatibility with ANSI SQL, SQL/DS, and DB2 datatypes. They have the same range of legal values as their base type, as displayed in Table 4-2. The NUMERIC, DECIMAL, and DEC datatypes can declare only fixed-point numbers. FLOAT, DOUBLE PRECISION, and REAL allow floating decimal points with binary precisions that range from 63 to 126.

Table 4-2. Predefined Numeric Subtypes

Subtype	Compatibility	Corresponding Oracle Datatype
DEC (prec, scale)	ANSI	NUMBER (prec, scale)
DECIMAL (prec, scale)	IBM	NUMBER (prec, scale)
DOUBLE PRECISION	ANSI	NUMBER
FLOAT (binary)	ANSI, IBM	NUMBER
INT	ANSI	NUMBER (38)
INTEGER	ANSI, IBM	NUMBER (38)
NUMERIC (prec, scale)	ANSI	NUMBER (prec, scale)
REAL	ANSI	NUMBER
SMALLINT	ANSI, IBM	NUMBER (38)

Prec, scale, and binary have the following meanings:

prec
  Precision for the subtype

scale
  Scale of the subtype

binary
  Binary precision of the subtype

Character Datatypes

Variables with character datatypes store text and are manipulated by character functions. Because character strings are "free-form," there are few rules concerning their content. You can, for example, store numbers and letters, as well as any combination of special characters, in a character-type variable. There are, however, several different kinds of character datatypes, each of which serves a particular purpose.

The CHAR datatype

The CHAR datatype specifies that the character string has a fixed length. When you declare a fixed-length string, you also specify a maximum length for the string, which can range from 1 to 32767 bytes (this is much higher than that for the CHAR datatype in the Oracle RDBMS, which is only 255). If you do not specify a length for the string, then PL/SQL declares a string of one byte. Note that this is the opposite of the situation with the NUMBER datatype. For example, a declaration of:

```
fit_almost_anything NUMBER;
```

results in a numeric variable with up to 38 digits of precision. You could easily get into a bad habit of declaring all your whole number variables simply as NUMBER, even if the range of legal values is much smaller than the default. However, if you try a similar tactic with CHAR, you may be in for a nasty surprise. If you declare a variable as follows:

```
line_of_text CHAR;
```

then as soon as you assign a string of more than one character to line_of_text, PL/SQL will raise the generic VALUE_ERROR exception. It will not tell you where it encountered this problem. So if you do get this error, check your variable declarations for a lazy use of CHAR.

Just to be sure, you should always specify a length when you use the CHAR datatype. Several examples follow:

```
yes_or_no CHAR (1) DEFAULT 'Y';
line_of_text    CHAR (80); --Always a full 80 characters!
whole_paragraph CHAR (10000); --Think of all the spaces...
```

Remember that even though you can declare a CHAR variable with 10,000 characters, you will not be able to stuff that PL/SQL variable's value into a database column of type CHAR. It will take up to 255 characters. So if you want to insert a CHAR value into the database and its declared length is greater than 255, you will have to use the SUBSTR function (described in Chapter 11, *Character Functions*) to trim the value down to size:

```
INSERT INTO customer_note
   (customer_id, full_text /* Declared as CHAR(255) */)
```

```
VALUES
   (1000, SUBSTR (whole_paragraph, 1, 255)));
```

Because CHAR is fixed-length, PL/SQL will right-pad any value assigned to a CHAR variable with spaces to the maximum length specified in the declaration. Prior to Oracle7, the CHAR datatype was variable-length; Oracle did not, in fact, support a fixed-length character string datatype and prided itself on that fact. To improve compatibility with IBM relational databases and to comply with ANSI standards, Oracle7 reintroduced CHAR as a fixed-length datatype and offered VARCHAR2 as the variable-length datatype. When a Version 6 RDBMS is upgraded to Oracle7, all CHAR columns are automatically converted to VARCHAR2. (VARCHAR2 is discussed in the next section.)

You will rarely need or want to use the CHAR datatype in Oracle-based applications. In fact, I recommend that you never use CHAR unless there is a specific requirement for fixed-length strings or unless you are working with data sources like DB2. Character data in DB2 is almost always stored in fixed-length format due to performance problems associated with variable-length storage. So, if you build applications that are based on DB2, you may have to take fixed-length data into account in your SQL statements and in your procedural code. You may, for example, need to use RTRIM to remove trailing spaces from (or RPAD to pad spaces onto) many of your variables in order to allow string comparisons to function properly. (These character functions are described in Chapter 11.)

The VARCHAR2 and VARCHAR datatypes

VARCHAR2 variables store variable-length character strings. When you declare a variable-length string, you must also specify a maximum length for the string, which can range from 1 to 32767 bytes. The general format for a VARCHAR2 declaration is:

```
<variable_name> VARCHAR2 (<max_length>);
```

as in:

```
DECLARE
   small_string VARCHAR2(4);
   line_of_text VARCHAR2(2000);
```

NOTE   In Version 1.1 of PL/SQL, which you use in Oracle Developer/2000 tools like Oracle Forms, the compiler does not insist that you include a maximum length for a VARCHAR2 declaration. As a result, you could mistakenly leave off the length in the declaration and end up with a variable with a maximum length of a single character. As discussed in the section on the fixed-length CHAR datatype, this can cause PL/SQL to raise runtime VALUE_ERROR exceptions. Always include a maximum length in your character variable declarations.

The maximum length allowed for PL/SQL VARCHAR2 variables is a much higher maximum than that for the VARCHAR2 datatype in the Oracle RDBMS, which is only 2000. As a result, if you plan to store a PL/SQL VARCHAR2 value into a VARCHAR2 database column, you must remember that only the first 2000 can be inserted. Neither PL/SQL nor SQL automatically resolves this inconsistency, though. You will need to make sure you don't try to pass more than the maximum 2000 (actually, the maximum length specified for the column) through the use of the SUBSTR function.

Because the length of a LONG column is two gigabytes, on the other hand, you can insert PL/SQL VARCHAR2 values into a LONG column without any worry of overflow. (LONG is discussed in the next section.)

The VARCHAR datatype is actually a subtype of VARCHAR2, with the same range of values found in VARCHAR2. VARCHAR, in other words, is currently synonymous with VARCHAR2. Use of VARCHAR offers compatibility with ANSI and IBM relational databases. There is a strong possibility, however, that VARCHAR's meaning might change in a new version of the ANSI SQL standards. Oracle recommends that you avoid using VARCHAR if at all possible, and instead stick with VARCHAR2 to declare variable-length PL/SQL variables (and table columns as well).

If you make use of both fixed-length (CHAR) and variable-length (VARCHAR2) strings in your PL/SQL code, you should be aware of the following interactions between these two datatypes:

- *Database-to-variable conversion.* When you SELECT or FETCH data from a CHAR database column into a VARCHAR2 variable, the trailing spaces are retained. If you SELECT or FETCH from a VARCHAR2 database column into a CHAR variable, PL/SQL automatically pads the value with spaces out to the maximum length. In other words, the type of the variable, not the column, determines the variable's resulting value.

- *Variable-to-database conversion.* When you INSERT or UPDATE a CHAR variable into a VARCHAR2 database column, the SQL kernel does not trim the trailing blanks before performing the change. When the following PL/SQL is executed, the company_name in the new database record is set to 'ACME SHOWERS········' (where · indicates a space). It is, in other words, padded out to 20 characters, even though the default value was a string of only 12 characters:

```
DECLARE
    comp_id#    NUMBER;
    comp_name   CHAR(20) := 'ACME SHOWERS';
BEGIN
    SELECT company_id_seq.NEXTVAL
        INTO comp_id#
        FROM dual;
```

```
        INSERT INTO company (company_id, company_name)
            VALUES (comp_id#, comp_name);
    END;
```

On the other hand, when you INSERT or UPDATE a VARCHAR2 variable into a CHAR database column, the SQL kernel automatically pads the variable-length string with spaces out to the maximum (fixed) length specified when the table was created, and places that expanded value into the database.

- *String comparisons.* Suppose your code contains a string comparison such as the following:

  ```
  IF company_name = parent_company_name ...
  ```

  PL/SQL must compare company_name to parent_company_name. It performs the comparison in one of two ways, depending on the types of the two variables:

  — If a comparison is made between two CHAR variables, then PL/SQL uses a blank-padding comparison. With this approach, PL/SQL blank-pads the shorter of the two values out to the length of the longer value. It then performs the comparison. So with the above example, if company_name is declared CHAR(30) and parent_company_name is declared CHAR(35), then PL/SQL adds five spaces to the end of the value in company_name and then performs the comparison. Note that PL/SQL does not actually change the variable's value. It copies the value to another memory structure and then modifies this temporary data for the comparison.

  — If at least one of the strings involved in the comparison is variable-length, then PL/SQL performs a nonblank-padding comparison. It makes no changes to any of the values, uses the existing lengths, and performs the comparison. This comparison analysis is true of evaluations which involve more than two variables as well, as may occur with the IN operator:

  ```
      IF menu_selection NOT IN
          (save_and_close, cancel_and_exit, 'OPEN_SCREEN')
        THEN ...
  ```

  If any of the four variables (menu_selection, the two named constants, and the single literal) is declared VARCHAR2, then exact comparisons without modification are performed to determine if the user has made a valid selection. Note that a literal like OPEN_SCREEN is always considered a fixed-length CHAR datatype.

These rules can make your life very complicated. Logic which looks perfectly correct may not operate as expected if you have a blend of fixed-length and variable-length data. Consider the following fragment:

```
DECLARE
    company_name CHAR (30) DEFAULT 'PC HEAVEN';
    parent_company_name  VARCHAR2 (25) DEFAULT 'PC HEAVEN';
```

```
BEGIN
   IF company_name = parent_company_name
   THEN
      -- This code will never be executed.
   END IF;
END;
```

The conditional test will never return TRUE because the value company_name has been padded to the length of 30 with 21 spaces. To get around problems like this, you should always RTRIM your CHAR values when they are involved in any kind of comparison or database modification.

It makes more sense to use RTRIM (to remove trailing spaces) than it does to use RPAD (to pad variable-length strings with spaces). With RPAD you have to know what length you wish to pad the variable-length string to get it in order to match the fixed-length string. With RTRIM you just get rid of all the blanks and let PL/SQL perform its nonblank-padding comparison.

It was easy to spot the problem in this anonymous PL/SQL block because all the related statements are close together. In the real world, unfortunately, the variables' values are usually set in a much less obvious manner and are usually in a different part of the code from the conditional statement which fails. So if you have to use fixed-length variables, be on the lookout for logic which naively believes that trailing spaces are not an issue.

The LONG datatype

A variable declared LONG can store variable-length strings of up to 32760 bytes— this is actually seven fewer bytes than allowed in VARCHAR2 type variables! The LONG datatype for PL/SQL variables is quite different from the LONG datatype for columns in the Oracle Server. The LONG datatype in Oracle7 can store character strings of up to two gigabytes or $2^{31}-1$ bytes; this large size makes the LONG column a possible repository of multimedia information, such as graphics images.

As a result of these maximum length differences, you can always insert a PL/SQL LONG variable value into a LONG database column, but you cannot select a LONG database value larger than 32760 bytes into a PL/SQL LONG variable.

In the Oracle database, there are many restrictions on how the LONG column can be used in a SQL statement; for example:

- A table may *not* contain more than one single LONG column.

- You may *not* use the LONG column in a GROUP BY, ORDER BY, WHERE, or CONNECT BY clause.

- You may *not* apply character functions (such as SUBSTR, INSTR, or LENGTH), to the LONG column.

PL/SQL LONG variables are free of these restrictions. In your PL/SQL code you can use a variable declared LONG just as you would a variable declared VARCHAR2. You can apply character functions to the variable. You can use it in the WHERE clause of a SELECT or UPDATE statement. This all makes sense given that, at least from the standpoint of the maximum size of the variables, there is really little difference between VARCHAR2 and LONG in PL/SQL.

Given the fact that a VARCHAR2 variable actually has a higher maximum length than the LONG and has no restrictions attached to it, I recommend that you always use the VARCHAR2 datatype in PL/SQL programs. LONGs have a place in the RDBMS, but that role is not duplicated in PL/SQL. This makes some sense since you will very rarely want to manipulate truly enormous strings within your program using such functions as SUBSTR or LENGTH or INSTR.

The RAW datatype

The RAW datatype is used to store binary data or other kinds of raw data, such as a digitized picture or image. A RAW variable has the same maximum length as VARCHAR2 (32767 bytes), which must also be specified when the variable is declared. The difference between RAW and VARCHAR2 is that PL/SQL will not try to interpret raw data. Within the Oracle RDBMS this means that Oracle will not perform character set conversions on RAW data when it is moved from one system (based, for example, on 7-bit ASCII) to another system.

Once again, there is an inconsistency between the PL/SQL maximum length for a RAW variable (32767) and the RDBMS maximum length (255). As a result, you cannot insert more than 255 bytes of your PL/SQL RAW variable's value into a database column. You can, on the other hand, insert the full value of a PL/SQL RAW variable into a column with type LONG RAW, which is a two-gigabyte container for raw data in the database.

The LONG RAW datatype

The LONG RAW datatype stores raw data of up to 32760 bytes and is just like the LONG datatype except that the data in a LONG RAW variable is not interpreted by PL/SQL.

Given the fact that a RAW variable actually has a higher maximum length than the LONG RAW and has no restrictions attached to it, I recommend that you always use the RAW datatype in PL/SQL programs. LONG RAWs have a place in the RDBMS, but that role is not duplicated in PL/SQL.

The ROWID datatype

In the Oracle RDBMS, ROWID is a *pseudocolumn* that is a part of every table you create. The rowid is an internally generated and maintained binary value which identifies a row of data in your table. It is called a pseudocolumn because a SQL statement includes it in places where you would normally use a column. However, it is not a column that you create for the table. Instead, the RDBMS generates the rowid for each row as it is inserted into the database. The information in the rowid provides the exact physical location of the row in the database. You cannot change the value of a rowid.

You can use the ROWID datatype to store rowids from the database in your PL/ SQL program. You can SELECT or FETCH the rowid for a row into a ROWID variable. To manipulate rowids in Oracle8, you will want to use the built-in package, DBMS_ROWID (see Appendix C, *Built-In Packages*). In Oracle7, you will use the ROWIDTOCHAR function to convert the rowid to a fixed-length string and then perform operations against that string.

In Oracle7, the format of the fixed-length rowid is as follows:

```
BBBBBBB.RRRR.FFFFF
```

Components of this format have the following meanings:

BBBBBBB
> The block in the database file

RRRR
> The row in the block (where the first row is zero, not one)

FFFFF
> The database file

All these numbers are hexadecimal; the database file is a number which you would then use to look up the actual name of the database file through the data dictionary.

In Oracle8, rowid have been "extended" to support partitioned tables and indexes. The new, extended rowids include a data object number, identifying the database segment. Any schema object found in the same segment, such as a cluster of tables, will have the same object number. In Oracle8, then, a rowid contains the following information:

- The data object number
- The data file (where the first file is 1)
- The data block within the data file
- The row in the data block (where the first row is 0)

Oracle8 provides functions in the DBMS_ROWID package to convert between the new formats of rowids.

Usually (and always in Oracle7), a rowid will uniquely identify a row of data. Within Oracle8, however, rows in different tables stored in the same cluster can have the same rowid value.

You are now probably thinking, "Why is he telling me this? Do I actually have to know about the physical blocks in the Oracle RDBMS? I thought the whole point of the relational approach is that I can focus on the logical design of my data and ignore the physical representation. Rowids are scary!"

Calm down. Very rarely would you want to use a rowid, and in those cases you probably wouldn't care about its internal structure. You would simply use it to find a row in the database. Access by rowid is typically the fastest way to locate or retrieve a particular row in the database: faster even than a search by primary key.

You could make use of the rowid in an Oracle Forms application to access the row in the database corresponding to the record on the screen. When you create a base-table block in Oracle Forms, it automatically includes the rowid in the block as an "invisible pseudoitem." You do not see it on your item list, but you can reference it in your triggers and PL/SQL program units. For example, to update the name of an employee displayed on the screen, you could issue the following statement:

```
UPDATE employee
   SET last_name = :employee.last_name
 WHERE rowid = :employee.rowid;
```

You can also use rowid inside a cursor FOR loop (or any other loop which FETCHes records from a cursor) to make changes to the row just FETCHed, as follows:

```
PROCEDURE remove_internal_competitors IS
BEGIN
   FOR emp_rec IN
      (SELECT connections, rowid
         FROM employee
        WHERE sal > 50000)
   LOOP
      IF emp_rec.connections IN ('President', 'CEO')
      THEN
         send_holiday_greetings;
      ELSE
         DELETE FROM employee
           WHERE rowid = emp_rec.rowid;
      END IF;
   END LOOP;
END;
```

The DELETE uses the rowid stored in the emp_rec record to immediately get rid of anyone making more than $50,000 who does not have known connections to the President or CEO. Note that the DBA controls who may have EXECUTE privilege to this stored procedure. So one must now wonder: does the DBA have connections to the President or CEO? Well, in any case, use of the rowid guarantees the fastest possible DELETE of that employee.

Of course, the above procedure could also simply have fetched the employee_id (primary key of the employee table) and executed a DELETE based on that real column, as in:

```
DELETE FROM employee WHERE employee_id = emp_id;
```

I am not convinced that the theoretical performance gains of searching by rowid justify its use. The resulting code is harder to understand than the application-specific use of the primary key. Furthermore, references to rowid could cause portability problems in the future.*

The Boolean Datatype

The Oracle RDBMS/SQL language offers features not found in PL/SQL, such as the Oracle SQL DECODE construct. PL/SQL, on the other hand, has a few tricks up its sleeve which are unavailable in native SQL. One particularly pleasant example of this is the BOOLEAN datatype.† Boolean data may only be TRUE, FALSE, or NULL. A Boolean is a "logical" datatype.

The Oracle RDBMS does not support a Boolean datatype. You can create a table with a column of datatype CHAR(1) and store either "Y" or "N" in that column to indicate TRUE or FALSE. That is a poor substitute, however, for a datatype which stores those actual Boolean values (or NULL).

Because there is no counterpart for the PL/SQL Boolean in the Oracle RDBMS, you can neither SELECT into a Boolean variable nor insert a TRUE or FALSE value directly into a database column.

Boolean values and variables are very useful in PL/SQL. Because a Boolean variable can only be TRUE, FALSE, or NULL, you can use that variable to explain what is happening in your code. With Booleans you can write code which is easily readable, because it is more English-like. You can replace a complicated Boolean expression involving many different variables and tests with a single Boolean variable that directly expresses the intention and meaning of the text.

---

* The rowid is not a part of the ANSI SQL standard; instead, it reflects directly the internal storage structure of the Oracle RDBMS. Use of this proprietary pseudo-column is akin to coding a clever trick in FORTRAN 77 which takes advantage of a loophole in the compiler to gain performance. The improvements could be wiped out in a future release of the software. If you are building applications which may need to work against both Oracle and non-Oracle data sources, you should avoid any references to the rowid pseudo-column and the ROWID datatype.

† The Boolean is named after George Boole, who lived in the first half of the 19th century and is considered "the father of symbolic logic." One therefore capitalizes "Boolean," whereas the other datatypes get no respect.

The Date-Time Datatype

Most of our applications require the storage and manipulation of dates and times. Dates are quite complicated: not only are they highly-formatted data, but there are myriad rules for determining valid values and valid calculations (leap days and years, national and company holidays, date ranges, etc.). Fortunately, the Oracle RDBMS and PL/SQL offer us help in many ways to handle date information.

The RDBMS provides a true DATE datatype which stores both date and time information. While you can enter a date value in a variety of formats, the RDBMS stores the date in a standard, internal format. It is a fixed-length value which uses seven bytes. You cannot actually specify this internal or literal value with an assignment. Instead you rely on implicit conversion of character and numeric values to an actual date, or explicit conversion with the TO_DATE function. (The next section describes these types of conversion.) PL/SQL provides a DATE datatype which corresponds directly to the RDBMS DATE.

An Oracle DATE stores the following information:

> century
> year
> month
> day
> hour
> minute
> second

PL/SQL validates and stores dates which fall between January 1, 4712 B.C. to December 31, 4712 A.D. The time component of a date is stored as the number of seconds past midnight. If you enter a date without a time (many applications do not require the tracking of time, so PL/SQL lets you leave it off), the time portion of the database value defaults to midnight (12:00:00 AM).

Neither the Oracle RDBMS DATE nor the PL/SQL DATE datatypes store times in increments of less than single seconds. The DATE datatype, therefore, is not very useful for tracking real-time activities which occur in subsecond intervals. If you need to track time at subsecond intervals, you could instead store this information as a number. You can obtain subsecond timings using the DBMS_UTILITY package's GET_TIME function described in Appendix C.

Because a variable declared DATE is a true date and not simply a character representation of a date, you can perform arithmetic on date variables, such as the subtraction of one date from another, or the addition/subtraction of numbers from a date. You can make use of date functions, described in Chapter 12, *Date Functions*, which offer a wide range of powerful operations on dates. Use the

SYSDATE function to return the current system date and time. You can also use the TO_CHAR conversion function (described in Chapter 14, *Conversion Functions*) to convert a date to character string or to a number.

In PL/SQL, a Julian date is the number of days since the first valid date, January 1, 4712 BC. Use Julian dates if you need to perform calculations or display date information with a single point of reference and continuous dating.

NLS Character Datatypes

When working with languages like Japanese, the 8-bit ASCII character set is simply not able to represent all of the available characters. Such languages require 16 bits (two bytes) to represent each character. Oracle offers National Language Support (NLS) to process single-byte and multibyte character data. NLS features also allow you to convert between character sets. PL/SQL8 supports two character sets which allow for the storage and manipulation of strings in either single-byte or multibyte formats. The two character sets are:

- Database character set: used for PL/SQL identifiers and source code
- National character set: used for NLS data

PL/SQL offers two datatypes, NCHAR and NVARCHAR2, to store character strings formed from the national character set.

The NCHAR datatype

Use the NCHAR datatype to store fixed-length NLS character data. The internal representation of the data is determined by the national character set. When you declare a variable of this type, you can also specify its length. If you do not provide a length, the default of 1 is used.

Here is the declaration of a NCHAR variable with a length of 10:

```
ssn NCHAR (10);
```

Here is the declaration of a NCHAR variable with a default length of 1:

```
yes_no NCHAR;
```

The maximum length for NCHAR variables is 32767.

But what does "a length of 10" actually mean? If the national character set is a fixed-width character set, then the length indicates length in characters. If the national character set is a variable-width character set (JA16SJIS is one example), then the length indicates length in bytes.

The NVARCHAR2 datatype

Use the NVARCHAR2 datatype to store variable-length NLS character data. The internal representation of the data is determined by the national character set. When you declare a variable of this type, you must also specify its length.

Here is the declaration of an NVARCHAR2 variable with a maximum length of 200:

```
any_name NVARCHAR2 (200);
```

The maximum length allowed for NVARCHAR2 variables is 32767. Length has the same meaning described above for NCHAR.

LOB Datatypes

Oracle8 and PL/SQL8 support several variations of LOB (large object) datatypes. LOBs can store large amounts (up to four gigabytes) of raw data, binary data (such as images), or character text data.

Within PL/SQL you can declare LOB variables of the following datatypes:

BFILE
> Declares variables that hold a file locator pointing to large binary objects in operating system files outside of the database.

BLOB
> Declares variables that hold a LOB locator pointing to a large binary object.

CLOB
> Declares variables that hold a LOB locator pointing to a large block of single-byte, fixed-width character data.

NCLOB
> Declares variables that hold a LOB locator pointing to a large block of single-byte or fixed-width multibyte character data.

There are two types of LOBs in Oracle8: internal and external. Internal LOBs (BLOB, CLOB, and NCLOB) are stored in the database and can participate in a transaction in the database server. External LOBs (BFILE) are large binary data stored in operating system files outside the database tablespaces. External LOBs cannot participate in transactions. You cannot, in other words, commit or roll back changes to a BFILE. Instead, you rely on the underlying filesystem for data integrity.

The BFILE datatype

Use the BFILE datatype to store large binary objects (up to four gigabytes in size) in files outside of the database. This variable gives you read-only, byte-stream I/O access to these files (which can reside on a hard disk, CD-ROM, or other such device).

When you declare a BFILE variable, you allocate memory to store the *file locator* of the BFILE, not the BFILE contents itself. This file locator contains a directory alias as well as a file name. See the section later in this chapter called "Working with BFILEs" for more information about the file locator.

Here is an example of a declaration of a BFILE variable:

```
DECLARE
    book_part1 BFILE;
```

The BLOB datatype

Use the BLOB datatype to store large binary objects "out of line" inside the database. This means that when a table has a BLOB column, a row of data for that table contains a pointer or a locator to the actual location of the BLOB data (so it is not "in line" with the other column values of the row).

A BLOB variable contains a locator, which then points to the large binary object. BLOBs can be up to four gigabytes in size, and they participate fully in transactions. In other words, any changes you make to a BLOB (via the DBMS_LOB built-in package) can be rolled back or committed along with other outstanding changes in your transaction. BLOB locators cannot, however, span transactions or sessions.

Here is an example of a declaration of a BLOB variable:

```
DECLARE
    family_portrait BLOB;
```

The CLOB datatype

Use the CLOB datatype to store large blocks of single-byte character data "out of line" inside the database. This means that when a table has a CLOB column, a row of data for that table contains a pointer or locator to the actual location of the CLOB data (so it is not "in line" with the other column values of the row).

A CLOB variable contains a locator, which then points to the large block of single-byte character data. CLOBs can be up to four gigabytes in size, and they participate fully in transactions. In other words, any changes you make to a CLOB (via the DBMS_LOB built-in package) can be rolled back or committed along with other outstanding changes in your transaction. CLOB locators cannot, however, span transactions or sessions.

Variable-width character sets are not supported in CLOBs.

Here is an example of a declaration of a CLOB variable:

```
DECLARE
    war_and_peace_text CLOB;
```

The NCLOB datatype

Use the NCLOB datatype to store large blocks of single-byte or fixed-width multi-byte character data "out of line" inside the database. This means that when a table has a NCLOB column, a row of data for that table contains a pointer or locator to the actual location of the NCLOB data (so it is not "in line" with the other column values of the row).

A NCLOB variable contains a locator, which then points to the large block of single-byte character data. NCLOBs can be up to four gigabytes in size, and they participate fully in transactions. In other words, any changes you make to a NCLOB (via the DBMS_LOB built-in package) can be rolled back or committed along with other outstanding changes in your transaction. NCLOB locators cannot, however, span transactions or sessions.

Variable-width character sets are not supported in NCLOBs.

Here is an example of a declaration of a NCLOB variable:

```
DECLARE
    war_and_peace_in japanese NCLOB;
```

LOBs and LONGs

LOB types are different from, and preferable to, LONG and LONG RAW. The maximum size of a LONG is two gigabytes, whereas the maximum size of a LOB is four gigabytes.

Oracle offers a powerful new built-in package, DBMS_LOB, to help you manipulate the contents of LOBs in ways not possible with LONGs. Generally, Oracle offers you random access to LOB contents, whereas with LONGs you have only sequential access. For example, with DBMS_LOB you can perform SUBSTR and INSTR operations against a LOB. This is not possible with LONG data.

Oracle recommends that you no longer use LONG or LONG RAW in your applications and instead take advantage of the new and improved features of the LOB datatypes. If you are going to be working with object types, you really don't have much choice: a LOB (except for NCLOB) can be an attribute of an object type, but LONGs cannot.

Working with LOBs

LOB values are not stored "in line" with other row data. Instead, a LOB *locator*, which points to the LOB, is stored in the row. Suppose that I have created the following table:

```
CREATE TABLE favorite_books
    (isbn VARCHAR2(50), title VARCHAR2(100), contents_loc CLOB);
```

I can then display the number of characters in the book, *The Bell Curve*, with the following code:

```
CREATE OR REPLACE PROCEDURE howbig (title_in IN VARCHAR2)
IS
    CURSOR book_cur
    IS
        SELECT contents_loc
          FROM favorite_books
         WHERE title = UPPER (title_in);
    book_loc CLOB;
BEGIN
    OPEN book_cur;
    FETCH book_cur INTO book_loc;
    IF book_cur%NOTFOUND
    THEN
        DBMS_OUTPUT.PUT_LINE
            ('Remember? You don''t like "' || INITCAP (title_in) || '".');
    ELSE
        DBMS_OUTPUT.PUT_LINE (title_in || ' contains ' ||
            TO_CHAR (DBMS_LOB.GETLENGTH (book_loc)) ||
            ' characters.');
    END IF;
    CLOSE book_cur;
END;
/

SQL> exec howbig ('the bell curve');
Remember? You don't like "The Bell Curve".
```

Here is an example of copying a BLOB from one row to another in SQL:

```
INSERT INTO favorite_books (isbn, title, contents_loc)
    SELECT isbn, title || ', Second Edition', contents_loc
      FROM favorite_books
     WHERE title = 'Oracle PL/SQL Programming';
```

In this situation, I have assigned a new LOB locator for my second edition. I have also copied the LOB value (the contents of my first edition) to this new row, not merely created another locator or pointer back to the same text.

Notice that I copied the entire contents of my book. DML operations such as INSERT and UPDATE always affect an entire LOB. If you want to change or delete just a portion of a LOB, you need to call the appropriate functions in the DBMS_ LOB package.

You cannot directly copy values between a character LOB and a VARCHAR2 variable, even if the LOB value is small and "fits" inside the specified VARCHAR2 variable. You can, however, use functions in the DBMS_LOB package to extract some or all of a CLOB value and place it in a VARCHAR2 variable (as the following example shows):

```
DECLARE
   big_kahuna CLOB;
   little_kahuna VARCHAR2(2000);
BEGIN
   /* I know it's in here. */
   SELECT contents_loc INTO big_kahuna
     FROM favorite_books
     WHERE title = 'WAR AND PEACE';

   /* Get first 2000 characters of book. */
   little_kahuna := DBMS_LOB.SUBSTR (big_kahuna, 2000, 1);
END;
```

Working with BFILEs

BFILEs are very different from internal LOBs in a number of ways:

- The value of a BFILE is stored in an operating system file, not within the database at all.

- BFILEs do not participate in transactions (i.e., changes to a BFILE cannot be rolled back or committed).

When you work with BFILEs in PL/SQL, you still do work with a LOB locator. In the case of a BFILE, however, the locator simply points to the file stored on the server. For this reason, two different rows in a database table can have a BFILE column which point to the *same* file.

A BFILE locator is composed of a directory alias and a file name. You use the BFILENAME function (see Chapter 13, *Numeric, LOB, and Miscellaneous Functions*) to return a locator based on those two pieces of information.

In the following block, I declare a BFILE variable and assign it a locator for a file named *family.ipg* located in the photos "directory":

```
DECLARE
   all_of_us BFILE;
BEGIN
   all_of_us := BFILENAME ('photos', 'family.ipg');
END;
```

But what precisely is "photos"? It doesn't conform to the format used for directories in UNIX, Windows NT, etc. It is, in fact, a database object called a DIRECTORY. Here is the statement I would use to create a directory:

```
CREATE DIRECTORY photos AS 'c:\photos';
```

You will need the CREATE DIRECTORY or CREATE ANY DIRECTORY privileges to create a directory. To be able to reference this directory you must be granted the READ privilege, as in:

```
GRANT READ ON DIRECTORY photos TO SCOTT;
```

For more information on directory aliases, see the section called "The BFILENAME function" in Chapter 13.

The maximum number of BFILEs that can be opened within a session is established by the database initialization parameter, SESSION_MAX_OPEN_FILES. This parameter defines an upper limit on the number of files opened simultaneously in a session (not just BFILEs, but all kinds of files, including those opened using the UTL_FILE package).

Conversion Between Datatypes

Both SQL and PL/SQL offer many different types of data. In many situations—more frequently than you perhaps might like to admit—you will find it necessary to convert your data from one datatype to another.

You might have one table which stores primary key information as a character string, and another table which stores that same key as a foreign key in numeric format. When you perform an assignment, you will need to convert the information:

```
:employee.department_num    -- the numeric format
   := :department.depno     -- the character format
```

You might wish to view a rowid value, in which case it is necessary to convert that value to character (hex) format, as follows:

```
ROWIDTOCHAR (:employee.rowid);
```

Or you might perform date comparisons by specifying dates as literals, as in the following:

```
IF start_date BETWEEN '01-JAN-95' AND last_sales_date THEN ...
```

Whenever PL/SQL performs an operation involving one or more values, it must first convert the data so that it is in the right format for the operation. There are two kinds of conversion: explicit and implicit.

Explicit data conversions

An *explicit conversion* takes place when you use a built-in conversion function to force the conversion of a value from one datatype to another. In the earlier example which demonstrated viewing a rowid value, I used the ROWIDTOCHAR conversion function so that the PUT_LINE function could display the resulting character string. PL/SQL provides a full set of conversion functions to enable conversion from one datatype to another. (These functions are explored more fully in Chapter 14.)

Implicit data conversions

Whenever PL/SQL detects that a conversion is necessary, it will attempt to change the values as necessary to perform the operation. You would probably be surprised to learn how often PL/SQL is performing conversions on your behalf. Figure 4-1 shows what kinds of implicit conversions PL/SQL can perform.

From \ To	BINARY_INTEGER	CHAR	DATE	LONG	NUMBER	PLS_INTEGER	RAW	ROWID	VARCHAR2
BINARY_INTEGER		•		•	•	•			•
CHAR	•		•	•	•	•	•	•	•
DATE		•		•					•
LONG		•					•		•
NUMBER	•	•		•		•			•
PLS_INTEGER	•	•		•	•				•
RAW		•							•
ROWID		•		•					•
VARCHAR2	•	•	•	•	•	•	•	•	

Figure 4-1. Implicit conversions performed by PL/SQL

With implicit conversions you can specify literal values in place of data with the correct internal format, and PL/SQL will convert that literal as necessary. In the example below, PL/SQL converts the literal string "125" to the numeric value 125 in the process of assigning a value to the numeric variable:

```
DECLARE
   a_number NUMBER;
BEGIN
   a_number := '125';
END;
```

You can also pass parameters of one datatype into a module and then have PL/SQL convert that data into another format for use inside the program. In the following procedure, the first parameter is a date. When I call that procedure, I pass a string value in the form DD-MON-YY, and PL/SQL converts that string automatically to a date:

```
PROCEDURE change_hiredate
   (emp_id_in IN INTEGER, hiredate_in IN DATE)

change_hiredate (1004, '12-DEC-94');
```

As shown in Figure 4-1, conversions are limited; PL/SQL cannot convert any datatype to any other datatype. Furthermore, some implicit conversions raise exceptions. Consider the following assignment:

```
DECLARE
    a_number NUMBER;
BEGIN
    a_number := 'abc';
END;
```

PL/SQL cannot convert "abc" to a number and so will raise the VALUE_ERROR exception when it executes this code. It is up to you to make sure that if PL/SQL is going to perform implicit conversions, it is given values it can convert without error.

Drawbacks of implicit conversions

There are several drawbacks to implicit conversion:

- Each implicit conversion PL/SQL performs represents a loss, however small, in the control you have over your program. You do not expressly perform or direct the performance of that conversion; you make an assumption that the conversion will take place, and that it will have the intended effect. There is always a danger in making this assumption: If Oracle changes the way and circumstances under which it performs conversions; your code could then be affected.

- The implicit conversion that PL/SQL performs depends on the context in which the code occurs. As a result, a conversion might occur in one program and not in another even though they seem to be the same. The conversion PL/SQL performs is not necessarily always the one you might expect.

- Implicit conversions can actually degrade performance. A dependence on implicit conversions can result in excessive conversions taking place, or in the conversion of a column value in a SQL statement instead of in a constant.

- Your code is easier to read and understand if you explicitly convert data where needed. Such conversions document variances in datatypes between tables or between code and tables. By removing an assumption and a hidden action from your code, you remove a potential misunderstanding as well.

As a consequence, I recommend that you avoid allowing either the SQL or PL/SQL languages to perform implicit conversions on your behalf. Whenever possible, use a conversion function to guarantee that the right kind of conversion takes place.

NULLs in PL/SQL

Wouldn't it be nice if everything was knowable, and known? Hmmm. Maybe not. The question, however, is moot. We don't know the answer to many questions. We are surrounded by the Big Unknown, and because Oracle Corporation prides itself on providing database technology to reflect the real world, it supports the concept of a null value.

When a variable, column, or constant has a value of NULL, its value is unknown—indeterminate. "Unknown" is very different from a blank or a zero or the Boolean value FALSE. "Unknown" means that the variable has no value at all and so cannot be compared directly with other variables. The following three rules hold for null values:

- *A null is never equal to anything else.* None of the following IF statements can ever evaluate to TRUE:

```
my_string := ' ';
IF my_string = NULL THEN ...--This will never be true.

max_salary := 0;
IF max_salary = NULL THEN ...--This will never be true.

IF NULL = NULL THEN ...--Even this will never be true.
```

- *A null is never not equal to anything else.* Remember: with null values, you just never know. None of the following IF statements can ever evaluate to TRUE.

```
my_string := 'Having Fun';
your_string := NULL;
IF my_string != your_string THEN ..--This will never be true.

max_salary := 1234;
IF max_salary != NULL THEN ...--This will never be true.

IF NULL != NULL THEN ...--This will never be true.
```

- *When you apply a function to a null value, you generally receive a null value as a result* (there are some exceptions, listed below). A null value cannot be found in a string with the INSTR function. A null string has a null length, not a zero length. A null raised to the 10th power is still null.

```
my_string := NULL;
IF LENGTH (my_string) = 0 THEN ...--This will not work.

new_value := POWER (NULL, 10);--new_value is set to null value.
```

NULL Values in Comparisons

In general, whenever you perform a comparison involving one or more null values, the result of that comparison is also a null value—which is different from TRUE or FALSE—so the comparison cannot help but fail.

Whenever PL/SQL executes a program, it initializes all locally declared variables to null (you can override this value with your own default value). Always make sure that your variable has been assigned a value before you use it in an operation.

You can also use special syntax provided by Oracle to check dependably for null values, and even assign a null value to a variable. PL/SQL provides a special reserved word, NULL, to represent a null value in PL/SQL. So if you want to actually set a variable to the null value, you simply perform the following assignment:

```
my_string := NULL;
```

If you want to incorporate the possibility of null values in comparison operations, you must perform special case checking with the IS NULL and IS NOT NULL operators. The syntax for these two operators is as follows:

```
<identifier> IS NULL
<identifier> IS NOT NULL
```

where <identifier> is the name of a variable, a constant, or a database column. The IS NULL operator returns TRUE when the value of the identifier is the null value; otherwise, it returns FALSE. The IS NOT NULL operator returns TRUE when the value of the identifier is not a null value; otherwise, it returns FALSE.

Checking for NULL Values

Here are some examples describing how to use operators to check for null values in your program:

- In the following example, the validation rule for the hire_date is that it cannot be later than the current date and it must be entered. If the user does not enter a hire_date, then the comparison to SYSDATE will fail because a null is never greater than or equal to (>=) anything. The second part of the OR operator, however, explicitly checks for a null hire_date. If either condition is TRUE, then we have a problem.

```
IF hire_date >= SYSDATE OR hire_date IS NULL
THEN
   DBMS_OUTPUT.PUT_LINE (' Date required and cannot be in  future.');
END IF;
```

- In the following example, a bonus generator rewards the hard-working support people (not the salespeople). If the employee's commission is over the target compensation plan target, then send a thank you note. If the commission is under target, tell them to work harder, darn it! But if the person has no commission at all (that is, if the commission IS NULL), give them a bonus recognizing that everything they do aids in the sales effort. (You can probably figure out what my job at Oracle Corporation was.) If the commission is a null value, then neither of the first two expressions will evaluate to TRUE:

```
    IF :employee.commission >= comp_plan.target_commission
    THEN
        just_send_THANK_YOU_note (:employee_id);
    ELSIF :employee.commission < comp_plan.target_commission
    THEN
        send_WORK_HARDER_singing_telegram (:employee_id);
    ELSIF :employee.commission IS NULL
    THEN
        non_sales_BONUS (:employee_id);
    END IF;
```

- PL/SQL treats a string of zero-length as a NULL. A zero-length string is two single quotes without any characters in between. The following two assignments are equivalent:

```
    my_string := NULL;
    my_string := '';
```

Function Results with NULL Arguments

While it is generally true that functions which take a NULL argument return the null value, there are several exceptions:

- *Concatenation.* There are two ways to concatenate strings: the CONCAT function (described in Chapter 11, *Character Functions*) and the concatenation operator (double vertical bars: | |). In both cases, concatenation ignores null values, and simply concatenates "around" the null. Consider the following examples:

```
    CONCAT ('junk', NULL) ==> junk
```

```
    'junk' || NULL || ' ' || NULL || 'mail' ==> junk mail
```

Of course, if all the individual strings in a concatenation are NULL, then the result is also NULL.

- *The NVL function.* The NVL function (described in Chapter 13) exists specifically to translate a null value to a non-null value. It takes two arguments. If the first argument is NULL, then the second argument is returned. In the following example, I return the string 'Not Applicable' if the incoming string is NULL:

```
    new_description := NVL (old_description, 'Not Applicable');
```

- *The REPLACE function.* The REPLACE function (described in Chapter 11, *Character Functions*) returns a string in which all occurrences of a specified match string are replaced with a replacement string. If the match_string is NULL, then REPLACE does not try to match and replace any characters in the original string. If the replace_string is NULL, then REPLACE removes from the original string any characters found in match_string.

Although there are some exceptions to the rules for null values, nulls must generally be handled differently from other data. If your data has NULLS, whether from the database or in local variables, you will need to add code to either convert your null values to known values, or use the IS NULL and IS NOT NULL operators for special case null value handling.

Variable Declarations

Before you can make a reference to a variable, you must declare it. (The only exception to this rule is for the index variables of FOR loops.) All declarations must be made in the declaration section of your anonymous block, procedure, function, or package (see Chapter 15, *Procedures and Functions*, for more details on the structure of the declaration section).

When you declare a variable, PL/SQL allocates memory for the variable's value and names the storage location so that the value can be retrieved and changed. The declaration also specifies the datatype of the variable; this datatype is then used to validate values assigned to the variable.

The basic syntax for a declaration is:

```
<variable_name> <datatype> [optional default assignment];
```

where <variable_name> is the name of the variable to be declared and <datatype> is the datatype or subtype which determines the type of data which can be assigned to the variable. The [optional default assignment] clause allows you to initialize the variable with a value, a topic covered in the next section.

Constrained Declarations

The datatype in a declaration can either be constrained or unconstrained. A datatype is *constrained* when you specify a number which constrains or restricts the magnitude of the value which can be assigned to that variable. A datatype is *unconstrained* when there are no such restrictions.

Consider the datatype NUMBER. It supports up to 38 digits of precision—and uses up the memory needed for all those digits. If your variable does not require this much memory, you could declare a number with a constraint, such as the following:

```
itty_bitty_# NUMBER(1);

large_but_constrained_# NUMBER(20,5);
```

Constrained variables require less memory than unconstrained number declarations like this:

```
no_limits_here NUMBER;
```

Declaration Examples

Here are some examples of variable declarations:

- Declaration of date variable:

  ```
  hire_date DATE;
  ```

- This variable can only have one of three values: TRUE, FALSE, NULL:

  ```
  enough_data BOOLEAN;
  ```

- This number rounds to the nearest hundredth (cent):

  ```
  total_revenue NUMBER (15,2);
  ```

- This variable-length string will fit in a VARCHAR2 database column:

  ```
  long_paragraph VARCHAR2 (2000);
  ```

- This constant date is unlikely to change:

  ```
  next_tax_filing_date CONSTANT DATE := '15-APR-96';
  ```

Default Values

You can assign default values to a variable when it is declared. When declaring a constant, you must include a default value in order for the declaration to compile successfully. The default value is assigned to the variable with one of the following two formats:

```
<variable_name> <datatype> := <default_value>;
<variable_name> <datatype> DEFAULT <default_value>;
```

The <default_value> can be a literal, previously declared variable, or expression, as the following examples demonstrate:

- Set variable to 3:

  ```
  term_limit NUMBER DEFAULT  3;
  ```

- Default value taken from Oracle Forms bind variable:

  ```
  call_topic VARCHAR2 (100) DEFAULT :call.description;
  ```

- Default value is the result of a function call:

  ```
  national_debt FLOAT DEFAULT POWER (10,10);
  ```

- Default value is the result of the expression:

  ```
  order_overdue CONSTANT BOOLEAN :=
      ship_date > ADD_MONTHS (order_date, 3) OR
      priority_level (company_id) = 'HIGH';
  ```

I like to use the assignment operator (:=) to set default values for constants, and the DEFAULT syntax for variables. In the case of the constant, the assigned value is not really a default, but an initial (and unchanging) value, so the DEFAULT syntax feels misleading to me.

NOT NULL Clause

If you do assign a default value, you can also specify that the variable must be NOT NULL. For example, the following declaration initializes the company_name variable to PCS R US and makes sure that the name can never be set to NULL:

```
company_name VARCHAR2(60) NOT NULL DEFAULT 'PCS R US';
```

If your code includes a line like this:

```
company_name := NULL;
```

then PL/SQL will raise the VALUE_ERROR exception. You will, in addition, receive a compilation error with this next declaration:

```
company_name VARCHAR2(60) NOT NULL;
```

Why? Because your NOT NULL constraint conflicts instantly with the indeterminate or NULL value of the company_name variable when it is instantiated.

Anchored Declarations

This section describes the use of the %TYPE declaration attribute to *anchor* the datatype of one variable to another data structure, such as a PL/SQL variable or a column in a table. When you anchor a datatype, you tell PL/SQL to set the datatype of one variable from the datatype of another element.

The syntax for an anchored datatype is:

```
<variable name> <type attribute>%TYPE [optional default value assignment];
```

where <variable name> is the name of the variable you are declaring and <type attribute> is any of the following:

- Previously declared PL/SQL variable name

- Table column in format "table.column"

Figure 4-2 shows how the datatype is drawn both from a database table and PL/SQL variable.

Here are some examples of %TYPE used in declarations:

- Anchor the datatype of monthly_sales to the datatype of total_sales:

```
total_sales NUMBER (20,2);
monthly_sales total_sales%TYPE;
```

- Anchor the datatype of the company ID variable to the database column:

```
company_id# company.company_id%TYPE;
```

Anchored declarations provide an excellent illustration of the fact that PL/SQL is not just a procedural-style programming language but was designed specifically as

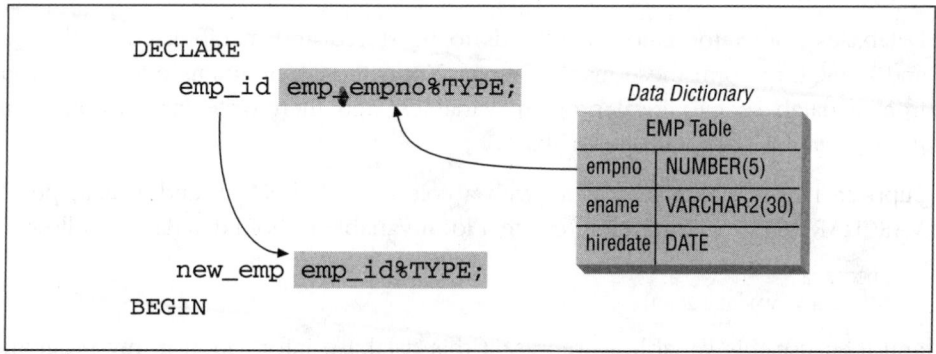

Figure 4-2. Anchored declarations with %TYPE

an extension to the Oracle SQL language. A very thorough effort was made by Oracle Corporation to tightly integrate the programming constructs of PL/SQL to the underlying database (accessed through SQL).

NOTE   PL/SQL also offers the %ROWTYPE declaration attribute, which allows you to create anchored datatypes for PL/SQL record structures.
%ROWTYPE is described in Chapter 9.

Benefits of Anchored Declarations

All the declarations you have so far seen—character, numeric, date, Boolean—specify explicitly the type of data for that variable. In each of these cases, the declaration contains a direct reference to a datatype and, in most cases, a constraint on that datatype. You can think of this as a kind of hardcoding in your program. While this approach to declarations is certainly valid, it can cause problems in the following situations:

* *Synchronization with database columns.* The PL/SQL variable "represents" database information in the program. If I declare explicitly and then change the structure of the underlying table, my program may not work properly.

* *Normalization of local variables.* The PL/SQL variable stores calculated values used throughout the application. What are the consequences of repeating (hardcoding) the same datatype and constraint for each declaration in all of my programs?

Let's take a look at each of these scenarios in more detail.

Synchronization with database columns

Databases hold information that needs to be stored and manipulated. Both SQL and PL/SQL perform these manipulations. Your PL/SQL programs often read data from a database into local program variables, and then write information from those variables back into the database.

Suppose I have a company table with a column called NAME and a datatype of VARCHAR2(60). I can therefore create a local variable to hold this data as follows:

```
DECLARE
    cname VARCHAR2(60);
```

and then use this variable to represent this database information in my program. Now, consider an application which uses the company entity. There may be a dozen different screens, procedures, and reports which contain this same PL/SQL declaration, VARCHAR2(60), over and over again. And everything works just fine...until the business requirements change or the DBA has a change of heart. With a very small effort, the definition of the name column in the company table changes to VARCHAR2(100), in order to accommodate longer company names. Suddenly the database can store names which will raise VALUE_ERROR exceptions when FETCHed into the company_name variable.

My programs have become incompatible with the underlying data structures. All declarations of cname (and all the variations programmers employed for this data throughout the system) must be modified. Otherwise, my application is simply a ticking time bomb, just waiting to fail. My variable, which is a local representation of database information, is no longer synchronized with that database column.

Normalization of local variables

Another drawback to explicit declarations arises when working with PL/SQL variables which store and manipulate calculated values not found in the database. Suppose my programmers built an application to manage my company's finances. I am very bottom-line oriented, so many different programs make use of a total_ revenue variable, declared as follows:

```
total_revenue NUMBER (10,2);
```

Yes, I like to track my total revenue down to the last penny. Now, in 1992, when specifications for the application were first written, the maximum total revenue I ever thought I could possibly obtain from any single customer was $99 million, so we used the NUMBER (10,2) declaration, which seemed like plenty. Then in 1995, my proposal to convert B-2 bombers to emergency transport systems to deliver Midwestern wheat to famine regions was accepted: a $2 billion contract! I was just about ready to pop the corks on the champagne when my lead programmer told me the bad news: I wouldn't be able to generate reports on this newest project and customer: those darn total_revenue variables were too small!

What a bummer...I had to fire the guy.

Just kidding. Instead, we quickly searched out any and all instances of the revenue variables so that we could change the declarations. This was a time-consuming job because we had spread equivalent declarations throughout the entire application. I had, in effect, denormalized my local data structures, with the usual consequences on maintenance. If only I had a way to define each of local total revenue variables in relation to a single datatype.

If only they had used %TYPE!

Anchoring at Compile Time

The %TYPE declaration attribute anchors the datatype of one variable to that of another data structure at the time a PL/SQL block is compiled. If a change is made to the "source" datatype, then any program which contains a declaration anchored to this datatype must be recompiled before it will be able to use this new state of the datatype.

The consequences of this rule differ for PL/SQL modules stored in the database and those defined in client-side tools, such as Oracle Forms.

Consider the following declaration of company_name in the procedure display_company:

```
PROCEDURE display_company (company_id_in IN INTEGER)
IS
   company_name company.name%TYPE;
BEGIN
   ...
END;
```

When PL/SQL compiles this module, it looks up the structure of the company table in the data dictionary, finds the column NAME, and obtains its datatype. It then uses this data dictionary-based datatype to define the new variable.

What, then, is the impact on the compiled display_company procedure if the datatype for the name column of the company table changes? There are two possibilities:

- If display_company is a stored procedure, then the compiled code will be marked as "invalid." The next time a program tries to run display_company, it will be recompiled automatically before it is used.

- If display_company is a client-side procedure, then the Oracle Server cannot mark the program as invalid. The compiled client source code remains compiled using the old datatype. The next time you execute this module, it could cause a VALUE_ERROR exception to be raised.

Whether stored or in client-side code, you should make sure that all affected modules are recompiled after data structure changes.

Nesting Usages of the %TYPE Attribute

You can nest usages of %TYPE in your declarations as well:

```
DECLARE
    /* The "base" variable */
    unlimited_revenue NUMBER;

    /* Anchored to unlimited revenue */
    total_revenue unlimited_revenue%TYPE;

    /* Anchored to total revenue */
    total_rev_94    total_revenue%TYPE;
    total_rev_95    total_revenue%TYPE;
  BEGIN
```

In this case total_revenue is based on unlimited_revenue and both variables for 1994 and 1995 are based on the total_revenue variable. There is no practical limit on the number of layers of nested usages of %TYPE.

Anchoring to Variables in Other PL/SQL Blocks

The declaration of the source variable for your %TYPE declarations does not need to be in the same declaration section as the variables which use it. That variable must simply be visible in that section. The variable could be a global PL/SQL variable (defined in a package) or be defined in an PL/SQL block which contains the current block, as in the following example:

```
PROCEDURE calc_revenue
IS
    unlimited_revenue NUMBER;
    total_revenue unlimited_revenue%TYPE;
BEGIN
    IF TO_CHAR (SYSDATE, 'YYYY') = '1994'
    THEN
        DECLARE
            total_rev_94    total_revenue%TYPE;
        BEGIN
            ...
        END;
    END IF;
END calc_revenue;
```

Anchoring to NOT NULL Datatypes

When you declare a variable, you can also specify the need for the variable to be NOT NULL This NOT NULL declaration constraint is transferred to variables declared with the %TYPE attribute. If I include a NOT NULL in my declaration of a source variable (one that is referenced afterwards in a %TYPE declaration), I must also make sure to specify a default value for the variables which make use of that source variable. Suppose I declare max_available_date NOT NULL in the following example:

```
DECLARE
    max_available_date DATE NOT NULL :=
            LAST_DAY (ADD_MONTHS (SYSDATE, 3));
    last_ship_date max_available_date%TYPE;
```

The declaration of last_ship_date will then fail to compile, with the following message:

```
a variable declared NOT NULL must have an initialization assignment.
```

If you use a NOT NULL variable in a %TYPE declaration, the new variable must have a default value provided. The same is not true, however, for variables declared with %TYPE where the source is a database column.

The NOT NULL column constraint does not apply to variables declared with the %TYPE attribute. The following code will compile successfully:

```
DECLARE
    -- Company name is a NOT NULL column in the company table.
    comp_name company.name%TYPE;
BEGIN
    comp_name := NULL;
```

You will be able to declare the comp_name variable without specifying a default, and you will be able to NULL out the contents of that variable.

Programmer-Defined Subtypes

With Version 2.1 of PL/SQL (available with Oracle Server Version 7.1), you can define your own unconstrained subtypes of predefined datatypes. In PL/SQL, a subtype of a datatype is a variation that specifies the same set of rules as the original datatype, but might allow only a subset of the datatype's values.

There are two kinds of subtypes: constrained and unconstrained. A *constrained subtype* is one that restricts or constrains the values normally allowed by the datatype itself. POSITIVE is an example of a constrained subtype of BINARY_INTEGER. The package STANDARD, which predefines the datatypes and the functions that are parts of the standard PL/SQL language, declares the subtype POSITIVE as follows:

```
SUBTYPE POSITIVE IS BINARY_INTEGER RANGE 1 .. 2147483647;
```

A variable that is declared POSITIVE can only store integer values greater than zero. The following assignment raises the VALUE_ERROR exception:

```
DECLARE
    pentagon_cost_cutting POSITIVE;--The report to Congress
BEGIN
    pentagon_cost_cutting := -100000000;--The inside reality
```

An *unconstrained subtype* is a subtype that does not restrict the values of the original datatype in variables declared with the subtype. FLOAT is an example of an unconstrained subtype of NUMBER. Its definition in the STANDARD package is:

```
SUBTYPE FLOAT IS NUMBER;
```

In other words, an unconstrained subtype provides an alias or alternate name for the original datatype.

In spite of the limitations of unconstrained subtypes, you should still use them wherever you can identify a logical subtype of data in your applications. Later, when you can implement constrained subtypes, you will only have to include a constraint in the SUBTYPE declaration, and all variables that are declared with this subtype will take on those constraints.

Declaring Subtypes

In order to make a subtype available, you first have to declare it in the declaration section of an anonymous PL/SQL block, procedure, function, or package. You've already seen the syntax for declaring a subtype used by PL/SQL in the STAN-DARD package. The general format of a subtype declaration is:

```
SUBTYPE <subtype_name> IS <base_type>;
```

where subtype_name is the name of the new subtype; this name is the identifier that will be referenced in declarations of variables of that type. The base_type, which specifies the datatype which forms the basis for the subtype, can be any of the categories shown in Table 4-3.

Table 4-3. PL/SQL Subtypes

Subtype Category	Description
PL/SQL datatype	Predefined PL/SQL datatype, including predefined subtypes, such as POSITIVE.
Programmer-defined subtype	Previously created with a SUBTYPE declaration.
variable_name%TYPE	The subtype is inferred from the datatype of the variable.
table_name column_name%TYPE	Determined from the datatype of the column in the table.
table_name %ROWTYPE	Contains the same structure as the table.

Table 4-3. PL/SQL Subtypes (continued)

Subtype Category	Description
cursor_name %ROWTYPE	Contains the same structure as the "virtual table" created by the cursor.
PL/SQL table	Contains the same structure as the PL/SQL table previously declared with a TYPE statement.

Examples of Subtype Declarations

Here are some examples of subtype declarations:

- A subtype based on a predefined datatype:

  ```
  SUBTYPE hire_date_type IS DATE;
  ```

- A subtype based on a predefined subtype:

  ```
  SUBTYPE soc_sec_number_type IS POSITIVE;
  ```

- Multiple subtypes based on a PL/SQL table:

  ```
  TYPE room_tab IS TABLE OF NUMBER(3) INDEX BY BINARY INTEGER;
  SUBTYPE hotel_room_tab_type IS room_tab;
  SUBTYPE motel_room_tab_type IS room_tab;
  SUBTYPE resort_room_tab_type IS room_tab;
  ```

- A general subtype based on NUMBER and then additional subtypes defined on that original subtype:

  ```
  SUBTYPE primary_key_number_type IS NUMBER;
  SUBTYPE company_key_type IS primary_key_number;
  SUBTYPE employee_key_type IS primary_key_number;
  ```

- A subtype based on the datatype of a table's column:

  ```
  SUBTYPE last_name_type IS employee.last_name%TYPE;
  ```

- A subtype based on the datatype of a record's column:

  ```
  SUBTYPE first_name_type IS emp_rec.first_name%TYPE;
  ```

- The following subtype declarations are invalid because they seek to apply a constraint to the subtype:

  ```
  SUBTYPE three_value_logic IS          -- Invalid constraint!
  VARCHAR2 IN ('YES', 'NO', 'MAYBE');

  SUBTYPE prefix_type IS CHAR(3);       -- Invalid constraint!
  ```

Emulating Constrained Subtypes

While you cannot directly constrain a subtype in PL/SQL at present you can, in effect, create a constrained subtype by anchoring a subtype to a constrained type declaration.

Suppose that the column big_line of table text_editor was set to VARCHAR2(200), as shown below:

```
CREATE TABLE text_editor
    (big_line VARCHAR2(200) NOT NULL, ...other columns...);
```

By applying this example, I can now create a subtype through a %TYPE reference to that column, as follows:

```
SUBTYPE paragraph_type IS text_editor.big_line%TYPE;
```

Like the original column declaration of big_line, this paragraph type is defined as VARCHAR2(200). If I use paragraph_type to declare character variables, then those variables will take on a maximum length of 200:

```
opening_paragraph paragraph_type;
```

You can also use %TYPE against a PL/SQL variable to constrain a datatype. Suppose I declare the following variables and a single subtype:

```
DECLARE
    /* A local PL/SQL string of length 10 */
    small_string VARCHAR2(10);

    /* Create a subtype based on that variable */
    SUBTYPE teensy IS small_string%TYPE;

    /* Declare two variables based on the subtype */
    weensy teensy;
    weensy_plus teensy(100);
BEGIN
```

The subtype is based on the small_string variable. As a result, the weensy variable, which is declared on the subtype, has a length of 10 bytes by default. So if I try to perform the following assignment, PL/SQL will raise the VALUE_ERROR exception:

```
weensy := 'morethantenchars';
```

When I declared the weensy_plus variable, on the other hand, I overrode the default subtype-based length of 10 with a maximum length of 100. As a result, this next assignment does not raise an exception:

```
weensy_plus := 'Lots of room for me to type now';
```

When you create a subtype based on an existing variable or database column, that subtype inherits the length (or precision and scale, in the case of a NUMBER datatype) from the original datatype. This constraint takes effect when you declare variables based on the subtype, but only as a default. You can always override that constraint. You will have to wait for a future version of PL/SQL, however, to actually enforce the constraint in a programmer-defined subtype.

Finally, an anchored subtype does not carry over the NOT NULL constraint to the variables it defines. Nor does it transfer a default value that was included in the original declaration of a variable or column specification.

Tips for Creating and Using Variables

How can you create, use, and maintain your variables and constants most effectively? This section pulls together a number of tips.

Establish Clear Variable Naming Conventions

Database administrators have long insisted on, and usually enforced, strict naming conventions for tables, columns, and other database objects. The advantage of these conventions is clear: at a single glance anyone who knows the conventions (and even many who do not) will understand the type of data contained in that column or table.

Many programmers, however, tend to get annoyed by such naming conventions. They regard them as just another bureaucracy that prevents them from "getting the job (the program) done." Of course, when it comes to tables and columns, most developers have no choice; they are stuck with what the DBA gives them. But when it comes to their own programs, they are free to name variables, programs, and other identifiers whatever they want. What a rush! Freedom! Room to express oneself!

Or rope with which to hang oneself. While those conventions are a bother to anyone who must follow them, they are a tremendous time- and eye-saver to anyone who must read and understand your code—even yourself.

If conventions for columns make sense in the database, they also make sense in PL/SQL programs—and in the development tools, such as Oracle Forms. In general I recommend that you follow the same guidelines for naming variables that you follow for naming columns in your development environment. In many cases, your variables simply represent database values, having been fetched from a table into those variables via a cursor. Beyond these database-sourced variables, however, there are a number of types of variables that you will use again and again in your code.

Generally, I try to come up with a variable name suffix that will help identify the representative data. This convention not only limits the need for additional comments, it can also improve the quality of code, because the variable type often implies rules for its use. If you can identify the variable type by its name, then you are more likely to use the variable properly.

Here is a list of variable types and suggested naming conventions for each.

Module parameter

A parameter has one of three modes: IN, OUT, or IN OUT. Attach the parameter mode as a suffix or prefix to the parameter name so that you can easily identify how that parameter should be used in the program. Here are some examples:

```
PROCEDURE calc_sales
    (company_id_IN IN NUMBER,
     in_call_type IN VARCHAR2,
     company_nm_INOUT IN OUT VARCHAR2)
```

See Chapter 15 for a more complete discussion of parameter naming conventions.

Cursor

Append a suffix of _cur or _cursor to the cursor name, as in:

```
CURSOR company_cur  IS ... ;
CURSOR top_sellers_cursor IS ... ;
```

I generally stick with the shorter _cur suffix; the extra typing (to spell out "cursor") is not really needed to convey the meaning of the variable.

Record based on table or cursor

These records are defined from the structure of a table or cursor. Unless more variation is needed, the simplest naming convention for a record is the name of the table or cursor with a _rec or _record suffix. For example, if the cursor is company_cur, then a record based on that cursor would be called company_rec. If you have more than one record declared for a single cursor, preface the record name with a word that describes it, such as newest_company_rec and duplicate_company_rec.

FOR loop index

There are two kinds of FOR loops, numeric and cursor, each with a corresponding numeric or record loop index. In a numeric loop you should incorporate the word "index" or "counter" or some similar suffix into the name of the loop index, such as:

```
FOR year_index IN 1 .. 12
```

In a cursor loop, the name of the record which serves as a loop index should follow the convention described above for records:

```
FOR emp_rec IN emp_cur
```

Named constant

A named constant cannot be changed after it gets its default value at the time of declaration. A common convention for such constants is to prefix the name with a c:

```
c_last_date CONSTANT DATE := SYSDATE:
```

This way, a programmer is less likely to try to use the constant in an inappropriate manner.

PL/SQL table TYPE

In PL/SQL Version 2 you can create PL/SQL tables which are similar to one-dimensional arrays. In order to create a PL/SQL table, you must first execute a TYPE declaration to create a table datatype with the right structure. I suggest that you use the suffix _tabtype to indicate that this is not actually a PL/SQL table, but a type of table. Here are some examples:

```
TYPE emp_names_tabtype IS TABLE OF ...;
TYPE dates_tabtype IS TABLE OF ...;
```

PL/SQL table

A PL/SQL table is declared based on a table TYPE statement, as indicated above. In most situations, I use the same name as the table type for the table, but I leave off the type part of the suffix. The following examples correspond to the previous table types:

```
emp_names_tab emp_names_tabtype;
dates_tab dates_tabtype;
```

You could also use the full table suffix for a high degree of clarity:

```
emp_names_table emp_names_tabtype;
dates_table dates_tabtype;
```

If you want to minimize confusion between PL/SQL tables and database tables, it is possible to call these constructs "arrays." In this case, switch your prefix:

```
emp_names_array emp_names_tabtype;
dates_array dates_tabtype;
```

Programmer-defined subtype

In PL/SQL Version 2.1 you can define subtypes from base datatypes. I suggest that you use a subtype suffix to make the meaning of the variable clear. Here are some examples:

```
SUBTYPE primary_key_subtype IS BINARY_INTEGER;
SUBTYPE large_string_subtype IS VARCHAR2;
```

Programmer-defined TYPE for record

In PL/SQL Version 2 you can create records with a structure you specify (rather than from a table or cursor). To do this, you must declare a type of record which determines the structure (number and types of columns). Use a rectype prefix in the name of the TYPE declaration, as follows:

```
TYPE sales_rectype IS RECORD ... ;
```

Programmer-defined record instance

Once you have defined a record type, you can declare actual records with that structure. Now you can drop the type part of the rectype prefix; the naming convention for these programmer-defined records is the same as that for records based on tables and cursors:

```
sales_rec sales_rectype;
```

Name Subtypes to Self-Document Code

One of the most compelling reasons for creating your own subtypes is to provide application- or function-specific datatypes that self-document your code. A programmer-defined subtype hides the generic "computer datatype" and replaces it with a datatype that has meaning in your own environment. In naming your subtype, you should consequently avoid references to the underlying datatype and concentrate instead on the business use of the subtype.

Suppose you are building a hotel reservation system. A very useful subtype would be a room number; it is a special kind of NUMBER and is used throughout the application. A room number is always an integer and is always greater than zero. So you could create the subtype as follows:

```
SUBTYPE room_#_pos_integer IS POSITIVE;
...
-- A declaration using the subtype:
open_room room_#_pos_integer;
```

The name, room_#_pos_integer, however, provides too much information about the subtype—this information is not needed by the developer. A much better name for the subtype follows:

```
SUBTYPE room_number_type IS POSITIVE;
...
-- A declaration using the subtype:
open_room room_number_type;
```

A word-processing screen might rely heavily on fixed-length, 80-character strings (full lines of text). Which of these subtype declarations would you prefer to use?

```
SUBTYPE line_fixlen_string IS CHAR;
```

```
SUBTYPE full_line_type IS CHAR;
```

Which of these next two subtypes makes more sense in the variable declarations?

```
DECLARE
    SUBTYPE use_details_flag_Boolean_subtype IS BOOLEAN;
    use_item_totals use_details_flag_Boolean_subtype;
    SUBTYPE use_details_type IS BOOLEAN;
    use_footers use_details_type;
```

In both examples, the second example is preferable. You can improve the readability of your subtypes if you include a standard prefix or suffix to all subtypes, explicitly defining the identifier as a type. As shown in the following example, you might use a concise _t or the full _type suffix; in either case, a glance at the code will reveal that identifier's nature:

```
DECLARE
    longitude coordinate_t;
    avail_room room_number_type;
    found_company t_entity_found;
```

If you set your standards before developers begin to define their subtypes, you will have a consistent naming convention throughout your application.

Avoid Recycling Variables

Do you hear yourself echoed in any of the following statements? I certainly do.

> Each variable and constant I use in your program takes up some amount of memory. I want to optimize memory usage in my program.

> It takes time to declare and document each variable and constant. I am under deadline pressures and need to work as efficiently as possible.

> As I write my program and run into the need for another variable, I can simply use an already declared but currently unused variable.

The one thing that all of the above statements have in common, besides the fact that they are poor excuses for writing poorly designed code, is that I avoid declaring separate variables and constants to meet the different needs in my program. Although I strongly support the idea of "reuse and recycle," both in my neighborhood and with procedures and functions, this principle produces hard-to-read code when applied to variables and constants.

Each variable and constant I declare should have one purpose and one purpose only. The name for that variable or constant should describe, as clearly as possible, that single-minded purpose.

The only reason to create generically-named variables and constants is to save you, the developer, typing time. That is always a terrible reason for a coding style or change in a programming effort. Reliance on a "time-saver" short-cut should raise a red flag: you are probably doing (or avoiding) something now for which you will pay later.

Use Named Constants to Avoid Hardcoding Values

Every application has its own set of special or "magic" values. These values are often configuration parameters, such as the maximum amount of time allowed before an order must be shipped or the name of an application (to be displayed in report and screen headers). Sometimes these special values will be relevant only for a particular program and not for the application as a whole, such as the character used as a string delimiter.

Whatever the scope and form of these values, programmers seem to believe that they will never change. The data in the database will certainly change and you might even need to add a column or two, but nobody will ever need to modify the naming scheme for reports, right? The value used to identify a closed request is always going to be "C," right? In a seemingly unconscious effort to prove this inviolability, we enter these values directly into the code, wherever it is needed, however often it is needed.

And then we are burned when the assumptions change—usually as the result of a change in business rules. Not only is our belief system undermined, our weekend is lost to minute changes to code. It's always better to be skeptical, with perhaps a tinge of cynicism. Assume that anything you do will have to be changed a week after you write it. Protect yourself in every way possible—particularly with your constants.

Follow these simple guidelines regarding literals in all of your applications:

- *Remove all literals (within reason) from your code.* Instead, declare constants which hold those literal values.

- *Allow the value of that literal (now a constant) to be set in only one place in your code, preferably with a call to a procedure.* This procedure can be run on startup of the application, or from the initialization section of a package.

- *Provide a single way to retrieve the literal value, preferably through a call to a function.* Don't let any program reference the literal directly. This way you reserve the right and ability to change at any time the data structures you use to store that literal—without affecting any of the programs which rely on that constant.

You can, of course, go overboard in your hunt for hardcoded values. Suppose you encounter this very common assignment to increment a counter:

```
number_of_orders := number_of_orders+ 1;
```

Should you really create a named constant called single_increment, initialize it with a value of one, and then change the above line to the following:

```
number_of_orders := number_of_orders+ single_increment;
```

I don't think so. The use of the literal value 1 in this situation is perfectly appropriate to the task at hand. Almost any other literal value hardcoded into your program should be replaced with a named constant.

Convert Variables into Named Constants

Every programming language provides a set of features to meet a set of requirements and needs. You should always try to use the most appropriate feature for a given situation.

There is a critical difference between a variable and a named constant. A variable can be assigned values; its value can be changed in the code. The value of a named constant is a constant; its value may not be altered after it has been declared. If you find that you have written a program in which a local variable's value does not change, you should first determine if that behavior is correct. If all is as it should be, you should then convert that variable to a constant.

Why should you bother converting "read only" variables to constants (and named ones at that)? Because when you "tell it and use it like it is," the program explains itself more clearly. The declaration of a named identifier as a constant gives you information about how it should be used in the program.

If you do convert a variable to a constant, you should also change its name. This will help to remind anyone reading the code that your identifier refers to a constant and cannot be changed. See the earlier tip on naming conventions for ideas on how to name your constants.

Directly related to improved readability, the declaration of a constant can also help with maintenance and debugging. Suppose you define and use a variable under the assumption that its default value will not change. You do not, however, go to the trouble of declaring that variable as a constant. You are aware of this assumption and use the variable properly. What happens, however, when a month or a year later another programmer has to perform maintenance on the code? This person might change the value of that variable in the course of making changes, and then cause a ripple effect of errors. If the variable was declared initially as a constant, such a change could not be compiled.

Remove Unused Variables from Programs

I have always been amazed at how quickly and easily a program can turn into spaghetti code. Consider this scenario. A program starts out with weak specifications. As a result, users change requirements at the same time that the developer implements the functions to support those requirements. A program evolves (or does it devolve?) rapidly, with whole sections of code moved, removed, or revamped. After many rounds of approximating a solution, the program works to the users' satisfaction. You wipe the sweat from your brow and gratefully move on to the next screen or report, hoping never to have to touch that program again.

Consider another scenario. After you wipe the sweat from your brow, you take a deep breath and dive into clean-up mode. There will never be a better time to review all the steps you took and understand the reasons you took them than immediately upon completion of your program. If you wait, you will find it particularly difficult to remember those parts of the program which were needed at one point, but were rendered unnecessary in the end. You should not view these "dead zones" in your code as harmless backwaters, never traveled so never a bother. In fact, unexecuted portions of code become sources of deep insecurity for maintenance programmers.

You should go through your programs and remove any part of your code that is no longer used. This is a relatively straightforward process for variables and named constants. Simply execute searches for a variable's name in that variable's scope. If you find that the only place it appears is its declaration, delete the declaration and, by doing so, delete one more potential question mark from your code.

Use %TYPE When a Variable Represents a Column

Always, always use the %TYPE attribute to declare variables which are actually PL/SQL representations of database values. When you think about it, this includes a lot of your variables; using %TYPE sometimes takes lots more typing, but it improves your code substantially.

Suppose you have a procedure in Oracle Forms that formats information about a customer. You need to declare a variable for each attribute of the customer: first name, last name, address, Social Security number, etc. "Hardcoded" declarations would look like this:

```
PROCEDURE format_customer
IS
    first_name  VARCHAR2 (30);
    last_name   VARCHAR2 (30);
    address     VARCHAR2 (60);
    city        VARCHAR2 (60);
    state       VARCHAR2 (2);
    soc_sec#    VARCHAR2 (11);
BEGIN
    ... interact with database customer information ...
END;
```

There are a few problems associated with this declaration style. As mentioned previously, these declarations are going to work only as long as the structure of the table does not change and the resulting changed data does not violate the above size constraints. Another drawback is that there is no documented relationship between the variables and the table columns. For example, is the city variable the city in which the customer lives or the city in which the sale was made? I need additional documentation here to guide my understanding of the ways these variables will be used.

These problems are all resolved with the %TYPE attribute. The declaration section shown in the preceding example has a very different look when explicit declarations are replaced with the referential %TYPE declarations:

```
PROCEDURE format_customer
IS
    first_name  customer.cust_fname%TYPE;
```

```
   last_name    customer.cust_lname%TYPE;
   address      customer.cust_addr_11%TYPE;
   city         customer.cust_city%TYPE;
   state        customer.cust_state_abbrev_cd%TYPE;
   soc_sec#     customer.cust_soc_sec_number%TYPE;
BEGIN
   ... interact with database customer information ...
END;
```

Using the %TYPE attribute ensures that my variables stay synchronized with my database structure. Just as importantly, though, this declaration section is more self-documenting now. The %TYPE attribute provides important information to anyone reviewing the code, stating: "These variables represent my columns in the program. When you see one of these variables, think 'database column'." This correlation makes it easier to understand the code, easier to change the code, and easier to recognize when one of those variables is used in an inappropriate manner.

Notice that the variable name does not have to match the column name. The %TYPE attribute guarantees only that the datatype of the variable matches the datatype of the column. While a name matchup is not required, I generally try to name my %TYPE variables the same as my column names. The identical name strongly reinforces the fact that this variable "represents" my column in this program. While name synchronization can be a nuisance (database administrators often insist on somewhat obscure and rigid naming conventions, such as cust_ state_abbrev_cd for the two-character abbreviation of a customer's state), you cannot escape a DBA's conventions. Because you must use that table, why not make your programs as consistent as possible with the underlying database?

Use %TYPE to Standardize Nondatabase Declarations

While it is true that many (perhaps even most) of your local PL/SQL variables are directly related to database columns, at least some of your variables are local-only, perhaps calculated values based on database columns. You can also use the %TYPE attribute to infer a variable's datatype from another, previously defined PL/SQL variable, as I'll explain in this section.

The following declarations use this alternative source:

```
DECLARE
   revenue_data NUMBER(20,2);
   total_revenue revenue_data%TYPE;
   --
   max_available_date DATE := LAST_DAY (ADD_MONTHS (SYSDATE, 3));
   last_ship_date max_available_date%TYPE;
```

The variable called revenue_data acts as the standard variable for revenue data. Whenever I declare my total_revenue variable (or any other revenue-related variables), I base it on the general revenue_data variable. By doing this, I can guarantee a consistent declaration of revenue variables. Furthermore, if I ever need to change my revenue datatypes again, I only have to change the way that revenue_data is declared and recompile. All variables declared with revenue_data%TYPE will automatically adjust.

Note that while max_available_date has a default value as well, it is not applied to last_ship_date. Everything up to the optional default value assignment (initiated with a DEFAULT keyword or assignment operator) in a declaration is used in the %TYPE declaration, such as NOT NULL and the datatype. The default value, if specified in the source variable declaration, is ignored.

To make it easiest for individual developers to be aware of and make use of standard variable declarations, consider creating a package that contains only standard variable declarations and any code necessary to initialize them, as follows:

```
PACKAGE std_vartypes
IS
    /* Source for all revenue-related declarations */
    revenue_data NUMBER(20,2);

    /* Source for any Y/N flags -- when you don't use Booleans */
    flag_data CHAR(1);

    /* Standard format for primary key columns */
    primary_key_data NUMBER (10);

END std_vartypes;
```

Use Variables to Hide Complex Logic

A variable is a chunk of memory that has a name. A variable can hold a simple value. It can also be assigned the value of the outcome of an arbitrarily complicated expression—either through a default value setting or an assignment. In this way a variable can represent that complex expression and thus be used in place of that expression in your code. The result is a program which is easy to read and maintain.

Consider the following code fragment:

```
IF (shipdate < ADD_MONTHS (SYSDATE, +3) OR
    order_date >= ADD_MONTHS (SYSDATE, -2)) AND
    cust_priority_type = 'HIGH' AND
    order_status = 'O'
THEN
    ship_order ('EXPRESS');
```

```
ELSIF (order_date >= ADD_MONTHS (SYSDATE, -2) OR
        ADD_MONTHS (SYSDATE, 3) > shipdate) AND
      order_status = 'O'
THEN
    ship_order ('GROUND');
END IF;
```

If I skip past the complicated Boolean expressions and look at the code executed in each IF and ELSIF clause I can "reverse-engineer" my understanding of the code. It looks like the IF statement is used to determine the method by which an order should be shipped. Well, that's good to know. Unfortunately, it would be very difficult to discern this fact from the conditions in the IF statement. Those Boolean expressions with multiple components are, in and of themselves, almost impossible to interpret without drawing a diagram. If there is an error in this logic, no one but the original author would be able to readily untangle the knot.

When you find yourself writing this kind of code (or having to maintain it) and, in the process, stumble through the logic—either not sure if you got it right or even wondering precisely what "right" is, it is time for a shift in your approach. Perhaps you are trying to understand the implementational details before you understand the business rules.

Build from high-level rules

You should, in general, avoid implementing complicated expressions and logic until you have mapped out and verified that logic independent of PL/SQL code. Are you working from specifications? Then for the above code, your specifications might say something like this:

Rule 1

   If the order is overdue and the customer priority is high, ship the products ordered using express delivery.

Rule 2

   If the order is not overdue or the order is overdue but the customer priority is normal, then use standard ground delivery.

Before you dive into the PL/SQL IF statement, write some pseudocode based on your specifications. Here is an example:

```
IF order-overdue
THEN
    IF customer-priority-is-high
    THEN
        ship-express;
    ELSE
        ship-ground;
    END IF;
ELSE
```

```
        ship-ground;
    END IF;
```

The next step would be to rewrite this nested IF statement as follows:

```
IF order-overdue AND IF customer-priority-is-high
THEN
    ship-express;
ELSE
    ship-ground;
END IF;
```

Even before writing a line of code, I have been able to simplify the logic which meets this specification. At this point I don't know what it means for an order to be overdue. I don't know how to tell if a customer's priority is high. I don't really need to know these details yet. My focus is to make sure I understand the logical requirements. Once this is done, I can recast the pseudocode as real PL/SQL.

Convert pseudocode to PL/SQL

My first pass in a conversion to PL/SQL would be a more-or-less direct translation:

```
BEGIN
    IF order_overdue AND high_priority
    THEN
        ship_order ('EXPRESS');
    ELSE
        ship_order ('GROUND');
    END IF;
END;
```

I don't know how ship_order will behave and, again, at this moment I don't care. I will employ top-down design to "fill in the blanks" and then work out the details later.

My conditional expression:

```
order_overdue AND high_priority
```

substitutes named variables for the pseudocode. To figure out exactly how these variables should be assigned their values, I need to look back at my requirements. Here is what I find:

Definition 1

An order is overdue if the shipping date is within the next three months or the order status is open and the order was placed more than two months ago.

Definition 2

A customer has a high priority if its priority type is equal to HIGH.

This last sentence is less a requirement than an implementation instruction. Be that as it may, instead of creating a function for each of these conditions, I can declare Boolean named constants and assign a value to those constants based on the variables representing the order and customer, as shown below:

```
DECLARE
    /* I hide my business rule behind this variable. */
    order_overdue CONSTANT BOOLEAN
        DEFAULT (shipdate < ADD_MONTHS (SYSDATE, +3) OR
                 order_date >= ADD_MONTHS (SYSDATE, -2)) AND
                 order_status = 'O';

    high_priority CONSTANT BOOLEAN
        DEFAULT cust_priority_type = 'HIGH';

BEGIN
    IF order_overdue AND high_priority
    THEN
        ship_order ('EXPRESS');
    ELSE
        ship_order ('GROUND');
    END IF;
END;
```

In this final version of the IF statement, I've used the order_overdue constant to abstract out or hide the two-part check against the order and ship dates. Now the IF-THEN code is much easier to read; in fact, it all but explains itself through the names of the constants. This self-documenting capability reduces the need for separate comments in the code.

By consolidating my redundant code, I also make it easier to maintain my application. If the conditions which make an order overdue change, I do not need to hunt through my code for all the places which perform the order_overdue test. I need only change the default value given to the order_overdue constant.

I can also take this approach a step further and place my business rule logic into a Boolean function. I can then call this function from any of my programs and avoid reproducing the logic in that declaration statement.

5

Conditional and Sequential Control

This chapter describes two types of PL/SQL control statements: conditional control statements and sequential control statements. Almost every piece of code you write will require conditional control: the ability to direct the flow of execution through your program based on a condition; you do this with IF-THEN-ELSE statements. Far less often, you will need to tell PL/SQL to transfer control unconditionally via the GOTO statement, or to do nothing via the NULL statement.

Conditional Control Statements

You need to be able to implement requirements such as:

> If the salary is between ten and twenty thousand, then apply a bonus of $1500.
> If the salary is between twenty and forty thousand, apply a bonus of $1000.
> If the salary is over forty thousand, give the employee a bonus of $500.

or:

> If the user preference includes the toolbar, display the toolbar when the window first opens.

The IF statement allows you to design conditional logic in your programs. The IF statement comes in three flavors:

IF THEN END IF;	This is the simplest form of the IF statement. The condition between the IF and THEN determines whether the set of statements between the THEN and END IF should be executed. If the condition evaluates to false, then the code is not executed.

IF
ELSE
END IF;
	This combination implements an either/or logic: based on the condition between the IF and THEN keywords, either execute the code between the THEN and ELSE or between the ELSE and END IF. One of these two sections of executable statements is performed.

IF
ELSIF
ELSE
END IF;
	This last and most complex form of the IF statement selects an action from a series of mutually exclusive conditions and then executes the set of statements associated with that condition.

The IF-THEN Combination

The general format of the IF-THEN syntax is as follows:

```
IF <condition>
THEN
    ... sequence of executable statements ...
END IF;
```

The <condition> is a Boolean variable, constant, or expression that evaluates to TRUE, FALSE, or NULL. If <condition> evaluates to TRUE, then the executable statements found after the THEN keyword and before the matching END IF statement are executed. If the <condition> evaluates to FALSE or NULL, then those statements are not executed.

Here are some examples of the simple IF-THEN structure:

- The following IF condition compares two different numeric values. Remember that if one of these two variables is NULL, then the entire Boolean expression returns NULL and the discount is not applied:

```
IF :company.total_sales > system_average_sales
THEN
    apply_discount (:company.company_id);
END IF;
```

- Here is an example of an IF statement with a single Boolean variable (or function—you really can't tell the difference just by looking at this line of code):

```
IF report_requested
THEN
    print_report (report_id);
END IF;
```

- In the previous example, I used a single Boolean variable in my condition. If the variable report_requested evaluates to TRUE, then the report prints. Otherwise, the print step is skipped. I could code that same IF statement as follows:

```
IF report_requested = TRUE
THEN
    print_report (report_id);
END IF;
```

While the code in the third example is logically equivalent to the IF report_ requested formulation, it is superfluous and works against the nature of a Boolean variable. A Boolean variable itself evaluates to TRUE, FALSE, or NULL; you don't have to test the variable against those values. If you name your Boolean variables properly, you will be able to easily read the logic and intent of your IF-THEN logic by leaving out the unnecessary parts of the statement.

The IF-THEN-ELSE Combination

Use the IF-THEN-ELSE format when you want to choose between two mutually exclusive actions. The format of this either/or version of the IF statement is as follows:

```
IF <condition>
THEN
    ... TRUE sequence of executable statements ...
ELSE
    ... FALSE/NULL sequence of executable statements ...
END IF;
```

The <condition> is a Boolean variable, constant, or expression. If <condition> evaluates to TRUE, then the executable statements found after the THEN keyword and before the ELSE keyword are executed (the "TRUE sequence of executable statements"). If the <condition> evaluates to FALSE or NULL, then the executable statements that come after the ELSE keywords and before the matching END IF keywords are executed (the "FALSE/NULL sequence of executable statements").

The important thing to remember is that one of these sequences of statements will always execute, because it is an either/or construct. Once the appropriate set of statements has been executed, control passes to the statement immediately following the END IF statement.

Notice that the ELSE clause does not have a THEN associated with it.

Here are some examples of the IF-THEN-ELSE construct:

- In this example, if there is a VIP caller, I generate an express response; otherwise, I use normal delivery:

```
IF caller_type = 'VIP'
THEN
    generate_response ('EXPRESS');
ELSE
    generate_response ('NORMAL');
END IF;
```

- You can put an entire IF-THEN-ELSE on a single line if you wish, as shown below:

```
IF new_caller THEN get_next_id; ELSE use_current_id; END IF;
```

- This example sets the order_exceeds_balance Boolean variable based on the order total:

```
IF :customer.order_total > max_allowable_order
THEN
```

```
        order_exceeds_balance := TRUE;
    ELSE
        order_exceeds_balance := FALSE;
    END IF;
```

In the last example, the IF statement is not only unnecessary, but confusing. Remember: you can assign a TRUE/FALSE value directly to a Boolean variable. You do not need the IF-THEN-ELSE construct to decide how to set order_exceeds_ balance. Instead, you can assign the value directly, as follows:

```
    order_exceeds_balance :=  :customer.order_total > max_allowable_order;
```

This assignment sets the order_exceeds_balance variable to TRUE if the customer's order total is greater than the maximum allowed, and sets it to FALSE otherwise. In other words, it achieves exactly the same result as the IF-THEN-ELSE and does it more clearly and with less code.

If you have not had much experience with Boolean variables, it may take you a little while to learn how to integrate them smoothly into your code. It is worth the effort, though. The result is cleaner, more readable code.

The IF-ELSIF Combination

This last form of the IF statement comes in handy when you have to implement logic which has many alternatives; it is not an either/or situation. The IF-ELSIF formulation provides the most straightforward and natural way to handle multiple, mutually exclusive alternatives. The general format for this variation of the IF statement is:

```
    IF <condition-1>
    THEN
        <statements-1>
    ...
    ELSIF <condition-N>
    THEN
        <statements-N>

    [ELSE
        <else_statements>]
    END IF;
```

Logically speaking, the IF-ELSIF implements the CASE statement in PL/SQL. The sequence of evaluation and execution for this statement is:

If <condition1> is true then execute <statements1>.
Otherwise ... if <condition *n*> is true then execute <statements *n*>.
Otherwise execute the <else_statements>.

Each ELSIF clause must have a THEN after its condition. Only the ELSE keyword does not need the THEN keyword. The ELSE clause in the IF-ELSIF is the "otherwise" of the statement. If none of the conditions evaluate to TRUE, then the statements in the ELSE clause are executed. But the ELSE clause is also optional. You can code an IF-ELSIF that has only IF and ELSIF clauses. In this case, if none of the conditions are TRUE, then no statements inside the IF block are executed.

The conditions in the IF-ELSIF are always evaluated in the order of first condition to last condition. Once a condition evaluates to TRUE, the remaining conditions are not evaluated at all.

IF-ELSIF examples

Here are some examples of the possible variations in the format of the IF-ELSIF structure:

- I have three different caller types to check. If the caller type is not one of VIP, BILL_COLLECTOR, or INTERNATIONAL, then send the response with normal delivery:

```
IF caller_type = 'VIP'
THEN
   generate_response ('EXPRESS');

ELSIF caller_type = 'BILL_COLLECTOR'
THEN
   generate_response ('THROUGH_CHICAGO');

ELSIF caller_type = 'INTERNATIONAL'
THEN
   generate_response ('AIR');

ELSE
   generate_response ('NORMAL');
END IF;
```

- Here is an IF-ELSIF without an ELSE clause. If none of the conditions are TRUE, then this block of code does not run any of its executable statements:

```
IF new_caller AND caller_id IS NULL
THEN
   confirm_caller;

ELSIF new_company AND company_id IS NULL
THEN
   confirm_company;

ELSIF new_call_topic AND call_id IS NULL
THEN
   confirm_call_topic;
END IF;
```

- Here's an IF-ELSIF with just a single ELSIF—and no ELSE. In this case, however, you could just as well have used an IF-THEN-ELSE structure because the two conditions are mutually exclusive. The ELSIF statements execute only if the IF condition is FALSE. The advantage to including the ELSIF is that it documents more clearly the condition under which its executable statements will be run.

```
IF start_date > SYSDATE AND order_total >= min_order_total
THEN
    fill_order (order_id);

ELSIF start_date <= SYSDATE OR order_total < min_order_total
THEN
    queue_order_for_addtl_parts (order_id);
END IF;
```

Mutually exclusive IF-ELSIF conditions

Make sure that your IF-ELSIF conditions are mutually exclusive. The conditions in the IF-ELSIF are always evaluated in the order of first to last. Once a condition evaluates to TRUE, the remaining conditions are not evaluated at all. If you have an overlap in the conditions so that more than one condition could be TRUE, you probably have an error in your logic. Either the conditions in the IF statement should be changed to make them exclusive, or you'll sometimes run the risk of not executing the right set of code in your IF statement. The following example illustrates these points. Translate the following rules:

> If the salary is between ten and twenty thousand, then apply a bonus of $1500.
> If the salary is between twenty and forty thousand, apply a bonus of $1000.
> If the salary is over forty thousand, give the employee a bonus of $500.

into this code:

```
IF salary BETWEEN 10000 AND 20000
THEN
    bonus := 1500;

ELSIF salary BETWEEN 20000 AND 40000
THEN
    bonus := 1000;

ELSIF salary > 40000
THEN
    bonus := 500;
END IF;
```

What if the salary is $20,000? Should the person receive a bonus of $1000 or $1500? The way the IF-ELSIF is currently written, a person making $20,000 will always receive a bonus of $1500. This might not be the intent of the specification, the overall approach of which seems to be "let the poorer catch up a little with the richer." Actually, the problem here is that the original phrasing of the specification is ambiguous—and even incomplete. It assumes that no one ever has a salary of less than $10,000 (or, if we did not want to give the author of this specification the benefit of the doubt, we would say, "Anyone with a salary under $10,000 gets no bonus").

We can close up the holes in this logic by moving away from the BETWEEN operator and instead relying on < and >. This clarifies those break-points in the salary:

```
IF salary < 10000
THEN
   bonus := 2000;

ELSIF salary < 20000
THEN
   bonus := 1500;

ELSIF salary < 40000
THEN
   bonus := 1000;

ELSE — same as ELSIF salary >= 40000
   bonus := 500;
END IF;
```

Now the conditions are mutually exclusive, and the people who make the lowest salary get the largest bonus. That seems fair to me.

Here is an example of an IF-ELSIF with a condition that will never evaluate to TRUE; the code associated with it, therefore, will never be executed. See if you can figure out which condition that is:

```
IF order_date > SYSDATE AND order_total >= min_order_total
THEN
   fill_order (order_id, 'HIGH PRIORITY');

ELSIF order_date < SYSDATE OR order_date = SYSDATE
THEN
   fill_order (order_id, 'LOW PRIORITY');

ELSIF order_date <= SYSDATE AND order_total < min_order_total
THEN
   queue_order_for_addtl_parts (order_id);

ELSIF order_total = 0
THEN
   MESSAGE (' No items have been placed in this order!');
END IF;
```

The only executable statement that we can say with complete confidence will never be executed is:

```
queue_order_for_addtl_parts (order_id);
```

An order is put in the queue to wait for additional parts (to boost up the order total) only if the third condition evalutes to TRUE:

The order was placed today or earlier and the total for the order is under the minimum.

The reason that queue_order_for_addtl_parts will never be executed lies in the second condition:

> An order is filled with LOW PRIORITY whenever the order date was no later than the system date.

The second condition is a logical subset of the third condition. Whenever the second condition is FALSE, the third condition will also be FALSE. Whenever the third condition evaluates to TRUE, the second condition will also evaluate to TRUE. Because it comes before the third condition in the evaluation sequence, the second condition will catch any scenarios that would otherwise satisfy the third condition.

When you write an IF-ELSIF, especially one with more than three alternatives, review your logic closely and make sure there is no overlap in the conditions. For any particular set of values or circumstances, at most one—and perhaps none—of the conditions should evalute to TRUE.

Nested IF Statements

You can nest any IF statement within any other IF statement. The following IF statement shows several layers of nesting:

```
IF <condition1>
THEN
   IF <condition2>
   THEN
      <statements2>
   ELSE
      IF <condition3>
      THEN
         <statements3>
      ELSIF <condition4>
      THEN
         <statements4>
      END IF;
   END IF;
END IF;
```

Nested IF statements are often necessary to implement complex logic rules, but you should use them carefully. Nested IF statements, like nested loops, can be very difficult to understand and debug. If you find that you need to nest more than three levels deep in your conditional logic, you should review that logic and see if there is a simpler way to code the same requirement. If not, then consider creating one or more local modules to hide the innermost IF statements.

A key advantage to the nested IF structure is that it defers evaluation of inner conditions. The conditions of an inner IF statement are evaluated only if the condition for the outer IF statement that encloses them evaluates to TRUE.

If the evaluation of a condition is very expensive (in CPU or memory terms), you may want to defer that processing to an inner IF statement so that it is executed only when absolutely necessary. This is especially true of code that will be performed frequently or in areas of the application where quick response time is critical.

The following IF statement illustrates this concept:

```
IF condition1 AND condition2
THEN
   ...
END IF;
```

The PL/SQL run-time engine evalutes both conditions in order to determine if the Boolean expression A AND B evaluates to TRUE. Suppose that condition2 is an expression which PL/SQL can process simply and efficiently, such as:

```
total_sales > 100000
```

but that condition1 is a much more complex and CPU-intensive expression, perhaps calling a stored function which executes a query against the database. If condition2 is evaluated in a tenth of a second to TRUE and condition1 is evaluated in three seconds to FALSE, then it would take more than three seconds to determine that the code inside the IF statement should not be executed.

Now consider this next version of the same IF statement:

```
IF condition2
THEN
   IF condition1
   THEN
      ...
   END IF;
END IF;
```

Now condition1 will be evaluated only if condition2 evaluates to TRUE. In those situations where total_sales <= 100000, the user will never have to wait the extra three seconds to continue.

Sequential Control Statements

Certain PL/SQL control structures offer structured methods for processing executable statements in your program. You use an IF statement to test a condition to determine which parts of the code to execute. You use one of the LOOP variations (described in Chapter 7, *Loops*) to execute a section of code more than once. In addition to these well-structured approaches to program control, PL/SQL offers two other statements to handle out of the ordinary requirements for sequential processing: GOTO and NULL. The GOTO statement allows you to perform unconditional branching to another executable statement in the same execution

---

Avoiding Syntax Gotchas

Keep in mind these points about IF statement syntax:

- *Always match up an IF with an END IF.* In all three variations of the IF statement, you must close off the executable statements associated with the conditional structure with an END IF statement.

- *You must have a space between the keywords END and IF.* If you type ENDIF instead of END IF, the compiler will get very confused and give you the following hard-to-understand error messages:

```
ORA-06550: line 14, column 4:
PLS-00103: Encountered the symbol ";" when expecting one of the following:
if
```

- *The ELSIF keyword does not have an embedded "E".* If you use type ELSEIF in place of ELSIF, the compiler will get very confused and not recognize the ELSEIF as part of the IF statement. It will interpret it as a variable name or program name.

- Place a semicolon (*;*) only after the END IF keywords. The keywords THEN, ELSE, and ELSIF should not have a semicolon after them. They are not standalone executable statements and, unlike END IF, do not complete a statement. If you include a semicolon after these keywords, the compiler will issue messages indicating that it is looking for a statement of some kind before the semicolon.

---

section of a PL/SQL block. The NULL statement gives you a way to tell the compiler to do...absolutely nothing.

The following sections explain the implementation of the GOTO and NULL statements in PL/SQL. As with other constructs in the language, use them with care and use them appropriately, and your programs will be stronger for it.

The GOTO Statement

The GOTO statement performs unconditional branching to a named label. The general format for a GOTO statement is:

```
GOTO label_name;
```

where label_name is the name of a label.

This GOTO label is defined in the program as follows:

```
<<label_name>>
```

You must surround the label name with double enclosing angle brackets (<< >>). In this case, the label names a loop. This label can then be appended to the END LOOP statement, making the termination of the loop more visible. You can also issue an EXIT statement for a particular labeled loop from within another (enclosed) loop. Finally, you can GOTO that loop label, even though it was "designed" for a loop. (Chapter 7 describes the details of loop processing.)

When PL/SQL encounters a GOTO statement, it immediately shifts control to the first executable statement following the label.

Contrary to popular opinion (including mine), the GOTO statement can come in handy. There are cases where a GOTO statement can simplify the logic in your program. On the other hand, PL/SQL provides so many different control constructs and modularization techniques that you can almost always find a better way to do something than with a GOTO.

There are several restrictions regarding the GOTO statement, described in the sections below.

At least one executable statement must follow a label

A label itself is not an executable statement (notice that it does not have a semi-colon (;) after the label brackets), so it cannot take the place of one. All of the uses of the loop label in the following blocks are illegal because the labels are not followed by an executable statement:

```
IF status_inout = 'COMPLETED'
THEN
   <<all_done>> /* Illegal! */
ELSE
   schedule_activity;
END IF;

DECLARE
   CURSOR company_cur IS ...;
BEGIN
   FOR company_rec IN company_cur
   LOOP
      apply_bonuses (company_rec.company_id);
      <<loop_termination>> /* Illegal! */
   END LOOP;
END;

FUNCTION new_formula (molecule_in IN NUMBER) RETURN VARCHAR2
IS
BEGIN
   ... construct formula for molecule ...
   RETURN formula_string;

   <<all_done>> /* Illegal! */

END;
```

Target labels and scope of GOTO

The target label must be in the same scope as the GOTO statement. In the context of the GOTO statement, each of the following constructs maintains its own scope: functions, procedures, anonymous blocks, IF statements, LOOP statements, and exception handlers. All of the code examples below generate the same PL/SQL error:

```
PLS-00375: illegal GOTO statement; this GOTO cannot branch to label
```

- *IF conditions.* The only way to enter an IF statement is through an evaluation to TRUE of an IF condition. Therefore, this code produces an error:

```
GOTO label_inside_IF;
IF status = 'NEW'
THEN
    <<label_inside_IF>> /* Out of scope! */
    show_new_one;
END IF;
```

- *BEGIN statements.* The only way to enter a block-within-a-block is through the sub-block's BEGIN statement. PL/SQL insists on orderly entrances and exits. This code produces an error because it doesn't comply with this structure:

```
GOTO label_inside_subblock;
BEGIN
    <<label_inside_subblock>> /* Crosses block boundary! */
    NULL;
END;
```

- *Scope of IF statements.* Each IF clause of the IF statement is its own scope. A GOTO may not transfer from one clause to another. This code produces an error:

```
IF status = 'NEW'
THEN
    <<new_status>>
    GOTO old_status; /* Crosses IF clause boundary! */
ELSIF status = 'OLD'
THEN
    <<old_status>>
    GOTO new_status; /* Crosses IF clause boundary! */
END IF;
```

- *Don't jump into the middle of a loop.* You cannot jump into the middle of a loop with a GOTO. This code produces an error:

```
FOR month_num IN 1 .. 12
LOOP
    <<do_a_month>>
    schedule_activity (month_num);
END LOOP;
GOTO do_a_month; /* Can't go back into loop. */
```

If <exception_name1> is raised, then execute its statements; if <exception_nameN> is raised, then execute its statements; and so on. The WHEN OTHERS clause handles any exceptions not handled in the previous WHEN clauses (it is just like the ELSE clause of the IF statement). You can use the NULL statement to make sure that a raised exception halts execution of the current PL/SQL block, but does not propagate any exceptions to enclosing blocks:

```
PROCEDURE calc_avg_sales
BEGIN
   :sales.avg := :sales.month1 / :sales.total;
EXCEPTION
   WHEN ZERO_DIVIDE
   THEN
      :sales.avg := 0;
      RAISE FORM_TRIGGER_FAILURE;

   WHEN OTHERS THEN NULL;

END;
```

If total sales are zero, then an exception is raised, the average is set to zero, and the trigger processing in Oracle Forms is halted. If any other exceptions occur (such as VALUE_ERROR, which would be raised if the number generated by the calculation is larger than the sales.avg item allows), then the procedure does nothing and processing continues.

Even though the WHEN OTHERS clause of the exception section is like the ELSE clause of an IF statement, the impact of a NULL statement is very different in each of these statements. The addition of an ELSE NULL clause to the IF statement has an impact only on the readability of the code. The IF statement executes in precisely the same way it would have without the ELSE NULL clause.

When you include an exception handler with the NULL executable statement, you are saying, in effect: "End processing in the current PL/SQL block and move to the enclosing block, but otherwise take no action." This is very different from leaving out the exception handler altogether. If there is no exception handler, then PL/SQL raises the exception in the enclosing block again, and continues to do so until the last block, at which point it becomes an *unhandled exception* and halts the program. A "null" exception handler passes control back to the enclosing block, but does not cause the exception to be raised again.

See Chapter 8, *Exception Handlers*, for more detailed information about exceptions.

Supporting top-down design of modules

With top-down design (also known as top-down decomposition), you move from a general description of your system through step-by-step refinements of that idea to the modules which implement that system, and finally to the code that implements the modules. By moving through levels of abstraction, your mind concentrates on a relatively small number of issues at a time and can better process the details.

From a programming perspective, you implement top-down design by creating "stubs," or dummy programs. A stub will have the name and parameter list you need, but not have anything under the covers. Using stubs you define the API (application programmatic interface), which indicates the way that the different modules connect to each other.

In order for a PL/SQL program to compile, it must have at least one executable statement. The smallest, most nonintrusive program you can build will therefore be composed of a single NULL statement. Here are sample stubs for both a procedure and a function:

```
PROCEDURE revise_timetable (year_in IN NUMBER) IS
BEGIN
   NULL;
END;

FUNCTION company_name (company_id_in IN NUMBER) RETURN VARCHAR2 IS
BEGIN
   RETURN NULL;
END;
```

The NULL statement gives you a way to quickly cobble together the programmatic interface you need to formulate the functional hierarchy of your application. I'd like to say that this is half the battle, but I am not really sure that is so. You still have to figure out how to fill in all of those stubs.

Using NULL with GOTO to avoid additional statement execution

In some cases, you can pair NULL with GOTO to avoid having to execute additional statements. Most of you will never have to use the GOTO statement; there are very few occasions where it is truly needed. If you ever do use GOTO, however, you should remember that when you GOTO a label, at least one executable statement must follow that label. In the following example, I use a GOTO statement to quickly move to the end of my program if the state of my data indicates that no further processing is required:

```
PROCEDURE process_data (data_in IN orders%ROWTYPE,
                        data_action IN VARCHAR2) IS
BEGIN
   -- First in series of validations.
   IF data_in.ship_date IS NOT NULL
   THEN
      status := validate_shipdate (data_in.ship_date);
      IF status != 0 THEN GOTO end_of_procedure;
```

```
    END IF;

    -- Second in series of validations.
    IF data_in.order_date IS NOT NULL
    THEN
        status := validate_orderdate (data_in.order_date);
        IF status != 0 THEN GOTO end_of_procedure;
    END IF;

    ... more validations ...

    << end_of_procedure >>
    NULL;
END;
```

With this approach, if I encounter an error in any single section, I use the GOTO to bypass all remaining validation checks. Because I do not have to do anything at the termination of the procedure, I place a NULL statement after the label because at least one statement is required there.

6

Database Interaction and Cursors

PL/SQL is tightly integrated with the Oracle database via the SQL language. From within PL/SQL, you can execute any DML (data manipulation language) statements, including INSERTs, UPDATEs, DELETEs, and, of course, queries. You can also join multiple SQL statements together logically as a *transaction*, so that they are either saved ("committed" in SQL parlance) together or rejected in their entirety (rolled back). This chapter examines the SQL statements available inside PL/SQL to manage transactions. It then moves on to cursors, which give you a way to fetch and process database information in your PL/SQL program.

Transaction Management

The Oracle RDBMS provides a very robust transaction model, as you might expect for a relational database. You (or more precisely, your application code) determine what constitutes a *transaction*, the logical unit of work that must be either saved together with a COMMIT statement or rolled back together with a ROLLBACK statement. A transaction begins implicitly with the first SQL statement issued since the last COMMIT or ROLLBACK (or with the start of a session).

PL/SQL provides the following statements for transaction management:

COMMIT

Saves all outstanding changes since the last COMMIT or ROLLBACK and releases all locks.

ROLLBACK

Erases all outstanding changes since the last COMMIT or ROLLBACK and releases all locks.

ROLLBACK TO SAVEPOINT

Erases all changes made since the specified savepoint was established.

SAVEPOINT

Establishes a savepoint, which then allows you to perform partial ROLLBACKs.

SET TRANSACTION

Allows you to begin a read-only or read-write session, establish an isolation level, or assign the current transaction to a specified rollback segment.

LOCK TABLE

Allows you to lock an entire database table in the specified mode. This overrides the default row-level locking usually applied to a table.

These statements are explained in more detail in the following sections.

The COMMIT Statement

When you COMMIT, you make permanent any changes made by your session to the database in the current transaction. Once you commit, your changes will be visible to other Oracle sessions or users. The syntax for the COMMIT statement is:

```
COMMIT [WORK] [COMMENT text];
```

The WORK keyword is optional and can be used to improve readability.

The COMMENT keyword specifies a comment which is then associated with the current transaction. The text must be a quoted literal and can be no more than 50 characters in length. The COMMENT text is usually employed with distributed transactions. This text can be handy for examining and resolving in-doubt transactions within a two-phase commit framework. It is stored in the data dictionary along with the transaction ID.

Note that COMMIT releases any row and table locks issued in your session, such as with a SELECT FOR UPDATE statement. It also erases any savepoints issued since the last COMMIT or ROLLBACK.

Once you COMMIT your changes, you cannot roll them back with a ROLLBACK statement.

The following statements are all valid uses of the COMMIT:

```
COMMIT;
COMMIT WORK;
COMMIT COMMENT 'maintaining account balance'.
```

The ROLLBACK Statement

When you ROLLBACK, you undo some or all changes made by your session to the database in the current transaction. Why would you want to erase changes? From an *ad hoc* SQL standpoint, the ROLLBACK gives you a way to erase mistakes you might have made, as in:

```
DELETE FROM orders;
```

"No, no! I meant to delete only the orders before May 1995!" No problem, just issue ROLLBACK. From an application coding standpoint, ROLLBACK is important because it allows you to clean up or restart from a "clean state" when a problem occurs.

The syntax for the ROLLBACK statement is:

```
ROLLBACK [WORK] [TO [SAVEPOINT] savepoint_name];
```

There are two basic ways to use ROLLBACK: without parameters or with the TO clause to indicate a savepoint at which the ROLLBACK should stop.

The parameterless ROLLBACK undoes all outstanding changes in your transaction.

The ROLLBACK TO version allows you to undo all changes and release all acquired locks which were issued since the savepoint identified by savepoint_name was marked (see the next section on the SAVEPOINT statement for more information on how to mark a savepoint in your application).

The savepoint_name is an undeclared Oracle identifier. It cannot be a literal (enclosed in quotes) or variable name.

All of the following uses of ROLLBACK are valid:

```
ROLLBACK;
ROLLBACK WORK;
ROLLBACK TO begin_cleanup;
```

All of the following uses of ROLLBACK are *invalid*:

```
ROLLBACK SAVEPOINT;
   -- ORA-02181: invalid option to ROLLBACK WORK
   -- Must use TO keyword before SAVEPOINT.
ROLLBACK WORK TO;
   -- ORA-02182: save point name expected
   -- Must specify savepoint name.
ROLLBACK TO SAVEPOINT 'favorite_movies';
   -- ORA-03001: Unimplemented feature
   -- Savepoint cannot be in quotes.
```

When you roll back to a specific savepoint, all savepoints issued after the specified savepoint_name are erased. The savepoint to which you roll back is not, however, erased. This means that you can restart your transaction from that point and, if necessary, roll back to that same savepoint if another error occurs.

Immediately before you execute an INSERT, UPDATE, or DELETE, PL/SQL implicitly generates a savepoint. If your DML statement then fails, a rollback is automatically performed to that implicit savepoint. In this way, only that last DML statement is undone.

The SAVEPOINT Statement

SAVEPOINT gives a name to and marks a point in the processing of your transaction. This marker allows you to ROLLBACK TO that point, erasing any changes and releasing any locks issued after that savepoint, but preserving any changes and locks which occurred *before* you marked the savepoint.

The syntax for the SAVEPOINT statement is:

```
SAVEPOINT savepoint_name;
```

where savepoint_name is an undeclared identifier. This means that it must conform to the rules for an Oracle identifier (up to 30 characters in length, starting with a letter, containing letters, numbers and #, $, or _), but that you do not need to (nor can you) declare that identifier.

Savepoints are not scoped to PL/SQL blocks. If you reuse a savepoint name within the current transaction, that savepoint is "moved" from its original position to the current point in the transaction, regardless of the procedure, function, or anonymous block in which the SAVEPOINT statements are executed. As a corollary, if you issue a SAVEPOINT inside a recursive program, a new SAVEPOINT is executed at each level of recursion, but you can only roll back to the most recently marked savepoint.

The SET TRANSACTION Statement

The SET TRANSACTION statement allows you to begin a read-only or read-write session, establish an isolation level, or assign the current transaction to a specified rollback segment. This statement must be the first SQL statement processed in a transaction and it can appear only once. This statement comes in the following four flavors:

```
SET TRANSACTION READ ONLY;
```

This version defines the current transaction as read-only. In a read-only transaction, all subsequent queries only see those changes which were committed before the transaction began (providing a read-consistent view across tables and queries).

This statement is useful when you are executing long-running, multiple query reports and you want to make sure that the data used in the report is consistent:

```
SET TRANSACTION READ WRITE;
```

This version defines the current transaction as read-write:

```
SET TRANSACTION ISOLATION LEVEL SERIALIZABLE|READ COMMITTED;
```

This version defines how transactions that modify the database should be handled. You can specify a *serializable* or *read-committed* isolation level. When you specify SERIALIZABLE, a data manipulation statement (UPDATE, INSERT, DELETE) which attempts to modify a table already modified in an uncommitted transaction will fail. To execute this command, you must set the database initialization parameter COMPATIBLE to 7.3.0 or higher.

If you specify READ COMMITTED, a DML which requires row-level locks held by another transaction will wait until those row locks are released:

```
SET TRANSACTION USE ROLLBACK SEGMENT rollback_segname;
```

This version assigns the current transaction to the specified rollback segment and establishes the transaction as read-write. This statement cannot be used in conjunction with SET TRANSATION READ ONLY.

The LOCK TABLE Statement

This statement allows you to lock an entire database table with the specified lock mode. By doing this, you can share or deny access to that table while you perform operations against it. The syntax for this statement is:

```
LOCK TABLE table_reference_list IN lock_mode MODE [NOWAIT];
```

where table_reference_list is a list of one or more table references (identifying either a local table/view or a remote entity through a database link), and lock_ mode is the mode of the lock, which can be one of the following:

ROW SHARE
ROW EXCLUSIVE
SHARE UPDATE
SHARE
SHARE ROW EXCLUSIVE
EXCLUSIVE

If you specify the NOWAIT keyword, Oracle will not wait for the lock if the table has already been locked by another user. If you leave out the NOWAIT keyword, Oracle waits until the table is available (and there is no set limit on how long Oracle will wait). Locking a table never stops other users from querying or reading the table.

The following LOCK TABLE statements show valid variations:

```
LOCK TABLE emp IN ROW EXCLUSIVE MODE;
LOCK TABLE emp, dept IN SHARE MODE NOWAIT;
LOCK TABLE scott.emp@new_york IN SHARE UPDATE MODE;
```

Now that you see know the "macro" commands for managing transactions from within a PL/SQL application, let's move on to cursors; you will use cursors (in one form or another) to *create* transactions (i.e., specify the SQL statements which make up the transaction).

Cursors in PL/SQL

When you execute a SQL statement from PL/SQL, the Oracle RDBMS assigns a private work area for that statement. This work area contains information about the SQL and the set of data returned or affected by that statement. The PL/SQL cursor is a mechanism by which you can name that work area and manipulate the information within it.

In its simplest form, you can think of a cursor as a pointer into a table in the database. For example, the following cursor declaration associates the entire employee table with the cursor named employee_cur:

```
CURSOR employee_cur IS SELECT * FROM employee;
```

Once I have declared the cursor, I can open it:

```
OPEN employee_cur;
```

And then I can fetch rows from it:

```
FETCH employee_cur INTO employee_rec;
```

and, finally, I can close the cursor:

```
CLOSE employee_cur;
```

In this case, each record fetched from this cursor represents an entire record in the employee table. You can, however, associate any valid SELECT statement with a cursor. In the next example I have a join of three tables in my cursor declaration:

```
DECLARE
   CURSOR joke_feedback_cur
   IS
      SELECT J.name, R.laugh_volume, C.name
        FROM joke J, response R, comedian C
       WHERE J.joke_id = R.joke_id
         AND J.joker_id = C.joker_id;
BEGIN
   ...
END;
```

Here, the cursor does not act as a pointer into any actual table in the database. Instead, the cursor is a pointer into the *virtual table* represented by the SELECT statement (SELECT is called a virtual table because the data it produces has the same structure as a table—rows and columns—but it exists only for the duration of the execution of the SQL statement). If the triple-join returns 20 rows, each row containing the three columns in the preceding example, then the cursor functions as a pointer into those 20 rows.

Types of Cursors

You have lots of options in PL/SQL for executing SQL, and all of them occur as some type of cursor. Generally, there are two types of SQL that you can execute in PL/SQL: static and dynamic. SQL is *static* if the content of the SQL statement is determined at compile time. A SQL statement is *dynamic* if it is constructed at runtime and then executed.

Dynamic SQL is made possible in PL/SQL only through the use of the DBMS_SQL built-in package (see Appendix C, *Built-In Packages*). All other forms of SQL executed inside a PL/SQL program represent static SQL; these forms of cursors are the focus of the remainder of this chapter.

Even within the category of static SQL, we have further differentiation. With the advent of PL/SQL Release 2.3, you can choose between two distinct types of cursor objects:

Static cursor objects

These are the really static cursors of PL/SQL. The SQL is determined at compile time, and the cursor always refers to one SQL statement, which is known at compile time. The examples shown earlier in this chapter are static cursors.

Unless otherwise noted, any reference to "static cursor" refers to this sub-category of static (as opposed to dynamic) cursors.

Cursor variables

You can declare a variable which references a cursor object in the database. Your variable may refer to different SQL statements at different times (but that SQL is defined at compile time, not run time).

The cursor variable is one of the newest enhancements to PL/SQL and will be unfamiliar to most programmers. Cursor variables act as references to cursor objects. As a true variable, a cursor variable can change its value as your program executes. The variable can refer to different cursor objects (queries) at different times. You can also pass a cursor variable as a parameter to a procedure or function. Cursor variables are discussed later in this chapter.

Static PL/SQL cursors have been available since PL/SQL Version 1. The static version of cursors "hardcodes" a link between the cursor name and a SELECT statement. The static cursor itself comes in two flavors: implicit and explicit.

PL/SQL declares and manages an *implicit cursor* every time you execute a SQL DML statement, such as an INSERT or a SELECT that returns a single row.

You, the programmer, define your own *explicit cursors* in your code. You must use an explicit cursor when you need to retrieve more than one row of data at a time through a SELECT statement. You can then use the cursor to fetch these rows one at a time. The set of rows returned by the query associated with an explicit cursor is called the *active set* or *result set* of the cursor. The row to which the explicit cursor points is called the *current row* of the result set.

The bulk of this chapter is devoted to the management of static, explicit cursors. All information about cursor variables is localized in the later section called "Cursor Variables." Any references to PL/SQL cursors and cursor characteristics outside of that section will pertain to static cursors.

Cursor Operations

Regardless of the type of cursor, PL/SQL performs the same operations to execute a SQL statement from within your program:

PARSE

> The first step in processing an SQL statement is to parse it to make sure it is valid and to determine the execution plan (using either the rule-based or cost-based optimizer).

BIND

> When you bind, you associate values from your program (host variables) with placeholders inside your SQL statement. For static SQL, the SQL engine itself performs these binds. When you use dynamic SQL, you explicitly request a binding of variable values.

OPEN

> When you open a cursor, the bind variables are used to determine the result set for the SQL statement. The pointer to the active or current row is set to the first row. Sometimes you will not explicitly open a cursor; instead the PL/SQL engine will perform this operation for you (as with implicit cursors).

EXECUTE

> In the execute phase, the statement is run within the SQL engine.

FETCH

> If you are performing a query, the FETCH command retrieves the next row from the cursor's result set. Each time you fetch, PL/SQL moves the pointer

forward in the result set. When working with explicit cursors, remember that if there are no more rows to retrieve, then FETCH does nothing (it does not raise an error).

CLOSE

The CLOSE statement closes the cursor and releases all memory used by the cursor. Once closed, the cursor no longer has a result set. Sometimes you will not explicitly close a cursor; instead the PL/SQL engine will perform this operation for you (as with implicit cursors).

Figure 6-1 shows how some of these different operations are used to fetch information from the database into your PL/SQL program.

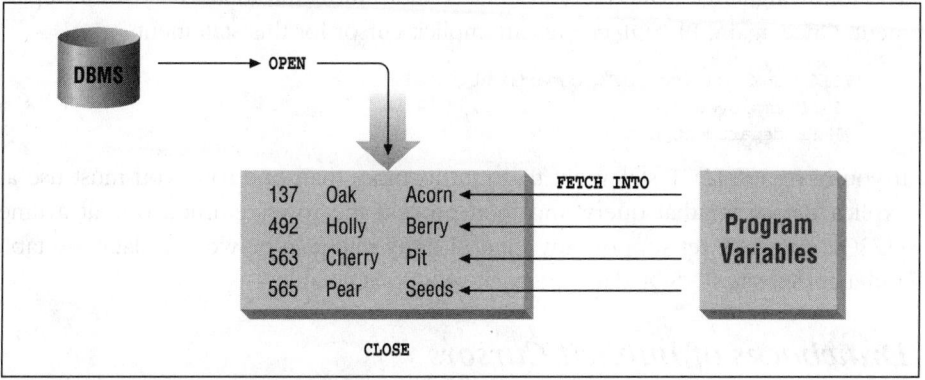

Figure 6-1. Using cursor operations to fetch database information into your program

Implicit and Explicit Cursors

Let's take a closer look at implicit and explicit cursors and the ways you can put them in your programs.

Implicit Cursors

PL/SQL issues an implicit cursor whenever you execute a SQL statement directly in your code, as long as that code does not employ an explicit cursor. It is called an "implicit" cursor because you, the developer, do not explicitly declare a cursor for the SQL statement.

If you use an implicit cursor, Oracle performs the open, fetches, and close for you automatically; these actions are outside of your programmatic control. You can, however, obtain information about the most recently executed SQL statement by examining the values in the implicit SQL cursor attributes, as explained later in this chapter.

PL/SQL employs an implicit cursor for each UPDATE, DELETE, or INSERT statement you execute in a program. You cannot, in other words, execute these statements within an explicit cursor, even if you want to. You have a choice between using an implicit or explicit cursor only when you execute a single-row SELECT statement (a SELECT that returns only one row).

In the following UPDATE statement, which gives everyone in the company a 10% raise, PL/SQL creates an implicit cursor to identify the set of rows in the table which would be affected by the update:

```
UPDATE employee
   SET salary = salary * 1.1;
```

The following single-row query calculates and returns the total salary for a department. Once again, PL/SQL creates an implicit cursor for this statement:

```
SELECT SUM (salary) INTO department_total
   FROM employee
  WHERE department_number = 10;
```

If you have a SELECT statement that returns more than one row, you must use an explicit cursor for that query and then process the rows returned one at a time. PL/SQL does not yet support any kind of array interface between a database table and a composite PL/SQL datatype such as a PL/SQL table.

Drawbacks of Implicit Cursors

Even if your query returns only a single row, you might still decide to use an explicit cursor. The implicit cursor has the following drawbacks:

- It is less efficient than an explicit cursor (in PL/SQL Release 2.2 and earlier)
- It is more vulnerable to data errors
- It gives you less programmatic control

The following sections explore each of these limitations to the implicit cursor.

Inefficiencies of implicit cursors

An explicit cursor is, at least theoretically, more efficient than an implicit cursor (in PL/SQL Release 2.2 and earlier). An implicit cursor executes as a SQL statement and Oracle's SQL is ANSI-standard. ANSI dictates that a single-row query must not only fetch the first record, but must also perform a second fetch to determine if too many rows will be returned by that query (such a situation will RAISE the TOO_MANY_ROWS PL/SQL exception). Thus, an implicit query always performs a minimum of two fetches, while an explicit cursor only needs to perform a single fetch.

This additional fetch is usually not noticeable, and you shouldn't be neurotic about using an implicit cursor for a single-row query (it takes less coding, so the temptation is always there). Look out for indiscriminate use of the implicit cursor in the parts of your application where that cursor will be executed repeatedly. A good example is the Post-Query trigger in the Oracle Forms.

Post-Query fires once for each record retrieved by the query (created from the base table block and the criteria entered by the user). If a query retrieves ten rows, then an additional ten fetches are needed with an implicit query. If you have 25 users on your system all performing a similar query, your server must process 250 additional (unnecessary) fetches against the database. So, while it might be easier to write an implicit query, there are some places in your code where you will want to make that extra effort and go with the explicit cursor.

NOTE   In PL/SQL Release 2.3 and above, the implicit cursor has been optimized so that it may, in isolation, run faster than the corresponding explicit cursor. Generally, the differences between these two approaches from a performance standpoint are negligible. On the other hand, if you use an explicit cursor, you are more likely (or at least *able*) to reuse that cursor, which increases the chance that it will be pre-parsed in shared memory when needed—thereby improving the performance of your application as a whole.

Vulnerability to data errors

If an implicit SELECT statement returns more than one row, it raises the TOO_MANY_ROWS exception. When this happens, execution in the current block terminates and control is passed to the exception section. Unless you deliberately plan to handle this scenario, use of the implicit cursor is a declaration of faith. You are saying, "I trust that query to always return a single row!"

It may well be that today, with the current data, the query *will* only return a single row. If the nature of the data ever changes, however, you may find that the SELECT statement which formerly identified a single row now returns several. Your program will raise an exception. Perhaps this is what you will want. On the other hand, perhaps the presence of additional records is inconsequential and should be ignored.

With the implicit query, you cannot easily handle these different possibilities. With an explicit query, your program will be protected against changes in data and will continue to fetch rows without raising exceptions.

Diminished programmatic control

The implicit cursor version of a SELECT statement is a black box. You pass the SQL statement to the SQL layer in the database and it returns (you hope) a single row. You can't get inside the separate operations of the cursor, such as the open and close stages. You can't examine the attributes of the cursor—to see whether a row was found, for example, or if the cursor has already been opened. You can't easily apply traditional programming control constructs, such as an IF statement, to your data access.

Sometimes you don't need this level of control. Sometimes you just think you don't need this level of control. I have found that if I am going to build programs in PL/SQL, I want as much control as I can possible get.

Always Use Explicit Cursors!

My rule of thumb is always to use an explicit cursor for all SELECT statements in my applications, even if an implicit cursor might run a *little* bit faster and even if, by coding an explicit cursor, I have to write more code (declaration, open, fetch, close).

By setting and following this clear-cut rule, I give myself one less thing to think about. I do not have to determine if a particular SELECT statement will return only one row and therefore be a candidate for an implicit cursor. I do not have to wonder about the conditions under which a single-row query might suddenly return more than one row, thus requiring a TOO_MANY_ROWS exception handler. I am guaranteed to get vastly improved programmatic control over that data access and more finely-tuned exception handling for the cursor.

Explicit Cursors

An explicit cursor is a SELECT statement that is explicitly defined in the declaration section of your code and, in the process, assigned a name. There is no such thing as an explicit cursor for UPDATE, DELETE, and INSERT statements.

With explicit cursors, you have complete control over how to access information in the database. You decide when to OPEN the cursor, when to FETCH records from the cursor (and therefore from the table or tables in the SELECT statement of the cursor) how many records to fetch, and when to CLOSE the cursor. Information about the current state of your cursor is available through examination of the cursor attributes. This granularity of control makes the explicit cursor an invaluable tool for your development effort.

Let's look at an example. The following anonymous block looks up the employee type description for an employee type code:

```
1    DECLARE
2       /* Explicit declaration of a cursor */
3       CURSOR emptyp_cur IS
4          SELECT emptyp.type_desc
5             FROM employees emp, employee_type emptyp
6             WHERE emp.type_code = emptyp.type_code;
7    BEGIN
8       /* Check to see if cursor is already open. If not, open it. */
9       IF NOT emptyp_cur%ISOPEN
10      THEN
11          OPEN emptyp_cur;
12      END IF;
13
14      /* Fetch row from cursor directly into an Oracle Forms item */
15      FETCH emptyp_cur INTO :emp.type_desc;
16
17      /* Close the cursor */
18      CLOSE emptyp_cur;
19   END;
```

This PL/SQL block performs the following cursor actions:

Action	Line(s)
Declare the cursor	3
Open the cursor (if not already open)	9, 11
Fetch one or more rows from the cursor	15
Close the cursor	18

The next few sections examine each of these steps in more detail. For the remainder of this chapter, unless noted otherwise, the word "cursor" refers to the explicit cursor.

Declaring Cursors

To use an explicit cursor, you must first declare it in the declaration section of your PL/SQL block or in a package, as shown here:

```
CURSOR cursor_name [ ( [ parameter [, parameter ...] ) ]
   [ RETURN return_specification ]
   IS SELECT_statement;
```

where cursor_name is the name of the cursor, return_specification is an optional RETURN clause for the cursor, and SELECT_statement is any valid SQL SELECT statement. You can also pass arguments into a cursor through the optional parameter list described in the section called "Cursor Parameters."

Once you have declared a cursor you can then OPEN it and FETCH from it.

Here are some examples of explicit cursor declarations:

*   *A cursor without parameters.* The result set of this cursor is the set of company ID numbers for each record in the table:

    ```
    CURSOR company_cur IS
        SELECT company_id FROM company;
    ```

*   *A cursor with parameters.* The result set of this cursor is the name of the company which matches the company ID passed to the cursor via the parameter:

    ```
    CURSOR name_cur (company_id_in IN NUMBER)
    IS
        SELECT name FROM company
        WHERE company_id = company_id_in;
    ```

*   *A cursor with a RETURN clause.* The result set of this cursor is all columns (same structure as the underlying table) from all employee records in department 10:

    ```
    CURSOR emp_cur RETURN employee%ROWTYPE
    IS
        SELECT * FROM employee
        WHERE department_id = 10;
    ```

The Cursor Name

The name of an explicit cursor is not a PL/SQL variable. Instead, it is an undeclared identifier used to point to or refer to the query. You cannot assign values to a cursor, nor can you use it in an expression.

As a result, both of the executable statements after the BEGIN line below are invalid:

```
DECLARE
    CURSOR company_cur IS
        SELECT company_id FROM company;
BEGIN
    company_cur := 15009; /* Invalid syntax */

    IF company_cur IS NOT NULL THEN ... ;   /* Invalid syntax */
```

In compiling either statement, you will receive the following error:

```
PLS-0321: expression 'COMPANY_CUR' is inappropriate as the left-hand side of
an assignment statement.
```

The name of a cursor can be up to 30 characters in length and follows the rules for any other identifier in PL/SQL.

PL/SQL Variables in a Cursor

Because a cursor must be associated with a SELECT statement, every cursor must reference at least one table from the database and determine from that (and from the WHERE clause) which rows will be returned in the active set. This does not mean, however, that a cursor's SELECT may only return database information. The list of expressions that appears after the SELECT keyword and before the FROM keyword is called the *select list*.

In native SQL, this select list may contain both columns and expressions (SQL functions on those columns, constants, etc.). In PL/SQL, the select list of a SELECT may contain PL/SQL variables, expressions, and even functions (PL/SQL Release 2.1 and above).

In the following cursor, the SELECT statement retrieves rows based on the employee table, but the information returned in the select list contains a combination of table columns, a PL/SQL variable, and a bind variable from the host environment (such as an Oracle Forms item):

```
DECLARE
    /* A local PL/SQL variable */
    projected_bonus NUMBER := 1000;
    /*
    || Cursor adds $1000 to the salary of each employee
    || hired more than three years ago.
    */
    CURSOR employee_cur
    IS
        SELECT employee_id,
                salary + projected_bonus new_salary, /* Column alias */
                :review.evaluation                   /* Bind variable */
          FROM employee
         WHERE hiredate < ADD_MONTHS (SYSDATE, -36);

    BEGIN
        ...
    END;
```

You can reference local PL/SQL program data (PL/SQL variables and constants), as well as host language bind variables in the WHERE, GROUP, and HAVING clauses of the cursor's SELECT statement.

Identifier Precedence in a Cursor

Be careful about naming identifiers when you mix PL/SQL variables in with database columns. It is, for instance, common practice to give a variable the same name as the column whose data it is supposed to represent. This makes perfect sense until you want to reference those local variables in a SQL statement along with the column.

In the following example, I want to fetch each employee who was hired more than three years ago and, using a local variable, add $1000 to their salary. The employee table has a column named "salary." Unfortunately, this procedure relies on a local variable of the same name to achieve its ends. Although this code will compile without error, it will not produce the desired result:

```
PROCEDURE improve_QOL
IS
    /* Local variable with same name as column: */
    salary NUMBER := 1000;

    CURSOR double_sal_cur
    IS
        SELECT salary + salary
          FROM employee
         WHERE hiredate < ADD_MONTHS (SYSDATE, -36);
BEGIN
```

Instead of adding $1000 to each person's salary, this code will instead double his or her salary. Inside the SQL statement, any unqualified reference to "salary" is resolved by using the column named "salary."

I could achieve the desired effect by qualifying the PL/SQL variable with the name of the procedure, as follows:

```
CURSOR double_sal_cur
IS
    SELECT salary + improve_QOL.salary
      FROM employee
     WHERE hiredate < ADD_MONTHS (SYSDATE, -36);
```

In this situation, you are informing the compiler that the second reference to salary is that variable "owned" by the improve_QOL procedure. It will then add the current value of that variable to the salary column value.

I do not, however, recommend that you make use of qualified local variable names in this way. If your local variable names conflict with database column or table names, *change the name of your variable*. Best of all, avoid this kind of duplication by using a standard naming convention for local variables which represent database information.

The Cursor RETURN Clause

One of the most significant new features in PL/SQL Version 2 is the full support for packages and the resulting modularization of code that is now possible with that construct. Packages introduce an enhancement to the way you can declare a cursor: the RETURN clause.

When you group programs together into a package, you can make only the specification, or header information, of those programs available to developers.

Although a developer can tell from the specification what the module is called and how to call it, he or she does not need to see any of the underlying code. As a result, you can create true black boxes behind which you can hide complex implementational details.

With Version 2 of PL/SQL you can accomplish the same objective with cursors by using the cursor RETURN clause. The RETURN clause allows you to create a specification for a cursor which is separate from its body (the SELECT statement). You may then place cursors in packages and hide the implementation details from developers.

Consider the following cursor declaration with RETURN clause:

```
CURSOR caller_cur (id_in IN NUMBER) RETURN caller%ROWTYPE
IS
    SELECT * FROM caller WHERE caller_id = id_in;
```

The *specification* of the caller_cur cursor is:

```
CURSOR caller_cur (id_in IN NUMBER) RETURN caller%ROWTYPE
```

while the *body* of the caller_cur cursor is:

```
SELECT * FROM caller WHERE caller_id = id_in;
```

Everything up to but not including the IS keyword is the specification, while everything following the IS keyword is the body.

You can include a RETURN clause for any cursor you write in PL/SQL Version 2, but it is required only for cursors which are contained in a package specification.

The RETURN clause may be made up of any of the following datatype structures:

- A record defined from a database table, using the %ROWTYPE attribute

- A record defined from a programmer-defined record

Here is an example of a cursor defined in a package. First, the package specification provides the name of the cursor and the RETURN datatype (an entire row from the company table):

```
PACKAGE company
IS
    CURSOR company_cur (id_in NUMBER) RETURN company%ROWTYPE;
END company;
```

Then the following package body repeats the cursor specification and adds the SQL statement:

```
PACKAGE BODY company
IS
    CURSOR company_cur (id_in NUMBER) RETURN company%ROWTYPE
    IS
        SELECT * FROM company
```

```
    WHERE company_id = id_in;

 END company;
```

The number of expressions in the cursor's select list must match the number of columns in the record identified by table_name%ROWTYPE or PLSQL_ record%ROWTYPE. The datatypes of the elements must also be compatible. If the second element in the select list is type NUMBER, then the second column in the RETURN record cannot be type VARCHAR2 or BOOLEAN.

Why place cursors in a package? For the same reasons you would place a procedure or a function in a package: a package is a collection of logically related objects. By grouping the code into a package you make it easier for a developer to identify and use the code (see Chapter 16, *Packages,* for more details). Packaged cursors are essentially black boxes. This is advantageous to developers because they never have to code or even see the SELECT statement. They only need to know what records the cursor returns, in what order it returns them, and which columns are in the column list.

When cursor information is limited on this kind of "need to know" basis, it protects developers and the overall application from change. Suppose that a year from now the WHERE clause of a query has to change. If a packaged cursor is not used, then each program that has a hardcoded or local cursor will have to be modified to meet the new specification. If, on the other hand, all developers simply access the same cursor, then changes will only need to be made to that packaged declaration of the cursor. The programs can then be recompiled to automatically support this change.

Opening Cursors

The first step in using a cursor is to define it in the declaration section. The next step you must perform before you try to extract or fetch records from a cursor is to open that cursor.

The syntax for the OPEN statement is simplicity itself:

```
 OPEN <cursor_name> [ ( argument [, argument ...] ) ];
```

where <cursor_name> is the name of the cursor you declared and the arguments are the values to be passed if the cursor was declared with a parameter list.

When you open a cursor, PL/SQL executes the query for that cursor. It also identifies the active set of data—that is, the rows from all involved tables that meet the criteria in the WHERE clause and join conditions. The OPEN does not itself actually retrieve any of these rows—that action is performed by the FETCH statement.

Regardless of when you perform the first fetch, however, the read consistency model in the Oracle RDBMS guarantees that all fetches will reflect the data as it existed when the cursor was opened. In other words, from the moment you open your cursor until the moment that cursor is closed, all data fetched through the cursor will ignore any inserts, updates, and deletes performed after the cursor was opened.

Furthermore, if the SELECT statement in your cursor uses a FOR UPDATE clause, then, when the cursor is opened, all the rows identified by the query are locked. (This topic is covered in the section called "SELECT FOR UPDATE in Cursors" later in this chapter.)

You should open a cursor only if it has been closed or was never opened. If you try to open a cursor that is already open you will get the following error:

```
ORA-06511: PL/SQL: cursor already open
```

You can be sure of a cursor's status by checking the %ISOPEN cursor attribute before you try to open the cursor:

```
IF NOT company_cur%ISOPEN
THEN
    OPEN company_cur;
END IF;
```

The section called "Cursor Attributes" later in the chapter, explains the different cursor attributes and how to make best use of them in your programs.

Fetching from Cursors

A SELECT statement creates a virtual table in SQL: its return set is a series of rows determined by the WHERE clause (or lack thereof) and with columns determined by the column list of the SELECT. So a cursor represents that virtual table within your PL/SQL program. In almost every situation, the point of declaring and opening a cursor is to return, or fetch, the rows of data from the cursor and then manipulate the information retrieved. PL/SQL provides a FETCH statement for this action.

The general syntax for a FETCH is shown below:

```
FETCH <cursor_name> INTO <record_or_variable_list>;
```

where <cursor_name> is the name of the cursor from which the record is fetched and <record_or_variable_list> is the PL/SQL data structure into which the next row of the active set of records is copied. You can fetch into a record structure (declared with the %ROWTYPE attribute or TYPE declaration statement) or you can fetch into a list of one or more variables (PL/SQL variables or application-specific bind variables such as Oracle Forms items).

The following examples illustrate the variety of possible fetches:

- Fetch into a PL/SQL record:

  ```
  FETCH company_cur INTO company_rec;
  ```

- Fetch into a variable:

  ```
  FETCH new_balance_cur INTO new_balance_dollars;
  ```

- Fetch into the row of a PL/SQL table row, a variable, and an Oracle Forms
  bind variable:

  ```
  FETCH emp_name_cur INTO emp_name (1), hiredate, :dept.min_salary;
  ```

Matching Column List with INTO Clause

When you fetch into a list of variables, the number of variables must match the
number of expressions in the SELECT list of the cursor. When you fetch into a
record, the number of columns in the record must match the number of expressions in the SELECT list of the cursor.

If you do not match up the column list in the cursor's query with the INTO
elements in the FETCH, you will receive the following compile error:

```
PLS-00394: wrong number of values in the INTO list of a FETCH statement
```

Let's look at variations of FETCH to see what will and will not work. Suppose I
have declared the following cursor, records, and variables:

- Cursor that selects just three columns from dr_seuss table and a record based
  on that cursor:

  ```
  CURSOR green_eggs_cur (character_in IN VARCHAR2)
  IS
      SELECT ham_quantity, times_refused, excuse
        FROM dr_seuss
       WHERE book_title = 'GREEN EGGS AND HAM'
         AND character_name = character_in;
  green_eggs_rec green_eggs_cur%ROWTYPE;
  ```

- Cursor for all columns in dr_seuss table and a record based on the dr_seuss
  table:

  ```
  CURSOR dr_seuss_cur
  IS
      SELECT * FROM dr_seuss;
  dr_seuss_rec dr_seuss_cur%ROWTYPE;
  ```

- Programmer-defined record type which contains all three of the green_eggs_
  cur columns, followed by declaration of record:

  ```
  TYPE green_eggs_rectype IS RECORD
      (ham# dr_seuss.ham_quantity%TYPE;
       saidno# dr_seuss.times_refused%TYPE,
       reason dr_seuss.excuse%TYPE);
  full_green_eggs_rec green_eggs_rectype;
  ```

- Programmer-defined record type which contains only two of the three cursor columns, following by declaration of record:

```
TYPE partial_green_eggs_rectype IS RECORD
    (ham# dr_seuss.ham_quantity%TYPE;
     saidno# dr_seuss.times_refused%TYPE);
partial_rec partial_green_eggs_rectype;
```

- A set of local PL/SQL variables:

```
ham_amount NUMBER;
refused_count INTEGER;
lousy_excuse VARCHAR2(60);
```

Now that everything is declared, I then OPEN the cursor for the "Sam I Am" character (passed as an argument) as follows:

```
OPEN green_eggs_cur ('Sam I Am');
```

All of the following fetches will compile without error because the number and type of items in the INTO clause match those of the cursor:

```
FETCH green_eggs_cur INTO green_eggs_rec;
FETCH green_eggs_cur INTO ham_amount, refused_count, lousy_excuse;
FETCH green_eggs_cur INTO full_green_eggs_rec;
FETCH dr_seuss_cur INTO dr_seuss_rec;
```

Notice that you can FETCH a cursor's row into either a table-based or a programmer-defined record. You do not have to worry about record type compatibility in this situation. PL/SQL just needs to be able to match up a cursor column/expression with a variable/field in the INTO clause.

As you can see from the above FETCHes, you are not restricted to using any single record or variable list for a particular FETCH—even in the same program. You can declare multiple records for the same cursor and use all those different records for different fetches. You can also fetch once INTO a record and then later INTO a variable list, as shown below:

```
OPEN green_eggs_cur ('Sam I Am');
FETCH green_eggs_cur INTO green_eggs_rec;
FETCH green_eggs_cur INTO amount_of_ham, num_rejections, reason;
CLOSE green_eggs_cur;
```

PL/SQL is very flexible in how it matches up the cursor columns with the INTO clause.

Fetching Past the Last Row

Once you open a cursor, you can FETCH from it until there are no more records left in the active set. At this point the %NOTFOUND cursor attribute for the cursor is set to TRUE.

Actually, you can even FETCH past the last record! In this case, PL/SQL will not raise any exceptions. It just won't do anything for you. Because there is nothing left to fetch, though, it also will not modify the values in the INTO list of the FETCH. The fetch will not set those values to NULL.

You should, therefore, never test the values of INTO variables to determine if the FETCH against the cursor succeeded. Instead, you should check the value of the %NOTFOUND attribute, as explained in the "Cursor Attributes" section.

Column Aliases in Cursors

The SELECT statement of the cursor includes the list of columns that are returned by that cursor. Just as with any SELECT statement, this column list may contain either actual column names or column expressions, which are also referred to as calculated or virtual columns.

A *column alias* is an alternative name you provide to a column or column expression in a query. You may have used column aliases in SQL*Plus in order to improve the readability of ad hoc report output. In that situation, such aliases are completely optional. In an explicit cursor, on the other hand, column aliases are required for calculated columns when:

- You FETCH into a record declared with a %ROWTYPE declaration against that cursor.

- You want to reference the calculated column in your program.

Consider the following query. For all companies with sales activity during 1994, the SELECT statement retrieves the company name and the total amount invoiced to that company (assume that the default date format mask for this instance is 'DD-MON-YYYY'):

```
SELECT company_name, SUM (inv_amt)
   FROM company C, invoice I
  WHERE C.company_id = I.company_id
    AND I.invoice_date BETWEEN '01-JAN-1994' AND '31-DEC-1994';
```

If you run this SQL statement in SQL*Plus, the output will look something like this:

```
COMPANY_NAME                           SUM (INV_AMT)
_____                           _____

ACME TURBO INC.                        1000
WASHINGTON HAIR CO.                    25.20
```

SUM (INV_AMT) does not make a particularly attractive column header for a report, but it works well enough for a quick dip into the data as an ad hoc query. Let's now use this same query in an explicit cursor and add a column alias:

```
DECLARE
   CURSOR comp_cur IS
```

```
        SELECT company_name, SUM (inv_amt) total_sales
          FROM company C, invoice I
         WHERE C.company_id = I.company_id
           AND I.invoice_date BETWEEN '01-JAN-1994' AND '31-DEC-1994';
    comp_rec comp_cur%ROWTYPE;
  BEGIN
     OPEN comp_cur;
     FETCH comp_cur INTO comp_rec;
     ...
  END;
```

With the alias in place, I can get at that information just as I would any other column in the query:

```
IF comp_rec.total_sales > 5000
THEN
   DBMS_OUTPUT.PUT_LINE
      (' You have exceeded your credit limit of $5000 by ' ||
       TO_CHAR (5000-company_rec.total_sales, '$9999'));
END IF;
```

If you fetch a row into a record declared with %ROWTYPE, the only way to access the column or column expression value is to do so by the column name—after all, the record obtains its structure from the cursor itself.

Closing Cursors

Early on I was taught that I should always clean up after myself. This rule is particularly important as it applies to cursors:

> *When you are done with a cursor, close it.*

Here is the syntax for a CLOSE cursor statement:

```
CLOSE <cursor_name>
```

where <cursor_name> is the name of the cursor you are closing.

An open cursor uses a certain amount of memory; the exact amount depends on the active set for the cursor. It can, therefore, use up quite a lot of the Shared Global Area of the RDBMS. The cursor can also cause the database to issue row-level locks when the FOR UPDATE clause is used in the SELECT statement.

Maximum Number of Cursors

When your database instance is started, an initialization parameter called OPEN_CURSORS specifies the maximum number of open cursors that a single-user process can have at once. This parameter does not control a system-wide feature, but rather the maximum address/memory space used by each process. If you are sloppy and do not close your cursors, you and all other users might encounter the dreaded error message:

```
ORA-01000:  maximum open cursors exceeded
```

You would rather not deal with this situation. For one thing, you will need to comb through your code and check for opened cursors which have not been closed. Even more frightening, your database administrator might insist that you tune your application so as to reduce the number of cursors you are using—real code changes! I say this in jest, but in fact 90% of all the tuning that can be done for an application has nothing to do with the database, and everything to do with the application. Are the SQL statements tuned? Are you closing all opened cursors? And so on.

When you close a cursor, you disable it. Because the cursor no longer has an active set associated with it, you cannot fetch records from the cursor. The memory for that cursor is released, and any locks caused by the cursor are removed. The RDBMS decreases by one the number of cursors currently open, pulling you and everyone else further away from the brink of error ORA-01000.

You should close a cursor only if it is currently open. You can be sure of a cursor's status by checking the %ISOPEN cursor attribute before you try to close the cursor:

```
IF company_cur%ISOPEN
THEN
    CLOSE company_cur;
END IF;
```

Closing Local Cursors

If you declare a cursor in a PL/SQL block (an anonymous block, procedure, or function), the cursor is only defined within (is "local to") that block. When execution of the block terminates, PL/SQL will automatically close any local cursors which were left open without raising an exception.

I recommend, however, that you still include CLOSE statements for any cursor you opened in your programs. Don't depend on the runtime engine to do your cleaning up for you.

In addition, if your cursor is defined in a package, then its scope is not limited to any particular PL/SQL block. If you open such a cursor, it will stay open until you CLOSE it explicitly or you disconnect your Oracle session.

Cursor Attributes

You can manipulate cursors using the OPEN, FETCH, and CLOSE statements. When you need to get information about the current status of your cursor, or the result of the last fetch from a cursor, you will access *cursor attributes*.

Both explicit and implicit cursors have four attributes, as shown in Table 6-1.

Table 6-1. Cursor Attributes

Name	Description
%FOUND	Returns TRUE if record was fetched successfully, FALSE otherwise.
%NOTFOUND	Returns TRUE if record was not fetched successfully, FALSE otherwise.
%ROWCOUNT	Returns number of records fetched from cursor at that point in time.
%ISOPEN	Returns TRUE if cursor is open, FALSE otherwise.

To obtain information about the execution of the cursor, you append the cursor attribute name to the name of your cursor. For example, if you declare a cursor as follows:

```
CURSOR caller_cur IS
    SELECT caller_id, company_id FROM caller;
```

then the four attributes associated with the cursor are:

```
caller_cur%FOUND
caller_cur%NOTFOUND
caller_cur%ROWCOUNT
caller_cur%ISOPEN
```

Some of the ways you can access the attributes of an explicit cursor are shown below in bold:

```
DECLARE
    CURSOR caller_cur IS
        SELECT caller_id, company_id FROM caller;
    caller_rec caller_cur%ROWTYPE;
BEGIN
    /* Only open the cursor if it is not yet open */
    IF NOT caller_cur%ISOPEN
    THEN
        OPEN caller_cur
    END IF;
    FETCH caller_cur INTO caller_rec;

    /* Keep fetching until no more records are FOUND */
    WHILE caller_cur%FOUND
    LOOP
        DBMS_OUTPUT.PUT_LINE
            ('Just fetched record number ' ||
            TO_CHAR (caller_cur%ROWCOUNT));
        FETCH caller_cur INTO caller_rec;
    END LOOP;
    CLOSE caller_cur;
END;
```

PL/SQL does provide these same attributes for an implicit cursor. Because an implicit cursor has no name, PL/SQL assigns the generic name SQL to it. Using this name, you can access the attributes of an implicit cursor. For more information on this topic, see the section entitled "Implicit SQL Cursor Attributes" later in the chapter.

You can reference cursor attributes in your PL/SQL code, as shown in the preceding example, but you cannot use those attributes inside a SQL statement. If you try to use the %ROWCOUNT attribute in the WHERE clause of a SELECT, for example:

```
SELECT caller_id, company_id
  FROM caller
 WHERE company_id = company_cur%ROWCOUNT;
```

then you will get a compile error:

```
PLS-00229: Attribute expression within SQL expression
```

The four explicit cursor attributes are examined in detail in the following sections.

The %FOUND Attribute

The %FOUND attribute reports on the status of your most recent FETCH against the cursor. The attribute evaluates to TRUE if the most recent FETCH against the explicit cursor returned a row, or FALSE if no row was returned.

If the cursor has not yet been opened, a reference to the %FOUND attribute raises the INVALID_CURSOR exception. You can evaluate the %FOUND attribute of any open cursor, because you reference the cursor by name.

In the following example, I loop through all the callers in the caller_cur cursor, assign all calls entered before today to that particular caller, and then fetch the next record. If I have reached the last record, then the %NOTFOUND attribute is set to TRUE and I exit the simple loop.

```
OPEN caller_cur;
LOOP
    FETCH caller_cur INTO caller_rec;
    EXIT WHEN NOT caller_cur%FOUND;

    UPDATE call
       SET caller_id = caller_rec.caller_id
     WHERE call_timestamp < SYSDATE;
END LOOP;
CLOSE call_cur;
```

In this next example, I keep a count of the total number of orders entered for a particular company. If I have fetched my last order (%FOUND is FALSE), then I display a message in Oracle Forms informing the user of the total number of orders:

```
OPEN order_cur;
LOOP
```

```
      FETCH order_cur INTO order_number, company_id;
      EXIT WHEN order_cur%NOTFOUND;
      do_other_stuff_then_keep_count;
      :order.count_orders := :order.count_orders + 1;
   END LOOP;
   CLOSE order_cur;

   IF :order.count_orders > 1
   THEN
      DBMS_OUTPUT.PUT_LINE
         ('A total of ' || TO_CHAR (:order.count_orders) ||
         ' orders have been found.');
   ELSE
      /*
      || I hate to code messages like 'A total of 1 orders was found.'
      || It makes me sound illiterate. So I will include a special-case
      || message when just one order is found.
      */
      DBMS_OUTPUT.PUT_LINE('Just one order was found.');
   END IF;
```

The %NOTFOUND Attribute

The %NOTFOUND attribute is the opposite of %FOUND. It returns TRUE if the explicit cursor is unable to fetch another row because the last row was fetched. If the cursor is unable to return a row because of an error, the appropriate exception is raised. If the cursor has not yet been opened, a reference to the %NOTFOUND attribute raises the INVALID_CURSOR exception. You can evaluate the %NOTFOUND attribute of any open cursor, because you reference the cursor by name.

When should you use %FOUND and when should you use %NOTFOUND? The two attributes are directly, logically opposed, so whatever you can do with one you can also do with a NOT of the other. In other words, once a fetch has been performed against the open cursor <cursor_name>, the following expressions are equivalent:

```
<cursor_name>%FOUND      = NOT <cursor_name>%NOTFOUND
<cursor_name>%NOTFOUND   = NOT <cursor_name>%FOUND
```

Use whichever formulation fits most naturally in your code. In a previous example, I issued the following statement:

```
EXIT WHEN NOT caller_cur%FOUND;
```

to terminate the loop. A simpler and more direct statement would use the %NOTFOUND instead of %FOUND, as follows:

```
EXIT WHEN caller_rec%NOTFOUND;
```

The %ROWCOUNT Attribute

The %ROWCOUNT attribute returns the number of records fetched from a cursor at the time that the attribute is queried. When you first open a cursor, its %ROWCOUNT is set to zero. If you reference the %ROWCOUNT attribute of a cursor that is not open, you will raise the INVALID_CURSOR exception. After each record is fetched, %ROWCOUNT is increased by one. This attribute can be referenced in a PL/SQL statement, but not in a SQL statement.

You can use %ROWCOUNT to limit the number of records fetched from a cursor. The following example retrieves only the first ten records from the cursor, providing the top ten companies placing orders in 1993:

```
DECLARE
   CURSOR company_cur IS
      SELECT company_name, company_id, total_order
        FROM company_revenue_view
       WHERE TO_NUMBER (TO_CHAR (order_date)) = 1993
       ORDER BY total_order DESC;
   company_rec company_cur%ROWTYPE;
BEGIN
OPEN company_cur;
LOOP
   FETCH company_cur INTO company_rec;
   EXIT WHEN company_cur%ROWCOUNT > 10 OR
             company_cur%NOTFOUND;

   DBMS_OUTPUT.PUT_LINE
      ('Company ' || company_rec.company_name ||
       ' ranked number ' || TO_CHAR (company_cur%ROWCOUNT) || '.');
END LOOP;
CLOSE company_cur;
```

The %ISOPEN Attribute

The %ISOPEN attribute returns TRUE if the cursor is open; otherwise, it returns FALSE. In most cases when you use a cursor, you open it, fetch from it, and close it, all within one routine. Most of the time it is easy to know whether your cursor is open or closed. In some cases, however, you will spread your cursor actions out over a wider area of code, perhaps across different routines (possible if the cursor is declared in a package). If so, it will make sense to use the %ISOPEN attribute to make sure that a cursor is open before you perform a fetch:

```
IF NOT caller_cur%ISOPEN
THEN
   OPEN caller_cur;
END IF;
FETCH caller_cur INTO caller_rec;
...
```

WARNING   Remember that if you try to open a cursor that has already been
             opened, you will receive a runtime error:

             ORA-06511: PL/SQL: cursor already open

Implicit SQL Cursor Attributes

When the RDBMS opens an implicit cursor to process your request (whether it is
a query or an INSERT or an UPDATE), it makes cursor attributes available to you
with the SQL cursor. This is not a cursor in the way of an explicit cursor. You
cannot open, fetch from, or close the SQL cursor, but you can access information
about the most recently executed SQL statement through SQL cursor attributes.

The SQL cursor has the same four attributes as an explicit cursor:

```
SQL%FOUND
SQL%NOTFOUND
SQL%ROWCOUNT
SQL%ISOPEN
```

Differences Between Implicit and Explicit Cursor Attributes

The values returned by implicit cursor attributes differ from those of explicit
cursor attributes in the following ways:

*   If the RDBMS has not opened an implicit SQL cursor in the session, then the
    SQL%ROWCOUNT attribute returns NULL instead of raising the INVALID_
    CURSOR error. References to the other attributes (ISOPEN, FOUND, NOT-
    FOUND) all return FALSE. You will never raise the INVALID_CURSOR error
    with an implicit cursor attribute reference.

*   The %ISOPEN attribute will always return FALSE—before and after the SQL
    statement. After the statement is executed (whether it is SELECT, UPDATE,
    DELETE, or INSERT), the implicit cursor will already have been opened and
    closed implicitly. An implicit cursor can never be open outside of the state-
    ment itself.

*   SQL cursor attributes are always set according to the results of the most
    recently executed SQL statement. That SQL statement might have been exe-
    cuted in a stored procedure which your program called; you might not even
    be aware of that SQL statement execution. If you plan to make use of a SQL
    cursor attribute, make sure that you reference that attribute immediately after
    you execute the SQL statement.

- The %FOUND attribute returns TRUE if an UPDATE, DELETE, or INSERT affected at least one record. It will return FALSE if those statements failed to affect any records. It returns TRUE if an implicit SELECT returns one row.

- The behavior of the %NOTFOUND attribute for UPDATE, DELETE, or INSERT statements is the opposite of %FOUND. The situation for an implicit SELECT is a bit different: when you use an implicit SELECT statement, never rely on the %NOTFOUND and %FOUND attributes.

- When an implicit SELECT statement does not return any rows, PL/SQL immediately raises the NO_DATA_FOUND exception. When an implicit SELECT statement returns more than one row, PL/SQL immediately raises the TOO_MANY_ROWS exception. In either case, once the exception is raised, control shifts to the exception section of the PL/SQL block.

Cursor Parameters

You are probably familiar with parameters for procedures and functions. Parameters provide a way to pass information into and out of a module. Used properly, parameters improve the usefulness and flexibility of modules.

PL/SQL also allows you to pass parameters into cursors. The same rationale for using parameters in modules applies to parameters for cursors:

- *A parameter makes the cursor more reusable.* Instead of hardcoding a value into the WHERE clause of a query to select particular information, you can use a parameter and then pass different values to the WHERE clause each time a cursor is opened.

- *A parameter avoids scoping problems.* When you pass parameters instead of hardcoding values, the result set for that cursor is not tied to a specific variable in a program or block. If your program has nested blocks, you can define the cursor at a higher-level (enclosing) block and use it in any of the subblocks with variables defined in those local blocks.

You can specify as many cursor parameters as you want and need. When you OPEN the parameter, you need to include an argument in the parameter list for each parameter, except for trailing parameters that have default values.

When should you parameterize your cursor? I apply the same rule of thumb to cursors as to modules: if I am going to use the cursor in more than one place, with different values for the same WHERE clause, then I should create a parameter for the cursor.

Let's take a look at the difference between parameterized and unparameterized cursors. First, a cursor without any parameters:

```
    CURSOR joke_cur IS
       SELECT name, category, last_used_date
          FROM joke;
```

The result set of this cursor is all the rows in the joke table. If I just wanted to retrieve all jokes in the HUSBAND category, I would need to add a WHERE clause as follows:

```
    CURSOR joke_cur IS
       SELECT name, category, last_used_date
          FROM joke
          WHERE category = 'HUSBAND';
```

I didn't use a cursor parameter to accomplish this task, nor did I need to. The joke_cur cursor now retrieves only those jokes about husbands. That's all well and good, but what if I also would like to see lightbulb jokes and then chicken-and-egg jokes and finally, as my ten-year-old would certainly demand, all my knock-knock jokes?

Generalizing Cursors with Parameters

I really don't want to write a separate cursor for each different category—that is definitely not a data-driven approach to programming. Instead, I would much rather be able to change the joke cursor so that it can accept different categories and return the appropriate rows. The best (though not the only) way to do this is with a cursor parameter:

```
    DECLARE
       /*
       || Cursor with parameter list consisting of a single
       || string parameter.
       */
       CURSOR joke_cur (category_in VARCHAR2)
       IS
          SELECT name, category, last_used_date
             FROM joke
             WHERE category = UPPER (category_in);

       joke_rec joke_cur%ROWTYPE;

    BEGIN
       /* Now when I open the cursor, I also pass the argument */
       OPEN joke_cur (:joke.category);
       FETCH joke_cur INTO joke_rec;
```

I added a parameter list after the cursor name and before the IS keyword. I took out the hardcoded "HUSBAND" and replaced it with "UPPER (category_in)" so that I could enter "HUSBAND", "husband", or "HuSbAnD" and the cursor would still work. Now when I open the cursor, I specify the value I wish to pass as the category by including that value (which can be a literal, constant, or expression) inside parentheses. At the moment the cursor is opened, the SELECT statement is parsed and bound using the specified value for category_in. The result set is identified and the cursor is readied for fetching.

Opening Cursors with Parameters

I can OPEN that same cursor with any category I like. Now I don't have to write a separate cursor to accommodate this requirement:

```
OPEN joke_cur (:joke.category);
OPEN joke_cur ('husband');
OPEN joke_cur ('politician');
OPEN joke_cur (:joke.relation || ' IN-LAW');
```

The most common place to use a parameter in a cursor is in the WHERE clause, but you can make reference to it anywhere in the SELECT statement, as shown here:

```
DECLARE
    CURSOR joke_cur (category_in VARCHAR2)
    IS
        SELECT name, category_in, last_used_date
          FROM joke
         WHERE category = UPPER (category_in);
```

Instead of returning the category from the table, I simply pass back the category_in parameter in the select list. The result will be the same either way, because my WHERE clause restricts categories to the parameter value.

Scope of Cursor Parameters

The scope of the cursor parameter is confined to that cursor. You cannot refer to the cursor parameter outside of the SELECT statement associated with the cursor. The following PL/SQL fragment will not compile because the program_name identifier is not a local variable in the block. Instead, it is a formal parameter for the cursor and is defined only inside the cursor:

```
DECLARE
    CURSOR scariness_cur (program_name VARCHAR2)
    IS
        SELECT SUM (scary_level) total_scary_level
          FROM tales_from_the_crypt
         WHERE prog_name = program_name;
BEGIN
    program_name := 'THE BREATHING MUMMY'; /* Illegal reference */
    OPEN scariness_cur (program_name);
END;
```

Cursor Parameter Modes

The syntax for cursor parameters is very similar to that of procedures and functions, with the restriction that a cursor parameter can be an IN parameter only. You cannot specify OUT or IN OUT modes for cursor parameters (see Chapter 15, *Procedures and Functions*, for more information on parameter modes).

The IN and IN OUT modes are used to pass values out of a procedure through that parameter. This doesn't make sense for a cursor. Values cannot be passed back out of a cursor through the parameter list. Information is retrieved from a cursor only by fetching a record and copying values from the column list with an INTO clause.

Default Values for Parameters

Cursor parameters can be assigned default values. Here is an example of a parameterized cursor with a default value:

```
CURSOR emp_cur (emp_id_in NUMBER := 0)
IS
   SELECT employee_id, emp_name
     FROM employee
    WHERE employee_id = emp_id_in;
```

So if Joe Smith's employee ID is 1001, the following statements would set my_emp_id to 1001 and my_emp_name to JOE SMITH:

```
OPEN emp_cur (1001);
FETCH emp_cur INTO my_emp_id, my_emp_name;
```

Because the emp_id_in parameter has a default value, I can also open and fetch from the cursor without specifying a parameter. If I do not specify a value for the parameter, the cursor uses the default value.

SELECT FOR UPDATE in Cursors

When you issue a SELECT statement against the database to query some records, no locks are placed on the selected rows. In general, this is a wonderful feature because the number of records locked at any given time is (by default) kept to the absolute minimum: only those records which have been changed but not yet committed are locked. Even then, others will be able to read those records as they appeared before the change (the "before image" of the data).

There are times, however, when you will want to lock a set of records even before you change them in your program. Oracle offers the FOR UPDATE clause of the SELECT statement to perform this locking.

When you issue a SELECT...FOR UPDATE statement, the RDBMS automatically obtains exclusive row-level locks on all the rows identified by the SELECT statement, holding the records "for your changes only" as you move through the rows retrieved by the cursor. No one else will be able to change any of these records until you perform a ROLLBACK or a COMMIT.

Here are two examples of the FOR UPDATE clause used in a cursor:

```
CURSOR toys_cur IS
    SELECT name, manufacturer, preference_level, sell_at_yardsale_flag
      FROM my_sons_collection
     WHERE hours_used = 0
       FOR UPDATE;

CURSOR fall_jobs_cur IS
    SELECT task, expected_hours, tools_required, do_it_yourself_flag
      FROM winterize
     WHERE year = TO_CHAR (SYSDATE, 'YYYY')
       FOR UPDATE OF task;
```

The first cursor uses the unqualified FOR UPDATE clause, while the second cursor qualifies the FOR UPDATE with a column name from the query.

You can use the FOR UPDATE clause in a SELECT against multiple tables. In this case, rows in a table are locked only if the FOR UPDATE clause references a column in that table. In the following example the FOR UPDATE clause does not result in any locked rows in the winterize table:

```
CURSOR fall_jobs_cur IS
    SELECT w.task, w.expected_hours,
           w.tools_required, w.do_it_yourself_flag
      FROM winterize w, husband_config hc
     WHERE year = TO_CHAR (SYSDATE, 'YYYY')
       FOR UPDATE OF husband_config.max_procrastination_allowed;
```

The FOR UPDATE OF clause only mentions the max_procrastination_allowed column; no columns in the winterize table are listed.

The OF list of the FOR UPDATE clause does not restrict you to changing only those columns listed. Locks are still placed on all rows; the OF list just gives you a way to document more clearly what you intend to change. If you simply state FOR UPDATE in the query and do not include one or more columns after the OF keyword, then the database will then lock all identified rows across all tables listed in the FROM clause.

Furthermore, you do not have to actually UPDATE or DELETE any records just because you issued a SELECT...FOR UPDATE—that act simply states your intention to be able to do so.

Finally, you can append the optional keyword NOWAIT to the FOR UPDATE clause to tell Oracle not to wait if the table has been locked by another user. In this case, control will be returned immediately to your program so that you can perform other work or simply wait for a period of time before trying again. Without the NOWAIT clause, your process will block until the table is available. There is no limit to the wait time unless the table is remote. For remote objects, the Oracle initialization parameter, DISTRIBUTED_LOCK_TIMEOUT, is used to set the limit.

Releasing Locks with COMMIT

As soon as a cursor with a FOR UPDATE clause is OPENed, all rows identified in the result set of the cursor are locked and remain locked until your session issues either a COMMIT statement to save any changes or a ROLLBACK statement to cancel those changes. When either of these actions occurs, the locks on the rows are released. As a result, you cannot execute another FETCH against a FOR UPDATE cursor after you COMMIT or ROLLBACK. You will have lost your position in the cursor.

Consider the following program, which assigns winterization chores:[*]

```
DECLARE
    /* All the jobs in the Fall to prepare for the Winter */
    CURSOR fall_jobs_cur
    IS
        SELECT task, expected_hours, tools_required, do_it_yourself_flag
          FROM winterize
         WHERE year = TO_CHAR (SYSDATE, 'YYYY')
           AND completed_flag = 'NOTYET'
          FOR UPDATE OF task;
BEGIN
    /* For each job fetched by the cursor... */
    FOR job_rec IN fall_jobs_cur
    LOOP
        IF job_rec.do_it_yourself_flag = 'YOUCANDOIT'
        THEN
            /*
            || I have found my next job. Assign it to myself (like someone
            || is going to do it!) and then commit the changes.
            */
            UPDATE winterize SET responsible = 'STEVEN'
             WHERE task = job_rec.task
               AND year = TO_CHAR (SYSDATE, 'YYYY');
            COMMIT;
```

---

[*] Caveat: I don't want to set false expectations with anyone, especially my wife. The code in this block is purely an example. In reality, I set the max_procrastination_allowed to five years and let my house decay until I can afford to pay someone to do something, or my wife does it, or she gives me an ultimatum. Now you know why I decided to write a book...

```
       END IF;
    END LOOP;
END;
```

Suppose this loop finds its first YOUCANDOIT job. It then commits an assignment of a job to STEVEN. When it tries to FETCH the next record, the program raises the following exception:

```
ORA-01002: fetch out of sequence
```

If you ever need to execute a COMMIT or ROLLBACK as you FETCH records from a SELECT FOR UPDATE cursor, you should include code (such as a loop EXIT or other conditional logic) to halt any further fetches from the cursor.

The WHERE CURRENT OF Clause

PL/SQL provides the WHERE CURRENT OF clause for both UPDATE and DELETE statements inside a cursor in order to allow you to easily make changes to the most recently fetched row of data.

The general format for the WHERE CURRENT OF clause is as follows:

```
UPDATE table_name
   SET set_clause
 WHERE CURRENT OF cursor_name;

DELETE
  FROM table_name
 WHERE CURRENT OF cursor_name;
```

Notice that the WHERE CURRENT OF clause references the cursor and not the record into which the next fetched row is deposited.

The most important advantage to using WHERE CURRENT OF where you need to change the row fetched last is that you do not have to code in two (or more) places the criteria used to uniquely identify a row in a table. Without WHERE CURRENT OF, you would need to repeat the WHERE clause of your cursor in the WHERE clause of the associated UPDATEs and DELETEs. As a result, if the table structure changes in a way that affects the construction of the primary key, you have to make sure that each SQL statement is upgraded to support this change. If you use WHERE CURRENT OF, on the other hand, you only have to modify the WHERE clause of the SELECT statement.

This might seem like a relatively minor issue, but it is one of many areas in your code where you can leverage subtle features in PL/SQL to minimize code redundancies. Utilization of WHERE CURRENT OF, %TYPE, and %ROWTYPE declaration attributes, cursor FOR loops, local modularization, and other PL/SQL language constructs can have a big impact on reducing the pain you may experience when you maintain your Oracle-based applications.

Let's see how this clause would improve the previous example. In the jobs cursor FOR loop above, I want to UPDATE the record that was currently FETCHed by the cursor. I do this in the UPDATE statement by repeating the same WHERE used in the cursor because (task, year) makes up the primary key of this table:

```
WHERE task = job_rec.task
  AND year = TO_CHAR (SYSDATE, 'YYYY');
```

This is a less than ideal situation, as explained above: I have coded the same logic in two places, and this code must be kept synchronized. It would be so much more convenient and natural to be able to code the equivalent of the following statements:

Delete the record I just fetched.

or:

Update these columns in that row I just fetched.

A perfect fit for WHERE CURRENT OF! The next version of my winterization program below uses this clause. I have also switched to a simple loop from FOR loop because I want to exit conditionally from the loop:

```
DECLARE
    CURSOR fall_jobs_cur IS SELECT ... same as before ... ;
    job_rec fall_jobs_cur%ROWTYPE;
BEGIN
    OPEN fall_jobs_cur;
    LOOP
        FETCH fall_jobs_cur INTO job_rec;

        IF fall_jobs_cur%NOTFOUND
        THEN
            EXIT;

        ELSIF job_rec.do_it_yourself_flag = 'YOUCANDOIT'
        THEN
            UPDATE winterize SET responsible = 'STEVEN'
             WHERE CURRENT OF fall_jobs_cur;
          COMMIT;
          EXIT;
        END IF;
    END LOOP;
    CLOSE fall_jobs_cur;
END;
```

Cursor Variables

In PL/SQL Release 2.3, available with the release of Oracle Server Release 7.3, you can create and use *cursor variables*. Unlike an explicit cursor, which names the PL/SQL work area for the result set, a cursor variable is instead a (Release 2.3) reference to that work area. Explicit and implicit cursors are both static in that they are tied to specific queries. The cursor variable can be opened for any query, even different queries within a single program execution.

The most important benefit of the cursor variable is that it provides a mechanism for passing results of queries (the rows returned by fetches against a cursor) between different PL/SQL programs—even between client and server PL/SQL programs. Prior to PL/SQL Release 2.3, you would have had to fetch all data from the cursor, store it in PL/SQL variables (perhaps a PL/SQL table), and then pass those variables as arguments. With cursor variables, you simply pass the reference to that cursor. This improves performance and streamlines your code.

It also means that the cursor is, in effect, shared among the programs which have access to the cursor variable. In a client-server environment, for example, a program on the client side could open and start fetching from the cursor variable, then pass that variable as an argument to a stored procedure on the server. This stored program could then continue fetching and pass control back to the client program to close the cursor. You can also perform the same steps between different stored programs, on the same or different database instances.

Cursor Variables in PL/SQL Release 2.2

Cursor variables first became available in PL/SQL Release 2.2. This first version of cursor variables allowed you to open and close the cursor objects within PL/SQL, but you could fetch through these cursor variables only within a host language (using the Oracle Call Interface—OCI—or a precompiler like Pro*C). It was not until Release 2.3 that the PL/SQL language made cursor variables available for "self-contained" execution, independent of any host language.

Because the focus of this book is on standalone PL/SQL development, I present cursor variables as a PL/SQL Release 2.3 enhancement. If you do have PL/SQL Release 2.2 and work with PL/SQL in a host language environment, you can still use cursor variables. Just don't try to FETCH within PL/SQL and don't expect any of the cursor attributes to be available for your cursor variables.

NOTE   The client-server aspect of this sharing will only really come into play when the Oracle Developer/2000 tools are converted to use PL/SQL Release 2.3 or above.

This process, shown in Figure 6-2, offers dramatic new possibilities for data sharing and cursor management in PL/SQL programs.

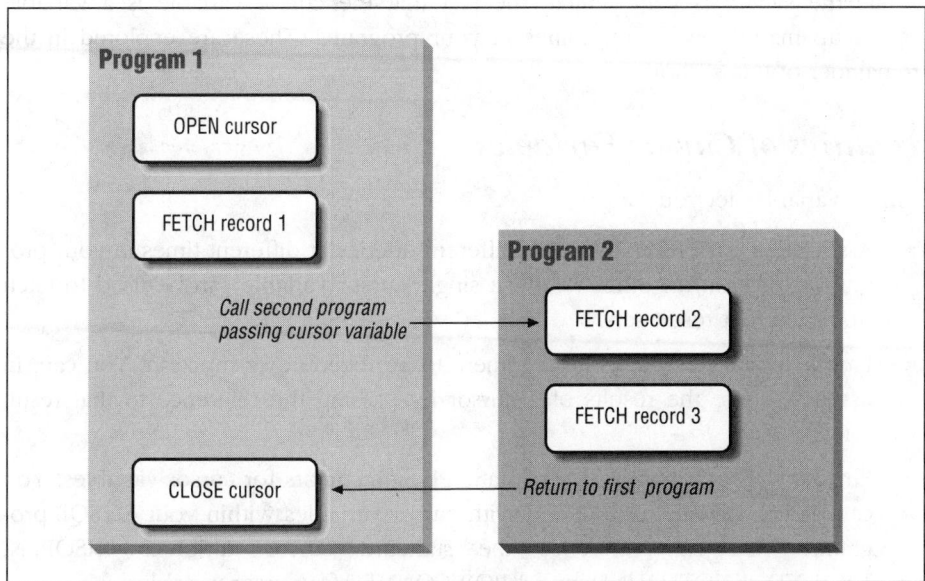

Figure 6-2. Referencing a cursor variable across two programs

The code you write to take advantage of cursor variables is very similar to that for explicit cursors. The following example declares a cursor type (called a REF CURSOR type) for the company table, then opens, fetches from, and closes the cursor:

```
DECLARE
    /* Create the cursor type. */
    TYPE company_curtype IS REF CURSOR RETURN company%ROWTYPE;

    /* Declare a cursor variable of that type. */
    company_curvar company_curtype;

    /* Declare a record with same structure as cursor variable. */
    company_rec company%ROWTYPE;
BEGIN
    /* Open the cursor variable, associating with it a SQL statement. */
    OPEN company_curvar FOR SELECT * FROM company;

    /* Fetch from the cursor variable. */
    FETCH company_curvar INTO company_rec;

    /* Close the cursor object associated with variable. */
    CLOSE company_curvar;
END;
```

That looks an awful lot like explicit cursor operations, except for the following:

- The REF CURSOR type declaration
- The OPEN FOR syntax which specified the query at the time of the open

While the syntax is very similar, the fact that the cursor variable is a variable opens up many new opportunities in your programs. These are explored in the remainder of this section.

Features of Cursor Variables

Cursor variables let you:

- Associate a cursor variable with different queries at different times in your program execution. In other words, a single cursor variable can be used to fetch from different result sets.

- Pass a cursor variable as an argument to a procedure or function. You can, in essence, share the results of a cursor by passing the reference to that result set.

- Employ the full functionality of static PL/SQL cursors for cursor variables. You can OPEN, CLOSE, and FETCH with cursor variables within your PL/SQL programs. You can reference the standard cursor attributes—%ISOPEN, %FOUND, %NOTFOUND, and %ROWCOUNT—for cursor variables.

- Assign the contents of one cursor (and its result set) to another cursor variable. Because the cursor variable is a variable, it can be used in assignment operations. There are, however, restrictions on referencing this kind of variable, addressed later in this chapter.

Similarities to Static Cursors

One of the key design requirements for cursor variables was that as much as possible the semantics used to manage cursor objects would be the same as that of static cursors. While the declaration of a cursor variable and the syntax for opening it are enhanced, the following cursor operations are unchanged for cursor variables:

- *The CLOSE statement.* In the following example I declare a REF CURSOR type and a cursor variable based on that type. Then I close the cursor variable using the same syntax as for that of a static cursor:

```
DECLARE
    TYPE var_cur_type IS REF CURSOR;
    var_cur var_cur_type;
BEGIN
    CLOSE var_cur;
END;
```

- *Cursor attributes.* You can use any of the four cursor attributes with exactly the same syntax as for that of a static cursor. The rules governing the use and values returned by those attributes match that of explicit cursors. If I have declared a variable cursor as in the previous example, I could use all the cursor attributes as follows:

```
var_cur%ISOOPEN
var_cur%FOUND
var_cur%NOTFOUND
var_cur%ROWCOUNT
```

- *Fetching from the cursor variable.* You use the same FETCH syntax when fetching from a cursor variable into local PL/SQL data structures. There are, however, additional rules applied by PL/SQL to make sure that the data structures of the cursor variable's row (the set of values returned by the cursor object) match that of the data structures to the right of the INTO keyword. These rules are discussed in the section called "Rules for Cursor Variables."

Because the syntax for these aspects of cursor variables remain unchanged, I won't cover them again in the remainder of this section. Instead I will focus on the new capabilities available and the changed syntax required for cursor variables.

Declaring REF CURSOR Types and Cursor Variables

Just as with a PL/SQL table or a programmer-defined record, you must perform two distinct declaration steps in order to create a cursor variable:

1. Create a referenced cursor TYPE.

2. Declare the actual cursor variable based on that type.

The syntax for creating a referenced cursor type is as follows:

```
TYPE cursor_type_name IS REF CURSOR [ RETURN return_type ];
```

where cursor_type_name is the name of the type of cursor and return_type is the RETURN data specification for the cursor type. The return_type can be any of the data structures valid for a normal cursor RETURN clause, defined using the %ROWTYPE attribute or by referencing a previously-defined record TYPE.

Notice that the RETURN clause is optional with the REF CURSOR type statement. Both of the following declarations are valid:

```
TYPE company_curtype IS REF CURSOR RETURN company%ROWTYPE;
TYPE generic_curtype IS REF CURSOR;
```

The first form of the REF CURSOR statement is called a *strong type* because it attaches a record type (or row type) to the cursor variable type at the moment of declaration. Any cursor variable declared using that type can only be used with SQL statement and FETCH INTO data structures which match the specified record type. The advantage of a strong REF TYPE is that the compiler can determine whether or not the developer has properly matched up the cursor variable's FETCH statements with its cursor object's query list.

The second form of the REF CURSOR statement, in which the RETURN clause is missing, is called a *weak type*. This cursor variable type is not associated with any record data structure. Cursor variables declared without the RETURN clause can be used in much more flexible ways than the strong type. They can be used with any query, with any rowtype structure—varying even within the course of a single program.

Declaring cursor variables

The syntax for declaring a cursor variable is:

```
cursor_name cursor_type_name;
```

where cursor_name is the name of the cursor and cursor_type_name is the name of the type of cursor previously defined with a TYPE statement.

Here is an example of the creation of a cursor variable:

```
DECLARE
    /* Create a cursor type for sports cars. */
    TYPE sports_car_cur_type IS REF CURSOR RETURN car%ROWTYPE;

    /* Create a cursor variable for sports cars. */
    sports_car_cur sports_car_cur_type;
BEGIN
    ...
END;
```

It is very important to distinguish between declaring a cursor variable and creating an actual cursor object—the result set identified by the cursor SQL statement. The cursor variable is nothing more than a reference or pointer. A constant is nothing more than a value, whereas a variable points to its value. Similarly, a static cursor acts as a constant, whereas a cursor variable points to a cursor object. These distinctions are shown in Figure 6-3. Notice that two different cursor variables in different programs both refer to the same cursor object.

Declaration of a cursor variable does not create a cursor object. To do that, you must instead use the OPEN FOR syntax to create a new cursor object and assign it to the variable.

Opening Cursor Variables

You assign a value (the cursor object) to a cursor when you OPEN the cursor. So the syntax for the OPEN statement is now modified in PL/SQL Release 2.3 to accept a SELECT statement after the FOR clause, as shown below:

```
OPEN cursor_name FOR select_statement;
```

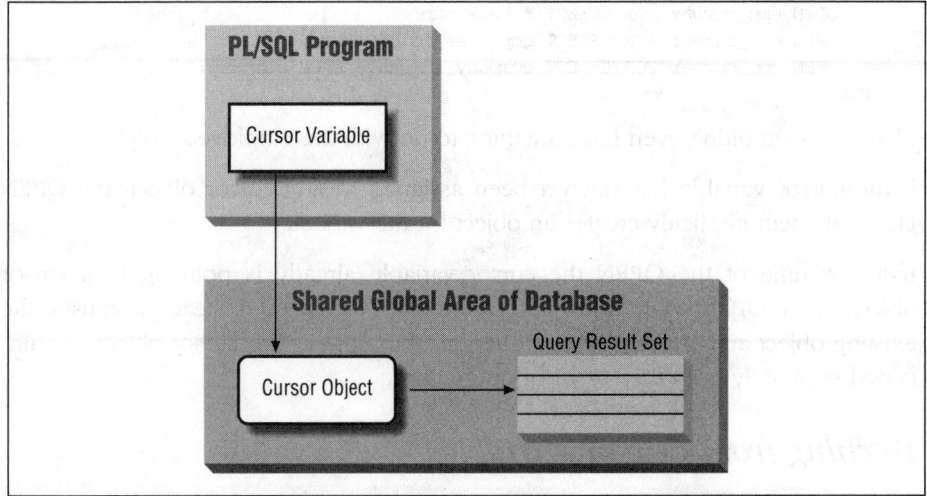

Figure 6-3. The referencing character of cursor variables

where cursor_name is the name of a cursor or cursor variable and select_statement is a SQL SELECT statement.

For strong REF CURSOR type cursor variables, the structure of the SELECT statement (the number and datatypes of the columns) must match or be compatible with the structure specified in the RETURN clause of the type statement. Figure 6-4 offers an example of the kind of compatibility required. "Rules for Cursor Variables" contains the full set of compatibility rules.

```
DECLARE
    TYPE emp_curtype IS
        REF CURSOR RETURN emp%ROWTYPE;
    emp_curvar emp_curtype;
BEGIN
    OPEN emp_curvar FOR
            SELECT * FROM emp;
END;
```

Figure 6-4. Compatible REF CURSOR rowtype and SELECT list

If cursor_name is a cursor variable defined with a weak REF CURSOR type, you can OPEN it for any query, with any structure. In the following example, I open (assign a value to) the cursor variable twice, with two different queries:

```
DECLARE
    TYPE emp_curtype IS REF CURSOR;
    emp_curvar emp_curtype;
```

```
BEGIN
    OPEN emp_curvar FOR SELECT * FROM emp;
    OPEN emp_curvar FOR SELECT employee_id FROM emp;
    OPEN emp_curvar FOR SELECT company_id, name FROM company;
END;
```

That last open didn't even have anything to do with the employee table!

If the cursor variable has not yet been assigned to any cursor object, the OPEN FOR statement implicitly creates an object for the variable.

If at the time of the OPEN the cursor variable already is pointing to a cursor object, then OPEN FOR does not create a new object. Instead, it reuses the existing object and attaches a new query to that object. The cursor object is maintained separately from the cursor or query itself.

Fetching from Cursor Variables

As mentioned earlier, the syntax for a FETCH statement using a cursor variable is the same as that for static cursors:

```
FETCH <cursor variable name> INTO <record name>;
FETCH <cursor variable name> INTO <variable name>, <variable name> ...;
```

When the cursor variable was declared with a strong REF CURSOR type, the PL/SQL compiler makes sure that the data structure(s) listed after the INTO keyword are compatible with the structure of the query associated with cursor variable.

Strong and weak REF CURSOR types

If the cursor variable is of the weak REF CURSOR type, the PL/SQL compiler cannot perform the same kind of check. Such a cursor variable can FETCH into any data structures, because the REF CURSOR type it is not identified with a rowtype at the time of declaration. At compile time, there is no way to know which cursor object (and associated SQL statement) will be assigned to that variable.

Consequently, the check for compatibility must happen at run time, when the FETCH is about to be executed. At this point, if the query and the INTO clause do not structurally match (and PL/SQL will use implicit conversions if necessary and possible), then the PL/SQL runtime engine will raise the predefined ROWTYPE_MISMATCH exception.

Handling the ROWTYPE_MISMATCH exception

Before PL/SQL actually performs its FETCH, it checks for compatibility. As a result, you can trap the ROWTYPE_MISMATCH exception and attempt to FETCH from the cursor variable using a different INTO clause—and you will not have skipped any rows in the result set.

Even though you are executing a second FETCH statement in your program, you will still retrieve the first row in the result set of the cursor object's query. This functionality comes in especially handy for weak REF CURSOR types.

In the following example, a centralized real estate database stores information about properties in a variety of tables, one for homes, another for commercial properties, etc. There is also a single, central table which stores an address and a building type (home, commercial, etc.). I use a single procedure to open a weak REF CURSOR variable for the appropriate table, based on the street address. Each individual real estate office can then call that procedure to scan through the matching properties:

1. Define my weak REF CURSOR type:

```
TYPE building_curtype IS REF CURSOR;
```

2. Create the procedure. Notice that the mode of the cursor variable parameter is IN OUT:

```
PROCEDURE open_site_list
   (address_in IN VARCHAR2,
    site_cur_inout IN OUT building_curtype)
IS
   home_type CONSTANT INTEGER := 1;
   commercial_type CONSTANT INTEGER := 2;

   /* A static cursor to get building type. */
   CURSOR site_type_cur IS
      SELECT site_type FROM property_master
       WHERE address = address_in;
   site_type_rec site_type_cur%ROWTYPE;

BEGIN
   /* Get the building type for this address. */
   OPEN site_type_cur;
   FETCH site_type_cur INTO site_type_rec;
   CLOSE site_type_cur;

   /* Now use the site type to select from the right table.*/
   IF site_type_rec.site_type =  home_type
   THEN
      /* Use the home properties table. */
      OPEN site_cur_inout FOR
         SELECT * FROM home_properties
          WHERE address LIKE '%' || address_in || '%';

   ELSIF site_type_rec.site_type =  commercial_type
   THEN
      /* Use the commercial properties table. */
      OPEN site_cur_inout FOR
         SELECT * FROM commercial_properties
          WHERE address LIKE '%' || address_in || '%';
   END IF;
END open_site_list;
```

3. Now that I have my open procedure, I can use it to scan properties.

In the following example, I pass in the address and then try to fetch from the cursor, assuming a home property. If the address actually identifies a commercial property, PL/SQL will raise the ROWTYPE_MISMATCH exception (incompatible record structures). The exception section then fetches again, this time into a commercial building record, and the scan is complete.[*]

```
DECLARE
    /* Declare a cursor variable. */
    building_curvar building_curtype;

    /* Define record structures for two different tables. */
    home_rec home_properties%ROWTYPE;
    commercial_rec commercial_properties%ROWTYPE;
BEGIN
    /* Get the address from the user. */
    prompt_for_address (address_string);

    /* Assign a query to the cursor variable based on the address. */
    open_site_list (address_string, building_curvar);

    /* Give it a try! Fetch a row into the home record. */
    FETCH building_curvar INTO home_rec;

    /* If I got here, the site was a home, so display it. */
    show_home_site (home_rec);
EXCEPTION
    /* If the first record was not a home... */
    WHEN ROWTYPE_MISMATCH
    THEN
        /* Fetch that same 1st row into the commercial record. */
        FETCH building_curvar INTO commercial_rec;

        /* Show the commercial site info. */
        show_commercial_site (commercial_rec);
END;
```

Rules for Cursor Variables

This section examines in more detail the rules and issues regarding the use of cursor variables in your programs. This includes rowtype matching rules, cursor variable aliases, and scoping issues.

Remember that the cursor variable is a reference to a cursor object or query in the database. It is not the object itself. A cursor variable is said to "refer to a given query" if either of the following is true:

---

[*] The "prompt" and "show" programs referenced in the example interact with users and are not documented here.

- An OPEN statement FOR that query was executed with the cursor variable.

- A cursor variable was assigned a value from another cursor variable that refers to that query.

You can perform assignment operations with cursor variables and also pass these variables as arguments to procedures and functions. In order to perform such actions between cursor variables (and to bind a cursor variable to a parameter), the different cursor variables must follow a set of compile-time and runtime rowtype matching rules.

Compile-time rowtype matching rules

These are the rules that PL/SQL follows at compile-time:

- Two cursor variables (including procedure parameters) are compatible for assignments and argument passing if any of the following are true:
  — Both variables (or parameters) are of a strong REF CURSOR type with the same <rowtype_name>.
  — Both variables (or parameters) are of some weak REF CURSOR type, regardless of the <rowtype_name>.
  — One variable (parameter) is of any strong REF CURSOR type, and the other is of any weak REF CURSOR type.

- A cursor variable (parameter) of a strong REF CURSOR type may be OPEN FOR a query that returns a rowtype which is structurally equal to the <rowtype_name> in the original type declaration.

- A cursor variable (parameter) of a weak REF CURSOR type may be OPEN FOR any query. The FETCH from such a variable is allowed INTO any list of variables or record structure.

In other words, if either of the cursor variables are of the weak REF CURSOR type, then the PL/SQL compiler cannot really validate whether the two different cursor variables will be compatible. That will happen at runtime; the rules are covered in the next section.

Run-time rowtype matching rules

These are the rules that PL/SQL follows at run time:

- A cursor variable (parameter) of a weak REF CURSOR type may be made to refer to a query of any rowtype regardless of the query or cursor object to which it may have referred earlier.

- A cursor variable (parameter) of a strong REF CURSOR type may be made to refer only to a query which matches structurally the <rowtype_name> of the RETURN clause of the REF CURSOR type declaration.

- Two records (or lists of variables) are considered structurally matching with implicit conversions if both of the following are true:

  — The number of fields is the same in both records (lists).

  — For each field in one record (or variable on one list), a corresponding field in the second list (or variable in second list) has the same PL/SQL datatype, or one which can be converted implicitly by PL/SQL to match the first.

- For a cursor variable (parameter) used in a FETCH statement, the query associated with the cursor variable must structurally match with implicit conversions the record or list of variables of the INTO clause of the FETCH statement. This is, by the way, the same rule used for static cursors.

Cursor variable aliases

If you assign one cursor variable to another cursor variable, those two cursor variables become aliases for the same cursor object. They share the reference to the cursor object (result set of the cursor's query). An action taken against the cursor object through one variable is also available to and reflected in the other variable.

The following anonymous block illustrates the way cursor aliases work:

```
 1  DECLARE
 2     TYPE curvar_type IS REF CURSOR;
 3     curvar1 curvar_type;
 4     curvar2 curvar_type;
 5     story fairy_tales%ROWTYPE;
 6  BEGIN
 7     /* Assign cursor object to curvar1. */
 8     OPEN curvar1 FOR SELECT * FROM fairy_tales;
 9
10     /* Assign same cursor object to curvar2. */
11     curvar2 := curvar1;
12
13     /* Fetch first record from curvar1. */
14     FETCH curvar1 INTO story;
15
16     /* Fetch second record from curvar2. */
17     FETCH curvar2 INTO story;
18
19     /* Close the cursor object by referencing curvar2. */
20     CLOSE curvar2;
21
22     /* This statement raises INVALID_CURSOR exception! */
23     FETCH curvar1 INTO story;
24  END;
```

The following table is an explanation of cursor variable actions.

Lines	Action
1-5	Declare my weak REF CURSOR type and cursor variable through line 5.
8	Creates a cursor object and assigns it to curvar1.
11	Assigns that same cursor object to the second cursor variable, curvar2.
14	Fetches the first record using the curvar1 variable.
17	Fetches the second record using the curvar2 variable. (Notice that it doesn't matter which of the two variables you use. The pointer to the current record resides with the cursor object, not any particular variable.)
20	Closes the cursor object referencing curvar2.
23	Raises the INVALID_CURSOR exception when I try to fetch again from the cursor object. (When I closed the cursor through curvar2, it also closed it as far as curvar1 was concerned.)

Any change of state in a cursor object will be seen through any cursor variable which is an alias to that cursor object.

Scope of cursor object

The scope of a cursor variable is the same as that of a static cursor: the PL/SQL block in which the variable is declared (unless declared in a package, which makes the variable globally accessible). The scope of the cursor object to which a cursor variable is assigned, however, is a different matter.

Once an OPEN FOR creates a cursor object, that cursor object remains accessible as long as at least one active cursor variable refers to that cursor object. This means that you can create a cursor object in one scope (PL/SQL block) and assign it to a cursor variable. Then, by assigning that cursor variable to another cursor variable with a different scope, the cursor object remains accessible even if the original cursor variable has gone out of scope.

In the following example I use nested blocks to demonstrate how the cursor object can persist outside of the scope in which it was originally created:

```
DECLARE
    /* Define weak REF CURSOR type, cursor variable
       and local variable */
    TYPE curvar_type IS REF CURSOR;
    curvar1 curvar_type;
    do_you_get_it VARCHAR2(100);
BEGIN
    /*
    || Nested block which creates the cursor object and
    || assigns it to the curvar1 cursor variable.
    */
    DECLARE
        curvar2 curvar_type;
    BEGIN
        OPEN curvar2 FOR SELECT punch_line FROM jokes;
```

```
        curvar1 := curvar2;
    END;
    /*
    || The curvar2 cursor variable is no longer active,
    || but "the baton" has been passed to curvar1, which
    || does exist in the enclosing block. I can therefore
    || fetch from the cursor object, through this other
    || cursor variable.
    */
    FETCH curvar1 INTO do_you_get_it;
END;
```

Passing Cursor Variables as Arguments

You can pass a cursor variable as an argument in a call to a procedure or function. When you use a cursor variable in the parameter list of a program, you need to specify the mode of the parameter and the datatype (the REF CURSOR type).

Identifying the REF CURSOR type

In your program header, you must identify the REF CURSOR type of your cursor variable parameter. To do this, that cursor type must already be defined.

If you are creating a local module within another program (see Chapter 15 for more information about local modules), then you can also define the cursor type in the same program. It will then be available for the parameter. This approach is shown below:

```
DECLARE
    /* Define the REF CURSOR type. */
    TYPE curvar_type IS REF CURSOR RETURN company%ROWTYPE;

    /* Reference it in the parameter list. */
    PROCEDURE open_query (curvar_out OUT curvar_type)
    IS
        local_cur curvar_type;
    BEGIN
        OPEN local_cur FOR SELECT * FROM company;
        curvar_out := local_cur;
    END;
BEGIN
    ...
END;
```

If you are creating a standalone procedure or function, then the only way you can reference a pre-existing REF CURSOR type is by placing that type statement in a package. All variables declared in the specification of a package act as globals within your session, so you can then reference this cursor type using the dot notation as shown below:

1. Create the package with a REF CURSOR type declaration:

```
PACKAGE company
IS
   /* Define the REF CURSOR type. */
   TYPE curvar_type IS REF CURSOR RETURN company%ROWTYPE;
END package;
```

2. In a standalone procedure, reference the REF CURSOR type by prefacing the name of the cursor type with the name of the package:

```
PROCEDURE open_company (curvar_out OUT company.curvar_type) IS
BEGIN
   ...
END;
```

See Chapter 16 for more information on this feature.

Setting the parameter mode

Just like other parameters, a cursor variable argument can have one of the following three modes:

IN
> Can only be read by program

OUT
> Can only be written to by program

IN OUT
> Read/write in program

Remember that the value of a cursor variable is the reference to the cursor object and not the state of the cursor object. In other words, the value of a cursor variable does not change after you fetch from or close a cursor.

Only two operations, in fact, may change the value of a cursor variable change, that is, the cursor object to which the variable points:

*   An assignment to the cursor variable

*   An OPEN FOR statement

If the cursor variable already pointed to a cursor object, then the OPEN FOR wouldn't actually change the reference. It would simply change the query associated with the object.

The FETCH and CLOSE operations affect the state of the cursor object, but not the reference to the cursor object itself, which is the value of the cursor variable.

Here is an example of a program which has cursor variables as parameters:

```
PROCEDURE assign_curvar
   (old_curvar_in IN company.curvar_type,
    new_curvar_out OUT company.curvar_type)
```

```
IS
BEGIN
   new_curvar_out := old_curvar_in;
END;
```

This procedure copies the old company cursor variable to the new variable. The first parameter is an IN parameter because it appears only on the right-hand side of the assignment. The second parameter must be an OUT (or IN OUT) parameter, because its value is changed inside the procedure. Notice that the curvar_ type is defined within the company package.

Cursor Variable Restrictions

Cursor variables are subject to the following restrictions; Oracle may remove some of these in future releases.

- Cursor variables cannot be declared in a package since they do not have a persistent state.

- You cannot use RPCs (Remote Procedure Calls) to pass cursor variables from one server to another.

- If you pass a cursor variable as a bind or host variable to PL/SQL, you will not be able to fetch from it from within the server unless you also open it in that same server call.

- The query you associate with a cursor variable in an OPEN-FOR statement cannot use the FOR UPDATE clause.

- You cannot test for cursor variable equality, inequality, or nullity using comparison operators.

- You cannot assign NULLs to a cursor variable.

- Database columns cannot store cursor variable values. You will not be able to use REF CURSOR types to specify column types in statements to CREATE TABLEs or CREATE VIEWs.

- The elements in a nested table, index-by table, or variable array (VARRAY) cannot store the values of cursor variables. You will not be able to use REF CURSOR types to specify the element type of a collection.

- Cursor variables cannot be used with dynamic SQL (through use of the DBMS_SQL package).

Working with Cursors

The following sections offer some practical applications of cursors. They are also designed to be programs you can put to use in your own environments with a few changes. The following files on the companion disk offer additional examples:

varcurs.doc
　　Explanation of how to emulate a cursor variable with local modules

unquein.doc
　　Explanation of how to guarantee unique entry with cursors

unquein.ff
　　Code required to guarantee unique entry with cursors

Validating Foreign Key Entry with Cursors

A hefty percentage of our code can be taken up with validating the entry or selection of foreign keys. Consider the example of an application which maintains companies and employees of that company. On the employee maintenance screen, I want to let my user enter the name or partial name of the company that employs a person. If the user has identified a unique company, the form displays that name and stores the company ID on the null canvas. If the user's entry finds more than one match, a message is displayed. If no matches are found, the entry is rejected.

How should I implement this requirement? Well, the first thing that comes to the minds of many programmers is the following:

> Use a cursor which, with a single fetch, employs the COUNT built-in to compute the total number of companies that match the entry.

This is, perhaps, the most obvious and direct solution to the requirement—when it is phrased as follows:

> To find out if the user's entry has more than one match, count up just how many matches there are.

Inefficiency of group functions in cursors

There are, however, two serious problems with using the COUNT group function in my cursor:

- *The cursor does far too much work on my behalf.* By using COUNT, the cursor must scan through all records (or, I hope, those identified by the index) and count up the total number of matching records. Yet, all I really need to know is whether more than one company matched the entry. The performance penalty on this COUNT could be severe if the query goes out over a network or if the user's entry matches many of the records. What if a user entered a percent sign (%)? All records would then match. An application should never punish a user for poorly thought-out data entry.

- *The cursor does not do enough for me.* If the COUNT-based query did return a value of 1, I would still have to go back to the company table and SELECT the ID for that company with another cursor. As a result, I would have coded the same query twice. This redundancy introduces maintenance and performance issues.

You should use COUNT only when you need to know or display the total number of matches for the user's entry. In this scenario, I don't really need that total; I need only to know if the total is greater than one (i.e., if there is more than one match). I can obtain this knowledge in a much more efficient and straightforward manner.

Using multiple fetches more efficiently

Use a cursor that, with multiple fetches, determines if there are at least two companies that match the entry. This approach takes a bit more sophistication and thought, but is always a better performer and offers more flexibility to programmers.

To employ the multiple-fetch technique, take the following steps:

1. Declare a cursor which returns the company_id of all companies that match the value in the item:

```
CURSOR company_cur
IS
    SELECT company_id
        FROM company
    WHERE company_name LIKE :company.company_name || '%';
```

2. Fetch twice against this cursor. If I can fetch twice successfully (company_cur%NOTFOUND is FALSE both times), that means that there is more than one match for the company name. If I can fetch only once before the %NOTFOUND cursor attribute returns FALSE, then I have found a unique match. If the very first fetch fails, then there is no match for the name.

3. Because my cursor returns the company_id, I do not have to perform another select once I have determined that I have a unique match. I simply use the ID that was provided in the first fetch.

The procedure in the following example supports the foreign key validation requirements with a double fetch against the cursor (it is coded for Oracle Forms, but can be adapted easily to other tool environments):

```
/* Filename on companion disk: fkval.fp */
PROCEDURE validate_company
    (comp_name_inout IN OUT company.company_name%TYPE,
    comp_id_out OUT company.company_id%TYPE)
IS
    /* Cursor as explained above */
```

```
        CURSOR company_cur IS
            SELECT company_id, company_name
              FROM company
             WHERE company_name LIKE comp_name_inout || '%';

        /* Declare two records against the same cursor. */
        company_rec company_cur%ROWTYPE;
        duplicate_rec company_cur%ROWTYPE;
    BEGIN
        /* Open and perform the first fetch against cursor. */
        OPEN company_cur;
        FETCH company_cur INTO company_rec;
        IF company_cur%NOTFOUND
        THEN
            /* Not even one match for this name. Display message and reject. */
            MESSAGE
                (' No company found with name like "' ||
                  comp_name_inout || '".');
            CLOSE company_cur;
            RAISE FORM_TRIGGER_FAILURE;
        ELSE
            /*
            || Found one match. Now FETCH again, but this time FETCH into the
            || duplicate_rec record. This is just a "place holder". I don't
            || need to see the contents of the record. I just need to know if
            || I can successfully retrieve another record from the cursor.
            */
            FETCH company_cur INTO duplicate_rec;
            IF company_cur%NOTFOUND
            THEN
                /*
                || Found 1 match, but not second. Unique! Assign values to
                || the OUT parameters and close the cursor.
                */
                comp_id_out := company_rec.company_id;
                comp_name_inout := company_rec.company_name;
                CLOSE company_cur;
            ELSE
                /*
                || At least two matches found for this name. I don't know how
                || many more and I do not care. Reject with message.
                */
                MESSAGE (' More than one company matches name like "' ||
                         comp_name_inout || '".');
                CLOSE company_cur;
                RAISE FORM_TRIGGER_FAILURE;
            END IF;
        END IF;
    END;
```

Call this procedure in the When-Validate-Item trigger so that any changes to the
company name can be validated. Here is an example of an actual call to validate_
company:

```
    validate_company (:employee.company_name, :employee.company_id);
```

Notice that the first parameter (the company name) is an IN OUT parameter. I want to let the user enter just a part of the name and let the application figure out if that entry is enough to uniquely identify a company. If a single match is found, the form replaces the partial entry with the full name.

I believe strongly that we should design our applications to allow the user to enter the minimal amount of information necessary to get the job done. Our applications should be smart enough to take advantage of the dumb, brute strength of our CPUs in order to lift some of the burden off the user.

Managing a Work Queue with SELECT FOR UPDATE

As discussed earlier, a cursor with a SELECT...FOR UPDATE syntax issues a row-level lock on each row identified by the query. I encountered a very interesting application of this feature while helping a client resolve a problem.

The client offers a distribution package which tracks warehouse inventory. The work queue screen assigns warehouse floor packers their next tasks. The packer opens the screen and requests a task. The screen finds the next unassigned task and assigns it to the packer. A task might involve collecting various products together for shipment or returning products to the shelf. Completion of this task can take anywhere between one and ten minutes. When the task is completed, the packer will commit the changes or close the screen, performing an implicit commit.

For the amount of time it takes a packer to finish the task, that record must be tagged as "assigned" so that no other packer is given the same job to do. The first attempt at implementing this feature involved the use of a status flag. Whenever a packer was assigned a task, the flag on that task was set to ASSIGNED and the task record committed. The screen then excludes that task from the work queue. The problem with this approach is that the status had to be committed to the database so that other users could see the new status. This commit not only interrupted the actual transaction in the screen, but also created a number of headaches:

- What if the user never completes the task and exits the screen? The form would have to detect this scenario (and there are generally many ways to cancel/exit) and update the status flag to AVAILABLE, which involves yet another commit.

- Worse yet, what if the database goes down while the user is performing the task? That task will disappear from the work queue until manual intervention resets the status.

My client needed a mechanism by which the task could be flagged as UNAVAIL-ABLE without having to perform commits, build complex checks into the form, and develop crash-recovery guidelines. They needed a program that would step through each of the open tasks in priority until it found a task that was unassigned. The SELECT...FOR UPDATE construct proved to be the perfect answer, in combination with two queries against the task table—an explicit cursor and an implicit cursor using a FOR UPDATE clause.

The function in the following example returns the primary key of the next unassigned task using a cursor against the task table to look through all open tasks in priority order. The tasks returned by this first cursor include those which are assigned but "in process" (and should therefore not be assigned again). For each task retrieved from this cursor, the function then tries to obtain a lock on that record using the FOR UPDATE...NOWAIT clause. If the SELECT statement cannot obtain a lock, it means that task is being handled by another packer. So the function fetches the next task and tries, once again, to obtain a lock, continuing on in this fashion until a free task is found or the last task is fetched.

Notice that the next_task function does not perform any commits, so it doesn't have to do any kind of complicated clean-up. It simply requests the lock and returns the primary key for that task. The calling program can then offer this task to the packer who will issue the commit, freeing the lock, when she or he is done with the task:

```
/* Filename on companion disk: selupdt.sf */
FUNCTION next_task RETURN task.task_id%TYPE
IS
    /* Cursor of all open tasks, assigned and unassigned */
    CURSOR task_cur IS
       SELECT task_id
         FROM task
        WHERE task_status = 'OPEN'
        ORDER BY task_priority, date_entered DESC;

    /* The record for the above cursor */
    task_rec task_cur%ROWTYPE;
    /*
    || An exception for error ORA-00054:
    || "resource busy and acquire with NOWAIT specified"
    */
    record_locked EXCEPTION
    PRAGMA EXCEPTION_INIT (record_locked, -54);
    /*
    || Variables which determine whether function should continue
    || to loop through the cursor's records.
    */
    found_unassigned_task BOOLEAN := FALSE;
    more_tasks BOOLEAN := TRUE;
```

```
        /* The primary key of the unassigned task to be returned */
        return_value task.task_id%TYPE := NULL;
BEGIN
        /* Open the cursor and start up the loop through its records */
        OPEN task_cur;
        WHILE NOT found_unassigned_task AND more_tasks
        LOOP
            /* Fetch the next record. If nothing found, we are done */
            FETCH task_cur INTO task_rec;
            more_tasks := task_cur%FOUND;
            IF more_tasks
            THEN
                /*
                || A record was fetched. Create an anonymous block within
                || the function so that I can trap the record_locked
                || exception and still stay inside the cursor loop.
                */
                BEGIN
                    /* Try to get a lock on the current task */
                    SELECT task_id INTO return_value
                      FROM task
                      WHERE task_id = task_rec.task_id
                     FOR UPDATE OF task_id NOWAIT;
                    /*
                    || If I get to this line then I was able to get a lock
                    || on this particular task. Notice that the SELECT INTO
                    || has therefore already set the function's return value.
                    || Now set the Boolean to stop the loop.
                    */
                    found_unassigned_task := TRUE;
                EXCEPTION
                    WHEN record_locked
                    THEN
                        /* Record was already locked, so just keep on going */
                        NULL;
                END;
            END IF;
        END LOOP;
        /*
        || Return the task id. Notice that if an unassigned task was NOT
        || found, I will simply return NULL per declaration default.
        */
        CLOSE task_cur;
        RETURN return_value;
EXCEPTION
        /*
        || General exception handler for the function: if an error occurred,
        || then close the cursor and return NULL for the task ID.
        */
        WHEN OTHERS
        THEN
            CLOSE task_cur;
            RETURN NULL;
END;
```

7

Loops

This chapter explores the iterative control structures of PL/SQL, otherwise known as *loops*, which let you execute the same code repeatedly. PL/SQL provides three different kinds of loop constructs:

- The simple or infinite loop

- The FOR loop (numeric and cursor)

- The WHILE loop

Each type of loop is designed for a specific purpose with its own nuances, rules for use, and guidelines for high-quality construction. As I explain each of the loops, I will include a table (based on the following one) describing the following properties of the loop:

Property	Description
How the loop is terminated	A loop executes code repetitively. How do you make the loop stop executing its body?
When the test for termination takes place	Does the test for termination take place at the beginning or end of the loop? What are the consequences?
Reason to use this loop	What are the special factors you should consider to determine if this loop is right for your situation?

Loop Basics

Why are there three different kinds of loops? To provide you with the flexibility you need to write the most straightforward code to handle any particular situation. Most situations which require a loop could be written with any of the three loop constructs. If you do not pick the construct best-suited for that particular requirement, however, you could end up having to write many additional lines of code. The resulting module would also be harder to understand and maintain.

Examples of Different Loops

To give you a feeling for the way the different loops solve their problems in different ways, consider the following three procedures. In each case, the procedure executes the same body of code inside a loop:

```
set_rank (ranking_level);
```

where set_rank performs a ranking for the specified level.

- *The simple loop.* My procedure accepts a maximum ranking as an argument and then sets the rank until the level exceeds the maximum. Notice the IF statement to guard against executing the loop when the maximum rank is negative. Notice also the EXIT WHEN statement used to terminate the loop:

```
PROCEDURE set_all_ranks (max_rank_in IN INTEGER)
IS
    ranking_level NUMBER(3) := 1;
BEGIN
    IF max_rank_in >= 1
    THEN
        LOOP
            set_rank (ranking_level);
            ranking_level := ranking_level + 1;
            EXIT WHEN ranking_level > max_rank_in;
        END LOOP;
    END IF;
END;
```

- *The FOR loop.* In this case, I rank for the fixed range of values, from one to the maximum number:

```
PROCEDURE set_all_ranks (max_rank_in IN INTEGER)
IS
BEGIN
    FOR ranking_level IN 1 .. max_rank_in
    LOOP
        set_rank (ranking_level);
    END LOOP;
END;
```

- *The WHILE loop.* My procedure accepts a maximum ranking as an argument and then sets the rank until the level exceeds the maximum. Notice that the condition which terminates the loop comes on the same line as the WHILE keyword:

```
PROCEDURE set_all_ranks (max_rank_in IN INTEGER)
IS
    ranking_level NUMBER(3) := 1;
BEGIN
    WHILE ranking_level <= max_rank_in
    LOOP
        set_rank (ranking_level);
        ranking_level := ranking_level + 1;
    END LOOP;
END;
```

In the above example, the FOR loop clearly requires the smallest amount of code. Yet I could only use it in this case because I knew that I would run the body of the loop a specific number of times (max_rank_in). In many other situations, the number of times a loop must execute varies and so the FOR loop cannot be used.

Structure of PL/SQL Loops

While there are differences among the three loop constructs, every loop has two parts: the *loop boundary* and the *loop body*. The loop boundary is composed of the reserved words that initiate the loop, the condition that causes the loop to terminate, and the END LOOP statement that ends the loop. The body of the loop is the sequence of executable statements inside the loop boundary which execute on each iteration of the loop.

Figure 7-1 shows the boundary and body of a WHILE loop.

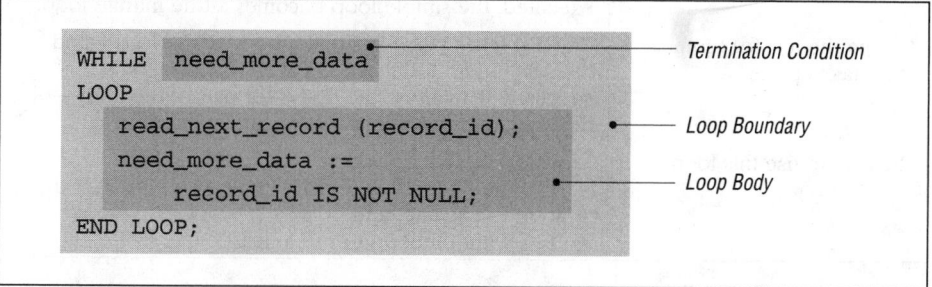

Figure 7-1. The boundary and body of the WHILE loop

In general, think of a loop much as you would a procedure or a function. The body of the loop is a black box, and the condition that causes loop termination is the interface to that black box. Code outside of the loop should not have to know about the inner workings of the loop. Keep this in mind as you go through the different kinds of loops and examples in the rest of the chapter.

In addition to the examples you will find in this chapter, I have included several lengthy code samples utilizing PL/SQL loops in the Oracle Forms environment in the following files on the disk:

highrec.doc and highrec.fp
   Demonstrate highlighting items in an Oracle Forms record.

ofquery.doc, postqry.fp, and preqry.fp
   Demonstrate automatic post- and pre-query processing in Oracle Forms.

The Simple Loop

The structure of the simple loop is the most basic of all the loop constructs. It consists of the LOOP keyword, the body of executable code, and the END LOOP keywords, as shown here:

```
LOOP
    <executable statement(s)>
END LOOP;
```

The loop boundary consists solely of the LOOP and END LOOP reserved words. The body must consist of at least one executable statement. The following table summarizes the properties of the single loop:

Property	Description
How the loop is terminated	The simple loop is terminated when an EXIT statement is executed in the body of the loop. If this statement is not executed, the simple loop becomes a true infinite loop.
When the test for termination takes place	The test takes place inside the body of the loop—and then only if an EXIT or EXIT WHEN statement is executed. Therefore, the body—or part of the body—of the simple loop will always execute at least once.
Reason to use this loop	Use the simple loop when: • You are not sure how many times you will want the loop to execute, and • You want the loop to run at least once.

This loop is useful when you want to guarantee that the body (or at least part of the body) executes at least one time. Because there is no condition associated with the loop boundary that determines whether or not it should execute, the body of the loop will always execute the first time.

The simple loop will terminate only when an EXIT statement is executed in its body (see "Terminating a Single Loop: EXIT and EXIT WHEN" below). Because this doesn't have to be the case, a simple loop can also become an infinite loop. This could cause difficulties in your program and is something to be avoided.

The following example shows a simple loop which is truly infinite; it keeps checking for messages from a particular pipe so that it can respond immediately and display the information in the pipe. (This is the central concept behind a DBMS_PIPE-based debugger for PL/SQL code—a prototype of which may be found in the *dbg.doc* file on the companion disk. See Appendix C, *Built-In Packages*, for details.)

```
DECLARE
    pipe_status INTEGER;
    message_text VARCHAR2
BEGIN
```

```
        LOOP
           pipe_status := DBMS_PIPE.RECEIVE_MESSAGE ('execution_trace');
           IF pipe_status = 0
           THEN
              DBMS_PIPE.UNPACK_MESSAGE (message_text);
              DBMS_OUTPUT.PUT_LINE (message_text);
           END IF;
        END LOOP;
     END;
```

Terminating a Simple Loop: EXIT and EXIT WHEN

Be very careful when you use simple loops. Make sure they always have a way to stop. To force a simple loop to stop processing, execute an EXIT or EXIT WHEN statement within the body of the loop. The syntax for these statements is as follows:

```
EXIT:
EXIT WHEN condition;
```

where condition is a Boolean expression.

The following example demonstrates how the EXIT forces the loop to immediately halt execution and pass control to the next statement after the END LOOP statement. The account_balance procedure returns the amount of money remaining in the account specified by the account ID. If there is less than $1000 left, the EXIT statement is executed and the loop is terminated. Otherwise, the program applies the balance to the outstanding orders for that account.

```
     LOOP
        balance_remaining := account_balance (account_id);
        IF balance_remaining < 1000
        THEN
           EXIT;
        ELSE
           apply_balance (account_id, balance_remaining);
        END IF;
     END LOOP;
```

You can use an EXIT statement only within a LOOP.

PL/SQL also offers the EXIT WHEN statement, which supports the concept of "conditional termination" of the loop. Essentially, the EXIT WHEN combines an IF-THEN statement with the EXIT statement. Using the same example I showed above, the EXIT WHEN changes the loop to:

```
     LOOP
        /* Calculate the balance */
        balance_remaining := account_balance (account_id);

        /* Embed the IF logic into the EXIT statement */
        EXIT WHEN balance_remaining < 1000;
```

```
    /* Apply balance if still executing the loop */
    apply_balance (account_id, balance_remaining);
END LOOP;
```

Notice that the loop no longer requires an IF statement to determine when it should exit. Instead, that conditional logic is embedded inside the EXIT WHEN statement.

EXIT WHEN is a very concise and readable way to terminate a simple loop; I recommend its use over the unconditional EXIT statement. After all, you should always have an EXIT statement nested within an IF-THEN. If you don't, then you either have an infinite loop or you have a loop that executes just once. In the latter case, it is better to execute the body of the loop without using a loop. If the EXIT is always included within the IF-THEN, you'd be better off using a language construct built specifically for the purpose. The EXIT WHEN construct also reduces the amount of code you need to write.

Emulating a REPEAT UNTIL Loop

PL/SQL does not provide a REPEAT UNTIL loop in which the condition is tested after the body of the loop is executed and thus guarantees that the loop always executes at least once. You can, however, emulate a REPEAT UNTIL with a simple loop, as follows:

```
LOOP
   ... body of loop ...
   EXIT WHEN boolean_condition;
END LOOP;
```

where boolean_condition is a Boolean variable or an expression that evaluates to a Boolean value of TRUE or FALSE.

The Numeric FOR Loop

There are two kinds of PL/SQL FOR loops: the numeric FOR loop and the cursor FOR loop. The numeric FOR loop is the traditional and familiar "counted" loop. The number of iterations of the FOR loop is known when the loop starts; it is specified in the loop boundary's range scheme. The number of times the loop executes is actually determined by the range scheme found between the FOR and LOOP keywords in the boundary.

The range scheme implicitly declares the loop index (if it has not already been declared), specifies the start and end points of the range, and optionally dictates the order in which the loop index proceeds (from lowest to highest or highest to lowest).

Here is the general syntax of the numeric FOR loop:

```
FOR <loop index> IN [REVERSE] <lowest number> .. <highest number>
LOOP
   <executable statement(s)>
END LOOP;
```

You must have at least one executable statement between the LOOP and END LOOP key words.

The following table summarizes the properties of the numeric FOR loop:

Property	Description
How the loop is terminated	The numeric FOR loop terminates unconditionally when the number of times specified in its range scheme has been satisfied. You can also terminate the loop with an EXIT statement, but this is not recommended.
When the test for termination takes place	After each execution of the loop body, PL/SQL checks the value of the loop index. When it exceeds the difference between the upper and lower bounds of the range scheme, the loop terminates. If the lower bound is greater than the upper bound of the range scheme, the loop never executes its body.
Reason to use this loop	Use the numeric FOR loop when you want to execute a body of code a fixed number of times, and you do not want to halt that looping prematurely.

Rules for Numeric FOR Loops

*   Do not declare the loop index. PL/SQL automatically and implicitly declares it as a local variable with datatype INTEGER. The scope of this index is the loop itself; you cannot reference the loop index outside the loop.

*   Expressions used in the range scheme (both for lowest and highest bounds) are evaluated once, when the loop starts. The range is not re-evaluated during the execution of the loop. If you make changes within the loop to the variables which you used to determine the FOR loop range, those changes will have no effect.

*   Never change the values of either the loop index or the range boundary from within the loop. This is an extremely bad programming practice. In most cases, PL/SQL will not let you compile such code.

*   Do not use an EXIT statement inside a FOR loop in order to cause early execution of the loop. If you are going to use a numeric FOR loop, then you should let the loop execute as it is designed: from start value to end value. If you need more control over how frequently a loop is to execute and, particularly, when it is to terminate, do not use the FOR loop. Instead, use the WHILE loop or simple loop with EXIT WHEN constructs.

- Use the REVERSE keyword to force the loop to decrement from the upper bound to the lower bound. You must still make sure that the first value in the range specification (the N in N .. M) is less than the second value. Do not reverse the order in which you specify these values when you use the REVERSE keyword.

Examples of Numeric FOR Loops

The following examples demonstrate some variations of the numeric FOR loop syntax:

- The loop executes ten times; loop_counter starts at 1 and ends at 10:

```
FOR loop_counter IN 1 .. 10
LOOP
    ... executable statements ...
END LOOP;
```

- The loop executes ten times; loop_counter starts at 10 and ends at 1:

```
FOR loop_counter IN REVERSE 1 .. 10
LOOP
    ... executable statements ...
END LOOP;
```

- Here is a loop that doesn't execute even once. I specified REVERSE so the loop index, loop_counter, will start at the highest value and end with the lowest. I then mistakenly concluded that I should switch the order in which I list the highest and lowest bounds:

```
FOR loop_counter IN REVERSE 10 .. 1
LOOP
    /* This loop body will never execute even once! */
END LOOP;
```

Even when you specify a REVERSE direction, you must still list the lowest bound before the highest bound. If the first number is greater than the second number, the body of the loop will not execute at all. If the lowest and highest bounds have the same value, then the loop will execute just once.

- Loop executes for a range determined by the values in the variable and expression:

```
FOR calc_index IN start_period_number ..
            LEAST (end_period_number, current_period)
LOOP
    ... executable statements ...
END LOOP;
```

Note that in this example we do not know the values for the lowest and highest bounds at the time of the writing of the code. The actual or dynamic range is determined at runtime and is fully supported by PL/SQL. In other words, the numeric FOR loop needs to know when it starts and how many times it will execute, but *you* do not have to know this when you write the program.

Handling Nontrivial Increments

PL/SQL does not provide a "step" syntax, whereby you can specify that the loop index increment. In all variations of the PL/SQL numeric FOR loop, the loop index is always incremented or decremented by one.

If you have a loop body which you want executed for a nontrivial (different from one) increment, you will have to write some cute code. For example, what if you want your loop to execute only for all even numbers between 1 and 100? You can make use of the numeric MOD function, as follows:

```
FOR loop_index IN 1 .. 100
LOOP
    IF MOD (loop_index, 2) = 0
    THEN
        /* We have an even number, so perform calculation */
        calc_values (loop_index);
    END IF;
END LOOP;
```

Or you can use simple multiplication inside a loop with half the iterations:

```
FOR even_number IN 1 .. 50
LOOP
    calc_values (even_number*2);
END LOOP;
```

In both cases, the calc_values procedure executes only for even numbers. In the first example, the FOR loop executes 100 times. In the second example, the FOR loop executes only 50 times.

Whichever approach you decide to take, be sure to document this kind of technique clearly. You are, in essence, manipulating the numeric FOR loop to do something for which it is not designed. Comments would be very helpful for the maintenance programmer who has to understand why you would code something like that.

The Cursor FOR Loop

A cursor FOR loop is a loop that is associated with (actually defined by) an explicit cursor or a SELECT statement incorporated directly within the loop boundary. Use the cursor FOR loop whenever (and only if) you need to fetch and process each and every record from a cursor, which is a high percentage of the time with cursors.

The cursor FOR loop is one of my favorite PL/SQL features. It leverages fully the tight and effective integration of the procedural constructs with the power of the SQL database language. It reduces the volume of code you need to write to fetch data from a cursor. It greatly lessens the chance of introducing loop errors in your programming—and loops are one of the more error-prone parts of a program. Does this loop sound too good to be true? Well, it isn't—it's all true!

Here is the basic syntax of a cursor FOR loop:

```
FOR record_index IN cursor_name
LOOP
    <executable statement(s)>
END LOOP;
```

where record_index is a record declared implicitly by PL/SQL with the %ROWTYPE attribute against the cursor specified by cursor_name.

The following table summarizes the properties of the cursor FOR loop where record_index is a record declared implicitly by PL/SQL with the %ROWTYPE attribute against the cursor specified by cursor_name:

Property	Description
How the loop is terminated	The cursor FOR loop terminates unconditionally when all of the records in the associated cursor have been fetched. You can also terminate the loop with an EXIT statement, but this is not recommended.
When the test for termination takes place	After each execution of the loop body, PL/SQL performs another fetch. If the %NOTFOUND attribute of the cursor evalutes to TRUE, then the loop terminates. If the cursor returns no rows, then the loop never executes its body.
Reason to use this loop	Use the cursor FOR loop when you want to fetch and process every record in a cursor.

Let's take a look at how you can use the cursor FOR loop to streamline your code and reduce opportunities for error.

Example of Cursor FOR Loops

Suppose I need to update the bills for all pets staying in my pet hotel, the Share-a-Din-Din Inn. The example below contains an anonymous block that uses a cursor, occupancy_cur, to select the room number and pet ID number for all occupants at the Inn. The procedure update_bill adds any new changes to that pet's room charges:

```
1   DECLARE
2       CURSOR occupancy_cur IS
3           SELECT pet_id, room_number
4           FROM occupancy WHERE occupied_dt = SYSDATE;
5       occupancy_rec occupancy_cur%ROWTYPE;
```

```
 6  BEGIN
 7     OPEN occupancy_cur;
 8     LOOP
 9        FETCH occupancy_cur INTO occupancy_rec;
10        EXIT WHEN occupancy_cur%NOTFOUND;
11        update_bill
12           (occupancy_rec.pet_id, occupancy_rec.room_number);
13     END LOOP;
14     CLOSE occupancy_cur;
15  END;
```

This code leaves nothing to the imagination. In addition to defining the cursor (line 2), you must explicitly declare the record for the cursor (line 5), open the cursor (line 7), start up an infinite loop, fetch a row from the cursor set into the record (line 9), check for an end-of-data condition with the cursor attribute (line 10), and finally perform the update. When you are all done, you have to remember to close the cursor (line 14).

If I convert this PL/SQL block to use a cursor FOR loop, then I have:

```
DECLARE
   CURSOR occupancy_cur IS
      SELECT pet_id, room_number
        FROM occupancy WHERE occupied_dt = SYSDATE;
BEGIN
   FOR occupancy_rec IN occupancy_cur
   LOOP
      update_bill (occupancy_rec.pet_id, occupancy_rec.room_number);
   END LOOP;
END;
```

Here you see the beautiful simplicity of the cursor FOR loop! Gone is the declaration of the record. Gone are the OPEN, FETCH, and CLOSE statements. Gone is the need to check the %FOUND attribute. Gone are the worries of getting everything right. Instead, you say to PL/SQL, in effect, "You and I both know that I want each row and I want to dump that row into a record that matches the cursor. Take care of that for me, will you?" And PL/SQL does take care of it, just the way any modern programming language should.

As with all other cursors, you can pass parameters to the cursor in a cursor FOR loop. If any of the columns in the select list of the cursor is an expression, remember that you must specify an alias for that expression in the select list. Within the loop, the only way to access a particular value in the cursor record is with the dot notation (cursor_name.column_name, as in occupancy_rec.room_number), so you need a column name associated with the expression.

The Cursor FOR Loop Record

The record which functions as the index for the cursor FOR loop is, like the loop index of a numeric FOR loop, defined only within the loop itself. You cannot reference that record outside of the loop. Furthermore, PL/SQL declares that record itself. You, the programmer, should never declare a record for use as the index in a cursor FOR loop. If you do include such a declaration, the effect will not be as you intended.

Consider the code shown below. This code contains explicit declarations for both the cursor (line 2) and a record for that cursor (line 5). The block then uses a cursor FOR loop with that cursor and specifies as its index a record with the same name as the declared record:

```
 1  DECLARE
 2  CURSOR occupancy_cur IS
 3     SELECT pet_id, room_number
 4       FROM occupancy WHERE occupied_dt = SYSDATE;
 5  occupancy_rec occupancy_cur%ROWTYPE;
 6
 7  BEGIN
 8   FOR occupancy_rec IN occupancy_cur
 9   LOOP
10     update_bill
11        (occupancy_rec.pet_id, occupancy_rec.room_number);
12   END LOOP;
13
14   DBMS_OUTPUT.PUT_LINE
15     ('Last pet ID updated: ' || TO_CHAR (occupancy_rec.pet_id));
16 END;
```

I frequently run across this kind of code. Every time I see it, I shudder because it is fraught with the potential for hard-to-trace bugs. In this example, the declaration of the occupancy_rec record on line 5 is completely unnecessary and completely ignored by the cursor FOR loop. Remember: the record named as the index of the cursor FOR loop index is always declared by PL/SQL—even if another record of the same name is defined in the declaration section. Inside the loop, any references to occupancy_rec refer to the record declared by the loop, which is completely different from the record defined explicitly in the declaration section.

The danger of this redundant declaration is that an inexperienced developer may try to reference the loop record outside of the loop. In this case, the code will compile anyway because a record is defined in the scope of that PL/SQL block. The contents of that record will, however, come as a big surprise. For example, lines 14-15 of the code above call the DBMS_OUTPUT.PUT_LINE built-in function to display (or so the developer thinks) the ID of that last pet updated by the cursor.

This block compiles successfully because a record called occupancy_rec is declared outside of the loop. The reference to occupancy_rec.pet_id in line 15 does not, however, return the value of the last pet ID from the cursor. It returns

NULL, because it refers to the record declared explicitly on line 5, which is not the same record as that used inside the loop to receive fetched rows.

If you really do need to refer to the contents of the loop's record outside of the loop, don't use a cursor FOR loop. Instead, use a WHILE loop or infinite loop. Then the record you defined on line 5 will be the same as the record used inside the loop and will contain the last row fetched by the cursor. If, on the other hand, you need to reference the record only inside the loop, strip out any declarations that match the loop indexes. Leave it to PL/SQL to handle all references correctly.

When to Use the Cursor FOR Loop

As you have seen, the cursor FOR loop offers many advantages when you want to loop through all of the records returned by a cursor. This type of loop is not appropriate, however, when you need to apply conditions to each fetched record to determine if you should halt execution of the loop. Suppose you need to scan through each of the records from a cursor and stop when a total accumulation of a column like the maximum number of pets exceeds a maximum, as shown in the code below. Although you can do this with a cursor FOR loop by issuing an EXIT statement inside the loop, that is an inappropriate use of this construct:

```
1   DECLARE
2      CURSOR occupancy_cur IS
3         SELECT pet_id, room_number
4            FROM occupancy WHERE occupied_dt = SYSDATE;
5      pet_count INTEGER := 0;
6   BEGIN
7      FOR occupancy_rec IN occupancy_cur
8      LOOP
9         update_bill
10            (occupancy_rec.pet_id, occupancy_rec.room_number);
11         pet_count := pet_count + 1;
12         EXIT WHEN pet_count > :GLOBAL.max_pets;
13      END LOOP;
14  END;
```

The FOR loop explicitly states: "I am going to execute the body of this loop *n* times" (where *n* is a number in a numeric FOR loop, or each record in a cursor FOR loop). An EXIT inside the FOR loop short-circuits this logic. The result is code which is difficult to follow and debug.

If you need to terminate a loop based on information fetched by the cursor FOR loop, you should use a WHILE loop or infinite loop in its place. Then the structure of the code will more clearly state your intentions.

The WHILE Loop

The WHILE loop is a conditional loop that continues to execute as long as the Boolean condition defined in the loop boundary evaluates to TRUE. Because the WHILE loop execution depends on a condition and is not fixed, use a WHILE loop if you don't know ahead of time the number of times a loop must execute.

Here is the general syntax for the WHILE loop:

```
WHILE <condition>
LOOP
   <executable statement(s)>
END LOOP;
```

where <condition> is a Boolean variable or an expression that evaluates to a Boolean value of TRUE, FALSE, or NULL. Each time an iteration of the loop's body is to be executed, the condition is checked. If it evaluates to TRUE, then the body is executed. If it evaluates to FALSE or to NULL, then the loop terminates and control passes to the next executable statement following the END LOOP statement.

The following table summarizes the properties of the WHILE loop:

Property	Description
How the loop is terminated	The WHILE loop terminates when the Boolean expression in its boundary evaluates to FALSE or NULL.
When the test for termination takes place	The test for termination of a WHILE loop takes place in the loop boundary. This evaluation occurs prior to the first and each subsequent execution of the body. The WHILE loop, therefore, cannot be guaranteed to always execute its loop even a single time.
Reason to use this loop	Use the WHILE loop when: • You are not sure how many times you must execute the loop body, and • You will want to conditionally terminate the loop, and • You don't have to execute the body at least one time.

The WHILE loop's condition is tested at the beginning of the loop's iteration, before the body of the loop is executed. There are two consequences to this pre-execution test:

- All the information needed to evaluate the condition must be set before the loop is executed for the first time.

- It is possible that the WHILE loop will not execute even a single time.

The Infinite WHILE Loop

One of the dangers of the simple loop is that it could be an infinite loop if the body of the loop never executes an EXIT statement. While this is less of a problem with the WHILE loop, you should be aware that it is certainly possible to construct a WHILE loop that is syntactically equivalent to the infinite LOOP. The most obvious version of an infinite WHILE loop is the following:

```
WHILE TRUE
LOOP
   <executable statement(s)>
END LOOP;
```

Sometimes, however, an infinite WHILE loop can be disguised by poor programming techniques. The following WHILE loop will terminate only when end_of_analysis is set to TRUE:

```
WHILE NOT end_of_analysis
LOOP
   perform_analysis;
   get_next_record;
   IF analysis_cursor%NOTFOUND AND
      next_analysis_step IS NULL
   THEN
      end_of_analysis := TRUE;
   END IF;
END LOOP;
```

In this WHILE loop, the end_of_analysis Boolean variable is set to TRUE only if the analysis_cursor fetches no data and we are at the last step of the analysis.

Unfortunately, both the cursor and the next_analysis_step variable are completely invisible in the loop itself. How is next_analysis_step set? Where is the cursor declared? How is a record fetched? This is a very dangerous way to structure code because if you do fall into an infinite loop, the information you need to resolve the problem is not readily available.

Managing Loop Execution

I've explained how to construct the different kinds of PL/SQL loops. The topics in this section address the following nuances of loop execution:

Labels

> You can associate a label with a loop and use that label to increase your control over loop execution.

Scope

> The loop boundary creates a scope similar to that of a PL/SQL block.

Termination

> There is only one way to enter a loop, but a number of ways you can exit your loop.

Loop Labels

You can associate a name with a loop by using a label. A *loop label* in PL/SQL has the following format:

```
<<label_name>>
```

where label_name is the name of the label. (By the way, this is the same format used for GOTO labels.) In order to associate a name with a loop, however, the loop label must appear just before the LOOP statement as shown below:

```
<<all_emps>>
FOR emp_rec IN emp_cur
LOOP
   ...
END LOOP;
```

The label can also appear optionally after the END LOOP reserved words, as the following example demonstrates:

```
<<year_loop>>
WHILE year_number <= 1995
LOOP

   <<month_loop>>
   FOR month_number IN 1 .. 12
   LOOP
      ...
   END LOOP month_loop;

END LOOP year_loop;
```

By providing a label for a loop, you give that loop a name. This allows you to use dot notation to refer to loop-related variables, such as the FOR loop index. In the following example of nested FOR loops, I qualify my reference to the year_number index with the loop name:

```
<<year_loop>>
WHILE year_number <= 1995
LOOP

   <<month_loop>>
   FOR month_number IN 1 .. 12
   LOOP
      IF year_loop.year_number = 1900
      THEN
         ...
      END IF;
   END LOOP month_loop;

END LOOP year_loop;
```

Benefits of loop labels

The loop label is useful in two particular situations:

- When you have written a loop whose code length exceeds a single page, use a loop label to tie the end of the loop back explicitly to its start. This visual tag will make it easier for a developer to maintain and debug the program. Without the loop label, it can be very difficult to keep track of which LOOP goes with which END LOOP.

- When you have nested loops, you can use the label to both improve readability and increase control over the execution of your loops. This capability is explored in the next section.

Loop termination using labels

You can affect loop execution by adding a loop label after the EXIT keyword in the EXIT statement of a loop, as follows:

```
EXIT loop_label;
EXIT loop_label WHEN condition;
```

When you specify a loop label with the EXIT statement, PL/SQL terminates the specified loop.

Consider the last example with nested year and month loops. You might encounter a condition in which both loops should be immediately terminated. The usual, unlabeled EXIT statement inside the month loop would simply halt the month processing for the current year. The year loop would, however, continue its iterations. If the EXIT statement includes the year_loop label, both loops will halt execution:

```
<<year_loop>>
WHILE year_number <= 1995
LOOP

    <<month_loop>>
    FOR month_number IN 1 .. 12
    LOOP
        calc_totals
            (year_number, month_number, termination_condition);

        /* If the termination condition is TRUE exit ALL loops. */
        EXIT year_loop WHEN termination_condition;

    END LOOP month_loop;

END LOOP year_loop;
```

In this way, the loop labels offer you added control. Nevertheless, don't use this variation of the EXIT WHEN statement unless absolutely necessary. This kind of

Tips for PL/SQL Loops

Loops are very powerful and useful constructs, but they are among the most complicated control structures in PL/SQL. The tips in this section will help you select the most efficient and easily maintained loops for your programs.

Naming Loop Indexes

How would you like to try to understand—much less maintain—code that looks like this?

```
FOR i IN start_id .. end_id
LOOP
   FOR j IN 1 .. 7
   LOOP
      FOR k IN 1 .. 24
      LOOP
         build_schedule (i, j, k);
      END LOOP;
   END LOOP;
END LOOP;
```

It is hard to imagine that someone would write code based on such generic integer variable names (right out of Algebra 101), yet it happens all the time. The habits we pick up in our earliest days of programming have an incredible half-life. Unless you are constantly vigilant, you will find yourself writing the most abominable code. In this case, the solution is simple: use variable names for the loop indexes that are meaningful and therefore self-documenting:

```
FOR focus_account IN start_id .. end_id
LOOP
   FOR day_in_week IN 1 .. 7
   LOOP
      FOR month_in_biyear IN 1 .. 24
      LOOP
         build_schedule (focus_account, day_in_week, month_in_biyear);
      END LOOP;
   END LOOP;
END LOOP;
```

Well, that cleared things up! Before I substituted the meaningless loop index names, I would wager that you were fairly sure the statement:

```
FOR j IN 1 .. 7
```

meant that "j" stood for the seven days of the week. And I bet further that you were equally confident that:

```
FOR k IN 1 .. 24
```

meant that "k" represented the hours in a day.

Now that I have provided descriptive names for those index variables, however, you discover that the innermost loop actually spanned two sets of twelve months (12 × 2 = 24). Your deduction about "k", while reasonable, was wrong, but it would have been completely impossible to determine this without looking at the build_schedule code. Given PL/SQL's ability to hide information within packages, this code might not even be available.

Software programmers should not have to make Sherlock Holmes-like deductions about the meaning of the start and end range values of the innermost FOR loops in order to understand their purpose. Use names that self-document the purposes of variables and loops. That way other people will understand your code and you will remember what your own code does when you review it three months later.

The Proper Way to Say Goodbye

No matter what kind of loop you are using, there is always only one entry point into the loop: the first executable statement following the LOOP keyword. Your loops should also have just one way of leaving the loop. The method of exit, furthermore, should be compatible with the type of loop you use. The following tips will help you write well-structured and easily maintained loops.

Premature FOR loop termination

The syntax of the FOR loop states your intent explicitly and should only be a FOR loop if you know in advance how many times the loop needs to execute. For example, the following loop is very clear:

```
FOR month_count IN 1 .. 12
LOOP
    analyze_month (month_count);
END LOOP;
```

It states: "I am going to execute the analyze_month procedure 12 times, once for each month in the year." Straightforward and easy to understand.

Now take a look at the next numeric FOR loop:

```
FOR year_count IN 1 .. years_displayed
LOOP
   IF year_count > 10 AND :store.status = 'CLOSED'
   THEN
      EXIT;
   END IF;
   analyze_month (month_count);
END LOOP;
```

In this case, the loop boundary states: "Run the loop for the number of years displayed in the form." Yet in the body of the loop, an IF statement allows a premature termination of the loop. If the year count (the loop index) exceeds 10

Avoiding the Phony Loop

As I have stated previously, you should not use a numeric FOR loop if you cannot specify in a range scheme of lowest and highest bounds the number of times the loop must execute. Just because you know the number of iterations of some code, however, doesn't mean that you should use a loop.

I have run across a number of programs which execute variations on this kind of FOR loop:

```
FOR i IN 1 .. 2
LOOP
   IF i = 1
   THEN
      give_bonus (president_id, 2000000);

   ELSIF i = 2
   THEN
      give_bonus (ceo_id, 5000000);
   END IF;
END LOOP;
```

This loop provides hefty bonuses to the president and CEO of a company that just went deep into debt to acquire a competitor. I need to use the loop so the code executes twice to make sure both the president and CEO receive their just compensation. Right? Wrong. This code should not be inside a loop. It does not need iteration to perform its job; the LOOP syntax just confuses the issue.

The two sections within the IF-THEN-ELSE construct in the previous example both need to be executed all the time; this is straight sequential code and should be written as follows:

```
give_bonus (president_id, 2000000);
give_bonus (ceo_id, 5000000);
```

PL/SQL Loops Versus SQL Processing

One of the indicators that a numeric FOR loop is being used incorrectly is that the loop index is not used for anything but traffic control inside the loop. The actual body of executable statements completely ignores the loop index. When that is the case, there is a good chance that you don't need the loop at all.

When should you use standard SQL to accomplish your task and when should you rely on PL/SQL loops? Sometimes the choice is clear: if you do not need to interact with the database, then there is clearly no need for SQL. In addition, SQL can't always provide the necessary flexibility to get the job done. Conversely, if you are performing a single record insert into a table then there is no need for a loop. Often, however, the choice is less obvious. For example, a SELECT statement queries one or more rows from the database. A cursor FOR loop also queries rows from the database based on a SELECT statement. In fact, PL/SQL and native SQL often can both accomplish the task at hand. Given that fact, you will need to choose your implementation according to more subtle issues like performance and maintainability of code.

Before we look at some examples of scenarios which call for one or the other approach, let's review the difference between the implicit looping of the SQL set-at-a-time approach and the PL/SQL loop.

SQL statements such as SELECT, UPDATE, INSERT, and DELETE work on a set of data. That set (actually, a collection of rows from a table or tables) is determined by the WHERE clause (or lack thereof) in the SQL statement. SQL derives much of its power and effectiveness as a database language from this set-at-a-time processing approach. There is, however, a drawback, as I mentioned earlier: SQL often does not give you the flexibility you might need to handle individual records and specialized logic which must be applied differently to different records.

The PL/SQL cursor offers the ability to access a record at a time and to take action based on the contents of that specific record. It is not always clear, however, which language component would best fit the needs of the moment. I have seen a number of programs where developers went overboard in their drive to PL/SQL-ize the SQL access to their data. This happens most frequently when using a cursor FOR loop.

The PL/SQL block in the code below moves checked-out pets from the pet hotel occupancy table to the pets_history table using a cursor FOR loop. For each record fetched (implicitly) from the cursor (representing a pet who has hit the road), the body of the loop first inserts a record into the pet_history table and then deletes the record from the occupancy table:

```
DECLARE
    CURSOR checked_out_cur IS
        SELECT pet_id, name, checkout_date
          FROM occupancy
         S checkout_date IS NOT NULL;
BEGIN
    FOR checked_out_rec IN checked_out_cur
    LOOP
        INSERT INTO occupancy_history (pet_id, name, checkout_date)
            VALUES (checked_out_rec.pet_id, checked_out_rec.name,
                    checked_out_rec.checkout_date);
        DELETE FROM occupancy WHERE pet_id = checked_out_rec.pet_id;
    END LOOP;
END;
```

This will work just fine. But do we really need to use a cursor FOR loop to accomplish this task? Suppose 20 animals checked out today. This block of code will then perform 20 distinct inserts and 20 distinct deletes. The same code can be written completely within the SQL language as shown below:

```
INSERT INTO occupancy_history (pet_id, name, checkout_date)
SELECT pet_id, name, checkout_date
  FROM occupancy
 WHERE checkout_date IS NOT NULL;
DELETE FROM occupancy WHERE checkout_date IS NOT NULL;
```

Here, a single insert (making use of the INSERT...SELECT syntax) and a single delete (which now checks for the checkout_date and not the employee_id) accomplish the transfer of the data to the history table. This reliance on native SQL, without the help of PL/SQL, allows you to take full advantage of array processing. It significantly reduces network traffic in a client-server environment because only two SQL statements (instead of 40) are passed to the RDBMS.

The cursor FOR loop was not really needed here; the body of the loop did not perform any procedural logic which could not be handled by SQL itself. If, on the other hand, the program needed to selectively reject records for the transfer, or otherwise perform procedural logic not possible within SQL, then either the cursor FOR loop or a WHILE loop would make sense.

8

Exception Handlers

In the PL/SQL language, errors of any kind are treated as exceptions—situations that should not occur—in your program. An exception can be one of the following:

- An error generated by the system (such as "out of memory" or "duplicate value in index")

- An error caused by a user action

- A warning issued by the application to the user

PL/SQL traps and responds to errors using an architecture of *exception handlers*. The exception-handler mechanism allows you to cleanly separate your error processing code from your executable statements. It also provides an event-driven model, as opposed to a linear code model, for processing errors. In other words, no matter how a particular exception is raised, it is handled by the same exception handler in the exception section.

When an error occurs in PL/SQL, whether a system error or an application error, an exception is raised. The processing in the current PL/SQL block's execution section halts and control is transferred to the separate exception section of your program, if one exists, to handle the exception. You cannot return to that block after you finish handling the exception. Instead, control is passed to the enclosing block, if any.

Here is an example of how you might use the exceptions table. Suppose that your program generates an unhandled exception for error ORA–6511. Looking up this error, you find that it is associated with the CURSOR_ALREADY_OPEN exception. Locate the PL/SQL block in which the error occurs and add an exception handler for CURSOR_ALREADY_OPEN, as shown below:

```
EXCEPTION
   WHEN CURSOR_ALREADY_OPEN
   THEN
      CLOSE my_cursor;
END;
```

Of course, you would be even better off analyzing your code to determine proactively which of the predefined exceptions might occur. Then you could decide which of those exceptions you want to handle specifically, which should be covered by the WHEN OTHERS clause, and which would best be left unhandled.

Table 8-1. Predefined Exceptions in PL/SQL

Name of Exception Oracle Error/SQLCODE	Description
CURSOR_ALREADY_OPEN ORA–6511 SQLCODE= –6511	You tried to OPEN a cursor that was already OPEN. You must CLOSE a cursor before you try to OPEN or re-OPEN it.
DUP_VAL_ON_INDEX ORA–00001 SQLCODE= –1	Your INSERT or UPDATE statement attempted to store duplicate values in a column or columns in a row which is restricted by a unique index.
INVALID_CURSOR ORA–01001 SQLCODE= –1001	You made reference to a cursor that did not exist. This usually happens when you try to FETCH from a cursor or CLOSE a cursor before that cursor is OPENed.
INVALID_NUMBER ORA–01722 SQLCODE = –1722	PL/SQL executes a SQL statement that cannot convert a character string successfully to a number. This exception is different from the VALUE_ERROR exception, as it is raised only from within a SQL statement.
LOGIN_DENIED ORA–01017 SQLCODE= –1017	Your program tried to log onto the Oracle RDBMS with an invalid username-password combination. This exception is usually encountered when you embed PL/SQL in a 3GL language.
NO_DATA_FOUND ORA–01403 SQLCODE= +100	This exception is raised in three different scenarios: (1) You executed a SELECT INTO statement (implicit cursor) that returned no rows. (2) You referenced an uninitialized row in a local PL/SQL table. (3) You read past end of file with UTL_FILE package.
NOT_LOGGED_ON ORA–01012 SQLCODE= –1012	Your program tried to execute a call to the database (usually with a DML statement) before it had logged into the Oracle RDBMS.
PROGRAM_ERROR ORA–06501 SQLCODE= –6501	PL/SQL encounters an internal problem. The message text usually also tells you to "Contact Oracle Support."

Table 8-1. Predefined Exceptions in PL/SQL (continued)

Name of Exception Oracle Error/SQLCODE	Description
STORAGE_ERROR ORA–06500 SQLCODE= –6500	Your program ran out of memory or memory was in some way corrupted.
TIMEOUT_ON_RESOURCE ORA–00051 SQLCODE= –51	A timeout occurred in the RDBMS while waiting for a resource.
TOO_MANY_ROWS ORA–01422 SQLCODE= –1422	A SELECT INTO statement returned more than one row. A SELECT INTO can return only one row; if your SQL statement returns more than one row you should place the SELECT statement in an explicit CURSOR declaration and FETCH from that cursor one row at a time.
TRANSACTION_BACKED_OUT ORA–00061 SQLCODE= –61	The remote part of a transaction is rolled back, either with an explicit ROLLBACK command or as the result of some other action.
VALUE_ERROR ORA–06502 SQLCODE= –6502	PL/SQL raises the VALUE_ERROR whenever it encounters an error having to do with the conversion, truncation, or invalid constraining of numeric and character data. This is a very general and common exception. If this same type of error is encountered in a SQL DML statement within a PL/SQL block, then the INVALID_NUMBER exception is raised.
ZERO_DIVIDE ORA–01476 SQLCODE= –1476	Your program tried to divide by zero.

Named Programmer–Defined Exceptions

The exceptions that PL/SQL has declared in the STANDARD package cover internal or system-generated errors. Many of the problems a user will encounter (or cause) in an application, however, are specific to that application. Your program might need to trap and handle errors such as "negative balance in account" or "call date cannot be in the past." While different in nature from "division by zero," these errors are still exceptions to normal processing and should be handled gracefully by your program.

One of the most useful aspects of the PL/SQL exception handling model is that it does not make any structural distinction between internal errors and application-specific errors. Once an exception is raised, it can and should be handled in the exception section, regardless of the type or source of error.

Of course, to handle an exception, you must have a name for that exception. Because PL/SQL cannot name these exceptions for you (they are specific to your application), you must do so yourself by declaring an exception in the declaration section of your PL/SQL block. You declare an exception by listing the name of

the exception you want to raise in your program, followed by the keyword
EXCEPTION, as follows:

```
exception_name EXCEPTION;
```

The following declaration section of the calc_annual_sales contains three
programmer-defined exception declarations:

```
PROCEDURE calc_annual_sales
   (company_id_in IN company.company_id%TYPE)
IS
   invalid_company_id   EXCEPTION;
   no_sales_for_company EXCEPTION;
   negative_balance     EXCEPTION;

   duplicate_company    BOOLEAN;
BEGIN
   ... body of executable statements ...
EXCEPTION
   WHEN invalid_company_id
   THEN
      ...
   WHEN no_sales_for_company
   THEN
      ...
   WHEN negative_balance
   THEN
      ...
END;
```

The names for exceptions are similar in format to (and "read" just like) Boolean
variable names, but can be referenced in only two ways:

- In a RAISE statement in the execution section of the program (to raise the
  exception), as in:

  ```
  RAISE no_sales_for_company;
  ```

- In the WHEN clauses of the exception section (to handle the raised exception), as in:

  ```
  WHEN no_sales_for_company THEN
  ```

Unnamed System Exceptions

What do you do when you want to trap an internal error raised by PL/SQL or the
SQL engine, but it is not one of the lucky errors that have been given a
predefined name? Although this error is identified only by its internal error
number, exception handlers need a name by which they can check for a match.
Sure, you can always use the WHEN OTHERS clause to simply catch any exceptions not previously handled. (This is covered in detail in the section entitled
"Using SQLCODE and SQLERRM in WHEN OTHERS Clause") In many cases,

however, you will want to trap specific errors in a way that clearly documents and highlights them in your code. To do this, you assign your own name to the Oracle or PL/SQL error that might be raised in your program, and then write a specific exception handler for that custom-named exception.

The EXCEPTION_INIT pragma

You can use a compiler construct called a pragma to associate a name with an internal error code. A *pragma* (introduced in Chapter 2) is a special instruction to the compiler that is processed at compile time instead of at runtime. A pragma called EXCEPTION_INIT instructs the compiler to associate or initialize a programmer-defined exception with a specific Oracle error number. With a name for that error, you can then raise this exception and write a handler which will trap that error. While in most cases you will leave it to Oracle to raise these system exceptions, you could also raise them yourself.

The pragma EXCEPTION_INIT must appear in the declaration section of a block, after the declaration of the exception name used in the pragma, as shown below:

```
DECLARE
   exception_name EXCEPTION;
   PRAGMA EXCEPTION_INIT (exception_name, error_code_literal);
BEGIN
```

where exception_name is the name of an exception and error_code_literal is the number of the Oracle error (including the minus sign, if the error code is negative, as is almost always the case).

In the following program code, I declare and associate an exception for this error:

```
ORA-2292 violated integrity constraining (OWNER.CONSTRAINT) -
         child record found.
```

This error occurs if I try to delete a parent record while there are child records still in that table. A child record is a record with a foreign key reference to the parent table:

```
PROCEDURE delete_company (company_id_in IN NUMBER)
IS
   /* Declare the exception. */
   still_have_employees EXCEPTION;

   /* Associate the exception name with an error number. */
   PRAGMA EXCEPTION_INIT (still_have_employees, -2292);
BEGIN
   /* Try to delete the company. */
   DELETE FROM company
    WHERE company_id = company_id_in;
EXCEPTION
   /* If child records were found, this exception is raised! */
   WHEN still_have_employees
```

```
    THEN
        DBMS_OUTPUT.PUT_LINE
            (' Please delete employees for company first.');
    END;
```

When you use EXCEPTION_INIT, you must supply a literal number for the second argument of the pragma call. By explicitly naming this system exception, the purpose of the exception handler is self-evident.

The EXCEPTION_INIT pragma improves the readability of your programs by assigning names to otherwise obscure error numbers. You can employ the EXCEPTION_INIT pragma more than once in your program. You can even assign more than one exception name to the same error number.

Unnamed Programmer–Defined Exceptions

The final type of exception is the unnamed, yet programmer-defined exception. This kind of exception occurs when you need to raise an application-specific error from within the server and communicate this error back to the client application process. This scenario is more common than you might at first imagine. For example, even when you run all your Oracle software in a single hardware environment (such as a character-based SQL*Forms applications running on UNIX against an Oracle server on the same UNIX platform), you still have a separation between your client (SQL*Forms screen) and your server (the RDBMS).

You will trap some, perhaps most, application-specific errors on the client side. On the other hand, the Oracle7 architecture allows you to embed many of your business rules directly into your database structure, using database triggers, constraints, and stored procedures. In many cases, you will want to let the RDBMS trap and reject invalid database actions. To do this, you need a way to identify application-specific errors and return information about those error back to the client. This kind of error communication is illustrated in Figure 8-2.

I have called this type of exception "unnamed" and "programmer-defined." The programmer-defined aspect should be clear: because the error is application-specific, you cannot expect PL/SQL to have already defined it for you. The reason this type of exception is also unnamed is that you cannot name or declare an exception within a server-based program or database trigger and have the client-side tool handle that named exception. This identifier simply doesn't cross the great divide between client and server.

To get around this problem, Oracle provides a special procedure to allow communication of an unnamed, yet programmer-defined, server-side exception: RAISE_APPLICATION_ERROR. (The use of this procedure and exception type is

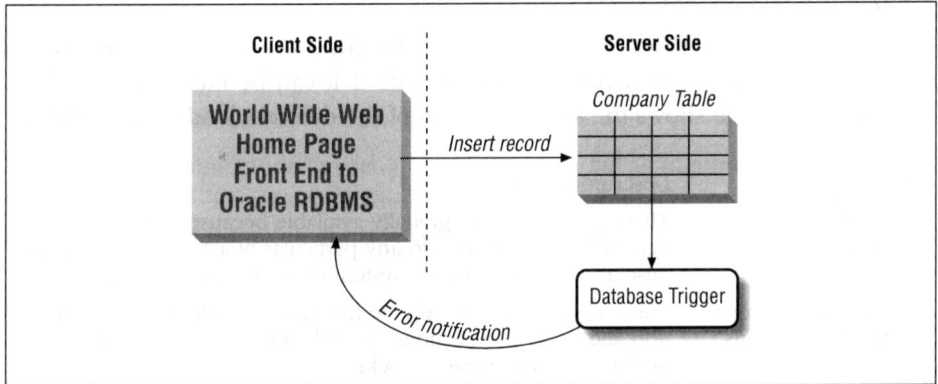

Figure 8-2. Error communication from server to client

discussed in the section entitled "Client-Server Error Communication" later in this chapter.) The specification for this procedure is as follows:

```
PROCEDURE RAISE_APPLICATION_ERROR
    (error_number_in IN NUMBER, error_msg_in IN VARCHAR2);
```

where error_number_in is the error number you have assigned to this error. The error_msg_in argument is the message that will be sent back with the error code to the client program.

Determining Exception-Handling Behavior

A PL/SQL program is an anonymous block, a procedure, or a function. This program, or "highest-level" block, can call other procedures or functions, or nest an anonymous block within that block. So at any given point in execution, there might be several layers of PL/SQL blocks nested within other blocks. Each PL/SQL block can have its own exception section, or it can be totally void of exception handlers.

To determine the appropriate exception-handling behavior, PL/SQL follows rules regarding:

Scope
    The PL/SQL block or blocks in which an exception can be raised and handled.

Propagation
    The way in which an exception is passed back through enclosing blocks until it is handled or is resolved to be an unhandled exception

Let's look at these two properties of exceptions.

one within the nested block on line 16 and one in the main body of the procedure on line 24. Finally, there is just a single exception section and one handler for overdue_balance on line 30.

Well, the overdue_balance exception is certainly declared in every block in which it is raised. Yet the exception-handling behavior of check_account may not be as you would expect. What happens, for example, when the RAISE statement on line 16 executes? Do you see this:

```
'Balance is overdue. Pay up!'
```

or this:

```
ORA-06501: PL/SQL: unhandled user-defined exception
ORA-6512: at "USER.CHECK_ACCOUNT", line N
```

You will, in fact, have raised an unhandled exception when you RAISE overdue_balance in the nested block. How can this be?

Remember that the nested block does not have its own exception section—yet it does have its own, locally declared exception. So when the exception is raised on line 16, the nested block cannot handle the exception. Instead, that exception (declared only in that nested block) is passed on to the enclosing block and PL/SQL tries to handle it there.

As soon as control passes to the enclosing block, however, the nested block terminates and all local identifiers are erased. This includes the exception which was just raised. It is no longer defined and therefore cannot be handled in the outer block, even though it seems to have an handler for precisely that exception.

But there is still a glitch: the enclosing block doesn't know anything about the local overdue_balance, only its own rendition. And even though they appear to have the same name, these exceptions are different exceptions as far as the compiler is concerned. As a result, the nested block overdue_balance exception goes unhandled.

How can you get around this problem? First of all, you should avoid such duplication of exception names. This only makes the code very hard to understand and follow. But if you insist on these overlapping names, you can take any of the following steps:

1. Raise the procedure-level overdue_balance exception within the subblock if the enclosing block has a name (if it is a procedure or a function). You can use dot notation to distinguish the local exception from its global counterpart as follows:

```
RAISE check_account.overdue_balance;
```

2. Make sure that the locally raised overdue_balance is handled by the main check_account exception section by including a WHEN OTHERS clause to trap any exceptions not otherwise handled.

3. Remove the local declaration of overdue_balance so this exception is declared only once in the program unit.

Propagation of an Exception

The scope rules for exceptions determine the block in which an exception can be raised. The rules for exception propagation address the way in which an exception is handled, once it has been raised.

When an exception is raised, PL/SQL looks for an exception handler in the current block (anonymous block, procedure, or function) for this exception. If it does not find a match, then PL/SQL *propagates* the exception to the enclosing block of that current block. PL/SQL then attempts to handle the exception by raising that exception once more in the enclosing block. It continues to do this in each successive enclosing block until there are no more blocks in which to raise the exception (see Figure 8-3). When all blocks are exhausted, PL/SQL returns an unhandled exception to the application environment that executed the outermost PL/SQL block. An unhandled exception halts the execution of the host program.

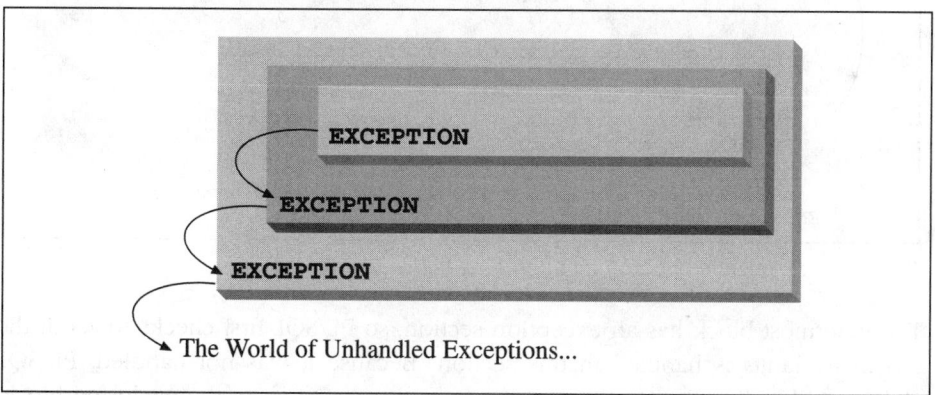

Figure 8-3. Propagation of exception through nested blocks

One very direct consequence of this propagation method is that if PL/SQL cannot locate an exception handler in the current block for a local, programmer-defined exception, the exception will not be handled at all. The exception is not recognized outside of the current block, so propagating to enclosing blocks will never cause the exception to be handled (unless you use the blanket WHEN OTHERS handler).

Let's look at a few examples of the way exceptions propagate through enclosing blocks.

Figure 8-4 shows the exception raised in the inner block too_many_faults is handled by the next enclosing block.

```
PROCEDURE list_my_faults IS
BEGIN
    ...
    DECLARE                                          Nested Block 1
        too_many_faults EXCEPTION;
    BEGIN
        ... executable statements before new block ...
        BEGIN                                        Nested Block 2
            SELECT SUM (faults) INTO num_faults FROM profile ... ;
            IF num_faults > 100
            THEN
                RAISE too_many_faults;
            END IF;
        EXCEPTION
            WHEN NO_DATA_FOUND THEN ... ;
        END;

        ... executable statements after Nested Block 2 ...

    EXCEPTION
        WHEN too_many_faults THEN ... ;
    END;
END list_my_faults;
```

Figure 8-4. Propagation of exception handling to first nested block

The innermost block has an exception section, so PL/SQL first checks to see if the too_many_faults is handled in this section. Because it was not handled, PL/SQL closes that block and raises the too_many_faults exception in the enclosing block, Nested Block 1. Control immediately passes to the exception section of Nested Block 1. (The executable statements after Nested Block 2 are not executed.) PL/SQL scans the exception handlers and finds that too_many_faults is handled in this block, so the code for that handler is executed, after which control passes back to the main list_my_faults procedure.

Notice that if the NO_DATA_FOUND exception had been raised in the innermost block (Nested Block 2), then the exception section for Nested Block 2 would have handled the exception. Then control would pass back to Nested Block 1 and the executable statements which come after Nested Block 2 would be executed.

In Figure 8-5, the exception raised in the inner block is handled by the outermost block.

```
PROCEDURE list_my_faults
IS
    too_many_faults EXCEPTION;
BEGIN
    ...                                                    Nested Block 1
    BEGIN

        BEGIN                                              Nested Block 2
            SELECT SUM (faults) INTO num_faults FROM profile ... ;
            IF num_faults > 100
            THEN
                  RAISE too_many_faults;
            END IF;
        END;

    END;
EXCEPTION
    WHEN too_many_faults THEN ... ;
END list_my_faults;
```

Figure 8-5. Exception raised in nested block handled by outermost block

The outermost block is the only one with an exception section, so when Nested Block 2 raises the too_many_faults exception, PL/SQL terminates execution of that block and raises that exception in the enclosing block, Nested Block 1. Again, this block has no exception section so PL/SQL immediately terminates Nested Block 1 and passes control to the outermost block (the list_my_faults procedure). This procedure does have an exception section, so PL/SQL scans the exception handlers, finds a match for too_many_faults, executes the code for that handler, and then returns control to whatever program called list_my_faults.

Raising an Exception

There are four ways that you or the PL/SQL runtime engine can raise an exception:

- *The PL/SQL runtime engine raised a named system exception.* These exceptions are raised automatically by the program. You cannot control when PL/SQL will raise a system exception. You can, however, write code to handle those exceptions when they are raised.

- *The programmer raises a named exception.* The programmer can use an explicit call to the RAISE statement to raise a programmer-defined or system-named exception.

- *The programmer raises an unnamed, programmer-defined exception.* These are raised with an explicit call to the RAISE_APPLICATION_ERROR procedure in the DBMS_STANDARD package.

- *The programmer re-raises the "current" exception.* From within an exception handler, you can re-raise the same exception for propagation to the enclosing block.

Who Raises the Exception?

The following sections show how you can let PL/SQL raise a system error or you can check for the error yourself and then raise that same system error.

PL/SQL raises ZERO_DIVIDE exception

In the following example, I raise my own exception, sales_domination, when the percentage of a customer's sales is over 50% of total sales. If, on the other hand, the total_sales is zero (as will be the case in the senseless code below), PL/SQL will automatically raise the ZERO_DIVIDE exception. Because I include a handler for that specific problem, the application does not abort when this code is executed. Instead, a message is displayed informing the user of a serious problem:

```
DECLARE
    total_sales NUMBER := 0;
    cust_sales NUMBER;
    sales_domination EXCEPTION;
BEGIN
    SELECT SUM (sales) INTO cust_sales
      FROM invoice WHERE customer_id = 1001;
    IF cust_sales / total_sales > .5
    THEN
        RAISE sales_domination;
    END IF;
EXCEPTION
    WHEN ZERO_DIVIDE
    THEN
        DBMS_OUTPUT.PUT_LINE
            (' We haven''t sold anything. We are bankrupt!');

    WHEN sales_domination
    THEN
        DBMS_OUTPUT.PUT_LINE
            (' Customer 1001 accounts for more than half of all sales!');
END;
```

Notice that there is no RAISE statement for the ZERO_DIVIDE exception in the body of the program. Instead, I leave it to PL/SQL to raise such internally generated exceptions. There is no restriction, however, on a programmer's raising a predefined exception.

Programmer raises ZERO_DIVIDE exception

I could recode the previous anonymous block as follows:

```
DECLARE
   total_sales NUMBER := 0;
   cust_sales NUMBER;
   sales_domination EXCEPTION;
BEGIN
   SELECT SUM (sales) INTO cust_sales
     FROM invoice WHERE customer_id = 1001;

   /* Check for zero divisor and raise exception if necessary */
   IF total_sales = 0
   THEN
      RAISE ZERO_DIVIDE;
   ELSIF cust_sales / total_sales > .5
   THEN
      RAISE sales_domination;
   END IF;
EXCEPTION
   ... unchanged ...
END;
```

Here, my own code raises the ZERO_DIVIDE exception because as author of the program I know that a total_sales of zero will result in a division by zero. With either approach, the result is the same. Regardless of how the ZERO_DIVIDE exception is raised, the same exception handler will trap the error.

Impact of unhandled exceptions

If an exception is raised in a PL/SQL block and goes unhandled, there are several consequences to consider. First, if the program contains OUT or IN OUT parameters, then the PL/SQL runtime engine does not assign values to those parameters. Any changes to those parameters made during the program execution are, in essence, rolled back. Second, the runtime engine does *not* roll back any database work performed by that PL/SQL block. Instead, you must issue an explicit ROLLBACK statement to achieve this effect.

Re-Raising an Exception

When you are inside an exception handler in an exception section, you can re-raise the exception that "got you there" by issuing an unqualified RAISE statement as follows:

```
RAISE;
```

Since you do not specify an exception, the PL/SQL runtime engine re-raises the current exception (whose error number would be returned by a call to the SQLCODE function).

Here is an example of using RAISE in this way:

```
EXCEPTION
    WHEN OTHERS
    THEN
        send_error_to_pipe (SQLCODE);
        RAISE;
END;
```

This re-raise functionality comes in very handy when you need to raise exceptions which have not been assigned a name through use of the EXCEPTION_INIT pragma.

Exceptions Raised in a Declaration

When an exception is raised in the declaration section of a block, control is passed immediately to the enclosing block, if there is one, not to the exception section of the current block, as shown in Figure 8-6.

The assignment of the default value to little_string is too big for the variable. This causes PL/SQL to raise the VALUE_ERROR exception. This exception will not, however, be handled by the VALUE_ERROR handler in the anonymous block's exception section. Instead, PL/SQL will terminate the anonymous block and try to handle the exception in early_failure's exception section. Because there is not one, the exception is unhandled.

The reason for this behavior is simple, as we describe in the next section.

Exceptions Raised in an Exception Handler

You can raise another exception from within an exception handler, but that exception can be handled only in the exception section of an enclosing block—never in the current block. The exception section of the current PL/SQL block will only handle exceptions raised in the execution section of that block.

When an exception is raised, the execution in the current block is immediately terminated, and control is passed in to the exception section, as shown in Figure 8-7. Once a match for the exception has been found, the rest of the exception section is inaccessible. At this point it is impossible to re-enter this same exception section because the corresponding execution section has been exited.

Why would you want to raise an exception *inside* an exception handler? You will find it useful to raise new exceptions from the current exception section when you do not want the enclosing block to continue normal processing after an

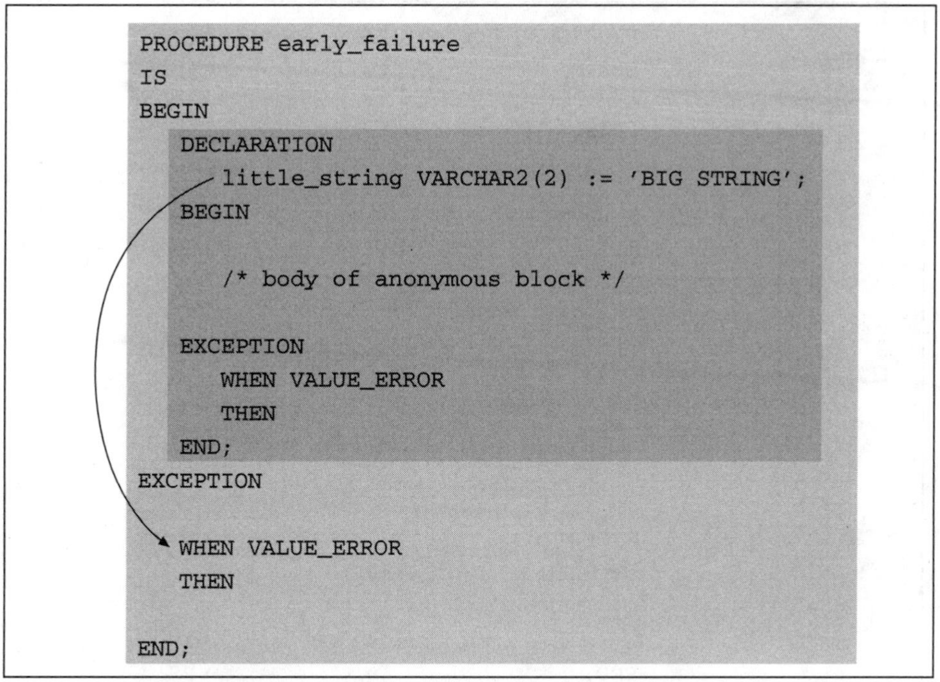

```
PROCEDURE early_failure
IS
BEGIN
   DECLARATION
      little_string VARCHAR2(2) := 'BIG STRING';
   BEGIN


      /* body of anonymous block */


   EXCEPTION
      WHEN VALUE_ERROR
      THEN
   END;
EXCEPTION

   WHEN VALUE_ERROR
   THEN


END;
```

Figure 8-6. VALUE_ERROR raised in nested block declaration section

exception in the subblock. You may instead want execution to branch off in a different direction, or to skip the rest of the enclosing block and move immediately to the enclosing block of that enclosing block.

In the following example, I have a triple nesting of anonymous blocks. When the innermost block raises an exception, I want to terminate both the second and third blocks, but continue normal processing in the outermost block. Raising an exception from within an exception block produces this behavior for me:

```
DECLARE -- Outermost block
BEGIN

   DECLARE -- First sub-block.
      -- An exception whose scope is the two sub-blocks.
      skip_sub_block EXCEPTION;
   BEGIN
   ... executable statements for first sub-block ...

   BEGIN -- Second sub-block.
      ... executable statements for innermost block ...
   EXCEPTION
      WHEN NO_DATA_FOUND -- A table fetch returned no values.
      THEN
         RAISE skip_sub_block; -- Raise exception in enclosing block.
   END;
```

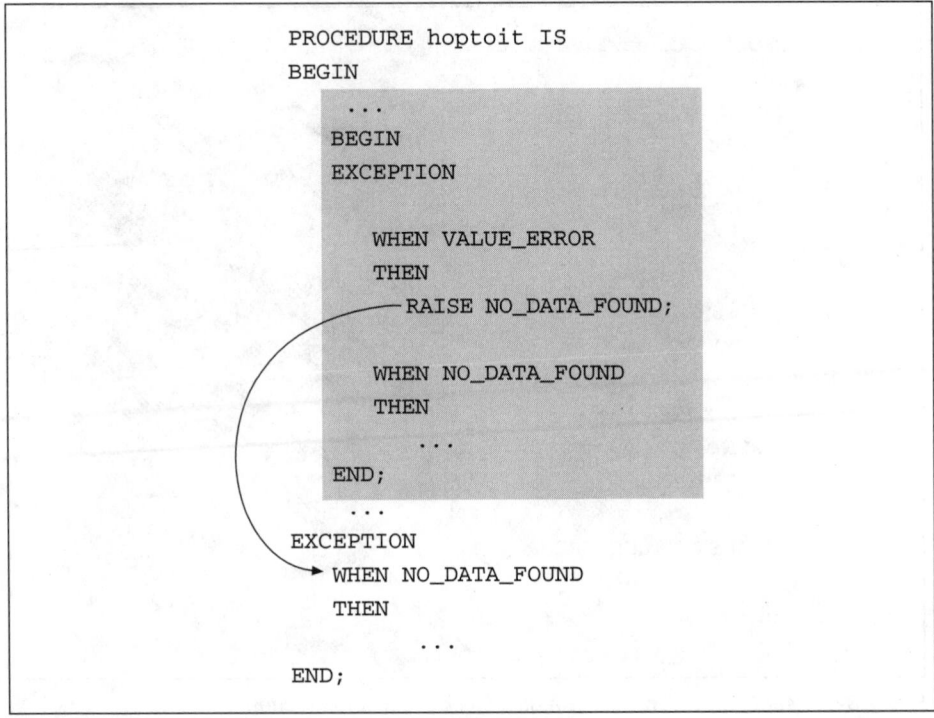

Figure 8-7. Exception raised in exception handler immediately exits the exception section

```
    EXCEPTION
       WHEN skip_sub_block
       THEN
           NULL; -- Terminate this sub-block, return to main block.
    END;

    -- Now continue with main block processing.
    ... executable statements ...

  END;
```

Handling Exceptions

Once an exception is raised, the current PL/SQL block stops its regular execution and transfers control to the exception section. The exception is then either handled by an exception handler in the current PL/SQL block or passed to the enclosing block.

Remember: once an exception is raised, the execution section is terminated. You cannot return to that body of code.

To handle or trap an exception once it is raised, you must write an exception handler for that exception. In your code, your exception handlers must appear after all the executable statements in your program but before the END statement of the block. The EXCEPTION keyword indicates the start of the exception section and the individual exception handlers.

The structure of the exception section is very similar to a CASE statement (which is not available in PL/SQL):

```
EXCEPTION
   WHEN exception_name1
   THEN
      <executable statements>

   WHEN exception_nameN
   THEN
      <executable statements>

   WHEN OTHERS
   THEN
      <executable statements>
END;
```

where exception_name1 is the name of the first exception handled in the section, exception_nameN is the name of the last named exception handled in the section, and the WHEN OTHERS clause provides the "otherwise" portion of the CASE statement. Of course, the code for each exception handler need not be on the same line, as shown in the preceding example. Every executable statement after a THEN and before the next WHEN or the final END statement belongs to the exception named by the previous WHEN statement, and is executed when that exception is raised.

The WHEN OTHERS clause must be the last exception handler in the exception section. If you place any other WHEN clauses after WHEN OTHER, you will receive the following compilation error:

```
PLS-00370: OTHERS handler must be last among the exception handlers
           of a block
```

Combining Multiple Exceptions in a Single Handler

You can, within a single WHEN clause, combine multiple exceptions together with an OR operator, just as you would combine multiple Boolean expressions:

```
WHEN invalid_company_id OR negative_balance
THEN
```

You can also combine application and system exception names in a single handler:

```
WHEN balance_too_low OR ZERO_DIVIDE
THEN
```

You cannot, however, use the AND operator, because only one exception can be raised at a time.

Unhandled Exceptions

If an exception is raised in your program and that exception is not handled by an exception section in either the current or enclosing PL/SQL blocks, that exception is "unhandled." PL/SQL returns the error which raised an unhandled exception all the way back to the application environment from which PL/SQL was run. That application environment (a tool like SQL*Plus, Oracle Forms, or a Powerbuilder program) then takes an action appropriate to the situation.

A well-designed application will not allow unhandled exceptions to occur. The best way to avoid unhandled exceptions is to make sure that the outermost PL/SQL block (whether it is an anonymous block in SQL*Plus or a stored procedure in the database) contains a WHEN OTHERS clause in its exception section.

Using SQLCODE and SQLERRM in WHEN OTHERS Clause

You can use the WHEN OTHERS clause in the exception section to trap all otherwise unhandled exceptions, including internal errors which are not predefined by PL/SQL. Once inside the exception handler, however, you will often want to know which error occurred. You can use the SQLCODE function to obtain this information.

Consider the following situation. My application maintains companies and orders entered for those companies. My foreign key constraint on company_id in the orders table guarantees that I cannot delete a company if there are still child records (orders) in the database for that company. The following procedure deletes companies and handles any exceptions which might arise:

```
PROCEDURE delete_company (company_id_in IN NUMBER)
IS
BEGIN
    DELETE FROM company WHERE company_id = company_id_in;

EXCEPTION
    WHEN OTHERS
    THEN
        DBMS_OUTPUT.PUTLINE (' Error deleting company.');
END;
```

Notice the generic nature of the error message. I don't have any idea what brought me there, so I cannot pass on much useful information to the users. Did the delete fail because there are orders still present? Then perhaps I would want to delete them and then delete the company. Fortunately, Oracle provides two functions, SQLCODE and SQLERRM, which return, respectively, the error code and the error message resulting from the most recently raised exception. (These two functions are described in detail in Chapter 13, *Numeric, LOB, and Miscellaneous Functions*.)

Combined with WHEN OTHERS, SQLCODE provides a way for you to handle different, specific exceptions without having to use the EXCEPTION_INIT pragma. In the next example, I trap both of the parent-child exceptions, –2292 and –2291, and then take an action appropriate to each situation:

```
PROCEDURE delete_company (company_id_in IN NUMBER)
IS
BEGIN
   DELETE FROM company
    WHERE company_id = company_id_in;
EXCEPTION
   WHEN OTHERS
   THEN
      /*
      || Anonymous block inside the exception handler lets me declare
      || local variables to hold the error code information.
      */
      DECLARE
         error_code NUMBER := SQLCODE;
         error_msg  VARCHAR2 (300) := SQLERRM;
      BEGIN
         IF error_code = -2292
         THEN
            /* Child records found. Delete those too! */
            DELETE FROM employee
             WHERE company_id = company_id_in;

            /* Now delete parent again. */
            DELETE FROM company
             WHERE company_id = company_id_in;

         ELSIF error_code = -2291
         THEN
            /* Parent key not found. */
            DBMS_OUTPUT.PUTLINE
               (' Invalid company ID: '||TO_CHAR (company_id_in));
         ELSE
            /* This is like a WHEN OTHERS inside a WHEN OTHERS! */
            DBMS_OUTPUT.PUTLINE
               (' Error deleting company, error: '||error_msg);
         END IF;
```

```
        END; -- End of anonymous block.

    END delete_company;
```

Continuing Past Exceptions

When an exception is raised in a PL/SQL block, normal execution is halted and control is transferred to the exception section. "You can never go home again," and you can never return to the execution section once an exception is raised in that block. In some cases, however, the ability to continue past exceptions is exactly the desired behavior.

Consider the following scenario: I need to write a procedure which performs a series of DML statements against a variety of tables (delete from one table, update another, insert into a final table). My first pass at writing this procedure might produce code like the following:

```
PROCEDURE change_data IS
BEGIN
    DELETE FROM employee WHERE ... ;
    UPDATE company SET ... ;
    INSERT INTO company_history SELECT * FROM company WHERE ... ;
END;
```

This procedure certainly contains all the appropriate DML statements. But one of the requirements for this program is that, in spite of the fact that these statements are executed in sequence, they are logically independent of each other. In other words, even if the delete fails, I want to go on and perform the update and insert.

With the current version of change_data, I cannot make sure that all three DML statements will at least be attempted. If an exception is raised from the DELETE, for example, then the entire program's execution will halt and control will be passed to the exception section (if there is one). The remaining SQL statements will not be executed.

How can I get the exception to be raised and handled without terminating the program as a whole? The solution is to place the DELETE within its own PL/SQL block. Consider this next version of the change_data program:

```
PROCEDURE change_data IS
BEGIN
    BEGIN
        DELETE FROM employee WHERE ... ;
    EXCEPTION
        WHEN OTHERS THEN NULL;
    END;

    BEGIN
        UPDATE company SET ... ;
    EXCEPTION
```

```
        WHEN OTHERS THEN NULL;
    END;

    BEGIN
        INSERT INTO company_history SELECT * FROM company WHERE ... ;
    EXCEPTION
        WHEN OTHERS THEN NULL;
    END;
END;
```

With this new format, if the DELETE raises an exception, control is immediately passed to the exception section. But now what a difference! Because the DELETE statement is in its own block, it has its own exception section. The WHEN OTHERS clause in that section smoothly handles the error by doing nothing. Control is then passed out of the DELETE's block and back to the enclosing change_data procedure.

Execution in this enclosing block then continues to the next statement in the procedure. A new anonymous block is then entered for the UPDATE statement. If the UPDATE statement fails, the WHEN OTHERS in the UPDATE's own exception section traps the problem and returns control to change_data, which blithely moves on to the INSERT statement (contained in its very own block).

Figure 8-8 shows this process for two sequential DELETE statements.

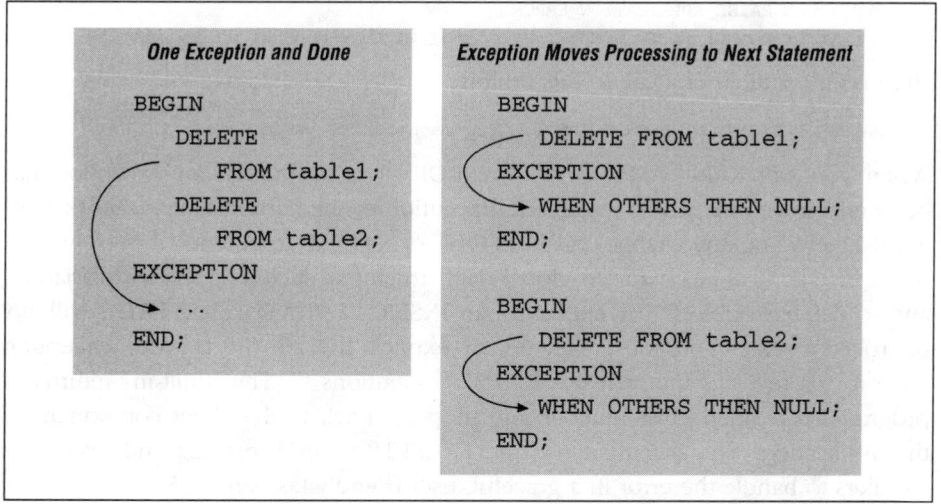

Figure 8-8. Sequential DELETEs, using two different approaches to scope

To summarize: a raised exception will always be handled in the current block—if there is a matching handler present. You can always create a "virtual block" around any statement(s) by prefacing it with a BEGIN and following it with an EXCEPTION section and an END statement. So you can control the scope of failure caused by an exception by establishing "buffers" of anonymous blocks in your code.

You can also take this strategy a step further and move the code you want to isolate into its own procedures or functions. These named PL/SQL blocks may also, of course, have their own exception sections and will offer the same protection from total failure. The advantage of using procedures and functions is that you hide all the BEGIN-EXCEPTION-END statements from the mainline program. The program is then easier to read, understand, and maintain.

Client-Server Error Communication

Oracle provides the RAISE_APPLICATION_ERROR procedure to communicate application-specific errors from the server side (usually a database trigger) to the client-side application. This built-in procedure is the only mechanism available for communicating a server-side, programmer-defined exception to the client side in such a way that the client process can handle the exception.

Using RAISE_APPLICATION_ERROR

Oracle provides the RAISE_APPLICATION_ERROR procedure to facilitate client-server error communication. The header for this procedure is shown below:

```
PROCEDURE RAISE_APPLICATION_ERROR
    (error_number_in IN NUMBER, error_msg_in IN VARCHAR2)
```

Here is an example of a call to this built-in:

```
RAISE_APPLICATION_ERROR (-20001, 'You cannot hire babies!');
```

When you call RAISE_APPLICATION_ERROR, it is as though an exception has been raised with the RAISE statement. Execution of the current PL/SQL block halts immediately, and any changes made to OUT or IN OUT arguments (if present) will be reversed. Changes made to global data structures, such as packaged variables, and to database objects (by executing an INSERT, UPDATE, or DELETE) will *not* be rolled back. You must execute an explicit ROLLBACK in your exception section to reverse the effect of DML operations. The built-in returns a programmer-defined error number and message back to the client component of the application. You can then use the EXCEPTION_INIT pragma and exception handlers to handle the error in a graceful, user-friendly fashion.

The error number you specify must be between −20000 and −20999 so you do not conflict with any Oracle error numbers.

The error message can be up to 2K bytes in length; if it is longer, it will not abort the call to RAISE_APPLICATION_ERROR; the procedure will simply truncate anything beyond the 2K.

The exception handler architecture, combined with RAISE_APPLICATION_ERROR and the On-Error trigger, allows your front-end application to rely on business rules embedded in the database to perform validation and communicate problems to the user. When you make use of RAISE_APPLICATION_ERROR, however, it is entirely up to you to manage the error numbers and messages. This can get tricky and messy. To help manage your error codes and provide a consistent interface with which developers can handle server errors, you might consider building a package.

RAISE_APPLICATION_ERROR in a database trigger

Suppose you need to implement a database trigger which stops records from being inserted into the database if the person is less than 18 years old. The code for this trigger would look like this:

```
CREATE OR REPLACE TRIGGER minimum_age_check
BEFORE INSERT ON employee
FOR EACH ROW
BEGIN
    IF ADD_MONTHS (:new.birth_date, 18*12) > SYSDATE
    THEN
        RAISE_APPLICATION_ERROR
            (-20001, 'Employees must at least eighteen years of age.');
    END IF;
END;
```

On the client side, I can write a program like the following to detect and handle this exception:

```
DECLARE
    /* Declare the exception. */
    no_babies_allowed EXCEPTION;

    /* Associate the name with the error number used in the trigger. */
    PRAGMA EXCEPTION_INIT (no_babies_allowed, -20001);

BEGIN
    /* Attempt to insert the employee. */
    INSERT INTO employee ... ;

EXCEPTION

    /* Handle the server-side exception. */
    WHEN no_babies_allowed
    THEN
        /*
        || SQLERRM will return the message passed into the
        || RAISE_APPLICATION_ERROR built-in.
        */
        DBMS_OUTPUT.PUT_LINE (SQLERRM);

END;
```

NO_DATA_FOUND: *Multipurpose Exception*

The NO_DATA_FOUND exception is raised under three different circumstances:

- An implicit query returns no data.

- You attempt to reference a row in a PL/SQL table which has not been defined. (PL/SQL tables are covered in Chapter 10, *PL/SQL Tables.*)

- You attempt to read past the end of an operating system file (using TEXT_IO in the Oracle Developer 2000 environment or UTL_FILE in PL/SQL Release 2.3).

This overlapping use of the same exception could cause some confusion and difficulty in your program. Suppose that in a single PL/SQL block I query from an implicit cursor and also make references to a PL/SQL table's rows. The NO_DATA_FOUND exception could be raised from either source, but the actual problem that caused the exception would be very different: bad data in the database (raised by the implicit cursor) versus an illegal memory reference (raised by the table access).

I want to be able to distinguish between the two situations. I can accomplish this by nesting the SELECT statement (the implicit cursor) inside its own PL/SQL block and thus trapping the NO_DATA_FOUND exception distinct from the PL/SQL table exception.

In the version of company_name shown in the following example, I have added a parameter to specify two types of access: from database (access type = DBMS) or from a PL/SQL table (access type = MEMORY). I want to check for NO_DATA_FOUND for each particular instance:

```
FUNCTION company_name
    (id_in IN NUMBER, access_type_in IN VARCHAR2)
RETURN VARCHAR2
IS
    /* Return value of the function */
    return_value VARCHAR2 (60);

    /* My own exception - used to represent bad data NO_DATA_FOUND. */
    bad_data_in_select EXCEPTION;

BEGIN
    /* Retrieve company name from the database */
    IF access_type_in = 'DBMS'
    THEN
        /* Place the SELECT inside its own BEGIN-END. */
        BEGIN
            SELECT name INTO return_value
              FROM company
             WHERE company_id = id_in;
            RETURN return_value;
```

```
                  /* Now it can have its OWN exception section too ! */
               EXCEPTION
                  /* This NO_DATA_FOUND is only from the SELECT. */
                  WHEN NO_DATA_FOUND
                  THEN
                     /*
                     || Raise my exception to propagate to
                     || the main body of the function.
                     */
                     RAISE bad_data_in_select;
            END;

         /* Retrieve company name from an in-memory PL/SQL table */
         ELSIF access_type_in = 'MEMORY'
         THEN
            /*
            || Direct access from table. If this ID is not defined
            || then the NO_DATA_FOUND exception is raised.
            */
            RETURN company_name_table (id_in);
         END IF;
      EXCEPTION
         /*
         || This exception occurs only when NO_DATA_FOUND was raised by
         || the implicit cursor inside its own BEGIN-END.
         */
         WHEN bad_data_in_select
         THEN
            DBMS_OUTPUT.PUT_LINE
               (' Unable to locate company in database!');
         /*
         || This exception occurs only when I have not previously placed
         || the company name for company id id_in in the table.
         */
         WHEN NO_DATA_FOUND
         THEN
            DBMS_OUTPUT.PUT_LINE
               (' Unable to locate company in memorized table!');
      END;
```

You can see how the scoping rules for exceptions provide a great deal of flexibility in managing the impact of exceptions. Whenever you want to isolate the
effect of a raised exception, just nest the statements inside their own BEGIN-END,
give them their own exception section, and then decide what you want to do
when the problem occurs. You are guaranteed to trap it there first.

Exception Handler as IF Statement

I pointed out earlier in this chapter the similarity between the CASE structure of
the exception section and the IF statement. Now let's draw on this similarity to
implement an interesting kind of exception handler. You can also use nested

the exception section. The RAISE statement, in other words, shifts the focus of the program from normal execution to "error handling mode." Both from the standpoint of code readability and also of maintenance, you should never use the RAISE statement as a substitute for a control structure, be it a GOTO or an IF statement.

If you have not tried to use RAISE in this way, you might think that I am building up a straw man in order to knock it down. Would that it were so. Just in the process of writing this book, I ran across several examples of this abuse of exception handling. Check out, for example, the function description for GET_GROUP_CHAR_CELL in Oracle Corporation's *Oracle Forms Reference Volume 1*. It offers a function called Is_Value_In_List, which returns the row number of the value if it is found in the record group, as an example of a way to use GET_GROUP_CHAR_CELL.

The central logic of Is_Value_In_List is shown in the following example. The function contains three different RAISE statements—all of which raise the exit_function exception:

```
1   FUNCTION Is_Value_In_List
2      (value VARCHAR2, rg_name VARCHAR2, rg_column VARCHAR2)
3      RETURN NUMBER
4   IS
5      Exit_Function EXCEPTION;
6   BEGIN
7      If bad-inputs THEN
8         RAISE Exit_Function;
9      END IF;
10
11     LOOP-through-record-group
12        IF match-found
13           RAISE Return_Value;
14        END IF;
15     END LOOP;
16
17     RAISE Exit_Function;
18
19  EXCEPTION
20     WHEN Return_Value THEN
21        RETURN row#;
22
23     WHEN Exit_Function THEN
24        RETURN 0;
25  END;
```

The first RAISE on line 8 is an appropriate use of an exception because we have an invalid data structure. The function should bail out.

The second RAISE on line 13 is, however, less justifiable. This RAISE is used to end the program and return the row in which the match was found. An exception is, in this case, used for successful completion.

Exception Handling—Quick Facts and Tips

Here are some facts and tips to remember about exception handling:

- The exception section of a PL/SQL block only handles exceptions raised in the execution section of that block.

- An exception raised in the declaration section of a PL/SQL block is handled by the exception section of the enclosing block, if it exists.

- An exception raised in the exception section of a PL/SQL block is handled by the exception section of the enclosing block, if it exists.

- Use WHEN OTHERS when you want to trap and handle all exceptions in a PL/SQL block.

- Once an exception is raised, the block's execution section is terminated and control is transferred to the exception section. You cannot return to that execution section after the exception is raised.

- After an exception is handled, the next executable statement in the enclosing block is executed.

- To handle a specific exception, it must have a name. You declare exceptions to give them names.

- Once you have handled an exception, normal program execution continues. You are no longer in an "exception" situation.

The third RAISE on line 17 is also questionable. This RAISE is the very last statement of the function. Now, to my mind, the last line of a function should be a RETURN statement. The whole point of the function, after all, is to return a value. In this case, however, the last line is an exception, because the author has structured the code so that if I got this far, I have not found a match. So raise the exception, right? Wrong.

"Row-not-found" is not an exception from the standpoint of the function. That condition should be considered one of the valid return values of a function that asks "Is value in list?" This function should be restructured so that the exception is raised only when there is a problem.

From the perspective of structured exception handling in PL/SQL, this function suffered from several weaknesses:

Poorly named exceptions

The exception names exit_function and return_value describe actions, rather than error conditions. The name of an exception should describe the error which took place.

Exceptions for valid outcomes

By using these "action" names, the developers are actually being very open about how they are manipulating the exception handler. They say, "I use exceptions to implement logic branching." We should say to them, "Don't do it! Use the constructs PL/SQL provides to handle this code in a structured way."

If you encounter either of these conditions in code you are writing or reviewing, take a step back. Examine the logical flow of the program and see how you can use the standard control structures (IF, LOOP, and perhaps even GOTO) to accomplish your task. The result will be much more readable and maintainable code.

9

Records in PL/SQL

Records in PL/SQL programs are very similar in concept and structure to the rows of a database table. A record is a *composite* data structure, which means that it is composed of more than one element or component, each with its own value. The record as a whole does not have value of its own; instead, each individual component or *field* has a value. The record gives you a way to store and access these values as a group.

If you are not familiar with using records in your programs, you might initially find them complicated. When used properly, however, records will greatly simplify your life as a programmer. You will often need to transfer data from the database into PL/SQL structures and then use the procedural language to further massage, change, or display that data. When you use a cursor to read information from the database, for example, you can pass that table's record directly into a single PL/SQL record. When you do this you preserve the relationship between all the attributes from the table.

Record Basics

This section introduces the different types of records and the benefits of using them in your programs.

Different Types of Records

PL/SQL supports three different kinds of records: table-based, cursor-based, and programmer-defined. These different types of records are used in different ways and for different purposes, but all three share the same internal structure: every record is composed of one or more fields. However, the way these fields are work at the level of the company itself, making changes to, deleting, or analyzing the status of a company. In all these cases I am talking about a whole row in the database, not any specific column. The company record hides all that information from me, yet makes it accessible when and if I need it. This orientation brings you closer to viewing your data as a collection of objects with rules applied to those objects.

Leaner, cleaner code

Using records also helps you to write clearer code and less of it. When I use records, I invariably produce programs which have fewer lines of code, are less vulnerable to change, and need fewer comments. Records also cut down on variable sprawl; instead of declaring many individual variables, I declare a single record. This lack of clutter creates aesthetically attractive code which requires fewer resources to maintain.

Guidelines for Using Records

Use of PL/SQL records can have a dramatic impact on your programs, both in initial development and in ongoing maintenance. To ensure that I personally get the most out of record structures, I have set the following guidelines for my development:

- *Create corresponding cursors and records.* Whenever I create a cursor in my programs, I also create a corresponding record (except in the case of cursor FOR loops). I always FETCH into a record, rather than into individual variables. In those few instances when it might involve a little extra work over simply fetching into a single variable, I marvel at the elegance of this approach and compliment myself on my commitment to principle.

- *Create table-based records.* Whenever I need to store table-based data within my programs, I create a new (or use a predefined) table-based record to store that data. I keep my variable use to a minimum and dynamically link my program data structures to my RDBMS data structures with the %ROWTYPE attribute.

- *Pass records as parameters.* Whenever appropriate, I pass records rather than individual variables as parameters in my procedural interfaces. This way, my procedure calls are less likely to change over time, making my code more stable. There is a downside to this technique, however: if a record is passed as an OUT or IN OUT parameter, its field values are saved by the PL/SQL program in case of the need for a rollback. This can use up memory and consume unnecessary CPU cycles.

Referencing a Record and its Fields

The rules you must follow for referencing a record in its entirety or a particular field in the record are the same for all types of records: table, cursor, and programmer-defined.

A record's structure is similar to that of a database table. Where a table has columns, a record has fields. You reference a table's column by its name in a SQL statement, as in:

```
SELECT company_id FROM company;
```

Of course, the fully qualified name of a column is:

```
<table_name>.<column_name>
```

This full name is often required in a SQL statement to avoid ambiguity, as is true in the following statement:

```
SELECT employee.company_id, COUNT(*) total_employees
   FROM company, employee
 WHERE company.company_id = employee.company_id;
```

If I do not preface the name of company_id with the appropriate table name, the SQL compiler will not know to which table that column belongs. The same is true for a record's fields. You reference a record by its name, and you reference a record's field by its full name using dot notation, as in:

```
<record_name>.<field_name>
```

So if I create a record named company_rec, which contains a company_id field, then I would reference this field as follows:

```
company_rec.company_id
```

You must always use the fully qualified name of a field when referencing that field. If you don't, PL/SQL will never be able to determine the "default" record for a field, as it does in a SQL statement.

You do not, on the other hand, need to use dot notation when you reference the record as a whole; you simply provide the name of the record. In the following example, I pass a record as a parameter to a procedure:

```
DECLARE
   TYPE customer_sales_rectype IS RECORD (...);
   customer_rec customer_sales_rectype;
BEGIN
   display_sales_data (customer_rec);
END;
```

I didn't make a single dotted reference to any particular field in the customer record. Instead I declared the record type, used it to create the record, used the

```
DECLARE
    comp_name company.name%TYPE;
    comp_rec   company%ROWTYPE;
BEGIN
    SELECT * FROM company INTO comp_rec
     WHERE company_id = 1004;
```

Notice that I do not need to specify the names of company's columns in either the record declaration or the SELECT statement. I can keep the code very flexible with the table record. If the DBA adds a column to the table, changes the name of a column, or even removes a column, the preceding lines of code will not be affected at all. (You would, however, need to recompile your programs in order to pick up the change in data structure.)

Of course, if my program makes an explicit reference to a modified column, that code would probably have to be changed. With a strong reliance on data manipulation through records, however, you can keep such references to a minimum.

Cursor-Based Records

A cursor-based record, or *cursor record*, is a record whose structure is drawn from the SELECT list of a cursor. (See Chapter 6, *Database Interaction and Cursors*, for more information on cursors.) Each field in the record corresponds to and has the same name as the column or aliased expression in the cursor's query. This relationship is illustrated by Figure 9-1.

The same %ROWTYPE attribute used to declare table records is also used to declare a record for an explicitly declared cursor, as the following example illustrates:

```
DECLARE
    /* Define the cursor */
    CURSOR comp_summary_cur IS
       SELECT C.company_id, name, city
         FROM company C, sales S
         WHERE c.company_id = s.company_id;

    /* Create a record based on that cursor */
    comp_summary_rec comp_summary_cur%ROWTYPE;
BEGIN
```

The general format of the cursor %ROWTYPE declaration is:

```
<record_name> <cursor_name>%ROWTYPE;
```

where <record_name> is the name of the record and <cursor_name> is the name of the cursor upon which the record is based. This cursor must have been previously defined, in the same declaration section as the record, in an enclosing block, or in a package.

Choosing Columns for a Cursor Record

You could declare a cursor record with the same syntax as a table record, but you don't have to match a table's structure. A SELECT statement creates a "virtual table" with columns and expressions as the list of columns. A record based on that SELECT statement allows you to represent a row from this virtual table in exactly the same fashion as a true table record. The big difference is that I get to determine the fields in the record, as well as the names for those fields. Through the cursor you can, therefore, create special-purpose records tailored to a particular program and need.

The query for a cursor can contain all or only some of the columns from one or more tables. A cursor can also contain expressions or virtual columns in its select list. In addition, you can provide aliases for the columns and expressions in the select list of a cursor. These aliases effectively rename the fields in the cursor record.

In the following example I create a cursor against the rain forest history table for all records showing a greater than average loss of species in 1994. Then, for each record found, I execute the publicize_loss procedure to call attention to the problem and execute project_further_damage to come up with an analysis of future losses:

```
DECLARE
   /*
   || Create a cursor and rename the columns to give them a more
   || specific meaning for this particular cursor and block of code.
   */
   CURSOR high_losses_cur IS
      SELECT country_code   dying_country_cd,
             size_in_acres  shrinking_plot,
             species_lost   above_avg_loss
        FROM rain_forest_history
       WHERE species_lost >
                (SELECT AVG (species_lost)
                   FROM rain_forest_history
                  WHERE TO_CHAR (analysis_date, 'YYYY') = '1994');

   /* Define the record for this cursor */
   high_losses_rec high_losses_cur%ROWTYPE;
BEGIN
   OPEN high_losses_cur;
   LOOP
      FETCH high_losses_cur INTO high_losses_rec;
      EXIT WHEN high_losses_cur%NOTFOUND;
      /*
      || Now when I reference one of the record's fields, I use the
      || name I gave that field in the cursor, not the original column
      || name from the table.
      */
```

```
            publicize_loss (high_losses_rec.dying_country_cd);
            project_further_damage (high_losses_rec.shrinking_plot);
      END LOOP;
      CLOSE high_losses_cur;
   END;
```

Setting the Record's Column Names

The column aliases change the names of the fields in the record. In the above example, the customized column names are more descriptive of the matter at hand than the standard column names; the code becomes more readable as a result.

A cursor's query can also include calculated values or expressions; in those cases, you must provide an alias for that calculated value if you want to access it through a record. Otherwise, there is no way for PL/SQL to create a named field for that value in the record—and that name is your handle to the data. Suppose, for example, I have a parameterized cursor and record defined as follows:

```
CURSOR comp_performance_cur (id_in IN NUMBER) IS
   SELECT name, SUM (order_amount)
     FROM company
    WHERE company_id = id_in;
comp_performance_rec comp_performance_cur%ROWTYPE;
```

I can refer to the company name with standard dot notation:

```
IF comp_performance_rec.name = 'ACME' THEN ...
```

But how can I refer to the sum of the order_amount values? I need to provide a name for this calculated column, as shown below:

```
CURSOR comp_performance_cur (id_in IN NUMBER)
IS
   SELECT name, SUM (order_amount) tot_sales
     FROM company
    WHERE company_id = id_in;
comp_performance_rec comp_performance_cur%ROWTYPE;
```

I can now refer to the sum of the order_amount values as follows:

```
IF comp_performance_rec.tot_sales > 10000 THEN ...
```

NOTE   Even though the same %ROWTYPE attribute is used in creating
            both table and cursor records and the declarations themselves
            look very similar, the record created from a table has a different record
            type from the record created from a cursor. Records of different
            types are restricted in how they can interact, a topic we will explore
            in the next section.

Programmer-Defined Records

Now you know how to create a record with the same structure as a table or a cursor. These are certainly very useful constructs in a programming language designed to interface with the Oracle RDBMS. Yet do these kinds of records cover all of our needs for composite data structures?

What if I want to create a record that has nothing to do with either a table or a cursor? What if I want to create a record whose structure is derived from several different tables and views? Should I really have to create a "dummy" cursor just so I can end up with a record of the desired structure? For just these kinds of situations, PL/SQL offers programmer-defined records, declared with the TYPE...RECORD statement.[*]

With the programmer-defined record, you have complete control over the number, names, and datatypes of fields in the record.

To declare a programmer-defined record, you must perform two distinct steps:

1. Declare or define a record TYPE containing the structure you want in your record.

2. Use this record TYPE as the basis for declarations of your own actual records having that structure.

Declaring Programmer-Defined Record TYPEs

You declare a record type with the record TYPE statement. The TYPE statement specifies the name of the new record structure, and the components or fields which make up that record.

The general syntax of the record TYPE definition is:

```
TYPE <type_name> IS RECORD
   (<field_name1> <datatype1>,
    <field_name2> <datatype2>,
    ...
    <field_nameN> <datatypeN>
    );
```

where <field_nameN> is the name of the Nth field in the record and <datatypeN> is the datatype of that Nth field. The datatype of a record's field can be any of the following:

- Pre-defined datatype (VARCHAR2, NUMBER, etc.)

- Programmer-defined subtype (PL/SQL Release 2.1 and above)

---

[*] Programmer-defined records are supported—but undocumented—in PL/SQL Release 1.1.

```
        FROM customer
       WHERE sold_on BETWEEN < ADD_MONTHS (SYSDATE, -3);
   cust_sales_rec cust_sales_cur%ROWTYPE;

BEGIN
   /* Move values directly into record by fetching from cursor */

   OPEN cust_sales_cur;
   FETCH cust_sales_cur INTO cust_sales_rec;

   /* or fetch values from the select list into individual fields. */

   OPEN cust_sales_cur;
   FETCH cust_sales_cur
      INTO cust_sales_rec.customer_id,
           cust_sales_rec.customer_name,
           cust_sales_rec.total_sales;
```

If you FETCH INTO the record without specifying the fields, you must be sure that the structure of the cursor's select list (columns or expressions) matches that of the record.

Aggregate Assignment

In this last and most powerful approach to record assignments, I change all the values of the record once, through an aggregate assignment or assignment of the group. When you SELECT INTO the entire record without listing its individual fields, you perform a type of aggregate assignment. But you can also change the values of every field in a record simultaneously with the assignment operator (:=). In the following example I declare two different rain_forest_history records and then set the current history information to the previous history record:

```
DECLARE
   prev_rain_forest_rec rain_forest_history%ROWTYPE;
   curr_rain_forest_rec rain_forest_history%ROWTYPE;
BEGIN
   ... initialize previous year rain forest data ...

   -- Transfer data from previous to current records.
   curr_rain_forest_rec := prev_rain_forest_rec;
```

The result of this aggregate assignment is that the value of each field in the current record is set to the value of the corresponding field record in the previous record. I could also have accomplished this with individual direct assignments from the previous to current records. This would require four separate assignments and lots of typing:

```
curr_rain_forest_rec.country_code := prev_rain_forest_rec.country_code;
curr_rain_forest_rec.analysis_date := prev_rain_forest_rec.analysis_date;
curr_rain_forest_rec.size_in_acres := prev_rain_forest_rec.size_in_acres;
curr_rain_forest_rec.species_lost := prev_rain_forest_rec.species_lost;
```

Which of these two types of assignments would you rather code? Which would you rather have to maintain?

I was able to perform this aggregate assignment because both of the records were based on the same rowtype. If the records are not compatible in this way, your assignment will not compile.

The next section on record types and record compatibility explores the restrictions on use of aggregate assignments and other record operations.

Record Types and Record Compatibility

As we have discussed, PL/SQL supports three types of records: table-based, cursor-based, and programmer-defined. A record is defined by its name, its type, and its structure. Two records can have the same structure but be of a different type. PL/SQL places restrictions on certain operations between different record types. This section explains these restrictions based on the records declared below:

- The table structure against which all the different types of records will be declared:

```
CREATE TABLE cust_sales_roundup
      (customer_id NUMBER (5),
       customer_name VARCHAR2 (100),
       total_sales NUMBER (15,2)
      );
```

- The table-based record:

```
cust_sales_roundup_rec cust_sales_roundup%ROWTYPE;
```

- The cursor-based record:

```
CURSOR cust_sales_cur IS SELECT * FROM cust_sales_roundup;
cust_sales_rec cust_sales_cur%ROWTYPE;
```

- The programmer-defined record:

```
TYPE customer_sales_rectype IS RECORD
   (customer_id NUMBER (5),
    customer_name customer.name%TYPE,
    total_sales NUMBER (15,2)
   );
top_customer_rec  customer_sales_rectype;
```

- A "manual" record: a collection of individual variables which the programmer can treat as a group by always making changes to and referring to all variables together:

```
v_customer_id NUMBER (5);
v_customer_name customer_name%TYPE;
v_total_sales NUMBER (15,2);
```

All three PL/SQL records defined above (cust_sales_roundup_rec, cust_sales_rec, and top_customer_rec) and the "manual" record have exactly the same structure. Each, however, is of a different type. Records of different types are incompatible with each other at the record level. As a result, you can't perform certain kinds of operations between them.

Assignment Restrictions

Using the previously defined records, the following sections describe the various restrictions you will encounter due to incompatible record types.

Manual records

You cannot assign a manual record to a real record of any type, and vice versa. If you want to assign individual variables to a record, or assign values in fields to individual variables, you must execute a separate assignment for each field in the record:

```
top_customer_rec.customer_id := v_customer_id;
top_customer_rec.customer_name := v_customer_name;
top_customer_rec.total_sales := v_total_sales;
```

Records of the same type

You can perform aggregate assignments only between records of the same type and same source. All of the aggregate assignments you saw in previous examples were valid because both the source and target records in the assignment were based on the same table, cursor, or TYPE statement.

The two assignments below are invalid and will fail because the record types do not match:

```
cust_sales_roundup_rec := top_customer_rec; /* Incompatible! */
cust_sales_rec := cust_sales_roundup_rec ; /* Incompatible! */
```

Even when both records in an aggregate assignment are the same type and same structure, the assignment can fail. Your assignment must, in addition, conform to these rules:

- Both cursor-based records in an aggregate assignment must be based on the same cursor.

- Both table-based records in an aggregate assignment must be based on the same table.

- Both programmer-defined records in an aggregate assignment must be based on the same TYPE...RECORD statement.

Setting records to NULL

You cannot "null out" a record with a record-level or aggregate assignment. The following syntax would be a convenient shorthand for "set my record to NULL." However, this statement will not compile:

```
comp_sales_rec := NULL; /* Invalid syntax */
```

Unfortunately, NULL is never interpreted by PL/SQL to mean "NULL record which automatically matches the structure of the record it is assigned to."

The NULL value is always treated as a scalar value. A NULL is not of the same record type as any kind of record so the aggregate assignment is not valid. You can use NULL in an assignment to set a single field of a record to NULL, but you cannot use it to set all of the fields of a record to NULL.

To set all fields of a record to NULL, perform a separate assignment to each field, as follows:

```
top_customer_rec.customer_id := NULL;
top_customer_rec.customer_name := NULL;
top_customer_rec.total_sales := NULL;
```

Record Initialization

When you declare a scalar variable (a variable with a scalar or noncomposite datatype), you can provide a default or initial value for that variable. In the following example, I declare the total_sales variable and initialize it to zero using both the DEFAULT syntax and the assignment operator:

```
total_sales NUMBER (15,2) := 0;
```

As you might expect based on the aggregate assignment discussed above, you can initialize a table or cursor record at the time of declaration only with another record of the same type and source.

If you want to initialize a record at the time of its declaration, you must use a compatible record to the right of the assignment operator (:=) or DEFAULT phrase. The following two examples show such initializations:

- Declare a local record with the same type and structure as the parameter and then set the default value of that local record to the incoming record:

```
PROCEDURE compare_companies
   (prev_company_rec IN company%ROWTYPE)
IS
   curr_company_rec company%ROWTYPE := prev_company_rec;
BEGIN
   ...
END;
```

Dot Notation with Nested Records

Although I still use the dot notation to refer to a field with nested records, now I might have to refer to a field which is nested several layers deep inside the structure. To do this I must include an extra dot for each nested record structure. Suppose that I have a record with two levels of nested records:

```
DECLARE
    TYPE level3_rectype IS RECORD (textline VARCHAR2(2000));
    TYPE level2_rectype IS RECORD (paragraph level3_rectype);
    TYPE level1_rectype IS RECORD (story level2_rectype);
    level1_rec level1_rectype;
```

Then the fully qualified name for the textline variable is:

```
level1_rec.story.paragraph.textline
```

Assignments with nested records follow the same rules as those for "flat" records. The following statement, for example, sets the fax phone number's area code to the home phone number's area code:

```
auth_rep_info_rec.fax_phone#.area_code :=
    auth_rep_info_rec.home_phone#.area_code;
```

Aggregate Assignments of Nested Records

I can also perform an aggregate assignment of one nested record to another. To set the fax number equal to the home phone number, I simply execute the following:

```
auth_rep_info_rec.fax_phone# := auth_rep_info_rec.home_phone#;
```

This is possible because both the fax_phone# and the home_phone# records have the same type, namely the phone_rectype. You can even perform this kind of assignment between records which are nested within different enclosing records, as the following example illustrates:

```
DECLARE
    /* Using the phone_rectype defined earlier in chapter... */
    TYPE contact_set_rectype IS RECORD
        (day_phone# phone_rectype,
         eve_phone# phone_rectype,
         fax_phone# phone_rectype,
         cell_phone# phone_rectype
        );
    TYPE emerg_contacts_rectype IS RECORD
        (emerg1_phone# phone_rectype,
         emerg2_phone# phone_rectype
        );
    auth_rep_info_rec contact_set_rectype;
    in_an_emergency_rec emerg_contacts_rectype;
```

```
    BEGIN
        in_an_emergency_rec.emerg1_phone# :=
            auth_rep_info_rec.day_phone#;
    END;
```

The emerg1_phone# and the day_phone# have the same record type: phone_rectype. So even though the enclosing records auth_rep_info_rec and in_an_emergency_rec have different record types, the nested record assignment works. A direct aggregate assignment between the two enclosing records as shown below would fail to compile:

```
    in_an_emergency_rec := auth_rep_info_rec; -- This would fail!
```

Denormalizing Program Data with Nested Records

At the beginning of this chapter I mentioned that nested records let you carry over the normalized data structures of your database to the memory structures in your programs. Using nested records I was able to avoid hardcoding the internal structure of a phone number multiple times in my contact set record. Oddly enough, you can also use nested records to take your normalized data from the database and denormalize that data inside your program so it is easier to manipulate.

Well-designed relational data structures are usually normalized, which means (roughly) that you eliminate redundant information and repeating groups. Consider a company entity. It might have four different kinds of addresses: receiving, shipping, accounts payable, and customer relations. Each address is made up of seven attributes or columns: address lines one through four, city, state, and zip code. Rather than burden the company table with 28 (7 × 4) columns for all four addresses, you would create a separate table of addresses with a foreign key back to the company table. By creating a separate table for company addresses, you also can easily add another kind of address for a company at a later date.

The denormalized nature of our world

While normalized data and foreign keys make sense enough inside a database, these concepts can be very confusing to users and actually present barriers to efficient and straightforward manipulation of the data within your programs. There is a simple reason for this seeming contradiction: real objects in the world are not normalized. Sure, in the most general sense a company can have four or more addresses. But in the real world, a particular company has only one or two addresses. And those addresses are not separate in any way from the company. They are a part of the definition of that company. Therefore, when data is in the database it is normalized, but whenever it is presented to or entered by the user it

10

PL/SQL Tables

A PL/SQL table is a one-dimensional, unbounded, sparse collection of homogeneous elements, indexed by integers. In technical terms, it is like an array; it is like a SQL table; yet it is not precisely the same as either of those data structures. This chapter explains these characteristics of the PL/SQL table in detail, so that you will understand the differences between PL/SQL tables and traditional arrays and SQL tables, and so that you will know how to use PL/SQL tables in your programs.

Like PL/SQL records, PL/SQL tables are composite data structures. Figure 10-1 shows a PL/SQL table composed of a single column named emp_name, with names saved to rows 100, 225, 226, 300, and 340.

Let's take a look at an example and then explore the characteristics of a table. The following procedure accepts a name and a row and assigns that name to the corresponding row in the PL/SQL table:

```
1   PROCEDURE set_name (name_in IN VARCHAR2, row_in in INTEGER)
2   IS
3
4      TYPE string_tabletype IS
5         TABLE OF VARCHAR2(30) INDEXED BY BINARY_INTEGER;
```

Row #	Emp_Name
100	Smith
225	Feuerstein
226	Silva
300	Russell
340	Ziemba

Figure 10-1. The single-column, one-dimensional PL/SQL table

```
 6
 7     company_name_table string_tabletype;
 8
 9  BEGIN
10     company_name_table (row_in) := name_in;
11  END;
```

The TYPE statement in lines 4–5 defines the structure of a PL/SQL table: a collection of strings with a maximum length of 30 characters. The INDEXED BY BINARY_INTEGER clause defines the integer key for the data structure. The table declaration in line 7 declares a specific PL/SQL table based on that table structure. In line 10, traditional array syntax is used to assign a string to a specific row in that PL/SQL table.

PL/SQL Tables and Other Collections

A PL/SQL table is one type of *collection* structure and, until Oracle8, it was the only one supported by PL/SQL. With Oracle8, there are now two additional types. This section briefly describes those types and includes information you need to know about using PL/SQL tables and other collections with different versions of PL/SQL. For detailed information about the new collection types, see Chapter 19, *Nested Tables and VARRAYs*.

PL/SQL Tables

PL/SQL tables are available only in releases of PL/SQL Version 2. PL/SQL tables reside in the private PL/SQL area of the Oracle Server database instance; they are not available as client-side structures at this time. As a result, you cannot declare and manipulate PL/SQL tables in your Oracle Developer/2000 environment.

You can, on the other hand, build stored procedures and packages which work with PL/SQL tables, but hide these structures behind their interface. You can then call this stored code from within Oracle Developer/2000 to take advantage of Version 2 features like PL/SQL tables.

Note that PL/SQL Release 2.3 offers several substantial enhancements to the PL/SQL tables, covered in the section called "PL/SQL Table Enhancements in PL/SQL Release 2.3" If you are using PL/SQL Release 2.3 (available with Oracle7 Server Release 7.3), make sure you read through this section and make use of these advanced features. All topics covered earlier in the chapter assume PL/SQL Release 2.2 or earlier and do not take advantage of these new features. (Where applicable, I will point you to the relevant Release 2.3 features.)

Nested Tables and VARRAYs

Like PL/SQL tables, the two collection types introduced under Oracle8—nested tables and variable arrays (VARRAYs)—can be used in PL/SQL programs. But these collection types offer something new: they can be used as the datatypes of fields in conventional tables and attributes of objects.

Both nested tables and VARRAYs can be used in PL/SQL and in the database (for example, as a column). They differ in certain ways, though, and you will find that each has pros and cons in certain situations, which I discuss in Chapter 19.

Characteristics of PL/SQL Tables

A definition worth repeating: A PL/SQL table is a one-dimensional, unbounded, sparse collection of homogenous elements, indexed by integers.

Let's examine each of these characteristics in detail:

One-dimensional
> A PL/SQL table can have only one column. It is, in this way, similar to a one-dimensional array. You cannot define a PL/SQL table so that it can be referenced as follows:
>
> `my_table (10, 44)`
>
> This is a two-dimensional structure and not currently supported.

Unbounded or Unconstrained
> There is no predefined limit to the number of rows in a PL/SQL table. The PL/SQL table grows dynamically as you add more rows to the table. The PL/SQL table is, in this way, very different from an array.
>
> Related to this definition, no rows for PL/SQL tables are allocated for this structure when it is defined.

Sparse

In a PL/SQL table, a row exists in the table only when a value is assigned to that row. Rows do not have to be defined sequentially. Instead you can assign a value to any row in the table. So row 15 could have a value of 'Fox' and row 15446 a value of 'Red', with no other rows defined in between.

In contrast, an array is a *dense* data structure. When you declare an array, all cells in the array are allocated in memory and are ready to use.

Homogeneous elements

Because a PL/SQL table can have only a single column, all rows in a PL/SQL table contain values of the same datatype. It is, therefore, homogeneous.

With PL/SQL Release 2.3, you can have PL/SQL tables of records. The resulting table is still, however, homogeneous. Each row simply contains the same set of columns.

Indexed by integers

PL/SQL tables currently support a single indexing mode: by BINARY_INTEGER. This number acts as the "primary key" of the PL/SQL table. The range of a BINARY_INTEGER is from $-2^{31}-1$ to $2^{31}-1$, so you have an awful lot of rows with which to work.[*]

Because the row number does not have to be used sequentially and has such enormous range, you can use this integer index in interesting ways. For example, the row number for a PL/SQL table could be the primary key of your company table, so that:

```
company_name (14055)
```

contains the name of the company whose company_id = 14055.

PL/SQL Tables and DML Statements

Tables are PL/SQL constructs. PL/SQL is a linguistic extension of the Oracle SQL language, but it is distinct from SQL. When PL/SQL executes a SQL DML statement (SELECT, INSERT, UPDATE, or DELETE), it actually passes control to the RDBMS or SQL kernel, so the PL/SQL statement containing the DML must conform to the SQL standards. Generally PL/SQL is designed to hide this distinction, but when you work with PL/SQL tables—just as when you work with records (the other PL/SQL composite data structure)—you will have to be aware of the differences between SQL and PL/SQL.

---

[*] Notice that the index of a row in the table can even be negative. In the PL/SQL table, a negative row number is no different from a positive one; it's just another integer. However, there are ways that you, the programmer, can take advantage of differences between positive and negative row numbers in your application. For example, the ps_global package, included on the companion disk, uses rows with positive numbers to store "globals-by-number" and uses negative row values to store "globals-by-name".

The PL/SQL table structure is clearly not a part of the SQL language and standards, in that it employs array-like syntax to access rows in the PL/SQL table. Keep the following restrictions in mind when you work with PL/SQL tables:

- There is no concept of transaction integrity with PL/SQL tables. You cannot commit information to a PL/SQL table or roll back changes from the table.

- You cannot SELECT from PL/SQL tables. There is no way to perform set-at-a-time processing to retrieve data from a PL/SQL table. This is a programmatic construct in a programmatic language. Instead you can use PL/SQL loops to move through the contents of a PL/SQL table, one row at a time.

- You cannot issue DML statements (INSERTs, UPDATEs, and DELETEs) against PL/SQL tables (though PL/SQL Release 2.3 does offer a DELETE operator).

Of course, you can always use the individual rows of a table anywhere in a SQL DML statement where you can use an expression of a compatible type.

In this stage of PL/SQL's evolution, PL/SQL tables remain relatively simple in structure and restricted in usage. You can expect to see rapid progress in the sophistication, performance, and flexibility of this data structure in the coming years, as is evidenced by the enhancements offered in PL/SQL Release 2.3.

Declaring a PL/SQL Table

As with a record, a PL/SQL table is declared in two stages:

- Define a particular PL/SQL table structure (made up of strings, dates, etc.) using the table TYPE statement. The result of this statement is a datatype you can use in declaration statements.

- Declare the actual table based on that table type. The declaration of a PL/SQL table is a specific instance of a generic datatype.

Defining the Table TYPE

The TYPE statement for a PL/SQL table has the following format:

```
TYPE <table_type_name> IS TABLE OF <datatype> [ NOT NULL ]
    INDEX BY BINARY_INTEGER;
```

where <table_type_name> is the name of the table structure you are creating and <datatype> is the datatype of the single column in the table. You can optionally specify that the table be NOT NULL, meaning that every row in the table that has been created must have a value.

You must always specify INDEX BY BINARY_INTEGER at the end of the TYPE...TABLE statement, even though it is the only type of index you can have currently in a PL/SQL table.

PL/SQL uses BINARY_INTEGER indexes because they allow for the fastest retrieval of data. (In this case, the primary key is already in the internal binary format, so it does not have to be converted before it can be used by the runtime environment.)

The rules for the table type name are the same as for any identifier in PL/SQL: the name can be up to 30 characters in length, it must start with a letter, and it can include some special characters such as underscore (_) and dollar sign ($).

The datatype of the table type's column can be any of the following:

Scalar datatype
> Any PL/SQL-supported scalar datatype, such as VARCHAR2, POSITIVE, DATE, or BOOLEAN.

Anchored datatype
> A datatype inferred from a column, previously defined variable, or cursor expression using the %TYPE attribute.

Here are some examples of table type declarations:

```
TYPE company_keys_tabtype IS TABLE OF company.company_id%TYPE NOT NULL
     INDEX BY BINARY_INTEGER;

TYPE reports_requested_tabtype IS TABLE OF VARCHAR2 (100)
     INDEX BY BINARY_INTEGER;
```

NOTE   Prior to PL/SQL Release 2.3, you may not use composite datatypes declaring a PL/SQL table's column. With Release 2.3, you can create PL/SQL tables of records.

Declaring the PL/SQL Table

Once you have created your table type, you can reference that table type to declare the actual table. The general format for a table declaration is:

```
<table_name> <table_type>;
```

where <table_name> is the name of the table and <table_type> is the name of a previously declared table type. In the following example I create a general table type for primary keys in PACKAGE and then use that table type to create two tables of primary keys:

```
PACKAGE company_pkg
IS
    /* Create a generic table type for primary keys */
    TYPE primary_keys_tabtype IS TABLE OF NUMBER NOT NULL
        INDEX BY BINARY_INTEGER;
```

```
/* Declare two tables based on this table type */
company_keys_tab primary_keys_tabtype;
emp_keys_tab primary_keys_tabtype;

END company_pkg;
```

Referencing and Modifying PL/SQL Table Rows

Remember that a row, given the single columnar structure of the PL/SQL table in Version 2, is a scalar value. You refer to a particular row in a PL/SQL table by specifying the name of the table and the primary key value for that row. The syntax is very similar to standard, one-dimensional arrays:

```
<table_name> ( <primary_key_value> )
```

where <table_name> is the name of the table and <primary_key_value> is a literal, variable, or expression whose datatype is compatible with the BINARY_INTEGER datatype. You assign values to a row in a table with the standard assignment operator (:=).

All of the following table references and assignments are valid:

```
company_names_tab (15) := 'Fabricators Anonymous';

company_keys_tab (-2000) := new_company_id;

header_string := 'Sales for ' || company_names_tab (25);
```

Automatic Conversion of Row Number Expressions

PL/SQL will go to great lengths to convert an expression or string to BINARY_INTEGER for use as a row number. Here are some examples:

- Store the string in row 16:
  ```
  requests_table (15.566) := 'Totals by Category';
  ```
- Store the string in row 255:
  ```
  company_keys_table ('25'||'5') := 1000;
  ```
- The expression will be evaluated and used as the row number:
  ```
  keyword_list_table (last_row + 15) := 'ELSE';
  ```

Referencing an Undefined Row

As I've mentioned, a key difference between arrays and PL/SQL tables is that a row in a PL/SQL table does not exist until you assign a value to that row. This makes sense, given the fact that PL/SQL tables are unconstrained in size. In a 3GL program like C or FORTRAN, you specify a maximum size or dimension to an array when you declare it. Once an array is declared, the memory is set aside for all the cells in the array, and you can read from or place a value in any cell within the bounds of the array.

PL/SQL tables, on the other hand, have no predefined number of values, so PL/SQL does not create the memory structure for the rows in the table until you need them. Instead, whenever you assign a value to a row in a PL/SQL table, PL/SQL creates that row.

If, however, you reference a row which does not yet exist, PL/SQL raises the NO_DATA_FOUND exception. (The exception is also raised when an implicit cursor SELECT statement does not return any rows, or when you attempt to read past the end of a file with the UTL_FILE package.)

The following PL/SQL block will cause the NO_DATA_FOUND exception to be raised (and go unhandled) because row 15 has not yet been assigned a value:

```
DECLARE
    new_request NUMBER;
    TYPE request_tabtype IS TABLE OF NUMBER INDEX BY BINARY_INTEGER;
    request_table request_tabtype;
BEGIN
    new_request := request_table (15);
END;
```

If you want to trap the NO_DATA_FOUND exception, then you will need to add the following exception handler to the exception section of the block:

```
EXCEPTION
    WHEN NO_DATA_FOUND
    THEN
        ... take appropriate action ...
END;
```

You pay a stiff penalty for referencing a row in a table that has not been assigned a value. To avoid this exception, you need to keep track of the minimum and maximum row numbers used in a PL/SQL table.

Nonsequential Use of PL/SQL Table

Of course, the idea of using a minimum and maximum row assumes that the rows in the table are used sequentially. That is, you fill row one, then row two, etc. This is a perfectly reasonable way to fill a table's rows; to do this you absolutely must know the value of the row last filled. You are not, however, required to fill rows in this way. You can place a value in any row of the table you wish, regardless of the primary key value of the last row you filled.

The following example illustrates filling a PL/SQL table's rows randomly rather than sequentially:

```
DECLARE
    TYPE countdown_tests_tabtype IS TABLE OF VARCHAR2(20)
        INDEX BY BINARY_INTEGER;
    countdown_test_list countdown_tests_tabtype;
BEGIN
    countdown_test_list (1) := 'All systems go';
    countdown_test_list (43) := 'Internal pressure';
    countdown_test_list (255) := 'Engine inflow';
END;
```

In this situation, the minimum and maximum values do not have much significance.

The ability to randomly place values in a table can come in very handy when the primary key value for the table's row is actually not sequentially derived, but is instead based on data in your application. This use of "intelligent" primary key values is explored in more detail in the section entitled "Data-Smart Row Numbers in PL/SQL Tables" later in this chapter.

Passing PL/SQL Tables as Parameters

You can also pass a PL/SQL table as a parameter in a procedure or function; with this approach you can, in a single call, pass all the values in a table into the module. In the following package specification I define two modules that pass PL/SQL tables as parameters. The send_promos procedure sends a promotional mailing to all the companies in my table. The companies_overdue function returns a table filled with the names of companies that have overdue bills.

```
PACKAGE company_pkg
IS
    TYPE primary_keys_tabtype IS TABLE OF company.company_id%TYPE NOT NULL
        INDEX BY BINARY_INTEGER;
    company_keys_tab primary_keys_tabtype;
    emp_keys_tab primary_keys_tabtype;

    /* Table type and table for company names */
    TYPE company_names_tabtype IS TABLE OF company.name%TYPE
        INDEX BY BINARY_INTEGER;
    company_names_tab company_names_tabtype;

    /* Parameter is a table of company primary keys */
    PROCEDURE send_promos (company_table_in IN primary_keys_tabtype);

    /* Function returns a table of company names */
    FUNCTION companies_overdue (overdue_date_in IN DATE)
        RETURN company_names_tabtype;

    /* Returns company ID for name. */
```

```
      FUNCTION id (name in IN company.name%TYPE)
         RETURN company.company id%TYPE

   END company_pkg;
```

Now that I have a package containing both the table type and the programs referencing those types, I can call these programs. The only tricky part to remember
here is that you must declare a PL/SQL table based on the type before you can
use any of the programs. Here is an example of returning a PL/SQL table as a
function's return value:

```
CREATE OR REPLACE PROCEDURE send_promos_for_overdue_companies
   (date_in IN DATE := SYSDATE)
IS
   v_row PLS_INTEGER;

   /* Declare a PL/SQL table based on the packaged type. */
   cnames company_pkg.company_names_tabtype;
BEGIN
   cnames := company_pkg.companies_overdue (date_in);

   /*
   || In PL/SQL 2.3 I can use navigation methods to traverse.
   || Notice that I do not assume that rows are filled sequentially.
   */
   v_row := cnames.FIRST;
   LOOP
      EXIT WHEN v_row IS NULL;
      DBMS_OUTPUT.PUT_LINE (cnames(v_row));
      v_row := cnames.NEXT (v_row);
   END LOOP;
END;
/
```

Notice that I could also have avoided declaring my own PL/SQL table, cnames, by
using the predefined table in the package:

```
   company_pkg.company_names_tab :=
   company_pkg.companies_overdue (date_in);
```

If I had taken this approach, however, any rows already defined in this "global"
table would have been erased.

Here is an example of calling a procedure, passing a PL/SQL table as an argument
in the parameter list:

```
DECLARE
   v_row PLS_INTEGER;

   /* Table of primary keys for company */
   company_ids company_pkg.primary_keys_tabtype;
BEGIN
   /* Populate the table with names of overdue companies. */
   company_pkg.company_names_tab :=
```

```
       company_pkg.companies_overdue (date_in);

    /* For each company name, look up the ID and pass it to the
    || PL/SQL table of company IDs.
    */
    v_row := company_pkg.company_names_tab.FIRST;
    LOOP
        EXIT WHEN v_row IS NULL;
        company_ids (NVL (company_ids.LAST, 0) + 1) :=
            company_pkg.id(company_pkg.company_name_tab(v_row));
        v_row := company_pkg.company_names_tab.NEXT (v_row);
    END LOOP;

    /* Now send out promotional flyers to those companies. */
    company_pkg.send_promos (company_ids);

    /* Delete all the rows from the company names table. */
    company_pkg.company_names_tab.DELETE;

END company_pkg;
```

Filling the Rows of a PL/SQL Table

You can assign values to rows of a table in several ways:

- Direct assignment

- Iterative assignment

- Aggregate assignment

These methods are described in the following sections.

Direct Assignment

As shown in previous examples, you can simply assign a value to a row with the assignment operator:

```
    countdown_test_list (43) := 'Internal pressure';
    company_names_table (last_name_row) := 'Johnstone Clingers';
```

Direct assignment makes sense when you need to make a change to a specific row. But what do you use when you want to fill a whole set of rows, for example, unloading a whole cursor-full of information from a database table? Here, iterative assignment may be more appropriate.

Iterative Assignment

In order to fill up multiple rows of a table, I recommend taking advantage of a PL/SQL loop. Within the loop you will still perform direct assignments to set the values of each row, but the primary key value will be set by the loop rather than hardcoded into the assignment itself.

In the following example, I use a WHILE loop to fill and then display a PL/SQL date table with the next set of business days, as specified by the ndays_in parameter:

```
/* Filename on companion disk: bizdays.sp */
CREATE OR REPLACE PROCEDURE show_bizdays
    (start_date_in IN DATE := SYSDATE, ndays_in IN INTEGER := 30)
IS
    TYPE date_tabtype IS TABLE OF DATE INDEX BY BINARY_INTEGER;
    bizdays date_tabtype;

    /* The row in the table containing the nth_day */
    nth_day  BINARY_INTEGER := 1;
    v_date DATE := start_date_in;
BEGIN
    /* Loop through the calendar until enough biz days are found */
    WHILE nth_day <= ndays_in
    LOOP
        /* If the day is not on the weekend, add to the table. */
        IF TO_CHAR (v_date, 'DY') NOT IN ('SAT', 'SUN')
        THEN
            bizdays (nth_day) := v_date;
            DBMS_OUTPUT.PUT_LINE (v_date);
            nth_day := nth_day + 1;
        END IF;
        v_date := v_date + 1;
    END LOOP;
END show_bizdays;
/
```

As you can see from this example, using the WHILE loop produces a neat, sequential load of the PL/SQL table.

Aggregate Assignment

Just as you can assign one entire record to another record of the same type and structure, you can perform aggregate assignments with tables as well. In order to transfer the values of one table to another, the datatype of the two tables must be compatible. Beyond that you simply use the assignment operator (:=) to transfer the values of one table to the other. The following example contains an example of an aggregate table assignment:

```
DECLARE
    TYPE name_table IS TABLE OF VARCHAR2(100) INDEX BY BINARY_INTEGER;
    old_names name_table;
    new_names name_table;
BEGIN
    /* Assign values to old_names table */
```

```
     old_names(1) := 'Smith';
     old_names(2) := 'Harrison';

     /* Assign values to new_names table */
     new_names(111) := 'Hanrahan';
     new_names(342) := 'Blimey';

     /* Transfer values from new to old */
     old_names := new_names;

     /* This assignment will raise NO_DATA_FOUND */
     DBMS_OUTPUT.PUT_LINE (old_names (1));
  END;
```

A table-level assignment completely replaces the previously defined rows in the table. In the preceding example, rows 1 and 2 in old_names are defined before the last, aggregate assignment.

After the assignment, only rows 111 and 342 in the old_names table have values.

Clearing the PL/SQL Table

What happens when you are done with a PL/SQL table and want to remove it from memory? If a PL/SQL table is like a table, we should be able to DELETE the rows of that table or DROP it entirely, right? It's a nice idea, but you can't perform a SQL DELETE statement on a PL/SQL table because it is not stored in the database. You also cannot DROP a PL/SQL table.

You can set a single row to NULL with the following kind of assignment:

```
     company_names_table (num_rows) := NULL;
```

But this assignment doesn't actually remove the row or make it undefined; it just sets the value of the row to NULL.

The only way to actually empty a PL/SQL table of all rows is to perform an aggregate assignment with a table that is empty—a table, that is, with no rows defined.

With this approach, for every PL/SQL table you want to be able to empty, you declare a parallel, empty table of the same table type. When you are finished working with your table, simply assign the empty table to the actual table. This will unassign all the rows you have used. The following example demonstrates this technique:

```
DECLARE
     TYPE company_names_tabtype IS TABLE OF company.name%TYPE
        INDEX BY BINARY_INTEGER;
     company_names_tab company_names_tabtype;

     /* Here is the empty table declaration */
     empty_company_names_tab company_names_tabtype;
```

```
BEGIN
    ... set values in company names table ...

    /* The closest you can come to "dropping" a PL/SQL table */
    company_names_tab := empty_company_names_tab;

END;
```

NOTE	PL/SQL Release 2.3 offers a DELETE operator so that you can delete all or some rows of a PL/SQL table.

PL/SQL Table Enhancements in PL/SQL Release 2.3

PL/SQL Release 2.3 offers significantly enhanced functionality for PL/SQL tables. These new features include:

- *Records supported as elements of PL/SQL tables.* Prior to Release 2.3, the element or single column of the PL/SQL table could only be a scalar datatype, such as VARCHAR2 or BOOLEAN or DATE. Release 2.3 allows you to define table types whose element datatype is defined with the %ROWTYPE declaration attribute or is a named RECORD type.

- *New operations on PL/SQL tables.* PL/SQL Release 2.3 offers a set of new built-in functions and procedures which return information about, or modify the contents of, a PL/SQL table. These operations are shown in Table 10-1.

These new features allow you to use PL/SQL tables for a wider range of applications and also manipulate the data in tables in a more natural and efficient manner. You can now create local PL/SQL data structures which mimic precisely the structure of a table stored in the database. You do not have to create separate tables and manage them in parallel to emulate the multiple-column SQL table structure.

You can use the built-ins to obtain PL/SQL table information that previously was unavailable. For example, you can use the COUNT function to determine the number of elements defined in a table. You no longer have to keep track of that number yourself.

Table 10-1. PL/SQL Release 2.3 Built-in Functions and Procedures for Tables

Operator	Description
COUNT	Returns the number of elements currently contained in the PL/SQL table.
DELETE	Deletes one or more elements from the PL/SQL table.

Table 10-1. PL/SQL Release 2.3 Built-in Functions and Procedures for Tables (continued)

Operator	Description
EXISTS	Returns FALSE if a reference to an element at the specified index would raise the NO_DATA_FOUND exception.
FIRST	Returns the smallest index of the PL/SQL table for which an element is defined.
LAST	Returns the greatest index of the PL/SQL table for which an element is defined.
NEXT	Returns the smallest index of the PL/SQL table containing an element which is greater than the specified index.
PRIOR	Returns the greatest index of the PL/SQL table containing an element which is less than the specified index.

These functions and procedures are described in detail later in this chapter.

PL/SQL Tables of Records

To declare a PL/SQL table, you must first declare a PL/SQL table TYPE. The syntax for the TYPE statement is as follows:

```
TYPE <type name> IS TABLE OF <datatype>
    INDEX BY BINARY_INTEGER;
```

With PL/SQL Release 2.3, the <datatype> may be a record type. This record type can be defined using the %ROWTYPE declaration attribute. You can also specify a previously defined record structure defined with the TYPE statement for records.

When you do create a PL/SQL table based on a record structure, that record may only be composed of scalar fields. A nested record type (in which a field in the record is yet another record type) may not be used to define a table type.

The following examples illustrate the different ways to declare table types based on records:

- Declare a PL/SQL table type with same structure as the employee table:

```
TYPE local_emp_table IS TABLE OF employee%ROWTYPE
    INDEX BY BINARY_INTEGER;
```

- Declare a PL/SQL table type to correspond to the data returned by a cursor:

```
CURSOR emp_cur IS SELECT * FROM employee;

TYPE cursor_emp_table IS TABLE OF emp_cur%ROWTYPE
    INDEX BY BINARY_INTEGER;
```

- Declare a PL/SQL table type based on a programmer-defined record:

```
TYPE emp_rectype IS
    RECORD (employee_id INTEGER, emp_name VARCHAR2(60));
```

```
TYPE emp_table IS TABLE OF emp_rectype
   INDEX BY BINARY_INTEGER;
```

Notice that when you use a programmer-defined record type you do *not* append the %ROWTYPE attribute to the record type. That is only done when you are using a table-based or cursor-based record.

Referencing fields of record elements in PL/SQL tables

References to fields of elements of PL/SQL tables which are records have the following syntax:

```
<table name>(<index expression>).<field name>
```

where <table name> is the name of the table, <index expression> is an expression (constant, variable, or computed expression) which evaluates to a number and <field name> is the name of the field in the record used to define the PL/SQL table.

If, for example, you have created a PL/SQL table named emp_tab based on a record structure with a field named emp_name, then the following assignment sets the employee name in the 375th row of the PL/SQL table to SALIMBA:

```
emp_tab(375).emp_name := 'SALIMBA';
```

The index to the table does not have to be a constant. In the following example, the index is calculated:

```
IF names_table (old_name_row + 1).last_name = 'SMITH'
THEN
```

You can define functions which return PL/SQL tables. As a result, you can also reference a field in a PL/SQL table's record with the following syntax:

```
<function name>(<argument list>)(<index expression>).<field name>
```

An example will make it easier to understand this complicated syntax. Suppose that I have defined a function as follows:

```
FUNCTION best_company (year_in IN INTEGER)
   RETURN company_tabtype;
```

where company_tabtype is a PL/SQL table type with a record structure for its element. Then the following call to PUT_LINE displays the name of the company found in the tenth row of the returned table:

```
DBMS_OUTPUT.PUT_LINE
   (best_company(1995)(10).company_name || ' was tenth best!');
```

To make sense of this expression, break it up into its components:

best_company(1995)

     Returns a table, each row of which contains information about a company.

best_company(1995)(10)

Returns the tenth row of that table.

best_company(1995)(10).company_name

Returns the name of the company found in the tenth row of the table.

You can improve the readability of such a statement by separating it as follows:

```
current_company_rec := best_company(1995)(10);

DBMS_OUTPUT.PUT_LINE
    (current_company.company_name || ' was tenth best!')
```

where current_company_rec is a record defined with the same type as the RETURN clause of the best_company function. Now you have two statements where only one is really needed, but the code can be more easily understood and therefore maintained.

Assigning records in PL/SQL tables

You can assign a whole record fetched from the database directly into the row of a PL/SQL table as shown below (where both the cursor and the PL/SQL table use the same company%ROWTYPE row type declaration):

```
FOR company_rec IN company_cur
LOOP
    /* Get last row used and add one. */
    next_row := NVL (company_table.LAST, 0) + 1;

    company_table(next_row) := company_rec;

END LOOP;
```

PL/SQL Table Built-ins

Each of the PL/SQL table built-in procedures and functions provides different information about the referenced PL/SQL table, except for DELETE, which removes rows from the PL/SQL table. The syntax for using the table built-ins for PL/SQL tables is different from the syntax I describe in Part III of this book. It employs a "member method" syntax, common in object-oriented languages such as C++.

To give you a feeling for member-method syntax, consider the LAST function. It returns the greatest index value in use in the PL/SQL table. Using standard function syntax, you might expect to call LAST as follows:

```
IF LAST (company_table) > 10 THEN ... /* Invalid syntax */
```

In other words, you would pass the PL/SQL table as an argument. In contrast, by using the member-method syntax, the LAST function is a method which "belongs to" the object, in this case the PL/SQL table. So the correct syntax for using LAST is:

```
IF company_table.LAST > 10 THEN ... /* Correct syntax */
```

The general syntax for calling these PL/SQL table built-ins is either of the following:

- An operation which takes no arguments:

  ```
  <table name>.<operation>
  ```

- An operation which takes a row index for an argument:

  ```
  <table name>.<operation>(<index number> [, <index_number>])
  ```

The following statement, for example, returns TRUE if the 15th row of the company_tab PL/SQL table is defined:

```
company_tab.EXISTS(15)
```

By using the member-method syntax, Oracle is able to distinguish the PL/SQL table functions such as EXISTS and DELETE from the SQL operations of the same name (which never appear with dot-qualified notation).

The following sections describe each of the table built-ins.

The COUNT function

The COUNT function returns the number of elements currently defined in the PL/SQL table. The specification for the function is:

```
FUNCTION COUNT RETURN INTEGER;
```

You call COUNT as follows:

```
total_rows := emp_table.COUNT;
```

Notice that if the emp_table structure were defined inside a package, then double dot notation would be needed to get the count:

```
total_rows := employee_pkg.emp_table.COUNT;
```

Prior to PL/SQL Release 2.3, the only way to determine this count was to manually keep track of the number of elements defined in the table.

The DELETE procedure

The DELETE procedure deletes elements from the specified PL/SQL table. The specifications for the procedure are overloaded, as shown in the following table.

Procedure Header	Description of Use
`PROCEDURE DELETE;`	Just as with SQL, this simplest form of the DELETE built-in (which takes no arguments at all) has the most sweeping impact: delete all rows from the PL/SQL table.
`PROCEDURE DELETE` `(index_in IN INTEGER);`	Deletes the row specified by that index.

`PROCEDURE DELETE`
`(start_index_in IN INTEGER,`
`end_index_in IN INTEGER);`
	Deletes all the rows defined between the start and end indexes. If end_index_in is less than start_index_in, then no rows are deleted.

If any of the arguments to DELETE is NULL, then the operation does not remove any rows at all.

You call DELETE as shown in the following examples:

- Delete all the rows from the names table:

  ```
  names_tab.DELETE;
  ```

- Delete the 77th row from the globals table:

  ```
  ps_globals.DELETE (77);
  ```

- Delete all rows in the temperature readings table between the 0th row and the −15,000th row, inclusive:

  ```
  temp_reading_tab.DELETE (-15000, 0);
  ```

Prior to PL/SQL Release 2.3, the only way to delete rows from a PL/SQL table was to assign an empty table to the existing PL/SQL table. The DELETE procedure gives you much finer control over the memory required by your PL/SQL tables.

The EXISTS function

The EXISTS function returns TRUE if an element is defined at the specified index in a PL/SQL table. Otherwise, it returns FALSE. The specification for the function is:

```
FUNCTION EXISTS (index_in IN INTEGER) RETURN BOOLEAN;
```

You call EXISTS as follows:

```
IF seuss_characters_table.EXISTS(1) THEN ...
```

Prior to PL/SQL Release 2.3, you could emulate the EXISTS function with your own function looking something like this:

```
/* Filename on companion disk: rowexist.sf */
FUNCTION row_exists
    (table_in IN <table type>, row_in IN INTEGER) RETURN BOOLEAN
IS
    stg VARCHAR2(20);
```

```
BEGIN
   stg := table_in (row_in);
   RETURN TRUE;
EXCEPTION
   WHEN NO_DATA_FOUND
   THEN
      RETURN FALSE;
END;
```

Unfortunately, you would need a different version of the function for each PL/SQL table TYPE, which makes this a very undesirable approach. The EXISTS function is a big improvement.

The FIRST function

The FIRST function returns the lowest value index for which an element is defined in the specified PL/SQL table. The specification for the function is:

```
FUNCTION FIRST RETURN INTEGER;
```

You call FIRST as follows:

```
first_entry_row := employee_table.FIRST;
```

If the PL/SQL table does not contain any elements at all, FIRST returns NULL.

The LAST function

The LAST function returns the highest value index for which an element is defined in the specified PL/SQL table. The specification for the function is:

```
FUNCTION LAST RETURN INTEGER;
```

You call LAST as follows:

```
last_entry_row := employee_table.LAST;
```

If the PL/SQL table does not contain any elements at all, LAST returns NULL.

If you plan to use the PL/SQL table to fill rows sequentially from, say, the first row, you will want to make sure to use the NVL function (see Chapter 13, *Numeric, LOB, and Miscellaneous Functions*) to convert the NULL to a zero, as shown in this example.

The following block uses a cursor FOR loop to transfer data from the database to a PL/SQL table of records. When the first record is fetched, the company_table is empty, so the LAST operator will return NULL. NVL converts that value to zero. I then add one and I am on my way:

```
FOR company_rec IN company_cur
LOOP
   /* Get last row used and add one. */
   next_row := NVL (company_table.LAST, 0) + 1;
```

```
       /* Set the (next_row) values for ID. */
       company_table(next_row).company_id :=
               company_rec.company_id;

   END LOOP;
```

The NEXT function

The NEXT function returns the next greater index after the specified index at which some element is defined in the specified PL/SQL table. The specification for the function is:

```
   FUNCTION NEXT (index_in IN INTEGER) RETURN INTEGER;
```

You call NEXT as follows:

```
   next_index := employee_table.NEXT (curr_index);
```

Remember that PL/SQL tables are sparse: if the tenth and 2005th rows are defined, there is no guarantee that the 11th row is also defined. NEXT gives you a way to find the next defined element, "skipping over" any undefined row numbers.

The table.NEXT procedure will return NULL if there aren't any elements defined after the specified row.

The PRIOR function

The PRIOR function returns the prior greater index after the specified index at which some element is defined in the specified PL/SQL table. The specification for the function is:

```
   FUNCTION PRIOR (index_in IN INTEGER) RETURN INTEGER;
```

You call PRIOR as follows:

```
   prev_index := employee_table.PRIOR (curr_index);
```

Remember that, as we described in the preceding section, PL/SQL tables are sparse. PRIOR gives you a way to find the previously defined element, "skipping over" any undefined row numbers.

The table.PRIOR procedure will return NULL if there aren't any elements defined before the specified row.

Working with PL/SQL Tables

The remainder of this chapter provides you with lots of examples of ways to use PL/SQL tables in your applications.

Transferring Database Information to PL/SQL Tables

You cannot use a SQL SELECT statement to transfer data directly from a database table to a PL/SQL table. You need to take a programmatic approach. A cursor FOR loop usually makes the most sense for this process, which requires the following steps:

1. Define a PL/SQL table TYPE for each datatype found in the columns of the database table.

2. Declare PL/SQL tables which will each receive the contents of a single column.

3. Declare the cursor against the database table.

4. Execute the FOR loop. The body of the loop will contain a distinct assignment of one column into one PL/SQL table.

In PL/SQL Release 2.3, this process would be much simpler. You could define a PL/SQL table with the same structure as the database table by creating a table-based record. Prior to that release, unfortunately, you need a separate PL/SQL table for each column. You do not, on the other hand, need a separate table TYPE for each column. If you have two date columns, for example, you can declare two separate PL/SQL tables both based on the same TYPE.

In the following example I load the company ID, incorporation date, and filing date from the database table to three different PL/SQL tables. Notice that there are only two types of PL/SQL tables declared:

```
/* Filename on companion disk: db2tab1.sql (see db2tab2.sql for the PL/SQL
   Release 2.3 version of same transfer) */
DECLARE
    /* The cursor against the database table. */
    CURSOR company_cur
    IS
        SELECT company_id, incorp_date, filing_date FROM company;

    /* The PL/SQL table TYPE and declaration for the primary key. */
    TYPE company_keys_tabtype IS
        TABLE OF company.company_id%TYPE NOT NULL
        INDEX BY BINARY_INTEGER;
    company_keys_table primary_keys_tabtype;

    /* Sincle PL/SQL table TYPE for two different PL/SQL tables. */
    TYPE date_tabtype IS
        TABLE OF DATE
        INDEX BY BINARY_INTEGER;
    incorp_date_table date_tabtype;
    filing_date_table date_tabtype;
```

```
        /* Variable to keep track of number of rows loaded. */
        num_company_rows BINARY_INTEGER := 0;
BEGIN
        /* The cursor FOR loop */
        FOR company_rec IN company_cur
        LOOP
            /* Increment to the next row in the two, coordinated tables. */
            num_company_rows := num_company_rows + 1;

            /* Set the row values for ID and dates. */
            company_keys_table (num_company_rows) := company_rec.company_id;
            incorp_date_table (num_company_rows)  := company_rec.incorp_date;
            filing_date_table (num_company_rows)  := company_rec.filing_date;

        END LOOP;
END;
```

Data-Smart Row Numbers in PL/SQL Tables

As I've mentioned, one of the most interesting and unusual aspects of the PL/SQL table is its sparseness. I can have a value in the first row and in the 157th row of the table, with nothing in between. This feature is directly related to the fact that a PL/SQL table is unconstrained. Because there is no limit on the number of rows in a table, PL/SQL does not set aside the memory for that table at the time of creation, as would normally occur with an array.

When you use the PL/SQL table to store and retrieve information sequentially, this sparse quality doesn't have any real significance. The ability to store data nonsequentially can, however, come in very handy. Because the row number does not have to be sequentially generated and used, it can represent data in your application. In other words, it can be "data-smart."

Suppose you want to use a PL/SQL table to store the text of messages associated with numeric error codes. These error codes are patterned after Oracle error codes, with ranges of values set aside for different aspects of the application: 1000–1999 for employee-related errors, 5000–5999 for company-related errors, etc. When a user action generates an error, the error number is passed to a procedure which then looks up and displays the message. By storing this information in PL/SQL tables, you avoid a lookup against the remote database.

Let's take a look at sequential and indexed access to implement this functionality.

Sequential, parallel storage

One possible way to implement this procedure is to create two tables: one that holds the error codes (stored sequentially in the table) and another that holds the messages (also stored sequentially). When an error is encountered, the procedure scans sequentially through the PL/SQL table of codes until it finds a match. The row in which the code is found is also the row in the PL/SQL message table; it uses the row to find the message and then displays it. Figure 10-2 shows the correlation between these two tables.

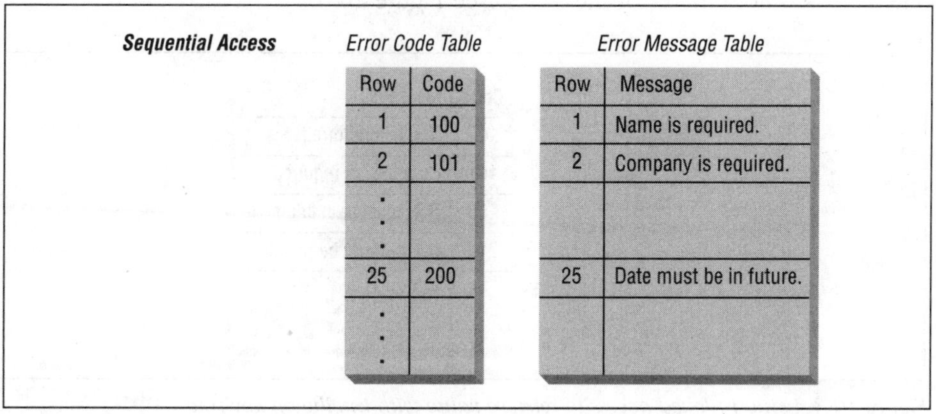

Figure 10-2. Using sequential access to correlate contents of two tables

The code needed to implement this algorithm is shown in the following procedure. The procedure assumes that the two PL/SQL tables have already been loaded with data. The error_pkg.last_row variable is the last row containing an error code:

```
/* Filename on companion disk: seqretr.sp */
PROCEDURE display_error (errcode_in IN NUMBER)
   IS
      matching_row BINARY_INTEGER := 1;
      keep_searching BOOLEAN := error_pkg.last_row > 0;
   BEGIN
      WHILE keep_searching
      LOOP
         /* Does the current row match the specified error code? */
         IF error_pkg.error_codes_table (matching_row) = errcode_in
         THEN
            DBMS_OUTPUT.PUT_LINE
               (error_pkg.error_messages_table (matching_row));
            keep_searching := FALSE;
         ELSE
            /* Move to the next error code in the table */
            matching_row := matching_row + 1;
            keep_searching := matching_row <= error_pkg.last_row;
         END IF;
      END LOOP;
   END;
```

A straightforward, sensible approach, right? Yes and no. Yes, it is straightforward. No, in the context of the PL/SQL table, it is not sensible. This module insists on performing a sequential scan when such a step is not necessary.

Using the index as an intelligent key

A much simpler way to accomplish this same task is to use the error code itself as
the primary key value for the row in the error messages table. Then I need only
one table—to hold the error messages (see Figure 10-3).

Indexed Access	Code	Message
	100	Name is required.
	101	Company is required.
	200	Date must be in future.
	210	Salary must be positive.
	•	
	•	
	•	

Figure 10-3. Using indexed access to retrieve value with intelligent key row

Instead of matching the error code and then using the primary key to locate the
corresponding message, the error code is itself the index into the PL/SQL table.
By using a single table and data-smart values for the primary key, the display_
error procedure boils down to the code shown below:

```
/* Filename on companion disk: indretr.sp */
PROCEDURE display_error (errcode_in IN NUMBER) IS
BEGIN
   /*
   || Deceptively simple: use the error code as the row, retrieve
   || the message, and display it. All in one statement!
   */
   DBMS_OUTPUT.PUT_LINE
           (error_pkg.error_messages_table (errcode_in));
EXCEPTION
   /*
   || Just in case an undefined error code is passed to the
   || procedure, trap the failure in the exception section.
   */
   WHEN NO_DATA_FOUND
   THEN
      DBMS_OUTPUT.PUT_LINE
         ('No match found for error code = ' || TO_CHAR (errcode_in));
END;
```

It has taken me a while to fully internalize the difference between a PL/SQL table
and an array. I have had to go back and rewrite several packages and procedures
once I realized that I had done it again, treating the PL/SQL table like a sequential
access data structure.

So if you ever find yourself reading sequentially through a PL/SQL table, take a step back and consider what data you need to obtain and how it is being stored. Sometimes you do need to store data sequentially (when you use a PL/SQL table, for example, to implement a stack data structure). Frequently, however, you can simplify your life and your code by using data-smart values in your PL/SQL table.

Displaying a PL/SQL Table

When you work with PL/SQL tables, you often want to verify the contents of the table. The usual verification method is to display the contents of each row using DBMS_OUTPUT. This sounds like a simple enough task. In the most basic scenario where you have a sequentially filled table, the code is indeed straightforward.

The following procedures shows the small amount of code required to display a table which has rows 1 through n defined, where n is passed as a parameter to the procedure. The procedure displays a VARCHAR2 table; to display DATE or NUMBER tables, you simply need to use TO_CHAR to convert the value in the call to PUT_LINE:

```
/* Filename on companion disk: disptab1.sp */
PROCEDURE display_table
     (table_in IN <the_table_type>, -- Placeholder for real table type.
      number_of_rows_in IN INTEGER)
  IS
  BEGIN
     /* For each row in the table ... */
     FOR table_row IN 1 .. number_of_rows_in
     LOOP
        /* Display the message, including the row number */
        DBMS_OUTPUT.PUT_LINE
           ('Value in row ' || TO_CHAR (table_row) || ': ' ||
            table_in (table_row));
     END LOOP;
  END;
```

To put this display_table module to use, you will need to create a different version of this procedure for each different type of table, because the table is passed as a parameter. That table's type must be declared in the parameter list in place of the <the_table_type> text.

Of course, not all PL/SQL tables can be filled in ways which are displayed as easily as the one shown above. To start with, the display_table procedure makes many assumptions about its table profile (although very few tables actually fit this profile). These include the following:

- The first defined row of the table is row one. The FOR loop always starts at one.

- All rows between one and number_of_rows_in are defined. There is no exception handler for NO_DATA_FOUND.

- The number_of_rows_in is a positive number. The loop does not even consider the possibility of negative row numbers.

Very few PL/SQL tables actually fit this profile. Even a traditional, sequentially filled table might start its rows at some arbitrary value; a PL/SQL table might be sparsely filled; you might know the starting row (lowest value) and the ending row (maximum value), but not really know which of the rows between those end points are defined. A table with the Oracle error codes would have all of these characteristics.

A flexible display_table procedure

It is possible to build a version of display_table which takes into account all of these variations in a PL/SQL table's structure. For example:

- The program must be supplied with both a starting and an ending row for the scan through the table.

- The program also needs to be told how many times it should encounter and handle an undefined row as it scans the table.

- display_table needs a parameter which specifies the increment by which it loops through the table. This increment can be negative, which would allow you to scan in reverse through the rows of the table.

By incorporating all of this input, the header for display_table becomes:

```
PROCEDURE display_table
    (table_in IN <the_table_type>,
     end_row_in IN INTEGER ,
     start_row_in IN INTEGER := 1,
     failure_threshold_in IN INTEGER := 0,
     increment_in IN INTEGER := +1)
```

where the parameters are defined as:

table_in

The table to be displayed. Again, you would need a different version of this program for each different table type you want to display.

end_row_in

The last row that is defined in the table. If sequentially filled from row 1, this value would simply be the maximum number of rows.

start_row_in

The starting row defined in the table. The default is 1.

failure_threshold_in

> The number of times the procedure will raise the NO_DATA_FOUND exception before it stops scanning through the table. The default is zero, which means that the first time it tries to access an undefined row it will stop.

increment_in

> The amount by which the row counter is incremented as the procedure scans through the table. The default is +1. If you know that every 15th row is defined, you can pass 15 and avoid the NO_DATA_FOUND exceptions. If your rows are negative, as with Oracle error codes, specify −1 for the increment and the procedure will then scan backwards through the table.

This version of display_table shown in the following example displays both sequentially filled and sparsely filled PL/SQL tables. When I use the new display_table to view the contents of a sequentially filled table, the call to the procedure looks exactly the same as in the first version:

```
display_table (customer_tab, num_customers);
```

If I store the Oracle error codes in my table, then I can take advantage of all these different parameters to view only the errors dealing with the date functions (−01800 through −01899) with the following command:

```
display_table (ora_errors_tab, -1899, -1800, 100, -1);
```

My end row is −1899 and my start row is −1800. I allow the procedure to access up to 100 undefined rows, because not all of these values are currently defined. I know that this is enough because the full range is only 100. Finally, I tell display_table to read backwards through the table, as is appropriate given the negative values of the rows.

Examples of display_table output

To test the display_table procedure I created a package named dt which declared a VARCHAR2 table type named string_tabletype and defined the procedure. I then built the SQL*Plus script shown in the example below. Notice that I use three substitution variables (&1, &2, and &3):

```
DECLARE
    t dt.string_tabletype;
BEGIN
    t(1)  := 'hello';
    t(2)  := 'world!';
    t(11) := 'I hope';
    t(21) := 'we make it';
    t(22) := 'to the year';
    t(75) := '2000.';
    dt.display_table (t, &1, &2, &3);
END;
/
```

Here are some of the results of my test scripts:

```
SQL> start disptab 100 1 100
Value in row 1: hello
Value in row 2: world!
Value in row 11: I hope
Value in row 21: we make it
Value in row 22: to the year
Value in row 75: 2000.

SQL> start disptab 100 1 50
Value in row 1: hello
Value in row 2: world!
Value in row 11: I hope
Value in row 21: we make it
Value in row 22: to the year
Exceeded threshold on undefined rows in table.

SQL> start disptab 2 1 0
Value in row 1: hello
Value in row 2: world!

SQL> start disptab 3 1 0
Value in row 1: hello
Value in row 2: world!
Exceeded threshold on undefined rows in table.

SQL> start disptab 50 10 50
Value in row 11: I hope
Value in row 21: we make it
Value in row 22: to the year
```

Implementation of display_table

The first argument in display_table is a PL/SQL table. Because there is no such thing as a generic PL/SQL table structure, you will need to create a version of this procedure for each of your tables. Alternatively, you could create a generic program which handles all the logic in this program which does not rely on the specific table. Then each of your PL/SQL table-specific versions could simply call that generic version.

```
/* Filename on companion disk: disptab2.sp */
PROCEDURE display_table
    (table_in IN <the_table_type>,
     end_row_in IN INTEGER ,
     start_row_in IN INTEGER := 1,
     failure_threshold_in IN INTEGER := 0,
     increment_in IN INTEGER := +1)
IS
    /* The current row displayed as I scan through the table */
    current_row INTEGER := start_row_in;

    /* Tracks number of misses, compared to threshold parameter. */
```

```
      count_misses INTEGER := 0;

      /* Used in WHILE loop to control scanning thru table. */
      within_threshold BOOLEAN := TRUE;

      /*---------------------- Local Module -----------------------*/
      || Determine if specified row is within range. I put this
      || into a function because I need to see which direction I
      || am scanning in order to determine whether I'm in range.
      */
      FUNCTION in_range (row_in IN INTEGER) RETURN BOOLEAN IS
      BEGIN
         IF increment_in < 0
         THEN
            RETURN row_in >= end_row_in;
         ELSE
            RETURN row_in <= end_row_in;
         END IF;
      END;
   BEGIN
      /* The increment cannot be zero! */
      IF increment_in = 0
      THEN
         DBMS_OUTPUT.PUT_LINE
               ('Increment for table display must be non-zero!');
      ELSE
         /*
         || Since I allow the user to pass in the amount of the increment
         || I will switch to a WHILE loop from the FOR loop. I keep
         || scanning if (1) have not reached last row and (2) if I have
         || not run into more undefined rows than allowed by the
         || threshold parameter.
         */
         WHILE in_range (current_row) AND within_threshold
         LOOP
            /*
            || I place call to PUT_LINE within its own anonymous block.
            || This way I can trap a NO_DATA_FOUND exception and keep on
            || going (if desired) without interrupting the scan.
            */
            BEGIN
               /* Display the message, including the row number */
               DBMS_OUTPUT.PUT_LINE
                  ('Value in row ' || TO_CHAR (current_row) || ': ' ||
                   table_in (current_row));

               /* Increment the counter as specified by the parameter */
               current_row := current_row + increment_in;

            EXCEPTION
               WHEN NO_DATA_FOUND
               THEN
                  /*
                  || If at the threshold then shut down the WHILE loop by
```

```
              || setting the Boolean variable to FALSE. Otherwise,
              || increment the number of misses and current row.
              */
              within_threshold := count_misses < failure_threshold_in;
              IF within_threshold
              THEN
                 count_misses := count_misses + 1;
                 current_row := current_row + increment_in;
              END IF;
           END;
        END LOOP;
        /*
        || If I stopped scanning because of undefined rows, let the
        || user know.
        */
        IF NOT within_threshold
        THEN
           DBMS_OUTPUT.PUT_LINE
              ('Exceeded threshold on undefined rows in table.');
        END IF;
     END IF;
  END;
```

By spending the time to think about the different ways a developer might want to display a table and the different kinds of tables to be displayed, and by adding the parameters necessary to handle these scenarios, I have transformed a very simple and limited procedure into a generic and useful program. While the more generic code is significantly more complex than that in the original display_table, I have to write it (and test it) only once. From then on, I simply substitute an actual table type.

Building Traditional Arrays with PL/SQL Tables

As I've mentioned, neither PL/SQL nor any other component of the Oracle product set supports true arrays. You cannot, for example, declare a two-dimensional array which is manipulated with statements such as the following:

```
company (2,3) := '100 Main St';
min_profits := financial_matrix (profit_row, min_column);
```

For years developers have complained about the lack of support for arrays. Although tables serve some of the same purposes as arrays, they are not equivalent. You can use a PL/SQL table as an array, but only one that is single-dimensional. If you need to make use of the more common two-dimensional array, such as a 10 × 10 array composed of 100 cells, then a PL/SQL table—all on its own—will not do the trick. You can, however, build a layer of code which will emulate a traditional *n* × *m* array based on the PL/SQL table data structure.

NOTE	This implementation relies on the PL/SQL package structure, which is covered in Chapter 16. If you are not familiar yet with packages, you may want to read through that chapter before diving into this exploration of array emulation.

Obstacles to implementing arrays

The first time I tried to implement such an array structure with PL/SQL tables, I gave up, thinking that it simply wasn't possible. My strategy had been to create a table for each of the *n* columns in the array. A 2 × 3 array would, in other words, consist of three different tables of the same type, as shown in Figure 10-4. The problem with this approach is that I could not dynamically generate the name of a PL/SQL table at runtime.

Suppose I supplied you with a function in which you specified the number of rows and columns in your array. You would expect to have a pointer to the array of that size returned to you. I can certainly return to you a pointer to a single PL/SQL table; it would simply be declared at the start of the function. If the array was made up of an arbitrary number of tables, however, I could not declare each of these as they were needed.

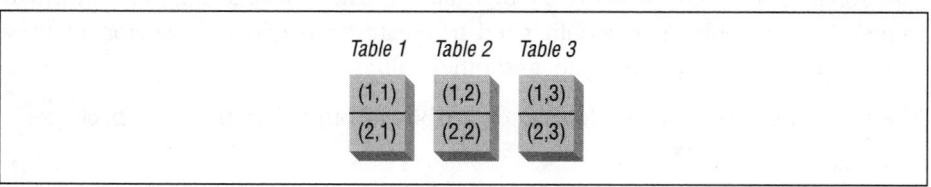

Figure 10-4. Three tables supporting a 2 × 3 array

I was about to give up when I realized that, oddly enough, the elements of the PL/SQL table which make it so different from an array—that it is both unconstrained and sparse—allow me to use a single PL/SQL table to implement the traditional *n* × *m* array, where *n* and *m* are virtually any positive integers. Because the PL/SQL table has no (practical) size limitation and I can use whichever rows in the table I desire, I can spread the *m* different columns of *n* rows across the expanse of the PL/SQL table. In other words, I can partition the single PL/SQL table so that it contains all the cells of a traditional array.

Partitioning a PL/SQL table to store an array

To understand how this partitioning works, consider a 3 × 4 array. This array contains a total of 12 cells. The cells would be spread among the rows of a PL/SQL table as shown in Figure 10-5. Using the distribution in the figure, we can see that cell (3,3) would be stored in row 9 of the table, that cell (2,4) would be stored in row 11, and so on.

Row	Column 1	Column 2	Column 3	Column 4
1	row 1	row 4	row 7	row 10
2	row 2	row 5	row 8	row 11
3	row 3	row 6	row 9	row 12

Figure 10-5. Distribution of 3 × 4 array cells in PL/SQL table

The general formula which converts the row and column of an array cell to the corresponding PL/SQL table row is this:

```
table_row := (cell_column - 1) * number_of_rows_in_array + cell_row;
```

where (cell_row, cell_column) is the cell in the array and number_of_rows_in_array is the total number of rows in the array.

Features of the array package

The array package I have developed (shown later in this section) implements traditional *n* × *m* arrays using PL/SQL tables. This package supports arrays of numeric values only. You would need to create an overloaded version of these same modules for character, date, and other values.

The following shows the modules and capabilities offered by the array package:

array.make
> Make or declare an array with specified numbers of rows and columns. You can optionally specify the default value you want placed in each cell.

array.cell
> Obtain the value of any cell in the array.

array.change
> Change the value of any cell in the array.

array.erase
> Erase the array from memory.

array.display
> Display the contents of the array. You can display the table contents in array style (matrix format) or inline style (one cell per line).

The package also provides two functions to return the number of rows and columns in the array (number_of_rows and number_of_columns, respectively). It does not, on the other hand, give programmers direct access to the variables which store these values. Instead, I hide the variables themselves in the package body and place the functions in the specification. There are two reasons for this layer of code:

- You cannot access stored package variables and PL/SQL Version 2 data structures such as PL/SQL tables directly from PL/SQL Release 1.1. The Version 1.1 layer cannot parse such references (see Appendix B, *Calling Stored Procedures from PL/SQL Version 1.1*). You can, however, call stored package functions from within Oracle Developer/2000.

- It is always better to hide the way you implement functionality, including variables names, data structures, and algorithms. By not exposing the details (in this case, the names of the variables which store this information), I can change the underlying implementation without affecting the way programmers use the data.

Most of the code needed to support arrays is straightforward. Oddly enough, the most complicated module in this package is the display procedure; its complexity is derived from the flexibility it offers. You can display the contents of an array in linestyle (one cell per line) or array style (all cells in each row on the same line, like a spreadsheet). You can also ask to display only selected columns and rows.

Examples using array package

The following four examples show how the array package is used.

- Create a 10 × 10 array with values all set to 0:

```
array.make (10, 10, 0);
```

- Set all the values in the first column of the array to 15:

```
FOR row_index IN 1 .. array.row_count
LOOP
    array.change (row_index, 1, 15);
END LOOP;
```

- Set the values in the third row to the values in the fifth row:

```
FOR col_index IN 1 .. array.column_count
LOOP
    array.change (3, col_index, array.cell (5, col_index));
END LOOP;
```

- Create and display contents of arrays:

```
SQL> execute array.make (10,10,25);

PL/SQL procedure successfully completed.

SQL>    execute array.display(4,6,2,4);
Row      Column 2  Column 3  Column 4
```

```
4          25        25        25
5          25        25        25
6          25        25        25

SQL>   execute array.display(4,6,2,4,'line');
Cell (4,2): 25
Cell (4,3): 25
Cell (4,4): 25
Cell (5,2): 25
Cell (5,3): 25
Cell (5,4): 25
Cell (6,2): 25
Cell (6,3): 25
Cell (6,4): 25
```

There are many possibilities for expanding the capabilities of the array package. You could, for example, offer a module which performs scalar operations against the specified column(s) and row(s) of the array, such as multiplying all cells in the first column by a value. If you implement a version of the array package which supports more than one array at a time, you could build array-level, aggregate operations, such as "multiply two arrays together" or "subtract one array from another," and so on.

I hope that you can see from this section that even if the current version of PL/SQL does not offer every single feature you might want or need, there is often a way to emulate the desired feature. The array package is not nearly as convenient or efficient as true, native arrays would be, but if you have a need right now for an array in PL/SQL Version 2, the package implementation is hard to beat!

Limitations in array implementation

There is one major limitation to the implementation of arrays in this package. You can use only one array at a time from this package. The reason for this restriction is that I need to keep track of the number of rows and columns in the array. To make an association between the array (a PL/SQL table) and those values, I would need to ask you for a name for this array and then create named globals with the number of rows and columns. I avoid those complications by "burying" the structure of the array inside the package.

On the positive side, there are several advantages to hiding the table. One is that you have an array which is very easy to use. You never have to declare a table yourself. You simply ask to create or make the array and then you can access the cells.

Another advantage of hiding the table is that you don't have to pass it as a parameter when you call the modules. A PL/SQL table parameter could harm performance, because all the rows of the table are copied into and out of local memory structures for manipulation in that module. In the array package, the number_array table is declared at the package level so it is available to all modules in the package without having to be passed as a parameter.

One final advantage is that you can call this array package (stored in the database) from within the Oracle Developer/2000 tools. If the table were exposed, then the array could only be used in a PL/SQL Version 2 environment. Wow! When I decided to build it this way, I had no idea it would make this much sense.

The array package specification

The package specification lists the modules which programmers can call to create and manipulate an array with PL/SQL tables. Notice that the statements in the specification only show the header information: module name and parameters. The code behind these headers is found in the package body (next section):

```
/* Filename on companion disk: array.sps */
PACKAGE array
IS
    /* Returns the number of rows in the array */
    FUNCTION row_count RETURN INTEGER;

    /* Returns the number of columns in the array */
    FUNCTION column_count RETURN INTEGER;

    /* Create an array */
    PROCEDURE make
        (num_rows_in IN INTEGER := 10,
         num_columns_in IN INTEGER := 1,
         initial_value_in IN NUMBER := NULL,
         conflict_action_in IN VARCHAR2 := 'OVERWRITE');

    /* Return the value in a cell */
    FUNCTION cell (row_in IN INTEGER, col_in IN INTEGER)
        RETURN NUMBER;

    /* Change the value in a cell */
    PROCEDURE change
        (row_in IN INTEGER, col_in IN INTEGER, value_in IN NUMBER);

    /* Erase the array */
    PROCEDURE erase;

    /* Display the array */
    PROCEDURE display
        (start_row_in IN INTEGER := 1,
         end_row_in IN INTEGER := row_count,
         start_col_in IN INTEGER := 1,
         end_col_in IN INTEGER := column_count,
         display_style_in IN VARCHAR2 := 'ARRAY');

END array;
```

The array package body

The package body provides the code which implements the modules listed in the array package specification. The longest module in this bunch is the display procedure. Because this code is basically the same as that shown in the section "Displaying a PL/SQL Table" I have not repeated it here. However, the full package body is found on the companion disk.

```
/* Filename on companion disk: array.spb */
PACKAGE BODY array
IS
    /*----------------------Private Variables ---------------------*/

    /* The number of rows in the array */
    number_of_rows INTEGER := NULL;

    /* The number of columns in the array */
    number_of_columns INTEGER := NULL;

    /* The generic table structure for a numeric table */
    TYPE number_array_type IS TABLE OF NUMBER
        INDEX BY BINARY_INTEGER;

    /* The actual table which will hold the array */
    number_array number_array_type;

    /* An empty table used to erase the array */
    empty_array number_array_type;

    /*----------------------Private Modules ---------------------*/

    FUNCTION row_for_cell (row_in IN INTEGER, col_in IN INTEGER)
        RETURN INTEGER
    /*
    || Returns the row in the table that stores the value for
    || the specified cell in the array.
    */
    IS
    BEGIN
        RETURN (col_in - 1) * number_of_rows + row_in;
    END;

    /*----------------------Public Modules ---------------------*/

    FUNCTION row_count RETURN INTEGER IS
    BEGIN
        RETURN number_of_rows;
    END;

    FUNCTION column_count RETURN INTEGER IS
    BEGIN
        RETURN number_of_columns;
    END;
```

```
PROCEDURE make
   (num_rows_in IN INTEGER := 10,
    num_columns_in IN INTEGER := 1,
    initial_value_in IN NUMBER := NULL,
    conflict_action_in IN VARCHAR2 := 'OVERWRITE')
/*
|| Create an array of the specified size, with the initial
|| value. If the table is already in use, it will be erased
|| and then re-made only if the conflict action is the
|| default value above.
*/
IS
BEGIN
   /*
   || If number_of_rows is NOT NULL, then the array is
   || already in use. If the conflict action is the
   || default or OVERWRITE, then erase the existing
   || array.
   */
   IF number_of_rows IS NOT NULL AND
      UPPER (conflict_action_in) = 'OVERWRITE'
   THEN
      erase;
   END IF;
   /*
   || Only continue now if my number of rows is NULL.
   || If it has a value, then table is in use and user
   || did NOT want to overwrite it.
   */
   IF number_of_rows IS NULL
   THEN
      /* Set the global variables storing size of array */
      number_of_rows := num_rows_in;
      number_of_columns := num_columns_in;
      /*
      || A PL/SQL table's row is defined only if a value
      || is assigned to that row, even if that is only a
      || NULL value. So to create the array, I will simply
      || make the needed assignments. Remember: I use a single
      || table, but segregate distinct areas of the table for each
      || column of data. I use the row_for_cell function to
      || "space out" the different cells of the array across
      || the table.
      */
      FOR col_index IN 1 .. number_of_columns
      LOOP
         FOR row_index IN 1 .. number_of_rows
         LOOP
            number_array (row_for_cell (row_index, col_index))
               := initial_value_in;
         END LOOP;
      END LOOP;
   END IF;
END;
```

```
FUNCTION cell (row_in IN INTEGER, col_in IN INTEGER)
   RETURN NUMBER
/*
|| Retrieve the value in a cell using row_for_cell.
*/
IS
BEGIN
   RETURN number_array (row_for_cell (row_in, col_in));
END;

PROCEDURE change
   (row_in IN INTEGER, col_in IN INTEGER, value_in IN NUMBER)
/*
|| Change the value in a cell using row_for_cell.
*/
IS
BEGIN
   number_array (row_for_cell (row_in, col_in)) := value_in;
END;

PROCEDURE erase
/*
|| Erase a table by assigning an empty table to a non-empty
|| array. Then set the size globals for the array to NULL.
*/
IS
BEGIN
   number_array := empty_array;
   number_of_rows := NULL;
   number_of_columns := NULL;
END;

PROCEDURE display
   (start_row_in IN INTEGER := 1,
    end_row_in IN INTEGER := row_count,
    start_col_in IN INTEGER := 1,
    end_col_in IN INTEGER := column_count,
    display_style_in IN VARCHAR2 := 'ARRAY')
IS
BEGIN
/*
|| See code on disk. This repeats, more or less, the code shown
|| above to display a table.
*/
END display;

END array;
```

Optimizing Foreign Key Lookups with PL/SQL Tables

Something you'll do again and again in your client-server applications is look up
the name or description of a foreign key from a database table that is resident on
the server. This lookup often occurs, for example, in the Post-Query trigger of

Oracle Forms applications. The base table block contains a database item for the company_id and a non-database item for company_name. What if you have to process a number of different records in your employee table? The SQL processing is very inefficient. When a record is queried from the database, the Post-Query trigger executes an additional SELECT statement to obtain the name of the company, as shown in the following example:

```
DECLARE
    CURSOR company_cur IS
        SELECT name FROM company
         WHERE company_id = :employee.company_id;
BEGIN
    OPEN company_cur;
    FETCH company_cur INTO :employee.company_name;
    IF company_cur%NOTFOUND
    THEN
        MESSAGE
            (' Company with ID ' || TO_CHAR (:employee.company_id)
             ' not found in database.');
    END IF;
    CLOSE company_cur;
END;
```

This SELECT statement is executed for each record queried into the form. Even if the first twelve employees retrieved in a query all work for the same company, the trigger will open, fetch, and close the company_cur cursor a dozen times—all to retrieve the same company name again and again. This is not desirable behavior in any application.

Is there a better way? Ideally, you'd want the company name to be already accessible in memory on the client side of the application—"instantly" available in the form.

One way to achieve this noble objective is to read the contents of the lookup table into a local memory structure on the startup of the form. Unfortunately, this simple solution has a couple of drawbacks:

- The data, such as the company name, might change during the user session. If you transfer all the names from an RDBMS table to memory and then another user changes the name in the database, your screen data is not updated.

- You have to set aside sufficient memory to hold all reference values, even if only a few will ever be needed. You will also pay the CPU price necessary to transfer all of this data. This pre-load approach seems like overkill to me.

Blending database and PL/SQL table access

A reasonable middle ground between RDBMS-only data and totally local data would store values as they are queried from the database. Then, if that value is needed again in the current session, the application could use the local value instead of issuing another SELECT statement to the database. This would minimize both the memory and the CPU required by the application to return the names for foreign keys.

In this section I offer an implementation of a self-optimizing foreign key lookup process based on PL/SQL tables. I chose PL/SQL tables because I could then store the resulting function in the database and make it accessible to all of my Oracle-based applications, whether they are based on Oracle Forms, PowerBuilder, or Oracle Reports. Let's step through this implementation.

Top-down design of blended access

Suppose that I stored company names in a PL/SQL table as they are retrieved from the database and returned to the form. Then, if that same company name is needed a second (or third, or fourth) time, I get it from the memory-resident PL/SQL table rather than from the database. The following example shows the pseudocode which would implement this approach:

```
 1   FUNCTION company_name
 2       (id_in IN company.company_id%TYPE)
 3   RETURN VARCHAR2
 4   IS
 5   BEGIN
 6       get-data-from-table;
 7       return-company-name;
 8   EXCEPTION
 9       WHEN NO_DATA_FOUND
10       THEN
11           get-data-from-database-table;
12           store-in-PL/SQL-table;
13           return-company-name;
14   END;
```

This function accepts a single parameter foreign key, id_in (line 2). It first attempts to retrieve the company name from the PL/SQL table (line 6). If that access fails—if, in other words, I try to reference an undefined row in the PL/SQL table—then PL/SQL raises the NO_DATA_FOUND exception and control is transferred to the exception section (line 9). The function then gets the name from the database table using a cursor (line 11), stores that information in the PL/SQL table (line 12), and finally returns the value (line 13).

As the user performs queries, additional company names are cached in the PL/SQL table. The next time that same company name is required, the function gets it from the PL/SQL table. In this way, database reads are kept to a minimum and the application automatically optimizes its own data access method. Figure 10-6 illustrates this process.

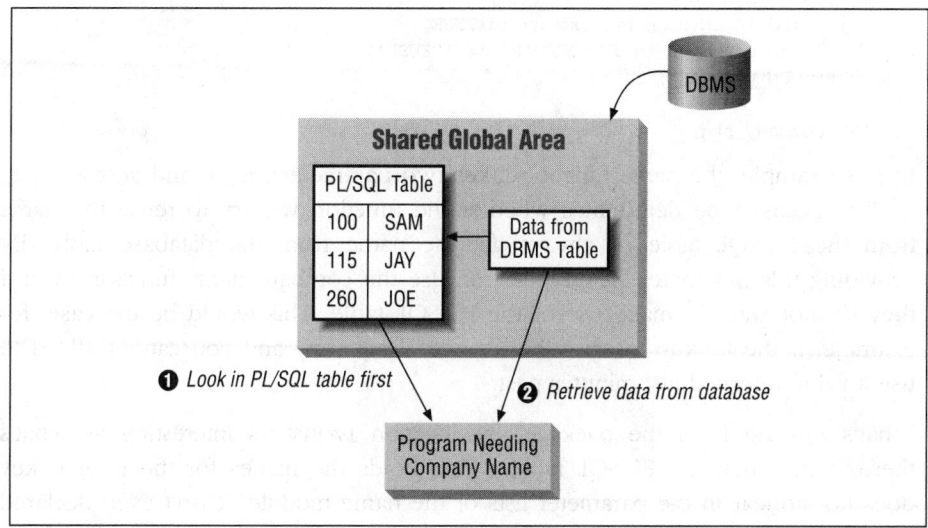

Figure 10-6. Blended method for lookup of foreign key descriptions

Let's see what it takes to actually write this pseudocode in PL/SQL. If I declare my PL/SQL table in a standalone function, then the scope of that PL/SQL table is restricted to the function. As soon as the function terminates, the memory associated with the PL/SQL table is lost. If, on the other hand, I declare the PL/SQL table in a package, that table remains in memory for the duration of my session (see Chapter 16 for more information about packages). I want my PL/SQL table to persist in memory for the duration of a user session, so I will use a stored package structure.

The package specification

The specification for my company package is shown in the following example. It contains a single module called name, which returns the name of the company. Does it seem silly to create a package for this single module? Not really. Beyond the technical justification I just provided, you should realize that in a production environment the company package would contain a number of other modules, such as procedures to return data about the company. And if it were the first module for the package, you are planning well for the future by starting with a package instead of a standalone module:

```
PACKAGE company_pkg
IS
    /*
    || Retrieve the name of the company. If you specify REUSE for
    || the access type, then it will try to get the name from
    || the PL/SQL table. Otherwise, it will just use the database
    || table and do a standard look-up.
    */
```

```
FUNCTION name
    (id_in IN company.company_id%TYPE,
     access_type_in IN VARCHAR2 := 'REUSE')
RETURN VARCHAR2;

END company_pkg;
```

In this example, the name function takes two parameters: id_in and access_type_in. The access type determines whether the function will try to reuse the name from the PL/SQL table or always get the name from the database table. By providing this parameter, developers can use the company.name function even if they do not want to make use of the PL/SQL table. This would be the case, for example, if the lookup information changes frequently and you cannot afford to use a value returned just minutes past.

What's missing from the package specification is just as interesting as what's there. Notice that the PL/SQL table which holds the names for the foreign key does not appear in the parameter lists of the name module. It isn't even declared in the specification. Instead, the PL/SQL table is declared in the body of the package—and is completely hidden to developers who make use of this function. By hiding the PL/SQL table, I make this package usable in the Oracle Developer/ 2000 environment, which, as I've mentioned, is based on PL/SQL Version 1.1 and does not directly support directly PL/SQL tables.

The package body

Let's now turn our attention to the package body. In the rest of this section I'll examine the various components of the body individually, listed below:

company_table_type
    PL/SQL table type declaration for the table which holds the company names.

company_table
    PL/SQL table declaration. The actual declaration of the table.

name_from_database
    Private function. Returns the name from the database if not yet stored in the PL/SQL table.

name
    Public function. Returns the name to a user of the package. The name might come from the PL/SQL table or the database table.

The body of the company package first declares the table type and table for the company names, as shown below. The datatype for the table's single column is based on the company name column, through use of the %TYPE attribute. This way if the column's length ever changes, this function will automatically adjust:

```
TYPE company_table_type IS
   TABLE OF company.name%TYPE
   INDEX BY BINARY_INTEGER;
company_table company_table_type;
```

The private function name_from_database shown in the next example retrieves the company name from the database. The name function calls name_from_database from two different locations. This function is essentially the same code as that shown in the Post-Query trigger at the start of the section:

```
FUNCTION name_from_database (id_in IN company.company_id%TYPE)
   RETURN company.name%TYPE
IS
   CURSOR comp_cur IS
       SELECT name FROM company
        WHERE company_id = id_in;
   return_value company.name%TYPE := NULL;
BEGIN
   OPEN comp_cur;
   FETCH comp_cur INTO return_value;
   CLOSE comp_cur;
   RETURN return_value;
END;
```

Notice that I do not check for %FOUND or %NOTFOUND after I have fetched a record from the cursor. If the FETCH fails, then the value of return_value is not changed. The initial value of NULL is returned by the function, which is what I want. Remember that the name_from_database function is only callable from within the package body. Programmers cannot call this function as they would call the company.name function.

Now that you have seen all the private components of the package, let's see how I use them to build the single public module of the company package: the name function. (whose full implementation is shown below). The body of the program consists of only six lines:

```
IF UPPER (access_type_in) = 'REUSE'
THEN
   RETURN company_table (id_in);
ELSE
   RETURN name_from_database;
END IF;
```

In other words, if reuse is specified then get the value from the PL/SQL table; otherwise get the name from the database. What if the name is not in the PL/SQL table? Then PL/SQL raises the NO_DATA_FOUND exception and the action moves to the exception section, which consists of the following:

```
EXCEPTION
   WHEN NO_DATA_FOUND
   THEN
      return_value := name_from_database;
```

```
    IF return_value IS NOT NULL
    THEN
        company_table (id_in) := return_value;
    END IF;

    RETURN return_value;
END;
```

I try to get the name from the database. If the function returns a non-NULL value, then I save it to the table. Finally, I return that company name. The result is simple, readable code.

In this exception handler you can see the random-access nature of the PL/SQL table. The id_in foreign key value actually serves as the row in the table. I do not have to store the values in the PL/SQL sequentially. Instead, I simply populate those rows of the table which correspond to the foreign keys.

The company.name function

The following function combines the various elements described earlier. This name function is defined within the company package:

```
/* Filename on companion disk: selftune.spp (contains the full code for the
package containing this function) */
FUNCTION name
    (id_in IN company.company_id%TYPE,
     access_type_in IN VARCHAR2 := 'REUSE')
    RETURN company.name%TYPE
IS
    return_value company.name%TYPE;
BEGIN
    /* If REUSE (default), then try to get name from PL/SQL table */
    IF UPPER (access_type_in) = 'REUSE'
    THEN
        RETURN company_table (id_in);
    ELSE
        /* Just get the name from the database table. */
        RETURN name_from_database;
    END IF;

EXCEPTION
    /* If REUSE and PL/SQL table does not yet have value ... */
    WHEN NO_DATA_FOUND
    THEN
        /* Get the name from the database */
        return_value := name_from_database;

        /* If name was found, save to PL/SQL table for next time. */
        IF return_value IS NOT NULL
        THEN
            company_table (id_in) := return_value;
        END IF;
```

```
      /* Return the company name */
      RETURN return_value;
  END;
```

Using the company package, the Post-Query trigger shown in an earlier example becomes simply:

```
:employee.company_name := company.name (:employee.company_id);
IF :employee.company_name IS NULL
THEN
   MESSAGE
      (' Company with ID ' || TO_CHAR (:employee.company_id)
       ' not found in database.');
END IF;
```

In this call to company.name, I did not provide a value for the second parameter, so it takes the default value of REUSE and checks to see if the company name is in the PL/SQL table. Alternatively, I could specify the access type using a GLOBAL variable as follows:

```
:employee.company_name :=
   company.name (:employee.company_id, :GLOBAL.access_type);
```

I could then modify the behavior and—I hope—the performance of my foreign key lookups without having to change my code. In other words, if I determine that the contents of a particular table are static throughout a session, I could set the GLOBAL to REUSE for that call. If, on the other hand, I determine that the data might change, I could change the GLOBAL to NOREUSE and then force the lookup to go against the database.

Performance impact of blended access

How much impact, you might ask, does the company.name function have on the lookup process? I tested the performance of this package with the SQL*Plus script shown in the following example.

The do package in the code below offers a substitution for the DBMS_OUTPUT package. The timer package makes use of DBMS_UTILITY and its GET_TIME function to measure elapsed time in 100ths of seconds. The do and timer packages are defined in Chapter 16.

```
DECLARE
   c VARCHAR2(100);
BEGIN
   timer.capture;
   FOR i IN 1 .. &num_iterations
   LOOP
      c := company.name (10, '&access_type');
   END LOOP;
```

```
        do.pl (c);
        timer.show_elapsed;
     END;
     /
```

I executed the script on a 100Mhz 486 workstation with a local Oracle7 for Windows database. The results of this comparison of database and PL/SQL table lookup performance are shown in Table 10-2.

Table 10-2. Comparison of Database and PL/SQL Table Lookup Performance

Access Type	Number of Accesses	Elapsed Time (100ths of seconds)
NOREUSE	100	22–28
REUSE	100	0–5
NOREUSE	1000	230–240
REUSE	1000	16–22

An access type of NOREUSE means that each access required a database query. An access type of REUSE means that the first request performed a database query, while all others worked with the PL/SQL table. Clearly, PL/SQL table access offers a significant performance savings—and this is with a local database. You can expect even more of an improvement with a remote database. The benefit of this approach is obvious: it is always faster to access local memory than the Oracle database shared memory.

III

Built-In Functions

Part III of this book presents the many built-in or predefined functions supported by PL/SQL. These chapters contain detailed descriptions and many extended examples of the dozens of built-in programs that you can use immediately in your PL/SQL applications.

- Chapter 11, *Character Functions*, describes the functions that allow you to parse names, concatenate strings, and perform many other character operations.

- Chapter 12, *Date Functions*, presents the functions that let you manipulate calendar dates in your PL/SQL programs.

- Chapter 13, *Numeric, LOB, and Miscellaneous Functions*, describes the functions you use to manipulate numbers and perform a variety of other operations.

- Chapter 14, *Conversion Functions*, discusses the functions that let PL/SQL convert from one datatype to another.

11

Character Functions

A character function is a function that takes one or more character values as parameters and returns either a character value or a number value. The Oracle Server and PL/SQL provide a number of different character datatypes, including CHAR, VARCHAR, VARCHAR2, LONG, RAW, and LONG RAW. In PL/SQL, the three different datatype families for character data are:

VARCHAR2

A variable-length character datatype whose data is converted by the RDBMS

CHAR

The fixed-length datatype

RAW

A variable-length datatype whose data is not converted by the RDBMS, but instead is left in "raw" form

When a character function returns a character value, that value is always of type VARCHAR2 (variable length), with the following two exceptions: UPPER and LOWER. These functions convert to upper- and lowercase, respectively, and return CHAR values (fixed length) if the strings they are called on to convert are fixed-length CHAR arguments.

PL/SQL provides a rich set of character functions that allow you to get information about strings and modify the contents of those strings in very high-level, powerful ways. Table 11-1 shows the character functions covered in detail in this chapter. The remaining functions (not covered in this chapter) are specific to National Language Support and Trusted Oracle.

Table 11-1. The Built-In Character Functions

Name	Description
ASCII	Returns the ASCII code of a character.
CHR	Returns the character associated with the specified collating code.
CONCAT	Concatenates two strings into one.
INITCAP	Sets the first letter of each word to uppercase. All other letters are set to lowercase.
INSTR	Returns the location in a string of the specified substring.
LENGTH	Returns the length of a string.
LOWER	Converts all letters to lowercase.
LPAD	Pads a string on the left with the specified characters.
LTRIM	Trims the left side of a string of all specified characters.
REPLACE	Replaces a character sequence in a string with a different set of characters.
RPAD	Pads a string on the right with the specified characters.
RTRIM	Trims the right side of a string of all specified characters.
SOUNDEX	Returns the "soundex" of a string.
SUBSTR	Returns the specified portion of a string.
TRANSLATE	Translates single characters in a string to different characters.
UPPER	Converts all letters in the string to uppercase.

Character Function Descriptions

The following sections briefly describe each of the PL/SQL character functions.

The ASCII function

The ASCII function returns the NUMBER code that represents the specified character in the database character set. The specification of the ASCII function is:

```
FUNCTION ASCII (single_character IN VARCHAR2) RETURN NUMBER
```

where single_character is the character to be located in the collating sequence. Even though the function is named ASCII, it will return the code location in whatever the database character set is set to, such as EBCDIC Code Page 500 or 7-bit ASCII. For example, in the 7-bit ASCII character set, ASCII ('a') returns 97. Remember that the collating code for uppercase letters is different from that for lowercase letters. ASCII ('A') returns 65 (in the 7-bit ASCII character set) because the uppercase letters come before the lowercase letters in the sequence.

If you pass more than one character in the parameter to ASCII, it returns the collating code for the first character and ignores the other characters. As a result, the following calls to ASCII all return the same value of 100:

```
ASCII ('defg') ==> 100
ASCII ('d') ==> 100
ASCII ('d_e_f_g') ==> 100
```

The CHR function

The CHR function is the inverse of ASCII. It returns a VARCHAR2 character (length 1) that corresponds to the location in the collating sequence provided as a parameter. The specification of the CHR function is:

```
FUNCTION CHR (code_location IN NUMBER) RETURN VARCHAR2
```

where code_location is the number specifying the location in the collating sequence.

The CHR function is especially valuable when you need to make reference to a nonprintable character in your code. For example, the location in the standard ASCII collating sequence for the newline character is ten. The CHR function therefore gives me a way to search for the linefeed control character in a string, and perform operations on a string based on the presence of that control character.

You can also insert a linefeed into a character string using the CHR function. Suppose I have to build a report that displays the address of a company. A company can have up to four address strings (in addition to city, state, and zipcode). I need to put each address string on a new line, but I don't want any blank lines embedded in the address. The following SELECT will not do the trick:

```
SELECT name, address1, address2, address3, address4,
       city || ', ' || state || ' ' || zipcode location
  FROM company;
```

Assuming each column (report field) goes on a new line, you will end up using six lines per address, no matter how many of these address strings are NULL. For example:

```
HAROLD HENDERSON
22 BUNKER COURT
SUITE 100


WYANDANCH, MN 66557
```

You can use the CHR function to suppress these internal blank lines as follows:

```
SELECT name ||
       DECODE (address1, NULL, NULL, CHR (10) || address1) ||
       DECODE (address2, NULL, NULL, CHR (10) || address2) ||
       DECODE (address3, NULL, NULL, CHR (10) || address3) ||
       DECODE (address4, NULL, NULL, CHR (10) || address4) ||
       CHR (10) ||
       city || ', ' || state || ' ' || zipcode
  FROM company;
```

Now the query returns a single formatted column per company. The DECODE statement offers IF-THEN logic within SQL and executes as follows: "If the address string is NULL then concatenate NULL; otherwise insert a linefeed character. Then concatenate the address string."

In this way, blank address lines are ignored. If I now use Wrap on the report field which holds this string, the address will be scrunched down to:

```
HAROLD HENDERSON
22 BUNKER COURT
SUITE 100
WYANDANCH, MN 66557
```

The CONCAT function

The CONCAT function concatenates by taking two VARCHAR2 strings and returning those strings appended together in the order specified. The specification of the CONCAT function is:

```
FUNCTION CONCAT (string1 IN VARCHAR2, string2 IN VARCHAR2)
               RETURN VARCHAR2
```

CONCAT always appends string2 to the end of string1. If either string is NULL, CONCAT returns the non-NULL argument all by its lonesome. If both strings are NULL, CONCAT returns NULL. Here are some examples of uses of CONCAT:

```
CONCAT ('abc', 'defg') ==> 'abcdefg'
CONCAT (NULL, 'def') ==> 'def'
CONCAT ('ab', NULL) ==> 'ab'
CONCAT (NULL, NULL) ==> NULL
```

I have a confession to make about CONCAT: I have never used it once in all my years of PL/SQL coding. In fact, I never even noticed it was available until I did the research for this book. How can this be? Did I never have to concatenate strings together in my programs? No, I certainly have performed many acts of concatenation in my time. Surprisingly, the answer is that PL/SQL (and the Oracle RDBMS) offers a second concatenation operator—the double vertical bars (||). This operator is much more flexible and powerful and is easier to use than CONCAT.

The INITCAP function

The INITCAP function reformats the case of the string argument, setting the first letter of each word to uppercase and the remainder of the letters in that word to lowercase. A word is a set of characters separated by a space or nonalphanumeric characters (such as # or _). The specification of INITCAP is:

```
FUNCTION INITCAP (string_in IN VARCHAR2) RETURN VARCHAR2
```

Here are some examples of the impact of INITCAP on your strings:

- Shift all lowercase to mixed case:

```
INITCAP ('this is lower') ==> 'This Is Lower'
```

- Shift all uppercase to mixed case:

```
INITCAP ('BIG>AND^TALL') ==> 'Big>And^Tall'
```

- Shift a confusing blend of cases to consistent initcap format:

```
INITCAP ('wHatISthis_MESS?') ==> 'Whatisthis_Mess?'
```

- Create Visual Basic-style variable names (I use REPLACE, explained later, to strip out the embedded spaces).

```
REPLACE (INITCAP ('ALMOST_UNREADABLE_VAR_NAME'), '_', NULL)
==>
    'AlmostUnreadableVarName'
```

When and why would you use INITCAP? Many Oracle shops like to store all character string data in the database, such as names and addresses, in uppercase. This makes it easier to search for records that match certain criteria.

The problem with storing all the data in uppercase is that, while it is a convenient "machine format," it is not particularly readable or presentable. How easy is it to scan a page of information that looks like the following?

```
CUSTOMER TRACKING LIST - GENERATED ON 12-MAR-1994
LAST PAYMENT WEDNESDAY: PAUL JOHNSON, 123 MADISON AVE - $1200
LAST PAYMENT MONDAY: HARRY SIMMERSON, 555 AXELROD RD - $1500
```

It is hard for the eye to pick out the individual words and different types of information; all that text just blends in together. Furthermore, solid uppercase simply has a "machine" or even "mainframe" feel to it; you'd never actually type it that way. A mixture of upper- and lowercase can make your output much more readable and friendly in appearance:

```
Customer Tracking List - Generated On 12-Mar-1994
Last Payment Wednesday: Paul Johnson, 123 Madison Ave - $1200
Last Payment Monday: Harry Simmerson, 555 Axelrod Rd - $1500
```

Can you see any problems with using INITCAP to format output? There are a couple of drawbacks to the way it works. First, as you saw earlier with the string "BIG AND TALL", INITCAP is not very useful for generating titles, since it doesn't know that little words like "and" and "the" should not be capitalized. That is a relatively minor problem compared with the second: INITCAP is completely ignorant of real-world surname conventions. Names with internal capital letters, in particular, cannot be generated with INITCAP. Consider the following example:

```
INITCAP ('HAMBURGERS BY THE BILLIONS AT MCDONALDS')
==>
    'Hamburgers By The Billions At Mcdonalds'
```

Use INITCAP with caution when printing reports or displaying data, since the information it produces may not always be formatted correctly.

The INSTR function

The INSTR function searches a string to find a match for the substring and, if found, returns the position, in the source string, of the first character of that substring. If there is no match, then INSTR returns 0. In Oracle7, if nth_appearance is not positive (i.e., if it is 0 or negative), then INSTR always returns 1. In Oracle8, a value of 0 or a negative number for nth_appearance causes INSTR to raise the VALUE_ERROR exception.

The specification of the INSTR function is:

```
FUNCTION INSTR
    (string1 IN VARCHAR2,
     string2 IN VARCHAR2
    [,start_position IN NUMBER := 1
    [, nth_appearance IN NUMBER := 1]])
    RETURN NUMBER
```

where string1 is the string searched by INSTR for the position in which the nth_appearance of string2 is found. The start_position parameter is the position in the string where the search will start. It is optional and defaults to 1 (the beginning of string1). The nth_appearance parameter is also optional and also defaults to 1.

Both the start_position and nth_appearance parameters can be literals like 5 or 157, variables, or complex expressions, as follows:

```
INSTR (company_name, 'INC', (last_location + 5) * 10)
```

If start_position is negative, then INSTR counts back start_position number of characters from the end of the string and then searches from that point towards the beginning of the string for the *n*th match. Figure 11-1 illustrates the two directions in which INSTR searches, depending on the sign of the start_position parameter.

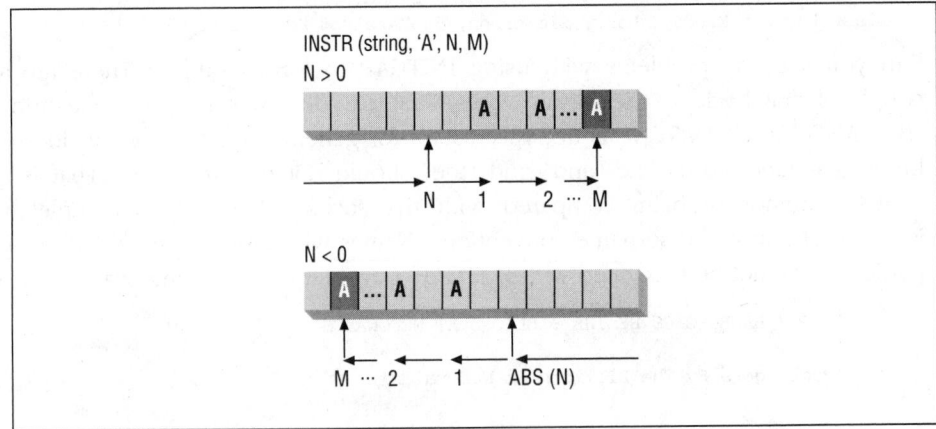

Figure 11-1. Forward and reverse searches with INSTR

I have found INSTR to be a very handy function—especially when used to the fullest extent possible. Most programmers make use of (and are even only aware of) only the first two parameters. Use INSTR to search from the end of the string? Search for the *n*th appearance, as opposed to just the first appearance? "Wow!" many programmers would say, "I didn't know it could do that." Take the time to get familiar with INSTR and use *all* of its power.

Let's look at some examples of INSTR. In these examples, you will see all four parameters used in all their permutations. As you write your own programs, keep in mind the different ways in which INSTR can be used to extract information from a string; it can greatly simplify the code you write to parse and analyze character data.

- Find the first occurrence of archie in "bug-or-tv-character?archie":

  ```
  INSTR ('bug-or-tv-character?archie', 'archie') ==> 21
  ```

  The starting position and the *n*th appearance both defaulted to 1.

- Find the first occurrence of archie in the following string starting from position 14:

  ```
  INSTR ('bug-or-tv-character?archie', 'ar', 14) ==> 21
  ```

  In this example I specified a starting position, which overrides the default of 1; the answer is still the same though. No matter where you start your search, the character position returned by INSTR is always calculated from the beginning of the string.

- Find the second occurrence of archie in the following string:

  ```
  INSTR ('bug-or-tv-character?archie', 'archie', 1, 2) ==> 0
  ```

  There is only one archie in the string, so INSTR returns 0. Even though the starting point is the default, I cannot leave it out if I also want to specify a nondefault *n*th appearance (2 in this case, for "second occurrence").

- Find the second occurrence of "a" in "bug-or-tv-character?archie":

  ```
  INSTR ('bug-or-tv-character?archie', 'a', 1, 2) ==> 15
  ```

  The second "a" in this string is the second "a" in "character," which is in the fifteenth position in the string.

- Find the last occurrence of "ar" in "bug-or-tv-character?archie".

  ```
  INSTR ('bug-or-tv-character?archie', 'ar', -1) ==> 21
  ```

  Were you thinking that the answer might be 6? Remember that the character position returned by INSTR is always calculated from the leftmost character of the string being position 1. The easiest way to find the last of anything in a string is to specify a negative number for the starting position. I did not have to specify the *n*th appearance (leaving me with a default value of 1), since the last occurrence is also the first when searching backwards.

- Find the second-to-last occurrence of "a" in "bug-or-tv-character?archie":

  ```
  INSTR ('bug-or-tv-character?archie', 'a', -1, 2) ==> 15
  ```

  No surprises here. Counting from the back of the string, INSTR passes over the "a" in archie, because that is the last occurrence, and searches for the next occurrence. Again, the character position is counted from the leftmost character, not the rightmost character, in the string.

- Find the position of the letter "t" closest to (but not past) the question mark in the following string: bug-or-tv-character?archie tophat:

  ```
  INSTR ('bug-or-tv-character?archie tophat', 't', -14) ==> 17
  ```

  I needed to find the "t" just before the question mark. The phrase "just before" indicates to me that I should search backwards from the question mark for the first occurrence. I therefore counted through the characters and determined that the question mark appears at the 20th position. I specified –14 as the starting position so that INSTR would search backwards right from the question mark.

  What? Did I hear you mutter that I cheated? That if I could count through the string to find the question mark, I could just as well count through the string to find the closest "t"? I knew that I couldn't slip something like that by my readers.

- A more general solution to the previous example: It is true that I "cheated." After all, when you are writing a program you usually do not know in advance the value and location of the string through which you are searching. It is likely to be a variable of some sort. It would be impossible to "count my way" to the question mark. Instead I need to find the location of the question mark and use that as the starting position. I need, in short, to use a second, or nested, INSTR inside the original INSTR. Here is a real solution to the problem:

  ```
  search_string := 'bug-or-tv-character?archie tophat';
  tee_loc :=
      INSTR (search_string, 't',
          -1 * (LENGTH (search_string) - INSTR (search_string, '?') +1));
  ```

  Instead of hardcoding 20 in my call to INSTR, I dynamically calculate the location of the question mark (actually, the first question mark in the string; I assume that there is only one). Then I subtract that from the full length of the string and multiply times –1 because I need to count the number of characters from the end of the string. I then use that value to kick off the search for the closest prior "t".

  This example is a good reminder that any of the parameters to INSTR can be complex expressions that call other functions or perform their own calculations. This fact is also highlighted in the final INSTR example.

- Use INSTR to confirm that a user entry is valid. In the code below, I check to see if the command selected by the user is found in the list of valid commands. If so, I execute that command:

```
IF INSTR ('|ADD|DELETE|CHANGE|VIEW|CALC|', '|' || cmd || '|') > 0
THEN
    execute_command (cmd);
ELSE
    DBMS_OUTPUT.PUT_LINE
        (' You entered an invalid command. Please try again...');
END IF;
```

In this case, I use the concatenation operator to construct the string that I will search for in the command list. I have to append a vertical bar (|) to the selected command because it is used as a delimiter in the command list. I also use the call to INSTR in a Boolean expression. If INSTR finds a match in the string, it returns a nonzero value. The Boolean expression therefore evaluates to TRUE and I can go on with my processing. Otherwise, I display an error message.

INSTR's flexibility allows you to write compact code which implements complex requirements. INSTRB is the multiple-byte character set version of INSTR. For single-byte character sets (such as American English), INSTRB returns the same values as INSTR.

The LENGTH function

The LENGTH function returns the length of the specified string. The specification for LENGTH follows:

```
FUNCTION LENGTH (string1 VARCHAR2) RETURN NUMBER
```

If string1 is NULL, then LENGTH returns NULL—not zero (0)! Remember, a NULL string is a "nonvalue." Therefore, it cannot have a length, even a zero length.

The LENGTH function, in fact, will never return zero; it will always return either NULL or a positive number. Here are some examples:

```
LENGTH (NULL) ==> NULL
LENGTH ('') ==> NULL -- Same as a NULL string.
LENGTH ('abcd') ==> 4
LENGTH ('abcd ') ==> 5
```

If string1 is a fixed-length CHAR datatype, then LENGTH counts the trailing blanks in its calculation. So the LENGTH of a fixed-length string is always the declared length of the string. If you want to compute the length of the nonblank characters in string1, you will need to use the RTRIM function to remove the trailing blanks (RTRIM is discussed later in this chapter). In the following example, length1 is set to 60 and length2 is set to 14.

```
DECLARE
   company_name CHAR(60) := 'ACME PLUMBING';
   length1 NUMBER;
   length2 NUMBER;
BEGIN
   length1 := LENGTH (company_name);
   length2 := LENGTH (RTRIM (company_name));
END;
```

LENGTHB is the multiple-byte character set version of LENGTH. For single-byte character sets (such as American English), LENGTH returns the same values as INSTR.

The LOWER function

The LOWER function converts all letters in the specified string to lowercase. The specifications for the LOWER function are:

```
FUNCTION LOWER (string1 IN CHAR) RETURN CHAR
FUNCTION LOWER (string1 IN VARCHAR2) RETURN VARCHAR2
```

As I noted earlier, LOWER and UPPER will actually return a fixed-length string if the incoming string is fixed-length. LOWER will not change any characters in the string that are not letters, since case is irrelevant for numbers and special characters, such as the dollar sign ($).

Here are some examples of the effect of LOWER:

```
LOWER ('BIG FAT LETTERS') ==> 'big fat letters'
LOWER ('123ABC') ==> '123abc'
```

LOWER and its partner in case conversion, UPPER, are useful for guaranteeing a consistent case when comparing strings. PL/SQL is not a case-sensitive language with regard to its own syntax and names of identifiers. It is sensitive to case, however, in character strings, whether found in named constants, literals, or variables. The string "ABC" is not the same as "abc", and this can cause problems in your programs if you are not careful and consistent in your handling of such values.

The LPAD function

By default, PL/SQL strips all trailing blanks from a character string unless it is declared with a fixed-length CHAR datatype. There are occasions, however, when you really want some spaces (or even some other character) added to the front or back of your string. LPAD (and its right-leaning cousin, RPAD) give you this capability. The LPAD function returns a string padded to the left (hence the "L" in "LPAD") to a specified length, and with a specified pad string. The specification of the LPAD function is:

```
FUNCTION LPAD
   (string1 IN VARCHAR2,
```

```
        padded_length IN NUMBER
        [, pad_string IN VARCHAR2])
    RETURN VARCHAR2
```

LPAD returns string1 padded on the left to length padded_length with the optional character string pad_string. If you do not specify pad_string, then string1 is padded on the left with spaces. You must specify the padded_length. If string1 already has a length equal to padded_length, then LPAD returns string1 without any additional characters. If padded_length is smaller than the length of string1, LPAD effectively truncates string1—it returns only the first padded_length characters of the incoming string1.

As you can easily see, LPAD can do a lot more than just add spaces to the left of a string. Let's look at some examples of how useful LPAD can be.

- Display the number padded left with zeros to a length of 10:

  ```
  LPAD ('55', 10, '0') ==> '0000000055'
  ```

- Display the number padded left with zeros to a length of 5:

  ```
  LPAD ('12345678', 5, '0') ==> '12345'
  ```

  LPAD interprets its padded_length as the maximum length of the string that it may return. As a result, it counts padded_length number of characters from the left (start of the string) and then simply returns that substring of the incoming value.

- Place the phrase "sell!" in front of the names of selected stocks, up to a string length of 45:

  ```
  LPAD ('HITOP TIES', 45, 'sell!')
  ==>
      'sell!sell!sell!sell!sell!sell!sell!HITOP TIES'
  ```

  Because the length of "HITOP TIES" is 10 and the length of "sell!" is 5, there is room for seven repetitions of the pad string. LPAD does, in fact, generate a repetition of the pattern specified in the pad string.

- Place the phrase "sell!" in front of the names of selected stocks, up to a string length of 43.

  ```
  LPAD ('HITOP TIES', 43, 'sell!')
  ==>
      'sell!sell!sell!sell!sell!sell!selHITOP TIES'
  ```

  Because the length of "HITOP TIES" is 10 and the length of "sell!" is 5, there is no longer room for seven full repetitions of the pad string. As a result, the seventh repetition (counting from the left) of "sell!" lost its last two characters. So you can see that LPAD does not pad by adding to the left of the original string until it runs out of room. Instead, it figures out how many characters it must pad by to reach the total, then constructs that full padded fragment, and finally appends the original string to this fragment.

- Place three repetitions of the string "DRAFT-ONLY" in front of the article's title. Put two spaces between each repetition.

```
LPAD ('Why I Love PL/SQL', 53, 'DRAFT-ONLY  ');
==>
        'DRAFT-ONLY  DRAFT-ONLY  DRAFT-ONLY  Why I Love PL/SQL'
```

You can specify any number of characters to be padded in front of the incoming string value. The 53 that is hardcoded in that call to LPAD is the result of some hard calculations: the title is 17 characters and the prefix, including spaces, is 12 characters. As a result, I needed to make sure that I padded to a length of at least 17 + 12*3 = 53. This is not a very desirable way to solve the problem, however; once again I have assumed that in my program I have access to all these specific values and can precompute the length I need. The section entitled "Frame String with Prefix and Suffix" shows how to generalize this kind of action in a procedure—without making any assumptions about lengths.

The LTRIM function

The LTRIM function is the opposite of LPAD. Whereas LPAD adds characters to the left of a string, LTRIM removes, or trims, characters from the leading portion of the string. And just as with LPAD, LTRIM offers much more flexibility than simply removing leading blanks. The specification of the LTRIM function is:

```
FUNCTION LTRIM (string1 IN VARCHAR2 [, trim_string IN VARCHAR2])
RETURN VARCHAR2
```

LTRIM returns string1 with all leading characters removed up to the first character not found in the trim_string. The second parameter is optional and defaults to a single space.

There is one important difference between LTRIM and LPAD. LPAD pads to the left with the specified string, and repeats that string (or pattern of characters) until there is no more room. LTRIM, on the other hand removes all leading characters which appear in the trim string, not as a pattern, but as individual candidates for trimming.

Here are some examples:

- Trim all leading blanks from ' Way Out in Right Field':

```
LTRIM ('   Way Out in Right Field') ==> 'Way Out in Right Field'
```

Because I did not specify a trim string, it defaults to a single space and so all leading spaces are removed.

- Trim '123' from the front of a string:

```
my_string := '123123123LotsaLuck123';

LTRIM (my_string, '123') ==> 'LotsaLuck123'
```

In this example, LTRIM stripped off all three leading repetitions of "123" from the specified string. Although it looks as though LTRIM trims by a specified pattern, this is not so, as the next example illustrates.

- Remove all numbers from the front of the string:

```
my_string := '70756234LotsaLuck';

LTRIM (my_string, '0987612345') ==> 'LotsaLuck'
```

By specifying every possible digit in my trim string, I ensured that any and all numbers would be trimmed, regardless of the order in which they occurred (and the order in which I place them in the trim string).

- Remove all a's, b's, and c's from the front of the string: 'abcabcccccI LOVE CHILI':

```
LTRIM ('abcabcccccI LOVE CHILI', 'abc') ==> 'I LOVE CHILI'
```

LTRIM removed the patterns of "abc", but also removed the individual instances of the letter "c". This worked out fine since the request was to remove any and all of those three letters. What if I wanted to remove only any instance of "abc" as a pattern from the front of the string? I couldn't use LTRIM since it trims off any matching individual characters. To remove a pattern from a string—or to replace one pattern with another pattern—you will want to make use of the REPLACE function, which is discussed next.

The REPLACE function

The REPLACE function returns a string in which all occurrences of a specified match string are replaced with a replacement string. REPLACE is useful for searching out patterns of characters and then changing all instances of that pattern in a single function call. The specification of the REPLACE function is:

```
FUNCTION REPLACE (string1 IN VARCHAR2, match_string IN VARCHAR2
                 [, replace_string IN VARCHAR2])
   RETURN VARCHAR2
```

If you do not specify the replacement string, then REPLACE simply removes all occurrences of the match_string in string1. If you specify neither a match string nor a replacement string, REPLACE returns NULL.

Here are several examples using REPLACE:

- Remove all instances of the letter "C" in the string "CAT CALL":

```
REPLACE ('CAT CALL', 'C') ==> 'AT ALL'
```

Because I did not specify a replacement string, REPLACE changed all occurrences of "C" to NULL.

- Replace all occurrences of "99" with "100" in the following string:

```
REPLACE ('Zero defects in period 99 reached 99%!', '99', '100')
==>
      'Zero defects in period 100 reached 100%!'
```

- Replace all occurrences of "th" with the letter "z":

```
REPLACE ('this that and the other', 'th', 'z') ==> 'zis zat and ze ozer'
```

- Handle occurrences of a single quote (') within a query criteria string. The single quote is a string terminator symbol. It indicates the start and/or end of the literal string. I ran into this requirement when building query-by-example strings in Oracle Forms. If the user enters a string with a single quote in it, such as:

```
Customer didn't have change.
```

and then I concatenate that string into a larger string, the resulting SQL statement (created dynamically by Oracle Forms in Query Mode) fails, because there are unbalanced single quotes in the string.

You can resolve this problem in one of three ways:

— Simply strip out the single quote before you execute the query. This is workable only if there really aren't any single quotes in the data in the database.

— If you do allow single quotes, you can then either replace the single quote with a single character wildcard (_) or:

— Embed that single quote inside other single quotes so that the SQL layer can properly parse the statement.

To replace the single quote with a wild card, you would code:

```
criteria_string := REPLACE (criteria_string, '''', '_');
```

That's right! Four single quotes in sequence are required for PL/SQL to understand that you want to search for one single quote in the criteria string. The first quote indicates the start of a literal. The fourth quote indicates the end of the string literal. The two inner single quotes parse into one single quote. That is, whenever you want to embed a single quote inside a literal, you must place another single quote before it.

This principle comes in handy for the final resolution of the single quote in query criteria problem: change the single quote to two single quotes and then execute the query.

```
criteria_string := REPLACE (criteria_string, '''', '''''');
```

as in:

```
REPLACE ('Customer didn''t have change.', '''', '''''')
==>
    Customer didn''t have change.
```

Now, even if you place single quotes at the beginning and end of this string, the internal single quote will not signal termination of the literal.

- Remove all leading repetitions of "abc" from the string:

    "abcabccccI LOVE CHILIabc"

This is the behavior I was looking at in the previous section on LTRIM. I want to remove all instances of the pattern "abc" from the beginning of the string, but I do not want to remove that pattern throughout the rest of the string. In addition, I want to remove "abc" only as a pattern; if I encounter three contiguous c's ("ccc"), on the other hand, they should not be removed from the string. This task is less straightforward than it might at first seem. If I simply apply REPLACE to the string, it will remove all occurrences of "abc", instead of just the leading instances. For example:

```
REPLACE ('abcabccccI LOVE CHILIabc', 'abc') ==> 'cccI LOVE CHILI'
```

That is not what I want in this case. If I use LTRIM, on the other hand, I will be left with none of the leading c's, as demonstrated in a previous example:

```
LTRIM ('abcabccccI LOVE CHILIabc', 'abc') ==> 'I LOVE CHILIabc'
```

And this is not quite right either. I want to be left with 'cccI LOVE CHILIabc' (please do not ask why), and it turns out that the way to get it is to use a combination of LTRIM and REPLACE. Suppose I create a local variable as follows:

```
my_string   := 'abcabccccI LOVE CHILIabc';
```

Then the following statement will achieve the desired effect by nesting calls to REPLACE and LTRIM within one another:

```
REPLACE
   (LTRIM
      (REPLACE (my_string, 'abc', '@'), '@'), '@', 'abc')
==>
      'cccI LOVE CHILIabc'
```

Here is how I would describe in English what the above statement does:

"First replace all occurrences of 'abc' with the special character '@' (which I am assuming does not otherwise appear in the string). Then trim off all leading instances of '@'. Finally, replace all remaining occurrences of '@' with 'abc'."

Voila, as they say in many of the finer restaurants in Paris. Now let's pull apart this single, rather complex statement into separate PL/SQL steps which correspond to my "natural language" description:

— Replace all occurrences of "abc" with the special character "@" (which I am assuming does not otherwise appear in the string). Notice that this only affects the pattern and not any appearance of "a", "b", or "c".

```
REPLACE ('abcabccccI LOVE CHILIabc', 'abc', '@')
     ==> '@@cccI LOVE CHILI@'
```

— Trim off all leading instances of "@".

```
LTRIM ('@@cccI LOVE CHILI@', '@') ==> 'cccI LOVE CHILI@'
```

Notice that LTRIM now leaves the c's in place, because I didn't ask it to remove "a" or "b" or "c"—just "@". In addition, it left the trailing "@" in the string since LTRIM deals only with characters on the leading end of the string.

— Replace all remaining occurrences of "@" with "abc".

```
REPLACE ('cccI LOVE CHILI@', '@', 'abc') ==> 'cccI LOVE CHILIabc'
```

And we are done. I used the first REPLACE to temporarily change the occurrences of "abc" so that LTRIM could distinguish between the pattern I wanted to get rid of and the extra characters which needed to be preserved. Then, a final call to REPLACE restored the pattern in the string.

The RPAD function

The RPAD function adds characters to the end of a character string. It returns a string padded to the right (hence the "R" in "RPAD") to a specified length, and with an optional pad string. The specification of the RPAD function is:

```
FUNCTION RPAD
    (string1 IN VARCHAR2,
     padded_length IN NUMBER
     [, pad_string IN VARCHAR2])
RETURN VARCHAR2
```

RPAD returns string1 padded on the right to length padded_length with the optional character string pad_string. If you do not specify pad_string, then string1 is padded on the right with spaces. You must specify the padded_length. If string1 already has a length equal to padded_length, then RPAD returns string1 without any additional characters. If padded_length is smaller than the length of string1, RPAD effectively truncates string1: it returns only the first padded_length characters of the incoming string1.

Let's look at some examples of RPAD:

• Display the number padded right with zeros to a length of 10:

```
RPAD ('55', 10, '0') ==> '5500000000'
```

I could also use TO_CHAR to convert from a number to a character (I don't know off-hand why you would do this, but it's good to be reminded that there are usually at least two or three ways to solve any problem):

```
TO_CHAR (55 * 10000000) ==> '5500000000'
```

• Display the number padded right with zeros to a length of 5:

```
RPAD ('12345678', 5) ==> '12345'
```

RPAD interprets its padded_length as the maximum length of the string that it may return. As a result, it counts padded_length number of characters from the left (start of the string) and then simply returns that substring of the incoming value. This is the same behavior as that found with LPAD, described earlier in this chapter. Remember: RPAD does not return the rightmost five characters (in the above case "45678").

- Place the phrase "sell!" after the names of selected stocks, up to a string length of 45:

```
RPAD ('HITOP TIES', 45, 'sell!')
==>
'  HITOP TIESsell!sell!sell!sell!sell!sell!sell!'
```

Since the length of "HITOP TIES" is 10 and the length of "sell!" is 5, there is room for seven repetitions of the pad string. RPAD does, in fact, generate a repetition of the pattern specified in the pad string.

- Place the phrase "sell!" after the names of selected stocks, up to a string length of 43:

```
RPAD ('HITOP TIES', 43, 'sell!')
==>
'HITOP TIESsell!sell!sell!sell!sell!sell!sel'
```

Because the length of "HITOP TIES" is 10 and the length of "sell!" is 5, there is no longer room for seven full repetitions of the pad string. As a result, the seventh repetition of "sell!" lost its last two characters.

- Create a string of 60 dashes to use as a border in a report:

```
RPAD ('-', 60, '-')
==>
'------------------------------------------------------------'
```

You can use RPAD (and LPAD as well) to generate repetitive sequences of characters. I have used this technique in SQL*Reportwriter V1.1, where graphical objects like boxes are not really available. I can include the RPAD in a SELECT statement in the report, and then use the corresponding field in Text elements to provide lines to break up the data in a report.

The RTRIM function

The RTRIM function is the opposite of RPAD, and the companion function to LTRIM. Where RPAD adds characters to the right of a string, RTRIM removes, or trims, characters from the end portion of the string. Just as with RPAD, RTRIM offers much more flexibility than simply removing trailing blanks. The specification of the RTRIM function is:

```
FUNCTION RTRIM (string1 IN VARCHAR2 [, trim_string IN VARCHAR2])
  RETURN VARCHAR2
```

RTRIM returns string1 with all trailing characters removed up to the first character not found in the trim_string. The second parameter is optional and defaults to a single space.

Here are some examples of RTRIM:

- Trim all trailing blanks from a string:

```
RTRIM ('Way Out in Right Field                    ')
==> 'Way Out in Right Field'
```

Since I did not specify a trim string, it defaults to a single space and so all trailing spaces are removed.

- Trim all the characters in "BAM! ARGH!" from the end of a string:

```
my_string := 'Sound effects: BAM!ARGH!BAM!HAM';
RTRIM (my_string, 'BAM! ARGH!') ==> 'Sound effects:'
```

This use of RTRIM stripped off all the letters at the end of the string which are found in "BAM!ARGH!." This includes "BAM" and "HAM," so those words too are removed from the string even though "HAM" is not listed explicitly as a "word" in the trim string. Also, the inclusion of two exclamation marks in the trim string is unnecessary, because RTRIM is not looking for the word "ARGH!", but each of the letters in "ARGH!".

The SOUNDEX function

The SOUNDEX function allows you to perform string comparisons based on phonetics (the way a word sounds), as opposed to semantics (the way a word is spelled).[*] SOUNDEX returns a character string which is the "phonetic representation" of the argument. The specification of the SOUNDEX function is as follows:

```
FUNCTION SOUNDEX (string1 IN VARCHAR2) RETURN VARCHAR2
```

Here are some of the values SOUNDEX generated and how they vary according to the input string:

```
SOUNDEX ('smith') ==> 'S530'
SOUNDEX ('SMYTHE') ==> ''S530'
SOUNDEX ('smith smith') ==> 'S532'
SOUNDEX ('smith z') ==> 'S532'
SOUNDEX ('feuerstein') ==> 'F623'
SOUNDEX ('feuerst') ==> 'F623'
```

Keep the following SOUNDEX rules in mind when using this function:

- The SOUNDEX value always begins with the first letter in the input string.

---

[*] Oracle Corporation used the algorithm in *The Art of Computer Programming*, Volume 3, by Donald Knuth, to generate the phonetic representation.

- SOUNDEX only uses the first five consonants in the string to generate the return value.

- Only consonants are used to compute the numeric portion of the SOUNDEX value. Except for a possible leading vowel, all vowels are ignored.

- SOUNDEX is not case-sensitive. Upper- and lowercase letters return the same SOUNDEX value.

The SOUNDEX function is useful for *ad hoc* queries, and any other kinds of searches where the exact spelling of a database value is not known or easily determined.

The SUBSTR function

The SUBSTR function is one of the most useful and commonly used character functions. It allows you to extract a portion or subset of contiguous (connected) characters from a string. The substring is specified by starting position and a length.

The specification for the SUBSTR function is:

```
FUNCTION SUBSTR
    (string_in IN VARCHAR2,
     start_position_in IN NUMBER
     [, substr_length_in IN NUMBER])
    RETURN VARCHAR2
```

where the arguments are used as follows:

string_in
   The source string

start_position_in
   The starting position of the substring in string_in

substr_length_in
   The length of the substring desired (the number of characters to be returned in the substring)

The last parameter, substr_length_in, is optional. If you do not specify a substring length, then SUBSTR returns all the characters to the end of string_in (from the starting position specified).

The start position cannot be zero. If the start position is less than zero, then the substring is retrieved from the back of the string. SUBSTR counts backwards substr_length_in number of characters from the end of string_in. In this case, however, the characters which are extracted are still to the right of the starting position. See Figure 11-2 for an illustration of how the different arguments are used by SUBSTR.

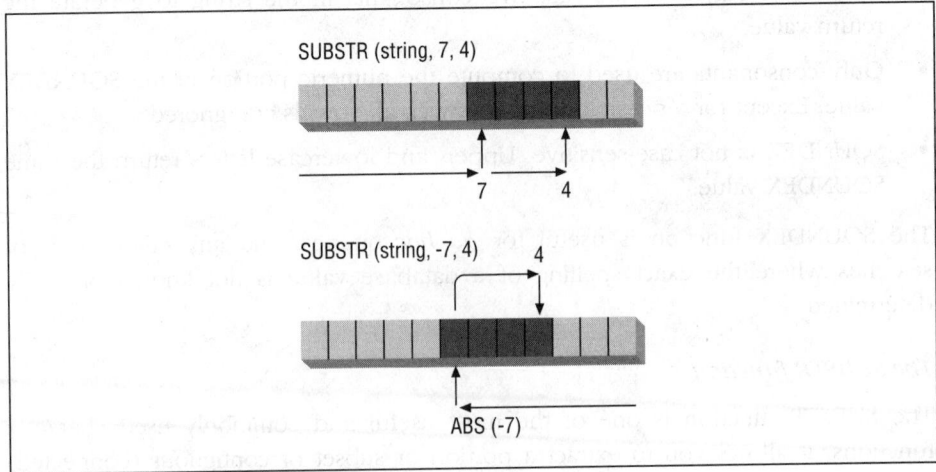

Figure 11-2. How arguments are used by SUBSTR

The substr_length_in argument must be greater than zero.

You will find that in practice SUBSTR is very forgiving. Even if you violate the rules for the values of the starting position and the number of characters to be substringed, SUBSTR will not generate errors. Instead, for the most part, it will return NULL—or the entire string—as its answer.

Here are some examples of SUBSTR:

- If the absolute value of the starting position exceeds the length of the input string, return NULL:

```
SUBSTR ('now_or_never', 200) ==> NULL
SUBSTR ('now_or_never', -200) ==> NULL
```

- If starting position is 0, SUBSTR acts as though the starting position was actually 1:

```
SUBSTR ('now_or_never', 0, 3) ==> 'now'
SUBSTR ('now_or_never', 0) ==> 'now_or_never'
```

- If the substring length is less than or equal to zero, return NULL:

```
SUBSTR ('now_or_never', 5, -2) ==> NULL
SUBSTR ('now_or_never', 1, 0) ==> NULL
```

- Return the last character in a string:

```
SUBSTR ('Another sample string', -1) ==> 'g'
```

This is the cleanest way to get the single last character. A more direct, but cumbersome, approach is this:

```
SUBSTR
    ('Sample string', LENGTH ('Sample string'), 1) ==> 'g'
```

In other words, calculate the LENGTH of the string and the one character from the string that starts at that last position. Yuch.

- Remove an element from a string list. This is, in a way, the opposite of SUBSTR: I want to extract a portion or substring of a string—and leave the rest of it intact. Oddly enough, however, I will use SUBSTR to perform this task. Suppose my screen maintains a list of selected temperatures, as follows:

```
|HOT|COLD|LUKEWARM|SCALDING|
```

The vertical bar delimits the different items on the list. When the user deselects "LUKEWARM," I now have to remove it from the list, which becomes:

```
|HOT|COLD|SCALDING|
```

The best way to accomplish this task is to determine the starting and ending positions of the item to be removed, and then use SUBSTR to take apart the list and put it back together—without the specified item. Let's walk through this process a step at a time. The list used in the above example contains 29 characters:

```
String:          |HOT|COLD|LUKEWARM|SCALDING|
Character index: 12345678901234567890012345679
```

As you can see, the item "LUKEWARM" starts on position 11 and ends on position 18. To extract this item from the list, I need to pull off the portion of the string before "LUKEWARM" as follows:

```
SUBSTR ('|HOT|COLD|LUKEWARM|SCALDING|', 1, 10)
```

and then I need to extract the trailing portion of the list (after "LUKEWARM"). Notice that I do not want to keep both of the delimiters when I put these pieces back together, so this next SUBSTR does not include the vertical bar at position 19:

```
SUBSTR ('|HOT|COLD|LUKEWARM|SCALDING|', 20)
```

Finally, then, to extract "LUKEWARM" from the list, I use the following concatenation of calls to SUBSTR:

```
SUBSTR ('|HOT|COLD|LUKEWARM|SCALDING|', 1, 10)
||
SUBSTR ('|HOT|COLD|LUKEWARM|SCALDING|', 20)
==>
    '|HOT|COLD|SCALDING|'
```

- Remove the middle word in a three-word string (in which each word is separated by an underscore) and switch the order of the first and last words. For example, change better_than_ever to ever_better. This is a bit different from the list_remove function because I do not have immediately available to me the length of the element I need to remove. Instead, I have to make use of INSTR twice to calculate that length. Here is the solution expressed as a function:

```
/* Filename on companion disk: bitesw.sf */
FUNCTION bite_and_switch (tripart_string_in IN VARCHAR2)
```

```
        RETURN VARCHAR2
    IS
        /* Location of first underscore */
        first_delim_loc  NUMBER := INSTR (tripart_string_in, '_', 1, 1);

        /* Location of second underscore */
        second_delim_loc NUMBER := INSTR (tripart_string_in, '_', 1, 2);

        /* Return value of function, set by default to incoming string. */
        return_value VARCHAR2(1000) := tripart_string_in;
    BEGIN
        /* Only switch words if two delimiters are found. */
        IF second_delim_loc > 0
        THEN
           /* Pull out  first and second words and stick them together. */
           return_value :=
               SUBSTR (tripart_string_in, 1, first_delim_loc - 1) || '_' ||
               SUBSTR (tripart_string_in, second_delim_loc + 1);
        END IF;

        /* Return the switched string */
        RETURN return_value;
    END bite_and_switch;
```

- Use SUBSTR to extract the portion of a string between the specified starting and ending points. I run into this requirement all the time. SUBSTR requires a starting position and the number of characters to pull out. Often, however, I have only the starting position and the ending position—and I then have to compute the number of characters in between. Is it just the difference between the end and start positions? Is it one more or one less than that? Invariably, I get it wrong the first time and have to scribble a little example on scrap paper to prove the formula to myself.

So to save all of you the trouble, I offer a tiny function below, called "betwnstr" (for: "BETWeeN STRing"). This function encapsulates the calculation you must perform to come up with the number of characters between start and end positions, which is:

```
end_position - start_position + 1
```

```
/* Filename on companion disk: betwnstr.sf */
FUNCTION betwnstr
    (string_in IN VARCHAR2, start_in IN INTEGER, end_in IN INTEGER)
    RETURN VARCHAR2
IS
BEGIN
    RETURN SUBSTR (string_in, start_in, end_in - start_in + 1);
END;
```

While this function does not provide the full flexibility offered by SUBSTR (for example, with negative starting positions), it offers a starting point for the kind of encapsulation you should be performing in these situations.

By the way, SUBSTRB is the multiple-byte character set version of SUBSTR. For single-byte character sets (such as American English), SUBSTRB returns the same values as SUBSTR.

The TRANSLATE function

The TRANSLATE function is a variation on REPLACE. REPLACE replaces every instance of a set of characters with another set of characters; that is, REPLACE works with entire words or patterns. TRANSLATE replaces single characters at a time, translating the *n*th character in the match set with the *n*th character in the replacement set. The specification of the TRANSLATE is as follows:

```
FUNCTION TRANSLATE
    (string_in IN VARCHAR2,
     search_set IN VARCHAR2,
     replace_set VARCHAR2)
RETURN VARCHAR2
```

where string_in is the string in which characters are to be translated, search_set is the set of characters to be translated (if found), and replace_set is the set of characters which will be placed in the string. Unlike REPLACE, where the last argument could be left off, you must include all three arguments when you use TRANSLATE. Any of the three arguments may, however, be NULL, in which case TRANSLATE always returns NULL.

Here are some examples of the effect of TRANSLATE:

```
TRANSLATE ('abcd', 'ab', '12') ==> '12cd'

TRANSLATE ('12345', '15', 'xx') ==> 'x234x'

TRANSLATE ('grumpy old possum', 'uot', '%$*') ==>   'gr%mpy $ld p$ss%m'

TRANSLATE ('my language needs the letter e', 'egms', 'X')
==>   '
    'y lanuaX nXXd thX lXttXr X';

TRANSLATE ('please go away', 'a', NULL) ==> NULL
```

You can deduce a number of the usage rules for TRANSLATE from the above examples, but I spell them out here:

- If the search set contains a character not found in the string, then no translation is performed for that character.

- If the string contains a character not found in the search set, then that character is not translated.

- If the search set contains more characters than the replace set, then all the "trailing" search characters that have no match in the replace set are removed from the string. In the following example, a, b, and c are changed to z, y, and x, respectively. But the letter "d" is removed from the return string entirely since it had no corresponding character in the replace set.

```
TRANSLATE ('abcdefg', 'abcd', 'zyx') ==> 'zyxefg'
```

In these cases, NULL is the matching "character" for all extra characters in the search set. When you replace a character with NULL it is the same as removing that character from the string.

- If any of the three arguments is NULL, then the result of the translation is NULL. This is consistent with a basic tenet of NULLs: apply an operation to an unknown value and you always get an unknown value.

The TRANSLATE function comes in handy when you need to change a whole set of characters in a string, regardless of the order in which they appear in the string. The section entitled "Verifying String Formats with TRANSLATE" demonstrates how handy this feature can be.

The UPPER function

The UPPER function converts all letters in the specified string to uppercase. The specifications of the UPPER function are:

```
FUNCTION UPPER (string1 IN CHAR) RETURN CHAR
FUNCTION UPPER (string1 IN VARCHAR2) RETURN VARCHAR2
```

As I noted at the beginning of this chapter, UPPER and LOWER will actually return a fixed-length string if the incoming string is fixed length. UPPER will not change any characters in the string which are not letters, since case is irrelevant for numbers and special characters such as $.

Here are some examples of the effect of UPPER:

```
UPPER ('short little letters no more') ==> 'SHORT LITTLE LETTERS NO MORE'

UPPER ('123abc') ==> '123ABC'
```

UPPER and its partner in case conversion, LOWER, are useful for guaranteeing a consistent case when comparing strings. PL/SQL is not a case-sensitive language as concerns its own syntax and names of identifiers. It is sensitive to case, however, in character strings, whether found in named constants, literals, or variables. The string "ABC" is not the same as "abc", and this can cause problems in your programs if you are not careful and consistent in your handling of such values.

Character Function Examples

Now that you have a solid grounding in all the different character functions, you should find the extended examples in the following sections easy to follow. I also hope that you'll find that the concepts embodied by the examples come in handy in your own applications.

Parsing a Name

Have you ever noticed that a person's name is a complicated data structure? You've got a first name, last name, middle initial, title, salutation, and who knows what else. It is also impossible to guarantee the uniqueness of a person's name, no matter how many attributes you plan to maintain. That's why I memorized my nine-digit Social Security number early in life.

The name of a human being is made up of many components. To make things even more complicated, though, there are at least two common formats for displaying and specifying a person's name:

- LAST, FIRST MIDDLE, as in Feuerstein, Eli S.

and:

- FIRST MIDDLE LAST, as in Eli Silva Feuerstein

But of course a name could also be formatted as follows:

- TITLE FIRST MIDDLE LAST1 LAST2 GENERATION SUFFIX

as in Mr. Eli S. Hamilton Feuerstein, III, PhD

Why should you care about these different formats? Suppose my application has a table of callers structured like this:

```
CREATE TABLE caller
    (caller_id NUMBER PRIMARY KEY,
    first_name VARCHAR2(30),
    last_name VARCHAR2(30),
    middle_name VARCHAR2(30)
    );
```

and that the caller_id column is a foreign key in a number of other tables.

I strongly believe that users should never have to see or enter the actual foreign key values, unless there is a specific application requirement to do so. Instead, the user should be able to work with the name of the caller and leave it to the PL/SQL code to get the key. Users don't need to know that the caller named "Steven Feuerstein" has called ID number 14067. They just know the name and they should be allowed to enter the name in whatever format they choose:

```
FIRST MIDDLE LAST
LAST, FIRST MIDDLE
LAST, FIRST
LAST
FIRST LAST
```

and so on. My application should be smart enough to figure out the intended name. To do this, I would have to parse the name entered by the user into its component parts, dynamically interpreting the type of format the user has employed. This parsing process is performed using a variety of string functions.

Now if you think I am going to provide you with code that will be able to make sense of a name like Mr. Eli S. Hamilton Feuerstein, III, PhD, then I would ask you to please lower your expectations. Instead, I will present several versions of a procedure that parses a name assuming a simpler format. I will then leave the more general and truly bewildering cases as, ahem, exercises for the reader.

Parsing first and last names only

The procedure that follows, parse_name, accepts a full name and returns the first and last names, separated out of that combined string. The first version of this procedure understands and interprets three different formats:

```
FIRST LAST
LAST, FIRST
LAST
```

The parse_name algorithm is straightforward, applying the following rules:

- If the full name has a comma, then everything to the left of the comma is the last name and everything to the right of the comma is the first name.

- If the full name does not have a comma but does have a space, then everything to the left of the space is the first name and everything to the right of the space is the last name.

- If the full name has neither a space nor a comma, then the entire string is the last name and the procedure returns a NULL value for the first name.

In all of these cases, the first and last names are returned in uppercase.

The following table shows how parse_name will interpret various name strings:

Full Name	First	Last
SANDRA BARKER	SANDRA	BARKER
QUINCE,HARRY	HARRY	QUINCE
JOG BOG, HOLLER	HOLLER	JOG BOG
Steve Samson	STEVE	SAMSON
Eli Silva Feuerstein	ELI	SILVA FEUERSTEIN
HALLY		HALLY

The following version of parse_name doesn't check for middle names and uses LTRIM, RTRIM, INSTR, and SUBSTR to separate a full name into its first and last name components:

```
/* Filename on companion disk: parsenm1.sp */
PROCEDURE parse_name
```

```
                 (fullname_in IN VARCHAR2,
                  fname_out OUT caller.first_name%TYPE,
                  lname_out OUT caller.last_name%TYPE)
   IS
      /* Trimmed and uppercased version of name. */
      fullname_int VARCHAR2(255) := LTRIM (RTRIM (UPPER (fullname_in)));

      /* The location of the comma delimiter in the name. */
      delim_comma NUMBER := INSTR (fullname_int, ',');

      /* Location of the first space delimiter in the name. */
      delim_space NUMBER := INSTR (fullname_int, ' ');

   BEGIN
      IF delim_comma = 0 AND delim_space = 0
      THEN
         /* No comma, no space: return whole string as LAST name. */
         lname_out := fullname_int;
         fname_out := NULL;

      ELSIF delim_comma != 0
      THEN
         /* Found a comma in the string! Use LAST, FIRST format.
         ||
         || Use SUBSTR to grab everything from the beginning of the
         || name to just before comma and assign it to last name.
         */
         lname_out := SUBSTR (fullname_int, 1, delim_comma-1);
         /*
         || Use SUBSTR to grab everything from just after the comma
         || and assign it to the first name. Use LTRIM to
         || get rid of any blanks between the comma and the first name.
         */
         fname_out := LTRIM (SUBSTR (fullname_int, delim_comma+1));

      ELSIF delim_space != 0
      THEN
         /* Found a space in the string! Use FIRST LAST format.
         ||
         || Use SUBSTR to grab everything from the beginning of the
         || name to just before the space and assign to first name.
         */
         fname_out := SUBSTR (fullname_int, 1, delim_space-1);
         /*
         || Use SUBSTR to grab everything from just after the space
         || and assign it to the last name. Use RTRIM to
         || get rid of any multiple spaces before the last name.
         */
         lname_out := LTRIM (SUBSTR (fullname_int, delim_space+1));
      END IF;
   END parse_name;
```

As you saw in the previous table, parse_name does not do such a great job with middle names when provided in the format FIRST MIDDLE LAST. In fact, it doesn't recognize middle names as a separate component in a person's name. In the next section we look at a version of parse_name that does handle middle names intelligently.

Parsing first, last, and middle names

In order to handle potential middle names, I need to come up with a new set of possible formats which will be recognized by the procedure. I can think of the following:

```
FIRST MIDDLE LAST
LAST, FIRST MIDDLE
LAST, FIRST
LAST
FIRST LAST
```

I could also try to handle MIDDLE LAST, FIRST—this would seem to me, however, to be a very unusual and awkward way to enter a name. I am going to ignore it.

Given these formats, I will enhance the parse_name procedure shown in the previous section so that it applies the following additional rules:

- If the format is FIRST MIDDLE LAST, then the last name is made up of everything after the last blank in the name, and the first name is everything up to the first blank.

- If the format is LAST, FIRST MIDDLE, then the last name is made up of everything up to the comma. The first name is everything after the comma and before the first blank after the comma (or the end of the string, in which case there is no middle name).

We've already seen how to find the first space in a string. How can we find the last occurrence of the space in a string? We will make use of the negative starting point for the INSTR function as follows (the INSTR function is discussed earlier in the chapter):

```
last_space_loc := INSTR (fullname_int, ' ', -1, 1);
lname_out    := SUBSTR (fullname_int, delim_space+1);
```

The enhanced version of parse_name is shown below. It takes the full name and returns up to three different components of that name. The three component parameters are given modes of IN OUT, rather than just OUT, because I make reference to the parameters in the program as I manipulate the values. Because of this they cannot be simply OUT parameters.

Here is the version of parse_name that checks for middle names:

```
/* Filename on companion disk: parsenm2.sp */
PROCEDURE parse_name
```

```
      (fullname_in IN VARCHAR2,
       fname_out IN OUT caller.first_name%TYPE,
       mname_out IN OUT caller.last_name%TYPE,
       lname_out IN OUT caller.middle_name%TYPE)
/*
|| Note: comments are provided only for new elements of code.
*/
IS
      fullname_int VARCHAR2(255) := LTRIM (UPPER (fullname_in));
      delim_comma NUMBER := INSTR (fullname_in, ',');

      /* Location of the first and last space delimiters. */
      first_space NUMBER := INSTR (fullname_in, ' ');
      last_space  NUMBER;

BEGIN
      IF delim_comma = 0 AND first_space = 0
      THEN
         /* Just one word, so it all goes to the last name */
         lname_out := fullname_int;
         fname_out := NULL;
         mname_out := NULL;

      ELSIF delim_comma != 0
      THEN
         /* LAST, FIRST or FIRST MIDDLE format:
         || Strip off last name, then do first and middle names
         */
         lname_out := SUBSTR (fullname_int, 1, delim_comma-1);
         /*
         || Assign the remainder of the name to the first name.
         || If there are no more spaces, there is no middle name
         || and the first name will be the rest of the name.
         ||
         || Find the first space after the comma. I use LTRIM
         || to remove any leading blanks between the comma and
         || the first name.
         */
         fname_out := LTRIM (SUBSTR (fullname_int, delim_comma+1));
         first_space := INSTR (fname_out, ' ');
         IF first_space = 0
         THEN
            /* No space, so there is no middle name. */
            mname_out := NULL;
         ELSE
            /* Split up the name into first and middle parts. */
            fullname_int := fname_out; -- hold a copy
            fname_out := SUBSTR (fullname_int, 1, first_space-1);
            mname_out := SUBSTR (fullname_int, first_space+1);
         END IF;

      ELSIF first_space != 0
      THEN
         /*
```

```
|| We have a "FIRST MIDDLE LAST" scenario. See if there is
|| another space, and make sure that there are non-blank
|| characters between the two blanks.  If this is the case,
|| we have a middle name. If not, just split up the name into
|| first and last. Well? Didn't I say that names are
|| complicated?
*/
last_space := INSTR (fullname_in, ' ', -1, 1);
IF first_space = last_space
THEN
    /* Just one space. Split name as in parse_name. */
    fname_out := SUBSTR (fullname_int, 1, first_space-1);
    lname_out := SUBSTR (fullname_int, first_space + 1);
/*
|| Check to see if there is anything besides blanks between
|| the first and last names. The user might have typed:
|| "JOE    SHMO" just to play games with your program. You
|| don't want to look silly, so you make the effort and
|| use RTRIM to squeeze out the blanks, leaving behind NULL
|| if that's all there was.
*/
ELSE
    /*
    || The hardest part about the middle name is that you have
    || to figure out its length. You need to subtract 1 from
    || the difference between last and first since the
    || first_space locator is actually always an offset from
    || zero. For example:
    ||        Loc = 12345678901234567890
    ||        String = thelma hoke peterson
    ||    first_space (7) ||-^    ^||- last_space (12)
    ||        Length of middle name "Hoke" = 12 - 7 - 1 = 4
    */
    mname_out :=
        LTRIM (RTRIM
                (SUBSTR (fullname_int,
                        first_space + 1,
                        last_space - first_space - 1)));

    /* Now the easy part. */
    fname_out := SUBSTR (fullname_int, 1, first_space - 1);
    lname_out := SUBSTR (fullname_int, last_space + 1);
    END IF;
END IF;
END;
```

You can see how the code grew considerably more complex just by adding the necessary parsing for middle name. You can see why I don't want to show you how to handle titles, suffixes, and salutations. Of course, in many data entry screens, these other elements of the name are isolated into separate fields or items on the screen.

Implementing Word Wrap for Long Text

Suppose you have a very long line of text and you need to wrap it to fit within a certain line length. Instead of breaking apart words, you want to fit as many separate words as you can onto a single line and then start a new line.

The wrap package contains the to_paragraph procedure,[*] which takes one long line of text and breaks it into separate lines, depositing those separate lines into a PL/SQL table. The procedure also contains calls to the built-in DBMS_OUTPUT package so it can display a trace of the way it performs the analysis to break apart the long text.

```
/* Filename on companion disk: wordwrap.spp */
create or replace PACKAGE wrap
IS
    TYPE paragraph_tabletype IS TABLE OF VARCHAR2 (80)
        INDEX BY BINARY_INTEGER;

    PROCEDURE to_paragraph
        (text_in IN VARCHAR2,
         line_length IN INTEGER,
         paragraph_out IN OUT paragraph_tabletype,
         num_lines_out IN OUT INTEGER,
         word_break_at_in IN VARCHAR2 := ' ');
END wrap;
/

create or replace PACKAGE BODY wrap
IS
    replace_string VARCHAR2(100) := NULL;

    PROCEDURE to_paragraph
        (text_in IN VARCHAR2,
         line_length IN INTEGER,
         paragraph_out IN OUT paragraph_tabletype,
         num_lines_out IN OUT INTEGER,
         word_break_at_in IN VARCHAR2 := ' ')
    IS
        len_text INTEGER := LENGTH (text_in);
        line_start_loc INTEGER := 1;
        line_end_loc INTEGER := 1;
        last_space_loc INTEGER;
        curr_line VARCHAR2(80);

        PROCEDURE set_replace_string IS
        BEGIN
            replace_string := RPAD ('@', LENGTH (word_break_at_in), '@');
        END;
```

---

[*] This example, including the wonderful test script, was provided by David Thompson. It contains a number of features of PL/SQL covered later in this book, including built-in package modules and programmer-defined packages. Thanks as well to Lawrence Pit for his help with this example.

```
      PROCEDURE find_last_delim_loc
      (line_in IN VARCHAR2, loc_out OUT INTEGER)
      IS
          v_line VARCHAR2(1000) := line_in;
      BEGIN
         IF word_break_at_in IS NOT NULL
         THEN
             v_line :=
                 TRANSLATE (line_in, word_break_at_in, replace_string);
         END IF;
         loc_out := INSTR (v_line, '@', -1);
      END;

   BEGIN
      set_replace_string;

      IF len_text IS NULL
      THEN
          num_lines_out := 0;
      ELSE
          num_lines_out := 1;
          LOOP
             EXIT WHEN line_end_loc > len_text;
             line_end_loc := LEAST (line_end_loc + line_length, len_text + 1);

             /* get the next possible line of text */
             curr_line := SUBSTR (text_in || ' ', line_start_loc, line_length +1);

             /* find the last space in this section of the line */
             find_last_delim_loc (curr_line, last_space_loc);

             /* When NO spaces exist, use the full current line*/
             /* otherwise, cut the line at the space.          */
             IF last_space_loc > 0
             THEN
                 line_end_loc := line_start_loc + last_space_loc;
             END IF;

             /* Add this line to the paragraph */
             paragraph_out (num_lines_out) :=
                 substr (text_in,
                         line_start_loc,
                         line_end_loc - line_start_loc);

             num_lines_out := num_lines_out + 1;
             line_start_loc := line_end_loc;
          END LOOP;
          num_lines_out := num_lines_out - 1;
      END IF;
   END to_paragraph;
END wrap;
/
```

The following script tests the to_paragraph procedure and provides a trace of the lines that are being placed in the table. Notice that David uses RPAD to generate a "ruler," which shows clearly how the long text will need to be broken up into the paragraph format:

```
/* Filename on companion disk: testwrap.sql */
DECLARE
    /* Declare a PL/SQL table to hold the lines of the paragraph. */
    loc_para wrap.paragraph_tabletype;

    /* The test text. */

    loc_text VARCHAR2 (2000) :=
        'This is a very long line of text which we will wrap to smaller lines';

    loc_line_length INTEGER := 10;
    loc_lines INTEGER;

BEGIN
    /* Display a header containing the text and ruler. */
    DBMS_OUTPUT.PUT_LINE ('====================');
    DBMS_OUTPUT.PUT_LINE (loc_text);
    DBMS_OUTPUT.PUT_LINE (RPAD('1',length(loc_text),'2345678901'));
    DBMS_OUTPUT.PUT_LINE
        ('Wrapping to: '||TO_CHAR(loc_line_length)||' characters.');
    DBMS_OUTPUT.PUT_LINE('====================');

    /* Wrap the long text into a paragraph. */
    wrap.to_paragraph(loc_text, loc_line_length, loc_para, loc_lines);

    DBMS_OUTPUT.PUT_LINE('====================');
END;
/
```

Here are two examples of the output from the test script. The first number in square brackets shows the position of the last space found before the line break. The second number in square brackets shows the starting position in the current line and location of the first character in the next line:

```
====================
This is a very long line of text which we will wrap to smaller lines
12345678901234567890123456789012345678901234567890123456789012345678
Wrapping to: 10 characters.
====================
"This is a v"[ 10][  1] [ 11]This is a
"very long l"[ 10][ 11] [ 21]very long
"line of tex"[  8][ 21] [ 29]line of
"text which "[ 11][ 29] [ 40]text which
"we will wra"[  8][ 40] [ 48]we will
"wrap to sma"[  8][ 48] [ 56]wrap to
"smaller lin"[  8][ 56] [ 64]smaller
"lines "     [  6][ 64] [ 70]lines
====================


====================
This is a very long line of text which we will wrap to smaller lines
12345678901234567890123456789012345678901234567890123456789012345678
Wrapping to: 6 characters.
```

```
=====================
"This is"[  5][  1] [  6]This
"is a ve"[  5][  6] [ 11]is a
"very lo"[  5][ 11] [ 16]very
"long li"[  5][ 16] [ 21]long
"line of"[  5][ 21] [ 26]line
"of text"[  3][ 26] [ 29]of
"text wh"[  5][ 29] [ 34]text
"which w"[  6][ 34] [ 40]which
"we will"[  3][ 40] [ 43]we
"will wr"[  5][ 43] [ 48]will
"wrap to"[  5][ 48] [ 53]wrap
"to smal"[  3][ 53] [ 56]to
"smaller"[  0][ 56] [ 62]smalle
"r lines"[  2][ 62] [ 64]r
"lines " [  6][ 64] [ 70]lines
=====================
```

Why would you want to break up text into paragraphs? One reason is to be able to place that text into a formatted document, such as a newsletter or newspaper. Such text usually needs to be filled out to the margins. The output from a call to wrap.to_paragraph would very naturally then become input to the fill_text function, described in the next section.

Filling Text to Fit a Line

It's very easy to left-align a string in PL/SQL—LTRIM it. It is also easy to right-align a string in a field or item—LPAD it with spaces to the full length of the field or item; that will force the string all the way to the right. But how would you justify the string to make it look like a line in a newspaper column, with the first word on the left margin and the last letter of the last word on the right margin?

To justify a string you need to add blanks to spaces between words until the line has been stretched to fill the field or item. You also want to space the blanks evenly across the column, so that it's as readable as possible. The fill_text function shown in the next example accepts a string and line size and returns a string of the specified length, with spaces distributed throughout the string.

In order to achieve an even distribution of spaces, fill_text employs two, nested loops. The inner loop moves from word to word in the string and adds a single blank space after each word. The outer loop calls the inner loop again and again until the string is filled to the specified size. A local module skips over contiguous spaces to find the location of the next nonblank character:

```
/* Filename on companion disk: filltext.sf */
FUNCTION filled_text (string_in IN VARCHAR2, linesize_in IN NUMBER)
RETURN VARCHAR2
/*
|| Parameters:
```

```
||    string_in  - the string to justify.
||    linesize_in - the length of the line to which string is justified.
*/
IS
    -- The length of the string.
    len_string NUMBER := LENGTH (string_in);

    -- I will give a name to the blank to make the code more readable.
    a_blank CONSTANT VARCHAR2(1) := ' ';

    -- The starting location for INSTR checks.
    start_loc NUMBER;

    -- Flag to control execution of the inner WHILE loop.
    keep_adding_blanks BOOLEAN;

    -- The location in the string of the next blank.
    nextblank_loc NUMBER;

    /*
    || The return value for the function is initially set to the incoming
    || string. I also LTRIM and RTRIM it to get rid of end spaces.
    || I am going to assume a max line size of 500. You could raise this
    || limit to 32K, but you will use more memory to do so.
    */
    return_value VARCHAR2 (500) :=
        LTRIM (RTRIM (SUBSTR (string_in, 1, 500)));

    /*--------------------- Local Module ---------------------------*/

    FUNCTION next_nonblank_loc (string_in IN VARCHAR2, start_loc_in IN NUMBER)
    RETURN NUMBER
    /*
    || Finds the location in a string of the next NON-BLANK character
    || from the starting location. Uses SUBSTR to examine the current
    || character and halts the loop if not a blank.
    */
    IS
        return_value NUMBER := start_loc_in;
    BEGIN
        WHILE SUBSTR (string_in, return_value, 1) = a_blank
        LOOP
            return_value := return_value + 1;
        END LOOP;
        RETURN return_value;
    END;

BEGIN
    /* The outer loop. */
    WHILE len_string < linesize_in
    LOOP
        /* Reset variables for inner loop. */
        start_loc := 1;
```

```
keep_adding_blanks := TRUE;
/*
|| Inner loop:
|| If I have filled the string or gone through the entire line,
|| halt this loop and go to the outer loop.
*/
WHILE len_string < linesize_in AND keep_adding_blanks -- Inner loop
LOOP
    /* Find the location of the next blank. */
    nextblank_loc := INSTR (return_value, a_blank, start_loc);

    /* If no more blanks, am done with line for this iteration. */
    keep_adding_blanks := nextblank_loc > 0;

    IF keep_adding_blanks
    THEN
        /*
        || Use SUBSTR to pull apart the string right where the
        || blank was found and then put the two pieces back together
        || after stuffing a space between them. Then add 1 to the
        || length and find the location of the next non-blank
        || character. This new starting location will be used by
        || INSTR to then find the next blank.
        */
        return_value :=
            SUBSTR (return_value, 1, nextblank_loc) ||
            a_blank ||
            SUBSTR (return_value, nextblank_loc+1);
        len_string := len_string + 1;
        start_loc := next_nonblank_loc (return_value, nextblank_loc);
    END IF;

    END LOOP;
END LOOP;

RETURN return_value;

END filled_text;
```

The *filltext.sf* file contains the function shown above as well as a procedure version of the function, which will show you through calls to DBMS_OUTPUT.PUT_LINE how the fill_text algorithm builds its string. After you run the script in that file, you will have a filled_text function and a fill_text procedure.

If you then execute the command:

```
SQL> exec fill_text ('this is not very long', 30)
```

You will see the following output from the procedure call:

```
123456789012345678901234567890
==============================
```

```
this is not very long
this is not very long
this is  not very long
this is  not  very long
this is  not  very  long
this  is  not  very  long
this  is   not  very  long
this  is   not   very  long
this  is   not   very   long
this   is   not   very   long
this   is   not   very   long
==============================
12345678901234567890123456789 0
```

You can see how the function dispersed the spaces evenly throughout the string. The final line is repeated twice because it was displayed from within the function and by the SQL*Plus script.

Counting Substring Occurrences in Strings

You now know how to use INSTR to find the location of a substring within a string. This means that you also know how to determine whether or not a certain substring is in that string (INSTR returns zero if the substring is not found). What if you want to figure out how many times a particular substring occurs within a string?

The first thing that you should do when asked to implement a request like this is to make sure that Oracle's SQL, PL/SQL, or some tool doesn't already provide what you need. I sure hate to spend an hour writing some convoluted program only to find out that a built-in program provided with the tool already does it. Become familiar with what is available, and don't be the least bit embarrassed to go back to the manuals for a refresher.

So, I ask myself, is there a character function that will return the number of times a substring occurs within a string? Afraid not—but checking was the right thing to do. Fortunately, the flexibility of INSTR makes it easy to build such a utility for ourselves. In fact, I use INSTR to produce two different versions of this freq_instr ("frequency in string") function.

The first version, freq_instr1, counts the number of occurrences of a substring by changing the starting location of the INSTR-based search to just past the location of the last match. From that point on, it always searches for the first occurrence.

The second version, freq_instr2, also counts the number of occurrences of a substring using INSTR as well. However, in this function, the starting location of the search always remains 1, and the nth_occurrence argument to INSTR (the fourth argument) is bumped up after each occurrence is found.

Here's the first version:

```
/* Filename on companion disk: freqinst.sf */
FUNCTION freq_instr1
    (string_in IN VARCHAR2,
     substring_in IN VARCHAR2,
     match_case_in IN VARCHAR2 := 'IGNORE')
RETURN NUMBER
/*
|| Parameters:
||    string_in - the string in which frequency is checked.
||    substring_in - the substring we are counting in the string.
||    match_case_in - If "IGNORE" then count frequency of occurrences
||                    of substring regardless of case. If "MATCH" then
||                    only count occurrences if case matches.
||
|| Returns the number of times (frequency) a substring is found
|| by INSTR in the full string (string_in). If either string_in or
|| substring_in are NULL, then return 0.
*/
IS
    -- Starting location from which INSTR will search for a match.
    search_loc NUMBER := 1;

    -- The length of the incoming substring.
    substring_len NUMBER := LENGTH (substring_in);

    -- The Boolean variable which controls the loop.
    check_again BOOLEAN := TRUE;

    -- The return value for the function.
    return_value NUMBER := 0;
BEGIN

    IF string_in IS NOT NULL AND substring_in IS NOT NULL
    THEN
        /* Loop through string, moving forward the start of search. */
        WHILE check_again
        LOOP
            IF UPPER (match_case_in) = 'IGNORE'
            THEN
                -- Use UPPER to ignore case when performing the INSTR.
                search_loc :=
                    INSTR (UPPER (string_in),
                            UPPER (substring_in), search_loc, 1);
            ELSE
                search_loc := INSTR (string_in, substring_in, search_loc, 1);
            END IF;

            /* Did I find another occurrence? */
            check_again := search_loc > 0;
            IF check_again
            THEN
                return_value := return_value + 1;
```

```
                /* Move start position past the substring. */
                search_loc := search_loc + substring_len;
           END IF;
        END LOOP;
     END IF;

     RETURN return_value;

  END freq_instr1;
```

Now let's take a look at the second version of freq_instr, which keeps the starting location of the call to INSTR at a constant value of 1 and increments the number of the occurrence we wish to extract from the string. Both approaches do the job, but this second version uses a little less code and relies more directly and naturally on INSTR to do the job.

```
/* Filename on companion disk: freqinst.sf */
FUNCTION freq_instr2
    (string_in IN VARCHAR2,
     substring_in IN VARCHAR2,
     match_case_in IN VARCHAR2 := 'IGNORE') RETURN NUMBER
IS
    substring_loc NUMBER;
    return_value NUMBER := 1;
BEGIN
    /*
    || Use the last argument to INSTR to find the Nth occurrence of
    || substring, where N is incremented with each spin of the loop.
    || If INSTR returns 0 then have one too many in the return_value,
    || so when I RETURN it, I subtract 1 (see code following loop).
    */
    LOOP
        IF UPPER (match_case_in) = 'IGNORE'
        THEN
            substring_loc :=
                INSTR (UPPER (string_in), UPPER (substring_in), 1, return_value);
        ELSE
            substring_loc := INSTR (string_in, substring_in, 1, return_value);
        END IF;

        /* Terminate loop when no more occurrences are found. */
        EXIT WHEN substring_loc = 0;

        /* Found match, so add to total and continue. */
        return_value := return_value + 1;

    END LOOP;

    RETURN return_value - 1;

END freq_instr2;
```

In freq_instr2, I use INSTR to keep on getting the next occurrence of the substring until there are no more, letting INSTR determine the number of occurrences. In freq_instr1, I explicitly move the starting point of the search through the string and then use INSTR to get the next occurrence. Will both functions always return the same values? And if not, which one returns the correct values?

In fact, freq_instr1 and freq_instr2 do not count the same number of occurrences of a substring in a string. This discrepancy relates back to the way INSTR works—consider the following results:

```
freq_instr1 ('abcdaaa', 'aa') ==> 1

freq_instr2 ('abcdaaa', 'aa') ==> 2
```

The first version, freq_instr1, only finds one match for aa because it moves the starting point for the next search for an aa past the second a in the string aaa, right to the last character of the string. The freq_instr2 function, on the other hand, uses the second a in the string aaa as the starting point for the second occurrence of aa and so returns 2 rather than 1. Which answer is correct? It depends on the detailed specifications for the function. Either answer could be right; it depends on the question.

Verifying String Formats with TRANSLATE

Oracle Forms allows you to specify a format mask on screen items that are numbers and dates. With a number mask of 999"-"99"-"9999, for example, a user could enter 123457890 and have Oracle Forms automatically convert the entry to 123-45-7890 for Social Security number formatting. With a date mask of MMDDYY, a user could enter 122094 and have Oracle Forms automatically convert that information to the internal date format for December 20, 1994. Unfortunately, you can use format masks only on number and date items. You cannot format a character item. You cannot use a mask, for example, to ensure that users enter the department code in the format AAANNN, where the first three characters are letters and the last three characters are numbers.

TRANSLATE offers an easy way to verify and enforce formats in character fields, which I will explore below. Suppose you need to make sure that users enter a value in the format AAANN99, where A is an uppercase letter (A through Z), N is a digit (0 through 9), and the two trailing nines are just that: two trailing nines. Given this format, the following entries would all be valid:

```
THR3399
ZYX1299
```

While these next entries violate the format:

1RR1299

First character is a digit, instead of a number

RRR8Q89

"Q" where number must be, second last digit not a nine

UUU1290

Last digit is not a nine

To validate and enforce this format in an Oracle Forms item, I create a When-Validate-Item trigger for that item. One approach I could take is to look at each character individually and make sure it has the right value. I could use SUBSTR to do this, as follows:

```
DECLARE
    /* The formatted value. */
    my_value VARCHAR2 (20) := UPPER (:company.industry_code);
BEGIN
    IF SUBSTR (my_value, 1, 1) NOT BETWEEN 'A' and 'Z' OR
        SUBSTR (my_value, 2, 1) NOT BETWEEN 'A' and 'Z' OR
        SUBSTR (my_value, 3, 1) NOT BETWEEN 'A' and 'Z' OR
        SUBSTR (my_value, 4, 1) NOT BETWEEN '0' and '9' OR
        SUBSTR (my_value, 5, 1) NOT BETWEEN '0' and '9' OR
        SUBSTR (my_value, 6, 2) != '99'
    THEN
        MESSAGE (' Please enter code in format AAANN99.');
        RAISE FORM_TRIGGER_FAILURE;
    END IF;
END;
```

This approach will work fine, in most cases, clearly stating the rules for each of the characters in the code item. Let's see how you would perform this same format check with TRANSLATE:

```
IF TRANSLATE (UPPER (:company.industry_code),
              '0123456789ABCDEFGHIJKLMNOPQRSTUVWXYZ',
              'NNNNNNNNNNAAAAAAAAAAAAAAAAAAAAAAAAAA') != 'AAANNNN'
    OR :company.industry_code NOT LIKE '_____99'
THEN
    MESSAGE (' Please enter code in format AAANN99.');
    RAISE FORM_TRIGGER_FAILURE;
END IF;
```

With TRANSLATE, I use the search and replace sets to replace all numbers with "N" and all letters with "A". If the user followed the specified format, then TRANSLATE will return AAANNNN. I then include a second check to see if the last two characters of the string are 99. Notice that I used five underscores as single-character wildcards to make sure the correct number of characters preceded the double nines.

I can also use TRANSLATE to support multiple formats on the same character item, and then determine action in the screen based on the format selected. Suppose that, if a user enters a string in the format NNNAAA, I need to execute a procedure to generate an industry profile. If the user enters a string in the format AAA, I need to execute a procedure to calculate annual sales for that specified department. TRANSLATE will easily sort through these formats as follows:

```
formatted_entry :=
    TRANSLATE (UPPER (:company.criteria),
               '0123456789ABCDEFGHIJKLMNOPQRSTUVWXYZ',
               'NNNNNNNNNNAAAAAAAAAAAAAAAAAAAAAAAAAAAA');

IF formatted_entry = 'NNNAAA'
THEN
    gen_ind_profile (:company.criteria);
ELSIF formatted_entry = 'AAA'
THEN
    calc_annual_sales (:company.criteria);
END IF;
```

If you need to perform pattern or format masking and analysis, TRANSLATE is generally the most efficient and effective solution.

12

Date Functions

This chapter contains detailed descriptions and extended examples of functions you can use to manipulate date information in PL/SQL programs.

Most applications store and manipulate dates and times. Dates are quite complicated: not only are they highly formatted, but there are myriad rules for determining valid values and valid calculations (leap days and years, national and company holidays, date ranges, etc.). Fortunately, PL/SQL and the Oracle RDBMS provide many ways to handle date information.

PL/SQL provides a true DATE datatype that stores both date and time information. Each date value contains the century, year, month, day, hour, minute, and second. The DATE datatype does not support the storage of fractions of time less than a second in length. The time itself is stored as the number of seconds past midnight. If you enter a date without a time (most applications do not require the tracking of time), the time portion of the database value defaults to midnight (12:00:00 AM). PL/SQL validates and stores dates which fall in the range January 1, 4712 B.C. to December 31, 4712 A.D.

Support for a true date datatype is only half the battle. You also need a language that can manipulate those dates in a natural and intelligent manner—as dates. PL/SQL offers a set of eight date functions for just this purpose, as shown in Table 12-1.

With PL/SQL you will never have to write a program which calculates the number of days between two dates. You will not need to write your own utility to figure out the day of the week on which a date falls. This information, and just about anything else you can think of having to do with dates, is immediately available to you through built-in functions. The date functions in PL/SQL all take dates, and, in some cases, numbers, for arguments, and all return date values. The only exception is MONTHS_BETWEEN, which returns a number.

Table 12-1. The Built-In Date Functions

Name	Description
ADD_MONTHS	Adds the specified number of months to a date.
LAST_DAY	Returns the last day in the month of the specified date.
MONTHS_ BETWEEN	Calculates the number of months between two dates.
NEW_TIME	Returns the date/time value, with the time shifted as requested by the specified time zones.
NEXT_DAY	Returns the date of the first weekday specified that is later than the date.
ROUND	Returns the date rounded by the specified format unit.
SYSDATE	Returns the current date and time in the Oracle Server.
TRUNC	Truncates the specified date of its time portion according to the format unit provided.

Date Function Descriptions

This section describes each date function and includes examples to give you a solid feel for how you can put the function to use in your programs.

NOTE   In the examples in this chapter, a date contained in single quotation marks is a character string. PL/SQL converts the string to a true date datatype when it applies the function. (This is an implicit conversion.) Date values that are displayed in the format DD-MON-YYYY and are not contained in single quotation marks represent actual date values in the database.

A true date value looks like this in the examples:

    12-DEC-1997

A character representation looks like this in the examples:

    '12-DEC-1997'

Remember, a date has its own internal storage format and cannot be viewed or entered directly. These examples also assume that the default format mask for dates is DD-MON-YYYY.

The ADD_MONTHS function

The ADD_MONTHS function returns a new date with the specified number of months added to the input date. The specification for ADD_MONTHS is as follows:

```
FUNCTION ADD_MONTHS (date_in IN DATE, month_shift NUMBER) RETURN DATE
FUNCTION ADD_MONTHS (month_shift NUMBER, date_in IN DATE) RETURN DATE
```

ADD_MONTHS is an overloaded function. You can specify the date and the number of months by which you want to shift that date, or you can list the month_shift parameter first and then the date. Both arguments are required.

Date Arithmetic

PL/SQL allows you to perform arithmetic operations directly on date variables. You may add numbers to a date or subtract numbers from a date. To move a date one day in the future, simply add 1 to the date as shown below:

```
hire_date + 1
```

You can even add a fractional value to a date. For example, adding 1/24 to a date adds an hour to the time component of that value. Adding 1/(24*60) adds a single minute to the time component, and so on.

If the month_shift parameter is positive, ADD_MONTHS returns a date for that number of months into the future. If the number is negative, ADD_MONTHS returns a date for that number of months in the past. Here are some examples that use ADD_MONTHS:

- Move ahead date by three months:

```
ADD_MONTHS ('12-JAN-1995', 3) ==> 12-APR-1995
```

- Specify negative number of months in first position:

```
ADD_MONTHS (-12, '12-MAR-1990') ==> 12-MAR-1989
```

ADD_MONTHS always shifts the date by whole months. You can provide a fractional value for the month_shift parameter, but ADD_MONTHS will always round down to the whole number nearest zero, as shown in these examples:

```
ADD_MONTHS ('28-FEB-1989', 1.5) same as
ADD_MONTHS ('28-FEB-1989', 1) ==> 31-MAR-1989

ADD_MONTHS ('28-FEB-1989', 1.9999) same as
ADD_MONTHS ('28-FEB-1989', 1) ==> 31-MAR-1989

ADD_MONTHS ('28-FEB-1989', -1.9999) same as
ADD_MONTHS ('28-FEB-1989', -1) ==> 31-JAN-1989

ADD_MONTHS ('28-FEB-1989', .5) same as
ADD_MONTHS ('28-FEB-1989', 0) ==> 28-FEB-1989
```

If you want to shift a date by a fraction of a month, simply add to or subtract from the date the required number of days. PL/SQL supports direct arithmetic operations between date values.

If the input date to ADD_MONTHS does not fall on the last day of the month, the date returned by ADD_MONTHS falls on the same day in the new month as in the original month. If the day number of the input date is greater than the last day of the month returned by ADD_MONTHS, the function sets the day number to the last day in the new month. For example, there is no 31st day in February, so ADD_MONTHS returns the last day in the month:

```
ADD_MONTHS ('31-JAN-1995', 1) ==> 28-FEB-1995
```

This is perfectly reasonable. However, what if the input date falls on the last day of the month and the new month has more days in it than the original month? If I shift two months forward from 28-FEB-1994, do I get back 30-APR-1994 (the last day of the month) or 28-APR-1994 (the same day in the new month as in the old month)? The answer is:

```
ADD_MONTHS ('28-FEB-1994', 2) ==> 30-APR-1995
```

If you pass to ADD_MONTHS a day representing the last day in the month, PL/SQL always returns the last day in the resulting month, regardless of the number of actual days in each of the months. This quirk can cause problems. I offer a solution in the section entitled "Customizing the Behavior of ADD_MONTHS" later in this chapter.

The LAST_DAY function

The LAST_DAY function returns the date of the last day of the month for a given date. The specification is:

```
FUNCTION LAST_DAY (date_in IN DATE) RETURN DATE
```

This function is useful because the number of days in a month varies throughout the year. With LAST_DAY, for example, you do not have to try to figure out if February of this or that year has 28 or 29 days. Just let LAST_DAY figure it out for you.

Here are some examples of LAST_DAY:

- Go to the last day in the month:

  ```
  LAST_DAY ('12-JAN-99') ==> 31-JAN-1999
  ```

- If already on the last day, just stay on that day:

  ```
  LAST_DAY ('31-JAN-99') ==> 31-JAN-1999
  ```

- Get the last day of the month three months after being hired:

  ```
  LAST_DAY (ADD_MONTHS (hiredate, 3))
  ```

- Tell me the number of days until the end of the month:

  ```
  LAST_DAY (SYSDATE) - SYSDATE
  ```

The MONTHS_BETWEEN function

The MONTHS_BETWEEN function calculates the number of months between two dates and returns that difference as a number. The specification is:

```
FUNCTION MONTHS_BETWEEN (date1 IN DATE, date2 IN DATE)
   RETURN NUMBER
```

The following rules apply to MONTHS_BETWEEN:

- If date1 comes after date2, then MONTHS_BETWEEN returns a positive number.

- If date1 comes before date2, then MONTHS_BETWEEN returns a negative number.

- If date1 and date2 are in the same month, then MONTHS_BETWEEN returns a fraction (a value between –1 and +1).

- If date1 and date2 both fall on the last day of their respective months, then MONTHS_BETWEEN returns a whole number (no fractional component).

- If date1 and date2 are in different months and at least one of the dates is not a last day in the month, MONTHS_BETWEEN returns a fractional number. The fractional component is calculated on a 31-day month basis and also takes into account any differences in the time component of date1 and date2.

Here are some examples of the uses of MONTHS_BETWEEN:

- Calculate two ends of month, the first earlier than the second:

  ```
  MONTHS_BETWEEN ('31-JAN-1994', '28-FEB-1994') ==> -1
  ```

- Calculate two ends of month, the first later than the second:

  ```
  MONTHS_BETWEEN ('31-MAR-1995', '28-FEB-1994') ==> 13
  ```

- Calculate when both dates fall in the same month:

  ```
  MONTHS_BETWEEN ('28-FEB-1994', '15-FEB-1994') ==>  0
  ```

- Perform months_between calculations with a fractional component:

  ```
  MONTHS_BETWEEN ('31-JAN-1994', '1-MAR-1994') ==> -1.0322581
  MONTHS_BETWEEN ('31-JAN-1994', '2-MAR-1994') ==> -1.0645161
  MONTHS_BETWEEN ('31-JAN-1994', '10-MAR-1994') ==> -1.3225806
  ```

If you detect a pattern here you are right. As I said, MONTHS_BETWEEN calculates the fractional component of the number of months by assuming that each month has 31 days. Therefore, each additional day over a complete month counts for 1/31 of a month, and:

```
1 divided by 31 = .032258065—more or less!
```

According to this rule, the number of months between January 31, 1994 and February 28, 1994 is one—a nice, clean integer. But to calculate the number of months between January 31, 1994 and March 1, 1994, I have to add an additional .032258065 to the difference (and make that additional number negative because in this case MONTHS_BETWEEN counts from the first date back to the second date.

The NEW_TIME function

I don't know about you, but I am simply unable to remember the time in Bombay when it is 3:00 P.M. in Chicago (and I really doubt that a lot of people in Bombay can convert to Midwest U.S. time). Fortunately for me, PL/SQL provides the NEW_ TIME function. This function converts dates (along with their time components) from one time zone to another. The specification for NEW_TIME is:

```
FUNCTION NEW_TIME (date_in DATE, zone1 VARCHAR2, zone2 VARCHAR2)
   RETURN DATE
```

where date_in is the original date, zone1 is the starting point for the zone switch (usually, but not restricted to, your own local time zone), and zone2 is the time zone in which the date returned by NEW_TIME should be placed.

The valid time zones are shown in Table 12-2.

Table 12-2. Time Zone Abbreviations and Descriptions

Time Zone Abbreviation	Description
AST	Atlantic Standard Time
ADT	Atlantic Daylight Time
BST	Bering Standard Time
BDT	Bering Daylight Time
CST	Central Standard Time
CDT	Central Daylight Time
EST	Eastern Standard Time
EDT	Eastern Daylight Time
GMT	Greenwich Mean Time
HST	Alaska-Hawaii Standard Time
HDT	Alaska-Hawaii Daylight Time
MST	Mountain Standard Time
MDT	Mountain Daylight Time
NST	Newfoundland Standard Time
PST	Pacific Standard Time
PDT	Pacific Daylight Time
YST	Yukon Standard Time
YDT	Yukon Daylight Time

The specification of time zones to NEW_TIME is not case-sensitive, as the following example shows:

```
TO_CHAR (NEW_TIME (TO_DATE ('09151994 12:30 AM', 'MMDDYYYY HH:MI AM'),
                   'CST', 'hdt'),
         'Month DD, YYYY HH:MI AM')
==> 'September 14, 1994 09:30 PM'
```

So, when it was 12:30 in the morning of September 15, 1994 in Chicago, it was 9:30 in the evening of September 14, 1994 in Bombay.

NOTE	By the way, I used TO_DATE with a format mask to make sure that a time other than the default of midnight would be used in the calculation of the new date and time. I then used TO_CHAR with another date mask (this one intended to make the output more readable) to display the date and time, because by default PL/SQL will not include the time component unless specifically requested to do so.

The NEXT_DAY function

The NEXT_DAY function returns the date of the first day after the specified date which falls on the specified day of the week. Here is the specification for NEXT_DAY:

```
FUNCTION NEXT_DAY (date_in IN DATE, day_name IN VARCHAR2) RETURN DATE
```

The day_name must be a day of the week in your session's date language (specified by the NLS_DATE_LANGUAGE database initialization parameter). The time component of the returned date is the same as that of the input date, date_in. If the day of the week of the input date matches the specified day_name, then NEXT_DAY will return the date seven days (one full week) after date_in. NEXT_DAY does not return the input date if the day names match.

Here are some examples of the use of NEXT_DAY. Let's figure out the date of the first Monday and Wednesday in 1997 in all of these examples.

- You can use both full and abbreviated day names:

```
NEXT_DAY ('01-JAN-1997', 'MONDAY') ==> 06-JAN-1997
NEXT_DAY ('01-JAN-1997', 'MON') ==> 06-JAN-1997
```

- The case of the day name doesn't matter a whit:

```
NEXT_DAY ('01-JAN-1997', 'monday') ==> 06-JAN-1997
```

- If the date language were Spanish:

```
NEXT_DAY ('01-JAN-1997', 'LUNES') ==> 06-JAN-1997
```

- NEXT_DAY of Wednesday moves the date up a full week:

```
NEXT_DAY ('01-JAN-1997', 'WEDNESDAY') ==> 08-JAN-1997
```

The ROUND function

The ROUND function rounds a date value to the nearest date as specified by a format mask. It is just like the standard numeric ROUND function, which rounds a number to the nearest number of specified precision, except that it works with dates. The specification for ROUND is as follows:

```
FUNCTION ROUND (date_in IN DATE [, format_mask VARCHAR2]) RETURN DATE
```

The ROUND function always rounds the time component of a date to midnight (12:00 A.M.). The format mask is optional. If you do not include a format mask, ROUND rounds the date to the nearest day. In other words, it checks the time component of the date. If the time is past noon, then ROUND returns the next day with a time component of midnight.

The set of format masks for ROUND is a bit different from those masks used by TO_CHAR and TO_DATE. (See Chapter 14, *Conversion Functions*, for more information on these functions.) The masks are listed in Table 12-3. These same formats are used by the TRUNC function, described later in this chapter, to perform truncation on dates.

Table 12-3. Format Masks for ROUND and TRUNC

Format Mask	Rounds or Truncates to
CC or SSC	Century
SYYY, YYYY, YEAR, SYEAR, YYY, YY, or Y	Year (rounds up to next year on July 1)
IYYY, IYY, IY, or I	Standard ISO year
Q	Quarter (rounds up on the sixteenth day of the second month of the quarter)
MONTH, MON, MM, or RM	Month (rounds up on the sixteenth day, which is not necessarily the same as the middle of the month)
WW	Same day of the week as the first day of the year
IW	Same day of the week as the first day of the ISO year
W	Same day of the week as the first day of the month
DDD, DD, or J	Day
DAY, DY, or D	Starting day of the week
HH, HH12, HH24	Hour
MI	Minute

Here are some examples of ROUND dates:

- Round up to the next century:

```
TO_CHAR (ROUND (TO_DATE ('01-MAR-1994'), 'CC'), 'DD-MON-YYYY')
==> 01-JAN-2000
```

- Round back to the beginning of the current century:

```
TO_CHAR (ROUND (TO_DATE ('01-MAR-1945'), 'CC'), 'DD-MON-YYYY')
==> 01-JAN-1900
```

- Round down and up to the first of the year:

```
ROUND (TO_DATE ('01-MAR-1994'), 'YYYY') ==> 01-JAN-1994
ROUND (TO_DATE ('01-SEP-1994'), 'YEAR') ==> 01-JAN-1995
```

- Round up and down to the quarter (first date in the quarter):

```
ROUND (TO_DATE ('01-MAR-1994'), 'Q') ==> 01-APR-1994
ROUND (TO_DATE ('15-APR-1994'), 'Q') ==> 01-APR-1994
```

- Round down and up to the first of the month:

```
ROUND (TO_DATE ('12-MAR-1994'), 'MONTH') ==> 01-MAR-1994
ROUND (TO_DATE ('17-MAR-1994'), 'MM') ==> 01-APR-1994
```

- Day of first of year is Saturday:

```
TO_CHAR (TO_DATE ('01-JAN-1994'), 'DAY') ==> 'SATURDAY'
```

So round to date of nearest Saturday for '01-MAR-1994':

```
ROUND (TO_DATE ('01-MAR-1994'), 'WW') ==> 26-FEB-1994
```

- First day in the month is a Friday:

```
TO_CHAR (TO_DATE ('01-APR-1994'), 'DAY') ==> FRIDAY
```

So round to date of nearest Friday from April 16, 1994:

```
TO_CHAR ('16-APR-1994'), 'DAY') ==> SATURDAY
ROUND (TO_DATE ('16-APR-1994'), 'W') ==> 15-APR-1994
TO_CHAR (ROUND (TO_DATE ('16-APR-1994'), 'W'), 'DAY') ==> FRIDAY
```

In the rest of the examples I use TO_DATE in order to pass a time component to the ROUND function, and TO_CHAR to display the new time.

- Round back to nearest day (time always midnight):

```
TO_CHAR (ROUND (TO_DATE ('11-SEP-1994 10:00 AM',
                'DD-MON-YY HH:MI AM'), 'DD'),
      'DD-MON-YY HH:MI AM')
==> 11-SEP-1994 12:00 AM
```

- Round forward to the nearest day:

```
TO_CHAR (ROUND (TO_DATE ('11-SEP-1994 4:00 PM',
                'DD-MON-YY HH:MI AM'), 'DD'),
      'DD-MON-YY HH:MI AM')
==> 12-SEP-1994 12:00 AM
```

- Round back to the nearest hour:

```
TO_CHAR (ROUND (TO_DATE ('11-SEP-1994 4:17 PM',
                'DD-MON-YY HH:MI AM'), 'HH'),
      'DD-MON-YY HH:MI AM')
==> 11-SEP-1994 04:00 PM
```

The SYSDATE function

The SYSDATE function returns the current system date and time as recorded in the database. The time component of SYSDATE provides the current time to the nearest second. It takes no arguments. The specification for SYSDATE is:

```
FUNCTION SYSDATE RETURN DATE
```

SYSDATE is a function without parameters; as a result, it looks like a system-level variable and programmers tend to use it as if it is a variable. For example, to assign the current date and time to a local PL/SQL variable, you would enter the following:

```
my_date := SYSDATE;
```

However, SYSDATE is not a variable. When you use SYSDATE, you are calling a function, which executes underlying code.

NOTE   In Oracle Version 6 and the earliest releases of the Oracle Server, when you called SYSDATE, PL/SQL issued an implicit cursor to the database to get the current date and time, as follows:

```
SELECT SYSDATE FROM dual;
```

Because this is no longer the case, you do not need to be as concerned about extra calls to SYSDATE as you would have in earlier releases.

The TRUNC function

The TRUNC function truncates date values according to the specified format mask. The specification for TRUNC is:

```
FUNCTION TRUNC (date_in IN DATE [, format_mask VARCHAR2]) RETURN DATE
```

The TRUNC date function is similar to the numeric FLOOR function discussed in Chapter 13, *Numeric, LOB, and Miscellaneous Functions*. Generally speaking, it rounds down to the beginning of the minute, hour, day, month, quarter, year, or century, as specified by the format mask.

TRUNC offers the easiest way to retrieve the first day of the month or first day of the year. It is also useful when you want to ignore the time component of dates. This is often the case when you perform comparisons with dates, such as the following:

```
IF request_date BETWEEN start_date AND end_date
THEN
   ...
```

The date component of date_entered and start_date might be the same, but if your application does not specify a time component for each of its dates, the comparison might fail. If, for example, the user enters a request_date and the screen does not include a time component, the time for request_date will be midnight or 12:00 A.M. of that day. If start_date was set from SYSDATE, however, its time component will reflect the time at which the assignment was made. Because 12:00 A.M. comes before any other time of the day, a comparison that looks to the naked eye like a match might well fail.

If you are not sure about the time components of your date fields and variables and want to make sure that your operations on dates disregard the time component, TRUNCate them:

```
IF TRUNC (request_date) BETWEEN TRUNC (start_date) AND TRUNC (end_date)
THEN
   ...
```

TRUNC levels the playing field with regard to the time component: all dates now have the same time of midnight (12:00 A.M.). The time will never be a reason for a comparison to fail.

Here are some examples of TRUNC for dates (all assuming a default date format mask of DD-MON-YYYY):

- Without a format mask, TRUNC sets the time to 12:00 A.M. of the same day:

```
TO_CHAR (TRUNC (TO_DATE ('11-SEP-1994 9:36 AM', 'DD-MON-YYYY HH:MI AM'))
==> 11-SEP-1994 12:00 AM
```

- Trunc to the beginning of the century in all cases:

```
TO_CHAR (TRUNC (TO_DATE ('01-MAR-1994'), 'CC'), 'DD-MON-YYYY')
==> 01-JAN-1900

TO_CHAR (TRUNC (TO_DATE ('01-MAR-1945'), 'CC'), 'DD-MON-YYYY')
==> 01-JAN-1900
```

- Trunc to the first of the current year:

```
TRUNC (TO_DATE ('01-MAR-1994'), 'YYYY') ==> 01-JAN-1994
TRUNC (TO_DATE ('01-SEP-1994'), 'YEAR') ==> 01-JAN-1994
```

- Trunc to the first day of the quarter:

```
TRUNC (TO_DATE ('01-MAR-1994'), 'Q') ==> 01-JAN-1994
TRUNC (TO_DATE ('15-APR-1994'), 'Q') ==> 01-APR-1994
```

- Trunc to the first of the month:

```
TRUNC (TO_DATE ('12-MAR-1994'), 'MONTH') ==> 01-MAR-1994
TRUNC (TO_DATE ('17-MAR-1994'), 'MM') ==> 01-APR-1994
```

In the rest of the examples I use TO_DATE to pass a time component to the TRUNC function, and TO_CHAR to display the new time:

- Trunc back to the beginning of the current day (time is always midnight):

```
TO_CHAR (TRUNC (TO_DATE ('11-SEP-1994 10:00 AM',
                   'DD-MON-YYYY HH:MI AM'), 'DD'),
      'DD-MON-YYYY HH:MI AM')
==> 11-SEP-1994 12:00 AM

TO_CHAR (TRUNC (TO_DATE ('11-SEP-1994 4:00 PM',
                   'DD-MON-YYYY HH:MI AM'), 'DD'),
      'DD-MON-YYYY HH:MI AM')
==> 11-SEP-1994 12:00 AM
```

- Trunc to the beginning of the current hour:

```
TO_CHAR (TRUNC (TO_DATE ('11-SEP-1994 4:17 PM',
                         'DD-MON-YYYY HH:MI AM'), 'HH'),
         'DD-MON-YYYY HH:MI AM')
==> 11-SEP-1994 04:00 PM
```

Date Function Examples

This section contains more detailed examples of some of the functions summarized in this chapter.

Customizing the Behavior of ADD_MONTHS

As noted earlier, if you pass a day to ADD_MONTHS which is the last day in the month, PL/SQL always returns the last day in the resulting month, regardless of the number of actual days in each of the months. While this may work perfectly well for many, if not most, Oracle installations, I have encountered at least one company in the insurance industry that definitely cannot use ADD_MONTHS the way it works by default. At this site, if I am on the 28th day of February and shift forward a month, I need to land on the 28th of March—not the 31st of March. What's a programmer to do?

The best solution is to write your own version of ADD_MONTHS that performs the way you want it to, and then use it in place of ADD_MONTHS. The following example shows a new_add_months function. It always lands you on the same day in the month, unless the original day does not exist in the new month, in which case the day is set to the last day in the new month.

This code uses the LAST_DAY function to see if the original date falls on the last day of that month:

```
/* Filename on companion disk: addmths.sf */
CREATE OR REPLACE FUNCTION new_add_months (date_in IN DATE, months_shift IN
NUMBER)
    RETURN DATE
IS
    /* Return value of function */
    return_value DATE;

    /* The day in the month */
    day_of_month VARCHAR2(2);

    /* The month and year for the return value */
    month_year VARCHAR2(6);

    /* The calculated end of month date */
    end_of_month DATE;
BEGIN
    return_value := ADD_MONTHS (date_in, months_shift);
```

```
        /* Is original date the last day of its month? */
        IF date_in = LAST_DAY (date_in)
        THEN
            /* Pull out the day number of the original date */
            day_of_month := TO_CHAR (date_in, 'DD');

            /* Grab the month and year of the new date */
            month_year := TO_CHAR (return_value, 'MMYYYY');

            /* Combine these components into an actual date */
            BEGIN
                end_of_month := TO_DATE (month_year || day_of_month, 'MMYYYYDD');
                /*
                || Return the earliest of (a) the normal result of ADD_MONTHS
                || and (b) the same day in the new month as in the original month.
                */
                return_value := LEAST (return_value, end_of_month);
            EXCEPTION
                WHEN OTHERS THEN NULL;
            END;
        END IF;

        /* Return the shifted date */
        RETURN return_value;
    END new_add_months;
```

Take a look at the difference between ADD_MONTHS and new_add_months:

```
ADD_MONTHS ('31-JAN-1995', 1) ==> 28-FEB-1995
new_add_months ('31-JAN-1995', 1) ==> 28-FEB-1995

ADD_MONTHS ('28-FEB-1994', 2) ==> 30-APR-1994
new_add_months ('28-FEB-1994', 2) ==> 28-APR-1995
```

The above function can be used in a PL/SQL program like the following:

```
IF new_add_months (order_date, 3) > SYSDATE
THEN
    ship_order;
END IF;
```

If you want new_add_months to also accept the two arguments in either date-number or number-date order, you need to place the function inside a package and then overload the function definition, as shown below; see Chapter 16, *Packages*, for more information on constructing packages and overloading module definitions.

```
PACKAGE date_pkg
IS
    FUNCTION new_add_months (date_in IN DATE, months_shift IN NUMBER)
        RETURN DATE;

    FUNCTION new_add_months (months_shift IN NUMBER, date_in IN DATE)
        RETURN DATE;
END;
```

If you are using PL/SQL Release 2.1 or beyond, you can use this substitute for ADD_MONTHS in your SQL DML statements, as well as your PL/SQL programs:

```
SELECT new_add_months (SYSDATE, 3) FROM dual;
```

A final observation: the unexpected behavior of ADD_MONTHS for the last day in a month demonstrates once again that it is always a good idea to test both your programs and the programs of others at their limits. Don't assume that a program will work in any particular fashion until you test it. In this case, if the program shifts dates by months, then be sure to test for the end and beginning of months.

Using NEW_TIME in Client-Server Environments

One issue to keep in mind with SYSDATE is that it will always reflect the date and time on the server and not on the individual client workstation or computer (unless, of course, your workstation is also the server). This may not be an issue when all machines are located in the same general vicinity, but when you have a server in New York and a client in Iowa, the times will definitely not match up. This is a more difficult problem to resolve.

You can use the NEW_TIME date function to convert the date and time returned by SYSDATE to the actual date and time in the client's location. To do this you need to know the time zones in each of these locations. The best way to be sure the time zones are available is to store them in a configuration table; the zones may then be read into some kind of global variables when an application is initiated. In PL/SQL, you would do this with package variables.

Note that this example relies heavily on the package structure, which is explained in Chapter 16.

In the following examples, I will store the client and server time zone values directly in PL/SQL variables and provide a way to change them if necessary. I will then build a function called system_date, which replaces the SYSDATE function. The objectives of this function are twofold:

1. Keep to a minimum the number of times that SYSDATE is called.

2. Adjust the time automatically to account for time zone changes.

The tz package shown below provides a set of procedures and functions to manage both the system date and the client and server time zones. Users of the package can access the package data only through the functions (retrieval) and the procedures (change values). The main module in the package is system_date; its specification follows:

```
FUNCTION system_date
    (refresh_in IN VARCHAR2 := 'NOREFRESH',
     server_time_zone IN VARCHAR2 := server,
     client_time_zone IN VARCHAR2 := client)
RETURN DATE;
```

This package-based version of SYSDATE takes up to three parameters:

refresh_in
> If you need the current time or want to update the global current date value, then you really do want SYSDATE to be called again. If you refresh, then SYSDATE is used to update the package globals.

server_time_zone
> The time zone of the server; the default is the packaged value.

client_time_zone
> The time zone of the client; the default is the packaged value.

The tz package relies on the following global variables inside the package to keep track of the current date/time and the default client and server time zones:

```
system_date_global DATE := SYSDATE;
client_tz   VARCHAR2(3) := 'AST';
server_tz   VARCHAR2(3) := 'PST';
```

The very first time the system_date function is called, the package will be loaded into memory and these variables assigned their default values. I can now call system_date using both of the default configuration time zones—and I will not get a new time computed each time I do so:

```
IF tz.system_date
   BETWEEN '15-JAN-1994' AND '22-JAN-1994'
THEN
   ...
END IF;
```

Or I can override the default time zones with Greenwich Mean and Newfoundland Standard times, also requesting a refresh of the time:

```
current_date :=
   tz.system_date ('REFRESH', 'GMT', 'NST');
```

If you do not want to have to specify the package name, tz, in front of the system_date function name, you can create a standalone stored procedure of the same name which, in effect, hides the package ownership:

```
FUNCTION system_date
   (refresh_in IN VARCHAR2 := 'NOREFRESH',
    server_time_zone VARCHAR2 := tz.server,
    client_time_zone VARCHAR2 := tz.client)
   RETURN DATE
IS
BEGIN
   RETURN tz.system_date
      (refresh_in, server_time_zone, client_time_zone);
END;
```

The following sections contain the code for the specification and body of the tz package.

The time zone package specification

```
/* Filename on companion disk:tz.spp */
PACKAGE tz
IS
    /* Return the client timezone */
    FUNCTION client RETURN VARCHAR2;

    /* Return the server timezone */
    FUNCTION server RETURN VARCHAR2;
    /*
    || Retrieve system date. Can ask to refresh the value
    || from the database and also over-ride the default
    || time zones, just as you would with NEW_TIME.
    */
    FUNCTION system_date
        (refresh_in IN VARCHAR2 := 'NOREFRESH',
         server_time_zone IN VARCHAR2 := server,
         client_time_zone IN VARCHAR2 := client)
        RETURN DATE;

    /* Change the client timezone */
    PROCEDURE set_client (tz_in IN VARCHAR2);

    /* Change the server timezone */
    PROCEDURE set_server (tz_in IN VARCHAR2);
END tz;
```

The time zone package body

```
/* Filename on companion disk: tz.spp */
PACKAGE BODY tz
IS
    /* The actual "global" variables stored in the package */
    system_date_global DATE := SYSDATE;
    client_tz VARCHAR2(3) := 'AST';
    server_tz VARCHAR2(3) := 'PST';

    FUNCTION client RETURN VARCHAR2
    IS
    BEGIN
        RETURN client_tz;
    END;

    FUNCTION server RETURN VARCHAR2
    IS
    BEGIN
        RETURN server_tz;
    END;

    FUNCTION system_date
        (refresh_in IN VARCHAR2 := 'NOREFRESH',
         server_time_zone IN VARCHAR2 := tz.server,
```

```
              client_time_zone IN VARCHAR2 := tz.client)
         RETURN DATE
      IS
      BEGIN
         /* Update the system date global if requested */
         IF UPPER (refresh_in) = 'REFRESH'
         THEN
            tz.system_date_global := SYSDATE;
         END IF;

         /* Use NEW_TIME to shift the date/time */
         RETURN NEW_TIME (system_date_global,
                          server_time_zone,
                          client_time_zone);
      END;

      PROCEDURE set_client (tz_in IN VARCHAR2)
      IS
      BEGIN
         assert (valid_time_zone (tz_in ));
         client_tz := tz_in;
      END;

      PROCEDURE set_server (tz_in IN VARCHAR2)
      IS
      BEGIN
         assert (valid_time_zone (tz_in ));
         server_tz := tz_in;
      END;

      PROCEDURE assert( condition_in IN BOOLEAN )
      IS
      BEGIN
         IF NOT condition_in THEN
            RAISE VALUE_ERROR;
         END IF;
      END;

      FUNCTION valid_time_zone( time_zone_in IN VARCHAR2 )
         RETURN BOOLEAN
      IS
         validation_tz VARCHAR2(3) := 'EST'; -- a valid time zone
         validation_date DATE;
         invalid_time_zone EXCEPTION;
         PRAGMA EXCEPTION_INIT(invalid_time_zone, -1857);
      BEGIN
         validation_date :=
            NEW_TIME( SYSDATE, time_zone_in, validation_tz );
         RETURN TRUE;
      EXCEPTION
         WHEN invalid_time_zone
         THEN
            RETURN FALSE;
      END;
   END tz;
```

13

Numeric, LOB, and Miscellaneous Functions

This chapter describes three sets of PL/SQL functions: the functions that manipulate numbers; the functions used to initialize large object (LOB) values; and a variety of miscellaneous functions which you will find useful. These sets of functions are listed in Tables 13-1 through 13-3.

Table 13-1. The Built-in Numeric Functions

Name	Description
ABS	Returns the absolute value of the number.
ACOS	Returns the inverse cosine.
ASIN	Returns the inverse sine.
ATAN	Returns the inverse tangent.
ATAN2	Returns the result of the tan2 inverse trigonometric function.
CEIL	Returns the smallest integer greater than or equal to the specified number.
COS	Returns the cosine.
COSH	Returns the hyperbolic cosine.
EXP (n)	Returns e raised to the nth power, where e = 2.71828183...
FLOOR	Returns the largest integer equal to or less than the specified number.
LN (a)	Returns the natural logarithm of a.
LOG (a, b)	Returns the logarithm, base a, of b.
MOD (a, b)	Returns the remainder of a divided by b.
POWER (a, b)	Returns a raised to the bth power.
ROUND (a, [b])	Returns a rounded to b decimal places.
SIGN (a)	Returns 1 if a is positive, 0 if a is 0, and −1 if a is less than 0.
SIN	Returns the sine.
SINH	Returns the hyperbolic sine.

Table 13-1. The Built-in Numeric Functions (continued)

Name	Description
SQRT	Returns the square root of the number.
TAN	Returns the tangent.
TANH	Returns the hyperbolic tangent.
TRUNC (a, [b])	Returns *a* truncated to *b* decimal places.

Note that the trigonometric and logarithmic functions are available only in PL/SQL Version 2.0 and subsequent releases. The inverse trigonometric functions are available only in PL/SQL Release 2.3. In these functions, all results are expressed in radians. Oracle Corporation did not implement pi itself, but it can be obtained through the following call:

```
ACOS (-1)
```

Table 13-2. The Built-in LOB Functions

Name	Description
BFILENAME	Initializes a BFILE column in an INSERT statement by associating it with a file in the server's filesystem.
EMPTY_BLOB	Returns an empty locator of type BLOB (binary large object).
EMPTY_CLOB	Returns an empty locator of type CLOB (character large object).

Note that the DBMS_LOB built-in package (See Appendix C, *Built-In Packages*) contains many more functions and procedures for manipulating LOB data.

Table 13-3. The Built-in MiscellaneousFunctions

Name	Description
DUMP	Returns a string containing a "dump" of the specified expression. This dump includes the datatype, length in bytes, and internal representation.
GREATEST	Returns the greatest of the specified list of values.
LEAST	Returns the least of the specified list of values.
NVL	Returns a substitution value if the argument is NULL.
SQLCODE	Returns the number of the Oracle error for the most recent internal exception.
SQLERRM	Returns the error message associated with the error number returned by SQLCODE.
UID	Returns the User ID (a unique integer) of the current Oracle session.
USER	Returns the name of the current Oracle user.
USERENV	Returns a string containing information about the current session.
VSIZE	Returns the number of bytes in the internal representation of the specified value.

Numeric Function Descriptions

The following sections briefly describe each of the PL/SQL numeric functions.

The ABS function

The ABS function returns the absolute value of the input. The specification for the ABS function is:

```
FUNCTION ABS (n NUMBER) RETURN NUMBER;
```

The ABS function can help simplify your code logic. Here's an example:

In one program I reviewed, line items and amounts for a profit and loss statement were footed or balanced. If the variance on the line amount was greater than $100, either positive or negative, that line item was flagged as "in error." The first version of the code that implemented this requirement looked like this (variance_ table is a PL/SQL table holding the variance for each line item):

```
IF variance_table (line_item_nu) BETWEEN 1 AND 100 OR
   variance_table (line_item_nu) BETWEEN -100 AND -1
THEN
   apply_variance (statement_id);
ELSE
   flag_error (statement_id, line_item_nu);
END IF;
```

There are two ways to express this logic. First, do not hardcode the maximum allowable variance; put the value in a named constant. Second, use ABS so that you perform the range check only once. With these changes, the above code can be rewritten as follows:

```
IF ABS (variance_table (line_item_nu))
   BETWEEN min_variance AND max_variance
THEN
   apply_variance (statement_id);
ELSE
   flag_error (statement_id, line_item_nu);
END IF;
```

The ACOS function

The ACOS function returns the inverse cosine. The specification for the ACOS function is:

```
FUNCTION ACOS (n NUMBER) RETURN NUMBER;
```

where the number *n* must be between –1 and 1, and the value returned by ACOS is between 0 and pi.

The ASIN function

The ASIN function returns the inverse sine. The specification for the ASIN function is:

```
FUNCTION ASIN (n NUMBER) RETURN NUMBER;
```

where the number n must be between −1 and 1, and the value returned by ASIN is between −pi/2 and pi/2.

The ATAN function

The ATAN function returns the inverse tangent. The specification for the ATAN function is:

```
FUNCTION ATAN (n NUMBER) RETURN NUMBER;
```

where the number n must be between −infinity and infinity, and the value returned by ATAN is between −pi/2 and pi/2.

The ATAN2 function

The ATAN2 function returns the result of the tan2 inverse trigonometric function. The specification for the ATAN2 function is;

```
FUNCTION ATAN (n NUMBER, m NUMBER) RETURN NUMBER;
```

where the numbers n and m must be between −infinity and infinity, and the value returned by ATAN is between -pi and pi.

As a result, the following holds true:

- atan2(−0.00001, −1) is approximately −pi.
- atan2(0,−1) is pi.

The CEIL function

The CEIL ("ceiling") function returns the smallest integer greater than or equal to the specified number. The specification for the CEIL function is:

```
FUNCTION CEIL (n NUMBER) RETURN NUMBER;
```

Here are some examples of the effect of CEIL:

```
CEIL (6) ==> 6
CEIL (119.1) ==> 120
CEIL (-17.2) ==> -17
```

I have found CEIL useful in calculating loop indexes for date ranges. Suppose that I need to calculate the net profit for sales activity in each month between two dates, and to store each value in a PL/SQL table. I don't really care where in the month the endpoints of the date range fall; I simply want to start from that month and loop through each month in between to the last month.

I could use a WHILE loop which increments a date variable until it is past the end date. That code would look like this:

```
PROCEDURE fill_profit_table (start_date_in IN DATE, end_date_in IN DATE)
IS
    /* Need local variables for loop condition and row in table. */
    curr_date DATE;
    month_index BINARY_INTEGER;
BEGIN
    /* Use TRUNC to always compare against first days of month. */
    curr_date := TRUNC (start_date_in, 'MONTH');
    month_index := 1;

    /* Loop until date exceeds  */
    WHILE curr_date <= TRUNC (end_date_in, 'MONTH')
    LOOP
        profit (month_index) := calc_profits (curr_date, 'NET');
        month_index := month_index + 1;
        curr_date := ADD_MONTHS (curr_date, 1);
    END LOOP;
END;
```

That works fine, but with CEIL I can produce a much simpler and cleaner implementation, as shown in the following code. I use both CEIL and MONTHS_BETWEEN to compute the number of months over which I need to calculate net profit. This number of months then bexcomes the upper limit of a fixed, numeric FOR loop. For each iteration of that loop, I call the calc_profits function and stuff the return value into the table:

```
PROCEDURE fill_profit_table (start_date_in IN DATE, end_date_in IN DATE)
IS
    number_of_months INTEGER :=
        CEIL (MONTHS_BETWEEN (end_date_in, start_date_in-1));
BEGIN
    FOR month_index IN 1 .. number_of_months
    LOOP
        profit (month_index) :=
            calc_profits (ADD_MONTHS (start_date_in, month_index - 1), 'NET');
    END LOOP;
END;
```

Notice that I subtract a day from the start_date_in in my computation of the number of months. I have to do this because if both the start_date_in and the end_date_in fall on the last days of their months, MONTHS_BETWEEN is one less than I need. In other words, if start_date_in = 28-FEB-97 and end_date is 31-MAR-97, MONTHS_BETWEEN (end_date_in, start_date_in) returns 1. For the purposes of this program, however, I need to generate profits for two months.

For a comparison of CEIL with several other numeric functions, see the section called "Rounding and Truncation with PL/SQL" later in this chapter.

The COS function

The COS trigonometric function returns the cosine of the specified angle. The specification for the COS function is:

```
FUNCTION COS (angle NUMBER) RETURN NUMBER;
```

where angle must be expressed in radians. A radian is equal to 180/pi or roughly 57.29578. If your angle is specified in degrees, then you should call COS as follows:

```
my_cosine := COS (angle_in_degrees/57.29578);
```

The COSH function

The COSH trigonometric function returns the hyperbolic cosine of the specified number. The specification for the COSH function is:

```
FUNCTION COSH (n NUMBER) RETURN NUMBER;
```

If n is a real number and $i = \sqrt{-1}$ (the imaginary square root of -1), then the relationship between COS and COSH can be expressed as follows:

```
COS (i * n) = COSH (h)
```

The EXP function

The EXP function returns the value e raised to the nth power, where n is the input argument. The specification for the EXP function is:

```
FUNCTION EXP (n NUMBER) RETURN NUMBER;
```

The number e (approximately equal to 2.71828) is the base of the system of natural logarithms.

The FLOOR function

The FLOOR function, the opposite of the CEIL function, returns the largest integer that is less than or equal to the input number. The specification for the FLOOR function is:

```
FUNCTION FLOOR (n NUMBER) RETURN NUMBER;
```

Here are some examples of the values returned by FLOOR:

```
FLOOR (6.2) ==> 6
FLOOR (-89.4) ==> -90
```

For a comparison of FLOOR with several other numeric functions, see the section called "Rounding and Truncation with PL/SQL" later in this chapter.

The LN function

The LN function returns the natural logarithm of the input. The specification for the LN function is:

```
FUNCTION LN (n NUMBER) RETURN NUMBER;
```

The argument *n* must be greater than or equal to 0. If you pass LN a negative argument, you will receive the following error:

```
ORA-01428: argument '-1' is out of range
```

The LOG function

The LOG function returns the base-*b* logarithm of the input value. The specification for the LOG function is:

```
FUNCTION LOG (b NUMBER, n NUMBER) RETURN NUMBER;
```

The argument *n* must be greater than or equal to 0. The base *b* must be greater than 1. If you pass LOG an argument that violates either of these rules, you will receive the following error:

```
ORA-01428: argument '-1' is out of range
```

The MOD function

The MOD function returns the remainder of one number when divided by a second number. The specification for the MOD function is:

```
FUNCTION MOD (dividend NUMBER, divisor NUMBER) RETURN NUMBER;
```

If the divisor is zero, then the dividend is returned unchanged. Here are some examples of MOD:

```
MOD (10, 5) ==> 0
MOD (2, 1) ==> 0
MOD (3,2) == 1
```

You can use MOD to determine quickly if a number is odd or even:

```
FUNCTION is_odd (num_in IN NUMBER) RETURN BOOLEAN
IS
BEGIN
   RETURN MOD (num_in, 2) = 1;
END;

FUNCTION is_even (num_in IN NUMBER) RETURN BOOLEAN
IS
BEGIN
   RETURN MOD (num_in, 2) = 0;
END;
```

The POWER function

The POWER function raises the first argument to the power indicated by the second argument. The specification for the POWER function is:

```
FUNCTION POWER (base NUMBER, power NUMBER) RETURN NUMBER;
```

If base is negative, then power must be an integer. The following expression calculates the range of valid values for a BINARY_INTEGER variable ($-2^{31}-1$ through $2^{31}-1$):

```
POWER (-2, 31) - 1 .. POWER (2, 31) - 1
```

or:

```
-2147483637 .. 2147483637
```

The ROUND function

The ROUND function returns the first argument rounded to the number of decimal places specified in the second argument. The specification for the ROUND function is:

```
FUNCTION ROUND (n NUMBER, [decimal_places NUMBER]) RETURN NUMBER;
```

The decimal_places argument is optional and defaults to 0, which means that *n* will be rounded to zero decimal places, a whole number. The value of decimal_places can be less than zero. A negative value for this argument directs ROUND to round digits to the left of the decimal point, rather than to the right. Here are some examples:

```
ROUND (153.46) ==> 153
ROUND (153.46, 1) ==> 153.5
ROUND (153, -1) ==> 150
```

For a comparison of ROUND with several other numeric functions, see the section called "Rounding and Truncation with PL/SQL" later in this chapter.

The SIGN function

The SIGN function returns the sign of the input number. The specification for the SIGN function is:

```
FUNCTION SIGN (n NUMBER) RETURN NUMBER;
```

This function returns one of the three values shown below:

−1 *n* is less than zero

0 *n* is equal to zero

+1 *n* is greater than zero

The SIN function

The SIN trigonometric function returns the sine of the specified angle. The specification for the SIN function is:

```
FUNCTION SIN (angle NUMBER) RETURN NUMBER;
```

where angle must be expressed in radians. A radian is equal to 180/pi or roughly 57.29578. If your angle is specified in degrees, then you should call SIN as follows:

```
my_sine := SIN (angle_in_degrees/57.29578);
```

The SINH function

The SINH trigonometric function returns the hyperbolic sine of the specified number. The specification for the SINH function is:

```
FUNCTION SINH (n NUMBER) RETURN NUMBER;
```

If n is a real number and $i = \sqrt{-1}$ (the imaginary square root of −1), then the relationship between SIN and SINH can be expressed as follows:

```
SIN (i * n) = i * SINH (h)
```

The SQRT function

The SQRT function returns the square root of the input number. The specification for the SQRT function is:

```
FUNCTION SQRT (n NUMBER) RETURN NUMBER;
```

where n must be greater than or equal to 0. If n is negative, you will receive the following error:

```
ORA-01428: argument '-1' is out of range
```

The TAN function

The TAN trigonometric function returns the tangent of the specified angle. The specification for the TAN function is:

```
FUNCTION TAN (angle NUMBER) RETURN NUMBER;
```

where angle must be expressed in radians. A radian is equal to 180/pi or roughly 57.29578. If your angle is specified in degrees, then you should call TAN as follows:

```
my_tane := TAN (angle_in_degrees/57.29578);
```

The TANH function

The TANH trigonometric function returns the hyperbolic tangent of the specified number. The specification for the TANH function is:

```
FUNCTION TANH (n NUMBER) RETURN NUMBER;
```

If n is a real number and i = $\sqrt{-1}$ (the imaginary square root of –1), then the relationship between TAN and TANH can be expressed as follows:

```
TAN (i * n) = i * TANH (h)
```

The TRUNC function

The TRUNC function truncates the first argument to the number of decimal places specified by the second argument. The specification for the TRUNC function is:

```
FUNCTION TRUNC (n NUMBER, [decimal_places NUMBER]) RETURN NUMBER;
```

The decimal_places argument is optional and defaults to 0, which means that n will be truncated to zero decimal places, a whole number. The value of decimal_places can be less than zero. A negative value for this argument directs TRUNC to truncate or zero-out digits to the left of the decimal point, rather than to the right. Here are some examples:

```
TRUNC (153.46) ==> 153
TRUNC (153.46, 1) ==> 153.4
TRUNC (-2003.16, -1) ==> -2000
```

Rounding and Truncation with PL/SQL

There are four different numeric functions that perform rounding and truncation actions: CEIL, FLOOR, ROUND, and TRUNC. It is easy to get confused about which of the functions to use in a particular situation. The following table compares functions. Figure 13-1 illustrates the use of the functions for different values and decimal place rounding.

Function	Summary
CEIL	Returns the smallest integer that is greater than the specified value. This integer is the "ceiling" over your value.
FLOOR	Returns the largest integer that is less than the specified value. This integer is the "floor" under your value.
ROUND	Performs rounding on a number. You can round with a positive number of decimal places (the number of digits to the right of the decimal point) and also with a negative number of decimal places (the number of digits to the right of the decimal point).
TRUNC	Truncates a number to the specified number of decimal places. TRUNC simply discards all values beyond the decimal places provided in the call.

LOB Function Descriptions

PL/SQL provides three functions to use within SQL DML statements to initialize a large object (LOB) locator.

Function	1.75	1.3	55.56	55.56	Input
	0	0	1	-1	Number of decimal places
ROUND	2	1	55.6	60	
TRUNC	1	1	55.5	50	
FLOOR	1	1	55	55	
CEIL	2	2	56	56	

Figure 13-1. Impact of rounding and truncating functions

The BFILENAME function

The BFILENAME function initializes a BFILE column in a database table or a BFILE variable in PL/SQL by returning a locator to a physical file in the server's filesystem. The header for BFILENAME is:

```
FUNCTION BFILENAME
    (directory_alias IN VARCHAR2, filename IN VARCHAR2
RETURN BFILE;
```

where directory_alias is a DIRECTORY database object which has already been defined with a CREATE DIRECTORY statement (see the following examples), and filename is the name of the file containing the large binary object.

This function will return NULL if you try to get a BFILE locator with a directory alias which does not yet exist.

You can use BFILENAME in SQL INSERT and UPDATE statements. You can also use it to initialize a BFILE locator in a PL/SQL program. Here are examples of both usages:

```
UPDATE school_report
    SET photo_op =
        BFILENAME ('projects', 'grasshoppers.atwork')
    WHERE title = 'REPRODUCTIVE CYCLES OF BUGS';

DECLARE
    pricelist BFILE;
BEGIN
    /* Now this is a BIG file. */
    pricelist := BFILENAME ('OraclePrices', '1997.all');
```

The BFILENAME function does *not* validate that the user has READ privileges on the specified file or directory alias. It also does not perform a physical check to see if the directory or file actually exist. Instead, these checks are performed when access against the BFILE object is attempted.

There are several issues to keep in mind with directory aliases:

- An alias is a database object, an "internal" name for an external, filesystem-based directory location.

- You must create a directory alias before you can use it.

- To create a directory alias, you will need the CREATE DIRECTORY or CREATE ANY DIRECTORY privileges.

- To access a directory alias, you must be the owner or be granted the READ privilege on that alias.

- Directory aliases *can be* case-sensitive!

Let's step through the creation and use of several directory aliases to drive home these points. Suppose I want to let the SCOTT account create directory aliases. I will connect to my DBA account and grant the privilege:

```
SQL> GRANT CREATE DIRECTORY TO SCOTT;
```

Then, connecting as SCOTT, I will create two directory aliases:

```
SQL> CREATE DIRECTORY projects AS 'm:\school\projects';
SQL> CREATE DIRECTORY "OraclePrices" AS '/oracle/prices';
```

Notice the double quotes around OraclePrices. By taking this approach, I have requested that this directory alias be stored in the database with mixed case. The PROJECTS directory alias, on the other hand, has been defined in the database using the default, uppercase method.

I want to let anyone access the OraclePrices directory, but let only ELI access the projects directory:

```
SQL> GRANT READ ON DIRECTORY projects TO SCOTT;
Grant succeeded.
SQL> GRANT READ ON DIRECTORY OraclePrices TO PUBLIC;
GRANT READ ON DIRECTORY OraclePrices TO PUBLIC;
                        *
ERROR at line 1:
ORA-22930: directory does not exist
```

What went wrong? I did not put double quotes around OraclePrices, so Oracle converted the identifier to uppercase and then could not find a match inside the ALL_DIRECTORIES data dictionary view.

Once I have defined the directory in mixed case, I need to continue to use the double quotes in my DDL statements for those statements to succeed. Within SQL DML and PL/SQL, the situation is a little bit different. When you call BFILENAME, you pass in a directory alias, either as an identifier or as a literal. In the call to BFILENAME, the case used to set that directory alias must match the case originally used to define the directory alias.

The following INSERT statement correctly identifies the OraclePrices alias:

```
INSERT INTO sw_budget
    (item_desc, price, source_lob)
VALUES
    ('ORACLE8', a_bargain, BFILENAME ('OraclePrices', '1997.rdbms'));
```

where a_bargain is a PL/SQL variable previously defined and set.

The following PL/SQL block incorrectly defines the projects directory alias:

```
DECLARE
    projects_dir VARCHAR2(30) := 'projects'; -- lower case!
    ants_scurrying BFILE;
BEGIN
    ants_scurrying := BFILENAME (projects_dir, 'ants_building.hill');

    /* FILEOPEN will fail because BFILE locator is NULL. */
    DBMS_LOB.FILEOPEN (ants_scurrying);
BEGIN
```

I have passed in a lowercase "projects", but the directory alias has been set to uppercase since I did not surround the directory alias name in double quotes in the CREATE DIRECTORY statement. This behavior differs from much of the rest of PL/SQL's interaction with the data dictionary. Usually, all names passed in for data dictionary access are by default uppercased. You will need to be careful how you define directory aliases and then reference them in your code.

The EMPTY_BLOB function

The EMPTY_BLOB function returns an empty locator of type BLOB (binary large object). The specification for the EMPTY_BLOB function is:

```
FUNCTION EMPTY_BLOB RETURN BLOB;
```

You can call this function without any parentheses or with an empty pair. Here are some examples:

```
INSERT INTO family_member (name, photo)
    VALUES ('Steven Feuerstein', EMPTY_BLOB());
```

```
DECLARE
    my_photo BLOB := EMPTY_BLOB;
BEGIN
```

Use EMPTY_BLOB to initialize a BLOB to "empty." Before you can work with a BLOB, either to reference it in SQL DML statements such as INSERTs or to assign it a value in PL/SQL, it must contain a locator. It cannot be NULL. The locator might point to an empty BLOB value, but it *will* be a valid BLOB locator.

The EMPTY_CLOB function

The EMPTY_CLOB function returns an empty locator of type CLOB. The specification for the EMPTY_CLOB function is:

```
FUNCTION EMPTY_CLOB RETURN CLOB;
```

You can call this function without any parentheses or with an empty pair. Here are some examples:

```
INSERT INTO diary (entry, text) VALUES (SYSDATE, EMPTY_CLOB());

DECLARE
    the_big_novel CLOB := EMPTY_CLOB;
BEGIN
```

Use EMPTY_CLOB to initialize a CLOB to "empty". Before you can work with a CLOB, either to reference it in SQL DML statements such as INSERTs or to assign it a value in PL/SQL, it must contain a locator. It cannot be NULL. The locator might point to an empty CLOB value, but it *will* be a valid CLOB locator.

Miscellaneous Function Descriptions

The following sections briefly describe the miscellaneous PL/SQL functions; these are functions that do not fall naturally into particular datatype categories.

The DUMP function

The DUMP function "dumps," or returns, the internal representation of the input expression. DUMP is an overloaded function, as is shown by its specification:

```
FUNCTION DUMP (expr_in DATE
    [, return_format_in BINARY_INTEGER
    [, start_position_in BINARY_INTEGER
    [, length_in BINARY_INTEGER
    )
RETURN VARCHAR2

FUNCTION DUMP (expr_in NUMBER
    [, return_format_in BINARY_INTEGER
    [, start_position_in BINARY_INTEGER
    [, length_in BINARY_INTEGER
    )
RETURN VARCHAR2

FUNCTION DUMP (expr_in VARCHAR2
    [, return_format_in BINARY_INTEGER
    [, start_position_in BINARY_INTEGER
    [, length_in BINARY_INTEGER
    )
RETURN VARCHAR2
```

where expr_in is the expression to be dumped, return_format_in is a numeric code specifying the format of the returned string, start_position_in is the starting position of the portion of the internal representation to be returned, and length_in is the length of the portion to be returned. The starting position and length arguments perform the same way as in the SUBSTR function described in Chapter 11, *Character Functions*.

Valid return format numbers are:

   8 Returns result in octal notation

   10 Returns result in decimal notation

   16 Returns result in hexadecimal notation

   17 Returns result as individual characters

The default for the return format is 10 (decimal), the default for the starting position is 1, and the default for length is the full length of the value. So, a fully default call to DUMP will return the full internal representation in decimal notation.

If expr_in IS NULL, then DUMP returns NULL.

The GREATEST function

The GREATEST function evaluates a list of values and returns the greatest value in that list. (The LEAST function, discussed below, returns the least value.) GREATEST accepts two or more arguments, and there is no upper limit on the number of values you can pass to GREATEST, which makes it especially useful. The specification for GREATEST is:

```
FUNCTION GREATEST (expr1, expr2 [, expr3 ...) RETURN DATE
FUNCTION GREATEST (expr1, expr2 [, expr3 ...) RETURN VARCHAR2
FUNCTION GREATEST (expr1, expr2 [, expr3 ...) RETURN NUMBER
```

The datatype of the return value of the GREATEST function is determined by the datatype of the first expression (expr1) in the list. In addition, PL/SQL must convert all the additional expressions in the list (expr2, expr3, and so on) to the same datatype as expr1, so they must all be compatible.

This example finds the greatest (most recent) of three dates:

```
GREATEST (SYSDATE, :emp.hire_date, '13-JAN-1994')
```

My first expression is a call to the SYSDATE function. My second expression is an Oracle Forms item of type DATE. My third expression is a literal string. This string is converted to a date by PL/SQL with an internal call to TO_DATE. The comparison of the values then proceeds.

The next example finds the greatest (last in alphabetical order) of two strings:

```
GREATEST (SUBSTR (text_chunk, INSTR (text_chunk, ';') + 1),
         last_command_entered)
```

The first expression is comprised of nested calls first to SUBSTR and then to INSTR, to find that part of the text_chunk variables that comes after the first semicolon (;).

The LEAST function

The LEAST function, the opposite of the GREATEST function, evaluates a list of values and returns the least value in that list. LEAST accepts two or more arguments; there is no upper limit on the number of values you can pass to LEAST, which makes it especially useful. The specification for LEAST is as follows:

```
FUNCTION LEAST (expr1, expr2 [, expr3 ...) RETURN DATE
FUNCTION LEAST (expr1, expr2 [, expr3 ...) RETURN VARCHAR2
FUNCTION LEAST (expr1, expr2 [, expr3 ...) RETURN NUMBER
```

The datatype of the return value of the LEAST function is determined by the datatype of the first expression (expr1) in the list. In addition, PL/SQL must convert all the additional expressions in the list (expr2, expr3, and so on) to the same datatype as expr1, so they must all be compatible.

The NVL function

The NVL function offers a concise way to return or substitute a non-NULL value if the specified value is NULL. You can think of NVL as an abbreviation for "if Null VaLue, then return X." The NVL function is massively overloaded because any type of data can also have a NULL value. Here is the specification:

```
FUNCTION NVL (string_in IN CHAR, replace_with_in IN CHAR)
    RETURN CHAR
FUNCTION NVL (string_in IN VARCHAR2, replace_with_in IN VARCHAR2)
    RETURN VARCHAR2
FUNCTION NVL (date_in IN DATE, replace_with_in IN DATE)
    RETURN DATE
FUNCTION NVL (date_in IN NUMBER, replace_with_in IN DATE)
    RETURN NUMBER
FUNCTION NVL (date_in IN CHAR, replace_with_in IN DATE)
    RETURN BOOLEAN
```

Note that the CHAR version of NVL also returns a CHAR, or fixed-length, value.

For dates, if date_in is NOT NULL, then return date_in; otherwise, return replace_with_in. The NVL function in this case is therefore equivalent to the following IF statement:

```
IF date_in IS NOT NULL
THEN
    RETURN date_in;
ELSE
    RETURN replace_with_in;
END IF;
```

NVL simply provides a much cleaner and more concise way of coding this functionality. And since it is a function, you can call it inline to provide substitution of NULL values where such a state of data would disrupt your program. For example, if you calculate the total compensation of an employee as salary plus compensation, then the expression:

```
salary + commission
```

will be NULL when commission is NULL. With NVL, however, you can be sure that the calculated value will make sense:

```
salary + NVL (commission, 0)
```

The next two examples show some other ways to use the NVL function:

- Check all IN parameters of a procedure and convert NULL values to 0 in the default value setting of the declarations of local variable copies of the parameters:

```
PROCEDURE no_nulls_allowed (number1_in IN NUMBER, number2_in IN NUMBER)
IS
    local_number1 NUMBER := NVL (number1_in, 0);
    local_number2 NUMBER := NVL (number2_in, 0);
BEGIN
    ...
END;
```

- After fetching the employee information from the database, return the employee's commission as 0 whenever it is NULL.

```
DECLARE
    CURSOR emp_cur IS
        SELECT first_name, last_name, salary, NVL (commission, 0)
            commission
        FROM employee
        WHERE employee_id = :emp.employee_id;
BEGIN
    ...
END;
```

The SQLCODE function

The SQLCODE function returns the number of the exception raised by PL/SQL. The specification for this function is:

```
FUNCTION SQLCODE RETURN INTEGER
```

SQLCODE returns values as follows:

- If you reference SQLCODE outside of an exception section, it always returns 0, which means normal, successful completion.

- If you explicitly raise your own user-defined exception, then SQLCODE returns a value of +1.

- If PL/SQL raises the NO_DATA_FOUND exception, then SQLCODE returns a value of +100.

- In all other cases, SQLCODE returns a negative value. In other words, if you try to convert a date to a string with TO_CHAR and use the wrong format mask, you might encounter the following error message:

```
ORA-01830: date format picture ends before converting entire input string
```

In this case, SQLCODE returns a value of –1830.

You will find SQLCODE and its sibling function, SQLERRM, most useful in the WHEN OTHERS exception handler. If an error is trapped by WHEN OTHERS, you do not know which exception was raised or which error was encountered. You can, however, use SQLCODE to find out, as shown in this example:

```
EXCEPTION
    WHEN NO_DATA_FOUND
    THEN
        MESSAGE ('No match found for entry!');

    WHEN OTHERS
    THEN
        MESSAGE
            ('Error ' || TO_CHAR (SQLCODE) || ': ' ||
            SQLERRM);
END;
```

The SQLERRM function

The SQLERRM returns the error message associated with the specified code. The specification for this function is:

```
FUNCTION SQLERRM (code_in IN INTEGER := SQLCODE) RETURN VARCHAR2
```

If you do not provide an error code when you call SQLERRM, it uses the value returned by SQLCODE (see the preceding section). If SQLCODE returns 0, then SQLERRM returns the following message:

```
ORA-0000; normal, successful completion
```

If PL/SQL has raised an internal Oracle error or you pass a negative value to SQLERRM, then the function returns the error message provided by Oracle Corporation. If you pass (or allow SQLCODE to pass) a value of +100 to SQLERRM, it returns this message:

```
ORA-01403: no data found
```

Any other positive value passed to SQLERRM will result in this message:

```
User-Defined Exception
```

The maximum length of a message returned by SQLERRM is 512 bytes. This length includes the error code and all nested messages that may have been flagged by the compiler.

The UID function

The UID function returns an integer that uniquely identifies the current user. This integer is generated by the Oracle RDBMS when a user connects to the database. The specification for UID is as follows:

```
FUNCTION UID RETURN NUMBER
```

When called inline, the UID function looks like a variable since it has no arguments. Remember that when you call UID you will actually issue a SQL call to the RDBMS to extract the UID information for the user. Furthermore, in a distributed SQL statement, the UID always returns the value identifying the user on the local database. You cannot obtain the UID for connections to other, remote databases.

The USER function

The USER function returns the name of the current account. The specification for USER is as follows:

```
FUNCTION USER RETURN VARCHAR2
```

Like UID, when called inline, the USER function looks like a variable since it has no arguments. Remember that when you call USER you actually issue a SQL call to the RDBMS to extract the account name for the user. Furthermore, in a distributed SQL statement, the USER always returns the value identifying the user on the local database. You cannot obtain the USER for connections to other, remote databases.

The most common use for the USER function is to initialize an application session with configuration for a user.

Most of the applications I build have a system configuration table (with one row for each system or application) and a separate user configuration table (with one row for each user in each application). This user configuration table might have the following columns:

RDBMS account name
    The name of the Oracle account, which matches the value returned by USER.

User name
    The actual name of the user, as in: STEVEN FEUERSTEIN.

Business data
    Information about the user that relates to the business of the application, such as the user's department and default printer.

Preference data

Information about the preferences of the user, such as "Display Toolbar" or "Automatically pop up a list of values boxes."

Assuming an Oracle Forms-based set of screens, each screen the user is able to enter from a Windows icon will contain a When-New-Form-Instance trigger. This trigger calls a procedure to transfer the information from the user configuration table to GLOBAL variables that are then available to all screens for the duration of the session. A sample initialization procedure follows:

```
PROCEDURE configure_user_globals
IS
   /*
   || I identify the row from the configuration table using the
   || USER function provided by PL/SQL.
   */
   CURSOR user_cur IS
      SELECT username, default_printer, toolbar_status, ... etc ...
        FROM user_configuration
       WHERE user_account_name = USER;
BEGIN

   OPEN user_cur;
   FETCH user_cur INTO
      :GLOBAL.username, :GLOBAL.default_printer ... etc ...;
   IF user_cur%NOTFOUND
   THEN
      CLOSE user_cur;
      MESSAGE (' You are not authorized to run this screen!');
      RAISE FORM_TRIGGER_FAILURE;
   ELSE
      CLOSE user_cur;
   END IF;

END configure_user_globals;
```

The USERENV function

The USERENV function returns information about the current user session or environment. The specification for USERENV is as follows:

```
FUNCTION USERENV (info_type_in IN VARCHAR2) RETURN VARCHAR2
```

where info_type_in can be one of these values (specified in a named constant or a literal string in single quotes). The following list gives options and descriptions of what they return:

ENTRYID

An auditing entry identifier

LANGUAGE

The language, territory, and character set used by your session. The value is returned in this format: language_territory.characterset

SESSIONID

An auditing session identifier

TERMINAL

The operating system identifier for your current session's terminal. The format of this information will clearly be dependent on your underlying operating system.

The VSIZE function

The VSIZE function returns the number of bytes used by the internal representation of the input expression. The specification for VSIZE is:

```
FUNCTION VSIZE (expr_in IN DATE) RETURN NUMBER
FUNCTION VSIZE (expr_in IN VARCHAR2) RETURN NUMBER
FUNCTION VSIZE (expr_in IN NUMBER) RETURN NUMBER
FUNCTION VSIZE (expr_in IN CHAR) RETURN NUMBER
```

If the expression is NULL, then VSIZE returns NULL.

I am not sure when I would use this function in a program, but it comes in very handy when I get a call like this on the phone: "How many bytes does a date value take up in the database?" I could try to remember the answer (it sure seems like something I once knew). I could try to hunt down the answer in one of the many database administration manuals from Oracle, or I could execute the following SQL statement:

```
SQL> SELECT VSIZE (hiredate) FROM emp WHERE ROWNUM=1

VSIZE(HIREDATE)
---------------
              7
```

I included the WHERE clause for ROWNUM equal to 1 so that I would receive the answer (7 bytes) only once. Otherwise, I would have had the "opportunity" to learn that the VSIZE of hiredate is 7—for every record in the emp table.

Interestingly, if you apply VSIZE to the SYSDATE function, you get a slightly different answer:

```
SQL> SELECT VSIZE (SYSDATE) FROM dual;

VSIZE(SYSDATE)
--------------
             8
```

Conversion Functions

Whenever PL/SQL performs an operation involving one or more values, it must first convert the data to be the right datatype for the operation. As Chapter 4, *Variables and Program Data*, describes, there are two kinds of conversion: implicit and explicit. An *implicit conversion* is performed by PL/SQL as needed to execute a statement. An *explicit conversion* takes place when you use a built-in conversion function to force the conversion of a value from one datatype to another. This chapter describes each of these functions.

If you do not use a conversion function to explicitly convert your data, or if you do use those functions and additional conversion is still needed, PL/SQL attempts to convert the data implicitly to the datatypes needed to perform the operation. I recommend that you avoid allowing either the SQL or PL/SQL languages to perform implicit conversions on your behalf. Whenever possible, use a conversion function to guarantee that the right kind of conversion takes place. Implicit conversion has a number of drawbacks, summarized in the section called in "Implicit data conversions" in Chapter 4.

Explicit conversions help you to avoid unpleasant surprises, maximize performance, and make your code more self-documenting. When you perform an explicit conversion involving dates or numbers (using TO_CHAR, TO_DATE, or TO_NUMBER), you can specify a conversion format mask. PL/SQL uses this mask to either interpret the input value or format the output value.

Table 14-1 summarizes the PL/SQL conversion functions described in this chapter.

Table 14-1. The Built-In Conversion Functions

Name	Description
CHARTOROWID	Converts a string to a ROWID.
CONVERT	Converts a string from one character set to another.

Table 14-1. The Built-In Conversion Functions (continued)

Name	Description
HEXTORAW	Converts from hexadecimal to raw format.
RAWTOHEX	Converts from raw value to hexadecimal.
ROWIDTOCHAR	Converts a binary ROWID value to a character string.
TO_CHAR	Converts a number or date to a string.
TO_DATE	Converts a string to a date.
TO_NUMBER	Converts a string to a number.

Conversion Formats

Several of the conversion functions (TO_CHAR, TO_DATE, and TO_NUMBER) use format models to determine the format of the converted data. Format models convert between strings and dates, and strings and numbers. This section discusses these format models, which are then put to use in the function descriptions.

Date Format Models

In Versions 6 and earlier of the Oracle RDBMS, the default format for dates as character values was DD-MON-YY, a cause of consternation for many developers and users. While this format is common in many parts of the world, very few people use it in the United States.

With Oracle7 you can specify your own default date format (which takes effect on the initialization or startup of the RDBMS instance) with the NLS_DATE_FORMAT[*] parameter as follows:

```
NLS_DATE_FORMAT = 'MM/DD/YYYY'
```

The default date format is also set implicitly with another initialization parameter, NLS_TERRITORY. When you specify an NLS_TERRITORY value, you set conventions for date format, date language, numeric formats, currency symbols, and week start day.

Even with this flexibility, the database still supports only a single default date format in a given instance. Both developers and users must be aware of this format when working with dates. Later sections of this chapter explore approaches in PL/SQL that give the user much more flexibility when entering dates in their applications.

As you can see, format masks (such as MMDDYY and Month DD, YYYY) play an important role in the conversion of date and character data. Table 14-2 provides

---

[*] NLS is an abbreviation for National Language Support.

the full set of date format masks and explains how to use them in all their variations. You can use the format elements in any combination, in any order. You can even use the same format element more than once in your format mask. Following the table are examples showing these variations.

Table 14-2. Date Format Model Elements

Mask	Description
SCC or CC	The century. If the SCC format is used, any B.C. dates are prefaced with a hyphen (–).
SYYYY or YYYY	The four-digit year. If the SYYYY format is used, any B.C. dates are prefaced with a hyphen (–).
IYYY	The four-digit ISO standard year.
YYY or YY or Y	The last three, two, or one digits of the year. The current century is the default.
IYY or IY or I	The last three, two, or one digits of the ISO standard year. The current century is the default.
Y,YYY	The four-digit year with a comma.
SYEAR or YEAR or SYear or Year	The year spelled out. The S prefix places a negative sign in front of B.C. dates.
RR	The last two digits of the year. This format is used to display years in centuries other than our own. See the section called "RR: Changing Millenia."
BC or AD	The B.C. or A.D. indicator, without periods.
B.C. or A.D.	The B.C. or A.D. indicator, with periods.
Q	The quarter of the year, from 1 through 4. January through March are in the first quarter, April through June in second quarter, etc.
MM	The number of the month in the year, from 01 through 12. January is month number 01, September is 09, etc.
RM	The Roman numeral representation of the month number, from I through XII. January is I, September is IX, etc.
MONTH or Month	The name of the month, either in upper- or mixed-case format.
MON or Mon	The abbreviated name of the month, as in JAN for January.
WW	The week in the year, from 1 through 53.
IW	The week in the year, from 1 through 52 or 1 through 53, based on the ISO standard.
W	The week in the month, from 1 through 5. Week 1 starts on the first day of the month and ends on the seventh.
DDD	The day in the year, from 1 through 366.
DD	The day in the month, from 1 through 31.
D	The day in the week, from 1 through 7. The day of the week that is decreed the first day is specified implicitly by the NLS_TERRITORY initialization parameter for the database instance.
DAY or Day	The name of the day in upper- or mixed-case format.

Table 14-2. Date Format Model Elements (continued)

Mask	Description
DY	The abbreviated name of the day, as in TUE for Tuesday.
J	The Julian day format of the date (counted as the number of days since January 1, 4712 B.C., the earliest date supported by the Oracle RDBMS).
AM or PM	The meridian indicator (morning or evening) without periods.
A.M. or P.M.	The meridian indicator (morning or evening) with periods.
HH or HH12	The hour in the day, from 1 through 12.
HH24	The hour in the day, from 0 through 23.
MI	The minutes component of the date's time, from 0 through 59.
SS	The seconds component of the date's time, from 0 through 59.
SSSSS	The number of seconds since midnight of the time component. Values range from 1 through 86399, with each hour comprising 3600 seconds.
TH	Suffix which converts a number to its ordinal format; for example, 4 becomes 4th and 1 becomes 1st. This element can appear only at the end of the entire format mask. The return value is always in English, regardless of the date language.
SP	Suffix which converts a number to its spelled format; for example, 4 becomes FOUR, 1 becomes ONE, and 221 becomes TWO HUNDRED TWENTY-ONE. This element can appear only at the end of the entire format mask. The return value is always in English, regardless of the date language.
SPTH	Suffix which converts a number to its spelled and ordinal format; for example, 4 becomes FOURTH and 1 becomes FIRST. This element can appear only at the end of the entire format mask. The return value is always in English, regardless of the date language.
FX	Element which requires exact pattern matching between data and format model. (FX stands for Format eXact.)
FM	Element which toggles suppression of blanks in output from conversion. (FM stands for Fill Mode.)
Other text	Any punctuation, such as a comma (,) or slash (/) or hyphen (–), will be reproduced in the formatted output of the conversion. You can also include text within double quotes (") and this text will then be represented as entered in the converted value. See examples in TO_CHAR for an illustration of this element.

Note that whenever a date format returns a spelled value (words rather than numbers, as with MONTH, MON, DAY, DY, AM, and PM), the language used to spell these words is determined by the National Language Support parameters, NLS_DATE_LANGUAGE and NLS_LANGUAGE, or by the optional date language argument you can pass to both TO_CHAR and TO_DATE.

Here are some examples of date format masks composed of the above format elements:

```
'Month DD, YYYY'
'MM/DD/YY Day A.M.'
'Year Month Day HH24:MI:SS'
'J'
'SSSSS-YYYY-MM-DD'
'"A beautiful summer morning on the" DDth" day of "Month'
```

See the description of the TO_CHAR and TO_DATE functions for more examples of the use and resulting values of these masks.

Number Format Models

The number formats are used in both TO_CHAR and TO_NUMBER. The number format in TO_CHAR translates a numeric value to a VARCHAR2 datatype. The number format in TO_NUMBER translates a VARCHAR2 value to a numeric datatype.

A number format mask can comprise one or more elements from Table 14-3. The resulting format of the character string (or the converted numeric value) will reflect the combination of the format elements. You will find examples of different applications of the format models in the descriptions of both the TO_CHAR and TO_NUMBER functions

Format elements with a description starting with "Prefix:" can be used only at the beginning of the complete format mask. Format elements with a description starting with "Suffix:" can be used only at the end of the complete format mask.

Table 14-3. Number Format Model Elements

Format Elements	Description
9	Each 9 represents a significant digit to be returned. Leading zeros in a number are displayed or treated as blanks.
0	Each 0 represents a significant digit to be returned. Leading zeros in a number are displayed or treated as zeros.
$	Prefix: puts a dollar sign in front of the number.
B	Prefix: returns a zero value as blanks, even if the 0 format element was used to show a leading zero.
MI	Suffix: places a minus sign (–) after the number if it is negative. For positive values it returns a trailing space, which is different from NULL.
S	Prefix: places a plus sign (+) in front of a positive number and a minus sign (–) before a negative number.
PR	Suffix: places angle brackets (< and >) around a negative value. For positive values it places leading and trailing spaces around the number.

Table 14-3. Number Format Model Elements (continued)

Format Elements	Description
D	Specifies the location of the decimal point in the returned value. All format elements to the left of the D will format the integer component of the value. All format elements to the right of the D will format the fractional part of the value. The character used for the decimal character is determined by the database initialization parameter NLS_NUMERIC_CHARACTERS.
G	Specifies the location of the group separator (for example, a comma to separate thousands as in 6,734) in the returned value. The character used for the group separator is determined by the database initialization parameter NLS_NUMERIC_CHARACTERS.
C	Specifies the location of the ISO currency symbol in the returned value.
L	Specifies the location of the local currency symbol (such as $) in the returned value.
, (comma)	Specifies that a comma be returned in that location in the return value.
. (period)	Specifies that a period be returned in that location in the return value.
V	Multiplies the number to the left of the V in the format model by 10 raised to the *n*th power, where *n* is the number of 9s found after the V in the format model.
EEEE	Suffix: specifies that the value be returned in scientific notation.
RN or rn	Specifies that the return value be converted to upper- or lowercase Roman numerals. The range of valid numbers for conversion to Roman numerals is between 1 and 3999. The value must be an integer.

Here are some examples of numeric format masks built from these elements:

```
9.999EEEE
00V99
S9,999,999
00009MI
999D99
9G999G999
L999.99
```

Conversion Function Descriptions

This section describes the various conversion functions provided by PL/SQL.

The CHARTOROWID function

The CHARTOROWID function converts a string of either type CHAR or VARCHAR2 to a value of type ROWID. The specification of the CHARTOROWID function is:

```
FUNCTION CHARTOROWID (string_in IN CHAR) RETURN ROWID
FUNCTION CHARTOROWID (string_in IN VARCHAR2) RETURN ROWID
```

In order for CHARTOROWID to successfully convert the string, it must be of the format:

```
BBBBBBBB.RRRR.FFFF
```

where BBBBBBBB is the number of the block in the database file, RRRR is the number of the row in the block, and FFFF is the number of the database file. All three numbers must be in hexadecimal format.

If the input string does not conform to the above format, PL/SQL raises the VALUE_ERROR exception.

The CONVERT function

The CONVERT function converts strings from one character set to another character set. The specification of the CONVERT function is:

```
FUNCTION CONVERT
    (string_in IN VARCHAR2,
    new_char_set VARCHAR2
    [, old_char_set VARCHAR2])
RETURN VARCHAR2
```

The old_char_set is an optional argument. If this third argument is not specified, then the default character set for the database instance is used.

The CONVERT function does not translate words or phrases from one language to another! CONVERT simply substitutes the letter or symbol in one character set with the corresponding letter or symbol in another character set. (A character set is not the same thing as a human language.)

Two commonly used character sets are US7ASCII (U.S. 7-bit ASCII character set) and F7DEC (DEC French 7-bit character set).

The HEXTORAW function

The HEXTORAW function converts a hexadecimal string from type CHAR or VARCHAR2 to type RAW. The specification of the HEXTORAW function is:

```
FUNCTION HEXTORAW (string_in IN CHAR) RETURN RAW
FUNCTION HEXTORAW (string_in IN VARCHAR2) RETURN RAW
```

The RAWTOHEX function

The RAWTOHEX function converts a value from type RAW to a hexadecimal string of type VARCHAR2. The specification of the RAWTOHEX function is:

```
FUNCTION RAWTOHEX (binary_value_in IN RAW) RETURN VARCHAR2
```

RAWTOHEX always returns a variable-length string value, even if its mirror conversion function is overloaded to support both types of input.

The ROWIDTOCHAR function

The ROWIDTOCHAR function converts a binary value of type ROWID to a string of type VARCHAR2. The specification of the ROWIDTOCHAR function is:

```
FUNCTION ROWIDTOCHAR (row_in IN ROWID ) RETURN VARCHAR2
```

The string returned by this function has the format:

```
BBBBBBBB.RRRR.FFFF
```

where BBBBBBBB is the number of the block in the database file, RRRR is the number of the row in the block, and FFFF is the number of the database file. All three numbers are in hexadecimal format.

The TO_CHAR function (date conversion)

The TO_CHAR function can be used to convert both dates and numbers to a variable-length string. The following specification describes TO_CHAR for dates:

```
FUNCTION TO_CHAR
    (date_in IN DATE
    [, format_mask IN VARCHAR2
    [, nls_language IN VARCHAR2]])
    RETURN VARCHAR2
```

where date_in is the date to be converted to character format, the format_mask is the mask made up of one or more of the date format elements, and nls_language is a string specifying a date language. Both the format mask and the NLS language parameters are optional.

If the format mask is not specified, then the default date format for the database instance is used. This format is DD-MON-YY, unless the initialization parameter NLS_DATE_FORMAT is included in the initialization file. The format of the specification of an alternative date mask is:

```
NLS_DATE_FORMAT = 'MM/DD/YYYY'
```

If the NLS language parameter is not specified, then the default date language for the instance is used. This is either the language for the instance specified by the NLS_LANGUAGE parameter, or the date language specified in the initialization file with the parameter NLS_DATE_LANGUAGE. Note that if you want to specify a date language, you also must include a format mask. You cannot skip over the intervening parameters.

Here are some examples of TO_CHAR for date conversion:

- Notice that there are two blanks between month and day and a leading zero for the fifth day:

```
TO_CHAR (SYSDATE, 'Month DD, YYYY') ==> 'February  05, 1994'
```

- Use the FM fill mode element to suppress blanks and zeros:

```
TO_CHAR (SYSDATE, 'FMMonth DD, YYYY') ==> 'February 5, 1994'
```

- Note the case difference on the month abbreviations of the next two samples. You get exactly what you ask for with Oracle date formats!

```
TO_CHAR (SYSDATE, 'MON DDth, YYYY') ==> 'FEB 05th, 1994'
TO_CHAR (SYSDATE, 'fmMon DDth, YYYY') ==> 'Feb 5th, 1994'
```

- Show the day of year, the month, and the week for the date:

```
TO_CHAR (SYSDATE, 'DDD DD D ') ==> '036 05 7'
TO_CHAR (SYSDATE, 'fmDDD DD D ') ==> '36 5 7'
```

- Some fancy formatting for reporting purposes:

```
TO_CHAR (SYSDATE, '"In month "RM" of year "YEAR')
==>
    'In month II   of year NINETEEN NINETY FOUR'
```

The TO_CHAR function (number conversion)

The TO_CHAR function converts numbers as well as dates. The specification of the TO_CHAR (number) function is:

```
FUNCTION TO_CHAR
    (number_in IN NUMBER
    [, format_mask IN VARCHAR2
    [, nls_language IN VARCHAR2]])
    RETURN VARCHAR2;
```

where number_in is the number to be converted to character format, the format_ mask is the mask made up of one of more of the number format elements, and nls_language is a string specifying one or more of the NLS parameters which affect the way numbers are displayed. Both the format mask and the NLS language parameters are optional.

If the format mask is not specified, then the default number format for the database instance is used.

Here are some examples of TO_CHAR for number conversion:

```
TO_CHAR (564.70, '$999.9') ==>  $564.7
TO_CHAR (564.70, '$0000999.9') ==> $0000564.7
```

The TO_DATE function

The TO_DATE function converts a character string to a true DATE datatype. The specification of the TO_DATE function is overloaded for string and number input:

```
FUNCTION TO_DATE (string_in IN VARCHAR2
    [, format_mask IN VARCHAR2
    [, nls_language IN VARCHAR2 ]]
    )
    RETURN DATE;
```

```
FUNCTION TO_DATE
   (number_in IN NUMBER
   [, format_mask IN VARCHAR2   [, nls_language IN VARCHAR2 ]])
   RETURN DATE;
```

The second version of TO_DATE can be used only with the format mask of J for Julian date. The Julian date is the number of days which have passed since January 1, 4712 B.C. Only in this use of TO_DATE can a number be passed as the first parameter of TO_DATE.

For all other cases, string_in is the string variable, literal, named constant, or expression to be converted, format_mask is the format mask TO_DATE will use to convert the string, and nls_language is a string which specifies the language which is to be used to interpret the names and abbreviations of both months and days in the string. The format of nls_language is as follows:

```
'NLS_DATE_LANGUAGE=<language>'
```

where <language> is a language recognized by your instance of the database. You can usually determine the acceptable languages by checking your installation guide.

Here are some examples of the TO_DATE function:

- Convert the string '123188' to a date:

  ```
  TO_DATE ('123188', 'MMDDYY') ==> 31-DEC-1988
  ```

- Convert a date using the Spanish language:

  ```
  TO_DATE ('Abril 12 1991', 'Month DD YYYY', 'NLS_DATE_LANGUAGE=Spanish')
     ==> 12-APR-1991
  ```

Any Oracle errors between ORA-01800 and ORA-01899 are related to the internal Oracle date function and can arise when you encounter date conversion errors. You can learn additional nuances of date conversion rules by perusing the different errors and reading about the documented causes of these errors. Some of these rules are:

- A date literal passed to TO_CHAR for conversion to a date cannot be longer than 220 characters.

- You cannot include both a Julian date element (J) and the day of year element (DDD) in a single format mask.

- You cannot include multiple elements for the same component of the date/ time in the mask. For example, the format mask YYYY-YYY-DD-MM is illegal because it includes two year elements, YYYY and YYY.

- You cannot use the 24-hour time format (HH24) and a meridian element (e.g., AM) in the same mask.

The TO_NUMBER function

The TO_NUMBER function converts both fixed- and variable-length strings to numbers using the associated format mask. The specification of the TO_NUMBER function is as follows:

```
FUNCTION TO_NUMBER
    (string_in IN CHAR
    [, format_mask VARCHAR2 [, nls_language VARCHAR2 ]])
RETURN NUMBER;

FUNCTION TO_NUMBER
    (string_in IN VARCHAR2
    [, format_mask VARCHAR2 [, nls_language VARCHAR2 ]])
RETURN NUMBER;
```

where string_in is the string containing a sequence of characters to be converted to a number, format_mask is the optional string directing TO_NUMBER how to convert the character bytes to a number, and nls_language is a string containing up to three specifications of National Language Support parameters, as follows:

NLS_NUMERIC_CHARACTERS

The characters used to specify the decimal point and the group separator in a number. The decimal point character for the American language is a dot (.) while the group separator is a comma (,).

NLS_CURRENCY

The character(s) used to specify the local currency symbol. The currency character for the American language is a dollar sign ($).

NLS_ISO_CURRENCY

The character(s) used to specify the international currency symbol in the string.

The format for nls_language in the call to TO_NUMBER is as follows:

```
'NLS_NUMERIC_CHARACTERS = ''string'''
'NLS_CURRENCY = ''string'''
'NLS_ISO_CURRENCY = ''string'''
```

Two contiguous single quotes are needed before and after the values for each string value so that PL/SQL will parse the entire parameter and leave behind a single quote around each value.

Conversion Function Examples

This section shows how you can use the conversion functions we've described in actual PL/SQL examples.

FM: Suppressing Blanks and Zeros

PL/SQL offers the FM element as a modifier to a format mask. FM (fill mode) controls the suppression of padded blanks and leading zeros in values returned by the TO_CHAR function.

By default, the following format mask results in both padded blanks and leading zeros (there are five spaces between the month name and the day number):

```
TO_CHAR (SYSDATE, 'Month DD, YYYY') ==> 'April     05, 1994'
```

With the FM modifier at the beginning of the format mask, however, both the extra blank and the leading zeros disappear:

```
TO_CHAR (SYSDATE, 'FMMonth DD, YYYY') ==> April 5, 1994'
```

The modifier can be specified in upper-, lower-, or mixed-case; the effect is the same.

The FM modifier is a toggle, and can appear more than once in a format model. Each time it appears in the format, it changes the effect of the modifier. By default (that is, if FM is not specified anywhere in a format mask), blanks are not suppressed and leading zeros are included in the result value. So the first time that FM appears in the format it indicates that blanks and leading zeros are suppressed for any following elements. The second time that FM appears in the format, it indicates that blanks and leading zeros are not suppressed for any following elements, and so on.

In the following example I suppress the padded blank at the end of the month name, but preserve the leading zero on the day number with a second specification of FM:

```
TO_CHAR (SYSDATE, 'fmMonth FMDD, YYYY') ==> April 05, 1994'
```

If you do not use FM in your mask, a converted date value is always right-padded with blanks to a fixed length (that length is dependent on the different format elements you use). When you do use FM, on the other hand, the length of your return value may vary depending on the actual values returned by the different format elements.

When you do not use FM to convert a number to a character string, the resulting value is always left-padded with blanks so that the number is right-justified to the length specified by the format (or declaration of the variable). When you do use FM, the left-padded blanks are suppressed and the resulting value is left-justified.

Here are some examples of the impact of FM on numbers converted with TO_CHAR:

```
TO_CHAR (8889.77, 'L9999D99')   ==> '     $8889.77'
TO_CHAR (8889.77, 'fmL9999D99') ==> '$8889.77'
```

The FM modifier can also be used in the format model of a call to the TO_DATE function to fill a string with blanks or zeros to match the format model. This variation of FM is explored in the discussion of FX.

FX: Matching Formats Exactly

PL/SQL offers the FX element as a modifier to a format mask. FX (format exact) specifies that an exact match must be performed for a character argument and date format mask in a call to the TO_DATE function.

If FX is not specified, the TO_DATE function does not require that the character string match the format precisely. It makes the following allowances:

* Extra blanks in the character string are ignored. Blanks are not significant data in any of the parts of a date value, except to delimit separate parts of the date and time:

```
TO_DATE ('Jan        15      1994', 'MON DD YYYY') ==> 15-JAN-1994
```

* Numeric values, such as the day number or the year, do not have to include leading zeros to fill out the mask. As long as the numbers are in the right place in the string (as determined, usually, by the delimiter characters in the string), TO_DATE can convert the numeric values properly:

```
TO_DATE ('1-1-4', 'DD-MM-YYYY') ==> 01-JAN-0004
TO_DATE ('7/16/94', 'MM/DD/YY') ==> 14-JUL-1994
```

* Punctuation and literals in the string to be converted can simply match the length and position of punctuation and quoted text in the format. In the following example, my format mask specifies hyphen (-) delimiters and the text "WhatIsaynotdo" between the day and the year. The string that I pass it, on the other hand, uses caret (^) delimiters and "the year of" for the embedded text. Because both of the two literals inside quotes have the same number of characters, TO_DATE has no problem making the match.

```
TO_DATE ('JANUARY^1^ the year of 94', 'Month-dd-"WhatIsaynotdo"yy')
==> 01-JAN-1994
```

This kind of flexibility is great—until you want to actually restrict a user or even a batch process from entering data in a nonstandard format. In some cases, it simply is not a reflection of everything being OK when a date string has a pound sign (#) instead of a hyphen (-) between the day and month numbers. For these situations, you can use the FX modifier to enforce an exact match between string and format model.

With FX, there is no flexibility for interpretation of the string. It cannot have extra blanks if none are found in the model. Its numeric values must include leading zeros if the format model specifies additional digits. And the punctuation and literals must exactly match the punctuation and quoted text of the format mask

```
Current Date  Year 88  Year 18
------------  -------  -------
  11/14/1994     1988     2018
```

```
SELECT TO_CHAR (SYSDATE, 'MM/DD/YYYY') "Current Date",
       TO_CHAR (TO_DATE ('10/14/88', 'MM/DD/RR'), 'YYYY') "Year 88",
       TO_CHAR (TO_DATE ('10/14/18', 'MM/DD/RR'), 'YYYY') "Year 18"
  FROM dual;
```

```
Current Date  Year 88  Year 18
------------  -------  -------
  11/14/2001     1988     2018
```

Of course, if you use the RR format after the year 2000 and want to enter a date that falls in the latter half of the 21st century, you will need to add special logic. Masks with the RR format model will always convert such two-digit years into the previous century.

There are a number of ways you can activate the RR logic in your current applications. The cleanest and simplest way is to change the default format mask for dates in your database instance(s). You can do this by changing the NLS_DATE_FORMAT initialization parameter as follows:

```
NLS_DATE_FORMAT = 'MM/DD/RR'
```

or:

```
NLS_DATE_FORMAT = 'DD-MON-RR'
```

depending on what the previous format was. Then, if you have not hardcoded the date format mask anywhere else in your screens or reports, you are done. Bring down and restart the database and then your application will allow users to enter dates in the 21st century. If you do have date format masks in the format property for an Oracle Forms item or in an Oracle Reports query or field, you will need to change those modules to reflect the new approach embodied by RR.

Using TO_CHAR to Create a Date Range

At times, users want information about activity on a specific date. In other situations, however, their interest lies in a range of dates. The user might enter the two dates and then expect to view all data that falls between them.

Suppose, for example, that in an Oracle Forms application the user enters 12/4/93 in the start date field and 4/8/96 in the end date field. The query that Oracle Forms executes against the database would need to have logic in it as follows:

```
hire_date BETWEEN '04-DEC-93' AND '08-APR-96'
```

or, more generally:

```
hire_date BETWEEN :criteria.start_date AND :criteria.end_date
```

where criteria is the name of the block containing the start_date and end_date fields. The colons (:) in front of the field names indicate to PL/SQL that these are bind variables from the host environment.

Sometimes this general logic can be passed directly to the SQL layer. In other situations, programmers must use the Pre-Query trigger or the SET_BLOCK_PROPERTY built-in to alter the SQL statement directly. In this case, they will need to create a string date range from the input dates.

Rather than write the application-specific code to handle this each time, you can build a generic utility, using TO_CHAR and TO_DATE conversion functions.

I offer below the date_range function. Its specification is as follows:

```
FUNCTION date_range
    (start_date_in IN DATE,
     end_date_in IN DATE,
     check_time_in IN VARCHAR2 := 'NOTIME')
RETURN VARCHAR2
```

The arguments to date_range are:

start_date_in

> The starting date in the range. If NULL then use the min_start_date. If that is NULL, range has form '<= end_date'.

end_date_in

> The end date in the range. If NULL then use the max_end_date. If that is NULL, range has form '>= start_date'.

check_time_in

> Flag indicating whether or not to include the time component of the dates in the range check. If TIME then use the time component of the dates as part of the comparison. If NOTIME then strip off the time.

If the start date is NULL or the end date is NULL, the string returned by date_range uses the <= and >= operators rather than the BETWEEN operator.

Here are some examples of the output from date_range. Note that date_range places two contiguous quote marks around each date because these are actually string literals. At runtime these two quotes are resolved into a single quote by PL/SQL:

```
date_range ('04-DEC-93', '08-APR-96')
==>
    BETWEEN TO_DATE (''04-DEC-93'') AND TO_DATE (''08-APR-96'')
```

```
date_range ('04-DEC-93', NULL)
==>
   >= TO_DATE (''04-DEC-93'')

date_range (NULL, '04-DEC-93')
==>
   <= TO_DATE (''04-DEC-93'')
```

If you do want to include the time component, then date_range will generate a string in this form:

```
date_range ('04-DEC-93', '08-APR-96', 'time')
==>
   BETWEEN TO_DATE (''04-DEC-93'', ''HHMMYYYY HHMISS'') AND
           TO_DATE (''08-APR-96'', ''HHMMYYYY HHMISS'')
```

Let's take a look at how you might use date_range in query processing in Oracle Forms. The Pre-Query trigger modifies the Default Where clause of a base table block. In Pre-Query, an assignment actually results in the addition of a WHERE clause in the SQL query for that block. Let's look at a simple example first. If Pre-Query contains a statement like this:

```
:customer.contact_date := '12-JAN-95';
```

then the query executed by the forms tool to fill the block contains a WHERE clause that looks like this:

```
WHERE <other clauses> AND (contact_date = '12-JAN-95')
```

So a simple assignment results in a straightforward comparison/restriction in the WHERE clause. You can also place complex SQL statements in the WHERE clause by appending a pound sign (#) at the beginning of the assignment string. When the forms tools detect the #, they know to substitute completely the equals sign (=) comparison with the text following the symbol. So if you place a statement like this in Pre-Query:

```
:customer.customer_id :=
   '# IN (SELECT customer_id FROM invoice WHERE invoice_total > ' ||
   TO_CHAR (:invoice.amount);
```

then the query executed by the forms tool to fill the block contains a WHERE clause that looks like this:

```
WHERE <other-where-clauses> AND
      customer_id IN (SELECT customer_id
                      FROM invoice WHERE invoice_total > 1000)
```

This very useful feature is documented in the *Advanced Oracle Forms Techniques* manual from Oracle Corporation. The syntax of a # assignment in Pre-Query for a date range would be like this:

```
:employee.hire_date :=
   '# BETWEEN ' || TO_CHAR (:criteria.start_date) || ' AND ' ||
   TO_CHAR (:criteria.end_date);
```

If I were to place literal dates inside this string assignment, then I would need to put two single quotes together in the string wherever I needed one single quote to appear in the actual value placed in that field, as follows:

```
:employee.hire_date := '# BETWEEN ''01-JAN-93'' AND ''01-DEC-94''';
```

Now if I apply the date_range function to this Pre-Query context, I have one of the following:

```
:customer.contact_date :=
    '# ' || date_range (:criteria.start_date, :criteria.end_date);
```

or:

```
:customer.contact_date :=
    '# ' || date_range (:criteria.start_date, :criteria.end_date, 'TIME');
```

In the first call to date_range, I rely on the default value of the check_time_in parameter of NOTIME to ignore the time component of the dates. In the second call, I explicitly request that the time component be included.

The SET_BLOCK_PROPERTY built-in in Oracle Forms offers another method of modifying the DEFAULT WHERE clause of a base table block. It allows you to directly pass a string of SQL syntax, which then replaces the DEFAULT WHERE clause specified at design time in the form. It is a much more structured approach than using the # syntax. In the following two calls to the built-in, I call date_range to generate a date range and attach that date range syntax to the contact_date column. In the second example I apply TRUNC to the contact date so that the time at which the contact_date was entered does not become a factor in the range check:

```
SET_BLOCK_PROPERTY
    ('customer', DEFAULT_WHERE,
     'contact_date ' ||
     date_range (:criteria.start_date, :criteria.end_date, 'TIME'));
```

or:

```
SET_BLOCK_PROPERTY
    ('customer', DEFAULT_WHERE,
     'TRUNC (contact_date) ' ||
     date_range (:criteria.start_date, :criteria.end_date));
```

Here is the code for the date_range function:

```
/* Filename on companion disk: daternge.sf */
FUNCTION date_range
    (start_date_in IN DATE,
     end_date_in IN DATE,
     check_time_in IN VARCHAR2 := 'NOTIME')
RETURN VARCHAR2
IS
    /* String versions of parameters to place in return value */
    start_date_int VARCHAR2(30);
    end_date_int VARCHAR2(30);
```

```
    /* Date mask for date<->character conversions. */
    mask_int VARCHAR2(15) := 'MMDDYYYY';

    /* Version of date mask which fits right into date range string */
    mask_string VARCHAR2(30) := NULL;

    /* The return value for the function. */
    return_value VARCHAR2(1000) := NULL;
BEGIN
    /*
    || Finalize the date mask. If user wants to use time, add that to
    || the mask. Then set the string version by embedding the mask
    || in single quotes and with a trailing paranthesis.
    */
    IF UPPER (check_time_in) = 'TIME'
    THEN
        mask_int := mask_int || ' HHMISS';
    END IF;
    /*
    || Convert mask. Example:
    ||        If mask is: MMDDYYYY HHMISS
    ||        then mask string is: ', 'MMDDYYYY HHMISS')
    */
    mask_string := ''', ''' || mask_int || ''')';

    /* Now convert the dates to character strings using format mask */
    start_date_int := TO_CHAR (start_date_in, mask_int);
    end_date_int := TO_CHAR (end_date_in, mask_int);

    /* If both start and end are NULL, then return NULL. */
    IF start_date_int IS NULL AND end_date_int IS NULL
    THEN
        return_value := NULL;

    /* If no start point then return "<=" format. */
    ELSIF start_date_int IS NULL
    THEN
        return_value := '<= TO_DATE (''' || end_date_int || mask_string;

    /* If no end point then return ">=" format. */
    ELSIF end_date_int IS NULL
    THEN
        return_value := '>= TO_DATE (''' || start_date_int || mask_string;

    /* Have start and end. A true range, so just put it together. */
    ELSE
        return_value :=
            'BETWEEN TO_DATE (''' || start_date_int || mask_string ||
                ' AND TO_DATE (''' || end_date_int || mask_string;
    END IF;

    RETURN return_value;

END;
```

Building a Date Manager

The Oracle Server offers the ability to set a default date format for each instance of a database with the NLS_DATE_FORMAT initialization parameter.[*] Oracle provides a ruthlessly efficient gatekeeper for its RDBMS: there is no way you will ever be able to enter an invalid date into the database. And there are lots of functions that enable you to perform arithmetic on dates once they are in the database. There are, however, obstacles to entering dates efficiently:

- Oracle tools do not make it easy for users to enter dates. Oracle Forms, for example, insists that when a user enters a date, it must conform to a single date format mask—either the system-wide default, or an override for that particular item.

- Users cannot enter partial date information and have the rest defaulted by the system. Shouldn't users be able to enter a date in any manner they please? That same date mask demands that you enter every part of the date, even if it is always going to be in the current month or year. It seems to me that users should be able to enter the smallest number of characters needed to specify their date, and let the application figure out the rest.

It is possible with PL/SQL to build a "date manager" that satisfies the above moral imperatives for our users. The rest of this section explores the implementation of a function, dm_convert, which converts a string entered by the user into an actual Oracle date value. It liberates the user from having to know the default/enforced format in the Oracle7 database, because the input can conform to any of a wide variety of formats. The function determines which format applies, and returns the date.

The dm_convert function date masks

Table 14-4 shows the different date masks which dm_convert supports. The user can enter a string conforming to any of these masks and dm_convert will return a date value. It will not issue such errors as:

```
ORA-01861 literal does not match format string
ORA-01858 a non-numeric character found where a digit was expected
```

In addition to supporting many different date formats, dm_convert also offers conversion of "shortcut" entries. Suppose the user wishes to enter the Monday (first day) of this week or the last day of the month. Rather than requiring that users figure out the dates for those days, dm_convert allows them to simply enter

---

[*] This is a big improvement over earlier versions, in which the default date format was hardcoded to be DD-MON-YY. In the Oracle RDBMS Version 6, for example, if your company happened to use something else, you would have to make extensive use of the TO_DATE and TO_CHAR functions (and set the mask on all date fields in your forms applications, as well).

a shortcut like "ew" for "end of week." Table 14-5 shows the shortcuts supported by dm_convert. You can easily add your own!

Here are some examples of the way dm_convert changes a string to a date (assuming today's date is December 15, 1994):

```
dm_convert ('12')    ==> 12-DEC-1994
dm_convert ('3/15')  ==> 15-MAR-1994
dm_convert ('em')    ==> 31-DEC-1994
```

Table 14-4. Different Masks Supported by dm_convert

Date Mask	User Input	Result (Assuming SYSDATE = 15-DEC-93)
DD	12	12-DEC-1993
MM/DD	12/1	01-DEC-1993
MM/DD/YY	2/5/92	05-FEB-1992
MM/DD/YYYY	4/12/1990	12-APR-1990
DD-MON	3-Jan	03-JAN-1993
DD-MON-YY	19-NOV-92	19-NOV-1992
DD-MON-YYYY	19-NOV-1992	19-NOV-1992
MON	JAN	01-JAN-1993
MON-DD	MAR-02	02-MAR-1990
MON-DD-YY	MAR-13-90	13-MAR-1990
MON-DD-YYYY	MAR-13-1990	13-MAR-1990
Mon-YYYY	MAR-1990	01-MAR-1990

Table 14-5. Shortcut Entries for dm_convert

Abbreviation	String	Result (Assuming SYSDATE = 14-MAY-93)
Beginning of Week	BW or bw	Monday in the current week: 14-MAY-93
End of Week	EW or ew	Friday in the current week: 18-MAY-93
Beginning of Month	BM or bm	First day in current month: 01-MAY-93
End of Month	EM or em	Last day in current month: 30-MAY-93

Using exception handlers to find the right format

You might be wondering how Steven gets around raising those nasty Oracle errors relating to invalid date formats when he tries to convert the string to a date. The answer is that I use both the procedurality and the exception handling of PL/SQL. In native SQL, I can use TO_DATE to convert a string to a date, but if the format doesn't match the string, I will get an error and the SQL statement will fail.

In fact, this is exactly what Oracle Forms does when a user enters a value in a date item.

In PL/SQL, I can use the EXCEPTION clause in my program to trap a conversion failure and handle that failure. Usually when you get such a failure you raise an error, as shown in the following trap conversion failure example:

```
FUNCTION convert_date (string_in IN VARCHAR2) RETURN DATE IS
BEGIN
    RETURN TO_DATE (string_in);
EXCEPTION
    WHEN OTHERS
    THEN
        DBMS_OUTPUT.PUT_LINE
            (' Invalid format for date conversion of ' || string_in);
END;
```

Clearly, this is not the behavior I want in dm_convert. In dm_convert, a conversion failure does not result from a user's error in entry. It is simply the first step in a search for the right date format mask. The behavior I need to create in dm_convert is the following:

1. Try to convert the string with a particular date mask.

2. If it fails, then try to convert the string with a different date mask.

3. Continue to do this until the string converts without an error or I run out of date masks.

I can use nested exception handlers, as shown in the following example, to implement this multiple-pass technique:

```
FUNCTION dm_convert (string_in IN VARCHAR2) RETURN DATE
IS
    my_date DATE;
BEGIN
    BEGIN
        my_date := TO_DATE (string_in, 'MM/DD');
    EXCEPTION
        WHEN OTHERS
        THEN
            BEGIN
                my_date := TO_DATE (string_in, 'MM/DD/YY');
            EXCEPTION
                WHEN OTHERS
                THEN
                    BEGIN
                        my_date := TO_DATE (string_in, 'MM/DD/YYYY');

    .. and so on for all the formats...

                    END;
            END;
    END;
END;
```

Here, the dm_convert function uses nested anonymous blocks, each with its own exception section, to trap a date conversion failure and pass it on to the next format. The sequence and variety of masks used dictate the range of valid user input and the precedence with which it is parsed. One problem you might notice with this approach is with indentation. When I use my indentation guidelines for these nested blocks and exception handlers, I quickly run out of room on my page! As a result, in the final version of dm_convert, you will see that I pointedly give up trying to properly indent the exception sections of the function. Instead, I structure the exception sections like a CASE statement:

```
/* Filename on companion disk: dmcnvrt.sf */
FUNCTION dm_convert (value_in IN VARCHAR2)      RETURN DATE
/*
|| Summary: Validate and convert date input of most any format.
||    dm_convert stands for "date manager conversion". Accepts
||    a character string and returns a fully-parsed and validated
||    date. If the string does not specify a valid date, the function
||    returns NULL.
*/
IS
    /* Internal, upper-cased version of date string */
    value_int VARCHAR2(100) := UPPER (value_in);

    /* The value returned by the function */
    return_value DATE := NULL;

    /* Transfer SYSDATE to local variable to avoid repetitive calls */
    today DATE := SYSDATE;
BEGIN
    /*
    || Handle short-cut logic before checking for specific date formats.
    || Supported short-cuts include:
    ||    EW - end of week
    ||    BW - beginning of week
    ||    EM - end of month
    ||    BM - beginning of month
    ||
    || Add shortcuts for quarters specific to your site.
    */
    IF value_int = 'EW'
    THEN
        /* End of week in this case is Friday of the week */
        return_value := NEXT_DAY (today, 'FRIDAY');

    ELSIF value_int = 'BW'
    THEN
        /* Beginning of week in this case is Monday of the week */
        return_value := NEXT_DAY (today, 'MONDAY') - 7;

    ELSIF value_int = 'BM'
    THEN
        return_value := TRUNC (today, 'MONTH');
```

```
        ELSIF value_int = 'EM'
        THEN
            return_value := LAST_DAY (today);

        ELSIF value_int IS NOT NULL
        THEN
            /* No known short-cut. The user must have entered a date string for
            || conversion. Now attempt to convert the value using a sequence
            || of calls to TO_DATE. If one attempt fails, pass it to the next
            || TO_DATE and format mask within a (very) nested exception section.
            */
            BEGIN    return_value := TO_DATE (value_int, 'DD');
            EXCEPTION WHEN OTHERS THEN
            BEGIN return_value := TO_DATE (value_int, 'MM/DD');
            EXCEPTION WHEN OTHERS THEN
            BEGIN return_value := TO_DATE (value_int, 'MM/DD/YY');
            EXCEPTION WHEN OTHERS THEN
            BEGIN return_value := TO_DATE (value_int, 'MM/DD/YYYY');
            EXCEPTION WHEN OTHERS THEN
            BEGIN return_value := TO_DATE (value_int, 'DD-MON');
            EXCEPTION WHEN OTHERS THEN
            BEGIN return_value := TO_DATE (value_int, 'DD-MON-YY');
            EXCEPTION WHEN OTHERS THEN
            BEGIN return_value := TO_DATE (value_int, 'DD-MON-YYYY');
            EXCEPTION WHEN OTHERS THEN
            BEGIN return_value := TO_DATE (value_int, 'MON');
            EXCEPTION WHEN OTHERS THEN
            BEGIN return_value := TO_DATE (value_int, 'MON-DD');
            EXCEPTION WHEN OTHERS THEN
            BEGIN return_value := TO_DATE (value_int, 'MON-DD-YY');
            EXCEPTION WHEN OTHERS THEN
            BEGIN return_value := TO_DATE (value_int, 'MON-DD-YYYY');
            EXCEPTION WHEN OTHERS THEN
            BEGIN return_value := TO_DATE (value_int, 'MON-YYYY');
            EXCEPTION WHEN OTHERS THEN return_value := NULL;
            END; END; END; END; END; END;
            END; END; END; END; END; END;
        END IF;

        /* Whether NULL or a real date, return the value */
        RETURN (return_value);

    END;
```

In the rest of this section I offer alternative implementations of dm_convert. These do not require nesting of exception handling sections and also avoid hardcoding the format masks into the function.

Table-driven date format masks

One drawback to the dm_convert procedure as implemented in the previous section is that everything is hardcoded. Sure, I offer lots of acceptable formats, but they still are all coded explicitly in the procedure. What if a new format needs to be added? In addition, the order of precedence of those formats in validating the date input is hardcoded. If a person enters a 1 and the system date is 12-FEB-95, then dm_convert will change the entry into 01-FEB-95. Suppose, however, that the user really wanted to enter 01-JAN-95 by entering a 1 and suppose further that such defaulted entry is a requirement of your application?

Generally, I like to avoid hardcoding any literal values (like the specific formats and their order of execution) in my routines. Any changes (additions or deletions from the supported date formats, or a request in a specific application to move a format up in the batting order) necessitate a change to the program itself, and then the recompilation of all affected modules. I can avoid this scenario by making the date formats and the order in which they are used data-driven. Here's what I would need to do:

1. Create a table to store the date formats:

   ```
   CREATE TABLE dm_date_mask
       (date_mask VARCHAR2(30), date_mask_seq NUMBER(5,2));
   ```

2. Build a screen in your choice of tools to enter and maintain records in this table. Note that users should be able to change the date_mask_seq. This sequence number determines the order in which the mask is applied to the date input.

3. Rewrite dm_convert to use the data in this table instead of the hardcoded sequence of masks. This new version of dm_convert, shown in the following example, replaces the nested exception sections with a simple loop that reads through the contents of the table and attempts to convert the entry with the next format in the table.

```
/* Filename on companion disk: dmcntab.sf */
FUNCTION dm_convert (value_in IN VARCHAR2) RETURN DATE

    /* I will only comment the new sections in the function */

IS
    value_int VARCHAR2(100) := UPPER (value_in);
    return_value DATE := NULL;
    today DATE := SYSDATE;

    /* Now set up a cursor to go through the table of formats */
    CURSOR mask_cur IS
        SELECT date_mask FROM dm_date_mask
        ORDER BY date_mask_seq;
    mask_rec mask_cur%ROWTYPE;
BEGIN
    /* Convert short-cut entry. Same as before. */
    IF value_int = 'EW'
    THEN return_value := NEXT_DAY (today, 'FRIDAY');
    ELSIF value_int = 'BW'
    THEN return_value := NEXT_DAY (today, 'MONDAY') - 7;
```

```
      ELSIF value_int = 'BM'
      THEN return_value := TRUNC (today, 'MONTH');
      ELSIF value_int = 'EM'
      THEN return_value := LAST_DAY (today);
      ELSIF value_int IS NOT NULL
      THEN
         /*
         || Open the cursor and loop through the date masks until one
         || of them is used successfully in a TO_DATE conversion.
         */
         OPEN mask_cur;
         LOOP
            /* Fetch a record. Exit loop if there aren't any more masks */
            FETCH mask_cur INTO mask_rec;
            EXIT WHEN mask_cur%NOTFOUND;
            /*
            || Still need separate PL/SQL block in the function to trap
            || a conversion failure, but I only need ONE!
            */
            BEGIN
               /* Try to convert the date */
               return_value := TO_DATE (value_int, mask_rec.date_mask);
               /*
               || If I made it this far, I have converted the string, so
               || EXIT the loop.
               */
               EXIT;
            EXCEPTION
               /*
               || Conversion failure. Reset value to make sure it is still
               || NULL and then keep going -- back to the loop!
               */
               WHEN OTHERS
               THEN
                   return_value := NULL;
            END;
         END LOOP;
         CLOSE mask_cur;
      END IF;

      /* Return the converted date */
      RETURN return_value;
   END;
```

This new version of dm_convert not only looks more elegant than the first version—it is considerably more flexible in its approach. If you no longer want to accept Month YYYY DD as a date format, simply pull up the maintenance screen, delete that entry from the table, or execute a DELETE from the dm_date_mask table directly in SQL*Plus. Poof! The users will no longer be able to enter January 1995 11 for a date value.

There is, of course, a downside to this solution, and it is a familiar one. The price of making your code more flexible (for the developer) is almost always to make

your code work less efficiently. Now, instead of executing a series of inline TO_
DATE conversion functions, we fetch a series of records from a table. The dm_
date_mask table could well be sitting on a remote server. This network traffic
could well make the application performance unacceptable to precisely the
people you are trying to help by providing flexible date formats. What's a developer to do? One answer is to transfer the table into a memory structure at the start
of each user session, as we describe in the next section.

Stashing date masks in memory

Say you moved the date masks to a table and that any changes made to the dm_
date_mask table will not happen very often. For all intents and purposes, the date
masks are constant for a particular user session. So it is not really necessary to
read the masks from the table every time you need to validate a date entry.
Instead, we can transfer the masks from the table into a memory structure at the
start of the user session. With this approach you add a little more time to the
startup execution of the form, but then speed up the validation and conversion
for each date item.

You have a number of options for storing these date masks in memory:

- *GLOBAL variables in Oracle Forms.* These variables persist across forms and
  menus in an application and so are good candidates to store information
  which should last for an entire user session.

- *A record group in Oracle Forms.* This structure takes less memory than GLO-
  BAL variables (which use a fixed 255 bytes regardless of the actual data
  stored in the variable) and can be manipulated more naturally with Oracle
  Forms built-ins. However, you cannot currently pass a record group from one
  form to another (except with a call to RUN_PRODUCT, which is not always
  appropriate). You might use the record group if the user performs date processing primarily within a single form. Or you might just be looking for an
  excuse to practice building and manipulating record groups.

- *Other tool-specific memory structures.*

- *A PL/SQL table in PL/SQL Version 2.* Oracle's version of a simple array structure is perfect for this application; unfortunately, PL/SQL tables are available
  only in the RDBMS (through stored procedures and triggers) and SQL*Plus
  scripts.

I provide the code for PL/SQL table-based alternatives in the following
sections. The technique based on Oracle Forms GLOBAL variables may be
found in the *dmcnvrt.doc* and *dmcnvrt.fp* files on the companion disk. In both
cases, there are two steps involved in using the memory-resident, data-driven
approach:

1. Initialize the data structure with the various format masks.

2. Revamp dm_convert to rely on that data structure.

Notice that the specification of the call to dm_convert does not change with any of these new implementations. I am changing the engine under the hood without making any alterations to the body style, dashboard, or steering controls. None of the triggers that call dm_convert would have to be modified if you did change the storage implementation for the date masks.

Storing and accessing date masks in a PL/SQL table

You can also store the date masks in a PL/SQL table (PL/SQL tables are explained fully in Chapter 10, *PL/SQL Tables*). The PL/SQL table structure, available only with PL/SQL Version 2, is similar to both a database table and a single-dimensional array. There are two steps to using date masks from the PL/SQL table: Initialize the date masks in the PL/SQL table structure, and revamp dm_convert to rely on the PL/SQL table. These are described below:

1. *Initialize the date masks in the PL/SQL table structure.* The best way to do this in PL/SQL tables is to build a package (see Chapter 16, *Packages,* for more information about this structure). This package contains the code to initialize the masks in the PL/SQL table by transferring them from the database table, to perform the date conversions, and to clean up the table when done.

   A package is made up of two parts: the specification and the body. The specification for the date manager (dm) package is:

```
/* Filename on companion disk: dmcnvrt.spp */
PACKAGE dm
IS
    /* The replacement for dm_convert */
    FUNCTION convert (value_in IN VARCHAR2) RETURN DATE;

    /* Clean-up program */
    PROCEDURE erase;

END dm;
```

   The body of the dm package shown in the following example contains all the code behind the specification. In addition to the definitions of the convert and erase modules, the body also contains an initialization section following the last BEGIN in the body. This section is run automatically the first (and only the first) time the convert or erase modules are called. This initialization code populates the PL/SQL table of masks.

```
/* Filename on companion disk: dmcnvrt.spp */
PACKAGE BODY dm
IS
    /*
    || Declare the structure of the PL/SQL table which will hold
```

```
|| the masks. Then declare the table itself.
*/
TYPE mask_tabtype IS TABLE OF VARCHAR2 (30) INDEX BY BINARY_INTEGER;
mask_table mask_tabtype;

/* Also declare an empty table for use in erasing the masks */
empty_table mask_tabtype;

/* Package variable which keeps track of number of rows in table */
mask_count NUMBER;

/* Replacement for dm_convert */
FUNCTION convert (value_in IN VARCHAR2) RETURN DATE
IS
   value_int VARCHAR2(100) := UPPER (value_in);
   return_value DATE := NULL;
   today DATE := SYSDATE;

   /* Loop index for the scan through the masks */
   mask_index INTEGER := 1;

   /* Boolean to terminate loop if date was converted */
   date_converted BOOLEAN := FALSE;
BEGIN
   /* Same old shortcuts! */
   IF value_int = 'EW'
   THEN return_value := NEXT_DAY (today, 'FRIDAY');
   ELSIF value_int = 'BW'
   THEN return_value := NEXT_DAY (today, 'MONDAY') - 7;
   ELSIF value_int = 'BM'
   THEN return_value := TRUNC (today, 'MONTH');
   ELSIF value_int = 'EM'
   THEN return_value := LAST_DAY (today);

   /* Now convert from masks in table */
   ELSIF value_int IS NOT NULL
   THEN
      /* Loop through the rows in the table... */
      WHILE mask_index <= mask_count AND
            NOT date_converted
      LOOP
         BEGIN
            /* Try to convert string using mask in table row */
            return_value :=
               TO_DATE (value_int, mask_table (mask_index));
            date_converted := TRUE;
         EXCEPTION
            WHEN OTHERS THEN
               return_value := NULL;
               mask_index:= mask_index+ 1;
         END;
      END LOOP;
   END IF;
   RETURN (return_value);
END convert;
```

```
      PROCEDURE erase IS
      BEGIN
         /*
         || Clear the table of any defined rows by assigning the empty
         || table to the mask table.
         */
         mask_table := empty_table;
      END;

   BEGIN
      /* ----------- Initialization Section of Package ------------*/

      /* Transfer values from RDBMS table to PL/SQL table */
      mask_count := 0;
      FOR mask_rec IN (SELECT date_mask
                         FROM dm_date_mask
                         ORDER BY date_mask_seq)
      LOOP
         mask_count := mask_count + 1;
         mask_table (mask_count) := mask_rec.date_mask;
      END LOOP;

   END dm;
```

2. *Revamp dm_convert to rely on the PL/SQL table.* The structure of the convert program in the dm package is very similar to that of the dm_convert program, which relied on global variables in Oracle Forms. In both cases, I replace the nested exception sections with a PL/SQL loop.

To call the conversion program in the dm package, you would use dot notation, as follows:

```
my_date := dm.convert ('12');
```

But dm.convert is not the same thing as dm_convert, which is what all my triggers are already calling. In order to make the conversion to PL/SQL table-based format masks completely transparent to my Oracle Forms applications, I will need to build another layer of code over the package. I do this by creating a stored procedure as follows:[*]

```
CREATE OR REPLACE FUNCTION dm_convert (string_in IN VARCHAR2)
   RETURN DATE
IS
BEGIN
   RETURN dm.convert (string_in);
END;
```

Now I can call dm_convert just as I did in the good old days:

```
my_date := dm_convert ('12');
```

---

[*] I could also create this function in a PL/SQL library and attach it to all of my forms.

IV

Modular Code

Part IV of this book goes beyond the individual components of the PL/SQL language and explains how to build complete PL/SQL applications using program modules.

- Chapter 15, *Procedures and Functions*, presents the basics of modular programming in PL/SQL using blocks, procedures, functions, and parameters.

- Chapter 16, *Packages*, describes how to build packages, one of the least understood and least utilized features of PL/SQL.

- Chapter 17, *Calling PL/SQL Functions in SQL*, describes how you can construct PL/SQL functions and call them from SQL.

15

Procedures and Functions

Previous parts of this book explored in detail all the components of the PL/SQL language: cursors, exceptions, loops, variables, etc. While you certainly need to know about these components when you write applications using PL/SQL, putting the pieces together to create well structured, easily understood, and smoothly maintainable programs is even more important. Because this module building process goes to the core of our purpose, it is absolutely the most critical technique for a programmer to master.

Few of our tasks are straightforward. Few solutions can be glimpsed in an instant and immediately put to paper or keyboard. The systems we build are, for the most part, large and complex, with many interacting, if not sometimes conflicting, components. Furthermore, as users deserve, demand, and receive applications that are easier to use and vastly more powerful than their predecessors, the inner world of those applications becomes correspondingly more complicated.

One of the biggest challenges in our profession today is to find a way to reduce the complexity of our environment. When faced with a massive problem to solve, a mind is likely to recoil in horror. Where do I start? How can I possibly figure out a way through that jungle of requirements and features?

A human being is not a massively parallel computer. Even the brightest of our bunch have trouble keeping track of more than seven or eight tasks at one time. We need to break down huge, intimidating projects into smaller, more manageable components, and then further decompose those components into individual programs with an understandable scope.

The best way to deal with having too much to deal with is to not deal with it all at once. Use top-down design, or "step-wise refinement," to break down a seemingly impossible challenge into smaller components. Computer scientists have developed comprehensive methodologies (for top-down design and other approaches) and performed studies on this topic—I urge you to study their findings. When it comes to developing applications in PL/SQL, however, there is a very clear path you must take to reduce complexity and solve your problems: modularize your code!

Modular Code

Modularization is the process by which you break up large blocks of code into smaller pieces—modules—which can be called by other modules. Modularization of code is analogous to normalization of data, with many of the same benefits (and a few additional advantages which accrue specifically to code). With modularization, your code becomes:

- *More reusable.* By breaking up a large program or entire application into individual components which "plug-and-play" together, you will usually find that many modules will be used by more than one other program in your current application. Designed properly, these utility programs could even be of use in other applications!

- *More manageable.* Which would you rather debug: a 10,000-line program or five individual 2,000 line programs that call each other as needed? Our minds work better when we can focus on smaller tasks. You can also test and debug on a smaller scale (unit test) before individual modules are combined for a more complicated system test.

- *More readable.* Modules have names and names describe behavior. The more you move or hide your code behind a programmatic interface, the easier it is to read and understand what that program is doing. Modularization helps you focus on the big picture rather than the individual executable statements.

- *More reliable.* The code you produce will have fewer errors. The errors you do find will be easier to fix because they will be isolated within a module. In addition, your code will be easier to maintain since there is less of it and it is more readable.

Once you have mastered the different control, conditional, and cursor constructs of the PL/SQL language (the IF statement, loops, etc.), you are ready to write programs. You will not really be ready, however, to build an application until you understand how to create and combine PL/SQL modules.

PL/SQL offers the following structures which modularize your code in different ways:

Procedure

A named PL/SQL block that performs one or more actions and is called as an executable PL/SQL statement. You can pass information into and out of a procedure through its parameter list.

Function

A named PL/SQL block that returns a single value and is used just like a PL/SQL expression. You can pass information into a function through its parameter list.

Anonymous block

An unnamed PL/SQL block that performs one or more actions. An anonymous block gives the developer control over scope of identifiers and exception handling.

Package

A named collection of procedures, functions, types, and variables. A package is not really a module (it's more of a meta-module), but is so tightly related to modules that I mention it here.

I use the term *module* to mean either a function, a procedure, or an anonymous block, which is executed as a standalone script. As is the case with many other programming languages, modules can call other named modules. You can pass information into and out of modules with parameters. Finally, the modular structure of PL/SQL also integrates tightly with exception handlers to provide all encompassing error checking techniques.

This chapter will first review the PL/SQL block structure and anonymous blocks, and then move on to procedures and functions. The final portion of the chapter is devoted to parameters and some advanced features of PL/SQL modules, including overloading and forward referencing.

Review of PL/SQL Block Structure

Chapter 1, *Introduction to PL/SQL*, provided a brief introduction to the PL/SQL block and its structure. Before we explore the construction of modules in PL/SQL, let's take a more detailed look at the PL/SQL block.

PL/SQL is a block-structured language. Each of the basic programming units you write to build your application is (or should be) a logical unit of work. The PL/SQL block allows you to reflect that logical structure in the physical design of your programs.

The block determines both the scope of identifiers (the area of code in which a reference to the identifier can be resolved) and the way in which exceptions are handled and propagated. A block may also contain nested sub-blocks of code, each with its own scope.

There is a common block structure to all the different types of modules. The block is broken up into four different sections, as follows:

Header
> Relevant for named blocks only, the header determines the way that the named block or program must be called. The header includes the name, parameter list, and RETURN clause (for a function only).

Declaration section
> The part of the block that declares variables, cursors, and sub-blocks that are referenced in the execution and exception sections. The declaration section is optional, but if you have one, it must come before the execution and exception sections.

Execution section
> The part of the PL/SQL block containing the executable statements, the code that is executed by the PL/SQL run-time engine. The execution section contains the IF-THEN-ELSEs, LOOPs, assignments, and calls to other PL/SQL blocks. Every block must have at least one executable statement in the execution section.

Exception section
> The section that handles exceptions to normal processing (warnings and error conditions). This final section is optional. If it is included, control is transferred to this section when an error is encountered. This section then either handles the error or passes control to the block that called the current block.

Figure 15-1 shows the structure of the PL/SQL block.

Sequence of Section Construction

The ordering of the sections in a block corresponds to the way you would write your programs and the way they are executed.

Step 1
> Define the type of block (procedure, function, anonymous) and how it is called (header).

Step 2
> Declare any variables used in that block (declaration section).

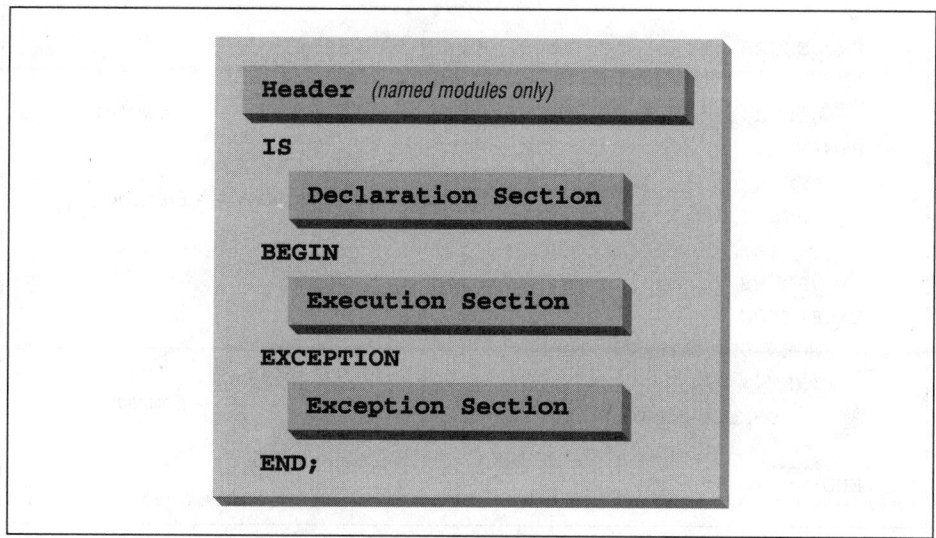

Figure 15-1. The PL/SQL block structure for procedures and functions

Step 3

> Use those local variables and other PL/SQL objects to perform the required actions (execution section).

Step 4

> Handle any problems that arise during the execution of the block (exception section).

The declaration and exception sections are optional in any PL/SQL block, but you must always have at least one executable statement in a block.

PL/SQL Block Structure Examples

Figures 15-2 through 15-4 illustrate several different ways that PL/SQL blocks can be constructed.

Now that you understand the basic components of a PL/SQL block, let's explore the ways you can use this structure in your programming.

The Anonymous PL/SQL Block

When someone wishes to remain anonymous, that person goes unnamed. So it is with the *anonymous PL/SQL block*. Unlike the other two types of PL/SQL blocks (the procedure and the function), the anonymous block has no name associated with it. In fact, the anonymous block is missing the header section altogether.

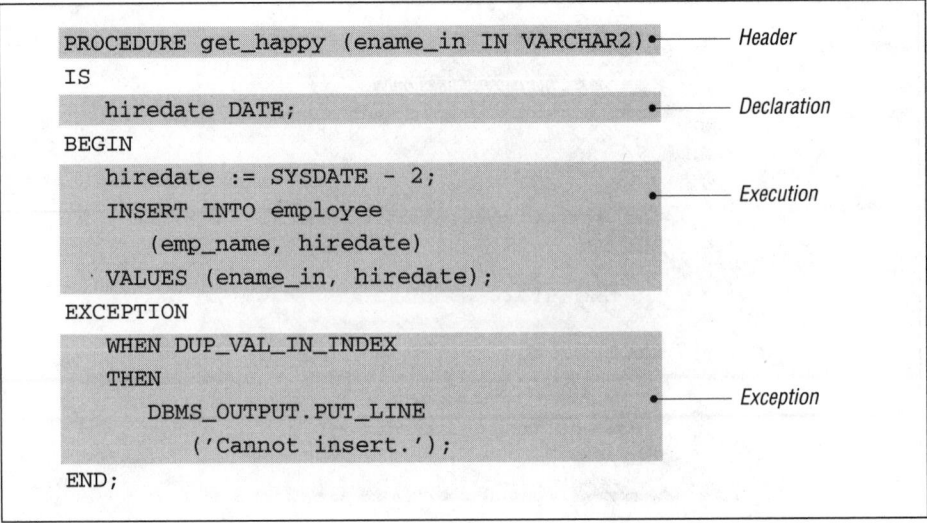

```
PROCEDURE get_happy (ename_in IN VARCHAR2)•——— Header
IS
   hiredate DATE;                             •——— Declaration
BEGIN
   hiredate := SYSDATE - 2;
   INSERT INTO employee
      (emp_name, hiredate)                    •——— Execution
 · VALUES (ename_in, hiredate);
EXCEPTION
   WHEN DUP_VAL_IN_INDEX
   THEN
      DBMS_OUTPUT.PUT_LINE                     •——— Exception
         ('Cannot insert.');
END;
```

Figure 15-2. A procedure containing all four sections

```
FUNCTION soft_pillow (type_in IN VARCHAR2)
   RETURN BOOLEAN                              •——— Header
IS
   CURSOR pillow_cur IS
      SELECT softness FROM pillow
      WHERE pillow_type = type_in              •——— Declaration
   pillow_rec pillow_cur%ROWTYPE;
BEGIN
   OPEN pillow_cur;
   FETCH pillow_cur INTO pillow_rec;
   CLOSE pillow_cur;                           •——— Execution
   RETURN pillow_rec.softness;
END;
```

Figure 15-3. A function without an exception section

Instead it simply uses the DECLARE reserved word to mark the beginning of its optional declaration section.

Without a name, the anonymous block cannot be called by any other block—it doesn't have a handle for reference. Instead, anonymous blocks serve as scripts that execute PL/SQL statements, including calls to procedures and functions. Anonymous blocks can also serve as nested blocks inside procedures, functions, and other anonymous blocks, as shown in Figure 15-5.

```
BEGIN                                      •——— Execution Only
    DBMS_OUTPUT.PUT_LINE ('Hello world');
END;
```

Figure 15-4. An anonymous block without declaration and exception sections

```
PROCEDURE get_happy IS
BEGIN
    DECLARE
        hiredate DATE;
    BEGIN
        ...
    END;
END get_happy;
```

Figure 15-5. An anonymous block defined inside a procedure

Because an anonymous block can have its own declaration and exception sections, developers use anonymous blocks to provide a scope for identifiers and exception handling within a larger program.

The Structure of an Anonymous Block

The general format of an anonymous PL/SQL block is as follows:

```
[ DECLARE
    ... optional declaration statements ... ]

BEGIN
    ... executable statements ...

[ EXCEPTION
    ... optional exception handler statements ... ]

END;
```

The square brackets indicate an optional part of the syntax. As you can see, just about everything in an anonymous block is optional. You must have BEGIN and END statements and you must have at least one executable statement.

Examples of Anonymous Blocks

The following examples show the different combinations of block sections, all of which comprise valid PL/SQL blocks:

- A block with BEGIN-END terminators, but no declaration or exception sections:

```
BEGIN
    hiredate := SYSDATE;
END
```

- An anonymous block with a declaration section, but no exception section:

```
DECLARE
    right_now DATE := SYSDATE;
BEGIN
    hiredate := right_now;
END
```

- An anonymous block containing declaration, execution, and exception sections:

```
DECLARE
    right_now DATE := SYSDATE;
    too_late EXCEPTION;
BEGIN
    IF :employee.hiredate < ADD_MONTHS (right_now, 6)
    THEN
        RAISE too_late;
    ELSE
        :employee.hiredate := right_now;
    END IF;
EXCEPTION
    WHEN too_late
    THEN
        DBMS_OUTPUT.PUT_LINE
            ('You no longer qualify for free air.');
    WHEN OTHERS
    THEN
        DBMS_OUTPUT.PUT_LINE
            ('Error encountered: ' || SQLCODE);
END;
```

Anonymous blocks execute a series of statements and then terminate, thus acting like procedures. In fact, all anonymous blocks are anonymous block procedures.

Anonymous Blocks in the Oracle Tools

Anonymous blocks are used in Oracle tools where PL/SQL code is either executed immediately (SQL*Plus) or attached directly to objects in that tool environment (see Table 15-1). That object then provides the context or name for the PL/SQL code, making the anonymous block both the most appropriate and the most efficient way to attach programmatic functionality to the object.

Table 15-1. Anonymous Blocks in Oracle Tools

Object Type	Environment	Description
Trigger	Oracle Developer/2000	Place PL/SQL code directly in the Oracle Forms or Oracle Reports trigger, which is then packaged as an anonymous block by the tool and sent to the PL/SQL engine.
Database trigger	Record or column of table	The body of the trigger is coded in PL/SQL. While the trigger has a name, the PL/SQL code itself is unnamed, hence anonymous.
Script	SQL*Plus and SQL*DBA	Ad hoc programs and batch processing scripts written in SQL*Plus are always anonymous blocks (which may then call procedures or functions).
Embedded PL/SQL programs	Pro* embedded languages	Embed PL/SQL blocks to execute statements inside the database server.

Whenever you attach PL/SQL code to a trigger or field in a tool, that code forms an anonymous PL/SQL block. When you write this code you can enter a fully specified PL/SQL block (declaration, execution, and exception sections), or you can enter only the executable section.

Nested Blocks

PL/SQL allows you to nest or embed anonymous blocks within another PL/SQL block. You can also nest anonymous blocks within anonymous blocks for more than one level, as shown in Figure 15-6.

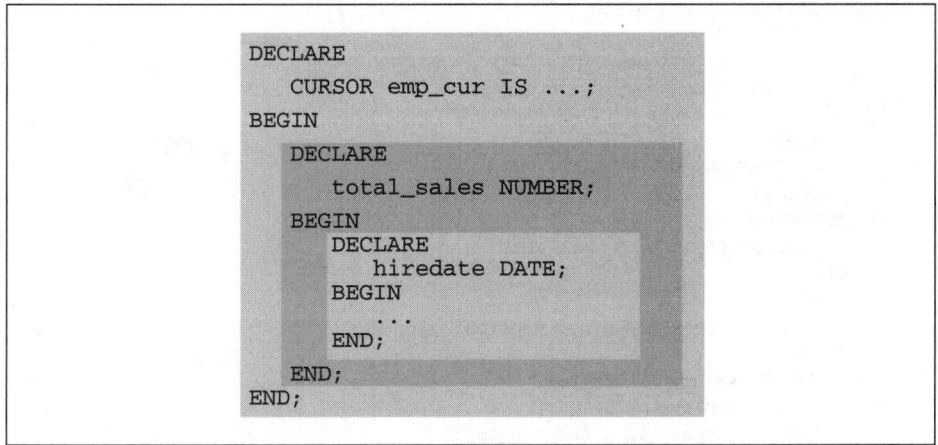

Figure 15-6. Anonymous blocks nested three levels deep

Nested block terminology

A PL/SQL block nested within another PL/SQL block may be called by any of the following: nested block, enclosed block, child block or sub-block.

A PL/SQL block that calls another PL/SQL block (anonymous or named) may be referred to as either the enclosing block or the parent block.

Nested blocks provide scope

The general advantage of a nested block is that you create a *scope* for all the declared objects and executable statements in that block. You can use this scope to improve your control over activity in your program. For a discussion, see "Scope and Visibility" later in this chapter.

Consider the following procedure, in which the president and vice-president of the specified company request their salaries be cut in half if their current salaries are more than ten times the average salary in the company. It's the sort of incentive plan that would encourage executives to "share the wealth."

```
PROCEDURE update_management
    (company_id_in IN NUMBER, avgsal_in IN NUMBER)
IS
BEGIN
    -- The vice-president shows his generosity...
    BEGIN
        SELECT salary INTO v_sal
          FROM employee
         WHERE company_id = company_id_in
           AND title = 'VICE-PRESIDENT';
        IF v_sal > avgsal_in * 10
        THEN
            UPDATE employee SET salary := salary * .50
              WHERE company_id = company_id_in
                AND title = 'VICE-PRESIDENT';
        ELSE
            DBMS_OUTPUT.PUT_LINE ('The VP is OK!');
        END IF;
    EXCEPTION
        WHEN NO_DATA_FOUND THEN NULL;
    END;

    -- The president shows her generosity...
    BEGIN
        SELECT salary INTO v_sal
          FROM employee
         WHERE company_id = company_id_in
           AND title = 'PRESIDENT';
        IF v_sal > avgsal_in * 10
        THEN
            UPDATE employee SET salary := salary * .50
              WHERE company_id = company_id_in
                AND title = 'PRESIDENT';
```

```
          ELSE
             DBMS_OUTPUT.PUT_LINE ('The Prez is a pal!');
          END IF;
       EXCEPTION
          WHEN NO_DATA_FOUND THEN NULL;
       END;
    END;
```

Each of the two SELECT-UPDATE combinations is embedded in its own anonymous PL/SQL block. Each block has its own exception section. Why go to all this trouble? Why couldn't the programmer just create a little script that will update the salary for a specified title? The following statement, saved to the updemp.sql file, would "do the trick" (&N is the syntax used to supply arguments to a SQL*Plus script):

```
UPDATE employee SET salary := salary * .50
  WHERE company_id = &1
    AND title = '&2'
    AND salary > &3 * 10;
```

and then execute the SQL script in SQL*Plus using the START command:

```
SQL> start updemp 1100 VICE-PRESIDENT
SQL> start updemp 1100 PRESIDENT
```

The programmer who was assigned this task took several things into account:

- The executives might decide they will want to take such actions repeatedly in the coming years; better to package the steps into a reusable chunk of code like a procedure than simply execute a series of SELECT-UPDATEs in SQL*Plus.

- Executives come and go frequently at the company. There is no guarantee that there will be a person in the employee table with a title of 'PRESIDENT' or 'VICE-PRESIDENT' at any given time. The first assumption argues for the encapsulation of these two SELECT-UPDATE steps into a procedure. This second assumption results in the need for embedded PL/SQL blocks around each UPDATE statement. Suppose that the procedure update_management did not make use of the embedded blocks. The code would then look like this:

```
PROCEDURE update_management
    (company_id_in IN NUMBER, avgsal_in IN NUMBER)
IS
BEGIN
    SELECT salary INTO v_sal
      FROM employee
     WHERE company_id = company_id_in
       AND title = 'VICE-PRESIDENT';
    IF v_sal > avgsal_in * 10
    THEN
        UPDATE employee SET salary := salary * .50
```

```
            WHERE company_id = company_id_in
               AND title = 'VICE-PRESIDENT';
      ELSE
         DBMS_OUTPUT.PUT_LINE ('The VP is OK!');
      END IF;
      SELECT salary INTO v_sal
        FROM employee
       WHERE company_id = company_id_in
         AND title = 'PRESIDENT';
      IF v_sal > avgsal_in * 10
      THEN
         UPDATE employee SET salary := salary * .50
          WHERE company_id = company_id_in
             AND title = 'PRESIDENT';
      ELSE
         DBMS_OUTPUT.PUT_LINE ('The Prez is a pal!');
      END IF;
   END;
```

If there is a record in the employee table with the title of "VICE-PRESIDENT" (for the appropriate company_id) and if there is a record in the employee table with the title of "PRESIDENT," then this procedure works just fine. But what if there is no record with a title of "VICE-PRESIDENT"? What if the Vice-President did not want to take a 50% cut in pay and instead quit in disgust?

When the WHERE clause of an implict SELECT statement does not identify any records, PL/SQL raises the NO_DATA_FOUND exception (for more details on this phenomenon see Chapter 6, *Database Interaction and Cursors*, and pay particular attention to the sections concerning implicit cursors). There is no exception handler section in this procedure. As a result, when there is no Vice-President in sight, the procedure will immediately complete (well, abort, actually) and transfer control to the calling block's exception section to see if the NO_DATA_FOUND exception is handled there. The SELECT-UPDATE for the President's salary is therefore not executed at all.

NOTE   You don't actually need a BEGIN-END block around the second
              SELECT-UPDATE. This is the last statement, and if it fails nothing
              will be skipped. It is good practice, however, to include an excep-
              tion statement for the procedure as a whole to trap errors and han-
              dle them gracefully.

Our programmer would hate to see an executive's wish go unfulfilled, so we need a mechanism to trap the failure of the first SELECT and allow PL/SQL procedure execution to continue on to the next SELECT-UPDATE. The embedded anonymous block offers this protection. By placing the first SELECT within a BEGIN-END envelope, you can also define an exception section just for the SELECT. Then, when the SELECT fails, control is passed to the exception handler for that specific block, not to the exception handler for the procedure as a whole (see Figure 15-7). If you then code an exception to handle NO_DATA_FOUND which allows for continued processing, the next SELECT-UPDATE will be executed.

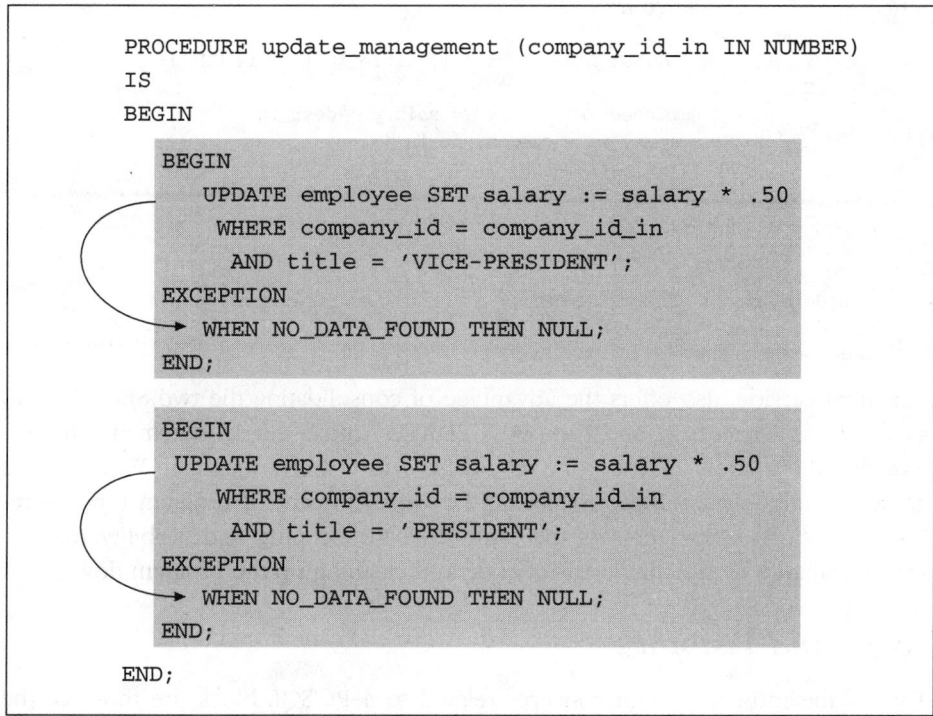

```
PROCEDURE update_management (company_id_in IN NUMBER)
IS
BEGIN
   BEGIN
      UPDATE employee SET salary := salary * .50
       WHERE company_id = company_id_in
         AND title = 'VICE-PRESIDENT';
   EXCEPTION
      WHEN NO_DATA_FOUND THEN NULL;
   END;

   BEGIN
     UPDATE employee SET salary := salary * .50
       WHERE company_id = company_id_in
         AND title = 'PRESIDENT';
   EXCEPTION
      WHEN NO_DATA_FOUND THEN NULL;
   END;
END;
```

Figure 15-7. An anonymous block "catches" the exception

Named modules offer scoping effect of nested block

You can also restructure the update_management procedure to avoid the problems addressed in the previous section, and also the redundancy in the code for that procedure. The following version of update_management uses an explicit cursor to avoid the problem of the NO_DATA_FOUND exception being raised. It also encapsulates the repetitive logic into a local or nested procedure.

```
PROCEDURE update_management
   (company_id_in IN NUMBER, avgsal_in IN NUMBER, decr_in IN NUMBER)
IS
   CURSOR salcur (title_in IN VARCHAR2)
   IS
     SELECT salary
       FROM employee
      WHERE company_id = company_id_in
        AND title = title_in
        AND salary > avgsal_in * 10;
```

```
      PROCEDURE update_exec (title_in IN VARCHAR2)
      IS
         salrec salcur%ROWTYPE;
      BEGIN
         OPEN salcur (title_in);
         FETCH salcur INTO salrec;
         IF salcur%NOTFOUND
         THEN
            DBMS_OUTPUT.PUT_LINE ('The ' || title_in || ' is OK!');
         ELSE
            UPDATE employee SET salary := salary * decr_in
             WHERE company_id = company_id_in
               AND title = title_in;
         END IF;
         CLOSE salcur;
      END;
   BEGIN
      update_exec ('VICE-PRESIDENT');
      update_exec ('PRESIDENT');
   END;
```

This final version also offers the advantage of consolidating the two SELECTs into a single explicit cursor, and the two UPDATEs into a single statement, thereby reducing the amount of code one would have to test and maintain. Whether you go with named or anonymous blocks, the basic concept of program (and therefore exception) scope remains the same. Use the scoping and visibility rules to your advantage by isolating areas of code and cleaning up the program flow.

Scope and Visibility

Two of the most important concepts related to a PL/SQL block are those of the scope and visibility of identifiers. An *identifier* is the name of a PL/SQL object, which could be anything from a variable to a program name. In order to manipulate a PL/SQL identifier (assign a value to it, pass it as a parameter, or call it in a module), you have to be able to reference that identifier in such a way that the code will compile.

The *scope* of an identifier is the part of a program in which you can make a reference to the identifier and have that reference resolved by the compiler. An identifier is *visible* in a program when it can be referenced using an unqualified name.

Qualified identifiers

A qualifier for an identifier can be a package name, module name (procedure or function), or loop label. You qualify the name of an identifer with dot notation, the same way you would qualify a column name with the name of its table.

The names of the following identifiers are qualified:

:GLOBAL.company_id

A global variable in Oracle Forms

std_types.dollar_amount

A subtype declared in a package

The scope of an identifier is generally the block in which that identifier is declared. The following anonymous block declares and then references two local variables:

```
DECLARE
    first_day DATE;
    last_day DATE;
BEGIN
    first_day := SYSDATE;
    last_day := ADD_MONTHS (first_day, 6);
END;
```

Both the first_day and last_day variables are visible in this block. When I reference the variables in the assignment statements, I do not need to qualify their names. Also, the scope of the two variables is precisely this anonymous block.

I cannot make reference to either of those variables in a second anonymous block or in a procedure. Any attempt to do so will result in a compile failure, because the reference to those variables cannot be resolved.

If an identifier is declared or defined outside of the current PL/SQL block, it is visible (can be referenced without a qualifier) only under the following conditions:

- The identifier is the name of a standalone procedure or function on which you have EXECUTE privilege. You can then include a call to this module in your block.

- The identifier is declared in a block which encloses the current block.

Scope and nested blocks

Let's take a closer look at nested blocks and the impact on scope and visibility. When you declare a variable in a PL/SQL block, then that variable is local to that block, but is visible in or global to any blocks defined within the first, enclosing block. For example, in the following anonymous block, the variable last_date can be referenced anywhere inside the block:

```
/* The enclosing or outer anonymous block. */
DECLARE
    last_date DATE;
BEGIN
    last_date := LAST_DAY (SYSDATE);

    /* The inner anonymous block. */
```

```
      BEGIN
         IF last_date > :employee.hire_date
         THEN
            ...
         END IF;
      END;
      ...
   END;
```

Even though last_date is not defined in the inner block, it can still be referenced there without qualification because the inner block is defined inside the outer block. The last_date variable is therefore considered a global variable in the inner block.

Figure 15-8 shows additional examples illustrating the concept of scope in PL/SQL blocks.

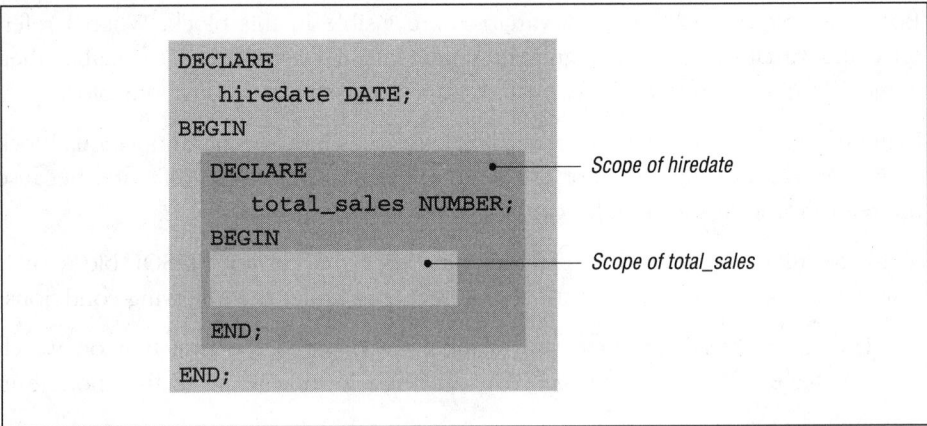

Figure 15-8. Scope of identifiers in PL/SQL blocks

Qualifying identifier names with module names

When necessary, PL/SQL offers many ways to qualify an identifier so that a reference to the identifier can be resolved. Suppose I create a package called company_pkg and declare a variable named last_company_id in that package's specification, as follows:

```
PACKAGE company_pkg
IS
   last_company_id NUMBER;
   ...
END company_pkg;
```

Then, when I reference that variable outside of the package, I must preface the identifer name with the package name:

```
IF new_company_id = company_pkg.last_company_id THEN ...
```

Because a variable declared in a package specification is global in your session, the last_company_id variable can be referenced in any program, but it is not visible unless it is qualified.

I can also qualify the name of an identifier with the module in which it is defined:

```
PROCEDURE calc_totals
IS
   salary NUMBER;
BEGIN
   ...
   DECLARE
      salary NUMBER;
   BEGIN
      salary := calc_totals.salary;
   END;
   ...
END;
```

The first declaration of salary creates an identifier whose scope is the entire procedure. Inside the inner anonymous block, however, I declare another identifer with the same name. So when I reference the variable "salary" inside the inner block, it will always be resolved first against the declaration in the inner block, where that variable is visible without any qualification. If I wish to make reference to the procedure-wide salary variable inside the inner block, I must qualify that variable name with the name of the procedure.

PL/SQL goes to a lot of trouble and has established many rules for determining how to resolve such naming conflicts. While it is good to be aware of such issues, you would be much better off never having to rely on these guidelines. Use unique names for your identifiers in different blocks so that you can avoid naming conflicts altogether.

Cursor scope

To use a cursor, you must declare it. But you cannot refer to that cursor—whether to OPEN, CLOSE, or FETCH from it—unless that cursor is accessible in your current PL/SQL block. The scope of a cursor is that part of a PL/SQL program in which you can refer to the cursor.

You can refer to a cursor in the code block in which it was declared and in all blocks defined within that declaring block. You cannot refer to the cursor outside of the declaring block unless the cursor is declared in a package (see Chapter 16, *Packages*, for more information on global variables and cursors). For example, if a cursor is declared in the get_employees procedure (see below) and within get_employees a second PL/SQL block is defined to calculate total compensation for each employee, the cursor and its attributes may still be referenced in that calculation block:

```
PROCEDURE get_employees
IS
    CURSOR emp_cur IS
        SELECT employee_id, sal + bonus FROM employee;
BEGIN
    OPEN emp_cur;
    DECLARE
        empid NUMBER;
        total_comp NUMBER;
    BEGIN
        FETCH emp_cur INTO empid, total_comp;
        IF total_comp < 5000
        THEN
            MESSAGE (' I need a raise!');
        END IF;
    END;
END;
```

If, on the other hand, the cursor is declared within an inner block, then that cursor cannot be referenced in an outer block. In the next procedure, the outer block declares the variables that receive the data fetched from the cursor. The inner block declares the cursor. While the inner block can open the cursor without error, the FETCH statement is outside the scope of the cursor-declaring block and will therefore fail:

```
PROCEDURE get_employees IS
    empid NUMBER;
    total_comp NUMBER;
BEGIN
    DECLARE
        CURSOR emp_cur IS
            SELECT employee_id, sal + bonus FROM employee;
    BEGIN
        OPEN emp_cur;
    END;

    /* This fetch will not be able to identify the cursor. */

    FETCH emp_cur INTO empid, total_comp; -- INVALID!
    IF total_comp < 5000
    THEN
        MESSAGE (' I need a raise!');
    END IF;
END;
```

The rules for cursor scope are, therefore, the same as those for all other identifiers.

Block Labels

Anonymous blocks don't have names under which they can be stored in the database. By using block labels, however, you can give a name to your block for the duration of its execution. A block label is a PL/SQL label which is placed directly in front of the first line of the block (either the DECLARE or the BEGIN keyword). You might use block labels for either of these reasons:

- Improve the readability of your code. When you give something a name, you self-document that code. You also clarify your own thinking about what that code is supposed to do, sometimes ferreting out errors in the process.

- Qualify the names of elements declared in the block to distinguish between references to elements with a different scope, but the same name.

A PL/SQL label has this format:

```
<<identifer>>
```

where identifier is a valid PL/SQL identifier (up to 30 characters in length, starting with a letter; see the "Identifiers" section in Chapter 2, *PL/SQL Language Fundamentals,* for a complete list of rules).

Let's look at a couple of examples of applying block labels. In the first example, I place a label in front of my block simply to give it a name and document its purpose:

```
<<calc_dependencies>>
DECLARE
    v_senator VARCHAR2(100) := 'THURMOND, JESSE';
BEGIN
    IF total_contributions (v_senator, 'TOBACCO') > 25000
    THEN
        DBMS_OUTPUT.PUT_LINE ('We''re smokin''!');
    END IF;
END;
```

In the next example, I use my block labels to allow me to reference all variables declared in my outer and inner blocks:

```
<<tobacco_dependency>>
DECLARE
    v_senator VARCHAR2(100) := 'THURMOND, JESSE';
BEGIN
    IF total_contributions (v_senator, 'TOBACCO') > 25000
    THEN
        <<alochol_dependency>>
        DECLARE
            v_senator VARCHAR2(100) := 'WHATEVERIT, TAKES';
        BEGIN
            IF tobacco_dependency.v_senator =
               alcohol_dependency.v_senator
            THEN
                DBMS_OUTPUT.PUT_LINE
                    ('Maximizing profits - the American way of life!');
            END IF;
        END;
    END IF;
END;
```

I have used my block labels in this case to distinguish between the two different v_senator variables. Without the use of block labels, there would be no way for me to reference the v_senator of the outer block within the inner block. Of course, I could simply give these variables different names, the much-preferred approach.

Procedures

A *procedure* is a module performing one or more actions. Because a procedure is a standalone executable statement in PL/SQL, a PL/SQL block could consist of nothing more than a single call to a procedure. Procedures are key building blocks of modular code, allowing you to both consolidate and reuse your program logic.

The general format of a PL/SQL procedure is as follows:

```
PROCEDURE name [ ( parameter [, parameter ... ] ) ]
IS
   [declaration statements]

BEGIN
   executable-statements

[ EXCEPTION
     exception handler statements]

END [ name ];
```

where each component is used in the following ways:

name
>   The name of the procedure comes directly after the keyword PROCEDURE.

parameters
>   An optional list of parameters that you define to both pass information into the procedure and send information out of the procedure, back to the calling program.

declaration statements
>   The declarations of local identifiers for that procedure. If you do not have any declarations, then there will not be any statements between the IS and BEGIN statements.

executable statements
>   The statements that the procedure executes when it is called. You must have at least one executable statement after the BEGIN and before the END or EXCEPTION keywords.

exception handler statements

The optional exception handlers for the procedure. If you do not explicitly handle any exceptions, then you can leave out the EXCEPTION keyword and simply terminate the execution section with the END keyword.

Figure 15-9 shows the apply_discount procedure, which contains all four sections of the named PL/SQL block, as well as a parameter list.

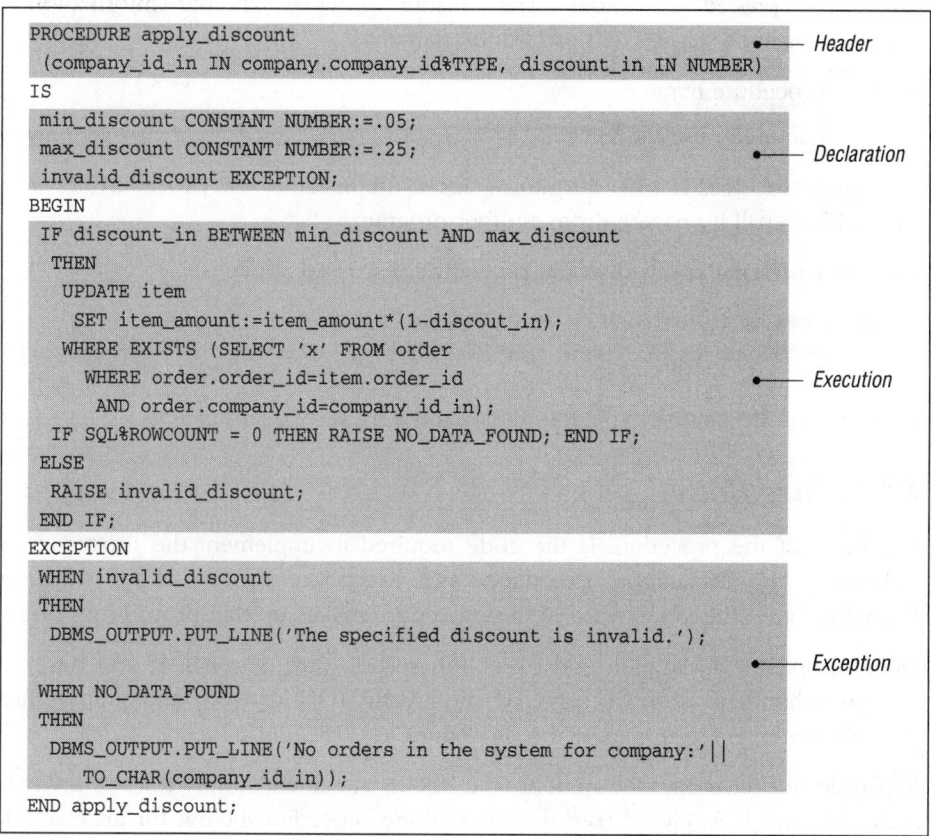

```
PROCEDURE apply_discount                                          •——— Header
  (company_id_in IN company.company_id%TYPE, discount_in IN NUMBER)
IS
  min_discount CONSTANT NUMBER:=.05;
  max_discount CONSTANT NUMBER:=.25;                              •——— Declaration
  invalid_discount EXCEPTION;
BEGIN
  IF discount_in BETWEEN min_discount AND max_discount
    THEN
      UPDATE item
        SET item_amount:=item_amount*(1-discout_in);
      WHERE EXISTS (SELECT 'x' FROM order
        WHERE order.order_id=item.order_id                        •——— Execution
          AND order.company_id=company_id_in);
    IF SQL%ROWCOUNT = 0 THEN RAISE NO_DATA_FOUND; END IF;
  ELSE
    RAISE invalid_discount;
  END IF;
EXCEPTION
  WHEN invalid_discount
  THEN
    DBMS_OUTPUT.PUT_LINE('The specified discount is invalid.');
                                                                  •——— Exception
  WHEN NO_DATA_FOUND
  THEN
    DBMS_OUTPUT.PUT_LINE('No orders in the system for company:'||
      TO_CHAR(company_id_in));
END apply_discount;
```

Figure 15-9. The apply_discount procedure

Calling a Procedure

A procedure is called as an executable PL/SQL statement. In other words, a call to a procedure must end with a semicolon (;) and be executed before and after other SQL or PL/SQL statements.

The following executable statement runs the apply_discount procedure:

```
apply_discount( new_company_id, 0.15 );   -- 15% discount
```

If the procedure does not have any parameters, then you must call the procedure without any parentheses:

```
display_store_summary;
```

Procedure Header

The portion of the procedure definition that comes before the IS keyword is called the procedure header. The header provides all the information a programmer needs to call that procedure, namely:

- The procedure name
- The parameter list, if any

A programmer does not need to know about the inside of the procedure in order to be able to call it properly from another program.

The header for the apply_discount procedure discussed above is:

```
PROCEDURE apply_discount
    (company_id_in IN company.company_id%TYPE,
     discount_in IN NUMBER)
```

It consists of the module type, the name, and a list of two parameters.

Procedure Body

The body of the procedure is the code required to implement the procedure. It consists of the declaration, execution, and exception sections of the function. Everything after the IS keyword in the procedure makes up that procedure's body.

Once again, the declaration and exception sections are optional. If you have no exception handlers, you will leave off the EXCEPTION keyword and simply enter the END statement to terminate the procedure.

If you do not have any declarations, the BEGIN statement simply follows immediately after the IS keyword (see the do_nothing procedure below for an example of this structure.).

You must supply at least one executable statement in a procedure. Here is my candidate for the procedure in PL/SQL with the smallest possible body:

```
PROCEDURE do_nothing IS
BEGIN
   NULL;
END;
```

Does the do_nothing procedure seem silly? A procedure that doesn't do anything can, in fact, be very useful when you are creating stubs for modules in a top-down design effort. I have also used this kind of procedure when building templates. My do_nothing procedure acts initially as a placeholder in my code, but then also provides a mechanism for customization of the templates.

The END Label

You can append the name of the procedure directly after the END keyword when you complete your procedure, as shown below:

```
PROCEDURE display_stores (region_in IN VARCHAR2) IS
BEGIN
   ...
END display_stores;
```

This name serves as a label that explicitly links up the end of the program with its beginning. You should as a matter of habit use an END label. It is especially important to do so when you have a procedure that spans more than a single page, or is one in a series of procedures and functions in a package body.

Functions

A *function* is a module that returns a value. Unlike a procedure, which is a standalone executable statement, a call to a function can only be part of an executable statement.

Because a function returns a value, it can be said to have a datatype. A function can be used in place of an expression in a PL/SQL statement having the same datatype as the function.

Appendix C, *Built-In Packages*, describes the built-in functions that PL/SQL provides to help you write your programs. You can also write your own functions—numeric functions, VARCHAR2 functions, and even functions that return a PL/SQL table or record. The programmer-defined function, a powerful addition to your toolchest, will aid greatly in making your code more flexible and easier to understand.

Structure of a Function

The structure of a function is the same as that of a procedure, except that the function also has a RETURN clause. The general format of a function follows:

```
FUNCTION name [ ( parameter [, parameter ... ] ) ]
   RETURN return_datatype
IS
   [ declaration statements ]

BEGIN
   executable statements
```

```
[ EXCEPTION
    exception handler statements ]

END [ name ];
```

where each component is used in the following ways:

name

>   The name of the procedure comes directly after the keyword FUNCTION.

parameters

>   An optional list of parameters that you define to both pass information into the procedure and send information out of the procedure, back to the calling program.

return_datatype

>   The datatype of the value returned by the function. This is required in the function header and is explained in more detail in the next section.

declaration statements

>   The declarations of local identifiers for that function. If you do not have any declarations, then there will not be any statements between the IS and BEGIN statements.

executable statements

>   The statements the function executes when it is called. You must have at least one executable statement after the BEGIN and before the END or EXCEPTION keywords.

exception handler statements

>   The optional exception handlers for the function. If you do not explicitly handle any exceptions, then you can leave out the EXCEPTION keyword and simply terminate the execution section with the END keyword.

Figure 15-10 illustrates the PL/SQL function and its different sections. Notice that the tot_sales function does not have an exception section.

The RETURN Datatype

The return_datatype is the datatype of the value returned by the function. This datatype can be any datatype (and many complex structures) supported by PL/SQL, including scalars like these:

- VARCHAR2
- NUMBER
- BINARY_INTEGER
- BOOLEAN

```
FUNCTION tot_sales
  (company_id_in IN company.company_id%TYPE,
    status_in IN order.status_code%TYPE:=NULL)         •———— Header
RETURN NUMBER
IS
  /*Internal upper-cased version of status code */
  status_int order.status_code%TYPE:=UPPER(status_in);

  /*Parameterized cursor returns total discounted sales. */
  CURSOR sales_cur (status_in IN status_code%TYPE) IS
   SELECT SUM (amount*discount)
     FROM item                                          •———— Declaration
   WHERE EXISTS (SELECT 'X' FROM order
       WHERE order.order_id=item.order_id
       AND company_id=company_id_in
       AND status_code LIKE status_in);

  /*Return value for function*/
  return_value NUMBER;
BEGIN
  OPEN sales_cur (status_int);
  FETCH sales_cur INTO return_value;
  IF sales_cur%NOTFOUND
  THEN                                                  •———— Execution
     CLOSE sales_cur;
     RETURN NULL;
  ELSE
     CLOSE sales_cur;
     RETURN return_value;
  END IF;
END tot_sales;
```

Figure 15-10. The tot_sales function

Functions can also return complex and composite datatypes, such as:

- PL/SQL table (Oracle7)

- Nested table or variable array (VARRAY) (PL/SQL8)

- PL/SQL record

- Object type (PL/SQL8)

- Large objects (LOBs) such as BFILEs and CLOBs (PL/SQL8)

The datatype of a function cannot be either of the following:

Named exception

> Once you declare an exception, you can reference that exception only in a RAISE statement and in the exception handler itself.

Cursor name

> You cannot return a cursor from a function. (Note that PL/SQL Release 2.2 and beyond provides a REF CURSOR TYPE declaration that will allow you to return a cursor and even declare a parameter as a cursor.)

The END Label

You can append the name of the function directly after the END keyword when you complete your function, as shown below:

```
FUNCTION tot_sales (company_in IN INTEGER) RETURN NUMBER
IS
BEGIN
   ...
END tot_sales;
```

This name serves as a label that explicitly links up the end of the program with its beginning. You should as a matter of habit use an END label. It is especially important to do so when you have a function that spans more than a single page, or is one in a series of functions and procedures in a package body.

Calling a Function

A function is called as part of an executable PL/SQL statement, wherever an expression can be used. The following examples illustrate the different ways that the tot_sales function demonstrated in Figure 15-10 might be called:

- Call tot_sales to assign a value to a local PL/SQL variable:

```
sales_for_1995 := tot_sales (1504, 'C');
```

- Use a call to tot_sales to set a default value for a variable:

```
DECLARE
   sales_for_1995 NUMBER DEFAULT tot_sales (1504, 'C');
BEGIN
```

- Use tot_sales directly in an expression:

```
IF tot_sales (275, 'O') > 10000
THEN
   ...
```

Functions without parameters

If a function has no parameters, then the function call must be written without parentheses, as the line below illustrates:

```
IF tot_sales THEN ...
```

Notice that you cannot tell just by looking at the above line of code whether tot_sales is a function or a variable. You would, in fact, have to check the declaration section of your PL/SQL block if you really needed to know. And that's the whole point. A function returns a value, as does a variable. The function just happens to execute some code to come up with that value, whereas a variable has that value as its very attribute, available for immediate return.

Function Header

The portion of the function definition that comes before the IS keyword is called the function header. The header provides all the information a programmer needs to call that function, namely:

- The function name
- The parameter list, if any
- The RETURN datatype

A programmer does not need to know about the inside of the function in order to be able to call it properly from another program.

The header for the tot_sales function discussed above is:

```
FUNCTION tot_sales
    (company_id_in IN company.company_id%TYPE,
     status_in IN order.status_code%TYPE := NULL)
RETURN NUMBER
```

It consists of the module type, the name, a list of two parameters, and a RETURN datatype of NUMBER. This means that the PL/SQL statement containing a call to tot_sales must be able to use a numeric value.

Function Body

The body of the function is the code required to implement the function. It consists of the declaration, execution, and exception sections of the function. Everything after the IS keyword in the function makes up that function's body.

Once again, the declaration and exception sections are optional. If you have no exception handlers, you will simply leave off the EXCEPTION keyword and enter the END statement to terminate the function.

If you do not have any declarations, the BEGIN statement simply follows immediately after the IS keyword (see the does_nothing function below for an example of this structure).

A Tiny Function

You must supply at least one executable statement in a function. Here is my candidate for the Boolean function with the smallest possible body in PL/SQL:

```
FUNCTION does_nothing RETURN BOOLEAN IS
BEGIN
    RETURN TRUE;
END;
```

You would call does_nothing as follows:

```
IF does_nothing
THEN
    NULL;
END IF;
```

The RETURN Statement

A function must have at least one RETURN statement in its execution section of statements. It can have more than one RETURN, but only one of those statements is executed each time the function is called. The RETURN statement that is executed by the function determines the value that is returned by that function. When a RETURN statement is processed, the function terminates immediately and returns control to the calling PL/SQL block.

The RETURN clause in the header of the function is different from the RETURN statement in the execution section of the body of the function. While the RETURN clause indicates the datatype of the return or result value of the function, the RETURN statement specifies the actual value that is returned. You have to specify the RETURN datatype in the header, but then also include at least one RETURN statement in the function.

Multiple RETURNs

In the tot_sales function shown in Figure 15-10, I used two different RETURN statements to handle different situations in the function, as follows:

```
IF sales_cur%NOTFOUND
THEN
    CLOSE sales_cur;
    RETURN NULL;
ELSE
    CLOSE sales_cur;
    RETURN return_value;
END IF;
```

In other words, if I could not obtain sales information from the cursor, I will return NULL (which is different from zero). If I do get a value from the cursor, I return it to the calling program. In both of these cases the RETURN statement passes back a value; in one case the NULL value, and in the other the return_value variable.

RETURN any valid expression

The RETURN statement can accept any expression for evaluation and return. This expression can be composed of calls to other functions, complex calculations, and even data conversions. All of the following usages of RETURN are valid:

```
RETURN 'buy me lunch';
RETURN POWER (max_salary, 5);
RETURN (100 - pct_of_total_salary (employee_id));
RETURN TO_DATE ('01' || earliest_month || initial_year, 'DDMMYY');
```

An expression in the RETURN statement is evaluated when the RETURN is executed. When control is passed back to the calling form, the result of the evaluated expression is passed along, too.

No RETURN is executed

What happens when you include one or any number of RETURN statements in your functions but none of them is executed? PL/SQL raises an error.

The following function:

```
FUNCTION company_type (type_code_in IN VARCHAR2)
    RETURN VARCHAR2 IS
BEGIN
    IF type_code_in = 'S'
    THEN
        RETURN 'SUBSIDIARY';
    ELSIF type_code_in = 'P'
    THEN
        RETURN 'PARTNER';
    END IF;
END;
```

is then called in this executable statement:

```
type_description := company_type ('R');
```

Because the RETURN statements are executed only when the type code is 'S' or 'P', the function never hits a RETURN. It does, however, execute to the end of the function and then raise an error, as follows:

```
ORA-6503: PL/SQL: Function returned without value
```

You can avoid this kind of problem (which you may never encounter in testing since you always pass a sensible value to the function) by restructuring your use of the RETURN statement.

RETURN as last executable statement

Generally, the best way to make sure that your function always returns a value is to make the last executable statement in the function your RETURN statement. Declare a variable named return_value, which clearly indicates that it will contain the return value for the function, write all the code to come up with that value, and then at the very end of the function RETURN the return_value:

```
FUNCTION do_it_all (parameter_list) RETURN NUMBER
IS
    return_value NUMBER;
BEGIN

    ... lots of executable statements ...

    RETURN return_value;
END;
```

The company_type function, for example, can be converted easily to this structure:

```
FUNCTION company_type (type_code_in IN VARCHAR2)
    RETURN VARCHAR2
IS
    return_value VARCHAR2 (25) := NULL;
BEGIN
    IF type_code_in = 'S'
    THEN
        return_value := 'SUBSIDIARY';

    ELSIF type_code_in = 'P'
    THEN
        return_value := 'PARTNER';
    END IF;

    RETURN return_value;
END;
```

Notice that, because I provided the return_value variable with a default value of NULL, I didn't have to code an ELSE clause in the IF statement to explicitly make that assignment (though doing so would probably make the code more readable). If the type_code_in does not match any of the values in the IF statement, there is no problem because each IF and ELSIF no longer performs its own RETURN. Instead, they just assign a value and then leave the RETURNing to the little RETURN section at the end of the function.

RETURN statement in a procedure

Believe it or not, RETURN statements can also be used in procedures. The procedure version of the RETURN does not take an expression; it cannot, therefore, pass a value back to the calling program unit. The RETURN simply halts execution of the procedure and returns control to the calling code.

You do not (should not, in any case) see this usage of RETURN very often, and for good reason. Use of the RETURN in a procedure usually leads to very unstructured code that is hard to understand and maintain. Avoid using both RETURN and GOTO to bypass proper control structures and process flow in your program units.

Parameters

Procedures and functions can both use *parameters* to pass information back and forth between the module and the calling PL/SQL block.

The parameters of a module are at least as important as the code that implements the module (the module's body). Sure, you have to make certain that your module fulfills its promise. But the whole point of creating a module is that it can be called, you hope by more than one other module. If the parameter list is confusing or badly designed, it will be very difficult for programmers to make use of the module. The result will be that few people will use that module. And it doesn't much matter how well you implemented a program that no one uses.

Many developers do not give enough attention to a module's set of parameters. Considerations regarding parameters include:

- *The number of parameters.* Too few parameters can limit the reusability of your program. Too many parameters, and no one will want to reuse your program.

- *The types of parameters.* Should you use read-only, write-only, or read-write parameters?

- *The names of parameters.* How should you name your parameters so that their purpose in a module is properly and easily understood?

- *Default values for parameters.* How do you set defaults? When should a parameter be given defaults and when should the programmer be forced to enter a value?

PL/SQL offers many different features to help you design parameters effectively. This section covers all elements of parameter definition. Chapter 22, *Code Design Tips*, offers a number of tips for designing your parameters for maximum readability and code reusability.

Defining the Parameters

Formal parameters are defined in the parameter list of the program. A parameter definition parallels closely the syntax for declaring variables in the declaration section of a PL/SQL block. There is one important distinction: a parameter declaration must be unconstrained.

A *constrained declaration* is one that constrains or limits the kind of value that can be assigned to a variable declared with that datatype. An *unconstrained declaration* is one that does not limit values in this way. The following declaration of the variable company_name constrains the variable to 60 characters:

```
DECLARE
    company_name VARCHAR2(60);
BEGIN
```

When you declare a parameter, however, you must leave out the constraining part of the declaration:

```
PROCEDURE display_company (company_name IN VARCHAR2) IS ...
```

%TYPE and %ROWTYPE

You can use the %TYPE and %ROWTYPE anchoring attributes in the parameter list, even if the %TYPE references a constrained declaration somewhere back along the line, as in a CREATE TABLE statement. The following parameter list will compile just fine:

```
PROCEDURE fun_and_games (ride_id_in IN rides.ride_id%TYPE)
```

If you are using PL/SQL Version 2, you can also declare parameters as PL/SQL tables through use of the TABLE type statement, as shown in this example:

```
PACKAGE pet_hotel
IS
    /* Define a table type and declare a table */
    TYPE breeds_type IS
       TABLE OF breed.breed_name%TYPE INDEX BY BINARY_INTEGER;
    TYPE avail_rooms_type IS
       TABLE OF room.room_number%TYPE INDEX BY BINARY_INTEGER;

    /* Specification of function which takes a table argument */
    FUNCTION room_by_breeds (breed_table_in IN breeds_type)
       RETURN avail_rooms_type;
END;
```

The %TYPE and %ROWTYPE attributes are allowed for parameters because both result in unconstrained declarations. The actual sizes of the parameters depend on the structures of the tables and columns to which the attributes point. This size is resolved only at compilation time.

Parameter Modes

When you define the parameter you also specify the way in which the parameter can be used. There are three different modes of parameters:

Mode	Description	Parameter Usage
IN	Read-only	The value of the actual parameter can be referenced inside the module, but the parameter cannot be changed.
OUT	Write-only	The module can assign a value to the parameter, but the parameter's value cannot be referenced.
IN OUT	Read-write	The module can both reference (read) and modify (write) the parameter.

The mode determines how the program can use and manipulate the value assigned to the formal parameter. You specify the mode of the parameter immediately after the parameter name and before the parameter's datatype and optional default value. The following procedure header uses all three modes of parameters:

```
PROCEDURE predict_activity
   (last_date_in IN DATE,
    task_desc_inout IN OUT VARCHAR2,
    next_date_out OUT DATE)
```

The predict_activity procedure takes in two pieces of information: the date of the last activity and a description of the activity. It then returns or sends out two pieces of information: a possibly modified task description and the date of the next activity. Because the task_desc_inout parameter is IN OUT, the program can both read the value of the argument and change the value of that argument.

Let's look at each of these parameter modes in detail.

IN mode

The IN parameter allows you to pass values in to the module, but will not pass anything out of the module and back to the calling PL/SQL block. In other words, for the purposes of the program, its IN parameters function like constants. Just like constants, the value of the formal IN parameter cannot be changed within the program. You cannot assign values to the IN parameter or in any other way modify its value.

IN is the default mode for parameters. If you do not specify a parameter mode, then the parameter is automatically considered an IN parameter. I recommend, however, that you always specify a parameter mode with your parameters. Your intended use of the parameter is then documented explicitly in the code itself.

IN parameters can be given default values in the program header (see the section called "Default Values").

The actual parameter for an IN parameter can be a variable, a named constant, a literal, or an expression. All of the following calls to display_title are valid:

```
DECLARE
    happy_title CONSTANT VARCHAR2(30)    := 'HAPPY BIRTHDAY';
    changing_title VARCHAR2(30) := 'Happy Anniversary';
    spc VARCHAR2(1) := ' ';
BEGIN
    display_title ('Happy Birthday');          -- a literal
    display_title (happy_title);               -- a constant

    changing_title := happy_title;

    display_title (changing_title);            -- a variable
    display_title ('Happy' || spc || 'Birthday'); -- an expression
    display_title (INITCAP (happy_title));     -- another expression
END;
```

What if you want to transfer data out of your program? For that, you will need an OUT or an IN OUT parameter.

OUT mode

An OUT parameter is the opposite of the IN parameter, but I suppose you already had that figured out. Use the OUT parameter to pass a value back from the program to the calling PL/SQL block. An OUT parameter is like the return value for a function, but it appears in the parameter list and you can, of course, have as many OUT parameters as you like.

Inside the program, an OUT parameter acts like a variable that has not been initialized. In fact, the OUT parameter has no value at all until the program terminates successfully (without raising an exception, that is). During the execution of the program, any assignments to an OUT parameter are actually made to an internal copy of the OUT parameter. When the program terminates successfully and returns control to the calling block, the value in that local copy is then transferred to the actual OUT parameter. That value is then available in the calling PL/SQL block.

There are several consquences of these rules concerning OUT parameters:

- You cannot assign an OUT parameter's value to another variable or even use it in a re-assignment to itself. An OUT parameter can be found only on the left side of an assignment operation.

- You also cannot provide a default value to an OUT parameter. You can only assign a value to an OUT parameter inside the body of the module.

- Any assignments made to OUT parameters are rolled back when an exception is raised in the program. Because the value for an OUT parameter is not actually assigned until a program completes successfully, any intermediate assignments to OUT parameters are therefore ignored. Unless an exception handler traps the exception and then assigns a value to the OUT parameter, no assignment is made to that parameter. The variable will retain the same value it had before the program was called.

- An OUT actual parameter has to be a variable. It cannot be a constant, literal, or expression, since these formats do not provide a receptacle in which PL/SQL can place the OUTgoing value.

OUT parameters are very restrictive in how they can and should be used. These restrictions place more of a burden on the programmer to understand the parameter modes and their impact. On the other hand, the OUT parameter provides a level of security and a narrowing of functionality which, when appropriate, is invaluable.

The IN OUT mode

With an IN OUT parameter, you can pass values into the program and return a value back to the calling program (either the original, unchanged value or a new value set within the program). The IN OUT parameter shares two restrictions with the OUT parameter:

1. An IN OUT parameter cannot have a default value.

2. An IN OUT actual parameter or argument must be a variable. It cannot be a constant, literal, or expression, since these formats do not provide a receptacle in which PL/SQL can place the outgoing value.

Beyond these restrictions, none of the other restrictions apply.

You can use the IN OUT parameter in both sides of an assignment, because it functions like an initialized, rather than uninitialized, variable. PL/SQL does not lose the value of an IN OUT parameter when it begins execution of the program. Instead, it uses that value as necessary within the program.

The combine_and_format_names procedure shown here combines the first and last names into a full name in the format specified ("LAST, FIRST" or "FIRST LAST"). It uses all three different modes of parameters: IN, IN OUT, and OUT.

```
PROCEDURE combine_and_format_names
    (first_name_inout IN OUT VARCHAR2,
     last_name_inout IN OUT VARCHAR2,
     full_name_out OUT VARCHAR2,
     name_format_in IN VARCHAR2 := 'LAST, FIRST')
IS
BEGIN
    /* Upper-case the first and last names. */
    first_name_inout := UPPER (first_name_inout);
    last_name_inout := UPPER (last_name_inout);
```

```
    /* Combine the names as directed by the name format string. */
    IF name_format_in = 'LAST, FIRST'
    THEN
        full_name_out := last_name_inout || ', ' || first_name_inout;

    ELSIF name_format_in = 'FIRST LAST'
    THEN
        full_name_out := first_name_inout || ' ' || last_name_inout;
    END IF;
END;
```

The first name and last name parameters must be IN OUT. I need the incoming names for the combine action, and I will uppercase the first and last names for future use in the program (thereby enforcing the application standard of all upper-case for names of people and things).

The full_name_out is just an OUT parameter because I create the full name from its parts. If the actual parameter used to receive the full name has a value going into the procedure, I certainly don't want to use it! Finally, the name_format_in parameter is a mere IN parameter since it is used to determine how to format the full name, but is not changed or changeable in any way.

Each parameter mode has its own characteristics and purpose. You should choose carefully which mode to apply to each of your parameters so that the parameter is used properly within the module.

Actual and Formal Parameters

When we talk about parameters, we need to distinguish between two different kinds of parameters: actual and formal parameters. The *formal parameters* are the names that are declared in the parameter list of the header of a module. The *actual parameters* are the values or expressions placed in the parameter list of the actual call to the module.

Let's examine the differences between actual and formal parameters using the example of tot_sales. Here, again, is tot_sales' header:

```
FUNCTION tot_sales
    (company_id_in IN company.company_id%TYPE,
     status_in IN order.status_code%TYPE := NULL)
RETURN std_types.dollar_amount;
```

The formal parameters of tot_sales are:

company_id_in
    The primary key of the company

status_in
    The status of the orders to be included in the sales calculation

They do not exist outside of the function. You can think of them as place holders for real or actual parameter values that are passed into the function when it is used in a program.

When you use tot_sales in your code, the formal parameters disappear. In their place you list the actual parameters or variables, whose values will be passed to tot_sales. In the following example, the company_id variable contains the primary key pointing to a company record. In the first three calls to tot_sales a different, hardcoded status is passed to the function. The last call to tot_sales does not specify a status; in this case the function assigns the default value (provided in the function header) to the status_in parameter:

```
new_sales       := tot_sales (company_id, 'N');
paid_sales      := tot_sales (company_id, 'P');
shipped_sales   := tot_sales (company_id, 'S');
all_sales       := tot_sales (company_id);
```

When tot_sales is called, all the actual parameters are evaluated. The results of the evaluations are then assigned to the formal parameters inside the function to which they correspond.

The actual parameters must be evaluated because they can be expressions, as well as pointers, to non-PL/SQL objects such as bind variables in the development tool.

The formal parameter and the actual parameter that corresponds to the formal parameter (when called) must be of the same or compatible datatypes. PL/SQL will perform datatype conversions for you in many situations. Generally, however, you are better off avoiding all implicit datatype conversions so you are sure of what is happening in your code. Use a formal conversion function like TO_CHAR or TO_DATE (see Chapter 14, *Conversion Functions*), so you know exactly what kind of data you are passing into your modules.

Matching Actual and Formal Parameters in PL/SQL

How does PL/SQL know which actual parameter goes with which formal parameter when a program is executed? PL/SQL actually offers you two different ways to make the association:

Positional notation
    Associate the actual parameter implicitly (by position) with the formal parameter.

Named notation
    Associate an actual parameter explicitly (by name) with the formal parameter.

Positional notation

In every example you've seen so far, I have employed positional notation in order
to guide PL/SQL through the parameters. With positional notation, PL/SQL relies
on the relative positions of the parameters to make the correspondence. PL/SQL
associates the nth actual parameter in the call to a program with the nth formal
parameter in the program's header.

With the tot_sales example shown below, PL/SQL associates the first actual parameter, :order.company_id, with the first formal parameter, company_id_in. It then
associates the second actual parameter, N, with the second format parameter,
status_in:

```
new_sales := tot_sales (:order.company_id, 'N');

FUNCTION tot_sales
    (company_id_in IN company.company_id%TYPE,
     status_in IN order.status_code%TYPE := NULL)
RETURN std_types.dollar_amount;
```

Now you know the name for the way compilers pass values through parameters
to modules. Positional notation, shown graphically in Figure 15-11, is certainly the
most obvious method.

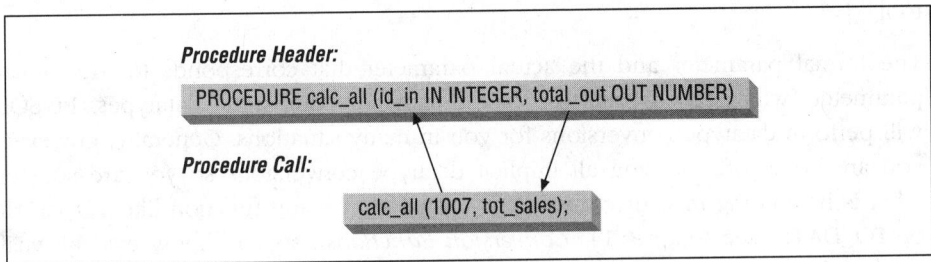

Figure 15-11. Matching actual with formal parameters (positional notation)

Named notation

With named notation, you explicitly associate the formal parameter (the name of
the parameter) with the actual parameter (the value of the parameter), right in the
call to the program, using the combination symbol =>.

The general syntax for named notation is:

```
formal_parameter_name => argument_value
```

Because you provide explicitly the name of the formal parameter, PL/SQL no
longer needs to rely on the order of the parameters to make the association from
actual to formal. So, if you use named notation, you do not need to list the param-

eters in your call to the program in the same order as the formal parameters are listed in the header. I can call tot_sales for new orders in either of these two ways:

```
new_sales :=
   tot_sales (company_id_in => :order.company_id, status_in =>'N');

new_sales :=
   tot_sales (status_in =>'N', company_id_in => :order.company_id);
```

You can also mix named and positional notation in the same program call:

```
:order.new_sales := tot_sales (:order.company_id, status_in =>'N');
```

If you do mix notation, however, you must list all of your positional parameters before any named notation parameters, as shown in the preceding example. Positional notation has to have a starting point from which to keep track of positions, and the only starting point is the first parameter. If you place named notation parameters in front of positional notation, PL/SQL loses its place. Both of the calls to tot_sales, shown below, fail. The first statement fails because the named notation comes first. The second fails because positional notation is used, but the parameters are in the wrong order. PL/SQL will try to convert 'N' to a NUMBER (for company_id):

```
:order.new_sales := tot_sales (company_id_in => :order.company_id, 'N');

:order.new_sales := tot_sales ('N', company_id_in => :order.company_id);
```

Benefits of named notation

Now you are aware of different ways to notate the order and association of parameters. One obvious question that you might ask is why you would ever use named notation. Here are some possibilities:

- *Named notation is self-documenting.* When you use named notation, the call to the program clearly describes the formal parameter to which the actual parameter is assigned. The names of formal parameters can and should be designed so that their use/purpose is self-explanatory. In a way, the descriptive aspect of named notation is another form of program documentation. If you are not familiar with all the modules called by an application, the listing of the formal parameters helps reinforce your understanding of a particular program call. In some development environments, the standard for parameter notation is named notation for just this reason.

- *Named notation gives you complete flexibility over parameter specification.* You can list the parameters in any order you want. You can also include only the parameters you want or need in the parameter list. Complex applications may at times require procedures with literally dozens of parameters. Any parameter with a default value can be left out of the call to the procedure. By using named notation, the developer can use the procedure, passing only the values needed for that usage.

Remember that whether you use named or positional notation, the actual module (both header and body) remains unchanged. The only difference is in the way the module is called.

Default Values

As you have seen from previous examples, you can provide a default value for IN parameters. If an IN parameter has a default value, you do not need to include that parameter in the call to the program. You must, of course, include an actual parameter for any IN OUT parameters, even if they have default values. A parameter's default value is used by the program only if the call to that program does not include that parameter in the list.

The parameter default value works the same way as a specification of a default value for a declared variable. There are two ways to specify a default value: either with the keyword DEFAULT or with the assignment operator (:=), as the following example illustrates:

```
PROCEDURE astrology_reading
    (sign_in IN VARCHAR2 := 'LIBRA',
     birth_time_in IN NUMBER DEFAULT 800) IS
```

By using default values, you can call programs using different numbers of actual parameters. The program uses the default value of any unspecified parameters. It also overrides the default values of any parameters in the list that have default values. Here are all the different ways you can ask for your astrology reading using positional notation:

```
astrology_reading ('SCORPIO', 1756);
astrology_reading ('SCORPIO');
astrology_reading;
```

The first line specifies both parameters explicitly. In the second call to astrology_reading, only the first actual parameter is included, so birth_time_in is set to 8:00 A.M. In the third line, no parameters are specified, so we cannot include the parentheses. Both the default values are used in the body of the procedure.

What if you want to specify a birth time, but not a sign? The following call to astrology_reading compiles properly since PL/SQL will convert NUMBER to VARCHAR2 automatically, but it results in assigning the string "1756" to the sign, and 8:00 A.M. to the birth time:

```
astrology_reading (1756);
```

Not exactly what you might have had in mind! You also cannot use a comma (,) to indicate a placeholder, as in, "There should be a parameter here so use the default value!" This next call does not even compile:

```
astrology_reading (,1756); -- Invalid skipped argument
```

If you wish to leave out leading and defaulted parameters from your program call, you need to switch to named notation. By including the name of the formal parameter, you can list only those parameters to which you need to pass (or retrieve) values. In this (thankfully) last request for a star-based reading of my fate, I have successfully passed in a default of Libra as my sign and an overridden birth time of 5:56 P.M.

```
astrology_reading (birth_time_in => 1756);
```

Local Modules

A *local module* is a procedure or function that is defined in the declaration section of a PL/SQL block (anonymous or named). This module is considered local because it is only defined within the parent PL/SQL block. It cannot be called by any other PL/SQL blocks defined outside of that enclosing block.

The syntax for defining the procedure or function is exactly the same as that used for creating standalone modules.

The following anonymous block, for example, declares a local procedure:

```
DECLARE
   PROCEDURE show_date (date_in IN DATE) IS
   BEGIN
      DBMS_OUTPUT.PUT_LINE (TO_CHAR (date_in, 'Month DD, YYYY'));
   END;
BEGIN
   ...
END;
```

Local modules must be located after all of the other declaration statements in the declaration section. You must declare your variables, cursors, exceptions, types, records, tables, and so on, before you type in the first PROCEDURE or FUNCTION keyword.

You can define both procedures and functions in the declaration section of any kind of PL/SQL block, be it anonymous, procedure, or function. You may not, however, define anonymous blocks (how would you call them?) or packages (maybe in a future release) in a declaration section.

The rest of this section explores the benefits of local modules and offers a number of examples.

Benefits of Local Modularization

There are two central reasons to create local modules:

- *Reduce the size of the module by stripping it of repetitive code.* This is the most common motivation to create a local module. You can see the impact by the next example. The code reduction leads to higher code quality because you have fewer lines to test and fewer potential bugs. It takes less effort to maintain the code, because there is less to maintain. When you do have to make a change, you make it in one place in the local module and the effects are felt immediately throughout the parent module.

- *Improve the readability of your code.* Even if you do not repeat sections of code within a module, you still may want to pull out a set of related statements and package them into a local module to make it easier to follow the logic of the main body of the parent module.

Reducing Code Volume

Let's take a look at an example. The calc_percentages procedure takes numeric values from the sales package (sales_pkg), calculates the percentage of each sales amount against the total sales provided as a parameter, and then formats the number for display in a report or form. The example you see here has only three calculations, but I extracted it from a production application that actually performed 23 of these computations!

```
PROCEDURE calc_percentages (tot_sales_in IN NUMBER)
IS
BEGIN
   :profile.food_sales_stg :=
      TO_CHAR ((sales_pkg.food_sales / tot_sales_in ) * 100,
               '$999,999');
   :profile.service_sales_stg :=
      TO_CHAR ((sales_pkg.service_sales / tot_sales_in ) * 100,
               '$999,999');
   :profile.toy_sales_stg :=
      TO_CHAR ((sales_pkg.toy_sales / tot_sales_in ) * 100,
               '$999,999');
END;
```

This code took a long time (relatively speaking) to write, is larger in code size than necessary, and is maintenance-intensive. What if I need to change the format to which I convert the numbers? What if the calculation of the percentage changes? I have to change each of the individual calculations.

With local modules, I can concentrate all the common, repeated code into a single function, which is then called repeatedly in calc_percentages. The local module version of this procedure is shown below:

```
PROCEDURE calc_percentages (tot_sales_in IN NUMBER)
IS
    /* Define a function right inside the procedure! */
    FUNCTION char_format (val_in IN NUMBER) RETURN VARCHAR2
    IS
    BEGIN
        RETURN TO_CHAR ((val_in/tot_sales_in ) * 100, '$999,999');
    END;
BEGIN
    :profile.food_sales_stg := char_format (sales_pkg.food_sales);
    :profile.service_sales_stg := char_format (sales_pkg.service_sales);
    :profile.toy_sales_stg := char_format (sales_pkg.toy_sales);
END;
```

All the complexities of the calculation, from the division by tot_sales_in to the multiplication by 100 to the formatting with TO_CHAR, have been transferred to the function, pct_stg. This function is defined in the declaration section of the procedure. By calling this function from within the body of calc_percentages, the executable statements of the procedure are much more readable and maintainable. Now, if the formula for the calculation changes in any way, I make the change just once in the function and it takes effect in all the assignments.

Improving Readability

Suppose I have a series of WHILE loops (some nested) whose bodies contain a series of complex calculations and deep nestings of conditional logic. Even with extensive commenting, it can be difficult for a person to follow the program flow over several pages, particularly when the END IF or END LOOP of a given construct is not even on the same page as the IF or LOOP statement that began the construct.

If you pull out sequences of related statements, place them in one or more local modules, and then call those modules in the body of the program, the result is a program that can literally document itself. The assign_workload procedure offers a simplified version of this scenario, which still makes clear the gains offered by local modules:

```
PROCEDURE assign_workload (department_in IN NUMBER)
IS
    /* Declare local variables first. */
    avg_workload NUMBER;
    case_number  NUMBER;

    /*---------------------Local Modules----------------------*/

    /* Define all the major tasks for workload assignment. */
    PROCEDURE assign_next_open_case
        (employee_id_in IN NUMBER, case_out OUT NUMBER)
    IS BEGIN ... END;
```

```
    FUNCTION average_cases (department_id_in IN NUMBER) RETURN NUMBER
    IS BEGIN ... END;

    FUNCTION caseload (employee_id_in IN NUMBER) RETURN NUMBER
    IS BEGIN ... END;

    FUNCTION next_appointment (case_id_in IN NUMBER) RETURN DATE
    IS BEGIN ... END;

    PROCEDURE schedule_case
        (employee_id_in IN NUMBER, case_in IN NUMBER, date_in IN DATE)
    IS BEGIN ... END;
/*
|| Now the execution section of assign_workload:
*/
BEGIN
    avg_workload := average_cases (department_in);
    FOR emp_rec IN (SELECT employee_id
                        FROM employee
                    WHERE department_id = department_in)
    LOOP
        /* If workload below average, assign next open case. */
        IF caseload (emp_rec.employee_id) < avg_workload
        THEN
            assign_next_open_case (emp_rec.employee_id, case_number);
            schedule_case (emp_rec.employee_id,
                        case_number,
                        next_appointment (case_number));
        END IF;
    END LOOP;
END assign_workload;
```

The assign-workload procedure has five local modules:

```
assign_next_open_case
average_cases
caseload
next_appointment
schedule_case
```

For the purposes of understanding the logic behind assign_workload, it doesn't really matter what code is executed in each of them. I can rely simply on the names of those modules to read through the main body of this program. Even without any comments, a reader can still gain a clear understanding of what each module is doing. Of course, if you want to rely on named objects to self-document your code, you'd better come up with very good names for the functions and procedures.

Bottom-Up Reading

Although it is not evident from the preceding example, one drawback of the extensive use of local modules is that the execution section of the program is pushed all the way to the bottom of the module's body. Most programmers are used to scanning a program's code from top to bottom. In trying to understand code with local modules, you should move to the execution section of the parent module and read that first to gain an understanding of the big picture. You can then move back up to dive into the details of the local module.

Scope of Local Modules

This modularized declaration section looks a lot like the body of a package, as you will see in Chapter 16. A package body also contains definitions of modules. The big difference between local modules and package modules is their scope: local modules can be called only from within the block in which they are defined. Package modules can—at a minimum—be called from anywhere in the package. If those modules are also listed in the package specification, they can be called by any other program in your application.

You should use local modules only to encapsulate code that does not need to be called outside of the current program. Otherwise, go ahead and create a package!

Spruce Up Your Code with Local Modules!

These days it seems that whenever I write a program with more than 20 lines, and with any complexity whatsoever, I end up creating several local modules. It helps me see my way through to a solution much more easily. I can conceptualize my code at a higher level of abstraction by assigning a name to a whole sequence of statements. I can perform top-down design and stepwise refinement of my requirements. Finally, by modularizing my code even within a single program, I make it very easy, if the need arises, to later extract a local module and make it a truly independent, reusable procedure or function.

I hope that as you read this, a program you have written (or one with which you are currently wrestling) comes to mind. Perhaps, you are thinking, you can go back and consolidate some repetitive code, clean up the logic, make the program actually understandable to another human being. Don't fight the urge. Go ahead and modularize your code.

Module Overloading

Two or more modules can, under certain conditions, have the same name with different parameter lists. Such modules are said to be *overloaded*. The code in these overloaded programs can be very similar or can be completely different.

Here is an example of two overloaded modules defined in the declaration section of an anonymous block (both are local modules):

```
DECLARE
   /* First version takes a DATE parameter. */
   FUNCTION value_ok (date_in IN DATE) RETURN BOOLEAN
   IS
   BEGIN
      RETURN date_in <= SYSDATE;
   END;

   /* Second version takes a NUMBER parameter. */
   FUNCTION value_ok (number_in IN NUMBER) RETURN BOOLEAN
   IS
   BEGIN
      RETURN number_in > 0;
   END;
BEGIN
```

When the PL/SQL run-time engine encounters the following statement:

```
IF value_ok (SYSDATE) THEN ...
```

the compile compares the actual parameter against the different parameter lists for the overloaded modules. It then executes the code in the body of the program with the matching header.

Overloading in PL/SQL Built-Ins

PL/SQL itself makes extensive use of overloading, as do various development tools such as Oracle Forms. An example of an overloaded program in PL/SQL is the TO_CHAR function. Module overloading allows developers to use a single function to convert both numbers and dates to character format:

```
date_string := TO_CHAR (SYSDATE, 'MMDDYY');
number_string := TO_CHAR (10000);
```

If overloading was not supported in PL/SQL (TO_CHAR is a function in the STAN-DARD package), then two different functions would be required to support conversions to character format. They might look and work as follows:

```
date_string := TO_CHAR_FROM_DATE (SYSDATE, 'MMDDYY');
number_string := TO_CHAR_FROM_NUMBER (10000);
```

You probably just always took it for granted that TO_CHAR automatically detects the difference in the argument (date versus number) and "does the right thing." There's nothing wrong with that. We should take an awful lot for granted in our hardware and software. (In fact, I think that our computers and software should function in more intelligent ways than they do today.) Coming back to the matter of overloading, however, PL/SQL actually examines the value you pass to TO_ CHAR. Based on the datatype of this value, it executes the appropriate TO_CHAR function.

There are, in other words, two different TO_CHAR functions defined in PL/SQL. Module overloading simply makes this fact transparent to developers. Fortunately, this is a feature that is available to developers as well as to the people who brought you PL/SQL. You, too, can overload!

Benefits of Overloading

Overloading can greatly simplify your life and the lives of other developers. This technique consolidates the call interfaces for many similar programs into a single module name. This process transfers the burden of knowledge from the developer to the software. You do not have to try to remember, for instance, the six different names for programs adding values (dates, strings, Booleans, numbers, etc.) to various PL/SQL tables. Instead, you simply tell the compiler that you want to add and pass it the value you want added. PL/SQL and your overloaded programs figure out what you want to do and they do it for you.

When you build overloaded modules, you spend more time in design and implementation than you might with separate, standalone modules. This additional up-front time will be repaid handsomely down the line. You and others will find that it is easier and more efficient to use your programs.

You will find many examples of how overloading is used in Chapter 16.

Where to Overload Modules

There are only two places in PL/SQL programs where you can overload modules:

- Inside the declaration section of a PL/SQL block
- Inside a package

You cannot, in other words, overload the names of standalone programs, nor can you create two completely independent modules with the same name but different parameter lists. For example if you attempt from SQL*Plus to "create or replace" the following two versions of chg_estimate, the second try will fail, as shown below:

```
CREATE OR REPLACE PROCEDURE chg_estimate (date_in IN DATE) IS
BEGIN
   ...
END chg_estimate;
/

Procedure created.
```

```
CREATE OR REPLACE FUNCTION chg_estimate (dollars_in IN NUMBER)
RETURN NUMBER
IS
BEGIN
   ...
END chg_estimate;

ORA-0955: name is already used by an existing object
```

Because the name was already used for a procedure, PL/SQL rejected the attempt to replace it with a function. The compiler would not interpret this second "create or replace" as an effort to create a second module of the same name.

Modules must be overloaded within a particular context. A PL/SQL block provides a scope: anything declared in its declaration section can only be accessed within the execution and exception sections. A PL/SQL package also provides a context for the overloaded modules.

Restrictions on Overloading

There are several restrictions on how you can overload programs. When the PL/SQL engine compiles and runs your program, it has to be able to distinguish between the different overloaded versions of a program; after all, it can't run two different modules at the same time. So when you compile your code, PL/SQL will reject any improperly overloaded modules. It cannot distinguish between the modules by their name, because by definition that is the same in all overloaded programs. Instead, PL/SQL uses the parameter lists of these sibling programs to determine which one to execute. As a result, the following restrictions apply to overloaded programs.

The datatype family of at least one of the parameters of overloaded programs must differ. INTEGER, REAL, DECIMAL, FLOAT, etc., are NUMBER subtypes. CHAR, VARCHAR2, and LONG are character subtypes. If the parameters differ only by datatype within the supertype or family of datatypes, PL/SQL does not have enough information with which to determine the appropriate program to execute. As a result, the following programs cannot be overloaded:

```
FUNCTION calculate_net_profit (revenue_in IN POSITIVE)
RETURN NUMBER IS
BEGIN
   ...
END calculate_net_profit;

FUNCTION calculate_net_profit (revenue_in IN BINARY_INTEGER)
RETURN NUMBER IS
BEGIN
   ...
END calculate_net_profit;
```

Nor can these programs be successfully overloaded, since CHAR and VARCHAR2 are both character datatypes:

```
PROCEDURE trim_and_center (string_in IN CHAR) IS
BEGIN
   ...
END;

PROCEDURE trim_and_center (string_in IN VARCHAR2) IS
BEGIN
   ...
END;
```

Another way of looking at this rule for users of PL/SQL Release 2.1 is that two programs cannot be overloaded if their formal parameters differ only by their subtypes and if those subtypes are based on the same datatype. This was already illustrated in the last example: POSITIVE is a subtype of BINARY_INTEGER.

With PL/SQL Release 2.1 (and beyond) you can now create your own subtypes, and the same rules apply for these subtypes as for the predefined subtypes. If you have declared the following subtypes:

```
SUBTYPE line_text_type IS LONG;
SUBTYPE atomic_type IS VARCHAR2;
SUBTYPE word_separator_type IS VARCHAR2;
```

then the following attempt at overloading will fail:

```
PROCEDURE count_occurrences
    (line_in line_text_type, fragment_in atomic_type);
PROCEDURE count_occurrences
    (line_in line_text_type, between_in word_separator_type);
```

because atomic_type and word_separator_type are two programmer-defined subtypes that share the same base datatype.

Overloaded programs with parameter lists which differ only by name must be called using named notation. If you don't use the name of the argument, how could the compiler distinguish between calls to the following two overloaded programs?

```
FUNCTION calculate_net_profit (revenue_in IN NUMBER)
RETURN NUMBER IS
BEGIN
   ...
END calculate_net_profit;

FUNCTION calculate_net_profit (total_revenue_in IN NUMBER)
RETURN NUMBER IS
BEGIN
   ...
END calculate_net_profit;
```

The only way to direct PL/SQL to the right version of calculate_net_profit is to explicitly identify the version as shown below:

```
calculate_net_profit (revenue_in => 197890);
```

The parameter list of overloaded programs must differ by more than parameter mode. Even if a parameter in one version is IN and that same parameter is IN OUT in another version, PL/SQL cannot tell the difference at the point in which the program is called. Suppose you overload the trim_and_center procedure as follows:

```
PROCEDURE trim_and_center (string_in IN VARCHAR2) IS
BEGIN
   ...
END;

PROCEDURE trim_and_center (string_in IN OUT VARCHAR2) IS
BEGIN
   ...
END;
```

How, then, could the compiler know which of trim_and_center to execute when it encounters this line of code?

```
trim_and_center ('ABC');
```

Overloaded functions must differ by more than their return type (the datatype specified in the RETURN clause of the function). At the time that the overloaded function is called, the compiler doesn't know what type of data that function will return. The compiler cannot, therefore, determine which version of the function to use if all the parameters are the same. The following attempt at overloading will fail once again with the PLS-00307 error:

```
FUNCTION calculate_net_profit (revenue_in IN NUMBER)
RETURN NUMBER IS -- How much did we make?
BEGIN
   ...
END calculate_net_profit;

FUNCTION calculate_net_profit (revenue_in IN NUMBER)
RETURN BOOLEAN IS -- Bankrupt or not?
BEGIN
   ...
END calculate_net_profit;
```

All of the overloaded programs must be defined within the same PL/SQL scope or block (anonymous block, module, or package). You cannot define one version in one block (scope level) and define another version in a different block. In the following example, I first define a chg_estimate procedure with a date parameter in the develop_analysis module. Then I define a chg_estimate procedure with a numeric parameter in the anonymous block in the body of develop_analysis:

```
PROCEDURE develop_analysis (quarter_end_in IN DATE, sales_in IN NUMBER)
IS
   PROCEDURE chg_estimate (date_in IN DATE) IS BEGIN ... END;
BEGIN
   DECLARE
      PROCEDURE chg_estimate
         (dollars_in IN NUMBER) IS BEGIN ... END;
   BEGIN
      chg_estimate (quarter_end_in);
      chg_estimate (dollars_in);
   END;
END develop_analysis;
```

When I try to compile this code I get the following error:

```
Error in line 8/column 3:
PLS-00306: wrong number or type of arguments in call to 'CHG_ESTIMATE'
```

Why do I get this error? I call chg_estimate with a date parameter (quarter_end_in) and it is defined in the declaration section of develop_analysis with a date parameter. I will answer this question ("Why do I get this error?") with another question: are these two procedures overloaded? The answer is no! Because they are defined in different PL/SQL blocks, they have a different scope and visibility. The scope of the date chg_estimate is the entire body of develop_analysis. The scope of the numeric chg_estimate is the anonymous block only, and it takes precedence over the date chg_estimate. There is no overloading going on here.

Forward Declarations

PL/SQL is rather fussy about its requirement that you declare a variable, cursor, or module before you use it in your code. Otherwise, how can PL/SQL be sure that the way you are using the object is appropriate? Since modules can call other modules, however, you can encounter situations where it is completely impossible to define all modules before any references to those modules are made. What if program A calls program B and program B calls program A? PL/SQL supports mutual recursion, where two or more programs directly or indirectly call each other.

If you do find yourself committed to mutual recursion, you will be very glad to hear that PL/SQL supports the *forward declaration* of local modules, which declares a module in advance of the actual definition of that program. This declaration makes that program available to be called by other programs even before the program definition.

Remember that both procedures and functions have a header and a body. A forward declaration consists simply of the program header, followed by a semi-colon (;). This construction is called the module header. This header, which must include the parameter list (and RETURN clause if a function) is all the information PL/SQL needs about a module in order to declare it and resolve any references to that module; a module should, after all, be a little black box.

The following example will illustrate the technique. I define two mutually recursive functions within a procedure. Consequently I have to declare just the header of my second function, total_cost, before the full declaration of net_profit:

```
PROCEDURE perform_calcs (year_in IN INTEGER)
IS
    /* Header only for total_cost function. */
    FUNCTION total_cost (. . .)  RETURN NUMBER;

    /* The net_profit function uses total_cost. */
    FUNCTION net_profit (. . .) RETURN NUMBER
    IS
    BEGIN
        RETURN tot_sales (. . .) - total_cost (. . .);
    END;

    /* The total_cost function uses net_profit. */
    FUNCTION total_cost (. . .)  RETURN NUMBER
    IS
    BEGIN
        IF net_profit (. . .) < 0
        THEN
            RETURN 0;
        ELSE
            RETURN . . .;
        END IF;
    END;
BEGIN
    . . .
END;
```

Here are some rules to remember concerning forward declarations:

- You cannot make forward declarations of a variable or cursor. This technique works only with modules (procedures and functions).

- The definition for a forwardly-declared program must be contained in the declaration section of the same PL/SQL block (anonymous block, procedure, function, or package) in which you code the forward declaration.

In some situations, you absolutely require forward declarations; in most situations, they just help make your code more readable and presentable. As with every other advanced or unusual feature of the PL/SQL language, use forward declarations only when you really need the functionality. Otherwise, the declarations simply add to the clutter of your program, which is the last thing you want.

Go Forth and Modularize!

As the PL/SQL language and Oracle tools mature, you will find that you are being asked to implement increasingly complex applications with this technology. To be quite frank, you don't have much of a chance of success in implementing such large-scale projects without an intimate familiarity with the modularization techniques available in PL/SQL.

While this book could not possibly provide a full treatment of modularization in PL/SQL, it should give you some solid pointers and a foundation from which to work. There is still much more for you to learn—the full capabilities of packages, the awesome range of package extensions Oracle Corporation now provides with the tools and database, and the various options for code reusability—and more.

Behind all of that technology, however, you must develop an instinct, a sixth sense, for modularization. Develop a deep and abiding allergy to code redundancy and the hardcoding of values and formulas. Apply a fanatic's devotion to the modular construction of true black boxes which easily plug-and-play in and across applications.

You will find yourself spending more time in the design phase and less time in debug mode. Your programs will be more readable and maintainable. They will stand as elegant testimonies to your intellectual integrity. You will be the most popular kid in your class and ... but enough already. I am sure you are properly motivated.

Go forth and modularize!

16

Packages

A *package* is a collection of PL/SQL objects that are packaged or grouped together within a special BEGIN-END syntax, a kind of "meta-block." Here is a partial list of the kinds of objects you can place in a package:

- Cursors

- Variables (scalars, records, tables, etc.)

- Constants

- Exception names

- PL/SQL table and record TYPE statements

- Procedures

- Functions

Packages are among the least understood and most underutilized features of PL/SQL. That is a shame, because the package structure is also one of the most useful constructs for building well-designed PL/SQL-based applications. Packages provide a structure in which you can organize your modules and other PL/SQL elements. They encourage proper structured programming techniques in an environment that often befuddles the implementation of structured programming.

Oracle Corporation itself uses the package construct to extend the PL/SQL language. Appendix C, *Built-In Packages*, contains descriptions of many of these predefined packages. In fact, the most basic operators of the PL/SQL language, such as the + and LIKE operators and the INSTR function, are all defined in a special package called STANDARD. If Oracle believes that packages are the way to go when it comes to building both fundamental and complex programs, don't you think that you could benefit from the same?

Packages are, by nature, highly modular. When you place a program unit into a package you automatically create a context for that program. By collecting related PL/SQL elements in a package, you express that relationship in the very structure of the code itself. Packages are often called "the poor man's objects" because they support some, but not all, object-oriented rules. For example, packages allow you to encapsulate and abstract your data and functions.

The PL/SQL package is a deceptively simple, powerful construct. You can in just a few hours learn the basic elements of package syntax and rules; there's not all that much to it. You can spend days and weeks, however, uncovering all the nuances and implications of the package structure. This chapter—and the next one filled with examples of packages—will help you absorb the features and benefits of the PL/SQL package more rapidly.

The Benefits of Packages

Before we explore all the aspects of working with packages, let's review some of the most important benefits of the package:

Enforced Information Hiding

When you build a package, you decide which of the package elements are public (can be referenced outside of the package) and which are private (available only within the package itself). You also can restrict access to the package to only the specification. In this way, you use the package to hide the implementational details of your programs. This is most important when you want to isolate the most volatile aspects of your application, such as platform dependencies, frequently changing data structures, and temporary workarounds.

Object-Oriented Design

While PL/SQL does not yet offer full object-oriented capabilities, packages do offer the ability to follow many object-oriented design principles. The package gives developers very tight control over how the modules and data structures inside the package can be accessed.

You can, therefore, embed all the rules about and access to your entities (whether they are database tables or memory-based structures) in the package. Because this is the only way to work with that entity, you have in essence created an abstracted and encapsulated object.

Top-Down Design

A package's specification can be written before its body. You can, in other words, design the interface to the code hidden in the package (the modules, their names, and their parameters) before you have actually implemented the modules themselves. This feature dovetails nicely with top-down design, in which you move from high-level requirements to functional decompositions to module calls.

Of course, you can design the names of standalone modules just as you can the names of packages and their modules. The big difference with the package specification is that you can compile it even without its body. Furthermore, and most remarkably, programs that call packaged modules will compile successfully— as long as the specification compiles.

Object Persistence

PL/SQL packages offer the ability to implement global data in your application environment. Global data is information that persists across application components; it isn't just local to the current module. If you designed screens with SQL*Forms or Oracle Forms, you are probably familiar with its GLOBAL variables, which allow you to pass information between screens. Those globals have their limitations (GLOBAL variables are always represented as fixed-length CHAR variables with a length of 254), but they sure can be useful.

Objects declared in a package specification (that is, visible to anyone with EXECUTE authority on that package) act as global data for all PL/SQL objects in the application. If you have access to the package, you can modify package variables in one module and then reference those changed variables in another module. This data persists for the duration of a user session (connection to the database).

If a packaged procedure opens a cursor, that cursor remains open and is available to other packaged routines throughout the session. You do not have to explicitly define the cursor in each program. You can open it in one module and fetch it in another module. In addition, package variables can carry data across the boundaries of transactions, because they are tied to the session itself and not to a transaction.

Performance Improvement

When an object in a package is referenced for the first time, the entire package (already compiled and validated) is loaded into memory (the Shared Global Area [SGA] of the RDBMS). All other package elements are thereby made immediately available for future calls to the package. PL/SQL does not have to keep retrieving program elements or data from disk each time a new object is referenced.

This feature is especially important in a distributed execution environment. You may reference packages from different databases across a local area or even a wide area network. You want to minimize the network traffic involved in executing your code.

Packages also offer performance advantages on the development side (with potential impact on overall database performance). The Oracle RDBMS automatically tracks the validity of all program objects (procedures, functions, packages) stored in the database. It determines what other objects that program is dependent on, such as tables. If a dependent object such as a table's structure changes, for example, then all programs that rely on that object are flagged as invalid. The database then automatically recompiles these invalid programs before they are used.

You can limit automatic recompiles by placing functions and procedures inside packages. If program A calls packaged module B, it does so through the package's specification. As long as the specification of a packaged module does not change, any program that calls the module is not flagged as invalid and will not have to be recompiled.

This chapter should provide you with all the information and examples you need to put packages to work immediately in your applications. If you are still unsure about packages after reading it, try out a couple of small packages. Test those hard-to-believe features like global package data to prove to yourself that they really work as advertised. Examine carefully the examples in Chapter 18. Do whatever you need to do to incorporate packages into every level of your application, from database server to client applications.

Overview of Package Structure

A package provides an extra layer of code and structure over that of an individual module. Many of the concepts needed to understand a package's structure will be familiar to you. In fact, a package is very similar in structure to a PL/SQL module that has local modules defined within it.

Whereas a module has a header and a body, a package has a specification and a body. Just as the module's header explains to a developer how to call that module, the package specification describes the different elements of the package that can be called. Beyond that, however, there are key differences between the constructs in the module and in the package.

A module's specification and body are connected by the IS keyword; both are required and one cannot be written without the other. The specification determines how you call the module. The body, after the IS keyword, contains the code that is executed when the function is used. These two components of a module are coded together and are completely inseparable.

A package also has a specification and a body, but the package's two parts are structured differently, and have a different significance, from those for a single module. With a package, the specification and body are completely distinct objects. You can write and compile the specification independently of the body. When you create and replace stored packages in the database, you perform this action separately for each of the specification and body.

This separation of specification and body allows you to employ top-down design techniques in a powerful way. Don't worry about the details of how a procedure or function is going to do its job. Just concentrate on the different modules you need and how they should be connected together.

The Specification

The package specification contains the definition or specification of all elements in the package that may be referenced outside of the package. These are called the public elements of the package (see the section entitled "Public and Private Package Elements" for more information). Figure 16-1 shows an example of a package specification containing two module definitions.

```
PACKAGE sp_timer
IS
    PROCEDURE capture (context_in IN VARCHAR2);
    PROCEDURE show_elapsed;
END sp_timer;
```

Figure 16-1. The specification of sp_timer package

Like the module, the package specification contains all the code that is needed for a developer to understand how to call the objects in the package. A developer should never have to examine the code behind the specification (which is the body) in order to understand how to use and benefit from the package.

The Body

The body of the package contains all the code behind the package specification: the implementation of the modules, cursors, and other objects. Figure 16-2 illustrates the body required to implement the specification of the sp_timer package shown in Figure 16-1.

```
PACKAGE BODY sp_timer
IS
    last_timing NUMBER := NULL;

    PROCEDURE capture
        (context_in IN VARCHAR2) IS
    BEGIN
        last_timing := DBMS_UTILITY.GET_TIME;
    END;

    PROCEDURE show_elapsed IS
    BEGIN
        DBMS_OUTPUT.PUT.LINE
            (DBMS_UTILITY.GET_TIME - last timing);
    END;
END sp_timer;
```

Figure 16-2. The body of sp_timer package

The body may also contain elements that do not appear in the specification. These are called the private elements of the package. A private element cannot be referenced outside of the package, since it does not appear in the specification.

The body of the package resembles a standalone module's declaration section. It contains both declarations of variables and the definitions of all package modules. The package body may also contain an execution section, which is called the *initialization section* because it is only run once, to initialize the package.

Package Syntax

The general syntax for the two parts of a package follows:

*   The package specification:

```
PACKAGE package_name
IS
[ declarations of variables and types ]

[ specifications of cursors ]

[ specifications of modules ]

END [ package_name ];
```

You can declare variables and include specifications of both cursors and modules (and only the specifications). You must have at least one declaration or specification statement in the package specification.

Notice that the package specification has its own BEGIN-END block syntax. This enables its independent existence and compilation from the package body.

- The package body:

```
PACKAGE BODY package_name
IS
[ declarations of variables and types ]

[ specification and SELECT statement of cursors ]

[ specification and body of modules ]

[ BEGIN
    executable statements ]

[ EXCEPTION
    exception handlers ]

END [ package_name ];
```

In the body you can declare other variables, but you do not repeat the declarations in the specification. The body contains the full implementation of cursors and modules. In the case of a cursor, the package body contains both specification and SQL statement for the cursor. In the case of a module the package body contains both the specification and body of the module.

The BEGIN keyword indicates the presence of an execution or initialization section for the package. This section can also optionally include an exception section.

As with a procedure or function, you can add the name of the package, as a label, after the END keyword in both the specification and package.

Public and Private Package Elements

A central concept of packages is the privacy level of its elements. One of the most valuable aspects of a package is its ability to actually enforce information hiding. With a package you can not only modularize your secrets behind a procedural interface, you can keep these parts of your application completely private.

An element of a package, whether it is a variable or a module, can either be private or public, as defined below:

Public

Defined in the specification. A public element can be referenced from other programs and PL/SQL blocks.

Private

Defined only in the body of the package, but does not appear in the specification. A private element cannot be referenced outside of the package. Any other element of the package may, however, reference and use a private element. Private elements in a package must be defined before they can be referenced by other elements of the package. If, in other words, a public procedure calls a private function, that function must be defined above the public procedure in the package body. You can, alternatively, use a forward declaration if you wish to keep your private programs at the bottom of the package body (see Chapter 15, *Procedures and Functions*).

If you find that a formerly private object such as a module or cursor should instead be made public, simply add that object to the package specification and recompile. It will then be visible outside of the package.

The distinct difference between public and private elements gives PL/SQL developers unprecedented control over their data structures and programs. Figure 16-3 shows a Booch diagram for the package that displays private and public package elements.

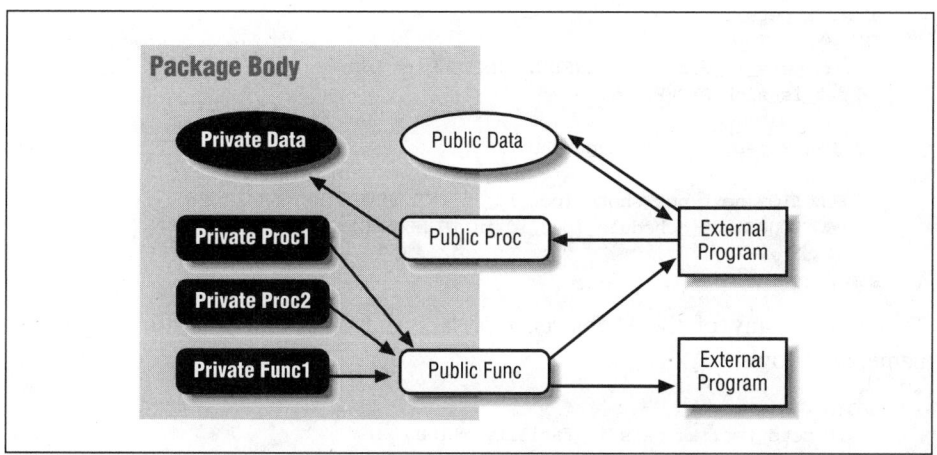

Figure 16-3. Booch diagram showing public and private package elements

The diagram offers a clear representation of the public/private character of PL/SQL packages. The large rectangle establishes the graphical boundary of the package. A program external to the package may only call a package element if a part of the element extends past the boundary of the package. Thus, all public elements defined in the specification straddle the package boundary. Part of the element is inside the boundary, and part lies outside, accessible to other programs.

---

* This diagram is named after Grady Booch, who pioneered many of the ideas of the package, particularly in the context of object-oriented design.

All the objects (data and modules) that are completely surrounded by the boundary of the package are private objects. These are defined only in the package body and do not appear in the specification. Because they are wholly contained, no external program can reference those elements.

Because the border of the public elements exists both outside and inside the package boundary, all elements in the package (private and public) can use those elements.

The next section offers a quick tour of a simple package which illustrates these concepts.

How to Reference Package Elements

A package owns its objects, just as a table owns its columns. You use the same dot notation to provide a fully qualified specification for a package's object as you would for a table's column.

The following package specification declares a constant, an exception, a cursor, and several modules:

```
PACKAGE pets_inc
IS
    max_pets_in_facility CONSTANT INTEGER := 120;
    pet_is_sick EXCEPTION;

    CURSOR pet_cur RETURN pet%ROWTYPE;

    FUNCTION next_pet_shots (pet_id_in IN NUMBER) RETURN DATE;
    PROCEDURE set_schedule (pet_id_in IN NUMBER);

END pets_inc;
```

To reference any of these objects, I preface the object name with the package name, as follows:

```
BEGIN
    IF pets_inc.max_pets_in_facility > 100
    THEN
        ...
    END IF;
EXCEPTION
    WHEN pets_inc.pet_is_sick
    THEN
        ...
END;

OPEN pets_inc.pet_cur;

:pet_master.next_appointment
        := pets_inc.next_pet_shots (:pet_master.pet_id);
```

If you do not preface the call to next_pet_shots with the package name, pets_inc, PL/SQL is not able to resolve the reference and the compile fails.

So, the rule for referencing package elements is simple and clear: *To reference a stored package element, use dot notation.* The one exception is that inside a package, you do not need to qualify references to other elements of that package. PL/SQL will automatically resolve your reference within the scope of the package.

Suppose, for example, that the set_schedule procedure of pets_inc references the max_pets_in_facility constant. Such a reference would be unqualified as shown here:

```
PROCEDURE set_schedule (pet_id_in IN NUMBER)
IS
   ...
BEGIN
   ...
   IF total_pets < max_pets_in_facility
   THEN
      ...
   END IF;
END;
```

Of course, if you want to reference the element of a second package inside the current package, you will need to include the name of that package.

Quick Tour of a Package

The pet maintenance package defined below is used by veterinarians to keep track of their patients and to determine when a pet needs another visit. Its specification identifies the public elements of the package. The body implements those elements and also creates two private elements.

The pets_inc package specification

The specification for the pets_inc package establishes the five public elements:

Name	Type	Description
petid_type	Subtype definition	Creates a programmer-defined subtype for the pet table primary key.
petid_nu	Variable declaration	Represents the primary key in pet table.
pet_cur	Cursor specification	Retrieves information about specified pet.
next_pet_shots	Function specification	Returns the date for next shots.
set_schedule	Procedure specification	Sets the schedule for the specified pet.

Here is the pets_inc package specification:

```
PACKAGE pets_inc
IS
   SUBTYPE petid_type IS pet.pet_id%TYPE;

   petid_nu petid_type;
```

```
CURSOR pet_cur (pet_name_in IN VARCHAR2) RETURN pet%ROWTYPE;

FUNCTION next_pet_shots (pet_id_in IN petid_type) RETURN DATE;

PROCEDURE set_schedule (pet_id_in IN petid_type)

END pets_inc;
```

The header for the package specification simply states PACKAGE. You do not explicitly indicate that it is the specification, as in PACKAGE SPECIFICATION. Instead, when you create the body of a package, you indicate explicitly in the first line of the definition that you are defining the body of the pets_inc package.

Since all of these elements are in the package, I can reference them in other programs, such as the following procedure:

```
PROCEDURE show_next_visit (pet_in IN VARCHAR2)
IS
    next_visit DATE;

    /* Declare record to receive row fetched from package cursor. */
    pet_rec pets_inc.pet_cur%ROWTYPE;
BEGIN
    /* Open the package-based cursor. */
    OPEN pets_inc.pet_cur (pet_in);

    /* Fetch from cursor into local record. */
    FETCH pets_inc.pet_cur INTO pet_rec;

    IF pets_inc.pet_cur%FOUND
    THEN
        /* Call packaged function to get next visit date. */
        next_visit := pets_inc.next_pet_shots (pet_rec.pet_id);

        /* Display the information. */
        DBMS_OUTPUT.PUT_LINE
            ('Schedule next visit for ' || pet_in || ' on ' ||
            TO_CHAR (next_visit));
    END IF;

    CLOSE pets_inc.pet_cur;
END;
```

The pets_inc package body

The package body for pets_inc contains elements shown in the following table:

Name	Type	Description
max_date	Constant declaration	Private variable. Maximum date allowed.
pet_cur	Cursor declaration	The cursor specification and SQL statement that retrieves information about specified pet.

Name	Type	Description
pet_status	Function definition	Private module. The specification and body for the function that returns the status of the pet.
next_pet_shots	Function definition	The specification and body for the function that returns date for next shots.
set_schedule	Procedure definition	The specification and body for the procedure that sets the schedule for the specified pet.

Here is the pets_inc package body:

```
PACKAGE BODY pets_inc
IS
    max_date CONSTANT DATE := SYSDATE + 10;

    CURSOR pet_cur (pet_name_in IN VARCHAR2) RETURN pet%ROWTYPE IS
        SELECT * FROM pet;

    FUNCTION pet_status  (pet_id_in IN petid_type) RETURN VARCHAR2
    IS
    BEGIN
        ... code behind the module ...
    END;

    FUNCTION next_pet_shots (pet_id_in IN petid_type) RETURN DATE
    IS
    BEGIN
        ... the code behind the module ...
    END;

    PROCEDURE set_schedule (pet_id_in IN petid_type)
    IS
    BEGIN
        ... the code behind the module ...
    END;

END pets_inc;
```

The body for the pet maintenance package contains the SELECT statement for the pet_cur cursor as well as the code required to implement all the modules.

This package body contains two private elements: max_date and pet_status. The max_date constant is used inside the package modules to validate dates that are manipulated in the package. The pet_status function is used by other modules to retrieve the status of the pet.

Because these elements are private, they can only be referenced by other elements of the package.

Observations about pets_inc

There are several interesting facts to point out about the previous two package components:

- The package specification does not contain any executable statements or exception handlers. A specification only specifies, or declares, those objects in the package that are public—that is, visible outside of the package and callable by other programs.

- The declaration of the petid_nu variable and the petid_type subtype are not repeated inside the body. The declaration in the specification is enough for the whole package. Any module in the body can reference variables declared in the specification.

- Both the body and the specification of pets_inc are actually extended declaration sections. The package body can, however, also contain execution and exception sections. These two parts of the package body make up the initialization section of the package, which is explored later in this chapter.

Now that you've had an introduction to the various parts of the package, let's take a closer look at each package component.

The Package Specification

The specification of a package lists all the objects in that package that are available for use in applications, and provides all the information a developer needs in order to use objects in the package. A package specification may contain any of the following object specification statements:

- *Variable declaration.* Any kind of variable declaration statement, from a Boolean variable to a character string to a number. This variable is then available outside of the package (as well as within the body of the package).

- *TYPE declaration* (PL/SQL Version 2 only). Any kind of valid TYPE statement, such as those to create a programmer-defined record type or a PL/SQL table. These complex data structures are then available outside of the package (as well as within the body of the package).

- *Exception declaration.* Declare exceptions in a package that can then be raised and handled outside of the package.

- *Cursor specification* (PL/SQL Version 2 only). Specify a cursor's name and its RETURN clause. This cursor can then be opened, fetched, and closed outside of the package (as well as within the body of the package). This is available only in PL/SQL Version 2 because Version 1 does not support the required RETURN clause for a cursor. For more information on cursors, see Chapter 6, *Database Interaction and Cursors.*

- *Module specification.* Place the full specification for a module in the package specification. A module specification is the module type (PROCEDURE or FUNCTION), module name, parameter list, and RETURN clause (for a function). This module can then be called both from within and outside of the package.

Of these object specification statements, only the cursor and the module need to be defined in the body of the package. The cursor and module, in other words, are not completely determined by the specification alone. The cursor needs its SELECT statement. The module needs its executable section.

The variable, TYPE, and exception declarations, on the other hand, do not need any additional code for completion—they need only their declaration statements. You can, therefore, write a package that consists solely of a specification and has no body at all, as you will see in the next section.

The specification is the API (Application Programmatic Interface) into the package's contents. A developer should never have to look at the actual code in a package in order to use an object in the specification.

The pets_inc package specification shown earlier contains a variable, cursor, and two modules. I do not need to know how the package function next_pet_shots determines the date when a pet will next need its shots. I need to know just the name of the function, its parameters, and the function's return datatype. Similarly, the package makes available a predefined cursor that gets me everything I need to know about a pet based on its primary key, pet_id. I, as a developer, do not have to understand the underlying data structures involved. The cursor might use a SELECT statement against a base table or against a three-way join with a sub-SELECT. None of that matters to me. In fact, my ignorance in these matters liberates my brain to work on how I can apply these package elements to good use in my application.

Packages Without Bodies

A package only requires a body if one of the following is true:

- You want to define private package elements
- You have included a cursor or module in your specification

A package may consist solely of declarations of public package elements. In this case, there is no need for a package body. This section offers two examples of scenarios where a bodiless package may be just the ticket.

A package of exceptions

The exception handler package in the next example declares a set of programmer-defined exception numbers and exceptions to go with them. It also declares a PL/SQL table to hold the associated error messages (see Chapter 8, *Exception Handlers*, for more information about exceptions and the pragma statement, EXCEPTION_INIT).

```
PACKAGE exchdlr
IS
    en_general_error NUMBER := -20000;
    exc_general_error EXCEPTION;
    PRAGMA EXCEPTION_INIT (exc_general_error, -20000);

    en_must_be_eighteen  NUMBER := -20001;
    exc_must_be_eighteen EXCEPTION;
    PRAGMA EXCEPTION_INIT (exc_must_be_eighteen, -20001);

    max_error_number_used NUMBER := -20001;

    TYPE error_msg_tabtype IS TABLE OF VARCHAR2 (240)
        INDEX BY BINARY_INTEGER;
    error_msg_table error_msg_tabtype;

END exchdlr;
```

Because this package does not specify any cursors or modules, I do not need to create a body for the exception handler package. In Chapter 8 I include a version of this package that does, in fact, specify two procedures in the package. That version does need a package body).

A package of magic values

A *magic value* is a literal that has special significance in a system. These values might be type codes or validation limits. Your users will tell you that these magic values never change. "I will always have only 25 line items in my profit-and-loss," one will say. "The name of the parent company," swears another, "will always be ATLAS HQ." Don't take these promises at face value, and never code them into your programs. Instead of writing code like this:

```
IF footing_difference BETWEEN 1 and 100
THEN adjust_line_item;
END IF;

IF cust_status = 'C'
THEN
    reopen_customer;
END IF;
```

you should instead replace the magic values with named constants, as follows:

```
IF footing_difference BETWEEN min_difference and max_difference
THEN adjust_line_item;
END IF;

IF cust_status = closed_status
THEN
   reopen_customer;
END IF;
```

The same magic values often appear in many different modules. Rather than declaring them repeatedly in each module, these magic values should be treated as global data in your application. And where can you create global data in PL/SQL? That's right, in a package! The bodiless package shown in the next example contains all the magic values in my application:

```
PACKAGE config_pkg
IS
   closed_status      CONSTANT VARCHAR2(1) := 'C';
   open_status        CONSTANT VARCHAR2(1) := 'O';
   active_status      CONSTANT VARCHAR2(1) := 'A';
   inactive_status    CONSTANT VARCHAR2(1) := 'I';

   min_difference     CONSTANT NUMBER := 1;
   max_difference     CONSTANT NUMBER := 100;

   earliest_date      CONSTANT DATE := SYSDATE;
   latest_date        CONSTANT DATE := ADD_MONTHS (SYSDATE, 120);

END config_pkg;
```

Using this package, my two IF statements above now become:

```
IF footing_difference
   BETWEEN config_pkg.min_difference and config_pkg.max_difference
THEN
   adjust_line_item;
END IF;

IF cust_status = config_pkg.closed_status
THEN
   reopen_customer;
END IF;
```

Notice that when you reference a package element you must use dot notation in the format package_name.object_name so the compiler can resolve the reference to the object's name. This is similar to prefacing a reference to a GLOBAL variable in Oracle Forms with the word GLOBAL, as in :GLOBAL.system_name.

If any of my magic values ever change, I need to modify only the assignment to the appropriate constant in the configuration package. I do not need to change a single program module. Just about every application I have reviewed (and many that I have written) mistakenly includes hardcoded magic values in the program. In every single case (especially those that I myself wrote), the developer had to make repeated changes to the programs, both during development and maintenance phases. It was often a headache, sometimes a nightmare; I cannot emphasize strongly enough the importance of consolidating all magic values into a single package, with or without a body.

Top-down design with bodiless packages

There is another motivation for writing a package without a body: you don't yet know what the body is going to look like. If you follow a top-down design methodology, you start with a general description of an application and gradually decompose into separate functional areas, programs, or individual statements. With the package structure you can immediately translate high-level refinements into code, while at the same time postponing a resolution of the actual implementation of that code. You can even compile references to unimplemented package modules as long as that module specification is available in a package specification.

Suppose I need to build an application to track calls about product quality. The functional areas of this application include call entry/maintenance, data validation, call analysis, and call assignment, and are represented in the packages shown below:

- Package to maintain support calls:

```
PACKAGE support
IS
    PROCEDURE add_call (call_id IN INTEGER);
    PROCEDURE remove_call (call_id IN INTEGER);
END support;
```

- Package to perform analysis on call workload:

```
PACKAGE workload
IS
    FUNCTION average (dept_id IN INTEGER)
        RETURN NUMBER;
    FUNCTION operator (operator_id IN INTEGER)
        RETURN NUMBER;
END workload;
```

Notice that I have only created package specifications. There is no body yet for these modules. Still, I can now implement the assigncall procedure below, referencing my "stubs." This procedure will compile successfully.

```
PROCEDURE assigncall
    (call_id IN INTEGER,
     operator_id IN INTEGER,
     dept_id IN INTEGER)
```

```
    IS
    BEGIN
       IF workload.operator (operator_id) <
          workload.average (dept_id)
       THEN
          support.add_call (call_id);
       END IF;
    END;
```

How can PL/SQL do this? It all goes back to the public/private boundary of packages. The package provides all the information you need to call package modules: name, parameters, RETURN type if a function. You should not need to know how a module is implemented. Conversely, the implementation of a module can change, and it should not affect your code—unless the module's header was affected (a parameter was removed, for example). When you write your own programs, the only thing PL/SQL needs to know at compile time is whether your call to a package module conforms to its specification. Of course, when you want to actually execute your application, you should throw some code into the package body.

The separation of specification and body in packages offers you tremendous flexibility in performing high-level design and implementation of your complex applications. See how great packages are? And we haven't even gotten to the body of the package yet!

Declaring Package Cursors

When you include a cursor in a package specification, you must use the RETURN clause of the cursor. It is an optional part of the cursor definition when that cursor is defined in the declaration section of a PL/SQL block. In a package specification, however, it is a necessary part of the structure.

The RETURN clause of a cursor indicates the data elements that are returned by a fetch from the cursor. Of course, these data elements are actually determined by the SELECT statement for that cursor, but the SELECT statement appears only in the body, not in the specification. The cursor specification must contain all the information a program needs to use that cursor; hence the need for the RETURN clause.

The RETURN clause may be made up of either of the following datatype structures:

- A record defined from a database table, using the %ROWTYPE attribute

- A record defined from a programmer-defined record (available in PL/SQL Version 2 only)

These variations are shown below, first with the specification and then with the body:

```
PACKAGE cursor_sampler
IS
    CURSOR caller_tab (id_in NUMBER) RETURN caller%ROWTYPE;
    /*
    || By placing this TYPE declaration in the specification, I give
    || access to the record outside of the package, so that other
    || programs can create caller records with this structure as well.
    */
    TYPE caller_rec IS RECORD (caller_id caller.caller_id%TYPE,
                               company_id company.company_id%TYPE);

    CURSOR caller_cur RETURN caller_rec;

END cursor_sampler;

PACKAGE BODY cursor_sampler IS

    /*
    || Notice that in the body I do not repeat the declarations of
    || the date variable and the custom record structure.
    */
    CURSOR hiredate_cur RETURN date_variable%TYPE
    IS
        SELECT hire_date FROM employee;

    CURSOR caller_key     RETURN caller.caller_id%TYPE
    IS
        SELECT caller_id FROM caller;

    CURSOR caller_tab (id_in NUMBER) RETURN caller%ROWTYPE
    IS
        SELECT * FROM caller WHERE caller_id = id_in;

    CURSOR caller_cur RETURN caller_rec
    IS
        SELECT caller_id, company_id FROM caller;

END cursor_sampler;
```

You have a lot to gain by creating cursors in packages and making those cursors available to the developers on a project. Crafting precisely the data structures you need for your application is hard and careful work. These same structures—and the data in them—are used in your PL/SQL programs, almost always through the use of a cursor. If you do not package up your cursors and provide them "free of charge and effort" to all developers, they will each write their own variations of these cursors. And they will write many, many different cursors, with different sets of columns and expressions in the SELECT list, and different WHERE clauses. This decentralized effort will result in increased development and debugging time. And then what do you do when your data structures change? You have to hunt down every one of those cursors and make changes as required by the alteration.

A much better solution is to think through in advance the common ways that developers will need to access data through cursors, and then place these in one or more packages. These cursors will not only provide the standard list of columns and expressions, but also perform the necessary joins, subselects, and so on required to retrieve that data. Publish the specification and perhaps even the body, so that everyone knows the SQL behind the cursors. Provide examples of how to reference and use the cursors. Build a mechanism for adding new cursors to the packages as developers discover new variations of data access.

Then, developers do not necessarily have to understand how to join three or six different highly-normalized tables to get the right set of data. They can just pick a cursor and leave the data analysis to someone else. This process is very similar to the view-building effort required to support real ease of use in an *ad hoc* query/EIS tool. Perhaps more importantly, everyone will be "singing from the same songbook." If the data structure changes and a new table must now be joined into an existing cursor in order to accurately query the correct rows, you simply change the cursor in the package. If the cursor specification (name, parameters, and RETURN clause) itself does not change, then you don't even have to recompile all the programs using that cursor.

See Chapter 6, *Database Interaction and Cursors*, for more information about the cursor RETURN clause.

NOTE   The file named *curs_ret.sp* on the companion disk contains a package of cursors for the employee and department tables; they should give you an idea of what will be possible in your own, more complex environments.

The Package Body

The package body contains all the code required to implement the package specification. As you saw in the previous section, some packages do not even need a body. A package body is required when any of the following conditions is true:

- *The package specification contains a cursor declaration.* You need to specify the SELECT statement in the package body.

- *The package specification contains a procedure or function declaration.* You need to define the module in the package body.

- *You wish to execute code in the initialization section of the package body.* The package specification does not support an execution section (executable statements within a BEGIN...END); you can do this only in the body.

The package body can have declaration, execution, and exception sections, just like a normal PL/SQL block. The declaration section contains the definition of any objects in public packages (listed in the specification) and also the definition of any private objects (not listed in the specification).

The execution section is the "initialization section" of the package. It is executed when the package is instantiated (which usually occurs the very first time you reference a package element) and is described in more detail below. The exception section handles any exceptions raised in the initialization section.

A package body could have an empty declaration section but include an initialization section (see the last section in the chapter). A package body could also have a declaration section without an initialization section—this is the format of most of the packages you will write.

Declare in Specification or Body

If you declare a variable, exception, TYPE, or constant in the package specification, you do not also declare that same object in the body. If you declare it in the specification, it is available in the package body without an explicit, local declaration. This can be a hard thing to get used to; the object is not declared in the immediately visible scope of code, yet your package modules compile just fine. Remember: objects declared in the package specification are global data, so they should certainly be available within the body of that same package!

If you do try to redeclare an object within the body, you receive the following kind of error:

```
PLS-00371 at one more declaration for 'PETID_NU' is permitted in the
          declaration section
```

If you declare objects in the package body that are outside of all the modules, but not in the package specification, then those objects are global within the package but invisible outside of the package. The values held by package variables persist from one call to a package module to another call to the same or a different package module. Such objects are called *package data*, since their scope is the package. Any module may reference such an object without explicitly declaring it in the module itself.

Synchronize Body with Package

The package specification and the package body of a package must be kept synchronized. Whenever you make a change in the package body to the name, parameter list, datatype, default value, or RETURN clause of a public object (to the portion of the object, in other words, that must be in the package specification), you must make that same change to the package specification. If the specifications for the objects do not match exactly, the body will fail to compile. In the PL/SQL language, the specification (like the proverbial customer) is always right.

Suppose that in my pet maintenance package, I decide to change the datatype of the pet_id_in parameter in next_pet_shot from the subtype for the primary key to simply NUMBER. My package body then looks like this:

```
PACKAGE BODY pets_inc
IS
   ...
   FUNCTION next_pet_shot (pet_id_in IN NUMBER) RETURN DATE
   IS BEGIN ... END;
   ...
END pets_inc;
```

while my package specification remains the same:

```
PACKAGE pets_inc
IS
   ...
   FUNCTION next_pet_shot (pet_id_in IN petid_type) RETURN DATE;
   ...
END pets_inc;
```

When I try to compile the package body, I receive the following error:

```
PLS-00323: subprogram 'NEXT_PET_SHOT' is declared in a package
           specification and must be defined in the package body.
```

This can be a very alarming and confusing error. The next_pet_shot subprogram must be "defined"? "But it's right there in the package body!" you exclaim. "What is wrong with that compiler?" The problem is that the parameter list of next_pet_shot in the body is different from that in the specification. Even if the datatype to which the petid_type subtype evaluates is a NUMBER, PL/SQL will not accept the version in the body as the implementation for the module in the specification.

When PL/SQL tries to compile a package body, it checks to see that everything defined in the package specification has a body (cursor or module) in the package body. If PL/SQL does not find an exact match for a specification in the body, then it decides that that object is not defined in the package body at all. PL/SQL doesn't look at the object named next_pet_shot in the body and say, "Gee, you really are so close to the version in the specification!" It just throws up its hands and points to the incriminating module. It would be nice to have PL/SQL automatically synchronize the body with the specification, but there are all sorts of complications and, anyway, it would probably destroy something you wanted left intact. So you just have to remember to make changes in both places.

Package Data

Some of the most interesting and useful features of packages have to do with package data. Package data is any data structure declared in a package body or specification. With package data you can:

- Create global variables that are accessible from any program in the current session.

- Create persistent data structures—data that retains its value throughout your Oracle session, even when no package programs are running.

This section describes the architecture of and uses for package data.

Architecture of Package-Based Data

The first time you reference a package element, the entire package (compiled) is loaded into the SGA of the Oracle database instance on the server. That code is then shared by all sessions having EXECUTE authority on the package.

The data that is declared by the package elements is also instantiated in the SGA, but it is not shared across all sessions. Instead, each Oracle session is assigned its own private PL/SQL area, which contains a copy of the package data (see Figure 16-4). This private PL/SQL area is maintained in the SGA for as long as your session is running. The values assigned to your packaged data structures also remain available in the SGA throughout your session. In other words, they persist for the duration.

Contrast this behavior with the variables instantiated in the declaration section of a standalone module. The scope of those variables is restricted to the module. When the module terminates, the memory and values associated with those variables are released. They are no more.

The scope of a package is, however, the entire schema in which it is defined. Any session that has EXECUTE authority on the package may access the package and use the data defined inside the package. Because the scope of the package data is the entire session, their values are maintained in the SGA. You are not, in other words, simply sharing the data structure among your programs. You share the values in those structures as well.

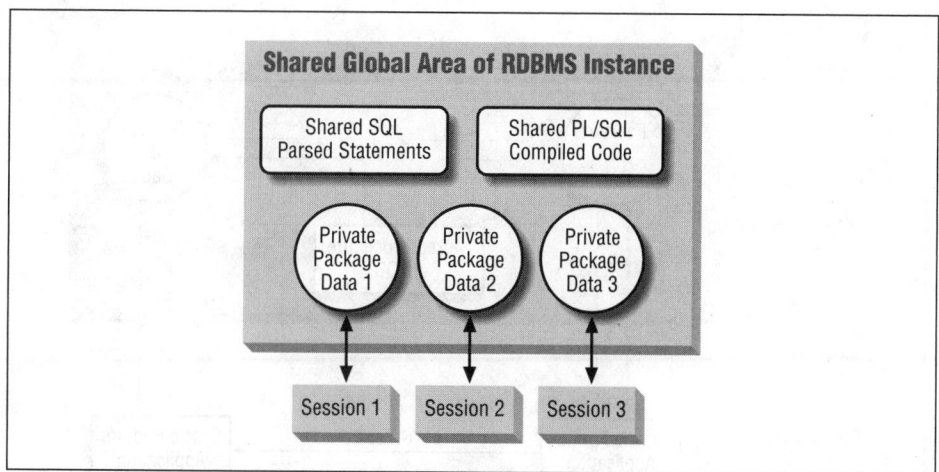

Figure 16-4. Private PL/SQL areas in shared memory

Global Within a Single Oracle Session

As a result of the SGA-based architecture, package data structures act as globals within the PL/SQL environment. Remember, however, that they are globals only within a single Oracle session or connection. Package data is not shared across sessions. If you need to share data between different Oracle sessions, you must use the DBMS_PIPE package (see Appendix C, *Built-In Packages*, for more information).

You need to be careful about assuming that different parts of your application do maintain a single Oracle connection. There are times when a tool may establish a new connection to the database to perform an action. If this occurs, the data you have stored in a package in the first connection will not be available.

Consider the scenario in Figure 16-5. An Oracle Forms application has saved values to data structures in a package. When the form calls a stored procedure, this stored procedure can access these same package-based variables and values as the form, because they share a single Oracle connection.

The form then uses the RUN_PRODUCT built-in to kick off a report using Oracle Reports. By default, Oracle Reports uses a second connection to the database (same user name and password) to run the report. So even if this report accesses the same package and its data structures, the values in those data structures will not match those used by the form. It is a different Oracle connection and a new instantiation of the data structures.

Just as there are two types of data structures in the package (public and private), there are also two types of global package data to consider: global public data

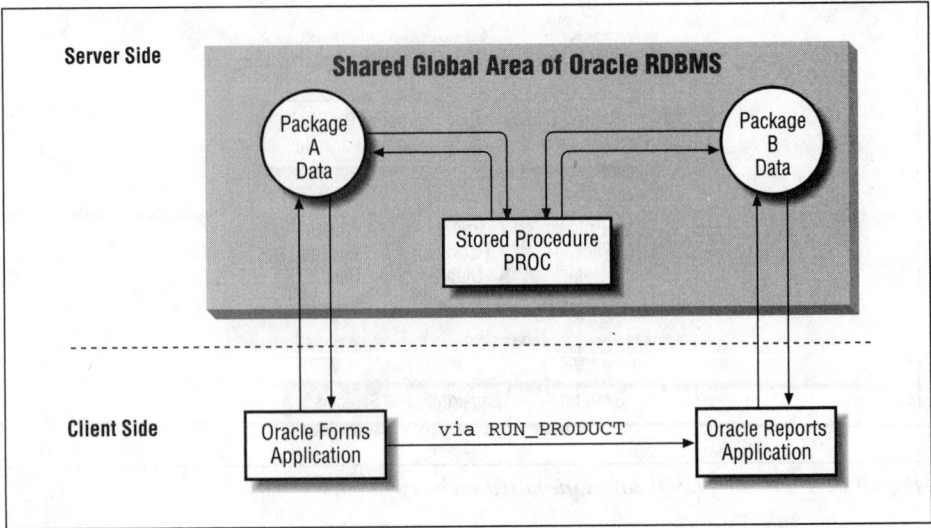

Figure 16-5. Two Oracle connections between Oracle Forms and Oracle Reports

and global private data. The next two sections explore the differences between these kinds of package data.

Global Public Data

Any data structure declared in the specification of a package is a global, public data structure. This means that any program outside of the package can access the data structure. You can, for example, define a PL/SQL table in a package specification and use it to keep a running list of all employees selected for a raise. You can also create a package of constants which are used throughout all of your programs. Then all developers will reference the packaged constants instead of hardcoding the values in their programs.

You can also change global public data structures, unless they are variables declared as CONSTANTs in the declaration statement.

Global data is the proverbial "loose cannon" of programming. It is very convenient to declare, and have available from any module at any point in time, all sorts of information. Reliance on global data structures, however, leads to unstructured code that is full of side effects.

Remember that the specification of a module should give you all the information you need to understand how to call and use that module. If the program reads and/or writes global data structures, you cannot tell this from the module specification. You cannot be sure of what is happening in your application and which program changes what data.

It is always preferable to pass data as parameters in and out of modules. In that way, the reliance on those data structures is documented in the specification and can be accounted for by the developer.

On the other hand, you should create named, global data structures for information that truly is global to an application, such as constants and configuration information.

Global Private Data

A global but private data structure, also called package-level data, is declared in the body of the package. Since it does not appear in the specification, this data cannot be referenced outside of the package—only from within the package, by other package elements. This data only exists on the level of the package.

A data structure declared in a package still does function as a global. Since it is not declared in any specific module's declaration section, it is available to all modules, cursors, and other elements of the package.

In the following example of the sp_timer package (the full version is on the disk), the last_timing variable is a package-level global. It is referenced in both of the modules, capture and elapsed. The capture procedures sets the value of last_timing. The elapsed function uses the value of last_timing to compute the elapsed time.

```
/* Filename on companion disk: sptimer.sps. */
PACKAGE BODY sp_timer
   IS
      /* Package variable which stores the last timing made */
      last_timing NUMBER := NULL;

      PROCEDURE capture (context_in IN VARCHAR2 := NULL)
      /* Save current time and context to package variables. */
      IS
      BEGIN
         last_timing := DBMS_UTILITY.GET_TIME;
      END;

      FUNCTION elapsed RETURN NUMBER IS
      BEGIN
         IF last_timing IS NULL
         THEN
            RETURN NULL;
         ELSE
            RETURN DBMS_UTILITY.GET_TIME - last_timing;
         END IF;
      END;

   END sp_timer;
```

Providing an Interface to Global Data

You will often want to build a programmatic interface around your global data, due to the following drawbacks of global data:

- *Loss of control.* When you declare a data structure in the package specification, that variable (or PL/SQL table or whatever) becomes fair game for any program that wants to change it (unless it is declared as a CONSTANT). If a program can make changes without any controls, then you lose the ability to apply rules to the way the data is used. It is impossible to provide an object orientation to your application if this happens.

- *Maintenance headaches.* When you allow programmers to make direct references to package data structures, you are limiting your ability to change those data structures over time. Suppose that last year I implemented an in-memory profit-and-loss statement as a string variable filled with numbers padded to a length of ten. Suppose too that the total profit entry in the statement is the fourteenth number in the string. If I declared this string in my package specification, programmers who needed access to the statement would write a line of code like this:

```
total_profit_loc := 14;
total_profit := SUBSTR (pl.stmt, (total_profit_loc-1)*10 + 1, 10);
```

Then along comes PL/SQL Release 2.3 and I can use PL/SQL tables of records to store my many P & L statements. Suddenly my hands are tied. If I change the underlying data structure of my P & L statement, every single program that directly accessed the filled string will have to be changed.

You can regain control of your package data and also ease your maintenance and enhancement frustrations by building a programmatic interface around your data. This interface is also referred to as "get and set programs" and "access routines," because they usually get and set the values of data and control access to those data structures.

In the preceding code, if I had instead declared the stmt string in the body of my pl package, I could have provided functions to retrieve the different elements of the statement as follows:

```
total_profit := pl.retrieve ('total_profit');
```

I would then be free to change the underlying data structure from filled string to PL/SQL table. As long as the interface to the pl.retrieve function did not change, none of the programs that relied on the old data would have to change. My programmatic interface would have protected both my data structure and all the programs that relied on it.

Consider the simple sp_timer package (the body of which was reviewed in the last section). The whole point of this package is to keep track of the elapsed time, down to the 100th of a second. It calculates the elapsed time by storing the starting point in a private global variable, last_timing. If a programmer could have direct access to this variable, he could change its value and disrupt the elapsed time calculation. So instead of defining last_timing in the specification, I place it in the body and instead provide two modules in the specification as follows:

```
PACKAGE sp_timer
IS
    PROCEDURE capture (context_in IN VARCHAR2 := NULL);

    FUNCTION elapsed RETURN NUMBER;

END sp_timer;
```

The only way a developer can change last_timing is through the capture procedure. The only way a developer can retrieve the elapsed time is through the elapsed function. My data structure is protected.

Package Initialization

The first time your application makes a reference to a package element, the entire package (in pre-compiled form) is loaded into the SGA of the database instance, making all objects immediately available in memory. You can supplement this automatic instantiation of the package code with the automatic execution of initialization code for the package. This initialization code is contained in the optional initialization section of the package body.

The initialization section consists of all statements following the BEGIN statement through the END statement for the entire package body. It is called the initialization section because the statements in this section are executed only once, the first time an object in the package is referenced (a program is called, a cursor is opened, or a variable is used in an assignment, to name a few possibilities). The initialization section initializes the package; it is commonly used to set values for variables declared and referenced in the package.

The initialization section is a powerful mechanism: PL/SQL detects automatically when this code should be run. You do not have to explicitly execute the statements, and you can be sure they are run only once.

Drawbacks of Package Initialization

There are some disadvantages to the initialization section.

- It can be dangerous to have your tool perform actions for you that are not explicitly triggered by a user or developer action.

- It is harder to trace actions triggered automatically by the tool ("Now where does that variable get set? How did that record get inserted into that table? I don't see it in any of my code!").

- Executable statements buried in initialization sections are much harder to maintain; what are the chances that a new developer will think to search the ends of packages for the cause of (or solution to) a problem?

In my experience, the initialization section is rarely used. By and large, you spend most of your package development time in the declaration area of the package body, since you use the package mostly to define modules, which can then be called outside of the package.

Use Initialization Section for Complex Logic

Use the initialization section only when you need to set the initial values of package elements using rules and complex logic that cannot be handled in the default value syntax for variables. You do not need an initialization section to set the value of the constant earliest_date to today's date. Instead, simply declare the variable with a default value. The straightforward declaration in the package specification looks like this:

```
PACKAGE config_pkg
IS
    earliest_date CONSTANT DATE := SYSDATE;
END config_pkg;
```

and should always be used in place of something like this:

```
PACKAGE config_pkg
IS
    earliest_date DATE;
END config_pkg;

PACKAGE BODY config_pkg
/*
|| This package body only exists to provide an initial value for the
|| earliest_date variable. This could have been done in the declaration
|| itself. This is not a justifiable use of an initialization section.
*/
IS
BEGIN
```

```
          earliest_date := SYSDATE;
     END config_pkg;
```

Side Effects

Avoid setting the values of package global data from other packages within the initialization section. This precaution could prevent havoc in code execution and confusion for maintenance programmers. As the following example demonstrates, keep the initialization section code focused on the current package so it can get its job done. Remember: this code is executed whenever your application first tries to use the package element. You don't want to have your users sitting idle while the package performs some snazzy, expensive setup computations that could be parceled out to different packages or even triggers in the application.

```
PACKAGE BODY company IS
BEGIN
   /*
   || Initialization section of company_pkg updates the global
   || package data of another package. This is a no-no!
   */
   SELECT SUM (salary)
     INTO employee_pkg.max_salary
     FROM employee;

END company;
```

If your initialization requirements do not fit within the above guidelines, you should consider alternatives to the initialization section, such as grouping your startup statements together into a procedure in the package. Give the procedure a name like init_environment. Then, at the appropriate initialization point in your application, call the init_environment procedure to set up your session.

Load Session Data in Initialization Section

A perfectly legitimate use of the initialization section is shown below for the session_pkg. This package contains information about the current user session—the name of the user, the Oracle account name, user preferences, and so forth. All the package global variables are set the very first time any of the variables are referenced in an application's code. I need to use an initialization section because most (but not all) of the user information is stored in a table.

The package specification declares all the variables and sets whatever values it can:

```
PACKAGE session_pkg
IS
   user_name VARCHAR2 (80);
   user_id VARCHAR2 (10) := USER;
```

```
    show_lov VARCHAR2 (1);
    show_toolbar VARCHAR2 (1);
    printer VARCHAR2 (30);

END session_pkg;
```

The package body selects the data from the table to fill in the remaining values. If
no match is found for the current user, an exception section traps that problem
and assigns default values for an "unregistered" user. If any other exception is
raised, then RAISE_APPLICATION_ERROR communicates the problem back to the
calling program and most likely halts execution of the application, as shown in
this example:

```
PACKAGE BODY session_pkg
/*
|| Look, Ma! No declarations in the package body at all!
|| Just an initialization section to support the specification.
*/
IS
BEGIN
    SELECT first_name || ' ' || last_name,
            show_lov_flag,
            show_toolbar_flag,
            default_printer
        INTO user_name, user_id, show_lov, show_toolbar, printer
        FROM user_config
       WHERE user_id = USER;

EXCEPTION
    WHEN NO_DATA_FOUND
    THEN
        /* No record in config table for this user. */
        user_name:= 'NOT REGISTERED';
        show_lov:= 'Y';
        show_toolbar:= 'Y';
        printer:= 'lpt1';

    WHEN OTHERS
    THEN
        /* Display generic error for unknown problem */
        RAISE_APPLICATION_ERROR
            (-20000, 'Problem obtaining user profile for ' || USER);

END session_pkg;
```

17

Calling PL/SQL Functions in SQL

PL/SQL is a procedural language extension to SQL, so you can also issue native calls to SQL statements such as SELECT, INSERT, and UPDATE from within your PL/SQL programs. Until Release 2.1 of PL/SQL (which comes with Oracle7 Release 7.1 of the RDBMS), however, you weren't able to place your own PL/SQL functions inside a SQL statement.

NOTE   The capabilities described in this chapter are available only in PL/SQL Release 2.1 and above.

Looking at the Problem

The restriction on putting PL/SQL functions inside an SQL statement often resulted in cumbersome SQL statements and redundant implementation of business rules. Suppose, for example, you need to calculate and use an employee's total compensation both in native SQL and also in your forms. The computation itself is straightforward enough:

```
Total compensation = salary + bonus
```

My SQL statement would include this formula:

```
SELECT employee_name, salary + NVL (bonus, 0)
   FROM employee;
```

while my Post-Query trigger in my Oracle Forms application would employ the following PL/SQL code:

```
:employee.total_comp := :employee.salary + NVL (:employee.bonus, 0);
```

In this case, the calculation is very simple, but the fact remains that if you need to change the total compensation formula for any reason (different kinds of bonuses, for example), you would then have to change all of these hardcoded calculations both in the SQL statements and in the front end application components.

A far better approach is to create a function that returns the total compensation:

```
FUNCTION total_comp
     (salary_in IN employee.salary%TYPE, bonus_in IN employee.bonus%TYPE)
     RETURN NUMBER
IS
BEGIN
     RETURN salary_in + NVL (bonus_in, 0);
END;
```

Then I could replace the formulas in my code as follows:

```
SELECT employee_name, total_comp (salary, bonus)
   FROM employee;

:employee.total_comp := total_comp (:employee.salary, :employee.bonus);
```

Until Release 2.1 of PL/SQL the above SELECT statement raised the following error:

```
ORA-00919: invalid function
```

because there was no mechanism for SQL to resolve references to programmer-defined functions stored in the database. Now, Oracle has made the relationship between PL/SQL and SQL more of a two-way street. This makes sense, since the functions are stored in the database (in tables, of course) and therefore easily accessible at the SQL layer via a SELECT statement.

With PL/SQL Release 2.1, you can now call stored functions anywhere in a SQL statement where an expression is allowed, including the SELECT, WHERE, START WITH, GROUP BY, HAVING, ORDER BY, SET, and VALUES clauses (since stored procedures are in and of themselves PL/SQL executable statements, they cannot be embedded in a SQL statement).

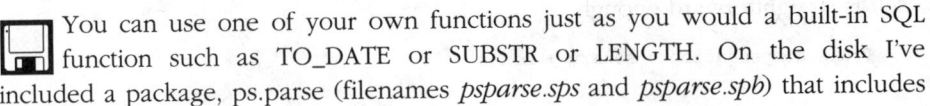 You can use one of your own functions just as you would a built-in SQL function such as TO_DATE or SUBSTR or LENGTH. On the disk I've included a package, ps.parse (filenames *psparse.sps* and *psparse.spb*) that includes

a function that returns the number of atomics (words and/or delimiters) in a string. I can employ this directly in a SQL statement to show the distribution of words in a series of textual notes, as follows:

```
SELECT line_number,
       ps_parse.number_of_atomics (line_text) AS num_words
  FROM notes
ORDER BY num_words DESC;
```

Notice that, in this case, I have assigned a column alias to my function call using the "AS" syntax. I can then use that alias in the ORDER BY without having to repeat the syntax for the function call itself.

The ability to place programmer-defined PL/SQL functions inside SQL is a very powerful enhancement to the Oracle development environment. With these functions you will be able to do the following:

- *Consolidate business rule logic into a smaller number of well tuned and easily maintained functions.* You do not have to repeat this logic across individual SQL statements and PL/SQL programs. This is probably the most far-reaching and important advantage of using functions in PL/SQL.

- *Improve the performance of your SQL statements.* SQL is a nonprocedural language, yet application requirements often demand procedural logic in your SQL. The SQL language is robust enough to let you get at the answer, but in some situations it is a very inefficient way to get that answer. Embedded PL/SQL can sometimes do the job much more quickly. There is also, of course, some overhead associated with calling these functions from within SQL. You will consequently need to evaluate carefully when and where PL/SQL functions in SQL will do you the most good.

- *Simplify your SQL statements.* All the reasons you have to modularize your PL/SQL code apply to SQL as well, particularly the need to hide complicated expressions and logic behind a function specification. From the DECODE statement to nested, correlated subselects, the readability of many SQL statements will benefit from programmer-defined functions.

- *Perform actions in SQL which are otherwise impossible.* SQL is a set-at-a-time language, identifying a set of rows and applying actions to those rows. It does not support iterative processing against an individual column value. Suppose you need to identify the number of occurrences of a substring within the names of companies. With pure SQL, you cannot do this. You can, on the other hand, apply a PL/SQL function to the company name in a SELECT list which can perform this kind of iterative processing.

You can place functions in a VALUES list, a SET clause, or a GROUP BY clause, as shown in the following:

- VALUES list. Consider the following example:

```
INSERT INTO notes
    (call_id, line_text, line_number)
VALUES
    (:call.call_id, :note.text, next_line_number (:call.call_id));
```

The next_line_number function obtains the next sequence number for the notes for that particular call (i.e., while you might use the sequence generator to obtain the next unique call ID number, the line_number for notes for a given call always starts from one, so a sequence generator is inapplicable).

- SET clause. The max_compensation function returns the maximum compensation possible for an employee's department.

```
UPDATE employee SET salary = max_compensation (department_id)
   WHERE employee_id = 1005;
```

In this case the max_compensation function replaces a subselect, which would use the SQL AVG function to compute the value.

- GROUP BY clause. My company has done a very poor job of normalizing its job titles; there are 15 different variations of VICE PRESIDENT, 20 different kinds of MANAGER, and so forth. The following SELECT statement cuts through all the confusion and displays the total salary for each "category" of job.

```
SELECT job_category (job_title_id) as title, SUM (salary)
   FROM employee
   GROUP BY title;
```

The function is used both in the SELECT list and in the GROUP BY.

Syntax for Calling Stored Functions in SQL

You call a stored function from within a SQL expression using the same syntax as in a PL/SQL expression:

```
[schema_name.] [pkg_name.] [func_name[@db_link_name] [parameter_list]
```

where schema_name is the optional name of the schema in which the function is defined (the schema is usually your own Oracle account), pkg_name is the optional name of the package in which the function is defined (if it is not a standalone function), func_name is the name of the function, db_link_name is the optional name of the database link if you are executing a remote procedure call, and parameter_list is the optional list of parameters for the function.

Suppose that the calc_sales function is defined as follows:

```
FUNCTION calc_sales
    (company_id_in IN company.company_id%TYPE,
     status_in IN order.status_code%TYPE := NULL)
RETURN NUMBER;
```

then here are some different ways it might be called inside SQL:

- As a standalone function:

```
SELECT calc_sales (1001, 'O')
   FROM orders;
```

- As a package-based function:

```
SELECT sales_pkg.calc_sales (1001, 'O')
   FROM orders;
```

- As a remote, package-based function call:

```
SELECT sales_pkg.calc_sales@NEW_YORK (1001, 'O')
   FROM orders;
```

- As a standalone function in a specific schema:

```
SELECT scott.calc_sales (1001, 'O')
   FROM orders;
```

SQL will properly parse all of these variations, but you should always avoid hard-coding the module's schema and database link directly in your SQL statements (as shown in the third and fourth bullets). Instead, you should create synonyms that hide this information. That way, if you ever need to change the owner of the function or move it to a different database instance, you will have to change only the synonym, as opposed to all the individual SQL statements that call that function.

When you use a stored function in a SQL statement, you must use positional notation; named and mixed notations are not allowed. You can only call calc_sales by listing both arguments in their positional order.

Requirements for Stored Functions in SQL

There are several requirements a programmer-defined PL/SQL function must meet in order to be callable from within a SQL statement:

- *The function must be stored in the database.* A function defined in an Oracle Developer/2000 PL/SQL library or in an individual form cannot be called from within SQL. There would be no way for SQL to resolve the reference to the function.

- *The function must be a row-specific function, not a column or group function.* The function can apply only to a single row of data, not an entire column of data that crosses rows.

- *All of the function's parameters must use the IN mode.* Neither IN OUT nor OUT parameters are allowed in SQL-embedded stored functions: You should never have IN OUT and OUT parameters in functions, period. Whether or not you are going to use that function inside a SQL statement, such parameters constitute side effects of the main purpose of the function, which is to return a single value.

- *The datatypes of the function's parameters,* as well as the datatype of the RETURN clause of the function, must be recognized within the Oracle Server. While all of the Oracle Server datatypes are valid within PL/SQL, PL/SQL has added new datatypes not (yet) supported in the database. These datatypes include BOOLEAN, BINARY_INTEGER, PL/SQL tables, PL/SQL records, and programmer-defined subtypes.

- Functions defined in packages must have a RESTRICT_REFEFRENCES pragma. If you want to call, from SQL, a function defined in a package, you will need to add a pragma to the package specification asserting explicitly that this function is valid for SQL execution. See the section called "Calling Packaged Functions in SQL" for more details on this step.

All of the following function specifications would be rejected if used within a SQL statement:

```
/* SQL doesn't know about PL/SQL tables. */
TYPE string_tabtype IS TABLE OF VARCHAR2(30) INDEX BY BINARY_INTEGER;
FUNCTION temp_table RETURN string_tabtype;

/* SQL doesn't know about Booleans. */
FUNCTION call_is_open (call_id_in IN call.call_id%TYPE) RETURN BOOLEAN;

FUNCTION calc_sales
    (company_id_in IN NUMBER, use_closed_orders_in IN BOOLEAN)
RETURN NUMBER;
```

Restrictions on PL/SQL Functions in SQL

Stored functions in SQL offer tremendous power. As you might expect, however, power introduces the possibility of abuse and the need for responsible action. In the context of SQL, abuse of power involves the rippling impact of side effects in a function. Consider the following function:

```
FUNCTION total_comp
    (salary_in IN employee.salary%TYPE, bonus_in IN employee.bonus%TYPE)
    RETURN NUMBER
```

```
    IS
    BEGIN
       UPDATE employee SET salary = salary_in / 2;
       RETURN salary_in + NVL (bonus_in, 0);
    END;
```

This simple little calculation, introduced at the beginning of the chapter, now also updates the salary of all employees to half of the specified value. This action affects the results of the query from which total_comp might originate; even worse, it affects any other SQL statement in this session.

Along with modification of database tables, modification of package variables is another side effect of stored functions in SQL. Package variables act as globals within a particular session. A function that changes a package variable could have an impact on another stored function or procedure, which in turn could affect a SQL statement using that stored function.

A PL/SQL function could also cause a side effect in the WHERE clause of a query. The query optimizer can reorder the evaluation of predicates in the WHERE clause to minimize the number of rows processed. A function executing in this clause could therefore subvert the query optimization process.

My general recommendation for a function is that it should be narrowly focused on computing and returning a value. But a recommendation is not enough when it comes to database integrity: in order to guard against nasty side effects and upredictable behavior, the Oracle Server makes it impossible for your stored function in SQL to take any of the following actions:

- The stored function may not modify database tables. It cannot execute an INSERT, DELETE, or UPDATE statement.

- A stored function that is called remotely or through a parallelized action may not read or write the values of package variables. The Oracle Server does not support side effects that cross user sessions.

- A stored function can update the values of package variables only if that function is called in a SELECT, VALUES, or SET clause. If the store function is called in the WHERE or GROUP BY clause, it cannot write package variables.

- Prior to Oracle8, you can call very few built-in packaged programs inside a function which will be used in SQL. This means that your PL/SQL function cannot contain calls to DBMS_OUTPUT.PUT_LINE, DBMS_PIPE, and DBMS_SQL, to name just a few. In some cases, this makes perfect sense. If you are not allowed to perform an UPDATE, you certainly shouldn't be able to use DBMS_SQL to sneak that UPDATE by "the censors." But with other packages, the restriction is unnecessary and present only because Oracle did not enable those programs. In Oracle8, some of these restrictions are removed. You *can* call DBMS_OUTPUT.PUT_LINE from within a function called in SQL. You can even send information to database pipes.[*]

- Prior to Oracle8, you cannot call RAISE_APPLICATION_ERROR from within the stored function.

- In Oracle Server 7.3, you cannot apply PL/SQL table methods (COUNT, FIRST, LAST, NEXT, PRIOR, etc.) in a stored function which is used in SQL (this is a "known bug" fixed in Oracle8). For example, if your function contains the following code, it cannot be used in SQL:

```
DECLARE
    TYPE emptabtype IS TABLE of emp%ROWTYPE INDEX BY BINARY_INTEGER;
    emptab emptabtype;
BEGIN
    IF emptab.COUNT > 0 THEN -- Causes rejection inside SQL
```

- The stored function may not call another module (stored procedure or function) that breaks any of the above rules. A function is only as pure as the most impure of any modules it, in turn, calls.

- The stored function may not reference a view that breaks any of the above rules. A view is a stored SELECT statement; that view's SELECT may use stored functions.

If your function violates any of these rules or is a function defined in a package and is missing its RESTRICT_REFERENCES pragma, you will receive the dreaded ORA-06571 error:

```
ORA-06571: Function TOTAL_COMP does not guarantee not to update database
```

As discussed in the section "Realities: Calling PL/SQL Functions in SQL," it can be very difficult at times (and sometimes impossible) to avoid this error. In other situations, however, there is an easy resolution (certainly do check the above list of restrictions).

Calling Packaged Functions in SQL

As I describe in Chapter 16, *Packages*, the specification and body of a package are distinct; a specification can (and must) exist before its body has been defined. This feature of packages makes life complicated when it comes to calling functions in SQL. When a SELECT statement calls a packaged function, the only information available to it is the package specification. Yet it is the contents of the package body which determine whether that function is valid for execution in SQL. The consequence of this structure is that you will have to add code to your package specification in order to enable a packaged function for calling in SQL.

---

[*] My book, *Oracle Built-in Packages*, contains a comprehensive discussion of the packaged functions which are available for use in SQL.

To use the official lingo, you must explicitly "assert" the purity level (the extent to which a function is free of side effects) of a stored function in a package specification. The Oracle Server can then determine when the package body is compiled whether the function violates that purity level. If so, an error will be raised and you then face the sometimes daunting task of figuring out where and how the violation occurs.

You assert a purity level for a function with the RESTRICT_REFERENCES pragma, explored in the next section.

The RESTRICT_REFERENCES Pragma

As I've mentioned, a *pragma* is a special directive to the PL/SQL compiler. If you have ever created a programmer-defined, named exception, you have already encountered your first pragma. In the case of the RESTRICT_REFERENCES pragma, you are telling the compiler the purity level you believe your function meets or exceeds.

You need a separate pragma statement for each packaged function you wish to use in a SQL statement, and it must come after the function declaration in the package specification (you do not specify the pragma in the package body).

To assert a purity level with the pragma, use the following syntax:

```
PRAGMA RESTRICT_REFERENCES
    (function_name, WNDS [, WNPS] [, RNDS] [, RNPS])
```

where function_name is the name of the function whose purity level you wish to assert, and the four different codes have the following meanings:

WNDS

Writes No Database State. Asserts that the function does not modify any database tables.

WNPS

Writes No Package State. Asserts that the function does not modify any package variables.

RNDS

Reads No Database State. Asserts that the function does not read any database tables.

RNPS

Reads No Package State. Asserts that the function does not read any package variables.

Notice that only the WNDS level is mandatory in the pragma. That is consistent with the restriction that stored functions in SQL may not execute an UPDATE, INSERT, or DELETE statement. All other states are optional. You can list them in any order, but you must include the WNDS argument. No one argument implies another argument. I can write to the database without reading from it. I can read a package variable without writing to a package variable.

Here is an example of two different purity level assertions for functions in the company_financials package:

```
PACKAGE company_financials
IS
    FUNCTION company_type (type_code_in IN VARCHAR2)
        RETURN VARCHAR2;

    FUNCTION company_name (company_id_in IN company.company_id%TYPE)
        RETURN VARCHAR2;

    PRAGMA RESTRICT_REFERENCES (company_type, WNDS, RNDS, WNPS, RNPS);
    PRAGMA RESTRICT_REFERENCES (company_name, WNDS, WNPS, RNPS);
END company_financials;
```

In this package, the company_name function reads from the database to obtain the name for the specified company. Notice that I placed both pragmas together at the bottom of the package specification—the pragma does not need to immediately follow the function specification. I also went to the trouble of specifying the WNPS and RNPS arguments for both of the functions. Oracle Corporation recommends that you assert the highest possible purity levels so that the compiler will never reject the function unnecessarily.

NOTE   If a function you want to call in SQL calls a procedure in a package, you must also provide a RESTRICT_REFERENCES pragma for that procedure. You can't call the procedure directly in SQL, but if it is going to be executed indirectly from within SQL, it still must follow the rules.

Pragma violation errors

If your function violates its pragma, you will receive the PLS-00452 error. Suppose, for example, that the body of the company_financials package looks like this:

```
CREATE OR REPLACE PACKAGE BODY company_financials
IS
    FUNCTION company_type (type_code_in IN VARCHAR2)
        RETURN VARCHAR2
    IS
        v_sal NUMBER;
    BEGIN
        SELECT sal INTO v_sal FROM emp WHERE empno = 1;
        RETURN 'bigone';
    END;
```

```
   FUNCTION company_name (company_id_in IN company.company_id%TYPE)
      RETURN VARCHAR2
   IS
   BEGIN
      UPDATE emp SET sal = 0;
      RETURN 'bigone';
   END;
END company_financials;
/
```

When I attempt to compile this package body I will get the following error:

```
3/4    PLS-00452: Subprogram 'COMPANY_TYPE' violates its associated pragma
```

because the company_type function reads from the database and I have asserted the RNDS purity level. If I remove that silly SELECT statement, I will then receive this error:

```
11/4   PLS-00452: Subprogram 'COMPANY_NAME' violates its associated pragma
```

because the company_name function updates the database and I have asserted the WNDS level. You will sometimes look at your function and say: "Hey, I absolutely do *not* violate my purity level. There is no UPDATE, DELETE, or UPDATE around." Maybe not. But there is a good chance that you are calling a built-in package or in some other way breaking the rules.

Asserting Purity Level with Package Initialization Section

If your package contains an initialization section (executable statements after a BEGIN statement in the package body), you must also assert the purity level of that section. The initialization section is executed automatically the first time any package object is referenced. So if a packaged function is used in a SQL statement, it will trigger execution of that code. If the initialization section modifies package variables or database information, the compiler needs to know about that through the pragma.

You can assert the purity level of the initialization section either explicitly or implicitly. To make an explicit assertion, use the following variation of the pragma RESTRICT_REFERENCES:

```
PRAGMA RESTRICT_REFERENCES
   (package_name, WNDS, [, WNPS] [, RNDS] [, RNPS])
```

Instead of specifying the name of the function, you include the name of the package itself, followed by all the applicable state arguments. In the following argument I assert only WNDS and WNPS because the initialization section reads data from the configuration table and also reads the value of a global variable from another package (session_pkg.user_id).

```
PACKAGE configure
IS
    PRAGMA RESTRICT_REFERENCES (configure, WNDS, WNPS);
    user_name VARCHAR2(100);
END configure;

PACKAGE BODY configure
IS
BEGIN
    SELECT lname || ', ' || fname INTO user_name
      FROM user_table
     WHERE user_id = session_pkg.user_id;
END configure;
```

Why can I assert the WNPS even though I do write to the user_name package variable? The answer is that it's a variable from this same package, so the action is not considered a side effect.

You can also implicitly assert the purity level of the package's initialization section by allowing the compiler to infer that level from the purity level(s) of all the pragmas for individual functions in the package. In the following version of the company package, the two pragmas for the functions allow the Oracle Server to infer a combined purity level of RNDS and WNPS for the initialization section. This means that the initialization section cannot read from the database and cannot write to a package variable.

```
PACKAGE company
IS
    FUNCTION get_company (company_id_in IN VARCHAR2)
       RETURN company%ROWTYPE;

    FUNCTION deactivate_company (company_id_in IN company.company_id%TYPE)
       RETURN VARCHAR2;

    PRAGMA RESTRICT_REFERENCES (get_company, RNDS, WNPS);
    PRAGMA RESTRICT_REFERENCES (deactivate_name, WNPS);
END company;
```

Generally, you are probably better off providing an explicit purity level assertion for the initialization section. This makes it easier for those responsible for maintaining the package to understand both your intentions and your understanding of the package.

Column/Function Name Precedence

If your function has the same name as a table column in your SELECT statement and it has no parameters, then the column takes precedence over the function.

The employee table has a column named "salary." Suppose you create a function named salary as well:

```
CREATE TABLE employee (employee_id NUMBER, ... , salary NUMBER, ...);

FUNCTION salary RETURN NUMBER;
```

Then a SELECT statement referencing salary always refers to the column and not the function:

```
SELECT salary INTO calculated_salary FROM employee;
```

If you want to override the column precedence, you must qualify the name of the function with the name of the schema that owns the function, as follows:

```
SELECT scott.salary INTO calculated_salary FROM employee;
```

This now executes the function instead of retrieving the column value.

Realities: Calling PL/SQL Functions in SQL

The ability to call PL/SQL functions in SQL has been around since Release 2.1, but in many ways (at least until Oracle8) it can still be considered "bleeding edge" technology. Why?

- You must manually apply RESTRICT_REFERENCES pragmas to all of your code—and you have to figure out where all those pragmas need to go. This process is described in a subsection below.

- Functions execute outside of the read consistency model of the Oracle database (!). This issue is also explored below in a subsection below.

- The overhead of calling a function from SQL remains high. The exact price you pay to call a function from within SQL (compared to, say, executing in-line SQL code) can be hard to pin down. It varies from computer to computer and even by instance or by the function being called; I have heard reports that range from an extra half-second to an astonishing additional 50 seconds (in that case, I suggested that they do some more analysis and debugging). Whatever the specific amount of time, the delay can be noticeable and you need to factor it into your design and test plans.

- Tuning mechanisms such as EXPLAIN PLAN do not take into account the SQL that may be called inside functions called in your SQL statement. PL/SQL functions are ignored by the EXPLAIN PLAN facility. This makes it very difficult to come up with a comprehensive understanding of performance bottlenecks and tuning needs.

- So much Oracle technology, especially that found in built-in packages, is declared "off limits" to functions in SQL. Just consider DBMS_OUTPUT. You can't use it in functions called in SQL. But ideally you will want to use those same functions in SQL *and* PL/SQL. Another issue may be that your standard debugging technique is to insert calls to a trace program at the beginning of each of your functions and procedures. Chances are that the trace program relies on DBMS_OUTPUT (or UTL_FILE or DBMS_PIPE or take your pick, they're all—at least until Oracle8—off limits). Sorry! You will not be able to use that function in SQL. So you have to *pull out* some of the code from the function. As a result, you can end up with two versions of your code: one for PL/SQL and one for SQL. That is one nasty scenario for software developers.

Let's examine two of these issues in more detail.

Manual Application of Pragmas

You must manually apply RESTRICT_REFERENCES pragmas to all of your code—and you have to figure out where all those pragmas need to go. This process is often similar to a Sherlock Holmes plot. You compile a package and get a pragma violation error. This can happen because your program breaks a rule (like trying to change data) or because it calls other programs which break a rule. You notice in this case that your function calls five or six other functions or procedures, so you must apply pragmas to each of these. By doing so, you assert purity levels where none had been asserted before, raising more errors and in some cases significant architectural issues.

For example, suppose that you suddenly have to apply a pragma to a procedure in package X and that package has an initialization section; you must then also pragma-tize the initialization section. A common practice in this section is to set up a PL/SQL table for in-memory manipulation of data. If you use any PL/SQL table methods to do this initialization, your pragma will fail.

This can be a very frustrating exercise, at times leading to abandoning the effort to enable your function for execution in SQL. In my experience, you will want to identify *in advance* (as much as possible) those areas of your application which you will want to call in SQL. You will then strive to keep this code very "clean" and focused, with limited entanglements with other packages, and with an absolutely minimal use of built-in packaged functionality. Neither an easy nor a particularly desirable task.

Read Consistency Model Complications

Yes, it is hard to believe, but quite true: unless you take special precautions, it is quite possible that your SQL query will violate the read consistency model of the

Oracle RDBMS, which has been sacrosanct territory for years at Oracle. To understand this issue, consider the following query and the function it calls:

```
SELECT name, total_sales (account_id)
  FROM account
 WHERE status = 'ACTIVE';

FUNCTION total_sales (id_in IN account.account_id%TYPE)
   RETURN NUMBER
IS
   CURSOR tot_cur
   IS
      SELECT SUM (sales) total
        FROM orders
       WHERE account_id = id_in
         AND year = TO_NUMBER (TO_CHAR (SYSDATE, 'YYYY'));
   tot_rec tot_cur%ROWTYPE;
BEGIN
   OPEN tot_cur;
   FETCH tot_cur INTO tot_rec;
   RETURN tot_rec.total;
END;
```

The account table has five million active rows in it (a very successful enterprise!). The orders table has 20 million rows. I start the query at 11 a.m.; it takes about an hour to complete. At 10:45 a.m., somebody with the proper authority comes along, deletes all rows from the orders table and performs a commit. According to the read consistency model of Oracle, the session running the query should see all those deleted rows until the query completes. But the next time the total_sales function executes from within the query, it finds no order rows and returns NULL—and will do so until the query completes.

So if you are executing queries inside functions which are called inside SQL, you need to be acutely aware of read-consistency issues. If these functions are called in long-running queries or transactions, you will probably need to issue the following command to enforce read-consistency *between* SQL statements in the current transaction:

```
SET TRANSACTION READ ONLY
```

You will find more information about this command in Chapter 6, *Database Interaction and Cursors*.

Working with functions in SQL is more difficult and more complicated than you might first imagine. Big surprise. You can say that about almost every aspect of Oracle technology, especially the newer additions to the stable. I hope that over time Oracle will make our lives easier (there are definitely some improvements in Oracle 8.0). Ultimately we need a utility that allows a developer to "point" to a function and request, "make that function usable in SQL." And that utility will then apply all the pragmas or at least generate a report of the steps necessary to get the job done.

We can dream, can't we?

Examples of Embedded PL/SQL

The more you think about stored functions in SQL, the more you come up with ways to put them to use in every single one of your applications. To prod your creativity and get you started, here are a number of examples of the ways stored functions in SQL can change the way you build Oracle-based systems.

Encapsulating Calculations

In just about any and every application, you will need to perform the same calculations over and over again. Whether it is a computation of net present value, mortgage balance, the distance between two points on a Cartesian plane, or a statistical variance, with native SQL you have to recode those computations in each of the SQL statements in which they are needed.

You can pay a big price for this kind of redundancy. The code that implements your business rules is repeated throughout the application. Even if the business rule doesn't change, the way you should implement the rule is almost sure to require modification. Worse than that, the business rule itself might evolve, which could necessitate fairly significant alterations.

To solve this problem, you can hide or encapsulate all of your formulas and calculations into stored functions. These functions can then be called from within both SQL statements and also PL/SQL programs.

One fine example of the value of encapsulated calculations arose when an insurance company needed to perform date-based analyses on its accounts. The last day of the month is, of course, a very important date for most financial institutions. To manipulate dates, the company's IS department planned to make use of the built-in LAST_DAY function to obtain the last day of the month, and ADD_ MONTHS to move from one month to the next. It soon uncovered a very interesting nuance to the way ADD_MONTHS worked: if you pass a day to ADD_ MONTHS which is the last day in the month, SQL always returns the last day in the resulting month, regardless of the number of actual days in each of the months.

In other words:

```
ADD_MONTHS ('28-FEB-1994', 2) ==> 30-APR-1993
```

This approach might make sense for some applications and queries. The requirement at the insurance company, however, was that when you move a month, you must always land on the same day of the month (or the last day, if the original month's day was past the last day of the target month). Without stored functions, the SQL required to perform this calculation is as follows:

```
SELECT
    DECODE (payment_date,
            LAST_DAY (payment_date),
            LEAST (ADD_MONTHS (payment_date, 1),
                TO_DATE (TO_CHAR (ADD_MONTHS (payment_date, 1),
                            'MMYYYY') ||
                        TO_CHAR (payment, 'DD'),
                        'MMYYYYDD')),
            ADD_MONTHS (payment_date, 1))
    FROM premium_payments;
```

which may be read as, "If the last payment date falls on the last day of the month, then return as the next payment date the earliest of either the result of adding one month to payment date (using ADD_MONTHS) or the same day in the new month as the day in the month of the last payment date. If the last payment was not made on the last day of the month, simply use ADD_MONTHS to get the next payment date."

Not only is that difficult to understand, but it required three different calls to the ADD_MONTHS built-in. And remember that this complex SQL would have to be repeated in every SELECT list where ADD_MONTHS was used to increment or decrement dates. You can well imagine how happy the programmers in this company became when they installed Oracle Server Version 7.1 and were able to use the following function inside their SQL statements (for a full explanation of the function's logic, see Chapter 12, *Date Functions*):

```
FUNCTION new_add_months (date_in IN DATE, months_shift IN NUMBER)
    RETURN DATE
IS
    return_value DATE;
BEGIN
    return_value := ADD_MONTHS (date_in, months_shift);
    IF date_in = LAST_DAY (date_in)
    THEN
        return_value :=
            LEAST (return_value,
                TO_DATE (TO_CHAR (return_value, 'MMYYYY') ||
                        TO_CHAR (date_in, 'DD') ,
                        'MMYYYYDD'));
    END IF;
    RETURN return_value;
END new_add_months;
```

With the stored function, the SELECT statement to obtain the next payment date is simply:

```
SELECT new_add_months (payment_date,1)
   FROM premium_payments;
```

The more you look through your SQL statements, the more opportunities you find for stored functions that can hide calculations and therefore improve the long-term stability of your code. While it is unlikely that you will have the time and resources to go back and rewrite wholesale the SQL underpinnings of your application, you can at least build the functions and roll them into any new product development.

Combining Scalar and Aggregate Values

This simple question is hard to answer in SQL: "Show me the name and salary of the employee who has the highest salary in each department, as well as the total salary for that person's department."

Broken into two separate queries, this question poses no problem. Here is the first part:

```
SELECT department_id, last_name, salary
   FROM employee E1
  WHERE salary = (SELECT MAX (salary)
                    FROM employee E2
                   WHERE E.department_id = E2.department_id)
  GROUP BY department_id;
```

and here is the second part:

```
SELECT department_id, SUM (salary)
   FROM employee
  ORDER BY department_id;
```

However, I cannot very easily combine them since that would require listing and obtaining both scalar (single row) and aggregate (across multiple rows) values from the same table. The following SELECT list contains the information I want to display. How could I construct my FROM, WHERE, and GROUP BY clauses to show both an individual's salary and the departmental total?

```
SELECT department_id, last_name, salary, SUM (salary)
   FROM ...?
  WHERE ...?
  GROUP BY ...?
```

The most straightforward solution prior to Release 2.1 of PL/SQL was to create a view that "presummarized" the salary for each department:

```
CREATE VIEW dept_salary
AS
   SELECT department_id, SUM (salary) total_salary
```

```
        FROM employee
     GROUP BY department_id;
```

Now, with this view, I can get at my answer with a single SQL statement as follows:

```
SELECT E.department_id, last_name, salary, total_salary
  FROM employee E, dept_salary DS
 WHERE E.department_id = DS.department_id
   AND salary = (SELECT MAX (salary)
                   FROM employee E2
                  WHERE E.department_id = E2.department_id);
```

This doesn't seem like such a bad solution, except that you have to create a customized view each time you want to perform this kind of calculation. In addition, this SQL is far less than straightforward for many programmers.

A better solution is to make use of a stored function in SQL. Instead of creating a view, create a function that performs exactly the same calculation, but this time only for the specified department:

```
FUNCTION total_salary (dept_id_in IN department.department_id%TYPE)
   RETURN NUMBER
IS
   CURSOR grp_cur
   IS
      SELECT SUM (salary)
        FROM employee
       WHERE department_id = dept_id_in;
   return_value NUMBER;
BEGIN
   OPEN grp_cur;
   FETCH grp_cur INTO return_value;
   CLOSE grp_cur;
   RETURN return_value;
END;
```

In this version I outer-join the department and employee tables. This way if a department does not exist (bad department ID number), I return NULL. If a department has no employees, I return 0; otherwise, I return the total salary in that department.

Now my query does not need to join to a view containing a GROUP BY. Instead, it calls the total_salary function, passing the employee's department ID number as a parameter:

```
SELECT E.department_id, last_name, salary, total_salary (E.department_id)
  FROM employee E
 WHERE salary = (SELECT MAX (salary)
                   FROM employee E2
                  WHERE E.department_id = E2.department_id);
```

The resulting SQL statement is not only easier to read; it also executes faster, especially for larger tables. I could simplify the SQL statement further by creating a function that returns the maximum salary in a particular department. The above SELECT would then become simply:

```
SELECT department_id, last_name, salary, total_salary (department_id)
   FROM employee E
WHERE salary = max_sal_in_dept (department_id);
```

Replacing Correlated Subqueries

You can also use stored functions in a SQL statement to replace correlated subqueries. A correlated subquery is a SELECT statement inside the WHERE clause of a SQL statement (SELECT, INSERT, or DELETE) which is correlated (or makes reference) to one or more columns in the enclosing SQL statement. In the preceding section I used a correlated subquery to determine the employee who receives the highest salary in each department:

```
SELECT E.department_id, last_name, salary, total_salary (E.department_id)
   FROM employee E
WHERE salary = (SELECT MAX (salary)
                  FROM employee E2
                  WHERE E.department_id = E2.department_id);
```

The last three lines in the query contain a SELECT statement matching the department ID number for the "inner" employee (E2) to the department ID number for the "outer" employee table (E1). The inner query is executed once for every row retrieved in the outer query.

The correlated subquery is a very powerful feature in SQL, since it offers the equivalent of a procedural language's nested loop capability, as in:

```
LOOP
   LOOP
   END LOOP;
END LOOP;
```

Two drawbacks with a correlated subquery are:

- The logic can become fairly complicated
- The resulting SQL statement can be difficult to understand and follow

You can use a stored function in place of a correlated subquery to address these drawbacks; in the above example, I would want a function that calculates the highest salary in a given department:

```
FUNCTION max_salary (dept_id_in IN department.department_id%TYPE)
   RETURN NUMBER
IS
   CURSOR grp_cur
   IS
```

```
        SELECT MAX (salary)
          FROM employee
         WHERE department_id = dept_id_in;
     return_value NUMBER;
BEGIN
   OPEN grp_cur;
   FETCH grp_cur INTO return_value;
   CLOSE grp_cur;
   RETURN return_value;
END;
```

I can now use both total_salary and max_salary in my SELECT statement that says, "Show me the name and salary of the employee who has the highest salary in each department, as well as the total salary for that person's department."

```
SELECT E.department_id, last_name, salary, total_salary (department_id)
  FROM employee
 WHERE salary = max_salary (department_id);
```

Compare that simple, self-documenting piece of SQL to the version requiring a view and correlated subquery:

```
CREATE VIEW dept_salary
AS
    SELECT department_id, SUM (salary) total_salary
      FROM employee
     GROUP BY department_id;

SELECT E.department_id, last_name, salary, total_salary
  FROM employee E, dept_salary DS
 WHERE E.department_id = DS.department_id
   AND salary = (SELECT MAX (salary)
                   FROM employee E2
                  WHERE E.department_id = E2.department_id);
```

and I am sure you will agree that stored functions in SQL can make your life much easier.

You may have noticed that the total_salary function from the previous section and the max_salary from this section look very similar. The only difference between the two is that the cursor in total_salary uses the SUM group function and the cursor in max_salary uses the MAX group function. If you are as fanatical about consolidating your code into the smallest possible number of distinct "moving parts," you might consider a single function that returns a different group-level statistic for a department based on a second parameter, as follows:

```
FUNCTION salary_stat
    (dept_id_in IN department.department_id%TYPE,
     stat_type_in IN VARCHAR2)
    RETURN NUMBER
IS
    v_stat_type VARCHAR2(20) := UPPER (stat_type_in);
```

```
      CURSOR grp_cur
      IS
         SELECT SUM (salary) sumsal,
                MAX (salary) maxsal,
                MIN (salary) minsal,
                AVG (salary) avgsal,
                COUNT (DISTINCT salary) countsal,
            FROM employee
           WHERE department_id = dept_id_in;

      grp_rec grp_cur%ROWTYPE;
      retval NUMBER;
   BEGIN
      OPEN grp_cur;
      FETCH grp_cur INTO grp_rec;
      CLOSE grp_cur;

      IF v_stat_type = 'SUM'
      THEN
         retval := grp_rec.sumsal;

      ELSIF v_stat_type = 'MAX'
      THEN
         retval := grp_rec.maxsal;

      ELSIF v_stat_type = 'MIN'
      THEN
         retval := grp_rec.minsal;

      ELSIF v_stat_type = 'COUNT'
      THEN
         retval := grp_rec.countsal;

      ELSIF v_stat_type = 'AVG'
      THEN
         retval := grp_rec.avgsal;
      END IF;

      RETURN retval;
   END;
```

The overhead of adding these additional expressions in the SELECT list—and the processing of the IF statement—is negligible. With this new, generic utility, my request for salary analysis shown above now becomes:

```
SELECT E.department_id, last_name, salary, salary_stat (department_id, 'sum')
   FROM employee
  WHERE salary = salary_stat (department_id, 'max');
```

If I ever have to change the SQL required to obtain departmental-level statistics for salary, I have to upgrade only this single function.

Replacing DECODEs with IF Statements

The DECODE function offers IF-like capabilities in the nonprocedural SQL environment provided by the Oracle Server. You can use the DECODE syntax to create matrix reports with a fixed number of columns and also perform complex IF-THEN-ELSE logic within a query. The downside to DECODE is that it can be difficult to write and very difficult to maintain. Consider the following example of DECODE to determine whether a date is within the prescribed range and, if it is, add to the count of rows that fulfill this requirement:

```
SELECT FC.year_number,
       SUM (DECODE (GREATEST (ship_date, FC.q1_sdate),
                    ship_date,
                    DECODE (LEAST (ship_date, FC.q1_edate),
                            ship_date, 1,
                            0),
                    0)) Q1_results,
       SUM (DECODE (GREATEST (ship_date, FC.q2_sdate),
                    ship_date,
                    DECODE (LEAST (ship_date, FC.q2_edate),
                            ship_date, 1,
                            0),
                    0)) Q2_results,
       SUM (DECODE (GREATEST (ship_date, FC.q3_sdate),
                    ship_date,
                    DECODE (LEAST (ship_date, FC.q3_edate),
                            ship_date, 1,
                            0),
                    0)) Q3_results,
       SUM (DECODE (GREATEST (ship_date, FC.q4_sdate),
                    ship_date,
                    DECODE (LEAST (ship_date, FC.q4_edate),
                            ship_date, 1,
                            0),
                    0)) Q4_results
  FROM orders O,
       fiscal_calendar FC
 GROUP BY year_number;
```

The result set for this query might look like this:

YEAR NUMBER	Q1 RESULTS	Q2 RESULTS	Q3 RESULTS	Q4 RESULTS
1993	12000	14005	22000	40000
1994	10000	15000	21000	55004

While it is very handy to use DECODE to produce such a report, the SQL required to accomplish the task is more than a little frightening. Here is how you might try to interpret the Q1 RESULTS nested DECODE: "If the ship date is greater than or equal to the first quarter start date and the shipdate is less than or equal to the first quarter end date, then add one to the sum of the total number of orders shipped in that quarter. Otherwise, add zero."

Unfortunately, unless you are experienced in interpreting DECODE statements, you will find it difficult to glean this understanding from that convoluted SQL statement. The repetition in that single SELECT also cries out for modularization, which we can supply with the following stored function (incr_in_range means "increment if in the range"):

```
FUNCTION incr_in_range
    (ship_date_in IN DATE, sdate_in IN DATE, edate_in IN DATE)
    RETURN INTEGER
IS
BEGIN
    IF ship_date_in BETWEEN sdate_in AND edate_in
    THEN
        RETURN 1;
    ELSE
        RETURN 0;
    END IF;
END;
```

Yep, that's all there is to it! With the incr_in_range function, that long and winding SELECT statement simply becomes:

```
SELECT FC.year_number,
       SUM (incr_in_range (ship_date, q1_sdate, q1_edate)) Q1_results,
       SUM (incr_in_range (ship_date, q2_sdate, q2_edate)) Q2_results,
       SUM (incr_in_range (ship_date, q3_sdate, q3_edate)) Q3_results,
       SUM (incr_in_range (ship_date, q4_sdate, q4_edate)) Q4_results
  FROM orders O,
       fiscal_calendar FC
 GROUP BY year_number;
```

This stored function gets rid of the code redundancy and makes the SELECT statement much more readable. In addition, this function could be used in other SQL statements to perform the same logic.

GROUP BY Partial Column Values

The GROUP BY clause in a SELECT statement allows you to collect data across multiple records and group them by one or more columns. The following SELECT statement, for example, calculates the total amount of salary paid to all workers with the same job description (or "title"):

```
SELECT job_title_desc, SUM (salary)
  FROM employee E, job_title JT
 WHERE E.job_title_id = JT.job_title_id
 GROUP BY job_title_desc;
```

A portion of the result set from this query might look like this:

```
ACCOUNT MANAGER        32000
OFFICE CLERK           4000
PROJECT MANAGER        10006
SHIPPING CLERK         4200
```

What if you wanted to see a total amount of salary for each type or category of job title? How much do all the various kinds of clerks in the company earn? What about all the different types of vice presidents and managers?

With native SQL, this is very difficult to write. In effect, you want GROUP BY to assess all the different categories, but those categories do not exist in a separate table. They are denormalized into the job title descriptions, and the GROUP BY clause can be applied only to whole column values. Fortunately, stored functions in SQL provide a straightforward solution to the problem. The following function, job_category, takes as its single parameter the primary key to the title table and returns the job category. It does so by performing a LIKE operation on the text for that job title—something you cannot do directly in the GROUP BY clause.

```
FUNCTION job_category (title_id_in IN job_title.job_title_id%TYPE)
    RETURN VARCHAR2
IS
    CURSOR title_cur IS
        SELECT job_title_desc FROM job_title
        WHERE job_title_id = title_id_in;
    title_rec title_cur%ROWTYPE;
BEGIN
    OPEN title_cur; FETCH title_cur INTO title_rec;
    IF title_cur%NOTFOUND
    THEN
        CLOSE title_cur;
        RETURN NULL;
    ELSE
        CLOSE title_cur;
        IF title_rec.job_title_desc LIKE '%CLERK%'
        THEN
            RETURN 'CLERK';
        ELSIF title_rec.job_title_desc LIKE '%VICE PRESIDENT%'
        THEN
            RETURN 'VICE PRESIDENT';
        ELSIF title_rec.job_title_desc LIKE '%MANAGER%'
        THEN
            RETURN 'MANAGER';
        END IF;
    END IF;
END;
```

I can now rewrite my query using the job_category function and cut through all the confusion of my denormalized job title descriptions:

```
SELECT job_category (job_title_id) as title, SUM (salary)
    FROM employee
    GROUP BY title;
```

I use the function in both the SELECT list and the GROUP BY. This query now produces a result set that looks like the following:

```
CLERK                 8200
MANAGER               42006
VICE PRESIDENT        75000
```

Sequential Processing Against a Column's Value

It is very easy for me to find out if a particular word or set of characters appears in a string with the INSTR function. It is also straightforward in SQL to determine which rows have a column that contains a certain word. It is much more difficult within native SQL to determine the number of times a particular word or set of characters appears in a string in a single row. The built-in set-at-a-time processing of SQL does not provide iterative or looping behavior within a row—just across rows.

If I want to perform iterative analysis or computation on a particular value in a single row, I need to apply a PL/SQL function. Let's see how this would come into play.

Here is the SQL that shows me all lines of text containing the word "the":

```
SELECT text
  FROM notes
 WHERE INSTR (text, 'the') > 0;
```

I can even use INSTR to find all the lines of text containing the word "the" at least three times:

```
SELECT text
  FROM notes
 WHERE INSTR (text, 'the', 1, 3) > 0;
```

I could, if pressed, also display all lines of text that containing the word "the" precisely three times:

```
SELECT text
  FROM notes
 WHERE INSTR (text, 'the', 1, 3) != 0
   AND INSTR (text, 'the', 1, 4) = 0;
```

In other words, if INSTR returns a nonzero number or location for a third occurrence of "the", but also returns a zero for a fourth occurrence of "the", that means that the string occurs precisely three times in the string.

If, however, I need to see a report that displays the number of occurrences of "the" in each of my notes, or if I want to GROUP BY the number of occurrences of "the", SQL comes up short. The best I can do is pseudocode to express my wish:

```
SELECT number-of-thes-in-text, text
  FROM notes
 GROUP BY number-of-thes-in-text;
```

As a nonprocedural language that deals with a set (multiple rows) of data at a time, SQL doesn't give me any way to programmatically analyze the contents of a particular column. PL/SQL, on the other hand, is perfectly equipped to solve these kinds of problems. The ps.parse package included on the disk demonstrates how to build a function that will return the number of atomics (words and/or delimiters) in a string. I will not repeat the implementation here, but will show how the function would be used in SQL:

- Show the number of occurrences of "the" in each line of text:

```
SELECT text,
       ps_parse.number_of_atomics (text, 'the')
  FROM notes;
```

- Show the distribution of the use of the word "urgent" across the days of the week for all text in which the word urgent appears at least once:

```
SELECT TO_CHAR (note_date, 'DAY'),
       ps_parse.number_of_atomics (text, 'urgent') urgent_count
  FROM notes
 WHERE urgent_count > 0;
```

Recursive Processing in a SQL Statement

The SQL language does not support recursion, yet this powerful programming method is at times crucial to solving a problem. PL/SQL does allow for recursive execution of function calls, however, so you can put it to use inside a SQL statement where recursion is needed.

Suppose your application needs to print checks. A check contains both the numeric version of the amount of the check (say, $99.70) and the written version of the amount of the check (ninety-nine dollars and seventy cents). You will not be able to use SQL to convert the numeric check amount (stored in the database) into the written version. You can, however, put PL/SQL to use, along with some of its more interesting features like recursion, global data, and PL/SQL tables, to provide a very elegant solution.

The package below offers a checks package to provide this conversion capability.[*]

```
/* Filename on companion disk: checks.spp */
PACKAGE checks
IS
   /* Convert number to words */
   FUNCTION num2words (number_in IN NUMBER) RETURN VARCHAR2;

   /* Since a package, must assert my purity level. */
```

---

[*] This implementation of "number-to-words" was first presented by Mike Burnside of Oracle Australia at the International Oracle User's Week in San Francisco in September 1994. I have made some minor modifications.

```
          PRAGMA RESTRICT_REFERENCES (num2words, WNDS);

END checks;

PACKAGE BODY checks
IS
     /* Table structure to hold names of numeric components. */
     TYPE numwords_tabtype IS TABLE OF VARCHAR2(20)
          INDEX BY BINARY_INTEGER;
     words_table numwords_tabtype;

     /* Used in initialization section. */
     v_date DATE;

     FUNCTION num2words (number_in IN NUMBER) RETURN VARCHAR2
     IS
          my_number NUMBER;
     BEGIN
          /* Sorry, I don't do cents in this program! */
          my_number := FLOOR (number_in);

          /* $1000+ */
          IF my_number >= 1000
          THEN
               /* Break up into two recursive calls to num2words. */
               RETURN num2words (my_number/1000) ||
                        ' Thousand ' ||
                        num2words (MOD (my_number, 1000));
          END IF;

          /* $100-999 */
          IF my_number >= 100
          THEN
               /* Break up into two recursive calls to num2words. */
               RETURN num2words (my_number/100) ||
                        ' Hundred ' ||
                        num2words (MOD (my_number, 100));
          END IF;

          /* $20-$99 */
          IF my_number >= 20
          THEN
               /* Break up into tens word and then final dollar amount. */
               RETURN words_table (FLOOR (my_number/10)) ||
                        ' ' ||
                        num2words (MOD (my_number, 10));
          END IF;

          /* Down to 19 or less. Get word from "upper register" of table. */
          RETURN words_table (my_number + 10);

     END num2words;

BEGIN
```

```
/* Initialization section of package. Run just once per session. */

/* Manually construct the tens names. */
words_table (1) := 'Ten';
words_table (2) := 'Twenty';
words_table (3) := 'Thirty';
words_table (4) := 'Forty';
words_table (5) := 'Fifty';
words_table (6) := 'Sixty';
words_table (7) := 'Seventy';
words_table (8) := 'Eighty';
words_table (9) := 'Ninety';

/* Return NULL for zero. */
words_table (10) := NULL;

/* Construct number names for one through nineteen. */
FOR day_index IN 1 .. 19
LOOP
   v_date := TO_DATE (to_char(day_index) || '-JAN-94');
   words_table (day_index+10) :=
      INITCAP (TO_CHAR (v_date, 'DDSP'));
END LOOP;

END checks;
```

Here are some examples of conversion from whole numbers to words:

```
checks.num2words (99)     ==> Ninety Nine
checks.num2words (12345) ==> Twelve Thousand Three Hundred Forty Five
checks.num2words (5)      ==> Five
```

I can also put this packaged function to use inside my SQL statement to query up all the information I need to print a check:

```
SELECT TO_CHAR (SYSDATE, 'Month DD, YYYY'),
       payee,
       amount,
       checks.num2words (amount),
       comment
  FROM bill
 WHERE bill_status = 'UNPAID'
```

V

New PL/SQL8
Features

Part V of this book contains the main discussion of the new features of Oracle8 that are relevant to PL/SQL.

- Chapter 18, *Object Types*, describes the Oracle "object-relational model" and how the object features work.

- Chapter 19, *Nested Tables and VARRAYs*, examines the two types of "collection" structures introduced in Oracle8.

- Chapter 20, *Object Views*, describes object views, which let you use object features with conventional relational tables.

- Chapter 21, *External Procedures*, discusses how you can call out to non-PL/SQL programs from within Oracle.

V

New PL/SQL Features

18

Object Types

In the last ten years, those of us who spend our lives with computers have probably seen and heard a lot about object-oriented (OO) programming and how it has revolutionized software development. Proponents cite the time-worn analogy with the integrated circuit (IC), which has allowed computer hardware manufacturers to bind together larger and larger reusable units into more and more powerful machines. "If only software people could match the pace of the hardware people," lament the advocates of objects. If we could build systems using reusable "software ICs," programming would be faster and more reliable, and we could address complex problems with relative ease. Detractors argue that, in contrast to relational theory, object approaches have no mathematical foundation, and they also shudder at the thought of turning the average corporate programmer into the rocket scientist needed to code in strangely popular OO languages. How many PL/SQL developers do you know, for example, who can also program in C++? For most of us, one look at the mysteriously juxtaposed punctuation marks gives us the heebie jeebies.

Of course, object orientation is much more than "programming in C++," just as relational databases are much more than "programming in SQL." The application programming language is only the last tool in the life cycle; techniques, methods, and user interfaces can now bear the object-oriented moniker. In fact, many Oracle users have been practicing at least some aspects of object orientation for years using solid engineering design principles, with SQL and PL/SQL as tools. If you model your system using entity-relationship diagrams, you have experience with "entities" that share many characteristics with objects. Not that I date from the Mesozoic era of computing history, but allow me to point out that the idea that programmers can modularize code into reusable fragments, and that data structures can include rich typing systems, predate Smalltalk and Simula, the first object languages.

Maybe you're a true believer in the software IC, or maybe your response is "objects, schmobjects, who needs 'em?", or maybe objects haven't even been on your radar screen because you're living with Oracle, and Oracle is, well, a relational database, with only rows and columns. That *used* to be true. Now with Oracle's objects option, the database can contain not only rows and columns, but also complex data structures which encapsulate both data and behavior.

Because objects may be new to many readers, this chapter will introduce objects concepts and terminology before plunging into the details of the Oracle objects option. First we'll look at the objects option in the context of the relational features of the Oracle server, and give some examples of places where objects can be used. To put the subject in the broader technology context, we'll also step back to look at what it means to be object-oriented, and how Oracle fulfills the object motif. Next, we'll show an extended example of creating and using Oracle objects for a hypothetical pet store, introducing salient points about using objects in a step-by-step fashion. Only then will we take a more in-depth look at the syntax and rules of usage in both PL/SQL and SQL. We'll also present four different technical strategies for applying object approaches in a new application. Finally, we'll look at housekeeping and the unpleasant business of modifying object designs, and conclude with a few words on making your object initiative work.

Although this chapter covers all aspects of using objects in PL/SQL, we don't have space to cover every possible aspect of using objects in the server. Some of the things we *don't* discuss in detail include: triggers on object tables (since objects do not alter what you already know about triggers from Oracle7); ways of using PL/SQL objects with the Oracle Call Interface (OCI) for C or C++; and some of the physical storage considerations of objects.

Introduction to Oracle8 Objects

When a mainstream vendor like Oracle Corporation ventures into new technology waters, it is virtually certain that the change will be evolutionary rather than revolutionary. True to form, Oracle8's relational capabilities are still the mainstay of Oracle Corporation's flagship database server, and these capabilities satisfy the need for compatibility with older Oracle versions. But with the objects option, Oracle8 allows programmers to use a new set of datatypes and models drawn from object programming languages, allowing *persistent objects*[*] to be created in the database and accessed, via an API, from C++, Smalltalk, Object COBOL, Java, and other languages.

Contrast this "object-relational" database approach with the true "object-oriented databases" (OODBs) that first appeared commercially in the mid-1980s. Pure OODBs are most successful in problem domains characterized by complex, often versioned, data (such as engineering, CASE, or CAD); they typically extend the type system of object-oriented languages to allow for persistent objects. Oracle8, on the other hand, extends the programming system of the database to allow for operations, and extends conventional datatypes to include complex structures. While these object extensions to SQL and PL/SQL sometimes look as if they were designed merely to confuse the programmer, object types in Oracle, properly implemented, can be the cornerstone of an overall object strategy. (And at least they don't use alien punctuation!)

Terminology

The first big hurdle to cross is the nomenclature; object technology in general, and Oracle8 in particular, seem to litter us with terms that seem familiar but aren't. For example, even prior to Oracle8, Oracle *did* have objects—that is, tables, indexes, packages, procedures, etc.—in fact, you can see them all in the USER_OBJECTS view. Now we have something most precisely called object *types,* which can have object *instances,* the latter of which are referred to simply as objects. Even more ironically, these objects don't show up in the USER_OBJECTS view (object types do, though). Confused? To keep things straight in this chapter, items you've always seen in USER_OBJECTS I'll call the *database objects,* and Oracle8 objects I'll call simply *objects.*

Rather than lob all the new terminology at you in eye-glazing detail, I'll introduce the most important terms first, and present the others as needed. These terms are not strictly from the lexicon of object-oriented purists, but are defined in an Oracle context.

Object type

    An Oracle database construct, managed via Data Definition Language (DDL) extensions, that defines a data structure (attributes) and the legal operations (methods) on the attributes. The type is only a template and holds no data itself; you may create variables, tables, columns, and other constructs of this

---

[*] "Persistence" is the characteristic illustrated when an object "sticks around" from one program session to the next, something taken for granted in the relational world. If all you have is an object-oriented language like Smalltalk or C++, you have to either do extensive custom programming to achieve object persistence, or use an OODB.

type. If you are familiar with object terminology, note that an object type is the closest thing to a *class*. It is also very similar to an *abstract data type* (ADT).

Object

An instance of an Oracle8 object type. The object is the place where the actual data resides. Objects may be stored within tables (in such cases, they are called *persistent*), or they may exist only temporarily in PL/SQL variables, in which case they are called *transient*.

Attribute

A structural part of an Oracle object, roughly akin to a column in a table. Each attribute must be of a single datatype, either scalar, like VARCHAR2 or INTEGER, or composite, like a user-defined nested table or another (nested) object. Scalar attributes are sometimes called *simple*, and composite attributes may be referred to as *complex*.

Method

A procedure or function, usually implemented in PL/SQL, that (typically) operates on an object's attributes. The methods for an object can only be invoked in the context of a specific object of that type. Similar to a program unit in a PL/SQL package, a method has a specification which is separate from its body. Method bodies can also be implemented in C (or other languages) and can be invoked as an Oracle "external procedure" (see Chapter 21, *External Procedures*). There is a special default method supplied by Oracle, a *constructor*, that initializes objects.

Some Simple Examples

To give you a better sense of how object technology works in Oracle, let's look at some specific code samples that use objects. The following examples use a simple object type, Pet_t. Don't worry too much about what all the syntax means yet; we'll review it in detail later. First, let's define the object type:

```
CREATE TYPE Pet_t AS OBJECT (
    tag_no INTEGER,
    name VARCHAR2(60),
    MEMBER FUNCTION set_tag_no (new_tag_no IN INTEGER)
        RETURN Pet_t
);
```

This object type has two attributes, tag_no and name, and one method, set_tag_no. But the method won't do anything until we create the associated body for the object type:

```
CREATE TYPE BODY Pet_t
AS
    MEMBER FUNCTION set_tag_no (new_tag_no IN INTEGER) RETURN Pet_t
```

```
    IS
        the_pet Pet_t := SELF;   -- initialize to "current" object
    BEGIN
        the_pet.tag_no := new_tag_no;
        RETURN the_pet;
    END;
END;
```

SELF is a way of referencing the object on which the method is invoked. This method returns an object with its tag_no attribute set to a new value.

Using this object type, here are some code fragments illustrating different applications of the type. Object types can serve as the datatype of any of a number of different entities.

An object type can serve as the datatype of each of the rows in a table. The table is then referred to as an object table, and it contains row objects; that is, each row is an object instance:

```
CREATE TABLE pets OF Pet_t;

-- Now we can create an object (object instance) of type Pet_t
INSERT INTO pets VALUES (Pet_t(23052, 'Mambo'));
```

An object type can serve as the datatype of a column. The column is then said to contain column objects. Different columns in a table could be of different object types. (The example below also uses Address_t, an object assumed to be already defined. Curiously enough, it contains attributes and methods appropriate to street addresses.)

```
CREATE TABLE families (
    surname VARCHAR2(50),
    favorite_pet Pet_t,
    address Address_t);
```

An object type can serve as the datatype of a local variable. Here, we declare and initialize an object variable in one statement. The initialization uses the automatically available constructor which has the same name as the datatype:

```
DECLARE
    my_pet Pet_t := Pet_t(23052, 'Mambo');
      ^       ^         ^
      |       |               constructor
      |       type
    variable
```

An object type can serve as the datatype of a PL/SQL return parameter. Functions may also return object types, as the example shows. The VALUE operator is needed to retrieve a table object:

```
CREATE FUNCTION find_pet (the_tag_no IN NUMBER) RETURN Pet_t
IS
```

```
      the_pet Pet_t;
      CURSOR pet_cur IS
         SELECT VALUE(p)
            FROM pets p
            WHERE tag_no = the_tag_no;
   BEGIN
      OPEN pet_cur;
      FETCH pet_cur INTO the_pet;
      CLOSE pet_cur;
      RETURN the_pet;
   END;
```

An object type can serve as the datatype of a nested table or VARRAY. This is possible as long as the object type has no TABLE or VARRAY attributes itself:

```
CREATE TYPE homeless_pet_t AS TABLE OF pet_t;
```

An object type can serve as the datatype of a "field" in a record variable. Nothing terribly exotic here:

```
DECLARE
   -- first define the type
   TYPE family_t IS RECORD (
      surname VARCHAR2(50),
      favorite_pet Pet_t);

   -- now declare a variable of that type
   family family_t;
```

Comparison: Oracle8 Objects and Earlier Features

In practical terms, object types live inside the Oracle database rather than inside PL/SQL programs. That is, you must issue the SQL DDL statement, CREATE TYPE ... AS OBJECT in order to create a type; only then can you use the type within PL/SQL. Once created, an object type defines an *interface* to a set of data. There is no good analogy for this behavior in Oracle7. An object type isn't really like a table, since it holds no data, but you can create tables *based on* the type.

An object type is a bit more like a package that contains only type declarations and functions that operate on those types. This is especially true since the object type, like the package, can have a separate "body" section in which to implement its procedures and functions (methods). There are key differences, though; perhaps most significantly, code in the object type body can only be invoked on a particular object. That is, you cannot call a method unless you also indicate an object instance on which to apply it. In addition, you can't create a table based on a package specification, the way you can create a table from an object type, and object types cannot include constants, exceptions, cursors, or datatypes. Table 18-1 compares the new object features with features of tables and packages.

Table 18-1. Comparing Oracle8 Objects to Earlier Oracle Features

Characteristic	Oracle7 Table	Oracle7 Package	Oracle8 Object
Stores data	Yes	Temporary only; package variables exist for duration of session	Object instance data may be persistent (stored in tables) or transient (stored in variables)
Serves as a template	No	No	Object types serve as a template for object instances
May contain complex data	No; normalized columns contain scalar values only	Yes; some datatypes such as RECORD and TABLE types do not require the objects option	Yes (requires objects option installed)
Contains procedural code	No (except for table triggers)	Yes	The code is in the object type definition, but can be invoked only on a specific instance
Has a body separate from its specification	N/A (in the case of triggers, the answer is no)	Yes	Yes (object type definition has separate body for method implementation)
May expose constants, exceptions, cursors, or datatypes	N/A (in the case of triggers, the answer is no)	Yes	No
Rights model (see "Privileges" later in this chapter)	Owner must explicitly grant DML privileges on table to user or role	If owner grants EXECUTE to invoker, latter inherits owner's DML privileges	Currently, if owner grants EXECUTE to invoker, latter inherits owner's DML privileges

Characteristics of Objects

Whether or not you have a background in the object-oriented world, you might find it useful to review some of the characteristics of objects and how they are implemented in Oracle. This section does not try to present a complete treatment of objects, but only a primer on the core principles.[*]

---

[*] The technically inclined who want more a detailed discussion of the technology can refer to Grady Booch's *Object-Oriented Analysis and Design with Applications*, Benjamin/Cummings, 1994. The managerially inclined might enjoy David A. Taylor's *Object-Oriented Technology: A Manager's Guide*, Addison-Wesley, 1990.

In a frequently cited work on the object approach, James Rumbaugh introduces four characteristics of objects: identity, classification, inheritance, and polymorphism.[*] Using this taxonomy as a starting point, let's dive in.

An object is a "thing," like a pet, or a contract, or a holiday, which is discrete and identifiable, which shares characteristics with other like objects. One of the major thrusts of object orientation is that its approach to modeling and implementing systems relies on an intuitive mapping of the problem space—the actual pet, for example—to a programmatic or database representation. The argument goes that the relational world is a bit artificial when it introduces one table to hold a list of animals, and another table to hold a list of vaccinations that the animal has received.

Identity

Since each object has identity, each object also has a unique identifier or *handle*. Even if all the properties of two different objects are identical, each has a different identity. Often, object-oriented programming systems assign invisible arbitrary numbers to serve as handles.

In Oracle8, unique object identifiers are automatically assigned to objects when they are stored as "table objects." It turns out that this identifier is stored in a hidden 16-byte RAW field. This "object identifier," or OID, can be referenced from columns in other tables, much as a primary key can be referenced from a foreign key.

Classification

Just as the human observer groups real-world objects into categories, so can the programmer in an object-oriented programming language. Objects are put into categories which share characteristics or properties, as well as legal operations on the category, or *methods*. In many languages, these categories are called *classes*. A more generic academic term for a class is an *abstract data type* or *ADT*; in fact, early beta versions of Oracle8 used the term "ADT" rather than "object type."

The actual object, such as the red-haired mutt named Mambo, is known as an *instance* of a class or object type Dog, in much the same way that a row in a relational table can be described as an instance of a relation.

In Oracle, objects are classified into *object types*, and properties are called *attributes*. Methods are either *member functions* or *member procedures*.

---

[*] See Rumbaugh, James., et al. *Object-Oriented Modeling and Design*, Prentice Hall, 1991.

Inheritance

Although there are few things that object practitioners agree on, one is that any language that claims to be object-oriented must support *inheritance*. Inheritance allows for hierarchies in which each *child* has characteristics of its *parent*. Each level in the type hierarchy has properties which can be shared by those beneath it; lower levels can have their own specialized attributes or functions as well.

As an example, our Dog type might exist as a subtype of a Pet type. So if a Pet has a name, each Dog would have a name, and you would not need to define this property a second time. The Dog type might extend the Pet type by including a dog-specific attribute such as is_house_trained. Note that this hierarchy allows the inheriting of properties and methods; it is *not* a hierarchy of data, like an Oracle CONNECT BY scheme.

From an object programming standpoint, the bad news is that Oracle 8.0 does not directly support inheritance. You cannot create a user-defined object type as a subtype of another. As a corollary, you cannot reuse method definitions. The good news, though, is that the ANSI and ISO committees working on object-oriented extensions to SQL are forming a position on how inheritance should behave in object-relational databases.[*] If history is any indicator, Oracle will move quickly to adopt as much of the new standard (known as SQL3), as possible. As we go to press, SQL3 is still a bit fluid, and the Oracle user community still has an opportunity to communicate to Oracle the most important inheritance features from a user perspective. Do we need multiple inheritance? Do we have to have late method binding? If you have an opinion, let Oracle know!

Although inheritance gets much attention in object technologies, it is one of several types of relationships that can be incorporated into an object model or, in some languages, an object implementation. Inheritance is often described as an *is-a* relationship; that is, a Dog *is-a* Pet.[†] Other prominent relationships include aggregation and association. *Aggregation* occurs where one object is composed, at least in part, of other objects; you could call it a *part-of* relationship: a Tail is *part-of* a Dog. *Association* is a more generic, usually named relationship, indicating some other link between object types, as in a Dog *gets examined by* a Veterinarian.

---

[*] A discussion of the committees' work on object extensions appears at *http://info.gte.com/ftp/doc/activities/x3b7/by_model/SQL3.html.*

[†] Viewing inheritance as synonymous with "is-a" relationships can sometimes be too simplistic. Martin Fowler describes a number of scenarios where doing so can lead to logical errors. See *UML Distilled: A Concise Guide for Applications Developers*, Addison-Wesley, 1997.

While these relationship types are common in object modeling nomenclatures such as the *Unified Modeling Language* (UML),[*] relational models rarely categorize them using these names. However, a kind of pseudo-inheritance is available in an entity-relationship (ER) model that uses supertype/subtype entities, which can be transformed into several different physical implementations. Aggregation and association can be represented as named relationships among entities and then transformed into foreign keys. The Oracle objects extension does give us the ability to create relationships using a new kind of pointer called a *reference* (REF), described later in this chapter.

Polymorphism

Polymorphism, by one definition, means that a given operation behaves consistently even when applied to different datatypes. You can implement polymorphism in at least two different ways, even without the Oracle objects option:

1. Module overloading (see Chapter 15, *Procedures and Functions*) allows a given PL/SQL module to have multiple specifications and bodies, distinguished by the datatype of the arguments supplied.

2. Programmers can implement a kind of *ad hoc* polymorphism in the way they program object types. For example, a Pet type might implement an operator called LIST_ME which gives a simple ability to display its contents on a report. This operator could be implemented in other object types as well.

The idea here is that a common core of functionality exists across the population of object types; each object knows how to respond to the requests sensibly. The classical form of polymorphism is one in which an object is not of a single type but actually represents many types, all of which are descendants of some common supertype; this behavior in fact exists in PL/SQL's implicit datatype conversions. For example, you can add a real number to an integer using a polymorphic "+" operator.

Object Programming Themes

While object-oriented programming languages have special features to support object identity, classification, inheritance, and polymorphism, software developers can adopt the general themes of object orientation in many languages. These themes[†] include:

---

[*] UML, the combined effort of Rational Corporation's object mavens Grady Booch, James Rumbaugh, and Ivar Jacobson, is expected to figure prominently in Oracle Corporation's object modeling conventions and tools. Visit *http://www.rational.com/uml/index.html* or *http://www.rational.com/uml/1.1/index.html* for documentation of the latest UML standard.

[†] Again, see James Rumbaugh.

- Information hiding
- Abstraction
- Combining data with behavior
- Decomposition of things, not processes

Information hiding

When I first learned about "information hiding," I said to myself, "Why in the world do we want to hide information? Isn't more better?" That was before I had worked on systems from the Jackson Pollock[*] school of design. Now I can say with conviction that hiding the internals of a software construct, and carefully limiting its public interface, is a *good* thing. Not only does it make for fewer unnecessary bits competing for attention in my limited biological CPU, it also brings clarity to application design, and keeps other modules from relying on the unsavory details.

One beautiful way that PL/SQL supports information hiding is by separating specifications from bodies and allowing separate recompilation. This separation is available to both packages (since Oracle7) and object types. In addition, package bodies can include "private" local variables, procedures, and functions which cannot be invoked outside the package.

Oracle 8.0.3 does not support private methods inside an object body, but we can hope that such a feature will appear in a future release.

Encapsulation

Encapsulation, a sister concept to information hiding, asserts that you can only "get at" an object's contents using predefined functions. The extreme degree of encapsulation asserts that no data can be viewed or modified except through explicitly defined (or inherited) methods. This allows the programmer to retain control of the data, and helps reduce the impact of schema changes. By establishing cleanly defined object interfaces, we can develop decoupled, reusable modules that can be made to fit together gracefully even when future requirements change.

Encapsulation was gracefully achievable as early as Oracle7 using packages. By putting all DML into procedures and functions and requiring applications to use these modules rather than issuing direct INSERT, UPDATE, or DELETE statements, developers can realize enormous long-term benefits. Oracle objects extend the encapsulation options available to programmers to include object methods.

---

[*] Jackson Pollock (1912-1956) was an American painter prominent in the Abstract Expressionist movement. His paintings abandoned the idea that composition should be expressed as the relationship among parts. Some say his paintings look as if he tossed paint cans at the canvas.

Oracle still allows server-side database triggers on object tables. In one sense, these triggers violate encapsulation because they allow PL/SQL code to modify object contents directly. However, in keeping with Oracle's hybrid object-relational strategy, you can use triggers if they make sense to your application.

Abstraction

The concept of abstraction includes both data abstraction and functional abstraction. An example of abstraction is a purchase order.[*] With a programming system that allows us to implement abstract datatypes, we can represent a purchase order as a purchase order object, rather than as a parent table, *plus* a child table of line items, *plus* a number of applications to manage the tables. In the real world, purchase orders can be created, edited, completed, and destroyed. In our object-oriented program, a single purchase order ADT would be defined using whatever complex data structures are appropriate, and would include methods for each of the corresponding real world operations.

One assumption about abstraction is that dealing with fewer "things" in the program can reduce the likelihood of errors. In addition, only by the practice of abstraction can we possibly build and maintain extremely large, distributed systems.

With the Oracle objects option, the essential structure we use to create an abstraction is the object type. While PL/SQL packages can also implement an ADT, programmers have typically used packages only for the abstraction of complex processing. Objects, on the other hand, are designed to encourage both process abstraction and data abstraction. These abstractions can encompass complex, multi-level structures. For example, an Oracle object may contain other embedded objects, collections (similar to arrays), and references (pointers) to other objects.

Combining data with behavior

In a typical relational application, there is a database schema consisting of a number of possibly normalized tables, plus a body of application code that manipulates the data. During design, analysts model the entity relationship graph separately from the module hierarchy, and this can result in the need for complex cross-reference matrices which can be costly to develop and more challenging to maintain.

In contrast, in an object model, the data and the legal operations on the data are co-located. In an object implementation, attributes and methods are welded into a single reusable part. A good object design means that there are fewer interconnections to deal with, increasing the likelihood of both reusability and adaptability.

---

[*] The purchase order example is particularly common in Larry Ellison speeches.

Oracle now directly supports this object programming theme, storing data in object attributes (persistent or not), with behavior defined by object methods.

Decomposition of things, not processes

It is common knowledge that changing a database's table design after the applications are built is a risky and expensive proposition. Database professionals have for years known that data structures are more stable than processes. That's why we require large scheduling windows (and expensive support tools) for entity-relationship modeling and database design.

Object programming carries this argument one step further, into the design of applications themselves. A well-designed object application, rather than being a hierarchy of sequential procedures exchanging flow of control, is more akin to a community of objects exchanging messages.

Non-object approaches, by contrast, often emphasize functional decomposition: breaking a problem, and its solution, into a series of processing steps. One problem with this type of approach is that, over time, the processes in the problem space are likely to change, and this will force extensive changes in the application. An object-oriented decomposition of the same problem, if properly designed, would require fewer changes.

Oracle Objects Example

Relative Pets, a combination pet store and animal hospital, is developing a database to help track their clientele. They tend to take an animal-centric view of the world, so their main entity is the Pet. They're also working on a web site where they can post photos of some critters that have been put up for adoption. Being on the foreleg of technology, they of course want to use an object-relational database like Oracle8.

Defining the Object Type Specification

We'll start simple. In this example, all of the attributes are primitive datatypes rather than objects or collections. The photo attribute is of the Oracle8 datatype BFILE, which is simply a reference to a file stored in the operating system (see Chapter 4, *Variables and Program Data*). We'll follow the convention that object type names start with a capital letter and end in "_t."

```
CREATE OR REPLACE TYPE Pet_t AS OBJECT (
    tag_no INTEGER,            -- pet license number
    name VARCHAR2(60),         -- name of pet
    animal_type VARCHAR2(30),  -- dog, cat, ferret,...
    sex VARCHAR2(1),           -- M/F
    photo BFILE,               -- JPG image in O/S file
```

```
    MEMBER FUNCTION set_tag_no (new_tag_no IN INTEGER)
        RETURN Pet_t,
    MEMBER FUNCTION set_photo (file_location IN VARCHAR2)
        RETURN Pet_t,
    MEMBER PROCEDURE print_me
);
/
```

This type contains scalar attributes and three methods. Note that the member functions return a value of type Pet_t. This affords flexibility in how the methods can be used later on.

NOTE   In SQL*Plus, you must enter the trailing slash after a CREATE TYPE
            or CREATE TYPE BODY statement. From this point forward in this
            text, we omit this trailing slash.

Defining the Object Type Body

To implement the methods, create the object type body, using a syntax that is remarkably similar to that used to create a package body:

```
CREATE OR REPLACE TYPE BODY Pet_t AS
    /* set_tag_no: Starting with the attributes of the "current"
    || pet object, return a new pet object with a new tag number.
    */
    MEMBER FUNCTION set_tag_no (new_tag_no IN INTEGER)
        RETURN Pet_t
    IS
        the_pet Pet_t := SELF;   -- initialize to current object
    BEGIN
        the_pet.tag_no := new_tag_no;
        RETURN the_pet;
    END;

    /* set_photo: Return new pet object with new photo filename.
    || Use BFILENAME, a built-in Oracle function that accepts
    || a directory alias and filename and returns a value of
    || type BFILE.
    */
    MEMBER FUNCTION set_photo (file_location IN VARCHAR2)
        RETURN Pet_t
    IS
        the_pet Pet_t := SELF;
    BEGIN
        the_pet.photo := BFILENAME('WEB_PHOTOS', file_location);
        RETURN the_pet;
    END;

    /* Do a simple listing of this object. Don't deal with the
    || contents of the photo, just its name.
    */
```

```
    MEMBER PROCEDURE print_me
    IS
        directory_alias VARCHAR2(60);
        file_name VARCHAR2(60);
    BEGIN
        DBMS_LOB.FILEGETNAME(SELF.photo, directory_alias, file_name);
        DBMS_OUTPUT.PUT_LINE('Tag No : ' || tag_no);
        DBMS_OUTPUT.PUT_LINE('Name   : ' || name);
        DBMS_OUTPUT.PUT_LINE('Type   : ' || animal_type);
        DBMS_OUTPUT.PUT_LINE('Sex    : ' || sex);
        DBMS_OUTPUT.PUT_LINE('Photo  : ' || file_name);
    END;
END;
```

This code introduces a couple of syntactic devices that we'll cover in detail later, namely the use of the "default constructor" to create an object of the designated type, and the use of the SELF parameter as a means of referring to the object and its component attributes. Notice that this code makes no mention of any tables in the database.

We haven't created a comprehensive implementation of this type yet, since we haven't coded methods for setting all of the attributes. Eventually, there could be quite a large number of new attributes, each of which could be managed by at least one method. Yes, an object approach can get a bit code-happy if you look at how the objects are implemented "under the covers." You may be asking yourself, why use these trivial procedures for setting attribute values? Why not expose the attributes and let application programs just set the value?

Although exceptions exist, a convention of the object approach is that *all* operations on object data must be implemented by methods. As soon as you allow the use of a back door to manipulate data, you have violated encapsulation, and you are asking for the same kind of trouble you'd get with excessive use of global variables: code that breaks easily, with low confidence that modifications will be free of errors, and, in general, high maintenance costs (see the discussion of global variables in Chapter 16, *Packages*). It's true enough that comprehensive object definitions can be code intensive; the payback comes later on, during maintenance and future development, when well implemented objects are less likely to break and more likely to facilitate reuse and resilience.

PL/SQL usage

To create an object based on a type—that is, to *instantiate* it—you can use a default *constructor,* a function that Oracle makes available as soon as you create a type. The constructor has the same name as the object type, and accepts each attribute as an argument, in the order in which attributes are declared in the object type definition. That is, Pet_t is both the name of an object type and the name of the corresponding default constructor:

```
DECLARE
    the_pet Pet_t;
BEGIN
    -- Instantiate the_pet using the default constructor
    the_pet := Pet_t(104525, 'Mambo', 'DOG', 'M',
        BFILENAME('WEB_PHOTOS','Mambo.jpg'));

    -- Invoke a method to change the tag number of the_pet
    the_pet := the_pet.set_tag_no(104552);

    -- Print a listing about the_pet
    the_pet.print_me();
END;
```

Notice the syntax for invoking the set_tag_no and print_me methods on the_pet. This *object.method* syntax is not uncommon in other OO languages. It's different from *package.procedure_or_function* syntax, because what you find on the left side of the dot is an object instance. That is, a correct call is:

```
the_pet.set_tag_no(104552)   -- the_pet is a variable of type Pet_t
```

rather than:

```
Pet_t.set_tag_no(104552)   -- invalid; what pet's no. are we changing?
```

You have to tell Oracle which particular object instance you want to use.

If you prefer, you can use a method invocation that is almost indistinguishable from a conventional packaged function or procedure call, with either named or positional notation. The following calls show how you can simply supply the object instance as the SELF parameter (more about SELF later):

```
Pet_t.set_tag_no (the_pet, 104552)
Pet_t.set_tag_no (SELF=>the_pet, new_tag_no=>104552)
```

DDL usage

To create a database structure that will hold persistent objects of a given type, it's blissfully easy to create an object table:

```
CREATE TABLE pets OF Pet_t
    (PRIMARY KEY (tag_no));
```

This creates a table with columns for the attributes. The table also has other special characteristics, such as a hidden object identifier column, on which Oracle automatically creates a unique index. As implied by the PRIMARY KEY clause, it also creates a relational primary key constraint—and therefore an additional unique index—on the tag_no column. (You cannot, by the way, use a nonscalar column such as a REF or a collection as the primary key.)

Encapsulation of Persistent Objects in Oracle?

A conceptually pure implementation of encapsulation would restrict all operations on the object's attributes, meaning that: (1) you would need to implement methods for every different read and write operation; and (2) it would be impossible to read or write object data without using these methods.

In practical terms, this means that *if* you design objects to be responsible for their own persistence—in other words, you program the methods to know how to perform DML on table(s) that implement the object type—you should not have to grant table-level INSERT, UPDATE, or DELETE privileges to anyone using the object. Instead, you should be able to simply grant EXECUTE on the object type to the Oracle user or role.

For improved reusability, however, there may be cases where you want public object methods to execute under the privilege set of the *invoker* rather than the object *owner*. How does this affect reuse? Remember that object types are only templates, not actual tables or columns. Under the owner rights model, if another Oracle user attempted to reuse a type definition "template," he might receive a load of inappropriate privileges, even if only during method execution. And he would wind up making a copy of the object type rather than reusing it—not an ideal situation, but not the end of the world.

By contrast, under an invoker rights model, you would have to grant SELECT, INSERT, UPDATE, and/or DELETE on the object table to every user who needs to perform these operations. Once you do that, encapsulation is lost, since these operations are perfectly happy to attack the data from the relational side, undermining object encapsulation.

By relying strictly on owner rights, Oracle 8.0.3 may limit reuse, but at least it does not require you to violate encapsulation. If you GRANT EXECUTE ON *object_type* TO *username*, the user will execute any object methods under the privilege domain of the owner. If the object type owner can delete a table, and writes a table deletion method, the user will also be able to execute that method to delete from the table.

If Oracle implements an invoker rights model, how should they do it? In my opinion, Oracle should give PL/SQL developers a choice: we should be able to decide which rights model a given method will use. This option would afford the designer both flexibility for reuse and the security of encapsulation.

Without such a choice, a strict invoker rights model could essentially mean that you would not want to read or write persistent objects directly from object methods. Instead, your methods would have to call modules in PL/SQL packages (or vice versa) which manipulate the database, presuming that packages still operated under the owner rights model.

—Continued—

The package-encapsulating strategy was available even in Oracle7; schematically, it looks like this:

```
CREATE TABLE foo (...);
/* foo can be a conventional table or an object table */

CREATE PACKAGE manage_foo AS ...
/* manage_foo contains stored procedures and functions that
|| encapsulate all DML on the foo table. It could also contain
|| REF cursors to encapsulate SELECTs.
*/

GRANT EXECUTE ON manage_foo TO taylor, fernando, kim;
/* Alternatively create an Oracle "role" and grant execute
|| on the role to the users
*/
```

Proving to ourselves that our table looks right, we can do a "describe" on it as follows:

```
SQL> desc pets
 Name                            Null?    Type
 ------------------------------- -------- ----
 TAG_NO                                   NUMBER(38)
 NAME                                     VARCHAR2(60)
 ANIMAL_TYPE                              VARCHAR2(30)
 SEX                                      VARCHAR2(1)
 PHOTO                                    BINARY FILE LOB
```

and we can insert a record object into the table:

```
INSERT INTO pets VALUES(Pet_t(1044526,'Socks','CAT', 'M',
    BFILENAME('WEB_PHOTOS', 'socks.jpg')));
```

The INSERT statement uses the constructor in the VALUES clause.[*] Now the object can continue its life more or less permanently in a database table. It can get retrieved by PL/SQL programs or referenced by other tables as needed. However, up to this point, we have not defined any methods that will manage the persistent data. We'll see later how to design these additional methods you have to invoke when programs need to change the state of a persistent object.

---

[*] This statement also assumes that we have already created the WEB_PHOTOS directory alias using the SQL CREATE DIRECTORY statement, as in: CREATE DIRECTORY web_photos AS '/u01/www/images/photos'.

Adding Complex Data Structures

As a dues-paying member of the SPCA, Relative Pets keeps a vaccination history on each animal. To introduce the rich data structures available to objects, we can create a nested table datatype to hold information about vaccinations. Each pet can have many vaccinations.

```
CREATE TYPE Vaccination_list_t AS TABLE OF VARCHAR2(30);
```

(See Chapter 19, *Nested Tables and VARRAYs,* for more information about this new collection type.) Since we are going to track the owners of the pets, we could benefit from having a "person" object. For now, we won't give this object type many attributes, but we will implement the RESTRICT_REFERENCES pragma so that we can use its "full_name" function in DML (see Chapter 17, *Calling PL/ SQL Functions in SQL,* for a full discussion of this pragma):

```
CREATE TYPE Person_t AS OBJECT (
    person_id INTEGER,
    last_name VARCHAR2(60),
    first_name VARCHAR2(30),
    MEMBER FUNCTION full_name RETURN VARCHAR2,
    PRAGMA RESTRICT_REFERENCES (full_name, RNDS, WNDS, RNPS, WNPS)
);
```

Here is a simple body that implements the full_name method:

```
CREATE TYPE BODY Person_t
AS
    MEMBER FUNCTION full_name RETURN VARCHAR2
    IS
    BEGIN
        RETURN first_name || ' ' || last_name;
    END;
END;
```

Finally, we can put a vaccination list and an owner in our "pet" object type:

```
CREATE OR REPLACE TYPE Pet_t AS OBJECT (
    tag_no INTEGER,             -- pet license number
    name VARCHAR2(60),          -- name of pet
    animal_type VARCHAR2(30),   -- dog, cat, ferret,...
    sex VARCHAR2(1),            -- M/F
    photo BFILE,                -- JPG image in O/S file
    vaccinations Vaccination_list_t,
    owner Person_t,
    MEMBER FUNCTION set_tag_no (new_tag_no IN INTEGER)
        RETURN Pet_t,
    MEMBER FUNCTION set_photo (file_location IN VARCHAR2)
        RETURN Pet_t,
    MEMBER PROCEDURE print_me
);
```

Although not illustrated here, after making this change, we might want to add new member functions in the type specification and body.

In this example, we are setting ourselves up to use a nested "person" object within the pet object. This is not necessarily a good idea, since the enclosed objects are not sharable by anything else. That is, if one person owned many pets, the information about the owner would have to be copied into each pet object. We're passing up an opportunity to control data redundancy, which is one of the reasons we are using a such a wonderful database system in the first place. Not to worry: we can use the REF keyword to tell Oracle that we want to store only a pointer or *reference* to another (persistent) object. That is, in our final version:

```
CREATE OR REPLACE TYPE Pet_t AS OBJECT (
    tag_no INTEGER,
    name VARCHAR2(60),
    animal_type VARCHAR2(30),
    sex VARCHAR2(1),
    photo BFILE,
    vaccinations vaccination_list_t,
    owner_ref REF Person_t,
    MEMBER FUNCTION set_tag_no (new_tag_no IN INTEGER)
        RETURN Pet_t,
    MEMBER FUNCTION set_photo (file_location VARCHAR2)
        RETURN Pet_t,
    MEMBER PROCEDURE print_me,
    MEMBER PROCEDURE vaccinate (vaccination VARCHAR2, on_date DATE),
    PRAGMA RESTRICT_REFERENCES (set_tag_no, RNDS, WNDS, RNPS, WNPS),
    PRAGMA RESTRICT_REFERENCES (set_photo, RNDS, WNDS, RNPS, WNPS)
);
```

we use REF Person_t to indicate that this attribute will store a pointer to an object rather than to its contents.

And we can build the tables:

```
CREATE TABLE persons OF Person_t
    (PRIMARY KEY (person_id));

CREATE TABLE pets OF Pet_t
    (PRIMARY KEY (tag_no))
    NESTED TABLE  vaccinations STORE AS pet_vaccinations_tab;
```

Using this separate persons table and the REF attribute will allow the existence of people outside the context of their pets (something the pet-obsessed may not envision, but probably a good idea from a design point of view). In this context, REF is called a *type modifier*.

Does a REF sound a lot like a foreign key? While there are important differences between REFs and foreign keys (see Table 18-2), Oracle actually claims that REFs, are "more reliable and persistent" than foreign keys—probably because REFs do not refer to user-changeable values, but rather to invisible internal values.

In fact, the problem with REFs is that they are *too* persistent. Oracle currently allows you to delete an object that is the target of a REF without deleting the reference to it. They even dignify this state with a name: a *dangling REF*. This is roughly equivalent to what would happen if you delete a department record without changing the records of employees in that department. There is no declarative way to prevent dangling REFs, but it should not be too challenging to do so by implementing pre-delete triggers on the table that contains the "parent" objects.[*] To make life somewhat easier, Oracle provides a predicate, IS DANGLING, to test for this condition:

```
UPDATE pets
    SET owner_ref = NULL
    WHERE owner_ref IS DANGLING;
```

Table 18-2. Chief Differences between Foreign Keys and REFs

Characteristic	Foreign Key	REF
Who defines the value used as the "pointer?"	User (programmer)	System
Requirements on the parent	Must have primary or unique key	Must be an object table or object view
Only allows insertions of child if parent exists (or if the referencing columns are null)?	Yes, when enabled	Yes, since you can only insert a "real" REF
Can be defined in such a way that the child may be associated with one of several possible parents?	No (although foreign keys have a little-known ability to point to *all* of several possible parents)	Yes; by default, a REF can refer to any row object of the given type
Can declaratively restrict the scope of the child so that it can point to only one given parent table?	No	Yes (by using the SCOPE clause in the CREATE TABLE command)
Restricts updates of the parent key when children exist?	Yes	Yes; object identifiers are not updateable
Can prevent the deletion of parent if children exist?	Yes	No
Can cascade deletions of the parent to child (objects)?	Yes, with ON DELETE CASCADE	No

---

[*] It is also possible to use a foreign key in combination with a REF. To do so, you would include an attribute for the foreign key in the Pet_t specification and include a FOREIGN KEY clause in the CREATE TABLE statement.

Table 18-2. Chief Differences between Foreign Keys and REFs (continued)

Characteristic	Foreign Key	REF
Default type of relation-ship between parent and child when joined via SQL	Equi-join	Outer join (when using dot navigation)
Parent and child can be on different databases?	No; must be enforced with table-level triggers	Not in Oracle 8.0.3

NOTE   In Table 18-2, we use the terminology "parent" and "child" only for convenience; these terms are not always accurate descriptions of objects linked via REFs.

Oracle has a special syntax for retrieving and modifying data in both SQL and PL/SQL using the REF operator; they also provide a DEREF operator (can you guess why?). We'll look at those operators a bit later.

Syntax for Creating Object Types

This section explains the syntax for CREATE TYPE, CREATE TYPE BODY, and some of the other statements you will use when working with Oracle objects.

About Object Types

A given object type can have all of the following:

- One default constructor method
- Zero or one comparison methods
- Any number of member methods

The default constructor, supplied automatically when you create an object type, allows you to create an object of the corresponding type. You have no direct control over this function (aside from how you have defined the attributes of the object type). The constructor is the only type of method that does not operate on an existing object.

Comparison methods are either MAP or ORDER methods (see the section "Comparing Objects" later in this chapter). They allow you to establish rules so that SQL statements and PL/SQL programs can order, group, and otherwise compare object instances. Comparison methods are always functions.

Member methods are either member functions or member procedures. These are where programmers define the bulk of the object's behavior.

CREATE TYPE and DROP TYPE: Creating and Dropping Types

The CREATE TYPE statement has the following general format:

```
CREATE [ OR REPLACE ] TYPE <type name> AS OBJECT
    <attribute name> datatype, ...,
    MEMBER PROCEDURE | FUNCTION <procedure or function spec>, ...,
    [ MAP | ORDER MEMBER FUNCTION <comparison function spec>, ... ]
    [ PRAGMA RESTRICT_REFERENCES (<what to restrict>, restrictions) ]
);
```

As you would expect, you can drop a type using a DROP statement as follows:

```
DROP TYPE <type name> [ FORCE ] ;
```

Parameters have the following meanings:

OR REPLACE

Tells Oracle that you want to rebuild the type if it should happen to already exist. This will preserve grants. (See "Schema Evolution" later in the chapter for information about the effect this option has on the object type's metadata.)

type name

A legal Oracle identifier that isn't already in use by any other Oracle database object such as another type, table, or package. May be expressed in "schema dot" notation (e.g., SCOTT.foo).

attribute name

A legal PL/SQL identifier for the attribute.

datatype

Any legal Oracle datatype *except* LONG, LONG RAW, NCHAR, NCLOB, NVARCHAR2, ROWID, BINARY_INTEGER, BOOLEAN, PLS_INTEGER, RECORD, REF CURSOR, %TYPE, %ROWTYPE, or types that exist only within packages.

comparison function

Defines a function that allows comparison of object values.

what to restrict

This is either the name of the function or procedure, or the keyword DEFAULT. Using DEFAULT tells Oracle that *all* member functions and procedures in the object type will have the designated restrictions, without having to list each one in its own RESTRICT_REFERENCES pragma.

restrictions

One or more of the following: RNDS, WNDS, RNPS, and WNPS (see Chapter 17).

FORCE++

> Tells Oracle that you want to drop a type even if there are other objects with dependencies on it. Even if you use FORCE, you can only drop a type if it has not been implemented in a table; you must first drop the table(s) before dropping the type.

Notice that the syntax for creating the specification is merely a comma-separated list of attributes and methods. There are no semicolons as you would find in a package specification.

You cannot impose NOT NULL or DEFAULT constraints at the attribute level. These constraints can, however, be applied to scalar attributes if you create an object table based on type. The syntax is:

```
CREATE TABLE <table name> OF <object type name>
   (<column constraint>, ... );
```

For example:

```
CREATE TABLE foos OF Foo_t
   (bar NOT NULL);
```

or, if you wish to name a constraint:

```
CREATE TABLE foos OF Foo_t
   (CONSTRAINT bar_not_null CHECK (bar IS NOT NULL));
```

CREATE TYPE BODY: *Creating a Body*

The syntax for the CREATE TYPE BODY statement is the following:

```
CREATE [ OR REPLACE ] TYPE BODY <type name> AS | IS (
   MEMBER PROCEDURE | FUNCTION <procedure or function body>, ...,
   [ MAP | ORDER MEMBER FUNCTION <comparison function body> ]
END;
```

Strictly speaking, type bodies are optional; you need a body only if you have created any methods in the specification. Similar to the rules for package specifications and bodies, the methods declared in the specification must match one for one the methods implemented in the body. Methods can be overloaded (see Chapter 15), and the standard rules about overloading apply.

Dot Notation

Even if you don't use the object extensions to Oracle, dot notation can be confusing. In SQL, for example, you may have references such as basil.meals.calories, referring to a column called calories in a meals table owned by basil. Add in remote database references, and you might get something like basil.meals.calories@mktg.ny.acme.com. In PL/SQL Version 2 and up, dots are found in record datatypes, table datatype operators, packaged procedure or function references, and elsewhere.

In the objects option, there are at least two new opportunities to get confused with dots: object data structures and object methods. (And the discussion below ignores the fact that object names can be preceded by the schema name, as in schema_name.object_name.)

Dots in data structures

In a PL/SQL program, you can refer to object attributes with dot notation, as in object_name.attribute_name. For example, after declaring and initializing an object my_pet of type Pet_t, we can do this:

```
IF my_pet.sex = 'M' THEN...
```

This variable means "the sex attribute of the object instance my_pet."

Referring to nested objects in PL/SQL using dot notation is almost intuitive, as long as you're using embedded objects (that is, the attribute is an object itself, not a REF to an object).

```
CREATE OBJECT Pet_t (
   ...
   owner Person_t,     -- embedded object, not a REF
   ...);

DECLARE
   the_dalmatian Pet_t;
BEGIN
   ...
   IF the_dalmatian.owner.first_name = 'Persephone'
   THEN...
```

The IF test above simply checks whether the first name of the owner of the Dalmatian is Persephone. In SQL statements, you can also use dots to navigate the components of nested objects. Even when you have nested objects with REFs, SQL graciously allows you to navigate to the referenced object without actually doing a join:

```
CREATE OBJECT Pet_t (
   ...
   owner_ref REF Person_t,
   ...);

CREATE TABLE pets of Pet_t;

SELECT name, p.owner_ref.first_name
   FROM pets p;
```

That's a pretty neat trick. No ugly join clause, just an intuitive "do the right thing" call. It works for attributes and member functions that are defined with the appropriate RESTRICT_REFERENCES pragma. But what do we do in PL/SQL? Is this legal?

```
DECLARE
    the_dalmatian Pet_t;
BEGIN
    SELECT VALUE(p) INTO the_dalmatian
      FROM pets p
     WHERE name = 'Cerberus';...
    IF the_dalmatian.owner_ref.first_name = 'Persephone'    -- invalid
    THEN...
```

It won't work! In Oracle 8.0.3, you cannot navigate the database through PL/SQL REF variables. Repeat this to yourself like a mantra. Dot notation doesn't help us in this case. For now, you can instead use DEREF, described in detail later on; a future version of Oracle will likely include a built-in package called UTL_REF that supports navigation in PL/SQL.

Dots in method invocations

When you invoke an object's member function or procedure, the dot syntax is straightforward, as in the following:

```
object_instance_name.function_name (args)
object_instance_name.procedure_name (args)
```

If you want to use the output from one method as the input to another, you don't have to use a temporary variable. You can actually chain methods together with dots, as long as they are type compatible:

```
object_name.function_name(args).function_name(args).procedure_name(args)
```

Before we can take a look at an example that chains our Pet_t methods, we'll want to change the specification of print_me. Instead of using the default IN OUT mode of the SELF parameter in a member procedure, we are going to make it an IN. That is, instead of:

```
MEMBER PROCEDURE print_me
```

we want to use:

```
MEMBER PROCEDURE print_me (SELF IN Pet_t)
```

(Remember that we have to make this change in both the object type specification and the object type body.)

Why did we make the change? The default IN OUT mode can only accept a SELF parameter that is writeable, and function return values are never writeable. But as an IN-only parameter, SELF can now accept a Pet_t object that is returned from one of the other functions.

```
DECLARE
    the_pet Pet_t := Pet_t(1949,'Godzilla','BIG MONKEY','M',
        NULL,NULL,NULL);
BEGIN
    the_pet.set_tag_no(1948).set_photo('gz105.jpg').print_me();
END;
```

This means "change the tag number of the pet variable to 1948, change its photo to gz105.jpg, and print the result." If you give a little thought to the implications of this convenience feature, you'll realize that it could be valuable to define member functions which return the base object type, so that you can chain them together later.

Here are some rules about chaining:

- Methods are invoked in order from left to right.

- The return value of a chained method must be of the object type expected by the method to its right.

- A chained call can include at most a single procedure.

- If your chained call includes a procedure, it must be the right-most method in the chain.

- Be sure that you don't try to use a function's return value (which is read-only) as an IN OUT input to the next method in the chain.

Attribute or method?

In PL/SQL, there is no automatic visual distinction between an object attribute and an object method unless the method has arguments. That is, in this code fragment:

```
IF my_pet.whatever = 'a value' THEN...
```

we can't immediately determine if "whatever" is an attribute or a method! In some cases, this ambiguity could be a feature, since one day we might want to replace an attribute by a method of the same name.

If we want to make our code less mysterious, we can add a trailing empty parameter list to method calls which have no parameters, as in the following:

```
my_pet.print_me();
```

The empty parentheses notation works for both member functions and member procedures.

NOTE   The situation is different in SQL statements. If you call a member
              function without parameters in a SQL statement, you *must* use empty
              parentheses notation. That is, if somefun is a function, don't do this:

```
SELECT p.somefun FROM pets p;   -- invalid
```

              The statement above fails with an ORA-00904, "invalid column
              name." The correct syntax is:

```
SELECT p.somefun() FROM pets p;
```

SELF: The Implied Parameter

Because a method can only be called within the context of a particular object
instance, it always has an object of the corresponding type as a "parameter." This
makes sense because the method will (almost) always need access to that object's
attributes. This implied parameter is called SELF. By default, SELF is an IN parameter in member functions, and an IN OUT parameter in member procedures.

If we create an object to hold American Kennel Club papers:

```
CREATE TYPE Akc_paper_t AS OBJECT(
    pet_ref REF Pet_t,
    issued_on DATE,
    contents BLOB);
```

the following member function specifications are equivalent:

```
MEMBER FUNCTION print_me RETURN BOOLEAN;
MEMBER FUNCTION print_me (SELF Akc_paper_t) RETURN BOOLEAN;
MEMBER FUNCTION print_me (SELF IN Akc_paper_t) RETURN BOOLEAN;
```

Similarly, member procedure SELF parameters default to IN OUT, so the following
are equivalent to one another:

```
MEMBER PROCEDURE reissue;
MEMBER PROCEDURE reissue (SELF Akc_paper_t);
MEMBER PROCEDURE reissue (SELF IN OUT Akc_paper_t);
```

Within the object type body, you can refer to the SELF object explicitly; if you do
not, PL/SQL name resolution rules will attempt to "do the right thing" with
attribute references. In the example below, the name and issued_on attributes will
resolve to attribute values even without the SELF parameter:

```
CREATE TYPE BODY Akc_paper_t
AS
    MEMBER FUNCTION print_me RETURN BOOLEAN
    IS
    BEGIN
        DBMS_OUTPUT.PUT_LINE('Name      : ' || name);
```

```
            DBMS_OUTPUT.PUT_LINE('Issued On: ' || issued_on);
            ...
        END;
    END;
```

The PUT_LINE statements above are equivalent to:

```
        DBMS_OUTPUT.PUT_LINE('Name      : ' || SELF.name);
        DBMS_OUTPUT.PUT_LINE('Issued On: ' || SELF.issued_on);
```

TIP   Including SELF explicitly can improve program clarity.

Forward type definitions

What would you do if you wanted to define object types that depend on each other? Suppose that we want to implement the following relationships:

- Each pet has an owner of type Person_t; owners can have one or more pets.

- A person can have one and only one *favorite* pet.

The solution is a *forward type definition*, similar to forward declarations in PL/SQL packages (see Chapter 16). A forward definition allows you to declare your intention to create a type before you actually define it:

```
/* Here is the incomplete type definition */
CREATE TYPE Person_t AS OBJECT;

/* Now owner_ref can make a "forward" reference to the
|| Person_t type
*/
CREATE TYPE Pet_t AS OBJECT (
   tag_no INTEGER,
   owner_ref REF Person_t,
   ...the rest of the attributes and methods...
);
/* Now we can complete the type definition we started
|| earlier.
*/
CREATE TYPE Person_t AS OBJECT (
   name VARCHAR2(512),
   favorite_pet REF Pet_t,
   ...
);
```

If you want to create a recursive type, that is, one which refers to itself, a forward type definition is not required. For example, the Relative Pets organizational hierarchy might be implemented with recursion:

```
CREATE TYPE organization_unit_t AS OBJECT (
   id NUMBER,
```

```
    parent REF organization_unit_t
       -- works fine without forward type def
);
```

Comparing Objects

In the "old days," when Oracle offered only scalar datatypes, the semantics for comparing values were clearly defined. For example, columns of type NUMBER are easily compared, ordered, and grouped. Ditto for dates, and even character types, despite differences in national language sorting conventions. NULLs have always given us some grief, but we can't argue that the rules about them were vague. Things got a little more interesting in PL/SQL programs, because there we can have complex data structures such as records and table datatypes, which offer very few comparison features within the language.

Now, if we are taking an object-oriented approach, it would be useful if Oracle allowed statements such as the following:

```
IF my_pet > your_pet THEN ... -- my_pet and your_pet are objects

SELECT ... FROM pets ORDER BY owner;    -- owner is an object column
```

But it is not at all obvious how Oracle would deal with statements like these. Should it do some sort of "munching" average on the objects' attributes, or what?

In fact, Oracle allows us to formulate our own comparison rules for the object types we create. By defining a special MAP or ORDER member function when we define an object type, we can tell Oracle how to compare objects of that type in both PL/SQL and SQL expressions.

The MAP and ORDER methods

Let's say that we have created an object type Appointment_t that will help us in scheduling visits to the veterinary offices of Relative Pets. We might need an application to compare appointments:

```
DECLARE
   my_appointment Appointment_t;
   your_appointment Appointment_t;
BEGIN
   ...initialize the appointments...

   IF my_appointment > your_appointment THEN ...
```

To perform this greater-than comparison, you'll need to define either a MAP or an ORDER function. MAP and ORDER methods are mutually exclusive; a given object type may have exactly one MAP method, or exactly one ORDER method (or zero comparison methods of either type).

MAP member functions. The MAP method simply translates or "maps" each object into a scalar datatype space that Oracle knows how to compare. For example, suppose we had a simple rule that says appointments are "greater than" others if they occur later in time. Then the MAP method is trivial:

```
CREATE TYPE Appointment_t AS OBJECT (
    pet REF Pet_t,
    scheduled_date DATE,
    with_whom REF Doctor_t,
    MAP MEMBER FUNCTION compare RETURN DATE
);

CREATE TYPE BODY Appointment_t
AS
    MAP MEMBER FUNCTION compare RETURN DATE
    IS
    BEGIN
        RETURN scheduled_date;
    END compare;
END;
```

MAP functions accept no parameters and must return a date, character, or number—that is, something that SQL and PL/SQL already know how to compare.

ORDER member functions. The alternative to MAP is an ORDER member function, which accepts two objects: SELF and another object of the same type. You must program the ORDER member function to return an INTEGER that is one of the values -1, 0, or 1, indicating the ordering relationship of the second object to SELF. That is, if you want:

- SELF < second object, return -1

- SELF = second object, return 0

- SELF > second object, return +1

- Undefined comparison, return NULL.

Let's look at an example of this type of function:

```
CREATE TYPE Location_t AS OBJECT (
    latitude REAL,
    longitude REAL,
    altitude REAL,
    ORDER MEMBER FUNCTION compare (the_location IN Location_t)
        RETURN INTEGER
);

CREATE TYPE BODY Location_t
AS
    ORDER MEMBER FUNCTION compare (the_location IN Location_t)
        RETURN INTEGER
    IS
```

```
    -- A very lame attempt at comparing geographic locations
    BEGIN
        IF the_location.latitude = SELF.latitude
           AND the_location.longitude = SELF.longitude
           AND the_location.altitude = SELF.altitude THEN
               RETURN 0;
        ELSIF SELF.latitude > the_location.latitude
           OR SELF.longitude > the_location.longitude
           OR SELF.altitude > the_location.altitude THEN
               RETURN 1;
        ELSE
            RETURN -1;
        END IF;
    END;
END;
```

This ORDER member function will allow us to make simple comparisons such as:

```
IF location1 > location2 THEN
    plant_a_flag;
END IF:
```

Although not recommended, your ORDER method can return NULL under certain situations, and the object comparison itself will evaluate to NULL. That is, if our object type body were rewritten as follows:

```
CREATE TYPE BODY Location_t
AS
    ORDER MEMBER FUNCTION compare (the_location IN Location_t)
        RETURN INTEGER
    IS
    -- An even more lame attempt at comparing geographic locations
    BEGIN
        IF the_location.latitude = SELF.latitude
           AND the_location.longitude = SELF.longitude
           AND the_location.altitude = SELF.altitude THEN
               RETURN 0;
        ELSE
            RETURN NULL;
        END IF;
    END;
END;
```

Then, if attributes of two locations are equal, the expression (location1 = location2) will evaluate to TRUE; but if any of the attributes differ, then you can detect the condition using the IS NULL operator. Using the second version of the Location_t body, the expression below will always be true!

```
IF (location1 < location2) IS NULL THEN...
```

Suffice it to say that returning NULL from a comparison function is not particularly helpful.

There is nothing magic about the name you give the MAP and ORDER functions. In fact, other than in the type definition statements, you may never refer to this name. An added bonus of using MAP or ORDER functions is that they enable you to do things like ORDER BY and GROUP BY the object in SQL statements.

Which should you use—MAP or ORDER? To some extent, it's a matter of what makes sense to your application, but keep in mind the following restrictions and qualifications:

- A MAP method is more efficient than the equivalent ORDER method.

- If you plan to perform hash joins on the object in SQL, you must use MAP, because this type of join requires a value to hash.

- A MAP method is particularly appropriate if you are sequencing a large series of objects, while an ORDER method is more useful if you are comparing two objects.

Equality comparisons

If you *don't* create a MAP or ORDER method, Oracle allows you to test only for *equality* of two different objects. Two Oracle objects are "equal" if and only if they (1) are of the same object type; and (2) both have attributes with identical values. Object attributes get compared one at a time, in order, and the testing stops when the first mismatch is discovered.

Here is an example of testing for equality:

```
DECLARE
    the_1997_spec Marketing_spec_t;
    the_1998_spec Marketing_spec_t;
BEGIN
    ...
    IF the_1997_spec = the_1998_spec THEN ...
```

Or, if we had one table of marketing specs per year:

```
CREATE TABLE marketing_1997 OF Marketing_spec_t;
CREATE TABLE marketing_1998 OF Marketing_spec_t;
```

then we could compare from within SQL by using the VALUE operator:

```
SELECT s97.make, s97.model
  FROM marketing_1997 s97,
       marketing_1998 s98
 WHERE VALUE(s97) = VALUE(s98);
```

Privileges

While there are two categories of users to whom object privileges may be granted,
programmers and end users, there is only one Oracle privilege that applies to
object types: EXECUTE. Let's look at how this privilege applies to DDL (typically
for programmers) and DML (typically for end users).

DDL

Let's say that you are the Oracle user named SCOTT and you have created an
object type Pet_t. You want to grant JOE permission to use this type in his own PL/
SQL programs or tables. All you need to do is grant the EXECUTE privilege to him:

```
GRANT EXECUTE on Pet_t TO JOE;
```

Joe can then refer to the type using *schema.type* notation:

```
CREATE TABLE my_pets OF SCOTT.PET_T;

DECLARE
   the_pet SCOTT.PET_T;
```

EXECUTE privileges are also required by users who simply need to run PL/SQL
anonymous blocks that use the object type.

DML

For object tables, the traditional SELECT, INSERT, UDPATE, and DELETE privileges still have meaning.   A user with SELECT on the object table may only
retrieve the relational columns and not the object-as-object.   That is, he cannot use

the VALUE operator. Similarly, the other three privileges, INSERT, UPDATE, and DELETE, apply only to the relational interpretation of the table.

In the same fashion, the grantee does not have permission to use the constructor or other object methods unless the object type owner has granted the user EXECUTE privilege on the object type.

Rights model

Suppose that the owner of a package grants me EXECUTE privileges on it in Oracle7. Whenever I execute the package, I am actually using the owner's privileges on tables, views, and the like. I need no privileges on the underlying structures. This *definer rights* model can be very useful in encapsulating the table data and protecting it from change except through the package.

As mentioned earlier in the chapter (see the Sidebar called "Encapsulation of Persistent Objects in Oracle"), the owner rights model may have a negative impact on object reuse, and it's conceivable that an object-relational database like Oracle could implement an *invoker rights* model for object methods. As with all new technology, we will simply have to wait and see whether such a change comes about, and if it does, what sort of impact it will have on existing applications.

Manipulating Objects in PL/SQL and SQL

In this section we look more deeply into the constructs and concepts you will need in order to master to use objects in your applications. There are three different ways you can initialize an object:

- Use the default constructor
- Make a direct assignment
- SELECT INTO or FETCH INTO

In addition, after an object is initialized, it can be stored in the database, and you can then locate and use that object using several new language constructs:

- REF
- VALUE
- DEREF

The Need to Initialize

The designers of the PL/SQL language have established a general convention that uninitialized variables are null.* Object variables are no exception; the term for this uninitialized object condition is "atomically null." Not only is the object null, but so are its individual attributes. To illustrate, let's take a trip back to the pet shop.

Since all pets need a home, we might want to create an address object type:

```
CREATE TYPE Address_t AS OBJECT(
    street VARCHAR2(40),
    city VARCHAR2(20),
    state VARCHAR2(10),
    country VARCHAR2(3)
);
```

In the example below, notice that the object itself is null, as well as the object's attributes:

```
DECLARE
    cerberus_house Address_t;   -- cerberus_house is not initialized here
BEGIN
    IF cerberus_house IS NULL ...        -- will evaluate to TRUE
    IF cerberus_house.street IS NULL... -- also TRUE
```

The nullity of the elements in PL/SQL follows somewhat unpredictable rules; uninitialized RECORD variables have null elements (as with objects), but uninitialized collections have elements whose nullity is not defined. As with collections, when an object is null, you cannot simply assign values to its attributes; if you do, PL/SQL will raise an exception. Before assigning values to the attributes, you *must* initialize the entire object.

Let's turn now to the three different ways a PL/SQL program can initialize an object.

Constructors

A constructor is a special method that allows the creation of an object from an object type. Invoking a constructor is a way to instantiate (create) an object. In Oracle 8.0, each object has a single default constructor that the programmer cannot alter or supplement.

The default constructor:

- Has the same name as the object type
- Is a function rather than a procedure

---

* One significant exception is the Version 2 table datatype, known as index-by tables in Version 3, which are non-null but empty when first declared. In PL/SQL8, uninitialized nested tables and uninitialized VARRAYs are, in fact, null

- Accepts attributes in named or positional notation

- Returns an object

- Must be called with a value, or the non-value NULL, for every attribute; there is no DEFAULT clause for object attributes

Notice how the name of the constructor matches the name of the object type, which may look odd at first glance (unless you're already an object-oriented programmer). The following declaration assigns an initial value to the cerberus_ house object:

```
DECLARE
    cerberus_house Address_t := Address_t('123 Main', 'AnyTown', 'TX', 'USA');
```

Direct assignment

When assigning one object to another, you create a new object that starts life as a copy of the original. In the following example, minotaurs_labyrinth gets initialized using direct assignment.

```
DECLARE
    cerberus_house Address_t := Address_t('123 Main', 'AnyTown', 'TX', 'USA');
    minotaurs_labyrinth Address_t;
BEGIN
    minotaurs_labyrinth := cerberus_house;
END;
```

The attributes of the two addresses start out identical, but subsequent modifications to one do not automatically apply to the other.

Assignment via FETCH (with SELECT)

Assuming that there is a "houses" table of Address_t objects, we can use a SELECT statement to retrieve from the database into a PL/SQL object. PL/SQL provides the VALUE keyword (described below) to retrieve the contents of the entire object:

```
DECLARE
    troubles_house Address_t;
    CURSOR h_cur IS
        SELECT VALUE(h)
          FROM houses h
         WHERE resident_cat = 'TROUBLE';
BEGIN
    OPEN h_cur;
    FETCH h_cur INTO troubles_house;
    ...
```

ACCESS_INTO_NULL exception

If your program attempts to assign a value to an attribute of an uninitialized object, PL/SQL will raise the predefined exception ACCESS_INTO_NULL:

```
DECLARE
    our_house Address_t;              -- not initialized
BEGIN
    our_house.street := '123 Main';   -- raises ACCESS_INTO_NULL
END;
```

While seeming quite reasonable, this kind of an assignment will clearly not achieve the desired result. It bears repeating: always initialize your objects!

OID, VALUE, REF, and DEREF

The Oracle objects option provides an initially bewildering set of constructs for locating and referring to persistent objects. Getting to know them may take some time, but understanding them will be essential to "doing objects right." Table 18-3 summarizes these schemes and the following sections look at them in more detail.

Table 18-3. Schemes for Referring to Persistent Objects

Scheme	Description	Applications
Object identifier (OID)	An opaque, globally unique handle, produced when the object is stored in the database as a table (row) object.	This is the persistent object's handle; it's what REFs point to. Your program never uses it directly.
VALUE	An operator. In SQL it acts on an object in an object table and returns the object's "contents." Do not confuse this keyword with the VALUES keyword that appears in the INSERT statement.	Used when fetching a table (row) object into a variable, or when you need to refer to an object table as an object instead of a list of columns.
REF	A pointer to an object. May be used within a SQL statement as an operator, or in a declaration as a type modifier.	Allows quasi-"normalizing" of object-relational databases and "joining" of object tables using "dot navigation." In PL/SQL, REFs serve as input/output variables.
DEREF	Reverse pointer lookup for REFs.	Helpful for retrieving the contents of an object when all you know is its REF.

Object identifiers (OIDs)

Have you ever used an arbitrary number (maybe an Oracle sequence) as a table's primary key? The benefits are many—chief among them that you can often hide it from the users and never have to worry about them wanting to change the key value! Object identifiers are a lot like your arbitrary numbers, except that they are assigned by Oracle. When you create a table of objects, Oracle adds a hidden field that will hold the object identifier for each object. Oracle also automatically creates a unique index on this column. When you insert an object into the table,

Oracle automatically assigns the object a rather large but hidden object identifier (OID). The OID is:

- *Opaque.* Although your programs can indirectly use the OID, you don't typically see its value.

- Potentially *globally unique* across databases. The OID space makes provisions for up to 2^{128} objects (definitely "many" by the reckoning of the Hottentots).[*]

- Capable of being *synthesized* from a primary key so that objects can be retrofitted onto relational schema using object views.

- *Preserved* after export/import by the owner, unlike ROWIDs. This could allow objects to be distributable across databases in the future (contrast with ROWIDs, which are tied to a particular database)..

In addition, unless you are using primary key-based OIDs in object views, OIDs are *immutable.* That is, even if you want to change the binary value of an OID, you can't do it unless you delete and recreate the object, at which point Oracle will assign a new OID.

Not all objects have an object identifier. In particular, objects stored in PL/SQL variables lack a referenceable OID, as do column objects. A column object only "makes sense" within the context of its row, and the row will have other means of unique identification. Implementors must sometimes choose between embedding an object and making it referenceable.[†]

REFs

Oracle8 "reference" datatypes are destined to cause more than a few knitted brows in the Oracle user community. The confusion starts with the fact that REF has two different yet related meanings, depending on context. Toss in the fact that some objects have REFs and some don't. It's best to invest a little extra time early on to understand REFs if you want to avoid increasing your gray hair count (or, in my case, the size of my forehead).

The main reason that the reference concept is so critical is that REFs are the best way of uniquely referring to object instances. REFs are the way that we "see" object identifiers. REFs are the basis of object relationships and object "joins."

---

[*] Oracle could one day use an OS-dependent function to make OIDs globally unique; that way, no two OIDs could have the same value, even on different machines that are configured identically. Perhaps object navigation will be possible without database links. (In case you're wondering, the Hottentots had a four-valued counting system: 1, 2, 3, and "many.")

[†] This approach is 180 degrees off from relational industry experts who assert that OIDs should not be used for row identification, and that only column objects should have OIDs. See Hugh Darwen and C. J. Date, "The Third Manifesto," *SIGMOD Record*, Volume 24 Number 1, March 1995.

Hidden Columns Exposed

The name of the column where Oracle8.0.3 stores object identifiers is SYS_NC_ OID$. This column is "hidden" in that you won't see it when you "describe" the table in SQL*Plus, but it exists for every object instance (row) in an object table. It contains a 16-byte binary value; although this value is selectable from SQL*Plus, it should never be stored or manipulated in your programs. Oracle has hidden the OID to prevent hardcoding memory addresses into programs— a dangerous practice in any environment. Moreover, the OID structure could change in future Oracle versions.

There's another hidden column, SYS_NC_ROWINFO$, which provides a representation of the constructor for the row object. The same caution applies— it's interesting to look at, but do *not* rely on it in any applications.

Just to get an idea of what these columns look like, let's say we had a type foo_t which includes two attributes: a number and a collection of type bar_t:

```
CREATE TYPE bar_t AS VARRAY(5) OF VARCHAR2(10)
/
CREATE TYPE foo_t AS OBJECT (
    id NUMBER,
    bars bar_t)
/
CREATE TABLE foos OF foo_t;

INSERT INTO foos VALUES (1, bar_t('apple','banana','cherry'));

SELECT SYS_NC_OID$ FROM foos;

SYS_NC_OID$
--------------------------------
5661E312079811D19F35006097646884

SELECT SYS_NC_ROWINFO$ FROM foos;

SYS_NC_ROWINFO$(ID, BARS)
----------------------------------------------
FOO_T(1, BAR_T('apple', 'banana', 'cherry'))
```

Oracle provides constructs such as REF() and VALUE() so you don't need direct access to these hidden columns. In fact, you can get the constructor out of SYS_NC_ROWINFO$ in an Oracle-supported manner as follows:

```
SELECT VALUE(f) FROM foos f;

VALUE(F)(ID, BARS)
----------------------------------------------
FOO_T(1, BAR_T('apple', 'banana', 'cherry'))
```

REF as operator. In a SQL statement, when you need to retrieve a table object's unique identifier, you will use REF. In this case, REF operates on a row object, accepting as its argument a *table alias* (also known as a *correlation variable*). As hinted earlier, REF cannot operate on column objects or otherwise nested objects, because such objects do not have an OID. REFs are constructed from (but are not identical to) OIDs; only objects with OIDs get to have REFs pointing to them.

Syntactically, to retrieve a pointer from a table of objects, you will use:

```
REF(table_alias_name)
```

as in

```
SELECT REF(p)
   FROM pets p       -- uses table alias "p"
   WHERE ...
```

While you can choose any unambiguous SQL identifier for the table alias, a short alias is generally more readable. In most cases in this book, we use a single letter.

But retrieving a REF is not terribly useful in and of itself unless you happen to like looking at long hex strings. More typically, REFs are used like a foreign key. To assign a value to a REF field, we must first retrieve the value from the object table:

```
DECLARE
     person_ref REF Person_t;
     CURSOR pref_cur IS
        SELECT REF(p)
          FROM persons p
          WHERE last_name = 'RADCLIFF';
BEGIN
     OPEN pref_cur;
     FETCH pref_cur INTO person_ref;
     CLOSE pref_cur;
     INSERT INTO pets VALUES (Pet_t(10234, 'Wally', 'Blue whale',
        'M', null, null, person_ref));
END;
```

Or, more concisely:

```
INSERT INTO pets
     SELECT Pet_t(10234, 'Wally', 'Blue whale',
        'M', null, null, REF(per))
       FROM persons per
      WHERE last_name = 'RADCLIFF';
```

Then, after your data is loaded, you *could* retrieve an attribute or member function of the referenced object via a join.

```
SELECT p.tag_no, per.full_name()
   FROM pets p,
        persons per
  WHERE p.owner_ref = REF(per);
```

But wouldn't you be happier using Oracle's ability to traverse REFs automatically?

```
SELECT tag_no, p.owner_ref.full_name()         -- cool!
   FROM pets p;
```

This illustration (which does work, by the way) shows how Oracle SQL elegantly supports object navigation across REFs, something not directly allowed in PL/SQL. This is some of "the neat stuff" that the object extensions provide. Most people will find this chained dot nomenclature much more intuitive and easier to maintain over the long run than the equivalent explicit join.

By the way, the two versions of this "join" are not *exactly* identical. The first, with the explicit join, performs an "equi-join," which means that if the owner_ref column is null or dangling, the record (object) will not appear in the result set. However, the second, with dot navigation, performs an "outer join," meaning that a null or dangling owner_ref will simply cause the full_name field to show up null.

WARNING   *REFs are not foreign keys.* As previously discussed and as illustrated in Table 18-2, the differences between REFs and foreign keys are significant. You will need to give some thought to how you are going to prevent dangling REFs.

REF as type modifier. To hold a REF in a local variable, declare the variable of type REF *object_name*, and assign it via fetch or assignment from another REF that points to the same type. This example of REF as a "type modifier" shows that you can assign REFs using fetches and direct assignment, as you would expect.

```
DECLARE
   pet_ref REF Pet_t;
   hold_pet_ref REF Pet_t;
BEGIN
   -- example of assignment via fetch
   SELECT REF(p) INTO pet_ref
     FROM pets p
    WHERE...

   -- example of direct assignment
   hold_pet_ref := pet_ref;
```

What about local object type variables? At first blush, it might seem that you should be able to do something like the following:

```
DECLARE
   our_house Address_t := Address_t('123 Main','AnyTown','TX','USA');
   house_ref REF Address_t;
BEGIN
   house_ref := REF(our_house);   -- invalid
```

You can't get the REF to an object variable which exists only in a PL/SQL program. REFs are constructed from an object's OID, and transient objects don't have such a pointer.

If they are so much trouble, what good are REFs? As mentioned earlier, REFs are the only supported way of getting at OIDs. And despite the dangling REF problem, if you want to "normalize" an object-oriented design so that objects can be shared, you will have to use REFs. In addition, a REF is an efficient and light-weight means of passing object information as a parameter. That is, if you pass only the pointer, you avoid the overhead of allocating memory for a copy of the object contents. Be aware that passing a REF can allow the called program to change the object's contents, something you may or may not intend.

VALUE

Like REF, the VALUE operator also accepts a table alias as its argument. However, VALUE retrieves the value of an object (for example, to create a copy of it) via SQL.

To understand what VALUE does, first consider what happens if you apply pre-Oracle8 techniques to an object table:

```
DECLARE
    CURSOR h_cur IS
        SELECT *
        FROM houses;              -- houses is an object table
    their_house h_cur%ROWTYPE;
BEGIN
    OPEN h_cur;
    FETCH h_cur INTO their_house;
```

These non-object calls work fine even though "houses" is an object table. This is one demonstration of the relational side of an "object-relational database." But their_house is a record variable, not an object.[*] If you later wanted to take advantage of objects in PL/SQL, your code would be ill-prepared.

To use a local variable that has been typed as an object, you must declare it to be of the same datatype on which you have defined the table object, and you must use the VALUE operator:

```
DECLARE
    some_house Address_t;
    CURSOR h_cur IS
        SELECT VALUE(h)
        FROM houses h;
BEGIN
    OPEN h_cur;
```

---

[*] If you wanted an object variable built from the their_house record variable, you could declare the variable of type Address_t, and initialize it, using the Address_t constructor, from the elements in their_house.

```
FETCH h_cur INTO some_house;
-- Attributes are available using dot notation
IF some_house.city IS NULL THEN ...
```

This code begs the question: What is the difference between the "value" of an object and the object itself? Why is VALUE necessary at all?

Without VALUE, the retrieval of data in object tables would be ambiguous. You therefore have to tell Oracle whether you want the attributes or the whole object. SELECTing a table object *without* the VALUE operator retrieves the attributes of the object, while using the VALUE retrieves the entire object as an object.

Omitting VALUE fails if we try to fetch *columns* directly into an object variable:

```
DECLARE
    some_house Address_t;
    CURSOR h_cur IS
        SELECT *
            FROM houses;
BEGIN
    OPEN h_cur;
    FETCH h_cur INTO some_house;    --invalid; type mismatch
...
```

It's worth pointing out that even if we fetch an object as an object from the database, we *still* can't get to the REF from the local object variable. This is unfortunate. In other words, I would like the following to be possible:

```
DECLARE
    some_house Address_t;
    some_house_ref REF Address_t;
    CURSOR h_cur IS
        SELECT VALUE(h)
            FROM houses h;
BEGIN
    OPEN h_cur;
    FETCH h_cur INTO some_house;
    some_house_ref := REF(some_house);  -- invalid
```

Perhaps Oracle will consider adding this functionality to a future release. Until then, the workaround is simple enough:

```
DECLARE
    some_house Address_t;
    some_house_ref REF Address_t;
    CURSOR h_cur IS
        SELECT VALUE(h), REF(h)
            FROM houses h;
BEGIN
    OPEN h_cur;
    FETCH h_cur INTO some_house, some_house_ref;
    CLOSE h_cur;
END;
```

NOTE   VALUE does not apply to column objects, since retrieving a column object unambiguously retrieves an object value.

DEREF

DEREF is the "dereference" operator. Like VALUE, it returns the *value* of an object; unlike VALUE, DEREF's input is a REF to an object. That is, if you have a REF column in a table and you want to retrieve the target instead of the pointer, you use DEREF. It "un-does" a REF. Consider the following example which, as we noted earlier, fails to compile:

```
DECLARE
    the_dalmatian Pet_t;
BEGIN
    SELECT VALUE(p) INTO the_dalmatian
      FROM pets p
     WHERE name = 'Cerberus';
    IF the_dalmatian.owner_ref.first_name = 'Persephone'  -- invalid
    THEN...
```

This can be "fixed" using DEREF as follows:

```
DECLARE
     the_owner Person_t;
BEGIN
    SELECT DEREF(owner_ref) INTO the_owner
      FROM pets
     WHERE name = 'Cerberus';
    IF the_owner.first_name = 'Persephone'
    THEN...
```

Modifying Persistent Objects

Just because you decide to use objects, don't think that your design decisions are over. On the contrary, the fun is just beginning. One of the core design options you must confront (consciously or not) is this: "Just how object-oriented do I want to make the PL/SQL in my applications?" When dealing with persistent data, this question translates (at least partially) into "Where should I allow modifications?" It is this second question that is the topic of this section.

There are four architectures discussed below, but they certainly don't represent all the possibilities.

Approach 1

Permit full use of conventional SELECT, INSERT, UPDATE, and DELETE statements on your persistent objects. Other than using complex datatypes, the objects option will, in this case, look a lot like conventional relational approaches. At this end of the spectrum, you don't even have to define any methods...but you pay a price.

Approach 2

Permit limited use of conventional SQL, but invoke the constructor method in INSERT, and create various UPDATE methods which will be invoked in clauses of UPDATE statements. Use DELETE as above. This is a better way to go, since you can rely at least partially on the core logic you embed in the methods. However, you still rely on application programmers to invoke the methods *properly*.

Approach 3

Implement all data manipulations via methods, including all DML on persistent object tables (or at least make an attempt to do so). If you come from an object shop, this might be your preferred approach. This approach absolutely commits you to an object bias in your applications. However, it ties the object type to a particular implementation, which *might* limit reuse.

Approach 4

Design the object methods to avoid references to persistent object tables, instead acting only on the SELF object and on data exchanged via method arguments. Construct PL/SQL "container" packages to manage your persistent object tables (this is similar to what you could do in Oracle7), but code these packages to reuse logic that is localized in the object type definition. When a PL/SQL application needs to manipulate persistent data, it must call the package; when it simply needs to perform an operation on a transient object variable, it will typically invoke a method. Approach 4 has a number of advantages over Approach 2 above; notably, it further increases the likelihood that application programmers will invoke the proper call in their code.

NOTE   Although the crystal ball isn't talking, a fifth approach may make a
            great deal of sense once Oracle supports inheritance. It might be
            possible to implement persistent object types as subtypes of the cor-
            responding transient object type. Doing so could potentially provide
            the benefits of encapsulation and reuse while circumventing difficult
            schema evolution problems. (That is, subtypes should be capable of
            specializing behavior of their supertypes so you don't have to re-
            build the entire dependency tree every time you make slight modifi-
            cations in object specifications.)

The examples that follow abandon our friends at the pet shop and move on to looking at documents as objects. We will use only a few attributes; the important thing to watch is how we use Oracle features to allow the manipulation of the object data, while still protecting it.

Approach 1: Permit Full Use of Conventional SQL

This scheme, illustrated in Figure 18-1, is characterized by ultimate flexibility. It allows any application to use whatever SQL the programmer feels is necessary to achieve the desired result. It requires little or no coordination among programmers, although they will (you hope) be coding against a shared database design.

```
CREATE OR REPLACE TYPE Doc_t AS OBJECT (
    doc_id INTEGER,
    name VARCHAR2(512),
    author VARCHAR2(60),
    url VARCHAR2(2000),
    publication_year INTEGER(4)
);

CREATE TABLE docs OF Doc_t
    (PRIMARY KEY (doc_id));
```

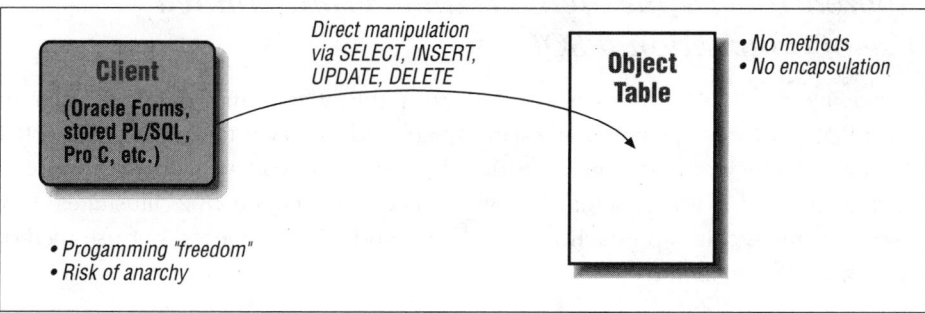

Figure 18-1. Approach 1 (full use of SQL)

It is certainly possible to go wild with SQL, as if we weren't using objects at all. Various applications might be issuing DML as they see fit.

An Oracle Forms application might be issuing inserts...

```
INSERT INTO docs VALUES (1001, 'Great Expectations', 'Charles Dickens',
    'http://www.literature.org/Works/Charles-Dickens/
    great-expectations/', 1861);

INSERT INTO docs VALUES(42, 'The Hitchhiker''s Guide to the Galaxy',
    'Douglas Adams', 'http://www.bxscience.edu/~grollman/trilogy/
    Hitchhikers.Guide.to.the.Galaxy', 1979);
```

...while an application programmer is working in SQL*Plus...

```
UPDATE docs SET author = 'Chuck Dickens' WHERE doc_id = 1001;

SELECT * FROM docs WHERE author LIKE '%Adams';
```

...and a Pro*C application is deleting data that's not in the mainframe any more:

```
DELETE docs WHERE doc_id = 42;
```

Does this possibly look a lot like what you've been doing for years? Consider for a moment the problems this might cause. First, allowing any application to issue any DML statement under the sun makes it difficult simply to assess the impact of a schema change, not to mention the actual cost and time to implement the change. Second, there is little hope of reusing DML statements since there is no central, controlled superstructure in place to facilitate code sharing. And what happens if you discover "bad data" in the database, which *might* be the result of a bug in an UPDATE statement in some application? Since DML can get mind-numbingly complex, simply locating buggy SQL can be a frustrating, costly process.

With an undisciplined approach, a database system of any substantial size—regardless of whether the database is relational or object-relational—may not survive the weight of its own maintenance.

Approach 2: Define Methods and Permit Limited Use of Conventional SQL

By adding methods to your objects, you can publicly announce to other programmers that you will maintain a standard, controlled interface to an object, and that if they use the methods you have defined, they and you will be less prone to getting slapped with maintenance work later on. Figure 18-2 illustrates how clients in this second approach invoke their own DML statements, but use method calls in these statements.

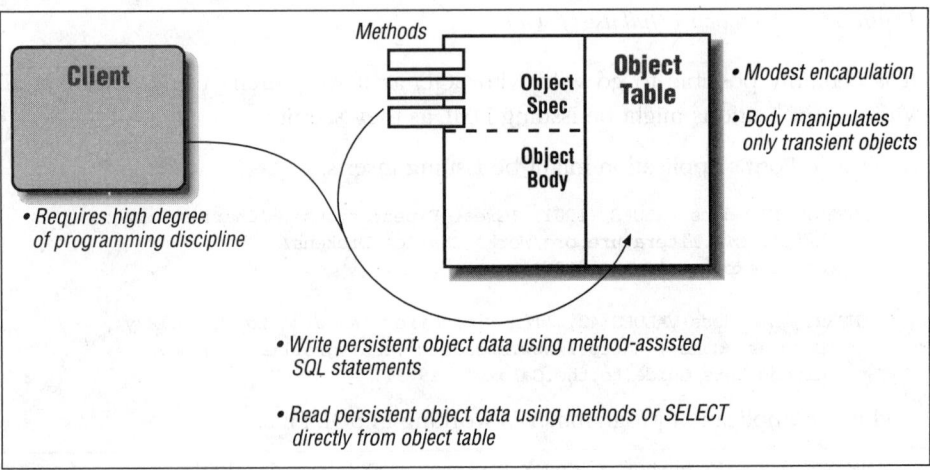

Figure 18-2. Approach 2 (methods and limited SQL)

Looking at a code sample, the set_author method below can be used in an UPDATE statement:

```
CREATE OR REPLACE TYPE Doc_t AS OBJECT (
    doc_id INTEGER,
    name VARCHAR2(512),
    author VARCHAR2(60),
    url VARCHAR2(2000),
    publication_year INTEGER(4),
    -- we return the entire object so methods can be chained if needed
    MEMBER FUNCTION set_author (new_author VARCHAR2) RETURN Doc_t,
    PRAGMA RESTRICT_REFERENCES (set_author, RNDS,WNDS,RNPS,WNPS)
);

CREATE OR REPLACE TYPE BODY Doc_t AS
    MEMBER FUNCTION set_author (new_author VARCHAR2) RETURN Doc_t
    IS
        the_doc Doc_t := SELF;
    BEGIN
        the_doc.author := new_author;
        RETURN the_doc;
    END set_author;
END;
```

Application DML might look like the following. Inserts are straightforward enough, using the default constructor:

```
INSERT INTO docs VALUES (Doc_t(1005, 'The Tempest',
    'William Shakespeare', 'http://the-tech.mit.edu/Shakespeare/Comedy/
    tempest/thetempest.html', 1611)));
```

Or even (just to illustrate the point):

```
INSERT INTO docs SELECT VALUE(d) FROM docs d;
```

Yes, the previous statement duplicates all the objects in the docs table.

In SQL, you can invoke a method in an UPDATE statement in a straightforward fashion. To change all of Shakespeare's documents so that I am the author, the following statement will do the job. Notice the use of the table alias *d* as the placeholder for the "current" object.

```
UPDATE docs d
    SET d = d.set_author('Bill')
    WHERE d.author = 'William Shakespeare';
```

Deleting a persistent object in this second approach is just like the first approach:

```
DELETE docs WHERE doc_id = 1001;
```

Or in PL/SQL, if we already have a REF in the doc_ref variable, we could delete as follows:

```
DELETE docs d WHERE REF(d) = doc_ref;
```

How does Approach 2 insulate applications from change? It's not hard to see that if we later implement a business rule regarding changing authors—for example, it's illegal to alter the author of anything written prior to 1900—we need only recode the method. When dealing with persistent objects, you will rightly point out, this sort of restriction can be coded using database triggers or stored procedures; however, triggers are no help at all if you want to enforce rules on transient objects.

Overall, this second approach, while improved, still leaves much to be desired, since it still relies heavily on programmer discipline to use the object methods in their DML statements.

Approach 3: Do Everything via Methods

If you are wedded to object technology, this approach (illustrated in Figure 18-3) may be for you, although it poses some challenges. In the sample code, notice that every DML statement will occur via a procedure call. Remember that DML can only be executed in member procedures because Oracle does not allow functions to modify the database.

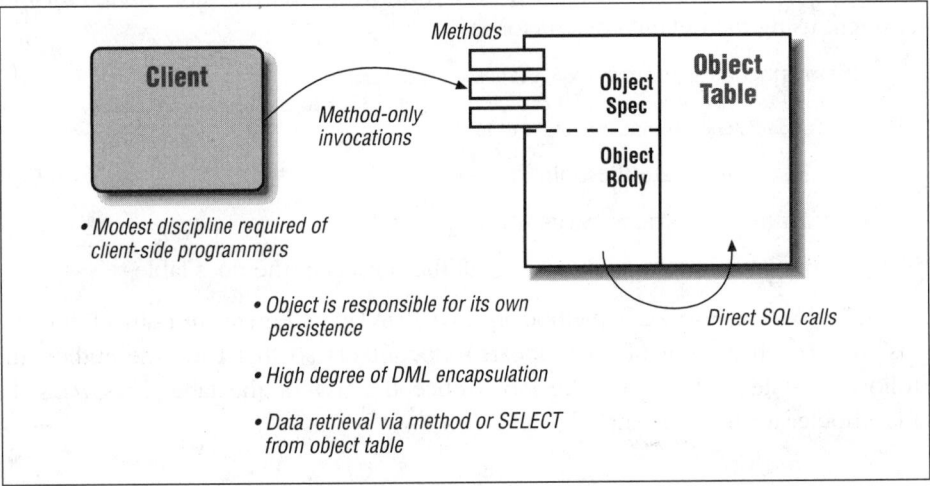

Figure 18-3. Approach 3 (everything via methods)

Rather than look at the full code of the object specification and body, let's look first at a client executing a single operation: change the name of the author. You would want a very simple call where you provide only the name of the new author. In other words, the call might ideally be invoked something like this:

```
DECLARE
    the_doc_ref REF Doc_t;
BEGIN
```

```
      SELECT REF(d) INTO the_doc_ref
        FROM docs d
        WHERE d.doc_id = 1001;
      the_doc_ref.set_author('me');  -- hypothetical call; is invalid
   END;
```

Here, "set_author" is a proposed method of the Doc_t object. Set_author would know how to update the database object corresponding to the_doc_ref. Whoops! Did you forget? *You cannot navigate the database through REF variables.* And the_doc_ref is certainly a REF variable, so you can't use it in place of an object.

Let's look at this from the other side now. What could we do in the object definition to make an update work easily?

Here again is the specification, which we won't change (yet):

```
CREATE OR REPLACE TYPE Doc_t AS OBJECT (
    doc_id INTEGER,
    name VARCHAR2(512),
    author VARCHAR2(60),
    url VARCHAR2(2000),
    publication_year INTEGER(4),
    MEMBER PROCEDURE set_author (new_author IN VARCHAR2)
);
```

And here is the body, with a new, but so far incomplete, UPDATE statement:

```
CREATE OR REPLACE TYPE BODY Doc_t
AS
    MEMBER PROCEDURE set_author (new_author IN VARCHAR2)
    IS
    BEGIN
       /* First update the transient object */
       SELF.author := new_author;

       /* Now update the persistent object  */
       UPDATE docs d SET author = new_author
         WHERE ???
    END;
END;
```

What exactly do we put in the WHERE clause? You could try this:

```
WHERE d = SELF;
```

But then you are doing an object comparison that could be problematic if you have defined a MAP member function. Think about it: MAP only provides some scalar mapping of some object characteristics, and it is possible to have different objects with the same MAPped value!

So what you might think of next is using a REF to the object:

```
WHERE REF(d) = REF(SELF);
```

The problem with this WHERE clause is that you can't get the REF of SELF, since SELF is not a table alias; logically, it also fails because it might not exist as a referenceable object in the database. (It kind of makes sense, but you don't have to like it.)

Now what? What about passing in a REF, something like this:

```
CREATE OR REPLACE TYPE Doc_t AS OBJECT (
    doc_id INTEGER,
    name VARCHAR2(512),
    author VARCHAR2(60),
    url VARCHAR2(2000),
    publication_year INTEGER(4),
    MEMBER PROCEDURE set_author (new_author IN VARCHAR2,
        doc_ref REF Doc_t)
);

CREATE OR REPLACE TYPE BODY Doc_t
AS
    MEMBER PROCEDURE set_author (new_author IN VARCHAR2,
        doc_ref REF Doc_t)
    IS
    BEGIN
        /* First update the transient object */
        SELF.author := new_author;

        /* Now update the persistent object */
        UPDATE docs d
            SET author = new_author
            WHERE REF(d) = doc_ref;
    END;
END;
```

There! That not only compiles, it does what we want. Here's an example of using the member procedure in PL/SQL to update the persistent object:

```
DECLARE
    my_doc Doc_t;
    my_doc_ref REF Doc_t;
BEGIN
    SELECT VALUE(d), REF(d) INTO my_doc, my_doc_ref
        FROM docs d
        WHERE doc_id = 1001;
    my_doc.set_author('Yogi Bear', my_doc_ref);
END;
```

It's a little ugly with the extra REF argument in there, but there is no easy way in Oracle8.0 to get to a more "pure" object approach.

Are we finished? What about the possibility that we want to update only the transient object, rather than the persistent object? For example, we might want to set_ author from within a SQL SELECT statement. For that, we can simply define a similar member function, which unfortunately cannot have the overloaded same name as the member procedure, since PRAGMA RESTRICT_REFERENCES will attempt to take effect on all modules of the supplied name.

```
CREATE OR REPLACE TYPE Doc_t AS OBJECT (
    doc_id INTEGER,
    name VARCHAR2(512),
    author VARCHAR2(60),
    url VARCHAR2(2000),
    publication_year INTEGER(4),
    MEMBER FUNCTION set_author (new_author IN VARCHAR2)
        RETURN Doc_t,
    PRAGMA RESTRICT_REFERENCES (set_author, RNDS,WNDS,RNPS,WNPS),

    /* We are changing the name of the procedure below to have "_p"
    ||   on the end, as a mnemonic for Persistent (or Procedure)
    */
    MEMBER PROCEDURE set_author_p (new_author IN VARCHAR2,
        doc_ref REF Doc_t)
);

CREATE OR REPLACE TYPE BODY Doc_t AS
    MEMBER FUNCTION set_author (new_author IN VARCHAR2)
        RETURN Doc_t
    IS
        l_doc Doc_t := SELF;
    BEGIN
        l_doc.author := new_author;
        RETURN l_doc;
    END;

    MEMBER PROCEDURE set_author_p (new_author IN VARCHAR2,
        doc_ref REF Doc_t)
    IS
    BEGIN
        SELF := SELF.set_author (new_author);
        UPDATE docs d
            SET author = new_author
         WHERE REF(d) = doc_ref;
    END;
END;
```

This code will definitely work. Because of the RESTRICT_REFERENCES, you can use the function in SQL:

```
SELECT d.set_author('me') FROM docs d;
```

...and you can use the function from PL/SQL:

```
DECLARE
    my_doc Doc_t := Doc_t(1,'OPP','Feuerstein',null,null);
BEGIN
    my_doc := my_doc.set_author('Steven Feuerstein');
END;
```

...and you can use the procedure in PL/SQL, as indicated earlier.

Think for a minute about the possibility that you code a method that changes more than one attribute at a time. You could get a bit more elegant by updating the entire object in the UPDATE statement, rather than using individual assignments in the SET clause.

```
MEMBER PROCEDURE set_name_and_author (new_name IN VARCHAR2,
    new_author IN VARCHAR2,
    doc_ref IN REF Doc_t) IS
BEGIN
    SELF.name := new_name;
    SELF.author := new_author;
    UPDATE docs d
       SET d = SELF
     WHERE REF(d) = doc_ref;
END;
```

WARNING   While this code is syntactically correct, it fails in Oracle8.0.3 due to a PL/SQL bug. At press time, summer of 1997, we don't know exactly when this will be fixed—soon, we hope!

The other "update" methods (for example, set_name, set_url, etc.) in our all-object approach would follow the general patterns we've established so far.

There are two more cases that you'll want to cover: persistent object construction and destruction. These are relatively simple INSERT and DELETE statements, as shown below:

```
CREATE OR REPLACE TYPE Doc_t AS OBJECT (
    doc_id INTEGER,
    name VARCHAR2(512),
    author VARCHAR2(60),
    url VARCHAR2(2000),
    publication_year INTEGER(4),
    MEMBER PROCEDURE construct_and_save (the_doc_id IN INTEGER,
        the_name IN VARCHAR2, the_author IN VARCHAR2,
        the_url IN VARCHAR2, the_year IN INTEGER,
        doc_ref_out OUT REF Doc_t),
    MEMBER PROCEDURE save (doc_ref_out OUT REF Doc_t),
    MEMBER PROCEDURE destroy (doc_ref IN REF Doc_t),
    MEMBER FUNCTION set_author (new_author IN VARCHAR2)
        RETURN Doc_t,
    PRAGMA RESTRICT_REFERENCES (set_author, RNDS,WNDS,RNPS,WNPS),
    MEMBER PROCEDURE set_author_p (new_author IN VARCHAR2,
        doc_ref REF Doc_t)
);

CREATE OR REPLACE TYPE BODY Doc_t AS
    MEMBER FUNCTION set_author (new_author IN VARCHAR2)
        ...as above
```

```
MEMBER PROCEDURE set_author_p (new_author IN VARCHAR2,
   ...as above

MEMBER PROCEDURE construct_and_save (the_doc_id IN INTEGER,
   the_name IN VARCHAR2, the_author IN VARCHAR2,
   the_url IN VARCHAR2, the_year IN INTEGER,
   doc_ref_out OUT REF Doc_t)
IS
/* Encapsulates the constructor and the INSERT. Note that the
|| values passed in via arguments need not match the initial
|| attributes of SELF. In fact, SELF can be atomically null
|| when you first invoke this method.
*/
BEGIN
   SELF := Doc_t(the_doc_id, the_name, the_author, the_url,
      the_year);
   SELF.save(doc_ref_out);
END;

MEMBER PROCEDURE save (doc_ref_out OUT REF Doc_t)
IS
/* Use this one for the INSERT if you have already invoked
|| the constructor and have a doc object in a variable.
|| The RETURNING clause returns the object's OID into the
|| host variable doc_ref.
*/
BEGIN
   INSERT INTO docs d VALUES (SELF)
      RETURNING REF(d) INTO doc_ref_out;
END;

MEMBER PROCEDURE destroy (doc_ref IN REF Doc_t)
IS
/* Note that we are passing in a REF that might not match
|| whatever might be in SELF. It is up to the calling module to
|| be aware of this idiosyncrasy.
*/
BEGIN
   SELF := NULL;
   DELETE docs d
     WHERE REF(d) = doc_ref;
END;
END;
```

When you store an object using the "save" procedure above, you will have already created an in-memory version of the object using the default constructor or other means. Contrast this with "construct_and_save."

As noted in the comments, the RETURNING clause of the INSERT statement returns the REF identifier of the newly created object into a program variable. Since this is a very useful value, we return it to the calling program using an OUT parameter. (RETURNING is a new feature of SQL in Oracle8 that allows us to retrieve data on INSERT, UPDATE, and DELETE statements. It's useful not only for returning a REF but also for returning other generated column values such as those computed by database triggers.)

When you "destroy" an object in a program, you simply assign NULL to the object. This returns its state to "atomically null," which is the nonvalue the object would have if you had never constructed it. Oracle does not supply any sort of "destructor" method.

Let's step back and think about the "method-only" approach. Making the object type responsible for its own persistence seems like a good idea. But this code assumes that your Doc_t object type will be intimately tied to the "docs" table. Is that a reasonable assumption? There is nothing in Oracle that forces you to implement the Doc_t object type only one time. If you ever decide to reuse the object types, which you probably will, our "method-only" approach could run into problems.

Maybe you could define an argument to indicate which table(s) needs to receive the data change. You could wind up with messy IF tests and multiple UPDATE statements or, at best, dynamic SQL to apply the change to multiple tables. Worse, you could end up having to drop and rebuild your object tables to accommodate the changes in method specifications (see the section called "Schema Evolution" later on). Very un-object-oriented.

But what is the alternative? Any way you code it, managing the persistent data in *multiple* object tables defined on the same object type will be more trouble than a *single* table. You could allow rampant DML statements, which we have already poo-poo'd as the moral equivalent of global variables. Perhaps we could make our code "more object-oriented" if the Oracle objects option allowed inheritance. That way, we might be able to have an object table managed by a child object type. The parent would manage only transient objects, and the children would manage persistent objects.

As we'll see in Approach 4, another method is to rely on the "other" object features of the language that you can find in packages. By using object types for nonpersistent transient data only, you can avoid a number of thorny issues, at the possible expense of clouding your abstraction.

Approach 4: Use an Object and a PL/SQL Container Package

If you typically program with packages, this approach (illustrated in Figure 18-4) will look familiar, and you should feel free to pat yourself on the back. If you don't use packages, you should seriously consider their benefits (see Chapter 16), which can include many of the same advantages of objects.

In this scheme, we eliminate all references to persistent data from the object definition and body. Instead, we write a PL/SQL package that will manage our object tables. By separating the layer that manages persistence (the package) from the layer that manages objects (the object type), we have a closer fit of PL/SQL with Oracle's object model, especially if we intend to reuse object type definitions. In addition, we gain access to REF CURSORs, which allow the encapsulation of complicated SELECT statements.

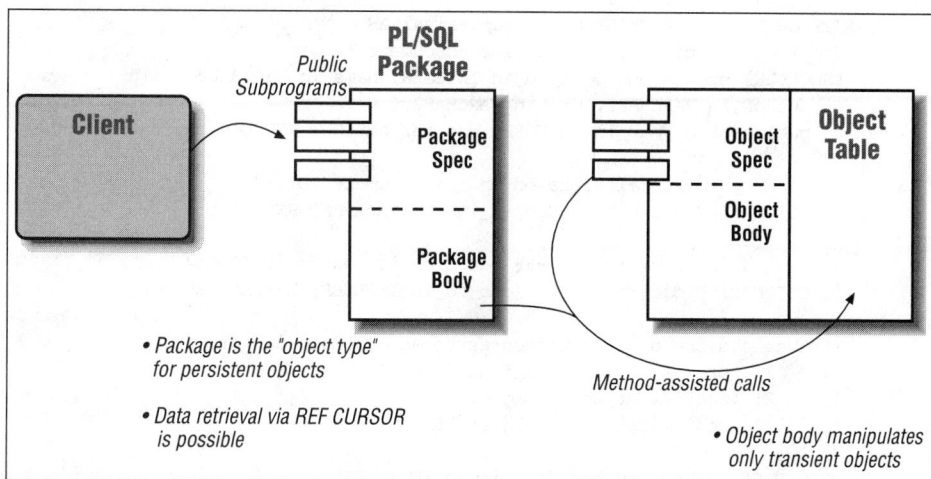

Figure 18-4. Approach 4 (object and PL/SQL container package)

Let's start with the type definition, with only the single archetypal set_author function illustrated:

```
CREATE OR REPLACE TYPE Doc_t AS OBJECT (
    doc_id INTEGER,
    name VARCHAR2(512),
    author VARCHAR2(60),
    url VARCHAR2(2000),
    publication_year INTEGER(4),
    MEMBER FUNCTION set_author (new_author IN VARCHAR2)
        RETURN Doc_t
);
```

And the body, which might be very familiar by now:

```
CREATE OR REPLACE TYPE BODY Doc_t AS
    MEMBER FUNCTION set_author (new_author IN VARCHAR2) RETURN Doc_t
    IS
        the_doc Doc_t := SELF;
    BEGIN
        the_doc.author := new_author;
        RETURN the_doc;
    END set_author;
END;
```

We can create an object table that will hold "appraisal" document objects, as long as they fit the Doc_t definition, and design the package without disturbing the object type:

```
CREATE TABLE appraisals OF Doc_t
    (PRIMARY KEY (doc_id));
```

The specification of our package to manage the persistent appraisal data could go something like this:

```
CREATE OR REPLACE PACKAGE manage_appraisal AS
    /* Allow creation of an appraisal document */
    PROCEDURE create_one (doc_id_in INTEGER, name_in VARCHAR2,
        author_in VARCHAR2, url_in VARCHAR2,
        publication_year_in INTEGER, doc_ref_out OUT REF Doc_t);

    /* Look up an appraisal based on its document ID  */
    FUNCTION find_doc_by_id (doc_id_in INTEGER) RETURN Doc_t;

    /* Look up an appraisal's REF based on its document ID  */
    FUNCTION find_doc_ref_by_id (doc_id_in INTEGER) RETURN REF Doc_t;

    /* Overload the update procedures to accommodate any of:
    ||    1) "primary key" style identification
    ||    2) identification by object
    ||    3) identification by object REF
    */
    PROCEDURE set_one_author (doc_id_in IN INTEGER,
        new_author_in IN VARCHAR2);
    PROCEDURE set_one_author (doc_in IN Doc_t,
        new_author_in IN VARCHAR2);
    PROCEDURE set_one_author (docref_in IN REF Doc_t,
        new_author_in IN VARCHAR2);

    /* You could define other "set_one" update procedures here
    || for other attributes...
    */

    -- don't forget about the deletions!
    PROCEDURE delete_one (doc_id_in IN INTEGER);
    PROCEDURE delete_one (doc_in IN Doc_t);
    PROCEDURE delete_one (docref_in IN REF Doc_t);
END;
```

And the body:

```
CREATE OR REPLACE PACKAGE BODY manage_appraisal AS
    PROCEDURE create_one (doc_id_in INTEGER, name_in VARCHAR2,
        author_in VARCHAR2, url_in VARCHAR2,
        publication_year_in INTEGER, doc_ref_out OUT REF Doc_t) IS
    BEGIN
        INSERT INTO appraisals a VALUES (Doc_t(doc_id_in, name_in,
            author_in, url_in, publication_year_in))
            RETURNING REF(a) INTO doc_ref_out;
    END create_one;
```

```
     FUNCTION find_doc_by_id (doc_id_in IN INTEGER) RETURN Doc_t IS
        doc Doc_t;
        CURSOR doc_cur IS SELECT VALUE(a) FROM appraisals a
           WHERE doc_id = doc_id_in;
     BEGIN
        OPEN doc_cur;
        FETCH doc_cur INTO doc;
        CLOSE doc_cur;
        RETURN doc;
     END find_doc_by_id;


     FUNCTION find_doc_ref_by_id (doc_id_in IN INTEGER)
        RETURN REF Doc_t IS
        doc_ref REF Doc_t;
        CURSOR doc_cur IS SELECT REF(a) FROM appraisals a
           WHERE doc_id = doc_id_in;
     BEGIN
        OPEN doc_cur;
        FETCH doc_cur INTO doc_ref;
        CLOSE doc_cur;
        RETURN doc_ref;
     END find_doc_ref_by_id;

     /* Unfortunately, the PL/SQL bug mentioned earlier prevents the
     || next three procedures from compiling. The error message is
     || "PLS-00382: expression is of wrong type." Until Oracle fixes
     || this problem, a conventional update statement will do the job,
     || although it will violate encapsulation and bypass the set_author
     || method.
     */
  PROCEDURE set_one_author (doc_id_in IN INTEGER,
        new_author_in IN VARCHAR2) IS
  BEGIN
        UPDATE appraisals a
           SET a = a.set_author(new_author_in)
          WHERE doc_id = doc_id_in;
     END set_one_author;


     PROCEDURE set_one_author (doc_in IN Doc_t,
        new_author_in IN VARCHAR2) IS
  BEGIN
        UPDATE appraisals a
           SET a = a.set_author(new_author_in)
          WHERE doc_id = doc_in.doc_id;
     END set_one_author;

     PROCEDURE set_one_author (docref_in IN REF Doc_t,
        new_author_in IN VARCHAR2) IS
  BEGIN
        UPDATE appraisals a
           SET a = a.set_author(new_author_in)
          WHERE REF(a) = docref_in;
     END set_one_author;
```

```
      PROCEDURE delete_one (doc_id_in INTEGER) IS
      BEGIN
         DELETE appraisals
          WHERE doc_id = doc_id_in;
      END delete_one;

      PROCEDURE delete_one (doc_in Doc_t) IS
      BEGIN
         DELETE appraisals
          WHERE doc_id = doc_in.doc_id;
      END delete_one;

      PROCEDURE delete_one (docref_in REF Doc_t) IS
      BEGIN
         DELETE appraisals a
          WHERE REF(a) = docref_in;
      END delete_one;

   END manage_appraisal;
```

An underlying assumption is that you want genuine encapsulation of the persistent data, and that you will grant users only EXECUTE privileges on the package and on the object type. You could further encapsulate the underlying data by declaring public REF CURSOR variables and creating associated procedures that will use them to open and fetch. See Chapter 6, *Database Interaction and Cursors*, for a discussion of how to do this.

Implications for Developer/2000

One of the challenges of encapsulating DML in packages is that the Oracle application development tools such as Developer/2000 assume that they have full use of SQL to navigate the database and manipulate tables. Oracle Forms' default block functionality relies heavily on this assumption.

Consistently using packages rather than Forms' default processing could force a lot of hand-coding of transactional triggers: on-insert, on-update, and on-delete. You will also need to hand-code your own on-lock trigger. (We haven't explicitly discussed locking in this chapter, but to support the Oracle Forms' transaction model, you would want to add methods or procedures to lock any persistent data that the user begins to change or delete.)

Using a PL/SQL container could be buying your future maintainability at the cost of immediate development productivity—a tough trade-off!

Object Housekeeping

In the business of working with objects, you will gain a familiarity with a number of ways of getting information about object types that you have created. These include making direct queries of the data dictionary and using the SQL*Plus "describe" command.

Another topic in the "housekeeping" category is how to deal with schema changes after you have already built tables on your object types. As the next section of the chapter explains, there are no easy answers to this question.

Data Dictionary

There are a few new entries in the data dictionary that will be very helpful in managing your object types. The shorthand dictionary term for object types is simply TYPE. Object type definitions and object type bodies are both found in the USER_SOURCE view (or DBA_SOURCE, or ALL_SOURCE), just as package specifications and bodies are. Table 18-4 summarizes the views.

Table 18-4. Data Dictionary Entries for Object Types

To Answer the Question...	Use This View	As In

What object types have I created?	USER_TYPES	`SELECT type_name`
		`  FROM user_types`
		`WHERE type_code = 'OBJECT';`

What are the attributes of type Foo_t?	USER_TYPE_ATTRS	`SELECT *`
		`  FROM user_type_attrs`
		`WHERE type_name = 'FOO_T';`

What are the methods of type Foo_t?	USER_TYPE_METHODS	`SELECT *`
		`  FROM user_type_methods`
		`WHERE type_name = 'FOO_T';`

What are the parameters of Foo_t's methods?	USER_METHOD_PARAMS	`SELECT *`
		`  FROM user_method_params`
		`WHERE type_name = 'FOO_T';`

What datatype is returned by Foo_t's method called bar?	USER_METHOD_RESULTS	`SELECT *`
		`  FROM user_method_results`
		`WHERE type_name = 'FOO_T'`
		`  AND method_name = 'BAR';`

What is the source code for Foo_t?	USER_SOURCE	`SELECT text`
		`  FROM user_source`
		`WHERE name = 'FOO_T'`
		`  AND type = 'TYPE'`
		`ORDER BY line;`

What is the code used in the object body of Foo_t?	USER_SOURCE	`SELECT text`
		`  FROM user_source`
		`WHERE name = 'FOO_T'`
		`  AND type = 'TYPE BODY'`
		`ORDER BY line;`

What are the object tables that implement Foo_t?	USER_TABLES	`SELECT table_name`
		`  FROM user_object_tables`
		`WHERE table_type = 'FOO_T';`

Table 18-4. Data Dictionary Entries for Object Types (continued)

To Answer the Question...	Use This View	As In

What columns implement Foo_t?	USER_TAB_ COLUMNS	SELECT table_name, column_name
		   FROM user_tab_columns
		   WHERE data_type = 'FOO_T';

What database objects are dependent on Foo_t?	USER_DEPENDEN-CIES	SELECT name, type
		   FROM user_dependencies
		   WHERE referenced_name = 'FOO_T';

SQL*Plus "Describe" Command

If you're like me and don't like to type any more than necessary, you'll appreciate a wonderful enhancement that Oracle has provided for the describe command in SQL*Plus. It will report not only the attributes of an object type, but also the methods and their arguments. To illustrate:

```
SQL> desc pet_t
 Name                             Null?    Type
 ------------------------------   -------- ----
 TAG_NO                                    NUMBER(38)
 NAME                                      VARCHAR2(60)
 ANIMAL_TYPE                               VARCHAR2(30)
 SEX                                       VARCHAR2(1)
 PHOTO                                     BINARY FILE LOB
 VACCINATIONS                             VACCINATION_LIST_T
 OWNER                                     REF OF PERSON_T

 METHOD
 ------
 MEMBER FUNCTION SET_TAG_NO RETURNS PET_T
 Argument Name                   Type                     In/Out Default?
 ------------------------------  -----------------------  ------ --------
 NEW_TAG_NO                      NUMBER                   IN

 METHOD
 ------
 MEMBER FUNCTION SET_PHOTO RETURNS PET_T
 Argument Name                   Type                     In/Out Default?
 ------------------------------  -----------------------  ------ --------
 FILE_LOCATION                   VARCHAR2                 IN
 MEMBER PROCEDURE PRINT_ME
```

Although the formatting could be improved, this is much easier than SELECTing the equivalent information from the data dictionary.

Schema Evolution

Let's say that you have created an object type and you need to make a change to its definition. What do you do? The answer is that *it depends*—on whether you have used the type, and on what type of change you want to make. Precious few modifications are easy; the rest will probably age you prematurely. Consider the implications of where you have used the type:

- *Type has no dependencies.* Using CREATE OR REPLACE, you can change the object type to you heart's content. Or drop and recreate it; who cares? Life is good.

- *Type is used only in PL/SQL modules.* In this case, since you don't have to rebuild any dependent tables, life is still easy. Oracle will automatically recompile dependent PL/SQL modules the next time they are called.

- *Type is used in one or more tables.* Consider what would be a simple change to a relational table: adding a column. If you try to add a column to an object table, you get an "ORA-22856 cannot add columns to object tables." The "Action" for this message says we need to "Create a new type with additional attributes, and use the new type to create an object table. The new object table will have the desired columns." Your frustrations are beginning.

OK, if you want to add an attribute, you're out of luck. What about methods? Oracle8.0 does include an ALTER TYPE statement that allows you to recompile an object specification or body. It also allows you to add new methods. It is extremely limited, however; it does not allow you to add or remove attributes, nor does it allow you to modify the quantity or datatypes of existing method arguments. The basic syntax is:

```
Form I
ALTER TYPE [ BODY ] type_name COMPILE [ SPECIFICATION | BODY ];
```

which does not solve our problem, or:

```
Form II
ALTER TYPE [ BODY ] type_name REPLACE
    <the entire new type or body definition>;
```

Using Form II, we can, in fact, add an entirely new method to an object type, even if there are dependencies on the type.

In the case of changing a method's specification (or deleting a method) in object type Foo_t which is implemented in table foo, you would think that export/import would work, using something like:

1. Export the foo table.

2. Drop the foo table.

3. CREATE OR REPLACE TYPE Foo_t with the new definition.

4. Import the foo table.

But alas, it doesn't work, because when you CREATE OR REPLACE the type, it actually assigns a new OID to the type, and the import fails with IMP-00063 when it sees that the OID is different. Huh? What do you mean, "assigns a new OID to the type?" For reasons apparently having to do with facilitating certain operations in the Oracle Call Interface (OCI), object types themselves have an OID. See for yourself—you can easily retrieve them from the USER_TYPES data dictionary view.

Neither can you "CREATE new_object_table AS SELECT ... FROM old_object_table." Even if you could, the REFs wouldn't match up to the OIDs of the new table.

It's even worse if you want to make any serious modifications to an object type and you have a dependency on the type from other types or tables. You cannot drop and recreate a parent object table unless you drop the child object types and object tables first. So maybe you could:

1. Create new object types and tables.

2. Somehow populate new from the old.

3. Drop the old object tables and types.

4. Rename the new types and object tables to the old names.

It is not obvious to me how to do the second step in a way that will preserve REFs to the type. The only way I see to do it in a guaranteed fashion is to rely on relational primary and foreign keys for tuple identification. That is, your schema will include not only REFs but also equivalent foreign keys. Then, when your OIDs change because you have rebuilt an object table, you can update all the REFs to that object table using foreign key values. Not a pretty picture.

Also, you cannot rename object types (number 4 above); attempting to do so fails with "ORA-03001: unimplemented feature."

WARNING   Requiring the dropping of *all* dependent types and objects before al-
             tering a type is not going to endear the Oracle objects option to the
             average database administrator (or to anyone else, for that matter).
             Object schema evolution is a significant area where Oracle could
             make a lot of improvements.

Making the Objects Option Work

This stuff isn't designed to be easy for the beginner, and the complexities are more than syntax-deep. In addition to the operational limitations we have discussed, the act of "thinking objects" is not a trait that comes naturally to programmers schooled in database or structured approaches. But if you feel intimidated, take heart from this advice: "There may be an OO revolution, but that does not mean you have to make the change all at once. Instead, you can incorporate what you know worked before, and bring in the best that OO has to offer, a little at a time as you understand it."[*]

If object technology is such a challenge, what is it that drives many organizations to consider object approaches in the first place? The overriding interest of managers seems to be their desire to *reuse* rather than *reinvent* the software needed to run their businesses.[†] In industries whose automation needs are not satisfied by off-the-shelf solutions, IS managers are continuously squeezed by the need to deliver more and more solutions while maintaining their legacy code, all while attempting to keep costs under control.

It may not be obvious from our examples just how the objects option is going to facilitate reuse, particularly given Oracle8.0's lack of inheritance and difficulties with schema evolution. Indeed, the benefits of an object approach do not *automatically* accrue to the practitioner; large systems, in particular, must exhibit other characteristics.[‡] Achieving reuse requires careful planning and deliberate execution.

Experts recommend not attempting object approaches just because someone says they are cool or because everyone else is doing it. Without a financial and time commitment to understanding, and without taking advantage of a different programming model, you are not likely to get much benefit, and yours will join the landscape of projects that didn't deliver.

Yes, object approaches can be a way to do more with less. In fact, computer industry pundits assert that "componentware" is becoming the dominant form of software, and that application development is evolving into a process of wiring together components—whether built in-house or procured—rather than developing software from scratch. These components are typically built using object design (to specify the component's interfaces, and what it will and won't do) and object-oriented programming languages. The game isn't over, though; we need look only as close as the nearest desktop computer to see both the benefits and the perils of componentware. Windows DLLs, for example, allow module sharing and dynamic loading, but lack a superstructure for managing multiple versions.

---

[*] See Rick Mercer and A. Michael Berman, "Object-Oriented Technology and C++ in the First Year: Ten Lessons Learned." Presented at the Northeastern Small College Computing Conference, April 18- 20, 1996, and on the web at *http://www.rowan.edu/~berman/tenLessons/paper.htm*.

[†] See Ivar Jacobson, "Reuse in Reality: The Reuse-Driven Software-Engineering Business." Presented at Object Expo Paris, available at *http://www.rational.com/support/techpapers/objex_ivar.pdf*.

[‡] See Grady Booch, *Object-Oriented Analysis and Design with Applications*, Addison-Wesley 1994.

Other component models exist (CORBA, ActiveX, COM, JavaBeans) in varying states of industry acceptance.

Almost certainly, Oracle Corporation will be adding needed features such as inheritance and schema evolution tools to their objects option. One day, objects may even be a standard part of the server. Until the technology matures, early adopters will enjoy the pleasures of finding workarounds, and will gain a deeper appreciation of features that appear later in the product.

19

Nested Tables and VARRAYs

In PL/SQL Version 2, Oracle introduced the TABLE datatype as a way of storing singly dimensioned sparse arrays in PL/SQL. Known as the "PL/SQL table," this structure is thoroughly documented in Chapter 10, *PL/SQL Tables*. PL/SQL8 introduces two new collection structures that have a wide range of new uses. These structures are *nested tables* and *variable-size arrays* (VARRAYs). Like PL/SQL tables, the new structures can also be used in PL/SQL programs. But what is dramatic and new is the ability to use the new collections as the datatypes of fields in conventional tables and attributes of objects. While not an exhaustive implementation of user-defined datatypes, collections offer rich new physical (and, by extension, logical) design opportunities for Oracle practitioners.

In this chapter we'll include brief examples showing how to create and use collection types both in the database and in PL/SQL programs. We'll also show the syntax for creating collection types. We'll present the three different initialization techniques with additional examples, and we'll discuss the new built-in "methods," EXTEND, TRIM, and DELETE, for managing collection content. This chapter also contains an introduction to the new "collection pseudo-functions" that Oracle8 provides to deal with nonatomic values in table columns. Although we can't cover every aspect of SQL usage, the examples will give you a sense of how important— and useful—these new devices can be, despite their complexity. We also include a reference section that details all of the built-in methods for collections: for each we'll show its specification, an example, and some programming considerations. The chapter concludes with a brief discussion of which type of collection is most appropriate for some common situations.

Types of Collections

Oracle now supports three types of collections:

- *PL/SQL tables* are singly dimensioned, unbounded, sparse collections of homogeneous elements and are available only in PL/SQL (see Chapter 10). These are now called *index-by tables*.

- *Nested tables* are also singly dimensioned, unbounded collections of homogeneous elements. They are initially dense but can become sparse through deletions. Nested tables are available in both PL/SQL and the database (for example, as a column in a table).

- *VARRAYs*, like the other two collection types, are also singly dimensioned collections of homogeneous elements. However, they are always bounded and never sparse. Like nested tables, they can be used in PL/SQL and in the database. Unlike nested tables, when you store and retrieve a VARRAY, its element order is preserved.

Using a nested table or VARRAY, you can store and retrieve nonatomic data in a single column. For example, the employee table used by the HR department could store the date of birth for each employee's dependents in a single column, as shown in Table 19-1.

Table 19-1. Storing a Nonatomic Column of Dependents in a Table of Employees

Id (NUMBER)	Name (VARCHAR2)	Dependents_ages (Dependent_birthdate_t)
10010	Zaphod Beeblebrox	12-JAN-1763 4-JUL-1977 22-MAR-2021
10020	Molly Squiggly	15-NOV-1968 15-NOV-1968
10030	Joseph Josephs	
10040	Cepheus Usrbin	27-JUN-1995 9-AUG-1996 19-JUN-1997
10050	Deirdre Quattlebaum	21-SEP-1997

It's not terribly difficult to create such a table. First we define the collection type:

```
CREATE TYPE Dependent_birthdate_t AS VARRAY(10) OF DATE;
```

Now we can use it in the table definition:

```
CREATE TABLE employees (
   id NUMBER,
   name VARCHAR2(50),
```

```
    ...other columns...,
    Dependents_ages Dependent_birthdate_t
);
```

We can populate this table using the following INSERT syntax, which relies on the type's *default constructor* to transform a list of dates into values of the proper datatype:

```
INSERT INTO employees VALUES (42, 'Zaphod Beeblebrox', ...,
    Dependent_birthdate_t( '12-JAN-1765', '4-JUL-1977', '22-MAR-2021'));
```

One slight problem: most of us have been trained to view nonatomic data as a design flaw. So why would we actually *want* to do this? In some situations (for those in which you don't need to scan the contents of all the values in all the rows), theoreticians and practitioners alike consider nonatomic data to be perfectly acceptable. Even the conscience of the relational model, Chris Date, suggests that relational domains could contain complex values, including lists.[*] Some database designers have believed for years that the large percentage of nonatomic data inherent in their applications demands a nonrelational solution.

Setting aside theoretical arguments about "natural" data representations, Oracle collections provide a dramatic advantage from an application programmer's perspective: you can pass an entire collection between the database and PL/SQL using a single fetch. This feature alone could have significant positive impact on application performance.

As we've mentioned, within PL/SQL both nested tables and VARRAYs are ordered collections of homogeneous elements. Both bear some resemblance to the PL/SQL Version 2 table datatype, the elder member of the "collection" family. The new types are also singly dimensioned arrays, but they differ in areas such as sparseness (not exactly), how they're initialized (via a *constructor*), and whether they can be null (yes).

One chief difference between nested tables and VARRAYs surfaces when we use them as column datatypes. Although using a VARRAY as a column's datatype can achieve much the same result as a nested table, VARRAY data must be predeclared to be of a maximum size, and is actually stored "inline" with the rest of the table's data.

Nested tables, by contrast, are stored in special auxiliary tables called *store tables*, and there is no pre-set limit on how large they can grow. For this reason, Oracle Corporation says that VARRAY columns are intended for "small" arrays, and that nested tables are appropriate for "large" arrays.

---

[*] See Hugh Darwen and C. J. Date, "The Third Manifesto," *SIGMOD Record*, Volume 24 Number 1, March 1995.

As we've mentioned, the old Version 2 table datatype is now called an *index-by table*, in honor of the INDEX BY BINARY_INTEGER syntax required when declaring such a type. Despite the many benefits of the new collection types, index-by tables have one important unique feature: initial sparseness. Table 19-2 illustrates many of the additional differences among index-by tables and the new collection types.

Table 19-2. Comparing Oracle Collection Types

Characteristic	Index-By Table	Nested Table	VARRAY
Dimensionality	Single	Single	Single
Usable in SQL?	No	Yes	Yes
Usable as column datatype in a table?	No	Yes; data stored "out of line" (in separate table)	Yes; data stored "in line" (in same table)
Uninitialized state	Empty (cannot be null); elements undefined	Atomically null; illegal to reference elements	Atomically null; illegal to reference elements
Initialization	Automatic, when declared	Via constructor, fetch, assignment	Via constructor, fetch, assignment
In PL/SQL, elements referenced via	BINARY_INTEGER (-2,147,483,647 .. 2,147,483,647)	Positive integer between 1 and 2,147,483,647	Positive integer between 1 and 2,147,483,647
Sparse?	Yes	Initially, no; after deletions, yes	No
Bounded?	No	Can be extended	Yes
Can assign value to any element at any time?	Yes	No; may need to EXTEND first	No; may need to EXTEND first, and cannot EXTEND past upper bound
Means of extending	Assign value to element with a new subscript	Use built-in EXTEND procedure (or TRIM to condense), with no predefined maximum	EXTEND (or TRIM), but only up to declared maximum size
Can be compared for equality?	No	No	No
Retains ordering and subscripts when stored in and retrieved from database?	N/A	No	Yes

The inevitable question is: Which construct should I use? This chapter reviews some examples of the new collections and offers some suggestions in this area. The short answer:

- Nested tables are more flexible than VARRAYs for table columns.

- VARRAYs are best when you need bounded arrays that preserve element order.

- Index-by tables are the only option that allows initial sparseness.

- If your code must run in both Oracle7 and Oracle8, you can use only index-by tables.

We'll revisit these suggestions in more detail at the end of the chapter. Before diving in, though, let's review a few of the new terms:

Collection
A term which can have several different meanings:

— A nested table, index-by table, or VARRAY *datatype*

— A PL/SQL *variable* of type nested table, index-by table, or VARRAY

— A table *column* of type nested table or VARRAY

Outer table
A term referring to the "enclosing" table in which you have used a nested table or VARRAY as a column's datatype

Inner table
The "enclosed" collection that is implemented as a column in a table; also known as a "nested table column"

Store table
The physical table which Oracle creates to hold values of the inner table

Unfortunately, the term "nested table" can be a bit misleading. A nested table, when declared and used in PL/SQL, is not nested at all! It is instead fairly similar to an array. Even when you use a nested table as a table column, in Oracle 8.0 you can only nest these structures to a single level. That is, your column cannot consist of a nested table of nested tables.

"Variable-size array" is also a deceptive name; one might assume, based on the fact that it is supposed to be "variable size," that it can be arbitrarily extended; quite the opposite is true. Although a VARRAY can have a variable number of elements, this number can never exceed the limit that you define when you create the type.

Creating the New Collections

There are two different ways of creating the new user-defined collection types:

1. You can define a nested table type or VARRAY type "in the database" using the CREATE TYPE command, which makes the datatype available to use for a variety of purposes: columns in database tables, variables in PL/SQL programs, and attributes of object types.

2. You can declare the collection type within a PL/SQL program using TYPE ... IS ... syntax. This collection type will then be available only for use within PL/SQL.

Let's look at a few examples that illustrate how to create collections.

Collections "In the Database"

Before you can define a database table containing a nested table or VARRAY, you must first create the collection's datatype in the database using the CREATE TYPE statement. There is no good analogy for this command in Oracle7; it represents new functionality in the server. If we wanted to create a nested table datatype for variables that will hold lists of color names, we'll specify:

```
CREATE TYPE Color_tab_t AS TABLE OF VARCHAR2(30);
```

This command stores the type definition for the Color_tab_t nested table in the data dictionary. Once created, it can serve as the datatype for items in at least two different categories of database object:

- A "column" in a conventional table
- An attribute in an object type

Defining a VARRAY datatype is similar to defining a nested table, but you must also specify an upper bound on the number of elements collections of this type may contain. For example:

```
CREATE TYPE Color_array_t AS VARRAY (16) OF VARCHAR2(30);
```

Type Color_array_t has an upper limit of 16 elements regardless of where it is used.

While these examples use VARCHAR2, collections can also consist of other primitive datatypes, object types, references to object types, or (in PL/SQL only) PL/SQL record types. To show something other than a table of scalars, let's look at an example of a VARRAY of objects. Here we define an object type that will contain information about documents:

```
CREATE TYPE Doc_t AS OBJECT (
   doc_id INTEGER,
```

```
      name VARCHAR2(512),
      author VARCHAR2(60),
      url VARCHAR2(2000)
);
```

We can then define a collection type to hold a list of these objects:

```
CREATE TYPE Doc_array_t AS VARRAY(10) OF Doc_t;
```

In this case, we've chosen to make it a variable-size array type with a maximum of ten elements.

Another useful application of collections is in their ability to have elements which are REFs (reference pointers) to objects in the database. That is, your collection may have a number of pointers to various persistent objects (see Chapter 18, *Object Types*, for more discussion of REFs). Consider this example:

```
CREATE TYPE Doc_ref_array_t AS TABLE OF REF Doc_t;
```

This statement says "create a user-defined type to hold lists of pointers to document objects." You can use a nested table of REFs as you would any other nested table: as a column, as an attribute in an object type, or as the type of a PL/SQL variable.

NOTE While Oracle 8.0.3 allows you to create homogeneous collections, in some cases we might want to build heterogeneous collections. It would be useful to be able to define a type like the following:

```
CREATE TYPE Generic_ref_t AS TABLE OF REF ANY; -- not in 8.0.3
```

This could allow you to make collections that hold references to more than one type of object in your database ... or, if OID's are globally unique, each REF could point to any object in any database on your entire network!

Collection as a "column" in a conventional table

In the following case, we are using a nested table datatype as a column. When we create the outer table personality_inventory, we must tell Oracle what we want to call the "out of line" store table:

```
CREATE TABLE personality_inventory (
   person_id NUMBER,
   favorite_colors Color_tab_t,
   date_tested DATE,
   test_results BLOB)
NESTED TABLE favorite_colors STORE AS favorite_colors_st;
```

The NESTED TABLE ... STORE AS clause tells Oracle that we want the store table for the favorite_colors column to be called favorite_colors_st.

You cannot directly manipulate data in the store table, and any attempt to retrieve or store data directly into favorite_colors_st will generate an error. The only path by which you can read or write its attributes is via the outer table. (See the later section called "Collection Pseudo-Functions" for a few examples of doing so.) You cannot even specify storage parameters for the store table; it inherits the physical attributes of its outermost table.

As you would expect, if you use a VARRAY as a column rather than as a nested table, no store table is required. Here, the colors collection is stored "in line" with the rest of the table:

```
CREATE TABLE birds (
    genus VARCHAR2(128),
    species VARCHAR2(128),
    colors Color_array_t
);
```

Collection as an attribute of an object type

In this example, we are modeling automobile specifications, and each Auto_spec_t object will include a list of manufacturer's colors in which you can purchase the vehicle. (See Chapter 18 for more information about Oracle object types.)

```
CREATE TYPE Auto_spec_t AS OBJECT (
    make VARCHAR2(30),
    model VARCHAR2(30),
    available_colors Color_tab_t
);
```

Because there is no data storage required for the object type, it is not necessary to designate a name for the companion table at the time we issue the CREATE TYPE ... AS OBJECT statement.

When the time comes to implement the type as, say, an object table, you could do this:

```
CREATE TABLE auto_specs OF Auto_spec_t
    NESTED TABLE available_colors STORE AS available_colors_st;
```

This statement requires a bit of explanation. When you create a "table of objects," Oracle looks at the object type definition to determine what columns you want. When it discovers that one of the object type's attributes, available_colors, is in fact a nested table, Oracle treats this table in a way similar to the examples above; in other words, it wants to know what to name the store table. So the phrase

```
...NESTED TABLE available_colors STORE AS available_colors_st
```

says that you want the available_colors column to have a store table named available_colors_st.

Collections in PL/SQL

Whether you use a predefined collection type or declare one in your program, using it requires that you declare a variable in a separate step. This *declare-type-then-declare-variable* motif should be familiar to you if you have ever used an index-by table or a RECORD type in a PL/SQL program.

Collection variables

Using the collection types we've declared above, the following shows some legal declarations of PL/SQL variables:

```
DECLARE
    -- A variable that will hold a list of available font colors
    font_colors Color_tab_t;

    /* The next variable will later hold a temporary copy of
    || font_colors. Note that we can use %TYPE to refer to the
    || datatype of font_colors. This illustrates two different
    || ways of declaring variables of the Color_tab_t type.
    */
    font_colors_save font_colors%TYPE;

    -- Variable to hold a list of paint colors
    paint_mixture Color_array_t;
```

But there is no reason you must use *only* types you have created in the database. You can declare them locally, or mix and match from both sources:

```
DECLARE
    /* As with Oracle7 index-by tables, you can define
    || a table datatype here within a declaration section...
    */
    TYPE Number_t IS TABLE OF NUMBER;

    /* ...and then you can use your new type in the declaration
    || of a local variable. The next line declares and initializes
    || in a single statement. Notice the use of the constructor,
    || Number_t(value, value, ...), to the right of the ":="
    */
    my_favorite_numbers Number_t := Number_t(42, 65536);

    /* Or you can just refer to the Color_tab_t datatype in the
    || data dictionary. This next line declares a local variable
    || my_favorite_colors to be a "nested" table and initializes it
    || with two initial elements using the default constructor.
    */
    my_favorite_colors Color_tab_t := Color_tab_t('PURPLE', 'GREEN');

BEGIN
    /* Once the local variables exist, usage is independent of whether
    || they were declared from local types or from types that live in
    || the data dictionary.
    */
```

```
        my_favorite_colors(2) := 'BLUE';    -- changes 2nd element to BLUE
        my_favorite_numbers(1) := 3.14159;  -- changes first element to pi
    END;
```

This code also illustrates *default constructors*, which are special functions Oracle provides whenever you create a type, that serve to initialize and/or populate their respective types. A constructor has the same name as the type, and accepts as arguments a comma-separated list of elements.

Collections as components of a record

Using a collection type in a record is very similar to using any other type. You can use VARRAYs, nested tables, or index-by tables (or any combination thereof) in RECORD datatypes. For example:

```
DECLARE
    TYPE toy_rec_t IS RECORD (
        manufacturer INTEGER,
        shipping_weight_kg NUMBER,
        domestic_colors Color_array_t,
        international_colors Color_tab_t
    );
```

RECORD types cannot live in the database; they are only available within PL/SQL programs. Logically, however, you can achieve a similar result with object types. Briefly, object types can have a variety of attributes, and you can include the two new collection types as attributes within objects; or you can define a collection whose elements are themselves objects.

Collections as module parameters

Collections can also serve as module parameters. In this case, you cannot return a user-defined type that is declared in the module itself. You will instead use types that you have built outside the scope of the module, either via CREATE TYPE or via public declaration in a package.

```
/* This function provides a pseudo "UNION ALL" operation on
|| two input parameters of type Color_tab_t. That is, it creates an
|| OUT parameter which is the superset of the colors of the two
|| input parameters.
*/
CREATE PROCEDURE make_colors_superset (first_colors IN Color_tab_t,
    second_colors IN Color_tab_t, superset OUT Color_tab_t)
AS
    working_colors Color_tab_t := Color_tab_t();
    element INTEGER := 1;
    which INTEGER;
BEGIN
    /* Invoke the EXTEND method to allocate enough storage
    || to the nested table working_colors.
    */
```

```
working_colors.EXTEND (first_colors.COUNT + second_colors.COUNT);

/* Loop through each of the input parameters, reading their
|| contents, and assigning each element to an element of
|| working_colors. Input collections may be sparse.
*/

which := first_colors.FIRST;
LOOP
   EXIT WHEN which IS NULL;
   working_colors(element) := first_colors(which);
   element := element + 1;
   which := first_colors.NEXT(which);
END LOOP;

which := second_colors.FIRST;
LOOP
   EXIT WHEN which IS NULL;
   working_colors(element) := second_colors(which);
   element := element + 1;
   which := second_colors.NEXT(which);
END LOOP;

superset := working_colors;
END;
```

As a bit of an aside, let's take a look at the loops used in the code. The general form you can use to iterate over the elements of a collection is as follows:

```
1    which := collection_name.FIRST;
2    LOOP
3       EXIT WHEN which IS NULL;
4       -- do something useful with the current element...
5       which := collection_name.NEXT(which);
6    END LOOP;
```

This works for both dense and sparse collections. The first assignment statement, at line 1, gets the subscript of the FIRST element in the collection; if it's NULL, that means there are no elements, and we would therefore exit immediately at line 3.

But if there are elements in the collection, we reach line 4, where the program will do "something useful" with the value, such as assign, change, or test its value for some purpose.

The most interesting line of this example is line 5, where we use the NEXT method on the collection to retrieve the next-higher subscript above "which" on the right-hand side. In the event that a particular subscript has been DELETEd, the NEXT operator simply skips over it until it finds a non-deleted element. Also in line 5, if NEXT returns a NULL, that is our cue that we have iterated over all of the collection's elements, and it's time to exit the loop when we get back to line 3.

You might also ask why we should use the local variable working_colors in the example above? Why not simply use the superset parameter as the working variable in the program? As it turns out, when we EXTEND a nested table, it must also read the table. So we would have to make superset an IN OUT variable, because OUT variables cannot be read within the program. It's better programming style to avoid using an IN OUT variable when OUT would suffice—and more efficient, especially for remote procedure calls.

Collections as the datatype of a function's return value

In the next example, the programmer has defined Color_tab_t as the type of a function return value, and it is also used as the datatype of a local variable. The same restriction about datatype scope applies to this usage; types must be declared outside the module's scope.

```
CREATE FUNCTION true_colors (whose_id IN NUMBER) RETURN Color_tab_t
AS
    l_colors Color_tab_t;
BEGIN
    SELECT favorite_colors INTO l_colors
      FROM personality_inventory
     WHERE person_id = whose_id;
    RETURN l_colors;
EXCEPTION
    WHEN NO_DATA_FOUND
    THEN
        RETURN NULL;
END;
```

This example also illustrates a long-awaited feature: the retrieval of a complex data item in a single fetch. This is so cool that it bears repeating, so we'll talk more about it later in this chapter.

How would you use this function in a PL/SQL program? Since it acts in the place of a variable of type Color_tab_t, you can do one of two things with the returned data:

1. Assign the entire result to a collection variable

2. Assign a single element of the result to a variable (as long as the variable is of a type compatible with the collection's elements)

The first option is easy. Notice, by the way, that this is another circumstance where you don't have to initialize the collection variable explicitly.

```
DECLARE
    color_array Color_tab_t;
BEGIN
    color_array := true_colors (8041);
END;
```

With option two, we actually give the function call a subscript. The general form is:

```
variable_of_element_type := function ( ) (subscript);
```

Or, in the case of the true_colors function:

```
DECLARE
   one_of_my_favorite_colors VARCHAR2(30);
BEGIN
   one_of_my_favorite_colors := true_colors (whose_id=>8041) (1);
END;
```

By the way, this code has a small problem: if there is no record in the database table where person_id is 8041, the attempt to read its first element will raise a COLLECTION_IS_NULL exception. We should trap and deal with this exception in a way that makes sense to the application.

In the previous example, I've used named parameter notation, *whose_id=>*, for readability, although it is not strictly required. The main syntactic rule is that function parameters come before subscripts. If your function has no parameters, you'll need to use the empty parameter list notation, (), as a placeholder:

```
variable_of_element_type := function () (subscript);
```

Syntax for Declaring Collection Datatypes

As noted earlier, you must first declare or create a collection datatype before you can create collections based on that type.

To create a nested table datatype that lives in the data dictionary, specify:

```
CREATE [ OR REPLACE ] TYPE <type name> AS
   TABLE OF <element datatype> [ NOT NULL ];
```

To create a VARRAY datatype that lives in the data dictionary:

```
CREATE [ OR REPLACE ] TYPE <type name> AS
   VARRAY (<max elements>) OF <element datatype> [ NOT NULL ];
```

To drop a type:

```
DROP TYPE <type name> [ FORCE ];
```

To declare a nested table datatype in PL/SQL:

```
TYPE <type name> IS TABLE OF <element datatype> [ NOT NULL ];
```

To declare a VARRAY datatype in PL/SQL:

```
TYPE <type name> IS VARRAY (<max elements>)
   OF <element datatype> [ NOT NULL ];
```

Where:

OR REPLACE

Allows you to rebuild an existing type as long as there are no other database objects that depend on it. This is useful primarily because it preserves grants.

type name

A legal SQL or PL/SQL identifier. This will be the identifier to which you refer later when you use it to declare variables or columns.

element datatype

The type of the collection's elements. All elements are of a single type, which can be most scalar datatypes, an object type, or a REF object type. If the elements are objects, the object type itself cannot have an attribute that is a collection. In PL/SQL, if you are creating a collection with RECORD elements, its fields can be only scalars or objects. Explicitly disallowed collection datatypes are BOOLEAN, NCHAR, NCLOB, NVARCHAR2, REF CURSOR, TABLE, and VARRAY.

NOT NULL

Indicates that a variable of this type cannot have any null elements. However, the collection can be atomically null (uninitialized).

max elements

Maximum number of elements allowed in the VARRAY. Once declared, this cannot be altered.

FORCE

Tells Oracle to drop the type even if there is a reference to it in another type. For example, if an object type definition uses a particular collection type, you can still drop the collection type using the FORCE keyword. Note that if you have a table that uses a particular type definition, you must actually drop the table before dropping the type; you cannot FORCE the drop.

Note that the only syntactic difference between declaring nested table types and index-by table types in a PL/SQL program is the absence of the INDEX BY BINARY_INTEGER clause.

The syntactic differences between nested table and VARRAY type declarations are:

- The use of the keyword VARRAY

- The limit on its number of elements

Using Collections

There are three main programming tasks you must understand when you are working with collections in PL/SQL:

- How to properly initialize the collection variable
- How to assign values to elements without raising exceptions
- How to add and remove "slots" for elements

In addition, to fully exploit the programming utility of collections, you will want to learn how to retrieve and store sets of data with them. This leads into our section on pseudo-functions, which allow you to perform magic tricks with collections. (Okay, maybe it's not *real* magic, but you're almost guaranteed to say "How did they *do* that?" the first time you try to program this stuff and find yourself bewildered.)

Initializing Collection Variables

With an index-by table datatype, initialization is a non-issue. Simply declaring an index-by table variable also initializes it, in an "empty" state. Then you can just assign values to subscripted table elements as you desire. Index values (subscripts) can be almost any positive or negative integer. A program can even assign subscripts to index-by tables arbitrarily, skipping huge ranges of subscripts without paying a memory or performance penalty.[*]

The allocation scheme for nested tables and VARRAYs is different from that of index-by tables. First off, if you don't initialize one of these collections, it will be "atomically null," and any attempt to read or write an element of an atomically null collection will generate a runtime error. For example:

```
DECLARE
    /* The variable cool_colors is not initialized in its
    || declaration; it is "atomically null."
    */
    cool_colors Color_tab_t;
BEGIN
    IF cool_colors IS NULL THEN          -- valid; will be TRUE
        ...
    IF cool_colors(1) IS NULL THEN       -- invalid
        ...
    cool_colors(1) := 'BLUE';            -- invalid
```

---

[*] This sparseness makes it possible to use an index-by table as an in-memory representation of almost any database table which uses an integer primary key. (See "Data-Smart Row Numbers in PL/SQL Tables" in Chapter 10 for a discussion of this eminently useful technique.)

You must initialize the collection before using it. There are three ways you can initialize a collection:

- Explicitly, using a constructor

- Implicitly, via a fetch from the database

- Implicitly, via a direct assignment of another collection variable

There is no requirement that you initialize any particular number of elements in a collection. Zero, one, or more are fine, and you can always add more values later. In particular, don't be confused by VARRAYs. Just because you specify a limit on the number of elements it can hold does not imply that you have to put that many elements in when you initialize it.

Initializing with a constructor

Earlier, we saw declarations that looked like this:

```
my_favorite_colors Color_tab_t := Color_tab_t('PURPLE', 'GREEN');
my_favorite_numbers Number_t := Number_t(42, 65536);
```

Color_tab_t() is the constructor function supplied by Oracle when we created the Color_tab_t collection type. This function accepts an arbitrary number of arguments, as long as each argument is of the "proper" datatype—which in this case is VARCHAR2(30), since our original type definition statement was the following:

```
CREATE TYPE Color_tab_t AS TABLE OF VARCHAR2(30);
```

At initialization, Oracle allocates to the variable an amount of memory necessary to hold the values you supply as arguments. Initialization both creates the "slots" for the elements and populates them.

So, if I want to "fix" the earlier invalid example, I can simply initialize the variable:

```
DECLARE
    cool_colors Color_tab_t := Color_tab_t('VIOLET');   -- initialize
BEGIN
    IF cool_colors(1) IS NULL THEN    -- This is OK now!
```

What do you suppose Oracle does with the following initialization?

```
working_colors Color_tab_t := Color_tab_t();
```

This is a way of creating an "empty" collection. Empty is a sort of enigmatic state in which the collection is not atomically null but still has no data. Whenever you create such an empty collection, you'll need to "extend" the collection variable later when you want to put elements into it. (The EXTEND built-in is explored later in this chapter.)

Initializing implicitly during direct assignment

You can copy the entire contents of one collection to another as long as both are built from the exact same datatype. When you do so, initialization comes along "for free."

Here's an example illustrating implicit initialization that occurs when we assign wedding_colors to be the value of earth_colors.

```
DECLARE
    earth_colors Color_tab_t := Color_tab_t('BRICK', 'RUST', 'DIRT');
    wedding_colors Color_tab_t;
BEGIN
    wedding_colors := earth_colors;
    wedding_colors(3) := 'CANVAS';
END;
```

This code initializes wedding_colors and creates three elements that match those in earth_colors. These are independent variables rather than pointers to identical values; changing the third element of wedding_colors to 'CANVAS' does not have any effect on the third element of earth_colors.

Note that assignment is not possible when datatypes are merely "type-compatible." Even if you have created two different types with the exact same definition, the fact that they have different names makes them different types. A collection variable cannot be assigned to another variable of a different datatype:

```
DECLARE
    TYPE Local_colors_t IS VARRAY(16) OF VARCHAR2(30);
    TYPE Remote_colors_t IS VARRAY(16) OF VARCHAR2(30);
    l_color Local_colors_t := Local_colors_t('THALO BLUE');
    r_color Remote_colors_t;
BEGIN
    r_color := l_color;   -- invalid
END;
```

This code will fail with the compile-time error "PLS-00382: expression is of wrong type," because r_color and l_color are of different types.

Initializing implicitly via fetch

If you use a collection as a type in a database table, Oracle provides some very elegant ways of moving the collection between PL/SQL and the table. As with direct assignment, when you use FETCH or SELECT INTO to retrieve a collection and drop it into a collection variable, you get automatic initialization of the variable. Collections can turn out to be incredibly useful!

Although we mentioned this briefly in an earlier example, let's take a closer look at how you can read an entire collection in a single fetch. First, we want to create a table containing a collection and populate it with a couple of values:

```
CREATE TABLE color_models (
    model_type VARCHAR2(12),
    colors Color_tab_t)
NESTED TABLE colors STORE AS color_model_colors_tab;

insert into color_models
    values ('RGB', Color_tab_t('RED','GREEN','BLUE'));
insert into color_models
    values ('CYMK',Color_tab_t('CYAN','YELLOW','MAGENTA','BLACK'));
```

Now we can show off the neat integration features. With one trip to the database
we can retrieve all of the values of the "colors" column for a given row, and
deposit them into a local variable:

```
DECLARE
    l_colors Color_tab_t;
BEGIN
    /* Retrieve all the nested values in a single fetch.
    || This is the cool part.
    */
    SELECT colors INTO l_colors FROM color_models
        WHERE model_type = 'RGB';

    /* Loop through each value and print it. This is only to demonstrate
    || that we really have the data in the local variable.
    */
    FOR element IN 1..l_colors.COUNT
    LOOP
        dbms_output.put_line (element || ' ' || l_colors(element));
    END LOOP;
END;
```

With SERVEROUTPUT turned on, SQL*Plus prints the following when this code
fragment executes:

```
1 RED
2 GREEN
3 BLUE
```

Pretty neat, huh? A few important points to notice:

- Oracle, not the programmer, assigns the subscripts of l_colors when fetched
  from the database.
- Oracle's assigned subscripts begin with 1 (as opposed to 0, as you may be
  used to in some other languages) and increment by 1.
- Fetching satisfies the requirement to initialize the local collection variable
  before assigning values to elements. We didn't initialize l_colors with a constructor, but PL/SQL knew how to deal with it.

You can also make changes to the contents of the nested table and just as easily move the data back into a database table. Just to be mischievous, let's create a Fuschia-Green-Blue color model:

```
DECLARE
    color_tab Color_tab_t;
BEGIN
    SELECT colors INTO color_tab FROM color_models
        WHERE model_type = 'RGB';
    FOR element IN 1..color_tab.COUNT
    LOOP
        IF color_tab(element) = 'RED'
        THEN
            color_tab(element) := 'FUSCHIA';
        END IF;
    END LOOP;
    /* Here is the cool part of this example. Only one insert
    || statement is needed -- it sends the entire nested table
    || back into the color_models table in the database.
    */
    INSERT INTO color_models VALUES ('FGB', color_tab);
END;
```

VARRAY integration

Does this database-to-PL/SQL integration work for VARRAYs too? You bet, although there are a couple of differences.

First of all, realize that when you store and retrieve the contents of a nested table in the database, Oracle makes no promises about preserving the order of the elements. This makes sense, because the server is just putting the nested data into a store table behind the scenes, and we all know that relational databases don't give two hoots about row order. By contrast, storing and retrieving the contents of a VARRAY *does* preserve the order of the elements.

Preserving the order of VARRAY elements is actually a fairly useful capability. It makes possible something you cannot do in a pure relational database: embedding meaning in the order of the data. For example, if you want to store someone's favorite colors in rank order, you can do it with a single VARRAY column. Every time you retrieve the column collection, its elements will be in the same order as when you last stored it. By contrast, abiding by a pure relational model, you would need two columns, one for an integer corresponding to the rank, and one for the color.

Thinking about this order-preservation of VARRAYs brings to mind some interesting utility functions. For example, you could fairly easily code a tool that would allow the insertion of a new "favorite" at the low end of the list by "shifting up" all the other elements.

A second difference between integration of nested tables and integration of VARRAYs with the database is that some SELECT statements you could use to fetch the contents of a nested table will have to be modified if you want to fetch a VARRAY. (See the "Collection Pseudo-Functions" section later for some examples.)

Assigning Values to Elements: Index (Subscript) Considerations

In contrast to index-by tables, you can't assign values to arbitrarily numbered subscripts of nested tables and VARRAYs; instead, the indexes, at least initially, are monotonically increasing integers, assigned by the PL/SQL engine. That is, if you initialize *n* elements, they will have subscripts 1 through *n*. And, as implied above, you cannot rely on the assignment of particular subscripts to particular element values in nested tables. Yes, any element can be null, but null is different from nonexistent (sparse).

Nested tables are initially dense, with no skipped subscripts. Once a nested table exists, however, it is possible to remove any element from it, even one in the "middle." This will result in a sparse array.

VARRAYs, on the other hand, are always dense. Elements of VARRAYs can only be removed from the "end" of the array, so VARRAYs cannot be coerced into being sparse.

However, if what you want is a sparse array in PL/SQL, you would be much better off using an index-by table. The real strength of nested tables and VARRAYs is their ability to move gracefully in and out of the database.

Adding and Removing Elements

With an old-style index-by table, Oracle automatically allocates memory for new elements. When you want to add an element, you simply pick a value for the subscript and assign a value to that element. To remove an element, you could use the DELETE method. To illustrate:

```
DECLARE
    TYPE color_tab_type IS TABLE OF VARCHAR2(30)
        INDEX BY BINARY_INTEGER;
    color_tab color_tab_type;
BEGIN
    color_tab(3845) := 'SEAFOAM GREEN';
    color_tab(702) := 'CERULEAN BLUE';
    color_tab.DELETE(3845);
END;
```

What would happen if you tried this assignment with a nested table? Aha, you say, knowing that subscripts start with 1 and are monotonically increasing, I'll just try:

```
DECLARE
    /* colors starts life initialized by empty */
    colors Color_tab_t := Color_tab_t();
BEGIN
    colors(1) = 'SEAFOAM GREEN'; -- invalid
```

But this code produces an "ORA-06533, Subscript beyond count" error. This is why you need EXTEND.

Adding elements using EXTEND

Adding an element to a collection requires a separate allocation step. Making a "slot" in memory for a collection element is independent from assigning a value to it. If you haven't initialized the collection with a sufficient number of elements (null or otherwise), you must first use the EXTEND procedure on the variable. (For the formal syntax and usage of this procedure, refer to the later section "Collection Built-Ins.")

```
DECLARE
    /* The colors variable begins life initialized but with
    || no elements allocated
    */
    colors Color_tab_t := Color_tab_t();
BEGIN
    colors.EXTEND;  -- allocate space for a single element
    colors(1) := 'GRANITE';   -- this works
    colors(2) := 'HUNTER GREEN';   -- invalid; we only extended by 1
END;
```

Removing elements using DELETE

When you DELETE an element, PL/SQL removes that element from the collection. Interestingly, it doesn't actually remove all traces of the element; in fact, a placeholder gets left behind. That means you can reassign the element later without having to re-allocate the space.

DELETE has three different forms depending on how much you want to remove: one, several (contiguous), or all of the elements. The section "Collection Built-Ins" describes all the forms of this procedure.

In physical terms, PL/SQL actually releases the memory only when your program deletes a sufficient number of elements to free an entire page of memory (unless you DELETE all of the elements, which frees all of the memory immediately). This de-allocation happens automatically and requires no accommodations or devices in your code.

...And what about TRIM?

TRIM is another built-in which lets you remove elements from a collection; it's equally applicable to nested tables and VARRAYs. (Again, refer to the "Collection Built-Ins" section for details.) As its name implies, TRIM drops elements off the end of a collection. Unlike DELETE, TRIM leaves no placeholder behind when it does its work.

Although my programming exercise above didn't need TRIM, this built-in, combined with EXTEND, can be very useful if you want to program a "stack" abstraction. In general, the syntax is simply the following:

```
collection_name.TRIM(n);
```

where n is the number of elements to remove. If you don't supply n, it defaults to 1.

Unfortunately, if you use TRIM and DELETE on the same collection, you can get some very surprising results. Consider this scenario: if you DELETE an element at the end of a nested table variable and then do a TRIM on the same variable, how many elements have you removed? You would think that you have removed two elements, but, in fact, you have removed only one. The placeholder that is left by DELETE is what TRIM acts upon.

TIP   To avoid confusion, Oracle Corporation recommends using either
                 DELETE or TRIM, but not both, on a given collection.

Comparing Collections

Unfortunately, there is no built-in capability to compare collections and determine whether one is "equal to" or "greater than" the other. Attempts to do so will produce compile-time errors. The *only* comparison that is legal for collections is a test for nullness, as we saw previously:

```
DECLARE
    cool_colors Color_tab_t;
BEGIN
    IF cool_colors IS NULL THEN          -- valid; will be TRUE
```

If comparing collections is important to your application, you could put an object "container" around the collection, and use objects instead of collections as the structure that your applications manipulate. Doing so allows you to define your own object comparison semantics. Although Chapter 18 provides a detailed discussion of defining your own object comparisons using the MAP and ORDER methods, we'll divert momentarily to illustrate how this technique will help us compare collections.

Without repeating a lot of descriptive detail that you'll find in Chapter 18, your object type specification might look quite simple:

```
CREATE TYPE Color_object_t AS OBJECT (
    crayons Color_array_t,
    ORDER MEMBER FUNCTION compare(c_obj Color_object_t) RETURN INTEGER);
```

This creates an object with a single attribute, crayons, and a special method that Oracle will use when it needs to compare instances of type Color_object_t.

The object type body could be implemented as follows:

```
CREATE TYPE BODY Color_object_t AS
    ORDER MEMBER FUNCTION compare(c_obj Color_object_t) RETURN INTEGER
        IS
    BEGIN
        /* If one object has more elements than the other, it is
        || by our convention defined to be "greater" than the other.
        */
        IF nvl(SELF.crayons.COUNT,0) > nvl(c_obj.crayons.COUNT,0)
        THEN
            RETURN 1;
        ELSIF nvl(SELF.crayons.COUNT,0) < nvl(c_obj.crayons.COUNT,0)
        THEN
            RETURN -1;
        ELSE
            /* Otherwise we compare the individual elements.
            || If the two arrays have the same number of elements,
            || we'll call them "equal."
            */
            RETURN 0;
        END IF;
    END compare;
END;
```

In PL/SQL, you can now compare objects of type Color_object_t to your heart's content, achieving a kind of *de facto* collection comparison:

```
DECLARE
    color_object_1 Color_object_t
        := Color_object_t(Color_array_t('BLUE','GREEN','RED'));
    color_object_2 Color_object_t := color_object_1;
BEGIN
    ...
    IF color_object_1 = color_object_2 THEN
        ...
END;
```

And if you needed this structure as a column in a table, it could go something like this:

```
CREATE TABLE kids_coloring_kits (
    NAME VARCHAR2(30),
    crayon_colors Color_object_t
);
```

Once the table is populated, you can then use SQL sorting features such as ORDER BY, GROUP BY, and DISTINCT on the crayon_colors column, since your ORDER member function tells Oracle how to compare values in the column.

Collection Pseudo-Functions

I've been working with Oracle's SQL for more than ten years and PL/SQL for more than five. My brain has rarely turned as many cartwheels over SQL's semantics as it has recently, when contemplating the "collection pseudo-functions" introduced in Oracle8.

These collection pseudo-functions exist to coerce database tables into acting like collections, and vice versa. Because there are some manipulations that work best when data are in one form versus the other, these functions give application programmers access to a rich and interesting set of structures and operations.

Note that these operators are not available in PL/SQL proper, but only in SQL. You can, however, employ these operators in SQL statements which appear in your PL/SQL code, and it is extremely useful to understand how and when to do so. We'll get to some examples shortly.

The four collection pseudo-functions are as follows:

THE

Maps a single column value in a single row into a virtual database table. This pseudo-function allows you to manipulate the elements of a persistent collection.

CAST

Maps a collection of one type to a collection of another type. This can encompass mapping a VARRAY into a nested table.

MULTISET

Maps a database table to a collection. With MULTISET and CAST, you can actually retrieve rows from a database table as a collection-typed column.

TABLE

Maps a collection to a database table. This is the inverse of MULTISET.

Oracle has introduced these pseudo-functions in order to manipulate collections that live in the database. They are important to our PL/SQL programs for several reasons, not the least of which is that they provide an incredibly efficient way to move data between the database and the application.

Yes, these pseudo-functions can be puzzling; but if you're the kind of person who gets truly excited by arcane code, these Oracle8 SQL extensions will make you jumping-up-and-down silly.

The THE Pseudo-function

If you have a column that's a nested table, and you want to insert, update, or delete from the contents of this column, you cannot do so with any SQL statement that is familiar to you from Oracle7. Instead, you will need to use the strangely named keyword THE, which helps tell Oracle which row from the outer table you want to deal with.

Earlier, we created the color_models table:

```
CREATE TABLE color_models (
    model_type VARCHAR2(12),
    colors Color_tab_t)
NESTED TABLE colors STORE AS color_model_colors_tab;
```

We had inserted a row with model_type ='RGB' and a colors column containing ('RED', 'GREEN', 'BLUE'). Imagine now that we've populated color_models with a half dozen or so records.

One question that might have come into your mind is: how can we retrieve all of the colors for a single model using a SELECT statement?

```
SELECT VALUE(c) FROM
    THE(SELECT colors FROM color_models
        WHERE model_type = 'RGB') c;
```

OK, you can exhale now. The meaning of this statement is "retrieve the individual elements of RGB color model." Or, more literally, "retrieve the value of each element of the colors nested table within the color_models outer table." Sure enough, it displays the following:[*]

```
VALUE(C)
-------------------------------
RED
GREEN
BLUE
```

I guess it's really not *that* weird; we're just substituting a subquery for a table in the FROM clause.

Why does the language use the keyword name THE instead of, say, OUTER? Oracle's documentation says "THE (*select expression*) identifies *the* nested table on which the DML operation is to be performed." I guess somebody at Oracle has a sense of humor!

Another way you could have expressed the previous query is to use the predefined alias COLUMN_VALUE:

---

[*] As of Oracle 8.0.4.

```
SELECT COLUMN_VALUE FROM
    THE(SELECT colors FROM color_models
        WHERE model_type = 'RGB');
```

COLUMN_VALUE is a way of referring to elements of a nested table of scalars. It is a syntactic shortcut to achieve the same result as the previous example.

The general structure of a SELECT statement with THE is shown here:

```
SELECT <expression list>
FROM THE(SELECT <outer column name>
             FROM <outer table>          -- which outer table row?
         WHERE <condition on outer table>)
WHERE <condition on inner table>;
```

Where:

expression list

Is COLUMN_VALUE or a SELECT-list, depending on whether the retrieved collection is a scalar or a composite. If it's a composite (such as an object), then the Select-list can include any of the object type's attributes.

outer column name

Refers to the name you've given the outer table column, which is a collection type.

The WHERE condition on the outer table must retrieve zero or one row(s); otherwise, you'll get the message "ORA-01427: single-row subquery returns more than one row."

You can also use a THE subquery as the target of an INSERT, UPDATE, and DELETE statements. Some brief examples:

```
-- change BLUE to BURGUNDY inside the collection
UPDATE THE(SELECT colors
                 FROM color_models
                 WHERE model_type = 'RGB')
    SET COLUMN_VALUE = 'BURGUNDY'
 WHERE COLUMN_VALUE = 'BLUE';

-- add a silly extra color
INSERT INTO THE(SELECT colors
                 FROM color_models
                 WHERE model_type = 'RGB')
VALUES ('EXTRA-COLOR');

-- show the current colors
SELECT COLUMN_VALUE FROM THE(SELECT colors
                              FROM color_models
                              WHERE model_type = 'RGB');


COLUMN_VALUE
-------------------
RED
GREEN
```

```
BURGUNDY
EXTRA-COLOR

-- delete the extra color
DELETE THE(SELECT colors
              FROM color_models
             WHERE model_type = 'RGB')
WHERE COLUMN_VALUE = 'EXTRA-COLOR';
```

The *Oracle8 Server Application Developers Guide* is a good source of more sample DML on collections.

The CAST Pseudo-function

The new THE pseudo-function does not work directly on VARRAYs. However, it is possible to use Oracle8's CAST function on a VARRAY so we can emulate the SELECT statement shown in the previous section.

Casting a named collection

Here is an example of casting a named collection. If we have created the color_ models table based on a VARRAY type as follows:

```
CREATE TYPE Color_array_t AS VARRAY(16) OF VARCHAR2(30);

CREATE TABLE color_models_a (
    model_type VARCHAR2(12),
    colors Color_array_t);
```

we can CAST the VARRAY colors column as a nested table and apply the THE pseudo-function to the result:

```
SELECT COLUMN_VALUE FROM
    THE(SELECT CAST(colors AS Color_tab_t)
          FROM color_models_a
         WHERE model_type = 'FGB');
```

CAST performs an on-the-fly conversion of the Color_array_t collection type to the Color_tab_t collection type.

NOTE   CAST is available only within SQL statements. That means you can't
           use it directly within PL/SQL. However, it is useful in SELECTs and
           DML statements that appear in your PL/SQL programs.

A subtle difference exists between what you can accomplish with CAST and what you can accomplish with THE. As we saw in the previous section, THE can serve on either the "left-hand side" or the "right-hand side" of an INSERT, UPDATE, or

DELETE statement. THE subqueries can be part of the source, or the target, of these DML statements. By contrast, CAST only works in SELECTs or on the right-hand side of DML statements.

Casting an "unnamed collection"

It is also possible to cast a "bunch of records"—such as the result of a subquery—as a particular collection type. Doing so requires the MULTISET function, covered in the next section.

The MULTISET Pseudo-function

This new Oracle8 function exists only for use within CASTs. MULTISET allows you to retrieve a set of data and convert it on-the-fly to a collection type. The simplest example is this:

```
SELECT CAST (MULTISET (SELECT field FROM table) AS collection-type)
    FROM DUAL;
```

So if we happened to have a relational table of colors:

```
CREATE TABLE some_colors (
    color_name VARCHAR2(30),
    color_classification VARCHAR2(30));
```

and we wanted to CAST to a collection so we could fetch a set of them at once, we could do this:

```
DECLARE
    some_hot_colors Color_tab_t;
BEGIN
    SELECT CAST(MULTISET(SELECT color_name
                         FROM some_colors
                         WHERE color_classification = 'HOT')
            AS Color_tab_t)
      INTO some_hot_colors
      FROM DUAL;
END;
```

Another way to use MULTISET involves a correlated subquery in the SELECT list:

```
SELECT outerfield,
   CAST(MULTISET(SELECT field FROM whateverTable
                 WHERE correlationCriteria)
     AS collectionTypeName)
   FROM outerTable;
```

This technique is useful for making joins look as if they include a collection. Going back to our birds example, suppose that we had a detail table that listed, for each bird, the countries where that species lives:

```
CREATE TABLE birds (
    genus VARCHAR2(128),
```

```
        species VARCHAR2(128),
        colors Color_array_t,
        PRIMARY KEY (genus, species)
    );

    CREATE TABLE bird_habitats (
        genus VARCHAR2(128),
        species VARCHAR2(128),
        country VARCHAR2(60),
        FOREIGN KEY (genus, species) REFERENCES birds (genus, species)
    );

    CREATE TYPE Country_tab_t AS TABLE OF VARCHAR2(60);
```

We should then be able to "smush" the master and detail tables together in a single SELECT that converts the detail records into a collection type. This feature has enormous significance for client/server programs, since the number of round trips can be cut down without the overhead of duplicating the master records with each and every detail record:

```
DECLARE
    CURSOR bird_curs IS
        SELECT b.genus, b.species,
            CAST(MULTISET(SELECT bh.country FROM bird_habitats bh
                            WHERE bh.genus = b.genus
                                AND bh.species = b.species)
                AS country_tab_t)
            FROM birds b;
    bird_row bird_curs%ROWTYPE;
BEGIN
    OPEN bird_curs;
    FETCH bird_curs into bird_row;
    CLOSE bird_curs;
END;
```

NOTE   In Oracle 8.0.3 this code produces the error "PLS-00201: identifier 'B.GENUS' must be declared." It works properly in 8.0.4. See Oracle's *SQL Reference Guide* for more information and examples. As with the CAST pseudo-function, MULTISET cannot serve as the target of an INSERT, UPDATE, or DELETE statement.

The workaround for this bug is to create a packaged function which will return the desired data expressed in the form of a collection. Then you can use this function, rather than the correlated subquery, in the SELECT statement. Here is the package specification that we need:

```
CREATE PACKAGE fixbug AS
    FUNCTION get_country_tab (p_genus IN VARCHAR2,
        p_species IN VARCHAR2)
        RETURN Country_tab_t;
```

```
        PRAGMA RESTRICT_REFERENCES (get_country_tab, WNDS, RNPS, WNPS);
    END;
```

And the body:

```
    CREATE PACKAGE BODY fixbug AS
        FUNCTION get_country_tab (p_genus IN VARCHAR2,p_species IN VARCHAR2)
          RETURN Country_tab_t
        IS
            l_country_tab Country_tab_t;
            CURSOR ccur IS
                SELECT CAST(MULTISET(SELECT bh.country FROM bird_habitats bh
                                WHERE bh.species = p_species
                                AND bh.genus = p_genus)
                    AS country_tab_t)
                FROM DUAL;

        BEGIN
            OPEN ccur;
            FETCH ccur INTO l_country_tab;
            CLOSE ccur;
            RETURN l_country_tab;

        END;
    END;
```

Note that the CAST above uses a selection from DUAL to substitute for the correlated subquery.

We can now rewrite our original PL/SQL fragment as follows:

```
    DECLARE
        CURSOR bird_curs IS
            SELECT b.genus, b.species,
                fixbug.get_country_tab(b.genus, b.species)
                FROM birds b;
        bird_row bird_curs%ROWTYPE;
    BEGIN
        OPEN bird_curs;
        FETCH bird_curs into bird_row;
        CLOSE bird_curs;
    END;
```

The TABLE Pseudo-function

Just what you were hoping for, another use of the TABLE keyword! In this case,
TABLE is operating as a function that coerces a collection-valued column into
something you can SELECT from. It sounds complicated, but this section presents
an example that's not too hard to follow.

Looking at it another way, let's say that you have a database table with a column
of a collection type. How can you figure out which rows in the table contain a

collection that meets certain criteria? That is, how can you select from the database table, putting a WHERE clause on the collection's contents?

Wouldn't it be nice if you could just say:

```
SELECT *
  FROM table_name
 WHERE collection_column
       HAS CONTENTS 'whatever';   -- invalid; imaginary syntax!
```

Logically, that's exactly what you can do with the TABLE function. Going back to our color_models database table, how could we get a listing of all color models which contain the color RED? Here's the real way to do it:

```
SELECT *
  FROM color_models c
 WHERE 'RED' IN
       (SELECT * FROM TABLE(c.colors));
```

which, in SQL*Plus, returns

```
MODEL_TYPE   COLORS
-----------  -------------------------------------------------------
RGB          COLOR_TAB_T('RED', 'GREEN', 'BLUE')
```

The query means "go through the color_models table and return all rows whose list of colors contains at least one RED element." Had there been more rows with a RED element in their colors column, these rows too would have appeared in our SQL*Plus result set.

As illustrated above, TABLE accepts an alias-qualified collection column as its argument:

```
TABLE(alias_name.collection_name)
```

TABLE returns the contents of this collection coerced into a virtual database table. Hence, you can SELECT from it; in our example, it's used in a subquery.

Does the TABLE function remind you vaguely of the THE pseudo-function? Recall our THE example:

```
SELECT VALUE(c) FROM
    THE(SELECT colors FROM color_models
        WHERE model_type = 'RGB') c;
```

which (in Oracle 8.0.4 and later) returns:

```
VALUE(C)
-------------------------------
RED
GREEN
BLUE
```

So what is the difference between the pseudo-functions THE and TABLE? Both return something that, for purposes of the rest of the SQL statement, serves as a "virtual database table." So the difference between the functions must lie in that on which they operate—their "inputs." The TABLE function operates on a (column-typed) nested table. By contrast, the pseudo-function THE operates on a SELECT statement's result set that contains exactly one row with one column which is a (column-typed) nested table.

As it turns out, the TABLE function gets called "under the covers" whenever you use THE as the target of an INSERT, UPDATE, or DELETE statement. This under-the-covers call coerces the results of the subquery into a virtual database table upon which the DML makes sense to operate.

TIP   To repeat an earlier admonition, none of the collection pseudo-func-
               tions are available from within PL/SQL, but PL/SQL programmers
               will certainly want to know how to use these gizmos in their SQL
               statements!

Personally, I find these new features fascinating, and I enjoy the mental calisthenics required to understand and use them. Maybe mine isn't a universal sentiment, but at least you can admit that Oracle hasn't let their language technology get tired!

Collection Built-Ins

As we've seen already, there are a number of built-in functions and procedures that apply to collection variables. These functions are collectively known as "collection methods" in honor of their object-like invocation syntax. That is, you invoke them using a "*variable*-dot-*method*" style. For functions, use this syntax:

```
result := collection_variable.function_method (method_argument);
```

where "result" must be of a datatype that is type-compatible with the method. For procedures, the syntax is:

```
collection_variable.procedure_method (method_arguments);
```

The following methods are not available from within SQL; they can only be used within PL/SQL programs. The first seven are functions (and are the same methods available for PL/SQL or index-by tables in PL/SQL Release 2.3), and the last three are procedures. For quick reference purposes, this section documents each method using a standard format, which includes an example.

COUNT function

Returns the current number of elements in a collection.

DELETE procedure

Removes one or more elements from the "middle" of a nested table. Reduces COUNT if the element is not already DELETEd. Does not apply to VARRAYs.

EXISTS function

Returns TRUE or FALSE to indicate whether the specified element exists.

EXTEND procedure

Increases the number of elements in a collection. Increases COUNT.

FIRST, LAST functions

Return the smallest (FIRST) and largest (LAST) subscripts in use.

LIMIT function

Returns the maximum number of allowed elements in a VARRAY.

PRIOR, NEXT functions

Return the subscript immediately before (PRIOR) or after (NEXT) a specified subscript. Useful for nested tables that might be sparse.

TRIM procedure

Removes collection elements at the "end" of the collection. Reduces COUNT if elements are not DELETEd.

COUNT

Specification

```
FUNCTION COUNT RETURN BINARY_INTEGER;
```

Example

```
FOR element IN 1..my_list.COUNT
LOOP
   DBMS_OUTPUT.PUT_LINE (my_list(element));
END LOOP;
/* Note: If my_list is a nested table with any deleted elements
|| in the middle, the my_list(element) reference above will
|| generate a NO_DATA_FOUND exception.
*/
```

Returns

Current number of elements in a collection. If elements have been DELETEd or TRIMmed from the collection, they are not included in COUNT.

Applies to

Nested tables, index-by tables, VARRAYs.

Boundary considerations

If applied to an initialized collection with no elements, returns zero. Also returns zero if applied to empty index-by table.

Exceptions possible

> If applied to an uninitialized nested table or a VARRAY, raises COLLECTION_
> IS_NULL predefined exception. (This exception is not possible for index-by
> tables, which do not require initialization.)

DELETE [(i [, j])]

Specification (overloaded)

```
PROCEDURE DELETE;
PROCEDURE DELETE (i BINARY_INTEGER);
PROCEDURE DELETE (i BINARY_INTEGER, j BINARY_INTEGER);
```

Example

```
CREATE PROCEDURE keep_last (the_list IN OUT List_t)
AS
    first_elt BINARY_INTEGER := the_list.FIRST;
    next_to_last_elt BINARY_INTEGER := the_list.PRIOR(the_list.LAST);
BEGIN
    the_list.DELETE(first_elt, next_to_last_elt);
END;
```

Action

> DELETE without arguments removes all the elements of a collection.
> DELETE(i) removes the ith element from the nested table or index-by table.
> DELETE(i,j) removes all elements in an inclusive range beginning with i and
> ending with j. When you use parameters, DELETE actually keeps a place-
> holder for the "removed" element, and you can later reassign a value to that
> element.

WARNING   Confusing behavior results if you TRIM and DELETE the same
collection.

Applies to

> Nested tables, index-by tables. Also, DELETE without arguments can be
> applied to VARRAYs.

Boundary considerations

> If i and/or j refer to nonexistent elements, DELETE will attempt to "do the
> right thing" and will not raise an exception. For example, if you have three
> elements in a TABLE item and DELETE(-5,1), the first element will be deleted.
> However, DELETE(-5) will do nothing.

Exceptions possible

> If applied to an uninitialized nested table or a VARRAY, raises COLLECTION_
> IS_NULL predefined exception.

EXISTS(i)

Specification
```
FUNCTION EXISTS (i IN BINARY_INTEGER) RETURN BOOLEAN;
```

Example
```
DECLARE
    my_list Color_tab_t := Color_tab_t();
    element INTEGER := 1;
BEGIN
    ...
    IF my_list.EXISTS(element)
    THEN
       my_list(element) := NULL;
    END IF;
END;
```

Returns
Boolean TRUE if *i*th element exists, FALSE otherwise. Never returns NULL. If you have used TRIM or DELETE to remove an element *i* that existed previously, EXISTS(*i*) returns false.

Applies to
Nested tables, index-by tables, VARRAYs.

Boundary considerations
If applied to an uninitialized (atomically null) nested table or VARRAY, or to an initialized collection with no elements, simply returns FALSE. You can use EXISTS beyond the COUNT without raising an exception.

Exceptions possible
If *i* is not an integer and cannot be converted to an integer, EXISTS will raise VALUE_ERROR. This exception is possible for any collection method which accepts an argument.

EXTEND [(n [,i])]

Specification (overloaded)
```
PROCEDURE EXTEND (n BINARY_INTEGER:=1);
PROCEDURE EXTEND (n BINARY_INTEGER, i BINARY_INTEGER);
```

Example
```
CREATE PROCEDURE push (the_list IN OUT List_t, new_value IN VARCHAR2)
AS
BEGIN
    the_list.EXTEND;
    the_list(the_list.LAST) := new_value;
END;
```

Action
Appends element(s) to a collection. EXTEND with no arguments appends a single null element. EXTEND(*n*) appends *n* null elements. EXTEND(*n*,*i*)

appends *n* elements and sets each to the same value as the *i*th element; this form of EXTEND is required for collections with NOT NULL elements.

Applies to

Nested tables, VARRAYs. Applying it to an index-by table will cause a compile-time error.

Boundary considerations

If you have deleted or trimmed from the end of a collection, EXTEND will "jump over" (skip) the deleted elements when it assigns a new index. If *n* is null, EXTEND will do nothing.

Exceptions possible

If applied to an uninitialized nested table or a VARRAY, raises COLLECTION_IS_NULL predefined exception. An attempt to EXTEND a VARRAY beyond its declared limit raises SUBSCRIPT_BEYOND_LIMIT. If the *i*th element does not exist, EXTEND will raise SUBSCRIPT_BEYOND_COUNT or, in the case of a VARRAY with a limit less than *i*, EXTEND will raise SUBSCRIPT_BEYOND_LIMIT.

FIRST, LAST

Specification

```
FUNCTION FIRST RETURN BINARY_INTEGER;
FUNCTION LAST RETURN BINARY_INTEGER;
```

Example

```
IF my_list.EXISTS(my_list.FIRST)
THEN
    my_list(my_list.FIRST) := 42;
ELSE
    my_list.EXTEND;
    my_list(my_list.FIRST) := 42;
END IF;
```

Returns

FIRST returns the lowest index in use in the collection; LAST returns the highest.

Applies to

Nested tables, index-by tables, VARRAYs.

Boundary considerations

FIRST and LAST return NULL when applied to initialized collections which have no elements. For VARRAYs which have at least one element, FIRST is always 1, and LAST is always equal to COUNT.

Exceptions possible

If applied to an uninitialized nested table or a VARRAY, raises COLLECTION_IS_NULL predefined exception.

LIMIT

Specification

```
FUNCTION LIMIT RETURN BINARY_INTEGER;
```

Example

```
IF my_list.LAST < my_list.LIMIT
THEN
    my_list.EXTEND;
END IF;
```

Returns

The maximum number of elements that is possible for a given VARRAY.

Applies to

VARRAYs only. Returns NULL if applied to nested tables or index-by tables.

Boundary considerations

None

Exceptions possible

If applied to an uninitialized nested table or a VARRAY, raises COLLECTION_IS_NULL predefined exception.

PRIOR(i), NEXT(i)

Specification

```
FUNCTION PRIOR (i BINARY_INTEGER) RETURN BINARY_INTEGER;
FUNCTION NEXT (i BINARY_INTEGER) RETURN BINARY_INTEGER;
```

Example

This function returns the sum of elements in a List_t collection of numbers:

```
CREATE FUNCTION compute_sum (the_list IN List_t) RETURN NUMBER
AS
    elt BINARY_INTEGER := the_list.FIRST;
    total NUMBER := 0;
BEGIN
    LOOP
        EXIT WHEN elt IS NULL;
        total := total + the_list(elt);
        elt := the_list.NEXT(elt);
    END LOOP;
    RETURN total;
END;
```

Returns

PRIOR returns the next lower index in use relative to *i*; NEXT returns the next higher.

Applies to

Nested tables, index-by tables, VARRAYs.

Boundary considerations

If applied to initialized collections which have no elements, returns NULL. If i is greater than or equal to COUNT, NEXT returns NULL; if i is less than or equal to FIRST, PRIOR returns NULL. (Currently, if the collection has elements, and i is greater than COUNT, PRIOR returns LAST; if i is less than FIRST, NEXT returns FIRST; however, do not rely on this behavior in future Oracle versions.)

Exceptions possible

If applied to an uninitialized nested table or a VARRAY, raises COLLECTION_IS_NULL predefined exception.

TRIM [(n)]

Specification

```
PROCEDURE TRIM (n BINARY_INTEGER:=1);
```

Example

```
CREATE FUNCTION pop (the_list IN OUT List_t) RETURN VARCHAR2
AS
    l_value VARCHAR2(30);
BEGIN
    IF the_list.COUNT >= 1
    THEN
        /* Save the value of the last element in the collection
        || so it can be returned
        */
        l_value := the_list(the_list.LAST);
        the_list.TRIM;
    END IF;
    RETURN l_value;
END;
```

Action

Removes n elements from the end of a collection. Without arguments, TRIM removes exactly one element. Confusing behavior occurs if you combine DELETE and TRIM actions on a collection; for example, if an element that you are trimming has previously been DELETEd, TRIM "repeats" the deletion but counts this as part of n, meaning that you may be TRIMming fewer actual elements than you think.

Applies to

Nested tables, VARRAYs. Attempting to TRIM an index-by table will produce a compile-time error.

Boundary considerations

If n is null, TRIM will do nothing.

Exceptions possible

Will raise SUBSCRIPT_BEYOND_COUNT if you attempt to TRIM more elements than actually exist. If applied to an uninitialized nested table or a VARRAY, raises COLLECTION_IS_NULL predefined exception.

Example: PL/SQL-to-Server Integration

To provide an(other) demonstration of how collections can ease the burden of transferring data between server and PL/SQL application program, let's look at a new example. The main entity in this example is the "apartment complex." We use a nested table of objects in order to hold the list of apartments for each apartment complex.

Each apartment is described by the following attributes:

```
CREATE TYPE Apartment_t AS OBJECT (
    unit_no NUMBER,
    square_feet NUMBER,
    bedrooms NUMBER,
    bathrooms NUMBER,
    rent_in_dollars NUMBER
);
```

And we can now define the nested table type which will hold a list of these apartment objects:

```
CREATE TYPE Apartment_tab_t AS TABLE OF Apartment_t;
```

Using this type as the type of a column, here is the definition of our database table:

```
CREATE TABLE apartment_complexes
    (name VARCHAR2(75),
    landlord_name VARCHAR2(45),
    apartments Apartment_tab_t)
NESTED TABLE apartments STORE AS apartments_store_tab;
```

If you're curious, the INSERT statements to populate such a table look like the following (note the use of nested constructors to create the collection of objects):

```
INSERT INTO apartment_complexes VALUES
    ('RIVER OAKS FOUR', 'MR. JOHNSON',
    Apartment_tab_t(
        Apartment_t(1, 780, 2, 1, 975),
        Apartment_t(2, 1200, 3, 2, 1590),
        Apartment_t(3, 690, 1, 1.5, 800),
        Apartment_t(4, 690, 1, 2, 450),
        Apartment_t(5, 870, 2, 2, 990)
    )
);
INSERT INTO apartment_complexes VALUES
    ('GALLERIA PLACE', 'MS. DODENHOFF',
```

```
        Apartment_tab_t(
            Apartment_t(101, 1000, 3, 2, 1295),
            Apartment_t(102, 800, 2, 1, 995),
            Apartment_t(103, 800, 2, 1, 995),
            Apartment_t(201, 920, 3, 1.5, 1195),
            Apartment_t(202, 920, 3, 1.5, 1195),
            Apartment_t(205, 1000, 3, 2, 1295)
        )
    );
```

Now, at last, we can show off some wonderful features of storing collections in the database.

Imagine that we are the new managers of the River Oaks Four apartments (hardly large enough to qualify as a complex) and we want to demolish any unit that rents for less than $500, and raise the rent on everything else by 15%.

```
DECLARE
    /* Declare the cursor that will retrieve the collection of
    || apartment objects. Since we know we're going to update the
    || record, we can lock it using FOR UPDATE.
    */
    CURSOR aptcur IS
        SELECT apartments
          FROM apartment_complexes
         WHERE name = 'RIVER OAKS FOUR'
           FOR UPDATE OF apartments;

    /* Need a local variable to hold the collection of fetched
    || apartment objects.
    */
    l_apartments apartment_tab_t;
    which INTEGER;
BEGIN
    /* A single fetch is all we need! */
    OPEN aptcur;
    FETCH aptcur INTO l_apartments;
    CLOSE aptcur;

    /* Iterate over the apartment objects in the collection and
    || delete any elements of the nested table which meet the
    || criteria
    */
    which := l_apartments.FIRST;
    LOOP
        EXIT WHEN which IS NULL;
        IF l_apartments(which).rent_in_dollars < 500
        THEN
            l_apartments.DELETE(which);
        END IF;
        which := l_apartments.NEXT(which);
    END LOOP;

    /* Now iterate over the remaining apartments and raise the
```

```
|| rent. Notice that this code will skip any deleted
|| elements.
*/
which := l_apartments.FIRST;
LOOP
    EXIT WHEN which IS NULL;
    l_apartments(which).rent_in_dollars :=
        l_apartments(which).rent_in_dollars * 1.15;
    which := l_apartments.NEXT(which);

END LOOP;

/* Finally, ship the entire apartment collection back to the
|| server -- in a single statement!
*/
UPDATE apartment_complexes
    SET apartments = l_apartments
  WHERE name = 'RIVER OAKS FOUR';

END;
```

To me, one of the most significant aspects of this example is the single-statement fetch (and store). This PL/SQL fragment emulates the creating of a "client-side cache" of data, which is an essential concept in many object-oriented and client-server architectures. Using this kind of approach with collections can reduce network traffic and improve the quality of your code.

Collections Housekeeping

Here are some not-so-obvious bits of information that will assist you in using nested tables and VARRAYS.

Privileges

When they live in the database, collection datatypes can be shared by more than one Oracle user (schema). As you can imagine, privileges are involved. Fortunately, it's not complicated; only one Oracle privilege—EXECUTE—applies to collection types.

If you are SCOTT and you want to grant JOE permission to use Color_tab_t in his programs, all you need to do is grant the EXECUTE privilege to him:

```
GRANT EXECUTE on Color_tab_t TO JOE;
```

Joe can then refer to the type using *schema.type* notation. For example:

```
CREATE TABLE my_stuff_to_paint (
   which_stuff VARCHAR2(512),
   paint_mixture SCOTT.Color_tab_t
);
```

EXECUTE privileges are also required by users who need to run PL/SQL anonymous blocks that uses the object type. That's one of several reasons that named PL/SQL modules—packages, procedures, functions—are generally preferred. Granting EXECUTE on the module confers the grantor's privileges to the grantee while executing the module.

For tables that include collection columns, the traditional SELECT, INSERT, UDPATE, and DELETE privileges still have meaning, as long as there is no requirement to build a collection for any columns. However, if a user is going to INSERT or UPDATE the contents of a collection column, the user must have the EXECUTE privilege on the type, because that is the only way to use the default constructor.

Data Dictionary

There are a few new entries in the data dictionary (shown in Table 19-3) that will be very helpful in managing your collection types. The shorthand dictionary term for user-defined types is simply TYPE. Collection type definitions are found in the USER_SOURCE view (or DBA_SOURCE, or ALL_SOURCE).

Table 19-3. Data Dictionary Entries for Collection Types

To Answer the Question...	Use This View	As In

What collection types have I created?	USER_TYPES	`SELECT type_name`
		`    FROM user_types`
		`  WHERE type_code = 'COLLECTION';`

What was the original type definition of collection Foo_t?	USER_SOURCE	`SELECT text`
		`    FROM user_source`
		`  WHERE name = 'FOO_T'`
		`    AND type = 'TYPE'`
		`ORDER BY line;`

What columns implement Foo_t?	USER_TAB_ COLUMNS	`SELECT table_name, column_name`
		`    FROM user_tab_columns`
		`  WHERE data_type = 'FOO_T';`

What database objects are dependent on Foo_t?	USER_DEPEN- DENCIES	`SELECT name, type`
		`    FROM user_dependencies`
		`  WHERE referenced_name = 'FOO_T';`

Call by Reference or Call by Value

Under certain circumstances that are beyond the control of the programmer, PL/SQL will pass collection arguments by reference rather than by value. The rationale is that since collections can be large, it is more efficient to pass only a pointer (call by reference) than to make a copy of the collection (call by value). Usually, the compiler's choice of parameter passing approach is invisible to the application programmer.

Not knowing whether the compiler will pass arguments by reference or by value can lead to unexpected results if all of the following conditions are met:

1. You have created a procedure or function "in line" in another module's declaration section (these are known as nested or local program units and are explained in Chapter 15, *Procedures and Functions*).

2. The inline module refers to a "global" collection variable declared outside its definition.

3. In the body of the outer module, this collection variable is passed as an actual parameter to the inline module.

This is a rather uncommon combination of affairs in most PL/SQL programs. If you are in the habit of using "in line" module definitions, it's probably not a good idea to rely on the value of global variables anyway!

Which Collection Type Should I Use?

It's not altogether obvious how to choose the best type of collection for a given application. Here are some guidelines:

- If you intend to store large amounts of persistent data in a column collection, your only option is a nested table. Oracle will then use a separate table behind the scenes to hold the collection data, so you can allow for almost limitless growth.

- If you want to preserve the order of elements that get stored in the collection column *and* your dataset will be "small," use a VARRAY. What is "small?" I tend to think in terms of how much data you can fit into a single database block; if you span blocks, you get row chaining, which decreases performance. The database block size is established at database creation time and is typically 2K, 4K, or 8K.

- Here are some other indications that a VARRAY would be appropriate: you don't want to worry about deletions occurring in the middle of the dataset; your data has an intrinsic upper bound; or you expect, in general, to retrieve the entire collection simultaneously.

- If you need sparse PL/SQL tables, say, for "data-smart" storage, your only practical option is an index-by table. True, you could allocate and then delete elements of a nested table variable as illustrated in the section on NEXT and PRIOR methods, but it is inefficient to do so for anything but the smallest collections.

- If your PL/SQL program needs to run under both Oracle7 and Oracle8, you also have only one option: index-by tables. Or, if your PL/SQL application requires negative subscripts, you also have to use index-by tables.

20

Object Views

Although Oracle's object extensions offer rich possibilities for the design of new systems, few Oracle shops with large relational databases in place will want to, or be able to, completely reengineer those systems to use objects. To allow established applications to take advantage of the new object features over time, Oracle8 provides *object views*. With object views, you can achieve the following benefits:

- *Efficiency of object access.* In PL/SQL, and particularly in Oracle Call Interface (OCI) applications, object programming constructs provide for the convenient retrieval, caching, and updating of object data. These programming facilities provide performance improvements, with the added benefit that application code can now be more succinct.

- *Ability to navigate using REFs (reference pointers).* By designating unique identifiers as the basis of an object identifier (OID), you can reap the benefits of object navigation. For example, you can retrieve attributes from related "virtual objects" using dot notation rather than via explicit joins.

- *Easier schema evolution.* In early versions of Oracle8, a pure object approach renders almost any kind of schema change at best ugly (see Chapter 18, *Object Types*). In contrast, object views offer more ways that you can change both the table structure and the object type definitions of an existing system.

- *Consistency with new object-based applications.* If you need to extend the design of a legacy database, the new components can be implemented in object tables; new object-oriented applications requiring access to existing data can employ a consistent programming model. Legacy applications can continue to work without modification.

Other new features of Oracle can improve the expressiveness of any type of view, not just object views. Two features which are not strictly limited to object views are collections and "INSTEAD OF" triggers. Consider two relational tables with a simple master-detail relationship. Using the Oracle objects option, you can portray the detail records as a single nonscalar attribute (collection) of the master, which could be a very useful abstraction. In addition, by using INSTEAD OF triggers, you can tell Oracle exactly how to perform inserts, updates, and deletes on any view. These two features are available to both object views and nonobject views. (I've described collections in Chapter 19, *Nested Tables and VARRAYs*, and I describe INSTEAD OF triggers later in this chapter.)

From an object-oriented perspective, there is one unavoidable "disadvantage" of object views, when compared to reengineering using an all-object approach: object views cannot retrofit any benefits of encapsulation. Insofar as old applications apply INSERT, UPDATE, and DELETE statements directly to table data, they will subvert the benefits of encapsulation normally provided by an object approach. As I discussed in Chapter 18, object-oriented designs typically prevent free-form access directly to object data.

Despite this intrusion of reality, if you do choose to layer object views on top of a legacy system, your future applications can employ object abstractions and enjoy many benefits of encapsulation and information hiding. And your legacy systems are no *worse* off than they were before! Figure 20-1 illustrates this use of object views.

This chapter discusses the nuances of creating and, to a lesser extent, using object views. The discussion of PL/SQL-specific aspects of object views is rather terse, for two reasons:

1. Object views are substantially similar to regular object types, which are covered in a Chapter 18.

2. As a topic, object views are closer to SQL than to PL/SQL.

However, PL/SQL developers who are interested in fully exploiting Oracle's object features must understand object views. This chapter pays close attention to the areas of difference between object tables and object views.

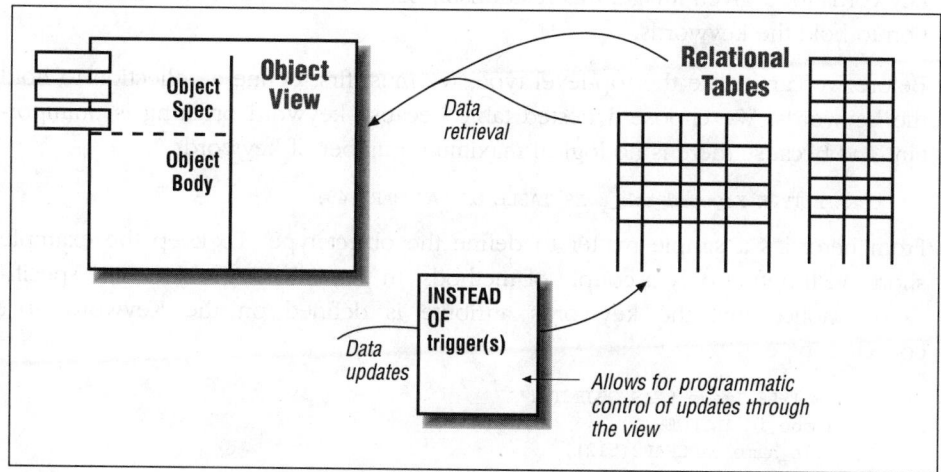

Figure 20-1. Object views allow you to "bind" an object type definition to (existing) relational tables

Example: Using Object Views

In our first example, let's look at how object views might be used at Planetary Pages, a fictitious firm that designs Web sites. Their existing relational application tracks JPEG, GIF, and other images that they use when designing client Web sites. These images are stored in files, but data about them are stored in relational tables. To help the graphic artists locate the right image, each image has one or more associated keywords, stored in a straightforward master-detail relationship.

Our legacy system has one table for image metadata:

```
CREATE TABLE images (
    image_id INTEGER NOT NULL,
    file_name VARCHAR2(512),
    file_type VARCHAR2(12),
    bytes INTEGER,
    CONSTRAINT image_pk PRIMARY KEY (image_id));
```

and one table for the keywords associated with the images:

```
CREATE TABLE keywords (
    image_id INTEGER NOT NULL,
    keyword VARCHAR2(45) NOT NULL,
    CONSTRAINT keywords_pk PRIMARY KEY (image_id, keyword),
    CONSTRAINT keywords_for_image FOREIGN KEY (image_id)
        REFERENCES images (image_id));
```

To create a more useful abstraction, Planetary Pages has decided to logically merge these two tables into a single object view. To do so, we must first create an object type with appropriate attributes. Since there are usually only a few keywords for a given image, this relationship lends itself to using an Oracle collection to hold the keywords.

Before we can create the top-level type, we must first define a collection to hold the keywords. We choose a nested table because keyword ordering is unimportant and because there is no logical maximum number of keywords.[*]

```
CREATE TYPE Keyword_tab_t AS TABLE OF VARCHAR2(45);
```

From here, it's a simple matter to define the object type. To keep the example short, we'll define only a couple of methods. In the following object type specification, notice that the keywords attribute is defined on the Keyword_tab_t collection type:

```
CREATE TYPE Image_t AS OBJECT (
     image_id INTEGER,
     file_name VARCHAR2(512),
     file_type VARCHAR2(12),
     bytes INTEGER,
     keywords Keyword_tab_t,
     MEMBER FUNCTION set_attrs (new_file_name IN VARCHAR2,
        new_file_type IN VARCHAR2, new_bytes IN INTEGER)
        RETURN Image_t,
     MEMBER FUNCTION set_keywords (new_keywords IN Keyword_tab_t)
        RETURN Image_t,
     PRAGMA RESTRICT_REFERENCES (DEFAULT, RNDS, WNDS, RNPS, WNPS)
 );
```

Here is the body:

```
CREATE TYPE BODY Image_t
AS
     MEMBER FUNCTION set_attrs (new_file_name IN VARCHAR2,
            new_file_type IN VARCHAR2, new_bytes IN INTEGER)
            RETURN Image_t
     IS
         image_holder Image_t := SELF;
     BEGIN
         image_holder.file_name := new_file_name;
         image_holder.file_type := new_file_type;
         image_holder.bytes := new_bytes;
         RETURN image_holder;
     END;
     MEMBER FUNCTION set_keywords (new_keywords IN Keyword_tab_t)
            RETURN Image_t
     IS
         image_holder Image_t := SELF;
```

---

[*] If ordering were important, or if there were a (small) logical maximum number of keywords per image, a VARRAY collection would be a better choice. See Chapter 19 for details.

```
      BEGIN
          image_holder.keywords := new_keywords;
          RETURN image_holder;
      END;
   END;
```

I've presented the body only for completeness; from this point forward, I'll discuss object views without regard for the details of their underlying type bodies.

At this point, there is no connection between the relational tables and the object type. They are independent organisms. It is when we build the object view that we "overlay" the object definition onto the tables.

Finally, to create the object view, we use the following statement:

```
CREATE VIEW images_v
    OF Image_t
    WITH OBJECT OID (image_id)
AS
    SELECT i.image_id, i.file_name, i.file_type, i.bytes,
        CAST (MULTISET (SELECT keyword
                        FROM keywords k
                        WHERE k.image_id = i.image_id)
        AS Keyword_tab_t)
      FROM images i;
```

Interestingly, there are only a couple of components of this statement that are unique to object views:

OF Image_t
> This means that the view will return objects of type Image_t.

WITH OBJECT OID (image_id)
> To behave like a "real" object instance, data returned by the view will need some kind of object identifier. By designating the primary key as the basis of a virtual OID, we can enjoy the benefits of referencing objects of this type from other object views.

In addition, the select-list has an important requirement unique to object views. The select-list must define the same number of columns as there are attributes in the object type Image_t. The datatype of each retrieved column matches the datatype of its corresponding object attributes.

You can use the CAST clause shown in the example in any view, not just in object views (but it does require the presence of the Oracle objects option). This subquery performs an "on-the-fly" conversion of the detail records into a collection type. For more details about the CAST and MULTISET operators, refer to the "Collection Pseudo-Functions" section of Chapter 19, *Nested Tables and VARRAYs*.

OK, now that we've created it, what can we do with it? Well, we can retrieve data from it just as if it were an object table. First, let's put some data into the underlying tables:

```
INSERT INTO images VALUES (100001, 'smiley_face.gif', 'GIF', 813);
INSERT INTO images VALUES (100002, 'peace_symbol.gif', 'GIF', 972);


INSERT INTO KEYWORDS VALUES (100001, 'SIXTIES');
INSERT INTO KEYWORDS VALUES (100001, 'HAPPY FACE');


INSERT INTO KEYWORDS VALUES (100002, 'SIXTIES');
INSERT INTO KEYWORDS VALUES (100002, 'PEACE SYMBOL');
INSERT INTO KEYWORDS VALUES (100002, 'JERRY RUBIN');
```

Now, from SQL*Plus, you can make a query like the following:

```
SELECT image_id, file_name, keywords
    FROM images_v;
```

Which yields:

```
IMAGE_ID FILE_NAME        KEYWORDS
-------- ---------------- -----------------------------------------------------------
  100001 smiley_face.gif  KEYWORD_TAB_T('HAPPY FACE', 'SIXTIES')
  100002 peace_symbol.gif KEYWORD_TAB_T('JERRY RUBIN', 'PEACE SYMBOL', 'SIXTIES')
```

Or, in a PL/SQL block, we can fetch and display a row of data very easily:

```
SET SERVEROUTPUT ON SIZE 100000
DECLARE
    CURSOR icur IS
        SELECT VALUE(v)
          FROM images_v v
         WHERE image_id = 100001;
    image Image_t;
BEGIN
    OPEN icur;
    FETCH icur INTO image;
    CLOSE icur;

    /* Print it out, just to prove that we got it */
    DBMS_OUTPUT.PUT_LINE('Image:    ' || image.image_id);
    DBMS_OUTPUT.PUT_LINE('File:     ' || image.file_name);
    DBMS_OUTPUT.PUT('Keywords: ');

    /* image.keywords is a nested table, and we can just loop
    || through it to print each keyword.
    */
    FOR key_elt IN 1..image.keywords.COUNT
    LOOP
        DBMS_OUTPUT.PUT(image.keywords(key_elt) || '   ');
    END LOOP;
    DBMS_OUTPUT.NEW_LINE;
END;
```

This results in:

```
Image:    100001
File:     smiley_face.gif
Keywords: HAPPY FACE   SIXTIES
```

See Chapter 19 for more examples of retrieving data from an object table.

Other things you can do with object views include the following:

- Define REFs that point to "virtual" objects (discussed in detail in the section "Differences Between Object Views and Object Tables" later in this chapter).

- Encapsulate an object view (more or less) using object methods and/or PL/SQL packages (discussed in-depth in Chapter 18).

- Write INSTEAD OF triggers that will allow direct manipulation of the view's contents (discussed in the next section).

INSTEAD OF Triggers

Some conventional views are "inherently modifiable." For example, even Oracle Version 6 allowed updates through a view of a single table which uses no aggregation clauses such as GROUP BY. While Oracle7 added to the family of modifiable views, even in Oracle8 there is still a class of views which are "inherently unmodifiable" if you limit yourself to standard SQL.

However, in Oracle8, if you can come up with the logic of how you want Oracle to interpret a particular operation on a view—however wacky that view might be—you can implement the behavior with INSTEAD OF triggers. Happily, this new type of trigger is available to all Oracle8 users; it is not a part of the Oracle objects option.

Conceptually, INSTEAD OF triggers are very simple. You write code that the Oracle server will execute when a program performs a DML operation on the view. Unlike a conventional BEFORE or AFTER trigger, an INSTEAD OF trigger *takes the place of,* rather than supplements, Oracle's usual DML behavior. (And in case you're wondering, you cannot use BEFORE/AFTER triggers on any type of view, even if you have defined an INSTEAD OF trigger on the view.)

For example, to allow applications to INSERT into our images_v view, we could write the following trigger:

```
CREATE OR REPLACE TRIGGER images_v_insert
INSTEAD OF INSERT ON images_v
FOR EACH ROW
BEGIN
    /* This will fail with DUP_VAL_ON_INDEX if the images table
    || already contains a record with the new image_id.
    */
```

```
        INSERT INTO images
            VALUES (:NEW.image_id, :NEW.file_name, :NEW.file_type,
                    :NEW.bytes);

        IF :NEW.keywords IS NOT NULL THEN
            DECLARE
                /* Note: apparent bug prevents use of :NEW.keywords.LAST.
                || The workaround is to store :NEW.keywords as a local
                || variable (in this case keywords_holder.)
                */
                keywords_holder Keyword_tab_t := :NEW.keywords;
            BEGIN
                FOR the_keyword IN 1..keywords_holder.LAST
                LOOP
                    INSERT INTO keywords
                    VALUES (:NEW.image_id, keywords_holder(the_keyword));
                END LOOP;
            END;
        END IF;
    END;
```

Once we've created this INSTEAD OF trigger, we can insert a record into this object view (and hence into *both* underlying tables) quite easily using:

```
INSERT INTO images_v
VALUES (Image_t(41265, 'pigpic.jpg', 'JPG', 824,
        Keyword_tab_t('PIG', 'BOVINE', 'FARM ANIMAL')));
```

This statement causes the INSTEAD OF trigger to fire, and as long as the primary key value (image_id = 41265) does not already exist, the trigger will insert the data into the appropriate tables.

Similarly, we can write additional triggers that handle updates and deletes. These triggers use the predictable clauses INSTEAD OF UPDATE and INSTEAD OF DELETE.

INSTEAD OF Triggers: To Use or Not to Use?

Before launching headlong into the business of updating complex views with triggers, let's step back and look at the bigger picture. Do we really *want* to use INSTEAD OF triggers in an Oracle environment? Particularly if we are migrating toward an object approach, isn't this new feature just a relational "throwback" which facilitates a free-for-all in which any application can perform DML?

Yes and no.

Let's consider arguments on both sides, and come up with some considerations so you can decide what's best for your application.

The "don't use" argument

On the one hand, you *could* use tools such as packages and methods to provide a more comprehensive technique than triggers for encapsulating DML. It is nearly trivial to take the logic from our INSTEAD OF trigger and put it into an alternate PL/SQL construct which has more universal application. In other words, if you standardize on some combination of packages and object methods as the means of performing DML, you could keep your environment consistent without using view triggers. You might conclude that view triggers are just another variable in an increasingly complex standards equation.

Moreover, even Oracle cautions against the "excessive use" of triggers, because they can cause "complex interdependencies." Imagine if your INSTEAD OF triggers performed DML on tables which had other triggers, which performed DML on still other tables...it's easy to see how this could get confusing.

The "use" argument

On the other hand, you can put much of the necessary logic into an INSTEAD OF trigger that you would normally put into a package or method body. Doing so in combination with a proper set of privilege restrictions could protect your data just as well as, or even better than, methods or packages.

What's more, if you use a client tool such as Oracle Forms, INSTEAD OF triggers allow you to use much more of the product's default functionality when you create a Forms "block" against a view rather than a table. This fact alone could make object views wildly popular.

Finally, if you use OCI, a more significant factor is that INSTEAD OF triggers are *required* if the object view is not inherently modifiable and you want to be able to easily "flush" cached object view data back to the server.

What to do?

One of the most important architectural decisions you will make for your object views is where to put SQL statements that insert, update, and delete data. Going on the assumption that you want to localize these operations on the server side, you have at least three choices: PL/SQL packages, object methods, and INSTEAD OF triggers.

Table 20-1 summarizes some of the major considerations of the three techniques. This table is not meant to compare these approaches "in general" but only as they apply to localizing DML on object views.

Table 20-1. Assessment of Techniques for Encapsulating DML on Object Views

DML Consideration	PL/SQL Package	Object Method	INSTEAD OF Trigger
Ability to adapt to schema changes	Excellent; can be easily altered and recompiled independently	Poor, especially if object types are responsible for their own persistence	Good, but still some areas where Oracle does not automatically recompile dependent structures
Risk of unexpected interactions	Low	Low	High; triggers may have unpredictable interactions with each other
Ease of use with client tool default functionality (specifically, Developer/2000)	Acceptable; programmer must add code for all client-side transactional triggers	Acceptable; programmer must add code for all client-side transactional triggers	Excellent (however, there is no INSTEAD OF LOCK server-side trigger)
Ability to use technique on transient objects	Very good, but not a "natural" use of packages	Excellent	Theoretically possible, but why bother?
Can be turned on and off at will	No	No	Yes (by disabling and enabling the trigger)

Chapter 18 discussed at some length architectural considerations of packages versus methods. While those considerations also apply to object views, we now need to compare packages and methods with INSTEAD OF triggers.

As you can see, there is no clear "winner." Each technique has benefits that may be of more or less importance to your own particular application.

And of course, you may decide that INSTEAD OF triggers make sense *in combination with* PL/SQL packages and/or object methods to provide layers of encapsulation. For example:

```
CREATE OR REPLACE TRIGGER images_v_insert
INSTEAD OF INSERT ON images_v
FOR EACH ROW
BEGIN
    /* Call a packaged procedure to perform the insertion.
    || (The called procedure is not presented in the text.)
    */
    manage_image.create_one(:NEW.image_id, :NEW.file_type,
        :NEW.file_name, :NEW.bytes, :NEW.keywords);
END;
```

In an ideal world, you will select an architecture and design approach before hurling every Oracle feature at your application. Use a feature if it make sense for your architectural approach. I tend to agree with Oracle's advice that if you do use triggers, you should use them in moderation.

Syntax for Object Views

Now that we've looked at one example and considered what INSTEAD OF triggers can offer, let's examine with more rigor the syntax required to create your own object views.

CREATE VIEW: Creating an Object View

This is the basic syntax for creating an object view:

```
CREATE [ OR REPLACE ] VIEW <view name>
   OF <object type name>
   [ WITH OBJECT OID DEFAULT | (<attribute list>) ]
   AS <query>
   [ WITH [ READ ONLY | CHECK OPTION ]];
```

Note that we've omitted some of the optional keywords, such as FORCE and CONSTRAINT, from this syntax discussion. The elements are as follows:

OF object type name
> The name of the preexisting user-defined object type that this view will emulate.

WITH OBJECT OID
> Indicates only that the OID specification follows. (It's a bit strange that the clause requires all three keywords. It seems grammatically sufficient to me to say WITH OID, which should mean "with object identifier," as opposed to WITH OBJECT OID, which means "with object *object* (sic) identifier." Must have been a late night at the syntax factory...

DEFAULT
> In the event that the object view is defined on an underlying object table or object view, you can tell Oracle to use the OID of the underlying object. If your view is eligible to use DEFAULT, the result is the same whether you include or omit the WITH OBJECT OID DEFAULT clause. That is, the default is DEFAULT (!).

attribute list
> Comma-separated list of type attributes which comprise a (usually unique) identifier.

query
> Your query must retrieve columns or expressions that match one for one, in order, the individual attributes of the object type. The datatype of each

SELECTed expression must also match, or be type-compatible with, the corresponding attribute defined in the object type. The maximum number of columns or expressions is 1000.

WITH CHECK OPTION

If your view is updateable—either because it is inherently updateable or because you have created an INSTEAD OF trigger—this option will prevent inserts or updates of data that cannot subsequently be selected (for example, because of a WHERE clause restriction).

WITH READ ONLY

Prevents any DML operation from being executed. This clause takes precedence over INSTEAD OF triggers.

It's also important to note what is missing. Conventional views may use an alias clause; that is, a comma-separated list of names that Oracle will assign, in order, to the columns of the view. By contrast, you cannot use an alias clause in an object view. Instead, the object view always derives its list of column (attribute) names from the attribute names of the underlying type.

DROP: Dropping Views and Triggers

There is no syntactic difference between dropping a conventional view and dropping an object view. Both are accomplished using the command:

```
DROP VIEW <view name>;
```

Dropping a view has the side effect of dropping any INSTEAD OF triggers that you have created on the view. Of course, you can drop INSTEAD OF triggers explicitly, using the following:

```
DROP TRIGGER <trigger name>;
```

MAKE_REF: Returning a Virtual REF

The MAKE_REF function returns a "virtual REF" for an object view. (REFs are described in Chapter 18.) Its syntax is:

```
MAKE_REF (<view name>, <value list>)
```

Where:

view name

The view from which you wish to derive a REF value (which other object views may reference).

value list

Comma-separated list of column values whose datatype must match one for one with the OID attribute(s) of <view name>.

As a generic example, let's say that we have a table foo, and we define a corresponding object type and object view:

```
CREATE TABLE foo (
    id NUMBER PRIMARY KEY,   -- defining it as a PK is optional
    name VARCHAR2(30)
);

CREATE TYPE Foo_t AS OBJECT (
    id NUMBER,
    name VARCHAR2(30)
);

CREATE VIEW foo_v
    OF Foo_t
    WITH OBJECT OID (id)
AS
    SELECT id, name
    FROM foo;
```

Now we can use MAKE_REF in an any statement, including something as simple as:

```
SELECT MAKE_REF(foo_v, 123) FROM DUAL;
```

This statement will return a REF to the virtual object with id = 123. (Although you will see a result for this query when you execute it from SQL*Plus, Oracle's earlier admonition still applies: don't attempt to store this value anywhere. Incidentally, this query causes the ORA-00932 error, "inconsistent datatypes," in SQL Worksheet.[*])

If you want to construct a REF via the foo_v view for object 123, the record in the foo table with id = 123 does not even need to exist! MAKE_REF merely applies an internal Oracle algorithm to the supplied arguments to derive a REF; it does not read the foo_v view to determine whether the object really exists in the underlying table.

One final note about MAKE_REF: you might be tempted to call MAKE_REF natively in PL/SQL:

```
DECLARE
    foo_ref REF Foo_t;
BEGIN
    foo_ref := MAKE_REF (foo_v, 123);    -- invalid
END;
```

---

[*] SQL Worksheet is an SQL interpreter that ships with Oracle Enterprise Manager. SQL Worksheet has one significant advantage over SQL*Plus: it retains in memory a good number of your recently issued statements, allowing you to retrieve and edit SQL statements or PL/SQL code easily. I developed many of the examples for the objects chapters of this book using this tool.

But that statement fails with the error PLS-00201, "identifier 'MAKE_REF' must be declared." You might also try the following:

```
DECLARE
    foo_ref REF Foo_t;
BEGIN
    SELECT MAKE_REF(foo_v, 123)    -- invalid
        INTO foo_ref
        FROM DUAL;
END;
```

But this too fails, at least in Oracle 8.0.3. This behavior is a suspected bug.

Differences Between Object Views and Object Tables

In addition to the obvious difference between a view and a table, more subtle differences exist between an object view and an object table. Areas of difference include the following:

- Uniqueness of object identifiers

- Use of REFs

- Storage of REFs

- REFs to nonunique OIDs

Lets look at each difference in turn.

OID Uniqueness

An object table will always have a unique, system-defined object identifier, whether or not the object type includes attribute(s) which can serve as a unique identifier. While this is seldom, if ever, good practice, it is technically possible to create an object table where two or more object instances (rows) contain duplicate values in every column; the instances will still be unique in their object identifier. And, as discussed in the previous chapter, OIDs of table objects are globally unique, even across databases.

By contrast, object views can give rise to two types of OID duplication:

- Duplication of OIDs within a single object view

- Duplication of OIDs across multiple views (or across an object view and an object table)

Duplicate OIDs in a single view

An object view can easily contain multiple object instances (rows) for a given OID. Let's look at how that can happen.

In our earlier example, we chose to "smush" the detail table into a collection and use the primary key of the parent table as the (unique) OID of the view. If for some reason we had used a simple join on the foreign key, a given value of the primary key of the parent could indeed yield a nonunique OID. This would require a different underlying object type where the "keywords" attribute is a scalar rather than a collection:

```
CREATE TYPE Image_keyword_t AS OBJECT (
    image_id INTEGER,
    file_name VARCHAR2(512),
    file_type VARCHAR2(12),
    bytes INTEGER,
    keywords VARCHAR2(45)
);
```

The object view could then be created as follows.

```
CREATE VIEW image_keyword_v
    OF Image_keyword_t
    WITH OBJECT OID (image_id)
AS
    SELECT i.image_id, i.file_name, i.file_type, i.bytes, k.keyword
      FROM keywords k, images i
     WHERE k.image_id = i.image_id;
```

This duplication of OIDs may make sense for some applications; however, in the more likely case that you want to avoid duplicate OIDs, simply include enough attributes to make it unique:

```
WITH OBJECT OID (image_id, keywords)
```

Duplicate OIDs across multiple views

There are other scenarios in which object views duplicate object identifiers used elsewhere. For example, if your object view is defined on an underlying object table or view *and* if you use the DEFAULT keyword to specify the OID, the view contains OIDs that match the OIDs of the underlying construct:

```
CREATE VIEW gif_images_v
    OF Image_t
    WITH OBJECT OID DEFAULT
AS
    SELECT *
      FROM images_v
     WHERE file_type = 'GIF';
```

In this case, all of the OIDs that Oracle uses for instances (rows) of gif_images_v will match existing OIDs of the images_v view.

Logically, this possibility of "duplication" makes a certain amount of sense. A view is often thought of as a "stored query." Used here, the query simply retrieves a subset of the underlying objects and does not modify them in any way.

NOTE   Just because your object view is defined on an object table, you
           don't *have* to use the underlying OID. If you want the OIDs of the
           objects in gif_images_v to be unique from those of the underlying
           object, you could simply specify the image_id attribute as the OID:

```
CREATE VIEW gif_images_v
    OF Image_t
    WITH OBJECT OID (image_id)
    AS SELECT *
        FROM images_v
        WHERE file_type = 'GIF';
```

           In this view, Oracle will use its internal algorithm to derive unique
           OIDs for the objects retrieved via gif_images_v.

Using REFs with Object Views

As we saw in Chapter 18, Oracle allows us to define a "reference" or REF datatype to designate relationships between two object tables. We also saw how REF types provide convenient navigation among families of persistent objects through dot notation rather than explicit relational joins.

In the same way that you can define a REF to link two object tables, you can create a "virtual REF" to link two object views. To see how this works, and to examine a critical difference between virtual REFs and "real" REFs, let's return to an example at our favorite Web design firm, Planetary Pages.

Defining virtual REFs

As it turns out, the table of images we mentioned earlier includes a column that designates the creator of the image, as a foreign key to a table of artists. Our intention is to make the images_v object view include a REF to an object view of the artists table.

The (admittedly simplistic) table of artists looks like this:

```
CREATE TABLE artists (
    id INTEGER NOT NULL,
    name VARCHAR2(60),
    CONSTRAINT artists_pk PRIMARY KEY (id)
);
```

Here's the images table definition, with the new foreign key defined:

```
CREATE TABLE images (
    image_id INTEGER NOT NULL,
    file_name VARCHAR2(512),
    file_type VARCHAR2(12),
    bytes INTEGER,
    artist_id INTEGER,
    CONSTRAINT image_pk PRIMARY KEY (image_id),
    CONSTRAINT image_created_by_artist FOREIGN KEY (artist_id)
        REFERENCES artists (id)
);
```

Because we will use the Oracle function MAKE_REF, which only works with object views, we will need to define an object type for artists:

```
CREATE TYPE Artist_t AS OBJECT (
    id INTEGER,
    name VARCHAR2(60)
);
```

Now we can layer the Artist_t type on the artists table using an object view:

```
CREATE VIEW artists_v
    OF Artist_t
    WITH OBJECT OID (id)
AS
    SELECT id, name
      FROM artists;
```

We need to redefine the image_t type to include the REF:

```
CREATE TYPE Image_t AS OBJECT (
    image_id INTEGER,
    file_name VARCHAR2(512),
    file_type VARCHAR2(12),
    bytes INTEGER,
    artist_ref REF Artist_t,
    keywords Keyword_tab_t,
    MEMBER FUNCTION set_attrs (new_file_name IN VARCHAR2,
        new_file_type IN VARCHAR2, new_bytes IN INTEGER)
        RETURN Image_t,
    MEMBER FUNCTION set_keywords (new_keywords IN Keyword_tab_t)
        RETURN Image_t,
    PRAGMA RESTRICT_REFERENCES (DEFAULT, RNDS, WNDS, RNPS, WNPS)
);
```

After all of this preparatory work, we can at last show the new version of the object view. This statement uses the built-in MAKE_REF function, which accepts a key value and returns a REF to an object view:

```
CREATE VIEW images_v
    OF Image_t
    WITH OBJECT OID (image_id)
AS
```

```
SELECT i.image_id, i.file_name, i.file_type, i.bytes,
    MAKE_REF (artists_v, i.artist_id),
    CAST (MULTISET (SELECT keyword
                       FROM keywords k
                       WHERE k.image_id = i.image_id)
          AS Keyword_tab_t)
    FROM images i;
```

The expression in bold above means "construct the REF that should point to the artists_v virtual object with artist ID of i.artist_id." I say "should" rather than "will" because Oracle does not check to make sure that the artist_id actually exists.

Let's take a closer look at the MAKE_REF in the example above:

```
MAKE_REF (artists_v, i.artist_id)
```

The first argument of this function, artist_v, is the target object view. The second argument, i.artist_id, is the value which MAKE_REF will convert into an OID to retrieve an instance of the virtual artist object.

It is not strictly necessary to have a foreign key, or even a primary key, in order to use MAKE_REF. But in almost all cases, it is highly desirable to make sure the target of the REF is a primary key-based OID, and that the REF is based on a foreign key.

Using virtual REFs

Where does all this get us? Once we have the view with its virtual REF, we can issue SQL statements that use dot navigation:

```
SELECT image_id, i.artist_ref.name
  FROM images_v i
  WHERE file_name = 'cheesefries.jpg';
```

On the surface, this statement is indistinguishable from what we might use with object tables. But there is a very important difference:

> *Using MAKE_REF in a view to convert a foreign key into a REF will produce an error if the foreign key value is NULL.*

To illustrate this inconvenient behavior, let's put some data in the underlying artist and image tables:

```
INSERT INTO artists VALUES (100, 'Sam Picasso');

/* Insert an image with a valid artist id (for Case 1) */
INSERT INTO images VALUES (1000, 'cheesefries.jpg', 'JPG', 2097, 100);

/* Insert an image with an invalid artist id (must first disable the
|| foreign key constraint.)  This is for Case 2.
*/
ALTER TABLE images
    DISABLE CONSTRAINT image_created_by_artist;
```

```
INSERT INTO images VALUES (1002, 'sodajerk.jpg', 'JPG', 813, 99);

/* Insert an image with a NULL artist id. This is for Case 3. */
INSERT INTO images VALUES (1001, '57chevy.gif', 'GIF', 3128, NULL);
```

Let's run each of three cases and assess the results.

Case 1 is the "normal" case in which the artist_id actually exists:

```
/* Case 1 */
SELECT image_id, i.artist_ref.name
  FROM images_v i
 WHERE file_name = 'cheesefries.jpg';

IMAGE_ID ARTIST_REF.NAME
--------- -------------------------------------------------------------
     1000 Sam Picasso
```

That works just fine—just as if images_v and artists_v were object tables. As long as there is a valid foreign key, we can use dot navigation until the cows come home.

Case 2 illustrates what happens when the artist_id in the images table is non-null, but does not point to a valid artist_id in the artists table. In other words, you have a referential integrity problem—we had to disable the foreign key to try this one out:

```
/* Case 2 */
SELECT image_id, i.artist_ref.name
  FROM images_v i
 WHERE file_name = 'sodajerk.jpg';

IMAGE_ID ARTIST_REF.NAME
--------- -------------------------------------------------------------
     1002
```

Here, Oracle simply returns i.artist_ref.name as a NULL. This behavior matches that of object tables; if the object corresponding to the REF doesn't exist, you get a NULL back. Another name for this unknown reference value is a *dangling REF.*

Case 3 is the problem child. For the 57chevy.gif record, the artist_id field in the images table is simply null. This might be a common occurrence if, for example, the artist is unknown.

```
/* Case 3 */
SELECT image_id, i.artist_ref.name
  FROM images_v i
 WHERE file_name = '57chevy.gif';
```

Oracle replies, somewhat unforgivingly:

```
ERROR at line 3:
ORA-22972: NULL value not allowed in PRIMARY KEY-based object identifier
```

We get the same Oracle error whether or not the foreign key constraint is enabled. This behavior is vastly different from that of object tables, which simply return a null (as in the previous case). Personally, I prefer the behavior of object tables, in which REF-based navigation is more like a relational "outer join."

Working around the ORA-22972 problem

One workaround for this behavior is to use a DECODE in the MAKE_REF so that null artist_ids get converted to some weird value that will never appear in the artists table. Since Oracle doesn't complain if an artist_id doesn't exist (as illustrated in Case 2) the silent response results in a null—which is the desired result.

```
CREATE VIEW images_v
    OF Image_t
    WITH OBJECT OID (image_id)
AS
    SELECT i.image_id, i.file_name, i.file_type, i.bytes,
            MAKE_REF (artists_v,
                DECODE(i.artist_id,
                        NULL, -1,
                        i.artist_id)),
        CAST (MULTISET (SELECT keyword
                          FROM keywords k
                         WHERE k.image_id = i.image_id)
                AS Keyword_tab_t)
        FROM images i;
```

The DECODE returns -1 if the artist_id is unknown; we are making the assumption that the artist_id will never, in fact, equal -1.

Seems like a lot of work just to use dot notation, doesn't it? There are other good reasons to use REFs, such as *complex object retrieval* (COR), but this feature is at present available only to OCI applications. (Note that OCI is beyond the scope of this book.) COR allows an application to efficiently retrieve an object and pre-fetch all objects REFerenced by that object to a predefined "depth level." It isn't yet clear whether Oracle will support some form of COR in a future version of PL/SQL.

DEREF: Interpreting a virtual REF

What should we do about updates to an object view that contains a REF if, for example, we are writing an INSTEAD OF trigger? How do we tell the view to deal with the constructed REF? Why, we use the DEREF function, of course. (Just what you were thinking, I bet.)

Here is the new version of our earlier INSTEAD OF trigger, modified to deal with the REF:

```
CREATE OR REPLACE TRIGGER images_v_insert
INSTEAD OF INSERT ON images_v
FOR EACH ROW
```

```
DECLARE
    /* The unrefcur cursor serves to "dereference" the artist_ref,
    || so that we can retrieve the object to which it refers.
    */
    CURSOR unrefcur IS
        SELECT DEREF(:new.artist_ref)
            FROM DUAL;

    /* We'll need a place to hold the object: */
    artist Artist_t;
BEGIN
    /* Go get the object... */
    OPEN unrefcur;
    FETCH unrefcur INTO artist;
    CLOSE unrefcur;

    /* This will fail with DUP_VAL_ON_INDEX if the images table
    || already contains a record with the new image_id.
    */
    INSERT INTO images
        VALUES (:NEW.image_id, :NEW.file_name, :NEW.file_type,
                :NEW.bytes, artist.id);

    IF :NEW.keywords IS NOT NULL THEN
        DECLARE
            /* Note: apparent bug prevents use of :NEW.keywords.LAST.
            || The workaround is to store :NEW.keywords as a local
            || variable (in this case keywords_holder.)
            */
            keywords_holder Keyword_tab_t := :NEW.keywords;
        BEGIN
            FOR the_keyword IN 1..keywords_holder.LAST
            LOOP
                INSERT INTO keywords
                VALUES (:NEW.image_id, keywords_holder(the_keyword));
            END LOOP;
        END;
    END IF;
END;
```

With this trigger defined, we can look briefly at an example of doing an INSERT:

```
INSERT INTO images_v                              -- invalid (bug?)
SELECT Image_t(451, 'library.jpg', 'JPG', 3092,
               REF(a),
               keyword_tab_t('BOOKS', 'LIBRARY', 'PUBLIC BUILDINGS'))
    FROM artists_v a
    WHERE id = 100;
```

which ought to work but fails with an ORA-00932 error, "inconsistent datatypes." (This is a suspected bug in Oracle 8.0.3.) As a workaround, you can either use the "relational equivalent" insert or issue an equivalent PL/SQL statement that does work.

The relational equivalent insert uses column values rather than the default constructor:

```
INSERT INTO images_v
SELECT 451, 'library.jpg', 'JPG', 3092,
       REF(a),
       keyword_tab_t('BOOKS', 'LIBRARY', 'PUBLIC BUILDINGS')
  FROM artists_v a
 WHERE id = 100;
```

The following PL/SQL snippet also works, with (or without) the constructor:

```
DECLARE
   image Image_t;
BEGIN
   SELECT Image_t(451, 'library.jpg', 'JPG', 3092,
                  REF(a),
                  keyword_tab_t('BOOKS', 'LIBRARY', 'PUBLIC BUILDINGS'))
     INTO image
     FROM artists_v a
    WHERE id = 100;
   INSERT INTO images_v VALUES (image);
END;
```

For more details about DEREF, refer to Chapter 18.

Storage of Virtual REFs

With object tables, REFs get physically stored in a table. That is, a column defined as a REF type can contain a binary value that Oracle can use as a "pointer" to an object.

However, when dealing with object views, Oracle does not yet allow you to store a REF pointing to a virtual object. In other words, even if you create a table with an appropriately typed REF column, you cannot actually save a value in this column. From one perspective, this is an irritant rather than a significant deficiency; as a workaround, create an object view of the table, and use MAKE_REF.

From another perspective, it's a bit unpleasant that we cannot intermingle object tables with object views; nor can we perform a simple transformation from an object view into an object table. I would like to be able to create an object table:

```
CREATE TABLE images2 OF image_t
   NESTED TABLE keywords STORE AS keyword_tab;
```

and then populate it from the view:

```
INSERT INTO images2                    -- invalid
   SELECT VALUE(i) FROM images_v i;
```

But alas, Oracle tells me I cannot: this request results in an ORA-22979 error, "cannot INSERT a REF from an object view into a table."

REFs to Nonunique OIDs

What do you suppose will happen if you create a REF to an object in an object view, but it has multiple object instances for the OID in question? Granted, this is a pretty weird case; you shouldn't be creating object views with ambiguous OIDs.

I won't keep you in suspense for this one. In my testing, DEREFing this type of virtual REF returned a null OID. That seems like an unusual result, so I don't think I would count on it in an application.

Not All Views with Objects Are Object Views

With the Oracle objects option installed, there are other interesting possibilities for views which do not necessarily qualify as "object views." For example, you can create a view that has an object as a column:

```
CREATE TABLE requisition (
    req_no INTEGER,
    image_id NUMBER
);

CREATE VIEW requisition_v
AS
    SELECT r.req_no, VALUE(i) image
      FROM requisition r,
           images_v i
     WHERE r.image_id = i.image_id;
```

The requisition view now has two columns: one for the req_no, of type INTEGER; and one for the image, of type Image_t.

You can combine many object features into an object view. For instance, you can define an object view that includes a column that contains a collection of objects. Just because the possibilities seem endless, though, there is no excuse to get carried away; objects should be restricted to "natural" representations of data; they shouldn't serve merely as the basis of intellectual calisthenics for the programmer.

Schema Evolution

One of the unsung heroes[*] of object views is their relative immunity from the problems of schema evolution that we discussed in Chapter 18. As the example below illustrates, object views do not impose the same "evolution penalty" as

---

[*] This feature is "unsung" from the point of view that Oracle does not seem to mention it in their documentation.

object tables. This resilience of object views is due at least in part to Oracle's refusal to let you store virtual REFs in a table (as discussed earlier in the section "Storage of Virtual REFs"). Since virtual REFs are computed on the fly, you can drop and rebuild underlying schema objects without affecting the way that object views reference each other.

Recall the earlier scenario about adding a table of artists. Let's pretend that we had to add the table of artists as a schema change, rather than rebuilding everything from scratch. Here's how we'll change the images table:

```
ALTER TABLE images
    ADD artist_id INTEGER;
```

The ability to execute this statement represents one significant advantage that object views provide over object tables. If images had been an object table defined directly on the images_t type, this statement would have failed with an ORA-22856 error, "cannot add columns to object tables."

Many DBAs do not like to use the ALTER TABLE statement in a production environment, but it's nice to know that it's possible. You could also recreate the table cleanly with the new column, drop the foreign key constraints to the old table, drop the old table, rename the new table, and rebuild the constraints. This, too, is impossible with object tables.

Proceeding with the rest of the schema change, here is the table of artists (just as we created it previously):

```
CREATE TABLE artists (
    id INTEGER,
    name VARCHAR2(60),
    CONSTRAINT artists_pk PRIMARY KEY (id)
);
```

To be "relationally correct," we'll add a foreign key to relate each image to an author:

```
ALTER TABLE images
    ADD CONSTRAINT image_created_by_artist
    FOREIGN KEY (artist_id)
    REFERENCES artists (id);
```

Now, as before, we can create the Artist_t type and its associated view:

```
CREATE TYPE Artist_t AS OBJECT (
    id INTEGER,
    name VARCHAR2(60)
);

CREATE VIEW artists_v
    OF Artist_t
    WITH OBJECT OID (id)
AS
```

```
SELECT id, name
   FROM artists;
```

and now it's a simple matter to replace the Image_t type definition (as long as we have not implemented any object tables or column objects using this type):

```
CREATE OR REPLACE TYPE Image_t AS OBJECT (
    image_id INTEGER,
    file_name VARCHAR2(512),
    file_type VARCHAR2(12),
    bytes INTEGER,
    artist_ref REF Artist_t,
    keywords Keyword_tab_t,
    MEMBER FUNCTION set_attrs (new_file_name IN VARCHAR2,
        new_file_type IN VARCHAR2, new_bytes IN INTEGER)
        RETURN Image_t,
    MEMBER FUNCTION set_keywords (new_keywords IN Keyword_tab_t)
        RETURN Image_t,
    PRAGMA RESTRICT_REFERENCES (DEFAULT, RNDS, WNDS, RNPS, WNPS)
);
```

Object Views Housekeeping

There are a few commands and facilities we haven't yet discussed that will help you to manage and control object views.

Data Dictionary

The USER_VIEWS (or ALL_VIEWS or DBA_VIEWS) view in the data dictionary includes several columns specific to object views. Table 20-2 lists some examples of using this information.

Table 20-2. Entries for Object ViewsData Dictionary

To Answer the Question...	Use This View	As In

What object views have I created?	USER_VIEWS	SELECT view_name
		    FROM user_views
		    WHERE type_text IS NOT NULL;

What object views have I created of the Foo_t type?	USER_VIEWS	SELECT view_name
		    FROM user_views
		    WHERE UPPER(type_text)
		        LIKE 'FOO_T%';

What is the virtual OID of the Foo_v view?	USER_VIEWS	SELECT oid_text
		    FROM user_views
		    WHERE UPPER(type_text)
		        LIKE 'FOO_T%';

Table 20-2. Entries for Object ViewsData Dictionary (continued)

To Answer the Question...	Use This View	As In

What is the query on which I defined the Foo view?	USER_VIEWS	`SET LONG 1000 -- or greater`
		`SELECT text`
		`    FROM user_views`
		`    WHERE view_name = 'FOO';`

What columns are in view Foo?	USER_TAB_COLUMNS	`SELECT column_name, data_type_`
		`        mod, data_type`
		`    FROM user_tab_columns`
		`    WHERE table_name = 'FOO';`

Another way of getting a quick listing of the columns in a view is to "describe" it in SQL*Plus:

```
SQL> desc images_v

Name                            Null?    Type
------------------------------- -------- ----
IMAGE_ID                                 NUMBER(38)
FILE_NAME                                VARCHAR2(512)
FILE_TYPE                                VARCHAR2(12)
BYTES                                    NUMBER(38)
ARTIST_REF                               REF OF ARTIST_T
KEYWORDS                                 KEYWORD_TAB_T
```

Privileges

As with conventional views, creating an object view requires the creator to have either the CREATE VIEW or the CREATE ANY VIEW system privilege.

If you are attempting to create an instance of an object type by using the default constructor, you must have the EXECUTE privilege on that type.

However, if a user has a DML privilege on a view that has an INSTEAD OF trigger for that DML operation, he doesn't need explicit EXECUTE privileges if the trigger invokes a constructor; the trigger runs with the "owner rights model" described in Chapter 18.

Forcing Compilation

As with conventional views, if you make changes to an underlying database object on which an object view is based, Oracle will mark the view as "invalid." When this happens, Oracle will also mark as invalid any other database objects (such as other views, INSTEAD OF triggers, or PL/SQL packages) that depend on the view. Then, the next time that you use the view, Oracle is supposed to attempt to "recompile" it first.

However, when you are modifying schema, there are some cases where Oracle does not seem to automatically recompile the view. One case in particular occurs when you CREATE OR REPLACE, or otherwise recompile, the object type on which the view is defined. When this happens, your view becomes invalid, leading to some disconcerting error messages (see the sidebar "A Comedy of Error Messages"); at this point, you must either recreate or recompile the object view. The command to compile the view is:

```
ALTER VIEW <view name> COMPILE;
```

If compilation fails, Oracle should return an error message, and the view will remain "invalid." You may need to redefine the view using, for example, CREATE OR REPLACE VIEW.

The ALTER VIEW ... COMPILE command has the side effect of marking as invalid all database objects that are dependent on the view, such as other views or types. Oracle does appear to automatically recompile these dependent database objects.

Similarly, INSTEAD OF triggers can be recompiled using the following:

```
ALTER TRIGGER <trigger name> COMPILE [ DEBUG ];
```

Postscript: Using the BFILE Datatype

A better abstraction for the Planetary Pages datatype Image_t would include a BFILE datatype rather than a VARCHAR2 file_name attribute. A BFILE is a file in the external operating system that Oracle can retrieve, but not store, using built-in packages. (We discuss the BFILE datatype in Chapter 4, *Variables and Program Data*.) We chose not to include this alternate representation in the core part of the chapter to avoid detracting from the basic themes of object views. However, let's look at it now.

The DDL follows for this alternate representation, with the changes highlighted in bold. First, here is the new version of the object type itself:

```
CREATE TYPE Image_t AS OBJECT (
    image_id INTEGER,
    image_file BFILE,
    file_type VARCHAR2(12),
    bytes INTEGER,
    keywords Keyword_tab_t,
    MEMBER FUNCTION set_attrs (new_image_file IN BFILE,
        new_file_type IN VARCHAR2, new_bytes IN INTEGER)
        RETURN Image_t,
    MEMBER FUNCTION set_keywords (new_keywords IN Keyword_tab_t)
        RETURN Image_t,
    PRAGMA RESTRICT_REFERENCES (DEFAULT, RNDS, WNDS, RNPS, WNPS)
);
```

```
CREATE TYPE BODY Image_t
AS
    MEMBER FUNCTION set_attrs (new_image_file IN BFILE,
        new_file_type IN VARCHAR2, new_bytes IN INTEGER)
        RETURN Image_t
    IS
        image_holder Image_t := SELF;
    BEGIN
        image_holder.image_file := new_image_file;
        image_holder.file_type := new_file_type;
        image_holder.bytes := new_bytes;
        RETURN image_holder;
    END;
    MEMBER FUNCTION set_keywords (new_keywords IN Keyword_tab_t)
        RETURN Image_t
    IS
        image_holder Image_t := SELF;
    BEGIN
        image_holder.keywords := new_keywords;
        RETURN image_holder;
    END;
END;
```

Now we need to create an "alias" known to Oracle for the directory that will contain the images. In this case, the alias is "webpix."

```
CREATE DIRECTORY webpix
AS
    '/files/web/pix';
```

The new version of the view uses the built-in BFILENAME to convert the filename in the underlying table into an Oracle BFILE datatype:

```
CREATE VIEW images_v
    OF Image_t
    WITH OBJECT OID (image_id)
AS
    SELECT i.image_id, BFILENAME('WEBPIX', i.file_name),
        i.file_type, i.bytes,
        CAST (MULTISET (SELECT keyword
                        FROM keywords k
                        WHERE k.image_id = i.image_id)
            AS Keyword_tab_t)
        FROM images i;
```

The INSTEAD OF trigger will need to make the inverse conversion—that is, accept a BFILE and extract a filename. This is easy to do using the built-in procedure DBMS_LOB.FILEGETNAME:

```
CREATE OR REPLACE TRIGGER images_v_insert
INSTEAD OF INSERT ON images_v
FOR EACH ROW
DECLARE
    l_file_name images.file_name%TYPE;
```

```
        l_directory VARCHAR2(30);
BEGIN
    /* Determine the directory name */
    DBMS_LOB.FILEGETNAME (file_loc => :NEW.image_file,
        dir_alias => l_directory,
        filename => l_file_name);

    /* This will fail with DUP_VAL_ON_INDEX if the images table
    || already contains a record with the new image_id.
    */
    INSERT INTO images
        VALUES (:NEW.image_id, l_file_name, :NEW.file_type,
                :NEW.bytes);

    IF :NEW.keywords IS NOT NULL THEN
        DECLARE
            /* Note: apparent bug prevents use of :NEW.keywords.LAST.
            || The workaround is to store :NEW.keywords as a local
            || variable (in this case keywords_holder.)
            */
            keywords_holder Keyword_tab_t := :NEW.keywords;
        BEGIN
            FOR the_keyword IN 1..keywords_holder.LAST
            LOOP
                INSERT INTO keywords
                VALUES (:NEW.image_id, keywords_holder(the_keyword));
            END LOOP;
        END;
    END IF;
END;
```

And finally, we can demonstrate how an insert would be made using the object view:

```
INSERT INTO images_v VALUES
    (Image_t (1002, BFILENAME('WEBPIX','abc.gif'), 'GIF', 1024,
            Keyword_tab_t('ALPHABET', 'LETTERS')));
```

Appendix C, *Built-In Packages*, contains information about these built-in packages.

21

External Procedures

I've lost count of how many times I've heard the question "Can I call *whatever* from within Oracle?" Typically, *whatever* is a program that interacts with the external environment: sending email, polling or controlling hardware, or invoking the C library functions that PL/SQL lacks. Until very recently, the standard answer was "No, you can't do that directly, but you can use a database pipe and write a daemon that responds to requests on the pipe." An early paper on this approach[*] describes pipes as an alternative to an even more primitive approach: using a temporary table as a sort of "bulletin board" for interprocess communication.[†]

Temporary tables have serious limitations for this use, and even database pipe-based daemons have their shortcomings. Packing and unpacking the contents of the pipe is a challenge; the daemon typically execute in a separate Oracle session (and thus can't participate in a transaction), and the solution is inherently single-threaded. Moreover, with the pipe solution, it's difficult to get return values back from the daemon to the caller. What we need from Oracle is a fast, reliable way of calling out to operating system commands or functions from within PL/SQL. Better yet, Oracle should allow external routines to serve as user-defined functions so that you can use them in SQL statements.

Enter *external procedures*. This long-awaited Oracle feature allows you to call anything that you can compile into the native "shared library" format of the operating system. Yes, the external procedures features is reliable; yes, it's multi-

---

[*] See Dan Bikle, "Inter-Application Communication Using Oracle7 Database Pipes," *Select* Vol. 1, No. 2, Winter 93/94, p. 34.

[†] The original paper did not present a true UNIX daemon (which has a specific definition to UNIX and C programmers), but rather discussed the generic idea of a continuously running process.

threaded; yes, communication is bidirectional; and yes, you can use external procedures as user-defined functions in SQL.

Under UNIX, a shared library is a shared object or *.so* file; under Windows NT, it's a DLL (dynamically linked library). You can write the external routine in any language you wish, as long as your compiler and linker will generate the appropriate shared library format that is callable from C. In Oracle 8.0, however, C will be the most common language for external procedures, since all of Oracle's support libraries are written in C. Curiously, Oracle has named this feature external "procedures," although the external routines you invoke are, technically speaking, C functions. (There is no such thing as a procedure in C.) If the C function returns a value, you map it to a PL/SQL function; if it returns no value, you map it to a PL/SQL procedure.

This chapter presents a few examples of external procedures (and functions). In addition, we review the preconditions you must establish before they will work, and present the syntax for creating and using this new feature. So, the next time you hear the question about calling *whatever*, you can answer, "You bet!...in Oracle8."

This chapter does *not* discuss "distributed external procedures," which are a way of accessing non-Oracle data sources from an Oracle server. Despite the name, these procedures are not closely related to external procedures. Neither do we discuss at length the programming techniques that allow your 3GL code to call back to Oracle (we'll leave that to the books on programming C language access to Oracle). But we do include some samples that you can use right away.

Introduction to External Procedures

How do external procedures work? How can I build my own? What are their advantages and disadvantages? Before answering in detail, let's take a look at a quick example.

Example: Determining Free Disk Space on Windows NT

Here is an external procedure that will discover the amount of free space on a given disk drive. This example is just to get you going. We won't try to explain all the details at this point. This example was designed for Windows NT 4.0, but the idea can be applied to any operating system that meets the requirements for external procedures. In this case, we simply make a call to the appropriate function in the Windows kernel, rather than writing our own DLL.

Windows NT's kernel, *kernel32.dll*, contains a routine called GetDiskFreeSpaceA, which accepts a drive letter as an input parameter and returns four statistics about the drive. When we register the routine with PL/SQL, we will provide mappings for each of these parameters to a PL/SQL parameter. Then, when we invoke the external procedure from a PL/SQL program, we'll use these statistics to compute the free disk space.

First, we need to define a "library" to tell Oracle where the DLL lives:

```
/* Filename on companion disk: nt_space.sql */
CREATE OR REPLACE LIBRARY nt_kernel
AS
    'c:\winnt\system32\kernel32.dll';
```

We'll create a package called disk_util that will contain our function, which we will call get_disk_free_space as shown here:

```
CREATE OR REPLACE PACKAGE disk_util
AS
    FUNCTION get_disk_free_space
       (root_path IN VARCHAR2,
        sectors_per_cluster OUT PLS_INTEGER,
        bytes_per_sector OUT PLS_INTEGER,
        number_of_free_clusters OUT PLS_INTEGER,
        total_number_of_clusters OUT PLS_INTEGER)
    RETURN PLS_INTEGER;
    PRAGMA RESTRICT_REFERENCES (get_disk_free_space,
        WNPS, RNPS, WNDS, RNDS);
END disk_util;
```

All the magic is in the package body, which uses the EXTERNAL clause rather than a BEGIN..END block. This clause is where we define the interface between PL/SQL and the external routine:

```
CREATE OR REPLACE PACKAGE BODY disk_util
AS
    FUNCTION get_disk_free_space
       (root_path IN VARCHAR2,
        sectors_per_cluster OUT PLS_INTEGER,
        bytes_per_sector OUT PLS_INTEGER,
        number_of_free_clusters OUT pls_integer,
        total_number_of_clusters OUT PLS_INTEGER)
    RETURN PLS_INTEGER
    IS EXTERNAL
        LIBRARY nt_kernel              -- our library (defined previously)
        NAME "GetDiskFreeSpaceA"       -- name of function in kernel32.dll
        LANGUAGE C                     -- external routine is written in C
        CALLING STANDARD PASCAL        -- uses Pascal parameter convention
        PARAMETERS                     -- map PL/SQL to C parameters by
                                       -- position
            (root_path STRING,
             sectors_per_cluster BY REFERENCE LONG,
             bytes_per_sector BY REFERENCE LONG,
             number_of_free_clusters BY REFERENCE LONG,
```

```
          total_number_of_clusters BY REFERENCE LONG,
       RETURN LONG); -- "return code" indicating success or failure
END disk_util;
```

Assuming that the DBA has set up the environment to support external procedures (see the section called "Step 1: Set Up the Listener" later in this chapter), we can make an easy call to compute free disk space on the C: drive:

```
SET SERVEROUTPUT ON SIZE 100000
DECLARE
    lroot_path VARCHAR2(3) := 'C:\';    -- look at C drive
    lsectors_per_cluster PLS_INTEGER;
    lbytes_per_sector PLS_INTEGER;
    lnumber_of_free_clusters PLS_INTEGER;
    ltotal_number_of_clusters PLS_INTEGER;
    return_code PLS_INTEGER;
    free_meg REAL;
BEGIN
    /* Call the external procedure. We ignore the return code
    || in this simple example.
    */
    return_code := disk_util.get_disk_free_space (lroot_path,
        lsectors_per_cluster, lbytes_per_sector,
        lnumber_of_free_clusters, ltotal_number_of_clusters);

    /* Using the drive statistics that are returned from the
    || external procedure, compute the amount of free disk space.
    || Remember Megabytes = (Bytes / 1024 / 1024)
    */
    free_meg := lsectors_per_cluster * lbytes_per_sector *
                lnumber_of_free_clusters / 1024 / 1024;

    DBMS_OUTPUT.PUT_LINE('free disk space, megabytes = ' || free_meg);
END;
```

On my machine, this fragment produces the following output:

```
free disk space, megabytes = 214.53515625
```

Of course, you could put this computation in a named function or procedure, and even make it part of the disk_util package.

Architecture

Let's take a look at what happens when you invoke an external procedure. As shown in Figure 21-1, the process flow starts with a PL/SQL application that calls a special PL/SQL "module body." In our example above, this body defines the get_disk_free_space function. PL/SQL then looks for a special Net8 listener[*] process,

---

[*] Net8 is the name for what was formerly the Oracle SQL*Net product. A Net8 listener is a background process, typically configured by the DBA, which enables other processes to connect to a given service such as the Oracle server.

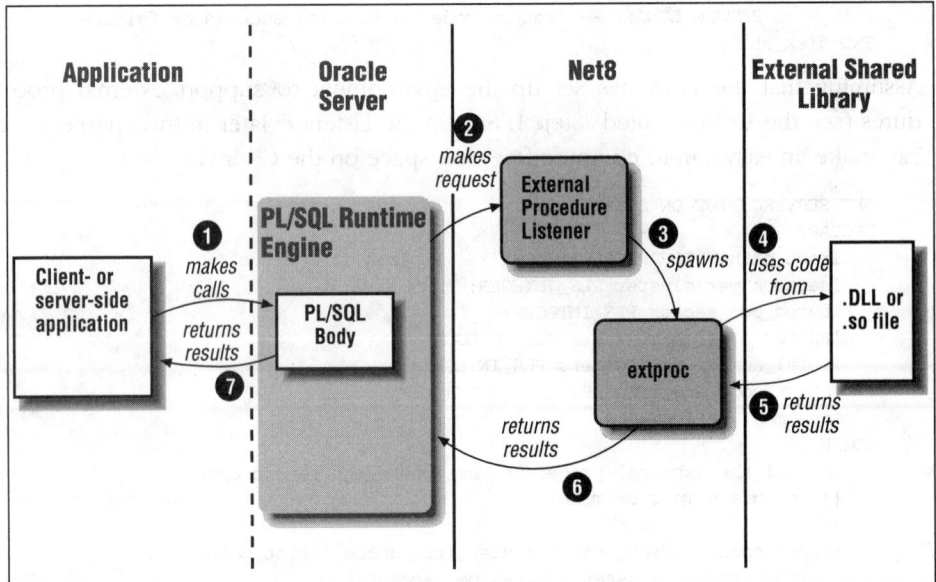

Figure 21-1. Invoking an external procedure

which should already be running in the background. At this point, the listener will spawn an executable program called extproc. This process loads the dynamic library and then invokes the desired routine in the shared library, whereupon it returns its results back to PL/SQL.

To limit overhead, only one extproc process needs to run for a given Oracle session; this process starts with the first external procedure call and terminates when the session exits. For each distinct external procedure you call, this extproc process loads the associated shared library, but only if it hasn't already been loaded.

In case you are unfamiliar with dynamic linking, we've provided a few words of explanation. Calling a dynamically linked routine simply maps the shared code pages into the address space of the "user" process. Then, when that process touches one of the pages of the shared library, it will be paged into physical memory, if it isn't already there. The resident pages of the mapped shared library file will be shared automatically between users of that library.* In practical terms, this means that heavy concurrent use of your external procedure often requires a *lot* less computer processing power and memory than, say, the primitive approach you might take with database pipes.

---

* This description applies to Sun's Solaris operating system as well as to Windows NT. For a more detailed discussion from a UNIX perspective, see Adrian Cockroft's performance column, "Which is Better—Static or Dynamic Linking?" in *SunWorld Online*, February 1996, at *http://www.tritec.de/sunworldonline/swol-02-1996/swol-02-perf.html*.

Advantages

Oracle has provided a number of features that make external procedures truly an industrial-strength resource. The four major features are summarized here.

- Oracle external procedures use shared libraries rather than executables. Requiring the external routine to be in a dynamically linked library, rather than in a statically linked module, helps prevent heavy use of the procedure from consuming your machine. By contrast, static linking means that all of the necessary libraries are actually copied into your compiled program, and each execution requires its own address space. By requiring a library rather than a program, Oracle further allows you to bundle many different external routines conveniently together into a single shared library file. Co-locating a family of related routines in one shared library provides the benefits of increased performance as well as manageability.

- Oracle external procedures run in a separate memory space from the main kernel processes. This is a good thing; it makes it easy to prevent your custom code from stepping on the memory used by the database server. While it is technically possible to write an external procedure that would crash the Oracle server, you have to set out to do so. If the external procedure crashes, the companion process, extproc, returns an error to the PL/SQL engine, which in turn reports it to the application.

- External procedures provide full transaction support; that is, they can participate fully in the current transaction. By accepting "context" information from PL/SQL, the procedure can call back to the database to fetch data, make SQL or PL/SQL calls, and raise exceptions. In the current release, utilizing these features requires some low-level Oracle Call Interface (OCI) programming...but at least it's possible!

- Oracle enforces the execution of external procedures with database-level security. At the first level of security, only the DBA can execute or grant privileges on the required CREATE LIBRARY statement that tells Oracle where the operating system file exists. At the next level of security, users may only invoke the external procedure if they are granted EXECUTE privilege on it.

Limitations

External procedures are not perfect, although their benefits far outweigh their shortcomings. I have no doubt that external procedures will find uses in many applications. Here are some of the current limitations of these procedures:

- Despite the wonders of shared libraries, Oracle's architecture requires an unavoidable amount of interprocess communication. Moreover, in Oracle 8.0, extproc is single-threaded; while there is only one external procedure process per session, each session does require its own process. (A future version may be multi-threaded, allowing sessions to share a smaller number of extproc processes.)

- External procedures (at least, as they are implemented in their first release) cannot pass parameters of any user-defined type. Arguments must be conventional scalars. If you wish to exchange objects or collections, a possible workaround is to write a PL/SQL module that would split them up into scalars before calling the external procedure, and reassemble them upon return.

- With Oracle's current implementation, extproc closes the shared library after it's called, meaning that libraries are not cached. Although this approach could save memory, it could also mean more of a CPU hit for subsequent calls. In addition, the overhead for the first external procedure call from a given session may result in a noticeable delay in response time; however, subsequent calls are much faster.

Steps in Creating an External Procedure

Before you try external procedures, be sure that the machine where you're running the Oracle server supports shared or dynamically linked libraries. Virtually all UNIX machines qualify, as do Windows NT machines. If your own machine doesn't qualify, you can stop here, or you can investigate the use of distributed external procedures.

These are your next tasks:

1. Ensure that your DBA has enabled a listener for external procedures in your Net8 environment. (This involves changes to *tnsnames.ora* and *listener.ora*.) This is a one-time job for a given server.

2. Identify or create the *.so* or *.DLL* file which contains the shared library.

3. In Oracle, issue the SQL statement CREATE LIBRARY..., which defines an alias in the data dictionary for the external shared library file. This registers the program with the database engine so that it knows where to find it when it is called.

4. Create the PL/SQL function or procedure body, typically within a package, that will register with PL/SQL the desired routine from the external library. The body of the procedure or function will use the EXTERNAL clause in place of a BEGIN...END block.

And that's it! Let's look at each step in more detail, focusing on the implementation of a random number generator for PL/SQL.

Step 1: Set Up the Listener

What actually happens when your code needs to use the external procedure? First, your code calls a predefined PL/SQL body. When the PL/SQL runtime engine notices such a call, it looks for the special Net8 listener named EXTERNAL_PROCEDURE_LISTENER, which in turn spawns a session-specific process called extproc. It is extproc that invokes your routine in the shared library.

You need to create a new listener with a specific name, EXTERNAL_PROCEDURE _LISTENER. This listener process will execute alongside other listener(s) that you already have running.

NOTE   You cannot change the names EXTERNAL_PROCEDURE_LISTENER or extproc. In the *listener.ora* fragment given, everything that's not in lowercase italics must match the listing.

In your *listener.ora* file, you will need the following entries:

```
/* filename on companion disk: lsnrfrag.ora /*
EXTERNAL_PROCEDURE_LISTENER =
    (ADDRESS_LIST =
        (ADDRESS =
            (PROTOCOL=IPC)
            (KEY=epsid)
        )
    )

SID_LIST_EXTERNAL_PROCEDURE_LISTENER =
    (SID_LIST =
        (SID_DESC=
            (SID_NAME=epsid)
            (ORACLE_HOME=full_directory_path)
            (PROGRAM=extproc)
        )
    )
```

Where:

epsid
> A short identifier that is used by Net8 to locate the listener. Its actual name is rather arbitrary, since your programs will never see it. *epsid* has to be the same identifier in the address list and in the SID list.

full_directory_path
> The full pathname to your ORACLE_HOME directory, such as */u01/app/oracle/product/8.0.3* on UNIX or *C:\ORANT* on Windows NT. Notice that there are no quotes around the directory name.

If desired, *listener.ora* can point the listener's log into your desired
directory:

```
LOG_DIRECTORY_EXTERNAL_PROCEDURE_LISTENER=/u01/app/
oracle/admin/SID/logbook
```

And, for debugging, you can control "tracing" for your new listener
with entries like this:

```
TRACE_DIRECTORY_EXTERNAL_PROCEDURE_LISTENER=/u01/app/
oracle/admin/SID/logbook
TRACE_LEVEL_EXTERNAL_PROCEDURE_LISTENER=user
```

The *tnsnames.ora* file on the machine where the server is running will need an
entry like the following:

```
EXTPROC_CONNECTION_DATA =
    (DESCRIPTION =
        (ADDRESS =
            (PROTOCOL=IPC)
            (KEY=epsid)
        )
        (CONNECT_DATA=
            (SID=epsid))
        )
    )
```

Again, *epsid* must match the key used in the *listener.ora* file.

TIP   If you intend to use external procedures on your server, remember
to modify your database startup and shutdown procedures to incorporate the listener start and stop commands. On UNIX, this typically
means editing a startup shell script.

On Windows NT, a Net8 listener is automatically installed as a system service the first time you start it from the command line. However, the listener will not launch automatically on boot unless you
configure it to do so. You can use the control panel to designate
which listeners launch on system startup.

To remove the external procedure service on NT, delete the entries
from *listener.ora* and *tnsnames.ora*, and use the NT command
instsrv <service name> remove as follows:

```
instsrv OracleTNSListener80external_procedure_listener
remove
```

(The instsrv utility is available in the NT 4.0 Server Resource Kit.
Without it, you'll probably have to edit the registry.)

After making these configuration file changes, you'll need to start the new listener process. In UNIX, this is typically performed from the command line:

```
lsnrctl start external_procedure_listener
```

If your database server is running on Windows NT, the first time you start the listener, you'll use the LSNRCTL80 command. From the command prompt, for example, the command would be:

```
LSNRCTL80 start external_procedure_listener
```

Thereafter (on NT) you can start and stop specific listeners from the Services component of the Control Panel.

Step 2: Identify or Create the Shared Library

Step 1 is completely independent of any external procedure that you may create on your system. The remaining steps, while specific to our random number procedure, include discussion that applies to almost any external procedure.

Although later examples will show how to create your own shared libraries, let's start with an example that requires no C language programming: calling a standard C library function, rand, which generates a 16-bit random number. On many platforms, rand already exists in a shared object library; on UNIX, it's often in */lib/libc.so*, and on NT, in *c:\winnt\system32\CRTDLL.DLL*.*

A bit of background is in order for folks who haven't played with random number generators. Random number algorithms have certain quirks you need to realize. First, such generators can be deterministic; that is, the algorithm may return the same sequence of "random numbers" every time unless first "seeded" with a quasi-random number. Often, the previous random number is stored and used as a seed. But for the very first call, your program provides the seed, perhaps using some function of the current system time. If you call rand later with an identical seed value, you will get an identical pseudo-random sequence.

rand has a companion "seeding" function, srand, that allows you to supply your own seed value. Calling srand before calling rand stores the seed value as a global in memory, for use by the next call to rand. Subsequent calls from the same session need not call srand, since rand will re-seed itself.

---

* Documentation on available library functions is commonly available in UNIX man pages or in SDK documentation on other platforms.

Step 3: Issue CREATE LIBRARY Statement

Now that we have identified */lib/libc.so* as the file containing our needed functions, the next thing we have to do is create a library in the Oracle database. This is the easy part!

Creating a library is a way of telling Oracle that we want to refer to a specific shared object file by a programmer-defined name. For many UNIX systems, */lib/ libc.so* will contain the needed function as shown here:

```
CREATE OR REPLACE LIBRARY libc_l
AS
    '/lib/libc.so';
```

Executing this command requires the CREATE LIBRARY privilege (see the "Syntax for External Procedures" section below for more details).

Note that we have to use a fully qualified pathname; attempting to use an environment variable such as $ORACLE_BASE in the filename will not work.

If your database server runs on Windows NT, your library would likely be created as follows:

```
CREATE OR REPLACE LIBRARY libc_l
AS
    'c:\winnt\system32\CRTDLL.DLL';
```

Regardless of platform, you only need to create a single library in this fashion for each shared object file you use. That is, even though you have only issued a single CREATE LIBRARY command for *libc.so* (or *CRTDLL.DLL*), you can define any number of external procedures that use routines from that file.

Step 4: Create the PL/SQL Body

The final step is to create a function or procedure definition which registers the desired routine from the shared library. This feature lets you write the body of a PL/SQL procedure or function in C instead of PL/SQL. To the caller it looks like any other PL/SQL subprogram.

Assuming that your C language skills are ready for any custom programming needed in Step 3, Step 4 is potentially the most complex one. Because of the differences between PL/SQL arguments and C language arguments (in datatype, character set, whether they can be null, etc.), Oracle provides a lot of "instrumentation" to allow you to properly map PL/SQL arguments to C language arguments. The details of this instrumentation are described in the section "Mapping Parameters" later in this chapter.

TIP   All of the samples in this chapter put the needed modules in a PL/SQL package. One of many benefits of packages is that they enable us to use the RESTRICT_REFERENCES pragma with our module(s). This pragma allows us to tell Oracle that the user-defined function is "safe" and can therefore be used in SQL statements. (See Chapter 17, *Calling PL/SQL Functions in SQL*, for a full discussion of this pragma.)

Returning once again to our random number example, the specification for an appropriate PL/SQL package might look like this:

```
/* Filename on companion disk: rand_utl.sql */
CREATE OR REPLACE PACKAGE random_utl
AS
     FUNCTION rand RETURN PLS_INTEGER;
     PRAGMA RESTRICT_REFERENCES (rand, WNDS, RNDS, WNPS, RNPS);

     PROCEDURE srand (seed IN PLS_INTEGER);
     PRAGMA RESTRICT_REFERENCES (srand, WNDS, RNDS, WNPS, RNPS);

END random_utl;
```

Notice that the package specification is completely devoid of clues that we intend to implement the two subprograms as external procedures. We can't yet tell that rand and srand are any different from conventional PL/SQL modules. And that is exactly the point! From a usage perspective, external procedures are interchangeable with conventional procedures.

Our package body is blissfully short. By the way, assuming that your library is defined correctly, this package will work as-is on either UNIX or Windows NT. (Even in cases where you can't use the same external code on different operating systems, it may be possible to make the PL/SQL specification the same. You could then make the external code the only thing that differs—which would be very desirable if you have to support multiple platforms.)

```
CREATE OR REPLACE PACKAGE BODY random_utl
AS
     /* Tested with: (1) Solaris 2.5.1 and Oracle 8.0.3
     ||              (2) Windows NT 4.0 and Oracle 8.0.3
     */

     FUNCTION rand RETURN PLS_INTEGER
     /* Return a random number between 1 and (2**16 - 1), using
     || the current seed value.
     */
     IS
          EXTERNAL         -- tell PL/SQL that this is an external procedure
          LIBRARY libc_1 -- specify the library that we created above
```

```
        NAME "rand"      -- function's real name is lowercase
        LANGUAGE C;      -- we are calling a function written in C

    PROCEDURE srand (seed IN PLS_INTEGER)
    /* Store a seed value used by external rand() function */
    IS
        EXTERNAL
        LIBRARY libc_1
        NAME "srand"     -- srand (lowercase) is function's real name
        LANGUAGE C
        PARAMETERS (seed ub4);  -- map to unsigned four-byte integer
    END random_utl;
```

In this example, we have chosen to make the names of the PL/SQL modules identical to those in the shared object library. It is not necessary that they match; in fact, you may wish to make them different so that you can talk about (or document) the parameters independently.

Notice the PARAMETERS clause in the body of srand. Each of the formal parameters to the PL/SQL module must have at least one corresponding entry in a PARAMETERS clause. Although there is an extensive set of defaults which can eliminate the need for this clause, this explicit PARAMETERS clause makes it perfectly clear how the parameters will be mapped between PL/SQL and C.

Using the rand External Procedure

Now that we've "registered" the external procedure with a PL/SQL package, we can test it:

```
SET SERVEROUTPUT ON SIZE 100000
DECLARE
    rnd_value    PLS_INTEGER;
    seed         PLS_INTEGER;
BEGIN
    /* Generate a seed value from the current system time. */
    SELECT TO_CHAR(SYSDATE, 'SSSSS') INTO seed FROM DUAL;

    /* Call the srand external procedure to store our seed in memory. */
    random_utl.srand (seed);

    /* Now demonstrate some random numbers. */
    FOR v_cnt IN 1 .. 10 LOOP
       rnd_value := random_utl.rand;
       DBMS_OUTPUT.PUT_LINE ('rand() call #' || v_cnt ||
                            ' returns ' || rnd_value);
    END LOOP;
END;
```

This brief test routine simply seeds the library routine with a quasi-random number derived from the current system time, then calls the random number generator ten times in a row.

One of our trial runs produced the following results:

```
rand() call #1 returns 27610
rand() call #2 returns 27964
rand() call #3 returns 27908
rand() call #4 returns 21610
rand() call #5 returns 14085
rand() call #6 returns 14281
rand() call #7 returns 9569
rand() call #8 returns 9397
rand() call #9 returns 24266
rand() call #10 returns 142
```

Limitations of rand

It doesn't take a rocket scientist to see that the numbers from our trial run are not totally random. This isn't Oracle's fault! The problem lies with the algorithm used in *rand*. Moreover, rand returns numbers only in the range 1 through 65535. Many C libraries include the XPG4 standard function rand48, which overcomes these limitations at the expense of mildly increased complexity. See the companion diskette for the source code of an external procedure that uses rand48 (the *rand48ut.c* and *rand48ut.sql* files).

Syntax for External Procedures

Now that we've gone through the basic steps and seen examples of the kind of code you must write in order to take advantage of external procedures, let's explore each syntactic element in more detail.

CREATE LIBRARY: Creating the External Procedure Library

Step 3 in the random number generator example we presented in the previous section uses the SQL statement CREATE LIBRARY. The general syntax for this command is:

```
CREATE [ OR REPLACE ] LIBRARY <library name>
AS
    '<path to file>';
```

Where:

library name

A legal PL/SQL identifier. This name will be used in subsequent bodies of external procedures that need to call the shared object (or DLL) file.

path to file
> The fully qualified pathname to the shared object (or DLL) file. As shown above, it must be enclosed in single quotes.

Here are some things to keep in mind when issuing a CREATE LIBRARY statement:

- The statement must be executed by the DBA or by a user who has been granted CREATE LIBRARY or CREATE ANY LIBRARY privileges.

- As with most other database objects, libraries are owned by a specific Oracle user (schema). Other users can refer to the library using *owner.library* syntax, or they can create synonyms for the library (or use a synonym) if desired.

- Oracle doesn't check whether the named shared library file exists when you execute the CREATE LIBRARY statement. Nor will it check when you later create an external procedure declaration for a function in that library (see Step 4). If you have a syntax error in the path, you won't know it until the first time you try to execute the function.

- Setting up a listener is typically a DBA task performed (in UNIX, anyway) when the DBA is logged on as the "oracle user." However, for security reasons, Oracle recommends setting up a different OS-level user with a limited profile to run the listener for external procedures.

EXTERNAL: Creating the PL/SQL Body

In lieu of a BEGIN..END block, the body of your PL/SQL function or procedure must contain an EXTERNAL clause. This section describes the content of this clause. Syntactically, it looks like this:

```
EXTERNAL LIBRARY <library name>
    [ NAME <external routine name> ]
    [ LANGUAGE <language name> ]
    [ CALLING STANDARD  C | PASCAL ]
    [ PARAMETERS (<external parameter list>) ]
    [ WITH CONTEXT ];
```

Where:

library name
> Name defined previously in the CREATE LIBRARY statement.

external routine name
> Name of the function as defined in the C language library. If the name is lowercase, you must put double quotes around it. You can omit this parameter; if you do, the name of the external routine must match your PL/SQL module's name (defaults to uppercase).

language name

Lets PL/SQL know the language in which the external routine is written. In early releases of Oracle8, this parameter can only be C, which is the default.

CALLING STANDARD

On Windows NT, your application may use the Pascal calling standard, which means that arguments are "reversed" on the stack and that your called function will deal with them accordingly. CALLING STANDARD defaults to C if omitted.

PARAMETERS

This section gives the position and datatypes of parameters exchanged between PL/SQL and C.

external parameter list

External parameters appear in a comma-delimited list. Each item in the list is one of three things:

— The keyword CONTEXT, which is a placeholder for the context pointer

— Information about a formal parameter's mapping between PL/SQL and C

— The keyword RETURN and information about its mapping

The syntax and rules are discussed in "Mapping Parameters" below.

WITH CONTEXT

The presence of this clause indicates that you want PL/SQL to pass a "context pointer" to the called program. The called program must be expecting the pointer as a formal parameter of type *OCIExtProcContext ** (defined in the C header file *ociextp.b*).

This "context" that we are passing via a pointer is a data structure that contains a variety of Oracle-specific information. The called procedure doesn't actually refer directly to the data structure's content; instead, the structure simply facilitates other Oracle Call Interface (OCI) calls which perform various Oracle-specific tasks. These tasks include raising predefined or user-defined exceptions, allocating session-only memory (which gets released as soon as control returns to PL/SQL), and obtaining information about the Oracle user's environment.

DROP: Dropping Libraries

The syntax for dropping a library is simply:

```
DROP LIBRARY <library name>;
```

The Oracle user who executes this command must have the DROP LIBRARY or DROP ANY LIBRARY privilege.

Oracle does not check dependency information before dropping the library. This is useful if you need to change the name or location of the shared object file to which the library points. You can just drop it and rebuild it, and any dependent routines will continue to function. (More useful, perhaps, would be a requirement that you use a DROP LIBRARY FORCE command, but such an option does not exist).

Before you drop the library permanently, you'll probably want to look in the DBA_DEPENDENCIES view to see if any PL/SQL module relies on the library.

Mapping Parameters

Consider for a moment the problems of exchanging data between PL/SQL and C. PL/SQL has its own set of datatypes that are only somewhat similar to those you find in 3GLs. PL/SQL variables can be NULL and subject to three-valued truth table logic; C variables have no equivalent concept. Your C library might not know which national language character set you're using to express alphanumeric values. And should your C functions expect a given argument by value, or by reference (pointer)?

Given these hurdles, it would be easy to conclude that the job is impossible or, at best, difficult. The good news, though, is that Oracle has thought of all these issues already, and has built a lot of options into the PARAMETERS clause to cover the possibilities. So the programmer's key task is to figure out how to apply the options to a given situation.

Datatype Conversion

Let's look first at the issue of datatype conversions. Oracle has kindly provided a useful set of default type conversions. Each PL/SQL datatype maps to an "external datatype," which in turn maps to an allowed set of C types as illustrated below:

   PL/SQL types ↔ External types ↔ C types

The external datatypes, which are included in the PARAMETERS clause, are case-insensitive. In some cases, the external datatypes have the same name as the C type, but in some others, they do not. For example, the STRING external datatype maps to a char * in C.

As another example, if you pass a PL/SQL variable of type PLS_INTEGER, the corresponding default external type is INT, which maps to an int datatype in C. Or if you prefer, you can override this conversion with an explicit mapping to other external types such as SHORT (maps to short in C) or UNSIGNED INT (maps to unsigned int in C).

Table 21-1 lists all the default datatype conversions, as well as alternative conversions, allowed by Oracle's PL/SQL to C interface. For brevity, in the cases where the external datatype and the C datatype are the same except for case sensitivity, we have listed the type name only once, in lowercase. Note that the allowable conversions depend on both the datatype and the mode of the PL/SQL formal parameter.

Table 21-1. Legal Mappings of PL/SQL and C Datatypes

| PL/SQL Datatype | C Datatype if PL/SQL Formal Parameters are... | | |
	IN or RETURN	IN BY REFERENCE or RETURN BY REFERENCE	IN OUT or OUT
"Long" integer family: BINARY_INTEGER, BOOLEAN, PLS_INTEGER	int, char, unsigned char, short, unsigned short, unsigned int, long, unsigned long, sb1, ub1, sb2, ub2, sb4, ub4, size_t	Same list of types as at left, but use a pointer (for example, the default is int * rather than int)	Same list of types as at far left, but use a pointer (for example, the default is int * rather than int)
"Short" integer family: NATURAL, NATURALN, POSITIVE, POSITIVEN, SIGNTYPE	Same as above, except default is unsigned int	Same as above, except default is unsigned int *	Same as above, except default is unsigned int *
"Character" family: VARCHAR2, CHAR, LONG, VARCHAR, CHARACTER, ROWID	STRING[a]	STRING[a]	STRING[a]
DOUBLE PRECISION	Double	Double	Double
FLOAT, REAL	Float	Float	Float
RAW, LONG RAW	RAW[b]	RAW[b]	RAW[b]
BFILE, BLOB, CLOB	OCILOBLOCATOR[c]	OCILOBLOCATOR	OCILOBLOCATOR
"User-defined" family: records, collections, objects, cursor variables	Disallowed in this Oracle release	Disallowed in this Oracle release	Disallowed in this Oracle release

[a] In the PARAMETERS clause, use the external datatype STRING, but in the C specification, use char *.
[b] In the PARAMETERS clause, use the external datatype RAW, but in the C specification, use unsigned char *.
[c] In the PARAMETERS clause, use the external datatype OCILOBLOCATOR; in the C specification, use OciLobLocator * for parameters of mode IN, RETURN, IN BY REFERENCE, or RETURN BY REFERENCE; use OciLobLocator ** for IN OUT or OUT.

In some simple cases where you are passing only numeric arguments and where the defaults are acceptable, you can omit the PARAMETERS clause entirely.

By contrast, any time you return a character parameter from an external procedure, you may need to include an explicit PARAMETERS clause. This is so that you can supply a "property" parameter such as INDICATOR, LENGTH, or MAXLEN that will tell PL/SQL the actual and maximum size of the character buffer. These properties apply both to arguments and to function return values. As it turns out, LENGTH is only needed for RAW datatypes since strings are null-terminated.

For example, if you had a generic procedure which accepted an operating system command and returned output from that command, your procedure body might look like this (notice the PARAMETERS clause):

```
PROCEDURE run_command
    (command IN VARCHAR2,
     result OUT VARCHAR2)
IS EXTERNAL
    LIBRARY libshell_1
    LANGUAGE C
    PARAMETERS
        (command STRING,
         result STRING,
         result INDICATOR,
         result MAXLEN);
```

INDICATOR and MAXLEN are two of five properties with which we can pass supplemental information for any given PL/SQL parameter. We pass the "indicator" in addition to the variable if it's important to detect whether the value is null. Once we specify that the indicator should be included, Oracle sets and interprets this value properly on the PL/SQL side. Our C application, though, will need to get and set this value programmatically. MAXLEN, on the other hand, is a read-only property that gets set automatically by the PL/SQL environment; MAXLEN communicates to the C program the maximum storage that can be used for an IN OUT, OUT, or RETURN parameter.

Each piece of supplemental information we want to exchange will be passed as a parameter, and will appear both in the PARAMETERS clause and in the C language function specification.

More Syntax: The PARAMETERS Clause

Three types of entries may appear in the PARAMETERS clause:

- Formal parameters of the PL/SQL module

- The function return value

- A placeholder for the context area

The syntax you use to map a PL/SQL formal parameter to a C parameter is:

```
<parameter name> [<property>] [BY REFERENCE] [<external datatype>]
```

For function return values, you use the keyword RETURN in lieu of a parameter name. RETURN must appear in the last position in the PARAMETERS clause:

```
RETURN <property> [BY REFERENCE] [<external datatype>]
```

Use the third variation of the external PARAMETER clause when you have specified WITH CONTEXT. In this case, the parameter is simply

```
CONTEXT
```

By convention, if you have specified WITH CONTEXT, you should make CONTEXT the first argument. That is its default location if you default all of the parameter mappings.

Parameter entries have the following meanings:

parameter name
> The name of the parameter as specified in the formal parameter list of the PL/SQL module. This name is not necessarily the name of the formal parameter in the C language routine. However, parameters in the PL/SQL parameter list must match one-for-one, in order, those in the C language specification.

property
> One of the following: INDICATOR, LENGTH, MAXLEN, CHARSETID, or CHARSETFORM. These are described in the "Properties" section below.

BY REFERENCE
> Pass the parameter by reference. In other words, the module in the shared library is expecting a pointer to the parameter rather than its value. BY REFERENCE only has meaning for scalar IN parameters that are not strings, such as BINARY_INTEGER, PLS_INTEGER, FLOAT, DOUBLE PRECISION, and REAL. All others (IN OUT and OUT parameters, as well as IN parameters of type STRING) are *always* passed by reference, and the corresponding C prototype must specify a pointer.

WARNING   The documentation for Oracle 8.0.3 erroneously states that the syntax for this option is "BY REF".

---

external datatype
> The C language datatype. If this is omitted, the external datatype will default as indicated in Table 21-1. Most conversions that make sense are legal; see the table for additional details.

TIP   When you are mapping parameters, you *must* use positional nota-
                tion in the PARAMETERS clause. That is, the parameters you supply
                in this clause must match those in the C language function specifica-
                tion one-for-one, and must appear in the same order.

Properties

This section describes each possible property you can specify in a PARAMETERS clause.

INDICATOR property

What it is
    "Flag" to denote whether the parameter is null

Allowed External Types
    short (the default), int, long

Allowed PL/SQL Types
    All scalars

Allowed PL/SQL Modes
    IN, IN OUT, OUT, RETURN

Call Mode
    By *value* for IN parameters (unless BY REFERENCE specified), and by *refer-*
    ence for IN OUT, OUT, and RETURN variables

You can apply this property to any parameter, in any mode, including RETURNs. If you omit an indicator, PL/SQL is supposed to think that your external routine will always be non-null (but it's not that simple; see the sidebar "Indicating Without Indicators?").

When you send an IN variable to the external procedure, and you've associated an indicator, Oracle will set its value automatically. However, if your C module is returning a value in a RETURN or OUT parameter and an indicator, your C code must set the indicator value.

For an IN parameter, an example of the indicator parameter in your C function might be:

```
sb2 pIndicatorFoo
```

Or for an IN OUT parameter, the indicator might be:

```
sb2 *pIndicatorFoo
```

In the body of your C function, you should use the #define constants OCI_IND_ NOTNULL and OCI_IND_NULL supplied in *oro.h* as values for the NOT NULL and NULL values. These are defined in *oro.h* as:

```
#define OCI_IND_NOTNULL 0          /* not NULL */
#define OCI_IND_NULL (-1)          /* NULL */
```

Indicating Without Indicators?

What happens if you don't specify an indicator variable for a string and then return an empty C string? We wrote a short test program to find out:

```
void myfunc(char *outbuff)
{
    outbuff[0] = '\0';
}
```

When invoked as an external procedure, PL/SQL interprets this parameter value as a NULL! The reason appears to be that the STRING external type is special; you can also indicate a NULL value to Oracle by passing a string of length 2 where the first byte is '\0'. (This only works if you *omit* a LENGTH parameter.)

But don't rely on this little-known behavior. Always use an indicator!

LENGTH property

What it is

Statistic indicating the number of characters in a character parameter

Allowed External Types

int (the default), short, unsigned short, unsigned int, long, unsigned long

Allowed PL/SQL Types

VARCHAR2, CHAR, RAW, LONG RAW

Allowed PL/SQL Modes

IN, IN OUT, OUT, RETURN

Call Mode

By *value* for IN parameters (unless BY REFERENCE specified), and by *reference* for IN OUT, OUT, and RETURN variables

The Oracle documentation states that you *must* include the LENGTH property for CHAR, RAW, LONG RAW, or VARCHAR2 parameters. In fact, LENGTH is only mandatory for RAW and LONGRAW. CHAR and VARCHAR2 are, in fact, passed on as STRING parameters for which the LENGTH parameter is redundant (since STRINGs follow null-termination semantics). For the external RAW datatype, a

LENGTH parameter is necessary to read the length of the RAW data for IN and IN OUT variable modes, and to tell PL/SQL the length of the raw data for IN OUT, OUT, and RETURN variable modes.

For an IN parameter, an example of the indicator parameter in your C function might be:

```
int pLenFoo
```

Or for an OUT or IN OUT parameter:

```
int *pLenFoo
```

MAXLEN property

What it is
>Statistic indicating the *maximum* number of characters in a string parameter

Allowed External Types
>int (the default), short, unsigned short, unsigned int, long, unsigned long

Allowed PL/SQL Types
>VARCHAR2, CHAR, RAW, LONG RAW

Allowed PL/SQL Modes
>IN OUT, OUT, RETURN

Call Mode
>By reference

MAXLEN is applied to IN OUT or OUT parameters and to no other mode. If you attempt to use it for an IN, you'll get a compile-time error "PLS-00250: Incorrect Usage of MAXLEN in parameters clause."

Unlike the LENGTH parameter, the MAXLEN data is always passed by reference.

An example of the C formal parameter follows:

```
int *pMaxLenFoo
```

CHARSETID and CHARSETFORM properties

What it is
>Flags denoting information about the character set

Allowed External Types
>unsigned int (the default), unsigned short, unsigned long

Allowed PL/SQL Types
>VARCHAR2, CHAR, CLOB

Allowed PL/SQL Modes
>IN, IN OUT, OUT, RETURN

Call Mode
> By reference

If you are passing data to the external procedure which is expressed in a nonde-fault character set, these properties will let you communicate its ID and form to the called C program. The values are read-only and should not be modified by the called program. For more information about national language support and how to accommodate it in an OCI program, refer to Oracle's *Programmer's Guide to the Oracle Call Interface*.

Correct Declaration of Properties

With one exception, every parameter-property combination that you list in the PARAMETERS clause must have an entry in the C function specification. For example, if you had the following body:

```
CREATE OR REPLACE PACKAGE BODY ext_utils
AS
    PROCEDURE my_foo (foo IN OUT VARCHAR2)
    IS EXTERNAL
        LIBRARY foobar_1
        PARAMETERS
            (foo STRING,
             foo MAXLEN,
             foo LENGTH);
END ext_utils;
```

then the C prototype would look like this:

```
void myFunction
    (char *pFoo,
     int *pMaxLenFoo,
     int *pLenFoo );
```

Notice that myFunction is declared void, which is appropriate when mapping to a PL/SQL procedure rather than a function. Also, since this PARAMETERS clause includes no explicit datatypes, we will get the default type mapping:

```
STRING → char *
MAXLEN → int *
LENGTH → int *
```

Char is typedefined as an unsigned char in *oratypes.h*.

The exception to the one-to-one correspondence rule occurs when explicitly declaring properties of the function return value. As an example, look at the parameter list below:

```
PARAMETERS
    (RETURN INT)
```

The corresponding C prototype could be:

```
int someFunction();
```

(OK, it's not really an exception; it's more a question of semantics.)

OCI Service Routines

There are four OCI routines that you can use in your external procedures. These require that you have passed context area information to the C function by including WITH CONTEXT in your PL/SQL body. The routines are:

OCIExtProcAllocCallMemory
> Allocates memory that will automatically de-allocate when control returns to PL/SQL.

OCIExtProcRaiseExcp
> Raises a predefined exception by its Oracle error number.

OCIExtProcRaiseExcpWithMsg
> Raises a user-defined exception, including a custom error message.

OCIExtProcGetEnv
> Allows an external procedure to perform OCI callbacks to the database to execute SQL or PL/SQL.

Refer to Oracle's *PL/SQL User's Guide and Reference* for detailed documentation and examples of using these routines.

External Procedure Housekeeping

Here are some not-so-obvious bits of information that will assist you in creating, debugging, and managing external procedures.

Data Dictionary

There are only a handful of entries in the data dictionary that help manage external procedures. As we have mentioned elsewhere, although Table 21-2 gives the USER_ version of the dictionary table, note that there are corresponding entries for DBA_ and ALL_.

Table 21-2. Data Dictionary Views for External Procedures

To Answer the Question...	Use This View	As In
What libraries have I created?	USER_LIBRARIES	`SELECT * FROM user_libraries;`

Table 21-2. Data Dictionary Views for External Procedures (continued)

To Answer the Question...	Use This View	As In
What packages depend on library foo?	USER_DEPENDENCIES	```SELECT * FROM user_dependencies WHERE referenced_name = 'FOO';```
What is the source code for the spec of my PL/SQL package "bar" that calls the library?	USER_SOURCE	```SELECT text FROM user_source WHERE name = 'BAR' AND type = 'PACKAGE' ORDER BY line;```
What is the source code for my PL/SQL package body bar that calls the library?	USER_SOURCE	```SELECT text FROM user_source WHERE name = 'BAR' AND type = 'PACKAGE BODY' ORDER BY line;```

Rules and Warnings About External Procedures

As with almost all things PL/SQL, external procedures come with an obligatory list of cautions:

- While the mode of each formal parameter (IN, IN OUT, OUT) may have certain restrictions in PL/SQL, C does not honor these modes. Differences between the PL/SQL parameter mode and the usage in the C module cannot be detected at compile time, and could also go undetected at runtime. The rules are what you would expect: don't assign values to IN parameters; don't read OUT parameters; always assign values to IN OUT and OUT parameters; always return a value of the appropriate datatype.

- Modifiable INDICATORs and LENGTHs are always passed by reference for IN OUT, OUT, and RETURN. Unmodifiable INDICATORs and LENGTHs are always passed by value unless you specify BY REFERENCE. However, even if you pass INDICATORs or LENGTHs for PL/SQL variables by reference, they are still read-only parameters.

- Although you can pass up to 128 parameters between PL/SQL and C, if any of them are float or double, your actual maximum will be lower. How much lower depends on the operating system.

- Since extproc might be a multithreaded process in future releases, your external code should avoid the use of "static" variables.

- Your external procedure may not perform DDL commands, begin or end a session, or control a transaction using COMMIT or ROLLBACK. (See Oracle's *PL/SQL User's Guide and Reference* for a complete list of illegal OCI routines.)

A Debugging Odyssey

Oracle supplies a script to facilitate the debugging of external procedures. The name of the script is *dbgextp.sql*, and it's found in *$ORACLE_HOME/plsql/demo* on UNIX (on Windows NT, it's in *<Oracle root directory>\pls80*).

dbgextp.sql builds a package needed for debugging, debug_extproc, and a library called debug_extproc_library. Don't look for a lot of documentation on *dbgextp.sql*—you won't find it. In fact, inline comments in the file itself are the only place that the debugging process is documented in any detail.

Although it wasn't exactly a cookbook process, I was able to demonstrate that the GNU debugger (gdb 4.16) can attach to a running process, as required to debug external procedures. Here's how I tried it.

First, I compiled the shared library file with the compiler option (-g) needed to include symbolic information for the debugger.

After running *dbgextp.sql*, I ran the "execute" command on DEBUG_EXT-PROC.STARTUP_EXTPROC_AGENT from SQL*Plus and it ran fine. However, I got a "permission denied" error every time I tried to attach the debugger to the extproc. The problem was that the extproc executable had file permissions of 0751 (i.e., -rwxr-x--x). This means that I cannot, by default, debug unless I am logged in as the "oracle" user or am in the dba group (this is somewhat intentional because Oracle says that the extproc listener shouldn't be started by a user that can write database files—that could be dangerous if you have a bug in your external procedure). So I issued the command:

```
chmod o+r $ORACLE_HOME/bin/extproc
```

which got me past the "permission denied" error.

I then loaded the extproc program into gdb and set a breakpoint on the "pextproc" symbol per the instructions in the *dbgextp.sql* file. Then I typed "@tz_utl" to call the timezone external procedure from the SQL*Plus session. When the external procedure was called, extproc hit the breakpoint.

After executing a gdb "share" command so gdb would read the symbols in my just-loaded external shared library, I was able to set a breakpoint on the get_timezone external procedure. It worked pretty well after that.

I did find that gdb seemed to get confused when I tried to debug one of our shared libraries after another. Detaching the extproc and restarting gdb fixed this problem.

Examples

This section contains several substantial examples of using external procedures.

Example: Retrieving the Time Zone

While it's trivial in Oracle to read the time on the system clock (by selecting SYSDATE from DUAL), Oracle provides no clue about the time zone in which the clock resides. I've seen how Oracle's silence on this matter can be a problem in a replicated environment where the Oracle servers were separated by thousands of miles. Without knowing the time zone, how can I write a conflict resolution routine that compares transaction execution time from different servers? Yes, I could set all the servers to a common time zone, but personally, I find that a painful solution at best.

External procedures to the rescue!

A useful application would return at least the name of the time zone in which the server is currently executing, allowing us to perform the time transformations— using, for example, Oracle's built-in NEW_TIME function.

Let's look first at the PL/SQL side of this external procedure. We are going to call our library *timezone_utl*. It doesn't exist yet, but we can tell Oracle to create the library anyway (for illustrative purposes):

```
/* filename on companion disk: tz_utl.sql /*
CREATE OR REPLACE LIBRARY timezone_utl_l
AS
    '/oracle/local/lib/libtz_utl.so';
```

Now we are going to create a procedure we call timezone. Again, we implement the external procedure in a package, and use RESTRICT_REFERENCES to tell Oracle that it does not affect database or package states:

```
CREATE OR REPLACE
PACKAGE timezone_utl
IS
    PROCEDURE timezone
        (local_timezone OUT VARCHAR2);
    PRAGMA RESTRICT_REFERENCES (timezone, WNDS, RNDS, WNPS, RNPS);
END timezone_utl;
```

Notice that we have chosen to retrieve the time zone into an OUT VARCHAR2 parameter. We will therefore include an explicit PARAMETERS clause, and it will include INDICATOR and MAXLEN properties. The routine is going to return a NULL if there is any problem.

```
CREATE OR REPLACE
PACKAGE BODY timezone_utl
```

```
IS
    PROCEDURE timezone
        (local_timezone OUT VARCHAR2)
    IS EXTERNAL
        LIBRARY timezone_utl_l
        NAME "get_timezone"
        LANGUAGE C
        PARAMETERS
            (local_timezone STRING,
             local_timezone MAXLEN sb4,
             local_timezone INDICATOR sb2);
END timezone_utl;
```

In our C module we write a function, get_timezone, that retrieves the current time zone string from the operating system. From the perspective of the C programmer, this function fills a caller-provided output buffer with the current time zone. If meaningful, the function can also return the alternate "daylight savings" time zone, since it is provided automatically by the localtime function.[*]

```
/* Filename on companion disk: tz_utl.c */
#include <stdio.h>
#include <time.h>
#include <oci.h>

/* Tested with Solaris 2.5.1 and Oracle 8.0.3.  */

void
get_timezone (char *pTimezone,
              sb4 *pMaxLenTimezone, /* not including NULL terminator */
              sb2 *pIndTimezone)
{
    if ( *pMaxLenTimezone > 0 )
    {
        time_t      tmpTime;
        struct tm   *pTimeInfo;
        char        timezoneBuff[BUFSIZ];
        size_t      lenCopied;

        /* Get the current time and extract the timezone string from it */
        tmpTime = time (0);
        pTimeInfo = localtime (&tmpTime);
        lenCopied = strftime (timezoneBuff,
                              sizeof(timezoneBuff),
                              "%Z",
                              pTimeInfo);

        /* If the timezone string fits, copy it into the output parameter */
        if ( (lenCopied > 0) && (lenCopied <= (size_
            t)*pMaxLenTimezone) )
        {
```

---

[*] The localtime and strftime functions are available in the C runtime libraries included with a number of standard implementations, such as SVID 3, POSIX, BSD 4.3, and ISO 9899.

```
                /* Copy the string and return the length */
                memcpy (pTimezone, timezoneBuff, lenCopied);

                /* Null-terminate the returned string. Note that the
                ** null-terminator byte is not included in MAXLEN */
                pTimezone[lenCopied] = '\0';

                *pIndTimezone = OCI_IND_NOTNULL;
            }
            else
            {
                /* it doesn't fit, so return a NULL */
                *pIndTimezone = OCI_IND_NULL;
            }
        }
        else
        {
            /* the output parameter is too small, return a NULL */
            *pIndTimezone = OCI_IND_NULL;
        }
    }
```

When this C function returns, the length parameter referenced by pLenTimezone will indicate the size of the returned string. If there is an error getting the timezone string, or if the maximum size of the buffer is too small for the timezone value, the indicator variable will be set to OCI_IND_NULL, indicating a NULL.

Compiling and linking this function as a shared library requires some special options. Here is the (slightly edited) log from a UNIX make command that illustrates the necessary include libraries and compiler options (the backslashes are continuation characters added here only for clarity). As mentioned before, this example is from Solaris 2.5.1 and Oracle 8.0.3.

```
gcc  -I/oracle/product/8.0.3/rdbms/demo \
     -I/oracle/product/8.0.3/network/public \
     -I/oracle/product/8.0.3/plsql/public \
     -fPIC -Wall -c tz_utl.c
gcc  -shared -o libtz_utl.so tz_utl.o
```

Briefly, these options have the following meanings:

-fPIC

Produce "position-independent code"

-Wall

Issue all "-W" compiler warnings

-c

Compile the source file (to produce a .so file), but do not link it

-shared

Produce a shared object file from a static library

-o libtz_utl.so

    Write the output file to libtz_utl.so

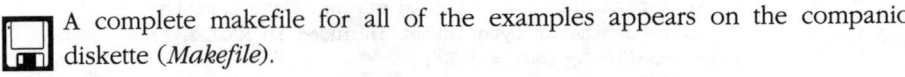 A complete makefile for all of the examples appears on the companion diskette (*Makefile*).

To test our routine, we can run the following PL/SQL block in SQL*Plus:

```
SET SERVEROUTPUT ON SIZE 1000000
DECLARE
    local_time   DATE;
    local_tz     VARCHAR2(3);
    target_time  DATE;
    target_tz    VARCHAR2(3) := 'GMT';
BEGIN
    /* Call the external procedure to discover the local time zone */
    timezone_utl.timezone (local_tz);

    IF ( local_tz IS NOT NULL ) THEN
      DBMS_OUTPUT.PUT_LINE ('timezone returned = "'
         || local_tz || '"');

        /* Convert the current time to the target time zone */
        local_time  := SYSDATE;
        target_time := NEW_TIME (local_time, local_tz, target_tz);

        /* Display original and converted times with their time zones */
        DBMS_OUTPUT.PUT_LINE (TO_CHAR (local_time,
           'DD-MON-YYYY HH24:MI:SS') || ' ' || local_tz );
        DBMS_OUTPUT.PUT_LINE ('=');
        DBMS_OUTPUT.PUT_LINE (TO_CHAR (target_time,
           'DD-MON-YYYY HH24:MI:SS') || ' ' || target_tz );
    ELSE
        DBMS_OUTPUT.PUT_LINE ('local_tz returned NULL');
    END IF;

END;
```

This block produced the following (correct) result:

```
timezone returned = "PDT"
08-JUL-1997 17:07:15 PDT
=
09-JUL-1997 00:07:15 GMT
```

Example: Sending Email

The last few versions of the Oracle server have included a built-in PL/SQL package which allows you to send email via Interoffice (née Oracle Mail). Unfortunately, this DBMS_MAIL package is of no use to the large number of Oracle shops that standardize on some other email server.

Using an external procedure, however, you can easily write a PL/SQL package that will call an operating system command such as mailx under UNIX. While it may not be the most elegant approach, it has one demonstrable benefit: it works!

Again, we'll look at the PL/SQL side first. In this case, we intend to create a separate shared object file for our library:

```
/* Filename on companion disk: mail_utl.sql */
CREATE OR REPLACE LIBRARY mail_utl_l
AS
    '/oracle/local/lib/libmail_utl.so';
```

The package specification contains a single function, send_mail, which accepts only four arguments: the sender, recipient(s), subject, and message body:

```
CREATE OR REPLACE
PACKAGE mail_utl
IS
    FUNCTION send_mail
        (return_address   IN VARCHAR2 DEFAULT NULL,
         recipient_list   IN VARCHAR2,
         subject_line     IN VARCHAR2 DEFAULT NULL,
         message_text     IN VARCHAR2 DEFAULT NULL)
    RETURN PLS_INTEGER;
    PRAGMA RESTRICT_REFERENCES (send_mail, WNDS, RNDS, WNPS, RNPS);
END mail_utl;
```

Before coding the body, let's dream up some interesting new requirements. First, if the return address, subject line, or message text is null, let's have the C function use some reasonable defaults. Second, if the recipient list is null, we want to raise a programmer-defined exception.

Mail on Windows NT

If your Oracle server is running on Windows NT, a rough equivalent to mailx is a public domain program called Blat, by Mark Neal and Pedro Mendes. It is available from several Internet sites, including *ftp://gepasi.dbs.aber.ac.uk/winnt/ blat12.zip* and *ftp://press.southern.edu/public/windowsnt/email/blat-nt-12.zip.* Like mailx, Blat assumes the presence of an SMTP mail server. (Unlike mailx, though, Blat doesn't assume that SMTP is running on the same machine on which you're running Oracle.) With Blat, you'll have to first save the text of the message to an operating system file.

If you have a non-SMTP mail server, it probably has a well-documented API that would allow your external procedure to call it directly.

To support the requirement of communicating nulls properly, the PARAMETERS clause shown below includes indicator variables for each of the parameters. To raise an exception, however, we must send "context" information to the function. We do so by including the WITH CONTEXT clause and including the CONTEXT keyword as the first argument in the PARAMETERS clause:

```
CREATE OR REPLACE
PACKAGE BODY mail_utl
IS
    FUNCTION send_mail
        (return_address  IN VARCHAR2,
         recipient_list  IN VARCHAR2,
         subject_line    IN VARCHAR2,
         message_text    IN VARCHAR2)
    RETURN PLS_INTEGER
    IS EXTERNAL
        LIBRARY mail_utl_l
        NAME "send_mail"
        LANGUAGE C
        WITH CONTEXT    -- passes context so we can raise exception
        PARAMETERS
            (CONTEXT,    -- keyword giving location of CONTEXT parameter
             return_address STRING,
             return_address INDICATOR,
             recipient_list STRING,
             recipient_list INDICATOR,
             subject_line   STRING ,
             subject_line   INDICATOR,
             message_text   STRING,
             message_text   INDICATOR,
             RETURN SB4);
    END mail_utl;
```

The corresponding C function sends mail by opening a pipe to the UNIX */bin/ mailx* program. If there are any errors during the call to */bin/mailx*, the function will return any error code returned by the operating system; otherwise it simply returns a value of zero, indicating normal, successful completion.

```
/* Filename on companion disk: mail_utl.c */
#include <stdlib.h>
#include <stdio.h>
#include <errno.h>
#include <oci.h>

/* Tested with Solaris 2.5.1 and Oracle 8.0.3. */

sb4
send_mail (OCIExtProcContext *pWithContext,
           char    *pReturnAddress,
           sb2     indReturnAddress,
           char    *pRecipientList,
           sb2     indRecipientList,
           char    *pSubject,
```

```
                   sb2     indSubject,
                   char    *pMessage,
                   sb2     indMessage)
    {
       char mailCmd[BUFSIZ];
       char returnAddrOption[BUFSIZ];
       sb4 errorStatus;
       FILE *pMailPipe;

       /* If there are NULL input parameters, try to "fill in the blanks"
       || and mail the message anyway.
       */
       if (indRecipientList == OCI_IND_NULL)
       {
           /* Raise an unnamed programmer-defined exception since a
           || recipients list is required to send a mail message.
           */
           if (OCIExtProcRaiseExcpWithMsg (pWithContext,
                                           (int)20101,
                                           "a recipient list is required",
                                           0) == OCIEXTPROC_SUCCESS)
           {
               /* Return immediately */
               return -1;
           }
           else
           {
       /* Error raising exception, abort this 'extproc' process. */
               abort();
           }
       }

       /* Test for null arguments and supply defaults where appropriate. */
       if (indMessage == OCI_IND_NULL)
       {
           pMessage = "<No Message>";
       }

       if (indSubject == OCI_IND_NULL)
       {
           pSubject = "<No Subject Given>";
       }

       if (indReturnAddress == OCI_IND_NULL)
       {
           /* No return address option requested */
           returnAddrOption[0] = '\0';
       }
       else
       {
           sprintf(returnAddrOption,
                   "-r '%s'",
                   pReturnAddress);
       }
```

```
/* Now format the mail command line */
sprintf(mailCmd,
        "/bin/mailx %s -s '%s' %s",
        returnAddrOption,
        pSubject,
        pRecipientList);

/* Reset the last system error value */
errno = 0;

/* Open a pipe to the mail program */
if ( (pMailPipe = popen (mailCmd, "w")) != NULL )
{
    if ( fwrite (pMessage, strlen (pMessage), 1, pMailPipe)
        == strlen (pMessage) )
    {
        /* Now close the pipe and return the termination status */
        errorStatus = pclose(pMailPipe);
    }
    else
    {
        /* We couldn't write the message buffer, return the error */
        errorStatus = errno;
        (void) pclose (pMailPipe);
    }
}
else
{
    /* We failed to open a pipe to the command, return the error */
    errorStatus = errno;
}
return errorStatus;
}
```

Compiling and linking this function into a shared object file is similar to the time zone example. Here, the OCI shared library is also included, and a separate call to ld is required:

```
gcc  -I/oracle/product/8.0.3/rdbms/demo \
     -I/oracle/product/8.0.3/network/public \
     -I/oracle/product/8.0.3/plsql/public \
     -fPIC -Wall -c mail_utl.c
ld -G -h libmail_utl.so -o libmail_utl.so mail_utl.o \
   /oracle/product/8.0.3/lib/libextp.a
```

Options have the following meaning:

ld

The link command on Solaris

-G

Produce a shared object

-h libmail_utl.so

Record *libmail_utl.so* as name used by runtime dynamic linker

To test our routine, we can run the following PL/SQL block in SQL*Plus:

```
SET SERVEROUTPUT ON SIZE 1000000
DECLARE
    exit_status  PLS_INTEGER;
BEGIN
    /* This call will succeed and "fill-in" the other NULL parameters */
    exit_status := mail_utl.send_mail (recipient_list => 'fred');
    DBMS_OUTPUT.PUT_LINE ('send_mail exit_status = ' || exit_status);

    /* This call will fail since the recipient list is NULL. Our unnamed
    || programmer-defined exception will be raised as a result.
    */
    exit_status := mail_utl.send_mail (recipient_list => NULL,
        subject_line   => 'Mail from PL/SQL!');
    DBMS_OUTPUT.PUT_LINE ('send_mail exit_status = ' || exit_status);
END;
```

When we run this test block, the first call should succeed, and we should get a message about exit_status being zero:

```
send_mail exit_status = 0
```

The next call fails with a user-defined exception—an exception generated by the external procedure:

```
DECLARE
*
ERROR at line 1:
ORA-20101: a recipient list is required
ORA-06512: at "USER8.MAIL_UTL", line 0
ORA-06512: at line 10
```

It's fortunate that Oracle gives us this ability to raise exceptions, so that our external procedures can participate fully in Oracle's SQL and PL/SQL error-handling model. Be sure to take advantage of it!

VI

Making PL/SQL
Programs Work

Part VI of this book describes how to make PL/SQL work most effectively and efficiently in the real world.

- Chapter 22, *Code Design Tips,* summarizes key advice for efficient PL/SQL programming, particularly in the use of procedures, functions, and parameters.

- Chapter 23, *Managing Code in the Database*, describes how you can store objects in the Oracle database most efficiently.

- Chapter 24, *Debugging PL/SQL*, describes how to debug your PL/SQL programs.

- Chapter 25, *Tuning PL/SQL Applications*, describes how to tune your PL/SQL programs so they run most efficiently.

- Chapter 26, *Tracing PL/SQL Execution*, describes how to trace the execution of your PL/SQL programs.

22

Code Design Tips

Syntax, syntax—is everything just a matter of syntax? You need literacy, a decent memory, and a good reference manual to master the syntax of a computer language like PL/SQL. But how far does that really get you? If you know the correct sequence of keywords to construct a valid procedure, does that mean that you also know how to design that procedure for maximum readability and minimum maintenance? Of course not.

Conquering PL/SQL's syntax is just the first leg of the journey you must take to develop the skills you need to modularize complex and effective applications. This chapter takes another step towards top quality module construction by offering a series of practical, directed tips. Many of these discussions repeat or summarize advice I've given elsewhere in this book, but I've collected it here for easy reference.

These tips cover both how to construct your procedures and functions and how to design your parameters. Once you have written a module and made it available in your development environment, very few people ever look at the code inside the program. Instead, users of your module refer to the module name and parameters, and to the documentation about the module.

The module parameters are far and away the most important part of a module's specification. They determine what information goes into the program and what information can be returned by it (as does the RETURN clause for a function). So this chapter includes a number of tips to help ensure that your parameter lists provide the most accurate information in the clearest manner possible.

Select Meaningful Module and Parameter Names

A name can make a big difference in the effectiveness of modules and parameters. The tips provided in this section should help you select names and define conventions for names that will improve the readability of your code.

Make Sure the Module Name Explains the Module

When you place code in a module, you hide it from view and give those executable statements a name (the name of the function or procedure). Information hiding is a good thing when it enhances your understanding of a program by letting you focus on a higher level of abstraction. Information hiding is a bad thing when it obscures your understanding of a program. This usually happens when you do not choose an accurate name for your module.

The name of your module should describe what it does in such a way that the replacement of code with the module call "self-documents" your program—that is, the name should describe the action performed by the module. In addition, the grammatical structure of the name you use is important.

A procedure is an executable statement, a command to the PL/SQL compiler. Consequently, the grammar of a procedure name should be similar to a command:

```
Verb_Subject
```

as in:

```
Calculate_P_and_L
Display_Errors
Confirm_New_Entries
```

A function is used like an expression in an executable statement. It returns or represents a value, so the grammar of a function name should be a noun:

```
Description_of_Returned_Value
```

as in:

```
Net_Profit
Company_Name
Number_of_Jobs
Earliest_Hire_Date
```

If I use the wrong grammatical structure for my names, they do not "read" properly. Consider the FOR loop below.

```
tabrow := 1;
FOR company_cur IN company_rec
LOOP
    profit_and_loss (company_cur.company_id);
    net_profit_table (tabrow) :=
        calculate_net_profit (company_cur.company_id);
    tabrow := tabrow + 1;
END LOOP;
```

Try reading this code out loud: "For every company in my cursor, profit-and-loss the company and then add the calculate-net-profit to the table." It doesn't sound right and it doesn't look right. If you simply name the procedure "profit_and_loss," you do not explain what you are doing with the profit and loss. And if you include a verb in the function name, you have one verb too many; the assignment operator itself already serves as the "action" for that statement.

I can make a few, minor adjustments in these module names and end up with much more readable code, as shown in this example:

```
tabrow := 1;
FOR company_cur IN company_rec
LOOP
    calculate_p_and_l (company_cur.company_id);
    net_profit_table (tabrow) := net_profit (company_cur.company_id);
    tabrow := tabrow + 1;
END LOOP;
```

The module names say it all: "For each company retrieved from the cursor, calculate the profit and loss and store the net profit for that company in the net profit PL/SQL table." Additional, formal documentation seems unnecessary. Can I say the same thing about the next version of the loop?

```
tabrow := 1;
FOR company_cur IN company_rec
LOOP
    calcpl (company_cur.company_id);
    net_profit_table (tabrow) := np (company_cur.company_id);
    tabrow := tabrow + 1;
END LOOP;
```

The module names in this code are excessively abbreviated. It is unrealistic to expect someone who didn't actually write the calcpl procedure and the np function to understand what those terms are supposed to mean. You should strike a happy medium between the above obscure identifiers and verbose names like these:

```
calculate_profit_and_loss_per_company
net_profit_for_single_company
```

Don't forget that you or someone else will have to type those program names!

Develop Consistent Naming Conventions for Your Formal Parameters

A parameter plays a specific role within a program; its name should indicate this difference. I recommend that in order to further distinguish parameters from other PL/SQL identifiers you include the parameter mode right in the name of the formal parameter.

A parameter has one of three modes: IN, OUT, or IN OUT. An IN parameter passes a value into the module, but its value cannot be modified. An OUT parameter passes a value out of the module, but its value cannot be referenced in the module. An IN OUT parameter can be both referenced and modified in the module.

By incorporating the parameter mode directly into the parameter name, its purpose in the module is self-documenting. Whenever you encounter that parameter in the code, you know that you are looking at a parameter, not a local variable, and you know exactly the ways in which that parameter can be used and/or changed.

In order for the parameter mode to stand out in the formal parameter name, you can include it either as a suffix or as a prefix. As a suffix, the mode is appended to the end of the parameter name, as follows:

```
PROCEDURE combine_and_format_names
   (first_name_inout IN OUT VARCHAR2,
    last_name_inout IN OUT VARCHAR2,
    full_name_out OUT VARCHAR2,
    name_format_in IN VARCHAR2 := 'LAST,FIRST');
```

The prefix standard would result in a parameter list for the above procedure as follows:

```
PROCEDURE combine_and_format_names
   (inout_first_name IN OUT VARCHAR2,
    inout_last_name IN OUT VARCHAR2,
    out_full_name OUT VARCHAR2,
    in_name_format IN VARCHAR2 := 'LAST,FIRST') ;
```

You could also opt for a minimum of typing by simply using the first letter of each parameter mode:

```
PROCEDURE combine_and_format_names
   (io_first_name IN OUT VARCHAR2,
    io_last_name IN OUT VARCHAR2,
    o_full_name OUT VARCHAR2,
    i_name_format IN VARCHAR2 := 'LAST,FIRST') ;
```

In any of these cases, a quick glance over the code identifies which objects represent parameters in the program. You can also more easily catch logic errors, such as the following case of an illegal update of an IN parameter:

```
in_name_format := 'FIRST MIDDLE LAST';
```

A parameter with an "in" suffix or prefix should never have its value changed. A parameter with an "out" suffix or prefix should never be used on the right-hand side of an assignment because its value is indeterminate in the program (until it is given a value).

Name Packages and Their Elements to Reflect the Packaged Structure

Given that a package provides a new layer or context over the normal variables and modules, you should take some special care in naming your packages and the elements within them. The name you use for a standalone module, in particular, will change when you move it inside a package. Consider the following example. If I develop a set of standalone procedures and functions to maintain lists of information, I might name them as follows:

```
PROCEDURE list_create (list_in IN VARCHAR2);
PROCEDURE list_get
    (list_in IN VARCHAR2, position_in IN NUMBER, item_out OUT VARCHAR2);
```

and so on. I need to use the "list_" prefix in front of each module name so that the name clearly identifies the structure for the action.

Suppose I now move modules like these inside the scope of a package called "list." The specification for the package looks like this:

```
PACKAGE list
IS
    PROCEDURE list_create (list_in IN VARCHAR2);
    PROCEDURE list_get
        (list_in IN VARCHAR2, position_in IN NUMBER, item_out OUT VARCHAR2);
END list;
```

At first glance this looks reasonable enough. The real test, however, comes when you try to use the modules. Let's try it. To create a list using the package procedure, I would execute a statement like this:

```
list_pkg.list_create ('company_names');
```

Now, that looks silly. The "list" is mentioned in both the package name and the module name. It didn't make much sense to carry over the standalone module names to the package names. A much cleaner naming scheme should produce executable statements that remove the redundancies:

```
PACKAGE list_pkg
IS
```

```
   PROCEDURE create (list_in IN VARCHAR2);
   PROCEDURE get
      (list_in IN VARCHAR2, position_in IN NUMBER, item_out OUT VARCHAR2);
END list_pkg;

list.create ('company_names');
```

As you define modules in a package, always think of them within the context of the package. If a package is supposed to maintain lists, then the name of the package should reflect that general purpose. The names of the individual modules ought to focus on their particular purpose—again, within the broader orientation of the package.

You might also consider setting as a standard the use of a _pkg suffix for all package names. With this approach, the list package and calls to the package look like this:

```
PACKAGE list_pkg
IS
   PROCEDURE create (list_in IN VARCHAR2);
   PROCEDURE get
      (list_in IN VARCHAR2, position_in IN NUMBER, item_out OUT VARCHAR2);
END list_pkg;

list_pkg.create ('company_names');
```

Personally, I have mixed feelings about this naming convention. It is important and useful to include information about the type of data in the name of the data, and I certainly encourage such a convention with cursors, records, tables, etc. A package, however, is a different sort of animal. It contains all those other language constructs. The way in which the package name is used to qualify the object already tells you what it is. It seems to me that inclusion of the _pkg suffix (or other indicator) reduces the readability of the code.

Build the Most Functional Functions

I like functions. They can replace an awful lot of complex logic in an expression with a simple statement of the result of all that logic. The following tips will help you construct functions that are as useful as possible.

Avoid Side Effects in Functions

Your function has one purpose in life: returning a single value via the RETURN statement. If it does anything else, such as update global or database information, then that function has potentially created a side effect. Side effects generally limit functions' usefulness. Let's look at a few examples and discuss how you can avoid side effects.

Do not use OUT and IN OUT parameters

Although a function returns its value with the RETURN statement, PL/SQL allows you to define OUT and IN OUT parameters for a function. If you do that, the function can actually pass changed data back through the parameter itself into the calling block of code through the parameters. This is generally not a good idea, and is a typical side effect in a function.

The format_name function below contains side effect parameters. Let's examine the impact of these parameters. The function takes a first name and a last name and returns a full name with the format LAST, FIRST. Because a requirement of the application happens to be that all names must be in uppercase, the function also converts the first and last names to their uppercase versions. It uses two IN OUT parameters to do this.

```
FUNCTION format_name
    (first_name_inout IN OUT VARCHAR2,
     last_name_inout IN OUT VARCHAR2)
    RETURN VARCHAR2
IS
BEGIN
    first_name_inout := UPPER (first_name_inout);
    last_name_inout := UPPER (last_name_inout);
    RETURN last_name_inout || ', ' || first_name_inout;
END;
```

If the application requires uppercase names, you may wonder, then, what is wrong with converting the first and last names to uppercase in format_name? First of all, this approach may be trying to meet the requirement a bit too enthusiastically. If the formatted name—the output, that is, of the function—must be in uppercase, you can certainly accomplish that without modifying the parameters, as follows:

```
FUNCTION format_name
    (first_name_in IN VARCHAR2,
     last_name_in IN VARCHAR2)
RETURN VARCHAR2
IS
BEGIN
    RETURN UPPER (last_name_in || ', ' || first_name_in);
END;
```

The second reason you would not want to automatically uppercase the name components is that you will make format_name less useful as a basic utility. Your current application may insist on uppercase, but there will be plenty of other applications that maintain entities having first and last names—and they do not have a similar requirement.

If you insist on the IN OUT parameters, the format_name utility could not be used in these other application development efforts.

Switch to a procedure with IN OUT parameters

If you do want a module that will convert both individual name components and the combined name to uppercase, then you would be better served with a procedure:

```
PROCEDURE combine_and_format_names
    (first_name_inout IN OUT VARCHAR2,
     last_name_inout IN OUT VARCHAR2,
     full_name_out OUT VARCHAR2)
IS
BEGIN
    first_name_inout := UPPER (first_name_inout);
    last_name_inout := UPPER (last_name_inout);
    full_name_out := last_name_inout || ', ' || first_name_inout;
END;
```

By using a procedure, you make it clearer that the module is applying changes to all the parameters. You avoid providing a function with side effects (i.e., other actions and impact beyond the return of a value). Let's take a look at the way these different modules would appear in your code.

- Let's first look at the function version. All our attention is focused on depositing the formatted name into the caller_name item:

  ```
  full_name := format_name (first_name, :last_name);
  ```

- Now let's look at the procedure version. The use of the plural of "name" in the name of the procedure indicates a change to more than one of the parameters:

  ```
  combine_and_format_names (first_name, last_name, full_name);
  ```

Generally speaking, when your function has a side effect such as the uppercasing of the parameter values, that function is less broadly useful. What if programmers don't want to have the other values uppercased? They would have to write their own function that does the same thing as format_name, but without the UPPER statements. This code redundancy will create nightmares down the road. If the function is supposed to return a formatted name based on the first and last names, then that is all it should do—never use OUT and IN OUT parameters with a function.

Don't interact with users

Such parameters are not the only kinds of side effects you may be tempted to slip into a function. Consider this Oracle Forms function, which retrieves the name of a company from its primary key:

```
FUNCTION company_name (company_id_in IN company.company_id%TYPE)
    RETURN VARCHAR2
IS
```

```
    CURSOR name_cur IS
        SELECT name FROM company
         WHERE company_id = company_id_in;
    name_rec name_cur%ROWTYPE;
BEGIN
    OPEN name_cur;
    FETCH name_cur INTO name_rec;
    IF name_cur%FOUND
    THEN
        CLOSE name_cur;
        RETURN name_rec.name;
    ELSE
        BELL;
        MESSAGE ('Invalid company ID: ' || TO_CHAR (company_id_in),
                 ACKNOWLEDGE);
        RAISE FORM_TRIGGER_FAILURE;
    END IF;
END;
```

When the company ID returns an existing company, the function properly closes the cursor and returns the company's name. When the SELECT statement comes up empty, however, I change my approach completely. Rather than return a value, I go into the equivalent of PL/SQL panic mode: ring the bell, display a message (and force the user to acknowledge that message), and then fail out of the calling trigger. I don't even close the cursor! Rather strong stuff, and very much out of place in this function.

My response to invalid data is a side effect in the function, made all the worse by the fact that my side effect completely substitutes for a RETURN. When the company ID does not find a match, I do not execute a RETURN statement at all.

The consequences of my error handling in this function are:

- This function can be called only in Oracle Forms. It is, however, a fairly generic task: take a primary key and return a name/description. It could be a function stored in the database and available to any program that needs to perform the lookup. I have now made that impossible.

- Anyone who calls this function gives up control over his or her own program. You cannot decide for yourself what to do if the name is not found. That message is displayed whether or not it is appropriate. That bell sounds even if users don't like to announce to everyone around them that they made a mistake. The best you can do is code an exception handler for FORM_TRIGGER_FAILURE in whatever trigger or program calls company_name.

A much better approach to the company_name function is simply to return a NULL value if the company is not found. Since the company name is a NOT NULL column, a NULL return value clearly indicates "no data found." This new approach is shown in the following example:

```
FUNCTION company_name (company_id_in IN company.company_id%TYPE)
    RETURN VARCHAR2
IS
    CURSOR name_cur IS
        SELECT name FROM company
         WHERE company_id = company_id_in;
    name_rec name_cur%ROWTYPE;

    no_company_found EXCEPTION;
BEGIN
    OPEN name_cur;
    FETCH name_cur INTO name_rec;
    IF name_cur%FOUND
    THEN
        CLOSE name_cur;
        RETURN name_rec.name;
    ELSE
        RAISE no_company_found;
    END IF;
EXCEPTION
    WHEN no_company_found OR OTHERS
    THEN
        CLOSE name_cur;
        RETURN NULL;
END;
```

This is now a nonjudgmental, mind-your-own-business function. It doesn't try to dictate the terms of surrender, or tell programmers who call it how they should handle a lack of data. It simply reports back the problem by returning a NULL value. Users of the function may then decide for themselves on an appropriate consequence, which might well consist of every action formerly embedded in the function itself:

```
new_company := company_name (:company.company_id);
IF new_company IS NULL
THEN
    BELL;
    MESSAGE
        ('Invalid company ID: ' || TO_CHAR (:company.company_id),
         ACKNOWLEDGE);
    RAISE FORM_TRIGGER_FAILURE;
END IF;
```

At least now the programmer has freedom of choice.

Side effects in functions come in many shapes and flavors. If you remember to keep the focus of the function on computing and returning its value, the resulting module will be more effectively and widely used.

Use a Single RETURN Statement for Successful Termination

A function exists to return a single value. The best way to structurally emphasize this single-minded focus in the body of the function is to make sure that the only RETURN statement in the execution section of the function is the last executable statement. Consider the following code-translating function:

```
FUNCTION status_desc (status_cd_in IN VARCHAR2) RETURN VARCHAR2
IS
BEGIN
   IF     status_cd_in = 'C' THEN RETURN 'CLOSED';
   ELSIF status_cd_in = 'O' THEN RETURN 'OPEN';
   ELSIF status_cd_in = 'A' THEN RETURN 'ACTIVE';
   ELSIF status_cd_in = 'I' THEN RETURN 'INACTIVE';
   END IF;
END;
```

Each of the different RETURN statements is actually a different exit point in this function. You are now probably saying to yourself, "This is such a simple program. What's wrong with using the different RETURN statements?"

Granted, the program is straightforward and short enough so that, at a glance, you understand its purpose and follow the exit flow. Unfortunately, it also is prone to failure. What if the status code that is passed into status_desc is not one of C, O, A, or I? Then the function does not even execute a RETURN statement, leaving the calling program with indeterminate results. Now examine the version of status_desc that relies on a single RETURN:

```
FUNCTION status_desc (status_cd_in IN VARCHAR2) RETURN VARCHAR2
IS
   return_value VARCHAR2 (20) := NULL;
BEGIN
   IF     status_cd_in = 'C' THEN return_value := 'CLOSED';
   ELSIF status_cd_in = 'O' THEN return_value := 'OPEN';
   ELSIF status_cd_in = 'A' THEN return_value := 'ACTIVE';
   ELSIF status_cd_in = 'I' THEN return_value := 'INACTIVE';
   END IF;
   RETURN return_value;
END;
```

Here, my IF statement assigns the description to a local variable. After the IF statement, the RETURN statement serves its purpose in life, which is to pass the value of the variable back to the calling program. Because I initialize the temporary description to NULL, if the status code is not one of the chosen four, then I return NULL. In any case, the result is that, by placing the RETURN statement at the last line of the execution section of the function, I always execute a RETURN statement when the function completes successfully. There are no holes in my return logic.

This approach is absolutely critical when your function is more elaborate and longer than 10 or 20 lines in length, perhaps even hundreds of lines long. It can be very difficult to follow multi-page complex logic, and nearly impossible to confirm, simply by reading the code, that the function always issues a RETURN statement for all branches of the logic. Your application works much more reliably if you build right into it the requirement that the only RETURN statement in the function occurs at the end of the program.

Build a function template

I realize that it is one thing to read through all of the tips in this book and, as you read them, nod in agreement with their wisdom. It is quite another thing to both remember the tips and make the time to put them to use in your code. The best way I have found to at least improve the chances that I follow even my own advice is to set hard and fast rules—and then stick to them. When it comes to "Use a single RETURN statement for successful termination," I try to always follow two simple rules when creating a function:

- Always declare a local variable named "return_value" with a datatype that matches the RETURN clause of the function. If I am returning a VARCHAR2, declare a VARCHAR2 local variable. If I am returning data with the same datatype as a table column, declare that. Here are two examples:

```
FUNCTION net_sales (company_id_in IN company.company_id%TYPE)
   RETURN NUMBER
IS
   return_value NUMBER;
BEGIN
   ...
END;
or:
FUNCTION company_name (company_id_in IN company.company_id%TYPE)
   RETURN company.name%TYPE
IS
   return_value company.name%TYPE;
BEGIN
   ...
END;
```

- Always make the last executable statement of my function the RETURN statement as follows:

```
RETURN return_value;
```

By following these two rules, the general structure of my function now looks like this:

```
FUNCTION function_name (parameter_list) RETURN datatype
IS
   return_value datatype;
BEGIN
```

```
    ... executable code of function ...

    RETURN return_value;
EXCEPTION
    ... optional exception section ...
END;
```

The name of the local variable states quite clearly that it is standing in for the data that is to be returned by the function. Any time this return_value variable is assigned a value in the function, you know that the function is fulfilling its purpose of generating a value to be returned with the RETURN statement. It provides a clean, understandable, and predictable structure for the function. I have even gone so far as to create a template script on disk that implements this guideline. It looks like this:

```
/* Filename on companion disk: functmpl.sf */
CREATE OR REPLACE FUNCTION fname () RETURN datatype
IS
    return_value datatype;
BEGIN
    RETURN return_value;
END fname;
```

Then I just have to search-and-replace on "fname" and "datatype" and I am all ready to go.

Exception handling

One exception to the rule of a single RETURN statement in a function concerns exception handling. A function should return a value, whether it completes successfully or it fails. Upon successful completion, you can use the above structure to guarantee that the RETURN executes. What if the function fails? Any exception handler in a function should have as its last executable statement a RETURN of its own, as this example shows:

```
FUNCTION present_value
    (FV IN NUMBER, interest_rate IN NUMBER, period IN NUMBER)
RETURN NUMBER
IS
    return_value NUMBER;
    negative_value EXCEPTION;
BEGIN
    return_value := FV / ((1 + interest_rate)**period);
    IF return_value < 0
    THEN
        RAISE negative_value;
    ELSE
        RETURN return_value;
    END IF;
EXCEPTION
    WHEN negative_value
```

```
    THEN
        RETURN 0;

    WHEN OTHERS
    THEN
        RETURN NULL;
  END;
```

When each handler has its own RETURN statement, you can be sure that the function returns a value regardless of the way it is terminated. The present_value function also illustrates another important principle: if the program encounters an error, always call an exception handler to deal with the problem. Do not process the error inline. PL/SQL provides a very structured distinction between the executable body of the program and the exception section. As soon as you hit an error or logical exception to normal processing, RAISE an exception to transfer control out of normal execution.

Avoid Exception Handlers for Normal Program Exits

There is always only one entry point for a module: the first executable statement is always the one that follows the BEGIN statement. PL/SQL does not allow you to enter a block at an arbitrary line of code. The same cannot be said, however, for the way in which a module terminates. A PL/SQL program unit may complete its execution either through the last executable statement, a RETURN statement, or the exception handler section, as is appropriate:

- The last executable statement in a program is the normal exit point for a procedure.

- The RETURN statement is the normal exit point for a function.

- The exception section is the way out of a module that has hit an error and raised an exception.

A programming language like PL/SQL is constructed very carefully: every keyword and element of syntax is chosen with a specific purpose. Although you can at times justify using a language construct in an unorthodox way, in most cases such an action will raise a red flag and be closely examined. One example of such linguistic abuse occurs when a programmer uses an exception handler to perform a normal program exit. Here is an example:

```
FUNCTION company_name (company_id_in IN company.company_id%TYPE)
    RETURN VARCHAR2
IS
    cname company.company_id%TYPE;
    found_it EXCEPTION;
BEGIN
    SELECT name INTO cname FROM company
    WHERE company_id = company_id_in;
```

```
        RAISE found_it;
   EXCEPTION
      WHEN NO_DATA_FOUND
      THEN
         RETURN NULL;
      WHEN found_it
      THEN
         RETURN cname;
   END;
```

In this function the programmer uses an implicit cursor to try to find the company that matches the incoming primary key. If no record is found, the program properly handles the NO_DATA_FOUND exception and returns NULL. But if a record is returned, then the program RAISEs an exception, which in turn returns the company name selected.

The found_it exception is not an exception at all. It indicates successful completion of the program. Rather than use an exception, the function should simply issue a RETURN with cname, indicating that the SELECT was successful:

```
   FUNCTION company_name (company_id_in IN company.company_id%TYPE)
      RETURN VARCHAR2
   IS
      cname company.company_id%TYPE;
   BEGIN
      SELECT name INTO cname FROM company
       WHERE company_id = company_id_in;
      RETURN cname;
   EXCEPTION
      WHEN NO_DATA_FOUND THEN     RETURN NULL;
   END;
```

In this case the replacement of the RAISE with a RETURN was obvious and straightforward; no other code changes were required. In other situations, it can take much more effort to undo the poor programming practices of others. It is much better to do the job right the first time!

Programmers are often tempted to use the RAISE statement because it acts like a GOTO: it immediately halts execution of the program and transfers control to the exception section. This GOTO-like behavior can be very convenient when a programmer cannot figure out how to use IF statements in a structured way to neatly end the program. In this case, the RAISE statement becomes an easy way out.

If you find yourself writing programs that rely on the RAISE statement to do something besides handle exceptions, take a step back. Examine the logical flow of the program and explore how you can use the standard control structures (IF, LOOP, and perhaps even GOTO as a last resort) to accomplish your task instead.

Use Assertion Modules to Validate Parameters and Assumptions

Just about every piece of software you write makes assumptions about the data it manipulates. For example, parameters may have only certain values or be within a certain range, or a string value should have a certain format. In both of these cases, an underlying data structure is assumed to have been created. It's fine to have such rules and assumptions, but it is also very important to verify or "assert" that none of the rules is being violated.

One approach you can take in this verification process is to make use of the IF statement at the beginning of your program. The status_desc function shown below uses the conditional construct to implicitly validate the value of the argument. The function does not actively or explicitly check to see if the status code argument is one of C, O, A, or I. Instead, the IF statement returns a non-null value only if a valid code is provided.

```
FUNCTION status_desc (status_cd_in IN VARCHAR2) RETURN VARCHAR2
IS
    return_value VARCHAR2 (20) := NULL;
BEGIN
    IF    status_cd_in = 'C' THEN return_value := 'CLOSED';
    ELSIF status_cd_in = 'O' THEN return_value := 'OPEN';
    ELSIF status_cd_in = 'A' THEN return_value := 'ACTIVE';
    ELSIF status_cd_in = 'I' THEN return_value := 'INACTIVE';
    END IF;
    RETURN return_value;
END;
```

The status_desc function does not really assert anything. If the programmer passes an invalid status code, the function returns NULL. Sometimes this kind of behavior makes sense. Perhaps a status code other than C, O, A, or I is a valid entry and a NULL description is useful information in the application. In that case, an assertion of argument validity is not needed.

On the other hand, what if a legal value should always be passed to status_desc? What if a different value means that a programmer has coded her use of the function improperly? If status_desc is an "internal" function accessed only by programmers and not intended to handle user input, then an illegal status code probably reflects a typographical error or a misunderstanding of the program's use. In this case, the lack of feedback by status_desc on the invalid argument results in hard-to-trace errors. Because the programmer is not informed of the typographical mistake when it happens, the problem propagates through other modules before it surfaces.

Trap invalid argument values

If the status_desc function is built to accept only four valid entries, then it should raise a red flag when that rule is broken. The following function shows a version of status_desc that adds an ELSE clause to trap an invalid entry:

```
FUNCTION status_desc (status_cd_in IN VARCHAR2) RETURN VARCHAR2
IS
    return_value VARCHAR2 (20) := NULL;
BEGIN
    IF    status_cd_in = 'C' THEN return_value := 'CLOSED';
    ELSIF status_cd_in = 'O' THEN return_value := 'OPEN';
    ELSIF status_cd_in = 'A' THEN return_value := 'ACTIVE';
    ELSIF status_cd_in = 'I' THEN return_value := 'INACTIVE';
    ELSE
        MESSAGE ('Invalid status code: ' || status_cd_in);
        RAISE FORM_TRIGGER_FAILURE;
    END IF;
    RETURN return_value;
END;
```

With this new version, programmers get immediate feedback if they pass an illegal value to status_desc. That problem is solved, but I personally find this solution less than totally satisfactory. Since it forces me to add several lines of code to the body of my program—lines that were added simply to handle values that never should have gotten into the program—this approach is somewhat intrusive and inelegant. Consider the alternative below:

```
FUNCTION status_desc (status_cd_in IN VARCHAR2) RETURN VARCHAR2
IS
    return_value VARCHAR2 (20) := NULL;
BEGIN
    /* Assert that the status code is valid */
    assert_condition (status_cd_in IN ('C', 'O', 'A', 'I'));

    /* Now perform processing of valid argument. */
    IF    status_cd_in = 'C' THEN return_value := 'CLOSED';
    ELSIF status_cd_in = 'O' THEN return_value := 'OPEN';
    ELSIF status_cd_in = 'A' THEN return_value := 'ACTIVE';
    ELSIF status_cd_in = 'I' THEN return_value := 'INACTIVE';
    END IF;
    RETURN return_value;

END;
```

The procedure, assert_condition, looks like this:

```
PROCEDURE assert_condition (condition_in IN BOOLEAN)
IS
BEGIN
    IF NOT condition_in
    THEN
        /* Uses generic PL/SQL exception */
```

```
            RAISE VALUE_ERROR;
        END IF;
    END;
```

Now the first line of my program is a call to a very general assertion module. I pass the condition, which must evaluate to TRUE in order for the assumptions to hold. In this case the condition was a fairly complex Boolean expression:

```
    status_cd_in IN ('C', 'O', 'A', 'I')
```

This kind of a program is called an *assertion module* because its single Boolean parameter asserts that a condition is true, and leaves it to the module to reject that claim. Clearly, there isn't much to assert_condition. It just hides an IF statement behind a procedural interface. Yet, by including the call to assert_condition, I can let the remainder of the body of my program concentrate on handling the valid data properly. I do not have to include special handling for illegal values.

Because assert_condition is very generic, I can use it in any program that has a condition I can express in a single Boolean expression. I don't have to code special nested logic repeatedly. I tell assert_condition what rule I want to test, and leave it to the module to take action (raise an exception) when necessary.

An application-specific assertion module

Of course, you can build less generic versions of assert_condition. The next function shows an assertion module for Oracle Forms that displays an optional message to the screen:

```
    PROCEDURE assert_condition
        (condition_in IN BOOLEAN, message_in IN VARCHAR2 := NULL)
    IS
    BEGIN
        IF NOT condition_in
        THEN
            /* Use NVL to substitute default message if not provided. */
            MESSAGE (NVL (message_in, 'Check Condition Failure!'));

            /* Raise an exception specific to Oracle Forms. */
            RAISE FORM_TRIGGER_FAILURE;
        END IF;
    END;
```

You can even produce assertion modules that handle very specific kinds of conditions. If you do a lot of work with record groups in Oracle Forms, you find yourself checking repeatedly at the beginning of your program to see that the name or handle for the record group points to a valid record group. You do this with the ID_NULL and FIND_GROUP built-ins, as follows:

```
    IF ID_NULL (FIND_GROUP ('monthly_sales'))
    THEN
        MESSAGE ('Record group does not exist!');
```

```
      RAISE FORM_TRIGGER_FAILURE;
   ELSE
      FOR month_count IN 1 .. GET_GROUP_ROW_COUNT ('monthly_sales')
      LOOP
         ... process monthly data ...
      END LOOP;
   END IF;
```

Again, rather than write these statements over and over in each of your programs, you can bundle them into a standalone module, as shown below:

```
assert_valid_group ('monthly_sales');
FOR month_count IN 1 .. GET_GROUP_ROW_COUNT ('monthly_sales')
LOOP
   ... process monthly data ...
END LOOP;
```

Then simply call that assertion program:

```
PROCEDURE assert_valid_group (rg_name_in IN VARCHAR2)
/*
|| Assertion: if there is not a valid Id for the record
|| group, display message and raise exception. This is a
|| "design" error; code should not continue executing.
*/
IS
   rg_id RECORDGROUP := FIND_GROUP (rg_name_in);
BEGIN
   IF ID_NULL (rg_id)
   THEN
      MESSAGE (' Record group  '||rg_name_in|| ' is not defined.');
   END IF;
END;
```

A big advantage of the assertion procedure over the ELSE clause is that it clearly states, at the very beginning of the module, the assumptions for that program. With the ELSE clause, a failure is a byproduct of the module's execution. The rule violation is only implied by the structure of the IF statement and not expressed explicitly.

Is an assertion module a side effect?

But wait. If I call assert_condition from within a function and the assertion fails, the function will not execute a RETURN statement. Doesn't the use of an assertion module violate my guideline to always return a value from a function? The assert_ condition procedure bails out of the calling module (or at least forces a transfer to the exception section) without any regard for whether a RETURN statement is needed. Even worse, doesn't the Oracle Forms version containing a MESSAGE statement contradict my suggestion to avoid side effects in a function?

Yes and no. Yes, I admit that when assert_condition RAISEs its exception, you do not issue a RETURN statement (unless you code for it yourself in the function, but then you would have to know which exception was RAISEd by assert_condition). I also admit that the MESSAGE is a side effect in the function, the main purpose of which is to return a row number in a table.

But I can explain everything, honest!

You see, the point of assert_condition is to test the underlying assumptions in the very structure of the module. If status_desc is called with an invalid code, that kind of error is very different from, say, a NO_DATA_FOUND when obtaining the name for a particular company ID number. The status_desc function as a whole is invalid if it is not passed a valid code. In this context, it doesn't even make sense to continue processing. The assert_condition procedure uncovers design level errors in the code that must be corrected before you can even worry about data entry errors or other application-level concerns.

The logic behind assert_condition is similar to the way Oracle Forms handles level 25 errors when it executes a form. No matter how high a value you have set for SYSTEM.MESSAGE_LEVEL, Oracle Forms always halts processing in a form when it encounters a level 25 error, which indicates a design error in the application.

Take Full Advantage of Local Modularization

A local module is a procedure or function that is defined within the declaration section of another module. The scope of a local module is the module in which it is declared. It is invisible to all other modules, and can be called only from within that defining module.

Few PL/SQL developers are aware of the local module feature, and fewer yet take full advantage of this capability. Yet I can think of few other aspects of the language that are more important to constructing clean, elegant, easily maintained programs. I strongly encourage you to use local modules at every possible opportunity, and offer several examples in this section to highlight their usefulness.

Local modules are very handy ways to "normalize" redundant code inside a program. If you perform the same calculation over and over again in a module, don't hardcode the calculation repeatedly. Instead, place it in its own function or procedure and then call that module. The power of such an approach is clear when you examine the following program. In the format_data procedure, I extract a value from the rg_sales record group, divide it by projected sales, and convert to a formatted string—over and over again. This code is taken from a production Oracle Forms application, and is actually just a small portion of the full set of more than two dozen repetitive calculations.

```
PROCEDURE format_data
   (projected_sales_in IN NUMBER, year_in IN INTEGER)
IS
   /* Declare local variables for calculations. */
   total_cost NUMBER (9);
   gross_profit NUMBER (9);
   crew_labor NUMBER (9);
   mgmt_labor NUMBER (9);
BEGIN
   :owner.total_cost_pc :=
      TO_CHAR((net_present_value ('total_sales', year_in) /
              projected_sales_in * 100),'999.99');
   :owner.gross_profit_pc :=
      TO_CHAR((net_present_value ('gross_profit', year_in) /
              projected_sales_in * 100),'999.99');
   :owner.crew_labor_pc :=
      TO_CHAR((net_present_value ('crew_labor', year_in) /
              projected_sales_in * 100),'999.99');
   :owner.mgmt_labor_pc :=
      TO_CHAR((net_present_value ('mgmt_labor', year_in) /
              projected_sales_in * 100),999.99');
END;
```

I suppose that when you work in a Windows environment, it isn't necessarily such a big deal to write code like this. You cut and paste, cut and paste ... who knows? You might even use Microsoft Recorder or some other utility to automate the process. However you manage it, though, you still end up with lots of repetitions of the same fragment of code. You still end up with code that is hard to maintain.

Because I have exposed the way I perform the calculation, I must upgrade each distinct calculation whenever a change is required (different numeric format, different numeric formula, etc.). If, on the other hand, I hide the calculation behind the interface of a callable module, then the calculation is coded only once. With the help of a local module, the format_data procedure is transformed as shown in this example:

```
PROCEDURE format_data
   (projected_sales_in IN NUMBER, year_in IN INTEGER)
IS
   total_cost      NUMBER (9);
   gross_profit    NUMBER (9);
   crew_labor      NUMBER (9);
   mgmt_labor      NUMBER (9);

   /*--------------------- Local Module ---------------------*/
   FUNCTION npv (column_in IN VARCHAR2) RETURN VARCHAR2 IS
   BEGIN
      RETURN
         TO_CHAR((net_present_value ('' || column_in, year_in) /
                 projected_sales_in * 100),'999.99');
   END;
```

```
BEGIN
    /* Perform direct, readable assignments using the function. */
    :owner.total_cost_pc    := npv ('total_cost');
    :owner.gross_profit_pc := npv ('gross_profit');
    :owner.crew_labor_pc    := npv ('crew_labor');
    :owner.mgmt_labor_pc    := npv ('mgmt_labor');
END;
```

The total amount of code is less than before and the body of format_data is so much more readable. Notice how the name of the procedure actually helps make the code self-documenting. The procedure name states precisely the nature of the calculation performed. Any additional documentation would in itself be redundant. With npv, if I ever need to change the format mask or the formula, I simply make a change to the npv function and then recompile. No fuss, no muss.

Notice that it doesn't make any sense to create npv as a standalone module outside of the format_data procedure. This calculation is very specific to the format_data program. Because no other module would ever call it, you needn't clutter up your stored procedure environment or your Oracle Forms program unit listing with this module-specific utility.

I have found that few developers are aware of the ability to create local modules. I have also found that these modules-within-a-module play an important role in allowing me to write well-structured, elegant programs.

These days it seems that whenever I write a program with more than 20 lines, and with any complexity whatsoever, I end up creating several local modules. It helps me see my way through to a solution in the following ways:

- Conceptualizing my code at a higher level of abstraction by assigning a name to a whole sequence of statements.
- Performing top-down design and step-wise refinement of my requirements.
- Extracting local modules at a later date, thus making truly independent, reusable procedures or functions if the need arises.

Take a look at any of your more complex programs and I guarantee you will quickly identify segments of the code that would serve you better bundled into a local module.

Be Wary of Modules Without Any Parameters

While you certainly shouldn't create parameters where you don't need them, I have found that a lack of parameters in a module usually reflects a limited vision of how the module will be used. That limited vision generally translates directly to a limited use of the module.*

In many of the cases, modules without parameter lists are fundamentally crippled—they force a programmer to know about the internals of the module and therefore cannot act as true black boxes. This situation arises most often from an overreliance on global variables.

Consider the example of the parameterless company_name function shown here. This program is driven by an Oracle Forms global variable. It returns the name of the company corresponding to the company ID number in the global.

```
FUNCTION company_name RETURN VARCHAR2
IS
   cname company.company_id%TYPE;
BEGIN
   SELECT name INTO cname FROM company
    WHERE company_id = :GLOBAL.company_id;
   RETURN cname;
EXCEPTION
   WHEN NO_DATA_FOUND THEN    RETURN NULL;
END;
```

This function works just fine, as long as I make sure that I have set the global variable to the appropriate company ID before I call the function. If I look only at the function's specification:

```
FUNCTION company_name RETURN VARCHAR2
```

there is no way for me to know that the function requires a particular global variable. It simply tells me, "I will give you a company name." But for which company? The lack of a parameter renders this function largely unusable.

Fortunately, the situation is easily remedied. The version of company_name below takes a company ID number and returns the corresponding company name:

```
FUNCTION company_name
    (company_id_in IN company.company_id%TYPE)
RETURN VARCHAR2
IS
   cname company.company_id%TYPE;
BEGIN
   SELECT name INTO cname FROM company
    WHERE company_id = company_id_in;
   RETURN cname;
EXCEPTION
   WHEN NO_DATA_FOUND THEN    RETURN NULL;
END;
```

---

* Very few modules truly have no input or output. Two examples of appropriate parameterless modules are a procedure that simply encapsulates a sequence of statements and a procedure that manipulates global variables. Such programs are the exception rather than the rule.

Now, compare the specifications for these two versions of company_name:

- First, a function that hides source of primary key:

```
FUNCTION company_name RETURN VARCHAR2;
```

- Next, a function that requires input of primary key:

```
FUNCTION company_name (company_id_in IN company.company_id%TYPE)
   RETURN VARCHAR2;
```

In the first case, I don't have any clue whatsoever about how I can provide the company ID to the function in order to look up the name. In order to use this version of company_name, I must either depend on external documentation, which states the reliance on :GLOBAL.company_id, or look at the body of the function. External documentation of modules is always something to be avoided, or at least kept to an absolute minimum. Because it is hard to maintain, it is often out of date. As for taking a peek at the body of the function, well, that simply isn't always possible and is never desirable. You should design your modules so that a developer needs nothing more than the specification in order to understand how to use that module.

In the second case, the specification is very explicit about needing a company ID number in order to look up the name. In the case of company_name, the company ID number is the "linkage" between the code calling company_name and the internal implementation of the function.

Whenever possible, you should make such linkages explicit and visible; the best way to do this is to place those items in the parameter list of the module.

Create Independent Modules

When you build modules, you need to be able to reuse them in as many different situations as possible, both within the current application and perhaps even in other, yet-to-be-developed systems. In order to do this, you will want to create modules that are as independent as possible both from other modules and from data structures defined in your current application.

Think of a module as a black box, which hides implementational complexities, often changing data structures, workarounds, and other sensitive elements of the application. Programmers using the module should not have to know how it does its job; they need only know the module's name, parameters, and return value (if a function). On the flip side (the inside of the module), the module should not be dependent on anything but the values coming in through the parameter list in order to do its job.

Personal computers move steadily towards an architecture of "plug and play:" the various components of the computer can be plugged together in different combinations and from different manufacturers. You will be certain that the result is a functioning computer because the hardware and software manufacturers agree on the standards that govern how the different components interact. They also (try to) make certain that nothing inside their own components causes a conflict with another component. Each product respects the boundaries around another's area of functionality.

The advantages of plug and play in the computer marketplace are many: lowered cost due to reduced reliance on proprietary technology, increased reliability, greater choice for consumers, and easier upgrades. All of these same advantages accrue to software following the same plug and play strategy. If you design your modules so that they are both tightly focused on a particular area of functionality and are simultaneously as generic as possible, and if those modules interact through well-defined interfaces, the resulting applications will:

- *Contain fewer bugs.* The more you rely on the same modules again and again, the less code you will write, and, as a result, there will be a narrower opportunity to introduce new problems into your code.

- *Adapt more easily to change* (enhancement and redesign). Change in one module is less likely to cause a ripple effect through all the rest of your code. As long as the interface through which calls are made to that module does not change, no other programs are affected.

- *Be developed more rapidly.* As the percentage of reusable code increases, you only need to concentrate on building additional layers of modules to add new functionality. If a module's design does not constrain its usefulness, you will use it more often.

But I suppose you have read all of this before. The question I'd like to address now concerns what you can do to improve the plug and play quality of your code. In this section I offer some general tips and examples that I have found helpful.

Stretch the Possibilities of the Module

You build a module to meet a requirement. A requirement is often stated in the most straightforward terms: "Calculate the total profits of a company," "Look up the description for a code," "Display the contents of a PL/SQL table," "Count the number of words in a string." Most developers proceed to implement these requirements in the most straightforward manner possible, without giving much thought to the full variety of ways in which the module might be used. The resulting program will probably work fine for the current requirement. Chances are great, however, that the requirement will expand or you will encounter a slightly different requirement in the next application—either of which will require a revamping of the module.

Whenever you build a module, take a moment to examine the motivation for the program. What immediate needs does it satisfy? Do you see other ways that the module might, could, or should be used? Can you incorporate these other areas of functionality into the module while still preserving the original purpose of the module? If so, you will end up with a module that, while requiring more code and is more complicated internally, will be more widely used and appreciated.

Keep the Focus of Your Module

Sure, I want you to stretch, to use your imagination, to think of the many different contexts in which a module might be used. I do not, however, want you to end up with a kitchen sink module that does everything, or does a little bit of everything for every situation. The trick is to "fill out" the module's applicability without expanding its scope.

If your function is supposed to count the number of separate "words" in a string, by all means broaden your concept of word to include punctuation. Give users of the module the option of counting just actual words, just punctuation, or all words. But don't also "enhance" the module to return the size of the largest word, the size of the smallest word, and the number of spaces in the word. Chances are that no one will use such a program.

A module should never be used as a dumping ground for miscellaneous actions, which otherwise do not seem to have a place to go. For a module to be applicable to many different situations in more than one application, it should do one thing and do it well.

Use Parameters Liberally

A direct consequence of making a module generic and flexible is that you will increase the length of your parameter list. Compare the parameter lists of the two procedures shown in the following example, in which two modules count the number of words in a string:

```
FUNCTION number_of_words (string_in IN VARCHAR2)
/*
|| Function returns the number of words in a string. A word
|| is any set of characters separated by a space.
*/
RETURN INTEGER;

FUNCTION number_of_atomics
/*
|| Function returns the number of atomics in a string. An atomic is
|| either a "word" (contiguous numbers or letters) or a delimiter.
||
|| Examples of results:
```

```
||    number_of_atomics ('this, is%not.') ==> 7
||    number_of_atomics ('this, is%not.', 'WORD') ==> 3
||    number_of_atomics ('this, is%not.', 'DELIMITER') ==> 4
||    number_of_atomics ('this, is%not.', 'WORD', ' ') ==> 2
*/
    (string_in IN VARCHAR2,
     count_type_in IN VARCHAR2 := 'ALL',
     delimiters_in IN VARCHAR2 := parse.std_delimiters)
   RETURN INTEGER;
```

The number_of_atomic function (drawn from the ps_parse package found on the disk) has two additional parameters. The second parameter, count_type_in, determines the type of count to perform on the string. The third parameter, delimiters_in, allows the programmer to specify the characters that act as delimiters in the string. The default values on these parameters not only allow me to call number_of_atomics as simply and easily as number_of_words, but when needed this function can do so much more for me.

Again, you can go too far with a good thing. The human mind seems to be fairly comfortable juggling up to seven items of information at a time. After that, we simply have trouble keeping it all straight. Modules with more than seven or eight parameters are difficult for programmers to use. If you create a module with an enormous parameter list, it will be intimidating and confusing to programmers. Because too much effort will be required to use the module, it is likely to be ignored or used improperly.

If you find that you are passing many attributes of the same entity as individual parameters, you might consider replacing all of those separate parameters with a single record parameter. Suppose you create a module to insert a company into the database. The company table has 25 columns. Are you going to create 25 parameters? Who wants to create all those separate variables and pass them into the module? You could instead create a record based on the table as follows:

```
DECLARE
    company_rec company%ROWTYPE;
BEGIN
    ... Fill the columns of the record as needed ...
    add_company (company_rec);
END;
```

Notice that the add_company module now just takes the record as a parameter, yet you can still pass all the company information you need to the INSERT statement inside add_company.

Avoid Global Variables and Data Structures

Global data sure is convenient. You can refer to it anywhere inside your application. You can transfer values from one module to another without having to expand the module's parameter lists. From the standpoint of plug and play, however, global data is a very bad idea.

When a module relies on a global variable, it is dependent on information from outside of that module, which is not passed to the module via the parameter list. As a result, the interface to that module does not completely describe the ways in which a programmer can use the module. In order to use the module, I must make sure that the global variable contains the proper value. If the module changes a global variable or data structure, I must ensure that this change does not affect my program. I cannot, in other words, call the module without worrying about side effects.

If your module relies on global data, it is also much less likely that the module could be reused in an entirely different application. A function that counts the number of atomics in a string could certainly apply to any number of completely distinct systems. If that function refers to a global variable, like a list of delimiters or a maximum size of string, then each system has to have a way to set those values. Who is going to bother with all of that? They'll just write their own version, perhaps making a copy of the original. Yuch!

There are times, however, when global data is both justified and necessary:

- Global variables containing system-wide named constants reduce the hardcoding of literal values in your programs.

- Global variables offer a way to communicate between application components that might otherwise be mutually deaf and mute.

- Global variables can sometimes improve performance over passing parameters, as happens with complex structures like PL/SQL tables.

For these reasons, very few applications succeed in completely resisting the use of global variables. If you are aware of the drawbacks of this kind of data, however, you will at least justify and keep your use of them to a minimum.

Construct Abstract Data Types (ADTs)

The term *abstract data type* is about as dry and technical sounding as you can get. Yet the concept of an abstract data type, or ADT, is something we apply—or should apply—in every single one of our application efforts, sometimes without even realizing that we are doing it. An abstract data type is a collection of information and operations that act on that information. An ADT can represent computer objects such as lists, records, stacks, arrays, and tables; but an ADT can also represent real-world objects, such as a company, a product, or the set of assembly line operations at a factory.

The power behind the ADT lies in the first word of its name: abstract. When you create an ADT, you work with objects as opposed to variables, columns, and other computer science items. You perform an abstraction from the implementation details to the "thing in itself" and work on a higher level.

PL/SQL offers several different constructs with which to build and manage ADTs, most importantly the package. The most general description of an ADT, in fact, sounds just like the description of a package: a collection of data and operations on that data.

Every application you build is filled with the need and potential for abstract data types. In order to construct an ADT, however, you first need to be able to identify which data is best represented at a new and higher level of abstraction. You then need to be able to build that ADT so that the programmatic interface to the underlying data is consistent and effective.

Build an ADT in Phases

You should build an ADT in four phases:

1. *Clarify the data to be represented by the ADT.* Make sure you understand all the attributes of the data and the way it is used in your application. When your ADT is based on a database table or entity, much of this phase is already done.

2. *List the key features and functions of the ADT as it relates to the underlying data.* Don't write any code until you have come up with a comprehensive list of all the operations on and by the ADT.

3. *Build the interface for the ADT.* This is equivalent to designing the specification of all the modules which are called by programmers to manipulate the ADT. Translate the list of features into procedure and function calls. You need to decide on module names and their parameter lists.

4. *Build the body of code behind the interface.* You know how programmers will manage the ADT, since they must work with the specification. The final phase is to actually implement the ADT. What internal data structures will you use? What code will you share among the different modules of the ADT? What data will you hide from view?

Some ADT Guidelines

Here are some guidelines you should follow when designing an ADT:

- *Maintain a consistent level of abstraction.* This is probably the most important aspect of your ADT implementation. All the modules you build to represent your abstract data structure should operate with the same level of data. If the ADT representing a company's product is implemented as a PL/SQL record, then all of the modules should accept or return this record structure. If there are alternative means of identifying a particular product (the product name, the ID number, the record as a whole), then provide functions that convert between the different identifier formats so that the programmer can easily shift to the ADT structure required by the main modules.

- *Provide a comprehensive interface to the abstract data type.* Make sure that the user (a programmer, in this case) can perform all necessary operations on the ADT without having to go around the interface you build to the ADT. Hide all the implementational details of your ADT behind calls to procedures and modules—without exception. If you implement a stack data structure as an ADT and forget to provide a way to pop a value off the stack, the programmer will have to invade your turf and mess around in your stack to retrieve the needed value. Of course, this is an obvious example. In many situations the gaps in an ADT's implementation are less obvious and sometimes discovered only when a programmer starts using the ADT in earnest.

- *Use the package structure, the most natural repository for ADT code.* The ADT represents a "thing" by presenting a layer of code that allows you to perform operations on that thing as a whole, rather than on its individual components. The package joins related objects together and so corresponds closely to the ADT. If your ADT represents a caller, then create a package named "caller" containing all the modules, variables, cursors, etc., needed to manipulate the caller. The package clearly distinguishes between the public and private parts of the code. The public objects make up the interface to the ADT. The private objects contain and hide the implementational details for the ADT.

Progress Box as ADT

The advantages of working with abstract data types should become clear from the following example of a "progress box". The development team of a financials application found that their Oracle Forms 4.0 application would not change the cursor from an arrow to an hourglass with long-running PL/SQL programs. With a wait-time of between three and five minutes, they were concerned that users would get impatient, click irresponsibly with the mouse, and possibly cause damage. Their solution was to construct a progress box aimed at keeping the user informed of the program's progress.

The progress box consisted of a window named progress_window, a canvas view named cv_progress, and the following three items, all defined in a block named b_progress:

process_name
    The description of the program currently executing

percent_done

A textual description of the percentage of the job completed

thermometer

A graphical representation of the percentage of the job completed

A very clever programmer found that by setting the visual attributes (specifically the font) of the thermometer in the item, the letter "n" would appear as a solid box (blue!) on the screen. Two letters would appear as two blocks and so on. Make the item ten characters long and you have a graphical representation of percentage completion in 10% increments.

Here are the four lines of code needed to show 20% completed:

```
:B_PROGRESS.PERCENT_DONE := '20 % Complete.';
:B_PROGRESS.THERMOMETER   := 'nn';
Show_View('CV_PROGRESS');
synchronize;
```

Actually, before any particular percentage of completion was displayed, it was necessary to initialize the progress box. The following five lines set the process name (in effect, the title for the bar) and initialized the other items:

```
SET_WINDOW_PROPERTY ('PROGRESS_WINDOW', Visible, Property_On);
:C_CONTROL.NBT_PROCESS_NAME := 'Updating Profit and Loss data...';
:C_CONTROL.NBT_PERCENT_DONE := '0 % Complete.';
:C_CONTROL.NBT_THERMOMETER  := 'n';
Show_View('CV_PROGRESS');
synchronize;
```

This progress box was also needed within a loop, which executed over a period of up to ten years. The development team was able to adapt their basic progress box code to dynamically adjust according to the loop index, year_count:

```
:B_PROGRESS.PERCENT_DONE :=
    TO_CHAR (round((year_count / years_displayed * 100),0)) ||
        ' % Complete.';
:B_PROGRESS.THERMOMETER   := :B_PROGRESS.THERMOMETER || 'n';
Show_View('CV_PROGRESS');
synchronize;
```

In this case, they simply concatenated another "n" onto the current value of the thermometer for each iteration of the loop.

Of course, they needed to hide the progress box when the program ended:

```
Hide_View('CV_PROGRESS');
SET_WINDOW_PROPERTY('PROGRESS_WINDOW', Visible, Property_Off);
synchronize;
```

Finally, there were also times when they would use the progress box to display a message, but not use the thermometer. The following code shows the lines required to implement this variation on the progress box:

```
SET_WINDOW_PROPERTY('PROGRESS_WINDOW', Visible, Property_On);
:B_PROGRESS.PROCESS_NAME := 'Building reports...';
:B_PROGRESS.PERCENT_DONE := null;
:B_PROGRESS.THERMOMETER  := null;
Show_View('CV_PROGRESS');
synchronize;
```

My first impression of their approach was that it was very clever. It had a nice look to it and definitely saved the users from wondering what was happening in their application. Then I took a look inside the form and found that the samples of code I presented previously were repeated over and over again in various forms in many different procedures, triggers, and functions.

Price Paid for Code Dispersion

The developers had not treated the progress box as a thing in itself, as an abstract data type. Instead, the progress was simply a series of executable statements: set the title, change the thermometer setting, make the view visible, etc. Because they did not abstract those individual statements into an object with rules and structure, they were forced to repeat those statements wherever a progress box of any form was needed. This approach not only required repetition of the statements, it also exposed the particular elements of the implementation (the fact that the letter "n" was needed to created a box on the screen, for example) throughout the application.

Well, the developers worked through these issues and got their application moved into production and everything seemed fine. Then a couple of things happened. First, I was asked to review the code with the objective of reducing code volume and improving performance. Second, we converted the application to Oracle Forms 4.5.

Replacing the sequence of executable statements used to produce the progress box with a procedure call was an obvious way to reduce the amount of code in the application. But the conversion to Oracle Forms 4.5 raised another whole issue: the font used to produce a graphical box from the letter "n" wasn't available any longer in the list of fonts for visual attributes! All the individual assignments of the thermometer to the letter "n" would now do little more than make a blue "n" appear on the screen.

These two factors forced us to completely revamp the progress box implementation. Instead of representing the progress box with the separate lines of code, we needed to create an object called a progress box, figure out the ways that progress box was used in the application, and create modules that would implement those different methods. I wanted to be particularly careful to not let individual programmers hardcode a letter or symbol, like "n", in order to achieve the desired effect in the thermometer item.

After some analysis, I determined that the application used the progress box in three ways:

- To display a message (which turns off the display of the thermometer bar)
- To display a percentage completion message with the thermometer
- To hide the box from view

I then converted this high-level specification to a package specification, as shown in the next section.

The progress package specification

```
/* filename on companion disk: progress.fpp */
PACKAGE progress
IS
    PROCEDURE msg (msg_in IN VARCHAR2);

    PROCEDURE bar
        (pct_in IN INTEGER,
         thermom_in IN INTEGER := 1,
         init_in IN VARCHAR2 := 'NOINIT',
         msg_in IN VARCHAR2 := NULL);

    PROCEDURE hide (item_prop_in IN INTEGER := PROPERTY_OFF);

END progress;
```

The msg procedure simply displays the provided message and hides the thermometer.

The bar procedures takes four parameters as follows:

pct_in

The percentage completed as a number. The module then converts the number to a string in the format "20% Completed."

thermom_in

The number of boxes to be added to the current thermometer setting.

init_in

Indicates whether the thermometer should be initialized with the thermom_in number of boxes ('INIT'), or if the thermometer should have that number of boxes concatenated to the current thermometer display.

msg_in

   The message to be displayed above the thermometer, if any.

The hide procedure hides the property box and optionally sets the property of
the thermometer item.

The package body needed to consolidate all of the formerly hardcoded executable statements in the application is shown in the next section. Notice that
programmers do not specify a character, like "n", when calling the progress.bar
procedure. Instead, they just indicate the number of boxes to add to the thermometer. Inside the package, a one-character string named thermom_char is set to a
value of "n". If the font requires a change, this single variable is modified and
none of the code that calls progress.bar is affected.

The progress package body

```
/* filename on companion disk: progress.fpp */
PACKAGE BODY progress
IS
    thermom_char VARCHAR2(1) := 'n';

    PROCEDURE msg (msg_in IN VARCHAR2) IS
    BEGIN
        SET_WINDOW_PROPERTY (handles.progress_window_id, Visible, Property_On);
        SET_ITEM_PROPERTY (handles.thermometer_id, DISPLAYED, PROPERTY_OFF);
        :b_progress.percent_done := msg_in;
        :b_progress.process_name := NULL;
        :b_progress.thermometer := NULL;
        SHOW_VIEW (handles.cv_progress_id);
        synchronize;
    END;

    PROCEDURE bar
        (pct_in IN INTEGER,
         thermom_in IN INTEGER := 1,
         init_in IN VARCHAR2 := 'NOINIT',
         msg_in IN VARCHAR2 := NULL)
    IS
        /* Create the string to be added to the thermometer. */
        bar_stg VARCHAR2(80) := LPAD (thermom_char, thermom_in, thermom_char);
    BEGIN
        SET_WINDOW_PROPERTY (handles.progress_window_id, Visible, PROPERTY_ON);
        SET_ITEM_PROPERTY (handles.thermometer_id, DISPLAYED, PROPERTY_ON);
        IF msg_in IS NOT NULL
        THEN
            :b_progress.process_name := msg_in;
        END IF;
        :b_progress.percent_done := TO_CHAR (pct_in) || ' % Complete';
        IF UPPER (init_in) = 'INIT'
        THEN
            :b_progress.thermometer := bar_stg;
        ELSE
```

```
                :b_progress.thermometer := :b_progress.thermometer || bar_stg;
          END IF;
          SHOW_VIEW (handles.cv_progress_id);
          synchronize;
      END;


      PROCEDURE hide (item_prop_in IN INTEGER := PROPERTY_OFF)
      IS
      BEGIN
          Hide_View (handles.cv_progress_id);
          SET_ITEM_PROPERTY (handles.thermometer_id, DISPLAYED, item_prop_in);
          SET_WINDOW_PROPERTY (handles.progress_window_id, Visible,
              PROPERTY_OFF);
          synchronize;
      END;


  END progress;
```

Now I can replace the cumbersome, virtually unmaintainable sequences of state-ments with a single call to the package modules. The following examples show the "before and after" of the progress box code.

- Initialize the thermometer with a title, empty thermometer, and 0% completed:

  Before:

  ```
  :B_PROGRESS.PROCESS_NAME := 'Updating profit and loss data...';
  :B_PROGRESS.PERCENT_DONE := '0 % Complete.';
  :B_PROGRESS.THERMOMETER   := NULL;
  Show_View('CV_PROGRESS');
  synchronize;
  ```

  After:

  ```
  progress.bar (0, 0, 'INIT', 'Updating Profit and Loss data...');
  ```

- Set the thermometer to 20% completion:

  Before:

  ```
  :B_PROGRESS.PERCENT_DONE := '20 % Complete.';
  :B_PROGRESS.THERMOMETER   := 'nn';
  Show_View('CV_PROGRESS');
  synchronize;
  ```

  After:

  ```
  progress.bar (20, 2);
  ```

- Adjust dynamically the contents of the progress box according to the loop index, year_count:

  Before:

  ```
  :B_PROGRESS.PERCENT_DONE :=
      TO_CHAR (round((year_count / years_displayed * 100),0)) ||
              ' % Complete.';
  ```

```
:B_PROGRESS.THERMOMETER   := :B_PROGRESS.THERMOMETER || 'n';
Show_View('CV_PROGRESS');
synchronize;
```

After:

```
progress.bar (ROUND((year_count / years_displayed * 100),0), 1);
```

- Hide the progress box when the program completed and control was returned to the user:

  Before:

```
Hide_View('CV_PROGRESS');
SET_WINDOW_PROPERTY('PROGRESS_WINDOW', Visible, Property_Off);
synchronize;
```

  After:

```
progress.hide;
```

By treating the progress box as an object with rules governing its use and appearance, I was able to greatly reduce the volume of code required. The resulting statements are also much more comprehensible and maintainable.

Tips for Parameter Design

This section offers tips for designing and using your parameters most effectively.

Document All Parameters and Their Functions

In the header of the program or directly next to each parameter, you should include comments explaining any assumptions about the parameter and the way it's used in the program. Such information would handle the following situations:

- The units of measure for a numeric parameter. If the parameter is speed_in, is the speed in miles-per-hour or kilometers-per-hour?

- The valid ranges for incoming parameter values. Remember that all parameters are unconstrained. You cannot, for example, declare a parameter as NUMBER(3). So if a parameter does have a valid range or list of values, explain that.

- Invalid or impossible values for the parameters. If the speed_in parameter cannot have a value less than 0 or greater than 200, a statement to that effect can help a person who is fixing a bug in that program or in a program that calls it.

- Error status and flag information. If the program returns a status flag, code, or message, you should indicate this at the start of the program so that anyone who reads the program is aware of the expected values.

It can be particularly handy to include these comments in the actual parameter list because that documentation then becomes part of the program's specification. Then, even when developers do not have access to the body of the program, as with packages like Oracle Developer/2000 PL/SQL libraries, they can still see important information about the parameters in the specification.

The following procedure specification illustrates some of these recommendations:

```
PROCEDURE calc_elapsed_time
    (start_time_in IN NUMBER /* Range: 0 through 24 */,
     start_loc_in  IN VARCHAR2 /* NY, CHI or SF */,
     end_loc_in    IN VARCHAR2 /* DC, LA, or NO */,
     valid_out     OUT VARCHAR2 /* VALID or INVALID */);
```

It can be hard to make time for this kind of documentation, but it can make a big difference in how easily your programs can be used by others.

Use Self-Identifying Parameters (Avoid Boolean Values)

A common parameter for a module is a flag that relies on two-valued logic (TRUE or FALSE) to pass information to the module. The temptation in such a case is to declare the parameter to be type BOOLEAN. With this approach, when you call the program, you will pass either TRUE or FALSE. You will find in these circumstances that while the specification for your program is very readable, the way you call it in other programs will be difficult to follow.

Consider the parameters for the following procedure, which is used to generate reports and optionally print the reports out on the specified queue:

```
PROCEDURE generate_report
    (report_id_in IN NUMBER,
     queue_in IN VARCHAR2,
     clean_up_log_files_in IN BOOLEAN := TRUE,
     print_file_in IN BOOLEAN := TRUE);
```

In order to make generate_report more flexible, the developer has provided two Boolean parameters:

clean_up_log_files_in
> TRUE if the procedure should clean up (remove) any log and listing files created in the process of generating the report; FALSE to keep the files in place, usually for purposes of debugging.

print_file_in
> TRUE if the output file of the report should be printed; FALSE to skip the print step.

When one glances over the procedure's specification, the purpose and usage of each parameter seems clear enough. But take a look at how I would call this procedure:

```
generate_report (report_id, 'PRINT_QUEUE1', TRUE, TRUE);
```

As you can see, these Boolean parameter values are not very descriptive. Without the context provided by their names, actual Boolean parameters are unable to self-document their effect. A developer (or, most importantly, a maintainer) of the code must go back to the source to understand the impact of a particular value. That completely defeats the information hiding principle of modular programming.

This problem is not restricted to true Booleans, either. You will be just as confused by parameters acting as "pseudo-Boolean" parameters. In the following version of generate_report, the BOOLEAN parameters are replaced by VARCHAR2 parameters, to little advantage.

```
PROCEDURE generate_report
    (report_id_in IN NUMBER, queue_in IN VARCHAR2,
     clean_up_log_files_in IN VARCHAR2:= 'Y',
     print_file_in IN VARCHAR2 := 'Y');
```

With these VARCHAR2 replacements, calls to generate_report now look like this:

```
generate_report (new_report_id, temp_queue_name,'Y', 'Y');
```

While it is true that I no longer have the obscure TRUE or FALSE to deal with in the call interface, it would be hard to argue that "Y" or "N" is any more illuminating. A much better approach replaces Boolean and pseudo-Boolean parameters with character parameters whose acceptable values are descriptions of the action or situation.

```
PROCEDURE generate_report
    (report_id_in IN NUMBER, queue_in IN VARCHAR2,
     clean_up_log_files_in IN VARCHAR2:= 'CLEANUP',
     print_file_in IN VARCHAR2 := 'PRINT');
```

Now a call to generate_report states clearly its intentions:

```
generate_report
    (report_id, queue_name, 'CLEANUP', 'PRINT');
```

or:

```
generate_report
    (report_id, queue_name, 'NO_CLEANUP', 'PRINT');
```

or:

```
generate_report
    (report_id, queue_name, 'NO_CLEANUP', 'NO_PRINT');
```

As you can see from these examples, I write my procedures to accept an unambiguous affirmative value (CLEANUP) and the most clearly-defined negative form (NO_CLEANUP). One complication to this style is that you need to validate the parameter values; if you were using a Boolean, the strong datatyping in PL/SQL would guarantee that a legal value is passed.

Assign Values to All OUT and IN OUT Parameters

Make sure that all OUT and IN OUT parameters are assigned values in your procedure (you should never have such parameters in a function, after all). Remember that any assignments made to OUT or IN OUT parameters in the body of a program are ignored when an exception is raised in that program. PL/SQL performs its own internal rollback of all incomplete changes. This can result in situations where the program that called the function or procedure with these parameters does not have reliable data with which to work.

Perform assignments within exception handlers

The way to make sure that you assign values to your OUT and IN OUT parameters whether the program succeeds or fails is to perform assignments within the exception handlers. Consider the generate_raise procedure:

```
PROCEDURE generate_raise
    (employee_id_in IN employee.employee_id%TYPE,
     salary_out OUT employee.salary%TYPE)
IS
    sal NUMBER;
    days_employed BINARY_INTEGER;
BEGIN
    -- Initialize the salary to zero.
    salary_out := 0;
    SELECT salary, SYSDATE - hire_date
      INTO sal, days_employed
      FROM employee
     WHERE employee_id = employee_id_in;
    salary_out := sal * (days_employed/365 + .15);
END;
```

Because the procedure does not have an exception section, any errors arising from the implicit cursor ("SELECT ... FROM employee ...") are not trapped in the program. As a result, generate_raise does not always return a valid amount in the salary_out parameter. By including an exception section, we can trap such errors and assign a value to salary_out, as shown in this example:

```
PROCEDURE generate_raise
    (employee_id_in IN employee.employee_id%TYPE,
     salary_out OUT employee.salary%TYPE)
IS
    sal NUMBER;
    days_employed BINARY_INTEGER;
BEGIN
    ... as shown above ...
EXCEPTION
    /*
    || Handle all exceptions in this single handler:
    || set the salary_out to zero.
    */
```

```
WHEN OTHERS THEN
    salary_out := 0;
END;
```

Now you can be sure that salary_out always has a value. Of course, it might not make sense to simply set the salary to zero when an error occurs. By doing so, you have placed a special, undocumented meaning on that value of zero. It doesn't just mean a very low salary. It means something went wrong.

It is generally not a good idea to load a variable with double meanings like that. It is hard to document and it makes the procedure difficult for people to use. Even if you changed the assignment in the exception handler to return NULL, you still have blurred the use of the salary_out parameter.

Use a flag to verify successful completion

A better approach is to pass back an explicit indication that the program has succeeded or failed; in this way the code that called the program can make an unambiguous check on the status of that procedure's results. This final version of generate_raise adds another OUT parameter whose sole purpose in life is to let me know how everything went inside the black box of the procedure.

```
PROCEDURE generate_raise
      (employee_id_in IN  employee.employee_id%TYPE,
       salary_out         OUT employee.salary%TYPE,
       found_emp_out   OUT VARCHAR2)
IS
   sal NUMBER;
   days_employed BINARY_INTEGER;
BEGIN
   ... as shown above ...
EXCEPTION
   /*
   || Now I set the salary to NULL, which is probably a better choice
   || for the error value, but I also set the status parameter to
   || "NOT FOUND" to show that something went wrong..
   */
   WHEN OTHERS THEN
      salary_out := NULL;
      found_emp_out := 'NOT FOUND';
END;
```

Now when I call generate_raise, I follow it immediately with a check of the status parameter and act accordingly (in this case of an Oracle Forms code fragment, I display an alert and then fail out of the trigger).

```
generate_raise (:employee.employee_id, :employee.salary, employee_around);
IF employee_around = 'NOT FOUND'
THEN
   alert_selection := SHOW_ALERT ('al_emp_not_found');
   RAISE FORM_TRIGGER_FAILURE;
END IF;
```

Ensure Case Consistency of Parameters

Procedures and functions will often take character values as parameters and use those strings in an IF statement to determine which code to execute. Parameters like action types, status flags, or selection codes often perform this kind of function. When a programmer calls a module with such a conditional parameter, the programmer must pass a value, which the program will recognize and process correctly.

Suppose I wrote a procedure that takes an action code as a parameter and then executes the appropriate code for that action. The routine might look like this:

```
PROCEDURE exec_action (action_in IN VARCHAR2)
IS
BEGIN
    IF action_in = 'DISPLAY_LEDGER'
    THEN
        ... the code to display the ledger.

    ELSIF action_in = 'CALC_PROFITS'
    THEN
        ... the code to calculate the profits.

    ELSIF ...
    END IF;
END;
```

This procedure will work correctly only when the argument for action_in is passed in uppercase. Yet, if you didn't happen to be the author of this program, you would have to be downright lucky to get the format of the value correct.

The exec_action module requires the user of the program—in this case, another programmer—to know and remember an aspect of the way the program was implemented. This is a violation of good coding style (make your program a black box). On top of that, the requirement that the parameter be uppercased is simply an avoidable bother. When people sense that they are being expected to follow a rule that is, well, dumb, they will at some level—consciously or unconsciously—rebel against that rule. The rebellion in this case will most likely take the form of truly annoying whines and sloppy code.

You show your respect for other people by not wasting their time and their brain cells. In the world of programming, you show this respect by freeing up your users (whether they are end users or other programmers) to concentrate on making important decisions and remembering key rules and information. In other words, you make your code smarter so your users don't have to worry over the details.

If you want to make the exec_action procedure as useful as possible, you will make it as easy and foolproof to use as possible. You will shift the burden of knowledge and effort from the user to the code. Programmers in particular shouldn't have to know or care about the format of the name of the requested action. You work it out for them.

In the version of exec_action that follows, I put some smarts in the code:

- Uppercasing the action as I copy it into a local (internal) variable, which I will then use for comparisons

- Checking for both full action strings and abbreviations, to save the programmer some typing

- Adding an ELSE clause to check for invalid actions

```
PROCEDURE exec_action (action_in IN VARCHAR2)
IS
    /* Uppercased copy of action. The "int" stands for "internal" */
    action_int VARCHAR2(30) := UPPER (action_in);
BEGIN
    /* Adds support for action abbreviations, too! */
    IF action_int IN ('DISPLAY_LEDGER', 'DL')
    THEN
        ... the code to display the ledger.

    ELSIF action_int IN ('CALC_PROFITS', 'CP')
    THEN
        ... the code to calculate the profits.

    ELSE
        MESSAGE (' Invalid action code: ' || action_in);
    END IF;
END;
```

Now, no matter how the user enters the action, exec_action can figure out what to do:

```
exec_action ('DL');
exec_action ('dl');
exec_action ('display_LEDGER');
exec_action ('calc_profits');
```

The ELSE clause also checks for an invalid value. While you, the author, may be sure that you would never enter an incorrect action, a new developer might be a lot less certain about the specific values. If you do not trap and report the mistake, this person would be at a tremendous disadvantage.

Never forget the Golden Rule when it comes to programming: trap mistakes for others as you hope they would trap them for you!

When checking for bad codes, you do have an alternative to performing the check at the end of a sometimes long IF-ELSIF sequence. That final ELSE clause is less than ideal since it can be hard to find in the code and, from a performance standpoint, you have to actually perform all the valid comparison checks before

you register the problem. I suggest that you develop a generic code_check procedure that takes the list of valid codes, the code entered by the user, and an
optional message text. If the code is not found in the list, code_check forces termination of the calling program.

```
PROCEDURE exec_action (action_in IN VARCHAR2)
IS
    action_int VARCHAR2(30) := UPPER (action_in);
BEGIN
    code_check ('|DISPLAY_LEDGE|DL|CALC_PROFITS|CP', action_int,
                'action code');
    IF action IN ('DISPLAY_LEDGER', 'DL')
    THEN -- the code to display the ledger.
    ELSIF action IN ('CALC_PROFITS', 'CP')
    THEN -- the code to calculate the profits.
    ELSIF ...
    END IF;
END;
```

Here is the code_check routine in Oracle Forms:

```
PROCEDURE code_check
    (valid_codes_in IN VARCHAR2,
     check_code_in IN VARCHAR2,
     code_name_in IN VARCHAR2 := 'code',
     delimiter_in IN VARCHAR2 := '|')
IS
BEGIN
    IF INSTR (valid_codes_in, delimiter_in || check_code_in) = 0
    THEN
        MESSAGE
        (' Invalid ' || code_name_in || ': "' || check_code_in || '"');
        RAISE FORM_TRIGGER_FAILURE;
    END IF;
END;
```

Using code_check, if I execute the following statement with an invalid action code:

```
exec_action ('dp');
```

the following text will appear on the message line or in an alert box:

```
Invalid action code: "dp"
```

Whether or not you go to the trouble of building a separate routine to check for
valid codes, as long as you do validate the input to your modules, programmers
will make fewer errors and be able to fix those faster. The more work your code
does for the programmer, the more productive that programmer will be.

Default Values and Remote Procedure Calls

If you are using Oracle Server Version 7.0, you will encounter a number of situations where you have to include a value for every parameter in your module's

parameter list. In Version 7.0, any call to a remote procedure must include all arguments, as indicated by the following error:

```
PLS-424: 'all arguments must be provided in remote procedure call;
            no defaults'.
```

You might say to yourself, "No problem. I do not have a distributed database. I am not performing any RPCs (remote procedure calls)." From the standpoint of PL/SQL, however, any of the following scenarios involves a remote procedure call:

- A Pro*C program that calls a stored procedure

- An Oracle Developer/2000 tool that calls a stored procedure

- An honest-to-goodness remote procedure call of the format:

  ```
  procedure_name@database_link;
  ```

One way you can get around this problem is to create a local procedure that supports default values by passing its own default to the stored procedure. Suppose I have a stored procedure as follows:

```
PROCEDURE calc_profits
    (company_id_in IN NUMBER,
     profit_type_in IN VARCHAR2 := 'NET');
```

If I try to use this procedure in Oracle Forms, I must include a value for both parameters, even if I use the default:

```
calc_profits (:company.company_id, 'NET');
```

Suppose I now create the following local procedure (either in the form itself or in a PL/SQL library):

```
PROCEDURE of_calc_profits
    (company_id_in IN NUMBER,
     profit_type_in IN VARCHAR2 := 'NET')
IS
BEGIN
    calc_profits (company_id_in, profit_type_in);
END;
```

I can now call this procedure using the default value of NET, since the Oracle Forms version of the procedure always passes a value to the stored procedure version:

```
of_calc_profits (:company.company_id);
```

(In Version 7.1 of the Oracle Server, by the way, you will be permitted to use default values in remote procedure calls.)

This situation with Oracle Server Version 7 reinforces one of my suggestions regarding default parameter values: always specify a value for each of the module's parameters, even if a value is the same as the default. You will find yourself less vulnerable to problems down the line.

23

Managing Code in the Database

You will either embed PL/SQL programs in your client-side application, as happens in the Oracle Developer/2000 tools, or you will store your code in the Oracle database.

The term *stored procedure* commonly refers to code that is stored in the database. Along with procedures, you can also store functions and packages, which can contain variables, cursors, record structures, etc. Whenever you hear the term stored procedures, you should think "stored objects."

There are a number of benefits to storing an object in the database:

- *The database manages dependencies between your stored objects.* For example, if a stored function relies on a certain table and that table's structure is changed, the status of that function is automatically set to INVALID and recompilation takes place, again automatically, when someone tries to execute that function.

- *Any session with EXECUTE authority can execute the stored object.* Whether you are in an Oracle Forms application, a database trigger, or a batch process, that stored object is accessible as long as the database is accessible. The compiled code for the object is made available from the shared memory of the database instance.

- *You can execute a module stored in another (remote) database.* This is known as a remote procedure call, or RPC. The ability to execute code on a different database means that you do not have to distribute application code to multiple databases in order to support distributed applications.

- *Stored modules offer transaction-level security,* which goes well beyond the table- and column-level data and referential integrity offered by the database. With a stored module you can make sure that transactions involving multiple tables and different steps are always performed properly. This was actually one of the original motivations for the development of the PL/SQL language.

- *Execution of a stored object shifts CPU load to the server.* Rather than run your code locally in a form or report, the stored object executes on the database server. Assuming that the server is sized to handle the load, this shift could improve overall application performance. This feature could be less of a benefit, of course, if the server is already heavily burdened.

Stored objects play an important role in today's client-server applications. The information in this chapter will help you make the best possible use of stored objects.

Executing Stored Code

To execute a stored program unit, you must first store this program in the database. I'll explain this CREATE OR REPLACE step later in this chapter. For now, let's take a look at what happens when you run a stored PL/SQL program.

Executing Procedures

If you are working in SQL*Plus, you can execute programs directly from the command line. Use the EXECUTE command to run procedures as follows:

```
SQL> execute calc_totals
```

Notice that you do *not* have to provide a semicolon. In fact, if you are going to use the EXECUTE command, the entire PL/SQL procedure call must fit on one physical line. As soon as you press the Enter key, the program executes.

You can also save a few microseconds (but accumulated over a whole year...) by providing only the minimum number of characters for the EXECUTE command:

```
SQL> exec calc_totals
```

When you are executing a procedure within a PL/SQL block, you do not use the EXECUTE syntax. You simply call the procedure, passing all necessary parameters within parentheses, and then terminate the line of code with a semicolon. Here is the syntax for calling the calc_totals procedure within a PL/SQL block:

```
BEGIN
    calc_totals;
END;
```

You can also execute PL/SQL procedures in various "front-end" tools, such as Oracle Forms, PowerBuilder, and many 3GL languages like C and COBOL. The syntax for calling procedures (and functions) will vary from tool to tool. Within the Oracle Developer/2000 environment, you can call stored programs from within a "native," albeit outdated, version of PL/SQL (see Appendix B, *Calling Stored Procedures from PL/SQL Version 1.1*, for more information). From a language like C, you will actually use a precompiler called Pro*C (from Oracle) and embed calls to PL/SQL programs within a SQL execution block like this:

```
EXEC SQL EXECUTE
    BEGIN
        calc_totals;
    END;
END-EXEC;
```

Executing Functions

The situation with functions is a little bit different. A function returns a value, so you can't just execute it directly. If you try to run a function as if it is a procedure, you will get the following error:

```
SQL> exec total_sales (1997)
begin total_sales (1997); end;
 *
ERROR at line 1:
ORA-06550: line 1, column 7:
PLS-00221: 'TOTAL_SALES' is not a procedure or is undefined
ORA-06550: line 1, column 7:
PL/SQL: Statement ignored
```

If you want to run a function simply to view its return value, you can execute it within a call to DBMS_OUTPUT.PUT_LINE as follows:

```
SQL> exec DBMS_OUTPUT.PUT_LINE (total_sales (1997))
```

Of course, this only works if the datatype of the return value of the function matches one of the datatypes supported by DBMS_OUTPUT: NUMBER, STRING and DATE. For anything else, you will need to execute the function within an anonymous block and then convert the value as necessary for display. In the following example, I declare a PL/SQL table of strings to retrieve the value from a function that returns all the foreign key information for a table. I then use a FOR loop to display that information:

```
/* Employs PL/SQL 2.3 syntax for PL/SQL tables. */
DECLARE
    TYPE strtabtype IS TABLE OF VARCHAR2(100) INDEX BY BINARY_INTEGER;
    strtab strtabtype;
BEGIN
    strtab := primary_keys.for_table ('emp');
    IF strtab.COUNT > 0
    THEN
        FOR tabrow IN strtab.FIRST .. strtab.LAST
        LOOP
            DBMS_OUTPUT.PUT_LINE (strtab.column_name);
        END LOOP;
    END IF;
END;
/
```

If I have saved this block in a file called *myscript.sql*, I can then execute this program and verify my function's behavior as follows:

```
SQL> @myscript
```

NOTE   You might wonder why I placed my FOR loop inside an IF statement. Surely, if there were no rows, the strtab.FIRST method would return NULL and the loop would not execute. Yes and no. The FIRST and LAST methods do return NULL if the PL/SQL table is empty, but oddly enough, if your numeric FOR loop range evaluates to:

```
FOR tabrow IN NULL .. NULL
```

then the PL/SQL runtime engine does enter the loop and try to process the body contents immediately. Then it raises an ORA-06502 VALUE_ERROR exception. So you really want to put some conditional logic around those FOR loops if you think the range endpoints might evaluate to NULL.

Now that you've seen how to execute programs "from the outside," let's move inside and take a look at the architecture Oracle employs to deliver that code to you for execution.

Memory-Based Architecture of PL/SQL Code

Whenever you start up an Oracle instance, a chunk (usually a rather large chunk) of memory is set aside for the System Global Area or SGA. Various Oracle processes manage this area of memory to do any of the following and more:

- Retrieve data from the database and deliver it to user processes (a PL/SQL procedure executing an explicit cursor, an Oracle Forms application querying records through a base table block, an Internet HTML page utilizing the Oracle WebServer interface, and so on).

- Change data and then manage the transaction processing (commits and rollbacks) based on those changes.

- Provide access to PL/SQL programs for execution in the server itself.

- Transfer information between Oracle sessions using database pipes and database alerts.

When you use a stored program element (by executing a procedure or function or by making reference to a nonexecutable part of a package like a constant or cursor), it must be accessible from the SGA. So when you reference a program element, its compiled version is loaded into the SGA's shared pool, if it is not already present. Then any program data associated with that element is instantiated in your Program Global Area (PGA). At that point, the code can be executed or otherwise used in your session.

The next time a session with execute authority on that program element references it, it will already have been loaded and will therefore be available for execution.

When the SGA shared pool area fills up, code in the pool will be aged out (that is, room will be made for newly requested programs) on a least-recently-used basis. Programs which are used often will therefore most likely be available immediately upon request. You can also *pin* programs into shared memory if you want to make certain that they will not be aged out. See Chapter 25, *Tuning PL/SQL Applications*, for more details on pinning.

Note that even if your compiled code is aged out of the SGA, any persistent, package-based data will remain available in your PGA. In other words, code may be swapped out of the SGA, but program data remains and persists for the duration of your session (or until you explicitly request a reinitialization of your schema).

Figure 23-1 illustrates a number of the points covered in this section.

Key Concepts for Program Execution

Here are some basic principles to remember about program execution:

- *Compiled PL/SQL code is shared among all users with EXECUTE authority on that code.* Usually you will set up your environment so that one account or schema owns all the code for an application. You then grant EXECUTE authority to other users on that code. When any of those schemas runs this code, they are working with the same compiled code. Again, the data instantiated and manipulated within those programs is specific to each connection.

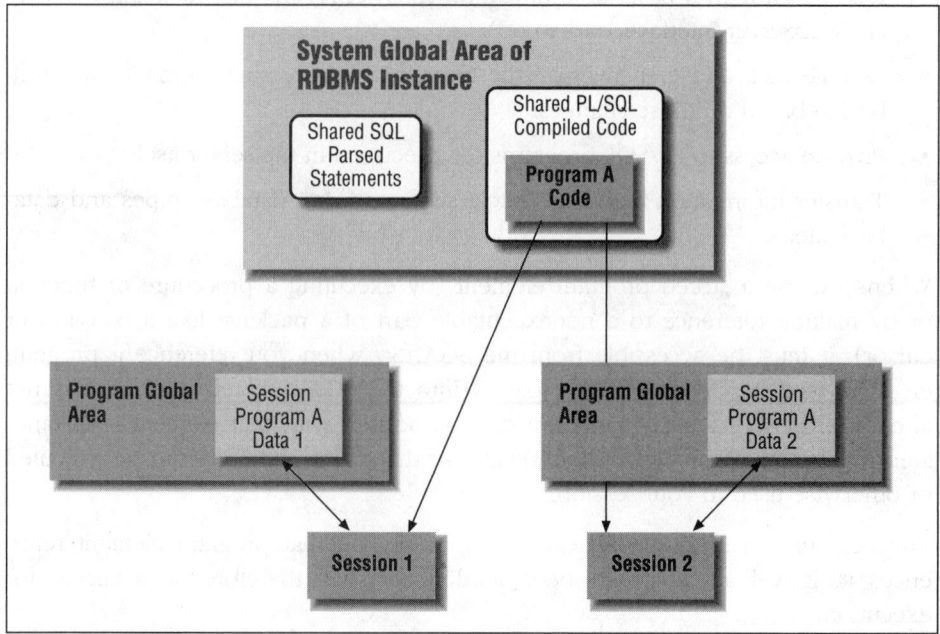

Figure 23-1. The System Global Area and Program Global Area

- *When you reference any individual element in a package, the entire package is loaded into shared memory.* This can be both an advantage and a disadvantage. If you group together (in a package) functionality which is usually executed in "close proximity," then you are more likely to find the program you need in shared memory. This will speed up the completion of your program.

  On the other hand, suppose that you build some very large packages which contain programs covering a disparate range of functionality. My application needs just one function out of the 100 procedures, functions, and cursors defined. Too bad! My SGA and my PGA must absorb the full punishment of the package (both the room needed for the shared, compiled code and all the package data instantiated in my PGA).

- *Program data instantiated within a program is stored in PGA for each user, rather than in the SGA.* This means that each user has his own copy of program data. If a procedure declares a PL/SQL table and stuffs it full of 1000 strings, every user who executes that procedure has his own copy of that table and its 1000 strings. The nice thing about this characteristic is that gives you a fair amount of flexibility in finding the delicate balance between those ever-competing resources: CPU and memory.

NOTE The architecture in the multi-threaded server (MTS) is a bit different, but the principle is the same: different users have their own copies of their program data.

- *Stored code runs under the authority of that code's owner, not that of the schema which is executing the code.* Suppose that you have stored all the code for your order entry application in the SYSTEM account (a *very* bad idea, as this example will illustrate). You then grant EXECUTE authority on that code to SCOTT, the traditional Oracle demonstration account, which has very little power outside of doing whatever it wants with the emp and dept tables.

  Now suppose further that the delall procedure of the ordent package allows you to delete all orders from the application table. The intention is that only administrators will have the ability to do that. In fact, the only account that can delete from the orders table at all is SYSTEM. Once you have granted EXECUTE authority on ordent to SCOTT, however, all heck can very decidedly break loose. For when a user logged in as SCOTT executes the ordent.delall procedure, that user is, for that moment, acting as though she were connected to SYSTEM. All rows are removed from the orders table!

  You must, consequently, very careful about (a) the authority of the schema owning your shared application code, and (b) to whom you grant EXECUTE authority on that code.

- *Even though stored code runs under the authority of that code's owner, the USER function still returns the name of the schema currently connected to Oracle.* The USER function does not, in other words, return the name of the schema which owns the code in which the USER function was called.

Transaction Integrity and Execute Authority

The RDBMS and SQL languages give you the capability to tightly control access to and changes in any particular table. With the GRANT command you can, for example, make sure that only certain roles and users have the ability to perform an UPDATE on a given table. This GRANT statement cannot, on the other hand, make sure that the UPDATEs performed by a user or application are done correctly.

In a typical banking transaction, you might need to transfer funds from account A to account B. The balance of account B must be incremented, and that of account A decremented. Table access is necessary, but not sufficient, to guarantee that both of these steps are always performed by all programmers who write code to perform a transfer. Without stored objects, the best you can do is require extensive testing and code review to make sure that all transactions are properly constructed. With stored objects, on the other hand, you can guarantee that a funds transfer either completes successfully or is completely rolled back, regardless of who executes the process.

Execute Authority on Stored Objects

The secret to achieving this level of transaction integrity is the concept of *execute authority* (also known as *run authority*). Instead of granting to a role or user the authority to update a table, you grant privileges to that role/user only to execute a procedure. This procedure controls and provides access to the underlying data structures (see Figure 23-2). The procedure is owned by a separate Oracle RDBMS account, which in turn is granted the actual update privileges on those tables needed to perform the transaction. The procedure therefore becomes the gate-keeper for the transfer transaction. The only way a program (whether an Oracle Forms application or a Pro*C executable) can execute the transfer is through the procedure, so the transaction integrity can be guaranteed.

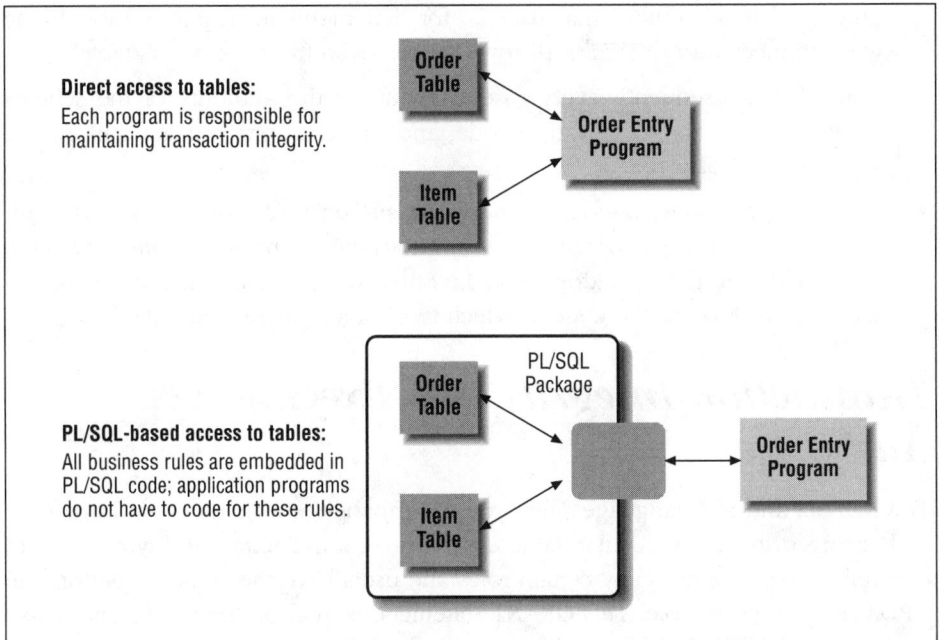

Figure 23-2. Transaction integrity with a PL/SQL code layer

In order for a stored procedure or package to compile (which occurs at the time of creation or replacement), the owner of that program must explicitly be granted all the necessary privileges to any objects referenced by the program. These privileges may not be granted simply to a role. If, for example, procedure disp_customer issues a SELECT statement against the customer table, then the owner of disp_ customer must be granted a minimum of SELECT privileges on that table with an explicit command:

```
GRANT privilege ON customer TO procedure_owner;
```

Requiring direct grants to individual Oracle users sometimes causes difficulty in environments where grants are controlled carefully and efficiently through the use of roles. After all, the whole idea of the role is to allow DBAs to move away from the onerous task of directly granting privileges to a myriad of individual users. Yet every one of those users must execute the stored procedures underlying an application. What's a DBA to do?

In some Oracle shops, a single account (user), which I'll call STOROBJ, is created in the production environment. This user owns all stored objects and has update privileges on all tables, as is appropriate. Other people who use the applications might have SELECT privileges on a number of tables, and perhaps even update privileges on certain tables that are maintained through Oracle Forms applications. But all complex transactions are bundled into stored procedures and stored functions, and users are granted EXECUTE authority only to those stored programs. If an Oracle Forms screen needs to perform a funds transfer, it calls the stored procedure and displays confirmation information on the screen. The logic and authority would, however, reside in the database and be controlled tightly by the STOROBJ account.

To grant execute authority on a stored object, you issue the following command (in SQL*Plus, SQL*DBA, or another product that supports the issuing of DDL calls):

```
SQL> GRANT EXECUTE ON object_name TO user_or_role;
```

NOTE   You can only grant EXECUTE authority to an entire package, not to individual programs within a package. Suppose that you build a single package to encapsulate all SQL-based access to a table; this package contains procedures which perform inserts, updates, and deletes, as well as cursors and functions to query data. There is no way to grant "read-only" EXECUTE authority. A schema can either run all programs in a package or none. As a result, you might want to build a single package encapsulating all SQL against a table or view, but then build additional packages *on top* of that "base" package which act as filters for certain classes of activity.

Creating Synonyms for Stored Objects

You should create public synonyms for each of the stored objects so that individual developers do not have to reference the STOROBJ account name in order to access the programs. Suppose, for example, that we have a funds transfer procedure, as follows:

```
PROCEDURE xfer_funds
    (from_account_in IN NUMBER, to_account_in IN NUMBER,
     transfer_amount_in IN NUMBER, transfer_status_out OUT NUMBER);
```

Without a synonym, you would have to execute this procedure in this way:

```
storobj.xfer_funds (:old_acct, :new_acct, :xfer_amt, :xfer_stat);
```

You should always avoid hardcoding the name of the owner of an object, be it a procedure or a table. What if you need to change the account name? What if you decide to move the procedure to an entirely different server and then need to execute this procedure as an RPC? Whenever you are working with stored objects, you should create synonyms, as follows:

```
SQL> CREATE PUBLIC SYNONYM xfer_funds FOR storobj.xfer_funds;
```

Now I can call the transfer procedure without making reference to its owner:

```
xfer_funds (:old_acct, :new_acct, :xfer_amt, :xfer_stat);
```

While it is possible to create a synonym for a standalone procedure, it is not possible to create a synonym for a packaged procedure or function. You can, however, create a synonym for the package itself. In effect, synonyms can be used to avoid having to provide the schema name of an object; you cannot use it to avoid specifying the package name in which a program is defined.

Module Validation and Dependency Management

Whenever you create or replace a stored object in the database, the PL/SQL engine compiles the code. If the compile succeeds, then the following information is stored in the database:

- The source code for the module, as you wrote it.

- The tree structure of the module, a hierarchical representation of the original source code, with a list of local and external references. The tree structure is used only by the compilation (and automatic recompilation) process.

- The pcode for the module, which is a list of instructions to the PL/SQL execution engine. The PL/SQL execution engine uses the pcode to execute the module when it is called by a host program.

When a module compiles, its status is set to VALID. This status is maintained in the SYS.OBJ$ table. Upon compilation, the PL/SQL engine also has resolved all references to other database objects such as tables and other stored programs.

Each of these references constitutes a dependency for that module. In other words, the validity of the module is dependent upon the validity of all objects on which it depends. All dependency information is stored in the SYS.DEPENDENCY$ table.

NOTE   The tree structure, pcode, and dependency information is maintained only for named modules. Anonymous blocks and database triggers are compiled only when (and each time that) they are executed. The generated pcode for these objects is stored directly in the shared pool of the database instance for as long as they are used, and until they are erased from the System Global Area, using a least-recently-used algorithm.

                Starting with Oracle Server Release 7.3, triggers are compiled and their pcode stored in the database.

Interdependencies of Stored Objects

A stored object must be VALID in order for its pcode to be loaded into the shared pool and executed by the host program. As noted above, if the compile succeeds at create/replace time, then the status is set to VALID. This status may, however, depend on other objects. Consider the following function:

```
FUNCTION full_name (employee_id_in IN NUMBER) RETURN VARCHAR2
IS
    first_and_last VARCHAR2(100);
BEGIN
    SELECT first_name || ' ' || last_name
      INTO first_and_last
      FROM employee
     WHERE employee_id = employee_id_in;
    RETURN first_and_last;
EXCEPTION
    WHEN NO_DATA_FOUND
    THEN
        RETURN NULL;
END;
```

Suppose that on Monday I save this function to the database. It compiles successfully and its status is set to VALID. The PL/SQL compiler also adds a record in the DEPENDENCY$ table to indicate that full_name is dependent on the employee table. Then on Tuesday, the DBA team adds another column to the employee table. The Oracle Server automatically checks the dependencies for the employee table and sets the status of all dependent objects to INVALID. This is a recursive process. Once full_name is set to INVALID, then any modules calling full_name are also set to INVALID.[*]

The next time a user runs the full_name function, the database notices that the status is INVALID. It then calls the PL/SQL engine to compile the function. If the compile succeeds, then the pcode is loaded to shared memory and the function runs.

Remote Procedure Calls

One of the most important enhancements contained in PL/SQL Version 2.0 and all subsequent releases is the ability to execute remote procedure calls or RPCs. A remote procedure (module) call occurs when you execute a program from within one database that is stored in another database. To execute a remote module, you simply attach a database link after the module name, as follows:

```
emp_name := full_name@new_york (:emp.employee_id);
```

The full specification for a remote module call is:

```
schema_name.[package_name.]module_name@database_link_name
```

where [package_name.] is the optional package name, necessary if the module is contained in a package.

Just as you should hide the owner of a module with a synonym, you should do the same thing for remote module calls. Programmers should never have to know where a module is located nor who owns it. You should never want them to know because if that information is placed in a program, that program is much more vulnerable to breakage. The very nature of a remote module call indicates that the code can be moved to a different remote database. Never let a programmer hardcode such information in a program.

When you call a remote module and it raises an exception, that exception is passed back as raised to the calling program—for all but user-defined exceptions. If your remote module raises a NO_DATA_FOUND exception, your exception handler traps that error. If, on the other hand, your module uses RAISE_APPLICATION_ERROR to raise a custom exception (error numbers between -20000 and -20999), then that specific exception is lost in the translation back to the calling program. Instead, error ORA-06510 is always returned to the local program.

---

[*] An important exception to this "chain reaction" occurs with packaged modules. If, for example, full_name was defined within a package called, say, "employee", then even if the status of the full_name module is set to INVALID, no modules that call full_name will be tagged invalid, unless the specification of full_name changed (which it does not in this case). See the package examples and documentation on the disk for more information about this extra protection provided by packages.

Automatic Versus Manual Compilation

It is easy to see that the database does a lot of work for you by maintaining the stored object dependencies and automatically recompiling objects as needed. You may not want to always depend on such recompilation, however. There are two potential drawbacks to automatic recompilation:

- The recompilation takes place at run time, when the user has requested an action. This means that the user waits while PL/SQL does its thing. The pause should not be very noticeable for small objects. Large packages can, however, take more than several seconds to compile. Do you want your users to wait while this happens?

- The recompilation can fail. What if the reason that the full_name function is INVALID is that the employee table was dropped? The database cannot recover from such an error, as far as full_name is concerned.

A much more sensible approach to take with stored object recompilation is to manually recompile all INVALID objects before the user tries to execute those objects. This way the compilation time is moved off-line and if any objects fail to compile, you can analyze and resolve the problem. To do this manual recompilation you need to coordinate closely with the DBA group (if it is separate from the application development team). You can determine which modules are INVALID by examining the contents of the USER_OBJECTS or ALL_OBJECTS views. You could even generate the commands necessary to recompile all INVALID PL/SQL objects with the following query:

```
SELECT 'ALTER ' || object_type || ' ' ||
       object_name || ' COMPILE;'
  FROM user_objects
 WHERE object_type IN
          ('PACKAGE', 'PACKAGE BODY', 'FUNCTION', 'PROCEDURE')
   AND status = 'INVALID';
```

Output from this query might look like:

```
ALTER PACKAGE PSGLOBAL COMPILE;
ALTER FUNCTION FULL_NAME COMPILE;
```

You could also force recompilation of a module by using the ALTER_COMPILE procedure in the DBMS_DDL package (see Appendix C, *Built-In Packages*, for more details), as follows:

```
DBMS_DDL.ALTER_COMPILE ('package', 'SCOTT', 'FULL_NAME');
```

It is easy, when you use stored objects, to take for granted automatic management of these objects by the database. You might scarcely notice the status of your objects and the recompilations that take place behind the scenes.

—Continued—

That's cool. That's the whole idea. As you move your applications into production, however, you would be well served to remember how the database works with your stored objects. That way, when something goes wrong (very slow execution time under certain circumstances, for example), you have some idea of how to fix it.

Managing Stored Objects with SQL*Plus

You can use SQL*Plus to manage stored objects like database triggers, procedures, functions, and packages. When Oracle7 was first released, SQL*Plus was the only way to create stored procedures. With the advent of CDE and Oracle Procedure Builder, however, you now have a number of choices for creating and updating your stored objects. Still, many of you will rely on SQL*Plus, especially if your DBA activities are performed on a UNIX (or other non-Windows) server.

Creating Stored Objects

The syntax to create stored objects is as follows:

```
CREATE [OR REPLACE] PROCEDURE proc_name (param_list) AS ... ;
CREATE [OR REPLACE] FUNCTION func_name (param_list) RETURN datatype AS ... ;
CREATE [OR REPLACE] PACKAGE pkg_name AS ... ;
CREATE [OR REPLACE] PACKAGE BODY pkg_name AS ... ;
CREATE [OR REPLACE] DATABASE TRIGGER trig_name AS ... ;
```

Everything from the object name onwards has the same syntax shown in the appropriate chapter on that object. The CREATE OR REPLACE syntax in front of the normal syntax indicates to SQL*Plus that you want to create the object in the database. This is a DDL (data definition language) statement in SQL, just like a CREATE TABLE statement.

You must create a package specification separately from the package body. In fact, you must create the specification first, or else you receive the following error:

```
PLS-00304: cannot compile body of 'pkg_name' without its specification
```

When an object is created, it is stored in a data dictionary table. The source for procedures, packages, functions, and package bodies is kept in the SOURCE$ table (owned by SYS). Views into the SOURCE$ table are:

ALL_SOURCE
> Source for all objects to which you have access, and therefore EXECUTE privilege on that object

USER_SOURCE
> Source for all objects you have created

The statements executed by a trigger are stored in the ACTION column of the TRIGGER$ table (owned by SYS). You can view all triggers you created by accessing USER_TRIGGERS, or all triggers to which you have access by viewing the contents of ALL_TRIGGERS.

Even though you store your modules in the database, you do not maintain your source code for these modules directly in their data dictionary tables. Instead, you must always keep the source code in text files. If you need to make a change to an object, make the changes in the source code and then replace the object in the database.

In order to distinguish regular SQL*Plus scripts from scripts that maintain stored objects, I employ a different file extension for them, as shown in the following table:

File Type	Extension
General SQL*Plus script	*<file>.sql*
Testing script	*<file>.tst*
Stored procedure	*<file>.sp*
Stored function	*<file>.sf*
Stored package body	*<file>spb*
Stored package specification	*<file>.sps*

Tips for Storing Code in Files

Here are some tips for storing code in files:

- Always keep your CREATE OR REPLACE statements for package specifications separate from those of your package bodies. That way you can compile each separately. If you keep them together, when you change something in the package body, you will recompile both specification and body. When you recompile your specification, the status of any programs referencing an element in that package will be marked INVALID. They will then have to be recompiled.

- When you construct installation scripts for your package-based applications, first compile all specifications and then compile all bodies. When package bodies are compiled, references to other package elements are resolved through the specification. With all the specifications "in place" in the database, you are much less likely to run into seemingly circular dependencies. Note that you will have to be careful about the order in which you compile specifications to resolve any dependencies in those specifications themselves. On the other hand, you can compile your bodies in any order you like.

Changing Stored Objects

There are two ways to change an existing object in the database:

- Drop the object and recreate it
- Use the CREATE OR REPLACE syntax instead of CREATE

With the first approach, I would issue a DROP command followed by a CREATE command, as follows:

```
DROP PROCEDURE calc_totals;
CREATE PROCEDURE calc_totals
    (company_id_in IN NUMBER, totals_out OUT NUMBER)
IS
BEGIN
    ... body of procedure ...
END;
/
```

Alternatively, I can use a single command to indicate that if the object already exists, replace it in its entirety with the new version found in the statement:

```
CREATE OR REPLACE PROCEDURE calc_totals
    (company_id_in IN NUMBER, totals_out OUT NUMBER)
IS
BEGIN
    ... body of procedure ...
END;
/
```

If you are replacing a very large procedure, you might at times encounter an error like the following:

```
CREATE OR REPLACE PACKAGE BODY PSGlobal
*
ERROR at line 1:
ORA-00604: error occurred at recursive SQL level 1
ORA-01562: failed to extend rollback segment (id = 2)
ORA-01547: failed to allocate extent of size 5 in tablespace 'ROLLBACK_DATA'
```

The RDBMS writes the rows being replaced (deleted) to the rollback segment; if the program is very large and your rollback segments are not commensurately massive, your CREATE OR REPLACE does not succeed. To get around this problem you can increase the size of your rollback segments or you can drop your object before you try to CREATE OR REPLACE. Because the DROP is a DDL statement, it will perform a commit upon completion. Then your rollback segments don't have to maintain the old, deleted rows while the INSERT is taking place.

Storing Versus Executing a Stored Program

An important point to remember with stored objects is that the command to CREATE OR REPLACE an object does not actually execute the stored object. It simply places the code for that object in the database and compiles it. To execute the program, you can then use the EXECUTE command at the SQL> prompt, or place a call to the program in a PL/SQL block. (This distinction is one reason I think that it is so important to use a different file extension (.sp) for the CREATE statements than for the normal SQL*Plus scripts (.sql).)

Say, for example, you create a file named calctot.sp, as follows:

```
CREATE OR REPLACE PROCEDURE calc_totals
    (company_id_in IN NUMBER, totals_out OUT NUMBER)
IS
BEGIN
    ... body of procedure ...
END;
/
```

Then, when you execute this file with the command:

```
SQL> start calctot.sp
```

you receive the following message:

```
Procedure created.
```

No totals will have been calculated. The procedure was simply created. To calculate and display those totals you can now create a .sql file with a PL/SQL block, as follows:

```
DECLARE
    mytot NUMBER;
BEGIN
    calc_totals (1005, mytot);
    DBMS_OUTPUT.PUT_LINE ('Totals for company 1005 is ' || TO_CHAR
(mytot));
END;
/
```

and then run the script:

```
SQL> start calctots.sql
```

If you do receive a compile error when creating a stored object, you see a message like this:

```
Warning: Package Body created with compilation errors.
```

*Viewing Compilation Errors in SQL*Plus*

When the PL/SQL engine encounters errors, it writes the generated error messages to the ERROR$ table (owned by SYS). To see these error messages, you can either write a query against the USER_ERRORS view, or you can type the following command at the SQL*Plus prompt:

```
SQL> show errors
```

The "show errors" command runs a script that formats the contents of USER_ ERRORS so you can easily scan the errors. Here is an example of the output from show errors:

```
Errors for PACKAGE BODY PS_GLOBAL:

SQL> show errors
LINE/COL ERROR
-------- ----------------------------------------------------------------
0/0      PL/SQL: Compilation unit analysis terminated
1/14     PLS-00304: cannot compile body of 'PSGLOBAL' without its
         specification
```

So you have a line number and an error message. Unfortunately, it is difficult to use these line numbers, since they do not correspond directly to the line numbers in your file. They are always relative to a specific program or PL/SQL block (remember that you can have more than one such program unit in a file). Even within that block, you will find it difficult to correlate the line number with a particular PL/SQL statement.

But, wait, there is hope for those line numbers! Even if they do not match your source code, they do match the line numbers saved with the text of that module in the data dictionary view of source code. The next section shows how to query this view to identify the line of code corresponding to a line number.

Using SQL to Examine Stored Objects

Since the stored objects are contained in tables in the data dictionary, you can use SQL itself to get information about the currently available programs. The following views are the most useful to familiarize yourself with:

USER_DEPENDENCIES
    The dependencies to and from objects you own

USER_ERRORS
    The current set of errors for all stored objects you own. This view is accessed by the SHOW ERRORS SQL*Plus command, described earlier in this chapter.

USER_OBJECTS
    The objects you own

USER_OBJECT_SIZE
  The size of the objects you own

USER_SOURCE
  The text source code for all objects you own

USER_TRIGGERS
  The database triggers you own

You can view the structures of each of these tables either with a DESC command in SQL*Plus or by referring to Appendix B in Oracle Corporations's *Oracle7 Server Administrator's Guide.* The following sections provide some examples of the ways you can use these tables.

Displaying Object Dependencies

The RDBMS keeps track of dependencies between stored objects so that it can make sure the compiled source code of an object is still valid. Whenever you create or replace a module, the PL/SQL engine compiles that program and stores both source and compiled code. When you execute the program, the compiled code is loaded into the shared pool and run. If procedure A calls procedure B, then whenever procedure B is modified, the compiled code for procedure A is no longer valid (this status is maintained in the USER_OBJECTS view, or at least in the underlying SYS.OBJ$ table). Use the USER_DEPENDENCIES view to see which objects reference or depend on a particular object, as shown in this example:

```
/* Filename on companion disk: userdpnd.sql */
SELECT referenced_name,
       referenced_type,
       referenced_owner,
       referenced_link_name
  FROM user_dependencies
 WHERE name = UPPER ('&1');
```

where &1 is a single parameter to the SELECT statement. If this statement were placed in a file named *dependon.sql,* then you could find all objects that reference the calc_totals procedure by entering the following command at the SQL> prompt:

```
SQL> start dependon calc_totals
```

Displaying Information About Stored Objects

The USER_OBJECTS view contains the following key information about an object:

OBJECT_NAME
  Name of the object

OBJECT_TYPE
  Type of the object

STATUS

> Status of the object: VALID or INVALID

Here are the types of objects that are accessible through this view:

```
SQL> select distinct object_type from user_objects;

OBJECT_TYPE
-------------
FUNCTION
INDEX
PACKAGE
PACKAGE BODY
PROCEDURE
SEQUENCE
SYNONYM
TABLE
TRIGGER

9 rows selected.
```

You can see that USER_OBJECTS does more than keep track of PL/SQL code. You can use USER_OBJECTS to obtain a list of all PL/SQL objects currently in the database. I created and ran the following SQL*Plus script in a file called *psobj.sql*:

```
/* Filename on companion disk: psobj.sql */
SET PAGESIZE 66
COLUMN object_type FORMAT A20
COLUMN object_name FORMAT A30
COLUMN status FORMAT A10
BREAK ON object_type SKIP 1
SPOOL psobj.lis
SELECT object_type, object_name, status
  FROM user_objects
 WHERE object_type IN ('PACKAGE', 'PACKAGE BODY', 'FUNCTION', 'PROCEDURE')
 ORDER BY object_type, status, object_name
/
SPOOL OFF
```

The output file from this script file contained the following list:

OBJECT_TYPE	OBJECT_NAME	STATUS
FUNCTION	DEVELOP_ANALYSIS	INVALID
	NUMBER_OF_ATOMICS	INVALID
	FREQ_INSTR	VALID
PACKAGE	CHECKS	VALID
	CONFIG_PKG	VALID
	DBG	VALID
	DO	VALID
	EXCHDLR_PKG	VALID
PACKAGE BODY	DBG	VALID
	DO	VALID
	EXCHDLR_PKG	VALID

```
PROCEDURE              ASSESS_POPULARITY              INVALID
                       ASSERT_CONDITION              VALID
```

Notice that a number of my modules are INVALID. This may be due to changes to the tables referenced in the modules, or by changes to other programs called by these modules. The RDBMS automatically recompiles these objects when a program tries to call them. In other words, this recompilation takes place at run time, when the user has caused these programs to be run, waiting while the compilation occurs. You can avoid this automatic recompilation (and impact on users) by manually compiling the INVALID modules yourself. The best way to do this is to generate the compile command for each invalid module, directly from the USER_OBJECTS table.

When I use SQL to generate a list of commands to be executed, I save the SQL statement into a file with a *.sql* extention. The output from this file is sent to another file, this time with a *.cmd* extention (since it contains CoMmanDs). I then execute that command file at the end of the SQL script.

The code below generates the SQL commands needed to force recompilation of any invalid PL/SQL objects. In addition to creating the ALERT...COMPILE command, it adds a SHOW ERRORS command after each compile attempt so that I can see any errors from an unsuccessful compile. I set the line size and lengths of the output strings so that each command goes on its own line in the command file. Finally, when I run the *recomp.cmd* file (generated by the SELECT statement), I spool the output to another file (*recomp.lis*) so that I can review the results.

```
/* Filename on companion disk: recomp.sql */
SET PAGESIZE 0
SET LINESIZE 80
COLUMN command_line1 FORMAT A75
COLUMN command_line2 FORMAT A75
SPOOL recomp.cmd
SELECT 'ALTER '||
       DECODE (object_type, 'PACKAGE BODY', 'PACKAGE', object_type) || ' '||
       object_name || ' ' ||
       DECODE (object_type,
           'PACKAGE', 'COMPILE SPECIFICATION;',
           'PACKAGE BODY', 'COMPILE BODY;' ,
           'COMPILE;') command_line1,
       'SHOW ERRORS' command_line2
  FROM user_objects
 WHERE object_type IN ('PACKAGE', 'PACKAGE BODY', 'FUNCTION', 'PROCEDURE')
   AND status = 'INVALID'
 ORDER BY
    DECODE (object_type,
        'PACKAGE', 1, 'PACKAGE BODY', 4, 'FUNCTION', 2, 'PROCEDURE', 3)
/
SPOOL OFF
SPOOL recomp.lis
START recomp.cmd
SPOOL OFF
```

Analyzing the Size of PL/SQL Code

In the Windows environment, you run into severe memory problems when your program size (for a standalone procedure or function, or an entire package) approaches and exceeds 32K. Now, thirty-two thousand-odd bytes is a very large size for a program. If you are writing a program this large, you should probably break it up into smaller pieces. You can use the USER_OBJECT_SIZE view to tell you about the size of your code, and use it as an early warning system for further code modularization.

This view also comes in handy when you want to balance the size of your programs and packages. The compiled code for a stored object must be present in the Shared Global Area of the database before it can be run. A certain amount of space is set aside in the SGA for program code. Suppose you have one program or package that is much larger than anything else and takes up much of the room in the shared pool. Whenever that program is executed or a reference is made to any of the package's objects, the RDBMS has to flush the other programs out of shared memory to make room for this single, massive chunk of code. Those other programs then have to be read back into the shared pool when next invoked. If you balance your code size, then you can minimize the disk I/O required to make stored objects available for execution.

The USER_OBJECT_SIZE view contains information about the size of the source code, the size of the parsed code, and the size of the compiled code. The following code shows the various sizes for each of your larger stored objects:

```
/* Filename on companion disk: pssize.sql */
SET PAGESIZE 66
COLUMN name FORMAT A30
COLUMN type FORMAT A15
COLUMN source_size FORMAT 999999
COLUMN parsed_size FORMAT 999999
COLUMN code_size FORMAT 999999
TTITLE 'Size of PL/SQL Objects > 2000 Bytes'
SPOOL pssize.lis
SELECT name, type, source_size, parsed_size, code_size
  FROM user_object_size
 WHERE code_size > 2000
 ORDER BY code_size DESC
/
SPOOL OFF
```

By only looking at PL/SQL objects with more than 2000 bytes, I can focus on the larger objects that might conceivably require attention. The output from *pssize.sql* is shown below:

```
Sun Dec 11                                              page    1
                   Size of PL/SQL Objects > 2000 Bytes
```

NAME	TYPE	SOURCE_SIZE	PARSED_SIZE	CODE_SIZE
PS_GLOBAL	PACKAGE BODY	23434	29199	22584
DBG	PACKAGE BODY	17011	23691	13793
PARSER_PKG	PACKAGE BODY	12367	11441	9795
PS_LIST	PACKAGE BODY	9893	11728	9488
COMPILER_PKG	PACKAGE BODY	5500	6262	4583
COMPILER	PACKAGE BODY	2374	4613	3650
NUMBER_OF_ATOMICS	FUNCTION	2106	4033	3056

I do have a wide disparity in the sizes of the packages and modules currently stored in the database. If I were running a production environment with this range of code size, I should look at balancing the code by breaking up the larger packages, particularly ps_global. In reality, however, these packages stand out mostly because my development database is devoid of the large application-specific modules and packages any normal production environment would include.

Regardless of whether you need to balance your code, you should never just build "one big package" to hold all of your programs. Break up your modules into logical sets of operations and data structures, and create packages for each of those.

Displaying and Searching Source Code

You should always maintain the source code of your programs in text files (or a development tool specifically designed to store and manage PL/SQL code outside of the database). When you have stored these programs in the database, however, you can take advantage of SQL to analyze your source code across all modules, which may not be a straightforward task with your text editor.

The USER_SOURCE view contains all of the source code for objects owned by the current user. The structure of USER_SOURCE follows:

Name	Null?	Type
NAME	NOT NULL	VARCHAR2(30)
TYPE		VARCHAR2(12)
LINE	NOT NULL	NUMBER
TEXT		VARCHAR2(2000)

where NAME is the name of the object, TYPE is the type of object (PROCEDURE, FUNCTION, PACKAGE, and PACKAGE BODY), LINE is the line number, and TEXT is the text of the source code.

So you could look for all programs containing a certain substring in its source code. You could return the text associated with a specific line number. You could get a list of all the packages defined in your schema, and so on. The following sections offer some concrete examples.

Cross-Referencing Source Code

Using SQL, for example, you can discover the set of programs that reference a particular global variable or even PL/SQL built-in. The SQL statement below uses a single parameter so that you can specify the string for which you want to search:

```
SELECT DISTINCT name
   FROM user_source
  WHERE INSTR (UPPER (text), '&1') > 0;
```

You can view the source code of a stored object with the SQL statement shown below. The column line is the sequence number of that line of text in the program:

```
SELECT text
   FROM user_source
  WHERE name = UPPER ('&1')
  ORDER BY line;
```

If the query in this code were stored in *pslist.sql*, then I could obtain the source code for the function called number_of_atomics by entering the following command at the SQL> prompt:

```
SQL> start pslist number_of_atomics
```

NOTE   The underlying SOURCE$ table (upon which the USER_SOURCE view is built) does not retain the blank lines of your original source file.

Finding the Code for a Line Number

As noted earlier in the chapter, the output from a call to SHOW ERRORS in SQL*Plus displays the line number in which an error occurred, but that line number doesn't correspond to the line in your text file. Instead, it relates directly to the line number stored with the source code in the USER_SOURCE view.

The source_at_line function that follows provides an easy mechanism for retrieving the text from a stored program for a specified line number. It takes three parameters:

name_in
> The name of the stored object

line_in
> The line number of the line you wish to retrieve (default value is 1)

type_in
> The type of object you want to view (default for TYPE is NULL)

The default values are designed to make this function as easy as possible to use. The following examples show the different ways source_at_line can be called:

- Retrieve the tenth line of code in the company package body:

```
the_text := source_at_line ('company', 10, 'package body');
```

- Retrieve the fifth line of code from the calc_totals procedure. Notice that I do not specify the type of object. Since I know that there is only a calc_totals procedure and no other type of object with that name, I can safely let the cursor scan through all of USER_SOURCE:

```
the_text := source_at_line ('calc_totals', 5);
```

- Retrieve the first line of the company_name function. I only supply the name of the function, so I use the default of the line = 1 and NULL type. This form of source_at_line would be handy for displaying the header of a module or package, which usually shows up on the first line.

```
DBMS_OUTPUT.PUT_LINE (source_at_line ('company_name'));
==>
    FUNCTION company_name (company_id IN INTEGER) RETURN VARCHAR2
```

Here, then, is the code for the source_at_line function:

```
/* Filename on companion disk: srcline.sf */
FUNCTION source_at_line
    (name_in IN VARCHAR2,
     line_in IN INTEGER := 1,
     type_in IN VARCHAR2 := NULL)
RETURN VARCHAR2
IS
    CURSOR source_cur IS
        SELECT text
          FROM user_source
         WHERE name = UPPER (name_in)
           AND (type = UPPER (type_in) OR type_in IS NULL)
           AND line = line_in;

    source_rec source_cur%ROWTYPE;

BEGIN
    /* Open and fetch the line of code. */
    OPEN source_cur;
    FETCH source_cur INTO source_rec;

    IF source_cur%NOTFOUND
    THEN
        CLOSE source_cur;
        RETURN NULL;
    ELSE
        CLOSE source_cur;
        RETURN source_rec.text;
    END IF;
END;
```

Changing Source Code in the Database

If you want to be truly adventurous you could also update your source code in the data dictionary. The only reason to do this would be to perform application-wide changes to source code in files which were not possible or practical through the editor. You might, for example, want to perform name replacements: every program that called number_of_atomics should now call parser.numatoms because I moved the standalone module into a package.

You cannot update source code through the USER_SOURCE view. Instead, you must make changes directly to the SOURCE$ table owned by SYS. The columns for SOURCE$ are:

OBJ$
> The object ID

LINE
> The line number

SOURCE
> The line of source code

You can obtain the object ID for a particular module from the USER_OBJECTS view, which contains the OBJECT_ID column. The code below offers a PL/SQL procedure that accepts an owner name, a program name, and the old and new versions of a string. The procedure then replaces all instances in that program of the old string with the new.

```
/* Filename on companion disk: srcupd.sp */
PROCEDURE src_update
    (owner_in IN VARCHAR2, program_in IN VARCHAR2,
     old_str_in IN VARCHAR2, new_str_in IN VARCHAR2)
IS
    /* Cursor uses all_objects since this is run from SYS */
    CURSOR obj_cur IS
       SELECT object_id
         FROM all_objects
        WHERE owner = owner_in
          AND object_name = program_in;
    obj_rec obj_cur%ROWTYPE;
BEGIN
    OPEN obj_cur;
    FETCH obj_cur INTO obj_rec;
    IF obj_cur%FOUND
    THEN
       UPDATE SOURCE$
          SET source = REPLACE (source, old_str_in, new_str_in)
        WHERE obj# = obj_rec.object_id;
    END IF;
    CLOSE obj_cur;
END;
```

If you ever do make changes like this, be sure to recompile all modified programs.

Encrypting Stored Code

It's kind of fun to watch a programming language like PL/SQL evolve over time. First there was Version 1.0—very useful for batch processing scripts, but not much else. And very buggy. Then with Version 2.0 we started to see the real promise of the language. Stored program units, packages, and more. Why, it was so useful that third-party vendors began to write applications in PL/SQL. And when they sold these applications to customers, they shipped them their software for installation—and then ran smack into a depressing discovery: there wasn't any way to hide their proprietary formulas, knowledge, and plain hard work from the eyes of competitors!

To install a PL/SQL-based application in another database instance, you must CREATE OR REPLACE those program units from the source code. Source code must, therefore, be supplied to each customer. "Wake up, Oracle!" came the cry from value-added resellers (VARs), "we can't let everyone see our secrets." Mostly in response to this basic need of VARs, Oracle added (with PL/SQL Release 2.2 and beyond) the ability to encrypt or "wrap" source code.

When you encrypt PL/SQL source (I prefer that word to "wrap," since the concept of wrapping code is common to many languages, but generally means "encapsulation"), you convert your readable ASCII text source code into *unreadable* ASCII text source code. This unreadable code can then be distributed to customers or regional offices or whatever for creation in new database instances. It is as portable as your original PL/SQL code, and is included in imports and exports. The Oracle database maintains dependencies for this encrypted code as it would programs compiled from readable text. In short, an encrypted program is treated within the database just as normal PL/SQL programs are treated; the only difference is that prying eyes can't query the USER_SOURCE data dictionary to extract trade secrets.

How to Encrypt Code

To encrypt PL/SQL source code, you run the wrap executable. This program may be found in the *bin* directory of the Oracle instance. In UNIX, this directory is located at *$ORACLE_HOME/bin*. In Windows NT, you can cd to *c:\OraNT\bin*, where "*c:*" denotes the drive on which Oracle has been installed. You will then find in your *bin* directory a program whose name has this format: *wrapNN.exe*, where *NN* is the version number of the database. So if you have Oracle 7.3 installed, you will have a *wrap73.exe* file in the *bin* directory.

The format of the encryption command is:

```
wrapNN iname=readablefile [oname=encryptedfile]
```

where *NN* is your version number (72, 73, 80, etc.), *readablefile* points to the original, readable version ("in" file) of your program, and *encryptedfile* is the name of the file which will contain the encrypted version of code ("out" file).

If *readablefile* does not contain a file extension, then the default of sql is assumed.

If you do not provide an *oname* argument, then *wrapNN* creates a file with the same name as *readablefile*, but with a default extention of plb, which stands for "PL/SQL binary" (a misnomer, but it gets the idea across: binaries are unreadable).

Here are some examples of using the *wrap73* executable:

1. Wrap a program relying on all of the defaults:

   ```
   c:\orant\bin\wrap73 iname=secretprog
   ```

2. Wrap a package body, specifying overrides of all the defaults. Notice that the encrypted file does not have to have the same filename or extension as the original:

   ```
   c:\orant\bin\wrap73 iname=secretbody.spb oname=shhhhh.bin
   ```

Working with Encrypted Code

I have found the following steps to be useful in working with encrypted code:

- Establish standard file extensions which clearly identify encrypted code. I use the following extensions:

Expression	Contents
sps	Readable package specifications
spb	Readable package bodies
pls	Encrypted package specifications
plb	Encrypted package bodies

- In Windows NT and Windows 95, you will have to open an MS-DOS window and then execute the *wrapNN* command from there. My suggestion is that you do *not* execute the program from within the Oracle *bin* directory, but instead cd to the directory containing your source code and execute the *wrapNN.exe* file from there.

- Create batch files so that you can easily, quickly, and uniformly encrypt one or more files. In Windows NT, I create *bat* files in the directories containing my source code which contain lines like this:

  ```
  c:\orant\bin\wrap73 iname=plvrep.sps oname=plvrep.pls
  ```

Of course, you can also create parameterized scripts and pass in the names of the files you want to encrypt.

Impact of Encrypting Code

There are several points to consider as you move to encrypting your PL/SQL code base:

- If you are an Oracle VAR, you probably are supporting multiple Oracle versions, from 7.0 or 7.1 to Oracle 8.x. If you are a lucky Oracle VAR, you will have (in many cases) one version of PL/SQL code which will work across all of these versions. If this is the case, then you can decide whether you want to have different encrypted versions of that same program for each Oracle release. You can do this (execute *wrap71*, *wrap72*, etc., for each of your versions) or you can simply encrypt at the highest version number (say, *wrap80*). This most recent encryption will compile in earlier versions. Earlier versions of encrypted code will not, however, compile properly in later versions of Oracle.

- To encrypt your source code, you must place that code in an operating system file. If you are working within a PL/SQL development environment which allows you to build and maintain source directly in the database, you will have to "dump" this code to a file, wrap it, and then compile it back into the database—thereby wiping out your original, readable, and maintainable source code. This is not an issue as you *deploy* software to customers, but it could cause some uncomfortable situations as you develop and maintain applications.

- You can only encrypt package specifications, package bodies, and standalone functions and procedures. You can run the *wrapNN* binary against any other sort of SQL and PL/SQL statement, but those files will not be changed.

- You can tell when a program is encrypted by examining the program header. If there are no comments in the program header, then you will see this text in the first line of USER_SOURCE for a encrypted package body:

```
PACKAGE BODY <package_name> WRAPPED
```

Even if you don't notice the keyword WRAPPED on the first line, you will immediately know that you are looking at encrypted code because the text in USER_SOURCE will look like this:

```
LINE TEXT
------- ----------------------
    45 abcd
    46 95a425ff
    47 a2
    48 7 PACKAGE:
```

and you know that no matter how bad your coding style, it surely isn't *that* bad.

- Comment lines are removed from the encrypted program (who's going to read them?) *except* for comment text which appears in the header of the program definition. That is, any comments that appear before the AS or IS keywords are preserved. This allows you to provide documentation on usage and copyright to all users of your software without revealing any proprietary information. For example, the following program description will appear in readable format in USER_SOURCE:

```
CREATE OR REPLACE PACKAGE
/*
|| Author: Steven Feuerstein
|| Overview: Collect all financial calcs together.
*/
financials WRAPPED
```

  I have found that when using large, complex comment blocks, the *wrapNN* program (at least through *wrap73*) either rejects valid source code for encryption, or encrypts successfully but then fails to compile. You may find that you need to simplify or shorten your standard headers when using the wrap utility.

- Encrypted code is much larger than the original source. I have found in my experience that a 57KB readable package body turns into a 153KB encrypted package body, while a 86KB readable package body turns into a 357KB encrypted package body. These increases in file size *do* result in increased requirements for storing source code in the database. The size of compiled code stays the same.

NOTE
: As of fall 1997, no one has yet admitted to having been able to (or bothering to) crack the encryption of wrapped PL/SQL code. But don't get your hopes up too high!

24

Debugging PL/SQL

When you test a program you find errors in your code. When you debug a program you uncover the cause of an error and fix it. These are two very different processes and should not be confused. In fact, you should probably have different people perform these steps. I have always found that the author of a program is the least effective tester of that program. Sure, you as the author should perform your unit tests and make a best effort to find bugs. But no project leader should ever rely on programmers for a complete test of their own programs. I have often found that a subtle, unconscious process takes place by programmers: they unknowingly follow steps through their code that avoid errors. They seem to know what it takes to make the program work and they execute those steps, rather than expose their own errors. (I stress that this is an unconscious process!)

Once a program is tested and bugs are uncovered, however, it is certainly the responsibility of the author to fix those bugs. And so the debugging begins!

Many programmers find that debugging is by far the hardest part of programming. This difficulty often arises from the following factors:

- *Lack of understanding of the problem being solved by the program.* Most programmers like to code—reading and understanding specifications are of less interest to them. They want to get down to it, doing what they do best and what they are most comfortable with: writing code. The chance of a program meeting its requirements under these conditions is slim at best.

- *Poor programming practice.* Programs that are hard to read (lack of documentation, too much documentation, inconsistent usage of whitespace, bad choices for identifier names, etc.), not properly modularized, or those that try to be too clever present a much greater challenge to debug than those programs that are well designed and structured.

- *The program simply contains too many errors.* Without the proper analysis and coding skills, you can end up with many more errors than is necessary. When you compile a program and get back five screens of compile errors, do you just want to scream and hide? It is easy to be so overwhelmed by your errors that you don't take the organized, step-by-step approach needed to fix those errors.

- *Limited debugging skills.* There are many different approaches to uncovering the causes of your problems. Some approaches only make life more difficult for you. If you have not been trained in the best way to debug your code, you can waste many hours, raise your blood pressure, and upset your manager.

The following section reviews the debugging methods that you will want to avoid at all costs, and then offers recommendations for more effective debugging strategies.

The Wrong Way to Debug

As I present the various ways you shouldn't debug your program, I expect that just about all of you will say to yourselves (some even without hypocrisy or the merest hint of shame), "Well, that sure is obvious. Of course, you shouldn't do that. I never do that."

And yet the very next time you sit down to do your work, unless you take a very disciplined approach and stick to your own (or your group's) rules, you will follow some of these obviously horrible debugging practices.

If you happen to see little bits of yourself in the paragraphs that follow, I hope you are inspired to mend your ways.

Disorganized Debugging

When faced with a bug, you become a whirlwind of frenzied activity. Even though the presence of an error indicates that you did not fully analyze the problem and figure out how the program should solve it, you do not now take the time to understand the program. Instead you place MESSAGE statements (in Oracle Forms) or SRW.MESSAGE statements (in Oracle Reports) or DBMS_OUTPUT.PUT_LINE statements (in stored modules) all over your program in the hopes of extracting more clues from the program.

You do not save a copy of the program before you start to make changes because that would take too much time; you are under a lot of pressure right now, and you are certain that the answer will pop right out at you. You will just remove your debug statements later.

You spend lots of time looking at information that is mostly irrelevant. You question everything about your program, even though most of it uses constructs you've employed successfully for years.

You skip lunch, but make time for coffee, lots of coffee, because it is free and you want to make sure your concentration is at its most intense level possible. Even though you have no idea what is causing the problem, you think that maybe if you try this one change it might help. You make the change and take several minutes to compile, generate, and run through the test case, only to find that the change didn't help—in fact, it seemed to have caused another problem because you hadn't thought through the impact of the change on your application.

So you back out of that change and try something else in hopes that it might work. But several minutes later you again find that it doesn't. A friend, noticing that your fingers are trembling, offers to help. But you don't know where to start explaining the problem because you don't really know what is wrong. Furthermore, you are kind of embarrassed about what you've done so far (turned the program into a minefield of tracing statements) and realize you don't have a clean version to show your friend.

So you snap at the best programmer in your group and call your family to let them know you aren't going to be home for dinner that night.

Why? Because you are determined to fix that bug!

Irrational Debugging

You execute your report and it comes up empty. You spent the last hour making changes both in the underlying data structures and the code that queries and formats the data. You are certain, however, that your modifications could not make the report disappear.

You call your internal support hotline to find out if there is a network problem, even though File Manager clearly shows access to network drives. You further probe as to whether the database has gone down, even though you just connected successfully. You spend another ten minutes of the support analyst's time running through a variety of scenarios before you hang up in frustration.

"They don't know anything over there," you fume. You realize that you will have to figure this one out all by yourself.

So you dive into the code you just modified. You are determined to check every single line until you find the cause of your difficulty. Over the course of the next two hours, you talk aloud to yourself—a lot.

"Look at that! I called the stored procedure inside an IF statement. I never did that before. Maybe you can't call stored programs that way." So you remove the IF statement and instead use a GOTO statement to perform the branching to or around the stored procedure. But that doesn't fix the problem.

"My code seems fine. But it calls this other routine that Joe wrote ages ago." He has since moved on, making him a ripe candidate for the source of all problems in the world. "It probably doesn't work anymore; after all, we did upgrade to a new voice mail system." So you decide to perform a standalone test of Joe's routine, which hasn't changed for two years and has no interface to voice mail. But his program seems to work fine—when it's not run from *your* program.

Now you are starting to get desperate. "Maybe this report should only run on weekends. Hey, can I put a local module in an anonymous block? Maybe I can use only local modules in procedures and functions! I think maybe I heard about a bug in this tool. Time for a workaround..."

You get angry and understand better why your eight-year old hits the computer monitor when he can't beat the last level of Mystic Conqueror. And just as you are ready to go home and take it out on your dog, you realize that you are connected to the development database, which has almost no data at all. You switch to the test instance, run your report, and everything looks just fine.

Except, of course, for that GOTO and all the other workarounds you stuck in the report.

Debugging Tips and Strategies

I do not pretend in this chapter to offer a comprehensive primer on debugging. The following tips and techniques, however, should improve upon your current set of error-fixing skills.

Gather Data

Gather as much data as possible about when, where, and how the error occurs. It is very unlikely that the first occurrence of an error will give you all the information you will want or need to figure out the source of that error. Upon noticing an error, the temptation is to show off one's knowledge of the program by declaring, "Got it! I know what's going on and I know exactly what to do to fix it." Such a move can be very gratifying when it turns out that you do have a handle on the problem, and that will be the case for simple bugs. Some problems can appear simple, however, and turn out to require extensive testing and analysis. Save yourself the embarrassment of pretending (or believing) that you know more than you actually do. Before rushing to change your code, take these steps:

1. *Run the program again to see if the error is reproducible.* This will be the first indication of the complexity of the problem. It is almost impossible to deter-

mine the cause of a problem if you are unable to get it to occur predictably. Once you work out the steps needed to cause the error to occur, you will have gained much valuable information about its cause.

2. *Narrow the test case needed to generate the error.* I recently had to debug a problem in one of my Oracle Forms modules. A pop-up window would lose its data under certain circumstances. At first glance, the rule seemed to be: "For a new call, if you enter only one request, that request will be lost." If I had stopped testing at this point, I would have had to analyze all code that initialized the call record and handled the INSERT logic. Instead, I tried additional variations of data entry and soon found that the data was lost only when I navigated to the pop-up window directly from a certain item. Now I had a very narrow test case to analyze and it was very easy to uncover the error in logic.

3. *Examine the circumstances under which the problem does not occur.* "Failure to fail" can offer many insights into the reason an error does occur. It also helps you narrow down the sections of code and the conditions you have to analyze when you go back to the program.

The more information you gather about the problem at hand, the easier it will be to solve that problem. It is worth the extra time it will take to assemble the evidence. So even when you are absolutely sure you are on to that bug, hold off and investigate a little further.

Remain Logical at All Times

Symbolic logic is the life-blood of programmers. No matter which programming language you use, the underlying logical framework is a constant. PL/SQL has one particular syntax. The C language uses different keywords and the IF statement looks a little different. The elegance of LISP demands a very different way of building programs. But underneath it all, symbolic logic provides the backbone on which you hang the statements that solve your problems.

The reliance on logical and rational thought in programming is one reason that it is so easy for a developer to learn a new programming language. As long as you can take the statement of a problem and develop a logical solution step by step, the particulars of a language are secondary.

With logic at the core of our being, it amazes me to see how often we programmers abandon this logic and pursue the most irrational path to solving a problem. We engage in wishful thinking and highly superstitious, irrational, or dubious thought processes. Even though we know better—much better—we find ourselves questioning code that conforms to documented functionality, has worked in the past, and surely works right at that moment. This irrationality

Get it Right the First Time

There can be no doubt that the best way to decrease the effort and time required to debug your application is to write code that has fewer bugs. Such code will have fewer errors, and the errors it does have are more likely to be typos and superficial mistakes. A single, fundamental logical flaw in a program can generate a multitude of other symptomatic errors.

We all have to accept the fact that it takes more effort and time to be careful and methodical. Yet we are almost always in a rush—to meet a deadline, to go home and play with the baby, to go bowling. And so we truly, deeply believe that "this next one is easy." Heck, why not just code it straight out?

The morning after such a lapse in judgment, however, is uniformly painful and embarrassing. If you have a reputation as a guru with a tool, you may not want to have to go through several rounds of test, debug, and fix to get your program to work. If you are just learning the tool and working hard for a promotion, you can't afford to reveal sloppy programming habits. If you are responsible for a complex project, which is bound to be behind schedule, you've got to make every hour, every line of code count.

There is no substitute for getting it right the first time. Here are a few of the things you can do to minimize the number of bugs you introduce into a program:

- Understand the purpose of the program and its logic. You should be thoroughly comfortable with the objective of your coding task. You should have a strong picture in your mind of the overall structure of the program and how that relates to the documented specifications before you write a single line of code. With this fundamental grounding, it will be much more difficult for you to introduce gross errors into the program.

- Use top-down design and stepwise refinement to help keep your eyes on the prize. It is difficult, especially with complicated programs, to translate specifications directly into code without getting a bit lost in the programming details. Before you start coding, use pseudo-code at a very high level to list the different steps or functions needed to build the program. Then, for each of these steps in turn, focus your attention just on the details needed to implement that step. In this way you isolate complexities behind your steps (which will, you hope, turn into modules) and concentrate more effectively on the structure of your program before you worry about its details.

—Continued—

> • *Modularize, modularize, modularize!* Once you are ready to code, avoid writing one large, amorphous program. Instead, break up your code into separate modules, each with a specific purpose, that you can implement and test individually.
>
> In addition to these high-level tips, follow the many pieces of advice offered throughout this book to improve the quality, readability, and maintainability of your code. Taken together and used together, these techniques should greatly improve your chances of bug-free programs.

almost always involves shifting the blame from oneself to "the other": the computer, the compiler, our spouse, the word processor, whatever. Anything and anybody but our own pristine selves!

When you attempt to shift blame, you only put off solving your problem. Computers and compilers may not be intelligent, but they are very fast and they are very consistent. All they can do is follow rules, and you write the rules for them in your program. So when you uncover a bug in your code, take responsibility for that error. Assume that you did something wrong. Don't blame the PL/ SQL compiler or Oracle Forms or the text editor.

If you do find yourself questioning a basic element or rule in the compiler that has always worked for you in the past (but maybe not in this precise circumstance, right?), it is time to take a break. Better yet, it is time to get someone else to look at your code. It is amazing how another pair of eyes can focus your own analytical powers on the real causes of a problem.

Strive to be the Spock of Programming. Accept only what is logical. Reject that which has no explanation.

Analyze Instead of Trying

So you have a pile of data, all the clues you could ask for in profiling the symptoms of your problem. Now it is time to analyze that data. For many people, analysis takes the following form: "Hmm, this looks like it could be the answer. I'll make this change, recompile, and *try* it to see if it works."

What's wrong with this approach? When you try a solution to see what will happen, what you are really saying is:

• You are not sure that the change really is a solution. If you were sure, you wouldn't "try" it to see what would happen. You would make the change and then test that change.

- You have not fully analyzed the error to understand what causes it to happen. If you know why an error occurs, then you know if a particular change will fix that problem. If you are unsure about the source of the error, you will be tempted to simply try a change and examine the impact. This is, unfortunately, very faulty logic.

- Even if the change stops the error from occurring, you cannot be sure that your "solution" really solved anything. Because you are not sure why the problem occurred, the simple fact that the problem does not appear with your particular test (or tests) does not mean that you fixed the bug. The most you can say is that your change stopped the bug from occurring under certain, perhaps even most, circumstances.

To truly solve a problem, you must completely analyze the cause of the problem. Once you understand why the problem occurs, you have found the root cause and you can take the steps necessary to make sure the problem goes away in all circumstances.

When you identify a potential solution, perform a walk-through of your code based on that change. Don't execute your form. Examine your program and mentally try out different scenarios to test your hypothesis. Once you are certain that your change actually does address the problem, you can then perform a test of that solution. You won't be trying anything; you will be verifying a fix.

Analyze your bug fully before you try solutions. If you say to yourself, "Why don't I try this?" in the hope that it will solve the problem, then you are wasting your time and debugging inefficiently.

Take Breaks and Ask for Help

We are often our own biggest obstacles when it comes to sorting out our problems, whether a program bug or a personal crisis. When you are stuck on the inside of a problem, it is hard to maintain an objective distance and, with that distance, a fresh look.

When you are making absolutely no progress and feel that you have tried everything, try these two radical techniques:

- Take a break

- Ask for help

When I have struggled with a bug for any length of time without success, I not only become ineffective, I also tend to lose perspective. I pursue irrational and superstitious leads. I lose track of what I have already tested and what I have assumed to be right. I get too close to the problem to debug it effectively.

My frustration level usually correlates closely to the amount of time I have sat in my ergonomic chair and perched over my wrist-padded keyboard and stared at my low-radiation screen. Often the very simple act of stepping away from the workstation will clear my head and leave room for a solution to pop into place. Did you ever wake up the morning after a very difficult day at work to find the elusive answer sitting there at the end of your dream?

Make it a rule to get up and walk around at least once an hour when you are working on a problem—heck, even when you are writing your programs. Give your brain a chance to let its neural networks make the connections and develop new options for your programming. There is a whole big world out there. Even when your eyes are glued to the monitor and your source code, the world keeps turning. It never hurts to remind yourself of the bigger picture, even if that only amounts to taking note of the weather outside your air-conditioned cocoon.

Even more effective than taking a break is asking another person to look at your problem. There is something entirely magical about the dynamic of adding another pair of eyes to the situation. You might have struggled without any result for an hour or two on a problem, and finally, out of desperation, asked a coworker to have a go at it. Then, at the exact moment that you explain the problem to your friend, the solution will jump out at you. It could be a mismatch on names, a false assumption, or a misunderstanding of the IF statement logic. Whatever the case, chances are that you yourself will find it (even though you couldn't for the last two hours) as soon as you ask someone else to find it for you.

If the error does not yield itself quite that easily, you still have lots to gain from the perspective of another person who (a) did not write the code and has no subconscious assumptions or biases about the code, and (b) isn't mad at the program.

Other benefits accrue from asking for help. You improve the self-esteem and self-confidence of other programmers by showing that you respect their opinions. If you are one of the best developers in the group, then your request for help demonstrates that you, too, make mistakes and need help from the team to move forward. This builds the sense (and reality) of teamwork, which will improve the overall development and testing efforts on the project.

Change and Test One Area of Code at a Time

One of my biggest problems when I debug my code is that I try to make too many changes at once. I am overconfident about my development and debugging skills. So I make five or ten changes, rerun my test, and get very unreliable and minimally useful results. I find that my changes cause other problems (a common phenomenon until a program stabilizes and a sure sign that lots more debugging and testing is needed), that some of the original errors are gone, but not all of them, and I have no idea which changes fixed which errors, and which changes caused new errors.

In short, my debugging effort is a mess and I have to back out of changes until I have a clearer picture of what is happening in my program.

Unless you are making very simple changes, you should fix one problem at a time and then test that fix. The amount of time it takes to compile, generate, and test may increase, but in the long run you will be much more productive.

One other aspect of incremental testing and debugging is performing "unit tests" on individual modules before you test a program which calls these various modules. If you test the programs separately and determine that they work, when you debug your application as a whole (in a system test), you do not have to worry about whether those modules return correct values or perform the correct actions. Instead, you can concentrate on the code that calls the modules.

Document and Back Up Your Efforts

Are you offended that I would even say this? Of course we all back up our programs. Of course we all document our efforts.

And pigs can fly.

What I personally cannot believe is that, as recently as September, 1994, I managed to delete the entire contents of my source code directory for a data transfer utility. Sure, there was a backup—on tape. It was already archived. It took the operations department five hours to recover my code and then I still lost three hours of work from that morning. You see, I hadn't bothered to back up my code to my own convenient refresh directory. And I had decided to clean up my UNIX subdirectories of old data files. My clean-up script, sad to say, had a bug in it, which caused it to remain in my source directory and remove all files.

You can snicker all you want, but the same thing has happened to you, and will happen again, unless you constantly remind yourself to:

- Archive your original program version
- Copy incremental versions to different files
- Save your current changes

Suppose you have finished development on a very complex and difficult program. You are not surprised when you discover many different bugs. You hunker right down to the task of analyzing and fixing the errors. As you complete a number of fixes, you should save that program out to a different file so that you have "frozen" a version to which you can return if necessary. Then if, as you continue debugging, you take a wrong turn and code yourself into a nonproductive corner, you do not have to spend time surgically removing your mistakes. You can instead shift back to an earlier version of the program.

Clearly, there are source code control programs such as PVCS that handle these functions for you. In many cases with Oracle software, however, these utilities are not used and it is completely up to you to take the steps necessary to protect yourself and your code.

Test All Assumptions

Every move you make, every test you take, every line of code you write has assumptions attached to it. You need to be conscious of those assumptions and, when you start your debug cycle, test those assumptions to make sure they are valid.

I recently wasted several hours debugging a problem. I could have solved it in about three minutes—if I'd properly tested my assumptions. A stored function accepted three parameters and returned a value as shown below:

```
new_rate := mortgage_rate (down_payment, prime_rate, mortgage_type);
```

The mortgage_rate function was, unfortunately, setting new_rate to NULL. After examining the function, it was clear to me that the only way it could return a NULL was if one of the inputs was NULL. I then used this information as follows:

1. I had just examined the global variable holding the mortgage type. That global value was transferred to the mortgage_type variable in an earlier program and passed to my current module, so I knew that it was OK.

2. I performed a walk-through of the code and could not identify how any of the other two variables could be NULL.

3. So I inserted a trace statement before and after the call to mortgage_rate. My code now looked like this:

```
DBMS_OUTPUT.PUT_LINE
    ('Inputs: ' || TO_CHAR (down_payment) || '-' ||
    TO_CHAR  (prime_rate));

new_rate := mortgage_rate (
    down_payment, prime_rate,
    bank, mortgage_type);

DBMS_OUTPUT.PUT_LINE ('Rate: ' || NVL (TO_CHAR (new_rate), 'Missing'));
```

4. I ran the program and no matter what data I entered on the screen, my trace statements remained the same:

```
Inputs: 55000-9.5
Rate: Missing
```

I wracked my obviously overwrought brain: what could cause a stored function to return a NULL value? I looked at the source code for the function again. There wasn't much to it. Just division and multiplication. How could it return a NULL without a NULL input?

After two hours of this nonsense, I finally said to myself, "Well, you know that you really haven't verified the value of the mortgage_type variable." I knew that it was OK, but, hey, it wouldn't hurt to check—and if I didn't solve this one soon I would have to actually ask for help.

So I modified my trace statement and, sure enough, the mortgage type was NULL. Turns out that while the global variable held the proper value, the previous program did not pass it to the local variable properly. My assumption did me in.

One of the first assumptions you will make in your testing is that you have valid inputs to your program. This can also be one of the most dangerous assumptions to make.

Data errors are perhaps the most frustrating of all the kinds of bugs you will encounter. You follow all the right steps for debugging and analyzing your code, only to discover that there is nothing actually wrong with your program. Instead, the data that drives your program is wrong.

I encounter this problem most often in the following situations:

- I am testing my code in multiple database instances. Never assume that the data structures and actual rows of data are identical in all instances. Never assume that all indexes have been defined the same way.

- The reference data is still unstable. What is the valid code for a "closed" call? What are the ten valid company types? If this data is still changing, your program is likely to break.

If you do not understand why your program is doing what it is doing, make a list of all your assumptions and then test those—including the data you rely on to run your program. There is a good chance that your error was introduced very early into the process.

Leverage Existing Utilities—Or Build Your Own

As you build more and more complex programs, you will find it increasingly difficult and incredibly frustrating to manage and debug these programs without a utility of some kind. Take the time to investigate what is available and what it will do for you.

Historically, Oracle Corporation has been very slow to offer debugging and other programmer-oriented utilities. Third-party vendors seem to have taken a clue from

Oracle and also have not hurried to provide a strong set of tools for PL/SQL developers. As of mid-year 1997, that situation is finally changing. You can now purchase debuggers from the following vendors:

- Oracle Corporation: Procedure Builder
- Platinum Technology: SQL Station Debugger
- Technosolutions: SQL Navigator
- Compuware: XPediter/SQL

All of these products greatly improve the ability to debug client-side PL/SQL; you will need to carefully examine the specific benefits and features before deciding which of these (and, I hope, by the time this book is published, others as well) fit your needs most closely.

If, on the other hand, you cannot find anything that will help (or you can't get the approval to buy the utility of your dreams), you might consider building your own. I have found in the past that it is relatively straightforward to implement utilities that have a significant impact on my debugging capabilities. I built XRay Vision, a debugger for SQL*Forms, implemented entirely in SQL*Forms itself, which gave me the ability to view and modify all variables in my programs. You'll find this debugger, *xrayvizn.zip*, on the RevealNet Web site. While you are unlikely to be using SQL*Forms at this point, you may find the source code of interest (stored in the good, old INP files).

When Oracle Forms 4.x (even the version in Oracle Developer/2000 that has its own source code debugger) came along, I realized that it was impossible to view and change data structures created at runtime (record groups, parameter lists, etc.). So I built a utility named Arjy (pronounced "RG" for Record Group), which gave me that access. The shareware version of Arjy, *arjy.zip* is also available at the RevealNet Web site.

The basic PL/SQL product from Oracle Corporation will never have everything you need. If you can't find what you need to get the job done, then get creative and take a crack at meeting your own needs. Dive in and build your own utility. Not only will you improve your productivity (and that of others), but you will gain a feeling of intense satisfaction from solving your own problems all by yourself.

Build Debugging Messages into Your Packages

If you do not use a GUI-based, source code debugger, you probably spend a fair amount of time throwing debug or trace messages into your code and then removing them when things are fixed. A much better approach is to leave these messages intact, but give yourself lots of flexibility in deciding when you want to see them.

The simplest model for this technique is actually built right into the DBMS_ OUTPUT package. The DBMS_OUTPUT.PUT_LINE procedure displays output from your PL/SQL program when that program completes execution. But it will not show anything unless the package itself is enabled with a call to DBMS_ OUTPUT.ENABLE and/or unless from within SQL*Plus you issue the SET SERVER-OUTPUT ON command. Furthermore, this is an all-or-nothing proposition: you either see no output, or you see output from every call to this procedure from every corner of your application. That can be overwhelming if you have inserted lots of trace messages.

You can easily come up with a more discerning technique when working with packages. Suppose I have developed a package to perform calculations for profit-and-loss statements. My p_and_l package maintains a last statement date as a global variable for use within the package. I build a "get and set" layer of code around the variable so that applications can retrieve and manipulate the variable—but only through my code layer. Here is the package:

```
CREATE OR REPLACE PACKAGE p_and_l
IS
    PROCEDURE set_lastdate (date_in IN DATE);
    FUNCTION lastdate RETURN DATE;

    /* Lots of other stuff, too! */
    . . .
END p_and_l;
/

CREATE OR REPLACE PACKAGE BODY p_and_l
IS
    g_lastdate DATE;

    PROCEDURE set_lastdate (date_in IN DATE)
    IS
    BEGIN
       /* Date cannot be in future. */
       g_lastdate := LEAST (SYSDATE, date_in);
    END;

    FUNCTION lastdate RETURN DATE
    IS
    BEGIN
        RETURN g_lastdate;
    END;
END p_and_l;
/
```

As I test this package as part of a large, complex application, suppose that I find that the last date variable is being set improperly, but I can't figure out what is

doing it and why. I can go into the p_and_l.set_lastdate procedure and insert a
call to DBMS_OUTPUT.PUT_LINE as follows:

```
PROCEDURE set_lastdate (date_in IN DATE)
IS
BEGIN
   DBMS_OUTPUT.PUT_LINE ('setting date to ' || TO_CHAR (date_in));
   /* Date cannot be in future. */
   g_lastdate := LEAST (SYSDATE, date_in);
END;
```

but then I have to see all the output in my application and try to find this one
statement among all the others. The approach I take instead is to provide a debug
"toggle" in my package which allows me to focus output to just the statements I
need to see. With the toggle technique, I add three programs to my package
specification:

```
CREATE OR REPLACE PACKAGE p_and_l
IS
   PROCEDURE set_lastdate (date_in IN DATE);
   FUNCTION lastdate RETURN DATE;

   PROCEDURE dbg;
   PROCEURE nodbg;
   FUNCTION debugging RETURN BOOLEAN;

   /* Lots of other stuff, too! */
   . . .
END p_and_l;
/
```

I also modify the package body to both implement this toggle and use it inside
the set_lastdate procedure:

```
CREATE OR REPLACE PACKAGE BODY p_and_l
IS
   g_lastdate DATE;
   g_dbg BOOLEAN := FALSE;

   PROCEDURE dbg IS BEGIN g_dbg := TRUE; END;
   PROCEDURE nodbg IS BEGIN g_dbg := FALSE; END;
   FUNCTION debugging RETURN BOOLEAN RETURN g_dbg; END;

   PROCEDURE set_lastdate (date_in IN DATE)
   IS
   BEGIN
      IF debugging
      THEN
         DBMS_OUTPUT.PUT_LINE ('before set ' || TO_CHAR (g_lastdate));
      END IF;

      /* Date cannot be in future. */
      g_lastdate := LEAST (SYSDATE, date_in);
```

```
      IF debugging
      THEN
          DBMS_OUTPUT.PUT_LINE ('after set ' || TO_CHAR (g_lastdate));
      END IF;
   END;

   FUNCTION lastdate RETURN DATE
   IS
   BEGIN
      RETURN g_lastdate;
   END;
END p_and_l;
/
```

Then if I want to see what is happening to the g_lastdate variable, I can issue the debug command in SQL*Plus for this package and see just the output I need:

```
SQL> exec p_and_l.dbg
SQL> exec testing_program
before set 12-JAN-97
after set 15-JAN-97
```

Of course, you'd probably want to see more information, such as the execution call stack to see what program called the p_and_l.set_lastdate procedure. You can add anything you want—all within the confines of the IF debugging clause—and that information will be available only on a need-to-know basis. You might even decide to free yourself from the confines of DBMS_OUTPUT by writing information out to a database pipe.

Furthermore, if you set as a standard in your group that every package is to have a debug toggle, then it will be much easier for users of those packages to debug their own use (or misuse) of that reusable code. They know that there will be a program named PKG.dbg which can be used to extract additional information about package processing.

This technique is explored in more detail and with a slightly different focus (production support) in Chapter 26, *Tracing PL/SQL Execution.*

In this chapter:
- *Analyzing Program Performance*
- *Tuning Access to Compiled Code*
- *Tuning Access to Your Data*
- *Tuning Your Algorithms*
- *Overview of PL/SQL8 Enhancements*

25

Tuning PL/SQL Applications

Tuning an application is a very complicated process. Really, it deserves a book of its own. Fortunately, there is such a book: *Oracle Performance Tuning* by Mark Gurry and Peter Corrigan.* Many of the ideas in this section are drawn from—and explored more thoroughly in—Gurry and Corrigan's book.

Before diving into the particulars, I want to be sure that you recognize the different aspects of tuning PL/SQL that you might want to perform:

- *Analyzing program performance.* Before you can tune your application, you need to figure out what is running slowly and where you should focus your efforts.

- *Tuning access to compiled code.* Before your code can be executed (and perhaps run too slowly), it must be loaded into the System Global Area (SGA) of the Oracle instance. This process can benefit from a focused tuning effort.

- *Tuning access to your data.* Much of the tuning you do will attempt to optimize the way PL/SQL programs manipulate data in the Oracle database, both queries and DML (updates, inserts, deletes). Lots of the issues here involve tuning SQL statements (out of the scope of this book), but there are certainly steps you can take in your PL/SQL code and environment to improve the performance of even an optimally constructed chunk of SQL.

- *Tuning your algorithms.* As a procedural language, PL/SQL is often used to implement complex formulas and algorithms. You make use of conditional statements, loops, perhaps even GOTOs and reusable modules (I hope) to get the job done. These algorithms can be written in many different ways, some of which perform very badly. How do you tune poorly written algorithms? A

---

* O'Reilly & Associates, Second Edition, 1996. There are other books on Oracle tuning as well.

tough question with no simple answers; I offer some case studies at the end of this chapter which will perhaps give you some fresh approaches to bring to bear on your own code.

The following sections address each of these areas of PL/SQL tuning.

Analyzing Program Performance

Before you can tune your application, you need to know what is causing it to slow down. To do this, you usually need to be able to analyze the performance of your application. Oracle offers a number of database monitoring and diagnostic tools, as do third-party vendors like Platinum Technology and Quest. Check Oracle documentation and Chapter 10 of *Oracle Performance Tuning* for more details, and be aware of the following major tools:

MONITOR
   A SQL*DBA facility that lets you look at various system activity and performance tables.

SQL_TRACE
   A utility that writes a trace file containing performance statistics.

TKPROF
   A utility that translates the SQL_TRACE file into readable output and can also show the execution plan for a SQL statement.

EXPLAIN PLAN
   A statement that analyzes and displays the execution plan for a SQL statement.

ORADBX
   An undocumented tool that allows you to track a running process and create a trace file in the same format as the SQL_TRACE trace file. You can then run TKPROF against the trace file to obtain the execution plan details, as well as disk I/O, parsing, and CPU usage.

ANALYZE
   A statement that compiles statistics for use by the cost-based optimizer to construct its execution plan. The statement also produces other useful information that can be used to detect chained rows and help with capacity planning.

UTLBSTAT (begin) and UTLESTAT (end)
   Scripts that produce a snapshot of how the database is performing from the time you start UTLBSTAT until you run UTLESTAT.

Enterprise Manager/Performance Pack
   An Oracle product introduced with Oracle7.3 that provides some excellent tuning tools, including Oracle Performance Manager, Oracle Trace, and Oracle Expert

Use the DBMS_UTILITY.GET_TIME Function

The tools listed in the previous section provide varying levels of detail and granularity; however, they all do require some effort—often on the part of a person other than the PL/SQL developer in need—to get them enabled. And then they require even more effort to interpret results. Don't get me wrong; I am not really complaining. It's just that, quite frankly, PL/SQL developers often want to examine the performance of a particular program and do not want to have to deal with all that other stuff.

No problem! PL/SQL provides a mechanism to obtain timings of code execution that are accurate to 100th of a second: the DBMS_UTILTY.GET_TIME function. Yes, that's right. I said 100th of a second. For those of you who have programmed in Oracle over the past few years, this should be a welcome surprise. Before the advent of the DBMS_UTILITY package, the only way to measure elapsed time was to use SYSDATE and examine the difference in the time component. Sadly, this component only records times down to the nearest second. This doesn't help much when you need to measure subsecond response time.

DBMS_UTILITY.GET_TIME returns the number of hundredths of seconds which have elapsed since some arbitrary point in time. I don't remember what that point is and, well, that's the whole point. A single value returned by a call to DBMS_UTILITY.GET_TIME is, by itself, meaningless. If, on the other hand, you call this built-in function *twice* and then take the difference between the two returned values, you will have determined the number of hundredths of seconds which elapsed *between* the two calls. So if you sandwich the execution of your own program between calls to DBMS_UTILITY.GET_TIME, you will have discovered how long it takes to run that program.

The anonymous block below shows how to use GET_TIME to determine the time it takes to perform the calc_totals procedure:

```
DECLARE
    time_before BINARY_INTEGER;
    time_after BINARY_INTEGER;
BEGIN
    time_before := DBMS_UTILITY.GET_TIME;
    calc_totals;
    time_after := DBMS_UTILITY.GET_TIME;
    DBMS_OUTPUT.PUT_LINE (time_after - time_before);
END;
```

I found myself relying on GET_TIME frequently as I developed the code in this book, because I wanted to analyze the performance impact of a particular approach or technique. Is it faster to raise an exception or execute an IF statement? Is it faster to load 100 rows in a table or concatenate 100 substrings into a long string?

There are two basic approaches you can take to using this handy function:

- Write again and again the kind of script you see above, changing the program or lines of code executed.

- Encapsulate the way DBMS_UTILITY.GET_TIME operates inside a package, which will hide the details and make it easier to use.

You will find on the companion disk an explanation and code for such a package, sp_timer, in the files *sptimer.sps* and *sptimer.spb*. In addition, you will find in *Advanced Oracle PL/SQL Programming with Packages* a more complete performance timing utility based on DBMS_UTILITY.GET_TIME in the PLVtmr package.

Once you have encapsulated your usage of DBMS_UTILITY.GET_TIME, it is very easy to put together scripts which not only analyze performance, but also compare different implementations. The following script, for example, executes two different versions of the is_number function (see "Tuning Your Algorithms" for more information on this function) and displays the resulting elapsed times (using the PLVtmr and p packages from the PL/Vision library; again, see *Advanced Oracle PL/SQL Programming with Packages*:

```
SET VERIFY OFF
DECLARE
   b BOOLEAN;
BEGIN
   PLVtmr.set_factor (&1)
   PLVtmr.capture;
   FOR repind IN 1 .. &1 -- Number of iterations
   LOOP
      b := isnum ('&2'); -- The string to test
      IF repind = 1
      THEN
         p.l (b);
      END IF;
   END LOOP;
   PLVtmr.show_elapsed ('TO_NUMBER Version');

   PLVtmr.set_factor (&1)
   PLVtmr.capture;
   FOR repind IN 1 .. &1
   LOOP
      b := isnum_translate ('&2');
      PLVtmr.last_timing := 15;
      IF repind = 1
      THEN
         p.l (b);
      END IF;
   END LOOP;
   PLVtmr.show_elapsed ('TRANSLATE Version');
END;
/
```

Tuning Access to Compiled Code

Before your code can be executed (and perhaps run too slowly), it must be loaded into the System Global Area (SGA) of the Oracle instance (described in more detail in Chapter 23, *Managing Code in the Database*). There are two elements to PL/SQL code in shared memory: the code segment and the data segment. This loading process can benefit from its own special tuning effort.

Tune the Size of the Shared Pool of the SGA

Before you can execute a stored package module or reference a stored package object, the compiled code for that package must be loaded into the SGA. Clearly, if the package is already present in shared memory, your code executes more quickly. An important element of tuning an application which is heavily dependent on stored packages (especially large ones) is to optimize package access so that the most often-used packages are always present when needed.

The default method for maintaining packages in the SGA (or "shared pool") is to let the RDBMS manage the code using its least-recently-used algorithm. The first time you reference a package, the compiled code is loaded into the shared pool. It is then available to anyone with EXECUTE authority on that package. It remains in the shared pool until the memory is needed by other memory-based resources and that package has not been used most recently. At that point, the package is flushed from the shared pool. The next time an object in the package is needed, the whole package has to be loaded once again into memory.

The larger your shared pool, the more likely it is that your programs will be resident in memory the next time they are needed. Yet if you make your shared pool too large, you will be wasting memory. You should monitor your shared buffer pool to make sure it is retaining all the parsed SQL cursors and PL/SQL code segments which are commonly referenced in your application. If you find that too much swapping is occurring, increase the size of the shared buffer pool (as physical memory permits) by adjusting the SHARED_POOL_SIZE parameter in your *INIT.ORA* file.

You can display all the objects currently in the shared pool that are larger than a specified size (in the example, 25KB) with the following statement (make sure you have SET SERVEROUTPUT ON in SQL*Plus before you make this call):

```
SQL> exec dbms_shared_pool.sizes (25);
```

Pin Critical Code into the SGA

To increase your ability to tune application performance, Oracle supplies the DBMS_SHARED_POOL package to pin a package in the shared pool. When a package is pinned, the RDBMS does not apply its least-recently-used algorithm to that package. The package remains in memory for as long as the database instance is available (or until you explicitly "unpin" the package, as described below).

At this time, only packages can be pinned in the shared pool; this fact provides added incentive to define your procedures and functions inside packages, rather than as standalone modules.

You will only want to pin code when absolutely necessary, since you can end up setting aside too much memory for code, resulting in a degradation in performance of other aspects of the application. In fact, Oracle Corporation warns that the KEEP and UNKEEP procedures may not be supported in future releases, since it might provide an "automatic mechanism" which replaces these procedures.

The usual candidates for pinning are particularly large programs. Prior to Oracle 7.3, Oracle requires contiguous memory in the SGA to store the code, so if sufficient space is not available at a given point of execution, Oracle will either raise an error or start swapping out other programs to make room. Neither scenario is optimal.

Usually you will pin programs right after the database is started up, so that all the critical elements of your application are in place for all users. Here is an example of the pinning of the order entry package (owned by the appowner schema):

```
DBMS_SHARED_POOL.KEEP ('appowner.ordentry');
```

Here is the code you would execute to unpin the same package from shared memory:

```
DBMS_SHARED_POOL.UNKEEP ('appowner.ordentry');
```

Keep the following factors in mind when working with the DBMS_SHARED_POOL package:

- When you call the KEEP procedure, the package is "queued" for pinning in the SGA. However, the KEEP procedure does not immediately load the package into the shared pool—that happens when the package is first referenced, either to execute a module or to use one of the declared objects, such as a global variable or a cursor.

- Oracle recommends that you pin all your packages in the shared pool soon after instance startup, when the SGA is still relatively unfragmented. That way it can set aside contiguous blocks of memory for large packages.

- If you pin a package which is not owned by SYS (DBMS_OUTPUT, for example, is owned by SYS), you must grant EXECUTE on the package to PUBLIC before you execute the KEEP procedure. Once you have pinned the package, you can revoke the PUBLIC access.

- The SQL DDL command, ALTER SYSTEM FLUSH SHARED_POOL, does not affect pinned packages. You must either explicitly UNKEEP a package or restart the database to release the package from the shared pool.

Candidates for pinning in the shared pool

You might consider pinning the following packages in the shared pool to improve performance:

STANDARD
Package which implements the core elements of the PL/SQL language.

DBMS_STANDARD
Package of standard database-level modules, such as RAISE_APPLICATION_ ERROR.

DBMS_UTILITY
Package of low-level database utilities which are used to analyze schemas and objects.

DBMS_DESCRIBE
Package containing a utility to describe the structure of a stored module.

DBMS_OUTPUT
Package which allows programmers to display output to the screen.

In addition, if you make frequent use of any other Oracle-provided "SYS" packages such as DBMS_LOCK or DBMS_PIPE, pinning those objects could improve performance as well.

You are probably getting the idea that the more you pin into the shared pool, the better off you are. Certainly that is true, at least as true as the statement: "If all your data is stashed in memory, your applications will run much faster." Memory is always quicker than disk access. The problem is making sure you have enough memory.

The more you pin into the shared pool, the less space is left in the SGA for other memory-based resources, such as data dictionary latches, application data, and shared SQL. Since a pinned object is never aged out of the SGA using a least-recently-used algorithm, other elements in the SGA are instead pushed out of the way.

You can use SQL to generate a script to KEEP packages in the SGA. You can use the following SQL statement to access the v$db_object_cache to generate a KEEP for each package currently in the shared pool:

```
SELECT 'EXECUTE DBMS_SHARED_POOL.KEEP('''||name||''');'
  FROM v$db_object_cache
 WHERE type='PACKAGE';
```

You can also generate a KEEP statement for every package currently stored in the database with these other SQL statements:

```
SELECT DISTINCT 'EXECUTE DBMS_SHARED_POOL.KEEP('''||name||''');'
  FROM user_source
 WHERE type='PACKAGE';

SELECT DISTINCT 'EXECUTE DBMS_SHARED_POOL.KEEP('''||object_name||''');'
  FROM user_objects
 WHERE object_type='PACKAGE';
```

Tune ACCESS$ Table to Reduce First Execution Time of Code

When a database object is first referenced in a PL/SQL program, the PL/SQL engine checks the ACCESS$ table (owned by SYS) to see if the executor of the program has authority on that database object. The structure of this table is shown here:

```
SQL> desc access$
 Name                                 Null?    Type
 ----------------------------------   -------- ----
 D_OBJ#                               NOT NULL NUMBER
 ORDER#                               NOT NULL NUMBER
 COLUMNS                                       RAW(32)
 TYPES                                NOT NULL NUMBER
```

The PL/SQL engine searches through this table on the D_OBJ# column, so if you create a nonunique index on the D_OBJ# column, you may in some cases reduce significantly the amount of time needed to perform this security check.

Creating Packages with Minimal Interdependencies

Design your code (preferably, most of it inside packages) so that you only load into memory the code you need at any given moment in time. To accomplish this objective, you should create more smaller packages, each of which is tightly focused on implementing functionality in a given area. The alternative, which too many of us employ without giving it much thought, is to create a few large packages that group together lots of different elements of functionality.

The problem with this approach is that if I need to execute one function in that 32K package, the entire package still must be loaded up into memory. Suppose that my application then touches another element of the package, such as a constant or perhaps a different function in a different functional area. The least-recently-used algorithm will then ensure that all the memory for that package continues to be set aside, perhaps crowding out other smaller programs. The result can be excessive swapping of code.

As you build your programs and design your package interfaces, be on the lookout for an opportunity to break up a single package into two or even more distinct packages with minimal interdependencies.

Reducing Memory Usage of Package Variables

Prior to PL/SQL8, any data declared in a package simply stayed around until the end of the session, whether or not it was needed any more by the application. This is an important feature of PL/SQL packages (persistent, global data), but it limits scalability since such memory grows linearly with the number of users.

To help applications better manage memory usage, PL/SQL8 provides the pragma SERIALLY_REUSABLE, which lets you mark some packages as "serially reusable." You can so mark a package if its state is needed only for the duration of a call to the server (for example, an OCI call to the server, a PL/SQL client-to-server, or server-to-server RPC).

The global memory for such packages is not kept in the memory area per user, but instead in a small SGA pool. At the end of the call to the server, this memory is returned to the pool for reuse. Before reuse, the package global variables are initialized to NULL or to the default values provided.

The pool is kept in SGA memory so that the work area of a package can be reused across users who have requests for the same package. In this scheme, the maximum number of work areas needed for a package is only as many as there are concurrent users of the package, which is typically much fewer than the total number of logged on users. The use of "serially reusable" packages does increase the shared-pool requirements slightly, but this is more than offset by the decrease in the per-user memory requirements. Further, Oracle ages out work areas not in use when it needs to reclaim shared pool memory.

The following example shows how global variables in a "serially reusable" package behave across call boundaries:

```
CREATE OR REPLACE PACKAGE sr_pkg
IS
  PRAGMA SERIALLY_REUSABLE;
  num NUMBER := 0;
  PROCEDURE print_pkg;
  PROCEDURE init_pkg (n NUMBER);
END sr_pkg;
/
CREATE OR REPLACE PACKAGE BODY sr_pkg
IS
    -- the body is required to have the pragma since the
    -- specification of this package has the pragma
  PRAGMA SERIALLY_REUSABLE;
    -- Print package state
```

```
   PROCEDURE print_pkg is
   BEGIN
     DBMS_OUTPUT.PUT_LINE ('num: ' || sr_pkg.num);
   END;
   -- Initialize package state
   PROCEDURE init_pkg(n NUMBER) IS
   BEGIN
     sr_pkg.num := n;
   END;
 END sr_pkg;
 /
```

Now I will exercise this package. First, I enable output from SQL*Plus:

```
SQLPLUS> set serveroutput on;
```

Next, I initialize the package with a value of 4 and then display package contents—all within a single PL/SQL block:

```
SQLPLUS> begin
            -- initialize and print the package
            SR_PKG.init_pkg(4);

            -- Print it in the same call to the server.
            -- We should see the new values.
            SR_PKG.print_pkg;
         end;
         /
Statement processed.
num: 4
```

And we see that initial value of 4. If I had not placed the call to sr_pkg.print_pkg *inside* the same PL/SQL block, however, that package variable would lose its setting, as you can see in the following steps:

```
SQLPLUS> begin
            -- We should see that the package state is reset to the
            -- initial (default) values.
            SR_PKG.print_pkg;
         end;
         /
Statement processed.
num: 0
```

Use this feature with care! Many of the packages I have constructed over the years absolutely rely on the persistent data feature.

Tuning Access to Your Data

Much of the tuning you do will attempt to optimize the way PL/SQL programs manipulate data in the Oracle database, both queries and DML (updates, inserts, deletes). Lots of the issues here involve tuning SQL statements, and I am not even going to attempt to show you how to tune SQL (definitely not my strong suit).

There are certainly steps you can take, though, in your PL/SQL code and environment to improve the performance of even an optimally constructed chunk of SQL.

Use Package Data to Minimize SQL Access

When you declare a variable in a package body or specification, its scope is not restricted to any particular procedure or function. As a result, the scope of package-level data is the entire Oracle session, and the value of that data persists for the entire session. Take advantage of this fact to minimize the times you have to access data from the SQL layer. Performing lookups against structures located in your own Program Global Area (PGA) is much, much faster than going through the SGA—even if the data you want is resident in shared memory.

This tip will come in handy most when you find that your application needs to perform multiple lookups which do not change during your session. Suppose, for example, that one of your programs needs to obtain a unique session identifier to avoid overlaps with other sessions. One of the ways to do this is to call DBMS_LOCK.ALLOCATE_UNIQUE to retrieve a unique lockname. Here is the inefficient way to do this: I need the ID or lockname in the calc_totals procedure. So I make the call to the built-in package right inside the procedure:

```
PROCEDURE calc_totals
IS
    v_lockname VARCHAR2(100);
BEGIN
    v_lockname := DBMS_LOCK.ALLOCATE_UNIQUE;

    /* Use the lock name to issue a request for data. */
    send_request (v_lockname);

    . . .
END;
```

The problem with this approach is that every time calc_totals is called, the built-in function is also called to get the unique value—a totally unnecessary action. After you get it the first time, you needn't get it again.

Packages provide a natural repository for these "session-level" pieces of data. The following sesspkg (session package) defines a variable to hold the lock name and then assigns it a value on initialization of the package:

```
PACKAGE sesspkg
IS
    lockname CONSTANT VARCHAR2(100) := DBMS_LOCK.ALLOCATE_UNIQUE;
END;
```

Now the calc_totals procedure can directly reference the package global in its call to send_request. The first time calc_totals is called, the sesspkg package is instantiated and the built-in function called. All subsequent calls to calc_totals within that session will not, however, result in any additional processing inside sesspkg. Instead, it simply returns the value resident in the constant.

```
PROCEDURE calc_totals
IS
BEGIN
    /* Use the lock name to issue a request for data. */
    send_request (sesspkg.lockname);
END;
```

You can apply a similar technique for lookups against database tables—both persistent and session-based. In the following example, the SELECT from v$parameter will be executed only once per session, regardless of how many times the db_ name function is executed. Since the database name will never change during the session, this is reasonable. Note also the judicious use of a function with side effects, where one side effect (modification of a persistent package variable) is used to gain the efficiency:

```
/* Filename on companion disk: dbdata.spp */

CREATE OR REPLACE PACKAGE db_data
IS
    /* function to return the name of the database */
    FUNCTION db_name RETURN VARCHAR2;
END db_data;
/
CREATE OR REPLACE PACKAGE BODY db_data
IS
    /* DB_name variable only manipulated by this function */
    v_db_name  VARCHAR2(8) := NULL;

    /* function to return the name of the database */
    FUNCTION db_name RETURN VARCHAR2
    IS
    BEGIN
        IF v_db_name IS NULL
        THEN
            SELECT SUBSTR(value,1,8) INTO v_db_name
              FROM v$parameter
             WHERE name = 'db_name';
        END IF;
        RETURN v_db_name;
    END db_name;
END db_data;
```

NOTE   You will need to have access to the v$parameter table granted to you from SYS if you want to compile and use this package outside of the SYS account.

For a final example of using package data to reduce SQL I/O and improve performance, Chapter 10, *PL/SQL Tables*, shows how you can use a PL/SQL table stored in a package to "remember" values which have already been queried in that session. If the value is in the PL/SQL table, the function returns that value. If not, it retrieves the value from the database table and, before returning the value, stores it in the PL/SQL table.

Call PL/SQL Functions in SQL to Reduce I/O

Chapter 17, *Calling PL/SQL Functions in SQL*, explains how to create and place functions inside SQL statements. There are many advantages to this approach, which can result in cleaner, easier to read SQL and performance improvements. The following example illustrates the use of packaged functions in SQL to minimize I/O in a SQL query (and thereby to improve performance); it also takes advantage of persistent package data to minimize data access.

Suppose we are given a table of address information, primary-keyed by a unique system-generated identifier as follows:

```
CREATE TABLE  addresses
    (id  NUMBER  NOT NULL PRIMARY KEY
    ,street VARCHAR2(200)
    ,city VARHAR2(200)
    ,state CHAR(2)
    ,ZIP VARCHAR2(20))
/
```

Suppose also that we have a complex view joining several tables and that one or more columns *may* contain address identifiers (or be NULL) and that we want to join in a single address according to some prioritization:

```
CREATE VIEW termination_notices
    (customer_id  NUMBER
    ,termination_reason VARCHAR2(10)
    ,customer_addr_id NUMBER
    ,employer_addr_id NUMBER)
AS
    SELECT ...
/
```

We want to assemble a new view (or PL/SQL cursor) which will de-reference one of the address ids as follows:

```
IF customer_addr_id IS NOT NULL
THEN
    use that address
ELSIF spouse_addr_id IS NOT NULL
THEN
    use that address
```

```
    ELSE
        no address
    END IF;
```

We can create a new view to meet these requirements using UNIONed SELECTs
each joining in different addresses, but this will be very complex and could
involve multiple scans through the termination_notices view. Another possibility
is to use PL/SQL functions to provide address lookups and then include these
functions directly in the new view or cursor SELECT statement. One possible
problem with this approach is that since we will want to provide all elements of
the address in multiple columns, we are in danger of doing address lookups four
times per row (once for each column of the addresses table). This can be avoided
by making use of the persistent state of package variables:

```
    CREATE OR REPLACE PACKAGE address_info
    IS
        /* these are the functions we will call in SQL */
        --
        FUNCTION streetaddr(addr_id_IN IN address.id%TYPE)
            RETURN address.street%TYPE;
        PRAGMA RESTRICT_REFERENCES (streetaddr,WNDS);
        --
        FUNCTION cityaddr(addr_id_IN IN address.id%TYPE)
            RETURN address.city%TYPE;
        PRAGMA RESTRICT_REFERENCES (cityaddr,WNDS);
        --
        FUNCTION stateaddr(addr_id_IN IN address.id%TYPE)
            RETURN address.state%TYPE;
        PRAGMA RESTRICT_REFERENCES (stateaddr,WNDS);
        --
        FUNCTION zipaddr(addr_id_IN IN address.id%TYPE)
            RETURN address.ZIP%TYPE;
        PRAGMA RESTRICT_REFERENCES (zipaddr,WNDS);
        --
    END address_info;
    /
    CREATE OR REPLACE PACKAGE BODY address_info
    IS
        /* curr_addr_rec is maintained by load_addr procedure */
        curr_addr_rec    address%ROWTYPE;
        --
        /* procedure to load curr_addr_rec by id            */
        PROCEDURE load_addr(addr_id_IN IN address.id%TYPE)
        IS
        null_addr_rec    address%ROWTYPE;
        BEGIN
            IF curr_addr_rec.id != addr_id_IN OR curr_addr_rec.id IS NULL
            THEN
                SELECT *
                    INTO curr_addr_rec
                    FROM address
                    WHERE id = addr_id_IN;
            END IF;
```

```
      EXCEPTION
         WHEN NO_DATA_FOUND THEN curr_addr_rec := null_addr_rec;
      END load_addr;
      --
      /* functions which return components of curr_addr_rec */
      FUNCTION streetaddr(addr_id_IN IN address.id%TYPE)
         RETURN address.street%TYPE
      IS
      BEGIN
         load_addr(addr_id_IN);
         RETURN curr_addr_rec.street;
      END streetaddr;
      --
      FUNCTION cityaddr(addr_id_IN IN address.id%TYPE)
         RETURN address.city%TYPE
      IS
      BEGIN
         load_addr(addr_id_IN);
         RETURN curr_addr_rec.city;
      END cityaddr;
      --
      FUNCTION stateaddr(addr_id_IN IN address.id%TYPE)
         RETURN address.state%TYPE
      IS
      BEGIN
         load_addr(addr_id_IN);
         RETURN curr_addr_rec.state;
      END stateaddr;
      --
      FUNCTION zipaddr(addr_id_IN IN address.id%TYPE)
         RETURN address.ZIP%TYPE
      IS
      BEGIN
         load_addr(addr_id_IN);
         RETURN curr_addr_rec.ZIP;
      END zipaddr;
      --
END address_info;
   /
```

Following is a version of the view built upon this package which gives us the addresses to which to mail termination notices.

```
CREATE VIEW termination_notice_mailing
IS
SELECT  customer_id
,DECODE(customer_addr_id,NULL,
                 DECODE(employer_addr_id,NULL,TO_CHAR(NULL)
                            ,address_info.streetaddr(employer_addr_id))
               ,address_info.streetaddr(customer_addr_id) )
        street
,DECODE(customer_addr_id,NULL,
                 DECODE(employer_addr_id,NULL,TO_CHAR(NULL)
                            ,address_info.cityaddr(employer_addr_id))
               ,address_info.cityaddr(customer_addr_id) )
```

```
        city
, DECODE (customer_addr_id, NULL,
               DECODE (employer_addr_id, NULL, TO_CHAR (NULL)
                       , address_info.stateaddr (employer_addr_id))
               , address_info.stateaddr (customer_addr_id) )
        state
, DECODE (customer_addr_id, NULL,
               DECODE (employer_addr_id, NULL, TO_CHAR (NULL)
                       , address_info.zipaddr (employer_addr_id))
               , address_info.zipaddr (customer_addr_id) )
        ZIP
  FROM termination_notices;
```

Notice that the DECODEs handle the prioritization of which address to use based on whether customer_addr_id and employer_addr_id are NULL. Notice also that the package ensures that we will hit the address table at most once per row selected. Certainly this is still a complex view, but we only have to scan the termination_notices view once, and we join in the correct address only when we need it.

As you can see, taking full advantage of all of this technology to improve performance doesn't always result in very attractive code. When you are faced with programs that do not meet minimal requirements, however, you must be ready to abandon elegance and even (as a last resort) simplicity to get the job done.

Avoid Client-Side SQL

Set as a goal for yourself or your entire development team that no one *ever* places a chunk of SQL code on the client side of the divide. Why? Because if you put all SQL or data access inside stored code in the database you get the following:

- You are much more likely to share that same SQL across multiple programs or even applications. This will result in a higher percentage of shared, preparsed SQL.

- Multiple SQL statements can be batched together into a single procedure or function, so that a single network access kicks off a sequence of SQL activity on the server without unnecessary network traffic.

Objections to this advice are often raised by Oracle Developer/2000 developers. When you create a form in Oracle Forms, the base table block takes care of an awful lot of the required SQL, including some very complex locking mechanisms. Am I saying that you should abandon all of that "automatic" stuff and write a large volume of code? Definitely not (though with Oracle Developer/2000 Release 2 you will be able to build "base table blocks" around stored procedures and functions *instead of* using tables). I would strongly recommend, though, that the *only* SQL you allow in your Oracle Forms modules is the stuff generated automatically for you.

You should most certainly *never* write POST-QUERY triggers (as an example) which contain multiple SELECT statements to do foreign key lookups. This is the most common place for additional SQL to show up in a form. Your tables are wonderfully normalized and you must, therefore, translate a key into a descriptor for display purposes. How do you do this? In the POST-QUERY trigger, you issue implicit SELECT after implict SELECT to get the data. Your trigger then looks like this:

```
BEGIN
    SELECT dept_name INTO :emp.dname
      FROM department
      WHERE dept_id = :emp.deptid;

    SELECT title_name INTO :emp.tname
      FROM titles
      WHERE title_id = :emp.title_id;

    /* and so on and so on... */
END;
```

This is very bad news for at least two reasons: First, chances are that you have this same or similar code in some other program. Surely this can't be the only place you look up a department name from a department ID. Second, you are forcing lots of unnecessary network activity.

Ideally, you should consolidate all the parts of your POST_QUERY triggers that contain SQL statements into a single procedure, preferably inside a package, as shown here:

```
BEGIN
    emppkg.lookups (:emp.deptid, :emp.dname, :emp.title_id, :emp.tname);
END;
```

The emppkg.lookups procedure bundles together each of the different foreign key lookups, which means that it requires just one network call to get the job done.

Take Advantage of DBMS_SQL Batch Processing

The PL/SQL8 version of DBMS_SQL allows you to perform bulk updates, inserts, deletes, and queries. The new version of this handy package (which allows for the execution of dynamic SQL and dynamic PL/SQL inside PL/SQL programs) offers the following programs to support "array processing":

DBMS_SQL.DEFINE_ARRAY
> This procedure allows you to associate a column in a cursor with a PL/SQL table. When you fetch from the cursor, you will be able to dump a specified number of values from multiple rows into that PL/SQL table.

DMBS_SQL.BIND_ARRAY

This procedure allows you to bind multiple values from a PL/SQL table to a DML statement, so that you can, say, insert 100 rows in a single call to DBMS_SQL.EXECUTE, instead of having to make 100 calls to this function.

See *Oracle Built-in Packages* for more information on this feature. It is the closest you can get to true array processing for SQL inside a PL/SQL program.

Avoid Procedural Code When Possible

Compared to Oracle SQL, PL/SQL is a slow language when it comes to processing SQL statements. So whenever possible, you should take advantage of set-oriented SQL statements instead of row-at-a-time cursor processing in PL/SQL. Consider the following block of code:

```
DECLARE
    CURSOR table_X_cur
    IS
        SELECT column_A,column_B,column_C
          FROM table_X
           FOR UPDATE of column_A;
    table_X_rec table_X_cur%ROWTYPE;
BEGIN
    OPEN table_X_cur;
    FETCH table_X_cur INTO table_X_rec;
    WHILE table_X_cur%FOUND
    LOOP
       UPDATE table_X
           SET column_A = table_X_rec.column_B * table_X_rec.column_C
         WHERE CURRENT OF table_X_cur;
         FETCH table_X_cur INTO table_X_rec;
    END LOOP;
    CLOSE table_X_cur;
END;
```

You can replace all of that stuff with this single UPDATE statement:

```
UPDATE table_X  SET column_A = column_B * column_C;
```

I hope you will find this tip to be self-evident; *you* would never be tempted to write a whole bunch of PL/SQL code when a simple UPDATE statement would suffice! It is worth the reminder, however, because as we spend more and more of our time cranking out PL/SQL code, we can easily lose perspective. We might find ourselves trying to do *everything* in PL/SQL and forget about our other options.

Use PL/SQL to Improve Performance
of IO-Intensive SQL

Now that I have finished telling you to use SQL whenever possible and avoid PL/SQL, it is time to urge you to use PL/SQL, particularly explicit cursors, to improve the performance of some types of SQL statements. Go figure!

Actually, it shouldn't be the least bit confusing. SQL is optimized for set-at-a-time processing. PL/SQL is designed for record-at-a-time logic. If your interaction with the database always occurs on an entire set, or between more than one set related through equi-joins, SQL is the obvious choice. If your requirements dictate that you must perform procedural-style logic on the data in order to produce the desired result, PL/SQL could have a dramatic impact on the performance of your program.

A good indicator of the potential for improvement with PL/SQL is the presence of a correlated sub-query. Consider the following query, which displays the department name followed by the name of the employee who receives the highest salary in that department:

```
SELECT 'Top employee in ' || D.name || ' is ' ||
       E.last_name || ', ' || E.first_name
  FROM department D, employee E
 WHERE D.department_id = E.department_id
   AND E.salary = (SELECT MAX (salary)
                     FROM employee E2
                    WHERE E2.department_id = E.department_id);
```

The records retrieved by the inner SELECT statement (which calculates the maximum salary for a department) is correlated to the department ID of the outer employee record. The maximum salary for a department is therefore calculated again and again for each employee record in the outer query. If the company has five departments and 1000 employees in those five departments, then the query will perform 1000 subqueries. Yet the maximum salary really needs to be computed only five times, once per department.

You can use PL/SQL and a cursor FOR loop to cut to a minimum the number of times the department maximum is calculated. The resulting execution time will be greatly reduced, especially for large numbers of records in the employee table:

```
PROCEDURE display_best_paid IS
/*
|| Display the name of the employee who makes the highest salary
|| in each department.
*/
   -- Cursor for each department (and its max salary) in the company.
   CURSOR dept_cur IS
      SELECT D.department_id, name, MAX (salary) max_salary
        FROM department D, employee E
```

```
                WHERE D.department_id = E.department_id
                GROUP BY D.department_id
                ORDER BY name;
        BEGIN
           <<dept_loop>>
           FOR dept_rec IN dept_cur
           LOOP
              DECLARE
                 CURSOR emp_cur IS
                    SELECT last_name || ', ' || first_name emp_name
                       FROM employee
                       WHERE department_id = dept_rec.department_id
                          AND salary = dept_rec.max_salary;
                 emp_rec emp_cur%ROWTYPE;
              BEGIN
                 OPEN emp_cur;
                 FETCH emp_cur INTO emp_rec;
                 DBMS_OUTPUT.PUT_LINE
                    ('Top employee in ' || dept_rec.name || ' is ' ||
                     emp_rec.emp_name);
                 CLOSE emp_cur;
              END;
           END LOOP <<dept_loop>>;
        END;
```

With the cursor FOR loop approach, the maximum salary is calculated once for each department through the use of a GROUP BY. This value is then used inside the loop to find the first employee whose salary matches the maximum. This program performs several hundred fewer logical reads than the correlated subquery version.

This technique also comes in handy when you have a very complex SQL statement involving a large number of tables. The rules-based optimizer—still used widely in Oracle shops around the world—does not use table size to determine which indexes should be applied to a query. So, for example, if you have a very small table in the query included to look up a description for a code, the optimizer might use the index on that table and ignore a much more useful index in a larger table. You can help avoid confusion and, at the same time, improve performance of the query by pulling that reference table out of the query and placing it in its own cursor. Your program then executes the cursor and fetches the description before the main query executes. You then reference the retrieved value directly in the query and simplify the main query.

Keep Database Triggers Small

Up until Oracle7 Server Release 7.1, database triggers are treated like anonymous blocks of code in the System Global Area (SGA). Compiled versions of triggers are not stored in the database. Instead, the source code is recompiled each time the trigger is referenced.

To minimize the overhead associated with these repeated compilations, you should keep your database triggers as small as possible. You should also tune your shared pool size so that it can accommodate most, if not all, of your compiled PL/SQL code without having to age out objects which are used repeatedly.

The best way to keep your triggers small is to transfer all of the procedural logic in the trigger to a procedure. This procedure's compiled version is stored in the database and can be managed more efficiently by the instance's SGA.

To change your trigger code to a procedure call, you move all of the code inside the procedure and create a parameter for each trigger-specific variable referenced in the code (such as :new and :old variables, which allow you to compare new and old values for columns in the affected row).

Let's convert a trigger's complex logic to a procedure. In the following trigger, I maintain a denormalized order total based on the line items for that order. This single trigger handles any changes to the line item amount, through an INSERT, UPDATE, or DELETE:

```
CREATE TRIGGER total_order
AFTER INSERT OR UPDATE OR DELETE OF line_amt ON line_item
FOR EACH ROW
BEGIN
    /*
    || If changed order for this line item or removing it,
    || then decrease the total in the old order.
    */
    IF (UPDATING AND :old.order_id != :new.order_id) OR DELETING
    THEN
        UPDATE orders
           SET order_total := order_total - :old.line_amt
         WHERE order_id = :old.order_id;
    END IF;
    /*
    || If a new line item or transferring line item to new order,
    || add the line amount to the new order.
    */
    IF (UPDATING AND :old.order_id != :new.order_id) OR INSERTING
    THEN
        UPDATE orders
           SET order_total := order_total + :new.line_amt
         WHERE order_id = :new.order_id;
    END IF;
    /*
    || If I have changed the amount of the line item and kept it
    || in the same order, adjust total by difference of old and
    || new line item amounts.
    */
    IF :old.order_id = :new.order_id AND
       :old.line_amt != :new.line_amt AND
```

```
        UPDATING
    THEN
        UPDATE orders
           SET order_total := order_total - :old.line_amt + :new.line_amt
        WHERE order_id = :new.order_id;
    END IF;
END;
```

Before I write the procedure, let's decide on the specification for the procedure—
that is, what the trigger should look like inside:

```
CREATE TRIGGER total_order
AFTER INSERT OR UPDATE OR DELETE OF line_amt ON line_item
FOR EACH ROW
BEGIN
    adjust_order_total
        (:old.order_id, :old.line_amt, :new.order_id, :new.line_amt,
         INSERTING, UPDATING, DELETING);
END;
```

The adjust_order_total contains many parameters, since it is a combined trigger
(handling all three DML states: INSERT, UPDATE, and DELETE) and also references the new and old values of two different columns. With this specification, I
can now create the procedure as a direct "translation" from the trigger:

```
PROCEDURE adjust_order_total
        (old_order_id_in IN orders.order_id%TYPE,
         old_line_amt_in IN line_item.line_amt%TYPE,
         new_order_id_in IN orders.order_id%TYPE,
         new_line_amt_in IN line_item.line_amt%TYPE,
         inserting_in IN BOOLEAN,
         updating_in IN BOOLEAN,
         deleting_in IN BOOLEAN)
BEGIN
    /*
    || If changed order for this line item or removing it,
    || then decrease the total in the old order.
    */
    IF (updating_in AND old_order_id_in != new_order_id_in)
        OR deleting_in
    THEN
       UPDATE orders
          SET order_total := order_total - old_line_amt_in
       WHERE order_id = old_order_id_in;
    END IF;
    /*
    || If a new line item or transferring line item to new order,
    || add the line amount to the new order.
    */
    IF (updating_in AND old_order_id_in != new_order_id_in) OR
        inserting_in
    THEN
       UPDATE orders
          SET order_total := order_total + new_line_amt_in
```

```
              WHERE order_id = new_order_id_in;
      END IF;
      /*
      || If I have changed the amount of the line item and kept it
      || in the same order, adjust total by difference of old and
      || new line item amounts.
      */
      IF old_order_id_in = new_order_id_in AND
         old_line_amt_in != new_line_amt_in AND
         updating_in
      THEN
         UPDATE orders
            SET order_total :=
                    order_total - old_line_amt_in + new_line_amt_in
            WHERE order_id = new_order_id_in;
      END IF;
   END;
```

By converting the trigger code to a procedure, I have not made the code more readable, nor is it more concise. The point of this conversion was, however, simply to improve transaction performance.

Finally, even if you are running Oracle Server 7.3 or above, you should still keep your trigger code to a minimum and instead place as much of your logic as possible in packages so that this code can be more easily reused throughout your application.

Tuning Your Algorithms

Tuning algorithms is a very application-specific activity. There is no general rule to be applied, and I have no generic tips. Instead, in this section I offer two "case studies" of tuning exercises I performed on some real-world code. Following those explorations are more general suggestions for writing optimized PL/SQL code.

There Are No Sacred Cows

In many places in this book, I recommend that you follow the principle of top-down design in building your applications and even single modules. This step-by-step process almost guarantees that you will come up with the most modular, logical solution to your problem. Unfortunately, that solution may not always be the most efficient performer. In such situations, you need to be ready to switch gears, tear down what you have built, and reconstruct it to improve performance.

In other words, you must be creative and, in some cases, even take a counter-intuitive approach to achieve the required performance levels in your application. Do not hang onto code just because you happened to have stayed up too late too many nights in a row to get it "just right." If it doesn't do the job, don't hesitate to scrap your implementation and try again.

Consider the build_pv_lease_schedule procedure shown below:

```
PROCEDURE build_pv_lease_schedule
/* Construct present value lease schedule over 20 years. */
IS
    /* Temporary variable to hold lease accumulation. */
    pv_total_lease NUMBER(9);
    /* Table structure to hold the lease accumulations. */
    TYPE pv_table_type IS TABLE OF NUMBER(9) INDEX BY BINARY_INTEGER;
    pv_table pv_table_type;
BEGIN
    FOR year_count in 1 .. 20
    LOOP
        /* Reset the lease amount for this year. */
        pv_total_lease := 0;
        /*
        || Build the PV based on the remaining years
        || plus the fixed and variable amounts.
        */
        FOR year_count2 in year_count..20
        LOOP
            /* Add annual total lease amount to cummulative. */
            pv_total_lease :=
                pv_total_lease +
                pv_of_fixed (year_count2) +
                pv_of_variable (year_count2);
        END LOOP;
        /* Add the annual PV to the table. */
        pv_table (year_count) := pv_total_lease;
    END LOOP;
END;
```

This module constructs a schedule of lease payments for a store and saves them in a PL/SQL table. For each of 20 years, the lease amount is calculated as the sum of lease amounts for the remaining years. The total lease for year 10, in other words, would consist of the lease amounts (fixed and variable) for years 10 through 20. The procedure reflects this logic directly and simply with nested loops:

```
FOR year_count IN 1 .. 20
LOOP
    FOR year_count2 IN year_count .. 20
    LOOP
        ... computation ...
    END LOOP;
END LOOP;
```

The build_pv_lease_schedule procedure is clean, direct, and to the point. The only problem with this code it that it took six seconds to calculate the 20 values in the lease schedule. This was simply too long a time, combined as it was with several other operations. A new approach was needed and I was asked to come up with alternatives.

One reason that I was brought in to perform the review is that it can be very difficult for a program's author to be creative about new ways of doing things. I have found that once I write something, once I feel I have reached a resolution, and once I see it in a printout, that particular approach entraps me, limiting my vision.

The nested loop technique was such a natural fit for this algorithm that it took an outsider to break away from this construct to tune the code. Now that you have seen this technique, can you see a more efficient way to perform this calculation?

My first step in analyzing and correcting the procedure was to be aware of just how many computations the program performed to come up with its answer. For each of the 20 years, the inner loop performs 20-N+1 calculations. So over 20 years, the nested loop performs:

20 + 19 + 18 + ... 3 + 2 + 1 = 210 calculations of annual lease amounts

to come up with the 20 accumulated lease amounts. Well, that's a lot of activity! No wonder it takes six seconds. The question in my mind then became: are all these calculations necessary? They would certainly all be required if each computation were unique, that is, not repeated during the nested loop execution. This is not, however, the case. In fact, many of the computations are exactly the same. For year 1, I calculate the annual lease amounts for years 1 through 20 to produce the year 1 accumulation. For year 2, I calculate the annual lease amount for years 2 through 20, and so on. For each year N, in other words, I calculate the annual lease amount for that year N times. Furthermore, within each execution of the inner loop, I am simply summing up the annual lease amounts for the subset of the full 20 years, as shown here:

Outer Loop Year Number	Years Over Which Lease Amounts are Summed in Inner Loop
1	Year 1 + Year 2 + ... + Year 20
2	Year 2 + ... + Year 20
...	
18	Year 18 + Year 19 + Year 20
19	Year 19 + Year 20
20	Year 20

From this table you can see that the difference between the total amount for year N and the total amount for year N-1 is the lease amount for year N. Starting with year 1, it then becomes clear that the total lease amounts are all reductions from that year 1 total. From this understanding, I found that I could generate the accumulated lease amounts for each year by substracting from the full 20-year accumulation, rather than having to build it up each time anew.

With this approach, I would build my lease schedule in two phases: first, for each year, calculate the annual lease amount and save that value. Simultaneously, add that value to the 20-year accumulation. In pseudo-code I have:

```
FOR year_count IN 1 .. 20
LOOP
   save annual lease amount
   add annual lease amount to 20-year accumulated total
END LOOP;
```

Once I have my 20-year accumulation and my 20 individual annual lease amounts, I can produce the 19 other accumulations as follows:

```
copy 20-year total to accumulated total variable
FOR year_count IN 2 .. 20
LOOP
   subtract annual lease amount from accumulated total
   save difference to PL/SQL table
END LOOP;
```

In other words, for year 2, subtract the annual lease amount of year 2 from the 20-year total. This is the 19-year accumulation. For year 3, subtract the annual lease amount of year 3 from the 19-year total. This is the 18-year accumulation. And so on.

With this approach, shown in full PL/SQL glory below, I perform only 20 lease computations and then another 20 simple subtractions, down from 210 lease computations:

```
PROCEDURE build_pv_lease_schedule
IS
   pv_total_lease NUMBER(9) := 0;
   TYPE pv_table_type IS TABLE OF NUMBER(9) INDEX BY BINARY_INTEGER;
   pv_table pv_table_type;
BEGIN
   /*
   || Build the 20-year accumulated total and save each
   || of the annual lease amounts to the PL/SQL table. Notice that
   || pv_table (N) is set to the annual lease amount for year N-1.
   */
   FOR year_count in 1 .. 20
   LOOP
      one_year_pv :=
         pv_of_fixed (year_count) + pv_of_variable (year_count);
      pv_total_lease := pv_total_lease + one_year_pv;
      IF year_count < 20
      THEN
         pv_table (year_count+1) := one_year_pv;
      END IF;
   END LOOP;

   /* Save the 20-year total in the first row. */
   pv_table (1) := pv_total_lease;
```

```
      /* For each of the remaining years... */
      FOR year_count IN 2 .. 20
      LOOP
         /* Subtract the annual amount from the remaining total. */
         pv_total_lease := pv_total_lease - pv_table (year_count);
         /*
         || Save the Nth accumulation to the table (this writes right
         || over the annual lease amount, which is no longer needed.
         || I get double use out of the pv_table in this way.
         */
         pv_table (year_count) := pv_total_lease;
      END LOOP;
   END;
```

By converting the nested loop to a sequence of two distinct loops, I cut down the elapsed time of this procedure from six seconds to three seconds. Both approaches produce the same number. The first technique was the more obvious and straightforward of the two. It did not, however, minimize the amount of effort required to produce the computations. It took careful analysis and rewriting both to preserve the correct values and to optimize the performance.

One should never underestimate the value of code review. In the process of having this chapter reviewed, both Eric Givler and Kannan Muthukkaruppan were quick to point out an even simpler and faster solution to this problem:

```
PROCEDURE build_pv_lease_schedule
IS
   pv_total_lease number(9) := 0;
   one_year_pv number(9) := 0;
   type pv_table_type IS TABLE OF NUMBER(9) INDEX BY BINARY_INTEGER;
   pv_table pv_table_type;
BEGIN
   FOR year_count IN REVERSE 1..20
   LOOP
      one_year_pv := pv_of_fixed(year_count) +
                     pv_of_variable(year_count);
      pv_total_lease := pv_total_lease + one_year_pv;
      pv_table (year_count) := pv_total_lease;
   END LOOP;
END build_pv_lease_schedule;
```

I was at first resistant to accepting that this use of a REVERSE FOR LOOP gets the job done. Eric, fortunately, did not give up and finally I was convinced. You just start from the last year and go backwards accumulating the values, completely eliminating the need for two different loops and much extraneous processing!

Zen and the Art of PL/SQL Tuning

My search for excellence and quality in PL/SQL coding takes me to many strange and wonderful places on our spanking-new virtual planet. It presents me with a myriad of challenges that can simultaneously make me despair of my fellow humans and also wonder at their capacity for renewal and creativity. In this section I share with you a journey of discovery I took in the arena of PL/SQL tuning.

It all started with a call from a valued customer and a very common opening line. "Steven," the gravely, despairing voice of Dave came over the line, "we've got a problem." Company X was massaging large volumes of data on a daily basis (an Oracle-to-Oracle conversion of gigabytes, actually, which involved a parse and denormalization of data to aid in query performance). The PL/SQL code used to perform the conversion was a bottleneck (or maybe the bottleneck was related to a limitation of the 24 hours normally encountered in each day).

When Dave first explained to me that his program parsed strings, I felt immediately certain that there would be many opportunities for improvement. PL/SQL string manipulation is, shall we say, not lightning fast. Furthermore, there are usually a number of paths one can take to meet the same requirements. Not all are equally desirable. When a particular action or program is performed thousands, or perhaps millions, of times, in a single pass of data, an improvement of even 10% in a low-level program can make a big difference.

Had Dave's developers chosen the highest quality route? It was time to find out.

I scanned the body of the main stored procedure. Deep within a series of nested loops, I encountered the following statement:

```
IF NOT is_number (stg)
THEN
    stg := remove_punctation (stg);
END IF;
```

In other words, if the current token was not a number, then remove the punctuation from the token. Straightforward enough—on the surface, anyway.

Now, this "is_number" function *sounded* like a PL/SQL built-in. Having written a book on PL/SQL, however, I knew immediately that is_number is not provided by Oracle, so instead it must be a low-level operator built by a developer at Company X. Since this function might be executed 20 or 30 million times a day, I decided it was as good a place as any to start. The following function shows the implementation of is_number I found stored in the database:

```
FUNCTION is_number (word_in IN VARCHAR2) RETURN BOOLEAN
IS
    BOOL_RC          boolean;
    ASCII_CHAR_VAL   number;
    WORD_LENGTH      number;
    CHAR_POS         number;
BEGIN
    BOOL_RC := TRUE;
    WORD_LENGTH := LENGTH(WORD_IN);
```

```
      for CHAR_POS in 1..WORD_LENGTH loop
         ASCII_CHAR_VAL := ASCII(SUBSTR(WORD_IN, CHAR_POS, 1));
         if  ASCII_CHAR_VAL < 48 or ASCII_CHAR_VAL > 57
             and  ASCII_CHAR_VAL != 46 then
            BOOL_RC := FALSE;
            return BOOL_RC;
         end if;
      end loop;
      return BOOL_RC;
   END is_number;
```

Granted, the programmer did not use my conventions for spacing within lines, line breaks, UPPER-lower case style, and the use of the RETURN statement. He even declared char_pos, which is unnecessary and dangerous, since it is actually the index variable of the FOR LOOP and is therefore implicitly declared by PL/SQL. I was ready to look past that, however, and focus on the inner life of the program: its logical flow. Here is what I found is_number doing:

> For each of the N characters in a string, isolate that character using SUBSTR and see if it is a digit or a period.

The programmer made use of the ASCII function to convert the character to its ASCII collating sequence number, and then checked to see if that value fell within the allowable range of values. If you are like me, you would also have broken out into a cold sweat. Where the heck could I get a copy of the ASCII collating sequence to verify the numbers in that program? Whoa! Why scan a book when you have PL/SQL? I quickly knocked out the following SQL*Plus script to spit out all the information I needed to know:

```
BEGIN
   FOR let_index IN &1 .. &2
   LOOP
      DBMS_OUTPUT.PUT_LINE ('Ascii ' ||
            TO_CHAR (let_index) ||
            ' = ' ||
            CHR (let_index));
   END LOOP;
END;
```

CHR is a built-in function which converts a number in the ASCII collating sequence to a character (the reverse of ASCII). Naming this script *showasci.sql*, I executed it as follows and got the output shown below:

```
SQL> start showasci 46 58
Ascii 46 = .
Ascii 47 = /
Ascii 48 = 0
Ascii 49 = 1
Ascii 50 = 2
Ascii 51 = 3
Ascii 52 = 4
Ascii 53 = 5
Ascii 54 = 6
```

```
Ascii 55 = 7
Ascii 56 = 8
Ascii 57 = 9
Ascii 58 = :
```

Who needs a printed chart, right? So far as I could tell, then, the programmer got it right. A number should not have any character whose ASCII value is *not* 46 or 48 through 57.

I had now completed the first stage of my journey: the is_number function seemed to do its job. This is a necessary, but not sufficent, condition for a successful module. I took a deep breath and a large, double-strength latte (Company X being in the Pacific Northwest), and prepared to grapple with a deeper question: *Was this implementation of is_number the best possible implementation?*

I was troubled, first of all, by the character-by-character scan through the string. Was this really necessary? The longer the string, the more work the program had to do. It would have been preferable to have a test for a number whose performance did not depend greatly on the input value. This scan also required lots of code to do its job (the loop, local variables, etc.). Finally, the use of ASCII to test the value of the individual character was obscure and "low level" (at least to a 4GL, 90s type of fellow like me!).

At times like this, I wonder if there might be a PL/SQL built-in function that could help out. Could I replace this loop through the string with a single call to a higher-level built-in?

I meditated about the various string functions available to me and my mind soon circled around TRANSLATE. This function *translates* individual characters in a string by matching up characters in a match string with those in a replacement string. If I could simply replace all digits and the decimal point with NULL, then the translated string should be NULL if the original string was a number. To test out my idea, I executed the following SQL statement:

```
SELECT TRANSLATE ('567.6', '0123456789.', '')
   FROM dual;
```

and the result in SQL*Plus was:

```
T
-
```

which means NULL (the name of the column was truncated to a single character to match this minimal value length). That was perfect! Then I tested the *negative* condition as follows:

```
SELECT TRANSLATE ('567A6', '0123456789.', '')
   FROM dual;
```

but I got the same result: NULL. What is going on? Well, the problem is that if you supply a NULL replacement string, it converts your string to NULL, regardless of the original string and the match string. If, on the other hand, I added the same "placeholder" letter at the start of both the match and replacement string, I would get the desired behavior. This statement:

```
SELECT TRANSLATE ('567.6', 'A0123456789.', 'A'),
       TRANSLATE ('567A6', 'A0123456789.', 'A')
  FROM dual;
```

results in:

```
T T
- -
A
```

In other words, '567A6' translates to 'A' and is NOT NULL. My technique validated, I then converted this "FROM dual" SQL statement into a PL/SQL function:

```
FUNCTION is_number (stg_in IN VARCHAR2)
   RETURN BOOLEAN
IS
BEGIN
   RETURN
      TRANSLATE
         (stg_in, 'A0123456789.', 'A')
      IS NULL;
END is_number;
```

This approach used *much* less code than the original is_number. I wondered how its performance would compare with the original, per-character scan. Rather than execute myriad individual calls to is_number within SQL*Plus, I decided to write a test script as shown below, saved to a file named *testnum.sql*:

```
SET SERVEROUTPUT ON
SET VERIFY OFF
DECLARE
   start_time BINARY_INTEGER;
   stg VARCHAR2(100) := '&2';
   bool BOOLEAN;
BEGIN
   start_time := DBMS_UTILITY.GET_TIME;
   FOR test_index IN 1 .. &1
   LOOP
      bool := is_number (stg);
      IF test_index = 1 AND bool
      THEN
         DBMS_OUTPUT.PUT_LINE ('TRUE');
      ELSIF test_index = 1 AND NOT bool
      THEN
         DBMS_OUTPUT.PUT_LINE ('FALSE');
      END IF;
   END LOOP;
```

```
        DBMS_OUTPUT.PUT_LINE (DBMS_UTILITY.GET_TIME - start_time);
    END;
    /
```

This script uses the DBMS_UTILITY.GET_TIME function to capture and display elapsed time in 100ths of seconds. It also displays the result of the first execution so I can verify correctness. This SQL*Plus script takes two parameters (&1 and &2):

1. The number of times the loop (and, therefore, is_number) executes

2. The input string

I can then CREATE OR REPLACE is_number before I call the script to try out my different version. The following call to testnum executes is_number 100 times for the string "12345R5".

```
    SQL> start testnum 100 12345R5
```

I ran this script for a number of different strings and made the following discovery: the TRANSLATE version is faster than the original version in almost every case and for many string values is *much* faster. In fact, the TRANSLATE version records the same performance, regardless of input (.44 seconds), while the performance of the original version varies greatly by length of string and value (if a non-numeric character appears early in the string, the original is_ number is similar in performance to the translate version). The results are shown in Table 25-1.

Table 25-1 Performance Comparison: Original vs. TRANSLATE[a]

String Value	Original	TRANSLATE
123456	181	44
1A3456	88	44
123456.8888	330	44
123	110	44
1	50	44
1A	77	44
A1	44	44

[a] All times are in 100ths of seconds for 100 iterations.

I had clearly come up with a superior version of is_number. Yet I couldn't help but wonder: was this the *best* implementation? I decided to continue on my journey. I treated myself to a cappuccino and settled into Company X's finest ergonomic swivel chair. I adjusted the lumbar support. I raised the arm rests to relieve stress to my wrists. And I thought about TRANSLATE. It was clearly a very efficient implementation. Regardless of the length of the input string, this built-in took the same amount of time to execute. Yet from a theoretical and aesthetic standpoint, I couldn't help but dwell on the fact that, however efficiently, TRANSLATE had to do a lot of work. For each character in the original string, it had to see if that character appeared in the match string and then replace it with the corresponding character in the replacement string. Was all that truly necessary?

When you came right down to it, what I wanted TRANSLATE to do was "throw away" all digits—and the decimal point—and see if anything was left. I didn't really need to *translate*. I needed to *trim*, and I had just the built-in to do it. Rather, I had my choice of two: RTRIM and LTRIM. And so my third attempt at fine-tuning is_number looked like this:

```
FUNCTION is_number (stg_in IN VARCHAR2)
   RETURN BOOLEAN
IS
BEGIN
   RETURN
      LTRIM (stg_in, '0123456789.')
      IS NULL;
END is_number;
```

Using this version, PL/SQL would start on the left and discard any characters found in the trim string. If there was nothing left when it was done, I had a number. There was a little less code using LTRIM instead of TRANSLATE. But what about performance? I ran the same battery of tests using my looping script and discovered that the LTRIM version achieved a steady state elapsed time of just .22 seconds—half the time of the TRANSLATE version!

So, given a string of "123456", my latest is_number returned TRUE in .22 seconds (for 100 iterations) compared with 1.81 for the original version. And for longer strings, the delta was even more dramatic: I had achieved an order of magnitude improvement.

I was very tempted to call in my friends at Company X to show them my results. But then I executed my test script one last time and accidently added another decimal point on my input as follows:

```
SQL> execute testnum 100 12345.56.6
```

I watched in horror as my script showed me that is_number returned TRUE for this value. Sure, it returned the value really quickly. But it was the *wrong* answer! I feverishly tried all my different versions of is_number and each one was happy to accept "123456.56.6" as a number. But that is *not* a number. Clouds seemed to cover the sun and darken every corner. I felt the walls of my cubicle closing in on me. Everything I had taken for granted about is_number had been cast into doubt.

What had gone wrong? The original algorithm and (since I did not challenge the basic approach) my subsequent replacements all treated the string as a *string*, not as a number. They then evaluated individual characters as candidates for being

part of a number. Yet none of my is_numbers ever bothered to check the validity
of the number as a whole.

When I looked at it from this angle, the solution to my problem was clear: forget
the string built-ins. Instead, use the TO_NUMBER built-in to try to convert the
string to a number. If the conversion worked, I would return TRUE. If an exception was raised, I would return FALSE. My fourth incarnation of is_number looked
like this:

```
FUNCTION is_number (stg_in IN VARCHAR2)
    RETURN BOOLEAN
IS
    val NUMBER;
BEGIN
    val := TO_NUMBER (stg_in);
    RETURN TRUE;
EXCEPTION
    WHEN OTHERS THEN RETURN FALSE;
END is_number;
```

I ran my performance test with some trepidation. I was certain that this version
would always return the correct value; that was, after all, the whole point of TO_
NUMBER. I was less certain of the performance, particularly when the string was
not a valid number. Raising and handling exceptions are not necessarily very efficient. It is a sad fact of life that the most elegant and correct solution is not always
the most efficient.

So you can imagine my joy when I discovered that the TO_NUMBER version was
far and away the fastest of the is_numbers. It registered a steady .17 seconds for
any and all inputs and 100 iterations. Feeling my oats, I then executed my test
script for 10000 iterations to check the string "123123.45". The elapsed times were
as follows:

A conversion process testing one million strings could require three hours just to
test for numbers with the original, per-character version, while the TO_NUMBER
version would consume just ten or twenty minutes! And it would return the
correct answer 100% of the time.

This was news I was ready to bring to the attention of Company X. I was sure
there were still other areas of improvement to discover in the PL/SQL conversion
code, but this was definitely a start.

Looking back

I learned a number of things about debugging, tuning, and my character in the
process of revamping is_number. My biggest surprise and most important lesson
regards making assumptions. When I started to analyze is_number, I was so sure
that I could improve performance that I didn't take the time to step back and fully

challenge all aspects of the program. I assumed that it performed properly, and I assumed that its basic approach to the problem was correct.

Both of these assumptions were wrong. There was a basic flaw in the program, and that flaw was directly related to an inappropriate strategy in the development plan. Once I no longer assumed the assumptions, it was easy to see my way through to a far better implementation.

Sure, I wasted some time exploring a variety of options for the design of is_ number. On the other hand, I was reminded once again of the need to identify and challenge all assumptions before proceeding. In any case, I ended up with some tightly tuned PL/SQL code.

Now let's look at some more specific actions you can take to tune your algorithms.

Rely on Local Variables to Improve Performance

When you are inside a PL/SQL block manipulating variable data, the PL/SQL runtime engine will work most efficiently with data structures declared locally (i.e., inside that block). You can use this fact to your advantage by working with local copies of parameters and also by minimizing references to host variables. Both of these topics are explored in this section.

Work with local copies

For anyone calling a procedure or function, the parameter list provides the interface into the program, which is otherwise a "black box." The parameter list acts as a boundary between the internals of the program and the outside world. It is also useful to extend this concept of the boundary inside the program.

The IN and IN OUT parameters carry data into the program. Often, these formal parameters are manipulated and modified during the execution of the program. Rather than act directly on those parameters, you should transfer the parameters to local variables and then manipulate those local variables. This transfer potentially gives the following advantages:

- Guarantees a consistent format for the incoming parameter value. In particular, you can use the local variable to avoid problems with different cases (upper, lower, mixed) of incoming text.

- Avoids repetitive execution of functions.

- Modifies the value of the parameter value, which may not be possible if it is an IN parameter.

Let's look at examples of each of these motivators to create local copies of parameters. The following program calculates different types of sales for a company:

```
PROCEDURE calc_sales (company_id IN NUMBER, action_in IN VARCHAR2)
IS
BEGIN
   IF UPPER (action_in) = 'ANNUAL' THEN ...
   ELSIF UPPER (action_in) = 'QUARTERLY' THEN ...
   ELSIF UPPER ...
   END IF;
END;
```

I need to uppercase the action code since it is being checked against all-caps literals. But it is wasteful to call the UPPER function repeatedly. Instead, I should copy the incoming action parameter in the declaration section, performing an UPPER conversion of the parameter at the same time. I then reference this internal variable, rather than the parameter itself, in the procedure's logic:

```
PROCEDURE calc_sales (company_id IN NUMBER, action_in IN VARCHAR2)
IS
   action_int VARCHAR2(10) := UPPER (action_in);
BEGIN
   IF action_int = 'ANNUAL' THEN ...
   ELSIF action_int = 'QUARTERLY' THEN ...
   END IF;
END;
```

Minimize references to host variables

Each time a PL/SQL program encounters a bind variable from the host environment which is using PL/SQL, the PL/SQL engine must halt execution and request from that host environment the current value of the bind variable. You can avoid these interruptions by passing a bind variable as a parameter to a procedure or function. You can also minimize the interruptions by copying bind variables to local variables, and then reference those local PL/SQL variables in the rest of the program. Consider the following code from a block-level Oracle Forms When-Validate-Item trigger:

```
-- Validate that a first and last name have been entered.
IF :SYSTEM.TRIGGER_ITEM = 'EMPLOYEE.LAST_NAME' OR
   :SYSTEM.TRIGGER_ITEM = 'EMPLOYEE.FIRST_NAME'
THEN
   IF :employee.first_name IS NULL OR
      :employee.last_name IS NULL
   THEN
      MESSAGE (' Enter a full name for employee ' ||
               TO_CHAR (:employee.employee_id));
      RAISE FORM_TRIGGER_FAILURE;
   ELSE
      -- Create full name and place in header.
      :header.name :=
```

```
                  :employee.first_name || ' ' || :employee.last_name;
      END IF;
-- Validate that a company has been entered.
ELSIF :SYSTEM.TRIGGER_ITEM = 'EMPLOYEE.COMPANY_NAME'
THEN
   IF :employee.company_name IS NULL
   THEN
      MESSAGE (' Enter a company for employee ' ||
               TO_CHAR (:employee.employee_id));
      RAISE FORM_TRIGGER_FAILURE;
   ELSE
      -- Look up the company id for this name.
      :employee.company_id := get_company_name (:employee.company_name);
   END IF;
-- Validate the entry of the employee's hire date.
ELSIF :SYSTEM.TRIGGER_ITEM = 'EMPLOYEE.HIRE_DATE'
THEN
   IF SYSDATE < :employee.hire_date
   THEN
      :employee.hire_date := SYSDATE;
   ELSIF ADD_MONTHS (SYSDATE, -120) > :employee.hire_date
   THEN
      MESSAGE (' Hire date ' ||
               TO_CHAR (:employee.hire_date, 'MM/DD/YY') ||
               ' more than ten years past.');
      RAISE FORM_TRIGGER_FAILURE;
   END IF;
END IF;
```

I obtain the value of bind variables from Oracle Forms (variables with a ":" in front of the name) repetitively, as follows:

Data Structure	Number of Touches
The SYSTEM variable TRIGGER_ITEM	4
Item last_name of employee block	2
Item first_name of employee block	2
Item company_name of employee block	2
Item employee_id of employee block	2
Item hire_date of employee block	3

If I apply all of the guidelines mentioned earlier in this section to the trigger logic you saw above—and consolidate some repetitive code as well—I end up with a procedure like validate_employee, which passes in many of the bind variables as arguments:

```
PROCEDURE validate_employee
   (empid IN INTEGER,
    fname IN VARCHAR2,
    lname IN VARCHAR2,
    cname IN VARCHAR2,
```

```
        item_in IN VARCHAR2,
        cid IN OUT INTEGER,
        hdate IN OUT DATE)
IS
    c_emp_id VARCHAR2(10) := TO_CHAR (empid_in);
    right_now DATE := SYSDATE;
BEGIN
    -- Validate that a first and last name have been entered.
    IF item_in IN ('EMPLOYEE.LAST_NAME', 'EMPLOYEE.FIRST_NAME')
    THEN
        IF fname IS NULL OR lname IS NULL
        THEN
           MESSAGE (' Enter a full name for employee ' || c_emp_id);
           RAISE FORM_TRIGGER_FAILURE;
        ELSE
           -- Create full name and place in header.
           :header.name := fname || ' ' || lname;
        END IF;

    -- Validate that a company has been entered.
    ELSIF item_in = 'EMPLOYEE.COMPANY_NAME'
    THEN
        IF company_name IS NULL
        THEN
           MESSAGE (' Enter a company for employee ' || c_emp_id);
           RAISE FORM_TRIGGER_FAILURE;
        ELSE
           -- Look up the company id for this name.
           cid := get_company_name (company_name);
        END IF;

    -- Validate the entry of the employee's hire date.
    ELSIF item_in = 'EMPLOYEE.HIRE_DATE'
    THEN
        IF right_now < hire_date
        THEN
           hdate := right_now;
        ELSIF ADD_MONTHS (right_now, -120) > hire_date
        THEN
           MESSAGE (' Hire date ' ||
                   TO_CHAR (hire_date, 'MM/DD/YY') ||
                   ' more than ten years past.');
           RAISE FORM_TRIGGER_FAILURE;
        END IF;
    END IF;
END;
```

The performance gain from each of these conversions may be slight. If they were the only tuning steps you took (or the only ones left to take) in your PL/SQL programs, I doubt that you would notice a difference. Combined with all the other tuning tips, however, avoidance of host variables in PL/SQL blocks will contribute to a more efficient PL/SQL layer in your application.

Use Package Data to Avoid Passing "Bulky" Parameter Values

With the exception of cursor variables, PL/SQL passes arguments by *value*, instead of reference, in the parameter lists of procedures and functions. If the argument can be changed (i.e., it is an OUT or IN OUT parameter), then the runtime engine makes a local copy of your structure and applies changes to that copy. If the program terminates without error, the local data is copied to your structure, which is then returned to the calling program.

This approach preserves the values of actual parameters against the possibility of program failure, but it introduces some potential performance problems. This is particularly the case when your OUT or IN OUT parameters are complex data structures such as records and PL/SQL tables.

Suppose that a record has 15 columns in it. Every time you pass that record into a procedure or function as an OUT or IN OUT parameter, PL/SQL copies the entire record into an internal record structure, column by column.

Suppose that a PL/SQL table has 100 rows defined in it. Every time you pass that table into a procedure or function as an OUT or IN OUT parameter, PL/SQL copies the entire table into an internal table structure, row by row.

Suppose, now, that you have a record with 15 columns in it, three of which are PL/SQL tables, each with 100 rows. Then, every time you pass that record into a procedure or function as an OUT or IN OUT parameter, PL/SQL copies the entire record into an internal record structure, column by column *and* row by row—for a total of 312 copies! And if that procedure calls another procedure, passing the record down to that inner procedure, well, PL/SQL executes the same copy process within the second procedure.

As you can easily imagine, this copying could consume a noticeable amount of memory and CPU cycles in your application.

So should you avoid using records and PL/SQL tables as parameters in programs? Absolutely not! These advanced, multi-component data structures are powerful constructs in your program—you definitely should take advantage of them. However, you should be aware of the kinds of problems you might encounter when using these kinds of parameters. And you should be ready to implement a workaround if you find that performance in your application is dragged down as a result of record or PL/SQL table copying.

The workaround for this problem is straightforward enough: don't pass the record or table as a parameter. But then how can you get your data inside your program? Replacing a record with a parameter list of 20 different parameters isn't really an answer, since PL/SQL will continue to execute 20 copies to internal variables. No, the answer is to stop PL/SQL from executing the copies altogether. To accomplish this, make use of package-level data, as explained in Chapter 16, *Packages*.

Here's an example of the steps you could take to avoid passing these data structures as parameters. Suppose you have a procedure which accepts both a record and a PL/SQL table as parameters, as follows:

```
PROCEDURE massage_mucho_data
    (io_columns_galore_rec IN OUT columns_galore%ROWTYPE,
     io_lotsarows_tab IN OUT lotsarows_tabtype);
```

To use this procedure, I first declare and populate both the row and table. Then, I call the procedure:

```
DECLARE
    galore_rec columns_galore%rowtype;
    TYPE lotsarows_tabtype IS TABLE OF VARCHAR2 INDEX BY BINARY_INTEGER;
    my_table lotsarows_tabtype;
BEGIN
    fill_table (my_table);
    massage_mucho_data (galore_rec, my_table);
END;
```

As PL/SQL executes the statements in massage_mucho_data, the contents of the record and PL/SQL table are copied into local structures. Upon successful termination of the program, the data in those local structures is copied back to galore_rec and my_table.

If, on the other hand, I create a package with the record and table types and instances in the specification as shown below, those data structures are "global" in my session. I can manipulate them directly in any procedure or function without passing them into those programs as parameters.

```
PACKAGE mucho_data_pkg
IS
    /* Declare the record in the package specification. */
    galore_rec columns_galore%rowtype;

    /* Define the table structure and declare the table. */
    TYPE lotsarows_tabtype IS TABLE OF VARCHAR2 INDEX BY BINARY_INTEGER;

    my_table lotsarows_tabtype;

END mucho_data_pkg;
```

After I populate the table, I can call the revised version of massage_mucho_data —which no longer has any parameter at all!

```
BEGIN
    fill_table;
    massage_mucho_data;
END;
```

I do not need to declare the package table. Nor do I need to declare the record. I simply modify the internals of massage_mucho_data to append the package name "mucho_data_pkg" to the names of the record and PL/SQL table. In other words, whereas a line in the original massage_mucho_data procedure might have looked like this:

```
FOR row_count IN 1 .. 100
LOOP
    io_lotsarows_tab (row_count) := row_count ** 2;
END LOOP;
```

this same loop in the new, parameter-less version of massage_mucho_data would appear as follows:

```
FOR row_count IN 1 .. 100
LOOP
    mucho_data_pkg.my_table (row_count) := row_count ** 2;
END LOOP;
```

I no longer pass the complex data structures as parameters. I reference them directly in the procedure. PL/SQL no longer copies the values to internal variables.

There are, by the way, a number of downsides to globalizing your data as shown above. When you use global data structures, you increase the dependencies between modules in your system. The massage_mucho_data is no longer a black box, completely independent of other elements of the application. Instead, it requires the data structures in the mucho_data_pkg. When I passed in the table as a parameter to fill_table, I gave myself the flexibility to call fill_table for any table of the correct table type. If I need this flexibility, then I cannot push the data structure down inside the package. If, on the other hand, these programs really will be run only for that record and that table, then package-level data would be the way to go.

The power of packages, particularly to provide package-level data, should make you want to place most, if not all, of your modules inside a package. You may not need to group additional modules into that package immediately. You may not need package-level data at this time. By using a package right from the start, however, you ensure that all references to the procedure or function are already prefaced with the package name. Otherwise, when you decide you need to wrap a package around a procedure, you either have to create a synonym for the newly-packaged object or change all references to the unqualified program name.

Given these drawbacks, you should convert from parameters to global variables only when you have verified that the parameter-copying of these data structures has an unacceptable impact on your application. Document clearly the changes you have to make and, most importantly, the data structures which have become globals in your system. A later release of PL/SQL might fix this problem by no longer insisting on performing the copies for OUT and IN OUT parameters. When this is the case, you will want to consider converting back to a parameter interface. This will be practical only if you have documented your workarounds.

Use PLS_INTEGER for All Integer Operations

When you need an integer variable, use the PLS_INTEGER type and not BINARY_INTEGER, INTEGER, or NUMBER. PLS_INTEGER is the most efficient implementation for integer types (available in PL/SQL 2.3 and above).

Numeric types such as INTEGER and NUMBER are represented in the 22-byte Oracle number format. Arithmetic operations on these types are implemented using Oracle number libraries. Furthermore, the INTEGER type is a constrained subtype of NUMBER with a precision of 0. On assignments to INTEGER variables precision checking is done at runtime.

Both PLS_INTEGER and BINARY_INTEGER are represented as a signed 4-byte quantity (sb4). But BINARY_INTEGER arithmetic is costly; the operands are first converted to an Oracle number, and then the Oracle number library is used to compute the result as another Oracle number. This results in increased use of temporaries, data conversion, and, hence, poor performance. On the other hand, arithmetic operations on PLS_INTEGERs are efficiently implemented using native integer arithmetic.

Unfortunately, it is not possible to fix all the implementation inefficiencies with INTEGER and BINARY_INTEGER datatypes without breaking backward compatibility of old applications. For instance, Oracle cannot simply implement these types the same way as PLS_INTEGER without changing the overflow/underflow semantics. (The sum of two BINARY_INTEGERs will result in an overflow only if the result exceeds the maximum value storable in an Oracle number. The sum of two PLS_INTEGERs will result in an overflow when the sb4 limit is exceeded.)

The numeric types NATURAL, NATURALN, POSITIVE, POSITIVEN, and SIGNTYPE are subtypes of BINARY_INTEGER with narrower range constraints. There is considerable overhead (about three or four byte-code instructions) in the enforcement of these range constraints on every assignment (or parameter passing) to variables of these types.

One caution about the use of PLS_INTEGER: this is a PL/SQL-specific datatype, so if you are constructing a function or procedure to be used in an environment which does not support that datatype, you could run into trouble. For example, a function which will be called inside SQL cannot have a PLS_INTEGER parameter. Instead, declare the parameter to be INTEGER, but then (if there is sufficient internal integer arithmetic) copy that value to a local variable of type PLS_INTEGER and perform computations on that variable.

Avoid NOT NULL Constraints

Using NOT NULL constraints in PL/SQL comes with a performance penalty. Consider the program fragment below:

```
procedure foo is
  m number not null;
  a number;
  b number;
begin
  m := a + b;
  m := m * 1.2;
  m := m * m;
  ..
end;
```

Since "m" is a NOT NULL constrained number, the result of the expression "a+b" is first computed into a temporary, and the temporary is then tested for NULLity, If the temporary is NULL an exception is raised; otherwise the value of the temporary is moved to "m".

On the other hand, if "m" were not constrained, then the result of the expression "a+b" could directly be computed into "m". So a more efficient way to rewrite the above fragment with reduced use of temporaries is:

```
procedure foo is
  m number;   -- Note: m doesn't have NOT NULL constraint
  a number;
  b number;
begin
  m := a + b;
  m := m * 1.2;
  m := m * m;
  -- enforce constraint programmatically
  if (m is null) then
    -- raise appropriate error
  end if;
  ..
end;
```

Another thing to note is that the types NATURALN and POSITIVEN are defined to be NOT NULL subtypes of NATURAL and POSITIVE, respectively; thus, you will incur the performance penalty described above when you use them.

Avoid Type Conversions When Possible

PL/SQL does implicit conversions between structurally different types at runtime. Currently, this is true even when the source item is a literal constant. A common case where implicit conversions result in a performance penalty, but can be avoided, is with numeric types. For instance, assigning a PLS_INTEGER variable to a NUMBER variable or vice-versa will result in a conversion since their representations are different. Such implicit conversions can happen during parameter passing as well.

Some examples of inefficient code and suggestions to fix them are shown below:

1. Prevent conversions between numeric types. Consider:

```
number_variable := number_variable + 1;
```

The literal constant 1 is represented as an sb4; it gets converted to Oracle number format before the addition. Instead, use:

```
number_variable := number_variable + 1.0;
```

The above is more efficient because literal floats (like 1.0) are represented as Oracle numbers, so no type conversion happens at runtime.

Or better still, when dealing with integer data, use:

```
pls_integer_variable := pls_integer_variable + 1;
```

2. Prevent numeric to character type conversion. Consider:

```
char_variable := 10;
```

The literal 10 is converted to CHAR at runtime, and then copied. Instead use:

```
char_variable := '10';
```

Use Index-By Tables of Records and Objects

In Oracle 7.3, PL/SQL added support for index-by tables of records. (Index-by tables were formerly known as PL/SQL tables.) Prior to that, users modeled the same as a bunch of index-by tables of scalars (one for each record attribute). Users should strongly consider rewriting such applications to use table of records (or objects). The effort will pay off in two major ways:

- *Better application performance*: The number of index-by table lookup, insert, copy, and similar operations will be reduced dramatically if the data is packaged into an index-by table of records.

- *Improved memory utilization*: There is memory overhead associated with each index-by table (primarily due to its tree structured implementation). Having fewer index-by tables will help cut this overhead, and also reduce memory fragmentation caused due to the varying size allocations in different tables.

Overview of PL/SQL8 Enhancements

Oracle Corporation has improved the peformance of PL/SQL programs with the release of Oracle8 and PL/SQL8. Without delving into detailed descriptions of the internal changes made to the engine, it is worth noting which elements of the technology have improved. This knowledge may well affect your choice of implementation for algorithms and your willingness to employ some features which in the past have come with a noticeable penalty.

PL/SQL8 offers improved performance in the following areas:[*]

- The memory required for PL/SQL code in the SGA has been reduced by about 20-25%. This will be especially important for large packages. In addition, Oracle8 uses a paging algorithm for code segments and data segments, leading to less fragmentation in the SGA.

- Large VARCHAR2 and RAW variables are dynamically allocated and resized as needed. For example, you might declare a package variable to be length 32,000 to handle all possible scenarios, but in most cases that variable only holds 255 bytes of data. You will no longer pay the penalty of all that extra memory.

- Anonymous blocks with bind variables execute much more rapidly. This is of special importance when you are working with DBMS_SQL or executing PL/SQL functions from within SQL. Oracle claims that the overhead of calling PL/SQL functions in SQL now is "negligible." If true, this will have significant implications for the deployment of PL/SQL code throughout SQL implementations.

- The use of temporary data structures has been minimized, resulting in performance improvements for such operations as concatenations and implicit conversions.

- PL/SQL records are now supported more efficiently for runtime operations. Prior to Oracle8, the compiler exploded records into individual scalar fields. Now, as you would expect with support for objects, PL/SQL provides native support for the RECORD composite type.

- The performance of index-by tables (formerly known as PL/SQL tables) has improved significantly due to a change in implementation from B*trees to a paged-array representation.

---

[*] This information has been provided by Oracle Corporation and has not been independently confirmed.

26

Tracing PL/SQL Execution

As you build more and more complex applications, it can be very difficult to keep track of which procedure calls which function; execution call stacks grow deep and bewildering. Yet there are times when it is very important to be able to trace the activity in your PL/SQL code base.

Oracle offers a trace facility for your PL/SQL code which allows you to generate voluminous information about the particular paths your programs take to get their job done. Of course, Oracle has for years offered a SQL trace facility which provides extensive data on the processing of your SQL statements. See *Oracle Performance Tuning* for more information on this feature, as well as other tuning/tracing utilities like TKPROF.

In addition to these standard Oracle facilities, you can build your own tracing utilities; the final section in this chapter offers an architecture and some implementational ideas for a utility designed specifically to trace execution within a running application. (Such a utility is particularly useful for production support.)

The PL/SQL Trace Facility

PL/SQL8 offers a tracing tool for server-side PL/SQL. You can use this tool to trace the execution of PL/SQL programs and the raising of exceptions within those programs. The output from the trace is written to the Oracle Server trace file. On Windows NT, you can find this trace file in the *\OraNT\RDBMS80\TRACE* directory. In UNIX, check the *$ORACLE_HOME\rdbms\trace* directory. The name of the file has the format *ORANNNNN.TRC*, where *NNNNN* is a left zero-padded number assigned internally by the Oracle Trace facility. Order your directory by date to find the latest trace file.

NOTE You cannot use the PL/SQL tracing tool with the multi-threaded server option (MTS).

Enabling Program Units for Tracing

In order to trace the execution of a program, you will first have to enable that program by recompiling it with the debug option. You can do this either by altering your session and then issuing a CREATE OR REPLACE statement, or by directly recompiling an existing program unit with the debug option.

To alter your session to turn *on* PL/SQL debug mode for compilation, issue this command:

```
SQL> ALTER SESSION SET PLSQL_DEBUG=TRUE;
```

Then compile your program unit with a CREATE OR REPLACE statement. That program unit will then be available for tracing.

You can also recompile your existing, stored program with debug mode as follows:

```
SQL> ALTER [PROCEDURE|FUNCTION|PACKAGE] <program_name> COMPILE DEBUG;
```

So if you wanted to enable the emp_pkg package for tracing, you would issue this command:

```
SQL> ALTER PACKAGE emp_pkg COMPILE DEBUG;
```

From within a PL/SQL program you can also turn on debug mode for a module by using DBMS_SQL as follows:

```
CREATE OR REPLACE PROCEDURE debugpkg (name IN VARCHAR2)
IS
    cur INTEGER := DBMS_SQL.OPEN_CURSOR;
    fdbk INTEGER;
BEGIN
    DBMS_SQL.PARSE (cur,
        'ALTER PACKAGE ' || name || ' COMPILE DEBUG',
        DBMS_SQL.NATIVE);

    fdbk := DBMS_SQL.EXECUTE (cur);

    DBMS_SQL.CLOSE_CURSOR (cur);
END;
/
```

For more information on DBMS_SQL, see Appendix C, *Built-In Packages*.

Turning On the Trace

Once you have enabled the desired program units for tracing, you can execute those programs (or the application code which makes use of those programs). To get trace output, however, you must turn on tracing for your session. You can request tracing of program calls and/or exceptions raised in programs.

You do this with the ALTER SESSION command as follows:

```
SQL> ALTER SESSION SET EVENTS='10938 TRACE NAME CONTEXT LEVEL <number>';
```

where 10938 is the event number for PL/SQL tracing and <number> is a number indicating the level of tracing you desire. Valid tracing levels are:

Level	Description
1	Trace all calls
2	Trace calls to enabled programs only
4	Trace all exceptions
8	Trace exceptions in enabled program units only

You can activate multiple event levels for tracing by adding the level values. For example, the following statement sets tracing for levels 2 and 8:

```
SQL> ALTER SESSION SET EVENTS='10938 TRACE NAME CONTEXT LEVEL 10';
```

while this next command activates tracing for levels 2, 4, and 8:

```
SQL> ALTER SESSION SET EVENTS='10938 TRACE NAME CONTEXT LEVEL 14';
```

Lower trace levels supersede higher levels. So if you activate tracing for level combination 12, level 8 will be ignored and trace output will be produced for all exceptions, not just exceptions in enabled program units.

As you can see, you have some control over the granularity of tracing. It is not possible, however, to activate tracing just within a specific program. It is either all programs or all programs in which tracing has been enabled with a debug-mode compile.

NOTE   You cannot turn on tracing for remote procedure calls (RPCs)—that is, programs which are stored in remote databases.

A Sample Tracing Session

To make it easier for me to test and use this facility I created the following scripts:

```
alter package &1 compile debug;
```

```
alter session set events='10938 trace name context level &1';
```

So I can now prepare a package for tracing with the following statement:

```
SQL> @compdbg PKGNAME
```

where PKGNAME is the name of my package. In the following session, I turn on tracing for all levels by passing 14 (2 + 4 + 8); then I call my PL/Vision substitute for DBMS_OUTPUT.PUT followed by the raising of an exception. The following code:

```
SQL> @trace 14
SQL> BEGIN
  2      p.1 (1);
  3      raise no_data_found;
  4  END;
  5  /
begin
*
ERROR at line 1:
SQL>
```

resulted in this trace file:

```
Dump file D:\ORANT\RDBMS80\trace\ORA00089.TRC
Wed Jun 11 13:22:52 1997
ORACLE V8.0.2.0.2 - Beta vsnsta=1
vsnsql=c vsnxtr=3
Windows NT V4.0, OS V5.101, CPU type 586
Oracle8 Server Release 8.0.2.0.2 - Beta
With the distributed, heterogeneous, replication, objects
and parallel query options
PL/SQL Release 3.0.2.0.2 - Beta
Windows NT V4.0, OS V5.101, CPU type 586
Instance name: orcl
Redo thread mounted by this instance: 1
Oracle process number: 11
pid: 59
Wed Jun 11 13:22:52 1997
*** SESSION ID:(11.18) 1997.06.11.13.22.52.431
------------ PL/SQL TRACE INFORMATION -----------
Levels set :   2    4    8
------------ PL/SQL TRACE INFORMATION -----------
Levels set :   2    4    8
Trace:    PACKAGE PLVPRO.P: P Stack depth = 2
Trace:    PACKAGE BODY PLVPRO.P: P Stack depth = 2
Trace:    PACKAGE BODY PLVPRO.P: L Stack depth = 2
Trace:    PACKAGE BODY PLVPRO.P: DISPLAY_LINE Stack depth = 3
Trace:    PACKAGE BODY PLVPRO.P: LINELEN Stack depth = 4
Trace:    PACKAGE BODY PLVPRO.P: PUT_LINE Stack depth = 4
Trace:    Pre-defined exception - OER 1403 at line 0 of ANONYMOUS BLOCK:
```

As you can see, trace files can get big fast, but they contain some extremely useful information.

Tracing for Production Support

You build a PL/SQL-based application. You debug it, probably by placing calls to some kind of trace procedure throughout your code.[*] Finally, after very careful QA and extensive testing with users, the application is deployed out into the field. You now have hundreds of people working with your code across the country (or maybe just in a single building).

And, of course, problems rear their ugly heads. A user calls the support line and says that his program is behaving in a certain way. You cannot easily reproduce the problem. You are not entirely sure that the environment in which you are running your code is the same as that of your user. What you would really like to do is connect into his session and watch what he is doing as he is doing it.

This section explores an implementation of a package architecture which allows you to "hook" into running programs and perform production support. You can also adapt it for use as a debugger/execution trace mechanism.

Features of a Real-Time Support Mechanism

First, let's come up with a concise definition of "real-time" support for PL/SQL-based applications: the ability to watch or analyze the activity of a currently connected Oracle user without disturbing that user's activity or otherwise affecting the behavior of the application. This is, obviously, very different from simply running the "same" code under the "same" circumstances—that is a *simulation* of what your users are doing.

To achieve this real-time support, you need to be able to get information out of your PL/SQL program and place it in some kind of repository where you can analyze what is going on and come up with fixes. You also need to be able to enable and disable the support mechanism while the user session is executing.

Based on my discussions with customers and my own experience, here are the kinds of features developers need to effectively support their applications:

- The mechanism should be completely transparent to the user—both when it is enabled and when it is disabled.

- A support person can enable the mechanism "remotely," that is, she can connect into a running session, turn on (or turn off) the real-time trace, and then analyze the application behavior.

---

[*] Unless you are lucky enough to be using one of the few PL/SQL debuggers out there in the marketplace like Platinum's SQL-Station or Oracle's Procedure Builder.

- When placing the trace inside the PL/SQL application code, the developer can specify a filter of some kind (nested levels, numeric ranges, categories, or some other type of filter) so that the support trace can be turned on selectively within the application.

- Output from the support mechanism can be changed and specified for each support session. In other words, sometimes you might want to write the trace information to a file, sometimes to a database pipe, and sometimes to a database table.

In this chapter, I can't provide a detailed implementation of all these features. Instead, I will discuss some of the more interesting challenges, and offer you ideas on building such a mechanism yourself.

Starting and Stopping a Support Session

How do you tell an Oracle session which is already up and running that you want to take a look around at its internal processing? How do you tell it that you are done and that it should stop feeding you information? Well, let's assume that you have put a call to the trace startup procedure at the beginning of each program. It would look something like this:

```
CREATE OR REPLACE PROCEDURE calctotals
IS
BEGIN
    trace.startup ('calctotals');
    . . .
END;
/
```

I could then have trace.startup check *something somehow* to see whether the trace mechanism should be turned on or off. I could do the same thing in any other trace procedure which is placed inside application code. Let's take the simplest and most direct approach: using a database table.

I create a table as follows:

```
CREATE TABLE tracetab_activate
    (username VARCHAR2(60),
     action VARCHAR2(20));
```

Then I add these constants and function to the trace package:

```
CREATE OR REPLACE PACKAGE trace
IS
        /* Just showing the part of the package that is relevant */
        /* for this functionality. */
        c_start CONSTANT CHAR(1) := 'Y';
        c_stop CONSTANT CHAR(1) := 'N';
```

```
        FUNCTION activated (username_in IN VARCHAR2) RETURN BOOLEAN;
    END trace;
    /

    CREATE OR REPLACE PACKAGE BODY trace
    IS
        /* Just showing the part of the package that is relevant
           for this functionality. */

        FUNCTION activated (username_in IN VARCHAR2) RETURN BOOLEAN
        IS
            CURSOR act_cur
            IS
                SELECT action FROM tracetab_activate
                WHERE username = UPPER (username_in);

            act_rec act_cur%ROWTYPE;
        BEGIN
            OPEN act_cur;
            FETCH act_cur INTO act_rec;
            RETURN (act_rec.action = c_start);
        END activated;

    END trace;
    /
```

With this function in place, I can modify my trace.startup procedure as follows:

```
    PROCEDURE startup (context_in IN VARCHAR2)
    IS
    BEGIN
        IF activated (USER)
        THEN
            log;
        ELSE
            nolog;
        END IF;

        /* Then the rest of the procedure activity. */
    END startup;
```

In other words, if the user should be activated, I call the trace.log procedure to turn on logging for that session. All calls to execution trace programs will then write their information out to the log specified by the PLVlog package (it can be an operating system file, database table, database pipe, etc.).

Normally, the activation table would be kept empty. If a user calls with a problem, the support person can get that user's Oracle account name and issue an insert (I hope through some sort of GUI interface) as follows:

```
    INSERT INTO tracetab_activate VALUES ('SAM_I_AM', 'Y');
```

The next time Sam I Am's session executes trace.startup, the trace will be activated and the analysis can commence. To deactivate the real-time trace, the support person can simply delete that record from the table. Then the next time trace.startup is executed, logging will be turned off.

This approach provides a straightforward mechanism to "get inside" an already-running session. One concern about using the trace.activated function in this way, however, is that a query against the tracetab_activate must be performed every time that trace.startup (and other trace "show" programs) is encountered. This could turn into an unacceptable amount of overhead if an application is well-modularized.

That's the difference between a prototype and a production-quality utility. To really make this architecture successful, it would very likely need to be fine-tuned. One refinement is to maintain a counter in the trace package and be able to specify that you want to check for activation of the trace logging only every 50 or 100 or 1000 calls to trace programs. This would cut down on the overhead by skipping lots of queries, but it would also mean that it might take longer to activate the trace.

Filtering Trace Information

Another critical element of a successful support mechanism is the ability to specify which trace information you want to see. If a system contains four main subsystems (with lots of interactions) and hundreds of programs, you're probably going to want to look at trace information from a particular area of functionality, based on the clues provided by the user.

There are many different approaches one can take to filtering out trace messages so the support person or developer (let's call this person the analyzer) sees only what is relevant at that time. Here are the ideas I have thought of:

Free format
> Allow the analyzer to provide a wildcard string which any trace message must be LIKE in order to actively logged during this connection. Knowing this in advance, a developer could concatenate a "context" or level or category to the beginning of the message string. This is the most primitive form of filtering and requires all developers to know about the way in which trace performs its filter check.

Structured interface
> Provide a separate argument in calls to programs like trace.startup and trace.show which would allow a developer to explicitly associate a level (integer) or category (string) with a given trace. With this approach, the trace message is kept distinct from the filter criteria. This is probably easier for developers to work with, but it requires more work within trace to provide an interface through which the analyzer can request a trace just for specific levels, ranges of levels, or one or more categories.

If you are going to try to design your own package to handle this kind of functionality, you will find yourself at a crossroads of sorts. How much effort do you want to put into something like this versus how much effort are you going to require that developers/analyzers make in order to take advantage of your package? It can sometimes be hard to justify the resources required to "do it right."

Obviously, I can't make that decision for you. In fact, I had trouble making that decision for myself as I designed the PLVxmn package of PL/Vision. I can, however, review what I think an appropriate interface would be to support these different approaches.

Free Format Filtering

With the free format approach, you could simply add a column onto the tracetab_ activate table which would contain the wildcard string:

```
CREATE TABLE tracetab_activate
   (username VARCHAR2(60),
    action VARCHAR2(20),
    matchto VARCHAR2(100));
```

Then when you insert into the table to "turn on" logging of trace information, you provide the string:

```
INSERT INTO tracetab_activate VALUES ('SAM_I_AM', 'Y', '%INVOICE%');
```

In this case, I am looking for trace messages which contain the word INVOICE. I would then modify the activated function shown earlier in the article to a *procedure* which returns a TRUE/FALSE value, to indicate whether or not the trace is activated for this user, as well as the match string. Here is the header for such a procedure:

```
PACKAGE trace
IS
   . . .
   PROCEDURE check_activation
      (turnon_out OUT BOOLEAN, match_out OUT VARCHAR2);
   . . .
END trace;
```

My trace.startup procedure would call the check_activation routine as follows:

```
PROCEDURE startup
IS
   v_turnon BOOLEAN;
   v_match VARCHAR2(100);
BEGIN
   check_activation (v_turnon, v_match);
   IF v_turnon
   THEN
      log (v_match);
```

```
    ELSE
        nolog;
    END IF;
    . . .
END:
```

The log procedure accepts the match string, setting flags internal to PLVlog so that the trace message is checked against the match string and is passed on to the log if a match is found.

Structured Interface Filtering

You get into a lot more code with this approach. Let's look at implementing an interface to support numeric levels. You will be able to ask to see trace information for one level, or a range of levels, or even a list of distinct levels. Because of the complexity and the need to maintain consistent formats of information, you would no longer perform your own direct inserts into the tracetab_activate table. Instead, you call a procedure which converts your request into the format necessary to store in the table. Here are some of those procedures:

```
PACKAGE trace
IS
    /* Just show the programs for this filtering. */
    PROCEDURE filter_by
        (username_in IN VARCHAR2, level_in IN INTEGER);

    PROCEDURE filter_by
        (username_in IN VARCHAR2, min_in IN INTEGER, max_in IN INTEGER);

    PROCEDURE filter_by
        (username_in IN VARCHAR2, list_in IN VARCHAR2);

END trace;
```

Notice that all three of these filtering programs have the same name. These are *overloaded* procedures; overloading is discussed in the section "Module Overloading" in Chapter 15, *Procedures and Functions*.

Here are some examples of these programs in use:

1. Request activation of trace on the SFEUERST account for level 16:

```
SQL> exec trace.filter_by ('sfeuerst', 16);
```

2. Request activation of trace on the LELLISON account for levels 16-25:

```
SQL> exec trace.filter_by ('lellsion', 16, 25);
```

3. Request activation of trace on the WGATES account for levels 2, 6, 10, and 55:

```
SQL> exec trace.filter_by ('wgates', '2,6,10,55');
```

Gee, that looks easy enough to use! Of course, the devil is in the details. In all three cases, the procedures must convert the levels provided into a string with a consistent format so that the trace.startup program (and others) can query the tracetab_activate table and properly interpret the request.

From Idea to Implementation

Sure, this section doesn't provide all of the code behind the interface. However, don't underestimate the importance of getting that interface right. Too many of us spend too little time thinking about how our programs will be used and how the interface to our functionality would be best constructed. Instead, we are eager to dive into the implementation of the programs. Without question, package bodies will be needed for most every package specification you ever write, but if your specification is poorly designed, it will be hard to understand and use—which means that most likely your code will *not* be used.

Quick-and-Dirty Tracing

I have found that in many situations, PL/SQL developers don't have the time or the access to tools to perform comprehensive tracing. Instead, they just need to get more information out of a specific package or program, and they need it *right away*.

Let's take a look at the options you have for some "quick-and-dirty" tracing. First of all, there is DBMS_OUTPUT.PUT_LINE, a built-in which generates output from within a PL/SQL program. For example, if I executed in SQL*Plus the following block:

```
BEGIN
    FOR emp_rec IN
        (SELECT ename, sal FROM emp ORDER BY sal DESC)
    LOOP
        DBMS_OUTPUT.PUT_LINE
            ('Employee ' || emp_rec.ename || ' earns ' ||
            TO_CHAR (emp_rec.sal) || ' dollars.');
    END LOOP;
END;
/
```

I would see the following output when the program terminated:

```
Employee KING earns 5000 dollars.
Employee SCOTT earns 3000 dollars.
Employee JONES earns 2975 dollars.
Employee ADAMS earns 1100 dollars.
Employee JAMES earns 950 dollars.
```

You will only see trace information from DBMS_OUTPUT in SQL*Plus if you issue the following command:

```
SQL> set serveroutput on
```

This will enable the package within SQL*Plus. You can also set the buffer which contains trace information to its maximum size of 1MB as follows:

```
SQL> set serveroutput on size 1000000
```

Finally, if you are running Oracle Server 7.3 and above, you can also request that output from DBMS_OUTPUT.PUT_LINE be "wrapped" so that leading blanks are not trimmed and long lines are wrapped within the SQL*Plus linesize:

```
SQL> set serveroutput on size 1000000 format wrapped
```

So DBMS_OUTPUT does give you the flexibility of embedding trace calls inside your program, but only seeing the output when you have SET SERVEROUTPUT ON. It is, unfortunately, an all-or-nothing proposition with this package. You see no messages or you see all messages. Using DBMS_OUTPUT.PUT_LINE "in the raw" as a trace mechanism therefore leaves much to be desired. (Well, to be honest, when talking about the inadequacies of DBMS_OUTPUT, one would also have to mention that it can only display a maximum of 255 bytes per call, that it does not display Booleans or combinations of data, and that it will not work in the Oracle Developer/2000 environment nor in Oracle WebServer.)[*]

Ideally, you would like to be able to set up a trace mechanism so that you can see information about only this package or that procedure. The best way to do that is to set up a "toggle" within a package. Let's step through a simple example to make the technique clear.

Suppose I have a package which assigns a value to a package variable (which must be defined in the package specification) using dynamic SQL execution. (This is similar to the indirect referencing available in Oracle Forms with COPY_IN.) The specification and body of such a package is shown below:

```
/* filename on companion disk: dynvar.spp */
CREATE OR REPLACE PACKAGE dynvar
IS
    PROCEDURE assign (var_in IN VARCHAR2, val_in IN VARCHAR2);
    FUNCTION val (var_in IN VARCHAR2) RETURN VARCHAR2;
END dynvar;
/
CREATE OR REPLACE PACKAGE BODY dynvar
IS
    PROCEDURE assign (var_in IN VARCHAR2, val_in IN VARCHAR2)
    IS
```

---

[*] See Chapter 7 of my book on packages, *Advanced Oracle PL/SQL Programming with Packages,* for details about the usage of DBMS_OUTPUT.PUT_LINE.

```
    cur INTEGER;
    fdbk INTEGER;
BEGIN
    cur := DBMS_SQL.OPEN_CURSOR;
    DBMS_SQL.PARSE (cur,
        'BEGIN ' || var_in || ' := :val; END;', DBMS_SQL.NATIVE);
    DBMS_SQL.BIND_VARIABLE (cur, 'val', val_in, 2000);
    fdbk := DBMS_SQL.EXECUTE (cur);
    DBMS_SQL.CLOSE_CURSOR (cur);
END;

FUNCTION val (var_in IN VARCHAR2) RETURN VARCHAR2
IS
    cur INTEGER;
    fdbk INTEGER;
    retval VARCHAR2(2000);
BEGIN
    cur := DBMS_SQL.OPEN_CURSOR;
    DBMS_SQL.PARSE
        (cur, 'BEGIN :val := ' || var_in || '; END;', DBMS_SQL.NATIVE);
    DBMS_SQL.BIND_VARIABLE (cur, 'val', var_in, 2000);
    fdbk := DBMS_SQL.EXECUTE (cur);
    DBMS_SQL.VARIABLE_VALUE (cur, 'val', retval);
    DBMS_SQL.CLOSE_CURSOR (cur);
    RETURN retval;
END;

END dynvar;
/
```

Here is a little test package and some program calls in SQL*Plus to give you a
sense of how it would work:

```
CREATE OR REPLACE PACKAGE TSTVAR
IS
    str1 varchar2(2000);
    str2 varchar2(2000);
END;
/

SQL> exec dynvar.assign ('tstvar.str1', 'abc')

SQL> exec dbms_output.put_line (tstvar.str1)
abc

SQL> exec dbms_output.put_line (dynvar.val ('tstvar.str1'))
abc
```

This package seems to work just fine. When working with dynamic SQL and PL/
SQL, however, the trickiest aspect of the package might not be building it, but
using it. The user of dynvar must construct the package variable's name properly
and if she gets it wrong, she will get all sorts of interesting but confusing errors.
Let's add a trace feature to dynvar so that when a user has trouble, she can very

selectively activate trace just for this package and the dynamic management of package globals.

First, I will add my toggle to the package specification:

```
CREATE OR REPLACE PACKAGE dynvar
IS
    PROCEDURE assign (var_in IN VARCHAR2, val_in IN VARCHAR2);
    FUNCTION val (var_in IN VARCHAR2) RETURN VARCHAR2;

    PROCEDURE trc;
    PROCEDURE notrc;
    FUNCTION tracing RETURN BOOLEAN;

END dynvar;
/
```

I turn on trace for this package with the following command:

```
SQL> exec dynvar.trc
```

Similarly, I can turn off trace with this command:

```
SQL> exec dynvar.notrc
```

The implementation of this toggle in the package body is very straightforward:

```
CREATE OR REPLACE PACKAGE BODY dynvar
IS
    g_trc BOOLEAN := FALSE;
    PROCEDURE trc IS BEGIN g_trc := TRUE; END;
    PROCEDURE notrc IS BEGIN g_trc := FALSE; END;
    FUNCTION tracing RETURN BOOLEAN IS BEGIN RETURN g_trc; END;

        . . .
END dynvar;
```

I establish a private global variable to hold the trace setting (default is "off"). When you call dynvar.trc, the variable is set to TRUE or "on." Now the question is this: how do I put this toggle to use inside the assign and val programs? Right after the BEGIN statement in each program, I will add a conditional clause. If tracing is turned on, then I display a message:

```
CREATE OR REPLACE PACKAGE BODY dynvar
IS
    PROCEDURE assign (var_in IN VARCHAR2, val_in IN VARCHAR2)
    IS
        cur INTEGER;
        fdbk INTEGER;
    BEGIN
        IF tracing
        THEN
            DBMS_OUTPUT.PUT_LINE
                ('dynvar assigning ' || val_in || ' to ' || var_in);
        END IF;
```

```
   /* same dynamic PL/SQL as before */
   END;

   FUNCTION val (var_in IN VARCHAR2) RETURN VARCHAR2
   IS
      /* same declarations as before */
   BEGIN
      IF debuging
      THEN
         DBMS_OUTPUT.PUT_LINE ('dynvar retrieving value of ' || var_in);
      END IF;

      /* same dynamic PL/SQL as before */
   END;

END dynvar;
/
```

With this new version of the dynvar package installed, I can then turn on trace and get feedback each time either of the package's programs are executed:

```
SQL> set serveroutput on
SQL> exec dynvar.trc

SQL> exec dynvar.assign ('tstvar.str1', 'abc')
dynvar assigning abc to tstvar.str1

SQL> exec p.l(dynvar.val ('tstvar.str1'))
dynvar retrieving value of tstvar.str1
abc
```

Of course in the "real world," you will want to enhance the information displayed with the context in which these programs were called (perhaps a date-time stamp and so forth). This should, however, give you a flavor of the basic technique and how to employ it.

NOTE   Intrigued by dynvar? You will find more information about dynamic PL/SQL in *Oracle Built-in Packages*. You can also overload the dynvar. package to perform assignments and retrievals for dates, numbers, and so on in their native formats.

VII

Appendixes

Part VII of this book contains summary and release-specific information.

- Appendix A, *What's on the Companion Disk?*, describes how to use the disk that accompanies this book.
- Appendix B, *Calling Stored Procedures from PL/SQL Version 1.1*, describes the mechanism for allowing Oracle Developer/2000-based applications to call stored procedures
- Appendix C, *Built-In Packages*, offers a quick reference to many of the Oracle built-in functions.

What's on the Companion Disk?

The disk that accompanies this book is a Windows disk containing the Oracle PL/SQL Programming Companion Utilities Guide, an online tool designed to help you easily find additional resources. The guide offers point-and-click access to nearly 100 files of source code and documentation prepared by the authors. The goal of providing this material in electronic form is to give you a leg up on the development of your own PL/SQL programs. Providing material on disk also helps us keep the size of this book under (some) control.

Installing the Guide

In a Microsoft Windows environment (3.1, 95, NT 3.5, or NT 4.0), you begin installation by double-clicking on the *setup.exe* file to run the installation program. If you are working in a non-Windows environment, please visit the RevealNet PL/SQL Pipeline Archives (*www.revealnet.com/plsql-pipeline*) to obtain a compressed file containing the utilities on this disk.

The installation script will lead you through the necessary steps. The first screen you will see is the install screen shown in Figure A-1.

You can change the default directory in which the files will be placed. Once this step is compete and the software has been copied to your drive, an icon will appear in the folder you specified. Double-click on the icon to start using the Companion Utilities Guide. You will then see the main menu shown in Figure A-2.

Figure A-1. Installing the companion utilities guide

Using the Guide

The three buttons on the main menu take you to the companion information for this book:

About the Utility Guide

   A brief description of the contents of this disk.

Package Examples

   Extended text and examples that explore the construction of complex packages in PL/SQL. Figure A-3 shows buttons available to you for exploration if you choose this. Once you select an example, you can scroll through text explaining how the package was designed and built. You can also choose to view the package specification and body, and copy either to the clipboard.

Source Code Index

   The guide gives you point-and-click access to each of the files on the companion disk. The files are listed in chapter order to make it easy for you to move between the book and guide. Source code listings in the book begin with comment lines keyed to the filenames on the disk. Figure A-4 shows a portion of the Source Code Index.

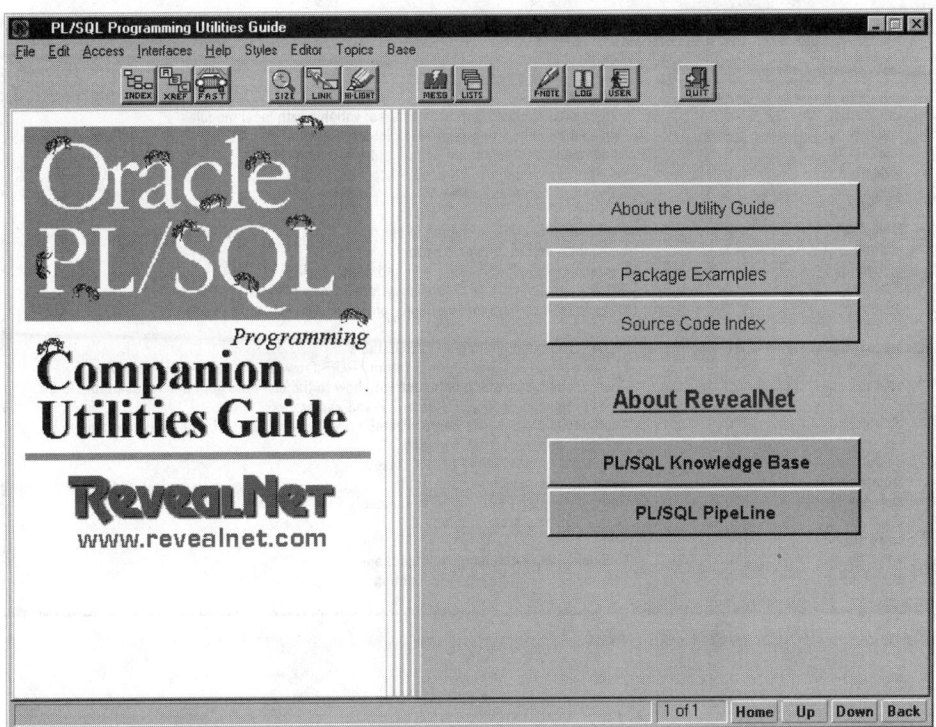

Figure A-2. The main menu

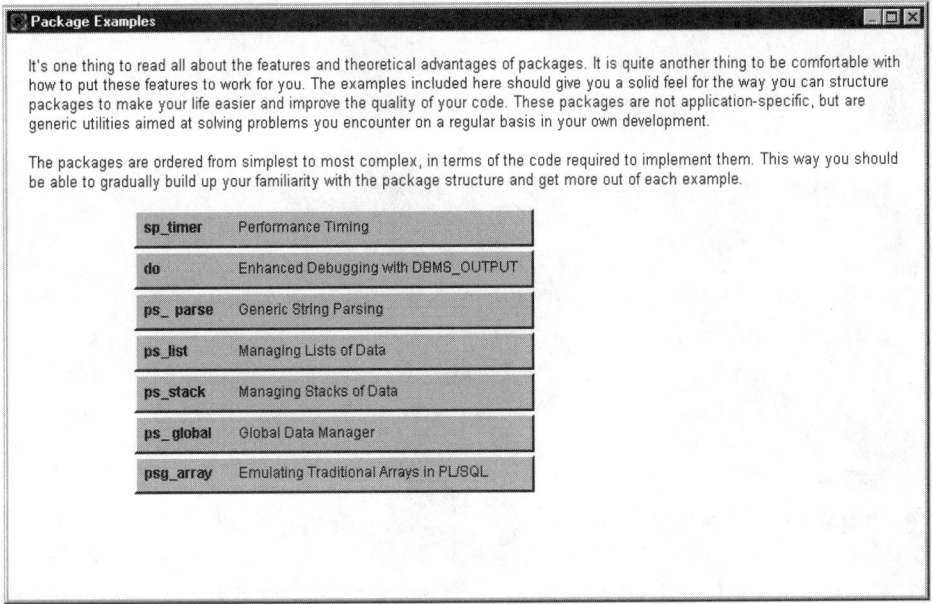

Figure A-3. The package examples

File Name	Chapter	Description
varcurs.doc	6	Explanation of how to emulate a cursor variable with local modules.
unquein.doc	6	Explanation of how to guarantee unique entry with cursors.
unquein.ff	6	Code required to guarantee unique entry with cursors.
fkval.fp	6	Foreign key validation with double fetch
selupdt.sf	6	Select for Update example
highrec.doc	7	Explanation of code in highrec.fp file.
highrec.fp	7	Highlight a record in Oracle Forms
ofquery.doc	7	Explanation of code in postqry.fp and preqry.fp files.
postqry.fp	7	Generic replacement for Post-Query foreign key lookups
preqry.fp	7	Generic replacement for Pre-Query processing or foreign keys.
bizdays.sp	10	Place business days into a PL/SQL table
rowexist.sf	10	Emulate the EXISTS operator to return TRUE if row is defined, FALSE otherwise.
db2tab1.sql	10	Anonymous block which demonstrates how to transfer data from a database table to a PL/SQL table in PL/SQL Release 2.2 and earlier.
db2tab2.sql	10	Anonymous block which demonstrates how to transfer data from a database table to a PL/SQL table in PL/SQL Release 2.3.
seqretr.sp	10	Sequential retrieval with PL/SQL table
indretr.sp	10	Indexed retrieval with PL/SQL table
disptab1.sp	10	Generic program to display a sequentially-filled table with little flexibility.
disptab2.sp	10	Generic display table program
array.sps		
array.spb	10	Traditional array emulation with package
selftune.spp	10	Self-tuning foreign key lookup function

Title bar: Source Code Index

Click on the file name to display its contents ...

Figure A-4. The Source Code Index

B

Calling Stored Procedures from PL/SQL Version 1.1

The Oracle Developer/2000 tools use PL/SQL Version 1.1, while the PL/SQL versions on the server range from 2.0 to 8.x. The PL/SQL version inside the Oracle Developer/2000 tools will be upgraded to PL/SQL Release 2.3 sometime in 1998 with Release 2 of Oracle Developer/2000. In the meantime, the tools group at Oracle Corporation has had to come up with a way to allow applications based on Oracle Developer/2000 to call stored procedures in the most transparent fashion possible. The end result is a mechanism which:

- Does not require any changes to the PL/SQL Version 1.1 base product
- Does allow the Oracle Developer/2000 application to find and execute stored procedures
- Does not require any special syntax to distinguish between stored and local PL/SQL modules

Achieving this effect, however, imposes several restrictions on the use of stored procedures:

- Only four datatypes are supported for module parameters: DATE, VARCHAR2, BOOLEAN, and NUMBER.
- You cannot directly reference a package object using the dot notation <schema>.<package>.<objname>.
- You cannot directly execute remote procedure calls using the standard syntax <procedure><dblink>
- You must provide an argument for each parameter in a stored module's parameter list, even if that parameter has a default value. (This restriction applies only to PL/SQL Version 2.0; this restriction goes away in Release 2.1 and beyond.)

- A stored procedure called from Oracle Developer/2000 cannot have only OUT argument types.

- From Oracle Developer/2000, you can call stored procedures, but you cannot debug them from within the Oracle Developer/2000 tool. (You will be able to do so with PL/SQL Release 2.2 and above; this release runs against Oracle7 Server Release 7.2, which contains the hooks for the step debugging in PL/SQL.)

- You cannot look up a remote subprogram via a synonym until RDBMS Version 7.1.1.

Using Stubs to Talk to Server-Side PL/SQL

The mechanism employed by the Oracle Developer/2000 tools to handle stored procedures is called *stub generation*. A stub is a PL/SQL procedure or function which has the same header as the actual procedure or function. A stub for a package contains a stub or specification for each module in the package.

When the Oracle Developer/2000 tool encounters an identifier in a PL/SQL code segment, it checks to see if it is a local PL/SQL variable, then a tool bind variable, table/view, synonym, sequence, and so on through the precedence order of object name resolution. If it is unable to resolve the reference, the PL/SQL compiler calls a stub generator to see if it can resolve the identifier as a stored function or procedure. In that case, a stub is generated for syntactical checking, and the compiler continues. Because the stub looks the same to the Oracle Developer/2000 tool as the stored module, the tool can continue to perform syntactical checks using that stub. Stub generation only occurs at compile time.

You can see what kind of stub PL/SQL generates in the Oracle Developer/2000 tool by executing the stub generator directly from SQL*Plus, as shown below:

```
VARIABLE not_needed VARCHAR2(2000);
VARIABLE stubtext VARCHAR2(2000);
DELETE FROM SYS.PSTUBTBL;
EXECUTE SYS.PSTUB ('&1', NULL, :not_needed, :stubtext);
PRINT stubtext;
DELETE FROM SYS.PSTUBTBL;
```

where "&1" is a substitution variable. Notice that I delete from the stub table, SYS.PSTUBTBL, before and after my call to the SYS pstub generator program. This is a temporary table and must be cleaned up manually if you are going to call the PSTUB program yourself.

Place this code in a file named *showstub.sql* and you can then call it as follows to show a module's stub:

```
SQL> start showstub calc_totals
```

The following is an example of the output from this showstub program:

```
SQL> CREATE PROCEDURE calc_totals
SQL>        (company_id_in IN NUMBER, type_inout IN OUT VARCHAR2)
SQL> IS
SQL> BEGIN
SQL>        ... all the code ...
SQL> END;
SQL> /

Procedure created.

SQL> start showstub calc_totals

STUBTEXT
---------------------------------------------------------------------
procedure calc_totals (COMPANY_ID_IN NUMBER, TYPE_INOUT in out CHAR) is
begin stproc.in('begin calc_totls(:COMPANY_ID_IN, :TYPE_INOUT); end;');
stproc.bind_i(COMPANY_ID_IN); stproc.bind_io(TYPE_INOUT);
stproc.execute;
stproc.retrieve(2, TYPE_INOUT); end;
```

If the output from showstub is '$$$ s_notv6Compat', you may be trying to use parameters with the %TYPE attribute, which are not allowed in the parameter list of a stored procedure called from Oracle Developer/2000 tools. If the output is '$$$ s_subp not found', the problem is that the stub generator cannot find the module. This will happen if you have not created a synonym for a module which is owned by another user. The stub generator cannot search across different users to resolve a named object reference. You will have to create a public synonym for this module and then grant EXECUTE authority on that module to PUBLIC.

Restrictions on Calling Stored Procedures

It's good to know why and how the Oracle Developer/2000 tools make stored procedures available, but the restrictions on use of those objects has the most direct impact on developers. Let's examine each restriction and the steps you can take to work around those restrictions.

No Server-Side PL/SQL Datatypes

Parameters in stored procedures, as well as the RETURN datatype of stored functions, can only have one of these datatypes if they are to be used by Oracle Forms. This rule applies both to standalone and package modules. Remember: when you work in a Oracle Developer/2000 tool, you are using PL/SQL Version 1.1; any code you write, including calls to stored modules, must conform to Version 1.1 compiler syntax rules. The specification or "public" side of a stored module must look like a Version 1.1 module. Behind the specification—in other words, the implementation of that module—can have all the server-side PL/SQL features you can pack into it. You just can't let any of that show outside of the body of the module or package.

Suppose you define a stored procedure as follows:

```
FUNCTION get_row RETURN BINARY_INTEGER;
```

If you try to execute the function inside an Oracle Forms PL/SQL block, the compiler will tell you:

```
Identifier 'GET_ROW' must be declared
```

It literally cannot even find a match for the function if the datatype does not conform to PL/SQL Version 1 valid datatypes. The SYS.PSTUB procedure will have been unable to generate a stub and so the name remains unresolved.

There are two ways to work around this problem:

- Do not use any server-side PL/SQL datatypes in the specifications of your stored modules.

- Write an overlay stored procedure which maps server-side PL/SQL datatypes to Version 1 datatypes (where possible).

I strongly urge you to employ the second workaround. If you have built stored objects which make use of server-side PL/SQL datatypes in the parameter list, and if that datatype is the most appropriate one for the parameter, you shouldn't change that module's specification. You should always try to take advantage of the most advanced features of a language. Don't choose a lowest common denominator solution unless there are no other options.

In many situations, you won't have the opportunity to change the specification (parameter list) of a stored module. It will have been written by others, perhaps for another application, and cannot be modified without possibly affecting those other applications.

In this case, the second workaround is annoying but thoroughly able to be implemented. If your Oracle Developer/2000 code must call the get_row function, for example, you can create another stored object (let's call it Oracle Developer/2000_ get_row) which does not return a BINARY_INTEGER, but instead returns a NUMBER. The specification and body for Oracle Developer/2000_get_row would be:

```
FUNCTION Oracle Developer 2000_get_row RETURN INTEGER IS
BEGIN
    RETURN get_row;
END;
```

The Oracle Developer/2000_get_row can be called from a Oracle Developer/2000 program because it returns one of the supported datatypes. In this case, PL/SQL will certainly perform the necessary implicit conversions because BINARY_ INTEGER and NUMBER are compatible datatypes.

No Direct Stored Package Variable References

This is the most serious drawback of the implementation for accessing stored objects from Oracle Developer/2000. You simply cannot use the dot notation to reference a package variable, whether it be a string, exception, or cursor. Consider the pet maintenance package which we discussed earlier in this book.

```
PACKAGE pet_maint
IS
    /*------------------ Global Variables ------------------*/
    max_pets_in_facility INTEGER := 120;
    pet_is_sick EXCEPTION;
    CURSOR pet_cur RETURN pet%ROWTYPE;

    /*------------------ Public Modules ------------------*/
    FUNCTION next_pet_shots (pet_id_in IN NUMBER) RETURN DATE;
    PROCEDURE set_schedule (pet_id_in IN NUMBER);
    PROCEDURE check_activity (pet_id_in IN NUMBER);

END pet_maint;
```

You can call the modules using dot notation, as in:

```
pet_maint.check_activity (1503);
```

but you cannot make reference to any of the package variables using this same dot notation. All of the statements shown in boldface will fail to compile:

```
BEGIN
    IF pet_maint.max_pets_in_facility < new_count
    THEN
        ...
        OPEN pet_maint.pet_cur;
        ...
    END IF;
EXCEPTION
    WHEN pet_maint.pet_is_stick
    THEN
        ...
END;
```

This restriction puts you in a tough situation. You really need to build packages; there are just too many advantages to this structure to ignore it. You also need to store as many of your objects as possible in the database. When you are done creating your elegant package, filled with overloaded programs and variables and exceptions, however, you find that you cannot use it in Oracle Forms or Oracle Reports or Oracle Graphics.

What can you do? You simply have to get rid of that dot notation. This is one instance where the workaround actually results in better code! Whenever you build a package with variables like pet_maint.max_pets_in_facility, you should avoid letting programmers directly reference those variables. Instead you are much better off building a pair of "get and set" modules around the package variable. This way, a programmer accesses the variable through a programmatic interface. This gives you more control over that variable. You can make sure that any changes to the variable are valid. You also retain the freedom to change the name or data structure of the variable. If programmers embed direct references to pet_maint.max_pets_in_facility in their code, you can never change how you store that value. If you hide it behind modules, you could decide to store that value in a PL/SQL table or record and not have any impact outside of the package.

The following example shows a new specification for the pet_maint package. In this version the max_pets_in_facility variable has been moved to the body of the package and is replaced by the get_max and set_max modules.

```
PACKAGE pet_maint
IS
    /*------------------ Global Variables ------------------*/
    pet_is_sick EXCEPTION;
    CURSOR pet_cur RETURN pet%ROWTYPE;

    /*------------------ Public Modules ------------------*/
    FUNCTION get_max_pets RETURN INTEGER;
    PROCEDURE set_max_pets (max_in IN INTEGER);
    FUNCTION next_pet_shots (pet_id_in IN NUMBER) RETURN DATE;
    PROCEDURE set_schedule (pet_id_in IN NUMBER);
    PROCEDURE check_activity (pet_id_in IN NUMBER);

END pet_maint;
```

The conversion to a programmatic interface is fairly straightforward for variables. However, it is considerably more complex to manipulate cursors through a procedural interface, and it is impossible to do so for exceptions.

Prior to PL/SQL Release 2.2, any reference to a cursor had to have the cursor name hardcoded. In subsequent releases, you can create cursor variables (explained in Chapter 6). Without cursor variables, you will need to build a set of modules in order to make reference to a cursor declared in a package.The following example contains examples of the kinds of modules you can write to hide the cursor and then access it from Oracle Developer/2000.

```
PROCEDURE open_pet_cur IS
BEGIN
    /* Open the cursor if not already open */
```

```
        IF NOT pet_maint.pet_cur%ISOPEN
        THEN
            OPEN pet_maint.pet_cur;
        END IF;
    END;

    PROCEDURE fetch_pet_cur
        (pet_rec_out OUT pet%ROWTYPE, fetch_status_out OUT VARCHAR2)
    /*
    || Fetch next record from the cursor. Also set a status variable
    || to indicate if a record was fetched (corresponds to
    || the %FOUND attribute).
    */
    IS
        BEGIN
        FETCH pet_maint.pet_cur INTO pet_rec_out;
        IF pet_maint.pet_cur%FOUND
        THEN
            fetch_status_out := 'FOUND';
        ELSE
            fetch_status_out := 'NOTFOUND';
        END IF;
    END;

    PROCEDURE close_pet_cur IS
    BEGIN
        /* Close the cursor if still open */
        IF pet_maint.pet_cur%ISOPEN
        THEN
            CLOSE pet_maint.pet_cur;
        END IF;
    END;
```

That wasn't a whole lot of fun, but at least it is doable. The last variable left exposed in the pet maintenance package is an exception: pet_is_sick. I do not know of any way to build a programmatic interface which would return an exception that you could then raise in your program and reference in an exception handler. A function cannot have an EXCEPTION as a RETURN datatype. The exception "datatype" is treated differently from true datatypes. As a result, you will not be able to trap and handle package-specific exceptions in a stored package unless the stored package uses the RAISE_APPLICATION_ERROR procedure with a user-defined exception number between -20000 and -20999.

No Direct Remote Procedure Calls

This very powerful feature is unavailable from Oracle Developer/2000. Instead, you will have to create a synonym for the remote procedure and then execute the synonym rather than the procedure directly. (Don't forget to grant EXECUTE authority on the synonym!)

Suppose I want to execute the following procedure from an Oracle Forms application:

```
new_schedule@HQ_repository;
```

I need to do the following:

1. Create a synonym:

   ```
   CREATE SYNONYM HQ_new_schedule FOR new_schedule@HQ_repository;
   ```

2. Grant EXECUTE authority on that synonym:

   ```
   GRANT EXECUTE ON HQ_new_schedule TO <user_or_role>;
   ```

3. Call the synonym in my Oracle Forms trigger or program unit:

   ```
   HQ_new_schedule;
   ```

No Default Parameter Values

PL/SQL Version 2.0 does not allow you to use default parameter values when you are performing a remote procedure call. (You must leave any arguments which have default values in the specification out of the module execution.) Even if you do not append an @ symbol on a call to a stored procedure, PL/SQL does consider that a remote procedure call because the client-side application is "remote" from the server.

Unfortunately, if you do try to call a stored object from a Oracle Developer/2000 component and rely on a default value, the PL/SQL error does not offer much help. It will not ask you to include values for all parameters. It will simply tell you:

```
Error at line N:
Identifier 'STORED_OBJECT' must be declared
```

The first time I encountered this error, I panicked. Why couldn't Oracle Forms find the stored procedure? I logged in through SQL*Plus and could run the module there. So I knew it was defined and stored in the database. Was it a security issue within Oracle Forms? Did I have to do something special to get Oracle Forms to realize it was looking for a stored object and not a local program unit? In the end, I discovered that Oracle Forms could find the object, it just couldn't use it (create a stub for it) because I hadn't passed the full set of arguments.

So when your Oracle Developer/2000 PL/SQL compiler tells you that an identifier "must be declared", make sure you that you included an argument for each parameter in the stored module parameter list. You should not consider this too much of a hardship; good programming practice dictates that you never rely on the default values anyway.

C

Built-In Packages

This appendix provides a quick summary of the most commonly used RDBMS-based packages built by Oracle Corporation and made available to all developers. Table C-1 shows the list of packages covered here. Unless otherwise noted, the packages are available in PL/SQL Release 2.1 and above.

Table C-1. Built-In Packages Stored in the Oracle Database

Package Name	Description
DBMS_ALERT	Provides support for notification of database events on an asynchronous basis. Registers a process with an alert and then waits for a signal from that alert.
DBMS_AQ	Offers an interface to Oracle/AQ, the Advanced Queueing Facility of Oracle8 (PL/SQL8 only).
DBMS_AQADM	Used to perform administrative tasks for Oracle/AQ (PL/SQL8 only).
DBMS_DDL	Provides programmatic access to some of the SQL DDL statements.
DBMS_JOB	Submits and manages regularly scheduled jobs for execution inside the database (PL/SQL Release 2.1)
DBMS_LOB	Provides a set of programs to manipulate LOBs (large objects) (PL/SQL8 only).
DBMS_LOCK	Lets you create your own user locks in the database.
DBMS_MAIL	Interfaces to Oracle Office (formerly known as Oracle*Mail).
DBMS_OUTPUT	Displays output from PL/SQL programs to the terminal.
DBMS_PIPE	Communicates between different Oracle sessions through a pipe in the RDBMS shared memory.
DBMS_ROWID	Encapsulates information about the structure of the ROWID datatype and allows for conversion between restricted and extended ROWIDs (PL/SQL8 only).

Table C-1. Built-In Packages Stored in the Oracle Database (continued)

Package Name	Description
DBMS_SESSION	Provides a programmatic interface to several SQL ALTER SESSION commands and other session-level commands.
DBMS_SNAPSHOT	Provides a programmatic interface through which you can manage snapshots and purge snapshot logs. You might use modules in this package to build scripts to automate maintenance of snapshots.
DBMS_SQL	Provides full support for dynamic SQL within PL/SQL. Dynamic SQL refers to statements that are not prewritten into your programs. They are, instead, constructed at run time as character strings and then passed to the SQL engine for execution. (PL/SQL Release 2.1)
DBMS_ TRANSACTION	Provides a programmatic interface to a number of the SQL transaction statements, such as SET TRANSACTION.
DBMS_UTILITY	The miscellaneous package. Contains various useful utilities, such as FORMAT_CALL_STACK, which returns the current stack of called modules.
UTL_FILE	Allows PL/SQL programs to read from and write to operating system files. (PL/SQL Release 2.3)

All of the packages in Table C-1 are stored in the database and can be executed both by client- and server-based PL/SQL programs. In addition to these packages, many of the development tools, like Oracle Forms, offer their own specific package extensions, such as packages to manage OLE2 objects and DDE communication.[*]

Using the Built-in Packages

In this appendix, I've provided a brief overview of each package, followed by a description and header for each program in the package. These headers are structured as follows:

```
PROCEDURE pkg.procname (<parameter list>);

FUNCTION pkg.funcname (<parameter list>) RETURN <return datatype>;
```

where pkg is the name of the package, procname and funcname are the names of the programs, <parameter list> is the list of parameters (if there are no parameters, then you do not provide parentheses either) and <return datatype> is the datatype of the value returned by the function.

Let's look at an example. Suppose that you want to receive a message from a pipe. The header for the built-in function which does this is:

---

[*] For more detailed information about these built-in packages, see my book, *Oracle Built-in Packages.*

```
FUNCTION DBMS_PIPE.RECEIVE_MESSAGE=20
    (pipename IN VARCHAR2, timeout INTEGER DEFAULT
    DBMS_PIPE.MAXWAIT)
RETURN INTEGER;
```

Note that all identifiers are in uppercase except for parameter names. This is consistent with my conventions: all keywords and other identifiers built by Oracle are in uppercase. The parameter names are lowercase because in many program headers, I have provided my own parameter names to make the headers more readable.

When I want to call a packaged program, I must use dot notation. For example to make use of the RECEIVE_MESSAGE built-in, I would write code like this:

```
DECLARE
    pipe_status INTEGER;
BEGIN
    pipe_status DBMS_PIPE.RECEIVE_MESSAGE (mypipe, 10);
END;
```

DBMS_ALERT

The DBMS_ALERT package provides support for notification of database events. You can use DBMS_ALERT to automatically detect that an event occurred, and then notify any process which is waiting for a signal from that alert. Many DBMS_ALERT programs perform at length, are not case-sensitive, and should not start with ORA$.

The REGISTER procedure

The REGISTER procedure adds your session and the specified alert to the master registration list. A session can register its interest in any number of alerts. The specification is:

```
PROCEDURE DBMS_ALERT.REGISTER (name IN VARCHAR2);
```

The REMOVE procedure

The REMOVE procedure removes the specified alert for the current session from the registration list. After a call to REMOVE, your application will no longer respond to the named alert when issued by SIGNAL. The specification is:

```
PROCEDURE DBMS_ALERT.REMOVE (name IN VARCHAR2);
```

The REMOVEALL procedure

The REMOVEALL procedure removes all alerts for the current session from the registration list. After a call to REMOVEALL, your application will no longer respond to any alerts issued by SIGNAL. The specification is:

```
PROCEDURE DBMS_ALERT.REMOVEALL;
```

The SET_DEFAULTS procedure

Use the SET_DEFAULTS procedure to set the amount of time (in seconds) for the POLLING_INTERVAL, which applies when DBMS_ALERT goes into a polling loop. The specification is:

```
PROCEDURE DBMS_ALERT.SET_DEFAULTS (sensitivity IN NUMBER);
```

The SIGNAL procedure

The SIGNAL procedure signals that an alert has been fired and passes a message to all sessions currently having registered interest in the alert. The specification is:

```
PROCEDURE DBMS_ALERT.SIGNAL (name IN VARCHAR2, message IN VARCHAR2);
```

The WAITANY procedure

The WAITANY procedure waits for a signal for any of the alerts in which the session has registered interest. The specification is:

```
PROCEDURE DBMS_ALERT.WAITANY
    (name OUT VARCHAR2,
     message OUT VARCHAR2,
     status OUT INTEGER,
     timeout IN NUMBER DEFAULT MAXWAIT);
```

The WAITONE procedure

The WAITONE procedure waits for a specified alert to be signaled. The specification is:

```
PROCEDURE DBMS_ALERT.WAITONE
    (name IN VARCHAR2,
     message OUT VARCHAR2,
     status OUT INTEGER,
     timeout IN NUMBER DEFAULT MAXWAIT);
```

Oracle AQ, the Advanced Queueing Facility

Oracle8 offers the Oracle Advanced Queuing facility (Oracle AQ) which implements deferred execution of work. There are two packages you will use to implement advanced queuing: DBMS_AQ, which contains the queuing procedures themselves, and DBMS_AQADM, which lets you perform administrative tasks. They make extensive use of PL/SQL record structures, as you will see in the individual program interfaces below. For more detail on these records and how to manipulate their contents, see *Oracle Built-in Packages*.

DBMS_AQ (PL/SQL 8 Only)

The DBMS_AQ package provides an interface to the messaging tasks of Oracle AQ. To use these procedures, you must have been granted the new role, AQ_ USER_ROLE.

The ENQUEUE procedure

The ENQUEUE procedure adds a message to an existing message queue. The target message queue must have had enqueuing enabled previously via the DBMS_ AQADM.START_QUEUE procedure. The specification is:

```
PROCEDURE DBMS_AQ.ENQUEUE
   (q_schema IN VARCHAR2 DEFAULT NULL
    q_name IN VARCHAR2,
    corrid IN VARCHAR2 DEFAULT NULL,
    transactional IN BOOLEAN:= TRUE,
    priority IN POSITIVE DEFAULT 1,
    delay IN DATE DEFAULT NULL,
    expiration IN NATURAL:= 0,
    relative_msgid IN NUMBER DEFAULT NULL,
    seq_deviation IN CHAR DEFAULT A,
    exception_queue_schema IN VARCHAR2 DEFAULT NULL,
    exception_queue IN VARCHAR2 DEFAULT NULL,
    reply_queue_schema IN VARCHAR2 DEFAULT NULL,
    reply_queue IN VARCHAR2 DEFAULT NULL,
    user_data IN any_object_type,
    msgid OUT RAW);
```

The DEQUEUE procedure

The DEQUEUE procedure can either remove or browse a message from an existing message queue. The target message queue must have had dequeuing enabled previously via the DBMS_AQADM.STOP_QUEUE procedure. The specification is:

```
PROCEDURE DBMS_AQ.DEQUEUE
   (q_schema IN VARCHAR2 DEFAULT NULL,
    q_name IN VARCHAR2,
    msgid IN RAW DEFAULT NULL,
    corrid IN VARCHAR2 DEFAULT NULL,
    deq_mode IN CHAR DEFAULT 'D',
    wait_time IN NATURAL DEFAULT NULL,
    transactional IN BOOLEAN:= true,
    out_msgid OUT NUMBER,
    out_corrid OUT VARCHAR2,
    priority OUT POSITIVE,
    delay OUT DATE,
    expiration OUT NATURAL,
    retry OUT NATURAL,
    exception_queue_schema OUT VARCHAR2,
    exception_queue OUT VARCHAR2,
```

```
        reply_queue_schema OUT VARCHAR2,
        reply_queue OUT VARCHAR2,
        user_data OUT any_object_type);
```

DBMS_AQADM (PL/SQL 8 Only)

The DBMS_AQADM package provides an interface to the administrative tasks of Oracle AQ. To use these procedures, a DBMS_AQADM user must have been granted the new role, AQ_ADMINISTRATOR_ROLE. You can verify the results of executing the DBMS_ AQADM package by querying the new Oracle AQ data dictionary views, USER_QUEUE_ TABLES and USER_QUEUES (DBA levels of these views are also available).

The CREATE_QUEUE_TABLE procedure

The CREATE_QUEUE_TABLE procedure creates a queue table. A queue table is the named repository for a set of queues and their messages. A queue table may contain numerous queues, each of which may have many messages. But a given queue and its messages may exist in only one queue table. The specification is:

```
    PROCEDURE DBMS_AQADM.CREATE_QUEUE_TABLE
      (queue_table IN VARCHAR2
      ,queue_payload_type IN VARCHAR2
      ,storage_clause IN VARCHAR2 DEFAULT NULL
      ,sort_list IN VARCHAR2 DEFAULT NULL
      ,multiple_consumers IN BOOLEAN DEFAULT FALSE
      ,message_grouping IN BINARY_INTEGER DEFAULT NONE
      ,comment IN VARCHAR2 DEFAULT NULL
      ,auto_commit IN BOOLEAN DEFAULT TRUE);
```

The DROP_QUEUE_TABLE procedure

The DROP_QUEUE_TABLE procedure drops an existing queue table. An error is returned if the queue table does not exist. The force parameter specifies whether all existing queues in the queue table are stopped and dropped automatically or manually. If manually (i.e., FALSE), then the queue administrator must stop and drop all existing queues within the queue table using the DBMS_AQADM.STOP_ QUEUE and DBMS_AQADM.DROP_QUEUE procedures. The specification is:

```
    PROCEDURE DBMS_AQADM.DROP_QUEUE_TABLE
      (queue_table IN VARCHAR2,
       force IN BOOLEAN default FALSE,
       auto_commit IN BOOLEAN default TRUE);
```

The CREATE_QUEUE procedure

The CREATE_QUEUE procedure creates a new message queue within an existing queue table. An error is returned if the queue table does not exist. The required queue_name parameter specifies the name of the new message queue to create. All queue names must be unique within the schema. The specification is:

```
PROCEDURE DBMS_AQADM.CREATE_QUEUE
    (queue_name IN VARCHAR2,
    queue_table IN VARCHAR2,
    queue_type IN BINARY_INTEGER default DBMS_AQADM.NORMAL_QUEUE,
    max_retries IN NUMBER default 0,
    retry_delay IN NUMBER default 0,
    retention_time IN NUMBER default 0,
    dependency_tracking IN BOOLEAN default FALSE,
    comment IN VARCHAR2 default NULL,
    auto_commit IN BOOLEAN default TRUE);
```

The ALTER_QUEUE procedure

The ALTER_QUEUE procedure modifies properties of an existing message queue. It returns an error if the message queue does not exist. Currently, you can alter only the maximum retries, retry delay, retention time, rentention delay and auto-commit properties; Oracle will augment this list in future releases. The specification is:

```
PROCEDURE DBMS_AQADM.ALTER_QUEUE (
    queue_name IN VARCHAR2,
    max_retries IN NUMBER default NULL,
    retry_delay IN NUMBER default NULL,
    retention_time IN NUMBER default NULL,
    auto_commit IN BOOLEAN default TRUE);
```

The DROP_QUEUE procedure

The DROP_QUEUE procedure drops an existing message queue. It returns an error if the message queue does not exist. DROP_QUEUE is not allowed unless STOP_QUEUE has been called to disable both enqueuing and dequeuing for the message queue to be dropped. If the message queue has not been stopped, then DROP_QUEUE returns an error of queue resource busy. The specification is:

```
PROCEDURE DBMS_AQADM.DROP_QUEUE_TABLE
    (queue_table IN VARCHAR2,
    force IN BOOLEAN default FALSE,
    auto_commit IN BOOLEAN default TRUE);
```

The START_QUEUE procedure

The START_QUEUE procedure enables an existing message queue for enqueuing and dequeuing. It returns an error if the message queue does not exist. The default is to enable both. The specification is:

```
PROCEDURE DBMS_AQADM.START_QUEUE (
    queue_name IN VARCHAR2,
    enqueue IN BOOLEAN DEFAULT TRUE,
    dequeue IN BOOLEAN DEFAULT TRUE);
```

The STOP_QUEUE procedure

The STOP_QUEUE procedure disables an existing message queue for enqueuing and dequeuing. It returns an error if the message queue does not exist. The default is to disable both enqueuing and dequeuing. The wait parameter specifies whether to wait for outstanding transactions or to return immediately. The wait option is highly dependent on outstanding transactions. If outstanding transactions exist, then wait will either hang until the transactions complete or return an error of ORA-24203, depending on whether the wait parameter is set to true or false. The specification is:

```
PROCEDURE DBMS_AQADM.STOP_QUEUE
   (queue_name IN VARCHAR2,
    enqueue IN BOOLEAN DEFAULT TRUE,
    dequeue IN BOOLEAN DEFAULT TRUE,
    wait IN BOOLEAN DEFAULT TRUE);
```

DBMS_DDL

The DBMS_DDL package provides access to some of the SQL DDL statements from within stored procedures.

The ALTER_COMPILE procedure

The ALTER_COMPILE procedure can be used to programmatically force a recompile of a stored object. The specification is:

```
PROCEDURE DBMS_DDL.ALTER_COMPILE
   (type VARCHAR2,
    schema VARCHAR2,
    name VARCHAR2);
```

The ANALYZE_OBJECT procedure

A call to ANALYZE_OBJECT lets you programmatically compute statistics for the specified object. The specification is:

```
PROCEDURE DBMS_DDL.ANALYZE_OBJECT
   (type VARCHAR2,
    schema VARCHAR2,
    name VARCHAR2,
    method VARCHAR2,
    estimate_rows NUMBER DEFAULT NULL,
    estimate_percent NUMBER DEFAULT NULL);
```

DBMS_JOB

The DBMS_JOB package provides a way for you to schedule jobs from within the Oracle RDBMS. A job is a call to a single stored procedure. You can submit a job to run once or on a recurring basis. Once a job has been submitted, you can check on the status of the job by viewing a data dictionary table. You can also change the parameters of the job with the CHANGE procedure. When you submit a job, you must provide a string that describes that job to the DBMS_JOB package and specify a job execution interval.

The BROKEN procedure

The Oracle Server considers a job to be broken if it has tried and failed 16 times to run the job. At this point, Oracle marks the job as broken and will no longer try to run the job until either (a) you mark the job as fixed or (b) you force the job to execute with a call to the RUN procedure. Use the BROKEN procedure to mark the job as fixed and specify the next date on which you want the job to run. The specification is:

```
PROCEDURE DBMS_JOB.BROKEN
    (job IN BINARY_INTEGER,
    broken IN BOOLEAN,
    next_date IN DATE DEFAULT SYSDATE);
```

The CHANGE procedure

Use the CHANGE procedure to change one or all of the attributes of a job. The specification is:

```
PROCEDURE DBMS_JOB.CHANGE
    (job IN BINARY_INTEGER,
    what IN VARCHAR2,
    next_date IN DATE,
    interval IN VARCHAR2);
```

The INTERVAL procedure

Use the INTERVAL procedure to change the interval for which a queued job is going to run. The specification is:

```
PROCEDURE DBMS_JOB.INTERVAL
    (job IN BINARY_INTEGER,
    interval IN VARCHAR2);
```

The ISUBMIT procedure

The ISUBMIT procedure submits a new job with a specified job number to the queue. The difference between ISUBMIT and SUBMIT (described later in this section) is that ISUBMIT specifies a job number, whereas SUBMIT returns a job number generated by the DBMS_JOB package. The specification is:

```
PROCEDURE DBMS_JOB.ISUBMIT
    (job IN BINARY_INTEGER,
    what IN VARCHAR2,
    next_date in DATE DEFAULT SYSDATE
    interval IN VARCHAR2 DEFAULT 'NULL',
    no_parse in BOOLEAN DEFAULT FALSE);
```

The NEXT_DATE procedure

Use the NEXT_DATE procedure to change when a queued job is going to run. The specification is:

```
PROCEDURE DBMS_JOB.NEXT_DATE
   (job IN BINARY_INTEGER,
    next_date IN DATE);
```

The REMOVE procedure

Use the REMOVE procedure to remove a job from the queue. If the job has started execution, you cannot remove it from the queue. The specification is:

```
PROCEDURE DBMS_JOB.REMOVE (job IN BINARY_INTEGER);
```

The RUN procedure

Use the RUN procedure to force a job to be executed immediately, regardless of the values for next_date and interval stored in the job queue. The specification is:

```
PROCEDURE DBMS_JOB.RUN (job IN BINARY_INTEGER);
```

The SUBMIT procedure

The SUBMIT procedure submits jobs to the queue. The specification is:

```
PROCEDURE DBMS_JOB.SUBMIT
   (job OUT BINARY_INTEGER,
    what IN VARCHAR2,
    next_date IN DATE DEFAULT SYSDATE,
    interval IN VARCHAR2 DEFAULT 'NULL',
    no_parse IN BOOLEAN DEFAULT FALSE);
```

The USER_EXPORT procedure

The USER_EXPORT procedure is used to extract the job string from a job in the queue. The specification is:

```
PROCEDURE DBMS_JOB.USER_EXPORT
   (job IN BINARY_INTEGER,
    mycall OUT VARCHAR2);
```

The WHAT procedure

Use the WHAT procedure to change what a queued job is going to run. The specification is:

```
PROCEDURE DBMS_JOB.WHAT
   (job IN BINARY_INTEGER,
    what IN VARCHAR2);
```

DBMS_LOB (PL/SQL8 Only)

Use the DBMS_LOB package to manipulate LOBs (large objects) from within a PL/SQL program and SQL statements. With DBMS_LOB you can read and modify BLOBs (binary LOBs), CLOBs (single-byte character data), and NCLOBs (fixed-width single-byte or multibyte character data), and you can perform read-only operations on BFILEs (file-based LOBs).

The APPEND procedure

Call the APPEND procedure to append the contents of a source LOB to a destination LOB. The specifications are:

```
PROCEDURE DBMS_LOB.APPEND
    (dest_lob IN OUT BLOB,
     src_lob IN BLOB);

PROCEDURE DBMS_LOB.APPEND
    (dest_lob IN OUT CLOB CHARACTER SET ANY_CS,
     src_lob IN CLOB CHARACTER SET DEST_LOB%CHARSET);
```

The COMPARE function

Use the COMPARE function to compare two LOBs in their entirety, or compare just parts of two LOBs. The specifications are:

```
FUNCTION DBMS_LOB.COMPARE
    (lob_1 IN BLOB,
     lob_2 IN BLOB,
     amount IN INTEGER := 4294967295,
     offset_1 IN INTEGER := 1,
     offset_2 IN INTEGER := 1)
RETURN INTEGER;

FUNCTION DBMS_LOB.COMPARE
    (lob_1 IN CLOB CHARACTER SET ANY_CS,
     lob_2 IN CLOB CHARACTER SET LOB_1%CHARSET,
     amount IN INTEGER := 4294967295,
     offset_1 IN INTEGER := 1,
     offset_2 IN INTEGER := 1)
RETURN INTEGER;

FUNCTION DBMS_LOB.COMPARE
    (file_1 IN BFILE,
     file_2 IN BFILE,
     amount IN INTEGER,
     offset_1 IN INTEGER := 1,
     offset_2 IN INTEGER := 1)
RETURN INTEGER;
```

The COPY procedure

The COPY procedure copies all or part of a source LOB to a destination LOB. The specifications are:

```
PROCEDURE DBMS_LOB.COPY
   (dest_lob IN OUT BLOB,
    src_lob IN BLOB,
    amount IN OUT INTEGER,
    dest_offset IN INTEGER := 1,
    src_offset IN INTEGER := 1);

PROCEDURE DBMS_LOB.COPY
   (dest_lob IN OUT CLOB CHARACTER SET ANY_CS,
    src_lob IN CLOB CHARACTER SET DEST_LOB%CHARSET,
    amount IN OUT INTEGER,
    dest_offset IN INTEGER := 1,
    src_offset IN INTEGER := 1);
```

The ERASE procedure

The ERASE procedure erases an entire LOB or part of a LOB. The specifications are:

```
PROCEDURE DBMS_LOB.ERASE
   (lob_loc IN OUT BLOB,
    amount IN OUT INTEGER,
    offset IN INTEGER := 1);

PROCEDURE DBMS_LOB.ERASE
   (lob_loc IN OUT CLOB CHARACTER SET ANY_CS,
    amount IN OUT INTEGER,
    offset IN INTEGER := 1);
```

The FILECLOSE procedure

Call the FILECLOSE procedure to close a BFILE which has previously been opened in your session or PL/SQL block. The specification is:

```
PROCEDURE DBMS_LOB.FILECLOSE (file_loc IN OUT BFILE);
```

The FILECLOSEALL procedure

The FILECLOSEALL procedure closes all BFILEs which have previously been opened in your session. The specification is:

```
PROCEDURE DBMS_LOB.FILECLOSEALL;
```

The FILEEXISTS function

The FILEEXISTS function returns 1 if the file you have specified via a BFILE locator exists. The specification is:

```
FUNCTION DBMS_LOB.FILEEXISTS (file_loc IN BFILE) RETURN INTEGER;
```

The FILEGETNAME procedure

Use the FILEGETNAME procedure to translate a BFILE locator into its directory alias and filename components. The specification is:

```
PROCEDURE DBMS_LOB.FILEGETNAME
    (file_loc IN BFILE,
     dir_alias OUT VARCHAR2,
     filename OUT VARCHAR2);
```

The FILEISOPEN function

The FILEISOPEN function returns 1 if the BFILE is already open. The specification is:

```
FUNCTION DBMS_LOB.FILEISOPEN (file_loc IN BFILE) RETURN INTEGER;
```

FILEOPEN procedure

The FILEOPEN procedure opens a BFILE with the specified mode. The specification is:

```
PROCEDURE DBMS_LOB.FILEOPEN
    (file_loc IN OUT BFILE,
     open_mode IN BINARY_INTEGER := FILE_READONLY);
```

The GETLENGTH function

Use the GETLENGTH function to return the length of the specified LOB in bytes or characters, depending on the type of LOB. The specifications are:

```
FUNCTION DBMS_LOB.GETLENGTH (lob_loc IN BLOB) RETURN INTEGER;

FUNCTION DBMS_LOB.GETLENGTH(lob_loc IN CLOB CHARACTER SET ANY_CS)
RETURN INTEGER;

FUNCTION DBMS_LOB.GETLENGTH (file_loc IN BFILE) RETURN INTEGER;
```

The INSTR function

The INSTR function returns the matching location of the nth occurrence of the specified pattern in the LOB. The specifications are:

```
FUNCTION DBMS_LOB.INSTR
    (lob_loc IN BLOB,
     pattern IN RAW,
     offset IN INTEGER := 1,
     nth IN INTEGER := 1)
RETURN INTEGER;

FUNCTION DBMS_LOB.INSTR
    (lob_loc IN CLOB CHARACTER SET ANY_CS,
     pattern IN VARCHAR2 CHARACTER SET LOB_LOC%CHARSET,
     offset IN INTEGER := 1,
     nth IN INTEGER := 1)
RETURN INTEGER;
```

```
FUNCTION DBMS_LOB.INSTR
   (file_loc IN BFILE,
    pattern IN RAW,
    offset IN INTEGER := 1,
    nth IN INTEGER := 1)
RETURN INTEGER;
```

The READ procedure

Call the READ procedure to read a portion of a LOB into a buffer variable. The specifications are:

```
PROCEDURE DBMS_LOB.READ
   (lob_loc IN BLOB,
    amount IN OUT BINARY_INTEGER,
    offset IN INTEGER,
    buffer OUT RAW);

PROCEDURE DBMS_LOB.READ
   (lob_loc IN CLOB CHARACTER SET ANY_CS,
    amount IN OUT BINARY_INTEGER,
    offset IN INTEGER,
    buffer OUT VARCHAR2 CHARACTER SET LOB_LOC%CHARSET);

PROCEDURE DBMS_LOB.READ
   (file_loc IN BFILE,
    amount IN OUT BINARY_INTEGER,
    offset IN INTEGER,
    buffer OUT RAW);
```

The SUBSTR function

The SUBSTR function returns the specified number of bytes or characters from a LOB. The specifications are:

```
FUNCTION DBMS_LOB.SUBSTR
   (lob_loc IN BLOB,
    amount IN INTEGER := 32767,
    offset IN INTEGER := 1)
RETURN RAW;

FUNCTION DBMS_LOB.SUBSTR
   (lob_loc IN CLOB CHARACTER SET ANY_CS,
    amount IN INTEGER := 32767,
    offset IN INTEGER := 1)
RETURN VARCHAR2;

FUNCTION DBMS_LOB.SUBSTR
   (file_loc IN BFILE,
    amount IN INTEGER := 32767,
    offset IN INTEGER := 1)
RETURN RAW;
```

The TRIM procedure

Use the TRIM procedure to trim the LOB value to the length you specify. The specifications are:

```
PROCEDURE DBMS_LOB.TRIM
     (lob_loc IN OUT BLOB,
      newlen IN INTEGER);

PROCEDURE DBMS_LOB.TRIM
     (lob_loc IN OUT CLOB CHARACTER SET ANY_CS,
      newlen IN INTEGER);
```

The WRITE procedure

Call the WRITE procedure to write a specified number of bytes or characters from a buffer variable into a LOB at a specified position. The specifications are:

```
PROCEDURE DBMS_LOB.WRITE
     (lob_loc IN OUT BLOB,
      amount IN OUT BINARY_INTEGER,
      offset IN INTEGER,
      buffer IN RAW);

PROCEDURE DBMS_LOB.WRITE
     (lob_loc IN OUT CLOB CHARACTER SET ANY_CS,
      amount IN OUT BINARY_INTEGER,
      offset IN INTEGER,
      buffer IN VARCHAR2 CHARACTER SET LOB_LOC%CHARSET);
```

DBMS_LOCK

The DBMS_LOCK package provides you with access to the Oracle Lock Management (OLM) services. With OLM, you can request a lock of a particular type, assign it a name that can then be used as a handle to this lock, modify the lock, and even release the lock. A lock you create with the DBMS_LOCK package has all the functionality of a lock generated by the Oracle RDBMS, including deadlock detection and view access through SQL*DBA and the relevant virtual tables.

The ALLOCATE_UNIQUE procedure

The ALLOCATE_UNIQUE procedure allocates a unique lock handle for the specified lock name. The specification is:

```
PROCEDURE DBMS_LOCK.ALLOCATE_UNIQUE
     (lockname IN VARCHAR2,
      lockhandle OUT VARCHAR2,
      expiration_secs IN INTEGER DEFAULT 864000);
```

The CONVERT function

The CONVERT function converts a lock from one type or mode to another. The specifications are:

```
FUNCTION DBMS_LOCK.CONVERT
    (id IN INTEGER,
     lockmode IN INTEGER,
     timeout IN NUMBER DEFAULT MAXWAIT)
RETURN INTEGER;

FUNCTION DBMS_LOCK.CONVERT
    (lockhandle IN VARCHAR2,
     lockmode IN INTEGER,
     timeout IN NUMBER DEFAULT MAXWAIT)
RETURN INTEGER;
```

The function returns the status of the attempt to change the mode, as shown below:

0   Success.

1   Timeout. The lock could not be converted within the specified number of seconds.

2   Deadlock. In this case, an arbitrary session will be rolled back.

3   Parameter error.

4   The session does not own the lock specified by lock ID or the lock handle.

5   Invalid lock handle. The handle was not found on the DBMS_LOCK_ALLO-CATED table.

The RELEASE function

The RELEASE function releases the specified lock. This specifications are:

```
FUNCTION DBMS_LOCK.RELEASE (id IN INTEGER) RETURN INTEGER;
FUNCTION DBMS_LOCK.RELEASE (lockhandle IN VARCHAR2) RETURN INTEGER;
```

In both cases, the RELEASE function returns a status with one of four values:

0   Successful release of lock

3   Error in the parameter passed to release

4   Session does not own lock specified by ID or lock handle

5   Illegal lock handle

The REQUEST function

The REQUEST function requests a lock of the specified mode. The specifications are:

```
FUNCTION DBMS_LOCK.REQUEST
    (id IN INTEGER,
```

```
      lockmode IN INTEGER DEFAULT X_MODE,
      timeout IN NUMBER DEFAULT MAXWAIT,
      release_on_commit IN BOOLEAN DEFAULT FALSE)
   RETURN INTEGER;

   FUNCTION DBMS_LOCK.REQUEST
      (lockhandle IN VARCHAR2,
       lockmode IN INTEGER DEFAULT X_MODE,
       timeout IN NUMBER DEFAULT MAXWAIT,
       release_on_commit IN BOOLEAN DEFAULT FALSE)
   RETURN integer;
```

The function returns the status of the attempt to obtain the lock; the codes are identical to those shown above for the CONVERT function.

The SLEEP procedure

The SLEEP procedure suspends the current session for a specified period of time (in seconds). The specification is:

```
   PROCEDURE DBMS_LOCK.SLEEP (seconds IN NUMBER);
```

DBMS_MAIL

The DBMS_MAIL package provides an interface to Oracle Office (formerly Oracle*Mail). To use this package you must first install the Oracle Office product.

The SEND procedure

The SEND procedure provides a programmatic interface to the Oracle*Mail send-message facility. Use the SEND module to send an Oracle*Mail message. The specification is:

```
   PROCEDURE DBMS_MAIL.SEND
      (from_str IN VARCHAR2, to_str IN VARCHAR2,
       cc IN VARCHAR2, bcc IN VARCHAR2,
       subject IN VARCHAR2, reply_to IN VARCHAR2,
       body IN VARCHAR2);
```

DBMS_OUTPUT

Of all the packages in this appendix, the DBMS_OUTPUT package is the one you will find yourself using most frequently. This package allows you to display information to your session's output device in a buffer as your PL/SQL program executes. As such, it serves as just about the only easily accessible means of debugging your PL/SQL Version 2 programs. DBMS_OUTPUT is also the package you will use to generate reports from PL/SQL scripts run in SQL*Plus.

The DISABLE procedure

The DISABLE procedure disables all calls to the DBMS_OUTPUT package (except for ENABLE, described next). It also purges the buffer of any remaining lines of information. After you execute this command, any calls to PUT_LINE and other modules will be ignored and you will not see any output. The specification is:

```
PROCEDURE DBMS_OUTPUT.DISABLE;
```

The ENABLE procedure

The ENABLE procedure enables calls to the other DBMS_OUTPUT modules. If you do not first call ENABLE, then any other calls to the package modules are ignored. The specification is:

```
PROCEDURE DBMS_OUTPUT.ENABLE (buffer_size IN INTEGER DEFAULT 2000);
```

The GET_LINE procedure

The GET_LINE procedure retrieves one line of information from the buffer. The specification is:

```
PROCEDURE DBMS_OUTPUT.GET_LINE
   (line OUT VARCHAR2,
      status OUT INTEGER);
```

The GET_LINES procedure

The GET_LINES procedure retrieves multiple lines from the buffer with one call. It reads the buffer into a PL/SQL string table. The specification is:

```
PROCEDURE DBMS_OUTPUT.GET_LINES
   (lines OUT CHARARR,
      numlines IN OUT INTEGER);
```

The NEW_LINE procedure

The NEW_LINE procedure inserts an end-of-line marker in the buffer. Use NEW_LINE after one or more calls to PUT in order to terminate those entries in the buffer with a newline marker. The specification is:

```
PROCEDURE DBMS_OUTPUT.NEW_LINE;
```

The PUT procedure

The PUT procedure puts information into the buffer, but does not append a newline marker into the buffer. Use PUT if you want to place information in the buffer (usually with more than one call to PUT), but not also automatically issue a newline marker. The specifications are:

```
PROCEDURE DBMS_OUTPUT.PUT (A VARCHAR2);
PROCEDURE DBMS_OUTPUT.PUT (A NUMBER);
PROCEDURE DBMS_OUTPUT.PUT (A DATE);
```

The PUT_LINE procedure

The PUT_LINE procedure puts information into the buffer and then appends a newline marker into the buffer. The specifications are:

```
PROCEDURE DBMS_OUTPUT.PUT_LINE (A VARCHAR2);
PROCEDURE DBMS_OUTPUT.PUT_LINE (A NUMBER);
PROCEDURE DBMS_OUTPUT.PUT_LINE (A DATE);
```

DBMS_PIPE

The DBMS_PIPE package provides a way for sessions in the same database instance to communicate with each other. One of the most useful aspects of Oracle pipes is that pipe communication is asynchronous: you need not COMMIT a transaction in order to initiate pipe-related activity, as is necessary with the DBMS_ALERT package. You can send a message through and receive a message from a pipe at any time. Indeed, more than one session can read or write to the same pipe.

The CREATE_PIPE function

With PL/SQL Release 2.2 only, the CREATE_PIPE function allows you to explicitly request the creation of a pipe, either public or private. The specification is:

```
FUNCTION DBMS_PIPE.CREATE_PIPE
    (pipename IN VARCHAR2,
     maxpipesize IN INTEGER DEFAULT 8192,
     private IN BOOLEAN DEFAULT TRUE)
RETURN INTEGER;
```

The function returns a numeric status code. If it returns 0, then the pipe was created successfully.

The NEXT_ITEM_TYPE function

The NEXT_ITEM_TYPE function returns the type of the next item in the local message buffer. Data is put in the message buffer with both the PACK_MESSAGE and the RECEIVE_MESSAGE procedures. Use NEXT_ITEM_TYPE to decide which kind of variable you should use to receive the data from the buffer with the over-loaded UNPACK_MESSAGE module. The specification is:

```
FUNCTION DBMS_PIPE.NEXT_ITEM_TYPE RETURN INTEGER;
```

where the return value for the function is one of the following:

0   No more items in buffer

9   VARCHAR2

5   NUMBER

12 DATE

The PACK_MESSAGE procedure

The PACK_MESSAGE procedure packs an item into the message buffer for your session. A pipe message item may have a datatype of VARCHAR2, NUMBER, or DATE. The specifications are:

```
PROCEDURE DBMS_PIPE.PACK_MESSAGE (item IN VARCHAR2);
PROCEDURE DBMS_PIPE.PACK_MESSAGE (item IN NUMBER);
PROCEDURE DBMS_PIPE.PACK_MESSAGE (item IN DATE);
```

The PURGE procedure

The PURGE procedure empties the contents of the named pipe. The specification is:

```
PROCEDURE DBMS_PIPE.PURGE (pipename IN VARCHAR2);
```

The RECEIVE_MESSAGE function

The RECEIVE_MESSAGE function receives a message from the named pipe and copies the contents of that message to the local message buffer. Once you receive the message into the buffer, you can use the UNPACK_MESSAGE procedure to extract the items from the buffer into local variables. The specification is:

```
FUNCTION DBMS_PIPE.RECEIVE_MESSAGE
    (pipename IN VARCHAR2, timeout IN INTEGER DEFAULT MAXWAIT)
RETURN INTEGER;
```

The function returns a status, which will be one of the following INTEGER values:

0   Successful receipt of message

1   Timed out waiting to receive a message

2   Record in pipe too big for buffer; this should never happen

3   Receipt of message was interrupted

The REMOVE_PIPE function

The REMOVE_PIPE function removes a pipe from shared memory. This function must be called to remove a pipe created explicitly with CREATE_PIPE. If your pipe is created implicitly, then it will be removed with a call to PURGE or whenever the pipe is emptied. The specification is:

```
FUNCTION DBMS_PIPE.REMOVE_PIPE (pipename IN VARCHAR2) RETURN INTEGER;
```

The RESET_BUFFER procedure

The RESET_BUFFER procedure clears the buffer so that both PACK_MESSAGE and UNPACK_MESSAGE will work from the first item. The specification is:

```
PROCEDURE DBMS_PIPE.RESET_BUFFER;
```

The SEND_MESSAGE function

The SEND_MESSAGE function sends the contents of the local message buffer to the named pipe. The specification is:

```
FUNCTION DBMS_PIPE.SEND_MESSAGE
    (pipename IN VARCHAR2,
     timeout IN INTEGER DEFAULT MAXWAIT,
     maxpipesize IN INTEGER DEFAULT 8192)
RETURN INTEGER;
```

The function returns a status code as follows:

0   Successful receipt of message

1   Timed out waiting to send a message

3   Sending of message was interrupted

The UNIQUE_SESSION_NAME function

The UNIQUE_SESSION_NAME function returns a name that is unique among the sessions currently connected to the database. You can use this function to obtain a name for a pipe that you know will not be in use by any other sessions. The specification is:

```
FUNCTION DBMS_PIPE.UNIQUE_SESSION_NAME RETURN VARCHAR2;
```

The UNPACK_MESSAGE procedure

The UNPACK_MESSAGE procedure unpacks the next item from the local message buffer and deposits it into the specified local variable. The specification is:

```
PROCEDURE DBMS_PIPE.UNPACK_MESSAGE (item OUT VARCHAR2);
PROCEDURE DBMS_PIPE.UNPACK_MESSAGE (item OUT NUMBER);
PROCEDURE DBMS_PIPE.UNPACK_MESSAGE (item OUT DATE);
```

DBMS_ROWID (PL/SQL8 Only)

Use the DBMS_ROWID package to work with ROWIDs from within PL/SQL programs and SQL statements. Remember that as of Oracle8, there are two types of ROWIDs: extended and restricted. Restricted ROWIDs are the ROWIDs available with Oracle Version 7 and earlier. Extended ROWIDs are used in Oracle8.

The ROWID_CREATE function

Call the CREATE function to create a ROWID (either restricted or extended as you request) based on the individual ROWID component values you specify. This should be used for test purposes only. The specification is:

```
FUNCTION DBMS_ROWID.ROWID_CREATE
    (rowid_type IN NUMBER,
```

```
      object_number IN NUMBER,
      relative_fno IN NUMBER,
      block_number IN NUMBER,
      row_number IN NUMBER)
   RETURN ROWID;
```

The ROWID_INFO procedure

The INFO procedure returns information about the specified ROWID. This procedure essentially "parses" the ROWID. The specification is:

```
PROCEDURE DBMS_ROWID.ROWID_INFO
   (rowid_in IN ROWID,
    rowid_type OUT NUMBER,
    object_number OUT NUMBER,
    relative_fno OUT NUMBER,
    block_number OUT NUMBER,
    row_number OUT NUMBER);
```

The ROWID_TYPE function

The TYPE function determines if the ROWID is restricted or extended. It returns 0 if the ROWID is restricted, and 1 if the ROWID is extended. The specification is:

```
FUNCTION DBMS_ROWID.ROWID_TYPE (row_id IN ROWID) RETURN NUMBER;
```

The ROWID_OBJECT function

Use the OBJECT function to return the data object number for an extended ROWID. The OBJECT function returns 0 if the specified ROWID is restricted. The specification is:

```
FUNCTION DBMS_ROWID.ROWID_OBJECT (row_id IN ROWID) RETURN NUMBER;
```

The ROWID_RELATIVE_FNO function

The RELATIVE_FNO function returns the relative file number (relative to the tablespace) of the ROWID. The specification is:

```
FUNCTION DBMS_ROWID.ROWID_RELATIVE_FNO (row_id IN ROWID) RETURN NUMBER;
```

The ROWID_BLOCK_NUMBER function

Use the BLOCK_NUMBER function to return the database block number of the ROWID. The specification is:

```
FUNCTION DBMS_ROWID.ROWID_BLOCK_NUMBER (row_id IN ROWID) RETURN NUMBER;
```

The ROWID_ROW_NUMBER function

The ROW_NUMBER function returns the row number of the ROWID. The specification is:

```
FUNCTION DBMS_ROWID.ROWID_ROW_NUMBER (row_id IN ROWID) RETURN NUMBER;
```

The ROWID_TO_ABSOLUTE_FNO function

Call the TO_ABSOLUTE_FNO function to return the absolute file number (for a row in a given schema and table) from the ROWID. The specification is:

```
FUNCTION DBMS_ROWID.ROWID_TO_ABSOLUTE_FNO
   (row_id IN ROWID,
    schema_name IN VARCHAR2,
    object_name IN VARCHAR2)
RETURN NUMBER;
```

The ROWID_TO_EXTENDED function

The TO_EXTENDED function converts a restricted ROWID to an extended ROWID. The specification is:

```
FUNCTION DBMS_ROWID.ROWID_TO_EXTENDED
   (old_rowid IN ROWID,
    schema_name IN VARCHAR2,
    object_name IN VARCHAR2,
    conversion_type IN INTEGER)
RETURN ROWID;
```

The ROWID_TO_RESTRICTED function

The TO_RESTRICTED function converts an extended ROWID to a restricted ROWID. The specification is:

```
FUNCTION DBMS_ROWID.ROWID_TO_RESTRICTED
   (old_rowid IN ROWID,
    conversion_type IN INTEGER)
RETURN ROWID;
```

The ROWID_VERIFY function

Use the VERIFY function to determine whether a restricted ROWID can be converted to an extended format. The VERIFY function returns 0 if the ROWID provided can be converted and 1 otherwise. The specification is:

```
FUNCTION DBMS_ROWID.ROWID_VERIFY
   (rowid_in IN ROWID,
    schema_name IN VARCHAR2,
    object_name IN VARCHAR2,
    conversion_type IN INTEGER)
RETURN NUMBER;
```

DBMS_SESSION

The DBMS_SESSION package provides you with a programmatic interface to several SQL ALTER SESSION commands and other session-level commands.

The CLOSE_DATABASE_LINK procedure

The CLOSE_DATABASE_LINK procedure closes the specified database link. The specification is:

```
PROCEDURE DBMS_SESSION.CLOSE_DATABASE_LINK (dblink VARCHAR2);
```

The IS_ROLE_ENABLED function

The IS_ROLE_ENABLED function determines whether the specified role is enabled for this session. The specification is:

```
FUNCTION DBMS_SESSION.IS_ROLE.ENABLED (rolename VARCHAR2) RETURN BOOLEAN;
```

The RESET_PACKAGE procedure

The RESET_PACKAGE procedure de-instantiates all packages in the current session. It comes in very handy for releasing all the memory associated with data structures and modules you may be using in your tests. However, this procedure should be used with extreme caution, since it literally wipes the slate clean for all packages in the session. The specification is:

```
PROCEDURE DBMS_SESSION.RESET_PACKAGE;
```

The SET_LABEL procedure

The SET_LABEL procedure changes the DBMS_SESSION label in Trusted Oracle. The specification is:

```
PROCEDURE DBMS_SESSION.SET_LABEL (lbl VARCHAR2);
```

The SET_NLS_LABEL procedure

The SET_NLS_LABEL procedure changes the default label format for your session in Trusted Oracle. The specification is:

```
PROCEDURE DBMS_SESSION.SET_NLS_LABEL (fmt VARCHAR2);
```

The SET_NLS procedure

The SET_NLS procedure provides you with a programmatic interface to change the value of a specified National Language Support parameter. The specification is:

```
PROCEDURE DBMS_SESSION.SET_NLS
    (param VARCHAR2,
    value VARCHAR2);
```

The SET_ROLE procedure

The SET_ROLE procedure enables or disables the role for the current session. The specification is:

```
PROCEDURE DBMS_SESSION.SET_ROLE (role_cmd VARCHAR2);
```

The SET_SQL_TRACE procedure

Use SET_SQL_TRACE to turn the trace facility on and off within your program. The specification is:

```
PROCEDURE DBMS_SESSION.SET_SQL_TRACE (sql_trace BOOLEAN);
```

The UNIQUE_SESSION_ID function

The UNIQUE_SESSION_ID function returns a name that is unique among the sessions currently connected to the database. The specification is:

```
FUNCTION DBMS_SESSION.UNIQUE_SESSION_ID RETURN VARCHAR2;
```

DBMS_SNAPSHOT

The DBMS_SNAPSHOT package provides a programmatic interface through which you can manage snapshots and purge snapshot logs. For detailed information about snapshots (read-only copies of tables), see Chapter 16 in the *Oracle7 Server Administrator Guide*.

The DROP_SNAPSHOT procedure

This procedures drops the specified snapshot. The specification is:

```
PROCEDURE DBMS_SNAPSHOT.DROP_SNAPSHOT
    (mowner VARCHAR2,
     master VARCHAR2,
     snapshot DATE);
```

The GET_LOG_AGE procedure

This procedures gets the oldest date entry in the log. The specification is:

```
PROCEDURE DBMS_SNAPSHOT.GET_LOG_AGE
    (oldest IN OUT date,
     mow VARCHAR2,
     mas VARCHAR2);
```

The PURGE_LOG procedure

This procedure purges the specified log of any unnecessary rows. The specifications are:

```
PROCEDURE DBMS_SNAPSHOT.PURGE_LOG
    (master VARCHAR2,
     num NUMBER);

PROCEDURE DBMS_SNAPSHOT.PURGE_LOG
    (master VARCHAR2,
     num NUMBER,
     flag VARCHAR2);
```

The REFRESH procedure

This procedure causes a manual refresh of the snapshot. The procedure is overloaded so that you can specify an optional refresh option. The specifications are:

```
PROCEDURE DBMS_SNAPSHOT.REFRESH (snapshot VARCHAR2);

PROCEDURE DBMS_SNAPSHOT.REFRESH
    (snapshot VARCHAR2,
     op VARCHAR2);
```

The REFRESH_ALL procedure

This procedure causes a refresh of all snapshots waiting to be refreshed automatically. The specification is:

```
PROCEDURE DBMS_SNAPSHOT.REFRESH_ALL;
```

The SET_UP procedure

This procedure prepares the specified master site to refresh a snapshot. The specification is:

```
PROCEDURE DBMS_SNAPSHOT.SET_UP
    (mowner VARCHAR2,
     master VARCHAR2,
         log IN OUT VARCHAR2,
     snapshot IN OUT date,
     snaptime IN OUT date);
```

The WRAP_UP procedure

The WRAP_UP procedure records a refresh at the master site. The specification is:

```
PROCEDURE DBMS_SNAPSHOT.WRAP_UP
    (mowner VARCHAR2,
     master VARCHAR2,
     sshot DATE,
     stime DATE);
```

DBMS_SQL

The DBMS_SQL package offers access to dynamic SQL from within PL/SQL. "Dynamic SQL" means SQL statements are not prewritten into your programs; instead, they are constructed at run time as character strings and then passed to the SQL engine for execution.

The BIND_ARRAY procedure

With PL/SQL8 you can perform bulk selects, inserts, updates and deletes to improve the performance of your application. You accomplish these by associating one or more index-by tables with columns in your cursor. The BIND_ARRAY procedure performs this step for you with this interface:

```
PROCEDURE DBMS_SQL.BIND_ARRAY (c IN INTEGER,
    name IN VARCHAR2,
    <table_variable> IN <datatype>,
   [,index1 IN INTEGER,
    ,index2 IN INTEGER)]);
```

The <table_variable> <datatype> pairing may be any of the following:

```
<number_table> DBMS_SQL.NUMBER_TABLE
<varchar2_table> DBMS_SQL.VARCHAR2_TABLE
<date_table> DBMS_SQL.DATE_TABLE
<blob_table> DBMS_SQL.BLOB_TABLE
<clob_table> DBMS_SQL.CLOB_TABLE
<bfile_table> DBMS_SQL.BFILE_TABLE
```

The BIND_VARIABLE procedure

The BIND_VARIABLE procedure lets you bind a specific value to a host variable which was placed in the SQL statement as a placeholder. Whenever you include a reference to a bind or host variable in the SQL statement that you pass to the PARSE procedure, you must issue a call to BIND_VARIABLE in order to bind or attach a value to that variable. The overloaded specification for this procedure supports multiple datatypes, as follows:

```
PROCEDURE DBMS_SQL.BIND_VARIABLE
    (c IN INTEGER,
    name IN VARCHAR2,
    value IN <datatype>);
```

The <datatype> may be any of the following:

```
BFILE
BLOB
CLOB CHARACTER SET ANY_CS
DATE
MLSLABEL /* Trusted Oracle only */
NUMBER
VARCHAR2 CHARACTER SET ANY_CS
```

The DBMS_SQL package also offers more specific variants of BIND_VARIABLE for less common datatypes:

```
PROCEDURE DBMS_SQL.BIND_VARIABLE
    (c IN INTEGER,
    name IN VARCHAR2,
    value IN VARCHAR2 CHARACTER SET ANY_CS,
    [,out_value_size IN INTEGER]);

PROCEDURE DBMS_SQL.BIND_VARIABLE_CHAR
    (c IN INTEGER,
    name IN VARCHAR2,
```

```
        value IN CHAR CHARACTER SET ANY_CS,
        [,out_value_size IN INTEGER]);

PROCEDURE DBMS_SQL.BIND_VARIABLE_RAW
    (c IN INTEGER,
     name IN VARCHAR2,
     value IN RAW,
     [,out_value_size IN INTEGER]);

PROCEDURE DBMS_SQL.BIND_VARIABLE_ROWID
    (c IN INTEGER,
     name IN VARCHAR2,
     value IN ROWID;
```

The CLOSE_CURSOR procedure

The CLOSE_CURSOR procedure closes the specified cursor and sets the cursor handle to NULL. It releases all memory associated with the cursor. The specification for the procedure is:

```
PROCEDURE DBMS_SQL.CLOSE_CURSOR (c IN OUT INTEGER);
```

The COLUMN_VALUE procedure

The COLUMN_VALUE procedure retrieves a value from the cursor into a local variable. Use this procedure when the SQL statement is a query and you are fetching rows with EXECUTE_AND_FETCH or FETCH_ROWS. You call COLUMN_VALUE after a row·has been fetched to transfer the value from the SELECT list of the cursor into a local variable. For each call to COLUMN_VALUE, you should have made a call to DEFINE_COLUMN in order to define that column in the cursor.

The overloaded specification is:

```
PROCEDURE DBMS_SQL.COLUMN_VALUE
    (c IN INTEGER,
     position IN INTEGER,
     value OUT DATE,
     [, column_error OUT NUMBER]
     [, actual_length OUT INTEGER ]);

PROCEDURE DBMS_SQL.COLUMN_VALUE
    (c IN INTEGER,
     position IN INTEGER,
     value OUT NUMBER,
     [, column_error OUT NUMBER]
     [, actual_length OUT INTEGER ]);

PROCEDURE DBMS_SQL.COLUMN_VALUE
    (c IN INTEGER,
     position IN INTEGER,
     value OUT VARCHAR2,
     [, column_error OUT NUMBER]
     [, actual_length OUT INTEGER ]);
```

The DBMS_SQL package also offers more specific variants of COLUMN_VALUE
for less common datatypes:

```
PROCEDURE DBMS_SQL.COLUMN_VALUE
    (c IN INTEGER,
     position IN INTEGER,
     value OUT MLSLABEL,
     [, column_error OUT NUMBER]
     [, actual_length OUT INTEGER ]);

PROCEDURE DBMS_SQL.COLUMN_VALUE
    (c IN INTEGER,
     position IN INTEGER,
     value OUT CHAR,
     [, column_error OUT NUMBER]
     [, actual_length OUT INTEGER ]);

PROCEDURE DBMS_SQL.COLUMN_VALUE
    (c IN INTEGER,
     position IN INTEGER,
     value OUT RAW,
     [, column_error OUT NUMBER]
     [, actual_length OUT INTEGER ]);

PROCEDURE DBMS_SQL.COLUMN_VALUE
    (c IN INTEGER,
     position IN INTEGER,
     value OUT ROWID,
     [, column_error OUT NUMBER]
     [, actual_length OUT INTEGER ]);
```

The DEFINE_COLUMN procedure

When you call DBMS_SQL.PARSE to process a SELECT statement, you want to
pass values from the database into local variables. To do this you must associate
the columns or expressions in the SELECT list with those local variables. You do
this with the DEFINE_COLUMN procedure, whose overloaded specification is:

```
PROCEDURE DBMS_SQL.DEFINE_COLUMN
    (c IN INTEGER,
     position IN INTEGER,
     column IN DATE);

PROCEDURE DBMS_SQL.DEFINE_COLUMN
    (c IN INTEGER,
     position IN INTEGER,
     column IN NUMBER);

PROCEDURE DBMS_SQL.DEFINE_COLUMN
    (c IN INTEGER,
     position IN INTEGER,
     column IN VARCHAR2,
     column_size IN INTEGER);
```

The EXECUTE function

The EXECUTE function executes the SQL statement associated with the specified cursor. It returns the number of rows processed by the SQL statement if that statement is an UPDATE, INSERT, or DELETE. If the SQL statement is not an UPDATE, INSERT, or DELETE, ignore the value returned by EXECUTE. If the SQL statement is a query, you can now call the FETCH_ROWS function to fetch rows which are retrieved by that query. The specification is:

```
FUNCTION DBMS_SQL.EXECUTE (c IN INTEGER) RETURN INTEGER;
```

The EXECUTE_AND_FETCH function

The EXECUTE_AND_FETCH function executes the SELECT statement associated with the specified cursor and immediately fetches the rows associated with the query. The specification is:

```
FUNCTION DBMS_SQL.EXECUTE_AND_FETCH
    (c IN INTEGER,
      exact_match IN BOOLEAN DEFAULT FALSE)
RETURN INTEGER;
```

The FETCH_ROWS function

The FETCH_ROW function corresponds to the FETCH statement for regular PL/SQL cursors. It fetches the next row from the cursor. The specification is:

```
FUNCTION DBMS_SQL.FETCH_ROWS (c IN INTEGER) RETURN INTEGER;
```

The IS_OPEN function

The IS_OPEN function returns TRUE if the specified cursor is already open, FALSE otherwise. This function corresponds to the %ISOPEN attribute for regular PL/SQL cursors. The specification is:

```
FUNCTION DBMS_SQL.IS_OPEN (c IN INTEGER) RETURN BOOLEAN;
```

The LAST_ERROR_POSITION function

The LAST_ERROR_POSITION function returns the byte offset in the SQL statement where the ERROR occurred. Call this function immediately after a call to EXECUTE or EXECUTE_AND_FETCH in order to obtain meaningful results. The specification is:

```
FUNCTION DBMS_SQL.LAST_ERROR_POSTITION RETURN INTEGER;
```

The LAST_ROW_COUNT function

The LAST_ROW_COUNT function returns the total number of rows fetched at that point. The specification is:

```
FUNCTION DBMS_SQL.LAST_ROW_COUNT RETURN INTEGER;
```

The LAST_ROW_ID function

The LAST_ROW_ID function returns the rowid of the row fetched most recently. The specification is:

```
FUNCTION DBMS_SQL.LAST_ROW_ID RETURN ROWID;
```

The LAST_SQL_FUNCTION_CODE function

The LAST_SQL_FUNCTION_CODE function returns the SQL function code for the SQL statement. The specification is:

```
FUNCTION DBMS_SQL.LAST_SQL_FUNCTION_CODE RETURN INTEGER;
```

The OPEN_CURSOR function

Use this function to open a cursor, which means that the Oracle Server will set aside memory for a cursor data area and return a pointer to that area. The specification is:

```
FUNCTION DBMS_SQL.OPEN_CURSOR RETURN INTEGER;
```

The PARSE procedure

The PARSE procedure immediately parses the statement specified. The specification for this procedure is:

```
PROCEDURE DBMS_SQL.PARSE
    (cursor_handle IN INTEGER,
    SQL_statement IN VARCHAR2,
    language_flag IN INTEGER);
```

PL/SQL8 offers a second, overloaded version of DBMS_SQL.PARSE, which comes in handy when you have very large SQL statements. If your SQL statement exceeds the largest possible contiguous allocation on your system (and it is machine-dependent) or 32K bytes (the maximum size for VARCHAR2), use this version of the PARSE procedure:

```
PROCEDURE DBMS_SQL.PARSE
    (cursor_handle IN INTEGER,
    SQL_statement IN DBMS_SQL.VARCHAR2S,
    lb IN INTEGER,
    ub IN INTEGER,
    lfflg IN BOOLEAN,
    language_flag IN INTEGER);
```

The VARIABLE_VALUE procedure

The VARIABLE_VALUE procedure lets you retrieve the value of a named variable from the specified PL/SQL block. The overloaded specification for this procedure supports three datatypes, as follows:

```
PROCEDURE DBMS_SQL.VARIABLE_VALUE
    (cursor_handle IN INTEGER,
     variable_name IN VARCHAR2,
     value OUT NUMBER);

PROCEDURE DBMS_SQL.VARIABLE_VALUE
    (cursor_handle IN INTEGER,
     variable_name IN VARCHAR2,
     value OUT DATE);

PROCEDURE DBMS_SQL.VARIABLE_VALUE
    (cursor_handle IN INTEGER,
     variable_name IN VARCHAR2,
     value OUT VARCHAR2);
```

DBMS_TRANSACTION

The DBMS_TRANSACTION package provides a programmatic interface to a number of the SQL transaction statements. The majority of these procedures (ADVISE_COMMIT through ROLLBACK_FORCE) have SQL equivalents that you can invoke directly from within PL/SQL. Thus, many PL/SQL programmers choose to use the SQL equivalents rather than these procedures. However, the last five procedures (BEGIN_DISCRETE_TRANSACTION through STEP_ID) have no equivalents and nicely abstract the PL/SQL programmer or database administrator from the internals of what is being accomplished.

The ADVISE_COMMIT procedure

The ADVISE_COMMIT procedure specifies that "commit" in-doubt transaction advice is sent to remote databases during distributed transactions.

The advice generated by this procedure appears on the remote database in the ADVICE column of the DBA_2PC_PENDING data dictionary view if the distributed transaction becomes in-doubt (i.e., a network or machine failure occurs during the commit). The remote database administrator can then review the DBA_2PC_PENDING information and manually commit or roll back in-doubt transactions using the FORCE clause of the COMMIT or ROLLBACK commands. Each call to an ADVISE procedure remains in effect for the duration of that connection or until a different ADVISE procedure call is made. This allows you to send different advice to various remote databases.

This procedure is equivalent to the SQL command, ALTER SESSION ADVISE COMMIT. The specification is:

```
PROCEDURE DBMS_TRANSACTION.ADVISE_COMMIT;
```

The ADVISE_NOTHING procedure

The ADVISE_NOTHING procedure specifies that no in-doubt transaction advice is sent to remote databases during distributed transactions. Advice is handled as described for ADVISE_COMMIT. This procedure is equivalent to the SQL command, ALTER SESSION ADVISE NOTHING. The specification is:

```
PROCEDURE DBMS_TRANSACTION.ADVISE_NOTHING;
```

The ADVISE_ROLLBACK procedure

The ADVISE_ROLLBACK procedure specifies that "rollback" in-doubt transaction advice is sent to remote databases during distributed transactions. Advice is handled as described for ADVISE_COMMIT. This procedure is equivalent to the SQL command, ALTER SESSION ADVISE ROLLBACK. The specification is:

```
PROCEDURE DBMS_TRANSACTION.ADVISE_ROLLBACK;
```

The COMMIT procedure

The COMMIT procedure ends the current transaction and makes permanent all pending changes. It also erases savepoints and releases all locks. It is provided primarily for completeness. It is equivalent to the COMMIT command, which is already implemented as part of PL/SQL. I recommend using the SQL command rather than the procedure. The specification is:

```
PROCEDURE DBMS_TRANSACTION.COMMIT;
```

The COMMIT_COMMENT procedure

The COMMIT_COMMENT procedure performs a commit and sends a "commit" in-doubt transaction comment to remote databases during distributed transactions. This comment appears on the remote database in the TRAN_COMMENT column of the DBA_2PC_PENDING data dictionary view if the distributed transaction becomes in-doubt (i.e., a network or machine failure occurs during the commit). The remote database administrator can then review the DBA_2PC_PENDING information and manually commit or roll back in-doubt transactions using the FORCE clause of the COMMIT or ROLLBACK commands. This procedure is equivalent to the SQL command, COMMIT COMMENT. The specification is:

```
PROCEDURE DBMS_TRANSACTION.COMMIT_COMMENT (cmnt VARCHAR2);
```

The COMMIT_FORCE procedure

The COMMIT_FORCE procedure manually commits local in-doubt, distributed transactions. Any decisions to force in-doubt transactions should be made after consulting with the database administrator(s) at the remote database location(s). If the decision is made to locally force any transactions, the database administrator should either commit or rollback such transactions as was done by nodes that successfully resolved the transactions. Otherwise, the administrator should query the DBA_2PC_PENDING views ADVICE and TRAN_COMMENT columns for further insight.* This procedure is equivalent to the SQL command, COMMIT FORCE. The specification is:

```
PROCEDURE DBMS_TRANSACTION.COMMIT_FORCE
   (xid VARCHAR2,
    scn VARCHAR2 DEFAULT NULL);
```

The READ_ONLY procedure

The READ_ONLY procedure establishes the current transaction as a read-consistent transaction (i.e., repeatable reads). Once a transaction is designated as read-only, all queries within that transaction can only see changes committed prior to that transactions start. Thus, read-only transactions let you issue two or more queries against tables that may be undergoing concurrent inserts or updates, and yet return results consistent as of the transaction's start. This procedure is equivalent to the SQL command, SET TRANSACTION READ ONLY. The specification is:

```
PROCEDURE DBMS_TRANSACTION.READ_ONLY;
```

The READ_WRITE procedure

The READ_WRITE procedure establishes the current transaction as a read-write transaction. This is the default transaction mode. This procedure is equivalent to the SQL command, SET TRANSACTION READ WRITE. The specification is:

```
PROCEDURE DBMS_TRANSACTION.READ-WRITE;
```

The ROLLBACK procedure

The ROLLBACK procedure ends the current transaction and undoes all pending changes. It also erases savepoints and releases all locks. It is provided primarily for completeness. It is equivalent to the ROLLBACK command, which is already implemented as part of PL/SQL. I recommend using the SQL command rather than the procedure. The specification is:

```
PROCEDURE DBMS_TRANSACTION.ROLLBACK;
```

---

* For more information on this topic, see "Manually Overriding In-Doubt Transactions" in *Oracle8 Server Distributed Systems.*

The ROLLBACK_FORCE procedure

The ROLLBACK_FORCE procedure manually rolls back local in-doubt, distributed transactions. The parameter identifies the transaction's local or global transaction ID. To find these transaction IDs, query the data dictionary view DBA_2PC_PENDING. Any decisions to force in-doubt transactions should be made after consulting with the database administrator(s) at the remote database location(s), as described for COMMIT_FORCE. This procedure is equivalent to the SQL command, ROLLBACK FORCE. The specification is:

```
PROCEDURE DBMS_TRANSACTION.ROLLBACK_FORCE (xid VARCHAR2);
```

The ROLLBACK_SAVEPOINT procedure

The ROLLBACK_SAVEPOINT procedure rolls back the current transaction to a previously declared savepoint. It is provided primarily for completeness. It is equivalent to the ROLLBACK SAVEPOINT command, which is already implemented as part of PL/SQL. I recommend using the SQL command rather than the procedure. The specification is:

```
PROCEDURE DBMS_TRANSACTION.ROLLBACK_SAVEPOINT;
```

The SAVEPOINT procedure

The SAVEPOINT procedure identifies a logical point within a transaction to which you can later roll back. It is provided primarily for completeness. It is equivalent to the SAVEPOINT command, which is already implemented as part of PL/SQL. I recommend using the SQL command rather than the procedure. The specification is:

```
PROCEDURE DBMS_TRANSACTION.SAVEPOINT;
```

The USE_ROLLBACK_SEGMENT procedure

The USE_ROLLBACK_SEGMENT procedure assigns the current transaction to the specified rollback segment. This option also establishes the transaction as a read-write transaction. The rollback segment specified must be online. You cannot use both the READ_ONLY and USE_ROLLBACK_SEGMENT procedures within the same transaction. Read-only transactions do not generate rollback information and thus cannot be assigned rollback segments. This procedure is equivalent to the SQL command, SET TRANSACTION USE ROLLBACK SEGMENT. The specification is:

```
PROCEDURE DBMS_TRANSACTION.USE_ROLLBACK_SEGMENT (rb_name VARCHAR2);
```

The BEGIN_DISCRETE_TRANSACTION procedure

The BEGIN_DISCRETE_TRANSACTION procedure streamlines transaction processing so short transactions can execute more rapidly. During discrete transactions, normal redo information is generated although it is stored in a separate location in memory. When the discrete transaction commits, the redo information is written to the redo log file and data block changes are applied directly. As such, there is no need for undo information in rollback segments. The block is then written to the database file in the usual manner. The call to this procedure is effective only until the transaction is committed or rolled back; the next transaction is processed as a standard transaction. Any PL/SQL using this procedure must be coded to ensure that the transaction is attempted again in the event of a discrete transaction failure.[*] The specification is:

```
PROCEDURE DBMS_TRANSACTION.BEGIN_DISCRETE_TRANSACTION;
```

The PURGE_MIXED procedure

The PURGE_MIXED procedure deletes information about a given in-doubt, distributed transaction that has had mixed outcomes due to a transaction resolution mismatch. This occurs when an in-doubt, distributed transaction is forced to commit or roll back on one node and other nodes do the opposite. Oracle cannot automatically resolve such inconsistencies, but it does flag entries in the DBA_2PC_PENDING view by setting the MIXED column to yes. When the database administrator is sure that any inconsistencies for a transaction have been resolved, he or she can call the PURGE_MIXED procedure.[†] The specification is:

```
PROCEDURE DBMS_TRANSACTION.PURGE_MIXED (xid VARCHAR2);
```

The PURGE_LOST_DB procedure

The PURGE_LOST_DB procedure deletes information about a given in-doubt, distributed transaction that has had mixed outcomes due to a lost database. This occurs when an in-doubt, distributed transaction is able to commit or roll back on one node and other nodes have either destroyed or recreated their databases. Oracle cannot automatically resolve such inconsistencies, as described in PURGE_MIXED. The specification is:

```
PROCEDURE DBMS_TRANSACTION.PURGE_LOST_DB (xid VARCHAR2);
```

The LOCAL_TRANSACTION_ID function

The LOCAL_TRANSACTION_ID function returns the unique identifier for the current transaction. The function returns NULL if there is no current transaction. The specification is:

```
FUNCTION DBMS_TRANSACTION.LOCAL_TRANSACTION_ID
    (create_transaction BOOLEAN := false)
RETURN VARCHAR2;
```

---

[*] For more information on this topic, see "Using Discrete Transactions" in *Oracle8 Server Tuning*.

[†] For more information on this topic, see "Manually Overriding In-Doubt Transactions" in *Oracle8 Serve Distributed Systems*.

The STEP_ID function

The STEP_ID function returns the unique positive integer that orders the DML operations of the current transaction. The specification is:

```
FUNCTION DBMS_TRANSACTION.STEP_ID RETURN VARCHAR2;
```

DBMS_UTILITY

The DBMS_UTILITY package includes several utility modules you might find useful when managing objects in the database.

The ANALYZE_SCHEMA procedure

This procedure analyzes all the tables, clusters, and indexes in the specified schema. The specification is:

```
PROCEDURE DBMS_UTILITY.ANALYZE_SCHEMA
    (schema VARCHAR2,
    method VARCHAR2,
    estimate_rows NUMBER DEFAULT NULL,
    estimate_percent NUMBER DEFAULT NULL);
```

The COMMA_TO_TABLE procedure

The COMMA_TO_TABLE procedure parses a comma-delimited list and places each name into a PL/SQL table. The specification is:

```
PROCEDURE DBMS_UTILITY.COMMA_TO_TABLE
    (list IN VARCHAR2,
    tablen OUT BINARY_INTEGER,
    tab OUT uncl_array);
```

The COMPILE_SCHEMA procedure

This procedure compiles all procedures, functions, and packages in the specified schema. The specification is:

```
PROCEDURE DBMS_UTILITY.COMPILE_SCHEMA (schema VARCHAR2);
```

The FORMAT_CALL_STACK function

This function formats and returns the current call stack. You can use this function to access the call stack in your program. The specification is:

```
FUNCTION DBMS_UTILITY.FORMAT_CALL_STACK RETURN VARCHAR2;
```

The FORMAT_ERROR_STACK function

This function formats and returns the current error stack. You might use this in an exception handler to examine the sequence of errors raised. The specification is:

```
FUNCTION DBMS_UTILITY.FORMAT_ERROR_STACK RETURN VARCHAR2;
```

The GET_TIME function

This function returns the number of 100ths of seconds which have elapsed from an arbitrary time. Without GET_TIME, Oracle functions can only record and provide elapsed time in second intervals, which is a very coarse granularity in today's world of computing. With GET_TIME, you can get a much finer understanding of the processing times of lines in your program. The specification is:

```
FUNCTION DBMS_UTILITY.GET_TIME RETURN NUMBER;
```

The IS_PARALLEL_SERVER function

This function helps determine if the database is running in Parallel Server mode. The specification is:

```
FUNCTION DBMS_UTILITY.IS_PARALLEL_SERVER RETURN BOOLEAN;
```

The function returns TRUE if the database is running in Parallel Server mode; otherwise it returns FALSE.

The NAME_RESOLVE procedure

This procedure resolves the name of an object into its component parts, performing synonym translations as necessary. The specification is:

```
PROCEDURE DBMS_UTILITY.NAME_RESOLVE
    (name IN VARCHAR2,
     context IN NUMBER,
     schema OUT VARCHAR2,
     part1 OUT VARCHAR2,
     part2 OUT VARCHAR2,
     dblink OUT VARCHAR2,
     part1_type OUT NUMBER,
     object_number OUT NUMBER);
```

The NAME_TOKENIZE procedure

The NAME_TOKENIZE procedure calls the PL/SQL parser to parse the given name that is in the following format:

```
a [ . b [. c]] [@dblink ]
```

where dblink is the name of a database link. NAME_TOKENIZE follows these rules:

- Strips off all double quotes

- Converts to uppercase if there are no quotes

- Ignores any inline comments

- Does no semantic analysis

- Leaves any missing values as NULL

The specification is:

```
PROCEDURE DBMS_UTILITY.NAME_TOKENIZE
    (name    IN VARCHAR2,
     a OUT VARCHAR2,
     b OUT VARCHAR2,
     c OUT VARCHAR2,
     dblink OUT VARCHAR2,
     nextpos OUT BINARY_INTEGER);
```

The PORT_STRING function

The PORT_STRING function returns a string that uniquely identifies the version of Oracle Server and the platform or operating system of the current database instance. The specification is:

```
FUNCTION DBMS_UTILITY.PORT_STRING RETURN VARCHAR2;
```

The TABLE_TO_COMMA procedure

The TABLE_TO_COMMA procedure converts a PL/SQL table into a comma-delimited list. The specification is:

```
PROCEDURE DBMS_UTILITY.TABLE_TO_COMMA
    (tab IN uncl_array,
     tablen OUT BINARY_INTEGER,
     list OUT VARCHAR2);
```

UTL_FILE

The UTL_FILE package allows your PL/SQL programs to both read from and write to operating system files. You can call UTL_FILE from within programs stored in the database server or from within client-side application modules, such as those built with Oracle Forms. You can, therefore, interact with operating system files both on the local workstation (client) and on the server disks.

Setting Up UTL_FILE

Before you can read and write operating system files on the server, you must make changes to the *INIT.ORA* initialization file of your database instance (this is generally a DBA task). Specifically, you must add one or more entries for the utl_file_dir parameter. Each line must have this format:

```
utl_file_dir = <directory>
```

where <directory> is either a specific directory or a single asterisk. If your entry has this format:

```
utl_file_dir = *
```

then you will be able to read from and write to any directory accessible from your server machine. If you want to enable file I/O for a restricted set of directories, provide separate entries in the *INIT.ORA* file as shown below:

```
utl_file_dir = /tmp/trace
utl_file_dir = /user/dev/george/files
```

The Oracle user must then have operating system privileges on a directory in order to write to it or read from it. Finally, any files created through UTL_FILE will have the default privileges taken from the Oracle user.

The FCLOSE procedure

Use FCLOSE to close an open file. The specification is:

```
PROCEDURE UTL_FILE.FCLOSE (file_in UTL_FILE.FILE_TYPE);
```

The FCLOSE_ALL procedure

FCLOSE_ALL closes all of the opened files. The specification is:

```
PROCEDURE UTL_FILE.FCLOSE_ALL;
```

The FFLUSH procedure

The FFLUSH procedure flushes the contents of the UTL_FILE buffer out to the specified file. You will want to use FFLUSH to make sure that any buffered messages are written to the file and therefore available for reading. The specification is:

```
PROCEDURE UTL_FILE.FFLUSH (file IN FILE_TYPE);
```

The FOPEN function

The FOPEN function opens the specified file and returns a file handle that you can then use to manipulate the file. The specification is:

```
FUNCTION UTL_FILE.FOPEN
    (location_in IN VARCHAR2,
     file_name_in IN VARCHAR2,
     file_mode_in IN VARCHAR2)
RETURN UTL_FILE.FILE_TYPE;
```

The GET_LINE procedure

The GET_LINE procedure reads a line of data from the specified file, if it is open, into the provided line buffer. The specification is:

```
PROCEDURE UTL_FILE.GET_LINE
    (file_in IN UTL_FILE.FILE_TYPE,
     line_out OUT VARCHAR2);
```

The IS_OPEN function

The IS_OPEN function returns TRUE if the specified handle points to a file that is already open. Otherwise it returns false. The specification is:

```
FUNCTION UTL_FILE.IS_OPEN
    (file_in IN UTL_FILE.FILE_TYPE)
RETURN BOOLEAN;
```

The NEW_LINE procedure

The NEW_LINE procedure inserts one or more newline characters in the specified file. The specification is:

```
PROCEDURE UTL_FILE.NEW_LINE
    (file_in IN UTL_FILE.FILE_TYPE,
     num_lines_in IN PLS_INTEGER := 1);
```

The PUT procedure

The PUT procedure puts data out to the specified file. The PUT procedure is heavily overloaded so that you can easily call PUT with a number of different combinations of arguments. The specifications are:

```
PROCEDURE UTL_FILE.PUT
    (file_in UTL_FILE.FILE_TYPE,
     item_in IN VARCHAR2);

PROCEDURE UTL_FILE.PUT (item_in IN VARCHAR2);

PROCEDURE UTL_FILE.PUT
    (file_in UTL_FILE.FILE_TYPE,
     item_in IN DATE);

PROCEDURE UTL_FILE.PUT (item_in IN DATE);

PROCEDURE UTL_FILE.PUT
    (file_in UTL_FILE.FILE_TYPE,
     item_in IN NUMBER);

PROCEDURE UTL_FILE.PUT (item_in IN NUMBER);

PROCEDURE UTL_FILE.PUT
    (file_in UTL_FILE.FILE_TYPE,
     item_in IN PLS_INTEGER);

PROCEDURE UTL_FILE.PUT (item_in IN PLS_INTEGER);
```

The PUTF procedure

Like PUT, PUTF puts data into a file, but it uses a message format (hence, the "F" in "PUTF") to interpret the different elements to be placed in the file. You can pass between one and five different items of data to PUTF. The specification is:

```
PROCEDURE UTL_FILE.PUTF
    (file_in UTL_FILE.FILE_TYPE,
    format_in IN VARCHAR2,
    item1_in IN VARCHAR2
    [, item2_in IN VARCHAR2 ... item5_in IN VARCHAR2]);
```

The PUT_LINE procedure

The third variation of the PUT feature in UTL_FILE is PUT_LINE. This procedure writes data to a file and then immediately appends a newline character after the text. The specification is:

```
PROCEDURE UTL_FILE.PUT_LINE
    (file_in UTL_FILE.FILE_TYPE,
    item_in IN VARCHAR2);
```

Index

Symbols

:= (assignment) operator, 43, 115, 290
- - (comment indicator), 50
<< and >> (label delimiters), 148
" (quotation mark), 48, 364, 47
; (semicolon), 49
/* and */ (comment block delimiters), 50
|| (concatenation) operator, 113, 354

A

ABS function, 412
absolute value, 412
abstract data types (see ADTs)
abstraction, 592
access
    to compiled code, tuning, 853–858
    to data, tuning, 858–871
    data structure, encapsulating, 38
    to SQL, minimizing, 859–861
ACCESS table, tuning, 856
actual parameters, 500–504
Ada programming language, xix
ADD_MONTHS function, 394–396
    customizing, 404–406
adding collection elements, 666–667
administration of Oracle databases, xxiv
administration, Oracle/AQ, 928–930
ADTs (abstract datatypes), 588
    building, 786–794
    (see also object types)
advanced queuing (see Oracle/AQ facility)

ADVISE_COMMIT procedure, 954
ADVISE_NOTHING procedure, 955
ADVISE_ROLLBACK procedure, 955
aggregate
    assignment into rows, 313–315
    operations, 279, 292, 294
        of nested records, 298
    values, combining with scalars, 566–568
aggregation, 589
alerts (see DBMS_ALERT package)
algorithms, tuning, 871–892
aliases
    column, 176–177, 286
    for cursor variables, 202
    directory, BFILENAME function
        and, 420–422
alignment of code (see coding, layout of)
ALLOCATE_UNIQUE procedure, 937
ALTER SESSION command, 895–896
ALTER TABLE command, 714
ALTER VIEW ... COMPILE command, 717
ALTER_COMPILE procedure, 930
ALTER_Q procedure, 929
ANALYZE statement, 850
ANALYZE_OBJECT procedure, 930
ANALYZE_SCHEMA procedure, 959
anchored datatypes, 32, 116–121
    anchoring to subtypes, 123
angle brackets (<<, >>) as label
        delimiters, 148
anonymous blocks, 469–482
    labels for, 482–484

About the Authors

Steven Feuerstein is considered one of the world's leading experts on the Oracle PL/SQL language. He is also the author of the sequel to *Oracle PL/SQL Programming, Advanced Oracle PL/SQL Programming with Packages* (O'Reilly & Associates, 1996) and the upcoming *Oracle Built-in Packages* (O'Reilly & Associates, 1998).

Steven has been developing software since 1980 and worked for Oracle Corporation from 1987 to 1992. He is a partner with RevealNet, Inc. (*www.revealnet.com*) and is the chief architect of the RevealNet products, PL/SQL Knowledge Base and PL/Vision (a code library of prebuilt PL/SQL packages which accelerates PL/SQL-based application development). Steven also sysops RevealNet's "PL/SQL Pipeline," an online community for PL/SQL developers (*www.revealnet.com/plsql-pipeline*). He can be reached through email at *feuerstein@revealnet.com*. Steven is also President of PL/Solutions, which offers training and consulting on both PL/Vision and PL/SQL (*www.plsolutions.com*). Finally (on the Oracle side of Steven's life), he serves as codirector of the Oracle Practice at SSC, a systems management consulting firm based in Chicago (*www.saraswati.com*).

Steven shares his Rogers Park, Chicago Georgian with his wife Veva, his youngest son Eli, two cats (Sister Itsacat and Moshe Jacobawitz), and Mercury (the Congo Red African Gray parrot). His older son, Chris, is busy making music and creating art nearby. Steven is a member of the Board of Directors of the Crossroads Fund, which provides grants to organizations in Chicago working for social change.

Bill Pribyl, founder and principal of DataCraft, Inc. (*www.datacraft.com*), has been learning and teaching about Oracle databases and applications for more than ten years. His work with object-oriented technology dates to the mid-1980s, when he coauthored a paper on the application of entity-relationship modeling to object-oriented analysis.

A self-avowed Oracle "generalist," Bill has served as an Oracle database administrator for several billion-dollar companies; led the development of web-based database applications for online commerce; configured an ultra-high availability database using Oracle replication; helped NASA apply database technology to space shuttle simulation software; and developed and taught classes in PL/SQL, Developer/2000, and the Oracle database. An ardent supporter of the Oracle user community, Bill is past chair of the South Central (USA) Oracle Users Group. He also served as Editor-in-Chief of *Select*, the quarterly publication of the International Oracle Users Group-Americas. His work has been published in Oracle user group publications worldwide. He also authored JavaScript programming examples for *The Official Netscape LiveWire Pro Book.*

Bill lives near his alma mater, Rice University, in Houston, Texas with his wife Norma, son Johnny, stepson Geoffrey, four cats, and a deaf Dalmatian. He volunteer teaches a class on the Internet and beginning HTML to children in public middle school.

Colophon

Ants are featured on the cover of *Oracle PL/SQL Programming, Second Edition.* At least 8,000 different species of ants can be found everywhere on Earth except the North and South Poles. Ants preserved in amber suggest that these insects existed 50 million years before humans.

Queen ants establish new communities, or nests, after their mating flight. On this flight the queen mates with several males. After mating, the males fall to Earth and die. In some species of red ant, the queen snaps the male in half after mating with him. The queen then finds an uninhabited nest, settles into it, and pulls her wings off. She will never fly again, and after removing her wings she is able to absorb the wing muscles as nutrients for her eggs. She will continue to lay eggs, thousands of them, for years.

During the three-stage development process, which takes about two months, the eggs, larvae, and pupae are cared for by the nurse ants, who feed, clean, and carefully move the young to warmer or cooler places in the nest, depending on the temperature. These nurse ants are, in turn, cared for by other worker ants, who feed the nurses with regurgitated food. The workers and the nurses will fight together to defend the young against enemies if the nest is invaded, either by another group of ants or by a larger animal.

Edie Freedman designed this cover and the entire bestiary that appears on the Nutshell Handbooks. The beasts themselves are adapted from 19th-century engravings from the Dover Pictorial Archive. The cover layout was produced with Quark XPress 3.3 using the ITC Garamond font. Whenever possible, our books use RepKover™, a durable and flexible lay-flat binding. If the page count exceeds RepKover's limit, perfect binding is used.

The inside layout was designed by Edie Freedman and Nancy Priest and implemented in FrameMaker 5.0 by Mike Sierra. The text and heading fonts are ITC Garamond Light and Garamond Book. The illustrations that appear in the book were created in Macromedia Freehand 5.0 by Chris Reilley and Robert Romano. This colophon was written by Clairemarie Fisher O'Leary.

 # *More Titles from O'Reilly*

Oracle

dvanced Oracle PL/SQL **Programming with Packages**

By Steven Feuerstein,
1st Edition Oct.1996, 690 pages,
plus diskette, ISBN 1-56592-238-7

This book explains the best way to construct packages, a powerful part of Oracle's PL/SQL procedural language that can dramatically improve your programming productivity and code quality, while preparing you for object-oriented velopment in Oracle technology. It comes with PL/Vision soft-re, a library of PL/SQL packages developed by the author, and es you behind the scenes as it examines how and why the Vision packages were implemented the way they were.

acle8 Design Tips

By Dave Ensor & Ian Stevenson
1st Edition September 1997
130 pages, ISBN 1-56592-361-8

The newest version of the Oracle DBMS, Oracle8, offers some dramatically different features from previous versions, including better scalability, reliability, and security; an object-relational model; additional datatypes; and more. To get peak performance out Oracle8 system, databases and code need to be designed these new features in mind. This small book tells Oracle ners and developers just what they need to know to use the e8 features to best advantage.

le Performance Tuning, 2nd Edition

By Mark Gurry & Peter Corrigan
2nd Edition November 1996
964 pages, Includes diskette
ISBN 1-56592-237-9

Performance tuning is crucial in any modern relational database management system. The first edition of this book became a classic for developers and DBAs. This edition offers 400 pages of aterial on new Oracle features, including parallel server, l query, Oracle Performance Pack, disk striping and ng, RAID, MPPs, SMPs, distributed databases, backup overy, and much more. Includes diskette.

Oracle Security

By Marlene Theriault & William Heney
1st Edition October 1998
446 pages, ISBN 1-56592-450-9

This book covers the field of Oracle security from simple to complex. It describes basic RDBMS security features (e.g., passwords, profiles, roles, privileges, synonyms) and includes many practical strategies for securing an Oracle system, developing auditing and backup plans, and using the Oracle Enterprise Manager and Oracle Security Server. Also touches on advanced security features, such as encryption, Trusted Oracle, and Internet and Web protection.

Oracle Design

By Dave Ensor & Ian Stevenson
1st Edition March 1997
546 pages, 1-56592-268-9

This book looks thoroughly at the field of Oracle relational database design, an often neglected area of Oracle, but one that has an enormous impact on the ultimate power and performance of a system. Focuses on both database and code design, including such special design areas as data models, enormalization, the use of keys and indexes, temporal data, special architectures (client/server, distributed database, parallel processing), and data warehouses.

Oracle Scripts

By Brian Lomasky & David C. Kreines
1st Edition May 1998
200 pages, Includes CD-ROM
ISBN 1-56592-438-X

A powerful toolset for Oracle DBAs and developers, these scripts will simplify everyday tasks—monitoring databases, protecting against data loss, improving security and performance, and helping to diagnose problems and repair databases in emergencies. The accompanying CD-ROM contains complete source code and additional monitoring and tuning software.

O'REILLY®

Oracle

Oracle Built-In Packages

By Steven Feuerstein
1st Edition March 1998
600 pages, Includes diskette
ISBN 1-56592-375-8

Oracle's built-in packages dramatically extend the power of the PL/SQL language, but few developers know how to use them effectively. This book is a complete reference to all of the built-ins, including those new to Oracle8. The enclosed diskette includes an online tool that provides easy access to the many files of source code and documentation developed by the authors.

Oracle PL/SQL Built-ins Pocket Reference

By Steven Feuerstein,
John Beresniewicz & Chip Dawes
1st Edition October 1998
78 pages, ISBN 1-56592-456-8

This companion to Steven Feuerstein's bestselling Oracle PL/SQL Programming and Oracle Built-in Packages provides quick-reference information on how to call Oracle's built-in functions and packages, including those new to Oracle8. It shows how to call all types of functions (numeric, character, date, conversion, large object [LOB], and miscellaneous) and packages (e.g., DBMS_SQL, DBMS_OUTPUT).

Web Programming

CGI Programming on the World Wide Web

By Shishir Gundavaram
1st Edition March 1996
450 pages, ISBN 1-56592-168-2

This book offers a comprehensive explanation of CGI and related techniques for people who hold on to the dream of providing their own information servers on the Web. It starts at the beginning, explaining the value of CGI and how it works, then moves swiftly into the subtle details of programming.

Web Programming

JavaScript: The Definitive Guide, 3rd Edition

By David Flanagan & Dan Shafer
3rd Edition June 1998
800 pages, ISBN 1-56592-392-8

This third edition of the definitive reference to JavaScript covers the latest version of the language, JavaScript 1.2, as supported by Netscape Navigator 4.0. JavaScript, which is being standardized under the name ECMAScript, is a scripting language that can be embedded directly in HTML to give web pages programming-language capabilities.

Learning VBScript

By Paul Lomax
1st Edition July 1997
616 pages, includes CD-ROM
ISBN 1-56592-247-6

This definitive guide shows web develop how to take full advantage of client-side scripting with the VBScript language. In addition to basic language features, it covers the Internet Explorer object mo and discusses techniques for client-side scripting, like adding ActiveX controls to a web page or validating data before sending to the server. Includes CD-ROM with over 170 code samples.

Web Client Programming with Perl

By Clinton Wong
1st Edition March 1997
228 pages, ISBN 1-56592-214-X

Web Client Programming with Perl sh you how to extend scripting skills to Web. This book teaches you the basi how browsers communicate with se and how to write your own customiz web clients to automate common ta It is intended for those who are motivated to develop softwa that offers a more flexible and dynamic response than a sta web browser.

Web Programming

ynamic HTML: The Definitive Reference

By Danny Goodman
1st Edition July 1998
1088 pages, ISBN 1-56592-494-0

Dynamic HTML: The Definitive Reference is an indispensable compendium for Web content developers. It contains complete reference material for all of the HTML tags, CSS style attributes, browser document objects, and JavaScript objects supported the various standards and the latest versions of Netscape vigator and Microsoft Internet Explorer.

Frontier: The Definitive Guide

By Matt Neuburg
1st Edition February 1998
618 pages, 1-56592-383-9

This definitive guide is the first book devoted exclusively to teaching and documenting Userland Frontier, a powerful scripting environment for web site management and system level scripting. Packed with examples, advice, tricks, and tips, *Frontier: The Definitive Guide* teaches you Frontier from the ground up. Learn how to automate repetitive processes, control remote computers across a network, beef up your web site by generating hundreds of related web pages automatically, and more. Covers Frontier 4.2.3 for the Macintosh.

How to stay in touch with O'Reilly

1. Visit Our Award-Winning Web Site

http://www.oreilly.com/

★ "Top 100 Sites on the Web" —*PC Magazine*
★ "Top 5% Web sites" —*Point Communications*
★ "3-Star site" —*The McKinley Group*

Our web site contains a library of comprehensive product information (including book excerpts and tables of contents), downloadable software, background articles, interviews with technology leaders, links to relevant sites, book cover art, and more. File us in your Bookmarks or Hotlist!

2. Join Our Email Mailing Lists

New Product Releases
To receive automatic email with brief descriptions of all new O'Reilly products as they are released, send email to:
listproc@online.oreilly.com
Put the following information in the first line of your message (*not* in the Subject field):
subscribe oreilly-news

O'Reilly Events
If you'd also like us to send information about trade show events, special promotions, and other O'Reilly events, send email to:
listproc@online.oreilly.com
Put the following information in the first line of your message (*not* in the Subject field):
subscribe oreilly-events

3. Get Examples from Our Books via FTP

There are two ways to access an archive of example files from our books:

Regular FTP
* ftp to:
  ftp.oreilly.com
  (login: anonymous
  password: your email address)
* Point your web browser to:
  ftp://ftp.oreilly.com/

FTPMAIL
* Send an email message to:
  ftpmail@online.oreilly.com
  (Write "help" in the message body)

4. Contact Us via Email

order@oreilly.com
To place a book or software order online. Good for North American and international customers.

subscriptions@oreilly.com
To place an order for any of our newsletters or periodicals.

books@oreilly.com
General questions about any of our books.

software@oreilly.com
For general questions and product information about our software. Check out O'Reilly Software Online at **http://software.oreilly.com/** for software and technical support information. Registered O'Reilly software users send your questions to: **website-support@oreilly.com**

cs@oreilly.com
For answers to problems regarding your order or our products.

booktech@oreilly.com
For book content technical questions or corrections.

proposals@oreilly.com
To submit new book or software proposals to our editors and product managers.

international@oreilly.com
For information about our international distributors or translation queries. For a list of our distributors outside of North America check out:
http://www.oreilly.com/www/order/country.html

O'Reilly & Associates, Inc.
101 Morris Street, Sebastopol, CA 95472 USA
TEL   707-829-0515 or 800-998-9938
      (6am to 5pm PST)
FAX   707-829-0104

International Distributors

UK, EUROPE, MIDDLE EAST AND NORTHERN AFRICA (EXCEPT FRANCE, GERMANY, SWITZERLAND, & AUSTRIA)

INQUIRIES
International Thomson Publishing Europe
Berkshire House
168-173 High Holborn
London WC1V 7AA
United Kingdom
Tel: 44-1-71-497-1422
Fax: 44-1-71-497-1426

ORDERS
International Thomson Publishing Services, Ltd.
Cheriton House, North Way
Andover, Hampshire SP10 5BE
United Kingdom
Tel: 44-1-264-342-832 (UK)
Tel: 44-1-264-342-806 (outside UK)
Fax: 44-1-264-364-418 (UK)
Fax: 44-1-264-342-761 (outside UK)
Email: itpint@itps.co.uk

FRANCE
GEODIF
61, Bd Saint-Germain
75240 Paris Cedex 05, France
Tel: 33-1-44-41-46-16 (French books)
Tel: 33-1-44-41-11-87 (English books)
Fax: 33-1-44-41-11-44
Email: distribution@eyrolles.com

ORDERS
SODIS
128, av.du Mal de Lattre de Tassigny
77403 Lagny Cédex, France
Tel: 33-1-60-07-82-00
Fax: 33-1-64-30-32-27

INQUIRIES
Éditions O'Reilly
18 rue Séguier
75006 Paris, France
Tel: 33-1-40-51-52-30
Fax: 33-1-40-51-52-31
Email: france@editions-oreilly.fr

GERMANY, SWITZERLAND, AUSTRIA

INQUIRIES
O'Reilly Verlag
Balthasarstr. 81
D-50670 Köln, Germany
Tel: 49-221-973160-0
Fax: 49-221-973160-8
Email: anfragen@oreilly.de

ORDERS
International Thomson Publishing
Königswinterer Straße 418
53227 Bonn, Germany
Tel: 49-228-970240
Fax: 49-228-441342
Email: order@oreilly.de

CANADA (FRENCH LANGUAGE BOOKS)
Les Éditions Flammarion ltée
375, Avenue Laurier Ouest
Montréal (Québec) H2V 2K3
Tel: 00-1-514-277-8807
Fax: 00-1-514-278-2085
Email: info@flammarion.qc.ca

HONG KONG
City Discount Subscription Service, Ltd.
Unit D, 3rd Floor, Yan's Tower
27 Wong Chuk Hang Road
Aberdeen, Hong Kong
Tel: 852-2580-3539
Fax: 852-2580-6463
Email: citydis@ppn.com.hk

KOREA
Hanbit Media, Inc.
Sonyoung Bldg. 202
Yeksam-dong 736-36
Kangnam-ku
Seoul, Korea
Tel: 822-554-9610
Fax: 822-556-0363
Email: hant93@chollian.dacom.co.kr

SINGAPORE, MALAYSIA, THAILAND
Addison-Wesley Longman Singapore Pte., Ltd.
25 First Lok Yang Road
Singapore 629734
Tel: 65-268-2666
Fax: 65-268-7023
Email: Daniel.Loh@awl.com.sg

PHILIPPINES
Mutual Books, Inc.
429-D Shaw Boulevard
Mandaluyong City, Metro
Manila, Philippines
Tel: 632-725-7538
Fax: 632-721-3056
Email: mbikikog@mnl.sequel.net

TAIWAN
O'Reilly Taiwan
No. 3, Lane 131
Hang-Chow South Road
Section 1, Taipei, Taiwan
Tel: 886-2-23968990
Fax: 886-2-23968916
Email: benh@oreilly.com

CHINA
China National Publishing
Industry Trading Corporation
504 AnHuiLi, AnDingMenWai
P.O. Box 782
Beijing 100011, China P.R.
Tel: 86-10-6424-0483
Fax: 86-10-6421-4540
Email: frederic@oreilly.com

INDIA
Computer Bookshop (India) Pvt. Ltd.
190 Dr. D.N. Road, Fort
Bombay 400 001 India
Tel: 91-22-207-0989
Fax: 91-22-262-3551
Email: cbsbom@giasbm01.vsnl.net.in

JAPAN
O'Reilly Japan, Inc.
Kiyoshige Building 2F
12-Bancho, Sanei-cho
Shinjuku-ku
Tokyo 160-0008 Japan
Tel: 81-3-3356-5227
Fax: 81-3-3356-5261
Email: japan@oreilly.com

ALL OTHER ASIAN COUNTRIES
O'Reilly & Associates, Inc.
101 Morris Street
Sebastopol, CA 95472 USA
Tel: 707-829-0515
Fax: 707-829-0104
Email: order@oreilly.com

AUSTRALIA
WoodsLane Pty., Ltd.
7/5 Vuko Place
Warriewood NSW 2102
Australia
Tel: 61-2-9970-5111
Fax: 61-2-9970-5002
Email: info@woodslane.com.au

NEW ZEALAND
Woodslane New Zealand, Ltd.
21 Cooks Street (P.O. Box 575)
Waganui, New Zealand
Tel: 64-6-347-6543
Fax: 64-6-345-4840
Email: info@woodslane.com.au

SOUTH AFRICA
International Thomson South Africa
Building 18, Constantia Park
138 Sixteenth Road
(P.O. Box 2459)
Halfway House, 1685 South Africa
Tel: 27-11-805-4819
Fax: 27-11-805-3648

LATIN AMERICA
McGraw-Hill Interamericana
Editores, S.A. de C.V.
Cedro No. 512
Col. Atlampa
06450, Mexico, D.F.
Tel: 52-5-547-6777
Fax: 52-5-547-3336
Email: mcgraw-hill@infosel.net.mx

O'REILLY™

O'Reilly & Associates, Inc.
101 Morris Street
Sebastopol, CA 95472-9902
1-800-998-9938

Visit us online at:
http://www.ora.com/
orders@ora.com

O'REILLY WOULD LIKE TO HEAR FROM YOU

Which book did this card come from?

_____

Where did you buy this book?
- ❏ Bookstore
- ❏ Direct from O'Reilly
- ❏ Bundled with hardware/software
- ❏ Other _____
- ❏ Computer Store
- ❏ Class/seminar

What operating system do you use?
- ❏ UNIX
- ❏ Windows NT
- ❏ Other _____
- ❏ Macintosh
- ❏ PC(Windows/DOS)

What is your job description?
- ❏ System Administrator
- ❏ Network Administrator
- ❏ Web Developer
- ❏ Programmer
- ❏ Educator/Teacher
- ❏ Other _____

❏ Please send me O'Reilly's catalog, containing a complete listing of O'Reilly books and software.

Name _____ Company/Organization _____

Address _____

City _____ State _____ Zip/Postal Code _____ Country _____

Telephone _____ Internet or other email address (specify network)

Nineteenth century wood engraving
of a bear from the O'Reilly &
Associates Nutshell Handbook®
Using & Managing UUCP.

BUSINESS REPLY MAIL

FIRST CLASS MAIL   PERMIT NO. 80   SEBASTOPOL, CA

Postage will be paid by addressee

O'Reilly & Associates, Inc.
101 Morris Street
Sebastopol, CA 95472-9902